The Joan Palevsky Imprint in Classical Literature

In honor of beloved Virgil—

"O degli altri poeti onore e lume . . ."

—Dante, *Inferno*

The publisher gratefully acknowledges the generous support
of the Classical Literature Endowment Fund of the
University of California Press Foundation, which was
established by a major gift from Joan Palevsky.

The publisher also thanks the following for generous
contributions to this book:
The Loeb Classical Library Foundation
The Committee on Research, University of California, Berkeley
The Abigail Reynolds Hodgen Publication Fund in the Social
Sciences at University of California, Berkeley

Creating a Common Polity

HELLENISTIC CULTURE AND SOCIETY
General Editors: Anthony W. Bulloch, Erich S. Gruen,
A. A. Long, and Andrew F. Stewart

Creating a Common Polity

Religion, Economy, and Politics in the
Making of the Greek Koinon

———

Emily Mackil

UNIVERSITY OF CALIFORNIA PRESS
Berkeley   Los Angeles   London

University of California Press, one of the most distinguished university presses in the United States, enriches lives around the world by advancing scholarship in the humanities, social sciences, and natural sciences. Its activities are supported by the UC Press Foundation and by philanthropic contributions from individuals and institutions. For more information, visit www.ucpress.edu.

University of California Press
Berkeley and Los Angeles, California

University of California Press, Ltd.
London, England

Library of Congress Cataloging-in-Publication Data

Mackil, Emily Maureen.
    Creating a common polity : religion, economy, and politics in the making of the Greek koinon / Emily Mackil.
        p.   cm. — (Hellenistic culture and society; 55)
    Includes bibliographical references and index.
    ISBN 978-0-520-27250-7 (cloth, alk. paper) — ISBN 978-0-520-95393-2 (ebook)
    1. Greece—Politics and government—To 146 B.C   2. City-states—Greece—History.   3. Religion and state—Greece—History.   I. Title.
    JC73.M337   2013
    320.938—dc23   2012012446

Manufactured in the United States of America

22   21   20   19   18   17   16   15   14   13
10   9   8   7   6   5   4   3   2   1

In keeping with its commitment to support environmentally responsible and sustainable printing practices, UC Press has printed this book on Cascades Enviro 100, a 100% post–consumer waste, recycled, de-inked fiber. FSC recycled certified and processed chlorine-free. It is acid-free, Ecologo-certified, and manufactured by BioGas energy.

For Max

CONTENTS

This book trades in a currency that is not widely accepted beyond the relatively small scholarly circle of classicists, ancient historians, and Greek epigraphers. Yet in the course of writing it I have learned a great deal from work done in fields well beyond theirs, including geography, economics, political science, anthropology, and sociology. I have therefore attempted to write in such a way as to keep my account accessible to the interested nonspecialist, in the hope that the intellectual exchange may be reciprocal. At the same time, the full scholarly apparatus of ancient historical research, especially that based in ancient documents, has been retained in the notes and above all in the appended epigraphic dossier, which collects, translates, and comments upon sixty-one Greek inscriptions of particular relevance to the argument that is sustained over the course of this book. I hope that, in offering this book for exchange with specialists and nonspecialists alike, I have not unwittingly debased my currency with both.

It is with a view to accessibility beyond classical circles that all Greek is transliterated (except in the epigraphic dossier), according to what I readily admit is a somewhat arbitrary system. I have preferred the Greek to the Latin system of transliteration, except where the result is an offense to normal English usage. So, for example, Achaia, Aitolia, Boiotia, Orchomenos, and Polybios are as close as possible to the Greek spelling, but Athens, Attica, Carthage, Cassander, Corinth, Crete, Macedonia, Thebes, and Thucydides are preferred over Athenai, Attike, Karchedon, Kassandros, Korinthos, Krete, Makedonia, Thebai, and Thoukydides, against which my spirit simply rebels.

The abbreviations of ancient authors and texts are in general those given in *The Oxford Classical Dictionary*, third edition (*OCD³*), occasionally with familiar variations; and references to secondary scholarship generally take the form of author-date citations, but abbreviated references have often been more convenient. For full details, see the headnote to the list of abbreviations used in this book.

This book has been more than a decade in the making, during the course of which time I have incurred significant debts. It is a great pleasure now to acknowledge them. Josiah Ober, who supervised the 2003 Princeton PhD dissertation to which this book is distantly related, has been an invaluable interlocutor, reader, critic, and friend. Nicholas Purcell, my first teacher of ancient history in Oxford, was also a member of the Princeton dissertation committee, and though he has not read a draft of this book and will, I am sure, not agree with everything I say here, the lessons I have learned from him, in tutorials, conversations, and print, have left their imprint on every page. Simon Hornblower, my tutor in Greek history in Oxford, first awakened my interest in the subject of Greek federal states by posing a question that I found impossible to answer in a tutorial essay.

The University of California, Berkeley, has been my academic home during the entire period of writing this book. Here I have been blessed with wonderful colleagues who have been cheerful discussants, critical readers, and friends: Susanna Elm, Erich Gruen, Leslie Kurke, Maureen Miller, Carlos Noreña, Michael Nylan, Nikolaos Papazarkadas, Andrew Stewart, and Ronald Stroud. Mary Elizabeth Berry has offered support and guidance of a different and invaluable kind. Three Berkeley graduate students—Eric Driscoll, John Lanier, and Michael Laughy—offered research assistance and saved me countless hours and the commission of innumerable mistakes. I have learned much from the comments and questions of Ryan Boehm, Lisa Eberle, Noah Kaye, and Joel Rygorsky, Berkeley graduate students with whom I have had the privilege to work closely. Their challenges and observations have significantly improved some of the ideas and arguments I have presented.

Many friends and colleagues beyond Berkeley have read and commented on one or more chapters of the book: Lisa Kallet, Barbara Kowalzig, Jack Kroll, Josh Ober, Gary Reger, Peter van Alfen, and Barry Weingast. Athanasios Rizakis has been a stimulating interlocutor on all things Achaian and has generously shared his unpublished work with me. The curatorial staff at the American Numismatic Society, above all Peter van Alfen and Ute Wartenberg Kagan, have welcomed me on repeated visits and generously made their holdings available to me for study. I am grateful to them also for permission to reproduce on the cover a photograph of an Achaian coin in their collection.

Some of the ideas and arguments of this book were presented in papers delivered at the American School of Classical Studies in Athens, Princeton University, the University of California, Berkeley, Stanford University, the University of Toronto, the University of Oxford, and the Westfälische Wilhelms-Universität

Münster, as well as at two annual meetings of the Association of Ancient Historians. I am grateful to the hosts who invited me and the audiences who, on all these occasions, offered comments and criticism. I express my profound and humble thanks to all, and absolve everyone but myself of responsibility for the errors and missteps that inevitably remain.

Thanks for financial support in the form of research leaves are due to the Department of History, the Townsend Center for the Humanities, and the Committee on Research, all of the University of California, Berkeley. A grant from the Loeb Classical Library Foundation contributed to an uninterrupted one-year sabbatical during which major portions of the book were written. Research travel was funded by a summer stipend from the National Endowment for the Humanities and the Aleshire Center for the Study of Greek Epigraphy at Berkeley. An early stage of my work in Greece was generously supported by the Fulbright Foundation and a Whiting Honorific Fellowship in the Humanities from Princeton University.

Erich Gruen first encouraged me to submit my book for consideration as part of the series *Hellenistic Culture and Society* published by the University of California Press. I owe him thanks not only because it is a privilege to see it become a part of this estimable series but also because everyone involved with the process at the Press has been so tremendously helpful. Alain Bresson and Jeremy McInerney took on the task of reviewing a massive manuscript for the University of California Press, and for their thoughtful and detailed comments and criticisms I am deeply grateful. Their suggestions have made this a much better book. My editor at U.C. Press, Eric Schmidt, has been unfailingly helpful and patient with an overly ambitious first-time author. His good advice and tireless advocacy at every stage are deeply appreciated. The work of Paul Psoinos, a meticulous and indefatigable copyeditor, has saved me from innumerable blunders. Cindy Fulton ushered the book through production carefully and thoughtfully. I am most grateful to Roberta Engleman for preparing the index and to Eric Driscoll for assistance with the proofreading. Subventions to meet the high cost of publishing a book of this size and complexity were generously granted by the Abigail Reynolds Hodgen Publication Fund and the Committee on Research, both of the University of California, Berkeley, and by the Loeb Classical Library Foundation.

My family never stopped offering encouragement, although they may have begun to believe that the project would never reach its completion, and whether they realized it or not, the regular queries about progress helped to keep me on track. My daughter, Lydia, has been an incomparably enlivening and enlightening companion since the day of her arrival. My husband, Max Christoff, has lived with this project virtually since its inception, listening patiently as I tried to work out innumerable problems and bearing the inevitable ups and downs with alacrity and good humor. It is in gratitude for all this and much more that I dedicate the book to him.

Throughout this book's footnotes and bibliography, the abbreviations used for the names of ancient authors and the titles of their works are in general those shown in the frontmatter list in Simon Hornblower and Antony Spawforth, eds., *The Oxford Classical Dictionary*, 3rd edition (*OCD*³: Oxford, 2003), supplemented where necessary by the corresponding list in Henry George Liddell, Robert Scott, and Henry Stuart Jones, eds., *A Greek-English Lexicon*, 9th edition (abbreviated LSJ: Oxford, 1996). Abbreviations used for the titles of modern works of scholarship or reference, or both, and for the titles of scholarly periodicals, are in general those given by *L'Année philologique*. Apart from these, the abbreviations listed below are used in this book.

AAA	Αρχαιολογικά Ανάλεκτα εξ Αθηνών
ANM	National Archaeological Museum, Athens, inventory
ANS	American Numismatic Society
ArchZeit	*Archaeologische Zeitung*
Arist. *Frag. Var.*	Aristotle, *Fragmenta Varia*
Barr.	*Barrington Atlas of the Greek and Roman World*, edited by R. J. A. Talbert (Princeton, 2000)
BE	*Bulletin épigraphique*, published annually in *Revue des études grecques*
BMC Peloponnese	Percy Gardner, *Catalogue of Greek Coins in the British Museum: Peloponnese* (London, 1887)
BNJ	*Brill's New Jacoby*, edited by Ian Worthington (Leiden, 2006)

BNP	*Brills New Pauly: Encyclopaedia of the Ancient World*, edited by Hubert Cancik, Helmuth Schneider, and Christine F. Salazar. 15 vols. (Leiden, 2006)
CID	*Corpus des inscriptions de Delphes* (Paris, 1977–2002)
comm.	commentary
ed.pr.	*editio princeps*
FDelph	*Fouilles de Delphes* (Paris, 1902–2003)
fr., frr.	fragment, fragments
IGCH	*Inventory of Greek Coin Hoards*, edited by Margaret Thompson, Otto Mørkholm, and Colin M. Kraay (New York, 1973)
IPArk	Gerhard Thür and Hans Taeuber, *Prozessrechtliche Inschriften der griechischen Poleis: Arkadien* (Vienna, 1994)
ISE	Luigi Moretti, *Iscrizioni storiche ellenistiche* (Florence, 1967–2003)
IThesp	Paul Roesch, *Les inscriptions de Thespies,* edited by Gilbert Argoud, Albert Schachter, and Guy Vottéro (Lyon, 2007). (http://www.hisoma.mom.fr/thespies.html)
Milet I.3	Georg Kawerau and Albert Rehm, *Das Delphinion in Milet.* Volume 3 of *Ergebnisse der Ausgrabungen und Untersuchungen seit dem Jahre 1899* (Berlin, 1914)
Milet VI.1	Albert Rehm, *Inschriften von Milet, Teil 1: Inschriften n. 187–406 (Nachdruck aus den Bänden I.5–II.3)*, with contributions by Hermann Dessau and Peter Herrmann (Berlin, 1997)
ML	Russell Meiggs and David M. Lewis, *A Selection of Greek Historical Inscriptions to the End of the Fifth Century* B.C. Revised edition (Oxford, 1988)
NCIG	Institut Fernand-Courby, *Nouveau choix d'inscriptions grecques* (Paris, 2005)
RO	Peter J. Rhodes and Robin Osborne, *Greek Historical Inscriptions, 404–323* (Oxford, 2003)
Σ	scholia
SNG Cop.	*Sylloge Nummorum Graecorum: The Royal Collection of Coins and Medals, Danish National Museum* (Copenhagen, 1942–79)
SNG Delep.	*Sylloge Nummorum Graecorum: France, Bibliothèque nationale, Cabinet des médailles, Collection Jean et Marie Delepierre* (Paris, 1983–)
Staatsverträge	Herrmann Bengston and Hatto H. Schmitt, *Die Staatsverträge des Altertums* (Munich, 1960–69)

MAPS

Full-color, high-quality versions of these maps may be downloaded from the book's permanent website: http://www.ucpress.edu/book.php?isbn=9780520272507.

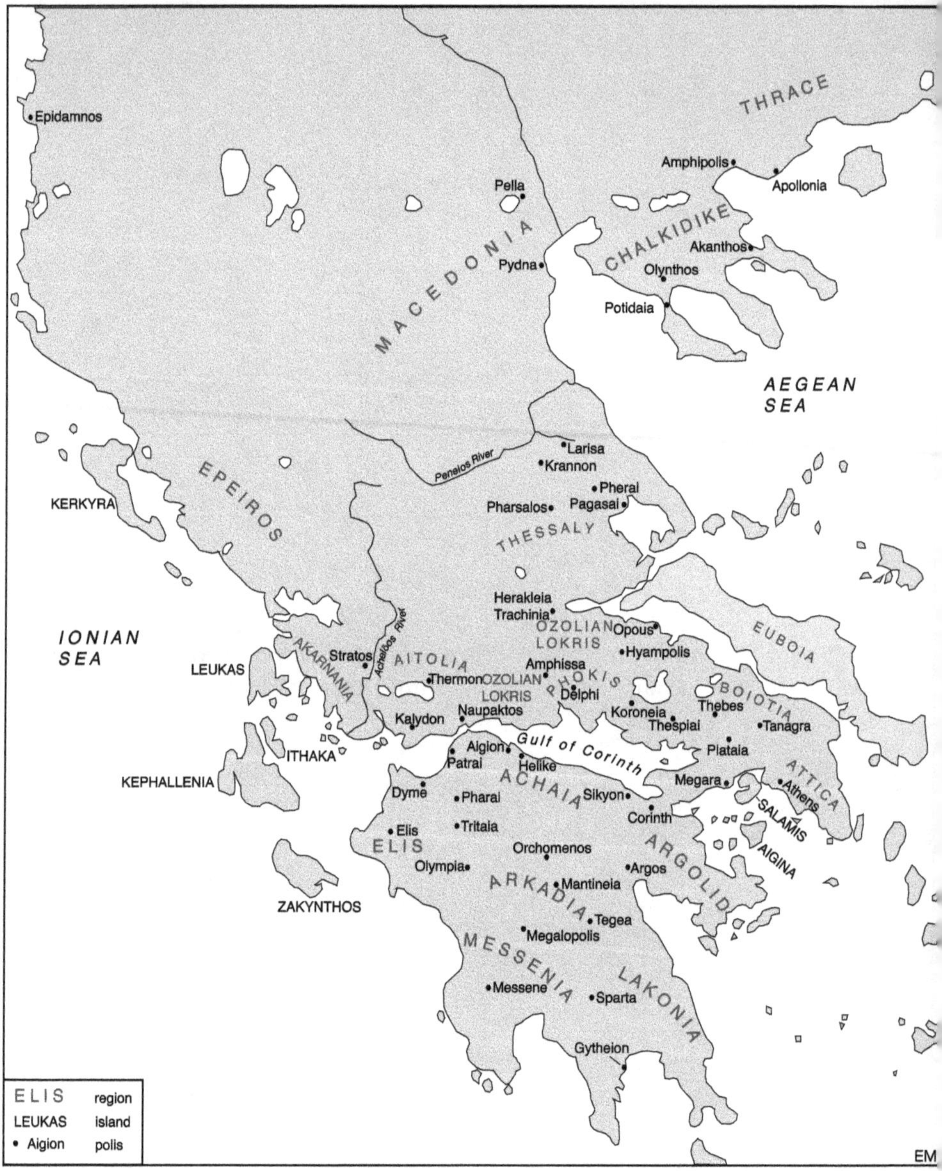

MAP 1. Mainland Greece and the Peloponnese in the classical and Hellenistic periods.

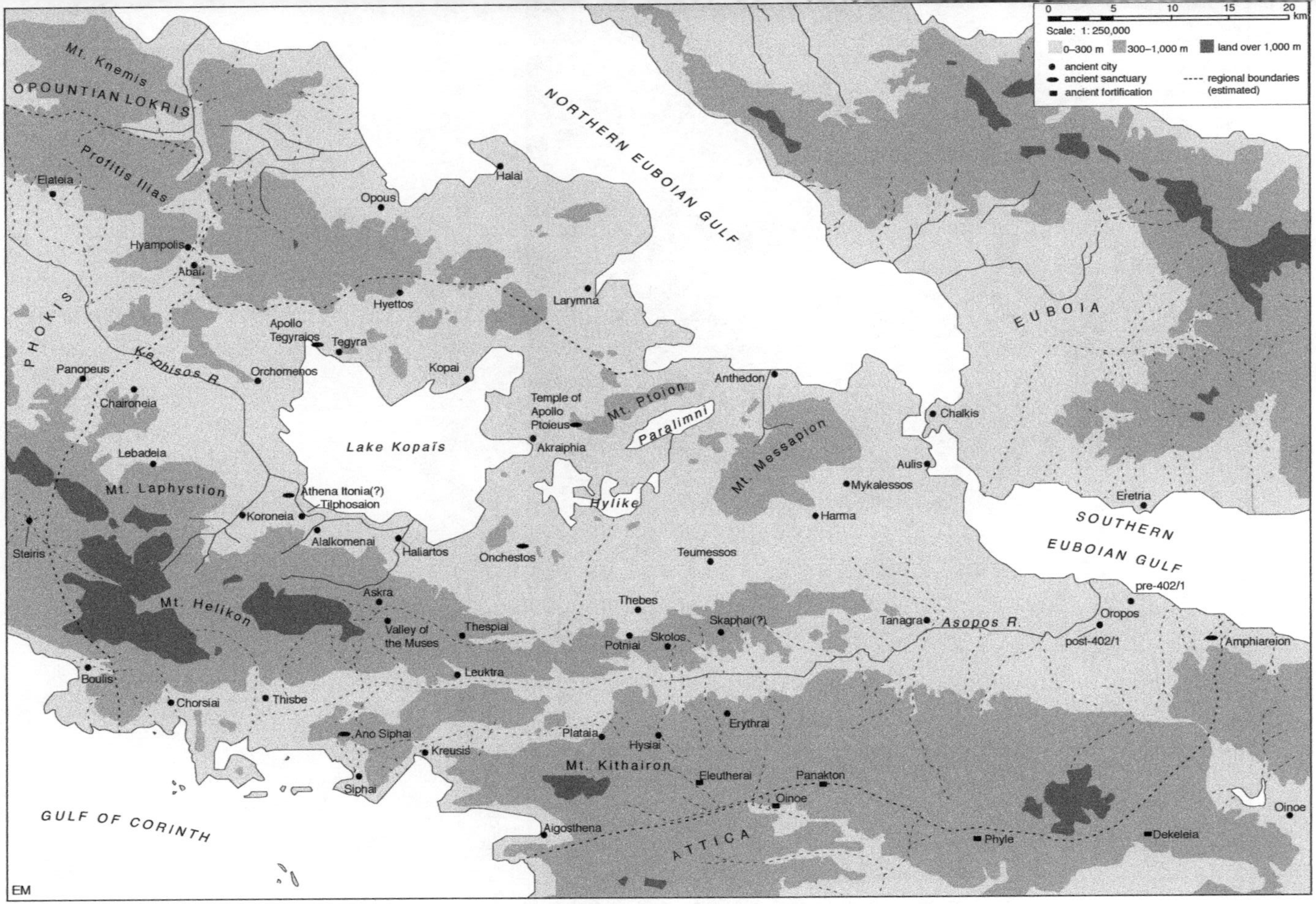

MAP 2. Boiotia in the classical and Hellenistic periods.

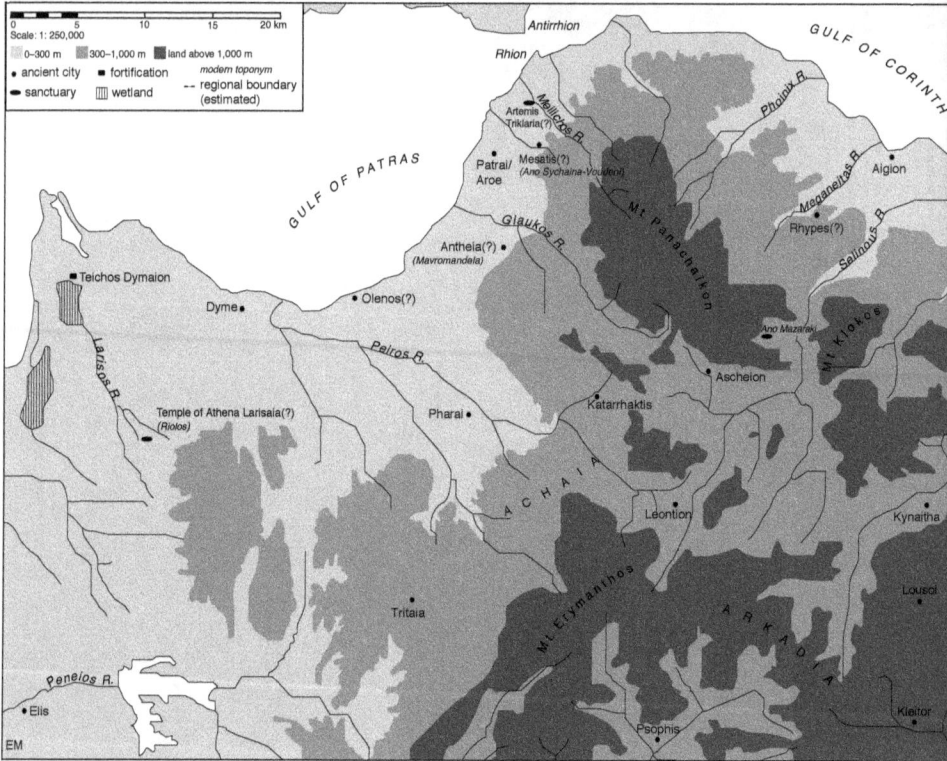

MAP 3. Achaia in the classical and Hellenistic periods.

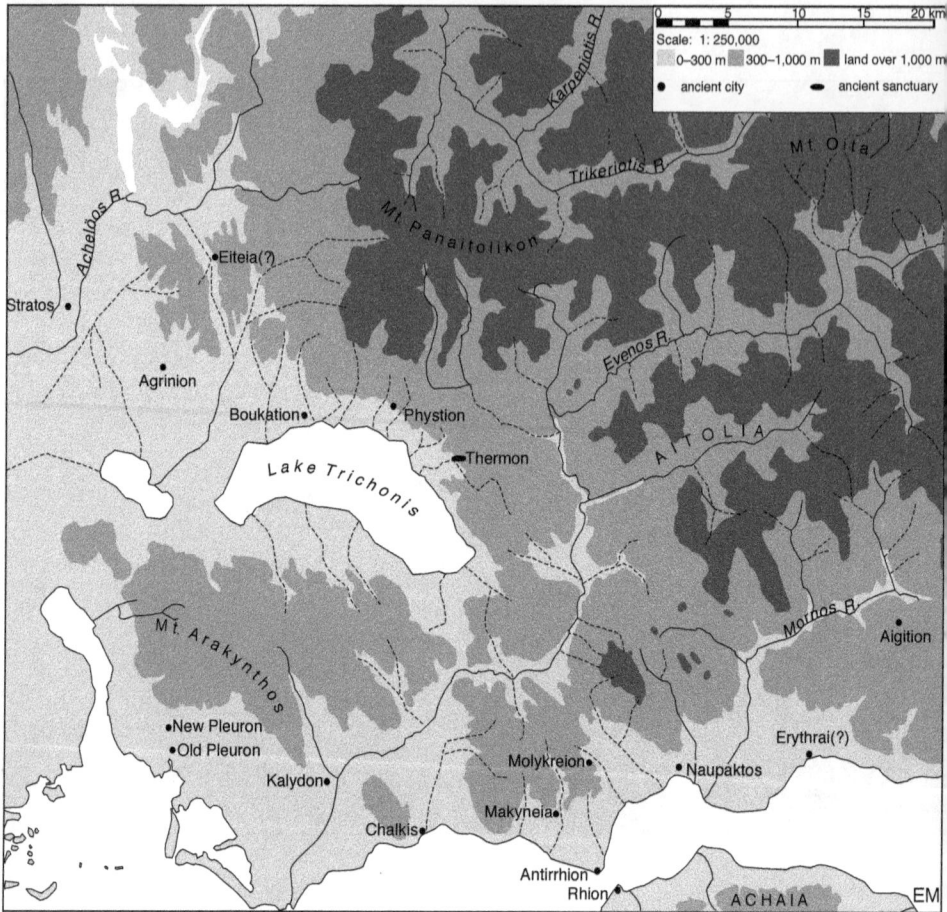

MAP 4. Aitolia in the classical and Hellenistic periods.

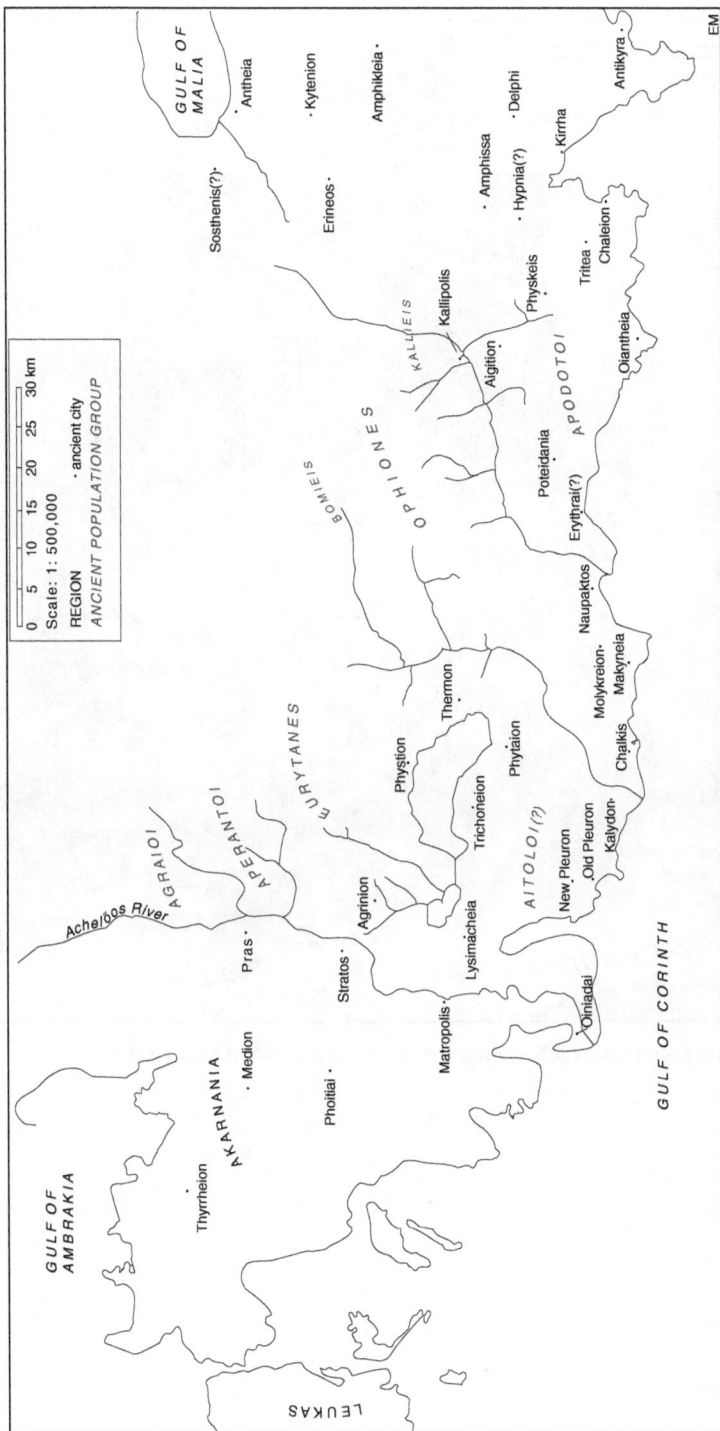

MAP 5. Aitolian population groups in the classical period.

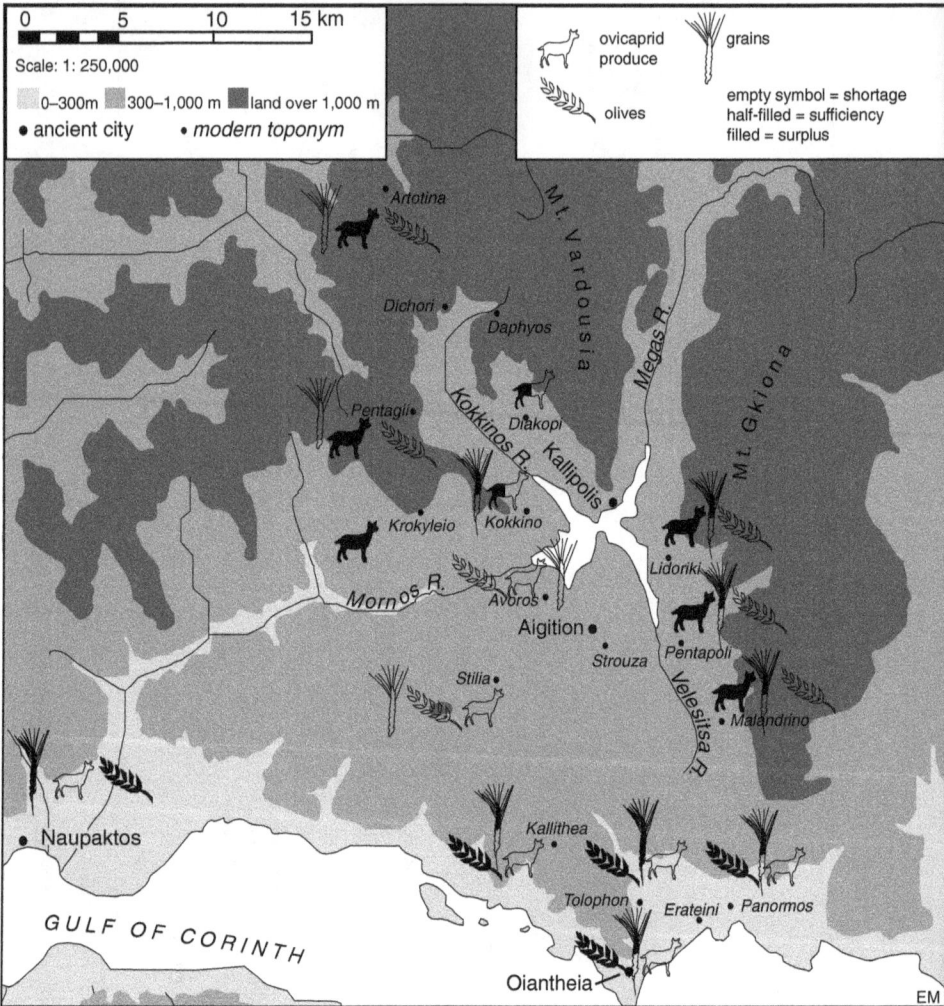

MAP 6. Resource complementarity in preindustrial modern eastern Aitolia, circa 1821–1940.

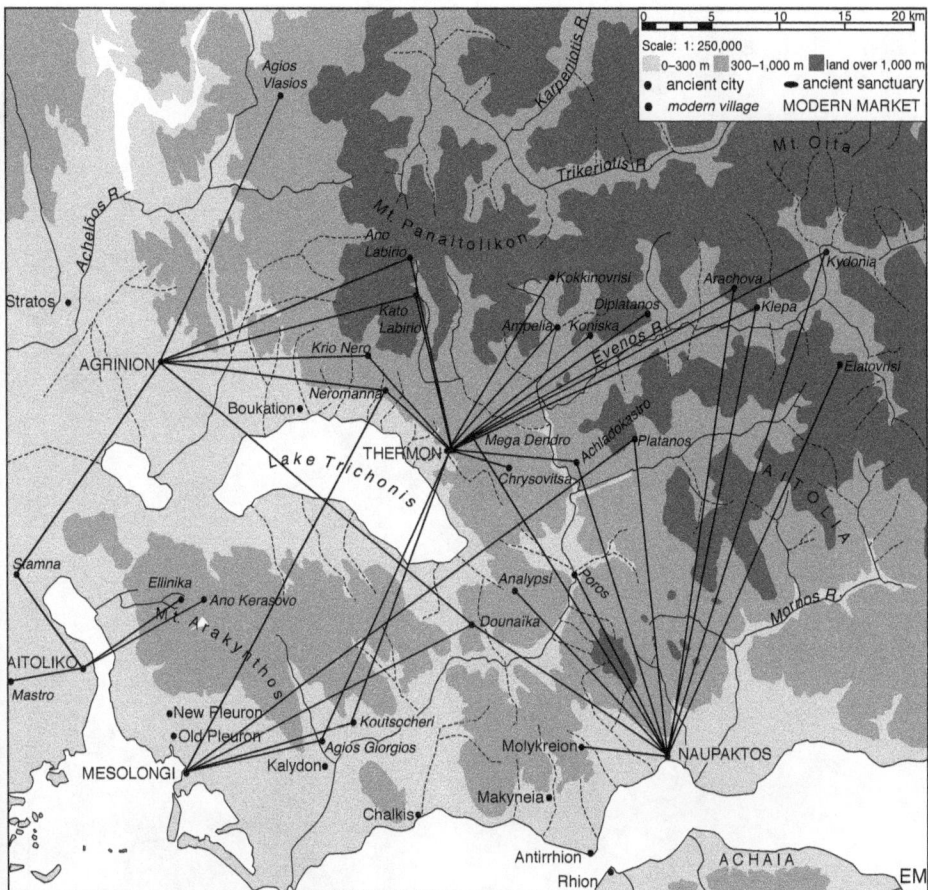

MAP 7. Market networks of preindustrial modern Aitolia, circa 1821–1940.

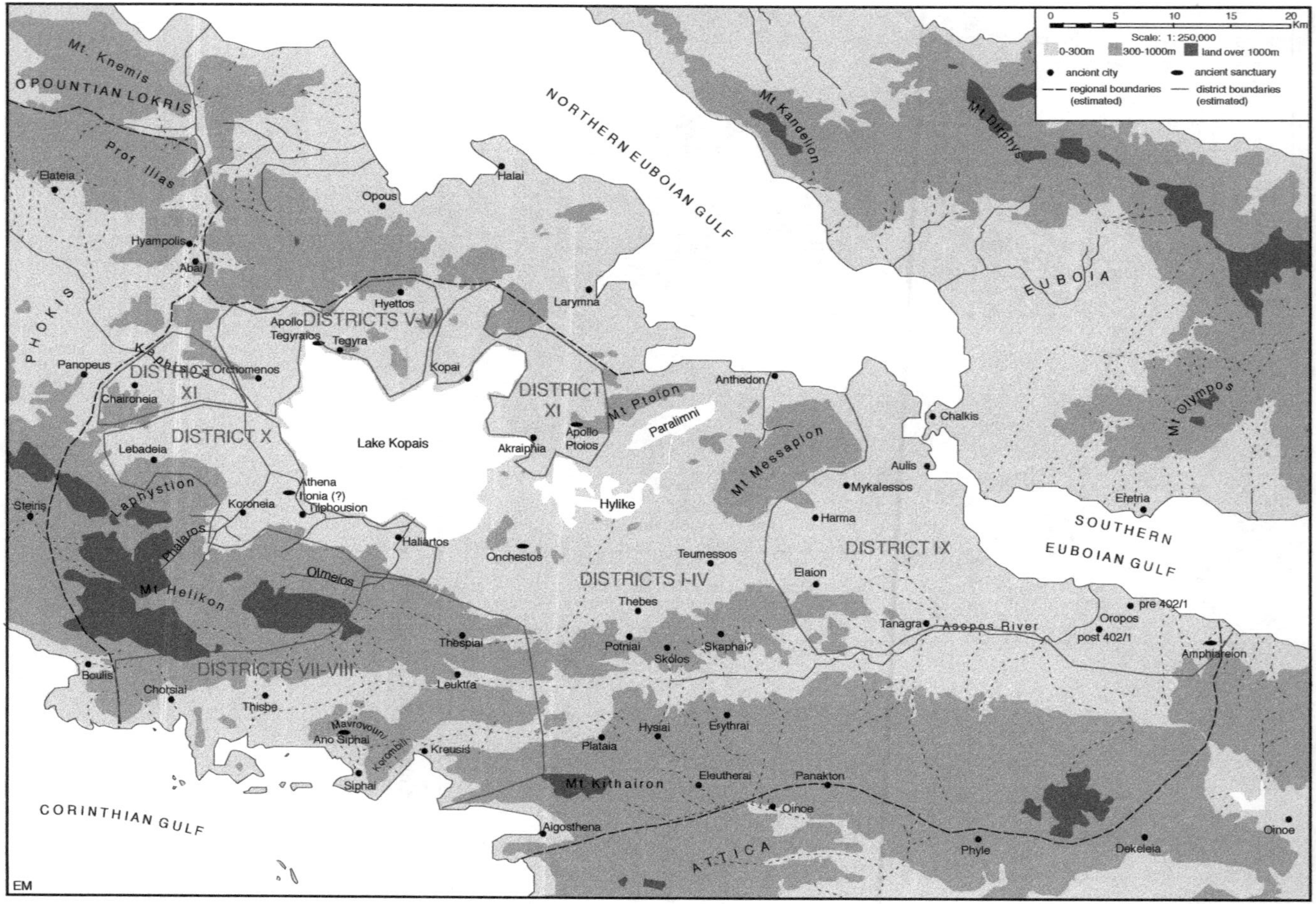

MAP 8. The Boiotian districts circa 395 BCE.

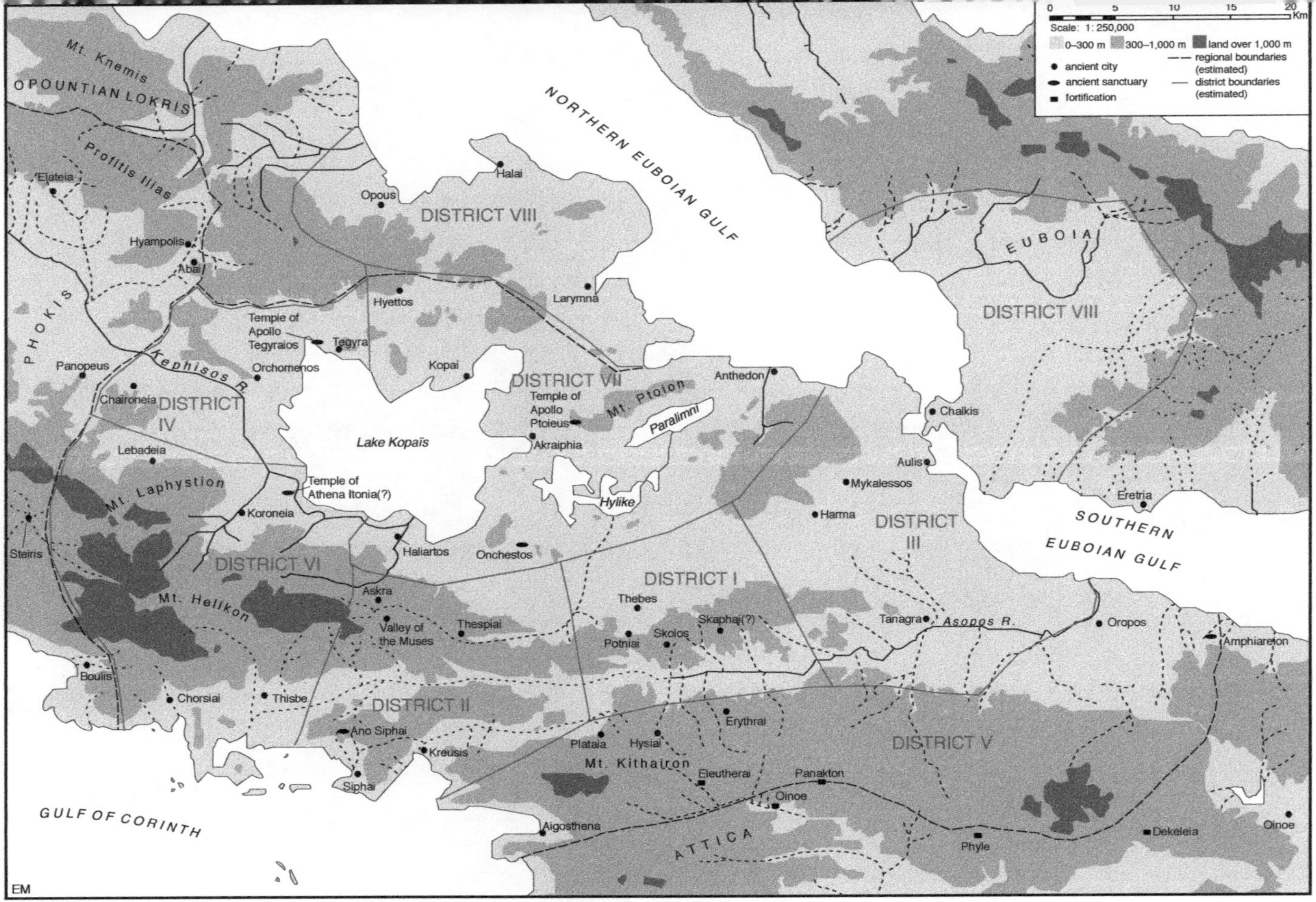

MAP 9. The Boiotian districts circa 287–171 BCE.

Introduction

Federal political structures, characterized by a division of sovereignty among multiple levels of government, have proved tremendously attractive in early modern and modern history for two basic reasons. First, their careful distribution of power gives them tremendous advantages for the governance of extremely large territories with disparate resources and highly localized economies; for this reason federalism has allowed the United States, Canada, and Australia to function successfully as single states.[1] Second, and more recently, the preservation of political entities below the national level has made them appealing to multiethnic states such as India, Belgium, and Spain; the ability to foster political cooperation and deliver public goods while nevertheless protecting the character, interests, and independence of different ethnic communities makes federalism a promising option for multiethnic states in transition.[2] And while federalism tends to be understood as a phenomenon of the modern world, it is widely recognized as having its origins in Greek antiquity.

Here, by the late fourth century, close to half the poleis of mainland Greece and the Peloponnese had become part of one federal state or another.[3] The scale of the

1. Riker 1987: 6–7.
2. G. Smith 1995; Stepan 1999; Kymlicka 2007. On the limitations of this approach see de Schutter 2011.
3. If we may use Hansen and Nielsen 2004 as a comprehensive list of poleis in existence by this period, 183 of the 456 poleis of mainland Greece and the Peloponnese (40%) certainly belonged to one koinon or another. This does not include poleis that were situated within regions where koina developed but whose participation is not clearly attested; in most cases their membership is likely, and if these cases were included, the total percentage would be in the range of 46–50 percent. Cf. Mackil 2012: 305–6. All dates are BCE unless otherwise noted.

1

phenomenon is truly remarkable. And yet we have no adequate understanding of why a federal political structure should have been so attractive to so many Greek communities. It is generally supposed that federalism arose among the small poleis of Greece as a means of achieving security that would otherwise have been unavailable to them against hostile neighbors and grew in the Hellenistic period as a defensive response to the volatile circumstances of this new world, providing an effective means for small poleis to deal with imperial superpowers.[4] While defense was certainly among the goods delivered by these states from the earliest stages and was indubitably one of the motives for poleis to cooperate with one another, this explanation on its own does not get us very far. For the Greeks had an admirable institution for the defensive (and offensive) military cooperation of states: the *symmachia* or military alliance. But the institutions that governed these states encompassed far more than the provision of defense, and the military-diplomatic explanation for their existence fails to account for numerous prominent features: their deep engagement in the religious practices of member communities and the region as a whole; their profound impact on the economic structures that influenced the welfare of their citizens, their constituent communities, and the entire region; and the extraordinarily fine-grained attention paid to the distribution of political powers throughout the state. Why, then, did so many Greek poleis find it so attractive to become part of a federal state in the classical and Hellenistic periods? And how do we account for the full range of these states' competencies and engagements as evidenced by the ancient sources?

STRATEGIES OLD AND NEW

This book is an attempt to answer the questions raised above. The scale of the phenomenon and the complexity of the evidence make the task a daunting one, and it is probably for this reason that no one has undertaken a systematic study of the subject, covering the whole of Greek antiquity, since 1968.[5] Instead, work has proceeded via focused studies of particular cases, often in particular periods.[6] While a

4. McInerney 1999: 156, 173–78 (Phokis, in response to Thessalian hostility); Lehmann 1983b (Boiotia, also in response to Thessalian hostility); Scholten 2000: 2 (Aitolia, in response to outside attacks from several quarters); F. W. Walbank 1976–77: 51; Roy 2003 (Hellenistic Achaia).

5. Larsen 1968, itself the first systematic approach to the subject since Freeman 1893. Beck 1997 provides a systematic analysis but does so largely case-by-case and limits his chronological scope to the fourth century. Note that a multiauthored volume attempting to update Larsen with fresh considerations of every federal state in Greek history is now in progress: Beck and Funke 2013.

6. E.g., Nottmeyer 1995a, b, Morgan and Hall 1996, Rizakis 2008b (Achaia); Funke 1985, Scholten 2000 (Aitolia); Schoch 1996, Dany 1999 (Akarnania); Nielsen 1996c (Arkadia); P. Salmon 1978, Buckler 1980b, R. J. Buck 1994 (Boiotia); Zahrnt 1971, Psoma 2001 (Chalkideis); Nielsen 2000 (Lokris); Behrwald 2000, Domingo Gygax 2001 (Lykia); McInerney 1999 (Phokis). The proceedings of several conferences on the topic, spurred by the emergence of the European Union, have also been published: Buraselis 1994; Aigner Foresti et al. 1994; Buraselis and Zoumboulakis 2003.

great deal of progress has thus been made on detailed and specific questions, this method produces scattered points of light while leaving the larger, pressing issues I have just outlined very much in the dark. The strategy adopted here is intended to blend the advantages of the analytic and synthetic approaches. While training my sights on the questions of the origins and true nature of the Greek federal state, I restrict my analysis to evidence from three regions: Achaia, in the northern Peloponnese; Aitolia, in western Greece; and Boiotia, in central mainland Greece (map 1).[7] These are the three best-attested instances, supported by rich literary, epigraphic, archaeological, and numismatic evidence. Federal institutions appear to have developed first in Boiotia, and this alone makes it a vital case for a larger study of how and why federalism emerged in the Greek world. These three were also the most powerful federal states to emerge in the classical period, and each for a time attained a leadership position within the wider Greek world. But they are also markedly different from one another. Urbanization and the entrenchment of statehood at the city scale, for example, occurred in Boiotia in the seventh and sixth centuries, while in Achaia and Aitolia it was a process of the fifth and fourth centuries.[8] The emergence of federal institutions in each region was the result of distinct sets of pressures and opportunities, and the economies of these three regions are highly differentiated. These three case studies provide rich but varied evidence for the adoption of similar (but not identical) political institutions that contributed—if it did not lead directly—to the achievement of hegemony in remarkably different geographical, economic, religious, and cultural contexts. The Boiotian, Achaian, and Aitolian koina also create a superregional cluster around the Gulf of Corinth; across and around its waters they interacted intensively, in both hostile and friendly contexts, and never more than in the Hellenistic period.[9] As such they yield an excellent set of data through which to examine the process by which federal institutions emerged, developed, and were maintained over time. This approach, in short, allows us to avoid overgeneralization while nevertheless pursuing the big questions that have proved so elusive. The conclusions I draw should not be assumed to apply to every koinon that was ever created in the Greek world, but I hope they may establish a set of questions that could profitably be applied to cases like the Lykian koinon, so rich in epigraphic evidence, or indeed the Thessalian koinon that was created near the end of the period I am studying.[10]

---

7. Sidelong glances will nevertheless be taken on occasion at other cases where the evidence is particularly rich or clear and seems for that reason to shed light on murkier hints in the evidence for our central case studies.

8. Bintliff 1999; Bintliff, Howard, and Snodgrass 2007; Morgan and Hall 1996; Petropoulos and Rizakis 1994; Funke 1987, 1991.

9. See Freitag 2000: 309–406 on the interactions and mobility facilitated by the Gulf of Corinth.

10. Graninger 2011 appeared too late for proper consultation.

I have thus far used the modern phrase "federal state" to refer to those states in which political power is distributed among at least two levels of government, but an unreflective application of the term to the Greek world has contributed to the deceptively narrow view of the topic that has prevailed in modern scholarship on the subject for so long. This is partly because we have no ancient analyses of the nature of a koinon to guide us, such as we have for democracy, oligarchy, and monarchy. If a few hints have been detected that there was some theoretical discussion about the koinon among Greek authors, most notably Aristotle and Polybios, these accounts have been lost, and we are left largely to fend for ourselves.[11] Whether implicitly or explicitly, ancient historians have fallen back on the assumption that ancient federal states are fundamentally like modern ones. They have, furthermore, been heavily influenced by what might be called the old institutionalist approach to modern federalism, marked by a preoccupation with the description of political institutions, which tend to be regarded as static entities. Thus the composition of assemblies and councils, the enumeration of magistracies, and the identification of meeting places and administrative calendars have remained the confining obsessions of the field.[12] And while political scientists studying modern federalism have expanded their approach to consider the impact of federal institutions on public economy, ancient historians have barely begun to take this cue.[13] There has also been a major transformation in the way that social scientists think about institutions in general, the development of the new institutionalism, which has wide-ranging implications for political historians; this will be addressed in detail below. The interest in federalism as a solution to the challenge of multiethnic nationalism in the modern world points

11. Larsen 1968: xi–xii and F. W. Walbank 1970a note the almost complete absence of federal theory. Lehmann 2000: 34–61 detects hints of a response to lost passages of Aristotle in lost passages of Polybios. Despite some expressions of enthusiasm about this "discovery" (Beck 2003: 188, "a quantum leap in the understanding of ancient perceptions of federalism"), it tells us nothing more than that the topic was on the agenda. It does not help us to understand what the Greeks thought a koinon really was. Cf. Funke 1998. The demonstration that particular ancient authors detected what we can see as fundamental political principles of the koinon, like the division of authority between polis and koinon, and the extension of the political power of a koinon by means of the integration of new member poleis (Beck 2001), is more productive.

12. Thus for many years the biggest debate about the Achaian federal state has been the composition of its assemblies: Aymard 1938; Larsen 1955: 165–88 and 1972; Giovannini 1969; F. W. Walbank 1957–79: III.406–14 and 1970b; O'Neil 1980; Lehmann 1983a: 251–61, 2000: 70–81. Similar efforts were expended on the Aitolian assemblies: Mitsos 1947; Larsen 1952. A recent preoccupation with the composition of the college of boiotarchs, the highest magistrates of the Boiotian federal state in the fourth century, shows that this focus persists: Knoepfler 1978: 379 and 2000; Buckler 1979 (reprinted in Buckler and Beck 2008: 87–98); Bakhuizen 1994; Beck 1997: 103.

13. Oates 1972, 1991, and 1999; Weingast 1995; Rodden 2007. Reger 1994: 165–66, 170, is exceptional in seeing the economic effects of an institution (the Koinon of the Islanders or Nesiotic League) that was created as a mechanism for political control.

to a fascinating potential for political institutions to address the desires of ethnic groups to retain their identities and deploy them in political contexts, an idea now being explored by ancient historians investigating the link between ethnic identity and political behavior in the ancient world. Although these developments have not yielded a systematic rethinking of the experience of federalism in the Greek world, there is progress, and ancient historians and political scientists studying federalism seem to be working along parallel lines that, in a Lobachevskian manner, intersect only at great distances. In one important respect, however, historical evidence points to a sphere of social action in which federal institutions were deeply embedded but that has drawn no attention from social scientists and little from ancient historians, namely religion. I shall return to this point.

We need to make room for ourselves to incorporate all the ancient evidence, to see the phenomenon for what it was rather than trying to fit it into a modern concept, and for this reason we should be cautious with our use of the word "federalism" and its cognates, deploying them only when there are truly clear and applicable parallels between modern federalism and ancient political structures. We should take our cue from the language of our sources, but the matter is (alas) not so simple, for the Greeks themselves had a variety of terms for this kind of state. By far the most common are *koinon, ethnos,* and the simple use of the plural ethnic of the citizen body, as for example "the Achaians" or "the Boiotians." Both *koinon,* a substantive adjective meaning "a common thing," and *ethnos* are nonspecific, being used for a variety of other things, and the semantic field of both words has been studied extensively.[14] In the Hellenistic period the Greeks' own political vocabulary expanded and became more technical, but even in the work of a writer such as Polybios, whose father was a high-ranking magistrate of the Achaian koinon and who was outstandingly well informed (if a little biased), we find an array of such words used almost interchangeably. Here we find not only *ethnos* and *koinon,* but also *koinōnia,* emphasizing the aspect of "community," and *sympoliteia,* conveying the sense of a shared state or a governing together; similar is *koinē politeia,* "a common polity," clearly an elaboration of the simpler, older *koinon.*[15] Polybios also refers to the

---

14. F. W. Walbank 1976–77: 29–32; Tréheux 1987; Sordi 1994: 4; C. P. Jones 1996; Lehmann 2000: 19–20; Bearzot 2001; Rzepka 2002; Vimercati 2003; Debord 2003. One of the more baffling uses of *ethnos* in an apparently political sense is Arist. *Pol.* 1261a27, a passage that has elicited a tremendous amount of inconclusive discussion (most recently Hansen 2000b; F. W. Walbank 2000: 21; Lehmann 2000: 35–36; Consolo Langher 2004: 316, with references to earlier work).

15. *Ethnos* and *koinōnia:* Polyb. 2.37.7–11, followed by the famous claim that the whole Peloponnese was united, as if in a single polis, by the shared institutions of the Achaians. *Sympoliteia:* Larsen 1968: 7–8 deemed this the only Greek word that properly describes a federal state but realized that it was a late development, appearing first in a Lykian inscription of the early second century (*SEG* 18.570) and in Polybios; recent work shows that it was not applied exclusively to federal contexts (Reger 2004). Giovannini 1971: 22–24; F. W. Walbank 1976–77: 32–35. *Koinē politeia:* Polyb. 2.50.8 (cf. Lehmann 2000: 35).

Achaian state as a "system," a word with organic, biological connotations, and an "ethnic standing together."[16] Most interesting of all, perhaps, is his single use of the phrase *polyeides politeuma*, "a constitution of many kinds."[17] We are left with the impression that here, as elsewhere, the Greeks themselves showed "a bold disregard for bureaucratic precision."[18] My solution has been to use the simple Greek word *koinon* throughout, primarily because this is the term that appears most frequently in the epigraphic sources for the regions that are the focus of this study. I use "federal" and its cognates only when it is absolutely clear that the ancient institutions and practices being discussed map closely onto the modern concept. This is a strategy of liberation, enabling consideration of the full range of ancient evidence pertaining to the phenomenon, without prejudicing the kinds of questions we should be asking or issues for which we should be looking.

This liberation has been indirectly facilitated by several important recent developments in ancient history. One is the argument that group identity among the Greeks, typically specified as ethnic identity, was socially constructed, not genetically determined, and that it was highly labile and negotiable, a discourse about the past that was heavily influenced by the present.[19] This set of ideas has been applied with great profit to specific case studies, including, in very different ways, the three regions that form the subject of this book.[20] The implications for the study of the koinon are significant. First, insofar as the construction of a shared identity functioned as a powerful mechanism for the integration of people into a single group, it is reasonable to expect that it played a role in encouraging poleis to participate in a koinon. Second, by demonstrating that claims of kinship and ethnic identity are socially constructed, not biologically determined, this set of ideas powerfully refutes the claim that federal states developed directly from tribal states, that the people who eventually participated in a single koinon did so because they belonged to a single population group that occupied, whether natively or by migration, a particular territory.[21] Although anthropologists discredited the tribal concept a generation ago, it has been the recent work on ethnic identity as a social construct that has caused historians of the koinon to rethink the process by which

16. *Systēma*: Polyb. 2.41.15, 9.28.2; cf. Str. 8.3.2, 14.2.25. Biological use: Arist. *Gen.An.* 740a20. *Ethnikē systasis*: Polyb. 30.13.6.

17. Polyb. 23.12.8. The phrase here seems to allude to the many communities of which the Achaian (or any other) koinon is composed. Cf. F. W. Walbank 1957–79: III.242.

18. R. Parker 2009: 187 on synoikism and sympolity.

19. Morgan 1991, 2003; J.M. Hall 1997, 2002; McInerney 1999; Malkin 2001; Derks and Roymans 2009.

20. Roussel 1976 is an early move in this direction, focused on the *genē*, phratries, and *phylai* of Attica but incorporating material from other poleis. Achaia: Morgan and Hall 1996; Morgan 2002. Aitolia: Antonetti 1987a, 1990; Antonetti and Cavalli 2004. Boiotia: Larson 2007; Kühr 2006a, b.

21. Larsen 1968: 3–7, 28, 40–42, etc.; Koerner 1974: 476; Grainger 1999: 29.

such identities emerged and were articulated, while the term "tribal state" continues to be applied to entities that appear to have state powers but are organized
along the lines of an ethnic group rather than a polis or a koinon.[22]

While these are undoubtedly important gains, the ethnicity approach still
leaves the wide gulf between the articulation of an ethnic identity and the formation of the institutions peculiar to the koinon completely unbridged.[23] A sense of
group identity will certainly have contributed to a sentiment of belonging and
perhaps enhanced a community's basic willingness to participate in a larger state
that would incorporate all members of that group. And its promulgation will certainly have assisted the leaders of a koinon in making claims about the legitimacy
of regional power structures that were either new or had come under attack once
established. These are themes we shall explore. But the emergence of group identity does not on its own explain why that group should become politicized, should
decide to create a particular set of political institutions or agree to proposals to that
effect. Nor does ethnic identity explain the shape of those political institutions or
their reach. We are left wondering, for example, how and why political powers
were so carefully divided among the member poleis and the koinon. There is in
this basic fact a need, or a desire, to distinguish poleis from the koinon, the local
from the regional group, even as the ethnic and the political groups have become
coextensive. And if a sense of identity somehow fostered the creation of regional
political institutions, then how do we explain the integration of communities
beyond the ethnic group into these states? The remarkable role of the koinon in
fostering and protecting a regional economy (a badly understudied phenomenon
that will be explored in depth in chapter 5) is likewise inexplicable from the perspective of ethnic identity.[24] These are only examples to illustrate the broader point

22. The tribal concept was discredited by anthropologists in the 1960s and 1970s as inherently
linked with a deeply flawed teleological view of the development of political organization and as neither logically nor theoretically necessary to bridge the gap between local settlement and larger-scale
power structures like nation-states and confederations: Fried 1968, 1975; Southall 1969, 1996. Persistence of tribal state (or *Stammstaat*) in this adjusted sense: Funke 1993; Freitag, Funke, and Moustakis
2004: 379 (Aitolia); Nielsen 1996b and 1997; Nielsen and Roy 1998 (Arkadia). Many scholars (above all
Morgan 2003) now prefer to use the Greek *ethnos*, which avoids the inevitable connotations of primi-
tiveness; cf. Archibald 2000; Davies 2000; Morgan 2000b. Cf. Yoffee 2005, who in a similar vein
exposes the problems with putative "chiefdoms" and their place in early state formation, rejecting the
argument that they were an early evolutionary stage and showing instead that they represent an alternative trajectory.

23. Beck 2003: 179–83, despite his enthusiasm for the work of the ethnicity school, notes (p. 182)
how much it leaves unanswered.

24. A. D. Smith, whose work heavily influenced that of Hall and others on ethnic identity in the
Greek world, after defining six criteria of an ethnic group (his *ethnie*), notes that economic unity, common legal rights, and a common polity are not among them (A. D. Smith 1986: 86).

that while the construction and articulation of ethnic identity certainly contributed to the process of koinon formation, it does not on its own explain that phenomenon.

The Greeks had other ways of grouping communities together, which had more to do with power than with a sense of belonging, and this brings us to a second development in ancient history that has indirectly facilitated the approach to the koinon developed in this book. The ability of one polis to subordinate another to its control resulted in the frequent creation of complex political entities that incorporated multiple poleis but never became more than a polis, a city-state. It has always been clear that becoming a member of a koinon significantly restricted a community's ability to determine its own laws, and whether or not *autonomia* was a formal juridical status of a polis, in modern terms it is clear that this meant a loss of partial autonomy.[25] This fact, combined with the orthodox principle that absolute autonomy was a central value of the polis, has always made the phenomenon of federalism in the Greek world seem particularly strange.[26] But recent work has shown that Greek poleis were quite frequently in positions of dependence and subordination to other poleis; becoming part of a koinon was only one way in which this happened.[27] If this work on the dependent polis changes the perspective from which we view the koinon, it still does not explain the phenomenon. Instead, it invites us to consider in detail the ways in which political power was distributed among member communities and the koinon and the processes by which such arrangements were produced. Were they the result of coercion, or of cooperation? And what role was played by the sense of belonging that stemmed from a shared identity?

If these major changes in our understanding of the Greek world have raised new questions and invited fresh perspectives on the development and nature of the koinon, so too has the discovery of a considerable amount of new evidence. Most of it is epigraphic. New inscriptions have been found and recently published that shed

---

25. The restrictions placed on poleis by membership in a koinon appear to have been much weaker for the Cretan koinon, which in many ways differs from the koina of mainland Greece and the Peloponnese studied here; see Ager 1994. For autonomy as a term in political discourse, not a definable juridical status: Ostwald 1982: 41–46; Raaflaub 2004: 147–60. Autonomy as a formal juridical status: Hansen 1995a: 34–39, 1995b, and 1997b; Hansen 1996 *contra* Keen 1996; Hansen and Nielsen 2004: 87–94. Beck 2003: 184 (cf. Beck 1997: 235–49) suggests that these views can be reconciled, with the result that "federalism and polis-autonomy were compatible." The debate then becomes one about the meaning of *autonomia*. My concern is to explain why so many poleis in the Greek world became willing to give up their ability to control certain aspects of their political lives, like determining foreign policy; whether this should be called *autonomia* or not is immaterial.

26. For autonomy as fundamental: Jehne 1994.

27. Hansen 1997b; Hansen and Nielsen 2004: 87–94 list fifteen different conditions under which a polis became dependent or nonautonomous.

light on each of the koina that form the core of this study. Texts discovered long ago but published in obscure and inaccessible journals and books are also beginning to receive fresh attention from scholars. Because of their detailed archival quality—their recording of the internal workings of koina that are rarely exposed by literary sources—these texts are of tremendous importance and provide clues that enable a complete reevaluation of the koinon as a phenomenon. And although archaeological evidence rarely exposes anything about institutional arrangements, new discoveries have significantly affected our understanding of the relationship between settlement patterns and the emergence of regional political structures. All this must be taken into account. The subject is ripe for fresh consideration.

There are two major questions before us: How did the koinon develop? And why did so many poleis become part of a koinon? They are, I suggest, best answered in tandem. The obvious way to approach the first question is simply to trawl through the ancient sources looking for evidence of political or military cooperation among communities in a region later known to have formed a koinon. The results of such an approach are, however, disappointing, not only because the sources make it impossible to determine what kind of political institutions lie behind such cooperative acts.[28] They are disappointing also because the approach works on the assumption that the koinon was a purely political entity that governed the joint military undertakings of its member communities; but the explicit evidence for the koinon in later years, when its institutions were fully developed, suggests that the koinon was much more than that, and we should entertain the possibility that it was also more complex from the beginning. This is where we return to the relationship between religion and the koinon. In Boiotia, Achaia, and Aitolia, we have clear evidence that sanctuaries served as archives for the koinon, repositories of its decrees, and frequently as meeting places for its deliberative assemblies. This is well known.[29] We also have evidence, less familiar, that these states themselves made dedications, in at least two cases extending the pervasive political strategy of representation into the sphere of ritual action, and seeking in religious practices both the legitimation and the protection of their institutional arrangements. Other evidence points to an engagement by the koinon in facilitating regional exchange and promoting a unified regional economy. These are hints that we should not be looking only for political and military cooperation, perhaps undergirded by myths promulgating a claim of ethnic unity. We should rather be asking how far back we can trace the evidence for interactions of all kinds—religious, economic, social, and political—among communities that later became part of a koinon. If we can detect

---

28. E.g., Larsen 1953, citing Th. 1.111.2–3, Diod. Sic. 11.85, and Plut. *Per.* 19, recording the participation of the Achaians in Perikles' expedition against Akarnanian Oiniadai in 455.

29. See R. Parker 1998, esp. 27–33.

this evidence prior to or coincident with early political and military cooperation and the emergence of the formal institutions of the koinon, then we shall have good reason to hypothesize that such interactions contributed significantly to the willingness of independent communities to become part of a larger state. But all hypotheses need to be tested, and the only way to do so in this case is to ask whether, on purely theoretical grounds, it would make sense for a state with an essentially federal character to have its origins in shared religious and economic interactions as well as a need or a desire to develop greater military strength. What, in other words, could religious and economic interactions between communities have done to encourage the formation of political institutions of a federal kind, and why should the state, having developed those institutions, have had an interest in becoming directly involved in regulating those interactions, whether by reinforcing them, shutting them down, or repatterning them?

Tracking the totality of interactions between communities prior to the emergence of the formal institutions of the koinon, analyzing their function and impact, and then asking how the koinon as an emergent state responded to that history of interactions is one productive way to proceed. But in order to understand why, we need to pause to think carefully about the nature of institutions and how they emerge and develop over time.

INSTITUTIONS

The emergence of formal institutions is tremendously complex, a process that is particularly difficult to understand when, as in the case of the Greek koinon, we have no direct account of it. The very complexity and precision of these institutions in their fully developed state belie the possibility that they developed in an entirely accidental and ad hoc manner. To take only the most obvious example, around the turn of the fourth century the Boiotian koinon was governed by a council, to which representatives were sent by districts. These districts were composed in such a way that they had roughly equal populations, and they formed the basis for the appointment of judges to Boiotian courts, the payment of taxes, and the provision of manpower to the Boiotian army.[30] This arrangement can only be the outcome of a deliberate and probably difficult process involving high-level planning by magistrates and political leaders as well as negotiation between the poleis and the koinon.[31] Yet there are good reasons to think that these institutions were rooted in a history of cooperative interactions and arrangements—indeed,

30. *Hell.Oxy.* 16.3–4 (Bartoletti).
31. Cf. Murray 1990: 10–11 for the view that the institutions of the polis were a product of the rational and self-conscious recognition of the reasons for change and the consequences of reform, not a "jumble of traditional practices."

that they could only have emerged from that history. In order to explain why, we need to dwell momentarily on the nature of institutions more generally and the processes by which they emerge and evolve.

Institutions are typically, and are certainly in our case, endogenous to the society that uses them. Where the old institutionalism treated institutions as static entities that affected outcomes, scholars working in the field of the new institutionalism have shown that they are highly dynamic, humanly devised constraints that structure and pattern social interactions of all kinds.[32] Sociologists have shown that institutions reflect the assimilation of cultural norms and practices into organizations of all kinds, including states; they are, in other words, socially embedded.[33] The economist Douglass North has argued that institutions are created by actors in order to guide or constrain human action, to secure the cooperation of others in collective action, and to reduce the inefficiencies (or transaction costs) that would ensue if they were to attempt a particular activity without such an institution.[34] Once created, on this view, institutions tend to structure individual behavior and are conceived as "the rules of the game in a society or, more formally, ... the humanly devised constraints that shape human interaction."[35] They are analyzed primarily as structural elements in society, and institutional development is rarely given another look.[36] While the idea that institutions are imposed from the outside, or from the top down, captures something of the process that must have lain behind the remarkably refined arrangements just described for Boiotia, in a political context such as the one that is our central concern it is difficult to accept the power implications of this claim. For actors to impose institutions that will govern the actions of others, they must either use (or have) overwhelming force, or they must secure the consent of others. But if they can secure the consent of others, should we not expect that those others would want to have a significant role in shaping the institutions? In a political context, in other words, institutions are more likely to be exogenous in imperial situations than in contexts of endogenous state formation.

One of the most intriguing facets of the process of state formation is the emergence of formal institutions from a situation in which there was no universally recognized system for the distribution of power or the resolution of disputes—

32. This demonstration has been approached from several different perspectives; see P. A. Hall and Taylor 1996.

33. J. W. Meyer and Rowan 1977; J. W. Meyer and Scott 1983; DiMaggio and Powell 1991: 1–40. Socially embedded: Parsons 1990 (a paper originally written ca. 1934–35 but published for the first time only in 1990); Williamson 1975; Granovetter 1985.

34. North 1990; cf. Williamson 1975.

35. North 1990: 1.

36. Cf. Thelen 2003: 208.

only competing individuals and, in the case of the koinon, competing poleis inter-acting in a world governed by norms but not laws.[37] In similar circumstances in the medieval Mediterranean, it has been shown that formal institutions emerged from arrangements made by merchant guilds, nonstate agents, to enforce con-tracts in the absence of state legal provisions. These institutions laid the framework for later economic growth.[38] And the conception of institutions as rules cannot account for this phenomenon, for it assumes that the state has a monopoly on coercive power and can enforce its rules. But the very ability for a state to do this can only be seen as an outcome of institutional development.[39]

In an important recent book, the economist and historian Avner Greif has pro-posed an alternative approach to institutions that lends itself extremely well to the problem of institutional dynamics—the emergence and change of institutions over time—as well as to thinking about how institutions affect the behavior of groups, not just of individuals. Greif defines institutions as systems "of rules, beliefs, norms, and organizations that together generate a regularity of (social) behavior."[40] This definition incorporates both informal (rules, beliefs, and norms) and formal (organizations) institutions under the central fact that they all contribute to producing regular behavior, eliciting predictable responses and choices from indi-viduals and groups. The claim that rules, beliefs, and norms play a role in generat-ing regular behavior is superficially obvious, but the role of such informal institutional elements is largely ignored by most economists and political scien-tists, which is why institutional dynamics have been so difficult to understand. But if we see these institutional elements as contributing to the regularity of behavior, then we can see individual actions and the social and political conditions to which they respond as being recursively related and mutually constitutive.[41] And this allows us in turn to see how institutions emerge gradually and endogenously. Change occurs when old institutions become inadequate, whether because of endogenous or exogenous factors. Yet those old institutions have a powerful effect on the direction of institutional change, for they provide "a cognitive frame-work, information, normative guidance, and a way to anticipate what others may do to coordinate their behavior with their responses."[42] Change tends thus to be

---

37. On the fundamental condition of interstate anarchy in classical Greece see A. M. Eckstein 2006: 37–78. On norms governing interactions between poleis see Sheets 1994; Chaniotis 2004.

38. Greif 1989, 1993; Greif, Milgrom, and Weingast 1994.

39. See Greif 2006: 8–9.

40. Greif 2006: 30.

41. Greif 2006: 187–216. In this way the model expands upon Giddens's structuration theory (Giddens 1984), the idea that agent and social structure are recursively related to each other, individual actions contributing to social structure while that structure in turn guides individual actions.

42. Greif 2006: 190.

incremental; the rootedness of institutions in the past, the way in which they are internalized by individuals such that they affect their understanding of the world, makes comprehensive, wholesale institutional change difficult and rare. Refinement will always be preferred to revolution.[43] For this reason institutions are path-dependent and sticky.[44] And the farther one travels along a particular path, the more attractive that path becomes relative to others, and the more costly it becomes to turn in another direction.[45] But revolution—wholesale change—can occur when crises reveal the complete deficiency of old institutions, and when it does the path ramifies; such moments are critical junctures.[46]

AN EXAMPLE

Let me return from theory to history and offer one example (undocumented and undetailed for now) that anticipates the argument sustained over the course of this book. The belief that the Boiotians were a distinct population group contributed to a norm of cooperation, despite significant competition, among the many communities that comprised this group in the archaic period. This belief was promulgated above all by myths and by rituals that enacted those myths in sanctuaries common to all Boiotians. The norm of cooperation in turn facilitated exchange between individuals from different Boiotian communities, despite the lack of any formal means of enforcing contracts or recourse in the event of goods being stolen or buyers or sellers being cheated. In the late sixth century exchange between Boiotian communities was facilitated by the production of a cooperative coinage, a coinage produced by multiple poleis on the same weight standard with a common type, again despite the lack of a state encompassing all these communities that could have demanded their cooperation in this matter or simply issued the coins itself. The norm of cooperation was reinforced by the same religious interactions that generated it as well as by the interactions and cooperation of individuals and communities in the economic sphere; it also contributed to military cooperation. Despite all this cooperation, the Boiotian communities were distinct state entities; they were poleis with their own laws, magistracies, and identities, although the details of these are rarely evident to us for the archaic period. And this fundamental fact strongly influenced the way in which the Boiotians cooperated; entrenched

43. Greif 2006: 194–99.
44. The concept of path dependence is drawn from evolutionary biology; see Gould 1985: 53. For its application to political and social life see Krasner 1988: 66; North 1990: 92–104; Levi 1997: 28; Pierson 2000.
45. This phenomenon is sometimes described as a process of increasing returns: Arthur 1994; Pierson 2000: 253–57.
46. Pierson 2000: 251. Cf. Pierson and Skocpol 2002; Thelen 2003.

polis interests made the possibility of a unified Boiotian state, or the political syn-oikism of all the Boiotian communities into a single polis on the Attic model, highly unlikely. Thus we find resistance to early proposals that communities should contribute to the Boiotians.

An exogenous shock exposed the profound deficiencies of the Boiotians' loose cooperative institutions: the region was conquered by the Athenians in 457, and at least some of its communities appear to have been subjected to tribute payment. At this critical juncture, it became apparent that the costs of developing new insti-tutions to strengthen the ties between Boiotian communities, to regularize their old habits of cooperation, and to prevent departures from these habits were less than the cost of attempting to operate in the old ways despite the dramatically changed environment. When the Athenians were expelled from the region a dec-ade later, the Boiotians developed a new set of institutions that regularized their cooperation. A new political entity, the koinon, was created that incorporated the old poleis. The poleis persisted as both states and social entities, but some of their powers were shifted to the koinon, which was governed by representatives of the poleis. Although this was a wholesale innovation, rather than an incremental change, the path was still influenced by the old institutions. Religion had always been a context for interaction, and it was by means of an essentially religious dis-course that the Boiotians had articulated their group identity; as a result, the new koinon quickly made itself a part of the religious life of Boiotia and availed itself of the power of religious ritual to integrate and legitimate. At the same time it used its powers to strengthen and facilitate old patterns of economic interaction that had occurred spontaneously but at some risk when there was no state entity to govern and protect exchange between individuals of different states. As the evidence becomes richer and more detailed over the course of the classical and Hellenistic periods, we see the Boiotian koinon investing its authority in these spheres of behavior in complex and fascinating ways. The biggest innovation, of course, lay in the way that public decisions were made, above all relating to the conduct of inter-state relations, diplomacy, and warfare. But the political innovation, the creation of what we can recognize as federal institutions, occurred against a backdrop of spontaneous cooperation and competition, frequent religious and economic inter-actions. It is for this reason that the koinon in Boiotia was never a narrowly politi-cal phenomenon: this was a state with a deep engagement in the religious and economic lives of its citizens and member communities.

This critical juncture of the mid-fifth century determined the path on which the Boiotians traveled for the rest of their independent political existence. There were incremental adjustments and refinements to the set of institutions established in this period, which accommodated both exogenous and endogenous change over the course of the fourth century and the early Hellenistic period. But the Boiotians had constructed their political reality as one in which poleis would retain local autonomy and an institutional presence in the direction of public affairs at the regional level, while the koinon would direct interstate relations and commit itself to protecting not only the political but also the religious and economic unity of the region. The process can be seen overall as one in which the behavior of individual agents generated norms of cooperation that became inadequate in the challenging political climate of fifth-century mainland Greece and were for that reason formalized in an innovative set of political, economic, and religious institutions. The behavior guided by these formal institutions recursively encouraged cooperation rather than competition among the Boiotian poleis.

Studying the institutional dynamics of the koinon, as revealed by a comprehensive analysis of the interactions of the communities that became its member poleis, reveals a great deal about how the koinon emerged and developed over time and about why being a member of a koinon was so attractive to so many poleis in the Greek world. Along the way, it exposes the koinon as a much more complex entity than previous studies have suggested: far from serving a narrowly political and military purpose, the koinon was a religious and an economic institution as well— a reality that was social as much as it was political. It is in this sense that the federal label is misleading, for it captures a part of the reality but misses the rest.

A ROAD MAP

All this needs to be explored and documented in detail, and in order to make any claims about koina in general the process needs to be examined in several other regions as well. The book is divided into two parts. Part I (chapters 1–3) provides a historical narrative of the development of the koinon in Boiotia, Aitolia, and Achaia. Widespread familiarity with the history of political cooperation in central Greece and the northern Peloponnese tends to be limited to one or two of several notorious periods: the so-called Theban hegemony of 371–362; and the wars of the Achaian and Aitolian koina with the Romans from the late third to the mid-second century BCE. Yet the internal histories of political cooperation in mainland Greece, and the relationship between those internal developments and the interstate relations that are the subject of the familiar grand narratives, have received less attention. Chapters 1–3 therefore present a narrative overview of the emergence and development of political cooperation that transcended polis boundaries and assumed the formal apparatus of a koinon, providing an historical context for the analysis and explanation of these developments in Part II.

Building on this narrative framework, Part II concentrates on exposing patterns and explaining them, isolating the religious (chapter 4), economic (chapter 5), and political (chapter 6) factors that contributed to an initial willingness to forge and participate in a koinon and that then went on to shape the nature of that state over time. These categories are in some ways artificial: they represent a strategy for breaking the problem up into manageable and intelligible pieces. But they have also been isolated in separate chapters because the ways in which interactions in these different spheres affected member communities and the koinon itself are qualitatively different. It is not enough simply to point, for example, to the presence of economic interactions between poleis prior to the emergence of koinon institutions, or to the engagement of the koinon in the management of a regional economy. We need to ask how and why such interactions would have facilitated the integration of member poleis while simultaneously requiring the maintenance of their identity as distinct states. We need to ask whether, why, and under what circumstances it would have been economically advantageous for poleis to become members of a koinon, and we need to understand how predatory or benevolent the koinon was with respect to the resources of its member poleis. Only then will we begin to answer our twin questions: How did the koinon develop, and why was it so attractive to so many Greek poleis? There are different questions to be asked about religion, economics, and politics. Their treatment in separate chapters facilitates the isolation of different factors that contributed to the larger phenomenon at the heart of this book. These threads are drawn together in the conclusion.

The arguments advanced in this book rely heavily on the evidence of inscriptions from areas of the Greek world that have not in recent years received sustained attention from epigraphers and historians. The fragmentary condition of many of the stones on which these documents are inscribed makes analysis of their content difficult; historical arguments based on such sources will be only as compelling as the readings of the documents are careful. Nor have these sources ever been collected in one place, although they are vital for our understanding of the koinon. For these reasons the epigraphic texts that are of central importance to the study of the koinon in Boiotia, Achaia, and Aitolia are gathered together in the epigraphical dossier comprised in the appendix. Throughout the book, references are made to texts in the dossier with the simple notation T (Text) and the number. (E.g., T23 indicates Text 23 in the dossier.)

The dossier does not make any pretensions to comprehensiveness. The selection is certainly idiosyncratic, reflecting those practices and institutions that seem to me most important for a full and nuanced understanding of both the nature of the Greek koinon and its developmental trajectory over the course of the archaic, classical, and Hellenistic periods. It is also selective in its geographical focus: excluding interesting and comparable texts from Lokris, Thessaly, and the Chalkidike, among other regions, in favor of a fairly representative collection of relevant documents from the three koina that form the focus of this study and that also happen to provide us with the richest epigraphic evidence. Nor have I attempted to place in the dossier every epigraphic source I discuss in the body of the book, but I have rather limited inclusion to those texts that are particularly important and revealing; or pose challenges of interpretation that require detailed discussion of issues that may be ancillary to the main argument and are therefore relegated to the commentary on the text in the dossier; or else are of such significance on a variety of issues that they are discussed at some length in several different places in the main body of the book. It is hoped that readers with a particular interest in the epigraphic evidence that is so central to this study will find in the dossier the technical and bibliographic details they seek, while more general readers and those interested in the larger argument will profit from a text relatively unencumbered by such technical details.

PART ONE

Cooperation, Competition, and Coercion

A Narrative History

1

The Archaic Period
and the Fifth Century

Signs of cooperation among communities within particular regions appear at different moments in the archaic and early classical periods. Across regions, however, evidence for an emergent group identity, articulated around descent from a common ancestor and the occupation of a shared territory, tends to precede evidence for active cooperation among communities. While this similarity is highly significant for our understanding of how the koinon developed, divergences in other respects command our attention. The process of urbanization that is a central part of polis development occurred differently in each of the three regions that form the core of this study, and this development appears to be correlated to the emergence of cooperation among communities, accounting at least in part for the distinct developmental trajectories we can trace in each region. We have glimmers of evidence for an active sense of group identity and for conflict as well as cooperation among the early-developing poleis of Boiotia in the archaic period. But in Achaia and Aitolia these are largely developments of the fifth century, during which time the Boiotians develop a sophisticated set of formal state institutions at the regional scale, incorporating established poleis as members of a koinon. Similar institutions appear in Achaia and Aitolia only in the fourth century, although there is much less evidence for these areas, and we can trace the process with considerably less detail than is possible for Boiotia. As a result, each region will be treated separately in the first chapter. It is only in the fourth century, the subject of chapter 2, that the histories of the mainland Greek koina can be integrated into a more coherent narrative.

BOIOTIA

Despite some evidence for an emerging Boiotian identity that comprised the region's many poleis as early as the eighth century (map 2), relations between those poleis were characterized as much by competition as by cooperation.[1] We shall see that both forms of engagement contributed to the development in the classical period of political institutions at the scale not of the single polis but of the region.

In the late eighth century a hierarchy of communities seems to have emerged, partially at least through the absorption and subordination of smaller communities.[2] This process is evident in Hesiod's *Works and Days*, which represents the village (*kōmē*) of Askra as being in some way subordinate to a larger polis, typically assumed to be Thespiai. All we can learn of the nature of this subordinate relationship from the poem is that judges in the polis had, or claimed, the authority to resolve disputes arising in the village.[3] If the polis alluded to by Hesiod was in fact Thespiai, it is likely that the subordination of Askra was accomplished by coercion rather than cooperation, for both Plutarch and Aristotle report the slaughter of its inhabitants by the Thespians sometime after the death of Hesiod.[4]

Whether it was by the absorption of smaller communities or other means, by the early sixth century the Thebans had enough strength to begin making claims to regional leadership. The *Shield of Herakles*, preserved among the manuscripts of Hesiod, provides good evidence for these claims. The last eight lines of the poem contain an allusion to the so-called First Sacred War, meaning that it must have reached the form in which we know it only after about 590.[5] Although details of the conflict are irretrievably lost and the literary sources for it reflect later

---

1. Hom. *Il.* 2.494–511, discussed in detail by Larson 2007: 32–40, with references to earlier literature.

2. Bintliff 1994 (cf. Bintliff 2002: 212) speculates that this hierarchy of settlements emerged out of a desire to create territories capable of supplying the needs of the largest settlement (or central place). There is much to recommend this view, but it is predicated on the assumption that such "central places" were virtually autarkic and had little interaction with the world beyond their territories, which does not fit with the fuller evidence from later periods in Boiotian history. See below, pp. 267–73.

3. Thespiai is not mentioned in Hes. *Op.*, but Σ Hes. *Op.* 631, citing both Aristotle and Plutarch, claims that the inhabitants of Askra were driven out by Thespiai after the death of Hesiod, so the inference is not unsound. Askra as *kōmē*: see *Op.* 639–40. Judges in the polis: *Op.* 37–41, 219–24. On the legal dispute see Gagarin 1974. On the relationship of Askra and Thespiai see Bintliff 1996: 197; Tandy 1997: 203–27; A. T. Edwards 2004: 166–73.

4. Σ Hes. *Op.* 631 with A. T. Edwards 2004: 171–72.

5. Hesiodic authorship, already questioned by Aristophanes of Byzantion (Hypothesis A line 2 of *Aspis*), has been rejected on linguistic grounds: McGregor 1976: 196–97; cf. Shapiro 1984a: 38. Cf. Hammond 1986: 155–56. Date: M. L. West 1985: 136; Shapiro 1984a: 40–47 *contra* Guillon 1963: 18–19; cf. Ducat 1964: 286; Jeffery 1976: 74–75. The poem as we have it is a complete whole; the final lines are not a late addition: Janko 1986: 38–40; R. P. Martin 2005 *contra* Russo 1965: 191–92, *comm. ad locum*.

traditions, we can still detect its basic contours. The First Sacred War began as a local Phokian conflict over Delphi but escalated to involve several other poleis and *ethnē* of central Greece.[6] The Thessalian victory in this conflict led to the subjugation of the entire region of Phokis and a significant increase in Thessalian influence in central Greece, which elicited a hostile response from the neighboring Boiotians.[7] This response was highly significant for the emergence of regional political cooperation in Boiotia, and the pseudo-Hesiodic *Shield* seems to represent a strategy for justifying Theban leadership of that cooperation. In the poem Herakles' slaughter of Kyknos (ll. 370–423), son of Ares and son-in-law of Keyx, the ruler of Trachis (ll. 353–56), is presented as an act of vengeance on behalf of Apollo, for Kyknos had been waylaying Apollo's pilgrims and stealing their hekatombs (479–80).

There is a heavy local accent about this poem, in the occasional use of epichoric forms and in the emphasis on place and the origins of both hero and antihero.[8] The sons of mighty gods, Herakles is nevertheless depicted as a Theban hero, and Kyknos as a Thessalian one. The conflict thus boils down to one between a Theban and a Thessalian over the right worship of Apollo, or at least over the manner in which his pilgrims and his sanctuary were treated. The poem also has a defensive tone: the Thessalians have corrupted the cult of Apollo, and the Thebans are its true defenders. In other respects, too, the poet is at pains to show that the gods favor Herakles, Thebes, and Boiotia: Apollo disregards Kyknos's prayer for victory over Herakles (68); and Iolaos reminds Herakles that both Zeus and "bullish Poseidon, who holds the turreted crown of Thebes and defends the city," honor him greatly,[9] a likely allusion to the cult of Poseidon at Onchestos, in central Boiotia.[10] If that is correct, it would suggest that in the early sixth century the Thebans had a proprietary interest in a rural sanctuary that in later periods at least was panregional and that was never, so far as we can tell, in the possession of a particular polis.

6. Davies 1994 *contra* Robertson 1978. For earlier treatments see Jannoray 1937; Forrest 1956. On the escalation from local to regional conflict see Kase and Szemler 1984; McInerney 1999: 165–72.

7. Cloché 1918; McInerney 1999: 174–78. Guillon 1963: 61–62 argued that the Boiotians were also directly attacked by the Thessalians during the war, prompted by signs of Theban aggression manifested in their "hostile takeover" of the Ptoion in the territory of Akraiphia ca. 600. But there is no evidence for this hostile takeover: Ducat 1964: 286–88, 1971: 439–42, and 1973: 64.

8. Persistence of epichoric forms: Peek 1933: 51–52; G. P. Edwards 1971: 196–97. Cf. Janko 1982: 14, 48; Shapiro 1984a: 43. It is thus striking that the *Shield* is so often read for the light it sheds on Athenian politics in the sixth century, frequently in relationship to the popularity of the subject on Athenian vases ca. 570–480; see Shapiro 1984a, b.

9. *Aspis* 104–5, trans. Athanassakis.

10. Poseidon at Thebes: *IG* VII.2465, found at Thebes, gives Poseidon the epithet *Empylēos*. The stone may in fact have come from Onchestos (Schachter 1981–94: II.224). Σ *Aspis* 105 suggests that the reference is to Onchestos, on which cult see below, pp. 163–67.

The poem as a whole reads like a claim, expressed in mythical terms, about the propriety of Boiotian relations with Delphi and the unwelcome aggressiveness of Thessalian interests in the shrine.[11] Indeed the description of the obliteration of Kyknos's tomb by Apollo, a detail in the myth apparently invented by the poet of the *Shield*, seems to echo the destruction of Krisa in the war.[12] The poem thus makes a powerful and menacing claim: those who mishandle Apollo's sanctuary and his pilgrims will be destroyed by his Theban protectors.

Other evidence confirms that hostility between the Thessalians and Boiotians escalated in the early sixth century. Plutarch mentions, in two conflicting accounts, a battle at Keressos in which the Boiotians drove out the Thessalians and thereby "liberated the Greeks."[13] It is impossible to date the battle precisely, but it probably belongs in the early sixth century.[14] Fortifications west of Orchomenos and on the akropolis of Chaironeia have been dated to the sixth century and make good sense as part of a defensive system constructed against the Thessalians, who probably occupied, or at least controlled, Phokis in that period.[15] It is thus possible that a military demonstration of the hostility between Boiotia and Thessaly manifested in the *Shield of Herakles* did occur in the first half of the sixth century. In this context the suggestion that the *Shield* may have been composed for the inaugural celebration of the Herakleia or Iolaeia in Thebes to celebrate and commemorate the victory over Thessaly at Keressos is particularly attractive.[16] The *Shield* articulates in mythic terms the Theban response to the Thessalian presence in central Greece after the First Sacred War. It reflects not only hostility toward Thessaly but also a Theban claim about the city's high status and power within the region. For if the Thessalians were perceived as abusing the cult of Apollo (probably at Delphi), then it was the Thebans who put them in their place, led by the hero Herakles and with

---

11. Ducat 1964: 284–86.

12. Russo 1965: 33 n. 35; Janko 1986: 45. Paus. 10.37.7–8 gives the only detailed account of Krisa's destruction. Other ancient sources are less specific about the fate of the city in the war, and all the sources are vague about the actual crimes committed by the inhabitants of Krisa (also known as Kirrha; for the confusion see Oulhen in Hansen and Nielsen 2004: 405), ranging from general impiety toward the shrine (Aeschin. 3.107) to insulting conduct toward the oracle (Plut. *Sol.* 11) to appropriation of sacred land (Paus. 10.37.5, clearly a retrojection of the charges leveled at the Phokians in the Third Sacred War).

13. Plut. *Cam.* 19.3 (ca. 571); Plut. *De mal. Her.* 33.4 (866F; ca. 480). The location of Keressos is uncertain.

14. Dates proposed: ca. 600 (Fossey 1990: 140; Helly 1995: 141 with n. 25), ca. 570 (Guillon 1963: 69 n. 83; Shapiro 1984a: 47 n. 52), ca. 520 (R. J. Buck 1979: 107–12), ca. 490 (Sordi 1953a: 257, 1958: 85–90; Larsen 1968: 30), and ca. 480 (Jeffery 1976: 76). Others (Forrest in *CAH²* III.3: 404; Schachter 1989: 81–82 with n. 35) are indecisive.

15. Lauffer 1985: 107; Fossey and Gauvin 1985: 64. The fortifications cannot be dated more precisely.

16. Shapiro 1984a: 48 with n. 62.

the support of Athena, Zeus, Poseidon, and Apollo themselves. That creates a fertile soil indeed for planting claims to regional hegemony in the future.

Yet for all the regional cohesion evoked by the *Shield*, there are reasons to believe that tension, conflict, and unrest were rife. The Boiotians participated in the settlement of Herakleia Pontike on the Black Sea in this period.[17] With the exception of a small contingent at Thourioi, this was the only occasion on which Boiotians participated in overseas settlement, and it may point to local tension and conflict as a motive for the departure of some Boiotians.[18] Ongoing unrest within Boiotia is attested for the second half of the sixth century by a series of arms dedicated as votives at Olympia to commemorate military victories. A bronze helmet of the period circa 550–525 records a victory of Orchomenos either over the Koroneians or from a battle that occurred at Koroneia.[19] A bronze greave from the end of the sixth century records a Theban victory over Hyettos.[20] And two bronze shields hint at fighting involving Tanagra, one recording a Tanagran victory and one recording a victory over Tanagra; neither shield preserves the name of Tanagra's opponent.[21] The greave recording a Theban victory over Hyettos has been cited as evidence of Thebes' expansion to the northwest in the late sixth century, and while that is indubitably true it is also only one piece of the puzzle: we do not know whether the Orchomenians won their victory over Thebes or some other enemy, and we certainly cannot ascertain what was happening at Tanagra in the period.[22] Four bronze plaques recently discovered in Thebes appear to record the settlement of land disputes between Boiotian poleis in the late sixth century; they may eventually shed some light on the conflicts that until now have been recorded for us only by the series of arms dedicated at Olympia.[23]

17. Herakleides Pontikos fr. 2 (Wehrli); Ephoros *FGrHist* 70 F 44; Ps.-Scymn. 1016–19 (Diller); A.R. 2.846; Paus. 5.26.7; Justin 16.3.4–6. See also Green 2006: 15–18; Avram, Hind, and Tsetskhladze in Hansen and Nielsen 2004: 956 for discussion of the circumstances surrounding Herakleia's foundation.

18. Thourioi: Diod. Sic. 12.11.3.

19. *SEG* 11.1208 (Jeffery 1990: 95 no. 11 with pl. 8; Lazzarini 1976: 322 no. 994).

20. *Ed.pr. AD* 17 (1961–62) 118 with pl. 134b (Kunze 1967: 98–100 with fig. 34.2 and photo pl. 47; *SEG* 24.300; Étienne and Knoepfler 1976: 215–16; Lazzarini 1976: 316 no. 957); cf. Kunze 1991: 128 no. 8.

21. *SEG* 11.1202 (Jeffery 1990: 95 no. 12; Lazzarini 1976: 316 no. 958); *SEG* 15.245 (Lazzarini 1976: 317 no. 968 with Étienne and Knoepfler 1976: 215–18).

22. Étienne and Knoepfler 1976: 217–18. The conclusion drawn from these dedications by Ducat 1973: 66, that there existed a formal Boiotian koinon at this time, which nevertheless permitted its members to wage separate wars, defies the evidence and reads too much into the coinage.

23. Whitley 2004/5: 46; Aravantinos 2006: 371; Angelos Matthaiou *per epist.* Aravantinos 2010: 166–67 publishes photographs of two of the plaques, now in the Thebes Museum. One is described as containing "an account of the receipt or payment of public money" and the other as "a list of properties that were confiscated or sold by the city for unknown reasons," suggesting that these two at least reflect internal Theban conditions rather than interpolis relations in Boiotia. Their full publication is eagerly awaited.

But before we conclude from these hints of interpolis competition that Boiotia was riddled with strife in the second half of the sixth century, we have to account for the appearance circa 525–500 of a series of coins minted in Boiotia on the same standard with similar types, and legends pointing to multiple polis mints.[24] Initially only Thebes, Tanagra, and Hyettos participated—precisely the cities that, along with Orchomenos, were engaged in active conflict in the previous quarter-century. Orchomenos remained aloof from the cooperative minting arrangement of the other Boiotian cities until the fourth century, but Hyettos may have been compelled to join this minting union by the Thebans in the victory they commemorated at Olympia, and the shields dedicated at Olympia from fighting over Tanagra may reflect the struggle that finally brought that city into the minting union. Within a short period, these three monetary partners were joined by Akraiphia, Koroneia, Mykalessos, and Pharai. Until quite recently this numismatic evidence has been interpreted by historians as incontrovertible proof of the existence of a fully functional Boiotian League or koinon.[25] Implicit in that argument is the claim that a coordinated coinage issued by multiple poleis can only have been produced by a fully developed political entity that encompassed them all. However, the assumption that coinage functioned primarily as a symbol of political autonomy is questionable, and it is clear that such coinages, whether produced under voluntary or compulsory conditions, must be understood as economic instruments above all, with their political import a secondary indicium of the coinage itself.[26] That argument is based in part on the underappreciated fact that coinages issued by multiple poleis with common types on a common standard are a widespread phenomenon of the classical Greek world, in no way limited to regions in which we know a koinon later developed. The coinage of late sixth-century Boiotia, then, cannot be taken as evidence for the existence of a koinon.[27]

It does, however, provide excellent evidence for economic cooperation among the Boiotian poleis in the same period. The purposes for which the coinage was initially created are unclear, but the usual guess is that coins were produced to meet military needs and state pay, as well as to facilitate exchange in those cases in which small denominations appear early.[28] In chapter 5 I shall discuss in detail

24. For full discussion see below, pp. 248–49.

25. E.g., Head 1881: 10; Larsen 1968: 29, 32; Ducat 1973: 71–72; R. J. Buck 1979: 111 and 2008: 26.

26. On sovereignty and coinage see T. R. Martin 1985. The argument that such coinages should be seen as economic instruments and indications of economic cooperation is developed in detail by Mackil and van Alfen 2006.

27. So Schachter 1989: 85: "It is not certain when the Boiotoi formed themselves into a federation: the date of the introduction of coinage can no longer be considered relevant to this question." Cf. Hansen 1995a: 31; Larson 2007: 68–72.

28. Crawford 1970; Howgego 1990; Kim 2001, 2002.

the kinds of interpolis, regional economic interactions that may lie behind this innovation, but for now two interesting passages in Herodotos may shed some light on the question and also begin to nuance our understanding of the development of regional cooperation. In 519 the Plataians were being pressed by the Thebans, Herodotos tells us, and sought assistance from a Spartan force led by Kleomenes that happened to be in the area.[29] Kleomenes refused the Plataians' request and referred them to the Athenians, on the grounds that they lived too far away to be helpful but really, Herodotos says (6.108.3), out of a desire to embroil the Athenians in a conflict with the Boiotians. The Plataians went to Athens as suppliants, and when the Thebans learned of this they marched against Plataia. The Athenians went to their assistance, but an engagement was avoided by an eleventh-hour Corinthian arbitration of the dispute by which the borders of Plataia were fixed (with the Asopos River as the basic natural boundary line) and the Thebans were prohibited from pressuring "any of the Boiotians who were not willing to contribute to the Boiotians," es Boiōtous teleein (6.108.5). This puzzling phrase has not attracted much attention; most scholars and translators assume that it means "to join the Boiotian League."[30] That is, however, to assume more about the nature of Boiotian interpolis relationships and regional power structures in the late sixth century than the evidence really permits, and I shall argue later (chap. 5) that it means rather "to make contributions to the Boiotians." For now I take it as certain that the Thebans were pressing the Plataians to contribute to the Boiotians in 519, but that is no indication of a fully fledged federal state in Boiotia in the period.[31] It is, however, an indication that the Thebans were attempting to create some kind of regional power structure, which they were calling "the Boiotians," rather than simply trying, as a polis, to subordinate their neighbors.

The possibility that armed fighting men may have been part of a community's contribution to the Boiotians is confirmed by a second passage in Herodotos. When the Spartan king Kleomenes invaded Athens in 506, he had among his allies the Boiotians and the Chalkidians from Euboia.[32] According to Herodotos (5.74.2),

29. Hdt. 6.108.2, Th. 3.68.5 with Wells 1905: 197–200; Gomme in Gomme, Andrewes, and Dover 1945–81: II.358; Prandi 1988: 27–41; Badian 1989: 103 n. 16; Hornblower 1991–2008: I.464–65 (with references to earlier scholars who emend the text of Thucydides and date the attack to 509 or 506).

30. How and Wells 1912: II.110; Scott 2005: 375–77. Waanders 1983: 111 compares the phrase to Hdt. 2.51.2, where it means "be counted amongst," and attributes the same meaning to this passage. But I suspect it is actually more complicated and refers in part to financial contributions; see below p. 295.

31. Contra Consolo Langher 2004: 320, who assumes the existence of a formal koinon under Theban hegemony by this period and supposes that it was already in place when the Homeric Catalogue of Ships was composed.

32. It was long argued that the alliance of Boiotia and Chalkis produced a coinage, known from only two specimens bearing the cutout shield on the obverse (one example of which has an epichoric

Kleomenes took Eleusis while the Boiotians seized Oinoe and Hysiai and the Chalkidians attacked other parts of Attica. But the Peloponnesian army, camped at Eleusis, crumbled with the sudden departure of the Corinthians and Kleomenes' fellow king, Demaratos, and the Athenians took quick vengeance on the Boiotians and Chalkidians. They engaged the former at the Euripos River, "killing large numbers and taking seven hundred prisoners," then crossed the strait, defeated the Chalkidians in battle, and took more prisoners.[33] With a tithe of the ransom from these prisoners the Athenians dedicated a victory monument on the akropolis, a four-horse chariot in bronze. The epigram on the base celebrates the "taming of the *ethnea* of the Boiotians and Chalkidians"; it is recorded by Herodotos (5.77.4), and fragments of two different copies have been found on the akropolis (T1). An inscribed votive column (T2) recently discovered on the outskirts of Thebes seems to confirm the broad outlines of Herodotos's account but suggests that the Boiotians may have taken Oinoe and Phyle, not Hysiai. The very fact that a monument was dedicated in this connection at Thebes at all suggests that the Boiotians may have had a victory that Herodotos fails to relate, or that they took their success in the outer demes of Oinoe and Phyle to be a victory worth commemorating, a territorial gain to be strengthened by ritual means. The Athenians' description of their enemy on this day as the *ethnea* of the Boiotians and Chalkidians shows that by the end of the sixth century outsiders could view Boiotia as an entity unified by a common identity and by concerted action on the part of its multiple poleis, if not by any formally institutionalized political structure.

Herodotos's continued narrative of the episode shows that the Boiotian *ethnos* was a loose organization existing at least in part for warfare and economic cooperation. The Thebans sought revenge for the defeat they had suffered and the added insult of heavy ransom fees. A Delphic oracle advised them not to act alone but to "ask those nearest." The Thebans, in an assembly at home, asked in puzzlement, "But are not those nearest to us the Tanagrans and Koroneians and Thespians? And these men, already fighting eagerly, wage war with us."[34] Herodotos's

---

chi) and a wheel on the reverse: Imhoof-Blumer 1883: 221; cf. W. P. Wallace 1962: 38 n. 2. But the association is actually quite uncertain: the variety of coin types produced by individual mints in the late sixth century, and by Chalkis in particular, means that we should be cautious about associating a specific type with a specific mint unless there is a much larger volume than two specimens, and these coins, minted in the last quarter of the sixth century, are so early that not even the Boiotians could have claimed the cutout shield as their distinctive device, which is a basic requirement for the old argument to hold any water. Along these lines see Kraay 1976: 109; MacDonald 1987–88. On the coalition against Athens see Tausend 1992: 118–23.

33. Hdt. 5.77.1–2. The Athenian dead from this battle may be commemorated in Simonides *Elegies* frr. 10–17 (West 1972).

34. Hdt. 5.79.2.

account of the assembly is ambiguous but seems to imply a deliberative body attended by multiple Boiotian poleis, hence the care to report that it was the Thebans who raised the question about the meaning of "those nearest," and the use of the demonstrative "these men" when mentioning the Tanagrans, Koroneians, and Thespians, as though the speaker were pointing toward men of those communities as he spoke. When several communities jointly undertake a war, it is absolutely necessary to assume some kind of economic arrangement for the joint funding of a campaign. The cooperative coinage described briefly above—in which Tanagra, Koroneia, and Thebes participated—was probably developed at least in part to facilitate the joint military action so clearly attested by Herodotos. The oracle puzzling the Thebans in 506 was finally interpreted as a suggestion that they should ally themselves with the Aiginetans, on the grounds that they were "those nearest to them," not in geographical but in genealogical terms.[35]

By the end of the sixth century, then, we can see the outlines of a loose regional organization centered on joint military action and the integration of local economies within the region. We shall see below (chap. 4) that there is clear evidence within the religious sphere of an emergent Boiotian identity in this period as well. Historical hindsight allows us to see that these were among the earliest stages in the process of regional state-formation in Boiotia, but it is important not to collapse a process that in fact took around three-quarters of a century into a single moment in the late sixth century when the Boiotian League suddenly emerged in the form in which we know it after the mid-fifth century. Rather, profound and violent disagreements between the poleis of Boiotia continued even as most of the region became aware of the need to square off against their Athenian neighbors.

It was, however, an even bigger if more distant neighbor that affected the course of Boiotian history in the early fifth century, putting the brakes on these cooperative developments. All the Boiotian cities except for Plataia and Thespiai supported the Persians when they invaded in 480, and if a small Theban presence at Thermopylai reflects internal divisions over the policy toward Persia, the Persian victory there decided matters for the Boiotians.[36] When Xerxes moved through Boiotia, the Thebans exposed the allegiance of Plataia and Thespiai to the allied cause, and their territories were ravaged as a result.[37] We do not know whether the rift between Thebes and Thespiai, which had been allies in 506,

35. Hdt. 5.80.1 explains the genealogy: Asopos (the river delimiting the territories of Thebes and Plataia after the Corinthian arbitration of 519) had two daughters, Thebe and Aigina.

36. Boiotian Medism: Hdt. 7.132.1; cf. Diod. Sic. 11.3.2. Thebans on Greek side at Thermopylai: Hdt. 7.205, 222; Diod. Sic. 11.4.7.

37. Hdt. 8.34, 50.2; cf. Diod. Sic. 11.14.5.

was caused only by the Persian question or whether it was the result of some local conflict.[38]

The pro-Persian party at Thebes continued to show its mettle after the Greek victory at Salamis. When Mardonios learned that Spartan forces were headed to occupied Athens to resist him, he withdrew his forces toward Thebes, where the territory was well suited to a cavalry battle and the city was friendly. He was met at Dekeleia, on the border between Attica and Boiotia, by men from the Asopos region, the Boiotian side of the border, who had been sent by the boiotarchs (according to Herodotos 9.15.1) and guided the Persians into Theban territory. What is the significance of these figures, evidently magistrates? The title signifies a leadership role for the whole region, which could point to the existence of formal political institutions comprising the entire region. Even if these boiotarchs are not an anachronism, it remains difficult to take them as incontrovertible evidence for the existence of a fully functional Boiotian federal state with developed state institutions and magistrates for the management of external affairs, fitting the model that is familiar to us from the later fifth century.[39] We saw in Herodotos's narrative of the events at Plataia in 519 that the Thebans at least had put energy behind the idea of the Boiotians as an organized group, and it should not surprise us to see it becoming gradually more formalized. It is thus possible that the boiotarchs were actually Theban magistrates, pursuing the Thebans' aspirations of regional political unification; the magistrates' title would then have been more normative than descriptive. We know from Herodotos only that in the spring of 479 boiotarchs had both the power to issue orders to inhabitants of the Asopos district and the authority to be obeyed.

After the battle of Plataia, the allies laid siege to Thebes and "demanded the surrender of those Thebans who had gone over to the Persians," in particular Timagenides and Attaginos, who are described as *archēgetai*. Perhaps the most neutral translation is "leaders"; the precise meaning is unclear, but we know that Attaginos hosted a banquet for Persians in Thebes and that Timagenides had

38. R.J. Buck 1979: 132 speculates that "a split had arisen in the League" after the abortive allied expedition to Tempe in 481 (Hdt. 7.173), in which Buck believes the Boiotians participated. His argument hinges on the dubious assumption that Plut. *De mal. Her.* 32 is based on Aristophanes the Boiotian (*FGrHist* 369), which even if true proves nothing about Boiotian participation in that expedition.

39. Boiotarchs in Herodotos as anachronism: Jacoby, *FGrHist* III *Kommentar* 162; Demand 1982: 18. But Herodotos's claim may now be corroborated: an unpublished bronze plaque records a dedication by a boiotarch (Aravantinos 2010: 233). The provenance is not reported, but if it is a dedication to Herakles it is certainly from Thebes. The epigraphic boiotarch is, in other words, highly likely to have been a Theban. Aravantinos places the inscription in the early fifth century, but the grounds for this date are not clear; on epigraphic grounds alone the text could belong anywhere in the first half of the fifth century. Many have taken Herodotos's boiotarchs as evidence for a full-fledged koinon: e.g., Waterfield 1998: 157; R.J. Buck 1979: 124 (cf. 89).

advised Mardonios before Plataia.[40] Whether ringleaders or appointed officials we cannot tell, but we know of them only in the context of this year. It is possible that it was to these individuals, and perhaps others like them, that the Thebans referred when, defending themselves to the Spartans in 427 over their seizure of Plataia, they described the Theban regime during the Persian Wars as a "*dynasteia* of a few men."[41] But that defense is rhetorically charged and exceedingly difficult to use as clear evidence for the nature of the Theban regime in 479. In fact Herodotos's narrative encourages us to think that Theban Medism was not the policy of a single clan, much less that of two individuals, who rather appear to have become scapegoats in a highly emotional event.

The Greeks besieged Thebes for twenty days before Timagenides addressed the Thebans with the suggestion that perhaps their demand for leaders was a pretense and that what the Greeks really wanted was money. "If they want money," he continued, "let's give them money from the common treasury [*ek tou koinou*], for it was with the koinon that we Medized, and not we alone."[42] The first use of the word *koinon* here certainly refers to the treasury, as is common.[43] The second, however, must refer to some state authority, and not again to the treasury.[44] The nature of that authority, its institutional structure, is unclear, however, and we should be wary of retrojecting later evidence. The word *koinon* is frequently used by Herodotos simply to indicate the government in places where there never was a confederate or federal polity, and this is how the word should be taken here.[45] The question of how developed Boiotian (not Theban) state institutions were in 479 cannot be answered with this puzzling passage. There is good reason to suspect that plenty of non-Theban Boiotians were within the walls of Thebes when they were besieged by the victorious Greek allied force: Diodoros (11.31.3) reports that "the Greeks serving with Mardonios withdrew to Thebes"; and Herodotos (9.87.2) has Timagenides express a desire that "Boiotia should not suffer further on our account." When the Greeks made it clear that they really did want traitors and not traitors' money, they led to Corinth those who were handed over, where they were all executed.[46]

40. Attaginos's banquet: Hdt. 9.115.4. Timagenides and Mardonios before Plataia: Hdt. 9.38.2.

41. Th. 3.62.3. Hornblower 1991–2008: I.457 translates the phrase as "small family clique."

42. Hdt. 9.87.2.

43. Cf. Hdt. 7.144.1 (Athens).

44. How and Wells 1912: II.326; Masaracchia 1978: 197.

45. Cf. Hdt. 1. 67.5 (Sparta); 3.80.6 (debate on constitutions, here used for an isonomic government that debates issues); 5.85.1 (Athens), 109.3 (Ionians, which may have a very similar connotation to the use of the word in the Boiotian context; some manuscripts read κοινὰ here instead of κοινὸν); 6.14.3 (Samos); 8.135.2 (Boiotia again); 9.117 (Athens). *Contra* Moretti 1962: 118, "con la parola *koinon* può intendersi non l'insieme dei Tebani, ma la federazione beotica, il *commune Boeotorum*."

46. Hdt. 9.88.

Herodotos's mention of boiotarchs and the reference to a koinon in the political sense in 480–479 cannot be taken as certain evidence for a regional state operating just like the one we know in much more detail from the period of the Peloponnesian War. These references do, however, point to the Persian Wars as a crisis in which the tentative moves toward the politicization of Boiotian regional and ethnic identity in the late sixth century received greater impetus, direction, and perhaps organization. The office of boiotarch and other institutions designed to lend authority and permanence to decisions and actions taken jointly by the Boiotians in military and economic matters may, in other words, have been created in this period as a solution, suggested by past experiences and the relational habits the Boiotian cities had to one another, to the immediate crisis of a Persian presence at the borders.

This impression is supported by an inscription (T3) from Olympia recording the outcome of a judicial appeal in a case that was probably judged originally by the Hellanodikai. The original suit found against the Boiotians and apparently also the Thessalians, and in favor of the Athenians and Thespians. The lineup points immediately to an issue arising from the Persian Wars. The appeal was heard by one Charixenos and a body of magistrates called the *mastroi*, who found that "the previous judgment was not rightly judged" and acquitted the Thessalians of the charges formerly brought against them. It is likely that behind the inscription lies an approach by the Athenians and Thespians to the Hellanodikai shortly after 479 to accuse the Thessalians and Boiotians of violating the Olympic peace of 480 by participating in the sack of the cities' territories.[47] For our purposes what is particularly important about this obscure text is its clue that the Boiotoi were recognized and dealt with as a political entity even at the moment when they were locked in conflict with another Boiotian city, Thespiai. The inscription shows that in a legal context, the Boiotoi constitute not only a recognizable but even a prosecutable group, despite the fact that they manifestly do not represent all the communities that regard themselves as Boiotian. But if the Boiotians were a prosecutable group, what was the nature of their common polity? I have already argued that political cooperation was loose and ad hoc prior to and probably throughout the Persian Wars, although we have seen signs that it was moving toward greater formalization under Theban leadership. Yet this is not enough to support the claim that the Boiotian League was dissolved after the allied reparations against Boiotia in 479.[48]

The extent to which cooperation—whether formal or informal—occurred after 479 is difficult to discern. Plataia became an autonomous, independent polis, but

47. Siewert 1981.

48. Busolt 1897: 312–13; Beloch 1912–27: II.1.58; Glotz 1925–41: II.92; Moretti 1962: 124 (both citing Diod. Sic. 11.81.2–3; Justin 3.6.10); Larsen 1968: 32; Sordi 1968: 66; Bradeen 1964: 217–18; R. J. Buck 1979: 141. The argument against this kind of analysis is well presented by Amit 1971, 1973: 86–87.

its geographical position, wedged precariously between Attica and Boiotia, made the long-term maintenance of that status a virtual impossibility.[49] There are some indications that the region was riven by *stasis* in this period, but the details are lost for about two decades.[50] In 458, the lights flicker on again, for Boiotia became a battleground for the Spartans and Athenians at Tanagra, where there was no decisive victory.[51] According to Thucydides, two months later the Athenians marched against the Boiotians and were victorious in battle at a place called Oinophyta, near Tanagra.[52] He ascribes no motive to the attack, which has been seen as part of the Athenians' brief attempt in the 450s to gain a land empire.[53] That may indeed be true but is only part of the story. Diodoros (11.81.1–2) claims that the Thebans, humiliated by their Medism and despised for it by the other Boiotians, sought some means to regain their former influence and prestige.[54] They approached the Spartans and made a compact whereby the Spartans would help the Thebans gain the complete hegemony of Boiotia and in exchange the Thebans would wage war against the Athenians on the Spartans' behalf.[55] If this diplomatic rapprochement in

49. Th. 2.71.2 for Plataian autonomy, with Hansen 1995a: 34–35, 1995b. There has been much inconclusive argument about whether Plataia now joined "the Boiotian League," but if it is correct that there were only informal cooperative structures and a Theban urge for more, then this is a moot point. Amit 1973: 87 tries to have it both ways, arguing that before the Persian Wars "the Boeotian League was a loose confederation based upon religion and common interests; it had no tight political organisation and no common foreign policy," and was not dissolved in 479, but also insisting that in the years after 479 Plataia had a formal "right of sending representatives to the federal council," which was appropriated by the Thebans in 446. Amit is clearly thinking here of the institution of federal districts, which probably dates back to 446 but not before.

50. Th. 3.62.5, a rhetorical remark, to be sure (Hornblower 1991–2008: I.455–58), should not be taken at face value (as does Bradeen 1964: 218); Arist. *Rhet.* 1407a2–6 may reflect on this period.

51. Th. 1.107.2–108.2; Diod. Sic. 11.79.4–11.80.2, 6, with variant details. Hdt. 9.35.2 and Plut. *Cim.* 17.6 claim victory for the Spartans. The Spartans too claimed it as a victory and dedicated a golden shield for the pediment of the Temple of Zeus at Olympia: Paus. 5.10.4 with Jeffery 1990: 129 no. 38 (photo pl. 21) and ML 36. The unstable outcome of the battle is what really matters. Athenian casualty list for the battle: *IG* I³ 1149 with a new fragment (Papazarkadas and Sourlas 2012).

52. Th. 1.108.2; Fossey 1988: 58–60 for the location of Oinophyta.

53. Compare the expedition to Thessaly in 454/3: Th. 1.111.1. So Hornblower 2002: 43; Hornblower 1991–2008: I.172.

54. This claim, combined with the hints of *stasis* within Boiotia between 479 and 457, may point to ongoing strife as the internal context in which the Athenian occupation should be situated; see Gehrke 1985: 165–67.

55. This section comes after Diodoros's principal narrative of the battle of Tanagra (for which see below), but he records, problematically, two battles at Tanagra, and the mention of the Theban-Spartan bargain is placed before the second one (11.81.4–82.5). But as Busolt 1897: 319 n. 2 made clear, the "second" battle of Tanagra in Diodoros matches Thucydides' narrative of Oinophyta (for which see below) so closely that we have to conclude Diodoros has made a mistake. Justin 3.6.10–11 likewise records the bargain, and it is accepted by Badian 1993: 213 n. 50. Whether the bargain was struck before or after the battle of Tanagra is unclear.

fact occurred after Tanagra, the most immediate cause for Spartan suspicion of Athens was probably the unclear outcome of that battle, as well as anxiety about Athens' control of Megara.[56] Such a bargain would make better sense of the Athenians' motivation for their invasion of Boiotia leading up to the battle of Oinophyta, as narrated by Thucydides. Before that engagement, however, Diodoros says that the Spartans "expanded the city wall of Thebes, and compelled the poleis in Boiotia to submit themselves to the Thebans."[57] This single sentence has prompted numerous historians to posit a refoundation of the Boiotian League, which, on this view, had been dissolved since 479.[58] Whatever gains the Thebans made with Spartan help were short-lived: the Athenian victory over the Boiotians at Oinophyta certainly put an end to the new arrangements. The Athenians pulled down the walls of Tanagra and, according to Diodoros, "going through all Boiotia cut and destroyed crops."[59] They took complete control of all the poleis in the region.[60] It is impossible to regard the two-month interval between Tanagra and Oinophyta as in any meaningful sense a period in which the Boiotian League was refounded.

For the Athenians, the victory at Oinophyta must have been enormously important. As we shall see below, there is epigraphic evidence to support the claim that the loss of Boiotia eleven years later constituted a very real blow to the Athenians. In the interim the region, one of the richest for agriculture in all Greece, certainly constituted a significant economic resource for Attica. So it was quite likely after Oinophyta that the Athenians set up on the akropolis a new copy of the bronze *quadriga* that they had dedicated to Athena in 506 following their retaliatory victory over the Boiotians and Chalkidians, which had been damaged in the Persian sack of Athens.[61]

56. Th. 1.103.4, 105.3–106.2. See Green 2006: 159 n. 329 for a different (and to my mind unpersuasive) chronology.

57. Diod. Sic. 11.81.3–4. R. J. Buck 2008: 26 supposes that the Athenians intervened in Boiotia in 457 because they saw a "League in stasis" as an invitation for conquest. But there is no good evidence for a formal "League" (by which Buck means a formal federal state), nor does this supposition take cognizance of the literary sources recording the context in which the Athenians invaded.

58. Busolt 1897: 312–13; Beloch 1912–27: II.1.169; Hammond 1986: 294; Moretti 1962: 126; Larsen 1968: 32.

59. Walls of Tanagra: Th. 1.108.2; Diod. Sic. 11.82.5. The cutting and destroying refer certainly to economic warfare (cutting down trees and vines, destroying crops), not to the carving up of Boiotia itself as a metaphor for the dismantling of a Boiotian league, which, as we have seen, was barely institutionalized in this period if it functioned at all, existing only in particular configurations of behavior.

60. Th. 1.108.3; cf. Diod. Sic. 11.83.3 (part of his second narrative of Oinophyta; the source of the repetition has been debated: R. J. Buck 1970: 220, following Busolt 1897: 319 n. 2; Barber 1935: 93–94; and Jacoby, *FGrHist* IIC 33 and comm. on 70 F 231).

61. T1a records the original dedication; T1b records a replacement, with a different word order, and this was the version seen by Hdt. (5.77) and Paus. (1.28.2).

The internal affairs of Boiotia in the period from 457 to 446 are quite obscure. Aristotle says that after Oinophyta "the democracy [at Thebes] was destroyed as a result of bad government." If correct, this would point to an unsuccessful attempt on the part of the Athenians to influence local governance at Thebes, but it is also true that, in this period as always, they were pragmatic enough to support whatever party would support them in return—including what must have been the vilest of political species to an Athenian, Boiotian oligarchs.[62] The Boiotians certainly felt some Athenian pressure: in 456/5 Tolmides settled the rebel Messenians at Naupaktos, and the Athenians probably felt that control of Boiotia was central to the security of that arrangement.[63] The Boiotians were required to serve in an Athenian expedition against Pharsalos, and at least some of the Boiotian poleis may have paid tribute to Athens.[64] Beyond this it is extremely difficult to say anything about Boiotian affairs, whether internal or external, in the period of Athenian control.

In the winter of 447/6, Thucydides tells us, Boiotian exiles seized Orchomenos, Chaironeia, and some other places.[65] These exiles had presumably been driven out by the Athenians as opponents to the new order they imposed, and it is important to recognize that the revolt was staged from the north by these outsiders. They established themselves so quickly and firmly as a group, with their action so focused on Orchomenos, that they became known as "the Orchomenizers."[66] In

62. Arist. *Pol.* 1302b29–32 with Ps.-Xen. *Ath.Pol.* 3.10–11 for Athenian support for Boiotian oligarchs. Diod. Sic. 11.83.1, claims that the Athenians gained control of all Boiotia except Thebes after Oinophyta; this may reflect the failure of democracy to take root in the city, as reported by Aristotle. See Larsen 1960b: 9–10.

63. Th. 1.103.3; Diod. Sic. 11.84.7; Badian 1990: 367–68.

64. Pharsalos: Th. 1.111.1 with *ATL* III.178; cf. Hornblower 2002: 81–82; R. J. Buck 1970: 223; T. R. Martin 1985: 74–75. Tribute: Lewis in *CAH* V²: 116 n. 72 suggests reading in the Athenian tribute list for 454/3 (*IG* I³ 259.III.20) not Ἀκρ[οτερίοι] : HHH but Ἀκρ[αιφνίο]ι: HHH, which would make Akraiphia a tributary ally. Lewis 1981: 77 n. 43 suggests restoring the tribute list for 453/2, *ATL* 2 col. IX line 9 (*IG* I³ 260.IX.9) as [ℎεϱχομ]ένιοι, which would make Orchomenos tributary. The editors of *ATL* I.2.IX.9 read [Κλαζομ]ένιοι, but Camp 1974: 314–18 published a new fragment of the same list, containing parts of cols. VII and VIII. In col. VIII.6 of this new fragment, Κλαζομέν[ιοι] is clearly read; an alternative must be found for col. IX.9; the stoichedon arrangement of text allows room for six letters. Camp 1974: 317 follows McGregor's suggestion that this could be restored [Κυζζικ]ενοί, questioning whether the first iota was really such or rather a stray mason's mark. This restoration was retained by McGregor 1976. Lewis's suggestion is the first proposed alternative; he points to *IG* I³ 73.23 as a parallel for the spelling of the name, but here too it is restored (again stoichedon). The Orchomenians themselves in this period began their name with ΕΡ, unaspirated (as shown by the coins and the earlier inscription from Olympia, *SEG* 11.1208).

65. Th. 1.113.1.

66. Hellanikos *FGrHist* 4 F 81; Theopomp. *FGrHist* 115 F 407; Aristophanes *FGrHist* 379 F 3. Larsen 1960b plays down the role of exiles from other communities, arguing that Orchomenos as a polis took the lead in the liberation. This relies on an inference that the text of Thucydides (1.113) does not support.

the spring of 446 the Athenians sent a force of a thousand hoplites under Tolmides to deal with the revolt; they managed to regain Chaironeia, at the cost of the citizens' freedom, and held it with a garrison. They must have been attempting to return to Athens, or to a base in a loyal part of Boiotia where they might await reinforcements, when they turned southeast and were met at Koroneia by the Orchomenizers and "others who were of the same mind."[67] In the battle that ensued the Boiotians and their allies had an overwhelming victory; the Athenian hoplites were all either killed or taken prisoner. This forced the Athenians' hand, and they surrendered control of Boiotia. Thucydides reports that the exiles returned and "all the others became autonomous again."[68]

The Athenians' defeat at Koroneia was a major blow, not only in itself but also because of its consequences, for it probably sparked the coordinated revolt of Megara and Euboia, which itself encouraged many other cities to follow suit.[69] In the same year the Athenians and Spartans concluded a thirty-year treaty that ended the First Peloponnesian War.[70] But the Athenians may have retained some friendships

---

Yet Dull 1977, arguing against Larsen's theory, falls into a different trap. His argument that the verb orchomenizein means not "to support the exiles who converged on Orchomenos" but rather the opposite, "to resist annexation, to be independent, to revolt," relies on three irrelevant facts: first, that Orchomenos is listed separately from the Boiotians in the Homeric Catalogue of Ships; second, that Orchomenos did not participate in the Boiotian cooperative coinage until the fourth century; and third, that Orchomenos preserved a mythological tradition about its population's origins distinct from that of the Boiotoi. What is clear is that Orchomenos was used as a base for the Boiotians who had been exiled by occupying Athenian forces in the rising that affected the expulsion of the Athenians from the region. Farinetti 2008: 286 explains the use of Orchomenos as a base for the anti-Athenian rising as a function of the city's strong oligarchic ideology.

67. Th. 1.113.1–2. It is odd that Tolmides would not have headed straight for Orchomenos after enslaving and garrisoning Chaironeia; R. J. Buck 1970: 225 may be correct in supposing that the Athenians were in the process of mustering a larger force when Tolmides' army was attacked (Diod. Sic. 12.6.2 uses the language of ambush), which would explain the move toward the southeast.

68. Th. 1.113.3–4. Cf. Diod. Sic. 12.6.1–2.

69. Th. 1.114.3; Diod. Sic. 12.7; Plut. Per. 22.1–2 for Pericles' quick and successful campaign against Euboia; ML 51–52. This was certainly provoked in part by the cleruchy set up on Euboia (Diod. Sic. 11.88.3, Paus. 1.27.5), but the date at which that occurred is quite unclear (Diod. Sic. puts it in 453, and Green 2006: 169–70 n. 364 defends his author's claim; Meiggs 1972: 122 puts it in 450, and Erxleben 1975: 85–86 leans back closer to Diodoros's date; but Meritt et al. in ATL III.294 and Brunt 1967: 81 argue for 447 or 446), and it is any case hard to see the orchestration of the Megarian and Euboian revolts except as a response to the Athenian defeat in Boiotia, the territory that lay between them. The sense of defeat is effectively conveyed by an epigram for Athenian war dead, which has been associated with Koroneia: IG I³ 1163d–f; casualty list: IG I³ 1163a–c, with Peek 1933 and 1955, Bowra 1938, Bradeen 1964 and 1969, Meiggs 1966, Clairmont 1983. But it may belong to Delion (Mattingly 1963, 1966a) or—and I think this is unlikely—to the Sicilian Expedition (Papagiannopoulos-Palaios 1965–66, Mastrokostas 1955a, Koumanoudes 1964, Tsirigoti-Drakotou 2000). See Papazarkadas 2009a: 76.

70. Th. 1.87.6, 115; 2.21; 4.21.3.

with Boiotians: an Athenian decree of roughly this period records the bestowal of proxeny on four individuals of Thespiai.[71] Without a more specific date it is difficult to place this evidence, but if it belongs after 446 it may reflect a new attempt on the part of the Athenians to maintain ties to those Boiotian cities with which they were closest. In this connection the sending out of settlers to reinforce Thourioi, in southern Italy, in 446–444 is of interest: in an Athenian-led expedition with participation from numerous Greek cities, the ten tribes of the new polis were comprised of the several ethnic groups represented by the colonists, including Boiotians.[72] We know too that Thourioi at its inception was governed by a democracy, and it is possible that pro-Athenian partisans in Boiotia opted to leave when the Athenians were expelled after Koroneia and most of the democracies were overturned.

The impact on Boiotia of the Athenian defeat at Koroneia was tremendous. In 427, when defending themselves to the Spartans on the charge of an unjust attack on Plataia, the Thebans spoke of Koroneia as a victory that liberated Boiotia (Th. 3.62.4; cf. 67.3), and though tendentious it is an unproblematic account of Theban perceptions of the importance and impact of the battle twenty years later. What happened in the interim? Freed of external constraints and imposed governments, the Boiotian poleis could pursue their own policies. In theory, they were free to pick up where they had left off in 457, before the Athenian victory at Oinophyta. Most historians have assumed that this meant refounding the koinon that was dismantled by the Athenians a decade before.[73] For neither part of that assumption, however, is there any solid evidence.[74] The Thebans, it is quite clear, were for much of the late sixth and early fifth century working to gain a leading position in the region and in any regional state apparatus that could be developed for the governance of the whole. The boiotarchs who make a brief appearance in Herodotos's narrative of 479 may be a reflection of such an apparatus at an early stage of development, if they are not a mere anachronism. The sources suggest, however, that the Thebans themselves had nothing to do with the liberation of Boiotia in 446, which was led rather by political exiles with strong support from Orchomenos, and this may reflect the weakness of Thebes after a series of failures—the attempt on Plataia in 519, the attack on Athens in 506, their shameful record in the Persian Wars, and the disaster at Oinophyta in 457.[75]

Thucydides' full and rich narrative of the Peloponnesian War reveals the existence and operation of institutions of a regional state in Boiotia that are described

71. *IG* I³ 23.

72. Diod. Sic. 12.11.3. For the various stages of the foundation process at Thourioi see Fischer-Hansen, Nielsen, and Ampolo in Hansen and Nielsen 2004: 304–6.

73. Larsen 1968: 31–33 (recognizing, however, the innovations of the post-447 government); Bruce 1968: 190; Hornblower 1991–2008: I.239 (who is more cautious); Hansen 1995a: 13, 35.

74. See in particular Amit 1971, followed by R. J. Buck 1979: 154.

75. Larsen 1960b: 11; cf. Larsen 1968: 32–33 *contra* Dull 1977.

yet more fully by the Oxyrhynchos Historian in his account of the year 395.[76] We must infer that at least some of those institutions were created immediately after 446 in order to promote and protect the tentative steps taken toward the formation of a regional state in the period from roughly 520 to 457. The victory at Koroneia certainly provided the regional security and independence that are necessary preconditions for this particular sort of institutional development, and the experience of an eleven-year Athenian occupation, combined with plentiful evidence of the ongoing imperialist aims and practices of their southern neighbor, must have provided the Boiotians with the motivation they needed to undertake it. The formal federal institutions that were established after 446 bear the hallmarks of voluntary participation and bargaining: the political rights and fiscal and military obligations of each polis were clearly established and protected by a system of districts, which went a long way toward preventing Boiotia from becoming a unitary state—like its southern neighbor Athens—under the hegemony of its single most powerful polis, Thebes.

The Boiotian cities, with the exception of Plataia and eventually Thespiai, were resolutely opposed to Athens during the Peloponnesian War and for that reason if for no other firmly allied with the Peloponnesian League. Their opposition was probably a response to the Athenian domination of Boiotia from 457 to 446 as well as being a function of oligarchic sympathies.[77] There was *stasis* in the cities of Boiotia during the Peloponnesian War, and Thucydides presents it as revolving around the political struggle between oligarchs (allied with the Thebans and favoring the strengthening of a regional state apparatus) and democrats (looking to the Athenians and seeking greater autonomy at the polis level). Thucydides' biggest Boiotian story is that of Plataia; it is well known, so a brief recounting will be sufficient here.

In early 431 a force of more than three hundred Thebans, led by their own boiotarchs, attacked Plataia by night, hoping to force the city out of its alliance with Athens and back into the Boiotian koinon that had started to take shape after 446.[78] When precisely the Plataians had left the koinon is unknown, but it is likely that the rupture occurred as tensions increased between Athens, with which Plataia was allied, and Sparta, with which most of the rest of Boiotia was. The Thebans certainly saw that a pro-Athenian Plataia increased Boiotia's vulnerability, and they were encouraged in the attack by some Plataians who wished to make the city over to the Thebans "for the sake of personal power," a phrase probably

---

76. *Hell.Oxy.* 16.3 (Bartoletti).

77. Pro-Peloponnesian stance before the war: Th. 1.27.2. Boiotian oligarchy: *Hell.Oxy.* 16.2 (Bartoletti).

78. Th. 2.2.1. The exact date of the Theban attack is controversial: see Gomme, Andrewes, and Dover 1945–81: 2.3; Smart 1986; Hornblower 1991–2008: I.237–38; Green 2006: 234–35 n. 195; Iversen 2007: 393–94, 410–11. On the participation of Plataia in the koinon in the years immediately after 446, see below, p. 336.

alluding to a desire to gain official positions within the koinon.[79] The attack was a Theban initiative, not an act of the Boiotian koinon; the other member poleis were either not privy or were uninvolved. Nevertheless it is clear that the Thebans were attempting not to subordinate Plataia to themselves but to make it part of "the Boiotians" (much as they had done in 519): the pro-Theban partisans in Plataia urged the Theban soldiers, once they had entered the city, to go immediately to the houses of their enemies (presumably to slaughter them), but the Thebans were unwilling. They preferred "to make friendly announcements and rather to lead the polis to an agreement and friendship." The herald accordingly announced that anyone who wished "to make an alliance in accordance with the ancestral customs [ta patria] of all the Boiotians" should lay down his arms.[80] The Plataians firmly resisted and managed to take 180 Theban prisoners, while the rest escaped; the prisoners were executed, according to the Thebans, contrary to an oath sworn by the Plataians.[81] The Athenians rallied to the aid of Plataia, installing a garrison in the city, and prepared for war with the Peloponnesians, since the attack on their ally constituted a breach of the terms of the Thirty Years' Peace.[82]

Theban resentment of Plataian recalcitrance lingered, and the Plataians became a natural target of Peloponnesian attack in the war between Athens and Sparta. The Spartan army arrived in 429, and Archidamos offered to leave the Plataians alone if they would abandon their alliance with Athens and remain neutral throughout the war. The offer was rejected, and the Peloponnesians, with Boiotian help, laid siege to the city.[83] The small force at Plataia held out, remarkably, until the summer of 427, when the place was surrendered.[84] In the sham trial of the defenders that followed, the Plataians speak only of Theban, not Boiotian, hostility: they accuse the Spartans of being willing "to efface the city, to its very last house, from the whole of Greece for the sake of the Thebans";[85] they fear that the

79. Th. 2.2.2–3.
80. Th. 2.2.4. Ta patria should perhaps not be taken literally. The appeal to tradition is in certain ways efficacious, but it would be overly simplistic to interpret it as a direct reference to an ancestral Boiotian confederacy along the lines known clearly only for the early fourth century. That there was a Boiotian tradition of interpolis cooperation is beyond doubt; it is certainly to this, and more normatively to the nascent confederation, that the Thebans refer here.
81. Th. 2.5.1–7.
82. Th. 2.6.1–7.1.
83. Th. 2.71.1–74.1 for negotiations and Plataia's rejection of neutrality; 74.2–78.4 for a remarkably detailed account of the stunningly laborious and ineffectual siege. Boiotian involvement: Th. 2.78.2.
84. Th. 3.52.1–3; cf. 3.20–24 for the breakout of 212 defenders in the winter of 428/7.
85. Th. 3.57.2. A remarkable phrase. "Efface" translates exaleiphein, which is used of whitewashing, wholesale obliteration. Its primary context is in the whitewashing of the written word, and so the obliteration of a record and a memory (Gomme, Andrewes, and Dover 1945–81: II.343). The same word is used to express fear of the obliteration of a city from the landscape by the Kytenians in the late third century: Bousquet 1988b, line 102; cf. Mackil 2004: 502–3.

Thebans have persuaded the Spartans to destroy them (Th. 3.58.1); they expect that
the Spartans intend to make the Plataian *chōra* Theban (3.58.5); and they speak
repeatedly of the Thebans as their most hated enemies (3.59.2–4).

The Theban response to the Plataians' defense speech reveals much about the
claims the Thebans were making in the mid-fifth century about the past, their
attempts to create their own version of Boiotian history, an attempt at ideological
leadership to match their attempt at the political leadership of the region.[86] Their
opening salvo is thus worth quoting in full (Th. 3.61.2):

> Differences first arose between us when we founded Plataia later than the rest of
> Boiotia, and other places with it, which we held after expelling the mixed population.
> But they did not think they deserved to be ruled by us, as was originally arranged,
> and so they stood outside the other Boiotians, contravening the traditions of their
> ancestors [*ta patria*]. But when they were pressed too severely, they went over to the
> Athenians, and with them they did us much harm, in exchange for which they also
> suffered.

The Thebans now claim responsibility for the settlement of all Boiotia, the expulsion of a mixed population upon their arrival from Thessalian Arne (cf. Th. 1.12.3),
and some almost primordial position of hegemony within the entire region.[87] They
claim too that cooperation of the poleis of Boiotia under Theban leadership was
ancestral; *ta patria* is an explicit attempt to place the political movement of the
present—toward the greater organization and institutionalization of Boiotian
interpolis cooperation under Theban leadership—in the deep past, to justify their
aggression on behalf of this cause. It echoes directly the offer made by the Thebans
to the Plataians in 431: if they were willing to make an alliance in accordance with
ta patria of all the Boiotians, they would not be attacked.[88] In the rest of the speech
the Theban strategy is to show that the Plataians are staunch allies of Athens and
therefore equally staunch enemies of the Peloponnesian alliance in the current
war, making the Athenians into latter-day Persians, enslaving the Greeks just as
the Persians had once tried to do. In the same vein the Thebans claim that the victory at Koroneia was won in order to bring Boiotia over to the Peloponnesians
(3.67.3). For our purposes their more interesting argument is that they were justified in invading the city in 431 because they were invited by Plataians who were
prominent both in wealth and in birth "to restore [the city] to the shared ancestral

---

86. As Hornblower 1991–2008: I.454 observes, some of this speech also reflects Thucydides'
attempt to square contemporary events with his own vision of the Greeks' distant past, as presented in
the Archaeology.

87. The Theban claim to have founded Plataia, as *mētropolis* to *apoikia*, is striking and not supported elsewhere. See Graham 1983: 40.

88. Th. 2.2.4; cf. 3.66.1.

traditions [*ta koina patria*] of all the Boiotians," which would have amounted to them "living among kin."[89] Plataia was, in other words, victim as much of its small size and geographical vulnerability as it was of internal *stasis,* with the oligarchic element favoring participation in a Boiotian regional government and the democratic majority favoring continued alliance with Athens.[90] The Plataians' pleas were unsuccessful, and the city met a brutal end: the defenders were executed by the Lakedaimonians, and the city itself came under direct Theban control, being quickly razed to the ground.[91]

If the Thebans had by 427 won a position of leadership within Boiotia, they fought hard to retain it within the institutional confines of the koinon established about 446, which by clearly establishing the rights and obligations of each member polis to the koinon restricted the Thebans' ability to act unilaterally or to efface the local autonomy of the other Boiotian poleis. In 426 they went to the assistance of the Tanagrans who were besieged by a full force of the Athenian army, an attack that started from Oropos (then in Athenian hands) and may have been motivated by the Athenians' anxiety over controlling the food supply from Euboia to Attica via Oropos.[92] Although the Thebans' assistance was ultimately ineffectual, it does point to their active commitment to the project of a regional state, for Tanagra was an independent Boiotian polis and member of the koinon in this period. And it was probably between 427 and 424 that the Thebans doubled the size of their territory and population by undertaking the synoikism of at least six small communities into Thebes: Erythrai, Skaphai, Skolos, Aulis, Schoinos, Potniai, and many others, the Oxyrhynchos Historian (17.3) tells us. This move was taken partially as a response to mounting Athenian aggression toward Thebes: in the frontier zone between northern Attica and southeastern Boiotia, these small communities were highly vulnerable. They had previously been in *sympoliteia* with Plataia, so it was ultimately the Theban destruction of that city that exposed them. The synoikism was not an act of Theban beneficence.[93] The reorganization of southern Boiotia in the mid-420s reveals how complex the political geography of Boiotia already was:

89. Th. 3.65.2–3.

90. On this aspect of the conflict see Gehrke 1985: 132.

91. Th. 3.68.2–3.

92. Th. 3.91.3–5.

93. *Hell.Oxy.* 16.3, 17.3 (Bartoletti). The date of the synoikism of the communities of the Parasopia into Thebes is controversial. It has been dated after the attack on Plataia in 519 (Grenfell and Hunt 1908: 225–27) or, more frequently, after the fall of Plataia in 427 (E. M. Walker 1913: 135–38; Cloché 1952: 72; Roesch 1965b: 40; Bruce 1967: 105, 161). The synoikism is sometimes explained as a measure to improve regional security at the outbreak of the Peloponnesian War in 431 (Demand 1990: 82–85) or in its early years (Moggi 1976: 197–204; Hansen 2004: 441, 452). But these scholars also accept that between 479 and 431 the towns of the Parasopia were part of the territory of Plataia, and it is difficult to see how the Thebans could have synoikized these poleis before they had defeated Plataia itself. P. Salmon (1956: 58

a region, recognized as such in ethnic terms, but only fitfully unified politically, and containing within itself subregions comprising multiple communities in various configurations of dependence and interdependence. This should provide us with an important indication of how and why the koinon came into existence.

But even as the regional government in Boiotia took on firmer and more stable institutions, internal unrest threatened the structure. In 424 democrats within the region, seeking closer Athenian relations and a weakening of this ever stronger and more centralized Boiotian regional state, encouraged the Athenians to invade. The Boiotian democrats, according to Thucydides (4.76.2), wished "to change the order of things and to set up a democracy, just like the Athenians." They were spread throughout the southern and western part of the region: their leader was a Theban exile, and some Orchomenians and Phokians were also involved.[94] These partisans planned three strategic points of betrayal: they would themselves hand over Siphai, the small Corinthian Gulf port of Thespiai, and Chaironeia, while the Athenians were to take the initiative in seizing Delion, a temple of Apollo in the territory of Tanagra.[95] Boiotia was thus to be invaded by Athenian and pro-Athenian forces from west, south, and east on the same day, appointed in advance.

But like many well-laid plans this one too was botched. There was confusion about the day on which the attack was to be made, and the plot was revealed to the Spartans and Boiotians. Siphai and Chaironeia were secured by the Boiotians because Hippokrates, the general who was supposed to seize Delion and thereby distract any possible defenders in the south and west, was planning his attack for the wrong day.[96] He did invade, unopposed, and with a large levy spent three days fortifying Delion. The Boiotians were not unaware of what was happening; during this time they were mustering their army at Tanagra, a slow process because the soldiers had to "come in from all the poleis." By the time they were prepared to fight, the Athenian forces had withdrawn just past the Boiotian border and into Oropos.[97] At this point we learn from Thucydides of a well-organized set of

---

and 1978: 82–83) dates the change to 447/6, supposing that it was a reward (from whom?) for the Thebans' leadership role in the expulsion of the Athenians; but that in itself was disproved by Larsen 1960b. The date of the synoikism of these communities is important insofar as it is wrapped up with the question of whether Plataia was a member of the koinon between 446 and sometime shortly before 432, which itself bears on the nature of the early formal institutions of the koinon. See below, pp. 336–37. Cf. Siewert 1977.

94. Th. 4.76.2; Gomme, Andrewes, and Dover 1945–81 and Hornblower 1991–2008 (*ad loc.*) for variant manuscript readings that would make Ptoiodoros an exile of Thespiai.

95. Th. 4.76.4. Delion is probably located at modern Dilesi, on the Boiotian coast opposite Euboia: Pritchett 1965–92: II.24–36 and III.295–97; P. W. Wallace 1979: 27–29; Fossey 1988: 62–66.

96. Th. 4.89.1–2.

97. Th. 4.90.1–91.1.

institutions for the control of the entire region: not only was there a regional levy, but the army was led by eleven boiotarchs, the same officials who cropped up so briefly in the narrative of the Theban attack on Plataia in 431 as representatives of the Thebans. We can combine these two pieces of evidence and assert with confidence that the college of boiotarchs was a regional, representative body by the time of the Peloponnesian War.

At Tanagra in 424 the boiotarchs were at odds: ten of the eleven urged that the army should be disbanded because the Athenians had already crossed out of Boiotia. One, Pagondas of Thebes, opposed them.[98] His speech to the assembled army, fascinating but generally neglected, is particularly interesting for our purposes. He begins by reminding the Boiotians of their tradition of opposing the invasion of foreigners (Th. 4.92.2) and asserts that freedom consists in readiness to contest with one's neighbors (4.92.4). The Boiotians' neighbors happen to be the Athenians, the worst neighbors one could possibly have, because they are trying to enslave everyone; by a sidelong allusion to Euboia (which had suffered the imposition of Athenian cleruchies in 446 after its revolt) he invokes the truly terrifying possibility that Boiotia could become, effectively, a part of Attica, with no meaningful boundary between them (4.92.4). He then reminds the Boiotians of their victory at Koroneia, which brought security to the entire region (4.92.6). In the battle that ensued the Boiotians were victorious, and after a protracted struggle over the fortifications the Athenians were resolutely chased out of Boiotia.[99] The human cost of this victory was heavy, but its significance was enormous, as is attested by the individual public funerary monuments for Boiotian casualties from Thespiai and Tanagra.[100]

The Thebans followed this victory with a move to shore up internal weaknesses threatening the integrity and success of an independent Boiotian regional state. In the summer of 423 the Thebans accused the Thespians of Atticism and tore down their walls.[101] This was certainly in part a response to the involvement of Siphai in the plot to betray Boiotia to Athens in the previous year, and according to Thucydides the Thebans took advantage of Thespiai's heavy manpower losses at Delion to attack the city.[102] Although Thucydides does not record any Theban

98. Pagondas the son of Aiolidas (Th. 4.91) may be the same Pagondas who in Pind. fr. 94b (Maehler) appears as the father of Agasikles, who served as *daphnēphoros* (laurel bearer) for Apollo Ismenios in Thebes (Hornblower 2004: 159; Kurke 2007: 65 with n. 3, following Lehnus 1984: 83–85). Cf. Hornblower 1991–2008: II.289.

99. Th. 4.96–101.

100. Thespian stelai: *IG* VII.1888a–i. Tumulus: Schilardi 1977; Pritchett 1974–91: IV.132–33; Low 2003: 104–9. Tanagran stelai: *IG* VII.585. Cf. Keramopoullos 1920.

101. Th. 4.133.1.

102. For severe Thespian losses at Delion see Th. 4.96.3.

response to the other leaders of the democratizing movement there is some evidence that they took measures to reduce the manpower base of Orchomenos and Chaironeia by reorganizing the districts and making coordination between the two poleis more difficult.[103]

When the Athenians and Lakedaimonians made peace in 421, the Boiotians refused to join.[104] A series of diplomatic negotiations resulted only in the conclusion in 420 of a separate treaty between Boiotia and Sparta that violated the terms of the Peace of Nikias and contributed to its speedy dissolution.[105] Until the end of the war the Boiotians remained loyal allies of Sparta.[106] There was, however, not complete internal harmony. In 414 some democrats at Thespiai attempted to stage a coup against the oligarchs in power, but a quick Theban response helped break it.[107] We hear little else of Boiotia until 413, when the Spartan fortification of Dekeleia, on the Boiotian-Attic frontier, gave the Boiotians an unsurpassed opportunity to ravage Attic land and harass their hated neighbors ceaselessly.[108] The Spartan-Boiotian alliance showed signs of pending rupture, too.[109] Yet the Boiotians remained staunchly opposed to Athens: in 404 they (along with the Corinthians and other Peloponnesians) proposed at a meeting of the Peloponnesian League that the great city should be razed to the ground and its land used as pasture. The proposal was so outrageously pugnacious that not even the Spartans could support it: they refused on the grounds that Athens had done too much for the Greeks when the Persians invaded, and this comment, with its silent allusion to Theban Medism, reveals that at least part of their refusal lay in fear that the Boiotians would simply replace Athens.[110]

The Boiotians' response to the civil war that erupted in Athens after the city's surrender to Sparta complicates the picture significantly and provides us with hints of internal discord in Thebes. When the Thirty Tyrants seized control in 404, the democrats in Athens were forced into exile, and the Spartans decreed that they should all be returned to the Thirty, the Thebans in response decreed that "every house and polis in Boiotia" should provide complete support for the exiles.[111] This shift of policy is certainly to be attributed in part to abhorrence of what unfolded

---

103. See below, p. 372.
104. The Boiotians' refusal to join the treaty (Th. 5.17.2) was grounded in their refusal to return the Attic border fort at Panakton and to return prisoners (Th. 5.18.7).
105. Negotiations: Th. 5.36–38. Separate treaty: Th. 5.39.3.
106. See Th. 5.57.2; 7.19.3; 8.3.2, 106.3. Xen. *Hell.* 1.3.15; Diod. Sic. 13.98.4, 99.5–6; Paus. 10.9.9.
107. Th. 6.95.2.
108. Th. 7.19.1–2, 27.8; Diod. Sic. 13.9.2.
109. Xen. *Hell.* 3.5.5; Plut. *Lys.* 27.4.
110. Xen. *Hell.* 2.2.19, cf. 3.5.8; Isocr. 14.31; Andoc. 3.21; Plut. *Lys.* 15.3.
111. Plut. *Lys.* 27.6. Cf. Plut. *Pelop.* 6.5; Diod. Sic. 14.6.3.

in Athens under the Thirty and a desire to prevent Sparta from becoming too strong by effectively ruling an oligarchic Athens. It is also to be attributed in part to a change in internal Theban politics, which we can detect only in outline. The Oxyrhynchos Historian (17.1) tells us that around 395 there was *stasis* in Thebes: one faction, led by Ismenias, Antitheos, and Androkleidas, was accused by the other of Atticizing. The other faction was led by Leontiades, Asias, and Koiratadas. In 395 "and a little before" the supporters of Ismenias were dominant in Thebes, but those of Leontiades had previously been in control of the city for a long time (12.2). The rise of Ismenias and his supporters clearly occurred sometime shortly after 404; their influence certainly lay behind the decree in favor of the exiled Athenian democrats.[112] Whoever was calling the shots in the very last years of the fifth century, they were charting a careful course, attempting to assert Boiotian independence from Sparta without stirring up a war against their former ally. The Oxyrhynchos Historian was also, however, right in saying that the faction of Ismenias, despite being accused of Atticism, was "not especially concerned for the Athenians" (17.1). For in 402 *stasis* erupted at Oropos, an important city and healing sanctuary of the hero Amphiaraos on the Attic-Boiotian border that was a regular bone of contention between the two states.[113] The exiles appealed to the Thebans, who sent an army and took the city by force. They then moved the whole community inland, and after a period in which they experimented with self-government, "gave them citizenship, and made their territory Boiotian."[114] It is important to emphasize that the Thebans did not make the territory Theban; they made it Boiotian: it now became a member polis of the Boiotian koinon.

With the exception of three brief democratic movements within Boiotia in the course of the Peloponnesian War, at Orchomenos and (twice) at Thespiai, the region was united in its opposition to Athens until the oligarchic coup that put the Thirty Tyrants in power. This hostile stance they carried forward from the shocking events of 506 and the even more painful Athenian occupation of the region from 457 to 446. The battle of Koroneia became a deeply significant event for both victor and defeated. Thucydides' detailed narrative reveals that by the early years of the Peloponnesian War the Boiotian regional state had created its central institutions, their significance recognizable from the fuller description of the Oxyrhynchos Historian of 395: eleven boiotarchs, serving as representatives of the various Boiotian communities; clusters of cities that facilitated the payment of taxes to the

112. Debate over the precise date at which Ismenias and his supporters gained ascendancy (e.g., Busolt 1908: 276–77; Cloché 1918; Morrison 1942: 76–77; E. Meyer and Stier 1953–58: V.213–14; Kagan 1961: 330–32; Perlman 1964: 65; Funke 1980: 47–48; Lendon 1989) is not important for our purposes.

113. Oropos had been independent since 412/1: Th. 8.60.1; Lys. 31.9; Gehrke 1985: 125. For its history to 323 see Hornblower 1991–2008: I.279; Hansen 2004: 448–49 (no. 215).

114. Diod. Sic. 14.17.1–3. Cf. Theopomp. *FGrHist* 115 F 12.

federal treasury and commitment of manpower to the Boiotian army; and four councils with final authority in deciding matters of regional and foreign policy. Of these institutions prior to the battle of Oinophyta we hear only of the boiotarchs, mentioned by Herodotos en passant; and we can see clear evidence of the clustering of communities in hierarchical relationships, a reflection of the process by which Boiotian poleis expanded. Clear evidence for moves toward regional cooperation appears in the late sixth century. But it was only after 446 that the Boiotians began to develop the institutions of a regional state to support and protect the relations of their poleis with one another, a move that was certainly taken (and accepted) as a response to the very real fear that the Athenians might return and occupy the region again, as indeed they tried to do in 424. By the 430s the Thebans were pushing hard for a position of leadership within Boiotia that was resisted with equal ferocity at Orchomenos, Thespiai, and Plataia. It is striking that by 404/3 the Thebans had the authority to issue decrees that were binding on every house and polis in Boiotia, and to incorporate the territory of Oropos into Boiotia. This is perhaps the most unmistakable mark of highly developed institutions of a regional state with an increasingly centralized political and legal structure concentrated primarily if not wholly in the hands of the Thebans.

ACHAIA

Our study of Boiotia began with the Hesiodic evidence for the growth of large poleis by the subordination of smaller ones. This pattern is in certain respects paralleled by developments across the Corinthian Gulf in Achaia (map 3), where we first find evidence for the organization of communities and their interactions in the classical period.[115] An important but elusive passage in Herodotos provides our earliest literary hint (1.145–46):

> It seems to me that the Ionians created for themselves twelve poleis and were not willing to introduce more, because when they lived in the Peloponnese they had twelve *merea*, just as now the Achaians, who drove out the Ionians, have twelve *merea*. Pellene is first after Sikyon, then Aigeira and Aigai, in which is situated the ever-flowing river Krathis, from which the river in Italy takes its name. Then there are Boura and Helike, to which the Ionians fled when they were worsted in battle by the Achaians, and Aigion and Rhypes and Patrai and Pharai and Olenos, in which is the great Peiros River, and Dyme and Tritaia. These last are the only Achaians who dwell inland. These are the twelve *merea* of the Achaians now, and in the past they belonged to the Ionians.

115. Numerous arguments were once advanced for the existence of an Achaian koinon, or something like it, in the archaic and early classical periods (e.g., Anderson 1954: 80; Larsen 1968: 83; Freitag 1996: 125), but they have been effectively disproved by Morgan and Hall 1996: 193–96, 201–14; Morgan and Hall 2000; cf. Moggi 2002.

There has been much discussion of the precise meaning of *merea* in this passage. Literally "parts," all these communities are later attested as poleis. It is exceedingly difficult to use Herodotos's description of Achaia as evidence for the precise status of these communities at the time when he was writing.[116] Rather than seeking positive evidence for a sociopolitical status that may have been meaningless to the Achaians of the early fifth century, it is perhaps more instructive to take the word literally: Achaia was comprised of "parts," a word that itself entails a whole. Indeed the region is elsewhere described by Herodotos as a whole occupied by the Achaian *ethnos* at the time of the Persian Wars.[117] The language of parts to describe the Achaian communities persists in later sources and may well reflect a local terminology. After giving a list of Achaian places that largely mirrors that of Herodotos, with changes in the region's political geography in the intervening centuries duly reflected, Strabo (8.7.5) reports that "each of the twelve parts [*merides*] consisted of seven or eight communities [*dēmoi*]."[118] Strabo is clear here: the twelve parts of Achaia that we know from later sources as poleis were comprised of multiple *dēmoi*, which may mean villages or simply communities. Here and elsewhere Strabo reports that the Achaian poleis familiar from later periods were formed by synoikism.[119] While none of the literary accounts allows us to date this process with any confidence, recent archaeological evidence suggests that it began in the fifth century.[120] Although Aigion appears to have been inhabited more or less continuously since the Mycenaean period, the area of occupation increased significantly over the course of the classical period.[121] To the southwest, excavations at Trapezá, identified as ancient Rhypes (map 3), have brought to light an acropolis fortified in the fifth century, with buildings and further fortifications to both the west and the

116. As Morgan and Hall 1996: 168 point out (and cf. Morgan and Hall 2004: 473), Herodotos is writing here about "the protohistoric period prior to the Return of the Herakleidai," and so it may be misleading to conclude (with Sakellariou 1991: 14) that the development of poleis in Achaia must postdate Herodotos. However, the verb of the very last sentence of the passage is emphatically in the present tense, making it difficult to accept Morgan and Hall's argument that the passage is a simple reflection of Herodotos's vision of protohistoric Achaia.

117. Hdt. 8.73.1.

118. Str. 8.7.4–5. One other such list survives, viz. the description of the Achaian coast by Ps.-Skylax 42, on which see Flensted-Jensen and Hansen 1996.

119. Str. 8.3.2 describes the communities of the Peloponnese mentioned by Homer as "systems of demes, each comprised of multiple [demes], from which later the well-known poleis were synoikized" and provides Aigion, Patrai, and Dyme as Achaian examples. *Systēma* is used by Strabo elsewhere (14.2.25) to describe the Chrysaoric koinon in Karia.

120. Koerner 1974: 467–69 dated the synoikism of the Achaian poleis between the "period of colonization" and the mid-fifth century. His argument has to be abandoned in the face of archaeological evidence that has since come to light. For discussion, primarily of the literary evidence, see Moggi 1976: 93, 124, 126; Demand 1990: 61–64.

121. Papakosta 1991.

east of this plateau.[122] The presence of a temple belonging to the sixth century at the site makes it clear that the classical period was one of intensification rather than settlement ex novo, and that is likely to have been achieved by a combination of demographic growth and synoikism.[123] Pausanias reports that Patrai was formed by the synoikism of Aroe, Antheia, and Mesatis (map 3).[124] A systematic extensive survey of the territory of Patrai has shown that the necropolis of Patrai was new in the fifth century, with the focus of classical settlement in the urban center.[125] And finally, near the western coast of the northern Peloponnese, while it is clear that the urban center of Dyme was settled more intensively in the classical period than before, this development does not appear to come at the expense of occupation of rural sites, so we may here have evidence of significant population growth in the classical period.[126] Over the course of the fifth century, then, the communities of Achaia were adopting increasingly urban forms, frequently but not always at the expense of rural habitation. Strabo reports that Dyme (formerly known as Paleia or Hyperesia) derived its name from the fact that it was the westernmost of the Achaian cities; if this is correct it would indicate that notions of an Achaian territory were becoming fixed in the same period.[127]

This implies a sense of Achaian identity, for which we also find our first clear evidence in the fifth century. Both Herodotos and Thucydides describe the Achaians as an *ethnos;* according to Herodotos, their sense of belonging stemmed from the belief that they had occupied the territory on the north coast of the Peloponnese under the leadership of Teisamenos the son of Orestes, a leader of the Homeric Achaians, after expelling the Ionians in the upheavals that followed the so-called Return of the Herakleidai.[128] The articulation of an Achaian ethnic identity based on territory and descent from Teisamenos may go back to the sixth century, when the Spartans purportedly took the bones of Teisamenos from

122. Vordos 2001, 2002. For the identification of Trapezá as Rhypes, on the grounds of Paus. 7.23.4, see D. Müller 1987: 841; Rizakis 1995: 193; Morgan and Hall 1996: 179.

123. Vordos 2002: 227–31.

124. Paus. 7.18.5. Mesatis has now been located at Voudeni: Petropoulos 2001–2.

125. Petropoulos and Rizakis 1994.

126. Morgan and Hall 1996: 186–89. The survey evidence is presented by Lakakis and Rizakis 1990, 1992a, b. There have been attempts to date the synoikism of Dyme more precisely on the basis of the use of ethnics reported in Pausanias (Paus. 5.9.1 = Moretti 1957: no. 171 with Koerner 1974: 469; Paus. 7.17.7, cf. 6.3.8 = Moretti 1957: no. 6 with Morgan and Hall 2004: 481). However, we have no ability to assess the relationship between synoikism and the use of the name Dyme, and indeed the archaeological record suggests that in this case synoikism was a gradual process, with rural sites in the surrounding area continuing to be inhabited throughout the classical and Hellenistic periods.

127. Str. 8.7.5; Steph. Byz. and *Etym. Magn.* s.v. *Dymē.* The name seems to appear for the first time in Ps.-Skylax 42. The idea that the region was unified by its inhabitants, rather than the other way around, is suggested also by Paus. 7.1.1. Cf. Gschnitzer 1955: 128; Koerner 1974: 458.

128. Hdt. 1.145; Th. 3.92.5; cf. Morgan and Hall 1996: 197; J.M. Hall 1997: 43, 52, 72–73, 137.

Helike, where he died in battle against the Ionians.[129] The use of *Achaios* as an ethnic, both collectively and for individuals, both internally and externally, on inscriptions of the fifth century provides clear evidence for the active relevance of this identity.[130] The question is when Achaian identity became politicized, contributing to political cooperation and the development of formal political institutions that encompassed all the Achaian communities.

A passage of Polybios describing the adoption by the people of Kroton, Sybaris, and Kaulonia of "Achaian customs and laws" and the use of a common sanctuary of Zeus Homarios as a political meeting place has been taken, above all by F. W. Walbank, as evidence that the Achaian koinon existed in the mid-fifth century, but the problems with that interpretation have been systematically exposed by Catherine Morgan and Jonathan Hall.[131] Walbank has recently defended his position, but problems remain.[132] Morgan and Hall's argument has three facets: first, we must suspect Polybios of retrojecting the existence of the Achaian koinon into hoary antiquity in order to prove his own contention that the Achaians had always been valued for their principles of equality and fairness; second, the inclusion of Sybaris in Polybios's report poses a problem, for we know that the city was destroyed by Kroton circa 511/0, some half-century before the burning down of the Pythagorean *synedria* in southern Italy; and third, it is not at all clear that the Achaians used the sanctuary of Zeus Homarios as a political meeting place in the mid-fifth century. Regarding the first, we can be either suspicious (Morgan and Hall) or accepting (Walbank); it depends largely on temperament, and nothing can be proven. Regarding the second, Walbank proposes that Polybios here refers to Sybaris on the Traeis, founded by those Sybarite survivors who had contributed to the settlement at Thourioi in 446/5 and were expelled.[133] That is possible, but it should be noted that this Sybaris too was destroyed soon after its foundation.[134]

129. Paus. 7.1.8. The episode can be dated only by its similarity to the Spartans' collection of the bones of Orestes from Tegea (Hdt. 1.67.2–68.6), ca. 560, both construed as a strategy for connecting to the pre-Dorian Spartan past as a means of expanding Spartan power in the Peloponnese. For discussion see Leahy 1955; Moreau 1990; Boedeker 1993; Malkin 1994: 28–30.

130. Collective and internal: Paus. 5.25.8 and below, pp. 176–77. Individual, internal use: Paus. 7.17.7, ca. 460. Individual, external use: *IG* I³ 174; *IG* II² 13 (*SEG* 40.54); *IG* V.1.1 with Loomis 1992: 297–308.

131. Polyb. 2.39.5–6 with Morgan and Hall 1996: 195–96 (cf. Morgan and Hall 2004: 474–75) *contra* F. W. Walbank 1957–79: I.224–26. Polybios gives *Homarios* as the epiklesis of Zeus at Aigion. *Hamarios* (T39 l. 8) and *Homagyrios* (Paus. 7.24.2) are also attested. I generally use *Homarios*, except where explicit discussion of the epiklesis requires use of the variant forms (e.g., T39 l. 8).

132. F. W. Walbank 2000.

133. Diod. Sic. 12.22.1.

134. Possible: Mele 1983: 86 n. 546; Giangiulio 1989: 177 n. 52, 197. Destruction of Sybaris on the Traeis: Diod. Sic. 12.22.1.

Regarding the third, I think we can gain more clarity. The political significance of the sanctuary of Zeus Homarios can be pushed back to the fourth century, for a decree of the Achaian koinon dating to this period has been discovered in the area (T41); the appearance of Zeus on an Achaian didrachma in the 360s confirms this impression.[135]

But for the fifth century Herodotos (1.145–46) indicates that insofar as the Achaians had a common sanctuary, it was that of Poseidon Helikonios, which at the very least remained of interest to the Achaians as late as 373.[136] This evidence for the regional, and possibly political, significance of Poseidon Helikonios is ignored by Walbank, who prefers to prioritize the claim of Livy (38.30.2) that the Achaians met at Aigion "from the beginning of the Achaian council."[137] It is on balance far likelier that the sanctuary of Zeus Homarios took on this regional political significance only after the destruction of Helike and the sanctuary of Poseidon Helikonios in 373. This is supported by Pausanias, who reports that the Achaians "resolved to gather themselves at Aigion. For after Helike was destroyed, from early on it surpassed the other cities in Achaia in reputation, and at the time it was also strong."[138] The date of the beginning of the Achaian council is itself far from clear, but I shall argue below (chap. 2) that we have evidence for it only in the early fourth century. On balance, we have no compelling reason to think that an Achaian koinon existed in the mid-fifth century.[139] Rather, the Achaian communities were in this period experiencing growth and urbanization, conditions that may have contributed later to a need, or a desire, for formal, cooperative political institutions.

The Achaians were only marginally involved in the Peloponnesian War, and although the evidence is limited, it is nevertheless clear that the Achaian poleis did not act with unanimity throughout the conflict. As the Spartans and Athenians assembled their allies in 431, the only Achaian polis to join either side was Pellene, the easternmost of the Achaian coastal communities, which became a Spartan ally.[140] Where we have evidence, it appears that other Achaian poleis were friendly to the Spartans but in every case acted independently, with no sign of an Achaian state that transcended polis boundaries in this period. So in 429

135. Didrachma: Kraay 1976: 101 with pl. 318.
136. Herakleides Pontikos fr. 46a (Wehrli 1953) and below, pp. 194–202.
137. Livy 38.30.2.
138. Paus. 7.7.2.
139. Th. 1.111.3 (cf. Diod. Sic. 11.85; Plut. Per. 19; Paus. 4.25) is inconclusive evidence for the existence of an Achaian state in the mid-fifth century. Cf. Th. 1.115.1, 4.21.3, regularly cited as evidence for an early Achaian koinon, but from which it is impossible to conclude anything. For a more accepting view see Larsen 1953.
140. Th. 2.9.2–3; cf. Ar. Lys. 996.

the Peloponnesian fleet took refuge at Patrai and Dyme, and later was allowed to anchor at Rhion while the land army assembled at Panormos.[141] These latter places appear both to have been in the territory of Patrai. Pro-Spartan sympathy in the Achaian poleis is further evidenced by the appearance of an "Achaian from Olenos" contributing to the Spartan war fund in the period 425–416.[142] Thus far the Achaian poleis appear to have been friendly to the Spartans, but every indication we have suggests that this orientation was assumed voluntarily and individually rather than collectively or under compulsion.[143] In 419, however, the situation changed. The Patraians accepted the overtures of Alkibiades and the Athenians to extend their city walls down to the sea in order to exclude the Peloponnesian fleet, which they had hosted only six years before, as part of the overall Athenian strategy of winning allies in the heart of the Peloponnese.[144] It seems likely that at least some other Achaian communities followed suit in establishing friendlier relations with Athens at the expense of Sparta, for in 417, Thucydides reports, the Spartans "arranged affairs in Achaia in a way more congenial to themselves than hitherto."[145] This may imply the Achaians' membership in the Peloponnesian League, but their status within that organization is entirely obscure. Equally unclear is the question of whether all Achaia as a political unit was a single member, or whether participation was formally conducted via the poleis.[146] In short, throughout the Peloponnesian War the Achaian cities were friendly to the Spartans, though only Pellene was a formal ally. The brief period of pro-Athenian sympathies, at least in western Achaia, is largely attributable to the energies and vision of Alkibiades. But while it is clear that other Greeks perceived of Achaia as a territory united by the shared ethnicity of its inhabitants, there is no reason to believe that the Achaians themselves had channeled

141. Th. 2.83–86.

142. IG V.1.1 ll. 6–8 with Matthaiou and Pikoulas 1989 (SEG 39.370); Loomis 1992.

143. That the Spartan relationship with Achaia was relatively weak (if generally positive) is suggested by the fact that Achaians were excluded by the Spartans, on ethnic grounds, from participation in the Dorian settlement of Herakleia Trachinia: Th. 3.92.5.

144. Th. 5.52.2; Plut. Alc. 15.4–6. Traces of these walls have been discovered: AD 52 (1997) Chron. B1: 273–75. The move followed the Athenian alliance with Elis, Mantineia, and Argos in 420 (Th. 5.47).

145. Th. 5.82.1, trans. Hornblower 1991–2008: III.208. This may imply the installation or promotion of oligarchies: cf. Th. 5.81.2 (with Hornblower 1991–2008: III.207–8) and Xen. Hell. 7.1.43 (with F. W. Walbank 2000: 23). However, Xenophon's account records the establishment of democracies in 371 under Theban auspices; it is in no way safe to conclude that the oligarchies that were implicitly toppled in the process had been set up by the Spartans nearly fifty years before. Indeed, as we shall see below, we know a good deal about Achaian political organization in the intervening time, and there are no further indications of behavior driven by allegiance or obligation to Sparta.

146. Freitag 2009: 16–17 seems undecided. If Achaia as a single entity were the member, it would be our earliest evidence for regional political unity.

this group identity into political institutions that transcended polis boundaries in the region.

AITOLIA

While archaeological evidence from the sanctuaries at Thermon and Kalydon (map 4) indicates communities in the region that were both prosperous and precocious in the early archaic period (see below, pp. 178–84), we know nothing about how these communities organized themselves or related to one another, and the little material evidence we have from other sites in the region offers little help. Fifth-century literary sources give us our first glimpse, but it is one that is narrowly restricted to the coastal area of eastern Aitolia and is for the most part refracted through the lens of Athenian and Messenian history.

In 456/5, the Athenians settled those Messenians who had survived the helot revolt on Mount Ithome, at Naupaktos (map 4), a place they had recently captured from the Ozolian Lokrians.[147] The Messenians and Naupaktians immediately began to cooperate with each other and acted as staunch allies to the Athenians.[148] Both groups made attacks on ethnically Aitolian communities: in 456/5, the Athenians seized Chalkis, which Thucydides describes as a polis of the Corinthians, although in early literary sources the city is resolutely Aitolian.[149] It is possible that Athenian control of Naupaktos and Chalkis entailed control of the smaller communities of Molykreion and Makyneia situated between them.[150] Around the same time the Messenians and Naupaktians dedicated a monumental pillar at Delphi as a tithe of spoils taken "from the Kalydonians" (T47), peopling a city central to the early mythic history of Aitolia.[151]

These attacks may have been the origin of the hatred that existed between the Aitolians and Naupaktians several decades later (Th. 3.94.3), and they may help to

147. Th. 1.103.3; Diod. Sic. 11.84.7. See Badian 1990 for detailed discussion of the seizure of Naupaktos.

148. This cooperation may be the result of a formal treaty by which the Messenians and Naupaktians established the terms of their cohabitation of Naupaktos, which has now been published by Matthaiou and Mastrokostas 2000–2003 (*SEG* 49.583). The editors place the inscription in the period ca. 430–420, primarily on the basis of letter forms and dialect. Luraghi 2008: 193 n. 73, however, suggests that because of the perfect stoichedon style and Ionian-influenced letter forms, the stone may have been inscribed by an Athenian stonecutter, which would require that we look for stylistic parallels in Attic inscriptions, with the result that "an earlier date, closer to the migration of the Messenians to Naupaktos, would be more likely."

149. Chalkis: Th. 1.108.5. Corinthian control of Chalkis may have been a function of Corinthian attempts to secure control of commercial traffic through the Corinthian Gulf: Freitag, Funke, and Moustakis 2004: 383; Freitag 2000: 55. The Athenians made another attack on Corinthian interests in this period with their unsuccessful attack on Oiniadai ca. 454/3 (Th. 1.111.3 with Diod. Sic. 11.85.2). Cf. Paus. 4.25 for the (perhaps confused) claim that the Messenians seized Oiniadai. Chalkis as Aitolian in early literary sources: Hom. *Il.* 2.639; Alcman fr. 24 Calame.

150. Larsen 1953: 799.

151. For Kalydon in Aitolian mythic history see Hom. *Il.* 2.640, 9.531, etc.

explain why Thucydides appears to report that Kalydon and Pleuron were not part of Aitolia in 426.[152] More immediately, the Athenian and Messenian attacks on coastal Aitolia may have been the occasion for the conclusion of a treaty between the Aitolians and the Spartans, an inscribed copy of which was discovered on the Spartan akropolis (T48).[153] The treaty establishes friendship, peace, and alliance between the Aitolians and Lakedaimonians (ll. 1–3), but the detailed terms of the treaty reveal an asymmetrical relationship that is in no way surprising:[154] the Aitolians must follow wherever the Lakedaimonians lead (ll. 4–7) and have the same friends and enemies as they do (ll. 7–10). They are further prohibited from concluding separate peace agreements (ll. 10–14). The only recorded obligation of the Lakedaimonians to the Aitolians is that they will succor them with all their strength if anyone should attack "the territory of the [–]rxadieis" (ll. 16–19). The identity of the [-]rxadieis is uncertain, but as we shall see below, they are probably a population group within Aitolia. One further clause in the treaty points to the period after 456/5 as a likely context: the Aitolians are prohibited from receiving "fugitives who have committed any wrongdoing" (ll. 14–16). The only group of fugitives whom the Spartans were concerned about, to our knowledge, was the rebel Messenians. Their residence in Naupaktos, on the border with Aitolia, may have made the Spartans concerned about Messenian flight into their territory. The treaty, it should be underscored, is a treaty of friendship and peace, which should entail some prior conflict. We have no information about such a conflict in any surviving source, but it seems possible that the Aitolians had harbored some rebel Messenians and brought on Spartan hostility, which was subsequently settled. In the midst of the larger conflict between Athens and Sparta in this period, it is not surprising that the Aitolians may have pursued or agreed to an alliance with the Spartans after experiencing the attacks of the Athenians and Messenians. The inscribed treaty between the Spartans and Aitolians raises one big question that we cannot satisfactorily answer: What kind of political entity is signified by "the Aitolians"? In the complete absence of any other evidence for a formally organized and institutionalized Aitolian state in the mid-fifth century, we can say only that the Aitolians were a juridically and diplomatically recognizable entity. We do not know the territorial extent of this entity or anything about its internal

152. Th. 3.102.5. We shall see below (p. 62) that Kalydon had come under the control of the Achaian koinon by 389; Bommeljé 1988: 314 suggests that Achaian control stemmed at least as far back as 426, the context of Thucydides' report. This seems highly unlikely given what we know of the limits on Achaian cooperation and action outside their own territory in the late fifth century.

153. The date of this inscription has been vigorously contested since its initial publication in 1974; see the commentary to T48 in the epigraphic dossier for full discussion.

154. On asymmetry as a characteristic of Spartan treaties in the early classical period see Bolmarcich 2005.

organization. Thirty years later, as we shall see below, we find the Aitolians adopting a kind of loose representative structure, again in the context of interstate diplomacy, combined with evidence of internal cooperation but none of formal state institutions; at this time Thucydides calls the Aitolians an *ethnos,* and we should probably follow suit; but it is worth specifying to the extent possible what that meant in practice. We should perhaps see the Aitolians' cooperation in the conduct of relations with foreign states as an early context in which their group identity was formalized in order to accomplish a shared goal, in this case one of preventing further territorial losses to the aggression of the Athenians, Messenians, and Naupaktians.

This situation appears not to have changed much by 426, when Thucydides' detailed narrative, along with several important but difficult inscriptions that seem to cluster around the same date, shed welcome light on conditions in Aitolia. In the summer of that year, the Athenian army and navy were at Leukas under the general Demosthenes, attempting to take the island for their Akarnanian allies. With all his forces assembled, Demosthenes' Messenian allies from Naupaktos approached and encouraged him to invade Aitolia, which they said was hostile to them. Buoyed by hopes of an easy victory that would pave the way to Athenian control of northwestern mainland Greece and provide him with an alternative land route into Boiotia, Demosthenes agreed.[155] At this point Thucydides pauses to give a description, from the Messenian perspective, of conditions prevailing in Aitolia, upon which their invasion strategy should be based (Th. 3.94.4–5):

> The *ethnos* of the Aitolians, they said, was great and warlike, but they lived in unwalled villages, which were widely scattered, and they used only light arms, so that it would not be difficult to overwhelm them before help could arrive. They bade him first to attack the Apodotoi, then the Ophiones, and after them the Eurytanes, which is the largest part [*meros*] of the Aitolians. They speak an unintelligible language and are eaters of raw meat, so they said.

While the report about linguistic isolation and an uncivilized diet can readily be understood as the bias of enemies exhorting their allies to attack, much of the rest of the passage appears credible.[156]

The Aitolians are perceived as an *ethnos* comprised of multiple parts; here three are listed, the Apodotoi, Ophiones, and Eurytanes (map 5). Later in the narrative of the same episode, Thucydides reports two more Aitolian population groups, the Kallieis and Bomieis, who belong to the Ophiones, from which we may infer that the *ethnos* of the Aitolians comprised *merē* that were themselves composite.[157] The

---

155. Th. 3.94.1–3.
156. Hornblower 1991–2008: I.510; Antonetti 1990: 79–84; Funke 1991: 315–17.
157. Th. 3.96.3.

Aitolian population groups mentioned by Thucydides may not be the only ones: Strabo likewise reports that the Bomieis belong to the Ophiones and agrees with Thucydides in placing the Eurytanes on the same organizational plane as the Ophiones, but he adds Agraioi, Kouretes, and others.[158] Strabo mentions these groups in his description of Aitolian geography and makes it clear that each group has its own territory. That we do not have the entire picture from Thucydides is further suggested by the appearance of the [-]rxadieis in the inscribed fifth-century treaty between the Spartans and the Aitolians (T48, l.17). This elusive document makes explicit what is only implied by Thucydides and Strabo: the Aitolian population groups have defined territories of their own (T48, ll. 16–18). The complexity of Aitolian political geography is further hinted at by two fourth-century inscriptions that marked the boundaries between the territories of the Arysaes and Nomenaeis (T50) and the Eiteaies and Eoitanes (T51), groups that are otherwise largely unknown.[159] In short, the Messenians' description of Aitolian sociopolitical organization in Thucydides appears to be accurate if incomplete and points to a region inhabited by distinct population groups with defined territories who nevertheless associated with one another as Aitolians.

But what of the Messenians' claim that the Aitolians lived in unwalled villages? For the fifth century it may be largely correct. Demosthenes' invasion of 426 ultimately targeted eastern Aitolia, home to the Ophiones. This area has been more systematically surveyed than others, and archaeological evidence points to the existence of some twenty-five settlements of various sizes in the classical and Hellenistic periods.[160] Of these, and indeed in all Aitolia, only one set of fortifications has been found that can be dated with any confidence to the fifth century. They cluster around a site identified as the polis Aigition (maps 4 and 5), which played an important role in the defense of Aitolia against the Athenian-Messenian attack.[161] So again Thucydides' Messenian characterization of the region is largely accurate, if somewhat overdrawn for rhetorical purposes.

The Messenians persuaded Demosthenes to launch the invasion from Ozolian Lokris and to proceed with haste, conquering village after village. While the Athenians and their allies captured three small settlements, the Aitolians organized

158. Str. 10.2.5. On the territory of the Agraioi see Antonetti 1987b, and for how they were figured by other Greeks as typical uncivilized nomads, Antonetti 1987a.

159. *Nomenaiewus* appears as an ethnic in third-century Akarnania: Antonetti 1987b: 97 (*SEG* 38.435); cf. *AD* 22 (1967) 322 (*BE* 1970: 325). The other three groups are otherwise unattested.

160. Bommeljé and Doorn 1985.

161. Th. 3.97.2; Funke 1997: 148. The fortifications are at the now abandoned village of Strouza: Bommeljé 1981–82; Bommeljé and Doorn 1984, 1985; Bommeljé, Doorn, Fagel, et al. 1981. The fortifications on Mount Boucheri may be related to those at Strouza. The polis status of Aigition has been a subject of debate: Funke 1997: 153–54 with n. 36, 173–76 (exchange between Funke and Hansen); Hansen 2000a: 200.

themselves to repulse the attack, "so that even the most distant of the Ophiones, living in the direction of the Malian Gulf, and the Bomieis and Kallieis all assisted."[162] Clearly the communities of eastern Aitolia were in close communication with one another and rallied to the defense of their territory, probably according to some preexisting agreement to defend other members of the group in the event of an attack. The invading force advanced as far as Aigition, which they found abandoned. Its inhabitants had taken refuge in the rugged hills above the settlement, from where they attacked the slow-moving Athenian hoplite army with javelins at a surprising speed. The invading army was eventually repulsed, with the death of some 120 hoplites whom Thucydides describes as "the best men in the city of Athens to die in this war," its survivors escaping into Lokris.[163] It is a fascinating episode, revealing the efficacy of communication and cooperation among the scattered population groups of eastern Aitolia.

That cooperation extended to the conduct of interstate diplomacy, for Thucydides tells us that after the Athenian army had been expelled, the Aitolians sent three ambassadors, representing each of the three major population groups—the Ophiones, Eurytanes, and Apodotoi—to Corinth and Sparta seeking support for a retaliatory attack on Naupaktos.[164] The Corinthian response is not reported, but the Spartans agreed.[165] Seeing an opportunity to dislodge the Athenians from central Greece, the Spartans sent an army into Ozolian Lokris, where along with the Aitolians they won over numerous communities that had been friendly to Athens. Lokrian forces swelled the ranks of the Spartan-Aitolian force, which then advanced on Naupaktos, cutting down crops in the territory and seizing an unfortified suburb but failing to take Naupaktos itself, which was defended by the remnants of Demosthenes' army. The principal gain for the Aitolians was the seizure of Molykreion, which had been subject to Athens and lay west of Naupaktos.[166] It was also probably at this time that they gained control of Makyneia in the same area.[167] Further west, however, Kalydon and Pleuron appear to have remained independent but must have been sympathetic to the Aitolians and Peloponnesians, for it was

162. Th. 3.96.3. The identification of Kallion (Kallipolis) with Velouchovo (*contra* Hornblower 1991–2008: I.513) is amply supported by new epigraphic evidence: Rousset 2006.

163. Th. 3.96.1–98.5, quotation at 3.98.4.

164. Th. 3.100.1.

165. This much is known from Thucydides. The treaty between the Spartans and Aitolians (T48) has been attributed by several scholars to this episode, which if correct would not change the Thucydidean picture radically; see the commentary to T48 in the epigraphic dossier.

166. Th. 3.100.2–102.5. Molykreion: 3.102.2.

167. Makyneia was certainly Aitolian by 329/8, when a decree of the Delphians bestowed proxeny upon an Aitolian from Makyneia (Bourguet 1899: 356–57 with La Coste-Messelière 1949: 229–36 for the date). That Makyneia was probably Aitolian by the fifth century is implied by Hellanikos (*FGrHist* F 118). Cf. Bosworth 1976: 168 with n. 35.

to these and other cities in the area that their combined army retreated after the failed retaliatory attack on Naupaktos.[168]

It is clear from Thucydides' narrative of the Athenian invasion that the Aitolians had in place some mechanism for coordination and cooperation in the face of external attacks, though it gives us precious little indication of the structure of their internal relations. While it would be quite unjustified to call this a koinon, the Aitolians' system of cooperation must directly or indirectly have affected their willingness to create a koinon in the fourth century. It is to this period that we now turn.

168. Th. 3.102.5.

2
—

The Fourth Century

During the first half of the fourth century the loose cooperative practices of the Achaians and Aitolians were transformed into a set of formal political institutions that bound the poleis and communities of each region together into regional states. Although the evidence is not plentiful, it is unmistakable. For Boiotia rich literary sources allow us to trace the struggle against Sparta and the unambiguous domination of the Boiotian koinon by Thebes, which itself begins to reveal the remarkable fragility of the koinon as a set of institutions, a theme we shall pick up in greater detail in chapter 6. The narratives of the fourth-century historians also allow us to trace, more broadly, the problem of the relationship between polis autonomy, hailed as a pan-Hellenic political goal in this period, and participation in a koinon. The creation of a common, regional polity was increasingly seen as a solution to the problem of how small poleis could survive in a world in which some states, and rulers, had grown exceptionally large, wealthy, and powerful. The story of the latter half of the fourth century, and indeed the Hellenistic period as well, can be seen as a story about the tremendous success of this solution, as well as about its limitations.

COMMON WARS, COMMON PEACES, COMMON POLITIES, 404–371

The end of the Peloponnesian War left the Aitolians and Achaians apparently independent but pro-Spartan. The Aitolians still lacked access to the Corinthian Gulf but had no immediate means of regaining it. Boiotian feelings toward Sparta, however, now ran tepid, and they grew even cooler in the first years of the fourth century. Of all the Spartans' Peloponnesian War allies, only the Boiotians and Corinthians refused to join the Spartans when they made war on the Elians in 398.[1] Relations between Sparta and Boiotia continued to deteriorate until outright hostility emerged in 395 in a series of engagements called by some sources the Boiotian War, which became only the first act in the longer play known as the Corinthian War. While there may have been lingering anger over the fallout of the Peloponnesian War, there were certainly more immediate causes for offense. The Spartans were interfering in factional Theban politics.[2] Farther afield, they were aggressively prosecuting a war with the Persians in the eastern Mediterranean that revealed imperialist ambitions, of which the Boiotians had expressed their disapproval.[3] They were also beginning to become involved in Thessaly (much to the alarm of the Boiotians), Sicily, and even Egypt.[4] These are the background conditions against which the Boiotians, according to Xenophon, were open to the suggestion, made by agents of the Persian king, that they should stir up a war against the Spartans in Greece in order to draw Agesilaos away from Asia. They were joined by the Corinthians and Argives, at least in part because of political divisions and strong anti-Spartan tendencies within each of the cities.[5] The Thebans took the lead in drumming up a war against Sparta indirectly, by exploiting an old conflict between the Lokrians, allies of the Boiotians and Athenians, and the Phokians, loyal allies of Sparta.[6] They were correct in their assumption that the Spartans would come to the aid of the Phokians if summoned, and their actions marked the beginning of the Corinthian War.

1. Diod. Sic. 14.17.7; cf. Xen. *Hell.* 3.2.25. Xenophon dates the war to 398/7, and Diodoros to 402/1. Diod. Sic. 14.17.9–10 reports that the Aitolians assisted their kin the Elians in this war, evidence, if in fact T48 (see comm.) belongs to the fifth century, that despite their alliance with Sparta they remained independent. The notice seems to reflect a troop commitment by a single Aitolian state authority, not mercenaries, but we have no contemporary evidence that might shed light on the nature of the Aitolian state that sent them out.

2. *Hell.Oxy.* 17.2 (Bartoletti) with Lendon 1989.

3. Spartan war against Persia: Xen. *Hell.* 3.1.1–2.20. Boiotian disapproval: Xen. *Hell.* 3.5.1–2; *Hell. Oxy.* 7.5 (Bartoletti) with Rung 2004. Spartan imperialism: Andrewes 1978; Hornblower 2002: 183–86; Cawkwell 2005.

4. Thessaly: Ps.-Herodes *Peri politeias* 6, 24 (advocating a Spartan-Thessalian war on Macedonia); Diod. Sic. 14.38.3–4 for Spartan involvement in *stasis* at Herakleia Trachinia (on which more will be said below) and 14.82 for a Spartan garrison at Pharsalos. Sicily: Diod. Sic. 14.10, 63, 70 (for Spartan support to Dionysius I, tyrant of Syracuse, in a local *stasis* and against the Carthaginians). Egypt: Diod. Sic. 14.79. On all this see Hornblower 2002: 181–91.

5. Xen. *Hell.* 3.5.1–2 reports bribery; *Hell.Oxy.* (Bartoletti) 7.5 with Rung 2004.

6. The accounts differ in their details, but the basic outlines are the same: Xen. *Hell.* 3.5.3–4 (dispute over taxes); *Hell.Oxy.* 16.1 (Bartoletti), 18.2–5 (rustling sheep); Paus. 3.9.8 (Lokrians harvesting crops and stealing sheep from Phokian territory). There is debate over which Lokris was involved, Ozolian (*Hell.Oxy.* 18.3 [Bartoletti]; Paus. 3.9.9) or Opountian (Xen. *Hell.* 3.5.3). See Lendon 1989: 311–13; R.J. Buck 1994: 30–35; Buckler 2004: 402–4.

It was probably around this time, when long-simmering discontent with the Spartans was about to boil over into outright conflict, that political divisions within Thebes affected all Boiotia.[7] According to Xenophon, it was a political faction led by Androkleidas and Ismenias that encouraged the Boiotians to invade Phokis in defense of their Lokrian allies. The Spartans agreed readily to a Phokian appeal for help, and the Boiotians (or at least some of them) had what they wanted: a war with Sparta.[8] In response to a damaging Boiotian invasion of western Phokis, the Spartans ordered a general mobilization and sent Lysander ahead to Phokis, from where he exploited the internal divisions of the Boiotians to Spartan advantage, inducing Orchomenos to revolt, once again, from Thebes.[9] While the main Spartan army was making its way north, the Thebans persuaded the Athenians to make an alliance with the entire Boiotian koinon.[10] This was probably part of the process of forming a larger coalition against Sparta, including Argos and Corinth, which only Diodoros recounts in detail, but which is implicit in several passages of Xenophon's account.[11]

Lysander, flushed with his success at Orchomenos, then moved on to Haliartos and had just persuaded the city to become autonomous when the Thebans got wind of his actions and attacked him there. A fierce battle took place beneath the walls of the city, in which Lysander himself was killed and the Boiotians emerged clearly victorious.[12] But they did not manage to regain Orchomenos, which was held by a Spartan garrison until the King's Peace in 386; the military burden of holding it was indeed one reason why the Spartans were eager for that settlement.[13] The complex events that unfolded in western Boiotia in 395 illustrate for us one reason why those Boiotians who were fighting for a regional state fought so hard: it is, geographically speaking, a relatively open region, and as soon as complete coherence breaks down, the entire region becomes exceptionally vulnerable. This defensive motive is thus an important part of the problem, but it should by no means be regarded as the only one.

---

7. *Hell.Oxy.* 17.2 (Bartoletti); cf. Gehrke 1985: 173–75.

8. Xen. *Hell.* 3.5.4–5. *Hell.Oxy.* 18.4 (Bartoletti) presents the Spartans as being rather more reticent, sending envoys to ask the Boiotians not to invade Phokis. (The Boiotians, of course, dismiss them, and the outcome is the same.)

9. Xen. *Hell.* 3.5.4, 6–16, with Bearzot 2004: 21–30; *Hell.Oxy.* 18.4 (Bartoletti). González 2006: 39 suggests that Orchomenos revolted because it shouldered a tax burden (18.18% of "federal dues") disproportionate to its territorial size (with Hysiai, 10.3% of "the federal territory"). The numbers are extrapolated from *Hell.Oxy.* 16.3–4 (Bartoletti), but the conclusion that every district paid the same amount in taxes is based on an uncertain assumption. See below, p. 298.

10. Xen. *Hell.* 3.5.6–16; RO 6. The Athenians also made an alliance with Lokris in the same year: Tod 102.

11. Diod. Sic. 14.82.1–4; Xen. *Hell.* 3.5.2, 4.2.10–14, 18.

12. Xen. *Hell.* 3.5.18–19; Diod. Sic. 14.81.1–3, 89; Plut. *Lys.* 28.1–30.1; Paus. 3.5.2–6. Cf. Westlake 1985.

13. Xen. *Hell.* 5.1.29.

From this point the Corinthian War assumes a familiar shape, and the issue of regional political organization and division receives no particular illumination from the sources, so a quick résumé of events should be sufficient. In 394 the Spartans enjoyed two important (but narrow) victories, one at Nemea and one at Koroneia, in the heart of Boiotia.[14] From 393 to 390 Corinth became the center of the allied struggle against Sparta.[15] In 392/1 the Spartans and their allies were sufficiently discontented with the pace of progress in the war, and alarmed by recent developments in the Aegean war, that they were willing to approach the negotiating table at Sardis. It is clear from Xenophon's account of the breakdown of peace talks at Sardis that the main principle of the proposed agreement was universal polis autonomy: the Argives were unwilling to surrender Corinth, which they had seized in 393; the Athenians feared the loss of their cleruchies on Lemnos, Imbros, and Skyros, and the implications of full autonomy for the Greek poleis of Asia Minor; and the Thebans were unwilling to allow the Boiotian poleis to become autonomous.[16] The Persian King Artaxerxes was likewise unwilling to accept Sparta's terms. Implementing the concept of autonomy in interstate agreements was always a slippery business, and the difficulty of it has led to debates over whether it was a clearly designated political status with legal backing or something more akin to an ideological concept around which partisans could rally.[17] The problem seems in fact to lie somewhere between these positions: as Martin Ostwald demonstrated, the concept developed over time, and the mistake seems to be in assuming that by the early fourth century it had assumed a fixed meaning independent of context. The Sardis negotiations were derailed in part by the Boiotians' refusal to grant the autonomy of their poleis, which would not have resulted in the immediate dissolution of the koinon, as is so often repeated, but in the Boiotians' being compelled to allow any member polis to break away if it no longer wished to be a part of the regional state. A second conference was apparently held at Sparta,

14. Nemea: Xen. *Hell.* 4.2.9–23; Diod. Sic. 14.83.1–2. Koroneia: Xen. *Hell.* 4.3.15–20; Diod. Sic. 14.84.1–2.

15. Corinth: Xen. *Hell.* 4.4.1–5.2.

16. Xen. *Hell.* 4.8.12–15 for the entire peace conference. For the Argive seizure of Corinth in 393, the subsequent civil war, and its resolution see Xen. *Hell.* 4.4.1–14, 5.1.34, 36; Diod. Sic. 14.86, 92.1; Andoc. 3.26–27. Cf. Bearzot 2004: 31–36.

17. Bickerman 1958 and Ostwald 1982 established the distinction in the language of interstate relations between *eleutheria* and *autonomia,* Bickerman placing the development of the latter concept in the context of the Greek cities under Persian rule, Ostwald in the context of the shift from Delian League to Athenian empire, but both agreeing that *autonomia* was a relative and restricted status that protected weaker communities from arbitrary abuses by stronger ones while at the same recognizing their ultimate authority in certain spheres. Hansen 1995b argues for a stronger, unrestricted view of *autonomia* as self-government, which he applies to Boiotia (Hansen 1995a). Cf. the debate between Hansen 1996 and Keen 1996.

where a concession was made to the Boiotians' understanding of polis autonomy: they would have only to renounce their claim to Orchomenos and allow the city to be autonomous.[18] This second attempt foundered too, at least in part because the Athenians refused to sign what had to be a multilateral agreement. The Boiotians could continue to fight for a unified regional state incorporating every polis that was conceived of as belonging (ethnically, culturally, politically, and economically) to Boiotia.

The Spartans were not opposed to koina in principle, for just as they were challenging the integrity of the Boiotian state, they actively supported what must have been a similar form of state in Achaia. In 389, Xenophon tells us, the Achaians were in possession of Kalydon, on the northern coast of the Corinthian Gulf in territory that was once Aitolian, and had made the Kalydonians Achaian citizens.[19] The place was attacked by the Akarnanians, Boiotians, and Athenians, so that the Achaians were compelled to garrison the city and summon Agesilaos for assistance. We do not know when Kalydon was taken by the Achaians, but it is clear that Naupaktos, formerly an Athenian stronghold occupied by both Messenians and Naupaktians, was likewise under Achaian control by 389.[20] The Achaians appealed to the Spartans for assistance, and together with other Peloponnesian allies they invaded Akarnania. This experience prompted the Akarnanians to make peace with the Achaians and alliance with the Spartans in the spring of 388.[21] With this Spartan assistance the Achaians were able to retain control of both Kalydon and Naupaktos until 367 but failed to achieve any further expansion, if indeed that was their purpose.[22] Behind the original Achaian seizure of Kalydon and Naupaktos, which the Aitolians had lost sometime in the fifth century but never surrendered their aspiration to regain, must lie hostility if not outright conflict between the Achaians and the Aitolians. We may detect a trace of this hostility in the tradition

18. Andoc. 3.13, 20; cf. Philoch. *FGrHist* 328 F 149b. See further Cawkwell 1976: 271–72 n. 13 with references.

19. Xen. *Hell.* 4.6.1.

20. Naupaktos: Xen. *Hell.* 4.6.14. Cf. Merker 1989; Freitag 2009: 17–19. It was probably in connection with the annexation of Kalydon and Naupaktos that the Achaians besieged and captured the Aitolian community Phana, an event described only by Pausanias (10.18.1) upon seeing the statue of Athena dedicated at Delphi by the Achaians to thank the god for the favorable oracle they received during the long siege of the city (with Jacquemin 1999: 85).

21. Xen. *Hell.* 4.6.4–7.1; Xen. *Ages.* 2.20; Plut. *Ages.* 22.9–11; Paus. 3.10.2 (a confused account that excludes the Achaians entirely and claims that the Spartans went to the assistance of the Aitolians in their own territory); Polyaenus, *Strat.* 2.1.1.

22. Diod. Sic. 15.75.2. Freitag 2009: 20 argues that the Achaians invaded Akarnania with expansionist intentions; he may be right. Note that the Aitolians granted Agesilaos passage through their territory in 389 as he withdrew from Akarnania "because they hoped that he would help them to regain Naupaktos" (Xen. *Hell.* 4.6.14). Kelly 1978 proposed that this was the context for the conclusion of the inscribed treaty between Sparta and Aitolia (T48).

recorded by the contemporary historian Ephoros that the Achaians controlled the sanctuary of Zeus at Olympia before being driven out by the Elians at the head of Oxylos and the Herakleidai.[23] The claim would have angered not only the Elians but also their constant allies and putative kin the Aitolians. Circulating such a claim in the early fourth century, when tensions between Achaia and Aitolia must have been elevated, would have been highly effective.

The episode reveals not only that the Achaians had by 389 developed a political organization in which citizenship was bound up with the political coherence of the entire region, comprising still multiple poleis, but also that it was robust enough to seize and incorporate non-Achaian communities.[24] If a sense of Achaian identity was all that bound the Achaian cities together throughout most of the fifth century, it clearly did not impose any restrictions on the limits of their new state, for Kalydon was an old Aitolian polis, and Naupaktos was inhabited by a mix of Lokrians and Messenians. Xenophon's description of the Achaians' response to this attack on their northern coastal possessions reveals a few clues about the operation of the Achaian koinon in the early fourth century: it maintained an alliance with Sparta, which may have gone back to the years of the Peloponnesian War, and had some institutional mechanism for the dispatch of ambassadors representing the entire Achaian state and for the levying of an army from all the Achaian member communities.[25]

The Corinthian War was fought primarily in the eastern Aegean, a contest more between Athens and Persia than between the allies at Corinth and the Spartans. Mainland activity centered around a struggle for control of the Corinthian Gulf, though none of these actions was decisive in bringing about a conclusion to the war. In 386 all parties were more committed to the peace, and the terms eventually dictated by Artaxerxes were essentially those offered in 392 at Sardis: the poleis in Asia were to belong to the king; all other Greek poleis both large and small were to be autonomous, with the exception of the Athenians' old cleruchies Lemnos, Imbros, and Skyros, which they were allowed to keep.[26] The Thebans were, infamously, hesitant to accept these terms and did so only in response to the real threat of a Spartan invasion of Boiotia.[27]

23. Ephoros *FGrHist* 70 F 115 (*ap.* Str. 8.3.33).

24. The political significance of the grant of Achaian citizenship to Kalydon has been cited by Larsen 1953: 809 and 1968: 81, 85; Koerner 1974: 485. The extent of the Achaian state in this period is indicated by Polyb. 2.41.7–8, providing a list of members before the reigns of Philip and Alexander: Olenos, Helike, Patrai, Dyme, Pharai, Tritaia, Leontion, Aigion, Aigeira, Pellene, Boura, and Karyneia.

25. Xen. *Hell.* 4.6.2–4.

26. Xen. *Hell.* 5.1.31; Diod. Sic. 14.110.2–4. See Cawkwell 1981 for speculation that the actual agreement had to contain more detailed provisions than are preserved in the royal rescript recorded by Xenophon.

27. Xen. *Hell.* 5.1.32–33.

The autonomy clause of the King's Peace is generally regarded as the death knell for states comprising multiple poleis like the Boiotian koinon and the recent *sympoliteia* of Argos and Corinth, as well as for nascent imperial structures like that being built in these years by the Athenian general Thrasyboulos. This is certainly an overstatement. We have already seen that the meaning of autonomy in this period was slippery. Precisely what Artaxerxes and Agesilaos expected would result from this agreement is unclear: Was polis autonomy at odds even with voluntary membership in a koinon or a *sympoliteia*? Probably not: Mogens Hansen has shown that the concept was contoured around consent.[28] The ambiguity of the term "autonomy," and as a result the difficulty of interpreting the actions surrounding its implementation, has prompted much debate about whether the actual treaty contained a full definition (like that in the Aristoteles Decree of 377) and what such a definition may have been.[29] But the problem of ambiguity is not all: the autonomy clause of the King's Peace actually affected only those political structures that had become involved in the war against Sparta, which in the immediate term meant only Boiotia.[30] It had no discernible effect on Achaia. It is, however, clear that it brought about some change in Boiotian political organization, but this change is typically described with undue confidence.[31] The college of boiotarchs may have been abolished, for in the period 382–379/8 officials called polemarchs appear to have held the highest office at Thebes, but this change is likely to have

28. Hansen 1995b: 28.

29. V. Martin 1944: 26 n. 7; Ryder 1965: 122–23; Cawkwell 1981: 72–74; Urban 1991: 110; Jehne 1994: 37–44. Beck 2001: 362 is right to conclude that "it is impossible to decide whether the federal principle was *eo ipso* in contradiction to the autonomy clause" and to insist on the importance of Spartan actions establishing a precedent that defined it in practical terms. It is certain that the issue was clarified in the next two decades. The Aristoteles decree of 377, which records the establishment of the Second Athenian League (RO 22 ll. 20–24), spells out the three facets of autonomy relevant to that context: being governed under whatever form of government a city wishes; neither receiving a garrison nor submitting to a governor; and not paying tribute (*phoros*). The common peace of 366/5 had as its principal condition that each signatory polis would "hold its own territory" (Xen. *Hell.* 7.6.10).

30. Larsen 1968: 171–72; Badian 1991: 39; Beck 2001: 363. The Olynthians, as aggressive leaders of the emergent koinon of the Chalkideis, were attacked by the Spartans in 382 in response to an appeal for help from Akanthos (Xen. *Hell.* 5.2.11–19), Amyntas (Diod. Sic. 15.19.1–3), or both. In Xenophon's account, the Akanthian speaker, Kleigenes, points to the efforts of the Spartans to "prevent Boiotia from becoming one" (5.2.16) and asks that they not ignore the repetition of the same phenomenon in the north. The Akanthians wished "to keep their ancestral laws [*patrioi nomoi*] and to be citizens of their own state [*autopolitai*]" (5.2.14). Whether Sparta's willingness to help was a direct response to the King's Peace (which was not a common peace; it was binding only on the actual signatories) is unclear and depends upon whether the Olynthians can be proved to have been involved in the Corinthian War, as is suggested by Isae. 5.46. Cawkwell 1973: 53 seems to assume that Olynthos was a signatory, and that the Spartan response to the Akanthian appeal was legally justified by a sanctions clause in the peace, which our sources do not record.

31. Larsen 1968: 171, 175; R. J. Buck 1994: 59–61; Beck 1997: 96.

been more a function of the Spartan occupation of Thebes in those years (on which more below) than of the demands of the King's Peace.[32] Our ignorance of what happened in the other Boiotian cities in the same period is so profound that we simply do not know how the King's Peace affected them.[33]

If the college of boiotarchs was in fact disabled in this period and the Boiotians were unable to make joint decisions and undertake joint actions within the frame-work of a regional state recognized as valid by outsiders, this does not mean that they were not interacting. Indeed, religious interactions and trade relations (about which there will be much more to say in chapters 4 and 5) must have continued almost undisturbed, and as we shall see these kinds of quotidian relations between individuals of different poleis within the region constituted the real core of the koinon; it was these relations that necessitated the development of state institutions to protect and promote them. So it is partly misleading to speak of the dissolution of the Boiotian koinon in 386; we should rather speak of a temporary institutional crip-pling enabled by the King's Peace but enforced by Agesilaos's interpretation of it.

The advantages that could stem from integrating poleis into a single regional state were apparently becoming clear, and the Chalkideis, under the strong leader-ship of Olynthos, were working hard in this period to expand theirs. The origin of this koinon is uncertain but may be associated with the synoikism of Olynthos in 432.[34] For the late fifth century we know only that the Chalkidian poleis cooperated militarily, made some treaties as a single state, and had ambassadors and proxenoi who represented them in their relations with other states.[35] It is only in the early fourth century that we begin to see how this state was organized and what made it powerful. The Chalkidians had joined the Boiotians, Athenians, Corinthians, and Argives in a treaty to fight against the Spartans at the outset of the Corinthian War,

32. Mention of polemarchs in Thebes, 382–379/8: Xen. *Hell.* 5.2.25, 30, 32 (382 BCE); 5.4.2, 7, 8 (379 BCE); Plut. *Pel.* 7.4, 9.8, 11.4; *Ages.* 24.2. The office is amply attested epigraphically in eight Boiotian poleis from the mid-third century BCE to the imperial period.

33. Numismatic evidence has sometimes been taken to prove the complete independence of the Boiotian poleis after 386. Coins minted with polis legends and types on the reverse, with the Boiotian shield on the obverse, have been assigned to the period 386–378 (Head 1881: 43–60; against Head's cir-cular reasoning note Hansen 1995a: 31–32). The magistrate staters were placed next in the series (Head 1881: 61–72; Kraay 1976: 113), but it has now been shown that they go back to the very earliest years of the fourth century (Hepworth 1989, 1998). The chronology of Boiotian coinage is so insecure, and its polit-ical significance so unclear, that the coins cannot be pressed into service as evidence for this argument.

34. Th. 1.58.2 with Hornblower 1991–2008: I.102–3; Zahrnt 1971: 49–66; Demand 1990: 77–83; Psoma 2001: 189–95.

35. Military cooperation: Th. 2.29, 58; 4.7, 78–79. The Chalkidian poleis were listed independently in the Peace of Nikias (Th. 5.18.5–8) but in 415 had concluded a ten-day truce with the Athenians (Th. 6.7.4). Ambassadors: Th. 4.83.3. Proxenos: Th. 4.78.1. There has been extensive debate about the nature of the Chalkidian state in the fifth century: Larsen 1968: 59 believed that it was federal, while Hampl 1935: 182 and Zahrnt 1971: 65–66 saw evidence only for a unitary state.

and probably around 393 they made a treaty with Amyntas, the Macedonian king.[36] So when in 382 a number of poleis in the Chalkidike resisted membership in the koinon of the Chalkideis, and Amyntas needed assistance to regain a number of Macedonian communities he had lost to them, the Spartans were an obvious source of help, not only because they had a history of opposition to the Chalkideis but also because in Boiotia they had demonstrated their willingness to apply the terms of the King's Peace in such a way as to restrict federal authority.[37] According to Xenophon, ambassadors were sent from Akanthos and Apollonia to alert the Spartans to the alarming growth of the Chalkideis and to seek their support in their efforts to avoid becoming part of the state. From a speech attributed by Xenophon to Kleigenes of Akanthos, we learn that the Chalkideis, under Olyn-thian leadership, had a single set of laws for all the poleis within the state, and a single citizenship just as the Achaians had in this period.[38] Diodoros, who makes no mention of the Chalkideis, claims that the appeal was made by Amyn-tas.[39] Whoever actually sent the embassy, the outcome was the same: the Spartans and their Peloponnesian allies launched a major expedition and an advance force to prevent any cities in the region from being brought by coercion into the koinon.[40] Kleigenes claims that the Olynthians sought an alliance with both Ath-ens and Thebes; diplomacy fell short of this aim, but the Thebans passed a decree prohibiting any Theban citizen from participating in an expedition against Olynthos.[41]

Internal support for the Thebans' decree was far from unanimous. Xenophon paints a picture of severe political infighting at Thebes that continues the story told by the Oxyrhynchos Historian about the opening years of the fourth century.[42]

36. Isae. 5.46; Diod. Sic. 14.82.3; RO 12.
37. The embassy from Amyntas is attested only by Diod. Sic 15.19.3, though Xen. *Hell.* 5.2.12–13 describes the hostilities between the Chalkideis and Amyntas.
38. Xen. *Hell.* 5.2.12. This speech and its arguments will be discussed in greater detail in chapter 5.
39. Diod. Sic. 15.19.1–3 with V. Parker 2003: 126–32.
40. Xen. *Hell.* 5.2.20–24. The Spartans authorized a levy of ten thousand Peloponnesian troops, augmented by allied forces. The size of this force is taken by Larsen 1968: 73–74 as an index of the strength of the Chalkideis.
41. Xen. *Hell.* 5.2.27. There has been some speculation that after the King's Peace the Thebans made an alliance with Sparta, but the only ancient evidence for the claim is in Isocr. 14.27, a passage full of tendentious factual errors, and Plut. *Pel.* 4–5.1, a passage that directly contradicts both Xenophon's (*Hell.* 5.2.4–6) and Diodoros's (15.5.3–5, 12.1–2) accounts of the same event and is tendentious in its own way, attempting to portray Epameinondas as a philosopher-warrior, the Sokrates to Pelopidas's Alkibi-ades. (Cf. Plut. *Alc.* 7.3.) The decree prohibiting Thebans from participating in an expedition against Olynthos would have been a clear violation of any such alliance, and this consideration along with the source problems tips the balance against the veracity of the claim. See Buckler 1980a; on Epameinondas as philosopher see Arist. *Rhet.* 1398b18; Vidal-Naquet 1986: 61–84.
42. On this aspect see Gehrke 1985: 175–77.

Ismenias led a group of anti-Spartan political *hetairoi*, while Leontiades led a group that was eager to cozy up to the Spartans.[43] When, therefore, part of the Spartan force being sent to Olynthos was encamped near Thebes, Leontiades approached the Spartan commander, Phoibidas, and offered to betray the Theban akropolis, the Kadmeia, to his forces during the Thesmophoria at Thebes, a festival during which the women took over the akropolis. Phoibidas took the opportunity, and once inside Leontiades approached the Theban council to report it as a fait accompli. He had certainly canvassed for support earlier, because he was immediately supported in the council and had Ismenias arrested as a warmonger. Ismenias's supporters fled the city in fear for their lives; many went to Athens. Ismenias faced a sham trial, defending himself unsuccessfully against charges of Medism and responsibility for every disturbance in Greece, and was executed.[44] Whether Phoibidas had acted on orders from Sparta or not was clearly debated in antiquity.[45] What matters for us is that the Spartans chose to hold the Kadmeia once it had been won, ushering in a period the Boiotians described as the time when the Spartan spear was dominant.[46]

The description is not at all inaccurate, for Thebes continued to be held by a Spartan garrison.[47] The impact on the rest of Boiotia is interesting. Plataia, destroyed by the Thebans in 427, was probably restored under Spartan sponsorship after 386 and became resolutely pro-Spartan, along with Thespiai.[48] The allegiance of Thespiai also made the Corinthian Gulf port at Kreusis available to the Spartans.[49] Spartan control of Boiotia was probably more widespread, managed through puppet governments and garrisons: Xenophon later tells us that they had, in the years prior to 378, established narrow oligarchies in all the poleis, which caused the *dēmos* in each city to withdraw to Thebes, becoming an unlikely haven for democrats, if not for democracy itself.[50] We know also that a pro-Spartan government was in place in Tanagra in 377 and probably had been for some years.[51] It

43. Xen. *Hell.* 5.2.25.
44. Betrayal: Xen. *Hell.* 5.2.26–31; cf. Plut. *Pel.* 5. Trial of Ismenias: Xen. *Hell.* 5.2.35–36 (jury composed of representatives of the Peloponnesian League); cf. Plut. *Pel.* 5.3; *De gen. Soc.* 576a (who places the trial in Sparta). See Landucci Gattinoni 2000.
45. Xen. *Hell.* 5.2.28, 32; Diod. Sic. 15.20.2.
46. T4.4.
47. Xen. *Hell.* 5.4.10–13; Diod. Sic. 15.20.2, 23.4, 25.1 and 3, 27.1 and 3; Plut. *Pel.* 12.3, 13.2; *De gen. Soc.* 598f.
48. The repopulation of Plataia is a necessary precondition to Xenophon's narrative about its pro-Spartan sympathies in the late 380s and early 370s. Paus. 9.1.4 places its restoration in the period of the King's Peace, and the same is implied by the hypothesis to Isocrates' *Plataikos*. Some have argued that Plataia was restored in 382, but Paus. 9.1.4 indicates that 386 is more likely; for full discussion see Amit 1973: 106–9.
49. Xen. *Hell.* 5.4.10, 14–16.
50. Xen. *Hell.* 5.4.46. For Spartan garrisons in Boiotia in this period see Wickersham 2007.
51. Xen. *Hell.* 5.4.49.

appears, then, that the Spartan seizure of Thebes in 382 had wider ramifications for the region than is typically realized; the regional takeover was certainly facilitated by political *stasis* in the Boiotian poleis. The blow dealt by the Spartans in 382 and facilitated by Theban dissidents resulted in deep fractures to the regional system and its institutions.

In 379 the Spartans and their allies finally took Olynthos and made it a member of the Peloponnesian League.[52] Surprisingly, however, the terms of their treaty contain not a single hint that the Spartans required the dismantling of the institutions that bound the Chalkideis together.[53] The issue of Sparta remained divisive in Thebes, where there was no similar softening of anticooperative sentiment. In the winter of 379/8 Theban exiles and several malcontents within the pro-Spartan Theban government murdered the polemarchs, described by Xenophon as tyrants, and immediately accomplished the adherence of the Theban hoplites and cavalry.[54] The Thebans immediately set about rebuilding the Boiotian koinon, conducting an election of boiotarchs to govern in place of the polemarchs. But the election was held by Thebans, not by all the Boiotians, and those elected were certainly Theban. This fact had profound effects on the nature of the koinon as it developed over the next decade.[55] The Spartan garrison on the Kadmeia was expelled with the help of the Athenians and other Boiotians, most of its members being treacherously killed.[56] Early in 378 the Spartans sent a force to Boiotia under the new king, Kleombrotos, who found the Plataians and Thespians still willing to help; after an ineffectual stay he left Sphodrias

---

52. Xen. *Hell.* 5.2.37–3.27; Diod. Sic. 15.20.3–23.3. The terms of the treaty (having the same friends and enemies, following wherever the Spartans might lead, and being *symmachoi*) are precisely those identified by Bolmarcich 2005 as belonging to subordinate allies of Sparta.

53. It is usually assumed, despite the absence of any clear evidence to support the claim, that the koinon of the Chalkideis was dissolved after the Spartan victory at Olynthos: Beck 1997: 241. Psoma 2001: 228–30 rightly dismisses the claim and summarizes the evidence for continued regional cooperation and economic and expansionist activities of the koinon in the decade after the Spartan victory.

54. Xen. *Hell.* 5.4.1–9. Cf. Diod. Sic. 15.25–27; Plut. *Pel.* 7–13 with varying details. Gehrke 1985: 177–80.

55. Diod. Sic. 15.28.1; Plut. *Pel.* 13.1. Sordi 1973 on the seizure of power by Thebans in this moment of political reconstitution.

56. Xen. *Hell.* 5.4.10–13; Diod. Sic. 15.25. Sources differ on the nature of Athenian support. Many have read Xenophon's account as evidence only for private Athenian support (noting especially the *dēmos*'s decision to execute the two generals who collaborated with the Theban rebels, *Hell.* 5.4.19, and the description of the supporters as "some Athenians from the frontiers" at *Hell.* 5.4.10, 12), but there is nothing in Xenophon that leads us ineluctably to that conclusion. Indeed several sources speak against it: Xen. *Hell.* 5.4.14; Diod. Sic. 15.25.4, 26.1–2; Din. 1.39; Isocr. 14.29. See Cawkwell 1973: 56–58; Cargill 1981: 56; Kallet-Marx 1985: 140–47; Stylianou 1998: 230–31; V. Parker 2007: 15–16, 24–25, 27–28. The evidence for other Boiotian poleis sending aid to expel the Spartan garrison in the winter of 379/8 is generally overlooked, but Diod. Sic. 15.26.3 is explicit. It is immediately plausible: we have every reason, from the accounts of the *Hellenica Oxyrhynchia* as well as Xenophon, to expect *stasis* in the Boiotian poleis in this period. On the high value of Diodoros's whole account of the Theban hegemony, based on Ephoros, see Momigliano 1935; Sordi 2005.

as harmost at Thespiai with a garrison, funds, and an order to hire mercenaries.[57] If nothing else Kleombrotos did manage to frighten both the Thebans, who did not relish the prospect of taking on the Spartan army alone, and the Athenians, who had no taste for the Spartan army traversing their territory. It was fear, then, that threw the Athenians and Thebans into alliance.[58] When Sphodrias attempted an unauthorized raid on Peiraieus, the Athenians felt their own vulnerability and probably saw that the King's Peace was now a mere sham.[59] Around this time the Athenians established their system of alliances known as the Second Athenian Confederacy; although the system was formalized and an allied synedrion established in spring 377 by the decree of Aristoteles, the recent alliance with Thebes provided a paradigm for the terms on which other states would join.[60] Whether this system of alliances was formalized before or after Sphodrias's attempt on Peiraieus in 378 has been debated.[61] The somewhat ominous clause stating that the Athenians should send three ambassadors "to persuade the Thebans of whatever good thing they can" may point to Athenian efforts to stave off the conflict between the Boiotian koinon, now being vigorously rebuilt, and the Spartans over the terms of the King's Peace.[62] According to Xenophon the Athenians now "assisted the Boiotians with great eagerness" (*Hell.* 5.4.34).

Thespiai continued to be friendly to the Spartans and became a base from which the Spartan army, again under Agesilaos, ravaged the territory of Thebes in the fall of 378 and spring of 377, doing enough damage to cause a grain shortage.[63]

57. Xen. *Hell.* 5.4.14–15.

58. Diod. Sic. 15.28.5.

59. Xen. *Hell.* 5.4.20–33 for the unsuccessful attempt and the sham trial of Sphodrias in absentia in Sparta that eventually acquitted him. Whether or not Sphodrias was bribed by the Thebans to make the attack is immaterial; for recent discussion of this point see Hodkinson 2007.

60. RO 22 ll. 24–25.

61. Xenophon, infamously, makes no mention. Diod. Sic. 15.28 places it in 377/6, after the liberation of Thebes from Sparta but before Sphodrias's raid on Peiraieus (Diod. Sic. 15.29.5–8). The liberation of the Kadmeia from its Spartan garrison occurred in winter 379/8, so Diodoros's absolute date must be wrong, but it is possible that his relative chronology is correct, viz. that the confederacy was founded before the seizure of Peiraieus (Cawkwell 1973; Cargill 1981: 57–60; Hornblower 2002: 233), which would help to understand the motives behind Sphodrias's raid. On the other hand, the raid on Peiraieus can be seen as precisely the sort of proof the Athenians needed to gain alliances in support of an Athenian role as the new enforcers of the King's Peace, taking over where the Spartans had so patently failed (Rice 1975; Badian 1995: 89–90 n. 34; Rhodes and Osborne 2003: 100).

62. RO 20 ll. 72–77. The full integration of Thebes into the allied *synedrion* may have been recorded in *IG* II² 40, but the text is so fragmentary that certain interpretation is impossible. See Cargill 1981: 52–56, 60.

63. Xen. *Hell.* 5.4.35–41, 46–56; cf. Diod. Sic. 15.34.1–3. The Thebans undertook a mission to Thessaly to purchase grain; the ships were captured by the Spartan garrison commander at Histiaia (Oreos) on Euboia, which shortly after revolted from Sparta and may have made an alliance with the Thebans that recognized their *hagemonia* in the war, recorded on a newly discovered inscription: Aravantinos and Papazarkadas 2012.

A third planned invasion, in spring 376, was thwarted by Athenian intervention. As a result, Xenophon reports, "the Thebans marched out boldly against the neighboring poleis and once again took control of them."[64] That process in fact took years. The Spartan garrison was expelled from Orchomenos in 375 by a small Theban force, which then led a victory over the Spartans at Tegyra, just east of Orchomenos.[65] Thespiai and Tanagra may have been persuaded to rejoin the koinon, but if that is right then Thespiai had rebelled again by 373, for in this year it was attacked by the Thebans, the city razed to the ground, its extended territory pillaged and depopulated.[66] Plataia, which had probably never been reintegrated, suffered the same fate for its stubborn refusal.[67]

Theban aggression in these years began to alarm the Athenians, who sought in 371 a reaffirmation of the terms of the King's Peace. They therefore sent an embassy to the Thebans, inviting them to join an embassy to Sparta.[68] The Thebans agreed and sent Epameinondas as ambassador.[69] Xenophon recounts a series of speeches given by the various Athenian ambassadors, and one of them, Kallistratos, rebukes the Spartans with the charge that as a result of their seizure of the Theban Kadmeia, "all those cities which you so much wanted to be independent are once again under Theban authority."[70] In Plutarch's version of the story, there was an aggressive confrontation at this conference between Agesilaos and the powerful Theban general Epameinondas, who charged the Spartan king with hypocrisy, arguing that the participation of the Boiotian poleis in a Theban-led koinon was no more a violation of autonomy than the subordination of the perioikic towns of Lakonia to Sparta.[71] Xenophon claims that when the allies agreed to renew the common peace and took their oaths, the Thebans did too, in their own name, but on the following day asked to change their oath, so that it would be in the name of all Boiotia. Agesilaos refused and sent orders to Kleombrotos, the Spartan general stationed in Phokis, to invade Boiotia.[72]

64. Xen. *Hell.* 5.4.63.

65. Orchomenos: Diod. Sic. 15.37.1–2 (who places the event, probably wrongly, in 376/5; cf. Beloch 1912–27: III.1.155); Plut. *Pel.* 16.2–3. Tegyra: Plut. *Pel.* 16–17.10, *Ages.* 27.3; Diod. Sic. 15.81.2.

66. Possible reintegration: Isocr. 14.9. Destruction of Thespiai: Xen. *Hell.* 6.3.1, 5; Diod. Sic. 15.46.6, 51.3; Isocr. 6.27; Dem. 16.4, 25, 28.

67. Xen. *Hell.* 6.3.1, 5; Plut. *Pel.* 25.7; Diod. Sic. 15.46.6; Paus. 9.1.8; Isocr. 14 passim. For discussion see Amit 1973: 114–18; Tuplin 1986. At the same time the Thebans apparently attacked Orchomenos, though the results were indecisive (Xen. *Hell.* 6.4.10). See below, pp. 366–67, for further discussion of the dynamics of these attacks.

68. Xen. *Hell.* 6.3.1–2.

69. Plut. *Ages.* 27.3–28.2.

70. Xen. *Hell.* 6.3.11.

71. Plut. *Ages.* 27.3–28.4; Paus. 9.13.2. Cf. Nep. *Epam.* 6.4. For discussion of the ambiguity of the concept of *autonomia* and its impact on this peace conference, see Rhodes 1999.

72. Xen. *Hell.* 6.3.18–4.3; cf. Plut. *Ages.* 28.2–3.

The implication is clear: the Spartans refused to recognize the Boiotian koinon as a state, insisting that it violated the autonomy clause of the King's Peace. As a result, all sources agree, the Thebans remained outside the peace, and we know of no other Boiotian poleis taking the oath in their own names. Kleombrotos, already in Phokis, could act quickly and launched an invasion of Boiotia, which led to a decisive engagement at Leuktra late in the year 371. The stunning defeat suffered by the Spartans at this battle is one of the major turning points in the history of fourth-century Greece. Leuktra led, undeniably, to a wholly different world, in which the Spartans were badly weakened and the Thebans wildly emboldened.[73] That different world is described by modern historians as the Theban hegemony, adopting the language of *hēgemonia* used by the ancient sources about Thebes' position vis-à-vis the rest of Greece for the next nine years. Yet this label captures only a part of the story that interests us, for these years also witnessed the burgeoning of formal koinon institutions throughout mainland Greece, a phenomenon that cannot be tied in every case to the energies of the Boiotians' brilliant statesman Epameinondas.

THEBAN HEGEMONY AND THE HEGEMONY OF THE KOINON, 371–346

The Athenians received Theban news of their victory at Leuktra with obvious distress; the herald was not even offered hospitality, much less a promise of aid.[74] Several attempts were made to arbitrate in the dispute between Thebes and Sparta, but the status of the Boiotian and the Lakonian perioikic poleis remained unresolved.[75] The Athenians soon took the lead in reaffirming the terms of the peace reached before the battle; the only difference appears to be that no one was prepared to force the issue of autonomy for the poleis of Boiotia.[76]

The Thebans now set about consolidating the Boiotian state and cementing alliances with central Greek neighbors. In 370 they punished the intransigence of Orchomenos, with which they had been in open conflict before Leuktra.[77] The original intention, according to Diodoros, was to enslave the city, but Epameinondas persuaded them of the political importance of *philanthrōpia*, so instead "they reckoned the Orchomenians among the territory of their allies," a mysterious

---

73. Xen. *Hell.* 6.4.14–15; Diod. Sic. 15.51–56; Plut. *Pel.* 20–23, *Ages.* 28.5–6; cf. Arist. *Pol.* 1269a34–1271b19 for analysis of Spartan weakness in the wake of this defeat.

74. Xen. *Hell.* 6.4.19 and Buckler 2000a: 328.

75. Polyb. 2.39.9 and Str. 8.7.1 report that the Achaians were asked to arbitrate in the dispute between Thebes and Sparta. For debate about the historicity of the report see von Stern 1884: 154–55; Grote 1906: VIII.189; Cary 1925; F. W. Walbank 1957–79: I.226–27; and Buckler 1978. I doubt the skepticism is justified.

76. Xen. *Hell.* 6.5.1–2; Ryder 1965: 70–71; Jehne 1994: 74–79.

77. Xen. *Hell.* 6.4.10.

phrase.[78] Whether that was equivalent to the treatment originally meted out to Thespiai in 373 (being compelled "to contribute to the Thebans"), or whether they allowed them independence from the koinon on condition of agreeing to an alliance, is unclear. They then established friendship with the Phokians, Lokrians, and Aitolians, all of whom turned out to be valuable supporters.[79] The Thebans now approached a hegemonic position within the mainland, which means in practice only that they tended to be the ones who were most effective at deciding disputes (usually by force) and received appeals for help by other states for that reason. Although Xenophon's account of these years focuses heavily on Theban relations with the Peloponnesian states, we know from other sources that they were also vigorously active in northern Greece and in the Aegean. The history of Thebes and Boiotia in the 360s thus demands a consideration of virtually the whole of the Greek world. But my aim is merely to show the outlines of the major events of the period in order to facilitate a better understanding of the developments of the institutions of the koinon and its internal workings.[80]

The Arkadians took the common peace reached in Athens, which implicitly sanctioned the existence of the Boiotian koinon, as an opportunity for political revolution. The Mantineians took it as a signal that they were free to resynoikize their city and did so despite Spartan anger, while in Tegea the first steps were taken toward the creation of an Arkadian regional state; it was proposed that whatever was decided in common would be binding upon all poleis.[81] But the proposal met with opposition in some places, at Tegea so strongly that a violent *stasis* erupted over the issue. As the Arkadian army grew with the adherence of each new member polis, it was used to compel recalcitrant poleis to join the koinon. It was probably in these earliest days of Arkadian unification after Leuktra, when there was heightened awareness of the need for physical security and institutional support for a newly created regional state, that the Arkadians began the process of creating their new Megalopolis by synoikism.[82] Spartan attempts to break what they clearly

78. Diod. Sic. 15.57.1.

79. Diod. Sic. 15.57.1; cf. Xen. *Hell.* 6.5.23 for Phokian and Lokrian support in 369.

80. Buckler 1980b provides a detailed account of these years.

81. Xen. *Hell.* 6.5.6. Diod. Sic. 15.59.1 attributes the political innovation to Lykomedes of Tegea, who persuaded the Arkadians "to arrange themselves in a single *synteleia* and have a common council made up of ten thousand men, with the authority to decide on matters of war and peace." The Arkadian origin of this koinon speaks against the idea that the Thebans were actively promoting federalism in this period: Beck 2000: 340–43 *contra* Beister 1989. For further discussion of the Arkadian regional state organized in 370 see Larsen 1968: 180–95; Beck 1997: 67–83; Nielsen 2002: 474–99.

82. The date of the foundation of Megalopolis has been contested; Diod. Sic. 15.72.4 places it after the Tearless Battle in 368, but Paus. 8.27.8 puts it in 371/0, and the Parian Marble (*IG* XII.5.444 l. 73) no earlier than 370. Roy 1971: 572 argues that the Thebans were uninvolved, and that is surely impossible given that it must have taken years for the city to get off the ground, but he may be right that we should not attribute to them the primary impetus for the project. See Hornblower 1990; Moggi 1976: 293–325.

saw as a very real threat were unsuccessful, but the Arkadians needed help and appealed to the Athenians in late 370. There they were rebuffed, but they received a much warmer reception in Thebes.[83]

The Boiotian army invaded the Peloponnese in late winter 370 to help the Arkadians, with virtually all central Greece in their alliance.[84] The army of Boiotians and Arkadians that invaded Lakonia was the first the Spartan women had ever seen, and the shock was so severe that the Spartans offered freedom to all helots who assisted in the defense of Lakonia.[85] After an indecisive battle at Sparta itself the Thebans attacked Gytheion, the southern port of Lakonia opposite Kythera, and won the support of Lakonian perioikoi.[86] It was probably at this juncture, in early spring 369, that they delivered a more significant blow to Sparta's ancient supremacy in the Peloponnese by helping to refound Messene as a city well situated, geographically and in a sense structurally, for opposition to Sparta.[87] The Messenian communities now formed themselves into a koinon, with the help not only of the Boiotians but also of the Arkadians and Argives.[88] The Thebans' invasion of the Peloponnese in winter 370/69 was focused primarily on damaging the Spartans indirectly by bolstering nascent Arkadian political union and strengthening the Messenians, and this was precisely what was accomplished before their withdrawal in the early spring of 369.[89] As they withdrew, however, they encountered Athenian forces, now allied with the Spartans, in the Corinthia. Fighting in the area, extending into summer 369, was indecisive.[90]

During the same period the Thebans became more heavily involved in northern Greece, and as they did so the Arkadians began to withdraw their support.[91] In Thessaly, one Alexander came to power in Pherai after a series of bloody power

83. Diod. Sic. 15.62.3; cf. Dem. 16.12. Athenian refusal to help the Arkadians is explained by their alignment with the Spartans implicit in the post-Leuktra peace conference: Buckler 1980b: 68–69 and 2000a: 328. I agree with Beck 2000 that the move in Arkadia toward federal institutions after Leuktra is not to be explained by some ideological penchant of the Thebans for federalism.

84. Xen. Hell. 6.5.22–24; cf. Diod. Sic. 15.62.4; Paus. 9.14.2.

85. Xen. Hell. 6.5.28; Diod. Sic. 15.65.6.

86. Xen. Hell. 6.5.30–32. This may have been the occasion for the Theban grant of proxeny to Timeas son of Cheirikrates, a Lakonian, recorded on a stele with a relief depicting inter alia the prow of a warship (T6 with commentary).

87. Diod. Sic. 15.66; Paus. 9.14.5.

88. Very little is known about this state, but it is attested epigraphically: IG V.1.1425 and FDelph III.4.5–6. See Luraghi 2009.

89. Xen. Hell. 6.5.50.

90. The Spartan-Athenian alliance: Xen. Hell. 6.5.33–49, 7.1–14; Diod. Sic. 15.67.1. Action in the Corinthia: Xen. Hell. 6.5.49–52 for the end of the first Theban invasion; 7.1.15–19 for the beginning of the second.

91. Arkadian independence under leadership of Lykomedes of Mantineia: Xen. Hell. 7.1.22–26; Diod. Sic. 15.67.2.

struggles, and the Boiotians responded to a call for help from Larisa, which Alexander held by force.[92] In Macedon similar dynastic struggles were unfolding, and the Thebans were asked to arbitrate. Most of the Boiotian army was in the Peloponnese with Epameinondas, so the Thebans sent their other star general, Pelopidas, at the head of a force that was able to expel Alexander's garrison from Larisa before continuing north to Macedon. The primary outcome of this first official Theban visit to Macedon was that Philip II, the brother of the reigning king, along with other noble youths, was taken back to Thebes as a hostage for the good behavior of the Macedonian ruler.[93]

Neither the Thessalian nor the Macedonian arrangement lasted long: Ptolemy assassinated Alexander II and took the throne for himself, sparking the complaints of Alexander's supporters, while the Thessalian poleis renewed their complaints against Alexander of Pherai.[94] Pelopidas returned to Macedonia, where he managed to extract a promise from Ptolemy that he would hold the throne only as regent for Alexander's heirs, but the agreement was made, according to Plutarch, more out of deference on Ptolemy's part to the prestige of the Thebans than as a result of military victory.[95] Indeed Pelopidas had been forced to hire mercenaries within Thessaly for his expedition to Macedonia, because the bulk of the Theban army was again in the Peloponnese with Epameinondas, but they were susceptible to Ptolemy's bribes. Pelopidas then entered Thessaly: whether he did so with the intention of punishing his treacherous mercenaries or to arbitrate again in the dispute between Alexander of Pherai and some of the Thessalian cities is not clear.[96] Whatever his intention, Pelopidas was seized by Alexander of Pherai and held at Pharsalos; it took two expeditions by the Thebans to rescue him, in the course of which Alexander of Pherai was so alarmed that he sought, and won, an alliance with the Athenians.[97]

The Athenian alliance first with Sparta and then with Alexander of Pherai in these years, and the Arkadians' increasing independence from the Boiotians, whom they had originally summoned in 370, suggest at first glance that the Boiotians suffered significant diplomatic isolation in these years. The long list of central Greek allies that they had built up in 371/0 was, however, for the most part still in place, and there is evidence to support the claim that Boiotian relations with some Thessalian communities continued to be warm.[98] As a means of persuading the Arkadians to remain loyal the Boiotians sought to develop stronger ties with the northern

---

92. Xen. *Hell.* 6.4.35; Diod. Sic. 15.67.3–4; Plut. *Pel.* 26.1.

93. Plut. *Pel.* 26.4–8; Diod. Sic. 15.67.4.

94. Plut. *Pel.* 27.1–2; Diod. Sic. 15.71.1.

95. Plut. *Pel.* 27.3–5; not reported by Diodoros.

96. The aim of punishment is underscored by Plut. *Pel.* 27.5.

97. Diod. Sic. 15.71.3, 75.2; Xen. *Hell.* 7.1.28.

98. Boiotian proxeny decree for a Perrhaibian: *IG* VII.2858.

Peloponnese, and this meant seeking the allegiance of the Achaians. Achaian Pellene had been a loyal Spartan ally since the invasion of 370, but it appears to have acted independently of the rest of Achaia and must not have been a member of the koinon in these years.[99] Although Achaia appears to have retained the institutions of a single state that allowed it to annex and integrate Naupaktos and Kalydon several decades before, Xenophon describes a condition of fairly serious regional *stasis*. When Epameinondas entered Achaia in 367 with his Boiotian and allied army, he was approached by "the best men from Achaia," a typical euphemism for those with oligarchic sympathies. He assured them that "the strongest" would not be exiled, nor would there be any changes in government, in exchange for a unilateral alliance.[100] Underlying Xenophon's account is significant tension, if not outright conflict, between oligarchs and democrats within Achaia, but there is no hint that these tensions ran along polis lines (as they had recently in Boiotia); the internal debate about how Achaia ought to be governed was clearly being conducted at the regional scale. The Thebans' aim was simply to achieve the Achaian alliance; they were apparently indifferent to the internal composition of the government, for almost immediately the oligarchs' political opponents objected that the arrangement was too favorable to Sparta. The Theban response was to send governors (harmosts) to each of the Achaian poleis; when they arrived these governors helped to oust the oligarchs and install democracies. We should probably infer that this was done on official orders from the Theban-led Boiotian koinon. The arrangement was ephemeral; the exiled oligarchs quickly regained control of their cities and rejected all allegiance to the Thebans, who had, according to Xenophon, so easily betrayed them.[101]

It was probably after this botched attempt to make an alliance with the Achaians that the Thebans under Epameinondas expelled the Achaian garrisons from Naupaktos and Kalydon, in Aitolia, and from Dyme itself, in the extreme west of coastal Achaia.[102] Diodoros, whose brief account is our only source for the supposed liberation of these cities, does not explain the Boiotians' motive, but it is perhaps not so difficult to divine. In a single blow they could take vengeance on the Achaians for their fickleness and reward the Aitolians, who had been their friends since 370 and had been hoping to regain Naupaktos since at least 389.[103]

99. Cf. Xen. *Hell.* 7.1.15–18; Diod. Sic. 15.68.2.

100. Xen. *Hell.* 7.1.42; cf. Diod. Sic. 15.75.2.

101. Xen. *Hell.* 7.1.43; Gehrke 1985: 14. Whether the harmosts should be seen as a Spartan-inspired strategy for subordination or an attempt to enforce some stability in the political settlement (so Buckler 1980b: 192–93) is unclear. In 367/6 the Thebans also had a harmost and garrison at Sikyon (Xen. *Hell.* 7.2.11, 7.3.4). The practice should probably be associated with the broader plan of gaining (by force if necessary) the adherence of the entire northern Peloponnese.

102. Diod. Sic. 15.75.2. Buckler 1980b: 188 for a slightly different chronology.

103. Aitolian friendship with Boiotia: Diod. Sic. 15.57.1. Aitolian aspirations for Naupaktos: Xen. *Hell.* 4.6.14 and above, n. 22. Cf. Buckler 1980b: 189–90.

It is additionally possible that winning over such coastal places was part of the planning stage of building a Boiotian navy, which got under way a few years later.[104] The liberation of Dyme may not have affected the Aitolians at all, but it may point to an ongoing struggle within Achaia to define the nature and boundaries of the power of the regional state.[105] The independence of Pellene in these years and the struggle between oligarchs and democrats point in the same direction.[106] The status of Naupaktos and Kalydon after their liberation is somewhat murky, but it is likely that Kalydon was handed over to the Aitolians while control of Naupaktos was returned to the Lokrian inhabitants of the town.[107] Even if the Aitolians did not gain what the Achaians lost, the expulsion of the Achaian garrisons from these places must have been a great benefit to them.

It is perhaps not a coincidence that we have our first incontrovertible evidence for the existence of formal koinon institutions in Aitolia in the very same year, 367/6. An Athenian decree (T52) records the decision to send a herald "to the koinon of the Aitolians" (ll. 16–17) to demand the release of sacred officials who had been seized by some Trichoneians while announcing the sacred truce for the Eleusinian Mysteries (ll. 11–14), which had been accepted by the Aitolian koinon before the seizure (ll. 8–10). There has been some debate about the meaning of "the koinon of the Aitolians" in this document, but it is clear that this entity was regarded by other states as having both authority over the behavior of the citizens of the polis Trichoneion (certainly inter alias) and responsibility for enforcing "the common laws of the Greeks" among them.[108] To put it another way, it was expected that the laws and decisions of the koinon, in this case accepting the truce for the Eleusinian Mysteries, were binding on its citizens. That the Aitolian koinon should first appear on the scene in the context of an illicit seizure has perhaps obscured the importance of the historical context of the decree. The Aitolians' Hellenistic reputation as plunderers seems to receive early confirmation here.[109] But while the act of seizure that lies behind the decree may have been the private act of a few Trichoneians, it is equally possible that it should be seen in the framework of

104. So Freitag 2009: 24.

105. Freitag 2009: 24 makes the attractive suggestion that the Achaians had garrisoned these places only in anticipation of the Boiotian attack, and that the language of liberation is pure Theban propaganda.

106. Gehrke 1985: 14–15.

107. Σ B *ad Il.* 2.494 reports that "Kalydon was given to the Aitolians, who were in a dispute with the Aiolians and called it their own on the grounds of the catalogue of the Aitolians," viz. the Aitolian entry in the Homeric Catalogue of Ships. Wilamowitz-Moellendorff 1921 suggested that the scholiast was a fourth-century historian whose report refers to the events of 367/6; cf. Jacoby, comm. to *FGrHist* 70 F 122. Kalydon was certainly Aitolian in the latter half of the fourth century: Ps.-Skylax 35 in *GGM* I.37. Buckler 1980b: 188–91; Bommeljé 1988: 298, 302–3, 310; Merker 1989: 305–6.

108. Sordi 1953b, 1969: 343–49. Rzepka 2002: 230–31 takes it as a reference to the Aitolian assembly.

109. See Polyb. 4.3.1 with Grainger 1999: 34–35; de Souza 1999: 70–76; Scholten 2000: 9–12.

broader hostilities between the Athenians and the Boiotians, with whom the Aitolians were in allegiance.

This inscription alone justifies the claim that the first decades of the fourth century witnessed political developments that formalized old patterns of cooperation among the different communities and poleis of Aitolia, committing them to a single authority through which interactions with foreign states would be conducted. We would like to know why this happened now. The Aitolians may have developed formal political institutions that created a single regional state at any time between the Peloponnesian War and 367/6. We have seen evidence of functional cooperation throughout that period but have lacked any evidence for formal institutions that may have supported or, indeed, required it. It has been argued that the Aitolian koinon was created by Epameinondas in 370, a hypothesis that could be supported by the Boiotians' efforts to liberate the old Aitolian city of Kalydon in 367.[110] But the Boiotian-Aitolian relationship in 370 is described only as a friendship, and there is no evidence to support the common view that the Boiotians were engaged in forging confederate polities outside their own borders.[111]

During the fourth century, however, we see another striking development in Aitolia that may be related, namely a significant increase in urbanization throughout the region. Although Kalydon had been occupied since at least the archaic period, in the early fourth century its inhabitants invested heavily in its defense, building a lengthy circuit wall with towers and gates to enclose the settlement.[112] With our inability to date fortification walls precisely comes uncertainty as to whether these should be associated with the period of the Achaian garrison or with Aitolian retrenchment following the city's probable return in 367, but the developments at Kalydon are in line with what we see in other parts of the region that were not subject to foreign control, suggesting that the Aitolians were indeed responsible for them. At nearby Chalkis, the fourth century saw the construction of a fortification above the city, which was itself defended by a circuit wall in the classical period.[113] The scant remains of a large fortified settlement of the classical period at modern Gavalou, south of Lake Trichonis, have long been associated

110. Schweigert 1939: 11; Klaffenbach 1939b: 191–92; Tod II.111.

111. Friendship: Diod. Sic. 15.57.1. Sordi 1953b, 1969: 343–49; Grainger 1999: 35 (though he is wrong to conclude that there was no Aitolian koinon at all in the first half of the fourth century); Beck 2000: 338–44.

112. Recent excavations conducted jointly by the Greek Archaeological Service and the Danish Institute at Athens have revealed the gates and towers, and clarified the overall plan of the town: *Archaeological Reports* 2001/2: 44–45; 2002/3: 41; 2003/4: 36; 2004/5: 42; 2005/6: 53; Dietz, Kolonas, Moschos, et al. 2007; Dietz and Stavropoulou-Gatsi 2009.

113. Bommeljé, Doorn, Deylius, et al. 1987: 112; Ober 1992: 165; Dietz, Kolonas, Moschos, et al. 1998: 255–57. Cf. Dietz, Kolonas, Houby-Nielsen, et al. 2000.

with ancient Trichoneion, the home of those accused by the Athenians of seizing the sacred heralds; they are an important corrective to any sense that urbanization and fortification were phenomena restricted to coastal Aitolia.[114] South again to the coast are the archaeological remains of a fortified settlement of the fourth century at Molykreion, with similar structures at nearby Makynea belonging to the late fourth or early third century.[115] Finally, Kallion (later known as Kallipolis), east of Naupaktos at the confluence of four rivers in the ancient Daphnos Valley, was planned and developed in the mid-fourth century with a defensive circuit wall and an independently fortified acropolis; over the course of the Hellenistic period urban forms proliferated here, despite the brutal sack of the city by the Gauls in 279.[116] When collected, this scattered evidence provides a clear picture of significant investments in urbanization and defense across southern Aitolia in the fourth century. The effort appears to have been systematic, and it should probably be associated with the internal development of the Aitolian koinon, which was itself prompted by the Aitolians' need for more effective cooperation in the face of their increasing involvement in the major conflicts of the Greek world.[117] Yet this implies that Aitolian cooperation was motivated solely by military vulnerability and aimed almost exclusively at eradicating it; we shall see later (chapters 4 and 5) that although this was certainly a factor, the story is rather more complex.

Growth in Boiotia was happening at an altogether different pace. With help from Euboian allies, the Thebans sought to detach Oropos from Athens and bring the city and its sanctuary back within the Boiotian fold. The city and its sanctuary were seized by the Boiotians, and the Athenian army sent to wrest it back was ill equipped to face the Thebans. The issue of possession of Oropos was turned over to arbitration.[118] The most significant outcome of this embarrassing encounter was that the Arkadians were emboldened to seek an Athenian alliance, and the Athenians nervous enough to accept it, going to lengths to ensure that it would not violate the terms of their alliance with Sparta.[119] It may also have been at this time that the Thebans voted to develop a navy by building a hundred triremes, with the stated aim of extending their hegemony on land to hegemony at sea in order to gain naval superiority over the Athenians.[120] The process took several years, but

---

114. The remains were first identified with Trichoneion by Leake 1835: 55. Cf. Woodhouse 1897: 232–35; Bommeljé, Doorn, Deylius, et al. 1987: 83, 110–11; Antonetti 1990: 238–40.

115. Molykreion: Woodhouse 1897: 328; Lerat 1952: I.84–86, 188–89; Bommeljé, Doorn, Deylius, et al. 1987: 112; Freitag 2000: 58–67.

116. Themelis 1979, 1999; Bakhuizen 1992.

117. Funke 1991: 330.

118. Xen. Hell. 7.4.1; Diod. Sic. 15.76.1; Isocr. 5.53; Σ Aeschin. 3.85. Cf. Buckler 1980b: 194–95, 250–51.

119. Xen. Hell. 7.4.2–4; Plut. Mor. 193c–d; Nep. Epam. 6.1–3.

120. So Buckler 1980b: 160–64 (most of which is overly speculative), 257–59, following Hammond 1967: 503, 665.

this seems the most logical juncture for its inception.¹²¹ The Corinthians were deeply discomfited by the Arkadian-Athenian alliance and, after the brief tyranny of Timophanes at Corinth and the persistent threat from Argos, they went to Thebes seeking a general peace. The agreement that was reached under Persian and Theban auspices included Thebes, Corinth, Phleious, Argos, and probably Athens, but the Spartans refused to join, preferring instead to fight for Messene, which the peace treaty would have required that they surrender.¹²²

Despite the strength of the Theban-led Boiotian koinon at this juncture—a navy in development, Persian support, and a general peace that excluded only Sparta—internal dissension wrought drastic and violent change in the region. A group of Theban aristocrats who had been expelled from their city sought to overthrow the democracy and enlisted the support of three hundred cavalry from Orchomenos. On the day of the planned attack, however, the instigators changed their minds and betrayed the plot to the boiotarchs, thus securing their own safety. The Orchomenian cavalry, by contrast, were arrested and brought before the popular assembly in Thebes, where the Thebans voted the most extreme measures imaginable: the cavalrymen guilty of conspiracy were to be executed; every remaining inhabitant of Orchomenos was to be sold into slavery; and the ancient city was to be razed to the ground.¹²³ The decree was carried out quickly, and the city was only resettled two decades later. It is tempting to see this act of overwhelming violence perpetrated against a member city as part and parcel with the destructions of Plataia and Thespiai, and to see in all these episodes evidence for Theban aggression. Yet when seen from the standpoint of a federal state responding to secession attempts that would yield major breaches of security, all these cases take on a rather different perspective.

Meanwhile, Alexander of Pherai was still causing trouble in Thessaly, and despite Pelopidas's narrow escape from the region in 367, he agreed to lead an army in 364 in response to a broad Thessalian appeal for help. Although Pelopidas died in the ensuing battle of Kynoskephaloi in 364, the Boiotians and their Thessalian allies enjoyed an overwhelming victory that led to the isolation of Alexander. He was compelled to surrender the other Thessalian cities he had subdued in war, and his rule was restricted to Pherai itself, under the further condition that he make

121. It is narrated only by Diod. Sic. 15.78.4–79.2 in the context of the year 364, an account that does not allow for the logical lapse of time between initial vote and readiness of the fleet for expeditions.

122. Xen. *Hell.* 7.4.6–11. Only Diod. Sic. 15.76.3 mentions Athenian involvement, and the issue has been a source of major controversy, which is tangential to my main purpose. Cawkwell 1961 (followed by Hornblower 2002: 230) and Jehne 1994: 86–88 argue that it was a common peace involving both Persia and Athens; *contra* Ryder 1965: 83, 137–39.

123. Diod. Sic. 15.79.3–6 for the main narrative; cf. Dem. 20.109; Paus. 9.15.3 (who absolves Epameinondas of any responsibility). Buckler 1980b: 182–84 suggests that the Orchomenian cavalry may have been motivated to join the conspiracy out of opposition to the move toward ever more democratic government in Thebes and in those cities outside Boiotia where the Thebans had some sway.

himself an ally of the Boiotians. The Magnesians and Phthiotic Achaians were recognized as Boiotian allies, an alignment that had important ramifications almost a
decade later.[124]

The initial decision to build a Boiotian fleet was mentioned above, and by
364 Epameinondas appears to have been in the Aegean working actively to further
Boiotian maritime interests. The primary motive here was to weaken Athenian
influence in the region.[125] The alliance between Arkadia and Athens in 366, regardless of whether the Athenians partook of the Theban-sponsored peace of that year,
was unsettling to the Boiotians, and Athenian support for the revolt of Ariobar-
zanes, the satrap of Hellespontine Phrygia, combined with a more aggressive
approach to their relations with the Aegean states under the Athenian admiral
Timotheos above all, meant that both the Thebans and the Persians were keen to
change the situation. The Thebans remained the most loyal allies of Persia, and it
was with Persian money that the fleet must have been funded. It is precisely in this
period that we find the Thebans issuing electrum coinage, a remarkable (and
ephemeral) phenomenon for fourth-century mainland Greece, and it can only be
associated with the Persian-funded naval program.[126] There is no doubt that the
appearance of a Boiotian fleet of one hundred triremes on the Aegean in 364 was a
remarkable novelty and may initially have been seen by disaffected Athenian allies
as potentially capable of improving their situation.

The actual success of the plan was, however, more limited. When the decision
was initially undertaken to build the fleet, the Boiotians planned to make overtures to Byzantion, Rhodes, and Chios.[127] After sailing past an Athenian fleet
unharassed, Epameinondas went to Byzantion, where he achieved the most signal
success of the entire campaign. Although Justin, our only detailed source for the
campaign, indicates that no formal alliance was made at Byzantion despite generally friendly feelings toward the Boiotians, we know that in this year a citizen of
Byzantion was made proxenos of the Boiotians. By 362 Byzantion had broken away
from the Athenian alliance and never returned to it, and in the 350s continued
to have a close relationship with the Boiotians.[128] The alignment was probably

124. Diod. Sic. 15.80; Plut. *Pel.* 31–35; Nep. *Pel.* 5. For detailed discussion of the battle see Buckler
1980b: 175–82.

125. Aeschin. 2.105.

126. Kraay 1976: 113.

127. Diod. Sic. 15.79.1.

128. Byzantine proxenos at Boiotia: T9. Separation from Athenian alliance by 362: Dem. 1.6. The
relationship in the 350s is deduced from RO 57 ll. 9–13, a record of contributions to the Boiotians for
the Third Sacred War in the period 354–352, in which the Byzantine contributions are made by
the Byzantine *synedroi;* the significance of this word has been a matter of some debate, hinging on the
question of how the Boiotians organized their allies. See below n. 146. Dem. 9.34 attests an alliance of
Byzantion and Thebes.

accomplished by Epameinondas in 364. Justin tells us that he had no success at Herakleia, Chios, or Rhodes, and no other source contradicts that report.[129] But in general Epameinondas's Aegean campaign must have been more complex than Justin reports. We know that the Athenian general Timotheos relieved a siege at Kyzikos, for which Epameinondas was probably responsible; it would have been a logical target if Byzantion was encouraging.[130] A newly discovered proxeny decree of Knidos for Epameinondas (T8) reveals that he had friendly relations with that city and was given the right to sail in and out of its harbor freely. And an Athenian inscription for Keos reveals that the island broke away from the Second Athenian Confederacy, probably in 364/3, and was brought back in only with real difficulty. It is usually inferred, probably rightly, that Epameinondas had something to do with it: the Boiotians had, after all, benefited from the Euboean revolt of 366 and supported the activities of Themison, tyrant of Eretria, at the expense of Athens. Keos, virtually equidistant from the southern tips of Euboia and Attika, would have been an attractive ally if the island could be won.[131] Although a careful study of the epigraphic evidence thus suggests a campaign far broader and more complex than literary sources let on, there is still no room to believe that Epameinondas achieved any lasting success in the Aegean in 364, and we never hear of renewed attempts by the Boiotians to exert any significant naval power.

Conflict in the Peloponnese, however, drew them back into action on land and presented the Thebans with another opportunity to show true leadership in Greece beyond the sheer military might they had demonstrated since Leuktra. In 363/2 they became involved in a war between the Arkadians and Elis that had broken out in 365 over the independent regional state of Triphylia and, later, over the use of sacred funds to pay the standing army of the Arkadians, the *Eparitoi*.[132] Claiming that the Arkadians had violated their agreement with the Boiotians by resolving on war with Elis independently, the Boiotians staged a massive invasion of Arkadia with their Euboian and Thessalian allies.[133] The defeat they suffered was totally unexpected. The battle of Mantineia in 362 resulted in enormous loss of life on both sides but, symptomatically for the mid-fourth century, had few decisive

129. Fossey 1994: 39 suggests that *SEG* 28.465 may provide evidence for Theban relations with Rhodes in this period, but the document (reused in antiquity) is so fragmentary that it offers no certainty, and the name "Rhodes" itself is restored. Cf. Buckler 1998: 197–98.

130. Diod. Sic. 15.81.6; Nep. *Timoth.* 1.3.

131. RO 39. In this connection it is interesting to note the hints of a koinonlike structure uniting the four poleis of Keos at this time: Tod 141; *SEG* 14.530 (*Staatsverträge* 232); *IG* XII.5.609 with Brun 1989. Two Athenian decrees reflect a desire to break up this structure: *IG* II² 404 (*SEG* 39.73) and 1128 (Tod 162; RO 40). See also Reger and Risser 1991, focused primarily on the Hellenistic koinon of the Keans.

132. Triphylian state: Nielsen 1997.

133. Xen. *Hell.* 7.4.38–40. Other allies from central Greece and the Peloponnese joined later: Xen. *Hell.* 7.5.4; Diod. Sic. 15.84.4.

implications.[134] Epameinondas himself was among those who died at Mantineia, and with him the Theban hegemony is conventionally thought to have ended.[135] This is overly schematic: the Thebans continued to lead affairs in Boiotia and retained the allegiance of many of their allies. That the Athenians concluded an alliance with the Thebans' Peloponnesian enemies after Mantineia comes as no surprise and should not be taken as an indication that Thebes was somehow finished. That the Spartans again remained outside the common peace that was concluded in 362/1, in order to fight for control over Messenia, further suggests that little had changed.[136] It is easier to argue that the battle of Mantineia itself changed the sociopolitical landscape by forcing upon the Greeks a realization that even with massive bloodshed the differences that divided them could not be reconciled. If indeed they had that realization (and Xenophon certainly did), however, it affected old patterns of behavior little. The experiment with the limits of power held by a regional state like the Boiotian koinon, which was arguably the most innovative attempt to solve the ills that plagued fourth-century Greece, was still being conducted in Arkadia, but the strength of Boiotia and, in the north, of the Chalkideis, could not be ignored.

The Thebans remained committed to their Arkadian allies and to the security of the new Megalopolis, and they were loyal to other allies like the Euboians.[137] Here *stasis* broke out in 357 over the issue of the island's stance toward Athens and Thebes, and the oligarchs sought help from Thebes. The background to the war can only be inferred: the cities of Euboia were among the first to join the Second Athenian Confederacy, but they had joined the Theban alliance shortly after Leuktra and apparently remained loyal.[138] A month of ineffectual fighting on Euboia was ended by the conclusion of an agreement in which the prodemocratic parties on the island clearly prevailed.[139] Loss of the Euboian alliance was certainly a blow to the Thebans, but they remained resolute in their attempt to retain a hegemonic position in the wider Greek world, as events of the next decade would clearly show.

134. Xen. *Hell.* 7.5.26–27.

135. Death of Epameinondas: Xen. *Hell.* 7.5.24–25; Diod. Sic. 15.87.5–6. Mantineia was the terminus for at least five different ancient historical accounts of the period: Diod. Sic. 15.89.3, 95.4. For its importance as both end and beginning in Xenophon see Dillery 1995: 17–40.

136. RO 41 = *IG* II² 112; Diod. Sic. 15.89.1–2; Plut. *Ages.* 35.3–4; Polyb. 4.33.8–9. Cf. Xen. *Hell.* 7.5.18.

137. Commitment to Megalopolis: Diod. Sic. 15.94.1–3.

138. Euboian cities in Second Athenian Confederacy: RO 22 ll. 80–84. Euboians in Theban alliance after Leuktra: Xen. *Hell.* 6.5.23.

139. Diod. Sic. 16.7.2; Aeschin. 3.85; Dem. 8.74–75; 21.174. The resulting alliance between Athens and Karystos (RO 48) alludes (lines 15–17) to the dispatch of embassies from Karystos to the other Euboian cities (viz. Eretria, Chalkis, and Histiaia) presumably in an attempt to persuade them too to make a formal alliance with Athens. There is a problem with the chronology of this conflict. Detailed discussion can be found in Cawkwell 1962 and the commentary to RO 48, which latter I follow. Whether the Euboian War occurred in 358/7 or 357/6 matters little for my purposes, but the Julian year 357 is more likely.

The Boiotians found another opportunity to strike at the Spartans and at their Phokian neighbors at the spring meeting of the council of the Delphic Amphiktyony in 356. With their strong Thessalian alliance, the Thebans persuaded the amphiktyony to renew an old indictment against the Spartans for their seizure of the Kadmeia sixteen years before and to pass a new indictment against the Phokians for cultivating the sacred plain of Kirrha. Both carried heavy penalties.[140] Both were largely political: the first was a strategy for the further humiliation of the Spartans, while the second was probably motivated by a desire to create a conflict that would allow the Thebans to present themselves as the undisputed hegemonic power of the Greek world—not so much by defeating the Phokians (who were not expected to be a formidable enemy) as by showing themselves to be the defenders of Delphi and the amphiktyony. In the next year the fines had not been paid, and the amphiktyonic council decreed that the territory of Phokis should be laid under a curse and that all who had not paid fines owed to the amphiktyony should incur the hatred of all the Greeks in common.[141] The Phokians claimed that the fine and the curse were both unjust and that they had an ancestral right to control the sanctuary of Apollo. Their general Philomelos sought the assistance of the Spartans, likewise implicated in the decrees of the council, but only covert monetary support was initially offered. With few other resources and a strong commitment to fighting the decrees, the Phokians seized the sanctuary at Delphi, and before the year was out they had begun to use the sacred treasuries to pay their mercenary army.[142] The Boiotians accepted a Lokrian appeal for help in defending the shrine, and in 354 the amphiktyony declared war on Phokis.[143] Most of central Greece supported the amphiktyons, while the Athenians and Spartans, along with the Achaians and some other Peloponnesians, decided to defend the Phokians and, implicitly, the claim that the charge leveled against the Spartans was unjust. Within the year the amphiktyonic forces had won a battle at Neon in Phokis, which appeared to be a decisive victory.[144] But the Phokians retreated to Delphi, which they still held, and met with their allies in an assembly that took on the guise of

140. Diod. Sic. 16.23.2–3, 29.2–3. We rely almost exclusively, by necessity, on Diodoros's account of the Third Sacred War, for which reason there has been much discussion of his sources. (See Markle 1994.) The date of the initial indictment of the Spartans has been debated: 371, directly after Leuktra (Harris 1995: 80; Lefèvre 2002: 455 n. 55), or 366 or 361 (Sordi 1957: 49–52) or 356 (Buckler 1985: 242–43 and 1989: 15). Diodoros, however, makes it clear that the charge was renewed in 356 when the fine had remained unpaid for many years. The matter cannot be settled with certainty, but the date is most likely sometime in the 360s (Hornblower 2007: 43–46).

141. Diod. Sic. 16.23.3.

142. Diod. Sic. 16.23.4–24.5, 30.1.

143. Diod. Sic. 16. 24.4, 25.1–3, 27.5, 28.3.

144. Diod. Sic. 16.28.4–31.5. The delay is to be explained by the Thessalians' reticence to act against Athens (a Phokian ally) until the outcome of the Social War (in 355) was clear.

what has been aptly termed a rebel amphiktyony.[145] The Phokians' use of the sacred treasuries to arm and fund their mercenary army protracted the conflict and made it expensive for the amphiktyony and its allies as well. The Boiotians accepted contributions for the war from a number of Greek states, including their steadfast ally Byzantion, and the Persian king.[146] But repeated Phokian attacks on western Boiotia exploited some internal divisions within the Boiotian poleis and in 349 resulted in the complete detachment of Koroneia, Tilphosaion, Chorsiai, and Orchomenos from the koinon.[147] These losses, combined certainly with financial exhaustion, led the Boiotians to appeal to Philip II of Macedon for help in the summer of 347.[148] The relationship was formalized as an alliance shortly thereafter.[149] The Thessalians made their own appeals to Philip, and in 346 his victories resulted in the surrender first of the Phokian leaders and then of the Phokian poleis, when they saw that they had been abandoned by their leaders. In the settlement, the Boiotians regained control of their western poleis.[150] Philip dismantled most of the Phokian poleis, scattered their populations into villages, and received control of the two Phokian votes in the amphiktyony.[151] Athenian fantasies notwithstanding, Philip did not use his upper hand to restore Plataia and Thespiai or to punish the Thebans in any way; the koinon was left fully intact and autonomous.[152] But Philip's now de facto leadership of the amphiktyony and his unique

145. Diod. Sic. 16.29.132 and *FDelph* III.5.19, a list of Delphic *naopoioi* that reflects fairly broad support for the Phokian position. Rebel amphiktyony: Ellis in *CAH* VI²: 741.

146. Greek contributions: RO 57. The Byzantines, who had supported the Theban naval initiative and now maintained the alliance out of hostility to Athens at the end of the Social War, made their contribution via *synedroi* (ll. 11, 24), implying a *synedrion* of which they were members (Lewis 1990b). It is doubtful that the Boiotians had created a formal deliberative body with representation from its allies, for if such an entity had existed we would expect that all contributions would have been made by the *synedroi* of each allied state, whereas the inscription indicates that only the Byzantines had them. See Buckler 1980b: 222–33 and 2000b; Jehne 1999: 328–44. Persian contribution: Diod. Sic. 16.40.1–2 with Buckler 1989: 100.

147. Phokian attacks on western Boiotia: Diod. Sic. 16.33.4, 56.2, 58.1; Dem. 3.27, 19.141 and 148; Theopomp. *FGrHist* 115 F 167. Opposition to the Boiotian koinon within Koroneia, exploited by the Phokian general Onomarchos: Ephoros *FGrHist* 70 F 94, Σ Arist. *Nic. Eth.* 3.8.9. Cf. Buckler 1989: 72, 82, 101–4; and Kallet-Marx 1989.

148. Diod. Sic. 16.58.2–3.

149. Diod. Sic. 16.59.2; Dem. 19.139, 318–25; Aeschin. 2.133.

150. The settlement had broad ramifications for the Athenians that are beyond my present concerns; for detailed discussion see Harris 1995: 82–106.

151. Phokian surrender: Diod. Sic. 16.59.3–4; Dem. 19.62, 123, 278. Western Boiotian poleis: Dem. 19.141. Punishment of the Phokians, inflicted by the amphiktyony, with Macedonian support: Diod. Sic. 16.60.1–4; cf. Dem. 19.60–61, 123. For the limited nature of the Macedonian destruction see Typaldou-Fakiris 2004: 326. This is not the place to enter into the debate about Philip's intentions toward Thebes and Athens, which now sought peace with Philip after their war over Amphipolis. See Buckler 1989: 121–24 with references.

152. Dem. 5.10, 19.112.

ability to settle an otherwise costly and unwinnable war had profound long-term consequences.

A NEW MACEDONIAN ORDER, 346–323

The settlement was ephemeral. Not only did Philip's peace with the Athenians break down quickly as a result of clashing interests in Thrace and the Hellespont, but his record of settling central Greek disputes appears to have made it unthinkable to combatants not to involve him. Between 346 and 340 relations between Philip and Athens became increasingly strained, rupturing completely when Philip seized Byzantion itself, thereby threatening the Athenian grain supply and eliciting a declaration of war from the Athenians.[153] Meanwhile, another amphiktyonic conflict was brewing, this time between Athens and Thebes. Probably shortly after 346 the Athenians had dedicated some shields in the new temple, with an inscription that declared them to have been taken "from the Medes and the Thebans, when they fought on the opposite side to the Greeks"; this was certainly a rededication of shields from the Persian Wars, destroyed in the fire that burned the temple in 373. The Thebans were displeased, and it was purportedly at their behest that amphiktyonic delegates from Lokrian Amphissa proposed that the amphiktyons should fine the Athenians fifty talents for having hung the shields on the walls of the temple before they had been properly purified or sanctified.[154] The orator Aeschines was one of the Athenian representatives at the meeting where the charge was leveled, and rather than deny the charge he sought to deflect it by accusing the Amphissans of cultivating the sacred plain and levying harbor taxes at Kirrha. These accusations triggered a minor conflict between the amphiktyony and Amphissa, the so-called Fourth Sacred War, in which the amphiktyons sought assistance from Philip.[155] From his base at Elateia Philip made overtures to the Thebans, and though they may have initially renewed their alliance, opinions on the matter were divided.[156] They had control of Lokrian Nikaia, just east of

153. Theopomp. *FGrHist* 115 F 292; Dem. 18.87–94; Plut. *Phok.* 14. Cf. Diod. Sic. 16.77. On Athenian politics in this period see Harris 1995: 107–23.

154. Aeschin. 3.116 with Sánchez 2001: 229. For the technicality upon which the Athenians are indicted by the Amphissans in Aeschines' account see Bommelaer and Bommelaer 1983: 21–26. Cf. Dem. 18.150.

155. Aeschin. 3.115, 117–33; Dem. 18.155–57. Demosthenes' claim (Dem. 18.143–51) that Aeschines fabricated the whole tradition about the consecration of Kirrha under a bribe from Philip, in order to have a war declared that would give Philip the right to be in central Greece with his army, is to be rejected in the face of earlier evidence for the duty of the amphiktyony to protect the sacred land (e.g., *CID* IV.1 with Sánchez 2001: 153–63 and Rousset 2002: 188–92). It is clearly intended to counter Aeschines' charge (3.113–14) that Demosthenes had taken bribes from Amphissa.

156. Dem. 18.167, 175; Plut. *Dem.* 18.1; Philoch. *FGrHist* 328 F 56; Diod. Sic. 16.85.3.

Thermopylai, which was tantamount to controlling the pass, and refused either to surrender it or to grant Philip unhindered passage.[157] News of Philip's proximity struck terror in the Athenians; when no one would come forward with a proposal in the Athenian assembly, Demosthenes braved the suggestion that the Athenians make an alliance with their long-reviled Theban neighbors, who stood between Philip and Athens and were therefore forced to take a stance on the matter.[158] Aeschines suggests that the Boiotians were so divided over the issue that some poleis threatened secession from the koinon if the Athenian alliance were accepted, and he quotes an Athenian decree promising help to any that might do so.[159] With the experience of having lost control of western Boiotia during the Third Sacred War still fresh, these threats of secession made the complete collapse of the Boiotian koinon a very real possibility. It was perhaps with the Athenian promise in mind that the Boiotians reversed themselves and accepted the Athenian alliance. The battle that ensued at Chaironeia in western Boiotia in August 338 was a terrible defeat for the allies and is regularly taken by historians to mark the end of Greek freedom.[160]

In the settlement that followed, the Thebans were punished by Philip while the Athenians received conciliations. Philip's evident intention was not to subordinate the Greeks but to secure their cooperation; but the Thebans' betrayal was evidently unforgivable. They were forced to ransom their dead; the city was garrisoned, and pro-Macedonian exiles were forcibly returned and put in control of a narrowly oligarchic regime.[161] Orchomenos, which had been lost to the koinon during the Third Sacred War and may have been one of the poleis that threatened secession over the question of the Macedonian alliance in the autumn of 339, was also forced to restore its exiles.[162] The Plataians were invited by Philip to return to their city.[163] But the koinon itself was certainly left intact, and this is no surprise if Philip wanted stability and cooperation from the Greeks.[164] By restoring pro-Macedonian exiles and putting them in power in the member poleis of the koinon, he could be sure to get both from Boiotia.

Before the Fourth Sacred War, Philip had been working to build alliances in central Greece. It was probably in this context that he had promised the

---

157. Aeschin. 3.140; Philoch. *FGrHist* 328 F 56b; Dem. 18.153. Cf. Harris 1995: 100. How the Boiotians had come to control Nikaia is unclear. Dem. 11.12 calls it a Theban *apoikia*. See Nielsen in Hansen and Nielsen 2004: 669–70 for its shadowy history.

158. Dem. 18.169–88; Diod. Sic. 16.84.2–85.1.

159. Aeschin. 3.142.

160. Dem. 16.169–79; Aeschin. 3.142–51; Diod. Sic. 16.85.5–86.6. See Harris 1995: 126–37.

161. Justin 9.4.6–8.

162. Paus. 4.27.10.

163. Plataia: Paus. 4.27.10, 9.1.8.

164. Arr. *Anab.* 1.7.11.

Aitolians that he would hand over Naupaktos to them; it was apparently back in Achaian hands.[165] The Aitolians duly fought on Philip's side at Chaironeia, but after the battle, when he was finally in a position to make good on his promise, he apparently failed to do so. Theopompos tells us that Philip captured Naupaktos and slaughtered the garrison at the behest of the Achaians, probably in the winter of 338/7; the certain implication is that it was now given to the Achaians. We are probably to infer that in the interim the Aitolians had seized Naupaktos on their own initiative when Philip reneged on his promise to give it to them.[166] The episode triggered a long-held Aitolian opposition to Macedonian kings.

Aside from the garrisoning of Thebes, Philip's efforts were focused on minor corrections and adjustments with the goal of securing a broad base of support in Greece for his planned campaign against Persia. His major innovation was the creation of the so-called League of Corinth, essentially a large military alliance in which the troop obligations of each member state were probably spelled out.[167] But Philip's sudden death in 336 created an opportunity for the Greeks to challenge these arrangements. In this effort the Thebans and Aitolians joined the Athenians in playing a leading role.

While the Aitolians undertook the restoration of anti-Macedonian exiles, the Thebans waited until they had heard a rumor of the death of Alexander, Philip's son and successor, in Illyria in 335 to attempt to expel the Macedonian garrison from their own city.[168] The Thebans sought help from several quarters, but they were matched in their enthusiasm only by the Aitolians.[169] Fearing that the revolt could easily spread, Alexander rushed into mainland Greece with terrifying speed at the head of his army. After inflicting a battlefield defeat the Macedonians entered the city of Thebes and destroyed it utterly. Women and children were raped and enslaved; men were slaughtered or captured, and following a vote by Alexander's Greek allies, who cited the Theban Medism of the previous century as an excuse, the ancient city was razed to the ground.[170] The Thespians, Plataians, and

---

165. Dem. 9.34.

166. Theopomp. *FGrHist* 115 F 235. Cf. Bosworth 1976: 169–74. Most assume that Dem. 9.34 simply anticipates Strabo (9.4.7), who says only that Naupaktos was Aitolian in his own time, that Philip must have actually made Naupaktos Aitolian, which he could only have done shortly after Chaironeia, and misread Theopompos as supporting this reconstruction, when in fact he (the best of the three sources) contradicts it. See Oldfather, *RE* XVI.2 *s.v.* "Naupaktos," col. 1990; Lerat 1952: II.49; Merker 1989: 306; Freitag 2000: 87–88; Rousset 2004: 396; *BNP* IX *s.v.* "Naupaktos," col. 547.

167. RO 76.

168. Diod. Sic. 17.3.3–4, 8.1–3; Arr. *Anab.* 1.1.3, 7.1–3.

169. Persian contributions: Din. 1.10, 18 with 1.20–22; Aeschin. 3.156–57, 239–40; Hyp. 5.17, 25. Uneven Arkadian support: Din. 1.19–20 with Arr. *Anab.* 1.10.1.

170. Arr. *Anab.* 1.7.4–8.8, 9.6–10; *Marm.Par.* (*IG* XII.5.444 ll. 103–4); Din. 1.24; Aeschin. 3.157; Diod. Sic. 17.9–14; Plut. *Alex.* 11.6–12.6.

Orchomenians, whose cities had all been destroyed by the Thebans in the last century, took the opportunity for revenge by participating in the Macedonian attack.[171] Survivors of the attack scattered, some going to Akraiphia and others to Athens, while at least a few able-bodied Thebans who sought some means of continuing their struggle against Alexander joined the Persian army.[172] The remains of the city were held by a Macedonian garrison, which presumably also policed the way in which the other Boiotians responded to the sudden appearance of this gaping hole in their political and economic landscape.[173] For Alexander portioned out the territory of Thebes to the neighboring Boiotians, who by 323 were deriving great revenues from it; in the same period a contemporary witness could report that "the city of Thebes . . . is being plowed and sown."[174]

The effects of the Theban revolt and destruction of the city rippled outward. Alexander advanced the process of rebuilding Orchomenos and Plataia begun by Philip after Chaironeia. In doing so he strengthened old opponents of Thebes and provided a vision of a Boiotia without its leading city.[175] The Athenians had, however, to be rewarded for staying out of it, and it was probably now that they received Oropos at Boiotian expense.[176] The Aitolians, conspicuous for their support of the Thebans, now sent embassies to Alexander "by *ethnos*, seeking pardon for having revolted, in response to the news brought from Thebes."[177] The dispatch of multiple embassies has signaled to some that the Aitolian koinon had been dismantled, perhaps by Philip in retaliation for the Aitolians' attempted seizure of Naupaktos after Chaironeia.[178] The conclusion is hardly inevitable: not only is the dismantling of a sovereign state by Philip otherwise unparalleled, but what Arrian, at a considerable remove, interpreted as separate embassies sent by *ethnos* may well have been simply a group of ambassadors who represented the several *ethnē* of which

---

171. Arr. *Anab.* 1.8.8 with Hurst 1989; Diod. Sic. 17.13.5; Justin 11.3.8.

172. Akraiphia: Paus. 9.23.5. Athens: Aeschin. 3.159; Paus. 9.7.1; Plut. *Alex.* 13.1; Munn 1998: 53–54 for a Theban among the ephebes at Panakton ca. 330–320. Persian army: Hofstetter 1978: nos. 89, 313 with Arr. *Anab.* 2.15.2–4; Plut. *Apophth. Alex.* 22 (*Mor.* 181B). Some of the Thebans' Boiotian enemies joined Alexander's army: *Anth.Pal.* 6.344.

173. Hyp. *Epit.* 17; Arr. *Anab.* 1.9.9.

174. Arr. *Anab.* 1.9.9; Diod. Sic. 18.11.3–5; Din. 1.24. Cf. Gullath 1982: 77–82.

175. Arr. *Anab.* 1.9.10; cf. Plut. *Alex.* 34.2; Plut. *Arist.* 11.9; Justin 11.3.8. The rebuilding of Plataia after 338 appears to have involved construction on an orthogonal plan: Konecny et al. 2008.

176. Paus. 1.34.1; Σ Dem. 18.99 (176 Dilts) suggest that it was made Athenian after Chaironeia, and this has been the dominant view until recently (e.g., Robert 1940–65: XI–XII.195). But now see Knoepfler 1993a: 295 and 2001a: 367–89 for 335 as the date when Oropos was handed over to the Athenians. After its transfer, the Athenians disputed how the territory would be divided up among the tribes; see Hyp. 4 and *Agora* I.6793 with Langdon 1987; Lewis 1990a; Papazarkadas 2009b.

177. Arr. *Anab.* 1.10.2.

178. Bosworth 1976: 166–67; Scholten 2000: 16.

the Aitolian koinon was composed.[179] We simply do not know enough about Aitolian diplomatic practices in the fourth century to conclude that embassies sent by *ethnos* are unusual and signal a collapse of the koinon. Ultimately what matters is that in their revolt, as in their attempt at conciliation, the Aitolians were united, and in these years were treated by outsiders as a single state. So the Aitolians received a collective grant of *promanteia* from the polis of Delphi in 335 or 334.[180] Although the real motives for the grant are difficult to divine, it is nevertheless significant as the first clear evidence we have for any relationship between the Aitolians and Delphi, and it helps to contextualize the apparent interest of the Aitolians in Delphi and the amphiktyonic world in the early third century, which will be explored in the next chapter. In short, if Philip had in fact dismantled the koinon, the measure had virtually no effect; we know that the Aitolian koinon, like the Arkadian and Boiotian koina, was very much in existence in 323.[181]

When Alexander left Greece to conquer the Persian empire in 334, he took the attention of Greek writers with him. We have little evidence for developments among the koina of mainland Greece in this period. The ephemeral revolt from Macedonian control led by the Spartan king Agis in 331/0 attracted some Peloponnesian support, including the participation of the Achaians, and it may have been as punishment that so many of the Achaian poleis were now saddled with tyrants installed by Alexander (or his agents).[182] The struggle to expel them is part of the story of the next chapter, inextricably bound up with the story of the redevelopment of the institutions of the Achaian koinon. Resistance to Macedonian rule remained strong in Aitolia.[183] The Boiotians were less restive, relieved to be rid of the Thebans who had determined regional politics since the end of the Peloponnesian War and grateful to Alexander for having brought about such a drastic change. The history of Boiotia in the fourth century is, effectively, a history of Thebes and the demands it placed on its fellow Boiotian poleis, which were, in the period after 379, virtually its subjects. The history of the region in the Hellenistic period is a different story altogether, a story of remarkably equitable institutions,

179. Sordi 1953b: 435. Compare the dispatch of three ambassadors by the Aitolians, one to represent each of the three major *ethnē*, to the Spartans in 426, after Demosthenes' invasion: Th. 3.100.1. See above, p. 56. For detailed discussion see Funke 1997: 159–60.

180. *FDelph* III.4.399 (*SEG* 17.228). The date of the grant is controversial. I follow Arnush 1995 (cf. Arnush 2000: 299–300) *contra* Bousquet 1988a: 58 n. 50. Even if we accept Arnush's argument for the Delphic archonship of Sarpadon belonging to the year 335/4, we cannot determine the relative chronology of the grant and the destruction of Thebes.

181. Hyp. 5.18.

182. Achaian participation in revolt of Agis: Aeschin. 3.165; Din. 1.34; Q.C. 6.1.20. This suggestion is hypothetical, and it is difficult to know how to square it with the claim of Hyp. 5.18 that the Achaian koinon was in existence in 323.

183. Mendels 1984: 129–49.

which included Thebes on an equal footing with the other poleis after the city was rebuilt and, eventually, accepted as a member of the koinon again. It is in the Hellenistic period that we finally begin to see the internal structures of the Achaian and Aitolian koina in some detail, just as we are at last able to follow much more closely the histories of their interactions with the rest of the Greek world, tracing lines of sight rather than simply noticing scattered points of light.

3

The Hellenistic Period

MAINLAND GREECE AND THE WARS
OF THE SUCCESSORS, 323–285

During the Hellenistic period, the koina of mainland Greece and the Peloponnese were strengthened and expanded both to achieve greater security against powerful enemies and to gain control over greater and more diversified sets of resources. Attempts to retain regional autonomy led to a series of shifting alliances, especially complex during the wars of Alexander's successors. The city of Thebes was rebuilt and eventually rejoined the Boiotian koinon, which became robust in this period, with a set of institutions refined to prevent the old hegemon from regaining its former position of dominance over the other member poleis and the koinon as a whole. The Aitolian koinon grew rapidly through much of the third century, acquiring members by an unusual variety of diplomatic means and experimenting with how—and how far—to integrate these newcomers into the Aitolian state. The Achaian koinon was refounded around 280 following the successful expulsion of Macedonian-installed tyrants from the Achaian cities and grew rapidly for the rest of the third century, eventually encompassing almost the entire Peloponnese. Resistance to integration came most notably from Sparta during the reign of Kleomenes, whom the Achaians defeated narrowly and only at the high price of forging an alliance with their longtime enemy Antigonos Doson. The short but bitter Social War (220–217) pitted the Achaians and Aitolians, former allies, against each other and paved the way for Roman intervention in Greece before the end of the third century. The koina of mainland Greece struggled, ultimately unsuccessfully, to retain their autonomy in the face of increasing Roman power over the next half-century. The means by which they were dismembered tell us a great deal both

about what made koina such effective states and about the nature of Roman ambitions in mainland Greece in the second century.

Despite their conciliatory embassies to Alexander after the destruction of Thebes,
the Aitolians remained resolutely hostile toward Macedonian rulers. If most Greek
cities were hard hit by Alexander's decree for the restoration of exiles, the Aitolians
and Athenians were united in their virulent resistance to the order. The Aitolians had
seized the Akarnanian polis of Oiniadai and expelled its entire population (a clear
illustration of the Aitolians' urgent need to gain greater access to the coast in this
period), while the Athenians worried that they would lose their cleruchy on Samos.[1]
When news of Alexander's death reached Greece, the Athenian general Leosthenes
"went to Aitolia to arrange a common undertaking. The Aitolians gladly acknowl-
edged his request and gave him seven thousand soldiers."[2] Whatever the constitutional details, which are unattested for this period, it is clear that the Aitolians were
engaged in a politics of cooperation. The aim of the ensuing Lamian War was
nothing short of the liberation of all Greece from Macedonian rule.[3] The Boiotians
initially refused to support the movement, fearing that if it was successful, the
Athenians would restore Thebes, but they were eventually persuaded to join.[4] The
Greek forces were finally defeated at the battle of Krannon in September 322.[5]

When Antipater and Krateros forced the Greek allies to come to terms city by city,
only the Aitolians and Athenians refused.[6] For their initial recalcitrance the Athenians paid with nothing less than the loss of their democracy, their Samian cleruchy,
and control of Oropos, which became independent until 304.[7] The Aitolians suffered
an abortive invasion of their territory by Antipater and gained and then lost control
of much of Thessaly. Two details emerge from the narrative of these years that are
important for our purposes: the Aitolians now had citizen forces, suggesting an
Aitolian army associated with a single Aitolian state, and they were already interested
in trying to acquire control of central Greece east of the Pindos Mountains.[8]

1. Diod. Sic. 18.8.2–7; Plut. *Alex.* 49.14. Mendels 1984: 130 discusses the strategic importance of
Oiniadai. Foundation of Athenian cleruchy on Samos: Isoc. 15.11; Dem. 15.9–10; Diod. Sic. 18.18.9; Nep.
Timoth. 1.2. Cf. Jehne 1994: 241–43.

2. Diod. Sic. 18.9.5.

3. Aim: Diod. Sic. 18.9.5, 10.2. Participants: Diod. Sic. 18.10.5, 11.1–2.

4. Diod. Sic. 18.11.3–5.

5. Melitaia: Diod. Sic. 18.15.1–7. Naval defeats: Diod. Sic. 18.15.8–9; Plut. *Demetr.* 11.4; *Marm.Par.* (*IG*
XII.5.444 l. 110). Krannon: Diod. Sic. 18.16.4–17.5.

6. Diod. Sic. 18.17.8.

7. Diod. Sic. 18.18.1–6. Moretti 1967–76: I.8 l. 14; Habicht 1997: 77.

8. Invasion: Diod. Sic. 18.24.1–5. Thessaly: Simpson 1958: 359 implies that they were motivated only
by stubborn opposition to those in power in Macedon; but the Aitolian occupation of the Parnassos
region by about 301 (to be discussed below) does require some background explanation. The two goals
are not mutually exclusive. Citizen forces: Diod. Sic. 18.38.5–6.

The Lamian War briefly united most of central Greece against Macedonian rule; thereafter they became divided by the wars of Alexander's successors. The Aitolians, believing in Polyperchon's declaration that the Greek cities were free to return to the governments they had known under Philip and Alexander, continued to support him even after the murder of his ally Olympias and the rise of Cassander.[9] They thus became willing allies of Antigonos Monophthalmos in 314/3, when he likewise promised freedom, autonomy, and freedom from garrisons in his bid to challenge Cassander.[10]

Cassander found a different strategy for gaining support, declaring his intention in 316/5 to rebuild Thebes.[11] Cassander probably had several motives. The only ancient explanation we have is that he acted out of hatred for Alexander. It was certainly, in part, a bid to gain further support in central Greece; his political enemies complained bitterly about it later.[12] The restoration promulgated the message that Cassander was committed to the freedom of the Greek cities, a message that he probably intended to spread beyond central Greece—at least to the Peloponnese, where many cities were under the control of his rival Polyperchon. The profile of supporters for the reconstruction of Thebes is interesting: the Athenians, probably motivated in part by a desire to see the many Theban exiles in Athens return home, were joined by the people of Messene and Megalopolis, two cities that owed their very existence to the Thebans.[13] Finally, the strategic position of Thebes, situated between the passes of Thessaly and the rest of central Greece, is obvious; the new city retained a Macedonian garrison for many years after its restoration.[14]

For our purposes there are two particularly important questions about the reconstruction of Thebes: How did the other Boiotian poleis feel about it, and how did it affect the Boiotian koinon? It is worth remembering that those cities that had most bitterly resented Theban hegemony in the fourth century—Plataia, Orchomenos, and Thespiai—all helped Alexander's forces to raze the city to the ground in 335. Diodoros says, somewhat ominously, that Cassander persuaded the Boiotians before he began to refound the city, implying that there was serious opposition. This was certainly political, but it was probably also economic: after the city was destroyed, Alexander had distributed the land among the neighboring

9. Declaration: Diod. Sic. 18.56.1–8. Aitolian support for Polyperchon: Diod. Sic. 19.35.2, 52.6, 53.1.

10. Declaration: Diod. Sic. 19.61.1–3; Justin 15.1.3. Alliance with Aitolia: Diod. Sic. 19.66.2. Cf. Simpson 1958: 359.

11. Diod. Sic. 19.53.2; *Marm.Par.* (*IG* XII.5.444) l. 117).

12. Hatred: Paus. 9.7.2. Complaints: Diod. Sic. 19.61.2; Justin 51.3.

13. Paus. 9.7.1. The importance of the message sent to the Peloponnesian cities has been stressed by Bearzot 1997. The enthusiasm of the Athenians for the project is to be explained in part by the fact that by this time Cassander had already wooed Athens away from Polyperchon (Diod. Sic. 18.74.3).

14. Knoepfler 2001c: 12.

Boiotians, who were "deriving great proceeds from the land."[15] It was probably the combination of Cassander's strategic intentions in refounding the city and the Boiotians' reticence toward its renewed existence that prevented it from immediately becoming a member of the Boiotian koinon upon its refoundation.[16] It is clear that in 313 the Thebans (still garrisoned by Cassander) and Boiotians were acting independently of each other. Indeed it is likely that it took nearly three decades for the Boiotians to accept the return of Thebes, the old hegemon, into the koinon. I shall return to this later.

The Peloponnesian cities became cruelly trapped between the shifting alliances of the successors in these tumultuous years. Both Polyperchon and Cassander held cities in the region by force, triggering a bloody series of events that resulted, ultimately, in the possession of all Achaia by Antigonos.[17] But the rivals who had garrisoned different cities in the region had violently splintered the recent political unification of Achaia; although we cannot trace that process in detail, these were the conditions that necessitated what Polybios later spoke of as a refoundation of the koinon in the late 280s.[18]

The Aitolians did not pin all their hopes on external support; they continued to attempt to build up their power in central Greece. A boundary dispute with their Akarnanian neighbors led to an Aitolian attack on the polis of Agrinion, which may at this time have been incorporated into the koinon.[19] Despite—or perhaps because of—a terrifying invasion by Cassander in 313, the Aitolians formalized their alliance with Antigonos, and the Boiotians followed suit.[20] But that was a difficult alliance to preserve with Thebes still garrisoned by Cassander. In a sham gesture of autonomy the Thebans now made a formal alliance with him, while Cassander managed only to squeeze an armistice out of the rest of the Boiotians.[21] The polis of Thebes and the koinon of the Boiotians remained distinct entities. In 312 Antigonos rewarded the Boiotians with Chalkis and Oropos, seized from Cassander, and then secured his control over the region by expelling Cassander's garrison from Thebes and professedly

15. Diod. Sic. 18.3–4. The comment is made by way of explanation for Boiotia's opposition to Athens in the Lamian War, for which see also Paus. 1.25.4. Boiotian opposition is highlighted by Knoepfler 2001c: 12.

16. *Contra* Beloch 1912–27: IV.2.427; Gullath 1982: 112. Contributions to the rebuilding effort were made by several kings and communities of mainland Greece and the Aegean: *IG* VII.2419.

17. *Stasis* at Dyme: Diod. Sic. 19.66.2–6. Antigonid victory: Diod. Sic. 19.74.1–2.

18. Polyb. 2.41.11.

19. Agrinion: Diod. Sic. 19.67.3–5, 68.1. It may be in connection with this attack that we have an epigram, found at Palairos, honoring Deinias the son of Learchos, who died defending the Akarnanians against the "hubris of the Aitolians": Peek 1955: I.1458 (*IG* IX.1² 462; Moretti 1967–76: II.89).

20. Invasion: Diod. Sic. 19.74.3–6, 75.6 with Billows 1990: 122 n. 52.

21. Diod. Sic. 19.77.4–6, 78.3.

freeing the city.[22] Although it has frequently been inferred that at this moment Thebes was reintegrated into the Boiotian koinon, there is in fact no solid evidence for the claim, and indeed there are good reasons for thinking that the reintegration occurred significantly later, in or shortly after 287.[23] The Boiotians and Aitolians then operated quite independently of Macedonian intervention, while the poleis of Achaia, under the close watch of Ptolemaic garrisons at Corinth and Sikyon, struggled individually to recover from the violence of the last two decades.[24] All were nominally free, but the events of 304 show that old Greece was still regarded as a source of power to the successors.

After abandoning his unsuccessful year-long siege of Rhodes, thanks at least in part to the diplomatic efforts of the Aitolian koinon and the Athenians, Demetrios Poliorketes sailed to central Greece with the intention of undermining Cassander's power in the region.[25] Again the propaganda was that he had arrived to protect the Greeks against the unmitigated depredations of Cassander and Polyperchon.[26] His arrival represented a blow to the Boiotian koinon, which lost both Chalkis and Oropos; the latter was given to the Athenians, who retained it until Demetrios lost his kingdom in 287.[27] The Boiotians were forced (perhaps without too much difficulty, given their history of hostility) to surrender their allegiance to Cassander and make a new alliance with Demetrios.[28] Having secured the allegiance of the Athenians as well, Demetrios moved on to Aitolia, where he found willing allies in his war against Cassander and Polyperchon.[29] He then moved into the Peloponnese, where their power was more firmly entrenched, and managed to take both Sikyon and Corinth as well as several Achaian and northern Arkadian poleis.[30]

22. Diod. Sic. 19.78.3–5, 20.100.6. Ptolemaios went on to dislodge Cassander's forces from the cities of Phokis and from Lokrian Opous. It is likely that he received Boiotian assistance at least for the latter campaign, to judge from a decree set up at Delphi to honor one Peisis of Thespiai for having liberated Opous: *FDelph* III.4.463 = Moretti 1967–76: II.71; cf. Flacelière 1937: 71–72.

23. Holleaux 1885, using the assumption to date the four aphedriate dedications that he found at the Ptoion (T16–19) to the period 312–304, which has now been proved too early. (See comm. *ad locum*.) Cf. Prandi 1988: 150, relying heavily on Paus. 9.3.6, which in fact allows no chronological specificity. The problems with the argument are discussed in detail by Knoepfler 2001c: 13–16.

24. Ptolemaic garrisons: Diod. Sic. 20.37.1–2.

25. Aitolian efforts: Diod. Sic. 20.99.3; Athenian efforts: Plut. *Dem.* 22.8. The claim of Aitolian diplomatic activity at Rhodes, if true, may provide some of the background to the otherwise surprisingly sudden prominence of the Aitolians in central Greece (particularly Phokis and Thessaly) after 301. See Mendels 1984: 178–79.

26. Diod. Sic. 20.100.6.

27. Chalkis: Diod. Sic. 20.100.6. Oropos: Moretti 1967–76: I.8 ll. 13–14; Habicht 1997: 77.

28. Diod. Sic. 20.100.6; Plut. *Dem.* 23.3.

29. Diod. Sic. 20.100.6.

30. Sikyon now became known for a brief period as Demetrias: Diod. Sic. 20.102; Paus. 2.7.1; Str. 8.6.25; Thür 1995. Corinth, Achaian Boura, Arkadian Skyros, and Orchomenos: Diod. Sic. 20.103.

The massive defeat suffered by Antigonos and Demetrios at Ipsos in 301 had important ramifications in central Greece. The Aitolians, guessing that it would yield great gains for their longtime enemy Cassander, seem to have in some way taken control of Phokis and forged an alliance "between the Boiotians and the Aitolians and the Phokians with the Aitolians"; fragmentary copies of the treaty were found at both Thermon and Delphi (T53, B10).[31] It was probably by this means that the Aitolians secured a foothold in the Parnassos region, and particularly at Delphi, which soon gave the persistent Demetrios a specious cause to declare war against them. It should be remembered, however, that the Aitolians' collective relations with Delphi had been quite close since around 335/4, when the Delphians granted all Aitolians the right of first consultation at the Delphic oracle.[32]

The independent alliance of the Boiotians and Aitolians, who now somehow included the Phokians in their state, presented a real threat to those Macedonian rulers now attempting to claim ultimate hegemony over the Greek cities, even as they fought one another to liberate them. The death of Cassander in 298/7, and the restoration of Pyrrhos to his Epeirote kingdom with the assistance of Ptolemy, changed the players on the field, though it did not change the rules of the game. By 294 Demetrios Poliorketes, having recovered from the loss at Ipsos, had himself declared king by the Macedonian army and set about securing control of central Greece, the largest single area of the Greek world not under his direct control.[33] The Boiotian-Aitolian alliance proved remarkably effective: the rebellion from Demetrios began in 293 in Boiotia and was supported by both the Aitolians and their new ally Pyrrhos. The death of Cassander may well have freed the Thebans to pursue a path of greater integration with the rest of Boiotia; if this was a gradual process, the details are lost. What is clear is that in 293 they participated so whole-heartedly in the rebellion that their city was once again besieged, this time by Demetrios. Although the sources focus on this effort, it is clear that the rebellion engaged the entire region.[34] And when it was finally quelled, Demetrios left garrisons not only in Thebes but also in the other Boiotian cities.[35] Although the

31. Flacelière 1930 and 1937: 49–91, esp. 57–68; Gullath 1982: 195–96. Knoepfler 2007a has proposed a later date for this treaty, ca. 274–272, on the grounds of his restoration of line 4, which would require the existence of a statue of Aitolia, known to have been erected at Thermon only after 279. If this is correct, we would need to find another way to explain the coordination between Boiotia and Aitolia in the war against Demetrios in 293 (in which the Aitolians rendered admittedly little material assistance to the Boiotians) and Aitolian support for the Boiotians in the matter of the Athenian inscription accompanying the rededication of Persian shields at Thermon ca. 291 (on which see below).

32. FDelph III.4.399 (SEG 17.228). See above, p. 89.

33. Plut. Demetr. 36–37 and 39.1, Pyrrh. 7.2; Justin 16.1.18–19.

34. Plut. Demetr. 39.2, 5 (on the leading role of Peisis of Thespiai in orchestrating and executing the revolt); Polyaenus, Strat. 4.7.11. Cf. Roesch 1982: 432–33.

35. Plut. Demetr. 39.4, Pyrrh. 7.3

Aitolians rendered minimal military assistance to the Boiotians, their opposition to Demetrios was clear, and their strong presence at Delphi, which had become a grievance to the Athenians, now gave him the pretext for an attack in the guise of a sacred war. Probably in 291, the Athenians became anxious about the dedication of the shields at Delphi, and passed a formal resolution to ask Demetrios, whom they called their savior, "how they might most piously, nobly, and swiftly achieve a restoration of the dedications."[36] The shields in question were the same ones that had been the subject of the dispute between the Athenians and Thebans in 339.[37] We have to infer that sometime after the Aitolians gained preeminence in if not control over Delphi, around 301, their Boiotian allies asked them to remove the offending shields. Demetrios arrived in Athens at about the time when the Athenians were worrying about this affront; this was the context in which they performed the famous ithyphallic hymn in his honor.[38] In it the Athenians plead for nothing less than war against the Aitolians: they wish to see them "flung down" and "reduced to dust."[39] That Demetrios accepted their plea is implied by the fact that he took the unprecedented step of celebrating the Pythian Games of 290 in Athens, "because the Aitolians had a tight hold on Delphi."[40] Demetrios accomplished a damaging invasion of Aitolia and negotiated a treaty with them that protected free access to Delphi.[41]

Demetrios lost his kingdom in 287, the result of a powerful alliance of his enemies and the exasperation of his own troops. It is a sign of the improvisational nature of early Hellenistic kingship, and its foundation in the support of communities, that the principal means by which he sought to regain power was to canvass support among the Greek cities. One of those we know he visited was Thebes, where according to Plutarch he "returned to the Thebans their *politeia*."[42] Hidden behind this terse allusion appears to be the full reintegration of the Thebans into the Boiotian koinon, contemporary with the revolt of Athens from Demetrios in the spring of 287.[43] This implies

36. Plut. *Demetr.* 13.1–3.
37. See above, p. 85. The shields were apparently left hanging, and the Thebans made their second appeal to have them removed ca. 291, hoping for support from the Aitolians.
38. Douris of Samos FGrHist 76 F 13 *apud* Ath. 6.253b–f. Habicht 1970: 232–33; Scholten 2000: 22 with n. 90.
39. Habicht 1970: 34–44 and 1997: 92–94.
40. Plut. *Demetr.* 40.7–8 with Kuhn 2006: 269–72.
41. Plut. *Demetr.* 41.1–3, *Pyrrh.* 7.4–10; Flacelière 1937: 76–78. The treaty has been fairly recently discovered, but the stone is highly fragmentary, and the text has been heavily restored: Lefèvre 1998 (*SEG* 48.588).
42. Plut. *Demetr.* 46.1.
43. Roesch 1982: 435–39; Knoepfler 2001c: 15–19, using epigraphic evidence to support the late date for reintegration. Ma 2008: 84 suggests that the lion monument built atop the burial mound for the Theban dead at Chaironeia was built either when Cassander refounded Thebes or now, when the city

either that Demetrios exercised power over Boiotia as a whole, which is unlikely given Demetrios's weak position at this date, or a remarkable unanimity on the part of the Boiotian cities toward the desirability of having Thebes as a part of the koinon again. We simply do not know by what mechanism or mechanisms this change was effected. What is clear is that from this point forward, the Boiotian koinon again included Thebes, but the Boiotians now adopted a strikingly different institutional architecture than the one that had facilitated the Theban hegemony of the fourth century, a change certainly made to prevent that outcome from repeating itself. It is now that we begin to see seven or eight (rather than the eleven of the early fourth century) districts, which ensured the active participation and sovereignty of even the smallest member poleis, and the aphedriates, those representatives of the districts who sacrificed on behalf of their constituencies in koinon-wide rituals and thereby reaffirmed the commitment of those communities to the larger state.[44] Only a few years later we see that the Boiotian koinon was deploying cavalry in the territories of both Thebes and Oropos, explicitly categorized as being in Boiotia (T15.31–37), which bespeaks not only the reintegration of Thebes and the Boiotians' commitment to its territorial integrity as part of the koinon, but also the return of Oropos to Boiotia after 287.[45]

INDEPENDENCE AND EXPANSION, 284–245

Demetrios's bid to regain power was, however, ultimately unsuccessful, and though he was eventually succeeded by his son, Antigonos Gonatas, in 277, the weakness of the interim period had a profound impact on the ability of the communities of mainland Greece and the Peloponnese to pursue a path of independence and, in many cases, of greater regional cooperation. Antigonos's weakness was quite apparent to the communities of old Greece, who now sought by various means to rebuild the political structures upon which their past glories and quiet periods of independence had rested.

For the Spartans under King Areus this meant a desire to rebuild the Peloponnesian League of the classical period by creating a network of alliances centered around Sparta.[46] The Aitolians quickly became a target for the energies of

---

rejoined the koinon. A date of 287 seems to me more likely, in that the monument was erected at Chaironeia and required the consent of the other Boiotians. It would be a splendid means for the Thebans to reestablish themselves as members of the koinon (they suffered heavily in the Boiotian attempt to defeat the Macedonians), in addition to the monument's immediate role in commemorating the battle itself.

44. The districts in general are discussed below, pp. 370–84; on the aphedriates, see below, pp. 221–24.

45. Cf. Roesch 1979: 246.

46. Justin 24.1.1–2.

Areus and his supporters, probably for several reasons: they perceived the Aitolians as having pro-Macedonian sympathies; they noted that their most powerful ally, Pyrrhos, had departed for Italy; and they knew that the freedom of Delphi, however specious, was a cause around which Greeks could be persuaded to rally. So the Spartans dredged up the usual claim—that the Aitolians had cultivated the sacred plain of Apollo at Kirrha—and with their allies declared a sacred war to dislodge them from Delphi.[47] But the Spartan alliance collapsed under suspicions of imperialist aims, and the war was a failure.[48] It was perhaps partly in retaliation for this Spartan-led attack that in 280 the Aitolians took control of Herakleia Trachinia, the old Spartan foundation in Malis, making it a member of their koinon. The background to this move is unclear; that there were simmering boundary disputes between the eastern Aitolian communities and Herakleia is likely, but the timing of the integration of Herakleia has also to be considered.[49]

During this same period, or perhaps immediately after the botched sacred war against the Aitolians, the Achaians sought to free themselves from the garrisons and tyrants installed and controlled by at least one of several Macedonian rulers since the reign of Alexander.[50] In a process that began in the extreme west in the period 284–280, the Achaian poleis gradually and quite voluntarily rebuilt the koinon they had created in the fourth century.[51] That it remained a very loose organization in its earliest years is suggested by the fact that the only Achaians to go to the aid of Delphi when it was attacked by the Gauls in 279 were the Patraians.[52] No Achaian federal army was sent, and the armed forces of each polis appear still to have been free to act independently.

The defense of Delphi against the Gauls was manned also by Phokians, Boiotians, and Athenians, but it was the Aitolians who claimed the leading role in saving the sanctuary, and it was they who suffered most directly when a band of the invaders broke off and attacked Kallipolis, in southeastern Aitolia, in an attempt to draw the defenders away from Delphi and Thermopylai.[53] In the aftermath of their victory, the Aitolians gained two seats on the amphiktyonic council, probably those formerly belonging to Herakleia Trachinia and to Ozolian Lokris, which were now

47. Justin 24.1.2–4.
48. Justin 24.1.7.
49. Paus. 10.20.9; Scholten 2000: 24. See below, p. 360.
50. Polyb. 2.41.10; cf. 9.29.5–6.
51. Polyb. 2.41.1, 11–12; cf. Str. 8.7.1.
52. Paus. 7.18.6; cf. F. W. Walbank 1957–79: I.233.
53. Paus. 10.3.4 (Phokian participation); IG VII.2537 = Moretti 1967–76: I.68 (Boiotian participation); Syll.³ 408 (Athenian participation). Paus. 10.19.5–23.14 is the fullest ancient narrative. The Aitolian defense of Delphi is treated in full by Flacelière 1937: 93–112; Nachtergael 1977: 137–75; Scholten 2000: 31–37.

part of an emergent "greater Aitolia."[54] Over the next decades, as we can discern from Delphic inscriptions, the Aitolians gained more seats on the amphiktyonic council, at the expense of traditional members, which may indicate the incorporation of those communities into the Aitolian koinon.[55] These included Dolopia (by spring 276), Ainis and Doris (by fall 272), and part of Eastern Lokris (by fall 272).[56] The means by which these regions were incorporated and the precise status they attained once they were is uncertain but will be discussed below.[57] What is clear is that the Aitolian presence at Delphi became increasingly dominant. The expulsion of the Gauls in 279 was celebrated by an annual amphiktyonic festival, the *Sōtēria*.[58] By 246/5, the Aitolians' control over Delphic politics and their own status around the Aegean led them to transform the festival into a penteteric pan-Hellenic one; embassies were sent throughout the Greek world seeking acceptance of the new *Sōtēria*, an effort that appears to have been broadly successful.[59] The decade of anarchy that intervened between the expulsion of Demetrios Poliorketes and the accession of his son Antigonos was vitally important for the koina of mainland Greece and the Peloponnese, for it had given them the incentive and the opportunity to regroup, expand, and refine the cooperative institutions by which they had in the classical period created their regional states.

Gonatas's recognition as king of the Macedonians in 277 was not enough to turn back this tide.[60] Around 275 a wave of rebellion motivated by a desire for independence rose over Achaia. Aigion, an important member of the fourth-century koinon and the seat of the regionally significant sanctuary of Zeus Homarios, expelled its Macedonian garrison and joined the western Achaian poleis in becoming part of the new koinon.[61] Further to the east, Boura was sufficiently encouraged by this rising to assassinate its tyrant, and then the tyrant of neighboring Keryneia

54. The phrase is Scholten's (2000: 29–58 passim). The status of Ozolian Lokris relative to Aitolia is difficult to determine, but it appears to have enjoyed greater independence than Herakleia did: *IG* IX.1² 1.12.

55. For the problems with this approach, and detailed analysis of the documents, see Grainger 1995: 318–20; Lefèvre 1995; Scholten 2000: 55, 235–52.

56. Scholten 2000: 240–43.

57. See below, p. 360.

58. *Syll.*³ 398.

59. Seven recognition decrees survive: *Syll.*³ 408 (Athens) and 402 with Robert 1933: 535–37 (Chios); *FDelph* III.1.481 (a Kykladic island), III.1.482 (Tenos), III.1.483 (Smyrna); Delph. inv. 6377 + 2872 (Abdera) and 6203 (unknown origin). The Smyrna decree must be slightly later than the first four, which all date to 246/5: Elwyn 1990. See Flacelière 1937: 133–38; Nachtergael 1977: 71–73 (for the date of the first four decrees), 435–37; Champion 1995.

60. Diog. Laert. 2.141; Nachtergael 1977: 167–68 with references to previous scholarship.

61. The sanctuary is discussed in greater detail below, pp. 199–200. T34, the only surviving decree of the koinon from the fourth century, was found at Aigion and is generally thought to have been set up in the Hamarion.

abdicated, sensing what was in store for him.[62] Polybios does not mention the status of the other three Achaian cities during this period, but inland Leontion and the large eastern coastal poleis of Aigeira and Pellene probably also joined at this time, returning the koinon to its fourth-century size, lacking only Helike and Boura, destroyed in 373.[63] Polybios (2.43.1) implies that until 251, membership of the Achaian koinon did not increase again; whether he should be taken literally, on the assumption that he explicitly listed all members, or not is unclear. In the intervening years there is evidence for concerted action on the part of the Achaians, directed consistently toward the goal of total independence from Macedonian control. They welcomed Pyrrhos, coming in 272 ostensibly to undermine Antigonid influence in the Peloponnese, and in 268 they joined the alliance of Greek states being formed against Antigonos, which led directly to the seven-year conflict known as the Chremonidean War.[64] The exact course of the war cannot be reconstructed with any detail, but Corinth was a major bone of contention and remained in Antigonid hands, making it a focal point in the Achaians' coordinated struggle for regional independence.[65]

Meanwhile, the persistent opposition of the Aitolians, who appear not to have taken part in the Chremonidean War, effected a remarkable, if ephemeral, change in their relationship with their Akarnanian neighbors, with whom they had a long history of antagonism. An inscription from Thermon (T57) records a treaty and alliance between the Aitolians and Akarnanians, of which no written source provides so much as a hint. The general paucity of evidence for Aitolian activities in this period, aside from the tangled and chronologically challenging evidence of the amphiktyonic decrees and other inscriptions from Delphi, makes this treaty difficult to place in context, but Günther Klaffenbach was probably right to place it at the end of the Chremonidean War and to explain it as a product of the attempt by Alexander of Epeiros, the son of Pyrrhos, to secure local support as a means of regaining his throne from Antigonos.[66] The treaty was evidently predicated upon a successful and mutually acceptable demarcation of the territories of the two koina, fixing the Achelöos River as the boundary; this meant that the Aitolians would surrender their claims to Oiniadai and Stratos, made by force in 314, but they were allowed to keep Agrinion.[67] What is truly striking

62. Polyb. 2.41.13–15.

63. Haussoulier 1917: 157; F. W. Walbank 1984a: 244; Rizakis 1995: 308 and 2008a: 146–47 (Leontion), 227 (Aigeira), 258 (Pellene).

64. Pyrrhos: Plut. Pyrrh. 26.14–24; Justin 25.4.4–7. Athenian alliance: IG II² 686–87 (Syll.³ 434–35; Staatsverträge III.476). Achaian embassy and participation: l. 24. Cf. Heinen 1972: 117–42; Knoepfler 1993b.

65. Heinen 1972: 95–212, esp. 167–81.

66. Klaffenbach 1955; see comm. to T57.

67. Diod. Sic. 19.67.3–68.1.

about the agreement, however, is the series of rights that in effect blurred those geographical boundaries: they extend to one another the rights of intermarriage (*epigamia*) and property ownership (*enktēsis*), as well as full citizenship, available to any individual who chose to domicile himself in the other region. It is an *isopoliteia* decree in all but name. The first two are rights that we have seen extended to all members of the expanding koinon of the Chalkideis in the early fourth century, and that, as I shall argue below, were widespread among other koina. They provide us with an important clue to the motivations behind the construction of cooperative political institutions beyond the polis, and their presence in the Aitolian-Akarnanian treaty suggests that the commitment to the idea of regional states not only was deep and widespread but was now beginning to transcend notions of the ethnic fixity of political boundaries to a degree that was previously almost unthinkable. This treaty may give us some indication of the terms upon which other non-Aitolian communities became members of the Aitolian koinon after 279, when our only evidence for the phenomenon consists of the shifting composition of the amphiktyonic council reflected in its now fragmentary and incomplete series of decrees. Throughout the 250s and 240s, the Aitolians pursued this logic of inclusion—or influence by potential inclusion—by granting both *isopoliteia* and *asylia* to several communities in western and mainland Greece.[68]

Whether out of an explicit awareness of what the Aitolians were doing in this period or not, the Achaians likewise began to extend beyond the ethnic boundaries of their koinon, as they had done in the 380s with the annexation of Kalydon and Naupaktos across the Corinthian Gulf. The immediate catalyst for this expansion was in both cases opposition to Macedonian control. But we shall see later that the expansion of koinon territories may also have had significant economic effects, which must be considered alongside the more traditional security concerns cited in narratives of third-century expansion.[69] In the ongoing struggle to dislodge the Macedonian-supported tyrants from the cities of the Peloponnese, the young and ambitious Aratos of Sikyon, the son of a former pro-Macedonian ruler of the city whose family had ties to Antigonos, seized control of his native city with the help of a private band of armed men.[70] Since the murder of Aratos's

---

68. *Isopoliteia* decrees: *SEG* 2.258 + *SEG* 18.245 (Chios = *FDelph* III.3.214 + *BCH* 23 [1959]: 435 with *BE* 77.231, 247/6?); possibly *Syll.*[3] 472 = *Staatsverträge* III.495 (*isopoliteia* between Phigaleia and Messene, shortly before 240, brokered by Aitolians, may imply existing *isopoliteia* between Messene and Aitolia, though ll. 19 and 25 speak only of *philia;* cf. Polyb. 4.6.11, ca. 220, for the claim that there existed "for a long time" a *symmachia* between Messene and the Aitolians). Kephallenia is perhaps to be added to this list: Flacelière 1937: 284 with n. 3.

69. See below, pp. 284–89.

70. Plut. *Arat.* 4.1–9.3; Paus. 2.8.3.

father, Kleinias, Sikyon had endured a series of tyrants and, along with them, significant sociopolitical upheavals that resulted in the exile of many citizens; hundreds poured back into the city upon learning of its liberation by Aratos and attempted to reclaim their property.[71] In response to the internal problems created by the return of some six hundred exiles as well as to the threat of external predation, particularly by Antigonos, Aratos orchestrated the integration of Dorian Sikyon into the Achaian koinon in 251.[72] Around the same time Megalopolis, the only node of Antigonid control near Sparta, ousted its own tyrant, constituting a further blow to Macedonian power in the Peloponnese.[73] Aratos energetically assumed the cause of the expansion of Achaian power. In 249 a new governor was appointed to man the Antigonid garrison at Corinth, and Aratos, sensing the weakness of a new appointee, launched an attack on Corinth.[74] Although it was unsuccessful, it made clear the commitment of the newly expanded Achaian koinon to a policy of independence.

The first half of the third century in mainland Greece was characterized by the reemergence and strengthening of the cooperative political institutions that developed in the fourth century and by a complete rupture of the idea that a regional polity had to be restricted to members of a single ethnic identity. And while these developments are clearly associated with resistance to Macedonian rule, they cannot be understood purely as a function of that political stance.

SHIFTING ALLIANCES, 245–229

Over the next sixteen years the Achaian koinon under the leadership of Aratos of Sikyon continued to pursue a vigorously anti-Antigonid politics and to welcome new communities into its ranks, while Aitolian ambitions set the two confederacies at odds until they joined forces for over a decade to battle Antigonid power. The Boiotian koinon, comparatively limited in its growth potential by the vigor of its western and southern neighbors as well as by the security of Macedonian

71. Plut. *Arat.* 9.4–5; Paus. 2.8.3.

72. Plut. *Arat.* 9.6–7; cf. Polyb. 2.43.3. The emphasis on *homonoia* as an Achaian virtue is especially Polybian; see Champion 2004: 122–29.

73. Polyb. 10.22.2; cf. Plut. *Arat.* 5.1, *Philop.* 1.3–4; Paus. 8.49.2, all with slight variations on the names. On the installation of Aristodemos see Paus. 8.27.11.

74. Plut. *Arat.* 12.1–14.4; Cic. *De off.* 2.23, 81–82. The attack may have been undertaken as an obligation to Ptolemy II, who had given Aratos forty talents (of 150 promised) to settle the demands of the returning Sikyonian exiles; might the attack on Corinth have been the condition for payment of the balance? The episode is cited by Bringmann 2001: 206 as an example of kings' inability to meet all their financial obligations at once. F. W. Walbank 1984a: 247–48 more optimistically (and politically) supposes that Ptolemy sought a demonstration of Aratos's good faith before the gift would be paid out in full.

control over nearby Athens, was more often than not caught in the middle of larger military and political contests. But its rich epigraphic record belies this impression of unimportance, at least to the history of political cooperation. This was, finally, the last period in which the koina of mainland Greece operated entirely free of the shadow of Rome, the arrival of which radically changed the dynamics of cooperation.

In 245 the Achaians under the leadership of Aratos of Sikyon adopted a policy of hostility toward the Aitolians, and in preparation for war they made an alliance with the Boiotians. The allies invaded Aitolia and Ozolian Lokris, now a part of the Aitolian koinon, but the Aitolians retaliated by invading Boiotia and destroying the Boiotian army at the old battle site of Chaironeia.[75] The Achaians arrived too late to help, and the Boiotians now joined the Aitolian koinon.[76] Refocusing, after this defeat, on Achaian expansion in the Peloponnese, Aratos seized Corinth in 243 and immediately brought it into the koinon.[77] He secured his prize by crossing the isthmus and bringing Megara, the near neighbor of now pro-Aitolian Boiotia, into the koinon, and protected Corinth's southeastern exposure by winning over Troizen and Epidauros, on the Saronic Gulf.[78] The introduction of four large poleis, including the vital stronghold of Acrocorinth, dramatically increased the Achaians' strategic power.

Sometime in the mid-240s, whether in response to the tremendous growth of the Achaian koinon in 243 or slightly before it, the Aitolians and Antigonos Gonatas reportedly "made an agreement to partition the Achaian *ethnos* between them."[79] The Achaians now faced pressure from both enemies on the periphery of their territory. The Aitolians, through the support of their Elian kin, gained influence without formal control in the western Peloponnese in these years.[80] They and the Elians may also have been involved in the tyrannical coup of one Lydiades at Arkadian Megalopolis.[81] But the Aitolians were still focused on expanding their

---

75. The motive of the Achaian attack on Aitolia is said to have been retribution for an Aitolian attack on Sikyon before 251: Plut. *Arat.* 4.1. The date of that attack is unclear, so interpretation is difficult. See Will 1979–82: I.316; Buraselis 1982: 171–72; Urban 1979: 14–16 with F. W. Walbank 1984a: 147; Scholten 2000: 85–86. Invasion of Boiotia: Plut. *Arat.* 16.1; Polyb. 20.4.5.

76. Polyb. 20.5.2. Boiotian membership in the Aitolian koinon did not entail the loss of Opous to the Aitolians: Étienne and Knoepfler 1976: 288–92, 331–37, *contra* F. W. Walbank 1984a: 249–50; Le Bohec 1993: 162–63.

77. Polyb. 2.43.4; Plut. *Arat.* 18.2–22.9, 23.4, 24.1.

78. Polyb. 2.43.5; Plut. *Arat.* 24.3 with T37, T38.

79. Polyb. 2.43.9–10; cf. 9.34.6, 38.9. For the date of the Aitolian-Antigonid agreement, see F. W. Walbank 1936: 69.

80. Aitolians as friends of Triphylian Phigaleia, now part of Elis: *IG* V.2.419 (*Staatsverträge* III.495); Ager 1996: 119–24; Harter-Uibopuu 1998: 47–50. Scholten 2000: 118–23 provides a detailed discussion of Aitolian influence in the western Peloponnese.

81. Polyb. 4.77.10; Urban 1979: 87 n. 412.

koinon in mainland Greece. Polybios twice mentions, in connection with the Aitolian-Antigonid agreement to partition Achaia, an agreement made between the Aitolians and Alexander, the king of Epeiros, to partition Akarnania.[82] This move was a direct violation of the earlier treaty between the Aitolians and Akarnanians (T57), which in the larger history of Aitolian-Akarnanian relations appears to have been truly exceptional. Antigonos may have countenanced such an aggressive strategy of territorial acquisition by both his Epeirote neighbors and the Aitolians in order to palliate any lingering Aitolian concerns about the benefits accruing to them from the agreement to attack the Achaians. It had thus far proved impossible for the Aitolians to exert anything but influence in the Peloponnese, and that only by way of their Elian kin; so what material benefits would they gain?[83] The sudden abandonment of the treaty with Akarnania, absent any provocation, may also reflect a change in Aitolian political leadership.[84] The process by which the acquisition of southern Akarnania was accomplished by the Aitolians is lost to us, but it is clear that by the 230s the important cities of Stratos and Oiniadai, along with lesser settlements like Matropolis, were part of the Aitolian koinon (T59).[85] The war between the Achaians and Aitolians that should have resulted from the purported Aitolian-Antigonid agreement never materialized. The Aitolians invaded the Peloponnese, but the Achaians refused to meet them in battle, defended Pellene from their attack, and by spring 240 succeeded in winning over Arkadian Kynaitha as a member of the koinon.[86] The Achaians made peace with the Aitolians and concluded a truce with Gonatas.[87]

The 230s were years of growth for the Achaian koinon under the continued leadership of Aratos, and they brought expansion, albeit on a smaller scale, for the Aitolians as well. This growth was, however, marked in both cases by hostilities with the new Macedonian king, Demetrios II. The Achaians focused on expanding

82. Polyb. 2.45.1–2, 9.34.7; cf. Justin 28.1.1. Cf. Staatsverträge III.485. Cabanes 1976: 91–93 dates the partitioning to the period 253–251, but this may be too early; it neglects the chronological hints given by Polybios. See F. W. Walbank 1957–79: I.240 with references. Schoch and Wacker 1996 date the partitioning very broadly, in the period ca. 258–230. Dany 1999: 87–89 finds it impossible to narrow down a date more precisely than the period 251–243; cf. Scholten 2000: 88–91. If Justin 28.1.1–4 is accurate, the partitioning must predate 239.

83. Flacelière 1937: 206; Will 1979–82: I.319; F. W. Walbank 1984a: 251.

84. Scholten 2000: 88–89 with Phlegon of Tralles FGrHist 257 F 36 II.

85. A statue group dedicated at Delphi (FDelph III.4.178 [FDelph II.312 with fig. 254]; Paus. 10.16.6 with Jacquemin 1999: 63–64 with cat. no. 290) may commemorate this victory over Akarnania.

86. Refusal to engage, associated by Plutarch with Achaian distrust of Agis's socioeconomic reforms: Plut. Agis 14.1–5, 31.1–2. Defense of Pellene: Plut. Arat. 31.3–32.3; Polyaenus, Strat. 8.59. See Urban 1979: 57 and Scholten 2000: 125–26 for the chronology of the attack; Plutarch's account is compressed. Kynaitha as member of Achaian koinon: F. W. Walbank 1936: 70.

87. Plut. Arat. 33.1–2; Polyb. 2.44.1; Justin 28.1.1–4. Cf. Larsen 1975.

their territory in the directions they had already staked out: the Argolid, which would complete Achaian control over the entire northern Peloponnese, and Arkadia, which would allow for southerly expansion. Peace with the Aitolians meant, at least ostensibly, that the Elians would be friendly, and there was no outright rupture in Achaian-Spartan relations. Opposition to the Achaians remained, however, in the presence of a number of local tyrants, most of them supported, if not installed, by Gonatas and now friendly to Demetrios. Chief among them was Lydiades of Megalopolis, who also controlled Alipheira, together perhaps with Heraia, Telphousa, and Kleitor, thereby extending his territory almost as far as Kynaitha.[88] This made conflict with the Achaians almost inevitable. Argos, too, was in the hands of a local Macedonian-supported tyrant, and Aratos made his first (unsuccessful) attempt on the city probably around 240.[89]

The peace between the Achaians and Aitolians was converted, around 239, into a formal alliance.[90] The change may have been motivated by a new alliance between Epeiros and Macedonia that was at least potentially anti-Aitolian.[91] No explicit statement of the terms of the alliance survives, but a careful reading of the slim record of Achaian-Aitolian cooperation over the next two decades suggests that there were at least two: first, that the allies would render military assistance to one another, and jointly to friends who sought it out; and second, that allied troops would be paid according to some predetermined wage.[92] It was probably in this year that the so-called Demetrian War broke out between the two sets of allies, but our sources are exceptionally scarce.[93]

Over the next decade the Achaian koinon grew vigorously, while our limited evidence suggests that the Aitolians lost ground in central Greece and struggled to gain it in Akarnania. In the Peloponnese, Aratos continued to lead the Achaians on attacks aimed at ousting the tyrants of Argos and attaching the city to the koinon, won over

88. Alipheira: Polyb. 4.77.10; Heraia, Telphousa, and Kleitor: F. W. Walbank 1936: 68.

89. Plut. *Arat.* 25.1–6, 27.1–3. The tyrant, Aristippos, having survived the attempt with his power intact, charged the Achaians with attacking the city in time of peace. The Mantineians were asked to arbitrate in the dispute, and the Achaians received a rap on the knuckles in the form of a tiny monetary fine. See Will 1979–82: I.305 for discussion of the date.

90. Polyb. 2.44.1; Plut. *Arat.* 33.1. Cf. Scholten 2000: 134–36.

91. Justin 28.1.1–4.

92. Scholten 2000: 141–44. The arrangement for payment of troops may have been similar to that preserved in T57.35–40; Scholten further suggests that such pay may explain the ephemeral Aitolian issue of Attic-standard tetradrachms, found mostly in Peloponnesian hoards, in this period.

93. The outbreak of the war is dated by *IG* II[2] 1299.56–7 to the archonship of Lysias at Athens, which is not securely dated: Habicht 1979: 134 and 1997: 164. Evidence for hostilities in Aitolia: Str. 10.2.4 claims that Old Pleuron was ravaged by Demetrios "Aitolikos," which caused the inhabitants to settle at New Pleuron—Demetrios II, or Demetrios Poliorketes? Attacks on Akarnania: Front. *Strat.* 1.4.4; Justin 28.1.1–2.14, on which see Holleaux 1921: 5–22; F. W. Walbank in Hammond et al. 1972–88: III.322; Dany 1999: 98–119; Scholten 2000: 147.

Kleonai, which now became a member, and accepted the adherence of Megalopolis, where Lydiades surrendered his tyranny in 235 and brought his city into the Achaian koinon.[94] In the previous year the Achaians had won Arkadian Heraia, which suggests that they had already won over Kleitor and Telphousa.[95] The admission of Megalopolis brought the Achaians further south into Arkadia, integrating a large and powerful city but one that had pursued, since its foundation in the 360s, a policy of implacable hostility toward the Spartans. It was inevitable that Megalopolis's membership in the koinon would embroil the Achaians in those same hostilities, particularly in the years 234–230, during which Lydiades was elected *stratēgos* three times, alternating in years of service with Aratos, and the ambitious young king Kleomenes III had recently come to power in Sparta.[96] Eastern Arkadia followed quickly, with Orchomenos, Mantineia, Tegea, and probably Kaphyai joining around 233.[97]

In central Greece, meanwhile, Demetrios II was attacking Aitolian interests. Around 234 he invaded Boiotia, which had been an Aitolian ally since the disastrous battle of Chaironeia in 245, and separated the Boiotian koinon from Aitolia.[98] It was probably during the same expedition that he wrested Opountian Lokris from the Aitolians and attached it to the now-allied Boiotian koinon, where it remained until circa 228.[99] The Aitolians may, however, have gained some ground against Demetrios in northeastern central Greece.[100] The Aitolian alliance with the Achaians prompted Demetrios to invaded the Peloponnese in 233. The Achaians under the leadership of Aratos suffered a serious defeat at Phylakia, just south of Tegea.[101] It may have been as a result of this defeat that the Achaians became willing to cede their newest Arkadian members—Orchomenos, Mantineia, Tegea, and Kaphyai— to the Aitolians, who may have offered to help the Achaians stabilize the area.[102]

94. Unsuccessful attacks on Argos: Plut. *Arat.* 28.1–3, 29.1–4. Lydiades' surrender and the introduction of Megalopolis into the Achaian koinon: Polyb. 2.44.5; Plut. *Arat.* 30.1–4, *Mor.* 552b.

95. Polyaenus, *Strat.* 2.36. Telphousians appear in the list of Achaian judges who arbitrated the dispute between Arsinoe and Epidauros (T40, A.9, B.19–33).

96. Plut. *Arat.* 30.5 for Lydiades' initial attempt to lead an Achaian expedition against Sparta.

97. Polyb. 2.46.2, reporting their seizure from the Aitolian koinon by Kleomenes in 229; see F. W. Walbank 1957–79: I.242–43. Mantineia was Achaian before it became Aitolian (Polyb. 2.57.1), as was Orchomenos (Polyb. 4.6.5; Livy 32.5.4; T38, which must postdate Megalopolis's entry to the koinon in 235). Cf. F. W. Walbank 1984b: 451.

98. Polyb. 20.5.3 with Moretti 1967–76: I.25, implying Aitolian control of Boiotia in 236/5. The precise date of the Macedonian invasion is not at all certain: Scholten 2000: 272–73.

99. Étienne and Knoepfler 1976: 331–41.

100. Lefèvre 1995: 194–95; Scholten 2000: 166 with n. 5 and 251 with n. 37.

101. Plut. *Arat.* 34.2–3; for the location see Beloch 1912–27: IV.2.529–30.

102. Polyb. 2.46.2 reports that the Aitolians controlled these cities in 229 but never explains how they achieved that control. Scholten 2000: 159–61 suggests that the defeat at Phylakia (Phylake) was the occasion for the transfer. There is some epigraphic evidence for pro-Aitolian sentiments in Tegea (*IG* V.2.10) and Orchomenos in these years (Blum and Plassart 1914: 454 no. 2).

Whatever the nature of their gains in Arkadia, the Aitolians continued to wage war against Demetrios's interests and to pursue their own agenda of westward expansion in mainland Greece. In 232 the Aiakid dynasty that had ruled Epeiros for centuries came to an end, and the inhabitants of both Epeiros itself and the Epeirote part of Akarnania chose to form independent koina by which they planned to govern themselves.[103] The Aitolians seized the moment to attack western Akarnania, hoping to gain access to the Adriatic. In the autumn of 231, they laid siege to Medion, a small Akarnanian polis south of the Ambrakian Gulf, having been "unable to persuade the Medionians to join their *politeia*."[104] But Medion was protected by the Illyrian king Agron, in the service of Demetrios, and the siege was unsuccessful.[105]

The Aitolians' failure to take Medion was not, however, decisive. Around the same time they gained control of Ambrakia, the capital of the old Aiakid dynasty, and with it Amphilochia, the territory east of the Ambrakian Gulf.[106] If they struggled to gain southwestern Akarnania, at least they now had complete access to the ports of the gulf. Illyrian forces now began to threaten the islands and coastal settlements of the Ionian Sea. Apollonia, Epidamnos, and Kerkyra appealed to the Achaians and Aitolians, whose combined fleet was defeated by the Illyrians in a naval battle off Paxos.[107] The Aitolian-Achaian alliance did not last much longer, and some historians have attributed the rupture to the losses they sustained at the battle of Paxos, but there is evidence that subsequent events in the Peloponnese down to 224 are rather to be blamed.[108] The Illyrians did not remain a threat to the western Greek communities for long, because their piratical raids drew the hostile attention of the Romans in 229. For a moment, though, they seemed to have replaced the threat of Macedon itself.

THE ROMAN ENTRANCE AND THE WAR
AGAINST KLEOMENES, 229-222

The accession of Antigonos Doson in 229 did not resolve the conflict between the allied koina and Macedon, and the threat posed by Illyrian piracy to seaborne

---

103. Dany 1999: 120–35; Scholten 2000: 149 with n. 74. Paus. 4.35.3–5, 6.12.3; Justin 28.3.1–8; Polyaenus, *Strat.* 8.52.

104. Polyb. 2.2.6.

105. Polyb. 2.2.7–4.5; Scholten 2000: 147.

106. Polyb. 4.61.6 reports that Ambrakia was Aitolian in 219, but we have no report of its initial acquisition, which must be determined only by historical context. See Scholten 2000: 151 with n. 81.

107. Polyb. 2.9.1–10.9.

108. Significance of Paxos: F. W. Walbank 1933: 68; Larsen 1968: 313. The argument that places Paxos at the fulcrum of the relationship seems to ignore the clear statement of Plut. *Arat.* 34.7. Peloponnesian events: Scholten 2000: 151–52, 183–92.

traffic in the Adriatic was in no way diminished. The Aitolians supported the revolt of Thessaly from Macedonian control, provoking a vigorous response from Doson that stripped them not only of their hopes of controlling Thessaly but also of eastern Phokis.[109] The Boiotians also lost Opountian Lokris.[110]

Phokis appears to have regained its political independence as a koinon and now made an alliance with the Boiotians. The first lines of the inscription recording the Boiotian-Phokian alliance (T28), which may have delineated obligations for defensive or offensive cooperation, are missing, but what survives is striking for its provision of safekeeping of goods in the other's territory, presumably in the event of a hostile invasion (ll. 1–6). Each koinon preserved its own officials, elections, and oaths; Phokis clearly preserved its independence from Boiotia, while both states essentially committed to preserving each other's autonomy in the tumultuous atmosphere of the early 220s. This alliance was strengthened by the inclusion of the Achaians not much later (T42). The Achaian polity continued to grow: Aigina, Hermione, and most of Arkadia, according to Plutarch, now joined the koinon.[111] After years of Achaian attempts, Argos finally joined and was followed by neighboring Phleious.[112]

In the spring of 228, the Aitolians and Achaians received embassies from unaccustomed visitors: the Romans sought to "explain the causes of the war and their crossing [to Illyria], and then gave an account of what they had done."[113] Both *ethnē*, according to Polybios, received the ambassadors with *philanthrōpia*. The episode provides our first evidence for direct contact between the Romans and the Aitolian and Achaian koina, at this time the most powerful states in mainland Greece. It is likely that the embassy was motivated in part by an awareness of the Aitolian-Achaian involvement in the Illyrian War, which preceded the Roman arrival, but it also reveals a cautious approach: the Romans were aware that they needed to explain their presence in an area where they had previously had no established interests.

---

109. Justin 28.3.14–16; Front. *Strat.* 2.6.5 with Will 1979–82: I.362; F. W. Walbank 1984b: 453; Le Bohec 1993: 154–59; Scholten 2000: 167. The Aitolians may have retained some part of Thessaly, though the evidence is very slim: Flacelière 1937: 253–55; Scholten 2000: 165–70. Doson's invasion of Doris and Phokis: Bousquet 1988b; for the date of the invasion in 228 (not 222, *contra* Bousquet) see F. W. Walbank 1989; *BE* 89.275; Le Bohec 1993: 159–62; Scholten 2000: 170–71. There is some indirect evidence for the following western Phokian communities remaining part of the Aitolian koinon after Doson's attack: Lilaia (*FDelph* II.2.224, one of purportedly four decrees of Lilaia honoring men sent by Attalos to protect the city against Philip V; cf. Flacelière 1937: 301 n. 5; Robert 1935a: 96 n.2); Drymos and Teithronion (Livy 28.7.12–13); probably also Tithoreia. See Flacelière 1937: 287, 301–2; M. Feyel 1942b: 124; Hennig 1977: 128.

110. Étienne and Knoepfler 1976: 331–37.

111. Plut. *Arat.* 34.7.

112. Polyb. 2.44.6, 60.4; Plut. *Arat.* 35.1–5.

113. Polyb. 2.12.4.

The resolution of the Illyrian conflict was well timed for the Achaians, for it freed them to focus on the new threat posed by Kleomenes III in Sparta. Sometime in 229, the Spartans seized the eastern Arkadian cities of Tegea, Mantineia, Orchomenos, and Kaphyai. These cities had joined the Achaian koinon in 235 but had then switched allegiance to become members of the Aitolian koinon perhaps around 233. According to Polybios, the Aitolians approved Kleomenes' seizure of these cities as a means of weakening Achaian power, but the claim is highly dubitable.[114] When Kleomenes attacked a fortification in the territory of Megalopolis, a prized part of Achaia since 235, the Achaians declared war.[115] The struggle focused initially around control of Arkadia, where the Achaians had limited success until spring 227.[116] Despite a serious setback in open battle against Spartan forces at Mount Lykaion, the Achaians managed to regain Mantineia, lay siege to Orchomenos, and protect Megalopolis against Spartan incursions, while Kleomenes dealt ruthlessly with ongoing challenges to his political authority at home and dramatically increased Spartan military strength.[117] Kleomenes put relentless pressure on Arkadia, and particularly Megalopolis, while political tensions were straining the hastily stitched seams of the Achaian koinon, which had expanded so rapidly in the previous decade and a half. In response to these pressures, Aratos took a step in winter 227/6 that had previously been unthinkable: he approached the reigning Macedonian king, Antigonos Doson, seeking his military support if the pressing need should arise. But political pressure made it impossible for him to do this directly, so he persuaded several family friends in Megalopolis, including the Cynic philosopher Kerkidas, to approach the Achaians and, citing the hardships being endured by the city, seek their permission to send an embassy to Antigonos.[118] Polybios claims that Aratos and the Achaians as a whole were motivated by the pressures of the war against Kleomenes and by fear of Aitolian territorial depredations in the Peloponnese.[119] It is difficult to determine how objective

114. Polyb. 2.45.1–46.3 with Fine 1940: 134; F. W. Walbank 1957–79: II.239; Champion 2004: 132–34.
115. Polyb. 2.46.5–6.
116. Plut. *Cleom.* 4.2–10: In 228 Aratos regained Kaphyai for the Achaians but failed in his attempt to take Tegea and Orchomenos.
117. Plut. *Arat.* 36.1–37.4, *Cleom.* 5.1–6.7; Paus. 8.28.7. The successful protection of Megalopolis from Kleomenes' forces came at the cost of significant Achaian losses, including the death of Lydiades, former tyrant of the city, erstwhile *stratēgos* of the Achaian koinon, and Aratos's only rival. It was probably his angry supporters who led the vote in the Achaian assembly to cut off funding for the war in 227/6 (Plut. *Arat.* 37.5). But there is no evidence that this measure was enacted, and its significance is probably purely political. Kleomenes in Sparta: Plut. *Cleom.* 8–11.
118. Polyb. 2.47.3–48.8; Plut. *Arat.* 38.7, 11–12
119. See esp. Polyb. 2.47.4, 7; 2.49.1–3, 7 (conceding Aitolian inaction, *hēsychia*). Note too Plut. *Cleom.* 10.11, where in the course of his coup Kleomenes cites the Aitolians (and Illyrians) as a significant threat to Sparta.

this claim is, for we have no independent evidence of Aitolian activity in the area in this period or of a rupture in the Achaian-Aitolian alliance concluded upon the accession of Demetrios in 239. In any case, the embassy was warmly received by Antigonos, who offered his help as soon as the Achaians should formally request it; Aratos nevertheless encouraged the Achaians to resolve the war on their own.[120]

In the summer and autumn of 226, however, the Achaians suffered three major setbacks that together made independent success in the war seem unlikely: Ptolemy withdrew the subsidies his kingdom had been providing since 251/0, choosing instead to fund the Spartans as being more likely than the Achaians, now, to oppose Antigonos; Kleomenes regained control of Mantineia, expelling the Achaians' mercenary garrison and slaughtering the entire population of Achaian settlers in the town; and finally, Kleomenes inflicted a heavy defeat on the full Achaian military levy at a site called Hekatombaion in western Achaia, in the territory of Dyme, thus moving the conflict out of Arkadia and into the heart of Achaian territory.[121] The Achaians spent the first half of 225 in negotiations, first with Kleomenes and then with Antigonos. Tension within the koinon was palpable. A pro-Spartan faction encouraged treating with Kleomenes, while other groups in Achaia were bitterly opposed to the pursuit of Macedonian support, and socioeconomic unrest was widespread.[122] In this atmosphere of factionalism, Aratos was either unable or unwilling to engage the Achaians in an open debate about inviting Doson to assist them; instead he is reported to have used covert methods to ensure a breakdown of the renewed negotiations between the Achaians and Kleomenes.[123] So it is not surprising that Kleomenes made so much headway in detaching member poleis from the koinon: in the summer and autumn of 225, he took control of Pellene, Pheneos, and Kaphyai, which sundered the territory of the koinon in two, and then worked systematically to seize the entire eastern portion of it, including Kleonai, Argos, Epidauros, Hermione, and Troizen.[124] Meanwhile the Achaians, under increasing pressure, consented to an alliance with Antigonos, but his demand for Acrocorinth, the old Macedonian garrison that Aratos had fought for years to take, was a sticking point. When, however, the citizens of Corinth ordered Aratos out of their

120. Polyb. 2.49.1–51.1.

121. Ptolemaic subsidy: Polyb. 2.51.2. There is also indirect evidence now for close relations between Ptolemy and the Aitolians, in the form of a dedication at Delphi by the Aitolian Lamios of statues of the Ptolemaic royal family (*FDelph* III.4.233; Jacquemin 1999: cat. no. 296), which may suggest a deepening rift between the Achaians and Aitolians. Mantineia: Plut. *Cleom.* 14.1, *Arat.* 39.1. Hekatombaion: Polyb. 2.51.3–4; Plut. *Cleom.* 14.4–5, *Arat.* 39.1; Paus. 7.7.3.

122. Pro-Spartan factions: Plut. *Arat.* 38.4, *Cleom.* 15.2. Cf. Plut. *Arat.* 40.1–2, *Cleom.* 19.1. Socioeconomic unrest: Kerkidas of Megalopolis *Meliambi* fr. 4, Powell 1925: 203–4; cf. Diehl 1949–52: III.141–52; Polyb. 4.17.4–5 (at Kynaitha).

123. Plut. *Arat.* 39.2, *Cleom.* 17.1; Gruen 1972.

124. Polyb. 2.52.2; Plut. *Arat.* 39.4; cf. *Cleom.* 19.6

city and invited Kleomenes in, the Achaians, further pressed by Kleomenes' three-month siege of Sikyon, felt justified in granting Antigonos what he wanted, thereby reversing the anti-Macedonian stance that had guided Achaian policy for more than twenty-five years.[125]

In the spring of 224, Antigonos arrived in the Megarid with a large force, but these were prevented from entering the Peloponnese by Kleomenes, who set up a strong line of defense across the isthmos and around Corinth, which Antigonos initially found impossible to break.[126] Megara, the most northerly of all the members of the Achaian koinon, was thus cut off from the larger regional state, and Antigonos transferred it to the Boiotian koinon, apparently after securing the consent of the Achaians.[127] The war against Kleomenes took a sudden and unexpected turn when the Argives decided to revolt from Kleomenes with an appeal to the Achaians and Antigonos, who immediately rallied to their aid. With hostile forces at his back, Kleomenes was forced to abandon Corinth and retreat to Sparta, while some other cities apparently returned to the Achaian koinon.[128]

The revolt of Argos from Kleomenes was a turning point in the war. At the Achaians' regular autumn council meeting in 224, according to Polybios, Antigonos was made *hēgemōn* of all the allies.[129] This is in all probability an allusion to the so-called Hellenic Alliance. All our evidence for the nature of this alliance comes from Polybios's narrative of the Social War (220–217), but it can be retrojected with some confidence to the Kleomenean War. In addition to the Macedonians and the Achaians, the members of this alliance were the other koina of mainland Greece that were already on good terms with the two principal members: the Epeirotes, Phokians, Boiotians, Akarnanians, and Thessalians.[130] It was, in other words, an alliance of koina. It is impossible to know who was responsible for developing this idea; one immediate inspiration may have been the realization, implicit in the consensual transfer of Megara from the Achaian to the Boiotian koinon, that interstate cooperation might be achieved on a very large scale indeed by a partnership of the several koina of mainland Greece. The organization is

125. Polyb. 2.51.4–52.4; Plut. *Arat.* 40.1–42.3, *Cleom.* 16.3–7 and 19.9. For discussion of Aratos's role in the conclusion of the Achaian-Macedonian alliance see Gruen 1972.

126. Plut. *Arat.* 43.1, *Cleom.* 20.1–4; Polyb. 2.52.9.

127. Polyb. 20.6.7.

128. Polyb. 2.53.1–54.1; Plut. *Arat.* 44.2–5, *Cleom.* 20.5–21.8. Plut. *Cleom.* 20.6 claims that the Argives were motivated to revolt by Kleomenes' failure to make good on his promise of abolishing debts. Specifics of the return of each city to Antigonos and the Achaians must be inferred from uncontextualized comments: Plut. *Arat.* 45.1 on Orchomenos; Plut. *Arat.* 45.6–9 on Mantineia; Plut. *Cleom.* 23.1 on Tegea.

129. Polyb. 2.54.4.

130. Polyb. 4.9.4; cf. 4.15.1. To this list are sometimes added the Euboians and Opountian Lokrians (so Fine 1940: 151–52) on the basis of Polyb. 11.5.4. But the Euboians were subjects of Macedon (Picard 1979: 274), and Opountian Lokris was probably reckoned part of Boiotia. See now Scherberich 2009.

sometimes compared to the League of Corinth developed by Philip II and to the Hellenic Alliance organized by Demetrios Poliorketes in conscious imitation of Philip's League, but those were both instruments of Macedonian domination, and it is clear that the new alliance left the autonomy of the allies intact and in the end worked more to the advantage of the Achaians than the Macedonians. Although a law was passed obligating the Achaian magistrates to summon an assembly upon the request of the Macedonian king, the allies had nevertheless to grant their consent to all common courses of action, including the integration of new members and the declaration and resolution of war.[131] And even when in an assembly the representatives of the allies met and issued a decree, it still required ratification by each member state, certainly at the level of the koinon rather than the polis.[132] Underlying this alliance is a strong awareness that the koinon rather than the polis had become the major political structure of Hellenistic mainland Greece; we can also detect an optimism that this building block, so much larger than the polis, might provide stability to structures of interstate cooperation in such a turbulent period.

In the short term, the alliance served as an instrument for the defeat of Kleomenes and his Spartan revolution. The struggle continued to revolve around control of Arkadia and the Argolid. In the spring of 223, Antigonos led the allied troops into Arkadia, where during the campaigning season they regained control of Tegea, Orchomenos, Mantineia, Heraia, and Telphousa.[133] In the autumn, Kleomenes learned that Antigonos had dismissed his Macedonian troops for the winter, and he took the opportunity to move against Megalopolis, which he seized by night and then systematically destroyed.[134] The Achaians and their allies were unable to act immediately in retaliation, and Kleomenes continued to move swiftly: in early spring 222 he ravaged the Argolid before retiring to Lakonia.[135] In early summer the Achaians, Macedonians, and other allies invaded Lakonia and defeated Kleomenes decisively at Sellasia.[136] Kleomenes fled to Egypt, while Antigonos seized Sparta, canceled Kleomenes' reforms, abolished the kingship by which the polis had been ruled for centuries, and appointed a Boiotian, Brachylles the son of Neon, as governor of the city.[137] Sparta now became a member of the alliance, but it was not made a member of a more restricted

131. Achaian law: Polyb. 4.85.3, 5.1.6–7; cf. Livy 27.30.6. Polyb. 4.9.3, 16.1, 22.2, 25; 5.102.9, 103.1, 7, 105.1–2.

132. Polyb. 4.26.2.

133. Polyb. 2.54.5–12 (cf. 2.56.6–8, 57.1–58.15); Plut. *Cleom.* 23.1, *Arat.* 45.6–9.

134. Polyb. 2.55.1–7, 61.4–63.6; Plut. *Cleom.* 23.1–25.1, *Philop.* 5.1–5.

135. Polyb. 2.64.1–7; Plut. *Cleom.* 25.2–8.

136. Polyb. 2.65.1–69.10; Plut. *Cleom.* 27.1–28.8, *Arat.* 46.1. The date of the battle has long been disputed, but 222 is most likely: F. W. Walbank 1957–79: I.272; Will 1979–82: I.360–61, 363.

137. Polyb. 2.69.10–70.3, 4.22.5, 5.9.9, 9.36.5, 20.5.12; Plut. *Cleom.* 29.1–30.1.

club—the Achaian koinon. It was inevitable that the issue would arise, insofar as many of the Achaians, having expanded their territory so significantly under Aratos, regarded the logical boundary of their polity as coterminous with the Peloponnese itself.

From its inception, however, there was a notable absence in the list of members of Antigonos Doson's alliance of koina: the Aitolians. This was certainly no accident. Antigonos must have harbored some resentment over the Aitolians' refusal to grant him passage through Thermopylai as he descended through mainland Greece with his army in 224 to answer the Achaians' call for help against Kleomenes.[138] And the Achaians cannot have forgotten the Aitolians' refusal to provide assistance against Kleomenes when they asked for it in 225, a refusal that may have been grounded in resentment over the Achaians' seizure of Triphylia from the Elians, age-old friends and allies of the Aitolians.[139] Polybios claims that the exclusion had left the Aitolians in a state of isolation with both economic and political implications. Economically, he claims that it prevented them from engaging in their customary acts of piracy and brigandage, with disastrous results at home.[140] But this picture may be overdrawn, for the Aitolians were wealthy enough to produce large quantities of both gold and silver coinage in these years.[141] There is more plentiful evidence to suggest that the Aitolians were not at all politically isolated during the 220s, though their attested activities took them beyond mainland Greece, suggesting that they may have been avoiding Doson and his powerful alliance. Other factors may also have been at work. We can detect three principal areas in which the Aitolians developed new relations, all probably in the course of the 220s: the Ionian island of Kephallenia; the island of Crete, and particularly the polis of Knossos, which was attempting at this time to unite the entire island under its hegemony; and the Attalid kingdom.

Around 223, the Aitolians sent a colony to Same, one of four poleis on Kephallenia; the inscription that records this settlement, entirely unique in the history of the Aitolian koinon, is regrettably fragmentary, and only limited information can be extracted from it.[142] But it appears that the Aitolians were taking measures to ensure the permanence of the settlement. Close relations with other Kephallenian poleis paved the way for the full integration of all the poleis on the island into the

---

138. Polyb. 2.52.8 with Scholten 2000: 188–89.

139. Plut. Arat. 41.3. For the seizure of Triphylia as a major motive in the Aitolians' refusal, see Urban 1979: 115–16; Scholten 2000: 187.

140. Polyb. 4.3.1–3.

141. Tsangari 2007: 253–54 contra Scholten 2000: 283–84 with nn. 105–7.

142. IG IX.1² 1.2. The document is dated by the first stratēgia of Pyrrhias of Herakleia (l. 8), which Klaffenbach (IG IX.1² 1, p.1) places ca. 223; but the stratēgia lists are not entirely secure.

koinon by 220.[143] The integration of Kephallenia may have been motivated by the Aitolians' experience of increased Illyrian piracy under Demetrios of Pharos, which probably began around 225 and eventually led the Romans, a few years later, to engage in the Second Illyrian War.[144] That the move also gave them access to a regular fleet can have been no disadvantage.

The Aitolians must also have developed close relations with some Cretan poleis in the 220s, for in 219 we find in operation a formal military alliance between the Aitolians and the powerful polis of Knossos.[145] And although the Knossians deployed their Aitolian allies to fight an unsavory war against the little polis of Lyttos, the Aitolians did have regular relations with some other Cretan poleis in this period.[146] The motive behind these alliances is unclear. Both the Cretans and the Aitolians were heavily engaged in piracy in this period, in ways that affected the direction of state affairs: Was the alliance born of an awareness that mutual assistance might be advantageous in this enterprise? Or were the Aitolians attempting to combat Doson's inroads on the island, made by treaties with both Hierapytna and Eleutherna?[147] Perhaps, but the chronology of these decrees is uncertain, and we cannot discern the direction of causation.[148] Aitolian connections with Crete are part of a broader pattern of granting *asylia* and *isopoliteia* to states in the eastern Aegean in the last two decades of the third century.[149]

Finally, the Attalids. While close Aitolian-Attalid relations are explicitly attested by 212/1, there are good reasons to think that they developed in the late 230s or 220s. In this period Attalos dedicated an enormous stoa at Delphi, still firmly under Aitolian control, and more important, in Polybios's narrative of 219 we learn of a fortification at Elaos, in the territory of Kalydon, that had been funded by Attalos I; its size suggests that it cannot have been built overnight.[150] It has been

143. Proxeny decree for Kallikrates son of Theodoros of Pale: *IG* IX.1² 1.31.74–81 (k). Scholten 2000: 196 infers from the fact that the magistrates involved in the colonization of western Same came from eastern Malis that the Aitolian koinon was strikingly united and committed to a unified Aitolia, devoid of regional factionalism.

144. Polyb. 3.16.2–3 for renewed piratical attacks by the Illyrians.

145. Polyb. 4.53.8, 55.5.

146. Eleutherna: *IG* IX.1² 1.31.48–50, 99–104. Oaxos: possibly Bousquet 1991: 175–76. The ethnic of the donor of the statue is lacunose, and Bousquet identifies it as Oaxos in Lokris, but we know that there were good relations between Aitolia and Cretan Oaxos: *IC* II.V.18–19, *koinopoliteia* and *isopoliteia* decrees of the Aitolian koinon for Oaxos, ca. 221–219 (or *post* 176). The earlier date is preferred by Funke 2008: 265–66.

147. *IC* III Hierapytna 1; *IC* II Eleutherna 20.

148. Scholten 2000: 195.

149. Funke 2008.

150. Stoa of Attalos at Delphi: Jacquemin 1999: 346 no. 388; *Syll.*³ 523. Elaos: Polyb. 4.65.6 with Pritchett 1965–92: VII.18–39; cf. Scholten 2000: 193.

surmised that the relationship could have been grounded in mutual distrust of Doson, sparked for the Attalids by his Karian expedition of 227.[151]

What is entirely clear is that, despite the almost complete silence of Polybios and Plutarch on Aitolian affairs in the 220s, and Polybios's implication of the Aitolians' total isolation by 222, they were in fact actively engaged in the broader Greek world, despite having largely withdrawn from the Peloponnese itself. This engagement was characterized by a cooperation that surpassed old ethnic boundaries to integrate new members of the Aitolian polity. The friends and alliances they made in this period, regardless of how murky their motivations are to us, remained staunch ones. As it turned out, that was a great boon, for in the next few years the alliance of koina organized by Doson turned against the Aitolians as its principal enemy.

THE RISE OF PHILIP V AND THE SOCIAL WAR, 221–217

We must rely for this development on the accounts of Polybios and Plutarch, in which anti-Aitolian bias is palpable.[152] Despite this difficulty, it is certain that the rupture between the Aitolians and Achaians was complete by 222/1 and led within a year to the conflict known as the Social War. Despite its brevity, the ramifications of the war endured: the Aitolians and Achaians never again regarded each other with anything but distrust or hostility; the fabric of the Achaian koinon was very nearly torn asunder, and the war was largely responsible for creating the conditions in Greece that paved the way for Roman intervention only a few years later.

Doson was succeeded by Philip V the son of Demetrios II, in the summer of 221.[153] The new king was young but showed himself—at least initially—to be a ruler of sound judgment and superb military skill. Along with the Macedonian throne he inherited the role of *hēgemōn* of the Hellenic Alliance and was immediately drawn into the maelstrom of Peloponnesian politics. The Aitolians and their Elian allies were plundering Achaian territories from Triphylian Phigaleia, which had remained friendly to the Aitolians since about 240.[154] Polybios's claim that these actions were prompted by Aitolian isolation during the 220s is probably overstated, as we have seen; that they regarded the accession of the young Philip as an opportunity to pursue a more aggressive agenda may well be true.[155] The Aitolians were probably motivated by a desire to protect their territory from Macedonian

151. Scholten 2000: 194 with n. 109. On Doson's Karian expedition see F. W. Walbank 1984b: 459–61.

152. On Polybios's anti-Aitolian bias see Champion 1996: 316 n. 5, 323 n. 45; Champion 2004: 129–37 and 2007.

153. Polyb. 4.2.5, 5.3.

154. For the Phigaleian-Aitolian relationship, see *IG* V.2.419 (*Staatsverträge* III.495); Ager 1996: 119–24.

155. Polyb. 4.3.1–4.

and allied depredations, a very real threat since the Akarnanians and Epeirotes were members of the Hellenic Alliance; it must have become more urgent when the Illyrian Demetrios of Pharos took refuge with Philip after violating his agreement with the Romans in 220.[156] But there is no denying the evident zeal of individual Aitolians for plundering Achaian territory or the willingness of the Aitolian koinon to be led in its public policy by these private economic demands.[157]

The Aitolians' aggressive policy in the Peloponnese was, according to Polybios, led by two politicians from Trichoneion, Dorimachos and Skopas. Dorimachos, "sent to Phigaleia on behalf of the koinon, on the pretext of guarding the territory and city, but in reality to spy on Peloponnesian affairs," found himself pressured by a group of Aitolian pirates who were looking for an excuse to plunder the area.[158] He granted them permission, and the raids extended even to the private houses of the Messenians, friends and allies of Aitolia. Dorimachos was upbraided by the Messenians and was reportedly so stung by a personal insult he received there that he went back to Aitolia and engineered a declaration of war against the Messenians, on the grounds that they were constantly threatening to ally themselves with the Achaians and Macedonians.[159] But the aim was clearly to declare war on the entire Hellenic Alliance, for their first acts of official hostility, late in 221, were to seize a Macedonian ship off the coast of Kythera, to plunder the coast of Epeiros with the help of the Kephallenian fleet, and to make an attempt on Akarnanian Thyrrheion.[160] In the Peloponnese, they moved against hard-won allied strongholds, including a fortification in the territory of Megalopolis and the garrison at Arkadian Orchomenos.[161] In the early spring of 220 the Aitolians, having mustered a full military levy, crossed the Gulf of Corinth and invaded western Achaia via Elis, plundering the territories of Patrai, Pharai, and Tritaia before moving on to Messenia, the alleged casus belli.[162] These westernmost of the old Achaian poleis bore the brunt of the invasion, as they did repeatedly throughout the Social War.

At a regular meeting of the Achaian assembly, after hearing complaints from the Patraians, Pharaians, and Messenians, the koinon voted to muster a full military levy, which went to the assistance of the Messenians but was completely routed by the Aitolians at Kaphyai, northwest of the garrison at Orchomenos.[163] Further outrages against the allies began to mount, and in summer 220 war was declared against the

156. Violation of the agreement: Polyb. 4.16.6.
157. Scholten 2000: 201–2.
158. Polyb. 4.3.7.
159. Polyb. 4.3.5–5.10.
160. Polyb. 4.6.1–2.
161. Polyb. 4.6.3–7.
162. Polyb. 4.6.7–12.
163. Achaian levy: Polyb. 4.7.1–11. Kaphyai: Polyb. 4.10.1–13.5.

Aitolians.[164] Polybios, certainly using the official decree of the alliance as his source, reports that it included the following declaration of intentions (Polyb. 4.25.6–7):

> that they would restore for the allies any territory or city held by the Aitolians since the death of Demetrios, the father of Philip; likewise concerning those who had been compelled by circumstances to join the *sympoliteia* of the Aitolians against their will, that they would restore all these to their ancestral constitutions [*patria politeumata*], and possessing their own territories and cities, these should be ungarrisoned, free from tribute, and independent, enjoying their ancestral constitutions and laws [*politeiais kai nomois . . . tois patriois*].

The decree has two distinct parts. The first clause refers explicitly and exclusively to fellow members of the alliance and can only apply to territories to which they believed they had a claim but that were seized by the Aitolians after 229. The only logical candidates are Ambrakia, formerly a part of Epeiros but which may, as we saw above, have joined the Aitolians when the Molossian dynasty crumbled around 230, and which was certainly in Aitolian hands in 219; and perhaps Phthiotic Achaia, in Thessaly, which they took upon the news of Doson's accession, and which he may never have managed to regain.[165] But the second clause appears to have a much broader rubric, applying to all those who had joined the Aitolian koinon unwillingly, regardless of the date at which they did so. Akarnania certainly applies here, as probably does western Phokis, both of which in their partitioned state belonged to the alliance. Most important, however, it left open the possibility of allied action on behalf of any member of the Aitolian koinon that now professed its participation to have been involuntary.

During the next three years, there were hostilities in each of these regions, but the Peloponnese remained the heart of the conflict. Here the Achaians were pressed from the northwest, by Aitolians invading from Elis and the Corinthian

---

164. Messenian membership in the alliance: Polyb. 4.15.1–4, 16.1–2. Outrages in Achaia: Polyb. 4.17–21 on Kynaitha, Kleitor, and Lousoi. (Scholten 2000: 205, 292–93, may be right to argue that this raid was not sanctioned by the Aitolian koinon and that Polybios's claim [4.16.11] that the Aitolian leaders "collected the Aitolians in full force" is untrue. What really matters, however, is that those who suffered these actions were either unable or unwilling to distinguish the difference. Compare T52 for Athenians holding the Aitolian koinon responsible for the acts of a few of its citizens.) Outrages against the allies include: the Aitolian sack of the sanctuary of Athena Itonia in Boiotia during peacetime (Polyb. 4.3.5, 25.2; 9.34.11; the sanctuary had been granted *asylia* by the Delphic Amphiktyony in the 260s: Rigsby 1996: no. 1); the Aitolian attempt to seize Phokian Ambryssos and Daulion; and the plundering of Epeiros. See also Polyb. 4.25.2–5.

165. Ambrakia in Aitolian hands in 219: Polyb. 4.61.1–63.3; cf. Scholten 2000: 151. Phthiotic Achaia: above, p. 109 , n. 109; Phthiotic Thebes was taken by Philip in 217 (Polyb. 5.99–100.8 and below, p. 120), necessitating the conclusion that it had been Aitolian prior to that date. The evidence for the status of Phthiotic Achaia in these years is very difficult, and more skepticism is in order than is accorded by Fine 1932; F. W. Walbank 1940: 11 n. 3 and 1957–79: I.472.

Gulf coast, and from the south by the Spartans, who were now fully committed to an alliance with the Aitolians.[166] In the spring of 219 the Spartans made an attack on southeastern Argos and then seized a fortification in the territory of Megalopolis, while the Aitolians invaded western Achaia, devastating the territories of Dyme, Pharai, and Tritaia, defeating a local force that marched out to oppose them, and seizing fortifications in the territories of Dyme and Telphousa.[167]

The Achaians' principal ally, Philip, was during this same period prosecuting the war in the northwest, returning towns in Epeiros and Akarnania that had been seized by the Aitolians, in accordance with the terms of the declaration of war, and then moved against Aitolia itself, ravaging the territories of Stratos and Kalydon and seizing Oiniadai.[168] In the winter of 219/8 he turned his attention to the Peloponnese, making small gains in northwestern Arkadia and conquering Triphylia, which had long been in the control of Elis.[169] The Macedonian army also managed to regain Teichos Dymaion.[170] Even Philip, however, was running short of both money and grain for his forces by the spring of 218, and the Achaians made a financial arrangement with Philip whereby the Achaians would pay salaries and provide grain for the Macedonian army during the entire period of campaigning in the Peloponnese.[171] The funding for the Macedonian army in accordance with this agreement came from taxes paid by the members of the Achaian koinon and from war booty; by late in the year, the burden on member poleis had become very heavy and led, temporarily, to significant military weakness.[172]

The year 218 was one of expensive, highly destructive, and ultimately ineffectual warfare. Western Achaia was repeatedly devastated; Messenia remained in the hands of the recalcitrant Spartans; and two venerable sanctuaries—that of Zeus at Dion, in Macedonia, and that of Apollo at Thermon, in Aitolia—were brutally sacked.[173] The result was widespread disaffection: the members of the Achaian koinon were disinclined to pay their *eisphora*, seeing no clear results from the contributions they had already made, and the soldiers, whose pay was in arrears, were not eager to serve.[174] Under these conditions the elder Aratos was again elected *stratēgos* for the year 217/6 and immediately deployed his political clout to

166. Formed in early 220: Polyb. 4.16.5, 34.1–36.6.

167. Argolid and Athenaion (Megalopolis): Polyb. 4.37.6, 60.3. Western Achaia and Telphousa: Polyb. 4.59.1–60.4.

168. Polyb. 4.61.1–8, 63–66.

169. Polyb. 4.67.6–75, 77.5–80.15.

170. Polyb. 4.83.1–5.

171. Polyb. 5.1.1–12.

172. *Eisphora*: Polyb. 5.30.5–6, 5.91.4; see below, pp. 299–302. War booty: Polyb. 5.94.9.

173. Western Achaia and Messenia: Polyb. 5.17.1–4. Spartan resistance: Polyb. 5.17.8–19.8, 20.11–24.12; 9.32.2, 35.6–8. Dion: Polyb. 4.62.1–5. Thermon: Polyb. 5.6.5–9.7, 13.1–14.7.

174. Polyb. 5.30.5–6, 91.4.

address the problem. He persuaded the Achaians to pass a decree (*dogma*) committing themselves to the maintenance of a specific military force: of mercenaries, eighty-five hundred infantry and five hundred cavalry; of citizens, three thousand infantry and three hundred cavalry; and a total of six ships with their crews, three to be stationed off the Argolid and three off the coast of Patrai and Dyme.[175] The resolution suggests that the problem was one of will rather than a true shortage of resources. The challenge of meeting the financial obligation implicit in such a troop commitment was not tested for long. In the late spring and summer of 217 the Achaians enjoyed a string of victories that yielded enough booty to obviate the need for another *eisphora* levy and at the same time brought the Aitolians to their knees.[176] Another Aitolian force invaded western Achaia but was forcefully attacked, with some two thousand men taken prisoner and their arms and baggage captured as plunder; the Achaian admiral crossed the Corinthian Gulf and seized a body of slaves and three ships with their crews.[177] The Achaians were now fighting fire with fire, using the very methods favored by their enemies to defeat them. They followed up these seizures with plundering expeditions to two of the richest and most strategic of the coastal poleis of Aitolia, Kalydon and Naupaktos.[178] Philip, meanwhile, made important gains in central Greece at the Aitolians' expense, winning control of Phthiotic Thebes, which he renamed Philippi, and by the late summer of 217 he had gained control of western Phokis, thus fulfilling some of the principal aims of the war on behalf of the allies.[179]

From a position of strength and expansion in the 220s, the Aitolians had suffered considerable losses by 217. Far from gaining a stronger foothold in the Peloponnese, they lost control of vital areas in central Greece and suffered depredations in Aitolia proper. It was in this context that they appear to have rewarded, if not directly commissioned, the work of several poets to promulgate a message of Aitolian unity throughout the koinon. Aristodama of Smyrna, an epic poetess, was praised by the city of Lamia in a decree of the Aitolian koinon dated to 218/7 for having "commemorated the *ethnos* of the Aitolians and the ancestors of the people."[180] Another decree in her honor, issued by the Lokrian polis of Chaleion, survives from a copy erected at Delphi and must belong to the same year.[181] It is clear, then, that Aristodama was making the rounds, performing poems that

175. Polyb. 5.91.5–8.
176. Polyb. 5.94.9.
177. Polyb. 5.94.2–8.
178. Polyb. 5.95.11–12.
179. Phthiotic Thebes: Polyb. 5.99–100.8. Phokis: Polyb. 5.96.4–8 (still in Macedonian hands in 198: Polyb. 10.42.2, 7; Paus. 10.34.3–4).
180. *IG* IX.2.62 + *SEG* 2.360 (Guarducci 1929: no. 17) ll. 3–6. The decree is dated by the Aitolian *stratēgia* of Hagetas of Kallipolis (Kallion), for which see Polyb. 5.91.1, 96.1, 96.4–8; *IG* IX.1² 59a.
181. *FDelph* III.3.145 (Guarducci 1929: no. 17a).

commemorated the Aitolians. The fact that both honorific decrees attesting to her activities survive from member poleis that were not ethnically Aitolian may suggest that a particular emphasis was placed on encouraging loyalty in these areas, where the risk of defection in the crisis conditions of the Social War was very high. But it would be surprising if she did not travel to the Aitolian heartland as well.[182] Similar work appears to have been carried out by the epic poet Nikander of Kolophon, who was active either in the last quarter of the third century, and so a contemporary of Aristodama, or in the second quarter, when the Aitolians capitalized on their victory over the Gauls to establish themselves at Delphi and expand their koinon vigorously.[183] He was the author of an *Aitolika*, a lost regional epic about the Aitolians, as well as other works that recounted traditional Greek myths in emphatically Aitolian settings, including not only ancient Aitolian places like Kalydon but also newer members of the koinon like Malis.[184] Whether Aristodama continued the work of Nikander or was his contemporary, the apparent content of her poetry and the evident itinerary she followed in performing it suggest that at the end of the Social War the Aitolians sought to bolster the unity and integrity of their koinon by elaborating, if not developing, a history of the Aitolian *ethnos* through poetic performance. It is a striking response to crisis.

At the Nemean Games in the summer of 217, Philip received a letter informing him of Hannibal's overwhelming victory over the Romans at Lake Trasimene. According to Polybios, the king showed the letter only to Demetrios of Pharos, who had taken refuge with him after violating his own treaty with the Romans in 220; it is likely that Demetrios had more experience with the Romans than anyone else present, and he had more than his share of ambition. The story goes that he whispered these ambitions into the ear of the still young king and urged him to end the war with the Aitolians.[185] The timing was fortuitous: the Achaians had not lost any ground in the war; Akarnania and Epeiros, although they had suffered a recent Aitolian invasion, were significantly better off than they had been in 220, and Philip had succeeded in wresting western Phokis and Phthiotic Achaia from the Aitolians. None of the Allies, then, had any significant motivation to continue what had turned out to be a costly war; the Aitolians, smarting from the recent Achaian depredations in their own territory and their losses in neighboring

182. Rutherford 2009 discusses these two texts but associates them only generally with the late third century, "the period when the Aetolian League was most powerful" (p. 248).

183. Uncertainty about the date stems from the fact that there appear to have been two Nikanders of Kolophon, the elder being Nikander the son of Anaxagoras (*Syll.*[3] 452), the younger, Nikander the son of Damaios, perhaps the grandson of the elder. For discussion see Cameron 1995: 194–206 with Crugnola 1971: 33–34; Pasquali 1913; Rutherford 2009: 244–48.

184. Rutherford 2009: 247 with Ant. Lib. *Met.* 22; cf. Cameron 1995: 204.

185. Polyb. 5.101.6–10.

regions, were also eager for peace. A conference was held at Naupaktos in the late summer of 217, at which peace was concluded on the simple condition that each party should retain those territories of which they were at that time in possession.[186] Polybios gives us few details, preferring instead to record a rousing speech by one Agelaos of Naupaktos, who warned the assembled Greeks to cease making war on one another, for there was a dark cloud rising in the west: whether Hannibal or the Romans won the war in which they were then engaged, the victor would not be content with sovereignty over Italy and Sicily.[187] If the speech is genuine, it was prophetic. But the Romans became involved in the affairs of the Greek koina long before they were able to end the war with Hannibal.

THE FIRST AND SECOND MACEDONIAN WARS: ROME, AITOLIA, AND PHILIP V, 215–196

The first Greek state with which the Romans made a treaty was the Aitolian koinon, but it was probably concluded, from the Roman perspective, for largely negative reasons: to break the power of Philip in Greece and the Adriatic, and to prevent the restoration of Demetrios of Pharos to Illyria.[188] It was only insofar as the Aitolians shared these aims, for entirely different reasons, that these strange bedfellows formed a partnership in 212 or 211.[189] The treaty, as recorded by Livy, committed the Aitolians to attacking Philip by land, while the Romans would support their efforts at sea. Akarnania was promised to the Aitolians, and both parties were effectively prohibited from making a separate peace with Philip.[190] A fragmentary copy of the inscribed treaty was found at Thyrrheion in Akarnania, and from it we learn important details: the Aitolians were free to act as their leaders (*archontes*) saw fit, and they were to gain possession of any poleis taken by the Romans in the war, while the Romans would control the territory (*chōra*) of such communities. The last complete clause of the inscription explicitly allows for expansion of the membership of the Aitolian koinon: "If any of these poleis revolt or advance against the Romans or the Aitolians, their men, cities, and territories shall be added to the Aitolian state [*politeuma*] for the sake of the Romans."[191] The promise of Akarnania and the recognized right of the Aitolians to expand their

---

186. Polyb. 5.103.7–8.

187. Polyb. 5.104.1–11 with Lévy 1994.

188. In 215 the Romans learned that Philip had concluded a treaty with Hannibal: Polyb. 5.109; Livy 23.32.17. In 214/3 the initial hostilities of the First Macedonian War broke out in the Adriatic: Livy 26.25.1–3.

189. Livy 26.24.7–15; Polyb. 9.39.2–3, 11.5.5, 18.38.7. For discussions of the date see Lehmann 1967: 10–50; Badian 1958: 56.

190. Livy 26.24.7–15.

191. *IG* IX.1² 241.15–21 (*Staatsverträge* III.536).

state, together with the Aitolians' continued isolation from the Hellenic Alliance, made the conflict almost a continuation of the costly but ineffective Social War. The only significant change was the presence of the Romans, who nevertheless committed few resources to the war against Philip, focusing their energies instead on the much nearer and more immediately threatening enemy, Hannibal.

The Aitolians immediately set about attacking the most strategic and valuable places in Akarnania, winning control of Oiniadai and Nasos as well as Zakynthos.[192] Philip's attacks on Aitolian interests centered on Thessaly, which experienced almost constant hostilities. The Romans' only significant intervention in the war came in 211/0, when by joint actions with the Aitolians the Opountian Lokrian coastal polis of Antikyra and the entire island of Aigina were seized. Although the Romans took the booty from these victories, the places themselves belonged to the Aitolians, who then sold Aigina to Attalos of Pergamon at the meager price of thirty talents.[193] The real price was perhaps higher, for in the autumn of 210 Attalos was elected *stratēgos* of the Aitolian koinon, an office that although honorific still signified a major development in the political alignments of the period.[194] Around the same time, the Aitolians persuaded the Spartans to join their alliance, which made Spartan opposition to the Achaian koinon explicit.[195] Like the Social War, this one inflicted significant collateral damage: over the next three years, Greeks who were not directly involved sought on two separate occasions to introduce negotiations to end the war but were unsuccessful.[196] Achaian military weakness was becoming costly even to Philip, who encouraged the Achaians to strengthen their own military, thereby reducing their dependence on his own forces.[197] It was through his Achaian supporter, Philopoimen, elected as *stratēgos* for the first time in 208/7, that a major reform of the Achaian military was undertaken.[198] This newly trained Achaian army inflicted a decisive defeat on the Spartans and their allies at Mantineia in 207, which proved the success of Philopoimen's military reforms and encouraged a waxing desire for

192. Livy 26.25.9–17; Polyb. 9.40.4–6.

193. Antikyra: Livy 26.26.1–4. Aigina: Polyb. 9.42.5–8, 11.5.8, 22.8.9; R. E. Allen 1971; Pollhammer 2002.

194. Livy 27.29.10–30.1. Livy's account of the Roman-Aitolian treaty suggests that explicit provision was made for the addition of Attalos to the alliance: Livy 26.24.9. Pro-Attalid sentiments in this period must also lie behind *IG* IX.1² 1.60, a list of names of Attalid soldiers (Catling 2004–9) inscribed on an exedra at Thermon.

195. Polyb. 9.28–39.

196. Embassies of 209: Livy 27.30; Polyb. 10.25. Embassies of 208: Livy 28.7.14; Polyb. 11.4.1; App. *Mac.* 3.1.

197. Achaian territorial vulnerability was made clear by the Roman seizure of Dyme in the period 210–205 (Livy 32.21.29, 22.10; Paus. 7.17.5) and the attack on Elis launched by Machanidas the tyrant of Sparta in 209/8: Livy 28.7.14–17.

198. Polyb. 11.9.1–10.9; Plut. *Philop.* 9; Paus. 8.50.1. Cf. Anderson 1967; Errington 1969: 62–66.

Achaian independence from Philip, reversing the policy of accommodation to Macedon that had been established by Aratos in order to save the Achaians from Kleomenes.[199] Philip's delicate bargain of promoting Achaian military self-sufficiency to enable him to wage war against the Romans had backfired. It may have been his own realization of this fact that made him refuse to hand over the western garrisons to the Achaians as he had promised.[200] The Achaian victory at Mantineia was of course also a defeat for Sparta's Aitolian allies, who earlier in the same year met with two signal reverses at the hands of Philip: they lost Zakynthos again and saw their regional sanctuary at Thermon plundered by Macedonian troops for a second time.[201] Having lost almost everything they had gained in the previous six years, and despairing of substantial help from the Romans, who remained heavily committed to the Hannibalic War, the Aitolians made a separate peace with Philip in the autumn of 206.[202] It was probably shortly after this treaty was concluded that the Aitolians, apparently overwhelmed by both public and private debt, appointed the leading politicians Dorimachos and Skopas as *nomographoi*, apparently to revise the laws in the direction of debt relief.[203] The war had clearly hit them hard; these measures suggest that their willingness to make peace with Philip in contravention of the terms of their alliance with the Romans was motivated at least in part by economic pressure. Nor were they to be coaxed from their new position of quietude by the Romans, who concluded peace with Philip in the following year at Phoinike, under Epeirote encouragement, with all the koina of mainland Greece and the Peloponnese on his side.[204]

Despite ongoing skirmishes, the broad-based coalition created by the Peace of Phoinike certainly facilitated the adoption of something like a common peace, but it also meant that as soon as any hostility flared up again, it was likely to consume the whole group in a single conflagration.[205] So when the Romans, after hearing complaints from the Athenians, Attalos, and the Rhodians, resolved on another Macedonian War, Philip's allies were faced with a new conflict.[206] The Roman legates paid visits to the Aitolian and Achaian koina. We have no record of the Achaians' response to the Roman embassy that visited Aigion in the spring of 200, but there are reasons to believe that it was divided, some remaining committed to the

199. Polyb. 11.1.1–18.10; Plut. *Philop.* 1.1–4; Paus. 8.50.2–3
200. Livy 28.8.6 with F. W. Walbank 1940: 96–97; Errington 1969: 62 n. 1 and 75.
201. Polyb. 11.7.1–3.
202. Livy 29.12.1, 4.
203. Polyb. 13.1–2; this is discussed in greater detail below, pp. 312–13.
204. Livy 29.12.11–16.
205. In the Peloponnese the Spartans continued to attack the southern border of Achaia, at Megalopolis in 204 (Polyb. 13.8.3–7) and Messene in 202/1 (Polyb. 16.13.3 with F. W. Walbank 1957–79: II.516; Plut. *Philop.* 12.4–5; Paus. 4.29.10, 8.50.5; cf. Livy 34.32.16).
206. Polyb. 16.25–27.

pro-Macedonian position that had prevailed since 235 while others saw alliance with Rome as a means of regaining independence from the Macedonian kings.[207] The latter group must have gained credibility when in the autumn of 200 Philip presented himself to the Achaian assembly and offered to fight the war against Nabis and the Spartans for them on the condition that they provide troops for his garrisons at Oreus, Chalkis, and Corinth. The Achaians quickly realized that his intention was to prevent them from siding with the Romans in the war he was already waging against them and that these troops would act as hostages to that end; they politely declined and raised a citizen levy to battle against Nabis's attacks on Achaian towns.[208]

The Roman army arrived in Greece in 199 under Flamininus to wage war against Philip. Hostilities unfolded around central Greece, with Thessaly bearing a particularly heavy burden, and Phokis, Lokris, and most of Euboia captured by the Romans by the spring of 198.[209] The Aitolians had been persuaded to join the Romans in 199; in Livy's portrayal their role was largely limited to plundering those territories still loyal to Philip. In the autumn of 198, while Flamininus was besieging Phokian Elateia, the Achaians received embassies from the Romans and their Greek allies. In an impassioned speech Aristainos, the Achaian *stratēgos*, reminded his assembled citizens of the Achaians' vulnerability if they should refuse to join the Roman cause: the Roman and allied fleet would attack the northern shore of the Peloponnese, where the oldest cities of the koinon were situated, driving the population into the interior, while Nabis and his forces would attack them from the south. After several days of discussion and negotiation, the Achaians voted to abandon Philip and conclude alliances with the Romans, Attalos, and the Rhodians.[210]

During the course of the war itself, the Achaians and Aitolians suffered only losses. Both Corinth and Argos were lost to Philip in the autumn of 198, and it was only when Nabis joined the Roman alliance in the spring of 197 that the threat from the south was temporarily neutralized.[211] The Aitolians lost Lysimacheia, Keos, and several Thessalian cities that had been members of their koinon since the early third century, including Phthiotic Thebes, Larisa, and Pharsalos. But by

207. The difference of opinion is reflected in the election of Kykliadas as *stratēgos* for 200/199 (Livy 32.19.2) and the Achaians' involvement in attempting to broker a peace between Philip and the Rhodians in order to prevent the war with Rome (Polyb. 16.35.1). Cf. Errington 1969: 70–75, 81–84.

208. Livy 31.25.2–11.

209. Livy 32.9.6–18.9.

210. Livy 32.19–23.

211. Corinth and Argos: Livy 32.25.1–12. Nabis joined the alliance only after having received Argos from Philip as a bribe to remain hostile to the Achaians, and with Flamininus he agreed only to an armistice with the Achaians: Livy 32.38.1–39.10.

that time the majority of central Greece was under the control of the Romans and their allies, including Boiotia, which joined with some reluctance.[212] The war ended on the battlefield at Kynoskephalai in the summer of 197, where Philip was soundly defeated by the Romans.[213] The terms of the peace treaty were on the whole favorable to the victor, but the Achaians received Corinth, having to accept the temporary presence of a Roman garrison in the citadel, while the Aitolians, who were now punished for abandoning their early alliance with the Romans, were allowed to keep only Phthiotic Thebes of all the Thessalian communities that had been members of their koinon.[214] Despite the mistrust that prevailed between them, the Romans allowed the Aitolians to control Phokis and Lokris, thus representing a return to the earlier third century.[215] It is worth noting that Aitolian control of these regions was regarded as being compatible with the public proclamation at the Isthmian Games that the Phokians and Lokrians would be "free, without garrison or tribute, and subject to their own laws."[216] "Their own laws" had become the laws of the Aitolian koinon.

The Boiotians had, during the war, remained loyal to Philip, but unanimous support for this pro-Macedonian position was lacking, and as soon as the Macedonian king was defeated at Kynoskephalai, the matter was violently disputed and brought a suspicion upon the Boiotians which the Romans were never able to dismiss. After the battle, the Boiotian koinon sent an embassy to Flamininus requesting the safe return of those Boiotian citizens who had fought on Philip's side. The request was granted, but rather than undertake a political shift in favor of the Romans, they quickly appointed as boiotarch a man named Brachylles, who like his father and grandfather was a staunch Macedonian partisan.[217] The leaders of the pro-Roman faction within Boiotia, led by one Zeuxippos, were struck with anxiety, anticipating that they would be harshly treated when the Romans withdrew from Greece, and upon Flamininus's advice sought the assistance of the Aitolian *stratēgos* Alexamenos in perpetrating the murder of Brachylles.[218] When the deed was done by some Italian and Aitolian assassins, Zeuxippos and his

212. Livy 33.1–2.

213. Polyb. 18.18–27; Livy 33.6–10 for accounts of the battle.

214. Corinth and Acrocorinth: Polyb. 18.45.12; Livy 33.31.1–11. Aitolian communities in Thessaly: Polyb. 18.38.3–9.

215. Polyb. 18.47.9; Livy 33.32.7–8. The return of Phokis to the Aitolians in 196 may be the context for the expulsion of the Elateians from their city, recorded in T43, though they would hardly have been in a position to act with such hostility before the departure of the Roman army from Greece in 194 (Livy 34.48.2–50.1). It is also possible that the expulsion is to be associated with Flamininus's occupation of the city in 198: Livy 32.24.1–7. For discussion and references see T43.

216. Polyb. 18.46.5; cf. Livy 33.32.5.

217. Cf. Polyb. 20.5.5.

218. Polyb. 18.43.1–12; Livy 33.27.5–11 avoids reporting Flamininus's sanction for the assassination.

supporters were immediately suspected and fled into exile.[219] The Boiotians, however, assumed that the Romans had actually incited the murder. "Having neither men nor a leader for rebellion," they simply began to rob and murder all the Roman soldiers they could find. A strategy that was initially motivated by political interest was soon driven by economics: brigandage against Roman soldiers was quite profitable. Enough men were killed to justify a Roman inquiry, in the course of which bodies were dredged up from the swamps of Kopaïs and "other crimes were found to have been committed at Akraiphia and Koroneia."[220] If the political dispute originated at Thebes, it is clear that it quickly occupied much of Boiotia. Outraged, Flamininus ordered the Boiotians to surrender those responsible and to pay a fine of five hundred talents, one talent for each of the Roman soldiers whom he claimed had been killed. To judge from the response, the order was issued to the koinon: "The cities made the excuse that no deed had been done by public resolution."[221] The consul declared war and moved troops against Akraiphia and Koroneia, apparently regarded as hotbeds of anti-Roman activity; it may not be coincidental that Koroneia was home to the sanctuary of Athena Itonia, which had retained its regional and political significance since the battle of Koroneia in 446 and may thus have represented a strike against the koinon itself.[222] The Boiotians quickly sought to come to terms and after negotiations they agreed to pay the Romans a fine of thirty talents; their rebellious polity was, however, left entirely intact, a measure of Flamininus's ideological commitment to the freedom of the Greeks.[223]

Since the beginning of the First Macedonian War, the foreign policies of both the Aitolian and the Achaian koina had undergone major changes. While the Aitolians persisted in their hostility to the Macedonian kingdom, their relations with Rome soured but were nevertheless still operable. In Achaia, an increasing commitment to the cause of Achaian independence from Macedon led to an alignment with the Romans. It was only in Boiotia that anti-Roman sentiment was strong enough to lead to direct hostilities. The treaty concluded after Kynoskephalai was on the whole advantageous to the koina of mainland Greece: although they lost many of their Thessalian possessions, the Aitolians regained control of Phokis and Lokris, while the Achaians at last were freed of Macedonian garrisons in the western portions of their territory, regained Corinth, and eagerly expected the departure of the Roman garrison troops from Acrocorinth. These changes were not, however, accompanied by institutional change or political reform. It was only the pressure of mounting

219. Livy 33.28.1–15.
220. Livy 33.29.1–7.
221. Livy 33.29.8.
222. Livy 33.29.9. For Koroneia and Athena Itonia see below, pp. 192–94.
223. Cf. Gruen 1984: 449–50.

debt in Aitolia that drove some legal reforms, the contours of which are entirely lost to us. There is little doubt that the Boiotian cities were experiencing similar problems, but we lack any evidence of a response at the level of the koinon. The relative stability of the koina of Achaia, Aitolia, and Boiotia in the midst of such massive upheavals was perhaps a testament, in Roman eyes, to the success of this form of state in the politically fragmented Greek mainland, for part of the settlement after Kynoskephalai involved the creation of a new koinon in Thessaly.[224]

THE FREEDOM OF THE GREEKS AND THE DISMANTLING OF REGIONAL COOPERATION, 196–167

The Achaians had successfully resisted the socioeconomic reforms championed by Spartan leaders since Agis and longed for by plenty of citizens within the Achaian koinon. But they had not solved a more immediate problem: by 196 the Achaian koinon incorporated virtually all the Peloponnese, with the notable exceptions of Elis, Sparta, Messene, and Argos, which were all aligned with one another in their hostility to Achaia. So when Flamininus, with authorization from the Roman senate as well as from the Hellenic Alliance, declared war against Nabis in 195, it was natural for the Achaians to be keen to help.[225] The war, which left Nabis in power in Sparta but in a significantly weakened state, returned Argos to the Achaian koinon and placed the coastal towns of Lakonia under Achaian control.[226] The Achaians were not, however, the only ones to feel discontented by the settlement of the Roman war against Nabis; for the Aitolians it was yet another piece of evidence to support their case that the Romans were trying to enslave the Greeks, not to liberate them. In response to the displeasure expressed by members of the Hellenic Alliance in the spring of 194, Flamininus announced his intention to evacuate the garrisons at Demetrias, Chalkis, and Acrocorinth, to hand the latter over to the Achaians, and to withdraw the entire Roman army from Greece.[227]

Not even this, however, was enough for the Aitolians, who began almost immediately to agitate for a war against the Romans. In the spring of 193 they sent ambassadors to those rulers whom they suspected would be most amenable to their plan: Nabis, Philip, and Antiochos III. The Spartan tyrant responded eagerly to their provocation and moved to regain the Lakonian coastal towns that had

224. Kramolisch 1978. The process of state building was ongoing in 194: Livy 34.51.4–6.
225. Authorization: Livy 34.22.5–24.7.
226. Livy 34.25.1–41.10. Argos: Livy 34.41.4, 35.13.2, 38.31.2. Coastal towns: Livy 34.35.5; 35.12.7, 13.2, 35.2. This may have been the context for the formation of the koinon of the free Lakonians (*Eleutherolakōnioi*): Str. 8.5.5; Paus. 3.21.7; Gitti 1939; Kennell 1999; Cartledge and Spawforth 2002 [1989]: 77 with n. 29 and further references.
227. Livy 34.49.1–51.4.

been stripped from him by Flamininus in 195. Philip had learned a harder lesson and was noncommittal. Antiochos, who had his own grievances against the Romans, was eventually won over to the Aitolian position and made an alliance with them for war against Rome.[228] The Achaians, incensed by Nabis's attacks on the Lakonian coastal towns and on their own land, voted once again to go to war. In a single campaign Nabis was defeated and driven back within the walls of the city, but it remained beyond their authority to strip him of his formal powers.[229] While Flamininus was making the diplomatic rounds in Greece, trying to prevent widespread disaffection, the Aitolians heard reports at the Panaitolika of 192 from their own ambassador to Antiochos, one Thoas, who had recently returned and brought with him an ambassador of Antiochos, and they voted "to invite Antiochos to liberate Greece and to arbitrate between the Aitolians and Romans."[230] As they awaited the king's arrival, according to Livy, in closed deliberations the *apoklētoi* of the Aitolian koinon resolved simultaneously to invade Demetrias and Chalkis, two of the old Macedonian fetters that had recently been evacuated by the Roman army, and Sparta itself.[231] They managed to capture Demetrias, but at Chalkis they had no success.[232] Nabis himself was of course no friend of the Romans, but the Aitolians plotted to assassinate him on the assumption that doing so would endear them to the Spartan populace and create in the city a certain ally for their war against Rome. After running the tyrant through with spears on an occasion when none expected hostility from this quarter, the small Aitolian force that had been sent to commit the murder turned to plundering Nabis's palace and the city of Sparta itself. It quickly became apparent that their promise of liberating the city was sham, and those Aitolians who were not killed in Sparta took flight into Achaia, where they were captured and sold into slavery by the Achaian magistrates.[233] Despite their coordinated opposition to the Aitolian assassins, the Spartans were in complete disarray following the sudden death of Nabis, and Philopoimen seized the opportunity to attach Sparta to the Achaian koinon.[234] Although the Achaians had for decades sought the incorporation of Sparta into the koinon, the circumstances by which it was accomplished almost guaranteed that Philopoimen's would be a pyrrhic victory.

Despite the limited success of their initial moves, the Aitolians pressed ahead with their war against the Romans and their Greek allies, placing most of their

228. Livy 35.12–13.3, 22.2, 23.
229. Livy 35.25.2–30.13; Plut. *Philop.* 14.2–12.
230. Livy 35.32.2–33.11 at 33.8.
231. Livy 35.34.1–6.
232. Livy 35.34.6–11, 37.4–14.
233. Livy 35.1–36.10; Plut. *Philop.* 15.3; Paus. 8.50.10.
234. Livy 35.37.1–3; Plut. *Philop.* 15.4–12; Paus. 8.51.1.

hope in the forces of Antiochos III, whom they persuaded to cross to Greece in the autumn of 192.[235] He arrived with a disturbingly small force and the promise of a much larger one in the following spring; the Aitolians welcomed Antiochos into their general assembly and voted to prosecute hostilities with Antiochos as their leader.[236] But few Greeks were persuaded by the claim that Antiochos had come to liberate them: the Chalkidians were resolutely unimpressed; the Boiotians remained neutral; the Achaians, instead of accepting the Aitolians' overtures, declared war on them; and their erstwhile enemy Philip V offered to assist the Romans.[237] The resistance effort ended in defeat at Thermopylai in April 191.[238]

The Aitolians had perhaps gone too far in their attempt to drive the Romans out of Greece to surrender the cause easily, enduring several sieges before realizing that they would have to resort to diplomacy with Rome in 190.[239] A terrifying round of negotiations ended when L. Cornelius Scipio arrived in Greece and, with his sights set on the incomparably richer target of Asia, granted the Aitolians a truce of six months.[240] Yet despite—or perhaps because of—the fear the Aitolians had experienced in their attempts to negotiate with the Romans, they were unable to remain at peace during the armistice. While Scipio and the Roman army were in Asia fighting Antiochos III in 189, the Aitolians intervened in a quarrel between Philip V and his former ally Amynander, who had taken refuge in Aitolian-controlled Ambrakia when his kingdom of Athamania was handed over to Philip.[241] Aitolian support for Amynander was regarded by the Romans as a rebellion not just against their ally Philip but against themselves as well.[242] Amynander sought to placate the Romans through diplomacy, but the Aitolians, having expelled some Macedonian garrisons for him, now regained some of the territories that they had incorporated into their koinon in the past—Amphilochia, Aperantia, and Dolopia.[243] The areas were strategic, creating a buffer zone between the Aitolian heartland, Macedonia, and the newly independent Thessaly. If the Aitolians derived some sense of security from these victories, it must have vanished with the news that the Romans had defeated Antiochos at Magnesia and were now sending an army under Marcus Fulvius Nobilior to attack them for their violation of the

235. Livy 35.42.1–43.6.
236. Livy 35.45.1–9.
237. Livy 35.48–50. Philip: Livy 36.4.1–4, 8.6; 39.23.10.
238. Garrison troops from Achaia: Livy 35.50.3–4.
239. Siege of Herakleia: Livy 36.22–24; siege of Naupaktos: Livy 36.30, 34.
240. Negotiations: Livy 36.27–28, 36.35, 37.1.4–5; Polyb. 21.2.2–4. Truce: Polyb. 21.5.4–13; Livy 37.6.4–7.7.
241. Livy 36.14.9.
242. Livy 38.1–2.
243. Polyb. 21.25.1–7; Livy 38.3.1–5.

armistice.[244] Fulvius laid siege to Aitolian-controlled Ambrakia while the Achaians and Illyrians harried coastal Aitolia and the Macedonians plundered Amphilochia and Dolopia.[245] The Aitolians, unable to defend themselves on so many fronts at once, sought to make peace. The terms that they finally accepted mandated a dramatic reduction of the territory of the koinon and a permanent prohibition on expansion: they were neither to retain nor to accept into their state in the future any of the communities that had been taken by the Romans or entered into alliance with them since 190, when Scipio had first crossed to Greece.[246] When this condition was presented to the Aitolian council, there was some dispute, for "they endured with difficulty the proposal that cities that had been under their jurisdiction should be torn off as if from their own body."[247] They had, however, no choice but to agree, consenting also to pay a war indemnity of five hundred Euboian talents, to restore all Roman prisoners and deserters, to surrender their control over the island of Kephallenia, and to have the same friends and enemies as the Romans.[248] In addition to major territorial losses, the Aitolians' ability to conduct interstate relations on an independent basis was entirely hobbled, and the war indemnity imposed a major economic hardship. Although the Aitolian koinon was not formally dismantled by the Romans, it was almost entirely subordinated to them and can from this historical moment no longer be analyzed as an independent state.

Most other Greeks, and above all the Achaians, had had nothing but scorn for the Aitolians, and it was perhaps this attitude that prevented them from seeing the fate of the Aitolian koinon as a warning sign. While the Aitolians had been rushing headlong to their ruin, the Achaians continued their struggle to incorporate the entire Peloponnese within their koinon. The main stumbling block was Sparta. Despite having been integrated into the Achaian koinon in 192 by Philopoimen after the assassination of Nabis, opposition remained in Sparta and sparked a brief rebellion in 191 when news came that Philopoimen had not been elected *stratēgos*.[249] The Spartans decided to involve the Romans in the winter of 191/0, establishing a pattern that persisted for nearly fifty years. They sought the restoration of hostages sent to Rome after Flamininus's war against Nabis in 195, the restoration of Spartans exiled

244. Polyb. 21.25.7–9; Livy 38.3.6.

245. Polyb. 21.25.10–11, 27.1–28.18; Livy 38.3.7–7.13.

246. Polyb. 21.30.4. Cf. Livy 38.9.10, 11.9 (who erroneously places the cutoff for expansion with the crossing of Titus Quinctius Flamininus, which would have meant 198, not 190; see F. W. Walbank 1957–79: III.129).

247. Livy 38.9.12. The rhetoric of dismemberment is strikingly similar to that used by Livy (45.30.2) to describe the Macedonian reaction to the division of their territory into four separate districts; see below, p. 264.

248. Polyb. 21.32.2–14; Livy 38.9.9–11, 11.2–7.

249. Plut. *Philop.* 16.1–3; Paus. 8.51.1.

by the Achaians, and the restoration of their traditional control over the coastal towns of Lakonia.[250] The hostages were returned by the Romans, but the other matters had more to do with Achaia than with Rome. Philopoimen, under some duress, agreed to allow the return of those Spartans who had been exiled by the Achaians.[251]

With the Spartans somewhat mollified, it remained only for the Achaians to persuade the Elians and Messenians to join the koinon in order to achieve the goal of a politically united Peloponnese. While the Elians expressed openness to the possibility, the Messenians refused, and the *stratēgos* of 191/0, Diophanes of Megalopolis, led the Achaian army against the city. Before hostilities had progressed very far the Messenians surrendered themselves to Flamininus, who was at Chalkis again in an unofficial diplomatic role. In a bizarre sequence of decisions that highlights both the ambiguity of the Romans' authority in Greece in this period and the distrust that prevailed among Greek states, Flamininus ordered the Achaians to withdraw and then ordered the Messenians to join the Achaian koinon.[252]

The pattern repeated itself in 189/8, when the Spartans again revolted from Achaia and handed their city over to Fulvius Nobilior. At his suggestion, both parties sent ambassadors to Rome, where it was resolved that "nothing should be changed with regard to the Lacedaemonians."[253] The Achaians took this to mean that they could deal with the Spartans as they would deal with any other member of their own polity, namely with complete autonomy. So Philopoimen, as *stratēgos,* led the Achaian army, its ranks swelled by pro-Achaian Lakedaimonian exiles, against Sparta in the spring of 188. As the force reached the city, the exiles attacked their compatriots, and some seventeen Spartans, held responsible for the revolt, were killed in a riotous encounter; on the following day an additional sixty-three were killed after a brief trial before some sort of Achaian tribunal. The Achaians demanded that the Spartans tear down their city wall and expel their mercenaries and those helots who had been liberated by the tyrants. Finally, they revoked the ancestral Lykourgan constitution and replaced the Spartan with Achaian laws.[254] If this seemed to Philopoimen and his supporters like a final settlement of the Spartan issue, they were mistaken. The Achaians had been unable to eradicate all opposition within Sparta, and those who still sought independence attempted

---

250. The details of the many embassies sent between Rome and Achaia regarding the Spartan exiles in the decades after 191 will for the most part not be discussed here, for they shed more light on Greek-Roman interactions, perceptions, and misperceptions than on the development of the Achaian koinon in this period. See Gruen 1984: 119–23 for discussion and references.

251. Plut. *Philop.* 17.4; Livy 36.35.7; Paus. 8.51.4.

252. Livy 36.31.1–9; cf. Polyb. 22.10.6; Paus. 4.29.11.

253. Livy 38.32.9.

254. Livy 38.33–34. For the murder of the purported leaders of the Spartan revolt, cf. Livy 39.36.9–37.8. The episode is reported more briefly by Plut. *Philop.* 16.3–9; Paus. 8.51.3; Polyb. 21.32c.3, 22.3.1.

to accomplish it by Roman intervention. In a series of embassies and letters, complaints were lodged with the Romans about the cruelty of the Achaians' behavior, requests were made by exiled Spartans for restoration, rebukes were sent from Rome to the Achaians, and the Achaians themselves became divided over the question of how they should respond to ostensible Roman requests. The emergence of this internal rift was perhaps more damaging to the Achaian koinon than anything else in this period, for it created political opportunities by which Achaian independence was eventually undermined.[255] The full cost of Philopoimen's decision to align the Achaians with Rome in order to secure their independence from Macedon was now being revealed. The Romans expected that their resolutions would be followed, but doing so sometimes required the Achaians to violate their own laws and reverse their own ratified decisions. They had indeed achieved independence from Macedon but were quickly becoming subordinated to the Romans.[256]

Although the Achaians had finally succeeded in creating a single state from the complex political mosaic of the Peloponnese, they did not succeed at quelling all disaffection among their newest members. Messene revolted in 183 in circumstances that are largely lost to us but was brought back into the koinon in the following year, in the course of which the great Achaian leader Philopoimen died.[257] Just as the Messenian War was being resolved, internal unrest at Sparta led to another temporary secession from the Achaian koinon. When Sparta's leaders sought to restore it, the major stumbling block in negotiations was the problem of how to handle a group of pro-Achaian Spartans who had been exiled when the city first revolted from the Achaian koinon in 189/8 and had been restored by the Achaians after the massacre of Spartan rebels at Kompasion in 188, but who subsequently sent embassies to Rome complaining of Achaian behavior and were therefore viewed by the Achaians as ungrateful.[258] Sparta was readmitted when its citizens agreed to bring back from exile those Spartans who "had not been guilty

255. Polyb. 22.7.1–7, 10.1–15, 11.5–12.10; 23.4.1–16; Livy 39.33.3–8, 35.5–37.21, 48.2–6; cf. Diod. Sic. 29.17. There were other threats to Achaian independence in this period, including Eumenes of Pergamon's offer to provide a salary for the members of the Achaian *boulē* (Polyb. 22.7.3, 7.8–8.13; cf. Diod. Sic. 29.17). The damage done by political infighting is most clearly revealed by the treacherous embassy of Kallikrates to the Romans, probably in 181/0: Polyb. 24.8.1–10.15.

256. On the pain of violating Achaian laws and reversing their own decisions, see Polyb. 23.4.14, 5.16–17; 24.8.4.

257. Revolt and Roman response: Polyb. 23.9.4–14 at 13, 24.9.12–13; Livy 39.48.5. Cf. Errington 1969: 185–87. Death of Philopoimen: Polyb. 23.12.3; Livy 39.50.7–8; Plut. *Philop.* 20; Paus. 8.51.7 with Errington 1969: 191–93. Reintegration of Messene: Polyb. 23.17.1. The terms of the settlement are discussed in greater detail below, pp. 368–69.

258. Polyb. 23.17.5–18.2. The exact date of this Spartan secession cannot be determined, but Polybios narrates the reintegration immediately after that of Messene, so it may belong to 182.

of any ingratitude to the *ethnos* of the Achaians." The decision was inscribed on a stele and had the binding force of law.[259]

The issue is highlighted by Polybios, for in his analysis it led to a deepening of the internal political rift in Achaia, which had disastrous results: his own father, Lykortas, as *stratēgos* of the koinon in 182, advocated and achieved the reintroduction of Sparta and the restoration only of those exiles who had not shown ingratitude to the Achaians, but in early 180 the Achaian council and assembly were called to a meeting to discuss a letter from the Roman senate requesting the restoration of all the exiles. Lykortas, according to Polybios, exhorted the Achaians to explain to the Romans that accommodating their request was impossible, for doing so would "violate our oaths, our laws, our stelai, which hold together our common polity."[260] His political opponents Kallikrates and Hyperbatos, however, argued that "neither law nor stele nor anything else is more compelling" than the Romans' request. The resolution of the debate is unclear, but Kallikrates went to Rome, exposed the political fault lines in Achaia, and urged the senate to express their disapproval of those Achaian leaders who valued their own laws and treaties as more binding than the will of the Romans. The Roman response was to ask the Achaians, once again, to restore the exiles; but this time the request was accompanied by letters to Aitolians, Epeirotes, Athenians, Boiotians, and Akarnanians, apparently requesting their assistance in putting pressure on the Achaians to comply with their demand.[261] The Romans' communication with the Achaians apparently also praised Kallikrates, according to Polybios increasing the esteem in which the Achaians held him; in 180/79 Kallikrates served as *stratēgos* of the Achaians and effected the return not only of the Spartan but also of the Achaian exiles.[262] Polybios charges Kallikrates with being the "instigator of great evils for all the Greeks, but especially for the Achaians" and with ushering in a "turn for the worse" in Achaia at the very moment when it had, at least in territorial terms, reached its greatest strength.[263] That assessment is clearly colored by a strong bias, and there is no doubt that Achaian internal affairs, as well as Achaian relations with Rome, had been flirting with disaster for at least a decade.[264] Assessing the immediate impact is, however, extremely difficult, for the texts of both Polybios and Livy are lacunose at this crucial juncture, and we can discern little of what happened in Achaia again until 174.

259. Polyb. 23.18.1–2.

260. Polyb. 24.8.4.

261. Polyb. 24.8.6–10.6. Cf. Paus. 7.9.6 with Lehmann 1967: 295–96 n. 317; Seibert 1979: 205–8.

262. Polyb. 24.10.14–15; cf. *IVO* 300 for honors paid by the Spartan exiles to Kallikrates at Olympia.

263. Polyb. 24.10.8, 10. Errington 1969: 201–5 for an analysis of the episode in terms of policies and politicians.

264. Cf. Errington 1969: 203–4.

We know, however, that in the intervening years Philip V died and was succeeded by his son Perseus, whose energetic attempts to regain the power and resources of the Macedonian kingdom before his father's defeat at Kynoskephalai had attracted the hostility and suspicion of the Romans. Among other strategies, Perseus courted the favor of the Greeks of the mainland, but in this he had mixed success: by 174 the Achaians and Athenians were staunchly opposed to him, but it was perhaps in the following year that the Boiotian koinon concluded an alliance with Perseus, a move that brought about the complete destruction of the oldest koinon in the Greek world.²⁶⁵ The Romans, having declared war on Perseus in 172, sent legates to Greece in advance of their forces to muster support for their cause. While in Thessaly, they received a number of envoys from the Boiotians, anxious about the Roman response to their alliance with Perseus. According to Polybios, ambassadors came from Thespiai, Chaironeia, Lebadeia, and several other cities seeking to hand their individual cities over to the Romans, while one Ismenias, a leader in the pro-Macedonian politics of Boiotia, sought "in accordance with the koinon to place all the poleis in Boiotia together at the discretion of the legates."²⁶⁶ The Roman legates, in Polybios's words, thought it "most suitable to break up the Boiotians into their constituent poleis," so they neglected Ismenias and received the other ambassadors warmly.²⁶⁷

The Romans had certainly learned from the endless internal disputes of the Achaians, their dodges and feints over the issue of the Spartan exiles, that in a large and complex state like one of the Hellenistic koina, unanimity of opinion, and therefore loyal allegiance to Rome, was exceedingly difficult to secure. Fragmentation would create a far more tractable political situation for the Romans. Word of the legates' position circulated in Boiotia, and a violent dispute arose over whether they should effectively dismantle their own state and present themselves to the Romans as individual cities or whether they ought to remain loyal to the Macedonian alliance and accept a war with Rome.²⁶⁸ Opinion gradually shifted toward making an alliance with the Romans, and in a final act of communal decision making the Boiotians resolved on a policy that they knew would lead directly to the dissolution of their koinon. Those leaders who had effected the Macedonian alliance were ordered to go to the Roman legates to explain and defend their actions, and the Boiotians in a

265. Achaian and Athenian opposition: Livy 41.23.1–24.20. The Boiotian alliance with Perseus is attested only for 172/1 (Livy 42.12.5–6) but was clearly established sometime previously: see Meloni 1953: 146 n. 1; Will 1979–82: II.121; F. W. Walbank 1957–79: III.292; Roesch 1982: 372–77.

266. Polyb. 27.1.2; cf. Livy 42.44.1.

267. Polyb. 27.1.3. Livy's compressed account (42.38.5) omits many of the details but conveys the same sense.

268. Livy 42.43.5 claims that at this point several Boiotian poleis effectively seceded from the koinon in order to demonstrate their opposition to the alliance with Perseus.

formal assembly tasked their magistrates with securing an alliance with the Romans.[269] Immediately thereafter, it appears that the cities began acting individually: we learn that the Thebans sent envoys to the legates to hand their city over and voted to recall those Thebans who had been exiled for their pro-Roman sympathies.[270] The legates received the envoys from Thebes and other cities "and exhorted them immediately to send embassies from the individual poleis to Rome, each one handing itself over to their care individually. . . . Everything proceeded according to their preference, this being to dissolve the Boiotian *ethnos* and weaken the goodwill of the masses toward the house of Macedon."[271] Polybios, a proud citizen of the Achaian koinon that later chose to fight to utter destruction rather than accept dissolution by fragmentation, had nothing but scorn for the Boiotians, who "having protected for a long time their common polity [*koinē sympoliteia*]" allowed the "Boiotian *ethnos* [to be] destroyed and dispersed among the several poleis."[272]

Unanimity was, however, evidently lacking in the vote that went in favor of a Roman alliance and the dissolution of the koinon. Perseus learned that some Boiotian cities were still favorably disposed toward him and sent an ambassador to Koroneia, Thisbe, and Haliartos, encouraging them to remain loyal, and they sought his protection against the powerful pressure being exerted by the Thebans to support the shift in favor of Rome.[273] Although Perseus was unable to offer these cities military aid, they continued to resist.[274] Haliartos was besieged in 171 by Roman and Boiotian pro-Roman forces; the city was captured and razed to the ground, its surviving citizens, some twenty-five hundred individuals, sold into slavery.[275] The siege and destruction of Haliartos put an end to active anti-Roman sentiment in Boiotia and informed the inhabitants of the region by its brutality and sheer efficacy that their ancient koinon, as an autonomous state, had been permanently dismantled.[276] This meant that the Boiotian poleis dealt on an individual basis with all foreign states as they did with the Romans, and there was no

---

269. Polyb. 27.1.10–11.

270. Polyb. 27.1.12–13.

271. Polyb. 27.1.6–7.

272. Polyb. 27.2.10.

273. Polyb. 27.5.3–6; cf. Livy 42.46.7, where *Thēbas* is probably an error for *Thisbas*.

274. Polyb. 27.5.7–8; Livy 42.46.9–10.

275. Livy 42.47.12, 56.3–5, 63.3–11; cf. Str. 9.2.30, Paus. 9.32.5, 10.35.2. In 167/6 (not 169 as Roesch 1965b: 63 n. 5 says) the territory of Haliartos was ceded to the Athenians, along with control of the islands of Delos and Lemnos: Polyb. 30.20.1–9. Two boundary stones found in excavations at Haliartos delineate Athenian territory (Austin 1926–27: 137–38 nos. 10 and 11); a third, once in the Thebes Museum (recorded by Pappadakis as MΘ 2290), is now lost (Nikolaos Papazarkadas, *per epist.*).

276. It has been claimed that the dissolution of the Boiotian koinon in 171 was only temporary (Niese 1893–1903: III.314 n. 5; Swoboda 1913: 289 n. 11; Barratt 1932: 96–97; Roesch 1965b: 69–71, with diffidence; Deininger 1971: 158; Touloumakos 1971: 38, 69–71; Accame 1972: 193, somewhat confused; Schwertfeger 1974: 21–22), relying heavily on Paus. 7.14.6, who reports on a boiotarch in the period

longer either instrument for joint decision making or regional laws that bound every Boiotian polis and its citizens alike. This meant, in short, political fragmentation and weakness, which the Romans had learned, especially from their experience with the Achaian koinon since 196, was most advantageous to them.

The Achaians must have been watching these events carefully. At the beginning of the Romans' war against Perseus, they had bristled at Roman behavior that carried hints of a desire to diminish the authority of the Achaian koinon, if not to dismantle it entirely, but after the defeat of Perseus at the battle of Pydna every caution was taken to avoid meeting a fate like the Boiotians'.[277] The Achaians now readily complied with a Roman request for a garrison force to hold Chalkis against Macedonian seizure until the arrival of the Roman army in the following spring.[278] Two years later, after the destruction of Haliartos but while the Romans' war against Perseus was still in full swing, Roman legates toured Greece with the object of stemming defections to Perseus and announcing the recent senatorial decree that "no one should contribute anything to Roman officials for the war except what the senate had approved."[279] In the Peloponnese the legates visited numerous individual cities, in each place announcing that they knew who was withdrawing from politics and who remained active, making clear that the former were suspected of using their withdrawal to mask anti-Roman sentiments.[280] The decision to visit individual cities was, strictly speaking, unnecessary, since the Romans should have interacted only with the Achaian koinon itself rather than its member states, which had no independent authority to conduct relations with foreign states. It is almost certain, particularly in the aftermath of Haliartos, that the Romans by this means sought if not to encourage secession then at least to express their preference for dealing with the poleis as individual states rather than as members of a koinon.[281]

167–146, and Paus. 7.16.9, claiming that the Boiotian *synedrion kata ethnos* was dismantled after the Achaian War of 146. Cf. Polyb. 30.13.3, 32.5.2, which provide no evidence for a regional state in Boiotia after 171. Larsen 1968: 463–64 expressed no doubt about the permanence of the dissolution, relying only on the primary literary sources. Étienne and Knoepfler 1976: 342–47 show that all the epigraphically attested Boiotian archons are to be placed before 171, providing clear support for the indications of the literary sources that the dissolution of 171 was permanent; cf. Holleaux 1938–68: I.58 n. 1, 257 n. 1; F. W. Walbank 1957–79: III.293; Roesch 1982: 376–77 (now expressing support for the conclusions of Étienne and Knoepfler). The numismatic evidence is inconclusive, not only because the late Boiotian coins cannot be dated precisely (Hackens 1969: 727–28, *contra* the indications of Head 1881: 91 and 1911: 353) but also because even when the chronology of emissions is clearer, they do not provide clear evidence for political organization; see below, pp. 247–55.

277. E.g., the Achaians' refusal of Perseus's offer to return runaway Achaian slaves who had taken refuge in Macedonia: Livy 41.22.2–25.8; cf. 42.6.1–2.

278. Polyb. 27.2.11–12; Livy 42.44.7–8.

279. Livy 43.17.2.

280. Polyb. 28.3.3–6.

281. Larsen 1968: 469.

According to Polybios, he himself, along with his father, Lykortas, and their supporter Archon, were suspected of anti-Roman sentiments when the legates came before a meeting of the Achaian assembly in 170, but with no pretext for making an accusation they kept quiet.[282] Similar suspicions arose when the legates subsequently visited Aitolia and Akarnania.[283] If indeed the Romans suspected Archon and his supporters in 170, the Achaians were extraordinarily bold to elect him *stratēgos* for 170/69, from which position he took what might be described as a soft pro-Roman policy.[284] After Pydna, the Achaians continued to wish to assert their authority to act as a fully autonomous state by conducting independent relations with foreign powers.[285] At the same time, the Romans persisted in their practice of visiting multiple cities in the koinon whenever legations took them to the Peloponnese, a not too subtle expression of mistrust and a stubborn preference to place political authority where local laws did not recognize it.[286] Suspicions of anti-Roman activity remained high throughout Greece, and the Romans conducted a series of inquiries in Aitolia, Akarnania, Epeiros, and Boiotia; names were provided, frequently by political enemies, and men were sent to Rome to stand trial.[287] In Achaia they allowed Kallikrates, the politician who had distinguished himself by his willingness to accuse his countrymen to the Romans, to provide the names of all those Achaians under suspicion. He provided a thousand names, including Polybios himself, and they were all deported to Italy, where instead of standing trial they lived as de facto hostages for the good behavior of the Achaian koinon.[288]

Yet all this was secondary to the main object of the Romans' presence in Greece in the early 160s: to put an end to the Macedonian threat. And their solution, in the aftermath of their victory on the battlefield at Pydna, reveals indirectly the remarkable strength of the koinon as a form of state in Hellenistic Greece. The Romans had forcibly extinguished the political authority of the Macedonian kingship, and in its place they fostered four Macedonian republics. And as they did so, they put in place prohibitions that would prevent these small Macedonian states from forming a state

---

282. Polyb. 28.3.7–10; Livy 43.17.4.

283. Polyb. 28.4.1–5.6; Livy 43.17.5–10.

284. Polyb. 28.7.1–14, 12.1–6, 12.7 (cf. *OGIS* 297); Livy 44.1.

285. E.g., Polyb. 29.23–25.

286. Polyb. 30.10.3–6 and Livy 45.28.1–5 both present Lucius Aemilius Paulus's trip through the Peloponnese as a sightseeing tour, but there is no doubt that the places he visited were of political significance to Achaia: Corinth, Sikyon, Argos, Epidauros, Sparta, Megalopolis, and Olympia in Elis. The exclusive authority of the koinon to conduct interstate relations is addressed in detail below, pp. 349–51.

287. Polyb. 30.13; Livy 45.31.1–15.

288. The most extensive account is Paus. 7.10.7–12; cf. Polyb. 30.13.1–11, Livy 45.31.9–11. Despite numerous embassies to Rome seeking their return (Polyb. 30.29.1–7, 166/5; 30.32.3–12, 165/4; 32.3.14–17, 160/59; 33.1.3–8, 3.2, 156/5; 33.14, 154/3), the detainees were not released until 150 (Polyb. 35.6 *apud* Plut. *Cato mai.* 9; Paus. 7.10.12).

like a koinon: not only were they subordinated to Rome in all their foreign affairs but they were prohibited from trading, intermarrying, or owning land in the other states, all distinctive practices of the koinon as a kind of state since at least the early fourth century, and which, as we shall see below (chapter 5), were central to its success.[289] The Romans' efforts to prevent the Macedonian kingdom from becoming a Macedonian koinon in 167 bespeaks the power and efficacy of the koinon as a state in the Hellenistic world. But it was now a dying breed in mainland Greece.

BARGAINING WITH ROME, THE STRUGGLE FOR SPARTA, AND THE END OF THE ACHAIAN KOINON, 167-146

The negotiations that took place between the Romans and Achaians throughout the course of the Third Macedonian War, including their surrender of hostages, carved out a space within which the Romans were apparently willing to allow the Achaian koinon to continue to function. Internally, the Achaians remained divided over the question of Roman involvement in their affairs.[290] The loss of the continuous narratives of both Polybios and Livy after 167 makes a detailed reconstruction of the history of this period impossible, but several episodes attest to the autonomy of the koinon, the lingering uncertainty on the part of both the Achaians and the Romans over the precise role the Romans should play in Achaian affairs, and the willingness of competing political agents in Achaia to exploit that uncertainty to further their own ends.

The eruption of a long-standing boundary dispute between Megalopolis and Sparta boiled over around 164, and both parties appealed to the Romans, who charged the legates of 163 with the task.[291] The Roman decision, effected as a third-party arbitration, was rejected by the Spartans.[292] Despite the fact that this was tantamount to a violation of Achaian laws, the koinon responded not with violence but rather with a second round of arbitration, in accordance with "the laws of the Achaians," this time between the koinon itself and Sparta.[293] The purpose of this legally required recourse to arbitration is made explicit in an inscription set up at Olympia: "so that the Achaians, having a democratic constitution and being in

---

289. Livy 45.29.10.

290. Cf. Polyb. 30.29.1–7. The vilification of Kallikrates in later sources (e.g., Paus. 7.11.2) reflects the anti-Roman side of the dispute.

291. Background to the dispute: Plut. *Cleom.* 4.1; Polyb. 2.54.3, 9.33.11–12; Livy 38.34.8; Paus. 7.11.1–2. Arbitration: T45.

292. Roman involvement: Polyb. 31.1.7; cf. Paus. 7.11.1–3, a problematic report. See Schwertfeger 1974: 8 n. 20; Gruen 1976: 50–51, 55; Bowman 1992; Nottmeyer 1995b: 201 with n. 20; Ager 1996: no. 135; Cartledge and Spawforth 2002: 86; Rizakis 2008b: 280.

293. T45.13–16.

agreement amongst themselves, may continue for all time to live in peace and good order."[294] The process by which the disputes between Megalopolis, Sparta, and the Achaian koinon were resolved demonstrates that the Achaians were not only fully autonomous in the aftermath of the Romans' war against Perseus but also that they continued to refine their institutions in the interests of achieving internal peace and civic order.

The Romans' settlement of Greece after Pydna instigated a series of local conflicts, in which we nevertheless find the Romans continuing to recognize and uphold Achaian autonomy. Two episodes illustrate the point. The first is a dispute between the Athenians and Achaians that was taken to Rome in 159/8 over the right of the Delians, who had been expelled when the Romans handed their island over to the Athenians in 166 and given citizenship in Achaia, to sue Athenians for loss of property in accordance with an existing *symbolon* between Athens and Achaia. The Romans found that "all arrangements made about the Delians by the Achaians according to their laws were valid," which amounts to an affirmation of the Delians' right as Achaian citizens to be covered by the existing Achaian-Athenian *symbolon*.[295] The Romans continued to uphold Achaian autonomy, but the episode must have soured Achaian-Athenian relations. They deteriorated further still when the Achaians responded to a call for help from the city of Oropos sometime shortly after 160. Oropos had been made independent when the Boiotian koinon was dismantled in 171, but for reasons that are unclear the Athenians invaded and sacked the city.[296] Outraged by this treatment, the Oropians sought redress from the Romans, who merely asked Sikyon, a member of the Achaian koinon, to arbitrate. When the Athenians balked at the fine imposed by the arbitrators and perpetrated further violence, it appears from an honorific decree of Oropos (T46) that the Achaians swung into action to restore the hapless Oropians to their city.[297] Again we see the Achaian koinon acting with full autonomy in relation to other states, with evident awareness of the Romans. In short, although our evidence for the period after 167 is scant, it all points to a fully autonomous Achaian koinon. Nothing, then, seems to have prepared the Achaians for the

---

294. T45.17–19; cf. ll. 38–40. On arbitration see below, pp. 313–20.

295. Polyb. 32.7.1–5 at 5. Cf. Gruen 1976: 51.

296. Motives: Paus. 7.11.4–8 with Gruen 1976: 51–53.

297. Athenian objection to the fine: Paus. 7.11.5, corroborated by Polyb. 33.2 (*apud* Aul. Gell. 6.14.8–10), a notice of the so-called philosophic embassy to Rome in 155, which is widely attested for other reasons by many sources: Cic. *Acad.* 2.137, *De or.* 2.155, *Tusc.* 4.5, *Att.* 12.23.2, *Fin.* 2.59; Plin. *NH* 7.112; Plut. *Cato mai.* 22; Aelian *Var. hist.* 3.17; Lact. *Hist.* 5.14.3–5; Macrob. 1.5.14. Cf. Ferrary 1988: 351–63. Paus. reports that the Achaian army was mobilized only after its general Menalkidas and the pro-Roman Kallikrates were bribed but that it arrived too late to be of assistance; whatever the veracity of this report, it is clear from T46 that the Achaians effected the Oropians' return, whether by diplomacy or military action or both.

overwhelmingly violent Roman response to a flare-up of the old quarrel between them and the Spartans.

Despite those long-standing tensions, Spartan commitment to the koinon must have appeared serious in 151/0, for in that year a Spartan, Menalkidas, was elected to the office of *stratēgos* for the first—and last—time in Achaian history.[298] With historical hindsight it is clear that the appointment exacerbated those tensions rather than soothing them. When Menalkidas laid down his office, he was accused by Kallikrates of having sought permission from the Romans for Sparta to secede from the koinon.[299] When precisely this happened is unclear, but it must have predated 150.[300] It is described by Pausanias as a capital charge, but Menalkidas was acquitted despite the hostility of most Achaians to his case. In order to deflect the Achaian suspicions that were incited by this acquittal, Diaios encouraged them to prosecute Spartan dissidents, those implicated in seeking Roman support for their cause in the still-simmering boundary dispute with Megalopolis. Diaios levied the Achaian army to make war "not on Sparta itself, but on those who were disturbing it."[301] He declared twenty-four leading Spartan citizens guilty of what he claimed was a capital crime, and the Spartans chose to exile them in an effort to prevent a war with Achaia. Both sides sent ambassadors to Rome, the Achaians represented by Diaios and Kallikrates (who died en route), the Spartans by Menalkidas, the erstwhile Achaian *stratēgos*. According to Pausanias, the Romans promised to send an arbitrator, but he was slow to arrive, so the ambassadors returned, and each told his home audience what it wanted to hear: the Achaians that they had been given permission to bring the Spartans under complete subjection; the Spartans that they had been separated from the koinon.[302]

Acting on this notion, the Achaians proceeded to levy their army against Sparta, now under the leadership of the *stratēgos* Damokritos, who ignored the stay of attack ordered by Roman envoys.[303] Damokritos won a victory in pitched battle against the Spartans but refused to attempt a siege of the city. For that failure he was fined by the Achaians, and his successor, Diaios of Megalopolis, appears to have persecuted those in Achaia whom he believed to have pro-Spartan sympathies.[304] In the spring or summer of 147 the Roman legate L. Aurelius Orestes, who had been promised in 149 to arbitrate in the dispute between Achaia and Sparta,

298. Paus. 7.11.7.

299. Paus. 7.12.2.

300. Gruen 1976: 55 n. 75 suggests that it was connected with the boundary dispute against Megalopolis; F. W. Walbank 1957–79: III.698 supposes that it occurred probably in 152/1.

301. Paus. 7.12.6.

302. Paus. 7.12.7–9.

303. Paus. 7.13.1–3.

304. Damokritos's victory and fine: Paus. 7.13.3–5. Persecution of pro-Spartan Achaians: Polyb. 38.18.6.

finally arrived in Corinth and summoned "those who held office in each city."[305] Orestes reported the decision of the Roman senate that Sparta, Corinth, Argos, Herakleia Trachinia, and Arkadian Orchomenos were to be immediately released from the *synedrion* of the Achaians on the grounds that they were not ethnically Achaian and had joined the koinon relatively recently.[306] This announcement was clearly a tremendous shock, for Sparta had been the only member polis in open dissent. After a hastily summoned assembly meeting, the Achaians arrested and imprisoned all the Spartans they could seize in Corinth. According to some sources, which Polybios regarded as exaggerated, Orestes and his colleagues themselves faced considerable personal danger, and their complaints to the senate on this score only further entrenched Roman hostility to the Achaians.[307]

In the autumn of 147, Diaios was succeeded as *stratēgos* by the resolutely anti-Roman Kritolaos. The Romans sent another embassy to the Achaians, with orders, according to Polybios, to deliver a mild reproof and to ask the Achaians to hold those directly responsible for mistreatment of the Roman ambassadors accountable for their crimes. Whether in fact they did not "wish to tear the [Achaian] *ethnos* asunder" at this point is unclear; Polybios finds himself in the awkward position of being an Achaian apologist for Rome, blaming his countrymen for allowing themselves to be misled by "the worst men, hated by the gods, bringing ruin upon the *ethnos*."[308] The Roman ambassadors sought to negotiate an end to the war between Achaia and Sparta, which was derailed by Kritolaos's refusal to cooperate.[309] That small war had been fully subsumed by a much larger one. Kritolaos spent the winter of 147/6 drumming up support for war against Rome and proposing financial measures that would enable the Achaians to fund the war that now appeared inevitable.[310]

By the spring of 146, Achaian opposition to Rome was widespread. Despite an apparently mollifying embassy from the Romans, war was declared by the

---

305. Paus. 7.14.1: *echontas tas archas*; cf. 7.14.2, where they are described as *hoi archontes tōn Achaiōn*. The latter phrase suggests that they were actually the elected magistrates of the Achaian koinon, who were summoned from their respective home cities.

306. Paus. 7.14.1.

307. Polyb. 38.9.1–3. Threats and insults to the legates themselves are reported by Str. 8.6.23; Livy *Epit.* 51; Dio 21.72; Justin 34.1.8; Eutrop. 4.14; Cic. *Pro lege Man.* 11. The reports clearly had some grounding in reality, for the Achaians sent representatives to Rome hoping to minimize the damage done (Polyb. 38.10.1–2; Paus. 7.14.3).

308. Polyb. 38.9.6, 10.8; cf. 38.10.3–7 for Roman apologetics. Champion 2004: 166–67 for Polybios's presentation of the errors of the Achaians in this war.

309. Polyb. 38.10.11–11.7.

310. Polyb. 38.11.10; *IG* IV.757. These measures, including a prohibition on debt imprisonment, were once interpreted as evidence that the Achaian War against Rome was motivated by social revolution; for a more balanced approach see Fuks 1970. The financial measures undertaken by the koinon are discussed in detail below, pp. 301, 311.

Achaians, "in word against the Spartans, but in reality against the Romans."[311] At the behest of Kritolaos, who stood to gain all as the current *stratēgos*, the Achaians voted extraordinary and complete authority to those who were elected as *stratēgoi*.[312] As the conflict shifted away from Sparta and toward Rome, the Achaians were joined by numerous other Greek cities.[313] Direct hostilities ensued so quickly, however, that if there was a formal alliance, it never had time to organize an effective defense. A Roman army was already present in Macedonia under the consul Quintus Caecilius Metellus, having finally quelled the revolt of Andriskos, a claimant to the Macedonian throne. Metellus, motivated by a desire to end the war before his successor, Mummius, should arrive, encouraged the Achaians to release Sparta and the other cities named by Orestes, and went himself to Herakleia Trachinia, which was under siege by Kritolaos and the Achaian army for its willingness to abandon the koinon after Orestes' embassy declared that it should be independent. As the Roman army descended across the Spercheios Valley, Kritolaos led the Achaians in flight to Skarpheia in Lokris, where he himself died and the Achaians suffered a massive defeat.[314] A full military levy was raised throughout Achaia, with orders to muster at Corinth. The peace overtures offered by Metellus were refused.[315] So the war with Achaia became the prize of Mummius, who mustered his massive force at Corinth and overwhelmed the Achaian defenders. The city was abandoned by its inhabitants and burned to the ground. The men who remained were killed; the women and children, sold into slavery. Ancient works of art, many of them sacred, were plundered and pillaged.[316] The walls of all those cities that had defied the Roman decrees were destroyed. Democracies were replaced by oligarchies. And just as they did when they sundered the Macedonian kingdom into four distinct republics, the Romans undermined the material foundations of political cooperation by making property ownership outside one's own polis illegal. Finally, not only the Achaian koinon but all ethnic confederacies throughout Greece were henceforth strictly prohibited.[317]

311. Polyb. 38.13.6.

312. Polyb. 38.13.7.

313. Polyb. 38.3.8, a corrupt text that cannot be fully restored, includes all the Peloponnesians (except the Spartans), the Boiotians (by which he appears to mean Thebans; cf. Polyb. 38.14.12, Paus. 7.14.6, 15.9), Phokians (Polyb. 38.14.3, Paus. 7.15.5), Lokrians, some communities on the Ionian Gulf, and the Macedonians. Livy *Epit.* 52 includes Chalkis.

314. Paus. 7.15.1–6; cf. Livy *Per.* 52, placing the battle at Thermopylai.

315. Paus. 7.15.9–11.

316. Paus. 7.16.1–8; Polyb. 39.2; Livy *Per.* 52. On the destruction of Corinth, considered in conjunction with the nearly contemporaneous sack of Carthage at the end of the Third Punic War, see Purcell 1995b.

317. Paus. 7.16.9.

PART TWO

Interactions and Institutions

4

Cultic Communities

Few would argue with the claim that religion was a powerful mechanism for social cohesion in the ancient Greek world, both within an individual state and between communities that retained distinct political identities. The former is captured, negatively perhaps but quite sharply, by the extreme reactions to perceived religious irregularities in moments of political crisis: the charges of impiety leveled against Alkibiades and others in connection with the Profanation of the Mysteries and the Mutilation of the Herms, actions interpreted by many as indicative of an attempt to overthrow the democracy, were made as the Athenians embarked on an expedition to Sicily that they probably knew could come at a grievous cost; and Socrates was accused of impiety in a time of democratic backlash against the Thirty Tyrants, with whom he was implicated by association.[1] The cohesive force of religion in interstate contexts is captured by the central importance of ethnic cults like the Ionian Apatouria and the Dorian Karneia, which marked participants as members of one ethnic group or another but did no more, as well as by the shared religious life of metropolis and *apoikia* or colonial settlement.[2] The role of religion in forging—or articulating—social bonds in the context of the Greek koinon has

---

1. Political interpretations of the Profanation of the Mysteries and the Mutilation of the Herms: Th. 6.28.1, 60–61; Andoc. 1.36; Diod. Sic. 13.2.3. Comprehensive discussions: R. Parker 1996: 199–217; Rubel 2000.

2. Hdt. 1.147.2 (Ionians and the Apatouria); Th. 5.54.2 (Dorians and the Karneia); J.M. Hall 1997: 39–40, 99–106. Cf. Hdt. 8.144.2 for shared shrines and sacrifices uniting all Hellenes. Religious links between *mētropolis* and *apoikia*: RO 93 for the example of Miletos and Olbia; Malkin 1987 more generally.

148   INTERACTIONS AND INSTITUTIONS

been explored for a few cases, almost exclusively in studies of the formation of an ethnic identity that served as a foundation on which federal institutions were later constructed.[3] This is a promising start to answering the central question of the role of religion in the formation and maintenance of Greek federal states. But it is only a start. For while the koinon was predicated on a notion of the connectedness of its member states, it was simultaneously characterized by their distinct social and political identities. We need to ask whether religion played a part in this second aspect of the federal experience and contributed to the differentiation of member communities as well as to their cohesion. That is not an easy question to answer: Can religious behavior simultaneously effect both cohesion and differentiation? And if so, how? This raises a second issue left untouched by previous approaches to what we can call koinon religion. The cohesive effect of religion is assumed, but it is rarely explained. Religion is effectively treated as a black box through which individuals pass and then exit as an integrated community. As a result the process itself, the precise ways in which individuals come to feel that they belong to the same group because they share certain religious experiences, has remained obscure. And when the group is politicized, when it takes the form of a state, the question of how religious behavior effects social cohesion becomes a question of the role of religion in state formation. The role of religious interaction and shared cults in the creation of bonds between communities and the role of religion in the establishment and maintenance of states (not just ethnic groups) that incorporated multiple distinct communities are the twin themes of this chapter.

The scholarly claim that shared religion promotes social cohesion can be traced back to Émile Durkheim and in the context of ancient Greece to N. D. Fustel de Coulanges, who argued that the ancient city was formed from religious associations and that all the city's institutions, laws, and practices were determined by religious practices and beliefs.[4] Durkheim's vision of social life as comprised of inextricably related religious, economic, and political experiences has been tremendously influential. Yet the twentieth-century study of ancient political history in particular took its cue, implicitly or explicitly, from Max Weber in seeing the political life of the Greek world as autonomous and isolated from religious behavior.[5] There are, however, such strong indications in the ancient evidence that religious interactions at shared sanctuaries played a significant role in the creation of group identities that an uneasy synthesis between these two great sociological approaches has frequently, if only implicitly, been adopted. This means that there

3. E.g., Schachter 1994 and Kühr 2006a for Boiotia; Nielsen 1996c; McInerney 1997 and 1999: 127–36 on Phokis.
4. Fustel de Coulanges 1980 with the forewords by Momigliano and Humphreys in Fustel de Coulanges 1980: ix–xxiii, and Humphreys 1983.
5. Murray 1990: 5–6.

has been a tendency to see religion as a significant force in state formation (where discussion has been focused on the polis), after which process, as Victor Ehrenberg put it in his classic study *The Greek State*, religion and cult, "though a necessary part of the life of the state, were confined to some special area of duties of a non-political kind."[6] Similar approaches have been applied to the world of the koinon.[7]

The bifurcation of religion and politics implicit in such accounts of course seemed to defy a rich array of sources attesting to the continued role of religion in political life beyond the process of state formation. So it was conceded that religious officials did in fact serve political functions, and it was recognized that the polis controlled both religious officials and the religious activities of its citizens.[8] This observation has been richly elaborated in the last two decades by scholars working with the so-called polis-religion model, which traces a fundamental isomorphism between religious and political structures in the Greek polis. In its strong form, as articulated by its initial proponent, Christiane Sourvinou-Inwood, the observed structural isomorphism of religion and politics led to the conclusion that "the polis anchored, legitimated, and mediated all religious activity."[9] In more nuanced forms, the model has provided an impetus to study religious practices and institutions at the level of a single polis in great depth and from a diachronic perspective.[10] Surveys of the cults, sanctuaries, and religious practices of several regions in which koina developed have been carried out, but the relationship of those activities to the emergence and development of federal political institutions has not been considered systematically.[11]

Understanding how religious practices contributed to state formation in the Greek world in general remains a live issue. It now seems unlikely that poleis initially demarcated their territories by the construction or monumentalization of rural sanctuaries at the borders. Rather, it appears that religious communities existed prior to the formation of particular political communities, and the former had a deep impact on the creation of the latter.[12] The role of religion in the formation of koina is more complex, for multiple communities, each with its own set of cults and religious practices, frequently quite well established, are necessarily

---

6. Ehrenberg 1960: 74; cf. pp. 16, 19–20.

7. E.g., Larsen 1968: 85.

8. E.g., Ehrenberg 1960: 74–77.

9. Sourvinou-Inwood 1990: 297. Cf. Sourvinou-Inwood 1988. For a recent overview of the model see Kindt 2009.

10. Above all R. Parker 1996, 2005.

11. E.g., Jost 1985 for Arkadia; Schachter 1981–94 for Boiotia.

12. J. M. Hall 1995 and Malkin 1996 *contra* Polignac 1995; cf. Polignac 1994 for a slight modulation of his earlier position.

involved. Most attempts to answer this question proceed by looking for the ethnic origins of koina in shared sanctuaries and common cult. Proponents of the idea that Greek federal states developed from tribal states emphasize evidence for a common shrine or religious center of a particular group and assume a direct and uncomplicated development from religious to political community, the details and process of which are never explored. In keeping with the tacit synthesis of Durkhe-imian and Weberian approaches, these scholars have tended to drop the subject of religion as soon as there is evidence for something more reassuringly constitu-tional, like magistracies, citizenship, and councils, except insofar as sanctuaries served as meeting places and repositories of decrees. Interest in the relationship between religion and political organization in the historical period of the koinon has thus been for the most part limited to passing references to these functional, paracultic aspects of shared sanctuaries.[13] Moving beyond the relationship between religious behavior and group (sometimes ethnic) identity to address the question of the relationship between cultic communities and political communities beyond the polis, Robert Parker has explored the "function of religion as the great focus for group identity in the Greek world, the rennet around which social groups coagulate," but has shown that it is rarely possible to take the next step by demon-strating that shared sacrifices led directly to political deliberation.[14] Yet insofar as social groups did form around religious practices, we should be considering how social groups were politicized: that is, how states emerged from social groups and what role religion played in that process.[15]

One way around this impasse is to privilege archaeological evidence for the identity and makeup of the worshipping group at a particular sanctuary, for ritual practices and changes in them over time. Catherine Morgan's recent study of *ethnē*,

13. E.g., Ehrenberg 1960: 7–16, 120–31; Larsen 1968: 3–8, 27–29 (Boiotia), 84–85 (Achaia); Tausend 1992: 21–34. Cf. Daverio Rocchi 1993: 108, 387, 394, etc. Cf. Demandt 1995: 248.

14. R. Parker 1998. Parker's insistence on drawing a distinction between group identity and the operation of a state is salutary but has not been widely followed. The emphasis in most scholarship continues to be on the role of religion in forming a group identity, and here analysis stops; see, e.g., Roy 2003: 90–92.

15. Horden and Purcell 2000: 456 point in a similar direction: "Various degrees of formality can be involved in the arrangement, which at its most political becomes a kind of federation; and sanctuaries on which regions focus in this way are often loosely called 'federal' in modern scholarship. These cen-tres express groupings and relationships on a scale far transcending the microregional. They are there-fore of the highest interest in the investigation of networks of interaction." The problem of the relation-ship between cults and communities beyond the polis is taken up from a variety of angles in a volume with the promising title *Kult—Politik—Ethnos* (Freitag, Funke, and Haake 2006). Yet most of the papers treat religion and ethnic identity or the social influence of the pan-Hellenic sanctuaries, which could be politicized in interstate relations and diplomacy but were not tied to the power of a single state. The one exception is Freitag 2006, on sanctuaries and the institutions of the Thessalian koinon after 146, to which I shall return below.

rooted in the understanding of "a community as a complex of relationships rather than a single organic entity," offers us among many other things a new picture of how the use of sanctuaries over time related to the constituency and development of political communities from the Iron Age to the archaic period.[16] By attending to archaeological evidence for the composition of the worshipping group and for ritual practices at particular sanctuaries, Morgan charts a history of sanctuary use marked by change rather than stable continuity.[17] This finding is extraordinarily important, for the claim that a particular group worshipped at the same sanctuary from the Iron Age to the classical period, at which time it served also as a political meeting place and archive, has been a linchpin in the argument that Greek federal states developed from tribal states. The shattering of this notion of long-term continuity of the worshipping group and its practices at a particular sanctuary effectively kicks the legs out from under the argument that federal states developed from tribal states, for which the claim of cultic continuity was always foundational.[18] In its place it is now possible to sketch at least the outlines of a history of regional religious and political behavior, their intersections, and their recursive relationship to each other.

But how, precisely, did religious practice—the creation and maintenance of sanctuaries, the performance of ritual, and the utterance of myth, especially in ritual contexts—contribute to the formation of communities and their politicization? This question has recently been addressed by Barbara Kowalzig in her rich and detailed study of the *pentēkontaetia*, which proceeds via close and deeply contextualized readings of the poetry of Pindar and Bacchylides.[19] Kowalzig considers a number of different political contexts, including the Athenian empire, the competing city-states of the Argolid, the independent Greek settlements of southern Italy, and the Boiotian koinon. Her study of the relationship between religious ritual and the creation of the Boiotian koinon is the first to look in detail at how the religious interactions of people from multiple communities related to the formation of political institutions of a federal sort, to show how ritual actually contributed to the construction of community and to explain why it did so. In this

16. Morgan 2003: 12.

17. Morgan 2003: 107–63, esp. 109; cf. Morgan 1997. The case of Phokis is particularly illustrative: the sanctuary at Kalapodi had a catchment area in the thirteenth century that extended across the later boundary between Phokis and Lokris (Morgan 2003: 175–79). The worshipping group split, however, around the middle of the tenth century, and at the same time large-scale construction began at the shrine, undertaken now by only part of the original group (Morgan 2003: 114–20). But in the Iron Age, Delphi was for southern Phokis what Kalapodi was for northern. It was hostility to Thessaly in the sixth century that unified the Phokians around Kalapodi as a single common sanctuary with regional and ethnic significance (Ellinger 1987; McInerney 1999: 177–78, 199–200).

18. E.g., Larsen 1968: 27.

19. Kowalzig 2007.

respect Kowalzig has blazed a new path for the study of koinon religion. By treating the Boiotian koinon as only one case in a broader study of the role of religion in the formation and articulation of communities and their occasional politicization, she has exposed the common threads that run through these processes regardless of the particular form of political institution that was adopted. We need, however, to examine the process in other regions in which koina developed, to see whether we can detect features that are distinctive to the koinon as a form of state. And we need to move beyond the context of foundation, for religious behavior continued to play an important role in the articulation, deployment, modification, and maintenance of political power by koina over the centuries of their existence. Because the koinon in every case incorporated multiple communities, its proponents faced the continuous challenge of justifying its authority even after its power had been legitimated in the earliest stages of institutionalized cooperation under the rubric of regional state power. In the following pages I shall explore these issues by analyzing the evidence for patterns of interaction at sanctuaries within koina as well as for the myths and rituals associated with those sanctuaries. These activities will be placed in their historical context so that we can assess their relationship to the processes of state formation, growth, and maintenance.

It is, in the end, rather unsatisfying merely to point to a correlation between, for example, a worshipping group and a political community, even if we can be far more detailed about it than Fustel or Louis Gernet or Jakob Larsen ever was, and even if we can provide a nuanced account of the process by which a particular group came to share one or more sanctuaries and articulate a sense of group identity in religious terms. We want to know why religion was important in this process at all, what it accomplished that other forms of interaction and communication could not, and to answer this question we need to think more carefully about the role of ritual—the most important and distinctive form of religious behavior in the Greek world—in the construction of political communities and their maintenance over time.

The issue was first addressed explicitly by Durkheim, who saw religion, very broadly speaking, as a means of making sense of the unknown.[20] For Durkheim one of the most fundamental puzzles for human beings is their own relationship to society, the fact of collective existence and its impact on the individual. He argued that ritual, as a principal component of religion (the other being belief), is the means by which collective experience is created and explained, so that participation in religious rituals becomes a principal mechanism for the reconciliation of individual and society.[21] In short, for Durkheim ritual promotes social

20. The issues in this section are treated in greater detail, but with a slightly different emphasis and different concerns, by Kowalzig 2007: 32–43.

21. Durkheim 1915: 205–14, 230–33. Cf. Bell 1992: 171–73.

solidarity and consensus. This basic view underlies much work on the social functions of ritual in all periods undertaken in the twentieth century, but there are at least two problems with it.[22] The first is that it does not adequately explain precisely how ritual promotes solidarity and consensus; Durkheim appealed to "collective effervescence," a shared emotional experience that binds those who participate in it to one another and to the ideas and institutions around which a ritual is performed. The effervescence of religion has become a celebrated phrase, but it is at best merely a dodge, not an explanation of how religion effects sociopolitical bonds.[23] The second problem with Durkheim's model is that it fails entirely to account for ritual innovation per se or for ritual's power to effect change in the prevailing social order—to be subversive and revolutionary.[24] Insofar as the social order partly comprises the political order, there is an implicit assumption that ritual behavior is related to political behavior only as a means of legitimating a particular, secular sociopolitical order. This view further implies the claim that ritual is wholly extrinsic to political behavior, and most political scientists agree. When political theorists have thought about ritual, they have regarded it either as a weapon to induce fear, awe, and compliance (insofar as the state is a Leviathan, with Thomas Hobbes), as a mask for material interests and conflicts (insofar as the state is a fraud, with Karl Marx or Vilfredo Pareto), as a celebration (insofar as the state is seen as an extension of community itself, with communitarians), or as a mask to cloak the arbitrary with an aura of legitimacy and justice (insofar as the state is a bundle of ongoing negotiations, with classical liberals). In sum, as Clifford Geertz puts it, rituals "exaggerate might, conceal exploitation, inflate authority, or moralize procedure. The one thing they do not do is actuate anything."[25]

Implicit in the Durkheimian (or neo-Durkheimian) view is the assumption that ritual has an inherently conservative role in political life, a notion that has been dismantled by sociologists and anthropologists in the last three decades.[26] Ritual, it is now realized, can exacerbate social conflict as effectively as it can promote socialization, or the integration of individuals into prevailing sociopolitical norms; any ritual that celebrates the victory of a dominant group over another group that nevertheless remains a part of the society in question will at

22. Durkheim's social-solidarity thesis strongly influenced sociologists throughout the twentieth century; see Lukes 1975: 293–301. It also underlies most work on the social and political functions of Greek religion: e.g., Sourvinou-Inwood 1990: 305; Polignac 1995: 39–40.

23. Ramp 1998; N. J. Allen 1998.

24. The view of ritual as fundamentally conservative persists (despite room for slight modulation and variance): Rappaport 1999: 36–37.

25. Geertz 1980: 123.

26. Kertzer 1988: 37

least have the potential to be explosive.[27] Ritual can also be used to foster a sense of legitimacy in a new government, sometimes by deploying old ritual forms for new purposes, leveraging the stabilizing effects of ritual's conservative properties.[28] By exposing the flip side of Durkheim's argument, sociologists have shown that ritual should be seen not simply as a means of promoting value integration but rather as a vital mechanism for the mobilization of bias, whether that happens to be conservative or subversive.[29] Through the deployment of symbols in rule-governed activities, ritual plays the cognitive role of marking out what is socially significant, focusing attention on particular activities and relationships while occluding the view of others: "Every way of seeing is also a way of not seeing."[30] One way this is accomplished is by uniting symbols of social reality with strong emotional attachment to that reality; whether the particular configuration of power that constitutes the social reality thus symbolized is traditional or revolutionary is irrelevant. For Victor Turner, famously, ritual "is precisely a mechanism that periodically converts the obligatory into the desirable," the process whereby "the irksomeness of moral constraint is transformed into the 'love of virtue.'"[31] This emphasis on the cognitive role of ritual, not entirely absent from Durkheim's own analysis but very much neglected by his followers, has the added advantage of breaking down the neo-Durkheimian notion of ritual as an inert, independent analytical object and points implicitly to the importance of contextual analysis of ritual action.

The subtle shift from thinking about ritual per se to thinking about ritual action, advocated in the clearest and most rigorous terms by Catherine Bell, entails enormous gains. It allows us to begin to see exactly how ritual behavior influences political behavior and to see what is distinctive and unique about that influence. Bell defines ritual action (or ritualization) as "the strategic production of expedient schemes that structure an environment in such a way that the environment appears to be the source of the schemes and their values."[32] As a specific kind of action, ritual is "situational; strategic; embedded in a misrecognition of what it is in fact doing; and able to reproduce or reconfigure a vision of the order of power in the world".[33] Insofar as it is situational, ritual action can only be understood in

27. The other side of ritual's cohesive force is that it excludes those who do not participate, an angle recently explored by Auffarth 2006 via the case of the Argive Heraion. This result, too, can be explosive; the difference lies in the inclusion of subordinated groups within the state versus their exclusion.

28. Kertzer 1988: 37–46.

29. See Kowalzig 2007: 39 with n. 86 for some examples of dissent and social transformation being expressed and achieved in religious contexts in Greek antiquity.

30. Lukes 1975: 301.

31. V. Turner 1967: 30.

32. Bell 1992: 140.

33. Bell 1992: 80.

the context in which it occurs; this means that there is much to be gained from an historical rather than a purely anthropological or sociological analysis of ritual action. The strategic nature of ritual action means, furthermore, that it is performed with the intention of accomplishing something specific within the context of its performance. That ritual action is embedded in a misrecognition means that there is a break between what it actually accomplishes in the world and what both ritual performers and their audiences explicitly claim that it accomplishes.[34] The ability of ritual action "to reproduce or reconfigure a vision of the order of power in the world," which Bell terms "redemptive hegemony," means that ritual action does not just reflect power (à la Durkheim); it constitutes it (à la Geertz).[35] Ritual action thus derives much of its unique and distinctive power from a recursive relationship between actor and observer, between symbol and reality, between agency and structure, that shares much in common with the broader view of the construction of society and community adopted throughout this book.[36] This suggests that ritual action—particularly, in the ancient Greek case, religious ritual action—played as prominent a role in the construction of political communities beyond the polis, as did the more familiar stuff of political history, though it did so in a wholly distinctive manner.

As I have already suggested, if in the modern world it is often difficult to see the state as a coherent and integrated body with full powers of agency, it is virtually impossible for the ancient world, despite the persistent historiographic practice of assigning will and agency to states ("Athens sought to exercise tighter economic control over her allies," etc.). And this is true a fortiori for emergent states in antiquity. For the formation of states is fundamentally a process by which social boundaries are created, and power both created and distributed. This process is accomplished, among other means, by the creation and propagation of images or perceptions of what the state is and can do. These images are recursively related to practices of all kinds—actions undertaken by a group of individuals in the name of the state that promote a commitment to the validity and reality of the images.[37] The process of state formation is thus intrinsically fraught with tension, for it creates a distinction between ruler and ruled that can appear, if not actually be, arbitrary. Ritual action that deploys religious symbols is especially effective at creating impressions of legitimacy, at generating and sustaining the image of the state

---

34. Cf. Bourdieu 1977: 5–6, 163–64; Sahlins 1976: 220.

35. Bell 1992: 83–85, 196; cf. Geertz 1980: 123–35; Cannadine 1987: 19; Bell 1997: 128–37.

36. So too Kertzer 1988: 4–5.

37. I draw here on Migdal 2001: 15–23, whose conception of states as fields of power shaped by both images and practices provides more traction with the problem of how states form than the Weberian ideal type of state (coherent, integrated, and goal-oriented) that so mightily dominated the social sciences throughout the twentieth century.

as a distinct entity with a specific set of powers within an established territory, by presenting the often revolutionary political order of the emergent future as a mere continuation of the traditions of the past and aligning that political order with divine order itself. The case of koinon formation is even more challenging, for it entails the struggle to achieve not just the consent of the individual poleis who become members but also their sense of participation in the larger, regional polity. Where fully autonomous poleis already existed, as in Boiotia and to some extent Achaia, the creation of a koinon necessarily entailed tensions over the redistribution of power that religious behavior, I shall argue, played an important role in defusing. In areas characterized by nonurban settlement, where *ethnē* rather than poleis were the norm, as in Aitolia, religious behavior was vital to the creation of shared social values and political arrangements. In every case ritual action played a significant role in creating a sense of belonging, of corporate existence and shared interests, that went well beyond the narrow confines of the individual community.[38] Ritual was not, however, sufficient on its own to accomplish this. As Bell points out, "ritualization cannot turn a group of individuals into a community if they have no other relationships or interests in common, nor can it turn the exercise of pure physical compulsion into participatory communality. Ritualization can, however, take arbitrary or necessary common interests and ground them in an understanding of the hegemonic order; it can empower agents in limited and highly negotiated ways."[39]

In this chapter I shall accordingly explore the role of religion in creating, articulating, and maintaining political communities beyond the polis in ancient Greece. I shall argue that in addition to creating a sense of community beyond polis boundaries, religious ritual also promoted a vision of the legitimacy of the koinon as it formed and, later, as it was challenged. But it will also become clear that ritual simultaneously protected and maintained the distinct identity of member communities as they participated in the religious life of the koinon. It should be said at the outset that there are many fascinating and well-documented religious practices in each of the regions treated here that will not enter at all into the discussion. This chapter does not purport to survey religious practices in toto throughout the world of the koinon; rather, it offers an attempt to explore, through careful attention to historical process, the role that religion played in building communities beyond the polis, in their politicization, and in the maintenance and development of the institutions distinctive to the koinon.

---

38. The role of ritual action in conferring meaning on shared experiences thus makes it a significant part of the package of social and cultural strategies for creating and articulating a sense of ethnic identity, as outlined by A. D. Smith 1986.

39. Bell 1992: 222.

BUILDING REGIONAL COMMUNITIES

In most of the koina that had their origins in the classical period, there is plentiful evidence to conclude that a developed sense of group identity emerged among the communities that later became members of a koinon prior to the development of formal political institutions at the regional level. Where this evidence is explicitly lacking (as in the Chalkidike), it would probably not be rash to infer a similar overlap, although caution must be taken and allowance given for divergent developmental trajectories, particularly between those that developed early in the period, like the Boiotians, and those that developed generations later, like the Achaians and Aitolians. Nevertheless, the identity of the social group and the later political group encourages us to ask how the social group formed in the first place. This complex question requires, of course, a complex answer; in this section I shall focus on the religious facet of this answer, exploring the role of ritual and religion in the formation of communities that extend beyond the reach of the individual polis. I shall suggest that, in koinon religion as in polis religion, shared ritual actions like making sacrifices to a common god, feasting, and making joint dedications were an essential part of the process by which people from different communities (whether poleis, villages, or nonnucleated population groups) came to associate with one another, to articulate a sense of a common past, and to conceive of a shared and meaningfully unified territory. I shall also suggest that investment by people of different communities in a common sanctuary through the funding and construction of monumental architecture and the dedication of valuable goods necessarily implicated them in the business of establishing formal relationships with one another, which entailed negotiations about hierarchy. The material is presented regionally, with a detailed exploration of religion and the construction of regional communities in Boiotia (where we enjoy the most detailed and plentiful evidence), Achaia, and Aitolia.

Boiotia

The Boiotians and Athena Itonia.   Two cults in Boiotia, that of Athena Itonia near Koroneia and that of Poseidon at Onchestos, appear to have played a major role in forging a Boiotian community that transcended polis boundaries and later formed the germ of a koinon. It has long been claimed that the cult of Athena Itonia was the tribal cult of the Boiotoi, a remnant of the group's habitation of Thessaly during the period before the so-called Dorian Invasion transformed the population history of mainland Greece.[40] This fact is taken to explain the Pamboiotia, a

---

40. Larsen 1968: 27–28; cf. Tausend 1992: 26–27. Kowalzig 2007: 328–401 offers an excellent historically situated analysis of Boiotian cults associated with their myths of migration.

festival celebrated at the Itonion but attested only for the Hellenistic period, although its existence is regularly retrojected into the archaic.[41] The evidence should be carefully considered.

The Boiotians claimed at least as early as the fifth century that they had brought Athena Itonia from Thessaly to her home near Lake Kopaïs when the Boiotoi occupied the territory after being driven out of Arne by the Thessalians, according to Thucydides' account, sixty years after the fall of Troy.[42] The classical Theban historian Armenidas reports in his *Thebaïka* a heroic genealogy that was clearly invented to explain the link: Iton the son of Amphiktyon was born in Thessaly, and both the Thessalian polis Iton and the goddess Athena Itonia were named after him.[43] The fact that Armenidas's remark is drawn from his *Thebaïka* suggests that the aetiological myth he preserves was in fact the Theban version current at the time he was writing.[44] It is likely that at this time, too, Boiotos himself was claimed to be the son of Iton, making Athena Itonia a goddess representing the entire population group.[45] Much later, Strabo (9.2.29) records a more elaborate version of the aetiological myth, according to which the Boiotoi founded the Itonion in commemoration of their seizure of the area from Orchomenos when they migrated south and west from Thessaly.

This myth, increasingly elaborated over time, in its simplest form associates the cult of Athena Itonia with a population group unified by a shared past (habitation of Thessaly) and the conquest of a now shared territory. The Arne to which Thucydides refers was called Kierion by the Thessalians and is located in the central Thessalian plain. The sanctuary of Athena Itonia in Thessaly was situated at Philia, some ten kilometers south of Arne (Kierion); the distinctive votive record of the sanctuary assembled by archaeologists suggests that it was a strictly local cult in Thessaly in which sacrifice, ritual dining, and the dedication of votives (including weapons, some apparently made on the site) characterized the worship of a warrior goddess conducted in the open air until the third century BCE.[46] The sanctuary of Athena Itonia in Boiotia has provided far less archaeological evidence, but what survives indicates that there was a temple on the site by the sixth century. The temple was restored in the Roman period, when two tripod bases of the fourth or third century were incorporated in its threshold; we do not know whether tripod dedications

41. Ziehen, *RE* 18 s.v. "Pamboiotia" cols. 288–89; Nilsson 1967: 434; R. J. Buck 1979: 77–78; Tausend 1992: 26; Mafodda 2000: 22. Schachter 1981–94: I.123 is appropriately cautious about retrojecting the Pamboiotia to the pre-Hellenistic period; cf. Schachter 1994: 81.

42. Th. 1.12.3 with Larson 2007: 52–64. Cf. Hekataios *FGrHist* 1 F 2.

43. Armenidas *FGrHist* 378 F 1; cf. Alexander Polyhistor *FGrHist* 273 F 97.

44. Armenidas's dates are uncertain. Jacoby placed him before 400 without further comment.

45. As reported by Paus. 9.1.1; cf. Paus. 9.34.1 with Kowalzig 2007: 363.

46. Papahatzis 1981, 1992; Morgan 2003: 141.

here occurred earlier, but it is a practice familiar from other sanctuaries in Boiotia (notably the Ptoion and the Ismenion, both of which will be discussed below) in the archaic period.[47] There is no votive assemblage from the Itonion, and no archaeological evidence for sacrifice or feasting at the sanctuary, so it is impossible to compare ritual practices with those attested for the Itonion at Philia in Thessaly. And the myth of a cultic transfer from Thessaly at the time of migration is attested only from the fifth century, when the Boiotian koinon was first formalized and acquired state powers. How does the picture change if we consider the evidence in historical context, refusing to retroject or assume anything?

A fragmentary poem of Alkaios, probably roughly contemporaneous with the construction of the sixth-century temple, addresses the goddess directly (Alkaios fr. 325 Campbell):

> Mistress Athena, war-sustaining goddess
> who rul[ing] over Koroneia
> before the temple . . .
> by the banks of the river Koralios

The poem was clearly written for performance as a hymn. The temple referred to in line three is probably the archaeologically attested sixth-century temple discussed above; if Alkaios was born in the last quarter of the seventh century, he would have been of the right age to compose a hymn for performance at its dedication, and we know that he traveled widely (if often involuntarily) from Lesbos. Significantly, for Alkaios Athena Itonia is the ruler of Koroneia, not of Boiotia as a whole, and we have no other evidence for patterns of participation in the cult during this period or for its pan-Boiotian significance before the fifth century.[48]

By the early fifth century, the rituals at the Itonion were clearly drawing a worshipping group beyond Koroneia, if they had not before. A fragmentary poem of

---

47. Spyropoulos 1975; Amandry 1978a. The attribution of this site to the Itonion is strengthened by Krentz 1989, and in my view there is no serious reason to doubt it (*contra* P. W. Wallace 1979: 115–16).

48. In line 2, "ru[ling]" (μεδ[έοισα]) is restored *exempli gratia*; see Lobel and Page 1955 and Campbell 1982 for textual variants and restorations. But the sense is quite clear from the first three, unrestored, letters. It is of course possible that in the lost portion of the poem mention is made of Boiotia as a whole, or of other communities within it relative to the cult; there is no way of knowing. Schachter 1994: 72 suggests that the Alkaios fragment may refer either to the Itonion or to the sanctuary of Athena at Alalkomenai, not far from the Itonion (though not certainly located). The fact, however, that Athena Alalkomeneïs is never associated with Koroneia in our (very meager) sources and the fact that the Alkaios fragment survives partly by quotation by Strabo in connection with his discussion of the Itonion together suggest that there is no real ambiguity in Alkaios's reference. There is no evidence to support Schachter's further suggestion (1994: 72) that the Alalkomenion was replaced by the Itonion; indeed in an earlier publication (Schachter 1981–94: I.113) he raised it only as a purely speculative hypothesis. As an outsider, Alkaios may have been well placed to give voice through poetic performance to an emergent sense of local identity: D'Alessio 2009a.

Bacchylides was certainly composed for ritual performance at the Itonion (Bacchylides fr. 15 Snell):[49]

> This is no time for sitting or delaying,
>   but we must go to the richly ornamented temple
> of Itonia of the golden aegis
>   to display a graceful [*habron*] ‹song and dance›

As in the Alkaios fragment, the temple is singled out as the locus of ritual, but here we learn slightly more about the nature of what went on. Bacchylides conveys a sense of *habrosynē* associated with the ritual—a sense of elegance, refinement, and luxury: not only is the song and dance (a plausible restoration of the lacunose last line of the fragment) *habron*, "graceful," but the temple is richly ornamented, and Athena wears a golden aegis.[50] The hortative, "we must go," points to a ritual procession to the temple.[51] We would like very much to know who participated in the rituals at the Itonion, whether as part of the chorus or as audience, but for even a partial answer to this question we have to look to yet another fragmentary poem.

Pindar wrote several poems for performance in the Daphnephoria, a ritual procession in honor of Apollo Ismenios in his hometown of Thebes, and several more survive that probably belong to other rituals at the same sanctuary.[52] One of these (fragment 94b Maehler) was written for the Daphnephoria led by the Theban Agasikles son of Pagondas, almost certainly the same Pagondas who commanded the Thebans at Delion in 424.[53] This would give us a rough date for the composition and performance of the poem in the period circa 445–440, making it one of Pindar's latest compositions.[54] The singer's voice is female; she is perhaps the sister

---

49. The poems are identified as *hyporchēmata* on the papyrus; the genre appears to belong to songs the performance of which involved dance in a more prominent form than usual (Kowalzig 2007: 363).

50. On *habrosynē* see Kurke 1992.

51. Bacchylides' hints of a procession to Athena, perhaps from some distance, is sometimes taken to be confirmed by a black-figure Boiotian lekane in the British Museum (BM B80), which has long been associated with the cult at the Itonion (Ure 1929: 167–71) and predates Bacchylides by perhaps half a century, but it is difficult to see in it anything other than an imagination of a ritual. Cf. Schachter 1981–94: I.119; Scheffer 1992.

52. Poems for the Daphnephoria: Pind. frr. 94a–c. Other poems for performance at the Ismenion: Pind. *Pae.* 1, 9, and possibly 7.

53. Th. 4.91–93; the identification of the Pagondas of the poem with the general at Delion was first made by Grenfell and Hunt 1904: 51; cf. Lehnus 1984: 77–78. The familial relations of the individuals named in the poem goes back to Wilamowitz-Moellendorff 1922: 435–36. For recent discussion see Calame 1997: 60–62.

54. The *daphnēphoria* was led by a *pais amphithalēs*, a boy with both parents still living (Procl. *ap.* Phot. *Bibl.* 321b). Assigning absolute ages to Greek age classes is notoriously difficult, but we can assume the *pais* was a child, not a youth (*neos*). Pagondas must have been at least twenty or twenty-five at the

or a close female relative of Agasikles. I shall return to consider the song in its entirety below, when I address the cult at the Ismenion, but here I should like to focus on what it tells us about the Itonion. Picking up near the middle of the preserved portion of the song, we get a quick snapshot of the role of Agasikles' family in several prominent Boiotian cults in addition to that at the Theban Ismenion, and simultaneously of their social importance (Pind. *Parth.* 2 [fr. 94b] 36–49 Maehler):

> Neither for a man nor a woman, to whose children   36
> I am devoted, must I forget a fitting song.
> As a faithful witness for Agasikles
> I have come to the dance
> and for his noble parents   40
> for the sake of their *proxeniai.* For
> both of old and now they have been honored
> by those who live around them [ἀμφικτιόνεσσιν]
> for their celebrated victories   44
> with swift-footed horses,
> for which on the shores of famous Onchestos
> and b[y the glori]ous temple of Itonia
> they adorned their hair with garlands   48
> and at Pisa . . .

On the simplest level, we learn from Pindar's song that elite Thebans who participated actively in rituals at the Ismenion in Thebes were also involved in ritual games at Onchestos, the Itonion, and Olympia (Pisa). We can thus be certain that by the time this poem was performed, the cult of Athena Itonia and its festival drew participants from at least as far afield as Thebes. Again we note the theme of the "[glorious] temple." What is especially interesting in this passage is the phrase in lines 41–43. The translation given above takes ἀμφικτιόνεσσιν at its most literal, "by those who live around them."[55] This sentence is, however, an expansion of the earlier assertion that the noble parents of Agasikles have rendered services to their neighbors as proxenoi. Proxeny, one of the most widespread diplomatic institutions of the classical and Hellenistic periods, in which a proxenos (always a foreigner) is honored by a community and obligated to look after its interests in his

---

time of Agasikles' service, and it seems unlikely that a man over sixty would serve as a general. It is thus difficult to assume a gap of more than twenty years between the battle of Delion in 424 and the earlier performance of the poem. It may have been less. Pindar's latest securely dated composition, *Pythian* 8, belongs to or shortly after 446.

55. The spelling with iota, observed by Pindar, points to the etymology of the word from the verb κτίζω, "inhabit, found, build, establish." According to Androtion (*FGrHist* 324 F 58) the more common spelling with upsilon, ἀμφικτύονες, supplanted the earlier spelling. See Sánchez 2001: 32–33.

own city, is rarely attested before the fifth century. Pindar's use of the phrase here is thus among the earliest, and it is difficult to know just how formalized these proxeny relationships were. But the earliest appearance of the word, on a funerary stele erected at Kerkyra in the last quarter of the seventh century, makes it clear that proxeny was from the beginning a status bestowed by a community, not by an individual.[56] If it is correct that proxeny originated with the practice of bearing witness for foreigners, then we should see serving as a proxenos, or offering *proxeniai* to others, as an inherently political act.[57] The institution of proxeny may have developed as an extension of the prepolitical institution of *xenia*, ties of friendship between elites of different communities, in response to the development of the polis.[58] In fragment 94b (lines 42–43) Pindar relates the services of the house of Agasikles as proxenoi to their being "honored by those who live around them."[59] It seems plausible that this elite household could have served as witnesses, protectors, hosts, and promoters of the interests of neighboring communities in Thebes. But the *amphiktiones* here are not ordinary neighbors; they are people who live in the region and participate in the same cult. Pindar's use of the term in this sense is consistent throughout his corpus, with the exception of clear applications to the more specific Delphic Amphiktyony.[60] Here, then, we find Theban elites being honored by people from other, neighboring communities for their services as proxenoi in Thebes and for their victories at the cultic contests staged at Onchestos and the Itonion.[61] These lines invert the normal order in which victories are mentioned in epinician poetry: typically Pindar mentions first the high-status pan-Hellenic victories and only then the more parochial victories in local or regional cults.[62] This is to be explained in part by the Theban cultic context of the *daphnēphorikon* and in part by the logic of this particular poem: the family of Agasikles is honored not just for its prominence in Theban society but for its

---

56. ML 4 l. 3; Marek 1984: 387; M. B. Walbank 1978.

57. Gauthier 1972: 33–41; Marek 1984: 387.

58. Herman 1987: 130–42 *contra* Marek 1984: 387. The political implications of the institution are clear in both accounts.

59. Kurke 2007: 90.

60. E.g., Pind. *Isthm.* 4.7–8; *Nem.* 6.39; cf. Kowalzig 2007: 130 n. 4, 386 n. 139. Delphic Amphiktyony: Pind. *Pyth.* 4.65–68, 10.8. I do not, however, wish to posit the existence of a formal Itonian Amphiktyony along the lines of the Delphic. So too Kowalzig 2007: 385–86.

61. Hence I agree to a point with the formulation of Schachter 1997: 103, who argues with Wilamowitz and Farnell that *proxenia* is a technical term, to be taken literally, "for an honour granted by a community to a person who was not a member of that community, in recognition of the fact that the person honoured—the proxenos—had furthered the interests of the granting state in his own community, or in the expectation that he would do so." I wish to emphasize, as Schachter does not, the importance of cultic activities in the creation of a community beyond the one he mentions here (the polis), the constitution of a civic reality by cultic means.

62. Kurke 2007: 90.

involvement and distinction in Boiotian society more broadly, as construed here by their participation in the cult of Athena Itonia.

The foregoing evidence, however fragmentary, makes it clear that by the mid-fifth century the cult of Athena Itonia near Koroneia was of broad regional significance; the warrior goddess received an elaborate temple, celebrated repeatedly in cult song and apparently the focus of ritual activity, sometime in the sixth century. Unfortunately we do not know who paid for the construction of that temple; if the *amphiktiones* mentioned by Pindar were an old organization, they would be likely candidates, and it would be possible to see the cult as an integrating force for the region; but there is no way to know whether they were. Our first evidence for the aetiological myth of the cult, which associates it with the migration of the Boiotoi from Thessaly into the territory known in the historical period as Boiotia, belongs to the fifth century, and this may or may not be coincidental. Certainly the fragments of Alkaios, Bacchylides, and Pindar demonstrate that the Itonion functioned as a locus for the articulation of group identity and for its institutionalization—in other words, as a force of social cohesion. That it also served to explain that group's boundaries may be why it played a central role in the politicization of the group, which I shall address below. Whether the Itonion had a regional catchment area before the fifth century is uncertain, but it is clear that as more people from more Boiotian communities participated in the rituals for Athena Itonia, to put it in theoretical terms, this ritual action structured their social environment in such a way that this new social environment appeared to be the source of their actions. To put it another way, participation in the rituals at the Itonion conveyed a sense of social cohesion beyond polis boundaries that simultaneously seemed to explain why they all participated in the first place. The rituals at the Itonion had this cohesive, community-building force only because the people who participated in them were at the same time—over the course of the sixth and into the fifth century—interacting with one another constantly for economic exchange and cooperation and for military undertakings, as we saw in chapter 1; however, until 446 the state apparatus by which those interactions were governed was minimal, if it existed at all. That such a recursive relationship between ritual action and social structure should be advantageous in the politicization of that sense of social cohesion would not be at all surprising. I shall turn in the next section to exploring how that worked.

Poseidon at Onchestos.   In his fragmentary *daphnēphorikon*, Pindar mentions Onchestos in the same breath as the "glorious temple of Itonia." Here the family of Agasikles won some of its "celebrated victories with swift-footed horses."[63] The sanctuary of Poseidon at Onchestos, situated to the southeast of Lake Kopaïs, was

_____

63. Pind. *Parth.* 2.44–46.

both an official meeting place and a repository of decrees of the Boiotian koinon in the Hellenistic period. It was probably for this reason that Strabo remarked, in the first century, that "Onchestos is where the amphiktyonic council used to meet."[64] Our earliest evidence for the cult is a passing mention by Homer, and then a much longer account in the *Homeric Hymn to Apollo*. The sanctuary is certainly quite ancient, then, and it has been supposed that cult activity on the site goes back to the Mycenaean period. While certainly not impossible, it is important to make a clear distinction between claims about hoary antiquity made in the classical period (which must always be understood in their historical context, so that the motivations for making them can be assessed) and clear archaeological or historical evidence for the antiquity of the cult and its catchment area.[65] How and why did it become a principal religious center of the Boiotian koinon in the Hellenistic period?

The *Homeric Hymn to* [Pythian] *Apollo*, usually dated about 585, narrates Apollo's journey across the Mediterranean in search of a place to found his own sanctuary.[66] In the hymn, the god moves from the Lelantine plain on Euboia, across the straits at Chalkis, to Boiotian Mykalessos, and then Teumessos. Thence he arrives at a still uninhabited Thebes and Onchestos, "the splendid grove of Poseidon" (l. 230), the site of elaborate rituals for the god associated with horse training.[67] It was also, the same hymn shows, the site of more general hippic contests. After leaving Onchestos, Apollo stops at the sacred spring belonging to the nymph Telphousa, west of Onchestos and rather near the temple of Athena Itonia, and finds the spot amenable for his temple and oracle. But as he lays the foundations for it, Telphousa warns him away: "The din of swift horses and mules drinking at my sacred springs will always be bothersome to you, and some men will prefer to look at the well-made chariots and the din of swift-footed horses than at your great temple and the many treasures within."[68] Apollo follows Telphousa's advice to build "below the folds of Parnassos" (l. 269) at Delphi, a place as ill suited to equestrian traffic as any. In the sacred context of the hymn and the activities of Telphousa and Apollo that it narrates, this hippic activity must have been overwhelmingly ritual, and it is tempting to suggest that the contests alluded to here are precisely those in which the family of Agasikles accomplished the "celebrated victories with swift-footed horses" for which they were "honored by the *amphiktiones*."

64. Str. 9.2.33.
65. Mafodda 2000: 22 is likewise cautious about retrojecting Strabo's claim as evidence for the archaic period, but he offers no further analysis.
66. For the date Janko 1982: 116–32.
67. *Hymn.Hom.Ap.* 225–30. Precisely the phrase used to describe the sanctuary in Hom. *Il.* 2.506. Horse-training rituals: Schachter 1976; cf. Schachter 1981–94: II.219; Teffeteller 2001.
68. *Hymn.Hom.Ap.* 262–66.

Our earliest archaeological evidence for the sanctuary at Onchestos again comes from the late sixth century, when a temple was built on the site.[69] Prior to this, it must have been an open-air sanctuary, which accords with the frequent description of the place, by Homer and the authors of the *Homeric Hymns*, as a "splendid sacred grove."[70] However little we know about this building, its very existence is evidence for an organized and relatively well-funded cult, which is all the more striking if Pindar's amphiktyonic language has not misled us. For Onchestos was never the site of settlement, nor did it ever belong exclusively to one polis, although it later probably fell within the territory of Haliartos. Two dedicatory inscriptions were also found on the site of the temple. One, dating to the late sixth or early fifth century, is a simple dedication to Poseidon, inscribed on a roughly worked limestone block at the top of which is a cutting for a votive object.[71] The second, a limestone stele from the late fifth or early fourth century with a cutting in the top for a votive object, also carries a dedication to Poseidon; it is additionally dated by the priesthood of one Pouthinas, whose identity is entirely uncertain.[72] The mere existence of such an official points to an organization imposed either by the state—which in this period would necessarily have been the koinon itself (since Onchestos was never under the control of a single polis)—or by a formalized amphiktyony. It is entirely likely that the two overlap in significant ways.

From Pindar again it is clear that there was broad Theban participation in the cult of Poseidon at Onchestos in the early fifth century. In two *Isthmian Odes*, both written for Theban athletes, Pindar implies that the victories won at Poseidon's Isthmian Games were due at least partly to the favor of Poseidon at Onchestos. The first is *Isthmian* 1, in honor of Herodotos of Thebes, winner of the chariot race; here the poet mentions Isthmia and Onchestos in the same breath as important cult places of the god, and later he describes Poseidon—surely at Onchestos—as the neighbor of the Thebans and patron of chariot racing.[73] In *Isthmian* 4, the Kleonymidai, the family of the Theban victor Melissos, "are said to have been honored at Thebes from the

69. Touloupa 1964: 200–201; *AD*22 (1967) *Chron.* 242; Spyropoulos 1973: 379–81; *Teiresias* 3 (1973): 4; *AR* 20 (1973–74): 20; Michaud 1974a: 644–45. Roesch 1982: 272. A boundary stone inscribed Βιασσθενῆο | Ποτιδάονος (*ed.pr.* Lauffer 1980: 162 no. 2; *SEG* 30.442) found in the village of Agios Demetrios is probably to be associated with this sanctuary. Habicht 1998: 36 accepts Spyropoulos's assertion that the bouleuterion also belongs to the sixth century, but there is no evidence for it, and indeed the inscription found in the structure identified as such (*SEG* 27.60) belongs to the period after 338.
70. Cf. *Hymn.Hom.Merc.* 186–87. The brief references in this poem convey a sense of rusticity and sparse habitation, which contrasts sharply with the loud and busy scene depicted in *Hymn.Hom.Ap.* 229–38.
71. *Ed.pr.* Spyropoulos 1973: 381 with photo (*AD* 28 B' 1 *Chron.* [1973] 270; Michaud 1974a: 644; Roesch, *Teiresias Epigraphica*, 1976: 10 no. 25; *SEG* 27.61): Ποτειδάονι Μ[..]ον ἀνέθεκε, "M[..]on dedicated it to Poseidon."
72. *SEG* 27.62. On the priesthood see Schachter 1981–94: II.216 n. 5, 218.
73. Pind. *Isthm.* 1.32–34, 52–54. Kurke 1988: 112 suggests that the poet's connection of these cult places is meant "to evoke the victor's own prayer of thanksgiving on his return."

beginning as *proxenoi* of the *amphiktiones*," a claim highly reminiscent of that made about the family of Agasikles in the *daphnēphorikon* considered above.[74] Melissos's victory at Poseidon's Isthmian Games, Pindar later implies, was granted by Poseidon at both Onchestos and Isthmia; the pan-Hellenic cult is here explicitly tied to the epichoric.[75] Again here, as in the *daphnēphorikon* for Agasikles, we see an elite Theban family acting as *proxenoi*—hosts, protectors, witnesses—of the neighboring communities. And here again the group of *amphiktiones* is defined by common participation in the cult of Poseidon at Onchestos. The reference to *amphiktiones* reminds us, too, that although the sanctuary continues to crop up in Theban contexts, it did not belong to Thebes; it was a common cult, and Poseidon at Onchestos was a neighbor of the Thebans. We would like to know in more concrete detail which other communities participated in the rituals and festivals at Onchestos, but here our sources are silent.

Geography can provide us with some plausible indications. Onchestos is situated on a slight rise along what is otherwise a natural thoroughfare, from the Euboian Gulf, around the southern shore of Lake Kopaïs, to the western border of Boiotia (and indeed beyond, well into Phokis). This route certainly brought northwestern Boiotia into communication with the central and eastern parts of the region, and we should perhaps not be surprised that two of the major sanctuaries situated on it, Onchestos and the Itonion near Koroneia, were frequented by *amphiktiones*, people from multiple communities who partook in common rituals. According to a myth with traces in the fifth century, the Thebans and the Minyans of Orchomenos both participated in the festival and rituals for Poseidon at Onchestos in the heroic, pre–Trojan War period.[76] At this festival, Pausanias reports, a few Theban men who had been angered by a minor affront killed Klymenos, the reigning king of Orchomenos. His eldest son, Erginos, who succeeded to the throne, led a successful attack on Thebes in retaliation for the murder of his father. In their defeat the Thebans were forced to pay tribute to the Minyans, until Herakles released them from the obligation by a successful attack on Orchomenos.[77]

---

74. Pind. *Isthm.* 4.7–8.

75. Pind. *Isthm.* 4.19–20.

76. This myth has to be taken as historical fact if Tausend's argument (1992: 27) for cultic and institutional continuity from the "Ionian" through the historical period is to be supported, as does the etymology of the cult of Poseidon Helikonios in Achaia as coming not from Achaian Helike but from Boiotian Helikon and, implicitly, from Onchestos (Aristarchos *ap.* Σ B Hom. *Il.* 5.422, *Etym. Magn.* 547.15–19 s.v. Κύπρις). Schachter 1981–94: II.214 rightly notes that this etymology "is not based on any evidence, but rather on purely morphological grounds." Cf. Veneri 1990; Katsonopoulou 1998; Mylonopoulos 2003: 381. Fifth-century traces of the myth: Pherekydes *FGrHist* 3 F 95; Eur. *HF* 47–50, 220.

77. Paus. 9.37.1–2; cf. Ps.-Apoll. *Bibl.* 2.4.11. Cf. Str. 9.2.29 for a slightly earlier version according to which the Theban seizure of Orchomenos is associated with the invasion of the Boiotoi from Thessaly. The Theban revolt from Orchomenos under Herakles' leadership was commemorated with a statue of Herakles *Rhinokoloustēs*, the Nose Clipper, at Thebes: Paus. 9.17.1–2, 25.4.

This myth can only be read as a way of making sense of the past, of the (correctly) remembered shared use of the sanctuary of Poseidon at Onchestos, of Theban supremacy, and of Orchomenos's resistance to it (which appears in the historical record in Orchomenos's delayed participation in the common monetary system of Boiotia and in the Orchomenians' support of Sparta against Thebes in the 370s and 360s). As we saw in chapter 1, several dedications at Olympia commemorating victories in wars between Boiotian cities reflect hostile conditions in the mid-sixth century, and the mythic war between Thebes and Orchomenos seems to be an attempt "to construe a 'memory' of the Thebans having taken control of the shrine from Orkhomenos at some point in the mythical past."[78]

The sanctuary of Poseidon at Onchestos, situated on the most widely and easily traveled east–west route through Boiotia, became a cult place of importance to several Boiotian communities, including Thebes, by the late sixth century, when it first received a temple and when archaeological evidence for dedications first appears. The shared interest in a cult and the logistical demands of building a temple on sacred ground not belonging to a single polis certainly acted as cohesive forces on the poleis of Boiotia in the late archaic and early classical periods. Whether the aetiological myth recorded in late sources actually dates from this period or not, Pindar makes it clear that the people who participated in the cult regarded themselves as a group. For this reason the rituals at Onchestos helped to build a broader Boiotian community. It may have been only within that community-building framework that the myth associating the sanctuary with Theban subordination of Orchomenos was promulgated, as a strategic deployment of symbols that caused Theban claims to political hegemony in the region (made first in the sixth century and more forcefully in the fifth) appear, to those who participated in the cult, to stem naturally from its mythic position. The existence of a priesthood in the late fifth or early fourth century points to cultic institutions that must have formalized these shared interests and reinforced the structures—whether a formal amphiktyony or the Boiotian koinon as a whole—built around them. This picture of gradual coalescence around a shared cult, which is integrated into civic, interpolis relations like proxeny as they develop and later into the institutions of the koinon itself, seems to follow a pattern similar to that we detected at the Itonion.

Apollo Ismenios, Thebes, and Boiotia.   The cult of Apollo Ismenios at Thebes was also associated with the occupation of the territory by the Boiotoi, and the ritual action associated with it contributed to the construction of a Boiotian community beyond the boundaries of the individual polis in which it resided, though it did so in a more hegemonic tone than anything we have seen at the Itonion or Onchestos.

<hr>

78. Kowalzig 2007: 366–67.

The cult of Apollo Ismenios was characterized by an oracle, the annual ritual of the Daphnephoria (the Carrying of the Laurel), and the practice of dedicating tripods. I shall concentrate my remarks on the Daphnephoria and the tripod dedications, for these are the two aspects of the cult that were bound up with community building in Boiotia. I shall discuss them in that order, because the political exploitation of the practice of dedicating tripods may be explained in part by the broader meaning of the cult revealed in the ritual of the Daphnephoria and the meanings attached to it by the Boiotians.

The sanctuary of Apollo Ismenios was situated on a low hill southeast of the Theban Kadmeia, near the river Ismenos, and appears to have been the site of continuous cultic activity from the geometric period, when the first temple was built on the site.[79] A second temple was built in the seventh or sixth century, with which the cedar cult statue crafted by Kanachos of Sikyon is probably to be associated.[80] A third was begun in the early fourth century but never completed, perhaps because of the destruction of Thebes; to this period belong the statues of Athena and Hermes Pronaoi by Skopas and Pheidias, which adorned the entrance to the sanctuary.[81] The archaeological record thus fits the pattern observed elsewhere in Boiotia of significant investment in sanctuaries in the late sixth century, when Boiotian cooperation first became widespread, and may be associated with a rise in prosperity, and again in the fourth century in the wake of the great military and political achievements of the 370s and 360s.

The Daphnephoria, the central ritual associated with the cult of Apollo Ismenios, was a sacred procession in which a boy chosen from the Theban elite to serve as priest of Apollo for one year bore laurel to the shrine of Apollo Ismenios, accompanied by a chorus of young girls.[82] This boy is described as a *pais amphithalēs*, a boy whose mother and father are both still alive.[83] Apollo Ismenios was closely bound up with the civic well-being of Thebes. The Daphnephoria itself, and the choruses sung to accompany it, ritualized the prevalence of civic virtues like justice and moderation, negotiating a place for elite competition within an emergent Theban state power and for Thebes in an emergent Boiotian state power.[84]

Further details of the Daphnephoria are preserved in the late account of Proklos, which despite some obvious late accretions has enough parallels to the hints we

79. Symeonoglou 1985: 132–33.
80. Paus. 9.10.2.
81. Keramopoullos 1917 for the sequence of structures. More recent excavations: *AD* 22 (1967 [1968]) *Chron.* B1: 232–33 and *AR* (1968/69) 18.
82. Paus. 9.10.4 and Procl. *ap.* Phot. *Bibl.* 321b, with Pind. fr. 94b (Maehler).
83. Procl. *ap.* Phot. *Bibl.* 321b; the phrase is first used with this meaning in Hom. *Il.* 22.496. Note that Pind. fr. 94b.36–45 (Maehler) emphasizes both the father and the mother of the *daphnēphoros*.
84. Pind. fr. 94b.61–65 (Maehler); cf. *Pae.* 1.5–10. Kurke 2007: 93–95 for a perceptive demonstration of the civic importance of the ritual.

find in Pindar to instill a certain guarded optimism about its utility as an historical source. According to Proklos, the Daphnephoria commemorated a truce reached between the Boiotoi who invaded the territory from Arne and the Pelasgians who had inhabited it before them. "Because there was a festival of Apollo in common to both groups, they made truces," and one group cut laurel branches for Apollo on Mount Helikon while the other took them from the nearby river Melas, in the territory of Orchomenos.[85] The truce, however, was ephemeral: the leader of the Boiotoi had a dream in which he saw a young man give him a panoply and order that *daphnēphoroi* pray to Apollo every nine years. Three days later, he attacked Thebes and overcame the Pelasgian enemy; in commemoration of their victorious seizure of Thebes, the Boiotoi instituted the ritual of the Daphnephoria.[86] This aition corresponds to those for the cults of Athena Itonia at Koroneia and of Poseidon at Onchestos, but whereas those emphasize the participation of (theoretically) the entire population of Boiotia in centrally located cults, the Daphnephoria brings the Boiotoi to Thebes to worship a god closely associated with civic order within the city in a ritual that conveys an inequality between Thebes and another Boiotian city that we have not seen before. The difference is to be explained at least in part by the fact that the Ismenion was a Theban cult, whereas the others were less closely related (if at all, in the case of Onchestos) to a single polis.

Proklos goes on to describe details of the ritual action that shed more light on the way in which ritual was used to unite the Boiotian communities under Theban leadership. The *pais amphithalēs* who, according to Pausanias, serves as priest of Apollo for the year, leads a procession that probably originated at his family's house.[87] He is followed in the procession by his closest male relative, who carries the so-called *kōpō*, an elaborately decorated log of olive wood wrapped in laurel, and behind this man follows the *daphnēphoros*, who holds the laurel.[88] These they convey to the sanctuary of Apollo Ismenios just outside the city walls and thence to another shrine, the location of which is uncertain.[89] It is striking that although

85. Procl. *ap.* Phot. *Bibl.* 321b. River Melas: Paus. 9.38.6; Plut. *Pelop.* 16.4. Cf. Str. 9.2.41; Σ Nic. *Ther.* 686a1.

86. Procl. *ap.* Phot. *Bibl.* 321b. The detail that the *daphnēphoroi* should pray every nine years suggests that by the time Proklos's source was writing the festival had become enneateric.

87. Kurke 2007: 98–99.

88. Proklos lavishes great detail on his description of the ornamentation of the *kōpō*, much of which reveals a post-Julian calendrical system and is thus a late superimposition: Nilsson 1906: 165, followed by Wilamowitz-Moellendorff 1922: 433 with n. 1 and Schachter 1981–94: I.84 n. 2. On the meaning of the *kōpō*, which does not concern me here, see Nilsson 1906: 164–65; Severyns 1938: II.218–19; Schachter 1997: 109–10.

89. The two manuscript traditions of Proklos preserve variant names: Chalazios or Galaxios. Schachter 1997: 110 explores the possibilities and suggests, rather tentatively, that the Galaxion was situated "near the western limit of Theban territory."

the aition for the cult offered by Proklos stresses the different locations from which the laurel was culled in the initial ritual event that sealed the truce between the Boiotoi and the Pelasgians, his description of the ritual reenactment of that event does not specify the source of the laurel borne in the procession. However, sacred processions involving the conveyance of branches culled from particular places appear to have been a feature of another cult in southern Boiotia. The name for the log, *kōpō*, is clearly related to Lake Kopaïs, and it plays an important role in the Daidala of Plataia, a festival that involved the creation of a unifying, dynamic sacred space from Alalkomenai, in the vicinity of Koroneia, all the way to Plataia.[90] The aetiological myth offered by Proklos for the Daphnephoria suggests that the Thebans believed the Ismenion and its ritual to have been used as a common cult to celebrate and solidify the Boiotian victory over the Pelasgians and their control over the territory between Phokis and the Parasopia. This territory is tolerably well defined by the locations from which the laurel was originally culled: the river Melas in the northwest and Mount Helikon in the southeast. The procession itself, however, demarcated the territory not of Boiotia but of Thebes.[91] The territorial aspect of the Daphnephoria is further reflected in the dedication of a tripod to Apollo Ismenios by the *daphnēphoros* to commemorate his service.[92] A symbol of his own prestige as an individual member of the Theban elite, the tripod also functioned, as has recently been shown, as a symbol of territorial control.[93]

Apollo Ismenios was regarded as the source of civic order at Thebes, because he was remembered as presiding over the Boiotian conquest of the region, including Thebes, and the truce achieved with the city's former inhabitants who were driven out to the Orchomenos region.[94] This myth postulates a distinction between the

90. Later it incorporated all Boiotia, as we shall see below.

91. Although the location of the Galaxion is uncertain (see above, n. 89), there is no reason to think that it lay outside the territory of Thebes.

92. Hdt. 5.59–61 describes tripods he saw in the Ismenion supposedly dedicated by heroic figures; these are frequently dismissed as forgeries but should probably be seen rather as attributions to the heroic past of ritual practices current by the fifth century: Papalexandrou 2008: 256–57. Paus. 9.10.4 records that in his day some *daphnēphoroi* dedicated tripods in commemoration of their service. It is no coincidence that Pindar describes the Ismenion as a treasury of golden tripods (Pind. *Pyth.* 11.4–5), though he does not say by what ritual they were dedicated. The Ismenion has only just begun to be excavated, and lack of archaeological evidence occludes our view of whether this is a late ritual accretion (so Schachter 1997: 110, 114), but the prevalence of tripod dedication in Boiotia, systematically studied by Papalexandrou 2008, and the fourth-century report that a group called the Thebageneis dedicated tripods to Apollo Ismenios (Ephoros *FGrHist* 70 F 21) suggest that the practice of dedicating tripods here may in fact be early.

93. Papalexandrou 2005: 37–42 and 2008: 267–68.

94. The aetiological myth for the Daphnephoria recorded by Proklos may be associated with the legends holding that Orchomenos was the only city in Boiotia not founded by the Boiotoi who invaded from Thessaly but rather was founded by Minyans, a myth complex itself probably developed to explain the serious rivalry between Thebes and Orchomenos in the historical period.

Boiotians who occupied Thebes and the surrounding territory on the one hand and the people of Orchomenos on the other, known as Minyans rather than Boiotoi and among the most resistant of the Boiotian cities to the project of unification (whether under the institutional umbrella of a koinon or in the moves toward integration signaled by economic and military cooperation in the late sixth century).⁹⁵ If the *kōpō* appears to be a strange accretion in the ritual of the Daphnephoria, that may be because it was added to a more straightforward, Delphic-influenced ritual in which laurel was carried to Apollo, in order to convey a sense of greater cohesion between Thebes and the territory west and south of it, where the procession of an adorned log was a feature of local ritual.⁹⁶ A structural similarity has been noted between the Apollo and hero cults at Thebes, Lebadeia, Tegyra, Perdikovrysi, and Kastraki, but this may be an indication not so much of common ancestry as of an intentional interweaving of communities through cultic means, a demonstration of Boiotia's unity seen in its ritual uniformity.⁹⁷

Apollo Ptoieus and the Boiotians.   One final cult appears to have played an important role in the construction of a Boiotian community, but here agency is extraordinarily difficult to detect. The sanctuary of Apollo Ptoieus, at modern Perdikovrysi, stands on the southern slope of Mount Ptoion, which runs like a high corridor between Akraiphia and Anthedon. From this hillside perch, Apollo looked out over the Teneric plain, which stretches south to Thebes itself over a distance of about twenty-three kilometers. The plain takes its name from Teneros, the son of Apollo and Melia who, Pindar claims, was the original prophet at both the Theban Ismenion and the Ptoion.⁹⁸ This prophetic link is not the only one between the two sanctuaries, as the archaeological evidence shows.

The Ptoion was systematically excavated by a series of teams from the late nineteenth to the mid-twentieth century.⁹⁹ As a result, the votive record is exceptionally full and reveals the complex role of the cult in Boiotia and in central Greece

95. Minyans: Hom. *Il.* 2.511–16; Th. 4.76.3; cf. Isocr. 14.10; Diod. Sic. 15.79.5. Cf. Kühr 2006a: 274–84; Larson 2007: 28.

96. Kurke 2007: 81 with n. 26.

97. On structural similarity see Schachter 1967 and 1981–94: I.78–79, who takes it to be a sign of common descent. I find the argument for similarity less compelling for Telphousa and Thourion than for the others.

98. Teneros as prophet at the Ismenion: Pind. *Pae.* 9.38–46, a paean for the Thebans to the Ismenion, usually dated to 463 by the reference to a solar eclipse in the opening lines of the poem; cf. Paus. 9.10.5–6. At the Ptoion: Str. 9.2.34, quoting Pind. frr. 51b, d (Race). The epithet of the god worshipped at the Ptoion appears in early sources as *Ptōieus,* but after the mid-fifth century as *Ptōios* (Schachter 1981–94: I.55–56). In order to avoid confusion with the hero Ptoios, worshipped at Akraiphia, I employ the earlier form of the epithet throughout, with the exception of the Hellenistic dedications to Apollo Ptoios treated in the appendix (T16–T21).

99. For a summary of excavations see Ducat 1971: 7–40.

more broadly, from its foundation in the late eighth century through the Hellenistic period.[100] In the archaic period Apollo Ptoieus received dedications of high artistic quality from worshippers throughout the Mediterranean. The kouroi dedicated in the sixth century alone point to participants in the cult not only from Boiotia but also from Attica, the southern Kyklades, Ionia, Paros, Naxos, Corinth, Argos, and Sparta.[101] The votive material from the early period of the sanctuary is frequently inscribed, but rarely is the origin of the dedicand recorded. This begins to occur only in the third quarter of the sixth century, showing us that Thebans as well as Akraiphians were making dedications at this sanctuary, but the Thebans were apparently employing Akraiphian sculptors or stonecutters to create the votives.[102] Unfortunately the mass of other inscribed dedications remains silent on the origins of its dedicators, so it is difficult to reconstruct with any detail the catchment area of the sanctuary, but its openness to the world beyond Boiotia (evidenced in the variety of local sculptural styles and materials found in the archaeological record) makes it extremely likely that it was open to, and frequented by, other Boiotians as well. Although the small finds from the sanctuary have never been published, several of the larger sculpted and inscribed votives are paralleled in other Boiotian sanctuaries, suggesting that votive practices were similar and may have been undertaken by similar groups.[103] Inscribed columns, serving as tripod supports, are closely comparable to those found in several other Boiotian sanctuaries, including Thebes and the Akraiphian hero shrine of Ptoios at Kastraki.[104] The numerous kouroi that have made the sanctuary famous were dedicated in other parts of Boiotia as well.[105] It thus appears that the sanctuary of Apollo Ptoieus received dedications similar to those made in other parts of

100. See above, p. 23 n. 7, for discussion (and rejection) of Guillon's theory that the sanctuary at Perdikovrysi was originally a hero sanctuary for Ptoios, who was expelled by the Thebans and supplanted with Apollo himself. The evidence suggests that Apollo was the recipient of the cult from the beginning. The earliest epigraphic evidence, which secures the cult as one of Apollo Ptoieus, belongs to the period ca. 640–620: Ducat 1971: 90 no. 50b; and *IG* VII.2729 (Ducat 1971: 77–83, no. 46 with photo, pl. XVIII).

101. Ducat 1971: part 3, 211–369.

102. Theban dedications: Ducat 1971: 379–84 nos. 232–35 with photos, pll. CXXVIII, CXXIX; Akraiphian dedications: Ducat 1971: 411 no. 260 with photo, pl. 142.

103. The material is in the Thebes Museum; a new catalogue contains photographs of many of these objects: Aravantinos 2010: 160–65.

104. Compare Ducat 1971: 391 no. 241 with photo, pl. 132 (sanctuary of Apollo Ptoieus, Perdikovrysi) with the kioniskos found northwest of Thebes (Aravantinos 2006 and below, T2). Photos of both in Aravantinos 2010: 148, 229. On tripod supports and the Boiotian practice of tripod dedication see Papalexandrou 2008.

105. For the Ptoion kouroi see Ducat 1971. Kouroi found elsewhere in Boiotia: Orchomenos, Richter 1960: nos. 33 (ca. 590–570), 99 (ca. 555–540); Tanagra, Richter 1960: no. 11 (ca. 615–590), C. Blümel 1940: A3; (ca. 590–570); Eutresis, Richter 1960: 156 (ca. 520–485).

Boiotia, alongside the frequent participation of outsiders in the activities of this oracular shrine in the sixth century. It was thus one of many sanctuaries that served as a locus of interactions between Boiotians of different communities. We shall see that in the late sixth and early fifth centuries the Ptoion became an important mechanism for the establishment a regional Boiotian state, for the politicization of Boiotian interactions, and was integrated fully and irreversibly into the region by heroic genealogies that sought to articulate Boiotian unity in terms that may not have been immediately recognizable or entirely uncontested in an exclusively and narrowly political discourse. As that process occurred, non-Boiotian interest in the sanctuary appears to have waned.

Plentiful and varied sources thus allow us to construct in considerable detail a picture of frequent interaction among the various Boiotian communities (with Thebes being invariably involved) at several sanctuaries throughout the region. In Boiotia several of the most regionally salient cults were those whose deities were associated with the occupation of the territory at the end of a period of migration, and participation in the rituals associated with these cults must have fostered a powerful sense of belonging, of group identity, among those who attended. The construction of a broad regional community can also be seen in the structural similarities noted in several Apollo cults in the region, most notably the Ismenion at Thebes, the Ptoion outside Akraiphia, and to a lesser extent the sanctuary of Apollo at Tegyra; but from the evidence available to us it is difficult to tell whether these similarities are the product of active creation or of a common catchment area for the cults. For no other region is the texture of our documentation comparable to that in Boiotia, but there are nonetheless important indications of some similar patterns.

Achaia

As we saw in chapter 1, the region known in the historical period as Achaia was unified only gradually, probably beginning to gain political salience in the fifth century, roughly coincident with the process of urbanization, as emerging archaeological evidence at Trapezá, Aigeira, and Patrai suggests.[106] If we are right to suggest that religious action played a central role in the construction of communities and their politicization generally, we may reasonably ask whether it did so in Achaia. Here the literary evidence, which contributed so much to the picture for Boiotia, is almost entirely absent for the sixth century and begins to pick up only in the late fifth. Later sources have been suggestive but must be handled with care. Archaeological evidence in Achaia is uneven but increasingly rich and vitally important for balancing the scarce and problematic literary sources.

---

106. Trapezá: Vordos 2001, 2002. Aigeira: Bammer 1996, 2002. Patrai: Petropoulos and Rizakis 1994. See above, chap. 1, for further discussion and references.

In 1972, during the construction of a road through a narrow upland valley (1,150 meters in altitude) on Mount Panachaïkon, the foundations of a remarkable building were exposed at Ano Mazaraki (sometimes called Rakita), an area that had previously shown no clear signs of occupation or use in antiquity (map 3). Excavation of the site has revealed a peripteral, apsidal temple built in the late eighth or early seventh century.[107] An inscription on a bronze mirror dedicated around 475 identifies the temple and its cult as belonging to Artemis Aontia.[108] The votive assemblage, as yet published in only a preliminary fashion, suggests that the sanctuary was in continuous use from its foundation until the early fourth century, when it was destroyed, probably by the same earthquake that destroyed Helike and Boura and leveled the temple of Apollo in Delphi in 373.[109] Although apparently on a much smaller scale, some cult activity appears to have continued at the site into the late Roman period, though at present there is no evidence for reconstruction of the temple.[110] Among the votive material, excavators discovered three small granary models, produced in the material and style of the distinctive Achaian impressed ware of the late geometric period, suggesting that the sanctuary belonged to a community heavily invested in agriculture.[111] Iron and bronze weapons of the late geometric period are also present, and these along with a bronze model tripod raise the question whether Apollo may indeed have been worshipped here alongside his sister.[112] Large quantities of terracotta fragments, belonging mostly to open-shaped vessels, and fragments of burned animal bones suggest that dining may have been a principal component of the cult here, but beyond this it is impossible to specify the nature of rituals that took place.[113]

The sanctuary is at a significant distance from any known Achaian and Arkadian communities of the late geometric, archaic, and classical periods, during all of which it was in regular use. What, then, was its catchment area? Our only clues are in topography and the votive assemblage. The Valley of Rakita stands

107. Mazarakis Ainian 1997a: 72–73.

108. Touchais, *BCH* 122 (1998): 790; Petropoulos 2001: 43–45 with fig. 3 and 2002: 154–55 with fig. 13 and pl. 4 (*SEG* 48.560, 52.489, 53.442). The identification with Artemis was postulated before discovery of the inscribed mirror on the basis of the small finds, particularly beads and fibulae: Petropoulos 1987–88; cf. Osanna 1996: 211–12, basing the attribution on the liminal location of the sanctuary, appropriate for Artemis.

109. Destruction: Petropoulos 1992–93: 154.

110. Petropoulos 2002: 155.

111. Granary models: Petropoulos 1987–88: 88–91 with pl. IA′ 9; Petropoulos 2002: pl. 3.4. The Achaian impressed ware is presented systematically by Gadolou 2003.

112. Weapons: Gadolou 1996–97. Model tripod: Petropoulos 2002: 150 with pl. 3.3. Indeed before discovery of the dedicatory inscription, Petropoulos 1992–93: 156 postulated a combined cult of Artemis and Apollo. The possibility should be left open.

113. Pottery: Gadolou 2002; cf. Gadolou 2000: 156. Bones: Petropoulos 1992–93: 156.

above the eastern tributary branch of the Meganeitas River, which runs down to meet the coast of the Corinthian Gulf just west of Aigion. Not far to the east of the sanctuary is the Selinous River, which runs to meet the coast between Aigion and Helike. To the southeast, Ano Mazaraki is easily accessed through the irregularly shaped valley created by Mount Panachaïkon to the northwest, Klokos to the northeast, and Erymanthos to the south (map 3). From the eastern end of this same valley the sanctuary of Artemis Hemera at Arkadian Lousoi is easily accessible. Michael Petropoulos reports the discovery of traces of an ancient road along the eastern bank of the Meganeitas River in the direction of Aigion and postulates that it extended to the southeast as well, connecting the sanctuary at Ano Mazaraki with Lousoi.[114] The same catchment area—Aigion to Lousoi—is indicated by the pottery and other small finds. The fine and quite distinctive local impressed ware of the late geometric period has also been found at Aigion, the site of Trapezá (probably to be identified with ancient Rhypes), and Lousoi, along with an isolated piece at Delphi. The ceramic evidence also suggests connections with Katarrhaktis (just southeast of Patrai) and Patrai as well as northeastern Achaia.[115] The association of Ano Mazaraki with Aigion is further underscored by the discovery of scarabs in both places, and it is likely that they came through the port at Aigion and were carried thence up to the sanctuary of Artemis on Mount Panachaïkon.[116] They are the only examples thus far known in Achaia.

The material evidence thus suggests that the sanctuary at Ano Mazaraki drew its worshippers from western and central Achaia as well as from Azania, the region around Lousoi, which was associated in historical times with northern Arkadia but appears to have been of importance to the Achaians throughout the archaic period. Indeed the boundary between Arkadia and Achaia appears not to have been salient in either cultural or political terms before the early fifth century.[117]

114. Petropoulos 2002: 157 with map, fig. 14, tracing postulated road.

115. Gadolou 2002; cf. Petropoulos 1987–88: 86–87 with pl. I´ 6–7. On the grounds of topography rather than ceramics, Vordos 2002: 226 suggests that the sanctuary at Ano Mazaraki may have belonged to Rhypes rather than Aigion.

116. Papapostolou 1982; Petropoulos 1987–88: 94 with pl. IΔ´ 24; Petropoulos 2002: 148 with pl. 1.2, 3. Cf. Morgan and Hall 1996: 179.

117. The clearest sign that the border became more significant in this period comes from *IG* V.2.410 (Jeffery 1990: 222–23; Thür and Taeuber 1994: no. 21; van Effenterre and Ruzé 1994: no. 57), a fragmentary bronze plaque preserving only a clause specifying a fine (100 drachmas) payable to a deity whose name begins with *E*- and another clause that makes reference to a polis. Nielsen and Roy 1998: 25–39; Morgan 2000a: 419–20 and 2003: 184–86. Yet the hardening of the political border by no means precluded the pursuit of old patterns of cultic interaction: note *IG* V.2.392, in which the polis of Lousoi makes a citizen of (Achaian) Pharai their proxenos and *thearodokos* in the late fourth or early third century, and *IG* V.1.1387 (Rizakis 1995: 382–83 no. 712), a victory list from Aigion attesting the participation of its citizens in the Hemerasia in the third century, with *BE* 55.115.

Small finds as well as topography suggest that the sanctuaries of Artemis at Ano Mazaraki and at Lousoi were frequented by the same group of people. This group, however, was made up of people who either inhabited several distinct communities at significant distances from one another, or were remarkably mobile, or both. I deem the last possibility most likely, for both sanctuaries are situated at natural crossroads, particularly for pastoralists, and it is in this connection no surprise to learn from Polybios that cattle were at least on occasion herded into Artemis's sanctuary at Lousoi with the hope of protecting them from plundering invaders.[118] Bacchylides' claim that from Lousoi Artemis Hemera "followed the Achaians dear to Ares to the horse-nourishing polis" of Metapontion suggests that the goddess was of broad significance to Achaians during the seventh century, when they established their settlements in southern Italy, and continued to be in the fifth century, when the ode was written.[119] The apparent connection of the sanctuaries at Ano Mazaraki and Lousoi, formed by the interactions of similar (if not necessarily identical) worshipping groups, points to the probability that both cults acted as vital mechanisms in the construction of an Achaian community in the late geometric and archaic periods.[120]

By the early fifth century, a sense of Achaian group identity was robust enough to be employed in the dedication of a monumental statue group to Zeus at Olympia. Pausanias describes in detail a dedication made "by the *ethnos* of the Achaians in common."[121] A group of bronze statues made by Onatas of Aigina depicted the nine Homeric Achaian heroes drawing lots for the duel with Hektor from a helmet held in his outstretched hand by Nestor, standing on a pedestal opposite the heroes. The bases of these statues still stand in situ before the Temple of Zeus and confirm both the number and arrangement of the statues described by Pausanias.[122] His claim that it was dedicated "by the *ethnos* of the Achaians in common" must derive from his own reading of the dedicatory epigram, inscribed on one of the bases in retrograde script:

> The Achaians dedicated these statues to Zeus,
> descendants of Pelops son of Tantalos, rival to the gods.

118. Polyb. 4.19.4 with the cautionary remarks of Sinn 1992 about the actual existence of sacred herds. Petropoulos 1987–88: 82 for the report that Ano Mazaraki was regularly used as a summer pasture for stockbreeders from Arvanites.

119. Bacchyl. 11.113–15. Kowalzig 2007: 267–327 discusses the ode and its Metapontine performance context, focusing on the construction of an Achaian identity for the cities of southern Italy.

120. Cf. Petropoulos 2002: 158; Gadolou 2002: 172.

121. Paus. 5.25.6–8.

122. F. Eckstein 1969: 27–32; Dörig 1977: 20–21. Onatas is further discussed by Walter-Karydi 1987: 19–32. The episode appears in Hom. *Il*. 7.123–205. The Riace bronzes have sometimes, probably erroneously, been attributed to this group: Stewart 1990: 147–48.

Our only means of dating the dedication is by the career of Onatas, who flourished about 470–460.[123] The trouble is that we cannot determine with any clarity who "the Achaians" were. We have already seen that there is no evidence for regional political institutions in Achaia before the late fifth century at the earliest, so there are no good grounds for seeing this as a political monument, at least in its origin, though it was almost certainly read as such by visitors to the sanctuary during the fourth century and Hellenistic period. The Achaians who dedicated the group to Zeus sought to present themselves as descendants of the Homeric Achaians through Pelops himself, grandfather or great-grandfather to Agamemnon and Menelaos, and recipient of cult at Olympia.[124] The dedication of ten larger-than-life-sized bronze statues must have been an expensive undertaking, and if it was indeed made by the *ethnos* of the Achaians in common, it would necessarily entail either a common treasury or a significant degree of organization to collect the funds from the many Achaian communities, not to mention some process for decision making. It is of course possible, but perhaps less likely, that it was dedicated not by the Achaians in common but by a group of elites as a strategy for strengthening an already existent Achaian identity and that it became a focal point for Achaian identity with respect to both their internal organization and their relationship to the wider Greek world that frequented Olympia. The dedication and its potent epigram symbolized at least the beginning of a revolutionary social order in Achaia clad in traditional, even heroic, garb. By deploying the Achaian heroes of the Trojan War as a symbol for the historical Achaians in the early fifth century in the sacred context of the cult of Zeus at Olympia, the dedicators (whether intentionally or unwittingly) enabled the creation of strong attachments on the part of individual Achaians to the emerging reality of a culturally if not politically unified Achaia.

Aitolia

If in Boiotia and to some extent in Achaia we have seen religious interactions building a sense of community beyond the boundaries of the individual polis, then in Aitolia, where polis formation was a phenomenon of the fifth and fourth centuries but where religious activity at the regional scale occurs much earlier, we should

---

123. The bases lay below a layer of stone chips, debris from the construction of the temple, which was probably completed in 457/6. That could suggest that the monument was dedicated before construction began in 470, but the fill could have been deposited at virtually any stage in the construction of the temple. See Dörig 1977: 21.

124. This association of the historical Achaians with the Homeric Achaians is equally explicit in Pausanias's claim (7.24.2) that the sanctuary of Zeus Homagyrios (also known as Homarios or Hamarios) in Aigion marked the gathering place of Agamemnon's forces prior to their departure for Troy, but the date when this aition first circulated cannot be determined. The panregional role of this cult cannot be demonstrated before the fourth century; see below, pp. 201–2.

expect to find a somewhat different pattern.[125] Indeed the sanctuary that appears to have developed earlier than any other in the region, the sanctuary at Thermon associated in the Hellenistic period with Apollo, shows signs of having been of regional interest from at least the seventh century. This impression, conveyed above all else by the puzzling combination of early monumental architecture and the certain lack of any single settlement that was responsible for it, is confirmed by striking similarities in the development of other Aitolian sanctuaries and their cults in a slightly later period, above all at Kalydon.

The sanctuary at Thermon, situated on a high plain above Lake Trichonis on the southern slopes of Mount Panaitolikon (map 4), is famous both as a site of monumental architecture from the Iron Age and as a principal sanctuary, meeting place, and archive of the Aitolian koinon in the Hellenistic period. Yet it is extremely difficult to determine the process by which Thermon became meaningful to all Aitolia. It appears never to have been a settlement on any scale. Its geographical situation is, however, certainly significant: it lies on the boundary of two geomorphologically distinct zones of Aitolia, the mountainous Pindos zone, an upland area unattractive for settlement and agriculture but valuable for pastoralism in the summer months, and the western Aitolian flysch zone, characterized by a fine-textured soil that makes it amenable to agriculture.[126] Thermon is also located on the only saddle of Mount Panaitolikon that makes the mountain traversable from east to west. It is safe to assume that in the archaic period, as demonstrably in the classical and later eras, the Aitolian economy was characterized by animal husbandry. Pastoralists would have relied equally on the mild, warm coastal plains and the cooler uplands at different times of year and would have had to pass through the saddle of Panaitolikon on which Thermon is situated.[127] Attempts to assign the area of Thermon to particular groups within the Aitolian *ethnos* known in the classical and Hellenistic periods do not help with the problem of who built and used the sanctuary in the archaic period.[128] The difficulty of tracing the role of Thermon in the region arises in part from the paucity of written evidence (whether epigraphic or literary) and in part from the lack of systematic and thorough publication of the excavations of the site, which began at the end of the nineteenth century and have continued intermittently ever since. So

125. On polis formation in Aitolia as a fifth- and fourth-century phenomenon, see above, pp. 55 and 77–78; and Funke 1987, 1997.

126. M. Deylius in Bommeljé, Doorn, Deylius, et al. 1987: 32–38.

127. Antonetti 1988, 1990: 152, 197–98.

128. Bommeljé, Doorn, Deylius, et al. 1987: 26, *contra* Bakhuizen 1982, who suggests that the area around Thermon was originally inhabited by the "Aetolians proper," who formed the basis of the *ethnos*. This answer, though, raises further questions: Who were the "Aetolians proper," and how extensive was their group? We can answer neither. Antonetti 1987b makes a more careful assessment for the late classical and Hellenistic periods, assigning the area north of Trichonis to the Aperantoi.

the suggestions made here will be necessarily tentative and will certainly need to be adapted as new evidence is discovered and published.

From the scattered summaries in annual archaeological reports, we can deduce prestige architecture at Thermon from the eleventh century, if not before.[129] The monumental building known as Megaron B and a surrounding wall associated with this period have been tentatively identified as an elite residence and cult center formed around early Iron Age burials.[130] An archaic temple (Temple C, probably for Apollo Thermios), the earliest example of Doric architecture in Greece, was built around 630 directly over the remains of Megaron B, which was destroyed in the late ninth or early eighth century.[131] Two other temples were built on the site in the seventh century: a small temple northwest of Temple C whose architectural terracottas point to a cult of Artemis or at least of a Mistress of Animals, built about 650; and a small building east of Temple C, identified as a second temple of Apollo, built probably at the end of the seventh century.[132]

The painted terracotta metopes of these temples, produced in local clay by local artists apparently with some Corinthian influence, provide an indication of the nature of the cults they housed as well as valuable hints about the nature of Thermon as a cult place in the archaic period.[133] The so-called Artemis temple, the earliest of the three built in the seventh century, was elaborated with a painted terracotta sima and antefixes in the form of bearded masculine heads and running gorgons; the result is the earliest example of a frieze of faces, which as we shall see is a characteristic feature of Aitolian architecture in the archaic period. Temple C was originally built about twenty years later with an entablature featuring antefixes

129. Bundgaard 1946 risks only the relative dates of Megaron B and the archaic Apollo temple; the former, a curvilinear apsidal building, was immediately replaced by the Apollo temple ca. 630. Rhomaios (*BCH* 57 [1933]: 275) dates the apsidal building to the twelfth or eleventh century. For a good summary of the evidence, with references to preliminary archaeological reports, see Antonetti 1990: 151–66.

130. Drerup 1969: 124–25; Mazarakis Ainian 1997a: 125–35. Papapostolou 2004 argues that there is evidence neither for curvature of the walls of Megaron B nor for an elliptical colonnade, contrary to the usual descriptions of Megaron B as a curvilinear apsidal structure.

131. Cook 1970; cf. Wesenberg 1982 for a summary of the Iron Age building sequence on the site. For the destruction date of Megaron B see Papapostolou 2004. The epiklesis Thermios is attested as early as ca. 500 on a dedicatory bronze plaque (*IG* IX.1² 1.91.1 [Lejeune 1945; Jeffery 1990: 227 no. 7).

132. Artemis temple: Rhomaios 1915: 47, with mid-seventh-century date provided by analysis of architectural terracottas by Mertens Horn 1978; Antonetti 1990: 167–68. The small Apollo temple is sometimes called the Temple of Apollo Lyseios, after a third-century boundary stone found near it in the excavations (*IG* IX.1² 1.81), but there is no secure evidence that Apollo had this epiklesis in an earlier period.

133. Bookidis in *PECS* 910–11; Mertens Horn 1978: 30–31; Winter 1990: 23 and 1993: 110–24. The old assertion, based on stylistic similarities and the (implicit) assumption that nothing so sophisticated could have been created by Aitolians themselves, has most recently been asserted by Palaiopanou 1991: 147; cf. Will 1955: 580–81, whose argument is overturned by the findings of Jeffery 1990: 225–26; J. Salmon 1984: 61, 120–21. Corinthian cultic connections with Aitolia, Akarnania, and Epeiros are discussed by Tsouvara-Souli 1991.

in the shape of female daedalic-style heads, and along the lateral sima beardless male heads and human heads wearing gorgon masks, which may point to a ritual involving masks, frequently a feature of coming-of-age rituals.[134] The result, again, is a frieze of faces. The original entablature of Temple C included painted metopes, which despite their fragmentary state provide further indications of the nature of the cult housed by the temple: among other things we find three seated deities, probably depicting Apollo, Artemis, and Leto; Perseus running to the right with the head of Medousa in a bag slung around his chest; a hunter with an antelope or other small deerlike animal tied to a staff slung over his shoulder; two female figures usually identified as the daughters of Proitis; and a gorgoneion.[135] Near the end of the seventh century what appears to have been a second temple of Apollo was built, smaller than Temple C and situated to the east of it. The painted terracotta metopes again provide interesting clues. One bears an image of two (or three) female figures standing face to face; between them is the legend *Charites*.[136] Two other fragments preserve the names of Iris and Eileithyia, and another seems to depict a centauromachy involving the centaur Pholos.[137] The Graces were, of course, frequently associated with Apollo, as in the *Homeric Hymn*, and Eileithyia was closely associated with the god's birth on Delos; her appearance in Thermon suggests that in Aitolia it was this version, in which the god is born into a preexisting divine structure, that was accepted and used to explain the rising prominence of Apollo at Thermon.[138] On the basis of the archaeological evidence, then, the sanctuary at Thermon appears to have belonged in its earlier stages to a Mistress of Animals figure who was later associated with Artemis, from which the introduction of her brother, Apollo, would follow easily. The metopes suggest a cult of the twin gods who together represented the concerns of both men and women in archaic Aitolian society: hunting, the clash between savage and civilized, song and dance, and childbirth.

At the end of the seventh century, while the second, small temple of Apollo was being built at Thermon, down near the coast of the Corinthian Gulf at Kalydon

---

134. The closest parallel is to the material from Tiryns (Gercke 1975) and the sanctuary of Artemis Orthia at Sparta (Dawkins 1929; Mertens Horn 1978; Burr Carter 1987). Burkert 1985: 103–4 on masks in coming-of-age rituals.

135. Letoids: ANM 13413; Perseus: ANM 13401; hunter: ANM 13409; Proitids: ANM 13407, identified as such by Dörig 1962: 88–91; gorgoneion: ANM 13402. Cf. Antonetti 1990: 174–85 with pls. 12–15 for discussion. Nerantzis's (1991) argument that the metopes of the three seated deities and Perseus with the head of Medousa provide evidence for the survival of a racial religion of matriarchy after the introduction of Apolline cult in the eighth century is certainly stretching the evidence too far.

136. *IG* IX.1² 1.86.2 (Antonetti 1990: 186 no. 1 and pl. 16.1); Harrison 1986: 193 cat. no. 6 with photo.

137. *IG* IX.1² 1.86.3–4.

138. *Hymn.Hom.Ap.* 182–206 on the Graces. The association of Eileithyia with the Delian cult of Apollo is suggested by Hdt. 4.35; cf. Paus. 1.18.5, 8.21.3, 9.27.2.

(map 4) a temple to Artemis was constructed, which in many of its features suggests that it was constructed by people who also participated in the cult at Thermon. Utilizing the same scheme of antefixes with daedalic-style heads to achieve a frieze of faces much like that from the original entablature of Temple C at Thermon, several of the surviving metopes feature representations of Herakles.[139]

During the sixth century both sanctuaries saw significant developments. At Kalydon in the first quarter of the century the temple of Artemis was restored with a new roof and accompanying terracotta entablature. One metope depicts a hunter quite similar to that from Apollo's Temple C at Thermon, and another has a bearded man carrying a boar over his shoulders, probably to be identified with Herakles and the Erymanthian Boar, an interesting echo of the mythical local boar and the problems it caused for the city of Kalydon, its king Oineus, and his son Meleager. The identification of the Thermon hunter remains uncertain, despite the temptation to assume that he too is Herakles.[140] This restored temple of Artemis was joined around the same time by a new temple of Apollo, probably to be identified as Apollo Lophrios after an inscribed *horos* immured in a modern building nearby.[141] The metopes from the new Apollo temple at Kalydon feature a pair of (or three) seated goddesses not unlike those from the first entablature of Temple C at Thermon, along with a variety of animals and a siren. The favored frieze of faces was deployed again here, and the temple was adorned with an akroterion in the shape of a running gorgon, a motif familiar from the mid-seventh-century Artemis temple at Thermon.[142] In the second half of the sixth century the entablature of Apollo's Temple C at Thermon was renovated, and the daedalic-style female heads were replaced with less formalized female heads, each wearing a *polos;* gutters were drained through gargoyles in the shape of bearded male heads and open-mouthed satyrs. At the end of the sixth and beginning of the fifth century, the Artemis temple at Kalydon received a thorough reworking, with another new roof and the addition of a colonnade around the cella to give it a canonical peripteral form; it was supported by the construction of a massive terrace, still among the most striking features of the site today.[143]

The small finds from Thermon have never been fully published, and even for Kalydon we rely on a preliminary presentation by the early excavators. Artemis is

139. For this, the so-called Temple B₁ at Kalydon, see Dyggve and Poulsen 1948: 138–64, 225–30; Mertens Horn 1978: 53–55.

140. The restorations ca. 600–575 at Kalydon resulted in the structure known as Temple B₂. For the hunter metope see Dyggve and Poulsen 1948: 160–61 (metope 2A) with fig. 164, pls. XIX, XXβ.

141. *IG* IX.1² 1.149 with Dyggve and Poulsen 1948: 295–97, 340–41 and figs. 275, 309 for the correct reading.

142. For the metopes and other architectural terracottas from this temple, the so-called Temple A, see Dyggve and Poulsen 1948: 214–25, esp. 219–25.

143. Renovations of the Artemis temple at Kalydon (known as Temple B₃ or the great Artemis temple): Dyggve and Poulsen 1948: 241–64.

represented in statuettes as a huntress, with bow and fawn, or as the Mistress of Animals, seated, with a lion on her knees. Figurines of animals of all kinds, domestic and wild, appear in large quantities, as do others of worshippers bearing gifts, including the typical doves, flowers, and apples as well as the more surprising gift of a cock, a sign that the cult had chthonic elements that appear at Thermon in the form of the frequent gorgoneia. Terracotta statuettes of pregnant women, two figurines of Baubo, and a figurine of a mother with infant point to the kourotrophic role of Artemis at Kalydon, which may be reflected at Thermon by the metope depicting Eileithyia.[144]

The archaic cults of Artemis and Apollo at Kalydon and Thermon thus share so many characteristics, from architecture to the particular concerns of the deities involved, as to suggest that their catchment areas were overlapping if not identical. Certainly there are differences: the presence of miniature anchors among the votive assemblage of Kalydon betrays a concern with seafaring that is, to our knowledge, wholly absent from inland, mountainous Thermon, and the architecture there is thought to display closer affiliations with Corinth than anything seen to the north.[145] Yet I would suggest that these distinctions point not so much to significant cultic differences as to the mobility of the Aitolians who worshipped at both sanctuaries: hunting motifs are prominent in both sanctuaries (and could hardly be avoided in the home of the Kalydonian Boar), and an Artemis who shares characteristics with the old Mistress of Animals would be vital to a community heavily involved with pastoralism, which required movement between coast and mountain, the two poles around which Aitolian economic—and religious—life rotated. For pastoralism usually implies a need for markets, for exchange, and Kalydon's position on the Gulf of Corinth, a vital trade and transportation route for mainland Greece, would have facilitated that process enormously.[146] The Corinthian influences detected in Aitolian cults and the Achaian influences detected in the archaic Aitolian script presume maritime interactions. So we should not be surprised by the anchors found at Kalydon. Nor should we be surprised that the vitality of both sanctuaries, the pace of development and the scale of investment, appears to have slowed down dramatically when the Aitolians lost control of their coastal territories at Kalydon and Pleuron by the early fourth century and the link between uplands and lowlands was broken; the community that had formed around these two sanctuaries may also have been fractured.[147]

144. Poulsen in Dyggve and Poulsen 1948: 335–54; Antonetti 1990: 253–56.
145. Anchors: Poulsen in Dyggve and Poulsen 1948: 345.
146. We shall see below (pp. 281-82) that in the late nineteenth and the early twentieth century the site of ancient Thermon was known as Old Bazaar and was an important regional marketplace. The place continued to be a locus of regional trade in the modern period, before industrialization reached Aitolia, because of its location on transportation and transhumance routes (map 7).
147. See above, p. 62.

There is one further reason to posit a regional, community-building role for the Laphrion at Kalydon, and that is the sanctuary's relationship to the myth of the Kalydonian Boar, which goes back at least to Homer. What began as the wrath of Artemis against Oineus, the king of Kalydon who had forgotten her in his sacrifices, became a war between neighboring groups in the region historically known as Aitolia. The boar, sent by Artemis to ravage the Kalydonians' crops and orchards, was killed by Meleager the son of Oineus, with help from a band of men he had gathered from the region. But Artemis, not ready to let go her wrath, caused the two groups—the Aitoloi, who lived at Kalydon, and the Kouretes, who lived in the region around Pleuron—to quarrel over the hide of the beast.[148] Apollo himself became involved in the quarrel, fighting on the side of the Kouretes against the Aitoloi and thus defending his sister's position according to the *Catalogue of Women* and the *Minyad*.[149] This sixth-century version of the myth was probably current around the time when we first see monumental architecture at the Laphrion and suggests that even from its origin the cult of Artemis and Apollo at Kalydon was associated with the eventual appeasement of Artemis and the resolution of the regional conflict between the Aitoloi and the Kouretes, an essential condition for the development of regional unity.[150] We have already seen that in the sixth century Apollo was certainly called Lophrios at Kalydon, and Pausanias records the belief that Artemis was called Laphria because her wrath "became lighter [*elaphroteron*] to the Kalydonians."[151]

Probably in the course of the fifth century Artemis Laphria received a chryselephantine cult statue, which represented her in the form of a huntress. That statue was made by two artists from neighboring Naupaktos, Menaichmos and Soïdas, a fact that may have interesting implications for the catchment area of the cult.[152] Several other indications suggest that the Naupaktians participated intensively in the cult of Artemis at Kalydon. Pausanias (10.38.2) tells us that there was a sanctuary of Artemis at Naupaktos with a marble statue depicting the goddess as an archer; she was worshipped under the epiklesis *Aitolē*. And elsewhere (4.31.7) he records the claim that the Messenians took the cult of Artemis Laphria with them from Naupaktos when they settled Messene, probably in the fourth century. A mid-fifth-century pillar monument at Delphi (T47) records a dedication of the Messenians and Naupaktians as a tithe to Apollo from spoils taken from the Kalydonians, and the rupture between the neighboring communities implied by

148. Hom. *Il.* 9.529–605; Bacchyl. 5.97–120. The Kouretes were at least remembered as having lived around Pleuron, for they were later associated with the town of Kourion in that area: Str. 10.2.4.

149. Paus. 10.31.3; Hes. *Cat.* fr. 25 (Merkelbach-West).

150. Sixth-century composition of the *Cat.*: M. L. West 1985: 130–37.

151. Paus. 7.18.10.

152. Paus. 7.18.10. For the statue and the problems of dating its production precisely see Lapatin 2001: 111–13, with references to earlier literature.

the dedication may have been long-lasting; it will be remembered that in 389 the Aitolians were prepared to make significant concessions to the Spartans in order to regain control of Naupaktos. All the evidence suggests that the cult complex at the Laphrion may have been the motive force behind the good relations of the period down to the mid-fifth century and points to a broad community participating in the cult, which appears to have retracted somewhat, or at least to have been reconfigured, when historical events led to a rupture between Kalydon and Naupaktos.[153] The later loss of Kalydon to the Achaians sometime before 389 will have prompted further changes to the configuration of the Aitolian community built by cult, particularly in the fracture it certainly created between coastal and inland Aitolia.

In Boiotia, Aitolia, and Achaia, we have seen that religious behavior contributed vitally to the construction of communities beyond the boundaries of a single polis or other relatively small locality. The interactions of people from these different cities and settlements at shared sanctuaries, their participation in common rituals, and the myths they articulated around both their rituals and the fact that they shared certain sanctuaries created a context in which claims of group identity could be expressed, frequently in terms of a common past and shared territory. In the case of Boiotia the sources afford us some glimpses of the process by which that sense of belonging developed, whereas in Achaia and Aitolia we can see only from the archaeological evidence that several large sanctuaries were frequented by a common worshipping group that inhabited several distinct local communities. The very visibility of these sanctuaries, however, their monumentalization, necessarily implicated those who participated in their cults in the business of forming relationships with one another in order to accomplish construction and dedication, a process that must have entailed negotiations about hierarchy. In Aitolia the mythic war between two population groups within what came to be known as Aitolia, both of which were certainly participating in the cult of Artemis and Apollo at Kalydon, serves as an aetiology for the cult and establishes its role in celebrating the resolution of a regional conflict and in protecting peace. In this it appears to have a similar function to the more obviously foundational Boiotian cults of Athena Itonia and Poseidon at Onchestos.

POLITICIZING REGIONAL COMMUNITIES

Having explored the ways in which ritual and the monumentalization of sacred space contributed to the articulation and reinforcement of a group identity that

---

153. See above p. 52.

incorporated the inhabitants of multiple distinct settlements within a region, we need now to consider the ways in which religious behavior, especially ritual action, contributed to the politicization of these regional communities, to the establishment of a relatively clear (if nevertheless still quite dynamic) political order within each region. In other words, we need to understand how religious behavior effected the formation of regional states around the outlines of the regional communities that we saw emerging in the previous section. In doing so it will be important to ask why religious behavior played such an important role in the process and whether it is able to accomplish something quite distinctive to the process of negotiation implicit in the creation of a new political order.

Becoming Theban: Thebes, Boiotia, and the Politicization of the Regional Community

The Struggle for Regional Unification and Leadership, 519–446. In the late sixth century the Boiotian community was only beginning to be politicized, a process that we know extended more than half a century before formal state institutions at the regional scale appear with any regularity in the sources. State formation, an inherently delicate process of negotiation between competing internal interests on the one hand and the interests of the entire community vis-à-vis external threats and opportunities on the other, seems to engender the need both for ways to construct and articulate power relations that will be relatively unobjectionable to those involved and for strategies for legitimating those relationships. This is nowhere more evident than in Boiotia from around 519 to 446, when the expulsion of the Athenians after a ten-year occupation gave the politicization process a massive boost and all the legitimation the koinon needed. But until that happened, and even after it did, religious action played an extremely important role in the politicization of the Boiotian community.

The first clear indication we have in the historical record of the Thebans' exerting pressure on their fellow Boiotian cities to form a single political entity comes in 519, when they sought to make Plataia "contribute to the Boiotians."[154] Although they failed at that particular enterprise, it was probably around the same time and in line with the same policy that they exerted some form of control over the small poleis of the Parasopia, the district between Thebes itself and the Asopos River, which was established as the boundary of Theban territory by the arbitrators in 519 (Hdt. 6.108.4). There are good indications that, whatever other methods they may have brought to bear (including force) to effect the adherence of these communities to "the Boiotians," ritual played a prominent part.

154. Hdt. 6.108.5; see above, p. 27.

In a poem that may have been composed for performance at the Daphnephoria, Pindar (*Pyth.* 11.4–5) describes the sanctuary as a "treasury of golden tripods,"
and other sources attest the frequency of this particular form of dedication at the
Ismenion as well as other Boiotian sanctuaries.[155] In a scholion to Pindar's *Pythian*
11, the commentator explains that the Ismenion was a treasury of golden tripods
"because the Thebageneis used to carry tripods there."[156] Ephoros himself corrobo-
rates this anonymous claim in a passage of vital importance for the problem before
us, providing some clues about how it can be historically contextualized (Ephoros
FGrHist 70 F 21 *apud* Ammon. *Diff.* 70 [Valckenaer = 231 Nickau]):

> Ephoros explains the difference between Thebageneis and Thebans in his second
> book: "These were annexed to Boiotia: the Thebans themselves added those com-
> munities that dwelt at the Athenian border many years later, but they were a mixed
> group that came from many places and inhabited the territory beneath Kithairon
> and opposite Euboia. These were called Thebageneis, because they were added to the
> other Boiotians by the Thebans."

Ephoros's testimony is the earliest source to mention the Thebageneis, and he
does not associate them with the rite of *tripodophoria*, bringing a tripod to
Apollo Ismenios in Thebes, as the Pindaric commentator does.[157] But the group
of people known to Ephoros as the Thebageneis are likely to have been formed
in a single historical event, almost certainly the integration of their territory
into Boiotia at the impetus of Thebes. The area identified by Ephoros, from
Kithairon to the Boiotian coast opposite Euboia, is more or less coincident with
the Parasopia, the territory around the Asopos River, which included the communities of Hysiai, Erythrai, Skaphai, Skolos, and perhaps Plataia. This area was,
we know, the object of intense Theban interest in the last quarter of the sixth
century, when Plataia was pressed by the Thebans to "take part in the Boiotians,"
and it seems quite likely that this was the period when the *tripodophoria*, the
ritual obligation for each community to dedicate a tripod to Apollo Ismenios at
Thebes, was instituted.[158]

155. Bernardini 1989 for the performance context. Hdt. 1.92.1, 5.59–61; Paus. 9.10.4 for tripod
dedications.

156. Σ B Pind. *Pyth.* 11.4–6; cf. Didymos *ap.* Ammon. *Diff.* 70 (Valckenaer = 231 Nickau).

157. For detailed discussion of the *tripodophoria* and the importance of tripods to Thebes and
the Ismenion, see Kowalzig 2007: 331–52 and Papalexandrou 2008. *Thēbageneis* clearly derives
from *Thēbaios* and the verb *gignomai*; since it clearly does not designate a population born in Thebes,
it must rather name a group who have become Theban: i.e., *Thēbaios* is predicated of the verb *gignomai*
(LSJ s.v. II).

158. Hdt. 6.108.4 for Theban pressure on the Plataians. Note Kowalzig 2007: 382 n. 129: "Are these
indications that the Ismenion already during the 6th cent. functioned as a 'Boiotian' cult, rallying those
cities who were keener on belonging to Thebes and Boiotia, rather than to Plataiai?" Cf. Papalexandrou
2008: 267 for the late sixth century as the date for the institution of the *tripodophoria*.

Epigraphic evidence from the Ismenion seems to support this reconstruction. A small limestone column of the sixth century, certainly a tripod support, bears the dedicatory inscription "The people of Potniai [dedicated it] to Apollo."[159] Two other inscribed dedications may be the product of later performances of the same ritual.[160] The ritual would then have served to articulate the membership of these communities in the broader social, cultural, and economic community known as Boiotia. And insofar as the collective dedication of a tripod was an act by which control over a territory was symbolically transferred to a god, the Thebageneis' dedication of tripods signaled their surrender of control over their territory to the Thebans' god, Apollo Ismenios, and thereby to the Thebans themselves.[161] As such it added a new religious dimension to the Boiotian community, along with shared cults like those of Athena Itonia at Koroneia and of Poseidon at Onchestos. Unlike those cults, however, the ritual of the *tripodophoria* made an implicit claim about Thebes' position of leadership within Boiotia not entirely unlike the claim of hegemony implicit in the fifth-century Athenians' demand for allied contributions to the City Dionysia and Panathenaia.[162] To impose on these small communities the religious obligation of carrying a tripod to Apollo Ismenios, the god of *eunomia*, civic order, in Thebes, was to extort from them a recognition of the rightness of the Thebans' claim to regional hegemony: they were "added to Boiotia" by "becoming Theban." Here ritual activity should be seen not as a simple expression of a political relationship but as a vital means of actually constituting a new political order in which the group of people who recognized themselves as Boiotian, in large part through their participation in the series of regional cults we studied in the previous section, began to take on political salience under the leadership of Thebes, Boiotia's largest polis. In other words, the role of ritual in the politicization of a community was by no means ancillary to the outcome: ritual, unlike any other mode of social behavior, has the power to make a claim about the rightness of a prevailing sociopolitical order that may or may not be embedded in reality. This is Bell's "misrecognition," which has the ability to reconfigure reality through the strategic deployment of symbols. To put this another way: the ritual obligation of dedicating a tripod to Apollo Ismenios was a mechanism by which the Thebans asked the Thebageneis to produce a symbol of their participation in the inchoate Boiotian regional state and to surrender control over their own territory to the

159. Keramopoullos 1917: 64, Ἀπόλ]λονι Ποτνιεῖς.

160. Late sixth-century kioniskos, again most likely a tripod support: AD 16 (1960) Chron. Β΄: 147 with photo pl. 125a (SEG 22.417): [Ἀπόλλον]ι hισμ[ενίοι - - -]| [- - -]εῖες κα[- - -]; cf. Roesch 1965a: 261–63 n. 1. Stone base of the fifth century (reinscribed in perhaps the mid-second century BCE): [Ἀπόλλονι] hισμεινίοι | [- - -]μο ἄρχοντος | [- - -]νεῖες ἀνέθειαν (Keramopoullos 1930–31: 106). The lacunose name of the dedicants is obviously the sticking point here.

161. Papalexandrou 2008: 266–67.

162. For discussion see R. Parker 1996: 142–43; Smarczyk 1990: 549–69.

Thebans without making a declarative statement of a political sort. As Pierre Bourdieu has written of pedagogy: "The whole trick . . . lies precisely in the way it extorts the essential while seeming to demand the insignificant."[163] That the obligation continued to be observed in the early years of the fourth century, when Ephoros was writing, eloquently supports one of the major themes of this chapter—that the same rituals and religious ties that build communities can also play a significant role in politicizing them.

If indeed the attempt to enforce Plataia's contribution to the Boiotians in 519 can be associated with the Thebans' move to secure the allegiance of the communities of the Parasopia, then it would appear that consolidation of the regional border with Athens was a major concern during this period and attests the ongoing process of building a regional state. The Boiotians' policy of supporting Kleomenes when he invaded Athens in 506 is therefore not surprising. (He had after all rebuffed the Plataians in their appeal for help.) The recent discovery of an inscribed votive column to the northwest of Thebes (T2) suggests that even this episode in the state-building effort was bolstered by ritual. The surviving portion of the text mentions Oinoe and Phylai, and the capture of Eleusis, for the most part in accordance with Herodotos's narrative. Because the column is broken and the left half of the text is missing, its precise meaning eludes us, but the parallels with Herodotos's narrative are enough to give us confidence that the text relates to the same episode. The final line assures us that the column was a dedication, but the name of the recipient is lost.[164] Inscribed columns frequently served as central supports for tripods dedicated in Boiotian sanctuaries, and if that is what we have here, then the significance of the dedication is much increased. The dedication has seemed puzzling in light of the Boiotians' eventual defeat at the hands of the Athenians. But Herodotos's narrative makes it clear enough that some time passed (how much we do not know) between the Boiotians' successful seizure of Oinoe and Hysiai (our stone indicates that it was Oinoe and Phylai) and the Athenians' defeat of the Boiotian and Chalkidian forces. The collective dedication of a tripod would make perfect sense in this interim period, a means of symbolically transferring their new control over this frontier area to a god as a means of securing it. If one firm conclusion can be drawn from this tantalizing fragment, it is that the Boiotoi, who undertook joint military actions against a neighboring state at a time when the existence of a Boiotian regional state was still being seriously questioned, made dedications at a Theban sanctuary to commemorate a victory and sanctify their

163. Bourdieu 1977: 94–95; cf. V. Turner 1967: 30.
164. The other contents of the cist in which the column fragment was found suggest that they belonged to debris from a sanctuary; the cist itself is similar in form to those discovered at Argos, Messene, and Epizephyrian Lokroi, which all served as sacred treasuries. Argos: Kritzas 2006; Lokroi: de Franciscis 1972; Costabile 1992.

control over this new territory, or at the very least to fulfill a vow. It was certainly the same group that made two small dedications at the Ptoion at the very end of the sixth century to Athena Pronaia, whose presence at the sanctuary is otherwise unattested for this period. These two dedications, one a small bronze statue (of which only the base survives) and the other a bronze vessel, were made by the Boiotoi.[165] These dedications at Thebes and the Ptoion made the will to politicize Boiotia evident to all, and implicitly justified the existence of a Boiotian regional state by demonstrating the piety of those who acted in the name of the Boiotians. There may have been some kickback: in the same period the Akraiphians made numerous collective dedications of tripods at their local sanctuary of the hero Ptoios at Kastraki, which have been interpreted as a means of articulating their autonomous control over their own territory in the face of emergent attempts to create a Boiotian state.[166]

The degree to which the Boiotians' response to the Persian Wars affected the process of regional state formation is not entirely clear, for the sources are almost entirely silent on the period between 479 and 458. I suggested above that the institutional apparatus of a Boiotian regional state was virtually nonexistent; functional cooperation in military action and the production of coinage can be seen in hindsight as the first steps in the development of the koinon, the practices that made the development of formal institutions attractive and, indeed, necessary. It is clear, however, that the Persian Wars drove a wedge between Thespiai and the rest of the Boiotian cities; Plataia had been alienated from the region since 519. And there are some indications that Boiotian Medism may be an oversimplification, but whatever the internal dynamics, the prestige of Thebes in particular, as the leading city of the region and host to the Persian army, suffered a dramatic setback in the years after 479.[167] Thucydides (3.62.5) has his Theban speaker, defending to the Spartans the Theban attack on Plataia in 427, claim that *stasis* prevailed throughout Boiotia after the departure of the Persians. There is, in other words, reason to expect that those who were pushing for full political unification of the region would have struggled to gain credibility in these years.

In this context, a story in Herodotos (6.118) about Theban-Tanagran cultic relations becomes particularly interesting. In his retreat after the battle of Marathon in 490, the Persian commander Datis stopped with his fleet at Mykonos, where he saw a vision in a dream. The vision itself was unknown to Herodotos, but it caused Datis to make a search of the ships in his fleet. On board a Phoenician ship he

165. Bronze statue base (4.95 cm × 5.5 cm), inscribed Βοιοτοὶ Προναίαι: Ducat 1971: no. 257 with photo pl. 141. Fragmentary bronze vessel, inscribed Βο[ιωτοὶ Ἀθαναῖ τ]αῖ Προναίαι (or perhaps better Βο[ιοτοὶ): Ducat 1971: no. 269a.
166. Papalexandrou 2008: 269.
167. See esp. Diod. Sic. 11.81.1–2.

found a gilded statue of Apollo; in response to his query he learned from what sanctuary the statue had come and then took it to Delos, where he instructed the Delians to return it "to the Delion of the Thebans," the sanctuary of Apollo Delios that was situated in the territory of Tanagra. The Delians neglected to do as they were told, and twenty years later, "the Thebans themselves conveyed it back to the Delion, in response to an oracle." We cannot conclude with any certainty from Herodotos's reference to the Delion of the Thebans that they controlled the Delion in any formal sense when they dedicated the statue around 470; Herodotos's narrative of Boiotian affairs elsewhere shows signs of having been informed from a strictly Theban point of view, and he shows little knowledge of Boiotia's internal relations.[168] Rather, what Herodotos's story reflects, in my judgment, is a move on the part of the Thebans to restore a statue stolen from the sanctuary of Apollo Delios by (some members of) the Persian fleet. As such, it was a move to redress a wrong suffered by the god, who had himself indicated by means of an oracle what should be done. If the Thebans themselves took the initiative, they could represent themselves as guardians of Apollo's cult, just as Herakles himself, their greatest hero, did when he slew Kyknos at the sanctuary of Apollo at Pagasai. And as guardians of sacred affairs they could boost their own reputation within the region and position themselves as its just and legitimate leaders. Indeed such a claim would be even stronger if the Thebans did not control the sanctuary of Apollo Delios but merely participated in its cult along with other Boiotians.

In a now-lost poem, Pindar described Apollo's journey from his birthplace on Delos to Delphi and included Tanagra on the god's route; it seems immediately plausible that this was offered as an aetiology for the fact that Apollo was worshipped along with Artemis and Leto at the Delion.[169] It appears to be a local version of the myth of Apollo's journey; the *Homeric Hymn to Apollo* has him take a more northerly route, as we have seen, from the Strait of Euripos to Mykalessos, Teumessos, and Thebes before reaching Onchestos.[170] In this light the return of the statue could have been seen as a return of the god himself, a restoration of the cult and the Apolline order it bestowed on the Boiotian community after the depredations of the Persians. It would also implicitly contribute toward a redemption of the Boiotian Medism that had encouraged the Persians to be in the area in the first place. Giovan Battista D'Alessio has recently argued that

---

168. This question has indeed been the focus of attention paid to the episode; cf. P. Salmon 1956: 62 n. 1; Schachter 1981–94: I.46; Demand 1982: 61. Note the Theban bias in the story about Mys's consultation of the oracles at the Ptoion and Amphiareion (Hdt. 8.134–35), as Schachter (*loc. cit.*) astutely observes.

169. Fr. 286 (Snell-Maehler) = Σ Aesch. *Eum.* 11. Cult configuration at Delion: Paus. 9.20.1; likewise in Tanagra: Paus. 9.22.1.

170. *Hymn.Hom.Ap.* 223–30.

several fragments of a Pindaric hymn, which opens with a catalogue of Theban heroes (fr. 29 Maehler) and continues with narratives of Herakles' attack (fr. 33a) on Kos and the birth of Apollo on Delos (frr. 33c, d), are dedicated not to Zeus, to whom they have been assigned since 1946, but to Apollo himself. D'Alessio further suggests—tentatively, to be sure, but provocatively—that this hymn to Apollo may have been written for the return of the statue from Delos to the Delion and performed as part of the ritual.[171] D'Alessio shows that the partial survival of these fragments on a single papyrus establishes the order in which the episodes were narrated in the hymn: fragment 33a appears to narrate Herakles' attack on the island of Kos during his return from Troy, while fragments 33b–d take up the theme of Apollo's birth on Delos.[172] The thread that connects these two episodes is lost in the lacuna, but other evidence suggests that it may have been a cultic link that prompted Pindar to associate them in a single narrative. In a fragmentary paean (fr. 140a Maehler), Pindar narrates Herakles' attack on Paros, another Ionian island, on his way to Troy.[173] The attack, Pindar indicates (fr. 140a.b26–31), was incited by Apollo himself and resulted in the establishment by the victorious hero of a cult of the god on the island. The episode seems a neat parallel to that of Herakles on Kos and may suggest how we may fill some of the gaps in our knowledge about the latter. Herakles and Apollo shared a sanctuary on Kos in the historical period, as we know from epigraphic evidence, and there is some indication that the Koans dedicated a statue to Apollo on Delos in the archaic period.[174] That there were cultic links between Herakles and Apollo on Kos and elsewhere in the Greek world is clear enough; the mythic association of the two figures is very strong, particularly in the pattern reflected in both the pseudo-Hesiodic *Shield* and Pindar fragment 140a whereby Herakles protects justice and establishes or corrects Apolline cults. D'Alessio's suggestion that a cultic association of the god and hero on both Kos and Delos may have provided the link between the two episodes in Pindar's fragmentary hymn (frr. 33a–d) is compelling on its own, but it is the link with Thebes that is of most interest for present purposes. As Bruno Snell realized, these fragments appear to belong to the same hymn as fragment 29, which begins with a veritable catalog of Theban deities and heroes: "Shall it be Ismenos, or Melia of the golden spindle, or Kadmos, or the holy race of the Spartoi, or Thebe of the dark-blue fillet, or the all-daring strength of Herakles, or the wondrous honor of Dionysos, or the marriage of white-armed Harmonia that we shall hymn?" (trans. Race). It is indeed difficult, as D'Alessio

171. Snell 1946; D'Alessio 2005 and 2009b: 142–44.

172. The episode is taken up elsewhere by Pindar (*Nem.* 4.25–26; *Isthm.*6.31–32), always after Troy.

173. D'Alessio 1997: 44–45; Rutherford 2001: 377–82.

174. Kos: Sherwin-White 1978: 319–20; R. Parker and Obbink 2001: 257 n. 8; *SEG* 45.1120. Koan dedication of statue of Apollo on Delos: Ps.-Plut. *De mus.* 14.

points out, to see hints of a hymn to Zeus in any of this material, and his attribution of the hymn to Apollo is quite persuasive.

The idea that the hymn was originally composed for performance at the rededication of the statue of Apollo, stolen from Delion by someone in the Persian
fleet and restored some twenty years later by the agency of the Thebans, merits
serious consideration. This cultic context makes excellent sense of the distinctly
Theban opening stanza (fr. 29) and of the narrative of Herakles on Kos and the
birth of Apollo on Delos, particularly since we know that in Boiotian myth Apollo
traveled through Tanagra from Delos on his way to Delphi. The performance of
such a hymn to Apollo on the occasion of the rededication of the statue would
have sent a powerful message: represented by Herakles himself, the Thebans
appear as protectors of the cult of Apollo not just in their own city but in Tanagra
too. It may have made an additional jab at the Athenians, for as leaders of the alliance that had its home on Delos, they may have been deemed at least partly
responsible for the failure to return the statue.[175] Such a ritual, performed to the
accompaniment of the powerful mythic narrative in the hymn, would present the
Thebans as leaders seeking to redress injustice and protect sacred property
throughout Boiotia. Could there have been a more effective strategy for regaining
some of the prestige lost in the failed policy of Medism, staking a claim to leadership within the region, and in the process perhaps implicitly articulating a stance
of independence from the Athenians, who at the time controlled Delos?

From Subordination to Regional Sovereignty, 446–394.   The political message
sent by the rededication of the pilfered statue was multifaceted, and it is difficult to
determine just how efficacious it was; if we can detect the strategy, we cannot see
the outcome clearly. The rededication conveyed a message of independence from
Athens, but that position was undermined by the Boiotian defeat at the battle of
Oinophyta and the ten-year period of Athenian control over Boiotia that followed.
In terms of formal institutions, Athenian domination was a major setback to the
formation of a regional state, but it lent the ideology of Boiotian unity perhaps
greater credence than any other single event in the preceding century. Athenian
rule underscored the vulnerability of the small poleis of Boiotia, and the manner
in which it was ended clarified the benefits to be captured from cooperation. The
revolt was begun, as we have seen, by a group of exiles from Orchomenos, Chaironeia, and other unnamed communities and was quickly supported by neighbors
and, certainly, by other Boiotians.[176] The decisive battle against the Athenian occupying army took place outside Koroneia, and though that may have been in part at

175. Cf. Schachter 1981–94: I.46 n. 6; Kowalzig 2007: 99 n. 120.
176. See above, p. 35.

least an accident of geography and the movements of the Athenian army, the Boiotians themselves appear to have regarded it as profoundly significant, for they erected a trophy directly before the temple of Athena Itonia at Koroneia. It must have been a trophy of the more permanent variety, for it was still there when Agesilaos led the Spartans against the Boiotians at the second battle of Koroneia, in 394, which we know was fought on the goddess's very doorstep.[177] The move would have been quite natural, for in the mid-fifth century we know that Athena Itonia was worshipped as a warrior goddess and drew people from some distance, at least as far as Thebes, to her temple and the festival celebrated there. The fragments of Alkaios and Bacchylides discussed above certainly predate the battle, and although the *daphnēphorikon* for Agasikles of Thebes, written by Pindar, may belong to the period immediately after the battle, it seems to refer to older practices and gives us no specific information about contemporary cultic innovations. It is, however, striking that our first evidence for the association of the cult of Athena Itonia with the migration of the Boiotoi from Thessaly appears after the mid-fifth century: Thucydides, Hekataios, and the Boiotian epichoric historian Armenidas are our earliest sources for this claim, and it would have been particularly powerful if promulgated in the aftermath of the decisive victory of 446.[178] It was also sometime after 446, but certainly before the second battle of Koroneia, that Athena Itonia received a new cult statue in bronze, made by the Parian sculptor Agorakritos, a pupil of Pheidias.[179]

The trophy, the new cult statue, and the assertion of the mythic link with the invasion of the Boiotoi and their occupation of the territory in the second half of the fifth century together suggest that Athena Itonia, the warrior goddess who presided over a victory that drove the Athenians out of central Greece and underscored the need for cooperation among the Boiotian poleis, was given a more explicitly ethnic, pan-Boiotian role and became the goddess who protected the claim of the Boiotoi to rule the territory around Lake Kopaïs. By situating contemporary claims in tales about the heroic past, those in Boiotia who brought about the formalization of old patterns of cooperation and community could situate the new social order in a deeply conservative framework, lending both stability and legitimacy to the innovative koinon that emerged in these same years. The defeat of the Athenians at Koroneia in 446 thus appears to have led the Boiotians to

177. Plut. *Ages.* 19.1–2; cf. Xen. *Hell.* 4.3.20. The topography of the Itonion and of the second battle of Koroneia is taken up by Pritchett 1965–92: II.85–95.

178. Larson 2007: 56–61.

179. Paus. 9.34.1. About Agorakritos little is known: Stewart 1990: 269 (contemporary of Alkamenes, active ca. 438–400). The appearance of the cult statue may be indicated by a series of rare obols issued by Koroneia in the early fourth century depicting the helmeted head of Athena in profile or the bust from a frontal perspective: Head 1881: 45 with pl. IV.2; Lagos 2001: 6 with pl. I.12–14.

endow the local cult of Athena Itonia, which already drew participants from other communities in the region, with broad regional meaning and to involve the goddess directly in the new Boiotian state.

The fact that the Boiotians were investing heavily in the Itonion and promulgating a myth that associated Athena Itonia with their occupation of the territory in the immediate aftermath of the expulsion of the Athenians in a battle that occurred near the sanctuary, and were at the same time developing formal institutions for a regional state, has not been sufficiently appreciated. For unlike any other mode of behavior, ritual actions of this sort in the highly charged political environment of Boiotia after the expulsion of the Athenians would have drawn people's attention to a vision of a unified Boiotia while at the same time deflecting it from visions of the divided politics of the recent past.[180] If Athena Itonia, a local warrior goddess, became celebrated as the goddess who helped the Boiotians to expel the Athenians from the region, she simultaneously became a goddess who promoted the political unification of the region that followed in the wake of the Athenians' departure and the strong sense of Boiotian ethnic identity that was articulated more clearly than ever before.

Achaians and Ionians

In the fourth century the Ionians of Asia Minor shared a cult of Poseidon Helikonios, which they claimed to have brought with them from the northern Peloponnese when they were expelled from the region by the Achaians in the series of upheavals known to the Greeks as the return of the Herakleidai. But the cult seems to have persisted, and the god's sanctuary was situated in what become the territory of the Achaian polis Helike. By the early fourth century, the koinon made some claim to control over the sanctuary of Poseidon at Helike, thus aligning the new political order with the conquerors who, at least in political legend, had created the territory of Achaia. In the course of the fourth century we also see the Achaian koinon associating strongly with the cult of Zeus Homarios at Aigion; this Zeus, a god of assemblies, was at some point associated with the assembly gathered by Agamemnon to organize his Achaian contingent for the attack on Troy. The emergent koinon's engagement with both cults appears to have been a strategy for fostering a sense of legitimacy in the new state by associating its rule with profoundly traditional cults that had acted in the past as crucibles of Achaian identity. There is no evidence for the nature of the rituals that took place at either sanctuary, but literary sources and coins of the period do provide vital indications of the strategic uses to which the ritual actions that must have taken place there were put.

That the cult of Poseidon at Helike had some renown in the archaic period is perhaps indicated by a single Homeric mention, but nothing more can be pressed

---

180. Cf. Lukes 1975: 301.

from it.[181] Herodotos (1.145) reports that the Ionians took refuge in the city of Helike when they were being besieged by the Achaians, suggesting that it may have been, or been remembered as, a central place for the Ionians before their expulsion, but although he has much to say about the cult of Poseidon Helikonios in Asia Minor, he never explicitly associates it with Achaian Helike.[182] The Ionians may well have sought refuge in Helike because the local Poseidon was a god of asylum.[183] Strabo (8.7.2) says that according to the Prieneans, the cult of Poseidon Helikonios in their territory was brought from Helike, and Pausanias (7.24.5) likewise reports that the Ionians transferred the cult to Asia Minor when they were expelled from the Peloponnese by the Achaians. The literary sources thus suggest that Poseidon Helikonios was an ethnic god for the Ionians, but they do not tell us that he played the same role for the Achaians who occupied the territory formerly held by the Ionians.[184] In geographical terms, Helike was undoubtedly central to the region of Achaia that was consolidated and unified over the course of the fifth century, stretching from Dyme to Pellene and inhabited overwhelmingly by coastal settlements.[185] That process of territorial definition may have been influenced by patterns of interaction at sanctuaries like that of Poseidon at Helike and perhaps even Artemis at Ano Mazaraki, but this is purely hypothetical.

Oddly, the most illuminating evidence about the position of the cult in the region has been the least discussed, but it points to a deep-seated tension between the polis of Helike and the koinon of the Achaians over control of the sanctuary shortly before its destruction by earthquake and tsunami in 373.[186] Strabo's full

181. Hom. *Il.* 8.203. Ongoing excavations have uncovered an altar and temple of the eighth century at Helike; this may in fact be the Temple of Poseidon Helikonios, but there is not yet any evidence to confirm that association. See Kolia 2011.

182. This detail is also reported by Paus. 7.1.8 and Str. 8.7.4, and is taken by Mylonopoulos 2006: 125 as evidence for his claim that Helike was "die bedeutendste Stadt in Achaia" before its destruction; but in fact it proves only that it was convenient, or central, or well fortified, or some combination of these.

183. Polyaenus, *Strat.* 8.46.

184. Prandi 1989 notes the close relations between Ionians, Achaians, Helike, and Sparta that underlay this episode; cf. Freitag 2009. Mylonopoulos 2006 suggests that all the purportedly amphiktyonic cults of Poseidon (Helike, Kalaureia, Samikon, and Tainaron) in the Peloponnese contributed to the articulation of non-Dorian identities for the worshipping group, whether they stressed Ionian or Achaian origins. See Rizakis forthcoming for the view that the cult of Poseidon Helikonios had regional preeminence in the Mycenaean period (relying on Hom. *Il.* 8.203, the recent excavations, and the late claims about the links between this cult and those in Ionia and Magna Graecia) but that this was eroded in the archaic period when the cult of Zeus Homarios at Aigion assumed its position. Although this hypothesis is attractive, I do not see that it is supported by the evidence.

185. Hdt. 1.145.

186. The date of destruction is given precisely by Polyb. 2.41.7. On the social response to the destruction of the city see Mackil 2004: 497–99. The manner of destruction, widely attested by literary sources, is now confirmed by archaeological evidence: Katsonopoulou 2002: 207.

account of the demise of Helike (8.7.2) derives directly from Herakleides Pontikos, the fourth-century Academic philosopher, and is worth quoting in full:[187]

> Herakleides says that in his own lifetime the disaster took place at night, and although the polis was twelve stades from the sea, the entire area along with the city was covered. Two thousand men were sent by the Achaians to collect the bodies of the dead, but they were unable to do so, and they distributed the territory among the neighbors. The disaster occurred because of the wrath of Poseidon. For some Ionians, who had been expelled from Helike, were sent to ask the people of Helike either for the wooden image of Poseidon or, failing that, for some sacred object that they could use in reestablishing the cult [aphidrysin]. When they refused to give either, they sent their sacred embassy to the Achaian koinon. Although the Achaians voted in favor of granting the request, the Helikeans were not willing. The disaster occurred during the following winter, and the Achaians later gave the relic [aphidrysin] to the Ionians.

Herakleides' account is, on some level, an attempt to explain a natural disaster as the result of divine wrath.[188] That does not, however, mean that the story of the Ionian ambassadors ought to be entirely discounted. There is good reason to believe that the Ionians did send an embassy seeking an *aphidrysis*, some physical relic of the cult that would allow them to transfer—or to replicate—it elsewhere.[189] For the Ionians had been forced by warfare in the region to move their sanctuary of Poseidon Helikonios from Mount Mykale to "a safe place near Ephesos."[190] It is quite likely that a memory of some contested embassy provided the motive for the claim about the cause of the disaster and could easily have been embellished. The sources preserve slightly different versions of this embassy. According to Herakleides, the Ionian ambassadors applied first to the people of Helike and then to the Achaian koinon. It is not clear from his account whether the Achaian koinon served as a kind of arbitrator or whether it was, in theory, ultimately responsible for the management of the sanctuary's affairs. According to Diodoros they did not present their case first to the city of Helike but made their request directly to the Achaian koinon, which voted in their favor. Both versions claim that the Helikeans refused to recognize the Achaian decision, and Diodoros explains that this was because an old oracle had prophesied danger for them when Ionians should sacrifice at the altar of Poseidon (Diod. Sic. 15.49.2),

---

187. Herakleides Pontikos fr. 46a (Wehrli 1953).

188. Gottschalk 1980: 94–95.

189. On *aphidrysis* and *aphidryma* see Malkin 1991; Anguissola 2006a, 2006b. While Brunel 1953 correctly understands the function of an *aphidryma*, his strict definition as relics taken from an altar is groundless. Cf. Katsonopoulou 1998.

190. Diod. Sic. 15.49.1, perhaps relying on Ephoros: Sen. *Quaest. nat.* 7.16.2 (*FGrHist* 70 F 212 with Jacoby's comments, *FGrHist* II.C: 98–99); cf. Gottschalk 1980: 95 n. 23.

saying that the sanctuary was not common [*koinon*] to the Achaians but was their own [*idion*]. The inhabitants of Boura also joined with them in this. But the Achaians having assented by a common decision, the Ionians sacrificed at the altar of Poseidon in accordance with the oracle [that they had received]. The Helikeans, however, scattered their possessions and seized the sacred ambassadors of the Ionians, thus committing sacrilege against the divine.

Both Herakleides and Diodoros make it clear that there was a tug-of-war going on between the Achaian koinon and the polis of Helike over control of the sanctuary's affairs and in particular over the question of who had the right to participate in the cult, whether by making sacrifices or by taking sacred relics.[191] Situated in the territory of Helike, the Helikeans deemed it their own and did not feel bound by the decision of the koinon. Diodoros's account, probably based on Ephoros, reveals the Helikeans' own awareness of the koinon's strategy here. By claiming to control a venerable sanctuary associated in myth with the Homeric Achaians, those who were working to advance the political unification of the region propagated and reinforced an image of the Achaian koinon as a legitimate state that should coexist with the Achaian poleis but rule in the name of all Achaians.

Their response to the Ionians' willful sacrifice at the altar of Poseidon Helikonios is also a beautiful illustration of Maurice Bloch's theoretical point about the arthritic nature of ritual communication.[192] With its limited vocabulary of repetitive symbolic actions and lack of syntactical rules by which arguments might be made about content and strategy, critical responses to specific ritual actions can only be made in the same register—by means of a competing ritual action. Bloch's famous point is that you cannot argue with a song, but in the Greek world we find many instances, of which the face-off between Helikeans and Ionians at the sanctuary of Poseidon is only one, in which an argument is in fact made about the justice and legitimacy of claims made by means of ritual action; this argument is always and can only be made in the same register of ritual action.[193] If despite the Helikeans' formal prohibition of the Ionians from sacrificing at their sanctuary the Ionian ambassadors committed the act nevertheless, then the Helikeans had no choice but to respond in subversive ritual terms, seizing the normally sacrosanct *theōroi* and scattering

---

191. In addition to responding to an oracle, Helikean resistance may be rooted in the notion that the removal of relics would be tantamount to the removal of the deity himself, whose presence was probably associated with the god's protection of Helike. One may compare the Athenians' conviction that Athena remained in protection of their city when, after the Persian sack, the sacred olive tree on the acropolis sprouted again (Hdt. 8.55), or the Homeric Achaians' idea that Troy would be taken only when the Palladion was removed from the city's acropolis (Frazer 1921: II.226–29 with n. 2). Cf. Sourvinou-Inwood 1990: 307.

192. Bloch 1977: 138

193. Bloch 1974: 71, an idea explored systematically throughout Kowalzig 2007.

their "possessions."[194] The Helikeans' position that the sanctuary of Poseidon belonged to them and not to the koinon is further articulated by the appearance of Poseidon on the fourth-century bronze coins of Helike, known from only three instances but each strikingly clear.[195] Regardless, the koinon was willing to hear the Ionian appeal (or, in Diodoros's account, the first and only request), which suggests that the koinon deemed that the matter did lie within its sphere of authority. This claim to sovereignty can date only to the late fifth or early fourth century, when the koinon developed as a state, but it may have been made at that time on the grounds that the sanctuary of Poseidon at Helike had always been a sanctuary in which Achaians from other communities also participated.[196]

This kind of disagreement, if not outright unclarity, about how authority was to be distributed among the member poleis and the koinon would not be at all surprising in the early stages of the process of formalizing the institutions of a federation of poleis. The fact that our earliest evidence for a formalized koinon in Achaia comes from 389 (or slightly before) suggests that the Achaians were in precisely this mode, sorting out how their koinon would work, when the Ionians came to Achaia seeking relics from the sanctuary that they claimed had been theirs in the distant past. The accounts of Herakleides and Diodoros assure us that the Achaian koinon claimed a stake in the sanctuary of Poseidon Helikonios, which suggests that as in Boiotia the incipient koinon sought to embed its own activities in a cult that stood as a symbol of the unification of the group in whose name it claimed to govern.

It is, however, certainly pressing the evidence too hard to claim, with Klaus Tausend and Ioannis Mylonopoulos, that the sanctuary of Poseidon Helikonios was the *Stammeskult* and *Stammesheiligtum* for the Ionians and was taken over as such by the Achaians, who organized themselves as an amphiktyony prior to the political unification of the region.[197] This argument implies a primordial tribal

194. It is not at all clear to what "possessions" (*chrēmata*) refers. There are linguistic parallels with Xenophon's description (*Hell.* 3.4.4) of the boiotarchs' disruption of Agesilaos's sacrifice at Aulis in 395, which may suggest that *chrēmata* here refers to sacrificial victims, as is clearly the case in the Xenophon passage.

195. Friedlaender 1861a, 1861b; Head 1911: 414; Jucker 1967. The third instance of this series appeared in an auction by LHS Numismatik on May 8, 2006 (auction 96, lot 497). Poseidon's role as a poliadic deity at Helike is briefly discussed by Mylonopoulos 2003: 418–19.

196. Cf. Morgan and Hall 1996: 196. Mylonopoulos 2006: 128 takes the consultation of the koinon as evidence that the sanctuary was a pan-Achaian concern (and had been since the sub-Mycenaean period, when the Ionians were driven out), and that the amphiktyony of Helike was identical with the Achaian koinon. The former entity is, to judge from the sources at our disposal, a figment of scholarly imagination. It is rather more illuminating to consider the role that the sanctuary played in the development of regional political institutions in the classical period.

197. Tausend 1992: 21–22; Mylonopoulos 2003: 424–27 and 2006: 127–29. Likewise dismissed by R. Parker 1998: 32 n. 79.

unity among the Achaians, which is undermined by archaeological indications that Achaia moved toward cultural unification only in the fifth century.[198] It also implies that the sanctuary and its cult were the sole motivations for the regional cohesiveness of Achaia, that the inhabitants of the region gathered at the sanctuary of Poseidon Helikonios only to discuss matters pertaining to it. The only evidence we have for the deliberative role of the Achaians in this period pertains precisely to a concern of the sanctuary, namely whether or not to fulfill the Ionians' request. But as we saw in chapters 1 and 2, from the late fifth century at the latest, other evidence points toward concerted Achaian actions in the military and political spheres, in matters that seem to have had nothing to do with the sanctuary at Helike. It clearly was important as a poliadic cult for Helike that attracted the attention of those who worked toward the politicization of the region and sought traditions about territory and ancestral practices by which to legitimate that move, as occurred in Boiotia with the cult of Athena Itonia, who was likewise associated with the invasion of the now-ruling group and its conquest of the territory. We have evidence neither for pan-Achaian participation in the sanctuary much before the destruction of Helike nor for the absolute priority of cultic over other (e.g., economic or military) interests, both of which would be required in order to have any confidence in the theory of an amphiktyony of Helike as the direct precursor to the Achaian koinon. What is clear is that some Achaians anyway were attempting to situate this sanctuary at the heart of the still-developing koinon, thus cloaking a revolutionary sociopolitical order in profoundly traditional garb.[199]

A passage of Pausanias has been taken as evidence that the destruction of Helike caused the Achaians to move their political deliberations to a new site, the polis of Aigion, and it is inferred from this that the sanctuary of Poseidon at Helike had previously been the site of political meetings.[200] Pausanias claims that "the Achaians gathered themselves at Aigion, for this was, after the submersion of Helike, the most prestigious polis in Achaia by reason of its antiquity and of the strength it had at the time."[201] Certainly Pausanias is here referring not just to Aigion in general but to the sanctuary of Zeus Homarios in Aigion, where we know the koinon did hold its meetings in the Hellenistic period, and it is possible that political meetings were similarly held at the Poseidonion in Helike before its

198. Morgan and Hall 1996: 197–99.

199. It is very much hoped that ongoing archaeological exploration of Helike, which has revealed the remains of early Helladic (Katsonopoulou 2002: 207–9), geometric (Kolia 2011), and Roman (Soter and Katsonopoulou1998) structures, as well as pottery, coins, and architectural fragments of the classical period (Katsonopoulou 2002: 207), will locate the sanctuary with certainty and shed some light on this dim corner of Achaian history.

200. Tausend 1992: 25.

201. Paus. 7.7.2.

destruction; but Pausanias's remark provides no certain proof.[202] The earliest surviving epigraphic evidence for a formalized Achaian koinon, a decree of the late
fourth century (T34), was found at Aigion and may well derive ultimately from the
Homarion.[203] This hint of Zeus Homarios's fourth-century political role is corroborated by his appearance on late fourth-century triobols and bronzes of the
Achaian koinon, which carry on the obverse a head of Zeus, laureate, and on the
reverse the monogram AX surrounded by a wreath.[204] This remains the standard
type for issues of the Achaian koinon in the Hellenistic period, but it appears not
to have been the first type adopted when the Achaians began minting cooperatively. A series of didrachmas, drachmas, and triobols known from only a few
specimens bears a goddess on the obverse, and most instances have Athena on the
reverse. The Zeus so familiar from the late fourth-century and Hellenistic coins of
Achaia is present only—but quite splendidly—on the reverse of the single speci-
men didrachma from the first half of the fourth century.[205] The numismatic evidence thus suggests that if Zeus Homarios was of political significance to the Achaian koinon, he was not alone in that role. The goddess on the obverse may be
Demeter Panachaia, who according to Pausanias was right next to the sanctuary of
Zeus at Aigion, along with Aphrodite and Athena, the goddess who usually appears
on the reverse of the early fourth-century coins of the Achaian koinon.[206]

The epiklesis of Zeus, Homarios, suggests that he was a god of assembly. Polybios uses the form *Homarios,* though *Hamarios* always appears in inscriptions.[207]
Hamarios and *Homarios* derive from the conjunction of the particles ἅμα or ὁμοῦ
, respectively, with the root ἀρ- of the verb ἀραρίσκω, making Zeus Homarios "he
who gathers at the same place" and Hamarios "he who gathers at the same time."[208]
Pausanias alone mentions a sanctuary of Zeus Homagyrios by the sea in the territory of Aigion, and it remains unclear whether it is to be identified with the

202. Str. 8.7.3, 5; Polyb. 5.93.10. The epiklesis of Zeus at Aigion is variously reported: Polybios (*loc.
cit.* and 2.39.6) has *Homarios,* which I prefer. Strabo's text has *Arnarios* and *Ainarios,* which has been
emended to *Amarios.* Third-century Achaian inscriptions have *Amarios* or *Hamarios:* T39 l. 8; *I.Magn.*
39.36–37; Breccia 1911: 70 no. 110 with photo, pl. XXXII no. 77 (Perdrizet 1921). Aymard 1935 gives an
excellent discussion of the problem of the epiklesis. Skepticism about the implications of Paus. 7.7.2:
R. Parker 1998: 32 n. 79.

203. So Bingen 1954: 402; cf. *BE* 55.221.

204. Triobols: Grose 1926: 6351–53; ANS 1944.100.37606, 1944.100.37608. Bronzes: Grose 1926:
6354–56. These coins cannot be dated with any precision.

205. Wroth 1902: 324–26 with pl. XVI.4; Head 1911: 416; photo in Mackil and van Alfen 2006:
pl. 14.40. For further discussion of these coins, see below, pp. 251–52.

206. Paus. 7.24.3. It is certainly significant that oaths to uphold a measure taken by the Achaian
koinon are sworn to Zeus, Athena, and Aphrodite: T39 line 8.

207. See above, n. 202.

208. This solution was first proposed by Schweighäuser 1792: 435–36 *ad* 2.39.6, and improved by
Welcker 1865: 120 with n. 144.

Homarion (or Hamarion) known from inscriptions and Polybios.[209] Pausanias (7.24.2) reports the tradition that "the cult name Homagyrios came to Zeus because Agamemnon gathered at this place the most worthy men in Greece in order that they might take part together in a deliberation about the best way to attack Priam's realm." Whether they refer to the same sanctuary or not, both epikleseis name a god of assemblies. Zeus is described in early Greek poetry as presiding over gatherings (*homēgyreis*) of the gods, and that role was at Aigion transferred to mortal assemblies.[210]

The earliest evidence that Zeus Homarios (or Homagyrios) was of significance not just to the polis of Aigion but to the Achaians as a whole is indirect but coincident with our earliest evidence for regional political institutions. The Zeus who appears on the Achaian didrachma of the early fourth century is probably Zeus Homarios, and the late fourth-century decree of the Achaian koinon found at Aigion is most easily understood as deriving from an archival context; we know that the Homarion played this role in the Hellenistic period. It is, however, sometimes argued that Zeus Homarios had regional political salience already in the fifth century, on the basis of an interesting but tricky passage in Polybios.[211] As an illustration of the political virtues of the Achaian koinon, Polybios claims that after the *synedria* of the Pythagoreans were burned down in southern Italy, the Achaian suggestions for a resolution to the conflict were so warmly accepted that the Krotoniates, Sybarites, and Kaulonians agreed to establish a common sanctuary of Zeus Homarios in which to hold assemblies and deliberations, and imitated in other ways Achaian political institutions.[212] Although there is much uncertainty about the dates of the attack on the Pythagorean *synedria* in southern Italy and of

209. Paus. 7.24.2–3. Aymard 1935: 466. Debate on the question of the identity of the Homarion and the sanctuary of Zeus Homagyrios has centered around the location of the latter but has borne little fruit (Aymard 1938: 286–87, 293; Osanna 1996: 205–6; cf. Lafond 1998b: 398; Rizakis 1995: 200–201), for Pausanias's specification "toward the sea" leaves ample room for interpretation. The discovery of several decrees of the Achaian koinon in northwestern Aigion (T34; Bingen 1953: 616–28 no. 1 [SEG 13.278]; Rizakis 1995: 201) may point to the location of the Homarion, where they are likely to have been erected.

210. Hom. *Il.* 20.142; *Hymn.Hom.Ap.* 187; Pind. *Isthm.* 7.46. Cf. Jessen *RE* VIII.1 s.v. "Homagyrios" col. 2143. The suggestion that *Homarios*, known to Polybios, is a shortened form of *Homagyrios*, is obvious and attractive. The appearance of *Homagyrios* in Pausanias could, then, be accounted for by a revival of the cult in the period after 146, when the archaic form may have been preferred as a means of emphasizing (if not exaggerating) the antiquity of the relationship between cult and koinon. See Pirenne-Delforge 1994: 244–47; Osanna 1996: 207. The Demeter Panachaia mentioned by Pausanias as being "right next to" Zeus Homagyrios may point to a cult complex associated with assemblies: Demeter Homaria is found at Chalkis on Euboia and seems to be associated with prepolitical (ethnic) assemblies: Breglia Pulci Doria 1984; Osanna 1996: 209–10.

211. E.g., Koerner 1974: 476.

212. Polyb. 2.39.1–6.

the Achaian arbitration of the dispute, the episode certainly belonged to the second half of the fifth century.[213] Polybios's report, however, is highly tendentious, part of an attempt not only to praise the justice of Achaian political institutions of the Hellenistic period but also to retroject that reputation for fairness onto a much earlier period, and it is not possible to claim with any confidence a regional political salience for the cult of Zeus Homarios at Aigion in the second half of the fifth century.[214] Zeus at Aigion was a god of assemblies and before the fifth century may have served to bring together the demes or parts of which the polis Aigion was later composed; the association of the sanctuary with Homeric Achaians and with the expelled Ionians cannot be dated precisely, but if early it will have attracted the attention of those who sought to politicize Achaian relations. By the end of the fourth century at the very latest Zeus the Gatherer had become the principal deity of Achaian political unity. Despite the fact that we are entirely in the dark about the nature of the rituals that took place at the cult, it is nevertheless quite clear that the koinon's adoption of the sanctuary as a meeting place and repository of decrees was a vital mechanism for the mobilization of bias, fostering an image of the new state as a deeply traditional, ethnically based structure aligned with divine favor.

The Aitoloi and the Aitolian Koinon at Thermon

The picture we have been able to develop from the relatively full sources for the role of ritual and religious behavior in the politicization of regional communities in Boiotia and Achaia may provide us with a blueprint for interpreting the rather scantier evidence that points, nevertheless, toward a strikingly similar process in Aitolia in the fourth century. We have already seen that Thermon probably attracted people from across the region to worship Apollo and Artemis. A few intriguing literary sources allow us to glimpse the importance of Thermon to the Aitolian koinon that emerged in the late fifth or early fourth century, an importance that was certainly sharpened by the Achaian annexation of Kalydon along with Naupaktos sometime before 389, which necessarily focused regional cultic interactions more narrowly on Thermon.[215] If Thermon's chief claim to fame is its early monumental architecture, it is known secondarily as "the meeting place of the Aitolian League" in the Hellenistic period.[216] Evidence for the nature of activity

213. F. W. Walbank 1957-79: I.225–26, with full references to earlier discussions of the problem, suggests that it occurred ca. 420, in the context of the war between Kroton and Thourioi, explaining the appearance of Sybaris in the list of cities as a reference to Sybaris on the Traeis, not the Sybaris destroyed in 510 (though note that according to Str. 6.1.14 it was a Rhodian, not an Achaian, colony, if Meinecke's restoration of the text is correct). Cf. Aymard 1935: 454; Anderson 1954: 80; Larsen 1968: 84.

214. Cf. Morgan and Hall 1996: 195–96.

215. Bommeljé 1988: 314 and above, p. 62.

216. Bookidis 1976: 911.

at the site in the fifth and fourth centuries has been elusive, but new epigraphic evidence confirms the testimony of fragmentary literary sources that the sanctuary played this role from the early fourth and perhaps even the fifth century: in other words, from the very earliest years of the koinon's existence.

In a long diatribe against Ephoros, Strabo preserves for us several precious fragments of the fourth-century historian's work on Aitolia. In support of his arguments that the Aitolians and Elians regarded themselves as kin, Ephoros records the texts of two inscriptions, one from Thermon and one from Olympia.[217] Only the former concerns us here [Ephoros *FGrHist* 70 F 122 apud Str. 10.3.2]:

> [Ephoros] gives as evidence of these claims two epigrams. One, in Thermon in Aitolia, where it is their ancestral custom [*patrion*] to hold elections, is inscribed on the base of a statue of Aitolos:
>
>> Founder of the country, reared by the eddies
>>   of the Alpheios, neighbor of the race courses of Olympia,
>> the Aitolians dedicated this statue of Aitolos
>> the son of Endymion, to look upon as a memorial of his virtue.

The phrase about the practice of holding elections at Thermon almost certainly belongs to Ephoros, not to Strabo. A fragmentary proxeny decree of the Aitolian koinon for an Athenian (T49), inscribed on a bronze tablet in the fourth century, was found near the temple of Apollo and proves that the sanctuary had become a site of regional political activity before the Hellenistic period. Furthermore, by the first century BCE cult activity at Thermon had ceased, and the area was used as a cemetery; the present tense in the phrase "it is their ancestral custom" cannot reasonably belong to an author of that era.[218] Aitolian elections are mentioned by Sophokles, and though the fragment does not specify a location, it is possible, especially in light of Ephoros's testimony, that they were held at Thermon in the second half of the fifth century as well.[219] Unfortunately we have no other

---

217. Kinship between Aitolians and Elians: Taita 2000. The earliest literary references to an Aitolian presence in Elis and Olympia are found in Pindar and Bacchylides. Strabo (8.3.3) claims that the Aitolians returned to their ancestral land of Elis under the leadership of Oxylos ten generations after Aitolos left Elis to conquer the land of the Kouretes, and he even says that they controlled Olympia and founded the games there. Strabo thus agrees with the testimony of Ephoros, whom he cites at 10.3.2. Tzetzes 12.363 explains Pindar's description (*Ol.* 3.12–13) of the *hellanodikai* as Aitolians by saying that the *hellanodikai* were drawn from "the amphiktyones, especially the Aitolians but also the Elians." Pindar's Aitolian *hellanodikai* may, then, be Elian Aitolians, and Siewert 1994b has suggested that they may represent at least part of the *symmachia* of the Elians that is now attested in a late sixth-century inscription (*SEG* 48.541; cf. Ebert and Siewert 1999: 391–412; Siewert 2006: 49 no. 4). In light of this, Pausanias (5.15.7) is certainly misled in trying to interpret the statue of Apollo Thermios at Olympia as *Thesmios*; it is rather more likely to be a reflection of the close ties between Aitolians and Elians in the archaic and early classical periods.

218. First-century graves at Thermon: Bookidis 1976: 910.

219. Soph. *Meleager*, *TrGF* IV F 404 (Radt), *Inachos*, *TrGF* IV F 288 (Radt) with Hsch. κ4343.

information about when the statue was dedicated, and only the floruit of Ephoros circa 350 provides a rough terminus ante quem. By this date, then, the Aitolians were holding elections and other political meetings and making collective dedications at a sanctuary of Thermon, where they celebrated their kinship as expressed through descent from a common heroic ancestor whom they regarded as founder of the country.[220] Although the rituals performed at the cult of Apollo and Artemis at Thermon are obscure to us, the epigram recorded by Ephoros reveals the practice of collective dedications in the sanctuary in the name of the entire *ethnos* at a time when it was first being politicized. In this sense the dedication is directly comparable to those of the Achaians at Olympia around 480 and of the Boiotians at the Ptoion in the fifth century. The epigram's emphasis on consanguinity and shared territory points to a deliberate promulgation of these ideas by the dedicators, and the dedicatory context of the now-lost statue suggests that as the Aitolians built the institutions of a regional state, they made direct appeal to mythic claims of group identity situated at the sanctuary where they held their elections and political meetings.

If we knew more about the date of the dedication, it would be possible to be more precise about the chronological relationship between the promulgation of an Aitolian identity in mythic terms, the cult at Thermon, and the creation of regional political institutions. It would be particularly interesting to know whether this happened before or after the Aitolians' loss of their coastal territory to the Achaians. It is nevertheless clear that the rituals at Thermon must have played a prominent role in effecting the political unification of Aitolia if the sanctuary itself became a locus not only for the expression of an Aitolian ethnic identity but also of its politicization in the late fifth and early fourth centuries. The very obvious antiquity of the site and its association with the eponymous hero of the Aitolians allowed those who were working toward the creation of new political institutions to couch their innovations in a stabilizing and reassuringly conservative environment. If there were objections to these political innovations, as there certainly were in other places (e.g., Boiotia and Arkadia), then this deeply traditional cultic and ethnic framework will have done much to deflect them.

The creation of a koinon, however sudden or gradual the process was (and we rarely have the evidence to tell), will necessarily have altered existing structures of

---

220. The genealogy of Aitolos persisted in the Hellenistic period, when it influenced diplomatic relationships motivated by kinship ties: *FDelph* III.3.444 (*IG* IX.1² 1.173), a decree of the Aitolian koinon ca. 259–255 bestowing citizenship upon the polis of Herakleia, reveals that the Herakleians had "renewed their kinship" with the Aitolians, on the grounds that they were *apoikoi* of the Aitolians. Robert 1978a: 477–90, adducing Paus. 5.1.4–5, concludes that the Herakleia in question was Herakleia on Latmos, purportedly founded by Endymion. Cf. Habicht 1998: 66–67.

power. Where previously poleis enjoyed complete autonomy at the local level, now they were being asked to transfer some of that power to a regional state in which they had a stake, but which they could never control absolutely. This process involved negotiations about hierarchy and the distribution of power, which we know were met in many instances with resistance. Ritual, with its distinctive ability to cloak innovation in the garb of tradition, to articulate the rightness of a sociopolitical order by connecting it with divine will, and to extort the essential while seeming to demand the insignificant, was a powerful mechanism for the mobilization of support for the emergent regional state.

Every piece of evidence we have reveals the central role of ritual action and of religious behavior more broadly speaking in the politicization of group identities, the development of states around ethnic groups in mainland Greece and the Peloponnese in the classical period. It is in late archaic and early classical Boiotia, when the first moves were made toward a politically unified Boiotia, that we have the clearest evidence for the deployment of ritual action to perform its distinctive social alchemy. The ritual of the *tripodophoria*, the carrying of tripods to Apollo Ismenios on Thebes, obligated the small cities of the Parasopia to participate in what had previously been a more narrowly Theban cult, but one strongly associated with civic order. We have no direct evidence for their resistance to Thebes, but the reaction of neighboring Plataia to Theban overtures to "take part in the Boiotians" in 519 is a guide to possible responses. Whether resistance was active, passive, or merely potential, the imposition of the tripodophoric rite must have transformed discontent and criticism into participation and acceptance of the rightness and justice of the emerging political unity. A gift to Apollo Ismenios on behalf of an entire small community carried with it the tacit recognition of his power as the source of sociopolitical order in the city of Thebes, which was responsible for making these cities Boiotian. After the Persian Wars, the Thebans sought ritual means to unite Boiotia once again, but after the shame of Theban Medism and its punishment at the hands of the allies, such heavy-handed and blatantly centralizing measures seem to have become unpalatable. Instead we see the Thebans seeking to support cults celebrated elsewhere in Boiotia, as with the restoration of the gilded statue of Apollo Delios, which was plundered by the retreating Persian navy after Marathon. More common, and less hierarchical, was the strategy of making dedications in the name of the entire group to deities who were strongly associated with its identity and cohesion: the Aitoloi to the eponymous hero Aitolos at Thermon, the Boiotians to Apollo Ptoieus and, probably shortly after their victory over the Athenians in 446, to Athena Itonia at Koroneia in the form of a new cult statue. The official presence of a koinon at a sanctuary with connections to the group identity of its populace was a powerful means of connecting the new political order to the uncontested and celebrated past. But things did not always go smoothly, as is amply illustrated by the dispute between the Achaian koinon and the city of Helike over the request of the Ionian ambassadors to sacrifice at the altar of Poseidon Helikonios. That conflict, with the literally cataclysmic outcome attached to it by ancient authors, suggests that the process of negotiation implicit in state formation was ongoing. That ritual should play a role in the continual legitimation of the power of the koinon long after it had been formed should, then, come as no surprise.

LEGITIMATING AND CELEBRATING
THE POWER OF THE KOINON

Regardless of the strength of the bonds that tie a community together, historical events both internal and external to it have the potential to weaken or even sever them. In the previous two sections I have explored the role of religion in the construction of communities at the regional scale and in the politicization of those communities in the form of a koinon. Both are historical processes: context is absolutely vital to a proper understanding of the actions explored. The promulgation of both local and regional myths at specific ritual moments and dedications made at certain sanctuaries by certain groups or at least in their name point to the powerful but complex role of religious behavior in effecting the development of the koinon. Yet even a community of poleis and other small settlements that shares a sense of belonging, that feels bound by its participation in common cults, and that has accepted the politicization of its group identity through the embedding of actions by an emergent regional state in a ritual context can be torn apart. In this section I turn to a consideration of the ways in which religious behavior contributed to a perception of the legitimacy of a regional state under pressure. This is particularly evident in the victorious aftermath of serious challenges to the legitimacy of a koinon's power, but it occasionally surfaces in the interstices of active conflict.

We have already seen that the Thebans as early as the 470s showed a strong interest in the sanctuary of Apollo Delios near Tanagra, to which they restored the gilded statue of Apollo pilfered by Persian troops in their retreat and left on Delos. When the Boiotian army under Theban leadership defeated the Athenians in a battle around the same sanctuary in 424, they used the proceeds from the sale of some of the booty to build a large new stoa in the Theban agora and decorated it with bronze statues, presumably of the generals who led the army to victory. But they went further, attaching the armor captured from the defeated Athenians to the new stoa and to temples in Thebes. It would be a mistake to regard this as a mere decorating choice: these suits of armor were dedicated to the gods in the Theban temples, just as the allies dedicated the Persian shields to Apollo Pythios at Delphi after the Persian Wars.[221] According

221. Diod. Sic. 12.70.5; cf. Plut. *De gen. Socr.* 33–34. Symeonoglou 1985: 138–39.

to Diodoros, the remaining proceeds from the sale of the booty were used to found a new festival, the Delia, for which otherwise our earliest evidence belongs to the late second century BCE.[222] If this date for the founding of the Delia is correct, the action would probably have reverberated beyond Boiotia, and intentionally so, for only two years before the Athenians had ostentatiously revived the Delia on Delos.[223]

A series of religious actions and innovations around the epochal battle of Leuktra in 371 illustrates clearly the vital role of religion in conveying a sense of the legitimacy of a regional state in the face of both internal and external opposition to its power. As we have seen, the Spartan occupation of Thebes in 382 created pockets of pro-Spartan, anti-Theban resistance within Boiotia that persisted in places for more than a decade. The Theban-led effort to rebuild the Boiotian koinon after the double blow of the King's Peace and the Spartan occupation was seriously hindered by opposition in every direction.[224] It is in this context of a decade of internal struggle over the issue of rebuilding the Boiotian koinon that had gained such strength in the early years of the fourth century that we should consider the intensity of religious actions and innovations in the name of the Boiotians around the battle of Leuktra.

According to Diodoros (15.52.3-6), those Thebans in favor of meeting the Spartans on the battlefield in 371 (most notably Epameinondas and his supporters) struggled against the perception of ill omens by the populace and the rank and file infantry as the army was marching out of Thebes. Fear of the signs lingered among the men and flared up again as they took cognizance of the size of the Spartan army encamped in the plain of Leuktra. Diodoros follows a source that imputes to Epameinondas a conscious, strategic deployment of religious symbolism, while Kallisthenes, ever fond of sensational details, reports as fact the omens that Diodoros claims Epameinondas conjured or persuaded people to fabricate: the arms in the temple of Herakles in Thebes had disappeared, being taken up by the hero for use in the upcoming battle against Sparta; and the oracle of Trophonios at Lebadeia, ensuring a Boiotian victory, ordered the Boiotians after the battle to establish a contest in honor of Zeus Basileus.[225] We do not know whether the tales about Herakles' arms were followed up with some kind of dedication or thank

<hr>

222. Brélaz, Andreiomenou, and Ducrey 2007 for new second-century epigraphic evidence for the Delia, and *IG* VII.20 (ll. 11-12).

223. Th. 3.104. Cf. R. Parker 1996: 150–51 with references.

224. See above, pp. 67–70.

225. Diod. Sic. 15.53.4; Kallisthenes *FGrHist* 124 F 22(a) *ap.* Cic. *Div.* 1.74. Polyaenus, *Strat.* 2.3.8 records a variant of Trophonios's utterance that addressed the problem of motivating soldiers to begin the battle; his version about Herakles' arms likewise shows Epameinondas as a conscious manipulator of local religious traditions and common beliefs. Cf. Jacquemin 2000: 40.

offering after the battle, but about Trophonios and Zeus Basileus we are well informed. Diodoros's report (15.53.4) that the Boiotians established a festival of Zeus Basileus at Lebadeia is confirmed by several fourth-century inscriptions recording dedications made in commemoration of victories at the new festival's contests. The stones were found at Thebes and Tanagra, thus confirming that from its earliest stages the Basileia drew contestants from across the region.[226] The sanctuary of Trophonios was managed by the polis of Lebadeia, and it seems likely that the Basileia was too, perhaps with some involvement by the koinon.[227] This changed when the temple for Zeus Basileus was begun at Lebadeia and the Basileia became a festival of the koinon.[228]

The circumstances in which the cult of Zeus Basileus at Lebadeia was founded would alone have marked it as a locus for anti-Spartan sentiment within Boiotia, but that association was strengthened in the years after the Boiotian liberation of Messenia and the foundation of Messene in spring 369. Pausanias alone reports the Thebans' claim that before Leuktra they consulted several oracles, including that of Trophonios at Lebadeia, and gives the text of the oracle's response to the Thebans, which was purportedly recorded along with others in Thebes: Trophonios ordered the Thebans to set up a trophy before the battle, adorned with the shield that Aristomenes, the Messenian hero, had placed in his temple; the god assured them that he would then destroy their enemies. Epameinondas readily obeyed, presumably to strike fear in the hearts of the Spartans, and later restored

226. *IG* VII.2532 (Thebes); *IG* VII.552 (Tanagra). *SEG* 23.332, from Delphi, commemorates victories at the Pythia and Isthmia; Ebert's (1972: 136-37 no. 42) restoration of the lacuna in line 3 would add a victory in an *agōn* for Zeus, but there is no clear connection with Zeus Basileus at Lebadeia. Cf. Schachter 1981-94: III.112 n. 3.

227. Roesch 1982: 290-95; Schachter 1981-94: III.109-18. That the Trophonion was in the hands of Lebadeia, not of the koinon, is indicated by an early fourth-century sacred law, *IG* VII.3055 (Prott and Ziehen 1896-1906: II.71; Sokolowski 1969: 74; new text by Vatin in Salviat and Vatin 1971: 81-94; revisions proposed by Schachter 1981-94: III.86-88, though all depend on the copies of Leake and Pococke, since the stone is lost), dated by the appearance of Amyntas son of Perdikkas, king of Macedonia (lines 7-8), first in the list of people who consulted the oracle and paid the fee established by the polis. This must be the Amyntas who reigned 393-370. Relevant too is *IG* VII.3086, a fragmentary dedication to Trophonios almost certainly by the polis of Lebadeia, and T14, the resolution of a dispute between Koroneia and Lebadeia in which the boundary between "the land sacred to Trophonios and belonging to Lebadeia" is demarcated from the territory of Koroneia. Bonnechere 2003: 27-28 deems it likely that the koinon managed the games from their inception in 371, but as he admits, the evidence does not allow certainty. On the administration of the Basileia see L. A. Turner 1996: 106-7.

228. Nafissi 1995 suggests that this was undertaken as a celebration of Boiotian participation in Antigonos Doson's Hellenic League against Kleomenes III, a conflict that was trumpeted as a renewal of the great fourth-century wars of Epameinondas and the Thebans against Sparta. Schachter 1981-94: III.85, 116-18, followed by L. A. Turner 1996: 111, places the reorganization earlier in the third century, perhaps shortly before 281/0 (*SEG* 25.90). It would then simply be connected to the reorganization of the Boiotian koinon after 335.

the shield to Trophonios.[229] The story makes sense only in the context of the Boiotian liberation of Messenia after Leuktra and must have been promulgated to heighten the anti-Spartan tone of the sanctuary as a whole, as well as the good political uses to which the Boiotians put the power they won at Leuktra. The war waged by the Hellenic League against Kleomenes may have been a particularly apt context for this particular evolution of the legend.[230] Yet it should be said that Diodoros's rather more sober and less detailed account likewise reports a consultation of the oracle before Leuktra and a link between Trophonios's statement and the establishment of the cult of Zeus Basileus, and the antiquity and prestige of Trophonios's oracle would have made it a likely point of consultation before such a momentous undertaking.

The consultation of the oracle of Trophonios in 371 and its outcome are, however, most interesting in the historical context of Thebes' decade-long struggle to unite Boiotia and promote its independence against the many stalwart supporters of Sparta in the region since the seizure of the Kadmeia in 382. The embattled Thebans who led this effort had recourse to the oracle as a means of demonstrating divine approval of their attempt to rebuild the Boiotian koinon against the wishes of the Spartans and their supporters within Boiotia; the establishment of the Basileia in accordance with the oracle can only have strengthened that position. In this context, the participation of athletes from Tanagra and Thebes (and probably elsewhere) in the new ritual games at Lebadeia implicitly constituted nothing short of a recognition of the legitimacy of the koinon's restored rule over the region and of the justice of the defeat of the Spartans and their Boiotian supporters. Lebadeia was also, however, a sensitive point in the broader political geography of Boiotia at the end of the 370s. The city had been sacked by Lysander in 395 for its refusal to revolt from the Boiotian koinon unlike its neighbor Orchomenos, so its allegiance to the Boiotians was perhaps natural but all the more important in the context of Leuktra.[231] The battle itself was fought in the territory of Thespiai and

<hr>

229. Paus. 4.32.5; cf. 4.16.7. The proleptic trophy is odd, and it has been argued by Beister 1973 that Pausanias's tale represents a distortion of a reality reflected in the Theban monument (probably funereal) set up after Leuktra: T4. But as Tuplin 1987: 103–7 has convincingly demonstrated, the trophy referred to in the epigram is easily understood as a regular post-battle trophy. The idea that the Boiotians were breaking rules about trophy erection around the battle of Leuktra may be behind the tradition recorded by Cic. *Inv. rhet.* 2.69 to the effect that the Thebans put up a bronze trophy after the victory, contrary to Greek practice, and that the Spartans tried to take them before the amphiktyonic council for the transgression. Sánchez 2001: 163–64 is probably right to dismiss it as a fiction. Ogden 2004: 59–60, 80–86 further discusses the shield of Aristomenes as it relates to Trophonios and the Boiotians.

230. I thus agree entirely with Tuplin 1987: 100 that "Pausanias' tale cannot be safely regarded as anything other than isolated."

231. Plut. *Lys.* 28.2.

not far from Plataia, which both stood in ruins at the time. Elevating the importance of an old shrine in the extreme west of the region was a mechanism for ensuring the allegiance of the entire central corridor of Boiotia, from the Phokian border, along the southern shore of Lake Kopaïs, through the sacred heart of the region at Koroneia, and east as far as Thebes. But in 371 Orchomenos, the northeastern neighbor of Lebadeia, continued to defy the Theban-led movement to rebuild the Boiotian koinon, and the establishment of the Basileia must have exerted powerful pressure on the recalcitrant city by aligning the success of the renascent koinon with the will of the gods.[232]

If the other Boiotian cities were the only communities whose adherence and support were absolutely essential for the advocates of renewed confederation in Boiotia, it is also true that in order to gain any prestige in interstate relations they also had to convince the rest of the Greek world that the new Boiotian koinon was a legitimate state and should be treated as such. If this was a struggle over the course of the Corinthian War and in the immediate aftermath of the King's Peace, it was a far easier case to make after the obvious and hypocritical breach of that treaty made by the Spartan seizure of the Kadmeia in 382. The Boiotian victory at Leuktra in a sense justified the existence of the koinon by right of force, and the string of successes that marks Boiotian military and political history in the 360s strengthened that claim to legitimacy in the wider Greek world. In the interests of promoting that claim by other means, the Boiotians dedicated a treasury at Delphi, paid for, according to Pausanias, by spoils taken from the battle in 371.[233] There is no reason to distrust this report; the treasury reuses blocks from the Alkmaionid temple destroyed in 373, which provides a clear terminus post quem.[234] The effort coincides nicely with other evidence for a higher Boiotian profile at the nearby pan-Hellenic sanctuary than is apparent in other periods. Sometime in the 360s, the Thebans received the right of *promanteia,* and when the Thessalians sought to

232. So too Schachter 1981–94: III.77, 112, though his emphasis on Theban motives is somewhat misleading: the need here was to deploy symbols that would facilitate the promotion of Boiotian unity and its institutionalization.

233. Paus. 10.11.5. Publication of the treasury: Michaud and Blecon 1973. On the basis of the discovery of blocks of tufa inscribed with personal names in archaic (sixth-century) letter forms beneath structure 226, immediately north of the treasury, Bourguet 1929: 219–20 suggested the possibility that the fourth-century treasury replaced one dedicated during the archaic period. The presence of a window in the building has raised some uncertainty as to whether the building actually functioned as a treasury, a secure storehouse for high-value dedications: Jacquemin 1999: 145; Neer 2001: 276.

234. Partida 2000: 195–98, without explaining why she rejects Pausanias's clear testimony, suggests that the treasury was erected to "commemorate the subversion of the oligarchic regime and the predominance of democratic ideals after the coup of Pelopidas and Epameinondas in 379." The suggestion is uncompelling and unduly speculative in the face of clear testimony to the contrary. Reuse of blocks from the Alkmaionid temple: Michaud and Blecon 1973: 24.

express their gratitude for the help rendered to them by the Boiotians, and in particular to commemorate the valor of Pelopidas, who died in the attempt to liberate them from the dominance of Jason of Pherai in 364, they dedicated a statue (probably of the general himself) made by Lysippos at Delphi (T10).[235] Although all the inscriptions that survive from the walls of the treasury date to the third and second centuries, the building's construction in the aftermath of Leuktra is rarely mentioned but provides an important indication of the wide array of religious strategies by which those working toward the political unification of Boiotia after the King's Peace sought to legitimate their actions.[236]

If the Boiotian presence at Delphi after Leuktra seems somewhat removed from the events to which it is related, the same cannot be said for the Aitolians' presence there after the Gallic invasion of 279. It is difficult to know whether the poor reputation that clung to the Aitolians throughout the fifth and fourth centuries preceded them into the third. Their opposition to Antipater during and after the Lamian War must have helped, but if the ithyphallic hymn chanted before Demetrios at Athens in 291 is any indication, the koinon of the Aitolians remained deeply suspect, if increasingly powerful, in central Greece.[237] Their repulse of an invading band of Gauls in 279 has rightly been seen as a major turning point in the Greek world's general perception of the Aitolians, a victory that lent them a moral authority not unlike that enjoyed by the Spartans after Thermopylae and the Athenians after Salamis. Although others had participated in the defense, the Aitolians were the leaders of the undertaking, and the cruel sack of Kallipolis (Kallion) meant that they paid more dearly than any other group for the victory; their suffering was collective, as was their victory.[238] But from an Aitolian perspective, although the sources are silent on this point, the suffering of Kallion and the settlements of the Mornos River Valley must have prompted a profound unease with the koinon, if not outright opposition to it. For it was the expansion of the koinon over the Parnassos massif that had placed them in harm's way. The Aitolians who were leading and promoting the koinon therefore had swift recourse to ritual action at both Delphi and Thermon as a means of legitimizing the regional state apparatus that was principally responsible both for the vulnerability of Kallion and the successful defense of Delphi. They needed to address two audiences: the suddenly grateful broader Greek world, which certainly still remembered their old criticisms of the Aitolians; and the Aitolians themselves, many of whom must have been deeply skeptical of the value of an expansionist Aitolian koinon. That we hear nothing about active dissent may be a function of the efficacy of the Aitolians' ritual actions in the immediate aftermath of the invasion.

235. *Promanteia: FDelph* III.4.375 (*Syll.*³ 176) with Sánchez 2001: 167 for discussion of date.
236. Inscriptions from the treasury walls: Bourguet 1929: 191–224.
237. See above, p. 97.
238. See above, p. 99.

Their first action at Delphi was likely the dedication of Gallic shields to Apollo, which they affixed to his temple on the western and southern entablatures, becoming a visual and symbolic pendant to the Persian shields dedicated by the Athenians after Marathon.[239] Some of the arms captured from the Gauls in their retreat were hung up on the interior walls of the enormous stoa just west of the temple of Apollo, a structure in such close relation to the temple that it has been described as an annex of it. Whether or not the stoa is to be identified with the *hoplothēkē* (repository for arms) that appears in the fourth-century building accounts from Delphi, a lacunose inscription on the interior rear wall of the stoa reveals that it was used as such by the Aitolians.[240] A series of cubic mortises appears to have been carved into the walls after construction of the stoa, into which timbers with tenons would have been slotted; onto these the arms themselves would have been easily mounted.[241] We can thus reconstruct a display of arms in two rows along the interior walls of the stoa, with the dedicatory inscription on the wall between the upper and the lower row.

In addition to arms, the Aitolians also dedicated a series of statues to Apollo. Pausanias describes a "trophy and a statue of an armed woman, Aitolia, [which] the Aitolians dedicated after they had punished the Gauls for their cruelty against the Kallieis."[242] The image of Aitolia personified, seated upon a pile of Gallic shields with a spear in her right hand, is the reverse type common to all the precious-metal coin issues of the Aitolian koinon in the second half of the third century, and it was on the basis of this image that fragments of the base, in the form of a shield trophy, were identified in 1911 near the southwest corner of the temple of Apollo at Delphi, just next to the stoa that housed the arms.[243] Pausanias makes brief

239. Paus. 10.19.4. One surviving block of the entablature preserves the traces of an elongated shield affixed to the metope, which must be either a Persian or a Gallic shield: *FDelph* II.2: 19 fig. 18 and p. 116; Flacelière 1937: 108 and n. 5; Nachtergael 1977: 197; Amandry 1978b: 578–79 with fig. 7; Jacquemin 1985: 29; Knoepfler 2007a: 1239–40. This dedication, which would have required little additional construction work, could have happened almost immediately after the battle and may be reflected in a decree of Kos issued in the period April–July 278 resolving to send a delegation from the city to make sacrifices to Apollo on behalf of the freedom of the Greeks: τὸ δὲ ἱερὸν διαπε|φυλάχθαι τε καὶ ἐπικεκοσμῆσθαι τοῖς| ὑπὸ τῶν ἐπιστρατευσάντων ὅπλοις (*Syll.*³ 398.8–10; Nachtergael 1977: 401–3 no. 1, with discussion p. 197).

240. For the west stoa as *hoplothēkē*: *FDelph* III.5.53 l. 11; III.5.71 l. 8; restored in III.5.48 l. 33 and III.5.61 IIB ll. 13–15 by Bousquet 1988a: 169–70 (= Bousquet 1985: 719–20). Against: Roux 1989: 36–62. Of the dedicatory inscription, estimated to have been at least 105 letters in length, all that survives is: Αἰτ[ω]λο[ί – 5-*meter lacuna* –]τὰ ὅπλα ἀπὸ Γαλατᾶν [– – –] (Amandry 1978b: 574–6 [*SEG* 28.496]; cf. Amandry 1981: 708; Jacquemin 1985: 29 n. 7) .

241. Amandry 1978b: 576–78; Roux 1989: 55 with fig. 12, p. 57.

242. Paus. 10.18.7; cf. Jacquemin 1985: 30.

243. Reinach 1911: 181–82. Position of the statue: Flacelière 1937 (SW corner of temple terrace); Nachtergael 1977: 204 ("sur la place de l'opisthodome, seule région qui ne fût pas encore trop encombrée au 3ᵉ siècle"); Amandry 1978b: 579–80 (on terrace before west stoa). Cf. Nachtergael 1977: 201–2; Knoepfler 2007a: 1240. Coins: de Laix 1973; Mørkholm 1991: 150–51; Tsangari 2007: 250–53; and below, pp. 252–53.

mention of a series of statues representing "many generals, Artemis, Athena, and two Apollos, which were made by the Aitolians to commemorate their war against the Gauls."[244] It is not entirely clear whether these represented a single statue group; if indeed they did, we may imagine that the two Apollos were Delphic Pythios and Aitolian Thermios; Artemis was of central importance at Thermon as well as at Kalydon, as we have seen, and she could be identified with the goddess of either sanctuary, or perhaps both. Pausanias mentions elsewhere a dedication by the Aitoloi of a statue of their general Eurydamos, leader of the army that fought the Gauls, and it may be that his mention of "many generals" is a summary remark.[245] But depicting the Aitolian generals as *symmachoi* of the gods themselves would have been a powerful integrating symbol, and that these statues were conceived and executed as a monumental group cannot be ruled out.[246]

There is a strong scholarly tendency to view such commemorative activities as mere political theater, the pan-Hellenic sanctuaries as parade grounds rather than sacred spaces. Although they certainly did function as contexts for display, it is important to remember that every dedication made was nevertheless a ritual act. To describe the flurry of Aitolian dedications at Delphi after 279 as an "obnoxious . . . display" or "political exploitation" is certainly to neglect the religious aspect of the act in favor of the political.[247] When we consider the Aitolians' dedications at Thermon, where no steady stream of non-Aitolian visitors muddies the waters, this perspective seems even more skewed. Here, at the ancestral sanctuary that had served as the site of their political assemblies since probably the late fifth century, the Aitolians appear to have dedicated a monumental statue similar if not identical to the one of Aitolia standing atop a pile of Gallic shields that was set up at Delphi. Numerous fragments of a stone base, again in the form of a shield trophy, have been found near the exedra in front of the east stoa at Thermon, and Konstantinos Rhomaios was certainly justified in suggesting that a statue of Aitolia herself stood atop this pile of shields.[248] The proximity of all the known fragments of this base to the exedra itself suggests that it was built precisely to house this precious monument. Behind it stood the enormous east stoa, 185 meters in length (2.5 times the size of

244. Paus. 10.15.2 with Blum 1914: 23–25 and Jacquemin 1985: 29.

245. Eurydamos: Paus. 10.16.4.

246. *IG* IX.1² 1.199, a highly fragmentary dedicatory inscription found at Delphi, has sometimes been thought (e.g., Blum 1914: 24–25) to be the base of a statue of Lakrates, one of the leaders of the Aitolian contingent (Paus. 10.20.4), but it is far too fragmentary to inspire confidence in the attribution. Cf. Nachtergael 1977: 199; Scholten 2000: 40 n. 39. Other examples of gods and humans together in victory monuments at Delphi: Paus. 10.1.10, 13.6 (Phokian offering); 10.10.1 (the Marathon commemoration).

247. Scholten 2000: 41; Nachtergael 1977: 175.

248. Rhomaios 1916: 188–89 with figs. 10 and 11; Rhomaios 1931: 66; cf. Béquignon 1931: 485; *BCH* 108 (1984) 781 with photo p. 783 fig. 83. Cf. Knoepfler 2007a: 1241–43.

the west stoa at Delphi), which was built in the early third century and may indeed have been constructed as part of a coherent plan of monumentalization in the wake of the victory over the Gauls. When Philip V sacked Thermon in 218, Polybios tells us that his army hauled away some fifteen thousand shields that had been laid up in the stoas.[249] Although the number is surely exaggerated, Polybios's report suggests that the Aitolians had decorated their stoas with armor taken from enemies, and Jean Bousquet is certainly correct to surmise that at least some of these were Gallic shields taken as booty in 279.[250] Yet the dedication of shields taken from defeated enemies appears to have been a traditional privilege of the Aitolian *stratagos,* and it would be misleading to assume that all or even most of the dedicated armor at Thermon was Gallic.[251] The construction date of the east stoa at Thermon seems to suggest that it was indeed built at least in part to house this massive dedication, with the statue of Aitolia personified immediately adjacent to it, a conscious repetition of the shields in the west stoa fronted by the statue of Aitolia at Delphi.[252]

In the face of significant internal and external challenges to the legitimacy of their koina, the Boiotians and Aitolians had recourse to ritual action as a strategy for answering them. By dedicating Gallic arms at Delphi and (probably) Thermon, by presenting the Aitolians as *symmachoi* of the gods in a monumental statue group at Delphi, by personifying the region of Aitolia itself as a fearsome warrior heroine the Aitolians undertook to draw the attention of both their fellow Aitolians and other Greeks to the close relationship between Aitolian regional cooperation and the will of the gods, and to deflect their attention from the plausible culpability of the Aitolians for the disastrous sack of Kallion and the region's generally poor reputation throughout the Greek world. These dedications symbolized a strong and coherent Aitolia; far from being an obnoxious display or mere political exploitation of a military victory, they were a vital mechanism in securing the allegiance of suspicious or resentful Aitolians as well as the rest of the Greek world insofar as they possessed the unique power of ritual to promote a strong sense of attachment to the social reality they symbolized. After their overwhelming victory against the Spartans at Leuktra, the Boiotians likewise found ritual action a powerful means of undergirding the new and hard-won but still compromised participation of the entire region in the koinon. The establishment of a new cult to Zeus

---

249. Polyb. 5.8.9.

250. Bousquet 1988a: 177; cf. Scholten 2000: 41 n. 42.

251. Polyb. 2.2.7–11.

252. This may be supported by the mention of a *pastas* on an inscribed block of the Doric epistyle of the stoa, which is dated by the generalship of Charixenos of Trichonis (*IG* IX.1² 1.54), perhaps the same Charixenos who held the office at least five times beginning in the mid-270s: Scholten 2000: 45. For the parallel placement of the statues and stoas containing arms see Knoepfler 2007a: 1241, based on his restoration of T53 fr. A l. 4.

Basileus at Lebadeia was embedded in the response of the venerable Boiotian oracle of Trophonios, the historical context of its founding making the cult ever after
a locus for anti-Spartan sentiment in the region. Significantly, though, this new
cult was not managed by the koinon itself or by the Boiotians as a whole: it
belonged to the polis of Lebadeia, a rich reward for the city's allegiance to the Boiotian cause and a mark of the koinon's ongoing (if limited) commitment to the
decentralized institutions by which it had been governed in the past. At the same
time the Boiotians' construction of a treasury at Delphi, funded by the spoils from
the battle at Leuktra, was an important strategy for making the rest of the Greek
world see that their opposition to Spartan arrogance had been both collective and
justified. The gods themselves, it appeared, were on the side of regional cooperation and independence. Where decades of diplomacy had failed, ritual action
worked its distinctive social alchemy.

REPRODUCING THE POWER OF THE KOINON

We have seen that shared rituals contributed significantly to the construction of
regional communities that spanned multiple poleis, in part by creating networks of
people who met and interacted at shared sanctuaries and developed shared interests
and in part through articulations of ethnic myths associated with those rituals,
myths that imputed to the larger community consanguinity, a shared territory, and
in many cases a common history of migration. Ritual action was vital to the process
of politicizing such regional communities, a process that unfolded through the
development of the koinon and its institutions, creating a complex political order
that could simultaneously recognize the political authority of its constituent communities while asserting the ultimate sovereignty of a new, central state power.
Ritual action also played an important role, hitherto virtually unrecognized, in
maintaining the koinon as it developed by a complex process of negotiation between
member states and central government, between unification and fragmentation.

A principal mechanism by which this delicate process was protected and its
ever-shifting outcome maintained was the ritualization of koinon institutions. By
this I mean the embedding of the formal political institutions of the koinon in
ritual practice, which both stabilized and protected them. Bloch's claim that ritual
communication is arthritic by virtue of its repetitive, symbolic, and nondialogic
nature helps us to see why this is so. For it is this characteristic that makes ritual
virtually impermeable to argument or reasoned contradiction and "protected . . .
from challenge, rapid modification, or evaluation against other statements or
empirical data."[253] Ritual's impermeability has the effect of stabilizing the positions

253. Bloch 1977: 138.

of its actors, and as a result it becomes a source of protection. And this, as Bloch realizes, is why ritual is vital to power, particularly in its institutionalized forms:[254]

> Those who acquire power institutionalize it to make it less vulnerable from the attacks of rivals, they put their power "in the bank of ritual." They do this by creating an office of which they are the legitimate holders, but which has reality beyond them. This is done by gradual ritualization of the power-holder's communication with the rest of the world and especially his inferiors. As this ritualization proceeds, communication loses the appearance of a creation on the part of the speaker and appears like repeats of set roles specified by the office which appears to hold him. Reality is thus reversed and the creation of the power-holder appears to create him. This process means two things: power having become authority appears less and less challengeable but at the same time it becomes less the power-holder's own.

In light of this, the need to ritualize power in monarchical contexts is immediately comprehensible; rituals of investiture not only demarcate the power holder from his subjects, but insofar as they are repetitions of similar rituals performed by and for previous power holders, they imbue in subordinate onlookers and participants a sense of the continuity, stability, and general rightness of the power holder's claims and undercut onlookers' ability to question a particular individual's possession of power.[255] Yet the ritualization of power and the institutionalization of ritual should also be vital to the creation and maintenance of more complex and fragile political orders like the koinon. Without the rule of a single leader, those who worked toward the politicization of regional communities in the ancient Greek world faced the constant threat of attacks on the federal state, in the form of either secessionist or centralizing movements. The rituals considered thus far, which contributed to the politicization of regional communities, may on their own have effaced the distinct identity and partial autonomy of the koinon's constituent members. From the fourth century onward, however, as koina across the Greek world developed a particularly robust set of institutions and as the resolution of our evidence is significantly increased by epigraphic sources, we find ritual practices that effected both integration and differentiation—that is, they articulated the essential persistence of the polis as a distinct and partly autonomous entity within the koinon while maintaining the unity and power of the koinon as a whole. In the koinon we find a distinctive response to the challenging imperative of simultaneous integration and differentiation, namely the deployment of a pervasive strategy of representation in the realm of ritual action.

As the koinon institutionalized its ritual practices, it simultaneously ritualized its own institutions. The extensive evidence we have for institutionalized ritual

254. Bloch 1977: 139; cf. Kertzer 1988: 51.
255. Bloch 1977; cf. Kertzer 1988, esp. 52–54.

action in the koinon points to its vital role in maintaining and strengthening the regional state, for the distinctive recursivity between ritualization and institution-alization reduced the vulnerability of the koinon as a power structure and dissi-pated impressions of the arbitrariness (or injustice) of the distribution of power in the koinon by enlisting the participation, and implicitly the assent and complicity, of all its member communities.

Ritual and the Maintenance of Local Distinction in the Koinon

Highly distinctive polis cults served in the framework of a city's membership in a koinon to articulate and reinforce the city's independent identity. One such cult can be found in the tiny coastal polis of Boiotian Anthedon, on the Strait of Euboia, where citizens derived their livelihood almost entirely from its maritime economy, the only one of its kind in Boiotia.[256] According to legend Anthas, eponymous hero of the polis, had a son, Glaukos, a fisherman who leapt into the sea and became both a *daimōn* and a prophet.[257] Anthedon's distinctive maritime economy was thus ritual-ized. Another example is the polis of Pellene, in eastern Achaia, which held an agonistic festival for Apollo Theoxenios that drew participants not only from the Peloponnese but also from central Greece and even the eastern Aegean.[258] The city rewarded victors with cloaks woven locally, presumably from sheep reared in the mountains that constituted the better part of Pellene's territory, cloaks that became a byword for quality textiles.[259] In both Anthedon and Pellene, local cults closely bound up with the local economy reinforced the distinct identities of poleis that were also members of a koinon, mitigating the erosion of boundaries between polis and koinon that could otherwise have led to the devolution of a koinon into a single unitary state.

Ritual also contributed to the maintenance of local identity and government in the koinon by articulating and reinforcing the distinctive history and social struc-ture of an individual polis.[260] The best example comes from Achaian Patrai, which, like the other poleis of Achaia, was formed by the synoikism of smaller settlements.[261]

256. See below, pp. 269–70.

257. Str. 9.2.13; Paus. 9.22.6–7; Mnaseas of Patrai *FHG* III.151 fr. 12 *ap.* Ath. 7.296b with Laqueur 1931. Pausanias mentions a monument on the shore commemorating the place of Glaukos's leap and hints at an annual ritual for him when he says that "those men who sail the sea most tell the tale every year of the soothsaying of Glaukos."

258. Rhodes: Pind. *Ol.* 7.83–87 (for Diagoras, 464 BCE). Argos *bis: IG* IV.510; Pind. *Nem.* 10.39–48 (for Theaios, 444[?] BCE). Corinth *bis:* Pind. *Ol.* 13.155–61 (for Xenophon, 464 BCE); *Anth.Pal.* XIII.19 = Simon. fr. 147D for Nikoladas.

259. Pind. *Ol.* 5.95–98, *Nem.* 10.49–52; Poseidippos *App. Anth.* 68 *ap.* Ath. 10.7.414; Str. 7.7.5.

260. This process is most familiar in Athens, where demes celebrated the cults of their local heroes and also participated as such in central polis cults: Sourvinou-Inwood 1990: 313–16.

261. Str. 8.3.2; Hdt. 1.145. On the synoikism and urbanization process in Achaia, see above, p. 48, and Moggi 1976: 89–95 (no. 15). Archaeological evidence surveyed in Morgan and Hall 1996; Vordos 2001, 2002 discusses the case of Trapezá (Rhypes).

Yet the rural communities from which the urban nucleus of Patrai was formed were not abandoned; their continuing vitality is shown by the fact that when the urban center of Patrai was temporarily abandoned after the Gallic invasion of 279 its inhabitants went back to the villages.[262] They attained a structural status rather like that of Patrai and the other Achaian poleis in relation to the koinon, distinct communities that were also part of a larger political community. This dual status clearly manifests itself in the rituals associated with the cult of Artemis Triklaria (Artemis of the Three Territories) and Dionysos Aisymnetes, which highlight for us at the scale of the polis the ritual practices deployed to stabilize the federal power structure.

According to Pausanias, "the Ionians who lived in Aroe, Antheia, and Mesatis had a sanctuary and temple of Artemis Triklaria in common, and the Ionians used to hold a festival for her and an all-night vigil every year."[263] Antheia and Mesatis were two of the communities from which Patrai was formed, and Aroe was the old name for the settlement that would become the nucleus of Patrai itself (map 3).[264] The associated ritual for Artemis was as follows. During the festival of Dionysos, a certain number of local children went to the sanctuary of Artemis Triklaria by the river later known as Meilichos, wearing grain garlands on their heads.[265] These they laid aside "by the goddess," perhaps meaning that they set them in front of her cult statue. After bathing in the river, they placed garlands of ivy on their heads and processed to the sanctuary of Dionysos in the urban center, near the theater, on the road from the agora to the western part of the city.[266] At some point during the festival, three images of Dionysos were brought into the sanctuary of Aisymnetes. These were, according to Pausanias, "equal in number to the ancient towns, and sharing their names: they are called Mesateus, Antheus, and Aroeus."[267] The civic and territorial associations of the ritual are clear: children wearing garlands of grain processed to a sanctuary of Artemis in the *chōra* of Patrai, which was

262. Persistence of rural occupation: Petropoulos and Rizakis 1994: 203. Return after 279: Paus. 7.18.6.

263. Paus. 7.19.1.

264. Paus. 7.18.2–5. According to local myth, after the expulsion of the Ionians, Patreus the son of Preugenes forbade anyone from settling at Antheia or Mesatis, fortified Aroe, and renamed it Patrai after himself. Despite the myth there is clear evidence for occupation of Mesatis, which has now been located at Voudeni by an inscription: Petropoulos 2001–2.

265. Paus. 7.20.1, 7.22.11. The sanctuary is probably to be identified with the sculptural fragments (now in the Patras Museum) found in the bed of the Meilichos (modern Velvitsianiko) River belonging to three marble statues, two naked males and one draped female, executed in the high classical style of the late fifth century BCE: Petropoulos 1991: 256 (with photo); Osanna 1996: 125–26, 130–31 with photo pl. 10.1. The discovery of ancient building foundations and the pavement of a Christian church on the left bank of the Velvitsianiko may further locate the site of the sanctuary of Artemis Triklaria: Petropoulos and Rizakis 1994: 198.

266. Paus. 7.20.1–2.

267. Paus. 7.21.6.

remembered as a sanctuary used by the Ionians who inhabited the region before the synoikism of Patrai; after bathing in the river, they adorned themselves with ivy and processed back to a sanctuary of Dionysos in the city, which held three images of the god, one for each community from which Patrai was composed, the three *klaroi* whose unification Artemis represented. The ritual thus reflects the fractal nature of the sociopolitical order at Patrai: separate communities that are nevertheless part of a larger single community, the polis of Patrai, which in its turn serves as a single member community of the yet larger koinon of the Achaians.[268]

Pausanias (7.19.2–10) also records the aetiological myth associated with this ritual, an aition inextricably bound up with the establishment of a new civic order in the synoikized polis. According to this myth, the priestess of Artemis Triklaria, outstanding for her beauty, was wooed by an equally handsome young man, and despite their love for each other, their parents forbade a marriage. As a result, they met secretly in the goddess's sanctuary and "used it as a bridal chamber." The virgin goddess in her anger inflicted famine and plague upon the people of Patrai, who in desperation consulted the oracle at Delphi. The god accused the priestess and her lover of being responsible for these plagues and ordered that they should be sacrificed to Artemis, to be followed every year by the sacrifice of the city's most beautiful *parthenos* and *pais*. The goddess's wrath led the people of Patrai to name the river that ran by her sanctuary Ameilichos, "Relentless." Before the incident with the priestess and the plague, however, the Patraians had received another oracle from Delphi, according to which "a foreign king would arrive in the land, carrying with him a foreign god, and this king would put an end to the sacrifice for Triklaria." The oracle was fulfilled by the arrival of Eurypylos the son of Euaimon, who had been wandering in madness upon his return from Troy after beholding an image of Dionysos created by Daidalos, kept in a chest, which had been given to him as a gift. In a moment of lucidity, Eurypylos too had consulted the oracle at Delphi and had been advised to make his home where he found people offering a strange sacrifice. His ships were subsequently blown to the coast of Aroe, where the human sacrifice to Artemis was about to take place. Both oracles were fulfilled: Eurypylos regained his sanity, the obligation of human sacrifice was ended, and the cult of Dionysos Aisymnetes, the foreign god inside the chest, was established in conjunction with that of Artemis. At the festival in their honor, Eurypylos received sacrifice as a hero, and the river that flowed by the sanctuary of Artemis was renamed Meilichos, "Gentle," "Kind."[269]

268. Cf. Polignac 1995: 68–71 for analysis of the procession as a symbolic reenactment of a synoikism in which the original settlements persist.

269. The lasting importance of Eurypylos in the construction and expression of Patrai's civic identity is revealed by his appearance on bronze coins of Patrai from the imperial period: Imhoof-Blumer and Gardner 1886: 79. For further discussion of Eurypylos see Nilsson 1906: 295; Kearns 1992: 89–91.

As so often, the myth both explains and interprets the ritual.[270] Pausanias explains (7.20.1) that the children wear grain garlands in imitation of the adornment of those who used to be sacrificed to Artemis before the advent of Eurypylos and Dionysos. The gift of grain garlands simultaneously commemorates harsher obligations once due to the goddess and celebrates the fact that they are now past. The children's bathing in the river is a ritual reenactment of the city's purification by the arrival of the foreign king and initiates the transition from one ritual object (Artemis) to another (Dionysos).[271] The ritual begins and ends with a procession from the urban center of Patrai to the edges of its eastern territory, and both deities simultaneously represent the unity of Patrai and its composite nature: Artemis of the Three Territories is yet a single deity, and the single god Dionysos Aisymnetes has three statues, each one representing a constituent community of Patrai. The crisis initiated by the priestess of Artemis was about improper union; Dionysos Aisymnetes, the epiklesis a title given to autocratic rulers selected to put an end to civil strife, resolved the crisis and restored civic order to the community.[272] It is impossible to date the origins of the ritual or even of the myth, although some elements are almost certainly elaborations of the Hellenistic or Roman period.[273] The sculptural fragments that are probably to be associated with the sanctuary of Artemis Triklaria on the banks of the river Meilichos belong to the fifth century, which suggests that when Patrai was being synoikized, this rural cult was receiving significant adornment and investment. A cultic pair symbolizing a unified sociopolitical order comprising multiple distinct entities would have created a powerful ritual context for the perpetual reinforcement of a synoikized city.

270. Cf. Redfield 1990.

271. Initiation ritual: Massenzio 1968; Calame 1997: 137. Purification: Nilsson 1906: 294–97.

272. *Aisymnētēs*: Arist. *Pol.* 1285a30–b4, 1295a12–14; *Frag.Var.* Category 8, Treatise 44; Hölkeskamp 1999: 12–13. It also appears as the name of a magistracy in Megara (*IG* 7.15) and Chalkedon (*GDI* 3045). In Hom. *Od.* 8.258, the *aisymnētēs* is an umpire in games, which reveals the basic function of autocratic arbitration belonging to this figure; cf. Hom. *Il.* 24.347; Theophr. fr. 127.1 *ap.* Dion. Hal. 5.73.3. Kearns 1992: 90 suggests that Dionysos earned his epiklesis as corrector of the sacrificial rites to Artemis; cf. Zunino 1994: 51. Nilsson 1951: 23 comments that "the epithet, which signifies 'ruler', 'judge', is singular and recorded nowhere else." But it appears (in feminine form) as an epithet of Athena in Call. fr. 238 Pfeiffer 1949 = Hollis 1990 fr. 17.10. At Miletos *aisymnētai* are not only the eponymous magistrates but also *molpoi* of Apollo Delphinios (*Milet* I.3 no. 122 with Herrmann, *Milet* VI.1 p. 166; *Milet* I.3 no. 133 with Herrmann, *Milet* VI.1 pp. 168–69). The question of whether they had anything more than symbolic political significance continues to be debated (de Sanctis 1930; Gehrke 1980: 20–24; Robertson 1987: 359–60; Faraguna 1995: 53–54, 2005: 325–26; Hölkeskamp 1999: 211–14), but the elision itself is interesting.

273. Nilsson 1951: 23 believes that the entire ritual complex embracing Artemis and Dionysos, the urban center and the territory of Patrai, was likely an invention of the Augustan age. But this belief stems from his skepticism about a pre-Hellenistic synoikism of Patrai, for which there is now plentiful archaeological evidence.

The examples of Anthedon, Pellene, and Patrai show the ways in which ritual action can reinforce the separate existence of member poleis at the local level, but the interdependence of polis, koinon, and formal clusters of poleis within a koinon known as districts was also stabilized and given permanence by the creation of formal ritual institutions that ensured the representation of all member communities in the cultic activities of the koinon. Evidence for such institutions in the Boiotian and Achaian koina will help to illuminate the ways in which ritual simultaneously effected integration and differentiation.

Ten inscriptions from the first half of the third century record the dedication of tripods by the Boiotian koinon to Apollo Ptoios (T16–21), the Muses of Helikon (T22), the Graces at Orchomenos (T23), and Zeus Eleutherios at Plataia (T24, T25).[274] Seven of the ten texts are complete or nearly so, and on these we find the name of the archon of the Boiotians followed by seven, and in one case eight, officials called *aphedriateuontes* or, more simply, "aphedriates," designated by name, patronymic, and city ethnic.[275] The title of the magistracy certainly derives from the verb *aphidruein*, "to set up," but we know nothing more about them than we can deduce from the epigraphic sources.[276] The only other text attesting to their existence is the magistrate list from Thespiai, where they appear as magistrates elected by the city in the *koinon synedrion* but are grouped among the magistrates of the koinon.[277] Their appearance there, alongside the boiotarchs, excludes the possibility that the aphedriates were simply a special name for boiotarchs acting in a religious capacity.[278] If the Thespian magistrate list proves that aphedriates were elected by the polis, a study of the corpus as a whole suggests that this was not true of every polis in Boiotia every year. Rather, the Boiotians extended their system of districts, clusters of poleis and other small communities that simplified the appointment of magistrates, collection of taxes, and provision of military levies to the koinon to facilitate the representation of every community in ritual actions made in the name of all Boiotians.[279]

274. Three additional documents belong to this series, raising the total number to thirteen, but they are not discussed in detail and have not been included in the epigraphic dossier because they are too lacunose to be of real assistance: *IG* VII.2724e, to Apollo Ptoios; *IG* VII.1674, to Zeus Eleutherios; Lauffer 1976: 33 no. 30 (*SEG* 26.588), to a hero at Orchomenos, perhaps to Minyas, whose cult included an *agōn* in the fifth century (Σ Pind. *Isthm.* 1.11c) and the Hellenistic period (*IG* VII.3218), and whose tomb in the city is described by Paus. 9.38.3–5.

275. The complete texts are T16–21 and T23.

276. Etymology: Szántó, *RE* I(2): 2712–13; Schultheß, *RE* VII(2): 1758.

277. Roesch 1965b: 135–41; *IThesp* 84.2–3, 67–68.

278. M. Feyel 1942b: 265 n. 7; Roesch 1965b: 136 *contra* Busolt and Swoboda 1920–26: 1437; Boeckh, *CIG* I.729; Wilamowitz-Moellendorff 1874: 438.

279. The system is most explicitly attested for the classical period by *Hell.Oxy.* 16.3–4 (Bartoletti) and will be discussed in greater detail below, pp. 371–72.

The corpus of aphedriate inscriptions shows that certain cities—Thebes, Thespiai, and Tanagra—are always represented, whereas other cities never appear together in the same text. The patterns of representation neatly and uniformly follow territorial lines, which suggests that the aphedriates represented not individual poleis but districts.[280] Orchomenos and Chaironeia, neighboring cities in the northwest, never appear together; nor do Lebadeia, Koroneia, and Thisbe, cities with contiguous territories in the southwest; nor Plataia and Oropos; nor Haliartos, Hyettos, Kopai, Akraiphia, and Anthedon.[281] If we group together the cities that never send representatives at the same time, the result is seven (and in one case eight) districts, each of which always has an elected aphedriate. (See table 1 and map 9.) The largest poleis, Thebes, Tanagra, and Thespiai, each comprised a district and therefore elected its aphedriates independently,[282] whereas smaller poleis like Anthedon, Haliartos, and Akraiphia must have elected theirs at the district level. Although we have no evidence for the procedure, provision of the magistrate was probably up to the polis members of the district and not mandated by the koinon, as is suggested by an agreement between Orchomenos and Chaironeia on the provision of cavalry to the Boiotian army (T15), an obligation they shared because they comprised a single district.[283]

When in the Hellenistic period the Boiotians consulted Apollo through an oracle, they made a collective dedication in the form of a tripod. Although the majority of the dedications are to Apollo Ptoios, whose oracle they consulted (T21 l. 2), the Boiotians also made dedications to the Muses (T22 ll. 2–3), the Graces (T23 ll. 2–3), and Zeus Eleutherios (T24 l. 2) "in accordance with the oracle of Apollo."[284] Unfortunately, we do not know the circumstances for any of these consultations,

280. Knoepfler 2000 and 2001b; Corsten 1999: 38–43. Roesch 1965b: 138–39, on the basis of the appearance of the aphedriates in the Thespian magistrate list, assumed that they were elected by cities as representatives to the federal government; he believed that the relatively consistent appearance of Tanagra, Thebes, Thespiai, Plataia, and Orchomenos indicated that they were cities "de premier rang," the remaining cities, less frequently represented, belonging to some "second rang," and he envisioned some unknown mechanism by which turns for representation were determined. But there are too many inconsistencies with this theory (not least the fact that Orchomenos and Plataia are not always represented), and Knoepfler's more systematic study of the corpus shows that Roesch's conclusions cannot stand.

281. In one list from the Ptoion (T19) we find Chalkis sending an unparalleled eighth representative, which as Roesch 1965b: 138 saw must belong to the brief period between 308 and 304 when Chalkis and Eretria formed part of the Boiotian koinon.

282. This, of course, is why an aphedriate appears on the magistrate list from Thespiai.

283. The evidence of this text for the structure and operation of the districts in the Hellenistic period will be discussed below, in chapter 6.

284. That all the texts were prompted by receipt of an oracle is shown by the presence of the *mantis* on many of the lists that lack the formula κατὰ τὰν μαντείαν τῷ Ἀπόλλω[νος]: T16 l. 5, T17 l. 8, T18 ll. 5–6, T19 l. 7, which all name the same individual, Onoumastos son of Nikolaios of Thespiai, although they belong to different archon years. It is not clear whether Apollo Ptoios or some other Apolline oracle is meant on the texts recording dedications to the Muses, the Graces, and Zeus.

TABLE 1 The districts of Hellenistic Boiotia as inferred from epigraphic evidence for patterns of representation by aphedriates in appendix texts 16–25

Polis	T16	T17	T18	T19	T20	T21	T22	T23	T24	T25	District[a]
Thebes	•	•	•	•	•	•	•	•	•	•	I
Thespiai	•	•	•	•	•		•	•	•	•	II
Tanagra	•	•	•	•	•	•	•	•			III
Orchomenos	•	•		•			•	•		•	
Chaironeia						•					IV
Plataia	•	•	•	•	•		•		•		V
Oropos								•			
Lebadeia	•										VI
Koroneia	•		•			•	•	•			
Thisbe				•	•						
Anthedon	•							•	•		VII
Haliartos		•		•			•				
Akraiphia			•		•						
Hyettos										•	
Kopai											
						•					
Opous											VIII
Chalkis				•							

[a] The districts as defined by these data are represented in map 9.

but all the texts belong in the period from 287 to roughly 240, a period of upheaval and frequent conflict for the region, as we have seen. The flurry of oracular consultations before Leuktra points to the kinds of contexts in which we may imagine these dedications to have been made, though we need not suppose that they all related to equally momentous decisions. The texts all contain the phrase "the Boiotians dedicated" or something similar. "Boiotians" must here signify the Boiotian koinon. The college of aphedriates, serving to represent all the member poleis of the koinon in an equitable fashion, was a means of ensuring that the dedications were in fact made by all the Boiotians. It complicated defection, implicitly securing the commitment and participation of every individual and community in the dedicatory act, which was performed in exchange for a good oracle from Apollo (T17 ll. 3–4). The broad range of the aphedriates' activities, from Akraiphia to Lebadeia, likewise suggests that the Boiotians sought to continually reinforce the unification of the region through systematic participation in many of its cults, capturing the cohesive effects of shared ritual action. We can also see the aphedriates and their collective dedications as a means of protecting the very system of districts by imbricating it in a ritual context. This would be particularly important if in fact, as has recently been suggested, the district system was recreated by the Boiotians in connection with the reintegration of Thebes in 287 as a means of protecting against the Theban abuses that led to their complete centralization of power in the years 379–335.[285]

Their practice of institutionalizing rituals to achieve full (if representative) pan-Boiotian participation and simultaneously to strengthen the institutions of the koinon may go beyond the dedicatory rituals evinced by the aphedriate inscriptions. By the late fourth or early third century the Itonion was used as a repository of decrees relating to the Boiotian koinon (T53 frag. A ll. 5–6). A Delphic decree of the 260s declared the Itonion inviolable, and by the 220s the festival celebrated there, known as the Pamboiotia, was protected by a sacred truce.[286] A series of four inscriptions from the second half of the third century commemorates victories achieved at the Pamboiotia in a variety of agonistic events, including a cavalry competition and a contest known as the *Euopliē*, in which men in arms were judged on their presentation according to military rank: elite infantry, light-armed infantry (*peltophoroi*), archers, slingers, and so on.[287] The inscriptions show that these competitors were, at least in some cases, not individuals but teams formed by Boiotian districts, which commemorated their victories by making dedications to the gods of their polis or dedicating statues with inscribed bases at the Itonion itself.[288]

This impression may be further supported by a decree of Haliartos recording the city's response to an embassy sent by their neighbors the Akraiphians. The embassy was sent to invite the Haliartians "to participate in the sacrifice in the *temenos* of Athana Itonia and Zeus Karaios," and "to send cavalry from the city for the contest by *telē* during the contest of the Ptoia."[289] Akraiphia's invitation to

285. C. Müller 2011.

286. Amphiktyonic decree recognizing *asylia* of the Itonion: Bousquet 1958: 74–77 with photo, fig. 10 (*SEG* 18.240; *FDelph* III.4.358) ll. 11–14. Pouilloux (*FDelph ad loc.*) rightly emphasizes the fact that the reference to Koroneia in line 14 is entirely restored and suggests that the decree could refer to the Thessalian Itonion. That is indeed possible, but literary references (Polyb. 4.3.5, 25.2; 9.34.11) suggest that in the latter part of the third century the Itonion at Koroneia had both *asylia* and a sacred truce for the Pamboiotia, both of which could of course be broken. Cf. F. W. Walbank 1957–79: I.452, 471; Schachter 1981–94:I.123.

287. *IG* VII.3087; *SEG* 26.551–52 and 3.354; Roesch, *IThesp* 201 (for the *Euopliē*). Although Ducat 1973: 60–61 detected an archaic character in these military contests, there is no evidence for their existence prior to the mid-third century, and they may be associated (Schachter 1978: 84 and 1981–94: I.124 n. 3) with the reform of the Boiotian army in exactly the same period (Beloch 1906: 34–51; M. Feyel 1942b: 188–218).

288. The clearest case is *SEG* 26.551–52, in which competitors from Koroneia, Lebadeia, and Thisbe commemorate the victory of the *telos* of the Koroneians.

289. *SEG* 32.456 (Lupu 2005: 227–37). It has been debated whether the cavalry contest here referred to was part of the festival for Apollo Ptoieus (Roesch 1982: 225–43) or whether it was part of a separate but concurrent festival for Athena Itonia and Zeus Karaios at Akraiphia (Rigsby 1987), but on balance the latter seems likelier.

Haliartos to participate in a contest by *telē* again suggests the Boiotian practice of ensuring pan-Boiotian representation and participation in regional cults by conducting rituals by districts. For Haliartos and Akraiphia, two small poleis that never appear together in the aphedriate lists, are therefore thought to have belonged to the same district. And the phrase "contest by *telē*" echoes the "*telos* of the Koroneians" that commemorated its victory at the Pamboiotia with a dedication at Thisbe. We know from the agreement between Orchomenos and Chaironeia on supplying cavalry for the federal military (T15) that the koinon left it up to poleis to determine how they would meet the obligations of their district, and the decree of Haliartos responding to the Akraiphian embassy may reflect a similar arrangement between members of a single district working out how they would fulfill their religious obligations. In particular, it has been proposed that the cavalry contest may best be understood as a kind of Pamboiotia in miniature, inasmuch as it is part of a festival held at a local sanctuary that honors precisely those gods celebrated at the regional sanctuary. May one purpose of such a festival have been to prepare the team for the upcoming high-profile competition at Koroneia itself? In any case the clustering of communities for participation in regional festivals is a structure that appears to be replicated even at smaller scales, pointing again to the full penetration of these institutions in the social life of the region.

If participation in the contests at the Pamboiotia was by district and perhaps by polis teams, then the festival is important not only in its obvious pan-Boiotian catchment area but in its replication of the sociopolitical structures that defined the Boiotian koinon. Individuals did not participate as Boiotians; rather they participated with fellow citizens as representatives of their districts, to which they belonged only as citizens of a polis. In this sense, then, the *agōnes* of the Pamboiotia simultaneously ritualized the institutions of polis, district, and koinon, insofar as each district team represented a polis or a cluster of poleis and participated in a regional cult managed by the koinon. The process of ritualization endowed these institutions with stability and permanence through reiteration and the deployment of symbols in a cultic context related in myth to the unity of the Boiotians by descent (from the Boiotoi who invaded from Arne) and in ritual to the community of the Boiotians by interaction (for we have seen that even in the early fifth century the Itonion drew worshippers from well beyond Koroneia). The games provided a framework for competitive displays of prowess, wealth, and training by each district, while simultaneously displaying the collective might of the Boiotian military, however badly it was in need of improvement following its defeat in the third battle of Chaironeia. Yet the existence of the college of aphedriates and the practice of making collective dedications at regional sanctuaries by district representatives on behalf of the koinon requires that we fully contextualize the practice of district-team competitions at the Pamboiotia. These ritual contests, although clearly related to military preparation, simultaneously adhered to broader practices by which the

Boiotians sought continuously to embed in a ritual context the institutions by which their koinon was structured, thereby strengthening and legitimating them.

Plataians and Boiotians at the Daidala

The rich evidence for Boiotian cult practices provides us with further insight into how the ritualization of institutions strengthened and perpetuated the socio-political order. At Plataia, the Daidala evolved from a ritual procession articulating the territory of the polis and celebrating the restoration of civic order in the polis into one in which the entire region participated, thus serving as another framework for ritualizing the institutions of the koinon.[290] Although epigraphic and archaeological evidence for the ritual is virtually nonexistent, we know that the cult of Hera at Plataia goes back to the late archaic period, for she was addressed by the Spartan Pausanias, with the epiklesis Kithaironia, during the epochal battle of 479.[291] When the Thebans finally captured Plataia in 427 and razed the city to the ground, they built an elaborate katagōgion (an inn or guest house for visitors to the sanctuary) and a new stone temple to Hera.[292] The trouble they took over the sanctuary, and particularly the katagōgion, which was two hundred feet long with rooms upstairs and downstairs, suggests that the Thebans were interested in perpetuating under their own control a festival that at least periodically drew a large crowd of visitors to a sanctuary of some prestige.[293] Pausanias (9.2.7) describes two statues in the Heraion at Plataia, one of Hera Nympheuomene, "the Bride," made by Kallimachos, and one of Hera Teleia, "the Wife," made by Praxiteles. Kallimachos was active in the final third of the fifth century BCE, and Praxiteles during the second and third quarters of the fourth century.[294] The dates are suggestive,

290. The Daidala festivals have attracted scholarly attention at least since Frazer, and I shall not attempt to provide a survey of the many variant approaches taken, for which see Chaniotis 2002 and 2005: 155–60.

291. Hdt. 9.52, 53, 61, 69. Terracotta figurines and small finds of the sixth century (Washington 1891: 402–3; Higgins 1954: 761–69, 775–80, 790–93; Mollard-Besques 1954: nos. B55–61, 72–76; cf. Riele and Riele 1966; Kossatz-Deismann 1988: 666; Simon 1997: 86; Iversen 2007: 382–83) suggest cult activity for a female goddess in that period but offer no specifics about ritual activity. A destruction layer noted beneath the foundations of the fifth-century temple at Plataia (Washington 1891: 403; Iversen 2007: 388) may represent the remains of an archaic temple destroyed by the Persians when they burned the town in 480. This evidence, even if it does pertain to a Hera cult at Plataia, simply does not support Prandi's (1982; 1983: 92; 1988: 22–24) inference that the ritual of the Daidala as described by Pausanias was a pan-Boiotian festival by the seventh century. Cf. S. Morris 1992: 369.

292. Th. 3.68.2–5. It is probably this temple that was discovered and partly excavated by Washington 1891. Though Pritchett 1965-92: I.119 n. 68 objects that the long, narrow dimensions do not suit a temple constructed in the late fifth century, Fossey 1971 suggests that this style prevailed in Boiotia much later than it did elsewhere on the Greek mainland.

293. Iversen 2007: 393.

294. Stewart 1990: 277–81; cf. Iversen 2007: 392, 398.

Kallimachos coinciding with the construction of the new temple and *katagōgion* at Plataia after 427 under Theban supervision, and Praxiteles with the short period between about 386 and 373, when the Plataians were restored to their city and were participating members of the Boiotian koinon, or with the restoration of the city after the battle of Chaironeia.[295]

The nature of the ritual at Plataia in the classical period and the patterns of participation in it are not clearly attested, but the fifth-century statue of Hera Nympheuomene is directly associated with the myth attached to the cult in the Roman period, which suggests that the rituals of the Lesser and Greater Daidala described in our later sources go back in some form to this period.[296] The rituals essentially enact the myth in which Hera, jealous of Zeus's amorous dalliances, separated herself from him. In despair Zeus consulted either Alalkomeneus or Kithairon, the tyrant of Plataia, who advised him to make a statue of oak, called a *daidalon*, adorn it like a bride, and lead it in a mock marriage procession.[297] Hera took the bait and approached in rage, but when she discovered his ruse she was delighted by it and reconciled herself to Zeus. In what follows I attempt to tease out the political and territorial implications of the ritual and the myths that sought to explain it.

According to Pausanias (9.3.3–5), the Plataians alone celebrated the Lesser Daidala. Every six years they would go to a grove near Alalkomenai where the largest oak trees in Boiotia were to be found, scatter about pieces of boiled meat, and wait, watching intently for a crow to seize a piece of the meat and land on one of the oak trees. That tree was then used to fabricate a new *daidalon*. Kallimachos's cult statue of Hera Nympheuomene must have been associated with preexisting cult practices and suggests that the Plataians worshipped Hera in connection with marriage before that time; it is thus probable that some form of ritual similar to what was later known as the Lesser Daidala predates the destruction of the city. The Theban occupation and reconstruction of the sanctuary may also be the historical moment when the Daidala became a regional festival: if the Thebans meant to maintain the cult, they would have had to find a new group of participants, and this would explain very well their reason for building such an enormous guest house.[298] Only four years later the Athenians, defending themselves against the Theban charge of having unlawfully occupied the sanctuary of Apollo at Delion,

295. Cf. Prandi 1988: 121–32; Iversen 2007: 398–99 favoring the post-338 date for Praxiteles' statue.
296. So too Iversen 2007: 391.
297. Alalkomeneus: Plut. fr. 157 (Sandbach 1967) *ap.* Euseb. *Praep. evang.* 3, prooem. = *FGrHist* 388 F 1; Kithairon: Paus. 9.3.1. On the *xoanon*, the *daidalon*, and Daidalos himself see Frontisi-Ducroux 1975: 193–216. Schachter 1981–94: I.245–47 gives a good overview of the many interpretations of the ritual, with full references. The marriage aspect is discussed by Clark 1998: 22–25 and Jost 1997: 89–92.
298. Iversen 2007: 395.

reminded them that "it is custom among the Greeks that conquest of a territory, whether large or small, always includes possession of its sanctuaries, and carries with it the obligation to maintain customary cultic practices as far as possible. Indeed the Boiotians themselves and many others, when they have taken some territory by force, now possess other people's sanctuaries, which they at first took by seizure."²⁹⁹ Could Thucydides' Athenians here be referring to the recent Theban occupation of the Plataian Heraion and their assumption of the maintenance of Plataia's customary cultic practices to the best of their abilities, namely by drawing participants from all over Boiotia to replace the now absent Plataians who once performed the rites?³⁰⁰ Yet it is not at all clear how closely the rituals of the Lesser Daidala described by Pausanias, which strictly speaking belongs to the Roman period but probably goes back to the Hellenistic, correspond to the Plataian-led rituals of the cult of Hera at Plataia before 427 and the Theban-led rituals between 427 and 386, and from 372 to a little after 338, when the Plataians were finally restored to their home. Ultimately Pausanias's account and the fragments of Plutarch's treatise on the Daidala tell us about a ritual complex of the period after 338.

The Greater Daidala was celebrated only once every sixty years, and all the cities of Boiotia joined the action.³⁰¹ Fourteen images (*xoana*) prepared at the Lesser Daidala that had occurred since the last Great Daidala were conveyed in a procession by representatives of the cities of Boiotia in an order determined by lot. The images were placed on wagons along with women serving as ritual bridesmaids, and the wagons were conveyed from the Asopos River to the peak of Kithairon, where the cities burned their images (*daidala*) along with a cow for Hera and a bull for Zeus.³⁰²

299. Th. 4.98.2–3.

300. If it is correct that the Theban construction of a *katagōgion* and new temple for Hera at Plataia after 427 catalyzed the transformation of a previously Plataian cult into a pan-Boiotian cult, then Schachter's (1981–94: I.248) suggestion that the Daidala became pan-Boiotian only in response to the pan-Hellenic appropriation of Plataia for the Eleutheria in the late fourth century under Macedonian hegemony (cf. Skias 1917: 160 no. 7) should be reevaluated.

301. There is a problem with the intervals of the Lesser and Greater Daidala, as Pausanias himself saw (9.3.3, 5). Knoepfler 2001b: 362–68 and Iversen 2007: 402–5 offer different but equally speculative solutions. For my purposes the point is immaterial.

302. Paus. 9.3.5–8. According to Pausanias the Thebans joined the ritual only after 316, when their city was restored by Cassander; the restoration of the city may, however, need to be separated from its reintegration in the koinon, which seems essential for participation in the Greater Daidala, so Theban participation may belong as late as 287 (Knoepfler 2001b: 373 and 2001c; and above, pp. 97–98). In this particular form the Greater Daidala must have had its origin in the final restoration of the Plataians to their city shortly after Chaironeia (Iversen 2007: 406). Indeed the symbolic homology between the reconciliation of Zeus and Hera on the one hand and of Plataia and Boiotia on the other would have become especially powerful after the reentry of Thebes, Plataia's once implacable enemy, into the koinon. (Cf. Knoepfler 2001b: 368–70.)

The ritual complex of the Lesser and Greater Daidala provides a clear illustra-tion, perhaps the best we have, of ritual's ability to accomplish both differentia-tion and integration, an essential condition for the viability of any federal sys-tem. The representative ritual institutions of the aphedriates and the Pamboiotian agonistic *telē* provided an unusual mechanism for the virtually simultaneous accomplishment of differentiation (at the scale of the polis and district) and integration (at the scale of the koinon) in a single ritual. More typically, these two effects are brought about only by "the orchestration of rituals in time," and this is precisely why the interrelation of the Lesser and Greater Daidala is so important.[303]

The Lesser Daidala is easily understood as a ritual of differentiation vis-à-vis the rest of the Boiotia, a performance of the unity and distinctiveness of the polis. The ritual's striking territorial aspect (map 2) has received scant attention: the Plataians traveled as far as Alalkomenai to select the oak from which to carve the *xoanon*, which required that they pass through the territory of either Thebes or Thespiai, and into that of Koroneia, which had absorbed Alalkomenai probably by the fourth century.[304] Hera cults, widespread in Thespiai and its extended territory, may have been associated by some formal institutional framework, if we have cor-rectly understood an early fourth-century inventory found at Chorsiai of "sacred possessions of the Thespians" that also included items held at the Heraia of Siphai and Kreusis.[305] If we are willing to believe two late sources, Hera was also wor-shipped at Thespiai under the epiklesis Kithaironia, precisely the epithet by which Pausanias addressed Hera before Plataia in 479; it is odd in the Thespian context because Thespiai and its subordinate communities lie on and around the spurs not of Kithairon but of Helikon.[306] The same sources claim that she was worshiped in the form of a branch or trunk, and if they have not simply confused Thespiai with Plataia, which is distinctly possible, then the cults seem to be closely associated, if not part of the same ritual system in which the deployment of "replicated symbols and gestures ... [creates] homologies among different ritual situations" to effect and reaffirm the close relationship between these two communities, bound together by their enmity to Thebes in the fourth century.[307] That association may have had something to do with the route taken to get to the oak grove at

303. Bell 1992: 125.

304. Hansen in Hansen and Nielsen 2004: 438.

305. *Ed.pr.* Platon and Feyel 1938 with photo (*BE* 39.132); text much improved by Taillardat and Roesch 1966 (*SEG* 24.361; *IThesp* 38). Cf. Vottéro 1996: 166 with French translation and commentary. A second text, very similar but highly fragmentary, was also found at Chorsiai: *ed.pr.* Michaud 1974a: 645 (based on the text of Roesch); *IThesp* 39.

306. Arn. *Adv.nat.* 6.11; Clem. Al. *Protr.* 4.46.3.

307. Bell 1997: 173.

Alalkomenai.[308] Plutarch's claim that it was Alalkomeneus who advised Zeus to undertake his ruse in the first place reflects the subregional cultic connection; the Plataian variant recorded by Pausanias, which held that Kithairon himself was the cunning advisor, situates the main events of the myth entirely within Plataian territory, thereby emphasizing the locality of the ritual.[309]

The ritual of selecting and harvesting the wood from which a *daidalon* is to be formed may thus enact Plataia's own cultic relations with its neighbors, but because it was performed by the Plataians alone, the ritual served to differentiate Plataia from its neighbors and from Boiotia as an integrated whole, enabling the Plataians to experience their own autonomy, however limited in scope it was by participation in the koinon. The Greater Daidala, however, functioned to integrate the city into the larger Boiotian system and allowed Plataia and the other Boiotian communities to experience simultaneously their interdependence and their collective integration in the region and the regional state.[310]

The sacred procession of the Greater Daidala began at the Asopos River, which from 519 separated the territories of Plataia and Thebes, and once the *daidala* were arranged on their wagons in the order appointed by lot, it proceeded to the summit of Kithairon, where the sacrificial holocaust was performed.[311] The procession therefore traversed much of Plataian territory, from the northern boundary, historically important and politically sensitive, to the peak of the mountain that probably served as the southern border of the polis. The random order of the wagons prevented any attempt to impose a hierarchy within the framework of the koinon, a feature of Hellenistic but not of classical Boiotia.[312]

Pausanias's list of cities that participated in the Greater Daidala deserves some closer scrutiny. Strictly speaking, it can pertain only to the second century CE.[313]

308. For Knoepfler 2001b: 370–71 the involvement of the grove near Alalkomenai signals "l'aveu des autorités fédérales," but this inference rests on the assumption that the grove was part of the sanctuary of Athena at Alalkomenai, and that is not entirely clear. It is certainly not proven by Plutarch's report (fr. 157 Sandbach) that Alalkomeneus (not Kithairon, Paus. 9.3.1) advised Zeus on the resolution of his quarrel with Hera.

309. Alalkomeneus: Plut. fr. 157 *ap.* Euseb. *Praep. evang.* 3, prooem. Kithairon: Paus. 9.3.1.

310. On the difficulty of understanding how the ritual itself, reenacting the reconciliation of Hera and Zeus by means of a botched sham sacred marriage of Zeus and Daidale, relates intrinsically to the practice of pan-Boiotian participation, note Prandi 1988: 23: "Il collegamento della ierogamia alla processione, con la dea che si trasforma, da sposa, in pronuba delle finte nozze, con la 'moltiplicazione' degli *xoana*—che rende incomprensibile il raconto originario (la finta sposa non poteva essere che una) ma tradisce un ampliamento dei partecipanti . . ."

311. Hdt. 6.108.6.

312. Compare the competition for first place in the process of the pan-Hellenic Eleutheria, also held at Plataia: Robertson 1986.

313. Alcock 1995: 333; Prandi 1988: 156. Schachter 1981–94: I.248 goes to considerable lengths to prove the point. Recent work on Pausanias by Alcock in particular (see also Alcock, Cherry, and

Although the intrinsically conservative nature of ritual action would keep relatively stable the composition of the group of cities that participated in the festival, the extraordinarily long interval of time between celebrations of the Greater Daidala means that there was probably more room for change than if the ritual were performed on a more typical cycle (annual, pentateric, or even heptateric). The ritual's obvious political significance also means that it was probably sensitive to changes in the composition of the koinon itself. Bearing these considerations in mind, Pausanias's list of participating cities (9.3.5–6) is in no way strange or problematic. Together they represent every part of Boiotia before the expansion of the Hellenistic period that brought into the koinon nearby but extraregional (viz. non-Boiotian) poleis like Opous, Chalkis, Eretria, Aigosthena, and Megara. Pausanias tells us that the small towns of lesser account "establish for themselves a common fund [*synteleia*]," certainly for provision of the sacrificial victims.[314] His concluding phrase, "the poleis and the *telē* sacrifice," echoes his earlier use of *synteleia* and may point to another way in which the political geography and institutions of the koinon were ritualized.[315]

The practice of smaller towns' pooling resources for participation in a pan-Boiotian cultic context is immediately familiar from the dedications made by the college of aphedriates on behalf of the Boiotian koinon. There are many points of overlap between the college of aphedriates as religious representatives of districts in the Boiotian koinon and Pausanias's list of cities and *telē* that participated in the Greater Daidala. In both contexts, Thebes, Thespiai, and Tanagra are always represented, as is Plataia, which appears to have shared an aphedriate only with Oropos during the period when it was part of Boiotia. According to Pausanias, both Orchomenos and Chaironeia received their own *daidalon* for the procession, whereas in the aphedriate texts these two neighboring cities never appear together and seem to have formed a single district that appointed its own aphedriate and made its own arrangements for meeting federal military obligations (T15). Likewise, Lebadeia and Koroneia are both mentioned by Pausanias as receiving their own *daidala,* whereas in the aphedriate dedications these cities never appear together and must have formed a district along with Thisbe, a polis not mentioned by Pausanias at all. Significantly, none of the small poleis that appear to have

---

Elsner 2001) puts such elaborate exercises in perspective as products of a period in which the periegete was taken for granted as a reliable guide for the political and religious landscape of a world that predated him by five hundred to seven hundred years.

314. Cf. Bakhuizen 1994: 312 n. 22; Knoepfler 2001b: 348, who prefers Hitzig's emendation of Pausanias's text to συντελέα ἀναιροῦνται.

315. Jones in the 1935 Loeb translates, "the cities and their magistrates." *Ta telē* can indeed have this meaning (LSJ s.v. τέλος I.3), but given the echo with *synteleia* and the description of small poleis pooling resources, I think it is more likely to refer to districts or clusters of cities than to magistrates.

formed the seventh district in Boiotia (Anthedon, Haliartos, Akraiphia, Hyettos, and Kopai) are mentioned by Pausanias, and these must have been among the small towns of lesser account that pooled their resources for provision of a sacrifice and received the four *daidala* not distributed to the larger cities, along with places in the procession up Mount Kithairon.[316]

The aphedriate dedications and the dedications made by teams at the Pamboiotia all belong to the third century BCE, and we should not expect exact correlations between the patterns they reveal and the cultic practices of the Daidala in the second century CE, but the practice of participating in regional cults by means of representatives of clusters of poleis continued in the period after 146, when the Boiotian koinon was reconstituted as an instrument of local government in the Roman empire.[317] Yet the overall consistency of practices is striking, and it seems likely that Pausanias's reference to pooling resources reflects the Hellenistic practice whereby the same small towns acted as coherent groups, districts, for a variety of regional activities, including the performance of cultic obligations.[318] In other words, the representative participation in the Greater Daidala attested by Pausanias is part of the Boiotian practice of ritualizing sociopolitical institutions to effect the regular reproduction and reaffirmation of the koinon not as a narrowly political constitution but as a broad-reaching social structure.

The Achaian Koinon and the Cult of Asklepios

As in Boiotia, so too in Achaia the koinon utilized its own institutions to ensure regional participation in common cults. Evidence for the practice in Achaia is meager by comparison with the Boiotian material, but what survives points to the deployment of similar strategies. An inscription (T41) found at Epidauros records a late third-century law of the Achaian *nomographoi*, the koinon's board of lawgivers, on sacrifices made to Hygieia (ll. 2–3), the mythical daughter of Asklepios and the recipient of cult at Epidauros alongside her father. The surviving portion of the inscription (ll. 4–30) lists the names of the twenty-four individuals serving on this board, identified by both patronymic and city ethnic. Together they represent seventeen communities, all members of the Achaian koinon. The law inscribed on the

316. Knoepfler 2001b: 351–56 too associates the distribution of *daidala* with the institution of districts in Boiotia, but he posits (pp. 353–56) a consistent assignment of two per district and argues that this is the real reason for the requirement that fourteen *daidala* had to be collected before the Greater Daidala. Although mathematically neat, only in two cases (Koroneia-Lebadeia and Chaironeia-Orchomenos) does Pausanias's description of the distribution correlate with the hypothesized two-per-district rule, and there are no parallels for the arrangement.

317. *IG* VII.1764, 2871, 4149.

318. Roesch 1965b: 104 makes only the slightest allusion to the possibility. At pp. 135–41 he analyzes the institution of the aphedriates in greater depth but does not bring the matter back to the Daidala. Cf. M. Feyel 1942b: 265. It is now explored by Knoepfler 2001b.

stele is unfortunately lacunose, but it is clear enough that it legislates the sacrifice of a cow to Hygieia, probably to be carried out by the priests of Asklepios, and arranges for the distribution of the victim's skin (ll. 31–36). The very fact that the koinon's board of lawgivers undertook to establish such a law suggests strongly that the sacrifice was to be made on behalf of the entire Achaian koinon.

We know from brief references in Pausanias and Strabo, as well as one dedicatory inscription of the fourth century, that the cult of Asklepios was widespread in Achaia.[319] In most instances we cannot put any chronological limits around each local cult, but there is one significant exception. At Aigion, a leading polis within the koinon, Pausanias describes a *temenos* of Asklepios with statues of both Asklepios and Hygieia—precisely the Epidaurian pair—made by the Messenian sculptor Damophon, active in the early second century.[320] It is tempting to suppose that Aigion either had a preexisting local cult of Asklepios and Hygieia, which the city sought to elaborate with a new pair of cult statues by a renowned artist in response to the koinon's new, official participation in the cult of Hygieia at Epidauros, or that it established the cult anew on the same occasion. Either way, the koinon's interest in the cult at Epidauros was multidirectional. Whatever the details of representation of the koinon at the actual sacrifice to Hygieia in Epidauros, this law provides a tantalizing hint that the Achaian koinon sought, like the Boiotians', if to a lesser extent, to continuously recreate itself and reassert the legitimacy of its power by employing its own institutions—in this case a board of lawgivers whose competence surely extended to matters other than sacred law—in the enactment of ritual.

The Boiotians and Achaians were not alone in deploying the politically pervasive strategy of representation in religious behavior. During the fourth century the members of the Ionian koinon sent representatives to the Panionia at Mykale, and in Thessaly in the same period individual representatives of member poleis of the Perrhaibian koinon made dedications on behalf of the koinon as a whole in an arrangement highly reminiscent of the Boiotian aphedriates.[321] These practices all point to the ritualization of institutions employed by a koinon to effect cooperation and unity while maintaining the distinct identities and powers of constituent

319. Aigeira: Paus. 7.26.7 with SEG 11.1268, a fourth-century dedicatory inscription on a base clearly designed for a bronze statue, found within *naiskos* D on the akropolis of Aigeira. Olenos: Str. 8.7.4 describes here "a notable temple of Asklepios," which must predate the destruction of the city sometime in the fourth century (on which see Mackil 2004: 501). Patrai: Paus. 7.21.14.

320. Paus. 7.23.7. For Damophon see Stewart 1990: 94–96, 221, 303–4; Themelis 1996, esp. pp. 167–78 for new epigraphic evidence supporting an early second-century date for Damophon's floruit.

321. Ionia: *ed.pr.* Hommel in Kleiner, Hommel, and Müller-Wiener 1967: 45–63; Sokolowski 1970. Perrhaibia: *ed.pr.* Helly 1979 (SEG 29.546); Lucas 1997: 80–81 no. 32; cf. Knoepfler 1983: 56–57 (SEG 33.457).

members in political affairs. The widespread nature of the phenomenon suggests that it served an important if not vital function in the koinon.[322] Embedding political institutions in ritual contexts, as anthropologists from Weber to Bloch have noted, puts power "in the bank of ritual," which reduces its vulnerability to attack by its association with the divine and its dissociation from individual agents and power holders.[323] We have seen that ritual has a unique ability to "reproduce or reconfigure a vision of the order of power in the world" and that the insertion of the koinon's institutions into numerous ritual actions was a powerful and efficacious mechanism for conveying over and over again, with the implicit consent of the participants and those whom they represented, a sense of the rightness of the koinon's power structure.[324]

Over the course of this chapter I have argued that religious action and interactions were central to both the formation of the koinon and to its maintenance and development over time. Little attention has been paid to the role of religion in the politicization of the regional community or in its maintenance over time; there has been a tendency to jump from observations about shared sanctuaries in the archaic period to evidence for their use as political meeting places and repositories of decrees of the koinon. But these paracultic activities at sanctuaries can be fully understood only in light of the ongoing, vital role played by religion in the maintenance of the regional state over time. Ritual action contributed to the construction of political institutions around the regional community that were widely accepted as legitimate and binding rather than arbitrary and unworthy of allegiance, even in the face of crisis and conflict. The ritualization of koinon institutions—the deployment of representative magistracies and civic subdivisions of the koinon used in other contexts for the mobilization of troops, the election of magistrates, and the payment of taxes—thus stabilized the fragile structure of the koinon by ensuring broad and representative regional participation in cultic acts

322. Freitag 2006 makes an argument in this direction as well, via a case study of the arbitration between Halos and Phthiotic Thebes, made almost certainly with some involvement by the Thessalian koinon after 146 (*FDelph* III.4.355; *SEG* 27.79; Ager 1996: 415–20). The decree survives only in six fragments from Delphi, but its publication clause reveals that copies were also to be erected at the sanctuary of Apollo Kerdoios in Larisa, at the sanctuary of Athena Polias in Thebes, in the sanctuary of Artemis Panachaia in Halos, and possibly in the Thessalian sanctuary of Athena Itonia, if this is rightly identified as the sacred land under dispute (line 29, with Robert 1935b: 208). Freitag argues that these particular sanctuaries were chosen as a means of accomplishing the simultaneous integration and distinction that is central to a koinon: one copy in the polis sanctuary of each party to the dispute (Thebes and Halos), one in the sanctuary of Larisa, the home of the single arbitrator whose decision is recorded, one in the pan-Thessalian sanctuary of Athena Itonia, and one at Delphi.

323. In at least one instance, the relationship between political institutions and ritual is inverted: in the koinon of the Chalkideis in the fourth century, documents recording property sales are dated by a federal priest: Hatzopoulos 1988, esp. 66–68 (*SEG* 38.637–39, 670–73).

324. Bell 1992: 81, elaborated at 83–88.

undertaken in the name and on behalf of the entire koinon. In short, religious action was essential to the formation and maintenance of regional states in the Greek world precisely because it could accomplish what no other form of social behavior can: it fosters social solidarity, cloaks revolutions of the sociopolitical order in the garb of tradition, and imbues in participants and onlookers a sense of the rightness of the power under which rituals are performed.

Only when we understand ritual's contribution over time to the formation and maintenance of the regional state can we fully understand the significance of the Hellenistic practice of using sanctuaries as centers for political deliberation. The Boiotians held their political meetings at Onchestos in the Hellenistic period and used the sanctuary of Poseidon there, along with the Itonion at Koroneia and its neighboring shrine of Athena Alalkomeneïs, as archives for the koinon's decrees and laws.[325] Although in the Hellenistic period they dated their decrees by the archon in Onchestos, the Boiotians went to lengths to ensure that the major shrines in the region received copies of documents, just as with their aphedriates and the institutions that governed participation in regional festivals, as a means of reinforcing the integration of the region and the strength of the regional state itself.[326] There is perhaps no clearer illustration of this than the clause of the treaty reached between the Phokians and Boiotians circa 228–218 that stipulates that the boiotarchs and the Phokian generals shall arrange for copies of the treaty to be deposited "each in their own sanctuaries, whichever one seems best."[327] The Aitolians held their elections and at least one annual meeting at Thermon and displayed their public documents at Thermon and at the Laphrion at Kalydon.[328] For several centuries the Achaians held elections and deliberations at the sanctuary of

325. Meetings: Str. 9.2.33; cf. Spyropoulos 1973 for report of (scant) archaeological evidence for a bouleuterion at the site.

326. Examples of documents dated by the archon in Onchestos include *IG* VII.27–28, 209–12, 214–18, 220, 222, 1747–48; *IThesp* 94–96, 98–106. Documents found at Onchestos: T12 and T13. Treaties recording orders for erection of copies at these shrines: T28 ll. 11–12, T53 fr. A ll. 4–6.

327. T28 ll. 19–21. The dominance of Onchestos as a central place tends, in other words, to be over-emphasized; cf. Roesch 1982: 268, who calculates that of the forty-nine surviving decrees of the Hellenistic koinon, twenty-three were found at the Amphiareion, twenty-two at the Itonion, and only two at Onchestos. This is, of course, partly a function of uneven excavation activities, but the importance of shrines other than Onchestos is nonetheless clear. It is odd, then, that Roesch proceeds, on the very same page, to describe Onchestos as the "'capitale' fédérale" and "siège légal du gouvernement fédéral."

328. The Aitolians' political meeting places rotated, but one was always at Thermon, coincidental with the Thermika festival: Ephoros *FGrHist* 70 F 122; Polyb. 4.15.8, 27.1, 37.2; 5.8.4; cf. Larsen 1952 and 1968: 198–99. Most meetings other than those at Thermon, where elections were held, seem to have taken place in military contexts: Polyb. 5.103.2, 16.27.4 (Naupaktos); Polyb. 20.10.14, Livy 36.26.1, 28.9 (Hypata); Livy 33.3.7 (Herakleia). Treaties recording orders for the erection of copies at particular shrines: T53 fr. A ll. 3–4, T57 ll. 14–16, T59 ll. 8–9. The rich corpora of Aitolian inscriptions from the excavations at both Thermon and Delphi provide ample broader testimony on the point.

236 INTERACTIONS AND INSTITUTIONS

Zeus Homarios, a god to whom oaths were also sworn upon the agreement of treaties and the admission of new members to the koinon, but as the koinon expanded
in the late third and early second centuries, a law was implemented that required
that political meetings be held in all the member cities in rotation.[329] Again these
practices go beyond the areas that serve as our case studies. The Phokian koinon
used the sanctuary of Athena Kranaia near Elateia as an archive for its documents
from the fourth century onward, as the koinon of the Epeirotes did with the sanctuary of Zeus at Dodona.[330] The koinon of the Chalkideis recorded major treaties
in a sanctuary, perhaps that of Artemis at Olynthos, and used a priest as its eponymous magistrate.[331] The Akarnanian koinon deposited its decrees at the sanctuary
of Zeus at Stratos and at the sanctuary of Apollo at Aktion, even before the latter
became an official sanctuary of the koinon in 216, and it appears that a cult of
Apollo Metthapios was likewise important to the koinon as a whole.[332] Finally,
when major interkoinon agreements were made, copies of the decrees were deposited not only at the several regional shrines of each party to the agreement but also
at the major pan-Hellenic shrines, including Delphi, Olympia, and Dodona.[333]

The koina of mainland Greece and the Peloponnese held political meetings and
elections at major regional sanctuaries and promulgated copies of their decrees in
numerous sanctuaries throughout their own territories, not simply because they
were convenient meeting places but also because these sanctuaries were the loci
for the establishment of regional communities as well as for their politicization
and legitimation. As the distinctive institutions of the koinon developed, which
were predicated upon the distribution of power and authority across multiple
scales, they were ritualized as a means of achieving greater stability for the state.
When a koinon held political meetings and displayed records of its actions and
decisions at sanctuaries throughout its territory, it did so because in a very real
sense it was in the sanctuaries and the activities performed within them that the
koinon had both its origin and its legitimacy.

329. Str. 8.7.3, 5; Polyb. 5.93.10. Oaths: T39 ll. 5, 8. Law on rotating meeting places: Livy 38.30.2.

330. Athena Kranaia at Phokis: *IG* IX.1.97.19–20; *IMagn.* 34.32, 98, 110–16 (*Syll.*³ 231–35) were all
found in the sanctuary. Epeirotes: *I.Magn.* 32.35; cf. Cabanes 1976: 375.

331. Publication of treaties: Robinson 1934: no. 1 (RO 50).

332. Stratos: Xen. *Hell.* 4.6.4; *IG* IX.1² 2.393. Aktion: *IG* IX.1² 2.583 (Habicht 1957). Apollo Metthapios: *IG* IX.1² 2.573. Cf. Corsten 2000 and 2006.

333. T53 l. 6, T57 l. 15.

5

Economic Communities

Shortly after the conclusion of the King's Peace, ambassadors from the northern Greek poleis of Akanthos and Apollonia went to Sparta to appeal for help in combatting the expansion of the koinon of the Chalkideis under the leadership of Olynthos. Having seized control of significant portions of Macedonia, including Pella itself, the leaders of the koinon were pressing on those poleis of the Chalkidic Peninsula, like Akanthos and Apollonia, that were not members. Xenophon gives us a speech by one Kleigenes, the Akanthian ambassador to Sparta, in which Kleigenes enumerates the resources and advantages that he believes make the koinon of the Chalkideis a threat to its neighbors and to the general peace so recently concluded:[1]

> And bear this in mind, too, how inappropriate it would be for you [Spartans], who went to great lengths to prevent Boiotia from becoming one, now to disregard the gathering of a much greater power, and that not only a land power but one that will also be strong at sea. What stands in their way, when there is plenty of timber in their territory for shipbuilding, the income of revenues from many harbors, many ports, and a large population produced by an abundance of food? . . . These poleis that have joined the koinon unwillingly, if they see that there is opposition, will revolt quickly. If however, they become closely connected by intermarriage [*epigamia*] and the right to acquire property [*enktēsis*] in one another's poleis, rights that have already been voted by them, and they recognize that it is beneficial to be on the side of the stronger, . . . it will perhaps not so easily be dissolved.

1. Xen. *Hell.* 5.2.16–19.

Kleigenes notes not only the extent of the koinon's territory but its variation and the wide range of natural resources it contained: grain, timber, ports, and plenty of manpower. He goes on to enumerate at least a few of the measures undertaken by the koinon to ensure the coherence of this large territory, comprised of multiple previously independent poleis: the rights of intermarriage (*epigamia*) and property ownership (*enktēsis*), enjoyed by all citizens of member poleis throughout the territory of the entire koinon, are expected to increase loyalty and the stability of the regional state over the long term. In short, for Kleigenes (and therefore certainly for Xenophon) the economic resources of the koinon of the Chalkideis, and the institutions implemented by the koinon to shape the interactions of its citizens with one another, are among the principal sources of its power.

Although we need look to no source more esoteric than Xenophon for this information, its significance has been almost entirely overlooked, perhaps because of the widespread assumption that the koinon was a narrowly political entity, and perhaps because in the broader field ancient historians have only begun to think seriously about the interactions between state power and economic behavior in the ancient world.[2] This is certainly due in part to Moses Finley's argument that ancient states acted not out of economic but out of political interests, although Finley conceded that virtually every action taken by a state in antiquity had economic consequences.[3] As Finley's substantivist model has been gradually discredited by specific arguments, historians have begun to return to questions of political economy and the intervention of states in economic activities.[4] Much of the focus

2. In his book on the koinon in the fourth century, Beck 1997: 172 dedicates a single paragraph to *Finanzwesen*. Recent discussions of the speech suggest that Xenophon, for whom Kleigenes acts a mouthpiece, recognized the economic, demographic, and military advantages presented by participation in a koinon but saw them as irrelevant in comparison with the political sacrifice of *autonomia*, of being *autopolitai* (Xen. *Hell.* 5.2.12, 14), explicitly contrasted with *sympoliteia*—that is, participation in a koinon. See Bearzot 1994: 174–79 and 2004: 47–52; Lehmann 2000: 22–23; Beck 2001: 360–62. Despite this recognition of Xenophon's own awareness of its material potential, no one has taken up the challenge of trying to understand the economic logic of the koinon. V. Parker 2003: 114–26 argues that the speech, if not the actual embassy, is a complete fiction designed to serve Xenophon's larger purpose of presenting the Spartans as protectors of the autonomy clause of the King's Peace, but he does not deny that this fabricated speech contains some verifiably true claims about the history and institutions of the koinon of the Chalkideis.

3. Finley 1985.

4. I. Morris 1994 (a review of Cohen 1992); Davies 1998; Eich 2006; Harris 2006: 143–62; Bresson 2007–8: I.7–26; I. Morris, Saller, and Scheidel 2007. The relationship between state power and economic behavior has been less explored for the Greek than for the Roman world; see, for example, Andreau, Briant, and Descat 1994 and Frier and Kehoe 2007, versus Davies 1998: 242 (a brief call for greater attention to public economy) and Möller 2007: 370–80 (comments limited almost exclusively to Athens). Two recent surveys by Migeotte (1995 and 2002) show that there is tremendous potential in the field, but these remain at a general level and present static models. He has also dedicated numerous studies to specific aspects of public economy in the Greek world, which will be cited passim where relevant.

has been on the extent to which states used their power to achieve reliable access to resources, especially grain, through either imports or imperialism; the framework for inquiry into this issue has always been either individual poleis or empires, whether Achaemenid, Athenian, or Roman.[5] Attention has begun to be paid recently to the economic consequences of political institutions. The guarantee afforded by poleis to private-property rights was a fundamental precondition for the development of market exchange, for it is only when producers are secure in their property rights that they feel free to dispose of their surplus in the market.[6] But the restriction of property rights to citizens and the occasional honored individual put a damper on economic mobility, which was further exacerbated by the highly limited legal protections afforded to traders operating in foreign ports.[7] Yet Kleigenes' speech shows that confederation—the creation of political institutions that incorporated but also superseded individual poleis—could lead to control over a significantly increased range of natural resources insofar as the regional state took steps to promote economic mobility throughout its territory, which brought together the varied resources of the territories of its member communities and broke down the economic barriers associated with the political fragmentation of the Greek world.

The relationship between state power and economic behavior is necessarily dynamic, changing constantly in response to new pressures and opportunities. In this chapter I shall argue that a crucial aspect of the koinon's development was its increasingly complex interaction with the economic affairs of its citizens, including intervention in economic crisis and dispute, and the more frequent exercise of the state's ability both to regulate exchange and to collect taxes from its citizens in order to fund the common undertakings of the state. In the previous chapter we saw that religious behavior was so closely imbricated with political power as to make the two virtually inseparable, primarily because ritual was a source of both

5. On the Greek side this debate has centered around the Athenian grain trade: Garnsey 1985 and 1988; Whitby 1998; Eich 2006: 150–74; Moreno 2007; Oliver 2007. Cf. Davies 1998: 235–36 and now Bissa 2009, who considers timber, gold, and silver in addition to grain. Eich 2006: 136–49 briefly considers politically integrated trade regions, but they are all products of the institutions and will of a single dominant polis.

6. Bresson 2007–8: II.107–15.

7. Another form of economic mobility, that of labor, is not in doubt for some professions; skilled artisans were in demand and were employed well beyond their own poleis. But individuals were hired to perform highly restricted tasks, and in many places states and temples that hired them required a third-party guarantor to inspect the work before releasing payment, a result certainly of the limited judicial protections that arose from their status as foreigners: C. Feyel 2006 and 2007. Cf. Archibald 2011. Hennig 1994 and 1995 has shown that even when foreigners were granted the right of property ownership on an ad hoc basis, the granting state found ways to take advantage of it. Measures were taken to address many of the restrictions created by political fragmentation, as will be discussed below.

power and legitimacy for the koinon, a sphere of social action in which the collectivity institutionalized in the koinon had both its origin and one source of its stability. It is equally difficult, and would perhaps be entirely misleading, to separate out economic behavior and state power. For states require revenues with which to fund their actions, including military campaigns most obviously, and perhaps primarily in developmental terms, but also the development of infrastructure like roads, bridges, market facilities at ports, and in the Greek world the construction and maintenance of temples and the performance of the many rituals explored in the previous chapter. Furthermore, exchange is a sphere of action in which the potential for conflict is omnipresent, and in the interests of minimizing both internal and cross-border conflicts, political leaders tend to deploy the state's legislative and regulatory authority in both intrastate and interstate trade.

The formal institutions created by the state tend in turn to influence the economic behavior of individuals, whether by responding to incentives, taking advantage of a good currency (i.e., one with a reputation for good weight and content, with a recognizable stamp that will be widely accepted within a trader's sphere of activities), or being more willing to trade in a state with both the strength and the willingness to enforce regulations and to do so fairly.[8] There is, in other words, a recursive relationship between economic behavior and state institutions, which makes it perhaps more helpful to think of state and economy not as "autonomous spheres of activity, but rather [as] mutually constitutive."[9] The dynamism of this relationship makes it an especially important part of any analysis of state formation and development. For formal institutions like laws and regulations can develop gradually from informal institutions like social conventions and cultural norms. These never go away, nor do they lose their importance in influencing and to some extent regulating behavior, but for an understanding of state formation it is the emergence of formal state institutions from informal ones that is important. Perhaps the most obvious instance of such a transformation in the economic sphere is the Athenian law against lying in the marketplace: deception is harmful to commerce, although its occurrence is widespread because the potential benefits of lying are high when there are no disincentives. In the interest of promoting commerce, the Athenian *dēmos* enacted a law that provided a disincentive to deception, combined with a credible commitment to the enforcement of the law.[10] In the context of the formation of a koinon and its development of state institutions influencing economic behavior, it is interesting to see the formalization of old Greek social norms like helping friends and neighbors in taxation structures,

8. Ober 2008 explores these issues for the case of classical Athens.
9. Block and Evans 2005: 520.
10. Hyp. 4.14; Dem. 20.9. Cf. Velissaropoulos-Karakostas 2002: 132; Cohen 2005: 292; Bresson 2007–8: II.18; van Alfen 2011: 204.

property rights, and regulatory mechanisms that benefit the friends and neighbors who are members of a koinon, while excluding outsiders.

In general terms, political federation almost necessarily entails what we might think of as economic federation: the opening up of trade boundaries, the creation of large common monetary systems, coordinated tax collection, and the pooling of risk. The Nobel prize-winning Austrian economist Friedrich Hayek observed in 1939 that[11]

> one of the great advantages of interstate federation [is] that it would do away with the impediments as to the movement of men, goods, and capital between the states and that it would render possible the creation of common rules of law, a uniform monetary system, and common control of communications. The material benefits that would spring from the creation of so large an economic area can hardly be overestimated, and it appears to be taken for granted that economic union and political union would be combined as a matter of course.

The resonances between Hayek's assertion and Kleigenes' urgent description of the many economic advantages enjoyed by the Chalkideis by virtue of their creation of a koinon are striking, but they are not accidental. As Hayek observes elsewhere in the same essay, there are at least three reasons why political federation has never existed without economic federation. The first is that if the central government has sole authority over relations with foreign states, it will necessarily have to control imports and exports, for economic relations with foreign states constitute a significant arena in which conflict can easily erupt. Second, a federation's common defense policy would be undermined by the presence of interstate (intrafederation) barriers to commerce, for these would "prevent the best utilization of the available resources and weaken the strength of the union" while "regional protectionism would inevitably raise obstacles to an effective defense policy."[12] Third, and finally, the absence of economic federation would seriously undermine the internal coherence of the political federation, for unequal treatment would tend to foster solidarity of interests at the level of the member state and lead thence to conflicts between their interests and those of other states.[13]

The relationship between political and economic federation is thus necessarily a close one, in theoretical terms, although the precise configurations of sovereignty, obligations, and rights have varied in different historical circumstances. Indeed the creation of an open economic zone has sometimes preceded and facilitated the creation of states within the same territory. Thus the Deutscher

11. Hayek 1948: 255 (reprinted from *New Commonwealth Quarterly* 1939).
12. Hayek 1948: 256.
13. Compare Hamilton, Jay, and Madison 1937: no. 7, exploring the causes of dispute that would inevitably arise between states if the confederacy were dissolved and each state were to become fully sovereign; they are all economic.

Zollverein of 1834, which eliminated customs within the union of participating states and distributed the revenues from customs collected at its borders according to agreed-upon principles, led to the adoption of a common currency, a common commercial law, and eventually to the development of the German Reich, forerunner of the modern German federal state.[14] Modern scholars of the political economy of federalism have consistently observed significant economic advantages to federation, to be found particularly in the creation of common currencies, the pooling of risk, and the achievement of economies of scale in the production of public goods. These are among the features recently described as contributing to "the promise of federalism," but insofar as the advantages of economic cooperation tend toward increasing centralization of power, paradoxically they are among the very same features that imperil the delicate balance struck by federal structures between centralization and complete fragmentation.[15]

This paradox immediately raises a normative question: How should economic powers, rights, and obligations be distributed among the various powers of a federal state in order to avoid the dismantling of federation by either centralization or fragmentation? In order to answer this question, economists and political scientists working in the field of fiscal federalism have explored the optimal design of federal institutions, whereby all the benefits of federation could be captured and its self-destructive tendencies minimized. One of the central issues in this work has been the assignment problem, the question of how economic authority should be distributed among central and local governments.[16] One principle tends to guide proposed solutions to the assignment problem, namely that goods and services should be provided by the government at the smallest possible scale. Known especially in European contexts as the principle of subsidiarity, the idea has its roots in late nineteenth-century Catholic social thought and in a modern federal context was enshrined as the guiding principle for the distribution of power in the 1992 Treaty on European Union ratified at Maastricht.[17] In federal applications, the principle of subsidiarity renders to the central government authority only over those affairs that will affect the entire federation or that cannot effectively be accomplished at the level of the member state. It is according to this principle that the provision and oversight of a common monetary system tends to belong

14. Fischer 1960; Dumke 1984.
15. Rodden 2007. Federalism's precarious structure is addressed by Riker 1964 in terms of an inherent set of dilemmas: What prevents complete centralization and the disintegration of member states as such? And what prevents member states from failing to cooperate and therefore leading to the fragmentation of power and the destruction of the federation? These questions, surpassing the narrower issue of fiscal practices in federal states, will be explored below, in chapter 6.
16. Musgrave 1959; Oates 1972 and 1999.
17. Inman and Rubinfeld 1998.

exclusively to the central government, along with responsibility for macroeconomic stabilization and measures for improving the welfare of the poor, while member states are expected to provide the "goods and services whose consumption is limited to their own jurisdiction."[18] More modern approaches to the economics of federalism, by relaxing the classical assumption of the state as a benevolent actor and considering the role of institutions in effecting the incentives of state agents, have tempered these generally laudatory conclusions about the economic effects of federalism while still arguing that the distribution of authority characteristic of federalism can have salutary results if the institutional design is right.[19]

While much of the work done by scholars in this field is explicitly normative, centered around the aim of influencing policies that could be beneficially implemented in modern federal states with all the complex financial instruments that characterize the modern market economy, the research on fiscal federalism retains significant interest for historians of federalism. For it tends to highlight in theoretical terms some of the pitfalls and advantages stemming from particular institutional structures, and comparison of those conclusions with historical instances of federation may help the historian to isolate features that led either to the success or to the failure of a particular federal experiment. It will be worth considering whether the institutional architecture of the Greek koinon promoted the economic welfare of its citizens to such an extent that it may help to explain why it became such a widespread political structure in fourth-century and Hellenistic Greece. But insofar as the work done on fiscal federalism can be construed as a model, it is not applied directly or wholesale to the Greek koinon. My aim is rather to analyze the economic life of the koinon on its own terms, to understand how its creation impacted the economic welfare of its member communities and its citizens, and to understand the ways in which the koinon deployed its power to regulate economic behavior. If in the end there is significant overlap with the way in which political and fiscal federalism have related in modern history, that will be important and interesting.

If, then, many modern political scientists and economists have realized a close relationship between political and economic federation, few historians have recognized that most koina were significantly engaged in the pooling not just of resources but also of risk and in the promotion (but certainly not the absolute attainment) of autarky at the regional level, and that they did so through the development of a series of formal institutions that regulated both intraregional and interregional economic interactions. The institutions of the koinon were, however, like all institutions, deeply embedded in the context in which they developed and

18. Oates 1999: 1121.
19. Weingast 1995 and 2005; De Figueiredo and Weingast 2005.

can be fully understood only as such.[20] Peregrine Horden and Nicholas Purcell have drawn our attention, in *The Corrupting Sea*, to the extreme ecological fragmentation of the Mediterranean and the microregions it created, small localities characterized by distinctive ecological features and highly localized natural resources that presented both opportunities and challenges to those who sought to extract them for survival or profit.[21] This kind of fragmentation means that at the scale of the individual polis complete autarky was generally impossible, a fact observed clearly and succinctly in the pseudo-Xenophontic treatise on the Athenian constitution, that in the Greek world "there is no polis that does not have to import or export something."[22] It is, however, in the intersection of this general phenomenon with the institutional architecture of the completely independent polis—the polis that is not part of a larger political structure—that things become particularly interesting and problematic. The economic and legal institutions of the polis tended to favor and promote internal exchange while creating hurdles and increasing the costs of transactions involving imported or exported goods. This can be seen in the production of local currency, always of local type but often on local weight standards as well; in the extraction of taxes on goods both imported into and exported from the territory of the individual polis; and in the often disadvantageous legal position of foreigners who might need access to local courts in order to resolve a commercial dispute.[23] One can, however, point to innovative practices that attempted to address each of these inefficiencies, to reduce transaction costs and promote the trade that was vital to the survival of every polis in the Greek world. Certain currencies, like the Athenian, became widely accepted far beyond the confines of the city in which they were produced, serving as trade coinages or, in Plato's words, a *nomisma koinon*, "common coinage."[24] In fifth-century Athens magistrates known as *nautodikai* were charged with resolving disputes arising over exchanges involving noncitizens. They were supplanted in the fourth century by maritime courts, *dikai emporikai*, which enabled the quick resolution of disputes arising between locals and foreigners, making it a more attractive place for traders to do business.[25] After the mid-fifth century, states began to

20. Social embeddedness of institutions: Granovetter 1985.

21. Horden and Purcell 2000.

22. Ps.-Xen. *Ath.Pol.* 2.3.

23. Taxes on import and export both: Bresson 2000: 109–49; Purcell 2005. The most famous (or most infamous) import duty was the *eikostē*, the 5-percent tax levied by the Athenians on all imported goods to replace the income that formerly derived from tribute in the changed political circumstances of 413: Th. 7.28.4. See Kallet 2004: 465–66.

24. Pl. *Leg.* 5.741e–742d. See Picard 1989; Marcellesi 2000.

25. *Nautodikai*, and the evidently similar *apologoi* of Thasos: Vélissaropoulos 1980: 251–62. Maritime courts: Cohen 1973; Vélissaropoulos 1980: 235–48; Todd 1993: 334–37; Laani 2006: 149–74; Ober 2008: 249–50.

draw up *symbola,* bilateral agreements that among other things created a legal framework within which exchange could be conducted between the citizens of the two signatory states, but their scope was inherently restricted.[26] In the same period we see an increase in the number of bilateral agreements between poleis, broader in nature, which leveraged the power of the state to promote economic mobility for citizens of both communities across their borders by abolishing import and export taxes, as in the agreement between Miletos and Olbia of circa 330.[27] Another example is an agreement between the small Aiolian polis Aigai and its even smaller neighbor Olympos or Olympe, situated above Aigai on the slope of Mount Aspordenos, which allowed the duty-free export of woolly lambs, she-goats, and yearling sheep from one community to the other.[28] Underlying this agreement is the ecologically determined need for mobility in a pastoral economy: the individual pastoralist requires upland pastures in summer, lowland pastures in winter, and a market in which to sell his produce.[29] Yet again, when Miletos and Sardis made an agreement in the third quarter of the fourth century, they included among the terms the right of the Sardians to import into and export goods from Miletos.[30] The general practice of Greek poleis to tax on the import and export of goods from their usually very small territories implies high transaction costs for an economic activity that demanded so much mobility. It is striking that many such agreements involve inland and coastal poleis.

Each of these institutions and agreements between poleis sought, in slightly different ways, to achieve the same end, namely to enlarge the territorial sphere within which vital economic activities could be pursued by removing high-cost deterrents and obstacles like import-export taxes and uncertain recourse to legal assistance in the event of a dispute. The enlargement and economic growth that certainly attended these agreements were still severely limited, however, to the two poleis that reached an agreement. Many of the economic institutions of the koinon were, I shall argue, responses to this same problem on a much larger scale.

<hr />

26. Gauthier 1972. It is always in the context of *symbola* that *nautodikai* appear outside Athens: Vélissaropoulos 1980: 253.

27. RO 93: Milesians shall be exempt from taxation in Olbia, unless any of them wishes to hold office there, in which case he must enroll and will become liable to taxation (*entelēs*), "just as the other citizens are" (ll. 6–11). The same is true for Olbians in Miletos (ll. 20–22).

28. *Staatsverträge* III.456 (late fourth or early third century).

29. See Chaniotis 1999 for a good overview of the demands of pastoralism, and civic responses to them, in mountainous Crete.

30. *Milet* I.3 (Delphinion) 135 with P. Herrmann, *Milet* VI.1: 169–70 (*Staatsverträge* 407), and Bresson 2007-8: 55–57, 64–66. Cf. the agreement between Magnesia on the Maiander and Phokaia, reached in the third century, which established reciprocal rights of import and export: *I.Magn.* 7b (*Syll.*³ 941); Migeotte 2004: no. 1.

246 INTERACTIONS AND INSTITUTIONS

Xenophon saw the power of the koinon of the Chalkideis residing both in its control over a diverse and complementary set of economic resources and in the formal institutions enshrined and protected by the koinon, which promoted economic mobility within the region. These advantages contributed to the power with which the koinon threatened the political principle of autonomy, which may be the only reason Xenophon was interested in how the Chalkideis organized their economy. Beginning from this Xenophontic cue, I shall argue in this chapter that the koinon cannot be fully understood unless we take cognizance of its impact on the economic behavior of its citizens and member states. The ancient evidence, both literary and numismatic, points to economic cooperation between poleis within a region prior to the development of formal state institutions at the regional level, which will suggest that economic considerations were part of the federal bargain from the start. I shall then explore the economic incentives created by the formal institutions of the state, particularly the rights of property ownership and intermarriage throughout the territory of a koinon, which at least according to Kleigenes contributed to the willingness of member states to participate in the koinon over the long term. In order to understand the importance and impact of these institutions that promoted economic cooperation, I shall then consider the distribution of resources within particular regions and consider the impact of their pooling in a koinon. There are limits here to what can be said; Kleigenes does not say that the koinon took steps to create a larger and more efficient market, and we know nothing from other sources about the institutions of market exchange within a koinon, but there is clear evidence for trade and for the pooling of complementary resources within this political framework that has been overlooked. The advantages deriving from relatively easy access to a wider range of resources than existed within the territory of any single polis, access created by the institutions of the koinon, suggest the possibility that the expansion of koina beyond their ethnic boundaries, a phenomenon that begins in the fourth century, may have been motivated at least in part by the desire for access to more—and different—resources. The economic rights and advantages accruing to citizens of a koinon were accompanied, crucially, by obligations; analysis of the taxation structures of the koinon—the occasions on which taxes were collected, by whom, and for what purposes—will suggest that these point not only to the facilitation of regional trade and the pooling of revenues for common expenses but also to an institutional architecture that contributed significantly to the stability of the federal system, insofar as it gave the poleis a powerful bargaining chip to be deployed against abuses of power by the koinon. In addition to pooling resources, I shall demonstrate that by the Hellenistic period poleis were also pooling risks, insofar as many koina had become engaged in the management of economic crises and disputes within their territories.

COOPERATIVE COINAGE AND EARLY FORMS
OF ECONOMIC COOPERATION

Although in the history of modern federations the adoption of a common monetary system was typically subsequent to the act of federation itself, the case of the
Deutscher Zollverein shows that it sometimes laid the foundation for federation,
and in the Greek world the same appears to be true for the earliest cases. The
cooperation of several entirely independent communities in minting coinage on a
common weight standard with a common type is a feature of the late sixth century. Such arrangements have been detected among several of the Greek cities of
Asia Minor, the Aegean islands of Lesbos and Chios, the Macedonian *ethnē*, and
the Achaian poleis of southern Italy. The phenomenon becomes even more
frequent in the fifth and fourth centuries and is by no means strictly tied to
federation or other forms of political alliance. This means that we need to consider the possibility that economic rather than political considerations may in
some instances have motivated the adoption of what Peter van Alfen and I
have called "cooperative coinages."[31] Often treated as little more than a badge of
political sovereignty, coinage is first and foremost an economic instrument for the
facilitation of trade and the payment of financial obligations, and it is only as such
that we can properly understand the adoption of cooperative coinages by states
that were not part of a larger political structure.[32] The same possibility should
remain open as we consider the coinages issued by the Greek koina. The evidence
for common coinages minted by Greek federal states has been recently and ably
surveyed.[33] What remains unclear is how the production of cooperative coinage
relates to the emergence of political structures beyond the polis and to the development of institutions at that scale over time. I shall suggest, first, that in several
cases cooperative coinages predate the appearance of formal institutions of a
regional state and point to economic cooperation as a preexisting and perhaps
catalyzing condition for koinon formation; and second, that as formal institutions
were developed for the governance of an entire region, control of monetary production was in many, but certainly not all, cases quickly arrogated to the central
government as a means of facilitating internal trade and financing the undertakings shared by the koinon as a whole.

In the last quarter of the sixth century, shortly after the adoption of coinage
in mainland Greece, several Boiotian poleis began to produce coins united by a
common type and common weight standard. Adopting the Aiginetan weight

---

31. Mackil and van Alfen 2006.

32. Finley 1985: 166–67 for Greek coinage as a political (and, frequently, economically irrational)
phenomenon.

33. Psoma and Tsangari 2003.

standard, Thebes, Tanagra, and Hyettos began in this period to issue silver coins with a cutout shield on the obverse and an incuse punch on the reverse. On the obverse, in the shield cutouts, were the initials Θ, T, and H, standing for the polis mint that produced each issue.[34] Shortly after the start of minting, apparently, these three cities were joined by four more: Akraiphia, Koroneia, Mykalessos, and Pharai, using the initials A, Ϙ, M, and Φ. These seven mints continued to produce this coinage on a common weight standard, united by the use of the heroic shield as the obverse type, until the mid-fifth century. Orchomenos is the only Boiotian polis in the late sixth and early fifth century that we know to have minted an independent type, deploying instead of the shield a device that has been variously interpreted as an amphora or a sprouting ear of grain, with the initials E or EP. Recent scholarship has broken the long-standing and once sturdy link between coinage and political sovereignty, and there are no compelling reasons to take these coins as evidence for a formal Boiotian federation.[35] Minted in the full range of denominations, from didrachmas to obols, they are best understood as monetary instruments for exchange and the facilitation of joint military endeavors undertaken by allied poleis who felt bound by a sense of shared identity, for which the shield type on the obverse may have served as a symbol.[36] The use of this cooperative coinage in regional trade is attested not only by the production of small denominations but by its voluminous appearance in hoards buried within Boiotia in the fifth century and its extreme rarity in hoards buried outside the region during the same period.[37] The larger-denomination coins issued by independent poleis on a common type and standard would serve well to meet expenses associated with joint military actions like that in which the Boiotians marched on Athens in 506 in support of Kleomenes, which required not only the usual pay for soldiers but also (though this would

34. Coins in the early series carrying the H legend used to be attributed to Haliartos (Head 1881: 10–11), but Étienne and Knoepfler 1976: 218–26, 383–91 suggested that they might rather belong to Hyettos, and Vottéro 1998: 33 n. 114, 53 makes the important point that Haliartos was locally called Ariartos until at least the fifth century; the change was based on a popular etymology associating the name of the polis with *hals* ("salt").

35. Mackil and van Alfen 2006: 221, 227–28. Cf. Schachter 1989: 85; Hansen 1995a: 31. T. R. Martin 1985 shows that nonsovereign poleis regularly minted coins. T. R. Martin 1995 argues that practical and economic considerations drove decisions about whether or not to mint, with more abstract concerns like the articulation or expression of a polis identity as a corollary.

36. Larson 2007: 67–109.

37. Hoards buried within Boiotia: *CH* V.10 (Agoriani 1972), I.17 with II.31 (Boiotia 1955), VIII.74 and *IGCH* 42 (Euboia or Boiotia 1951). Only three non-Boiotian hoards buried during the fifth century contained Boiotian coins, and these in very small numbers: *IGCH* 1644 (*CH* II.17), the Asyut hoard, buried ca. 475 (Price and Waggoner 1975) contained two anepigraphic Boiotian drachmas and two Tanagran drachmas; *IGCH* 37 (Agrinion 1931?) contained a single Tanagran stater; *IGCH* 40 (Arkadia? 1932) contained a single drachma and two triobols of Thebes (American Numismatic Society archive).

have been unforeseen) a significant monetary outlay to regain the seven hundred Boiotians who were taken prisoner by the Athenians in their swift retaliatory raid and ransomed for two mnas a head.[38]

The early Boiotian coinage suggests that economic cooperation on a regional scale preceded the development of the formal institutional apparatus by which we can recognize a koinon. Similar patterns can be seen in the early cooperative coinages of Phokis, the Chalkidike, and Arkadia. The case of Boiotia is the clearest, for here the coins were demonstrably minted by the three, and then seven, poleis that participated, and the weight and value of the metal used were backed by the authority of the polis whose abbreviated name appears on the coins, whereas in the other three cases we simply find coins issued in the name of the Phokians, the Chalkidians, and the Arkadians.[39] What is clear in all these cases is that cooperative monetary production, certainly the result of a need for economic cooperation at a regional scale, predated the formation of regional states, suggesting that the advantages to be derived from the existence of a single state that could promote and protect economic cooperation may have been a significant motivating factor in the development of more formal state institutions at the regional scale. This hypothesis is supported by the fact that in most other koina, cooperative coinages appear coincidentally with our earliest evidence for state institutions at the regional level. Centralized minting practices, in which coins are minted not by member states but by (or in the name of) the koinon itself, are typically coincident with the strength of the central authority in a koinon, while decentralized minting, the production of coins by polis mints participating in a common type and weight standard, is characteristic of places and periods in which the authority of the koinon was more limited. But distinct arrangements situated from one end of this spectrum to the other are attested.

In the second half of the fifth century strongly centralized minting practices were implemented in Boiotia. Around the mid-fifth century, the cooperative,

---

38. Hdt. 5.74.2–77.1 and above, pp. 27–28.

39. Phokis: R. T. Williams 1972: 9–12 dates the earliest Phokian coins (with the legend ΦΟ or ΦΟΚΙ) ca. 510, associating them with the immediate aftermath of the expulsion of the Thessalians, which he believed triggered the foundation of the Phokian koinon. But as in Boiotia so in Phokis there is no corroborating evidence for formal political institutions at this early date. The ΑΡΚΑΔΙΚΟΝ coinage of fifth-century Arkadia has likewise been taken as evidence for an Arkadian koinon (R. T. Williams 1965), which is nowhere else supported, and it is now thought to be either a coinage issued for the festival of Zeus Lykaios (Nielsen 1996c) or an instrument for mercenary pay and other fiscal needs (Psoma 1999 and 2001: 260; Psoma and Tsangari 2003: 112). In the Chalkidike, a coinage with the legend ΧΑΛΚ was issued decades before the synoikism of Olynthos that is associated with the establishment of the Chalkidian koinon (Robinson and Clement 1938: pl. XXXIVa, b); these coins were probably minted to meet a joint tribute obligation to the Athenian empire in the mid-450s: Psoma 2001: 257 with *IG* I³ col. V.6–8, 10–12.

decentralized approach to monetary production was replaced by a coinage issued exclusively by Thebes. Retaining the Boiotian shield as obverse type, the reverse of these coins depicts Herakles in a range of belligerent poses with legends of various lengths referring explicitly to Thebes, not to the Boiotians.[40] The aggressive stance of Herakles, combined with Thebes' apparently exclusive control over monetary production, points to the period after the expulsion of the Athenians in 446 and the Thebans' exploitation of the koinon to acquire greater control in the region over the following decade. In the last quarter of the fifth century the full-body depictions of Herakles are replaced by profile heads of Dionysos and Herakles, but the earlier Heraklid types reappear in the first decade of the fourth century (including the short-lived electrum issues).[41] Around 395 or 390, a change occurs. Instead of the reverse types with Herakles or Dionysos, we find an amphora along with the first letters of a magistrate's name, in a series that extends to the destruction of Thebes in 335.[42] This so-called magistrate coinage was produced primarily in the large denomination of didrachmas, but obols and bronzes of analogous type survive and must be contemporaneous.[43] Sometime before the mid-fourth century, a series of staters was issued in a style similar to the magistrate coinage, except that the magistrate name on the reverse was replaced by the letters BOIΩ and a small device such as a thunderbolt, club, ivy leaf, amphora, or crescent.[44] The significance of these coins is difficult to determine.[45] But it is certain that for at least the first quarter of the fourth century the magistrate staters were produced simultaneously with issues from thirteen polis mints in every denomination between the didrachma and the

40. *BMC Central Greece* 70–72 nos. 29–40 with pl. XII.1–8; Kraay 1976: 111 with pls. 351–55.

41. Kraay 1976: 111–13 with pls. 356–58, 361–62.

42. Head 1881: 61–63 places the series in the period 379–338, and Kraay 1976: 113, for the most part following Head, places the magistrate coinage in the period 371–338, but both dates need to be revised. Hepworth's die study of the series shows that it must begin in the period 400–390 (Hepworth 1998: 63 n. 16). The terminus is certainly the destruction of Thebes in 335, not its garrisoning by Philip in 338, as T. R. Martin 1985: 167–69 has shown.

43. Head 1881: 68–71.

44. These were placed by Head 1881: 73–79 in the period 338–315 but were subsequently discovered in quantity (77 specimens) in the Myron hoard, which was buried in the first half of the fourth century and certainly before 364: Svoronos 1916: 312–14, nos. 987–1063 with pls. E.26–30 and ΣT.1–6, with Hepworth 1989 for the burial date. It was generally assumed that there could be no minting overlap between the BOIΩ issues and the magistrate issues, and that the magistrate issues could not have begun before 371; they were accordingly squeezed into the period 379–371, for which date cf. Kraay 1976: 113. But as we have seen the magistrate staters must have begun in the 390s, and there is no reason to assume that there could have been no overlap.

45. With the exception of the crescent, which is always associated with Thespiai (*BMC Central Greece* pls. v.11, xvi.5–9), the other small devices can all be associated with Herakles and Dionysos, and could be taken as proof that the BOIΩ coins were issued by Thebes, perhaps in the period 379–371, as Kraay suggested. But the crescent raises the possibility that the devices are the mint marks of various poleis, which would lead to a radically different conclusion.

tetartemorion.[46] Still, the overall picture of Boiotian coinage from circa 446 to 335 is of tight Theban control of emissions, sometimes minted in the name of the Thebans and sometimes of the Boiotians, with the magistrate coinage probably reflecting Thebes' hegemonic position within the Boiotian koinon in the fourth century.

In early fourth-century Achaia, roughly coincident with our first glimpse of the formal institutions of a koinon, we find that polis mints issued small denominations and bronzes while the koinon issued larger-denomination silver, all conforming to consistent, markedly cooperative types. Although we have specimens of triobols and bronzes only from Dyme, Helike, Aigai, Aigeira, and Pellene, the geographical spread of these cities, from the western to the eastern edge of Achaia, suggests that every polis member had at least the right to produce its own coins on the shared Aiginetan weight standard, with a reverse type bearing a wreath. In each case, the obverse bears the head of a local deity; inside the wreath on the reverse are found either the initial letters of the name of the polis or a small image related to the cult of the deity represented on the obverse.[47] The wreath serves as the unifying device on these coins and persists as a feature of Achaian coinage throughout the Hellenistic period. While none of the poleis appears to have minted any silver denomination larger than a triobol, the koinon produced didrachmas, drachmas, and triobols. All three denominations have on the obverse a goddess in profile, an elaborately detailed and well-executed type. On the reverse of the drachmas and triobols is an armed Athena with the legend ΑΧΑΙΩΝ.[48] The reverse of the didrachma has a remarkable enthroned Zeus, who holds in his outstretched right hand an eagle and in his left a long scepter, resting on the ground, with the legend ΑΧΑΙΩΝ in the field to the right.[49] The didrachma, and with it the smaller-denomination coins in the name of all the Achaians, tends to be dated after 373, on the grounds that it establishes the cultic predominance of Zeus Homarios

46. The types are most easily seen together in Head 1881: 43–60 with pl. IV. Head does not include Akraiphia (which makes thirteen); see Brett 1955: 137 no. 1011 with plate 53 (unique).

47. Dyme bronzes: SNG Cop. Phliasia-Laconia 145–46; SNG Fitzwilliam 3559. Helike bronzes, certainly predating the destruction of the city in 373: Lambros 1891: 16, pl. 1.15; Babelon 1907: no. 831, pl. 223.3; A. Walker 2006: 134 lot 497. Pellene triobols: Bloesch 1987: 2150; ANS 1944.100.39485; SNG Cop. Phliasia-Laconia 209–10; Boutin 1979: 4040; SNG Lockett 2350; SNG Fitzwilliam 3567–69; SNG Manchester 1069; SNG Delep. 1968; Babelon 1925: 2239. Two known specimens of obols from Pellene have a kithara on the reverse in place of, or in addition to, the legend: SNG Cop. Phliasia-Laconia 212; SNG Fitzwilliam 3569a. Aigai silver triobols: SNG Cop. Phliasia-Laconia 125; SNG Fitzwilliam 3553; ANS 1944.100.37614. Imhoof-Blumer 1883: 157 attributed coins of this type to Aigion, but see now Rizakis 1995: 304; Kroll 1996: 52 n. 14. The coins of Aigai appear to cease ca. 370: Head 1911: 412. Aigeira: SNG Cop. Phliasia-Laconia 127.

48. Drachma: ANS 1950.53.6 (cover illustration). Triobols: SNG Cop. Phliasia-Laconia 226; Imhoof-Blumer 1883: 156.2; BMC Thessaly to Aetolia p. 48 with pl. X.17 (where it is wrongly attributed to Phthiotic Achaia).

49. Wroth 1902: 324–26 with pl. XVI.14; Head 1911: 416; Kraay 1976:101 with pl. 318.

in the aftermath of the destruction of the sanctuary of Poseidon at Helike; a striking similarity of the deity on the obverse with female heads on coins from Messene, Pheneos, and Stymphalos has also led scholars to the assumption that these
coins belong to the second quarter of the fourth century.[50] But the costly collective
undertaking of imposing and manning garrisons at Kalydon and Naupkatos for
over two decades is a more plausible motive for the production of a relatively high-
denomination silver coinage in the name of all the Achaians.[51] And there is reason
to believe, as we have seen, that the cult of Zeus Homarios was important before
the destruction of Helike.[52]

The chronological relationship between the earliest appearance of cooperative
coinage and of formal institutions of the koinon differs in Boiotia and in Achaia.
While the Boiotians were minting cooperatively for over fifty years before we are
certain that they had regional magistrates, council, and courts, with carefully articulated obligations of the member poleis to the koinon, in Achaia the two phenomena appear to coincide. Why? In the fifth century few Achaian poleis appear to have
minted coins of their own, and the majority were perhaps content to use the Aiginetan issues or those of the other Peloponnesian or central Greek mints that
adopted the same standard. The predominance of Aiginetan-standard coins
throughout the Peloponnese may have resulted in less pressure to coordinate than
was experienced in Boiotia, wedged between Athens and Euboia and with each
minting on a different standard. No hoards have been discovered in Achaia that
were buried in the fifth century, so it is difficult to tell what was in circulation. We
also know that some of the Boiotian cities were trying to coordinate their military
and political activities from the late sixth century, when the earliest cooperative
coinage appears, and the economic coordination may have been part of that effort.
Our few glimpses of fifth-century Achaian history point to a region with less interest in integration. But by the early fourth century it must have been clear from
observation of the Boiotians, the Phokians, and even the Chalkidians that coordinating minting practices was an essential part of being a koinon, although the
reverse was certainly not true.

Aitolia presents yet another pattern. Although, as we have, seen, there was an
Aitolian koinon in the early 360s and there was significant, and remarkably successful, coordination and military cooperation in the region as early as the 420s,
the Aitolians, like their Lokrian neighbors, appear to have been content to use
other people's money until the second half of the fourth century, and perhaps

50. Cf. *BMC Peloponnese* pls.xxii.1 (Messene), xxxvi.7 (Pheneos), xxxvii.4 (Stymphalos). Kraay
(1976: 101) looking for "the occasion of the issue," of the Achaian didrachma suggests the alliance
between Boiotia and Achaia in 367.

51. Mackil and van Alfen 2006: 233.

52. See above, pp. 199–202.

after 338.[53] At that time, however, they began to issue not a splashy high-denomination coin like most other koina but an apparently small issue of silver triobols
and a larger bronze coinage valued at a quarter-obol. Both issues have similar
types: a female head on the obverse, usually identified as Aitolia herself but more
recently as the mythical heroine Atalante, and on the reverse the legend ΑΙΤΟΛΩΝ
with charging boar and spearhead, all alluding to the important local and regional
myth of the Kalydonian Boar Hunt.[54] These bronze coins have been found at Thermon, at Medeon in Phokis, and at Livanates in Opountian Lokris.[55] Silver triobols
and bronzes proliferate in the late fourth century and are found from Akarnania to
Phokis.[56] It was only, however, after 240 that the Aitolians began to mint high-
denomination silver and gold coins, evidently to be associated with their war
against Demetrios, bearing types associated with the Aitolian victory over the
Gauls in 279.[57] Unlike the rest of the Aitolians' silver coinage, struck on the reduced
Aiginetan or Kerkyraian standard common to northwest Greece, these issues were
minted on the Attic standard and were clearly produced to meet large extraregional expenses.[58] These coins always carry the regional legend, along with initials
referring not to polis mints but to magistrates responsible for overseeing minting
activity during their (apparently annual) terms in office. At the same time, the
member poleis of the koinon were producing bronze coins of their own, which
though marked with the name of the issuing polis mint are united by the common
reverse type of spear and jawbone familiar from the late fourth-century bronze
types.[59] Akin to centralized management of monetary production is control of the

53. The earliest hoard that has been found in Aitolia, buried in the fifth century, was uncovered at
Agrinion and included one Tanagran stater, nineteen Aiginetan staters, and twelve staters of Elis
(*IGCH* 37). The only other is the massive, much more famous Agrinion hoard buried ca. 145–135:
Thompson 1968 (*IGCH* 271). For the date of the earliest silver and bronze issues see Tsangari 2007: 249.
Poleis of Ozolian Lokris did not mint before the Hellenistic period: T. R. Martin 1995: 275. A fifth-century Lokrian hoard (*IGCH* 19) points to use of Elian coins.
54. Atalante: Tsangari 2007. See above, pp. 183–84, for the regional significance of the myth of the
Kalydonian Boar Hunt.
55. Tsangari 2007: 249.
56. Picard 1984: 284–86 with n. 15; Tsangari 2007: 39–51, 249–50.
57. Tsangari 2007: 250–52 *contra* Scholten 2000: 25, 102, and Psoma and Tsangari 2003: 118, who
place the beginning of the gold coinage at 270 and the high-denomination silver in the mid-240s.
58. Scholten 2000: 102, 143; Tsangari 2007: 251.
59. Poteidania: Liampi 1996. Apollonia: *BMC Thessaly to Aetolia* 200 with pl. XXX.14. Amphissa:
BMC Central Greece 13. Thronion: *BMC Central Greece* 12 with pl. II.15. Oiantheia: Imhoof-Blumer 1883:
147 no. 69. Ainianes: Milne 1953: 22 no. 4 with pl. I.4; cf. Liampi 1994 and 1995–96: 98–100. Oitaioi:
Svoronos 1911: 274 no. 425 with pl. X.26. Scheu 1960: 49, without knowledge of the issues from Poteidania or Apollonia, suggested that the bronze coins should all be placed after 205, with those bearing
common types belonging to the period between the treaty with Rome in 189 and the final defeat at
Pydna in 167. His attempt to explain the issues as a reflection of Aitolian nationalist feeling in former
members after the treaty of 189 is not compelling, and through a survey of the Aitolian bronze coins

weight standard observed regionally for exchange. Two mna weights found at Thermon and inscribed "of Apollo Thermios" attest the koinon's investment in regulating exchange and overseeing the usual triad of weights, measures, and coinage, as well as the importance of Thermon as a commercial center.[60] If, then, the Aitolians are exceptional in their late start to minting relative to their development of state institutions at the regional level, they are entirely typical in their approach to monetary production as soon as they adopt the practice; certainly by the early third century the arrangement was so well proven in other koina as to have become almost formulaic. The late start to cooperative minting is, I think, simply a function of the late start to any kind of minting in the region; like the Achaians and the Lokrians, the Aitolians were content to use others' coins. In Aitolia as in Achaia, the extent of monetization of the economy before the fourth century is exceedingly difficult to judge. It is nevertheless possible that in Aitolia the facilitation of regional trade was a less important motivating factor for the development of a regional state than other considerations, most notably defense.[61] That does not, however, mean that economic considerations did not play a role; analysis of the structure of the Aitolian economy will suggest that they almost certainly did.

In most cases, then, the production of a currency in the name of the entire region was typically undertaken by a koinon around the same time that we can first detect the existence of formal state institutions at the regional level and probably as soon as it had demonstrable public financial needs, ranging from the payment of garrison and mercenary troops to the collection of taxes. The persistent appearance of small change and bronze coinage among these issues points ineluctably toward the facilitation of regional trade as an additional motivating factor.[62] The appearance in many regions of a cooperative coinage decades before the development of those formal institutions by which a koinon can be recognized suggests that regional economic cooperation among poleis is to be explained not as an accidental by-product of the development of state power at

found in securely datable hoards and in excavations, Liampi 1995–96 shows that they had certainly begun in the early third century.

60. Weights: *IG* IX.1² 1.83 (now in the Athens National Museum); Antonetti 1990: 201 pl. 18; cf. Antonetti 1999: 301–2. Compare the inscribed weights found at Olynthos (Robinson 1931: 56), clearly issued under the authority of the koinon of the Chalkideis, and the two Phokian weights, one bronze and one lead, that deploy the Phokian badge of the bull's head (Pernice 1894: 180 no. 701; Kroll 1971: 90–93).

61. The total absence of early hoards found in Aitolia also makes it difficult to assess whether limited monetization of the economy played a role: Tsangari 2007.

62. On the facilitation of trade as one important motive in coin production see Howgego 1990; Schaps 2004; Bresson 2005. This does not, of course, mean (as Schaps seems to think it does) that trade was not already vigorous before the introduction of coinage, being conducted via weighed bullion: Kroll 1998 and 2008; Kim and Kroll 2008.

the regional scale but as the intentional product of real economic interactions and the consent of multiple poleis to cooperate in the facilitation of those interactions. When that cooperation was formalized in a federal political structure, the assumption of responsibility by the koinon for minting higher-denomination coins bespeaks not only the koinon's higher expenses (for it was the koinon, not the member cities, that met the high costs associated with military expeditions) but also the greater financial importance attached to the security of the high-denomination monetary supply. Small change, vital for trade, was necessary but costly; its production could without any real loss of power be hived off to the poleis.[63] We can be certain that the cooperative structures of earlier periods were replaced by legal requirements to adhere to a common weight standard and type. After all, according to Polybios, under the Achaian koinon it was in part through the use of common laws, weights, measures, and coins that the "entire Peloponnese differed from a single polis only in that there was no single wall around all its inhabitants."[64]

PROTECTING AND PROMOTING
ECONOMIC MOBILITY

Yet if weights, measures, and coins are frequently cited together by ancient authors as the main spheres in which Greek states regulated the economic activities of their citizens, they are certainly not the only such measures taken.[65] Through Kleigenes' speech to the Spartan assembly in 382, Xenophon highlights the economic advantages of belonging to a koinon and suggests that the rights that ensured these advantages were among the first measures to be passed by the koinon of the Chalkideis as it reemerged in the years after the King's Peace. For Xenophon, the advantages were an incentive to membership, and this, in his view, only heightened the threat posed by the koinon to the world of the polis.[66] He reveals the information almost grudgingly, but the glimpse he gives us is highly informative. Kleigenes suggests that rights of intermarriage (*epigamia*) and property ownership (*enktēsis*), which had already been voted by the koinon of the Chalkideis and were upheld across its entire territory regardless of polis boundaries, would tend to strengthen the social bonds between member poleis

---

63. On the expense and attendant problems of producing small change see Sargent and Velde 2002.

64. Polyb. 2.37.10–11. The coinage of the Hellenistic Achaian koinon is well studied and will not be treated in detail here; see Thompson 1939 and 1968; Chantraine 1972; Warren 1991, 1993, 1999, and 2007.

65. Regulation of weights, measures, and coins regarded as a standard responsibility of states: Pl. *Leg.* 746d; Ps.-Arist. *Ath.Pol.* 10.1–2 with Plut. *Sol.* 15.3–4 and Rhodes 1981: 164–68; the same concern is of course at the heart of the Athenian Standards Decree (ML 45).

66. Bearzot 2004: 45–56.

and make it more difficult to dissolve the regional state.[67] It is not clear precisely when these rights had been formally approved; we can say only that they were in place by 382.[68] Xenophon attempts in Kleigenes' speech to present regional property rights as contributing to political cohesiveness and says nothing about their economic impact. If, however, the rights contributed to political unification, that is because they were economically advantageous. Property ownership in the ancient Greek world was bound up with political rights and status in complex ways, many poleis retaining a property qualification for service in certain magistracies and membership in civic councils. The impact of land distribution and access to landownership has been debated primarily insofar as it has a significant impact on our assessment of the egalitarianism of the Greek polis.[69] My concern here is rather different: to document and analyze the economic implications of a policy of opening up rights of property ownership across polis boundaries, which appears to be characteristic of the koina of mainland Greece and the Peloponnese. One would like to know about other institutions that may have been established by the koinon that would have promoted the economic integration of the region. Were there any special structures governing exchange between member poleis of the koinon that would have facilitated the flow of resources, or did this occur in much the same way as it did between completely independent poleis? Was labor more mobile within a koinon than it was between independent poleis? For neither question do we have any explicit evidence. There is, however, plenty to suggest that Xenophon emphasized institutions that were widespread and characteristic of the koinon, and it is to these that we can turn our attention.

Kleigenes' speech about the koinon of the Chalkideis provides the first explicit evidence for the rights of *enktēsis* and *epigamia* as an integral part of citizenship in

67. As Schwahn 1931b showed (*contra* Swoboda 1924), the possession of citizen rights in a single member polis of a koinon ("der sympolitischer Bundesstaat") necessarily entailed citizen rights in every other member polis of the same koinon. These include political rights like voting and standing as a candidate for a magistracy, which could be exercised only in a single polis at any given time, while the economic right of property ownership was not thus exclusive. Cf. Szántó 1892; Kolbe 1929. The issue is explored by Larsen 1957 for Lykia, but the majority of the evidence he presents dates from the second century CE; cf. Larsen 1971 for the Achaian case, which will be discussed in detail below.

68. Even if Kleigenes' speech is a fiction in the sense that it was composed by Xenophon for a specific historiographic purpose (V. Parker 2003), this does not mean that his description of the institutions of the koinon are likewise fictional; his audience was not ignorant of current affairs. Indeed the economic details are at least partly verifiable: see below.

69. Concentration of land in the hands of a small elite, with nonegalitarian political consequences: Foxhall 1992 and 2002; Osborne 1992 *contra* Ober 1989: 192–247; Hanson 1995; I. Morris 1996, for the view, each articulated in different terms and supported on different grounds, that regimes of property ownership should not affect our assessment of political egalitarianism in the Greek polis.

a member state of a koinon. Beyond this speech, evidence for the right of inter-marriage is slim, but for property ownership there is much more to say. Both rights, according to Kleigenes, extended to individuals of communities that agreed to become part of the Chalkidic koinon, and were thus one incentive for participa-tion. Kleigenes himself makes it clear why *enktēsis* should be so appealing: the koinon of the Chalkideis was virtually unstoppable because its territory included mountains, whence the invaluable large timber for ships derived (along with the products of pastoralism that he does not mention); it included coastal communi-ties that controlled harbors and benefited from import and export duties, in addi-tion to having the capacity to exploit the resources of the sea; and it included a large population with an abundance of food, implying the membership of com-munities that had access to fertile plains for grain production. As Horden and Purcell have shown, in the physically fragmented Mediterranean, where the small-est localities must exploit highly specialized extractive and productive strategies to survive, there is a need for easy, regular access to a variety of microregions.[70] If that is achieved and the resources from a number of microregions are put to common use, the authority that controls all those resources becomes very powerful indeed. The right of *enktēsis* was an institutional response to the ecological condition of highly localized and varied resource distribution that was intended to promote economic mobility across microregions, without the barriers typically created by polis boundaries.[71]

For the case of the koinon of the Chalkideis, Kleigenes' speech is perhaps our most explicit evidence, but there is a tantalizing epigraphic hint that a federal law on property ownership impacted property sales. Twenty-six deeds of sale survive from poleis within the koinon of the Chalkideis, all dating to the first half of the fourth century. It is frustrating that not a single one mentions the city ethnic of either buyer or seller, which might allow us to document citizens of one member polis acquiring property in another, but all the documents are dated by a federal priest, and although not identical in the formulas used to record the sale, they are

70. Horden and Purcell 2000.
71. The degree of control exerted by Greek cities over entrances into and departures from their territories and markets is made evident by Bresson 2007, a study that also highlights (pp. 51–57) through both positive and negative cases the advantages yielded by the close economic cooperation of coastal and inland cities. While Bresson's concern is with the juridical status of traders (rather than landowners) from separate communities with complementary resources, the structural issue is fundamentally similar. Oliver 2011 has highlighted the economic opportunities and intentionality behind individual relocation in the world of the Greek polis, as well as steps taken by poleis to attract new residents; *enktēsis* is not mentioned in this connection but would surely have contributed at least as much as grants of *ateleia*. From this perspective, the right of *enktēsis* encouraged long-term economic mobility and contributed to the economic integration of the region.

strikingly similar.[72] In addition to their formulaic similarity, the use of a federal magistrate—in this case a priest—to date all the transactions may point to their being carried out under a law of the koinon, precisely the one mentioned by Kleigenes to the Spartans, that all citizens had the right to purchase property throughout the territory of the koinon. This hypothesis may be strengthened by the fact that several deeds of sale from Amphipolis, never a member of the koinon, observe rather different formulas.[73]

The Chalkideis were not alone in creating regional rights of property ownership, but for other regions the evidence has to be pieced together primarily from inscriptions, mostly but not exclusively proxeny decrees, because we lack in the literary sources comparable explicit discussions of economic rights within a koinon.[74] In the late 330s the Boiotian koinon issued a decree (T13) honoring one Oïkles son of Antiphatas of Pellene as proxenos, and in so doing made him exempt from taxation and seizure, and granted him the right to acquire land and house, along with all the other privileges belonging to proxenoi. There is no evidence to suggest that the privileges bestowed on proxenoi were empty phrases devoid of legal import; these were real and potentially very meaningful privileges.[75] Because the rights were bestowed by the koinon of the Boiotians, presided over by its highest magistrate, the archon, and because the proxenos was not enrolled in a specific community, we must assume that he could exercise his rights anywhere in the koinon.[76] That raises the more troubling possibility that, if citizens of member poleis did not themselves have rights of intermarriage and property ownership throughout the territory of the koinon, the highest magistrates of the koinon could bestow on a foreigner rights that affected all member communities but that they did not themselves share. It is for this reason difficult to maintain the position that in the Boiotian koinon the citizens of member poleis did not have the

72. Sixteen are known from Olynthos and are now collected by Game 2008: 43–74 nos. 13–28. The Olynthian deeds of sale are discussed as a corpus by Cahill 2002: 276–80 with app. 2, pp. 293–99. Inscribed deeds of sale survive from four other poleis of the Chalkidike: Torone, Game 2008: no. 38; Sermylia, Pelekides 1924–25; Stolos (modern Kellion) Game 2008: nos. 29–33; Polichne (modern Smixi?), Game 2008: nos. 34, 35.

73. Game 2008: nos. 1–12.

74. Economic mobility appears to have been a prominent feature of Lokrian life. In the early fifth century the Hypoknemidian Lokrians envisioned and facilitated movement between their territory and their new settlements at Naupaktos and Chaleion (ML 20 ll. 6–7, 19–28, 46–47); IG IX.1² 3.717 assumes reciprocal rights of residence, if not citizenship, between Chaleion and Oiantheia (ca. 500–450). It is only in the mid-fourth century that we have clear evidence of a koinon of the Hesperian Lokrians (IG IX.1² 3.665); shortly thereafter, two members, Chaleion and Tritea, drew up an agreement providing mutual rights of property ownership and agricultural activity (Vatin 1968). Clearly the Lokrian koinon had not drawn up a law like the Chalkidian one, leaving it instead to the poleis.

75. Contra Schwahn 1931b.

76. Roesch 1973 and 1982: 303.

right to acquire property in other member poleis, though the evidence is not utterly incontrovertible. Paul Roesch pointed out that of the thirty-five then-extant proxeny decrees of the Boiotian koinon that are sufficiently intact to be legible, every one records the right of the foreigner to acquire land and a house.[77] Four proxeny decrees of the mid-fourth century show that the institution goes back at least to the period 371–335.[78] The creation of these rights of economic mobility in the classical period may be explained by the fact that it was precisely then that Boiotia as a whole experienced its highest population levels, with intensification of land use that pushed the maximum limits of the region's agricultural potential.[79] The creation of regional economic mobility may have been one response to this situation, an attempt to relieve the extreme pressure placed on the largest poleis. It certainly will have been a meaningful concession to the citizens of other Boiotian poleis when after 379 power was evidently concentrated so exclusively in Theban hands.[80]

The existence of these rights in the Hellenistic Achaian koinon is clearer. When Arkadian Orchomenos joined the Achaian koinon shortly after 235, the detailed terms of its membership were recorded on a stele (T39). Lines 11–13 make it clear that Achaians could acquire a parcel of land (*klaros*) or a house (*oikia*), or both, in Orchomenos, but they were forbidden from selling such acquired property for twenty years. The prohibition against sale was certainly made in the interests of establishing a firm Achaian presence in this important Arkadian polis, a tactic similar to that adopted by the Opountian Lokrians when they sent settlers to Naupaktos in the early fifth century.[81] Two things are immediately striking about the Achaian regulation: first, the right to own property in Orchomenos was open to all Achaians—that is, to all individuals who were citizens of a member polis of the koinon—which suggests that they typically enjoyed the right of property ownership

77. Roesch 1973; cf. C. Müller 2007: 34–39.
78. T6.7; T7.6–8; T9.9–11; T11.7–8. Roesch 1973 argued that the absence of any mention of *eppasis* in proxeny decrees of one Boiotian city for another was an indication that they already had the right, simply by virtue of being members of the koinon. But it has now been shown that all such decrees belong after 171 and are irrelevant to the question; see C. Müller 2007 and the commentary to T33. Knoepfler 1999a: 242 n. 66 and C. Müller 2007: 41 approach it from the other direction: Boiotian poleis did not bestow proxeny on one another during the period before 171 precisely because they already had the rights that usually went along with that status, including property ownership, by virtue of koinon laws.
79. Bintliff 2005: 10; cf. Bintliff, Howard, and Snodgrass 2007: 143–51.
80. Beck 2000: 338, citing Nep. *Pelop.* 3.3 on the popularity of Theban leadership. My interpretation of the distribution of political power in Boiotia in this period is less optimistic than Beck's; see below, chapter 6.
81. ML 20 ll. 16–19: The Lokrians attempted to ensure the maintenance of a strong presence at Naupaktos by requiring the next of kin among the Lokrians to take up any property in Naupaktos that belonged to a Lokrian colonist who died without an heir.

throughout the territory of Achaia. Second, there is no clause explicitly recognizing the right of the citizens of Orchomenos to acquire property in other poleis of the koinon. It is possible that the agreement was simply not reciprocal; *isopoliteia* treaties between Hierapytna and a number of Cretan poleis in the Hellenistic period reveal a consistent lack of reciprocity on this issue, but that may be a result of Hierapytna attempting to settle or simply rid themselves of a surplus, landless population.[82] However, at least in the mid-second century, Achaia was suffering not from overpopulation but from lack of manpower, and it is equally possible that the right of property ownership was not mentioned because it was a fundamental part of koinon citizenship.[83] Mention of the right to acquire property in Orchomenos may have been motivated by a need to stipulate the unusual mandate against selling property, a measure certainly taken to stabilize the population of Orchomenos and return its fields to productivity. The apparent lack of reciprocity in this decree was thus probably not about the right to acquire property but about the right to sell it once it had been acquired. Other Achaian evidence for comprehensive rights of *enktēsis* supports this argument.

Aratos of Sikyon owned a house at Corinth,[84] and though it remains theoretically possible that this was an honorific privilege rather than a universal right of citizens of the koinon, a mid-second-century decree of Oropos honoring Hieron of Aigeira (T46) makes it clear that he owned a house at Argos, at that time also a member of the Achaian koinon (ll. 16–17). An Epidaurian casualty list from the grim battle at the isthmos in 146 lists 156 names. Of these, 53 are citizens of Epidauros and are listed according to civic subdivisions; the remaining 103 are listed under the rubric "Achaians and *synoikoi*."[85] The individuals are listed with patronymic and not poliadic or ethnic. It would be strange, even if only half of these were citizens of Achaian-koinon cities, to see so many Achaians settled at Epidauros if they were not allowed to own property there. There is no doubt that the sanctuary at Epidauros provided an attractive economic incentive for nonresidents even if they could not own land, but there is no evidence for that kind of economic disability in the Achaian (or indeed any other) koinon, however familiar it is from classical Athens. The Achaians are not equated with the *synoikoi*, though they are listed with them, suggesting that like them they were residents of the city.[86]

Although the mechanisms for the integration of new citizens (whether from outside the koinon or within) are not entirely clear in every case, the manner in

82. Chaniotis 1999: 230.
83. Population shortage in Achaia: Polyb. 36.17.5–8.
84. Plut. *Arat.* 41.4, 42.3; *Cleom.* 19.
85. *IG* IV² 1.28 line 59.
86. Larsen 1971: 81–86 marshals as further evidence for population mobility within the Achaian koinon *IG* V.2.357, a *symbolon* between Stymphalos and another city that among other things establishes the legal rights enjoyed by the citizens of each polis in the other and the judicial procedures to be

which this was accomplished is attested in rather full detail by a third-century decree of Achaian Dyme (T35). The text opens with the declaration that it has been decided to grant citizenship to the residents (*epoikoi*) who want it and goes on to establish the process by which their enrollment can be achieved. It is difficult to know just how similar the *epoikoi* at Dyme and the *synoikoi* at Epidauros were.[87] The Dyme decree stipulates that once the residents have become citizens they are to be enrolled in one of three civic subdivisions (*phylai*) and are eligible to become priests and magistrates of both the city and the koinon. The status and rights of these foreign residents clearly changed, then, when they were registered as citizens of Dyme. Although the decree is issued by the polis of Dyme, the regulations it sets forth are also those of the Achaian koinon, which suggests that there were limits on local variation: the first step in attaining citizenship was the submission of payment "to the secretary of the Achaians," in two installments on a schedule in accordance with the Achaian calendar (ll. 4–6, 33–34). The payment entitled the individual and his or her family to registration in the polis of Dyme, but it was paid to the koinon itself, suggesting regulation of the process from above.[88] The last surviving lines of the document are too lacunose to admit certain interpretation, but one can expect that after having described the process of enrollment and the rights of the new citizens, a description of their obligations should follow in these lines. The appearance of the koinon in these difficult lines raises the tantalizing possibility that the new citizens had an obligation to pay the same taxes and contributions

---

followed in case of dispute. Larsen, following the restorations of Hiller (*IG* V.2.357) and Heberdey (in Wilhelm 1940) believed that the other partner to the alliance was Aigeira, and saw in ll. 173–74 a reference to "residents from Keryneia." Accepting the traditional date of ca. 219 for the agreement, Larsen pointed out that both parties would at that time have been members of the Achaian koinon. After a new study of the stone, however, Taeuber 1981 showed that there is no reference at all to "residents from Keryneia," and that Stymphalos's partner was not Aigeira but Demetrias, which then imposes an earlier date for the document, 303–300, the short period when Sikyon, having been relocated by Demetrios Poliorketes, was renamed in honor of its founder (Diod. Sic. 20.102.2–4; Plut. *Demetr.* 25). In that period the Achaian koinon was effectively nonexistent. A complete new edition with extensive commentary is given by Thür and Taeuber 1994: 158–251 no. 17. The document can no longer be accepted as evidence for the rights of cities within the Achaian confederacy.

87. Hiller von Gaertringen *ad Syll.*³ 531 n. 1 remarks that the *epoikoi* "sine dubio inquilini intelleguntur, qui Athenis et in aliis civitatibus μέτοικοι alibi πάροικοι aut σύνοικοι dicuntur." Rizakis 1990b: 112 discusses the slight gradations of meaning between these words insofar as they can be discerned.

88. The Dyme decree may suggest the terms upon which other foreigners were enrolled as citizens in the Achaian koinon; cf. Polyb. 32.7.1–5 for the enrollment of Delians as Achaian citizens after their expulsion from Delos in 166. Dyme's authority to issue its own decree, in which the procedures and regulations of the koinon are inserted, reflects one facet of the power of a member polis within the Achaian koinon. See below, pp. 384–90, for detailed treatment of this issue.

to the koinon as all normal citizens paid, an issue to which I shall return.[89] The *epoikoi* referred to in this decree were certainly non-Achaians; citizenship was effectively sold to them, and that sale was overseen by the koinon itself; the remainder of the decree may well have spelled out the financial obligations that the new citizens were expected to meet.[90]

It is clear that noncitizen residents in Achaia, as in most Greek political communities, did not have the right to stand for political offices or priesthoods until they went through the procedure of becoming citizens, though elsewhere not even that is certain. In Aitolia, new members of the koinon (whether admitted by treaty or by honorary decree) became functional participants in the economic community of the region with full rights only by degrees. Our earliest surviving proxeny decree of the Aitolian koinon, from the fourth century, bestows on an Athenian proxeny, citizenship, freedom from taxation, security, and immunity from seizure (T49). The bronze tablet on which the decree was inscribed is fragmentary, and it is possible that we have lost some reference to the right of *enktēsis*. In the first quarter of the third century the Aitolian koinon honored Aristion son of Androkles, a citizen of Chaleion, granting him and his sons "proxeny and all the other privileges that are given to proxenoi"; the comparatively unspecific terms of this decree are quite striking, especially in light of the fairly full set of privileges bestowed on the fourth-century proxenos, and suggest that the package of benefits was already well established.[91]

From around 275 we have an amphiktyonic decree from Delphi (T55) honoring two individuals who donated money to the sanctuary; one of them is Alexeinides son of Philonidos, who is further described as an Elian living in Aitolia (l. 5). A series of *asylia* decrees issued by the Aitolian koinon during the third century guarantee that neither the Aitolians themselves, nor those living in Aitolia, nor those living as citizens in Aitolia will plunder the possessions of citizens of a particular polis.[92] The two categories of people living in Aitolia and living as citizens in Aitolia, distinct from the Aitolians themselves, suggest the existence of foreigners resident in Aitolia, similar to the *epoikoi* and *synoikoi* of Achaia. The apparent interchangeability of the two terms in *asylia* decrees throughout the third century, clearly serving the same function, may point to

89. Rizakis 1990b: 123.

90. Gauthier 1985: 199–201. On the sale of citizenship in the Hellenistic period see Robert 1940–65: I.37–42; Savalli 1985.

91. *IG* IX.1² 1.5 ll. 4–5.

92. Living in Aitolia, τῶν ἐν Αἰτωλίαι κατοικεόντων: *IG* IX.1² 1.179 l. 19, ca. 260; *IG* IX.1² 1.4c l. 18; *IG* IX.1² 1.135 ll. 2–3, ca. 220; *IG* IX.1² 1.192 ll. 9–10, 204/3(?). Living as citizens in Aitolia, τῶν ἐν Αἰτωλίαι πολιτευόντων: *IG* IX.1² 1.176 l. 5, shortly after 228; *IG* IX.1² 1.169a ll. 2–3, b ll. 1–2, ca. 222; *IG* IX.1² 1.189 ll. 3–4, ca. 214/3(?).

their synonymity. What is perhaps more important for the present argument is to note that Alexeinides son of Philonidos is not a foreigner living in Kalydon or any other Aitolian community; rather, he is living in Aitolia, a status that points to the existence of open boundaries for residency within a koinon. This situation itself requires either a formal law of the koinon or an informal but uniformly accepted practice of allowing settlement mobility. The presence of resident foreigners in third-century Aitolia must have been considerable to merit special mention in so many decrees of the koinon. Whatever their political rights, these residents were nevertheless bound by the decisions of the central Aitolian authority, but they must also have had a motive for taking up residence there, and that may have been economic. Although this decree does not make explicit whether their economic rights extended to the possession of land, other (somewhat earlier) decrees make it clear that they did.

The right to acquire real property in Aitolia is consistently bestowed upon proxenoi of the koinon in the third century; it was typically accompanied by other rights, the precise configuration of which varies from one decree to the next for reasons that are usually indiscernible. So a fragmentary decree of 273/2 from Thermon grants the right to acquire land and a house, *asylia,* and all the other rights and privileges belonging to other proxenoi (T54 ll. 1–4). The same right of property ownership was granted by the Aitolian koinon along with proxeny to four citizens of Phthiotic Achaia in the second quarter of the third century (T56), and in the mid-third century a proxenos of the Aitolian koinon received in addition the right to import and export goods, perhaps free of any customs or tolls (T58 ll. 4–9). Because such grants were made by the koinon and not by any individual polis, we must infer that the right could be exercised anywhere in the territory controlled by the koinon.[93] The alliance between the Aitolians and Akarnanians made in the second quarter of the third century, which was in fact an agreement of complete and reciprocal *isopoliteia* between the communities of the two regions (T57), grants the Aitolians and the Akarnanians the right to intermarry and to own land and houses in each other's territory. Again there is no indication that the right to acquire property was limited to just one polis in either region, and given that the decree goes on to stipulate that every Aitolian shall have equal citizenship in Akarnania, and every Akarnanian in Aitolia (ll. 12–13), it is necessary to infer that Aitolians had the right to own property in any polis within the koinon, just as was the case in the Chalkidike in the fourth century and in Boiotia and Achaia in the third, if not earlier.

93. By contrast, a proxeny decree of Kallion for a citizen of Aigion grants him inter alia the right to acquire property "and all the other privileges belonging to other *proxenoi* and benefactors *of the polis*" (*IG* IX.1² 3.721B, my italics); those privileges could certainly have been exercised only within the jurisdiction of the polis of Kallion.

The strong integrative effect of rights of intermarriage and property ownership on an extended population, with trickle-down salutary effects on the political organization of that population, are perhaps best revealed by a negative case: when after the defeat of Perseus at Pydna the Romans sought to dismantle Macedonia as a political entity, they divided it into four regions and abolished the old rights of intermarriage and the sale of land and buildings among them.[94] Although its political structure differed radically from that of the mainland Greek koina, the existence of multiple poleis within Macedonia, bound together by a single regional government as well as by economic interdependence, makes it an interesting comparandum. According to Livy, the Macedonians had some cause for relief (the grant of freedom and a 50-percent reduction in their tax burden), but "to those who were cut off from trading between regions, their country seemed as mangled as an animal disjointed into parts, each of which needed the other."[95] The partitioning of Macedonia by the Romans and the prohibition of economic mobility between the new regions itself demonstrates a general perception that rights of intermarriage and property ownership contributed significantly to regional political cohesion. But the desperately dismayed response of the Macedonians shows that such rights also protected an economic mobility that was vital to the flourishing of both individual citizens and the region as a whole. We need to look next at the reasons why the sudden loss of these rights, which had been fully protected by a viable state with sovereignty over an entire region, could make a population feel as if its country had been brutally dismembered and left to die.

RESOURCE COMPLEMENTARITY
AND ECONOMIC INTERDEPENDENCE

Despite Aristotle's theoretical commitment to the idea that the accomplishment of autarky, economic self-sufficiency, was the final purpose of the polis, few Greeks can have experienced this "state of ecological grace."[96] Alain Bresson has shown that pseudo-Xenophon's assertion that "there is no polis that does not have to import or export something" comes far closer to reality than Aristotle's position, which can be construed, depending upon one's perspective, as either a myth or an ideal.[97] And while it is true that most Greeks exploited the resources of their polis

94. Livy 45.29.10, with Hatzopoulos 1996: 227–30 for full discussion of the partition. Hatzopoulos (pp. 354–55) raises the possibility that "some restrictions on *commercium* and *connubium* already existed under the kings," and while this cannot be ruled out, it seems unlikely. The right appears also to have been abolished in Achaia in 146, only to be restored later: Paus. 7.16.10.

95. Livy 45.30.2, trans. A. C. Schlesinger.

96. Arist. *Pol.* 1252b28–1253a2. The quote is from Horden and Purcell 2000: 115.

97. Ps.-Xen. *Ath.Pol.* 2.3. Bresson 2000: 109–30, reprinted from Bresson 1987. See above, n. 23.

territories to the fullest extent possible, finding value even in marshlands, maquis, and mountains, that in itself does not necessarily entail material self-sufficiency.[98] In place of the myth of settlement autarky, Horden and Purcell propose that "if a norm must be envisaged, let it be that of the tentacular settlement": the settlement, on whatever scale, that extends its reach in all directions by trade.[99] If the Athenian and Roman empires have sometimes been explained, at least in part, as elaborate structures for meeting the needs of the large populations of each urban agglomeration, it is worth thinking about the ways in which other states in antiquity may have utilized their power to achieve something closer to autarky, to exert control over a large and diversified set of resources as a means of reducing vulnerability. Horden and Purcell argue that we should not attribute so much agency to states in the organization of regional economies.[100]

> Just as the site of a town should be reconceived as a number of overlapping ecologies, so should its hinterland be thought of as a complex set of smaller entities, an accumulation of short distances and definite places. If the dynamics of the extended hinterlands that supported an Athens or a Genoa could be considered in detail, rather than by overview, what at first appeared a grand system, operating as if by careful plan, would be revealed as a huge accumulation of very local phenomena. The often tiny communities within the Athenian empire did not have to function in a wholly novel way when they became part of "the power that rules the sea." The larger entity was simply a direction, or impetus, given to the previously less formed, less patterned, ecological interaction of several hundred settlements, several thousand microregions.

It is precisely the last point that Horden and Purcell touch on in this passage, the direction or impetus given by a larger entity to "the previously less formed, less patterned ecological interaction" of settlements and microregions, that interests me. It is rather simpler to argue that hunger for resources was a significant motor for imperial growth in the ancient world, in part because the power structure of empires is so clear—to rulers and subjects as well as to their historians. Asking whether we can see the same dynamic at work in the development of the koinon presents particular interest, and particular challenges. For in almost every iteration in almost every period (with the probable exception of Boiotia from 379 to 335 and perhaps of Hypoknemidian Lokris in the early fifth century), power remained distributed and shared by member poleis and the regional state, resulting in a

98. Cf. Rougement 1991, who ranges over a variety of sources to show that Greeks exploited the hinterlands of their territories as well as the cultivable fields; but his conclusion that this practice led to self-sufficiency is unjustified, and he makes no mention of the equally well-documented trading activities of the cities he studies, which point to the desire, if not the need, for imported goods.

99. Horden and Purcell 2000: 121.

100. Horden and Purcell 2000: 121.

remarkable system of political interdependence that will be explored in detail in the next chapter. If achieving access to a larger and more diversified set of resources in order to meet the economic needs of a region's population was indeed a significant component of the koinon's activities and one of the factors that drove its formation and expansion throughout the Greek world, then we are faced with the complex but fascinating situation in which a relatively large group of poleis cooperated and made the federal bargain in order to promote not just their own survival but perhaps their flourishing. The existence of cooperative coinage prior to federation suggests, as we have seen, the creation of monetary institutions that facilitated trade between poleis within a region as well as any joint undertakings they may have wished or needed to make, and it points to existing economic interactions between poleis, perhaps "less formed, less patterned" than they became later under the framework of the koinon. It was relatively early in the history of the koinon of the Chalkideis—just how early we cannot tell, but certainly within the first or second generation since its formation in 432—that the central state gave "direction or impetus" to the economic interactions of its member poleis by granting rights of property ownership and intermarriage throughout its territory. Other koina put in place similar sets of institutions as they developed in the later fourth century and the Hellenistic period. We need to look at the ecological conditions in which these emergent institutions were embedded in order to understand what drove their development.

We have already seen that one of the principal sources of power for the koinon of the Chalkideis was its ability to draw on the varied wealth of its constituent microregions. Its territory was annexed by Philip II to become part of Macedonia, and when that kingdom was in turn dissolved by the Romans in 167 and split into four distinctly separate regions, Livy describes the resources of each. The second region of Macedonia included the territory formerly controlled by the Chalkideis: "Those highly flourishing cities Thessalonica and Cassandrea, and in addition, Pallene, fertile and fruitful land; facilities for seafaring are also furnished it by the harbours at Torone, Mount Athos, Aenea, and Acanthus, some of which conveniently face Thessaly and the island of Euboea, and others the Hellespont."[101] Cassandrea, of course, was formerly Poteidaia, a member of the koinon of the Chalkideis from at least the 380s, as was Torone, until both were seized by the Athenians in 364/3.[102] Poteidaia was restored to the Olynthians by Philip in 356 but probably remained dependent upon the goodwill of the Macedonian king.[103]

101. Livy 45.30.4, trans. A. C. Schlesinger.

102. Poteidaia: Xen. *Hell.* 5.2.15, 24. Poteidaia and Torone seized: Isocr. 15.108, 113; Din. 1.14, 3.17; Diod. Sic. 15.81.6.

103. Dem. 6.20, 7.10, 20.61 (with Hammond, Griffith, and Walbank 1972–88: II.361), 23.107–8; Diod. Sic. 16.8.5.

Akanthos, as we have seen, strenuously resisted the pressure to join the koinon in the 380s. Its participation was certainly attractive to the Chalkideis for precisely the reason cited by Livy—it had a port that conveniently faced the Hellespont—but its motives for resistance were certainly complex. The disposition of resources within the territory of the koinon of the Chalkideis, as described by Xenophon's Kleigenes and, much later, by Livy, points to two related phenomena that will be addressed in turn in this section: resource complementarity and the need for economic mobility.

Specialization and Resource Complementarity: The Case of Boiotia

Theban: *Where am I supposed to get payment for [the eel]?*

Dikaiopolis: *I presume you'll be giving that to me in lieu of market tax. Tell me, are you selling any of these other things?*

Theban: *I'm selling them all.*

Dikaiopolis: *Let me see, how much for, do you say? Or will you take some other goods from here to Thebes?*

Theban: *Will I? Yes, something that's found in Athens and not in Boiotia.*

Dikaiopolis: *Then you'll buy some Phaleron whitebait and take it with you, or some pottery.*

Theban: *Whitebait or pottery? But we have them at home. No, something that there isn't any of where we are, but plenty here.*

Dikaiopolis: *I know then: export an informer, packing him up like a piece of crockery.*

Theban: *By the Twin Gods, I would make a great profit taking one, filled with lots of mischief like a monkey!*

ARISTOPHANES, *ACHARNIANS* 885–907, TRANS. SOMMERSTEIN

The small Boiotian polis Akraiphia stands today over the fertile Kopaïc Basin, densely planted with tobacco, cotton, and melons. The landscape in antiquity, however, was at least seasonally quite different. Mycenaean engineering works to drain the Kopaïc Basin and reclaim its fertile soil seem not to have been functional for long, and throughout the historical period until the nineteenth century the plains, which are now so agriculturally productive, ranged from marsh to lake, the latter especially renowned for its eels.[104] According to local etymologies the poleis

---

104. Drainage works: Lauffer 1986; Argoud 1987: 31–36; Knauss 1990; Horden and Purcell 2000: 245–46 with map 16. Eels: Ar. *Ach.* 878–84 (Dikaiopolis shows no initial interest in the other commodities offered for sale by the Theban, but at the mention of Kopaïc eels he is delighted), 962 (Lamachos offers to buy a single Kopaïc eel for three drachmas); *Lys.* 35–36 (Kalonike submits that all the Boiotians may be destroyed, with the exception of the eels), 702 (the leader of the women's chorus complains that she was forbidden from serving a Boiotian eel, "from the neighbors, a good girl and one of my favorites" because of the Athenians' decrees); *Peace* 1005 (where great baskets of Kopaïc eels are counted as one of the blessings of peace); Hellanikos *ap.* Σ Ar. *Lys.* 36; Matron, the fourth-century parodist, *ap.* Ath. 4.135c–d; Antiphanes, the fourth-century comic poet, *ap.* Ath. 1.27e = *CAF* II.15

surrounding Lake Kopaïs received their names from it; they exploited not only the edible resources of the lake but also, certainly, its fertile soil when the bed became dry in summer and its waters as a transportation resource during the wet season.[105] One of the most significant implications of the fame of Boiotian eels is that they were widely exported. Aristophanes' exchange between the Theban merchant and Dikaiopolis, which forms the epigraph to this section, reveals the mutually advantageous arrangement of trade between microregions with complementary resources. Dikaiopolis suggests that he should be given an eel in exchange for exempting the Theban from payment of the market tax; the notion that certain goods were valuable enough that they should be imported duty-free, in order to provide an extra incentive for traders to deliver the precious goods, seems to have been institutionalized, predictably enough, at Sybaris, where eel merchants and eel fishermen, like purple merchants and murex fishermen, were exempt from taxation.[106] The very mention of Kopaïc eels made the mouths of Athenian gourmands water, but the lake's less famous denizens were of some value as well.

A remarkable inscription from Akraiphia records a list of prices for the sale of saltwater and freshwater fish.[107] The decree was issued by the three agonarchs named at the start of the document along with the archon Aristokles; these are magistrates of the polis, not of the koinon, although the koinon did appoint a college of agonarchs, and these officials are known in other Boiotian poleis as well.[108] They are the Boiotian equivalent of the *agoranomoi* so widely attested throughout the Greek world from the fourth century on, who were responsible for overseeing

---

(where eels are mentioned as the specialty product of Boiotia); Ptolemy Euergetes *Hypomnēmata ap.* Ath. 2.71b; cf. Ath. 14.622f; Nonn. *D.* 13.64–65; Hsch. s.v. Κωπαΐδες; Eust. *Il.* IV.516 (van der Valk). According to Agatharchides (*FGrHist* 86 F 5), eels were sacrificed to the gods in Boiotia, in a ritual complete with a sprinkling of barley groats on the head of the victim. On the Greek love of fish generally see Davidson 1997: 3–35, 144–47.

105. Etymologies: Eust. *Il.* I.409 (van der Valk). Local consumption of Kopaïc fish and eels: Vika, Aravantinos, and Richards 2009.

106. Phylarchos *FGrHist* 81 F45. Contrast the 5-percent tax levied on murex, perhaps as they were brought into the harbor, in the Customs Law of Asia: Cottier, Crawford, et al. 2008: line 20 §7 with commentary, p. 109. The rate was probably increased in the revision of 5 CE, but the amount is lost: lines 122–23 §5.

107. *Ed.pr.* M. Feyel 1936b: 27–36 (fragment B only); Salviat and Vatin 1971: 95–109 (frr. A and B, new readings in B); Lytle 2010 for a new edition. The prices are rendered by an acrophonic monetary system that contains redundancies; see Schaps 1987 and Sosin 2004 for different attempts to solve the problem.

108. Thespiai, as magistrates of the polis in a college of three: *IG* VII.1817; *IThesp* 84.51–53 (Roesch 1965b; *SEG* 23.271). Single agonarch as magistrate of the koinon: *IThesp* 84.3, 68 (Roesch 1965b; *SEG* 23.271). Local decree: Lytle 2010: 261 with references.

trade, protecting against extortionate prices, and adjudicating minor disputes between buyers and sellers.[109]

The fish listed in the Akraiphia tariff under the category "From the Lake" (fr. B.20) derive, without a doubt, from Lake Kopaïs, which stretched south and west from Akraiphia, and the two smaller lakes lying just south and east of the city; the famous eels are included, though their price is lost. The value of lake fish should not be underestimated: in his description of Aitolian Kalydon, Strabo tells us that the lake nearby, which was large and rich in fish, was managed by the Romans at Patrai, presumably a group of *negotiatores*.[110] The majority of the Akraiphia tariff, however, is concerned with the prices of saltwater fish, which had to be imported over some distance to the small landlocked polis. The most obvious point of origin for these saltwater fish is Anthedon, the northernmost of the eastern coastal poleis of Boiotia; it is the closest harbor to Akraiphia, and the route was an easy one, passing between Lake Paralimni and Mount Ptoion (map 2).[111]

Anthedon is not, however, simply the nearest Boiotian polis with a harbor and a reputation for good cod. Its economy was unusually dominated by the extraction of marine resources, an occupation that was in most poleis decidedly part-time and supplemental.[112] A vivid and detailed picture of the economy of Anthedon is painted by the third-century-BCE travel writer Herakleides Kritikos, of whose treatise *On the Cities in Hellas* only the portions covering Attica, Athens, Boiotia,

109. Agonarchs as Boiotian equivalent of *agoranomoi:* Salviat and Vatin 1971: 95–109 l. 1. Σ *Il.* 24.1b (Erbse); Eust. *Il.* IV.857 (van der Valk). *Agoranomoi* are attested in Boiotia only in the imperial period: Robert 1935b: lines 53–54 and pp. 448–49; Roesch 1965b: 145 with n. 1, who suggested that the more common term was adopted when the Boiotian dialect was abandoned around 172. But see Vottéro 2001: 15–16 for the problems associated with identifying a fixed date when the dialect was abandoned. On the powers of the *agoranomos* in general, see Migeotte 2005, with references to earlier scholarship. The price list has been associated with the Ptoia (Vatin in Salviat and Vatin 1971: 109, comparing *SEG* 23.326, from Delphi; Migeotte 1997: 40–41). But price regulation was probably a widespread part of ancient political economy; see Bresson 2000: 151–82 and 2007–8: II.39–44; Lytle 2010: 293–95.

110. Str. 10.2.21. Strabo's lake is actually a coastal lagoon; for this and other examples of productive lagoon fisheries in the ancient Mediterranean see Horden and Purcell 2000: 192.

111. Cf. Vatin 1966: 279.

112. The role of fish in the ancient diet is debated. Bintliff 1977: 117–22, 216–18, 240–44 believes that fish was a major food source. Gallant 1985 argues for a staunchly reductionist position based on a comparison with modern statistics. He is certainly correct that fish was never as central to the ancient diet as cereals; his argument that fish was eaten as a supplement is in essence probably correct, but he perhaps underestimates the role of supplementary food in the environment of Mediterranean unpredictability, on which see Purcell 1995a. Cf. Jameson, Runnels, and van Andel 1994: 311–16 for the case of the Argolid and support for Gallant's position. Bresson 2007–8: II.155–56 cites Tenedos, Anthedon, and Aigina, along with modern Trikeri, on the Magnesian Peninsula, as examples of the unusual city whose economy was almost exclusively oriented toward the sea.

and Euboia survive.[113] This unusual work, neglected until quite recently, offers a fascinating and detailed picture of the principal monuments of the cities described, much as Pausanias did five hundred years later; but Herakleides is also, unlike his imperial successor, deeply interested in the economies of the places he visited and the traveling conditions between points of interest. His description of Anthedon is remarkable and worth quoting in full (Her. Krit. 23–24, trans. McInerney, adapted):

> The polis [of Anthedon] is not a big city measured by size. It is located right by the edge of the Euboian Sea. It possesses an agora that is entirely full of trees, supported by two stoas. The city is well supplied with both wine and fish but short of grain because of the poor quality of the soil. The inhabitants of Anthedon are almost all fishermen, making their living from hooks and fish as well as from purple and sponges. They have grown old on this seashore amid their huts and the seaweed. They have a ruddy complexion, and all of them are slender. They have worn down the tips of their nails being entirely consumed by their nautical work. Most of them work as ferrymen and shipwrights, and the land is not such that they could work it; but they have none. They claim to be the descendants of Glaukos the sea god, who is agreed to have once been a seaman.

The territory of Anthedon did not support grain cultivation on any significant scale, though vines may have tolerated its poor soil.[114] Although it is possible that Herakleides was writing a description that aimed to amuse, the basic picture cannot be far from the mark, and to judge from his remark about the general lack of landed property, he does seem to have taken the trouble to ask about the city's economy. Fish, murex, sponges, ferrying (presumably to Euboia and back), and shipbuilding seem to have sustained the inhabitants of Anthedon, an economic pattern that may go back at least in part to the early archaic period.[115]

113. Pfister 1951; McInerney in *BNJ* 369A for text, translation, and commentary. See also Arenz 2006.

114. Pfister 1951: 171 regards Herakleides' description of Anthedon as "having plenty of wine" (*euoinos*) strange; he cites Plut. *Quaest. Graec.* 19.295d for a diametrically opposed claim, though he does not bear in mind the possibility of a change in the regional economy over four centuries. Pfister also, I think, puts too much weight on the declaration of Ulrichs 1840–63: II.36 that "im Tal von Anthedon sah ich keinen Weinstock," for he is led by it to assume that Herakleides' account was based not on autopsy but on written sources, a claim that seems to me implausible in view particularly of the highly visual details of the appearance and living conditions of the fishermen at Anthedon and of the lack of any relevant comparanda pointing to a possible source. As for the weight of Ulrichs's testimony, the likelihood of a shift in the productive regime of a place between the third century BCE and the nineteenth century CE is very high indeed. It should perhaps be noted that Herakleides (26) describes the north end of Mount Messapion, the region between Anthedon and Salganeus, as "grovey and well-watered," suggesting that vinestock is not so impossible. Cf. Rackham 1983: 327.

115. Fishing on this coast in the early archaic period is attested by an inscribed fishing weight from the second half of the eighth century BCE at Skala Oropou: Mazarakis Ainian 1997b: 33 (*SEG* 47.508); Petrakos 1997: no. 768; archaeological context and full publication by Mazarakis Ainian and Matthaiou 1999.

The dominance of fishing at Anthedon necessarily implies export of the catch. Other coastal poleis have little need for a resource to which they have their own access, just as Aristophanes' Theban had no interest in Athenian whitebait and pottery. But fish, unless they are salted, do not make good terrestrial travelers, so it is to nearby inland communities that they are generally exported.[116] Although the citizens of Akraiphia had a taste for saltwater fish, they had no direct access to it except by trade with citizens of other poleis. The territory of Akraiphia did, however, incorporate a good deal of arable and pasturable land. Roughly contemporaneous with the Akraiphia tariff is an inscription recording a public debt of Akraiphia to a certain Kallon son of Sosiphanos (probably a native son of the polis), who released the city from part of its debt to him; in exchange, the polis granted to Kallon and his descendants the right to pasture fifty of his own animals on what is either public or sacred land (T29). Another text inscribed on the same block records a similar cancellation of public debt by the Theban E[. . .]idas, who had received as security on a loan an unspecified amount of the sacred land of Apollo, certainly Ptoios (T30).

The cities of the Kopaïs region in particular seem to have had plenty of land for pasturage, which may reflect a condition of localized population shortage; as at Akraiphia, however, the land was transformed into a source of revenue by being used as surety for loans to the polis by wealthy individuals and entrepreneurs or to reward them for their benefactions. The city of Orchomenos borrowed from Eubolos of Phokian Elateia, situated in the mountains just above the Kopaïs region; when the city had repaid its debt in full, it granted to Eubolos the right to graze 220 cows or horses and 1,000 sheep or goats for four years.[117] Not only is the wealth of Eubolos implied by the permission for such a large herd surprising, but his desire to use the land of Orchomenos attests once again the need for economic mobility and the advantages derived from breaking down the economic barriers created by political boundaries.

Details of the two loan agreements made between Eubolos and Orchomenos reveal in a subtle way another advantage of membership in a koinon. Several witnesses are listed for each of the two contracts made between Eubolos and the city of Orchomenos, individuals who received copies of the contract: these include Phokians (lines 3, 9, 16, 20) and Orchomenians (lines 9–10, 22), as one would expect, but it is interesting that we find a Chaironeian (lines 9–10, 21–22) as well. His role as one of the guarantors and a recipient of a copy of the contracts has not been directly remarked upon but is an unusual piece of evidence for the regional

116. Overland transport of fish: Boiotia to Athens (above, n. 103); Argos to Tegea (*SEG* 11.423 ll. 21–29 with Simonides fr. 163 [Bergk] *apud* Arist. *Rhet.* 1365a20–28, 1367b18–19; cf. Dillon 1994: 253, 260; Roy 2000: 338–39); to Stymphalos: H. Williams 1996.

117. *IG* VII.3171 (Migeotte 1984: no. 12).

context and impact of what appear to be strictly local transactions. The Chaironeian's role in the affair is akin to that of an arbitrator: he is presumably a neutral third party whose presence would mitigate concerns of corruption and reduce the chances of either party's defaulting on the agreement. As a citizen of Chaironeia he is ideally suited to this role: he is involved at the scale of the koinon and of the district insofar as he participates in the same regional economic system and power structure as his Orchomenian counterparts, but he is disinterested as a nonparticipant in the financial transaction to which he bears witness.[118] In a slightly different arrangement at Kopai, the city granted to two women the right to graze two hundred head of cattle each on public land for the full duration of the loan they made to the city.[119] Finally, a series of nine land leases from Thespiai in the Hellenistic period together demonstrate the existence of a very considerable amount of public and sacred land.[120]

From all these agreements, it seems that the cities of the Kopaïs region had a surplus of land at their disposal, much of it apparently public or sacred (or both), the lease of which created a regular source of public revenue.[121] Some of that revenue may have been destined for funds with which grain was purchased, as occurred at Thespiai.[122] The resources that they had at their disposal are thus directly complementary to those controlled by the inhabitants of Anthedon. Yet another set of resources was exploited at Tanagra, complementary to both the coastal resources of Anthedon and the land wealth of the cities of the Kopaïs region in western Boiotia. Here, according to Herakleides, there is a surplus of vines and olives, but the land did not "produce nourishing fruits in abundance." He also notes, however, that there was no manufacturing at Tanagra, an odd claim in light of the city's fame as a center of pottery production in the region.[123] Despite the fact that the district to which Tanagra belonged in the fourth century was relatively small, it was always closely associated with Delion and Aulis, which had two harbors, so it will have had easy access to the kinds of marine resources we have seen at Anthedon.[124]

118. For Chaironeia and Orchomenos as part of the same district in the Hellenistic period, see above, p. 222, and below, pp. 374–76, with map 9.

119. M. Feyel 1942a: 148–55 (Pleket 1964: no. 32; SEG 22.432; Migeotte 1984: no. 15).

120. Osborne 1985 lists and discusses all the documents.

121. Migeotte 1994: 4–7.

122. The *sitōnai*, annual magistrates attested in the Thespiai magistrate list (Roesch 1965b: 220–24), purchased grain with revenues from two funds, one sacred, the other made up of royal bequests.

123. Her. Krit. 8–10.

124. The size of the Tanagran district is inferred from the fact that it sent only one boiotarch in the early fourth century: Hell.Oxy. 16.3 (Bartoletti). P. Salmon 1978: 94–95 envisions a shrinking of the territory of Tanagra after 457, but this is predicated on an insupportable assumption of regional dominance for Tanagra between 479 and 457; see in particular Fowler 1957. Delion and Aulis: Th. 4.76.4; Str. 9.2.7 (who mentions the two harbors).

The combination of a relatively rich and detailed epigraphic record and the narrative of Herakleides Kritikos provides enough evidence to piece together a clear picture of the complementarity of resources available in different parts of Boiotia in the third century. None of the Boiotian poleis was particularly large in the Hellenistic period, nor was the territory they controlled; without considerable economic interactions with other communities, these poleis would regularly if not constantly have experienced shortages of crucial goods. They did not individually control enough territory to comprise all the complementary resources that would have made them autarkic. Anthedon was probably not the only small coastal polis whose economy was particularly oriented toward the sea but that lacked an ability to grow grain on a scale sufficient to feed its own population. The poleis of central Boiotia, by contrast, commanded plentiful land for both pasture and agriculture, whereas Tanagra, and perhaps other poleis in the southeastern part of the region, produced olives and vines but no grain, while manufacturing certainly created a source of revenues. It was by interacting extensively with individuals from other Boiotian (and occasionally allied) communities, in trade as well as in loans, leases, and land-use grants, that the region as a whole became relatively autarkic. The rights of *enktēsis* and to a lesser extent *epigamia* set out in the previous section can only be an indication of the desire to safeguard regional autonomy by facilitating these kinds of interpolis economic transactions. While interpolis exchange was widespread throughout the Greek world, in the absence of koinon institutions the right to own property beyond one's own polis was not. The creation of that right alone promoted the economic—as well as the political—integration of the region; we would like to know whether the koinon took steps, beyond producing a common coinage, to facilitate interpolis regional exchange. Even if there were no tax advantages, the shared legal framework of the koinon must have created a more secure environment for exchange between citizens of different member poleis.[125]

Although Boiotia has several small mountains, Helikon, Kithairon, and Ptoion, its landscape is dominated by the Kopaïc Basin and by low plains, and the picture that emerges here of resource complementarity is embedded in ecological conditions that are, by Greek standards, relatively rare. Several of the regions in which koina developed in mainland Greece and the Peloponnese are characterized by their mountainous terrain, which poses a different set of opportunities and requires different economic strategies, but as in the low microregions of Boiotia in these regions too mobility is vital, and the impact of political boundaries on such movement needs to be assessed.

125. On taxes see below, pp. 290–95; and on federal law see below, pp. 351–55.

Upland Economies and the Need for Interaction

In local myth, Mount Kithairon, in southern Boiotia, was personified as "the tyrant of Plataia."[126] Mountains tyrannize populations, making distances seem twice or thrice as great as they are on flat ground, distorting space itself, and rejecting attempts to cultivate nourishing crops like olives and grains, fostering only maquis, grasses, and bitter herbs. So mountains were regarded in Greek myth as wild places, where gods lived and not men, where the normal social order was inverted, where painful transitions occurred.[127] There is no better visual representation of this perception than the third-century dedication by one Euthykles to the Muses of Helikon, depicting Helikon himself as a wild man, with savage, furrowed brow, bushy hair, and a decidedly unkempt beard.[128] If this wild tyrant could be persuaded to share power, however, if the mountain and its resources could be brought into cooperation with the plains and the coast, his hostile, threatening reign could be, and often was, mollified. One of the most valuable products of Mediterranean mountains is timber, the first resource of the Chalkideis listed so nervously by Kleigenes: "What stands in their way, when there is plenty of timber in their territory for shipbuilding?" An alliance reached between the koinon of the Chalkideis and the Macedonian king Amyntas III in the 390s or 380s records the right of the koinon, despite its own timber supplies, to export even the most valuable timbers from the king's territory.[129] The clause in the alliance granting rights to resources in the ally's territory underscores two important facts: the value of the resources found in mountains is generally predicated upon an ability to export them, and political boundaries can have a deleterious impact on this economic mobility.

Although Macedonia and the Chalkidic Peninsula tend to be regarded as the most important timber-producing areas in mainland Greece, other regions were likewise rich in this precious resource. Absolutely central to the successful exploitation of mountain resources was in every case a careful structural organization that enabled easy export and the import of other crucial but nonlocal goods. Mountain economies are by necessity closely bound up with the economies of the littoral and its plains.[130] The dominant notion that mountain communities are (and were) isolated flies in the face of this structurally determined logic.

126. Paus. 9.3.1.
127. Buxton 1992 and 1994: chap. 6.
128. *IG* VII.4240 (National Archaeological Museum, Athens, inv. 1455); Peek 1977; Hurst 1996; Veneri 1996. For the iconography see Palagia, "Helikon," *LIMC* IV.1.572.
129. RO 12.
130. Linking interior and coastal communities was vitally important, whether the interior was mountainous or not (though it usually is in the Greek world). See Bresson 2007: 49–57.

The connectivity of mountains and plains is well illustrated by an exchange involving the southern and northern coasts and uplands of the Gulf of Corinth. A Delphic inscription recording the purchase of timber for the final stages of construction of the fourth-century temple records payment by the *naopoioi* to three individuals, from Arkadian Kleitor, Achaian Ascheion, and Italian Kroton, who together sold 28,550 drachmas' worth of hewn fir.[131] The Krotoniate and Achaian together contributed half, and after the tithe each can be calculated to have put up over 6,423 drachmas in capital, an enormous sum for any individual. Ascheion and Kleitor are entirely landlocked, but the timber these men sold probably derived from the mountains in precisely that area; the only feasible transportation route would have been down to the coast through the transportation corridor along the Selinous River Valley and from the port at Aigion (map 3) across the Corinthian Gulf to the sacred port at Kirrha.[132] If precisely that route were followed (and that is only a suggestion based on the partnership of individuals from Kleitor and Ascheion, situated at either end of the high intermontane valley between Panachaïkon, Erymanthos, and Aroania), the merchants would have had to convey their timber through the territories of Rhypes and Aigion. The timber was exported shortly before the Achaian koinon was weakened if not dismantled by Alexander, and if here fiscal federalism accompanied the political federalism that is relatively well attested, we should expect that transit was significantly eased and the cost of the transaction reduced by the existence of the koinon. But what we really need to know is whether each city within the koinon could impose taxes on goods being transported through its territory, and for this question we have no evidence.

Achaian involvement in maritime import and export may be attested in the late fifth century by an Athenian proxeny decree for one Lykon the Achaian.[133] In exchange for his unspecified benefaction to Athens, Lykon is granted the right to import and export goods throughout the territories controlled by Athens. Like the Achaian timber traders, Lykon used the Corinthian Gulf as a vital conduit for trade, but unless he came from a coastal polis (which is of course possible) that use in itself requires the right to move freely across the many polis boundaries of Achaia. Indeed the need for goods from the interior to be exported via coastal communities is mentioned by the Corinthian delegate to the meeting of the

131. Bousquet 1977: 96–100 (*SEG* 27.108–9) and 1988a: 90–94.

132. Meiggs 1982: 432 for the mountains of northern Arkadia and southern Achaia as the likeliest origin for the timber; Freitag 2000: 250–56, 268–75, 309–29 for transportation routes into and across the gulf.

133. *IG* I³ 174. There has been debate about whether Lykon is a Peloponnesian Achaian or a Phthiotic (Thessalian) Achaian: Mattingly 1966b: 214; M. B. Walbank 1978: 283. Reference in the inscription to trading in the gulf points to the Corinthian Gulf and to Peloponnesian Achaia as Lykon's home.

Peloponnesian League in 432 during the debate about entering into war with Athens. He warns those living inland that if they fail to assist their maritime allies they will be unable to export their produce or to import those goods conveyed by maritime trade.[134]

Timber is just one of the precious commodities of mountain economies; most others are associated with pastoralism and stock rearing. The importance to participants in mountain economies of having regularized and easy access to harbors and coastal plains is clearly attested by the conclusion of bilateral agreements between poleis aimed at reducing the costs imposed by political boundaries that needed to be traversed for economic reasons.[135] In addition to needing access to the resources of coastal plains and harbors, individuals engaged in exploiting the resources of the mountains rely on fairs and markets to sell their surplus pastoral products and purchase other goods.[136] Regrettably, explicit evidence is lacking for mainland Greece in the same period, but the existence of similar structures there can be teased out of the sources. At Pellene, in eastern Achaia, as we have seen, woolen cloaks were given as prizes in the festival of Apollo Theoxenios, binding his sanctuary and its rituals closely to one of the principal economic activities of Pellene.[137] There are a few clear indications of pastoralism in Achaia in the fifth to third centuries, but none of them is detailed enough to elucidate the nature of the relationship between upland and lowland or coastal communities in the region.[138] Across the Corinthian Gulf in Aitolia, cloaks made at Kalydon from the wool of goats were as notorious (for their offensive smell) as the Pellenean cloaks were admired, but where and to whom they were sold is unknown.[139]

Aitolia's rugged, mountainous terrain is well known in general terms, but the economic strategies of its inhabitants, and the relationship between ecology, economy, and state structure is almost entirely unfamiliar. Strabo characterizes the region, macroscopically, as "rather rough and wretched."[140] He dedicates a full

---

134. Th. 1.120.2. Cf. Roy 2000: 339 with nn. 129, 130; Bresson 2007 on inland–coastal economic cooperation.

135. E.g., *Staatsverträge* III.456 (Aigai and the Olympenoi in Aiolis); *Staatsverträge* III.554 (Hierapytna and Praisos); *IC* III.3.4 (Hierapytna and Priansos). Cf. Chaniotis 1995, 1996a, 1996b; Guizzi 1999.

136. Cf. Forbes 1994: 192, "Pastoralism in Greece (and elsewhere) has been an activity primarily designed to generate goods via exchange, not for subsistence consumption." On the distinction between fairs (low frequency, volume irrelevant) and markets (high frequency, volume irrelevant) see de Ligt 1993: 14 and Andreau 2002: 119.

137. See above, p. 217, for Pellenean cloaks and the Theoxenia.

138. The sacred herds at Lousoi attest the use of the intermontane valley in which Lousoi, Kleitor, Kynaitha, Ascheion, and Leontion were all situated for pastoralism: Sinn 1992. The epic name for Dyme, "Bouprasion" (Hom. *Il.* 2.615–24), must mean something like "Cow Pasture."

139. Hsch. s.v. Καλυδώνιος αἴξ.

140. Str. 10.2.3.

paragraph to Aitolian orography; there are Korax ("the biggest mountain"), Oita, Arakynthos, Taphiassos, and Chalkis ("fairly tall mountains"), and Kourion.[141] Despite the presence of places like Trichoneion, which Strabo describes as having good soil, it is the relentlessly high landscape that seems to have affected Aitolian economic behavior as well, perhaps, as many of its strategic and military policies.[142] From antiquity to the present people have blamed this rough terrain for a supposed Aitolian backwardness. Modern scholars have even suggested that the Aitolians were slow to employ many typical Greek sociopolitical structures such as coinage and urban settlements because by the last quarter of the fifth century they had lost access to the Corinthian Gulf, an important artery of transportation, communication, and exchange, and failed to regain it until the third century.[143] But the production of coinage, as we have seen, actually began in the late fourth century, becoming voluminous in the early third, and a hoard buried in Agrinion shows that coins of Aigina, Elis, and Boiotia were circulating in the region in the fifth century.[144] And urbanization, as Peter Funke has shown, began in the fifth century, not the third, as had been previously assumed.[145] While Kalydon and Naupaktos were detached from Aitolia, Molykreion was gained in 426 and retained until the second century, along with nearby Makyneia (map 4).[146] In other words, the isolation of the region and its lack of access to the sea, with its commerce in goods and ideas, have been somewhat overstated.

This part of western Greece is relatively well watered, and it is certainly due in part to that fact that it was renowned for horse rearing from the classical period to the Roman.[147] However, ancient evidence for Aitolian economic practices, beyond piracy and raiding, simply does not survive, and it is difficult to proceed beyond tentative

141. Str. 10.2.4.

142. F. W. Walbank 1940: 28 n. 4: "In judging Aetolian piracy, one must always bear in mind the lack of resources, which drove the Aetolians to piracy and mercenary-service."

143. Th. 1.5.3, 3.94.5 for early statements about Aitolian backwardness. Loss of the coast by the 420s: Th. 3.102.5 with Bommeljé 1988. Freeman 1893: I.326–27 for the idea that the Aitolians' rusticity was determined by their isolation from the coast. Cf. Scholten 2000: 12.

144. *IGCH* 37.

145. Funke 1987, 1991, 1997.

146. Th. 3.102.2; see above, p. 56.

147. Oineus, king of Kalydon, is described as "horse-driving" (Bacchyl. 5.97). Polyb. 18.22.5 asserts that the Aitolian cavalry were as superior to that of other Greeks as their infantry forces were inferior. Str. 8.81 compares the value of Aitolian land for horse rearing to that of Thessaly. Str. 5.1.9 mentions a cult of Aitolian Artemis (clearly Laphria) associated with that of Diomedes among the Eneti in Italy; the goddess is associated with horse breeding. Malkin 1998: 253 suggests that the cults of Diomedes and Artemis Laphria may have reached this area via Aitolian sailing voyages up the Adriatic in the archaic period. The water resources of Aitolia vary considerably; the survey of eastern Aitolia suggests a general increase in water wealth as altitude increases, a result of the presence of plentiful mountain springs: Bommeljé and Doorn 1985: 24.

reconstructions of stock rearing and pastoralist practices in the region in antiquity.[148] But comparative modern evidence, which may provide hints of the situation in antiquity, can be gleaned from the report of the Strouza Region Project, a survey of eastern Aitolia by a team of Dutch scholars undertaken in the 1980s. The aim of the project was to establish settlement patterns and hierarchies, the economic structure of the region, and the ancient territory of the group known as the Ophiones.[149] A combination of intensive and extensive survey was employed to determine the settlement structure of the entire region and to gain some understanding of the nature and distribution of ancient sites in this previously unexplored area. In an attempt to develop a picture of the economic structure of the region as it existed in antiquity, the team sought information about the local economy prior to World War II, when Aitolia was still almost entirely preindustrial. They gathered this information by interviewing the elderly inhabitants of numerous villages about economic strategies, patterns of exploitation, and trade in the region. They also collected detailed demographic data for the area from census reports and similar official documents for the period circa 1821–1940. The project's findings suggest an economic structure so similar to what we have seen in ancient Achaia, and will see glimpses of in third-century Aitolia, that they indicate at least the horizon of possibility within which we should situate our understanding of the ancient Aitolian economy. They are nevertheless modern data and must be interpreted with care by the historian of antiquity.

The area surveyed in the Strouza Region Project was of roughly rectangular shape, forty kilometers east to west and fifty kilometers north to south, from the Gulf of Corinth just east of modern Erateini to the western end of the Bay of Efpalio, to the modern village Artotina in the northwest and the westernmost slopes of Mount Gkiona in the northeast (map 6). At the heart of this region lies the confluence of four rivers: the Kokkinos, Megas, Velesitsa, and Mornos. The damming of the Mornos River in the late 1970s has dramatically altered the landscape from its character in antiquity, and the resultant drowning of some low areas prevented surveying (though it indirectly prompted the excavation of ancient Kallipolis under rescue conditions). Because this survey area comprises both coastal plains and some of the highest mountains in Greece, connected by the river valleys that provide obvious transportation routes, it is well suited to address the problem of economic interdependence between coastal and upland communities. In addition to locating the presence of settlements based on pottery scatters and the presence of fortifications or other built remains datable to antiquity, the Strouza team established site intervisibility and distances on foot between the ancient settlements.

---

148. Pastoralism in Aitolia: Doorn and Bommeljé 1990; cf. Antonetti 1987a.

149. Th. 3.96.2–3. The data from the Strouza Region Project were published in Bommeljé, Doorn, Deylius, et al. 1987, though the discussion of territorial groups and economic structures in this region is included only in the privately published volumes (Bommeljé and Doorn 1984, 1985).

The Strouza region was not well known prior to the Dutch survey, but the few literary testimonia we do have suggest the kinds of questions we should be asking. According to Thucydides, the territory of the Ophiones reached north toward the Malian Gulf; he also tells us that there were two subgroups within this territory, the Kallieis and the Bomieis, though it is not clear whether any other subgroups existed (map 5).[150] We have already seen that this part of Aitolia participated in the process of urbanization that Peter Funke has documented for the fifth and fourth centuries, but it is still not clear how these preurban population groups divided up their territory and what effect their territorial divisions, if any, had on political organization.[151] By analyzing site distribution, settlement hierarchy, intervisibility, and regional geography together it is possible to develop a plausible answer to these questions. The valleys of the Kokkinos and Megas rivers (map 6) were a focus of settlement in the classical and Hellenistic periods. At their juncture stood Kallipolis itself, which was the site of cult activity, if not settlement, from the eighth century, becoming a fortified urban center by the fourth century.[152] In the two valleys north of Kallipolis surveyors located fifteen settlements occupied in the classical or the Hellenistic period or both. In addition, two fortified sites near the (now abandoned) village of Strouza, south of Kallipolis at an altitude of 953 meters, have been identified with the polis Aigition mentioned by Thucydides.[153] Apparently associated with the settlement near Strouza was a fortification on Mount Vouchori, which is connected by intervisibility with every other site in the valleys of the Kokkinos and Megas rivers and probably functioned as the nodal point in the network of communications in this area.[154]

The geography of the area facilitates interaction between these settlements beyond intervisibility. The deep river valleys, separated by the southern reaches of Mount Vardousia, with a summit of 2,383 meters, create corridors of transportation, with travel time between settlements in these valleys and their confluence (the area of Kallipolis and Strouza [Aigition]) averaging about two hours on foot, though a few are as far as six or seven hours from Kallipolis.[155] The archaeological

150. Th. 3.96.3.

151. See above, pp. 54–55, 77–78.

152. Cult activity from the geometric to the Hellenistic period: Themelis 1983: 237–44; cf. the fifth-century *lex sacra* found built into the wall of a house in Kallion, Mastrokostas 1955b: 72; Sokolowski 1969: 214 n. 128. Funke 1997: 171–72 on the development of Kallipolis as an urban center.

153. Local ceramic products are so little known that surveyors were unable to put very fine chronological distinctions on the scatters they located, though these were nevertheless taken to indicate settlement. For discussion of the problem see Vroom 1993 and Vroom in Bommeljé and Doorn 1985: 38–41. Aigition: Th. 3.97.2; located at Strouza by Bommeljé 1981–82; Bommeljé, Doorn, Deylius, et al. 1987: 75.

154. Bommeljé and Doorn 1984: 29–30 with figs. 30 and 34.

155. See Bommeljé and Doorn 1984: fig. 11.

remains of Kallipolis reveal a city of evident importance, which along with its situation at the nodal point in this network of communication led the Strouza survey
team to suggest that the entire region should be identified as the territory of the
Kallieis.[156]

The Strouza area was thus at least potentially a functional region in antiquity,
created and maintained by the interactions of its inhabitants. On several occasions
in the fifth and fourth centuries its inhabitants were able to mobilize troops quickly
against invaders and use the difficult mountainous terrain to their own advantage,
clear indications of the cooperative and cohesive nature of settlement in this
region, at least during hostile invasions.[157] Comparative evidence for the nature of
the region-forming interactions in eastern Aitolia may help to fill the gap between
the settlement data and historical evidence for intersettlement cooperation, which
brings us back to firmly economic problems.

The village interviews conducted by the Strouza Region survey team reveal a
complex network of exchange between early modern settlements in this region,
driven by the variety of surpluses and shortages in its microregions. In the eastern
part of the survey region, all the inland villages regularly experienced a surplus of
ovicaprid produce and a shortage of grains, olives, and garden produce (map 6).[158]
The villages in the northwestern part of the interior (e.g., Diakopi and Kokkino)
regularly had just enough ovicaprid produce for their own consumption, or a
slight surplus; to the southwest several villages (e.g., Avoros and Stylia) typically
had a shortage. These latter seem always to have been short of all basic foodstuffs
(ovicaprid produce, grains, olives, and garden produce), suggesting that in order
to survive they relied on imported goods. Shortage of ovicaprid produce was also
reported in the coastal villages of Kallithea and Erateini. All the coastal villages
regularly experienced a surplus of olives, though only one (Tolophon) had a grain
surplus. Garden produce existed in surplus in many of the inland and even upland
villages, though these tend to be situated along the rivers (Krokyleio, Pentagii,
Diakopi, Daphnos, Dichorio, and Lidorikio). The general situation, then, in the
early modern period was an almost panregional surplus of ovicaprid produce balanced by a microregional surplus of garden produce where the exploitation of animal resources was less successful, and a surplus of olives on the coast, where there
was also a regular shortage of the products of pastoralism. Grains seem to have
been grown in quantities that oscillated slightly between surplus and shortage in
the interior river valleys.

156. Bommeljé and Doorn 1984: 29–30 and fig. 32.
157. Th. 3.97.2; Diod. Sic. 18.24.2, 19.74.6.
158. The published data do not provide any details about the ovicaprid produce and issues of transportation of those goods. Whether wool and dairy products, meat, or live animals (for purposes of
breeding, milking, etc.) were being bought and sold is not recorded.

The macroscopic picture is of a vulnerable region on the verge of criticality, with a need for integration, or at least cooperation, with coastal settlements in order to survive, for vulnerability is determined by a complex, recursive relationship between ecology and institutions.[159] Cooperation between montane and coastal settlements facilitated the export of surplus ovicaprid produce to the coastal settlements themselves and through their harbors to other communities, particularly those along the Gulf of Corinth. The grain, olive, and vegetable shortages of so many upland communities could at the same time be met by importing the surplus of these goods from the coast. And indeed this seems to have been the pattern in the century or so before World War II.[160] Although both the geography and the specific resources are rather different, the overall picture of resource complementarity between microregions is similar to that we have drawn for Boiotia.

In western Aitolia the picture is, again, very similar. When the Strouza survey was completed, the same team of scholars took on a more extensive survey of the rest of Aitolia and conducted similar village interviews, the results of which were tabulated but never fully analyzed. One of the most effective ways to gauge microregional economic interdependence is to assess the catchment areas of market centers. Knowing how far people travel, in what direction, to exchange what sorts of goods, provides a clear, if necessarily coarse-grained, picture of patterns of economic interaction. The Dutch team designed a set of questions for villagers in order to gather precisely this kind of information.[161] Although the interviews were conducted primarily around Naupaktos and Thermon, and the results do not therefore accurately reflect the economic systems of the entire region, they are nonetheless extremely suggestive. In preindustrial western Aitolia there were five main market centers: Thermon, Naupaktos, Agrinion, Mesolongi, and Aitoliko (map 7).

Prior to excavation, the sanctuary of Thermon was the site of a village known as Old Bazaar, which had served as a market center for people traveling as far as nine hours on foot.[162] Most of them came from the area northeast of Thermon, including the villages of Klepa, Arachova, and Kydonia, which is the northeasternmost limit of the catchment area of the market at Thermon. Villagers from Klepa, as well as from Achladokastro to the east, sold their cattle at Thermon, but

159. Environmental criticality is defined by Kasperson et al. 1995: 25 as referring "to situations in which the extent or rate of environmental degradation precludes the continuation of current use systems or levels of human well being, given feasible adaptations and societal capabilities to respond." See Adger 2000 on vulnerability.

160. Bommeljé and Doorn 1984: 13–18 with figs. 9.I–II, 10B–C, 12A–B.

161. Bommeljé, Doorn, Deylius, et al. 1987: 123 table 7.4.

162. Bommeljé, Doorn, Deylius, et al. 1987: 59.

Thermon was also used as a general market center by the inhabitants of coastal communities like Agios Giorgios, Koutsocheri, Kokori, and Vlachomandra, as far as six hours away.

Naupaktos exerted an even stronger centripetal force, probably by virtue of its coastal location. Villagers from Arachova and Klepa, at least ten to twelve hours away, used it as a general market center as well as a place to sell their livestock and dairy produce. Villagers from Elatovrisi, situated above a river valley to the northeast of Thermon, and to the northwest of the Strouza region, traveled fourteen hours by foot to Naupaktos, where they sold livestock and dairy produce and bought agricultural goods, including grain. They reported using no other market—not even Thermon, several hours closer, which may suggest that they used the valley of the Platanos or the Mornos River to access the coast rather than following the western valley situated north of their village, which would have led them to Thermon. People from Mega Dendro frequently traveled eleven hours to sell their livestock at Naupaktos.

Agrinion, situated in the rich plain northwest of Lake Trichonis, was the focal point of an exchange network quite distinct from those revolving around Naupaktos and Thermon. Villagers from Agios Vlasios, lying on the northwestern slope of Mount Panaitolikon, traveled a full day on foot to sell their livestock and buy agricultural products at Agrinion. Inhabitants of Ano and Kato Labirio, on the southern reaches of Panaitolikon, went to Agrinion in order to exchange livestock and agricultural products but also used Thermon as a general market center; the former is eight hours on foot, the latter five. Villagers from Neromanna, ten hours east of Agrinion above Lake Trichonis, reported using Agrinion as well as Thermon and Mesolongi as market centers; the trip to Thermon was only four hours, that to Mesolongi two full days. This kind of trading flexibility, or perhaps variability, must have been an effective means of achieving resilience: individuals willing to travel long distances could tap into several different trading networks and their various sets of resources. People from the coastal village Stamna reported traveling six hours to Agrinion in order to buy livestock and dairy products.

Patrai was also used relatively frequently as a destination for sales of livestock and their produce by Aitolians; there is likewise some record of wholesalers from Patrai going directly to some of the Aitolian coastal villages between Mesolongi and Naupaktos to purchase livestock. Although political hostility may have precluded or occluded exchanges of this sort through much of the Hellenistic period, the brief alliance between the Aitolian and Achaian koina in the third century may well have provided opportunities for these sorts of exchanges. Aitolia's long history of friendly relations, bound by kinship, with Elis suggests that there was always considerable interaction between the northwestern Peloponnese and Aitolia, an impression supported by the few coin hoards found in Aitolia and neighboring

Akarnania, which frequently contain coins of Elis.[163] The modern practice of market exchanges between Patrai and the Aitolian pastoral economy is emblematic of the fact that the Corinthian Gulf unified the populations living around it more than it divided them.

Several important conclusions need to be extracted from this morass of unfamiliar detail. First, a willingness to travel up to two full days (or even eight to ten hours, a more normal figure) on foot implies extreme resource specialization and complementarity; these are the basic components of economic interdependence.[164] If resource complementarity and interdependence are the motives for movement and economic interactions between communities, then these should also be seen as factors that contribute to regionalization. What we can see in the results of the Aitolian village interviews is the existence of three distinct but highly interrelated trade regions. One, centered on Agrinion, comprises both coastal communities like Stamna and distant mountain villages like Agios Vlasios and Labirio, as well as places such as Neromanna that lie between Lake Trichonis and the steep slopes of Panaitolikon. To the east, Thermon and Naupaktos overlap significantly, but both draw on villages from a similar range of environmental conditions. We have already seen that Naupaktos seems to have exerted a greater attractive force, which may be accounted for both by the scale of its offerings (impossible to determine) and by its coastal position. This series of trade networks, viewed macroscopically, presents a striking structural similarity to the koinon itself, comprised of individual communities grouped together into districts and participating likewise in the regional system. The details that can be resurrected of the modern preindustrial economy of Aitolia are merely comparative, but they are suggestive of the range of possibilities we should envision for antiquity. If even roughly the same patterns of behavior prevailed in antiquity, it should be no surprise that the institutions of the koinon had an almost fractal quality, in that behavioral patterns were repeated at ever smaller scales, and institutional structures (in the loosest sense of the word) were created to protect and promote them.

The communities that became members of the several koina of mainland Greece and the Peloponnese were typical of ancient Mediterranean communities in that the resources they had at their disposal tended to be highly localized and highly specialized, with few achieving anything close to autarky and relying on imports only for the provision of nonessential or luxury commodities. But unlike independent, fully autonomous poleis, their membership in koina that either

---

163. *IGCH* 37; *CH* VII.45 and IX.136.

164. The distances traveled to market in Aitolia are much higher than the standard 2–3-hour, 10–15-km distances tolerated in most historical and prehistoric cases (Bintliff 2002). This is probably to be explained in part by the mountainous terrain of the region, making travel slower and more difficult. Resource specialization and complementarity are the corollaries of this geographical situation.

directly or indirectly promoted economic mobility meant that their resources were effectively pooled with those of neighboring member communities. We do not have the quantitative evidence to determine what percentage of the population of a koinon actually took advantage of the right of *enktēsis* and acquired property outside of the home polis, but it is clear enough that the more frequently it happened, the more evenly resources tended to be distributed throughout the koinon. And this has a bearing on the question of political stability, insofar as the even distribution of resources and the mobility of production throughout a state have been seen to mitigate incentives for fragmentation and separation.[165] I have suggested that the emergence of institutions to protect and promote regional economic mobility, resulting in greater access to a wider array of resources, was an important part of the institutional development of the koinon. Thus far, however, I have considered resource complementarity only within the original, ethnic boundaries of each koinon. If this argument about the economic incentives for participation in a koinon is correct, it would not be surprising if we were to see in the expansion of koina beyond these boundaries some evidence for economic motives, in particular for access to resources that were lacking entirely or in short supply within the koinon's own territory.

WINNING THE BATTLE FOR RESOURCES

If resource complementarity and something approaching regional autarky were characteristic of the third-century Boiotian koinon, the situation was not always the same. There are hints of economic motives behind Thebes' attack on Plataia at the outbreak of the Peloponnesian War. When, at Theban urging, the Spartans showed up in 429 to besiege Plataia, Archidamos attempted to persuade the Plataians to remain neutral, at least until the end of the war. He advised the Plataians, who were visibly anxious about their own resources, "to hand over the city and houses to us Lakedaimonians and point out the boundaries of the land and the number of your trees and whatever else it is possible for you to enumerate."[166] The Spartans would, he promised, hand it all back at the end of the war. The Plataians must have recognized the ominous sign of vultures circling overhead. When the city was finally taken in 427 after three years of siege, the Thebans declared its territory public land and leased it out to Thebans for ten-year terms.[167] There were, however, bigger rewards in play: it was certainly with the attack on Plataia and its seizure in 427 that Thebes gained full control of Skolos, Erythrai, Skaphai, and the

165. Bolton and Roland 1997.
166. Th. 2.72.3.
167. Th. 3.86.3.

other communities of the Parasopia that had, according to the Oxyrhynchos Historian, been in *sympoliteia* with Plataia.[168] It is also possible that control of Plataia brought with it control of Kreusis, one of only two Boiotian ports on the Corinthian Gulf, which is often assumed to have been the port of Thespiai but which, by 371 and probably before, was certainly in Theban hands.[169]

Ephoros praised Boiotia as *trithalattos*, a territory with access to three seas: "It receives the produce of Italy and Sicily and Libya into the Krisaian and Corinthian Gulf ports, while in the part that faces Euboia ... it has access to the sea, which stretches in one direction all the way to Egypt and Cyprus and the islands, and in the other direction toward Macedonia, the Propontis, and the Hellespont."[170] Ephoros, of course, wrote this passage sometime after Epameinondas's attempt to build up a Boiotian navy in the 360s, an episode in Boiotian history that bespeaks not only military but also economic motives. We have already seen that the Boiotians courted Byzantion heavily in this period and achieved its lasting allegiance in 364.[171] In light of the grain shortage experienced at Thebes in 377, after two years of war with Sparta, good relations with the city that controlled exports of grain from the Black Sea were advantageous.[172]

If the Boiotians under Theban leadership were making efforts to gain greater access to the sea and to maritime trade, the Chalkideis under Olynthian leadership appear to have been interested in landward expansion. Diodoros reports that after being defeated by the Illyrians, Amyntas made a gift of some Macedonian land to the Olynthians in the hope of securing their alliance or at least their support; but when shortly thereafter he asked that they surrender the land again, the Olynthians refused.[173] The treaty and alliance concluded between the koinon of the Chalkideis and Amyntas in this same period attests their desire for the resources of Macedonia,

168. *Hell.Oxy.* 16.3 (Bartoletti); cf. Hansen in Hansen and Nielsen 2004: 450.

169. Xen. *Hell.* 6.4.3 (Bartoletti). The impressive fortifications at Kreusis appear to belong to the second or third quarter of the fourth century; Cooper 2000 sees Epameinondas's hand in their construction.

170. Ephoros *FGrHist* 70 F 119 *apud* Str. 9.2.2. The "produce of Libya" is probably not an exaggeration: Boiotian cities were among the recipients of grain from Cyrene ca. 330–326: RO 96 ll. 32 (Tanagra) and 44 (Plataia); and the fact that the Boiotians bestowed proxeny on a Carthaginian in these years (T11) may well point to a desire to facilitate trade with North Africa. On the grain sent from Cyrene see now Bresson 2011.

171. Diod. Sic. 15.79.1; Isocr. 5.53; T9. The permanence of the Byzantine allegiance is implied by *IG* VII.2418 (RO 57), recording contributions to Thebes for the Third Sacred War. For the chronology of the Boiotian naval expedition see above, pp. 78–79, and Mackil 2008: 181–85.

172. Xen. *Hell.* 5.4.56.

173. The same episode appears to be narrated twice by Diodoros, once under 393/2 (14.92.3–4) and once under 383/2 (15.19.2–3). In the latter passage, he appeals to the Spartans for help at around the same time as the Akanthians and Apolloniates made their appeal. It therefore seems better to place the land grant sometime not too long before 383/2.

above all timber, and their strength in leveraging terms that were economically advantageous.[174]

Although the expansion of the Achaian and Aitolian koina in the Hellenistic period is inextricably bound up with the struggle first against Macedon, then against each other, and finally against Rome, we can nevertheless detect traces of economic motives for growth in both regions from the fourth century onward. In both cases, the struggle lay primarily but not exclusively in gaining greater access to the sea. No source ventures to explain why the Achaians annexed Kalydon, and probably Naupaktos, sometime before 389, but the two together may have allowed them to control, for over two decades, the heavy traffic moving through the Corinthian Gulf.[175] The Delphic record of a large sale of timber to the *naopoioi* by individuals from Ascheion and Kleitor, although two decades after the loss of these coastal poleis, attests the kind of trans–Corinthian Gulf economic traffic that we should probably envisage throughout this period.[176] The Achaians began to expand beyond their ethnic boundaries again only in the mid-third century. The first step was taken in securing the allegiance of Sikyon in 251, a move that was motivated not by economic considerations but by the hostility of the young Aratos and many inhabitants of the northern Peloponnese to the Macedonian-sponsored tyrants in Sikyon and neighboring cities. But it did pave the way to the inclusion of the Corinthia and Argolid in the koinon, a process that began when Aratos took Corinth in 243 with its Corinthian and Saronic Gulf ports, followed by the adherence of Megara (with Aigosthena), Epidauros , and Troizen.[177]

Having lost control of the northern coast of the Corinthian Gulf, including Kalydon and Pleuron, sometime before 426, the Aitolians spent the next century trying to regain it.[178] In the aftermath of the botched Athenian invasion of Aitolia in 426, the Aitolians sought Spartan help to take Naupaktos from the Athenians and Messenians; but the attempt failed, and they settled for Molykreion.[179] It is possible that the Achaians were responsible for the Aitolians' loss of Kalydon and Pleuron in the fifth century; certainly by 389 they were Achaian possessions along with Naupaktos.[180] Kalydon and, probably, Pleuron were liberated by

174. RO 12.
175. Xen. *Hell.* 4.6.1, 13; Diod. Sic. 15.75.1–2 shows that they were still garrisoned by the Achaians in 367/6. On Corinthian Gulf traffic see Freitag 2000. Cf. Merker 1989.
176. *SEG* 27.108–9 and above, p. 275.
177. Corinth and Megara: Polyb. 2.43.4–5 with T38; Megara was ceded to Boiotia in 223 (Polyb. 20.6.7) but went back to the Achaians in 192. Epidauros and Troizen: Plut. *Arat.* 24.3 with T37; Paus. 2.8.5.
178. Th. 3.102.5 with Bommeljé 1988.
179. Th. 3.102.2.
180. Xen. *Hell.* 4.6.1, 14 with Diod. Sic. 15.75.2.

Epameinondas in 367 and probably became Aitolian again.[181] Naupaktos, however, continued to be a goal, and the Aitolians won it only after Chaironeia but were unable to hold it for long.[182] The gradual reconquest of this Aitolian coast appears, however, not to have been enough, for sometime before 323 the Aitolians had also seized Akarnanian Oiniadai, which in addition to its excellent harbor had good agricultural land, enriched by alluviation from the Acheloös River.[183] Surrendered in accordance with Alexander's exiles decree, the Aitolians regained Oiniadai when they seized southern Akarnania, probably in the late 240s.[184] It is certainly no accident, as Joseph Scholten has observed, that the Aitolians first became seriously active at sea after their successful seizure of southern Akarnania.[185] Between these two violent seizures was, of course, the ephemeral alliance of Akarnania and Aitolia in the late 260s or early 250s (T57). The terms of the alliance respected the territorial autonomy of Akarnania, with the exception of Pras and Demphis, which the Aitolians claimed as their own (ll. 6–7). Located west of the Acheloös River, between Stratos and Agrai (map 5), Pras gave the Aitolians access to the Ambrakian Gulf and all its economic opportunities.[186] If, then, for political reasons the Aitolians could not control Oiniadai directly, they found other ways to gain access to the Ionian Sea.

In the previous section we saw that the Aitolian settlements around Kallipolis and Aigition had highly localized economic resources and in the preindustrial modern period depended upon exchange with one another, including the settlements at the coast (Kallithea, Tolophon, and Panormos) that produced sufficient or surplus quantities of grain and were the only source of surplus olives for the region (map 6). These coastal settlements cluster around the ancient city of Oiantheia, which was originally a part of Ozolian (West) Lokris, although Kallipolis and Aigition were always Aitolian. The Aitolians' relationship with Oiantheia should, then, be a particularly interesting case study in political expansion motivated by economic concerns, for its incorporation into Aitolia, or at least its consistent cooperation, would have provided an economic missing link for the entire region around Kallipolis and Aigition. The sources suggest that this suspicion is well founded. Oiantheia cooperated with the West Lokrians' decision in 426 to ally themselves with the Spartan general Eurylochos in advance of his attack on

181. Diod. Sic. 15.75.2.

182. High hopes: Xen. Hell. 4.6.14. Naupaktos regained by the Aitolians: Theopomp. FGrHist 15 F 235; Str. 9.4.7; Lerat 1952: II.54–55; Bosworth 1976; Freitag 2000. See above, pp. 86–87.

183. Seizure of Oiniadai: Diod. Sic. 18.8.6; Plut. Alex. 49.8. The soil was good enough to motivate a Messenian attack on the place in the 450s: Paus. 4.25.1.

184. Polyb. 2.45.1, 9.34.7.

185. Scholten 2000: 90 n. 108.

186. Berktold, Schmidt, and Wacker 1996: 127–28; Schoch and Wacker 1996: 127–28; Schoch 1997: 77–78.

Naupaktos in the same year; that attack was prompted by the request of the Aitolians, who had suffered at the hands of Demosthenes earlier in the year.[187] Although part of Lokris, Oiantheia was in practice cooperative with the eastern Aitolians in the fifth century. In the 270s the Aitolian koinon had a close relationship with several Lokrian communities but still seems to have respected their autonomy; the exact process of integration cannot be traced.[188] By 219, however, Oiantheia had been integrated into the Aitolian koinon and was used as a mustering point for troops headed across the Gulf of Corinth to Aigeira.[189] Facilitating military expeditions of this kind must have been one motivation for Aitolian expansion to the gulf, but it is essential to appreciate the economic impetus behind such a move. In addition to the import and export of goods, regularized relations with coastal communities gave the pastoralist communities of the mountains a greater range of pasturage. That they took full advantage of it is shown by Philip's invasion of Aitolia in 207 by way of Erythrai, on the Lokrian coast east of Naupaktos. The men who saw his landing fled into the mountains, the familiar Aitolian strategy; the cattle that they could not herd away in time were seized by the Macedonians.[190] In other words, the Aitolians were using the coastal area either as pasture for their cattle or as an emporium to sell their produce; the harbor at Oiantheia must have been valuable for the export of regional surpluses and the import of other commodities.[191] Scholten suggests that it was only a desire to secure their own borders that motivated Aitolian expansion, but it would appear that economic motives driven by human geography also played an important role.[192] Gaining control of the coast, or at least easy access to it, enabled the eastern Aitolians to realize the full potential of their dominantly upland economic system and to augment their own resilience by tapping into the complex network of redistribution centered on the Gulf of Corinth.

Although the evidence is not extensive, these hints suggest that attempts to expand the membership of a koinon were in many cases motivated at least in part by a desire to gain access to economic resources that were otherwise lacking within

187. Th. 3.101.

188. Koinon relations with citizens of various West Lokrian communities: *IG* IX.1² 1.5 records a grant of proxeny to Aristion son of Androkles, probably of Chaleion; *IG* IX.1² 1.12a grants *isopoliteia* to several citizens of Amphissa. Proxeny and *isopoliteia* may not have been granted to citizens of a community that had been fully integrated into the koinon. Both texts are dated to the 270s. Cf. Scholten 2000: 29 n.1, 44, 54.

189. Polyb. 4.57.2. Lokris seems to have continued to function as a unit once it had been integrated into the Aitolian koinon; it is referred to in several decrees as *to Lokrikon telos*; see below, p. 380 and T61.

190. Livy 28.8.9–10.

191. *IG* IX.1² 717 l. 4.

192. Scholten 2000: 29–58 passim.

the koinon's territory. In the case of Aitolia we can trace a desire to gain coastal territory to the south and west through the clearer and better-documented motive of securing borders to the north and east. Land hunger in late sixth-century Thebes may have been one motive in the attempt to press the Plataians "to take part in the Boiotians"; and the hegemonial politics of the mid-fourth century, including the attempt to build a navy and win allies in the eastern Aegean, can be understood to have had an economic incentive, particularly in light of the grain shortage experienced at Thebes in the 370s. But while the Aitolians, Achaians, and Boiotians were all putting expansionist pressure in maritime directions, the Chalkideis, who had plenty of ports, sought land and timber in their attempt to annex southeastern Macedonia in the early fourth century. In each instance we can detect a desire to control new resources. Combined with the numismatic evidence for economic cooperation prior to or simultaneous with the emergence of state institutions at the regional scale, the epigraphic evidence for institutions that worked to open up economic boundaries between poleis within a koinon and thereby to create a true regional economy, and the highly localized distribution of varied resources within each region, the hints of economically motivated expansion explored in this section suggest that the koinon was born from and developed in response to economic needs as much as the religious interactions considered in the previous chapter. Having established this fact, we need to turn from the question of natural resources to consideration of the public revenues of the koinon and their relationship to these highly localized resources and relatively open internal economic boundaries.

TAXATION AND REGIONAL STATE REVENUES

In federal governments throughout history, the apportionment of the tax burden has been a tremendously contentious issue, for reasons that have varied from case to case. In America after the Revolutionary War, the economic impact of slavery divided northern and southern states over how taxes should be levied by the Continental Congress, and then the United States Congress.[193] In the modern industrial world a cleavage tends to form between wealthy, urbanized industrial areas and the poorer agricultural periphery. But in each of these cases, the apportionment problem resides in variations—in economic structure, or welfare, or both— among member states or other constituent communities. Structures of taxation are important not only because they are situated at the intersection of institutions and practices but also because they reveal the strengths and weaknesses of the states that impose them, their priorities and limitations, all of which have a bearing on questions of the equity, justice, and stability of a state.

193. Einhorn 2006a and 2006b.

We have very little evidence for how koina raised revenues apart from booty collection in war, which was episodic and inherently unpredictable, and taxation; whereas their member poleis pursued a broader range of strategies for generating revenue that was typical of Greek poleis. Although the evidence is not especially plentiful, there is enough to outline the tax structures of Greek koina, which should help us to understand how they raised the revenues with which they paid their expenses, and how they adapted their fiscal policies to regional resources and economic practices. It should also, crucially, allow us to see how the taxes levied by the koinon impacted its member states.

The evidence suggests that koina, like poleis, tended to levy two kinds of taxes: regular, indirect taxes on individual economic actors, associated primarily with customs, imposts or duties levied on the import and export of goods through harbors within the territory of the koinon, and with land use; and an irregular, direct tax, usually known as an *eisphora* or *telos*, to be paid by poleis or districts to the koinon itself, apparently levied episodically to meet the expenses of war. Member poleis, meanwhile, continued to extract taxes from their own citizens and from foreigners with business in their territories. These tax revenues were used to provide services within the polis—the provision of sacrifices and festivals, the maintenance of public buildings, and services such as the military training of youths, the production and maintenance of public records, and the provision of rewards to civic benefactors. Given that the *eisphora* or *telos*, when levied, was paid to the koinon by poleis and districts, it is almost certain that the obligation was met from revenues raised by taxes at the level of the polis, but the evidence for this is indirect. The two contexts within which koina extracted taxes tell us a great deal about the nature and limitations of their power.

Harbor Dues, Imposts, and Taxes Paid by Individuals

When Kleigenes of Akanthos warned the Spartans about the economic resources that made the koinon of the Chalkideis so menacingly powerful, he reminded them that they had "the income of revenues from many harbors and ports," which suggests that the koinon itself collected duties on goods imported and exported through all the ports within its territory.[194] This impression is confirmed by the treaty reached in the early fourth century between the koinon of the Chalkideis and Amyntas, the king of Macedon. In addition to the standard clauses of bilateral alliances committing each party to come to the aid of the other in the event of an attack, the treaty establishes the economic rights of Amyntas and of the Chalkidians in each other's territory. We have already seen that the treaty granted the Chalkideis the right to export timber from Amyntas's territory. The agreement

194. Xen. *Hell.* 5.2.16.

further establishes the reciprocal right of export and transport of goods out of the ally's territory, but each must pay the duties levied on the export or transport by the other state.[195] The clear implication here is that the koinon of the Chalkideis controlled export and transport duties levied at all the harbors and ports within its territory. The territory of the koinon was conceived as a whole, and the transportation of goods out of it was taxed. If these duties were actually collected by magistrates of the poleis in whose territories the ports were situated, the treaty with Amyntas and Kleigenes' remark suggest that the revenues were then handed over to the koinon. We are in the dark as to collection mechanisms. The pseudo-Aristotelian treatise *Oikonomika*, probably written in the late fourth century, reports that at Mende the revenues from harbor taxes were so plentiful that the city did not need to impose direct property taxes; Mende was, of course, not part of the koinon of the Chalkideis at the time when the treaty with Amyntas was struck.[196] Yet the report in the *Oikonomika* suggests that the volume of trade through the harbors of the Chalkidike was high and therefore particularly profitable for those cities that controlled them. The decision of the koinon of the Chalkideis to arrogate to itself "the income of revenues from many harbors and ports" is a reflection not only of the value of these revenues but also, certainly, of the fact that if they remained in the hands of poleis, significant economic inequalities would arise as a simple function of geography: inland poleis would lack those revenues, but their citizens were equally the producers of goods exported through the harbors and consumers of those brought in. The profits of harbor cities would be parasitic on the activities of inland communities, a situation that could quickly become explosive in a koinon, which brought both into the same political entity and required their cooperation.

The taxation structure of Thessaly in the fourth century was apparently similar to that in the koinon of the Chalkideis: in 349/8 Demosthenes reported to the Athenians having heard that the Thessalians "will no longer hand over to Philip the revenues from their harbors and markets. For it is appropriate to administer the common affairs of the Thessalians from these, not for Philip to take them. If he is deprived of these revenues, he will be in a tight spot for the payment of his mercenaries."[197] If Philip was in fact relying on these Thessalian harbor revenues to pay his mercenaries, they must have been quite considerable. The background to their revocation is provided only by Justin's epitome of Trogus, but that report seems to cohere well with the indications given by Demosthenes and may well be trustworthy: the Thessalians had surrendered to Philip "all their taxes and revenues" at

195. RO 12 l. 16.
196. Ps.-Arist. *Oec.* 2.2.21a with van Groningen 1933: 142–44; Migeotte 2003: 300. RO 12 ll. 18–23.
197. Dem. 1.22; cf. 6.22.

some undisclosed time, but probably in 353 or 352 in connection with the help he rendered them in the Third Sacred War. Just a few years later, they resolved that these revenues should pay not for Philip's mercenaries but for "the common affairs of the Thessalians."[198] The Thessalians' claim that their tax revenues should be used to administer their own affairs, not to fill Philip's coffers, suggests that the koinon, rather than the individual poleis, controlled harbor taxes throughout the region and at least claimed to actually use the revenues to administer their own affairs; there is, in other words, no evidence to suggest that this control over regional taxes was a form of rent seeking by the Thessalian koinon.[199] But its control over these taxes was probably a relatively new phenomenon and was also an index of its increasing complexity and power; in the fifth century, when the Thessalians cooperated only intermittently and in order to meet external threats, the cities controlled their own tax revenues.[200] After the Thessalian koinon was reestablished by the Romans in 196, it was likewise in control of all harbor taxes, levied on exports and imports alike, and it is possible that it was a decree of the koinon that prohibited the Thessalian cities from granting complete tax immunity to anyone.[201] The mechanism by which such taxes were collected is unclear: while we know that the koinon was willing to send its magistrates out to member poleis to effect its decrees, it is also possible that those Thessalian poleis with harbors simply collected the taxes and were responsible for rendering the revenues to the treasury of the koinon.[202]

The situation in Boiotia is somewhat unclear. Herakleides Kritikos berates the Oropians for their rapacious collection of duties, and the polis of Thespiai had harbor officials (limenarchs) who were certainly responsible for collecting duties at the Thespian harbor of Kreusis.[203] It has recently been argued that the list of fish prices at Akraiphia originated in a list of values drawn up at the port of Anthedon

198. Justin 11.3.1–2; Sordi 1958: 251–52.

199. Cf. Brennan and Buchanan 1980.

200. *IG* IX.2.257 (C. D, Buck 1955: 225 no. 35), a decree of Thetonion granting *ateleia*, among other privileges, to a Corinthian benefactor. Cf. Larsen 1968: 20. Larsen 1968: 43 argues for federal tax collection in early sixth-century Phokis on the basis of the claim (Aeschin. 3.119) that the First Sacred War was provoked by Phokians levying harbor dues at Krisa. But other sources level different charges against the Phokians in connection with these hostilities, and the veracity of the entire tradition has been called into serious question (Robertson 1978; Davies 1994, urging caution). The late and tendentious speech of Aeschines can hardly be used as good evidence for tax collection by a Phokian koinon in the early sixth century, although it is now clear that the Delphic Amphiktyony itself did collect harbor dues at Kirrha in the fourth century: Lefèvre 1994.

201. Decree of Larisa on the export of grain to Athens, 190s: Helly 2008: 29 Decree B ll. 41–42, 45–46, with discussion pp. 95–96.

202. Helly 2008: 96.

203. Her. Krit. 1.7 with Arenz 2006: 145–46; McInerney in *BNJ* 369A F I.7. Thespiai: Roesch 1965b: 214–19.

for the purposes of taxing fishermen on their catch.[204] Whether the revenues from these duties went to the poleis, or whether the poleis were collecting them on behalf of the koinon, with the result that the situation would be directly comparable to that in Thessaly and the Chalkidike, is not clear. If in fact the harbor dues were simply collected by poleis directly, rather than as agents for the koinon, it would reflect a different approach to regional revenues in Boiotia than that taken in Thessaly and the Chalkidike, and might be explained by a lower frequency and volume of trade through the ports of Boiotia, which would result in lower revenues for those poleis. The smaller discrepancy between the revenues from indirect taxes levied by the coastal and inland poleis of Boiotia would have led to a less politically explosive situation than what may have faced the koinon of the Chalkideis as they sought to bring the rich coastal poleis of the Chalkidike under the same political structure as its inland poleis.

The Thessalians and Chalkidians clearly treated harbors and their revenues as resources common to the entire koinon for both political and economic reasons. We have a tantalizing epigraphic hint that the same basic logic applied in Hellenistic Achaia. In the late third century two member poleis of the Achaian koinon, Hermione and Epidauros, sought arbitration from Rhodes and Miletos in a dispute over land that lay between their territories.[205] The arbitrators ruled that the land should be common (*koinē*), and at the end of the document we learn that those who pasture their goats on this land will be subject to taxation by tax farmers (*telōnai*).[206] As the land is common, there would be no legal basis for either polis to collect taxes on its use. The koinon could, however, have done so, for it would have been a logical continuation of the policy of using the power of the koinon to promote economic mobility and the pooling of common resources.[207]

The two clear cases of Thessaly and the Chalkideis prompted Jakob Larsen to remark that "their financial organization may have followed the pattern of [neighboring] kingdoms rather than that of normal Greek federal states" and to wonder why "most Greek federal states did not allow the central government to collect taxes throughout the confederacy and forced it to rely on sums collected and transmitted by the cities."[208] As a parallel to the taxation structures of Thessaly and the Chalkidike, Larsen cites a short decree of "the *symmachoi* of the Epeirotes,"

---

204. Lytle 2010: 272–73. Lytle (p. 275 with n. 83) argues against the idea that poleis claimed or protected fishing rights in specific areas, which entails the conclusion that all maritime fish were potentially subject to import duties.

205. *SEG* 11.377 (Ager 1996 no. 63; Chandezon 2003 no. 5). For the date Mitsos 1979: 215–16.

206. *Koinē chōra*: l. 15. *Telōnai*: ll. 22–23. Robert 1940–65: VII.157 infers from the presence of the *telōnai* that the original dispute had been over the collection of pasturage taxes in this area.

207. The *telōnai* in this document have mystified: Chandezon 2003: 32.

208. Larsen 1960a: 245–46.

granting tax immunity (*ateleia*) and full rights (*enteleia*) to an Illyrian in the late fourth century.[209] Insofar as "the *symmachoi* of the Epeirotes" were in this period ruled by a *basileus*, Neoptolemos, the Epeirote case certainly reinforces Larsen's theory about monarchical economic practices influencing the taxation structures of koina that were themselves monarchic (of which Epeiros provides our only example) or bordered on the kingdom of Macedon. He is quite correct to infer that tax immunity granted by a koinon (if indeed the phrase "those of the Epeirotes who are allied" signals something like a koinon in the late fourth century) to an outsider implies that the koinon had control over taxation structures, whether directly or indirectly.[210] What is puzzling about Larsen's argument is that there is nothing even slightly exceptional about the Epeirote decree. Fourth-century decrees of the koinon of the Molossians grant the same combination of tax immunity and full rights to foreign benefactors, but such grants are by no means limited to this hybrid monarchical koinon.[211] The Boiotian koinon granted tax immunity to proxenoi and other foreign benefactors in the fourth century (T9, T11, T13), and in the third century sometimes granted them a status of taxation at a level equal to that paid by Boiotians themselves (*isoteleia*, T26), suggesting that there were differential rates for citizens and noncitizens.[212] The granting of both kinds of privilege suggests that the Boiotian koinon did have the right to place limits or exemptions on the taxation practices of its member poleis, just as the Epeirotes and Molossians did, even if it does not prove that the koinon was actually collecting these taxes. An Aitolian decree of the fourth century (T49) and an Achaian decree of the third (T42) point to the same ability of the koina in these regions to impose limits and exemptions on taxes levied by their member communities.[213] The tax immunity thus granted must in each case have been comprehensive: the recipients of such privileges would pay no taxes at harbors, for use of pasture land,

209. Cabanes 1976: 545 no. 12 (*GDI* 1336; Cabanes 2004: 52 no. 8).

210. The "*symmachoi* of the Epeirotes" must designate a state rather than a simple alliance: Will 1977; Cabanes 2004: 38. Cabanes (pp. 38–41) associates them with the union of the Molossoi, Aiakidai, and Chaones under Neoptolemos, an alliance that was quickly transformed into the Epeirote koinon. As he points out, our understanding of the meaning of *symmachoi* may need to be revised in light of this text and of the late sixth-century inscribed bronze plaque mentioning the "Elians and the *symmachia*" (Ebert and Siewert 1997, 1999).

211. Cabanes 1976: 536 no. 2 (*SEG* 23.471, 26.697), 539–40 no. 3 (*SEG* 26.698, 50.542, 54.576 with Cabanes 2004: 23, 49 no. 3).

212. Compare the grant of *isoteleia* made by the polis of Thespiai to an Athenian: T27 ll. 5–6.

213. *Ateleia* may have been among the privileges granted to proxenoi and benefactors of the Aitolian koinon in the third century; the formula of most of these decrees grants *enktēsis, asylia*, "and all the other privileges belonging to proxenoi" (e.g., T55). The first explicit mention of *ateleia* in an Aitolian decree of the Hellenistic era belongs to the period after the dismantling of the koinon by the Romans (Antonetti 1994, reprinted in Rizakis 1995: 367 no. 676).

or in the purchase or sale of property or commodities, whether exacted by the koinon or by the constituent poleis. The Epeirote case, then, is not exceptional and need not be explained away as a by-product of monarchical government in the region. It was, rather, typical for federal governments to make exceptional exemptions to foreigners, which seems to have required member poleis to recognize the privilege as well. The implication is that in each of these cases the koinon had ultimate sovereignty over the taxation policies of its poleis, although typically it appears not to have intervened.

War Levies and Taxes Paid by Member Poleis

The harbor dues and other taxes explored in the previous section were all levied on individuals, whether by a koinon or by its member poleis. In this respect they are broadly comparable to the taxation structures of autonomous poleis, except that the koinon claimed the authority to exempt honored individuals even from taxes collected by member poleis. The other principal source of revenue for the koinon came from a distinctive practice that is perhaps most closely paralleled by the exaction of tribute in imperial and symmachic contexts—the collection of taxes by the koinon not from individuals but from its constituent communities. When in 519 the Corinthians arbitrated the dispute between Thebes and Plataia, the Thebans were forbidden from pressuring "any of the Boiotians who were not willing to contribute to the Boiotians"—*es Boiōtous teleein,* a phrase that seems to reveal not just a prohibition on compelling membership but more specifically a prohibition on exacting *telē,* taxes or resource contributions of some sort.[214] Although the phrase is typically interpreted to mean "join the Boiotian league," Herodotos uses the verb *teleein* only once to refer unambiguously to group belonging in which monetary issues played no part.[215] On the other hand, Herodotos uses *teleein* at least six times to mean "pay" or "spend," and twice to mean "perform [an action of some kind]."[216] In the case of Boiotia, "to be counted among the Boiotians" very likely required some kind of contribution, whether in the form of resources or of action, particularly if, as was patently the case with Plataia, pressure needed to be exerted. Thebes' willingness to resort to coercion to achieve adherence to regional power structures is paralleled by the case of the koinon of the Chalkideis in the 380s, but until the Boiotians began to expand outside ethnic boundaries (as in the case of Hellenistic Achaia), koinon membership appears to have been largely voluntary. The significance of this voluntarism lies in the fact that in most cases a group of poleis agreed

214. Hdt. 6.108.4.

215. Hdt. 2.51.2, where the Athenians were counted among the Pelasgians in the distant past. The passage is cited as a parallel to Hdt. 6.108.4 by Waanders 1983: 111.

216. "Pay, spend": Hdt. 2.109.2, 125.6; 3.137.5; 7.118, 187.2; 9.93.4 (with also the possible meaning "perform"). "Perform [an action]": Hdt. 1.206.1; 3.134.4. Cf. Waanders 1983: 111.

to pool their resources via a tax paid by each polis to the koinon to meet expenses associated with their "common affairs," to use a Thessalian phrase.

From the Oxyrhynchos Historian we learn that as early as the second half of the fifth century the Boiotian poleis had an obligation to pay a tax (*eisphora*) to the koinon at a level tied indirectly to population size, via the clusters of communities called *merē*, the districts that we have already seen operative in the religious sphere:[217]

> They continued to run their internal [polis] affairs thus, but Boiotian affairs were managed in the following way. All who lived in the region were arranged in eleven districts [*merē*], and each of these provided one boiotarch as follows: [details about district allocations and representation]. . . . In this way the districts sent their magistrates. They provided sixty councillors for each boiotarch, and they paid their daily expenses. For the organization of the army, each district provided about a thousand hoplites and a hundred cavalry. To put it simply, depending on the number of its magistrates, each community shared in the common treasury, paid its taxes [*eisphoras*], sent judges, and shared likewise in public burdens and benefits. Thus the entire *ethnos* governed itself, and the councils and the treasury of the Boiotians were situated in the Kadmeia.

From this passage it is abundantly clear that federal taxes were collected in proportion to representation, which was in turn tied somehow to population size (a fact that can be inferred from the variable number of poleis comprising a district, small ones clustered together while large ones like Thebes alone made up a single district). A number of small Boiotian communities are described as having been in a relationship of *synteleia* to larger ones—Chaironeia to Orchomenos, and the villages of the Parasopia to Thebes—and the meaning of this has never been clear.[218] I suggest that one aspect of *synteleia* was the joint obligation to meet a fixed fiscal obligation; they were, from the koinon's perspective, tax units (among other things).[219] But it is uncertain whether the tax they were obligated to pay was a regular tax, paid perhaps on an annual basis, or whether it was an exceptional levy that could be raised to meet

217. *Hell.Oxy.* 16.3–4 (Bartoletti), trans. McKechnie and Kern, lightly adapted. Glotz 1908: 272 n. 1 (*contra* Grenfell and Hunt 1908: 242) rightly interprets the phrase τῶν κοινῶν ἀπέλαυον to mean "enjoyed a share of the federal treasury," not "enjoyed the privileges of the league." Cf. Bruce 1967: 109, 163; McKechnie and Kern 1988: 83. For detailed discussion of the districts and their political powers, see below, pp. 370–77.

218. Chaironeia-Orchomenos: Th. 4.76.3. Hornblower 1991–2008: 2.252 remarks rightly that "the idea of financial contributions seems to be present." Parasopia-Thebes: *Hell.Oxy.* 16.3 (Bartoletti). Bakhuizen 1988 argues that in Boiotia *synteleia* refers to a formal relationship of dependence or subordination, particularly toward Thebes, but this interpretation does not seem to capture the sense of the word in this passage.

219. González 2006: 36–37 argues for a more comprehensive definition of *synteleia,* likewise rooted in the concept of contribution. For him, so-called syntelic poleis were essentially a specific category of dependent poleis (cf. Hansen 1995a: 38–39). While I do not disagree with this characterization, the more specific inferences he draws are too hypothetical to inspire complete confidence.

the expenses of war.[220] Certainly the *eisphora* in fourth-century Athens was exceptional, but the arrangement in Boiotia may well have been different.[221] Another tax levied by the koinon is adduced in several leases of public and sacred land at Thespiai from the second half of the third century: "If it is necessary to pay a *telos* to the polis or to the koinon of the Boiotians, the farmer will pay it."[222] A rare and valuable piece of evidence for federal taxation in the Hellenistic period, the conditional phrase makes it clear that *telos* levies were occasional; that such a clause should be included in the terms of a lease of sacred land to a private individual may suggest that the *telos* was, at least in part, a tax levied on sacred land in the territory of member poleis. It is possible that the third-century *telos* and the fifth- and fourth-century *eisphora* are entirely different taxes, levied by different mechanisms according to different principles.[223] But given that the *telos* attested in the third-century lease would have been levied on sacred land, it is possible that sacred land may somehow have formed the basis of the tax assessment for a polis. An individual who chose to lease such land could simply have shouldered the tax burden associated with the property, an arrangement akin to tax farming in a situation in which the levy was irregular.[224]

The fact that the *eisphora* in Boiotia was paid not by individual citizens or by individual poleis but by districts, some of which comprised multiple cities, necessarily entails a tremendous coordination effort on the part of the several poleis that made up a single district. The districts also had to coordinate in the matter of meeting their military levies, and an early third-century text recording an agreement between Orchomenos and Chaironeia on supplying cavalry to the Boiotian army (T15) shows that the poleis had considerable latitude in how they met the requirements imposed by the koinon. It is probable that in the classical period as in the Hellenistic, the poleis had the same freedom to determine the procedures by which the requisite funds would be collected, but we have no evidence that sheds any light on the procedures actually adopted.[225]

220. Roesch 1982: 297 is confident that the *eisphora* was a regular tax, though he cites no further evidence than the current passage, which does not seem to me to admit of certainty.

221. On the Athenian *eisphora* see Brun 1983.

222. *IThesp* 55 (*ed.pr.* Keramopoullos 1931–32: 19–25, with facsimile and text in pls. 2 and 2a; M. Feyel 1936a: 181–83) ll. 26–27, providing the basis of restoration for *IThesp* 55 ll. 1–2; *IThesp* 48 ll. 14–15 (*IG* VII.1739). It is impossible to determine whether this means that the farmer might have to pay taxes to both polis and koinon for the same harvest, or whether, depending on circumstances, he might be liable to one but not the other.

223. Pernin 2004: 227.

224. It does not appear to me, in other words, inescapable that the *telos* was paid by individuals rather than by poleis (*contra* Roesch 1982: 298; Pernin 2004: 227), for the only instances in which we learn of its existence are in connection with the lease of land owned by poleis and their sanctuaries.

225. There is, however, plentiful evidence for taxes collected by the Boiotian poleis in the Hellenistic period, the revenues of which were probably funneled, at least in part, into the federal treasury. See Migeotte 1994: 7–11.

Whether this was the principal motive for its creation or not, the district system in Boiotia contributed significantly to the equity of the distribution of the tax burden. If one assumes that each district paid a fixed and identical amount in taxes, it becomes possible to calculate the tax burden of each district, or cluster of districts, as a percentage of the total. José Pascual González has recently correlated these percentages with the percentage of total Boiotian territory belonging to each district. The result is strikingly equitable: Thebes (Districts I–IV, map 10) held 37.82 percent of the total territory and paid 36.36 percent of total taxes; Akraiphia, Chaironeia, and Kopai (District XI) held 9.19 percent of territory and paid 9.09 percent of taxes. The largest inequity between territory and tax burden, on this hypothesis, was that faced by the districts centered on Orchomenos and Hyettos (Districts V and VI), which held between 8.18 and 10.30 percent of the territory and paid 18.18 percent of the tax burden.[226] If the koinon had simply required a fixed and equal sum from each polis, small poleis like Akraiphia would certainly have paid more per capita than large poleis like Tanagra or Thebes, without reaping benefits proportional to their heavier fiscal burden. The other obvious strategy, an assessment of the resources of each polis, based perhaps on annual polis revenues, or property values whether public or private, might have been suggested by the experience of the Delian League, but the contentious responses to such assessments, which could only with tremendous difficulty have been accurate and equitable, may also have posed a serious warning about the danger of fragmentation stemming from such specific assessments. The solution was rather to assess at the scale of the district, which became an instrument for the pooling of resources by smaller poleis. And unlike the tribute assessments of the Delian League and the Athenian empire, the constituent communities of Boiotia paid into a common treasury to which they had access through representation and participation in the regional political process. In sum, the Oxyrhynchos Historian says, the Boiotian poleis shared "likewise in public burdens and benefits."

The issue of how tax revenues were used is of vital importance for assessing the political economy of the koinon, for if member poleis were liable to pay taxes to the koinon but enjoyed no benefits in the distribution of those revenues, it would be quite difficult to argue that the koinon served as an effective mechanism in promoting the economic welfare of those who participated in it. The issue also pertains to one of the central problems in the modern study of federalism: What

226. González 2006: 38–39. González rejects Wilamowitz-Moellendorf's emendation of *Hell.Oxy.* 16.3 (Bartoletti) to read *Hyettos* rather than *Hysiai*, but he assumes that Hyettos was in *synteleia* to Orchomenos and so already in the district. If Hysiai (in the Parasopia) was in fact part of the two districts centered on Orchomenos, the district's percentage of total territory is 10.30 percent. If, as I have mapped them, Districts V and VI belong to Orchomenos and Hyettos, it is only 8.18 percent. The inequity of the tax burden would thus be slightly greater in González's scheme. This inequity is proposed as a reason for the revolt of Orchomenos from the koinon in 395: see above, p. 60.

prevents both the fragmentation of the federal state into a number of single unitary states and the complete absorption of the member states by the federal state? What, in other words, holds each party to the federal bargain, promoting the stability of the compromise?[227] We shall see in the next chapter that the single most important factor contributing to stability is the engagement of all parties in the state in enforcing the terms of the bargain.

We see this at work in fourth-century Arkadia, when the Mantineians, soon followed by other Arkadian poleis, refused to use sacred monies pillaged from the Temple of Zeus at Olympia to fund their war against Elis, leading to a common Arkadian resolution against the practice.[228] It was also happening in late third-century Achaia. As we have seen, western Achaia was extremely hard hit by the successive Kleomenean and Social wars in the period 226–217, during which the territories of Dyme, Pharai, and Tritaia, together comprising the entire fertile basin of the Peiros River, were overrun first by a Spartan and then by an Aitolian army.[229] When the Aitolian army ravaged western Achaia in 219, the *hypostratēgos* of the Achaian koinon was one Mikkos of Dyme. He gathered full levies of armed men from each of the three cities that had been attacked and marched out to meet the Aitolian general, Euripidas; the small Achaian force was defeated with heavy losses, and Euripidas pushed his position further by capturing Teichos Dymaion, a fortification above the plains of the Dymaia, near the border with Elis (map 3).[230] Dyme, Tritaia, and Pharai sent a messenger directly to the younger Aratos of Sikyon, then serving as *stratēgos* of the koinon, and also sent a formal embassy to the koinon itself requesting assistance. According to Polybios, the request was denied, because the Achaians had at that time still not paid their mercenary forces from the Kleomenean War (although they were at about the same time actively recruiting a mercenary force); implicit is the claim that they did not have enough citizen-soldiers either.[231] The response of the three cities to this refusal is extremely important (Polyb. 4.60.4–5):

> The Dymaians, Pharaians, and Tritaians, despairing of help from the *stratēgos*, agreed with one another not to pay [*telein*] their common taxes [*koinas eisphoras*] to the Achaians, and privately to fund a mercenary force, of three hundred infantry and fifty cavalry, with which to secure their own land.

227. Riker 1964. The federal bargain will be discussed more fully in chapter 6.
228. Xen. *Hell.* 7.4.33–34.
229. Polyb. 2.51.3–4 (Kleomenean War, 225), 4.59–60 (Social War, 217). For details see above, pp. 111, 117–19.
230. Rizakis et al. 1992: 102–7 with references for description of the archaeological record of the site.
231. Cf. Plut. *Arat.* 37 with Grandjean 2000: 318–19 for the Achaian koinon's use of federal funds to hire mercenaries. Polyb. 4.37.6 for the Achaians' active recruitment efforts in 219. We get some idea of the cost of levying troops in Achaia from Polyb. 28.13.7, 13: the dispatch of five thousand men to Epeiros would cost the koinon more than 120 talents.

The help they requested was military, but the concerns were economic: to protect their own territory and the resources in it, and to pay professional soldiers to do it. The solution was both political and economic: refusing to pay the taxes they normally owed to the koinon on the grounds that it was not providing the services it was obligated to render in exchange for the tax revenues it collected, the cities of western Achaia prevented the koinon from breaking its obligations with impunity.[232] A decree of Dyme recording the city's grant of citizenship to fifty-two individuals of unknown origin who "fought the war with us and together saved the city" is certainly to be associated with this event and shows that the cities that had withdrawn found means in addition to payment to honor those who assisted them in their hour of need.[233] Polybios certainly interpreted the move, angrily, as an act of secession from the koinon that set dangerous precedents and contributed to its weakness. Although he does not blame the cities for hiring a mercenary force on their own initiative, he does reproach them for their refusal to pay their taxes, "especially as according to the laws of the koinon they were certain of recovering their outlay."[234] This tantalizing hint points to a law that pertained to all members of the koinon, ensuring them of reimbursement in the event that they had to pay out of their own funds for the defense of their city or their territory.[235]

In 217, with the Social War dragging on, western Achaia was again subjected to an Aitolian raid from Elis, which on this occasion traversed the entire territory of Pharai and reached as far as Aigion. This was the year when Lykos of Pharai served as *hypostratēgos* of the koinon, and he was finally given a mercenary force hired by the koinon to defend his city's territory. With this force he managed to kill four hundred men and take two hundred prisoner, including a number of prominent Aitolians, and seized the invading army's baggage train and armor. Meanwhile, the Achaian admiral had crossed the Gulf of Corinth and taken nearly a hundred captives at Molykreion, two long ships with their crews at Chalkis, and another at Antirrhion.[236] The Achaians' response to this respectable haul of booty is extremely illuminating: "Plunder flowing in by land and by sea around the same time, and sufficient revenue [*prosodou*] and supplies for war being provided by it, there was joy among the soldiers because of the provision of pay and hope among the poleis because they would not be burdened by taxes [*eisphorai*]."[237] Not only do we learn that despite their refusal to pay taxes two years before the Pharaians were still

232. See below, pp. 392–93, for further discussion of this episode and its political significance.

233. *Syll.*[3] 529; Rizakis 1990b: 123–29 no. 2, with commentary (*SEG* 40.393), and 2008a: 49–54 no. 4, with complete and up-to-date references. See below, p. 387.

234. Polyb. 4.60.10.

235. Cf. F. W. Walbank 1957–79: I.514.

236. Polyb. 5.94.1–8. Polybios calls Antirrhion "Aitolian Rhion."

237. Polyb. 5.94.9.

members of the koinon with enough standing to have one of their citizens elected second in command, but in this passage Polybios also hints that there were ongoing complaints among the cities about the fiscal burdens of the long war. It is abundantly clear that the *eisphora* in late third-century Achaia was levied on member poleis to meet the costs of war, and was driven by need: if the revenues could be raised in any other way, the poleis would not be asked to contribute.[238] For a brief moment, the Social War seemed to fund itself.

One further episode in the tax history of the Hellenistic Achaian koinon points toward self-enforcing institutions as a source of the state's stability. When Messene was restored to the koinon in 182/1 after its revolt, the terms of the settlement included the grant of "tax immunity [*ateleia*] for three years, so that the destruction of the territory [inflicted during the war] would harm the Achaians no less than the Messenians."[239] The tax immunity thus granted to the Messenians will have covered the *eisphora* as well as any other taxes for which member poleis were liable to the koinon. What is important here is that the koinon appears to have voluntarily surrendered its claim to these revenues in order to take responsibility for the economic impact of its own struggle to bring Messene back into the koinon. At a moment when the justice and credibility of the Achaian state was under scrutiny, the move made it clear that the Achaians treated their member states with equity rather than arrogance.[240]

That the *eisphora* in Hellenistic Achaia was collected irregularly, on the basis of need, is further demonstrated by a measure taken at the very end of its history, as the koinon faced war with Rome in 146. An Achaian and allied force had already been annihilated by the Roman army under Metellus at Skarpheia, and the Achaian *stratēgos*, Diaios, sought some means of shoring up the Achaians' position. Polybios describes the financial aspect of his strategy (38.15.6–11):

> Seeing that there was a serious shortage in the common treasuries [*en tois koinois*] as a result of the past war against the Lakedaimonians, he compelled them to make pledges [*epangeliai*] and to exact a tax on wealthy individuals [*eispherein tous euporous*], not only men but even women. . . . The men were compelled to contribute [as a tax], contrary to their own self-assessment, whatever someone supposed they had; and the women, stripping themselves and their own children of their jewelry, contributed to their very destruction as though of some set purpose.

It is clear that the particulars of this levy were atypical: self-assessment was the norm, and in normal circumstances only men were liable to the *eisphora*. The

---

238. Compare Ps.-Arist. *Oec.* 2.2.1350a5–11 for taxation driven by need at Mende. This practice is highlighted through a series of examples by Migeotte 2003.

239. Polyb. 24.2.3. On the ravaging of Messene by Lykortas, Polyb. 23.15.1–3.

240. That the Achaians were at pains to show how equitable the koinon was at the end of the Messenian War is stated explicitly by Lykortas in Polybios's account (23.16.11).

urgency of the situation in 146, after the first major defeat, is certainly part of the explanation for the departure from these norms; but Polybios's hostility to Diaios also lurks just beneath the surface of the passage. There is also a striking difference between this incident and the events of 218–217 just discussed: the *eisphora* was levied on individuals, not on poleis. It is difficult to know whether this is also a product of crisis (though it is hard to see why collection would have been facilitated by a transgression of existing practices) or whether the mechanism for collection of the *eisphora* had changed by the mid-second century. The pledges were apparently something other than the contributions made by individuals, and it is likely that they were pledges of resources made by nonpolitical groups and organizations in each city. A decree of Troizen, a member of the Achaian koinon in 146, seems to record precisely this process.[241] Although highly fragmentary, the decree (ll. 14, 32–33) is explicitly issued in accordance with a prior decree of the koinon, which must have required these pledges. Polybios's implication that Diaios was somehow personally responsible for an outrage against the Achaian populace thus has little credibility. These three passages from Polybios and the inscription from Troizen are invaluable, because no other source sheds any light on the fiscal obligations of Achaian poleis to the koinon.[242]

There are hints that other koina levied similar taxes on their constituent poleis, but the evidence is not full enough to ascertain the purpose for which revenues were being collected. A document (T60) recording the arbitration of the Aitolian koinon in a boundary dispute between two member communities, Pereia and Melitaia, reveals the collection of taxes by the koinon from its poleis on a proportional basis tied to their representation in the Aitolian council. Although at the time of the arbitration Pereia and Melitaia had formed a *sympoliteia* and participated in the Aitolian koinon as though they were a single polis, the arbitration itself preserves the right of the smaller polis, Pereia, to separate itself again from Melitaia and establishes the terms on which it would in that event participate in the koinon: the Pereians would send a single councillor to the Aitolian council, and "join in paying whatever expenses the polis might owe, according to the proportion of their representation on the council, and . . . pay these expenses to the Aitolians in proportion with their representation on the council" (ll. 18–21). At the time the arbitration was recorded, in 213/2, Pereia and Melitaia apparently joined together in meeting a single tax obligation to the koinon at a rate somehow

---

241. Fraenkel, *IG* IV.757; Fuks 1970: 83; F. W. Walbank 1957–79: III.711.

242. We might expect that a description of the obligations of new citizens, perhaps including payments of *eisphora*, would have been included among the regulations for enrolling new citizens at Dyme (T35 l. 34), but the stone breaks off at this point. The beginning of the decree recording the admission of Arkadian Orchomenos into the Achaian koinon (T39), in which the terms of the membership were laid out, is likewise lost.

proportional to the number of councillors they sent to the Aitolian council. There are two important implications of the conditions on which Pereia was given permission to reassert its independence from Melitaia. The first is that representation and taxation were made by poleis in Aitolia, not by districts as in classical Boiotia. The second is that by some calculation now lost, members of the Aitolian koinon paid taxes in proportion to the strength of their voice and their vote on the council, which means, at least in theory, that the more influence a polis had over the direction of Aitolian affairs, the more taxes it had to pay.

Insofar as taxation stands precisely at the intersection of state power and economic behavior, its history has the potential to reveal a state's priorities, the extent and limits of its powers, and its relationship to the resources within its territory.[243] The taxation history of the Greek koinon has never before been written, and although the evidence is rarely as explicit and never as plentiful as one would wish, there is nevertheless enough material to draw several conclusions. Two things are particularly striking.

The first is that member communities for the most part remained in control of their tax revenues, apparently with the freedom to adopt whatever structures they wished for local taxation. There are two significant exceptions to this general rule. The first is the claim by the koina of Thessaly and the Chalkideis to control the revenues from ports and harbors throughout their territory. The existence of harbor officials as magistrates of the polis of Thespiai requires us to conclude either that the Boiotian harbor poleis were in full control of the revenues from their harbors and ports or that they collected those taxes on behalf of the koinon, although the latter seems less likely. Thessaly and the Chalkidike in the fourth century may truly be exceptional. But if they are, their practice of controlling the revenues from harbors and ports conforms both to the normative theoretical claim of fiscal federalism that interstate commerce should be controlled by the central government rather than by each individual member state and to the practice of federal states throughout history.[244] In these cases, the koinon's control over taxes on goods imported to and exported from the region as a whole extends the economic logic of federation and is another means of pooling highly varied but complementary resources. For not every polis in a koinon has a port (and in some cases, like Aitolia, very few have one), but not every polis with a port has control of goods that are worth exporting, as we have seen. The second exception to the general rule about polis autonomy over local tax revenues is the practice of granting *ateleia* to honored individuals like proxenoi, a status that was operative throughout the territory of the koinon. In these cases, the member poleis must have been required to honor

243. Cf. Purcell 2005: 200–201.
244. Cf. Hayek 1948.

the koinon's decision to grant the exemption and to refrain from taxing such individuals if they took up residence or engaged in any normally taxable activities in their polis.[245]

The second striking pattern to emerge from the taxation history of the koinon is that it collected taxes from its member communities only, so far as we can tell, in order to fund military activities. In the next chapter we shall see that defense is one of the major responsibilities of the koinon. It is what political scientists call a "nonrivalrous public good," one that benefits all member states equally, and the consumption or enjoyment of which by one member state does not affect the ability of others to consume it.[246] The restriction of the koinon's own tax collection practices thus maps directly the distribution of authority within the state. Revenues are collected by the koinon only to fund those activities over which it has special, exclusive control; the member communities are otherwise left in control of their resources. Although the levying of contributions from member states by the koinon appears reminiscent of the exaction of imperial tribute, our only evidence for objections to the tax obligation to the koinon comes from a historical context in which the koinon failed to meet its obligation to provide defense for its member poleis. The taxes levied by the koinon were not, in other words, strictly centripetal—and if they failed to flow from the center out to the states again in the form of protection, strenuous objections were raised. The member communities' tax obligation became, in the case of both fourth-century Arkadia and third-century Achaia, a powerful bargaining chip that was deployed against abuses (of rather different kinds) by the koinon. The koinon's strategy of exceptional direct levies on constituent communities also served an important political purpose: by paying, these members committed themselves openly and credibly to the joint undertaking, and they complicated defection from the koinon. If a particular conflict threatened only one part of a koinon's territory, every member nevertheless had an obligation to contribute. In so doing, they committed themselves, polis by polis, to the security of their koinon's entire territory and of the economic resources contained within it.

MANAGING ECONOMIC CRISES AND DISPUTES

We have seen that koina regularly and legitimately extracted resources from their member states in the form of taxation in ways that reflected the power of the regional state and its limits. The Thessalians and Chalkideis appear to have controlled duties levied on imports and exports through the harbors and ports of their

245. The economic benefits of *ateleia* grants were quite real (Oliver 2007: 30–37 on Hellenistic Athens) and did yield some reduction in revenues for the cities affected.

246. On defense as a nonrivalrous public good and its significance in federal governments see McKinnon and Nechyba 1997: 5–6.

entire territories, which was a means not only of controlling interstate commerce and preventing (or attempting at least to mitigate) trade conflicts with outsiders but also of pooling the complementary resources of their member communities. The facilitation of economic mobility across polis boundaries and within the territory of a koinon, which was a feature the economic life of koinon members and was promoted by the extension and protection of property rights throughout the region, was a means not only of maximizing access to highly varied sets of natural resources but also of buffering against localized shortages. The logic of this system is simple, and its implementation was so effective that I would suggest its achievement may be at least partly responsible for the remarkable spread of confederation in the Greek world in the fourth and third centuries, if it was not a conscious motive among the poleis of central Greece that first created regional state institutions. But how does this system function when normal conditions break down? Is it responsive to stress? And if so, on what level? We have seen that the shortage of particular goods, and the surplus of others, within particular communities was actually a fundamental structural component of the cooperative economy of a koinon; it remains to be seen how the system responded to crisis, to widespread shortage of something crucial like grain, to demographic and ecological pressures on constituent settlements, or to serious but localized shortages of money. Were the taxes collected by the koinon from its member poleis and from certain individual exchanges conducted within its territory (especially at ports) deployed to the benefit of those communities when they experienced pressures of various kinds? The following pages will assess the role of the koinon in managing economic crises and disputes within its borders.

Responding to Regional Crises

Although Boiotia ranks among the most fertile agricultural areas of mainland Greece, signs of food shortage and pressure on land emerge in the fourth century and become more frequent over the course of the Hellenistic period. This is certainly a result of strong demographic growth in the classical period with attendant agricultural intensification at unsustainable levels yielding soil exhaustion by around 200, combined with the deleterious effects of frequent and large-scale warfare.[247] After expelling the Spartan garrison from the Theban Kadmeia in 379,

---

247. On demographic growth in this period in Boiotia see Bintliff 2005: 10; Bintliff, Howard, and Snodgrass 2007: 143–51 (on the territory of Thespiai in particular). For Greece generally, see Scheidel 2003, who estimates that the decline began in the fourth or third century, and Reger 2003: 334–36 and 2007: 462, who in correlating the literary and archaeological evidence posits an end to growth only at the end of the third century. See also Corvisier and Suder 2000. Literary evidence for population decline: Polyb. 36.17.5–6. Archaeological evidence for decline in rural habitation: Alcock 1992: 33–92, interpreted differently by Corvisier and Suder 2000: 112–17; Bintliff 1997; Bintliff, Howard, and Snodgrass 2007: 151–55 for the case of Thespiai in the late Hellenistic–early Roman period.

several years of war in the region followed as the Thebans and Boiotian loyalists fought to dislodge remaining pockets of Spartan support in the region.[248] In 377/6 there was a grain shortage in Thebes, sparked by the war that had cost them two harvests. They sent men with two triremes and ten talents to Thessalian Pagasai to purchase grain, although the small amount of money suggests that the intention was only to supplement supplies within Thebes proper.[249]

Pressure on agricultural land in the region continued, and sometime in the period 336–323 the Boiotians hired the engineer Krates of Chalkis to drain Lake Kopaïs in order to reclaim some of the land for agricultural use; the effort was undermined, according to Strabo, by internal quarreling among the Boiotians, although a significant portion of the work had already been done.[250] The implication is certainly that the effort was undertaken by the koinon and that disagreements over details ultimately obstructed completion. So many poleis bordered Kopaïs that a draining operation could not have been undertaken by any one of them; the cost of the project would furthermore have been prohibitive for a single small polis.[251] The situation was certainly ripe for disagreement, and it is perhaps no surprise that this was the ultimate cause of the failure. Which poleis would control the land gained by the drainage project? Would it be doled out in proportion to each polis's tax burden? If so, how would poleis situated away from the lake, like Tanagra, benefit directly? Would any of it be public and common to the koinon, perhaps to be used as pasturage or rented out, the revenues going into the federal treasury? It would not have been entirely astonishing if the project had succeeded, because the koinon was relatively well suited to manage such projects, but the particular challenge of equitably distributing a benefit that was ultimately determined by geography among poleis whose participation in the koinon was determined by other means was particularly difficult. It is notable, furthermore, that these were the first years during which the Boiotian koinon was operating without Thebes, and the lack of a recognized voice of leadership—however resented it was by some—may have caused negotiations to break down more quickly.

In the early second century central Greece was hard hit by a grain shortage, probably due at least as much to crop failure or drought as to warfare. Around 180, Oropos bestowed proxeny and other privileges upon a man from Tyre and another from Sidon for importing grain to the city upon its request.[252] A few years later,

---

248. See above, pp. 68–70.

249. Xen. *Hell.* 5.4.56.

250. Str. 9.2.18. Cf. Argoud 1987: 34–35.

251. Chandezon 2003: 44 with n. 17 remarks (without citing Strabo) that efforts to manage the water level of Lake Kopaïs were more likely to have been undertaken by a common effort than by each city individually.

252. Petrakos 1997: 210 (*IG* VII.4262). The document is dated by the federal archon Agathokles, whose magistracy is placed ca. 180 by Étienne and Knoepfler 1976: 318, 350.

around 175, Euboian Chalkis likewise granted proxeny to a citizen of Sidon, among other reasons because he assisted them with the provision of grain.[253] Around the same time, Thespiai created an annual magistracy of *sitōnai*, officials responsible for the provision of grain for the city, and opened a public subscription for the creation of a fund for the purchase of grain, a sign not only of localized grain shortage but also of a serious shortfall in civic revenues.[254] Contemporary documents from Athens and Thessaly reflecting a grain shortage attest to the extent of this central Greek crisis.[255] According to a Boiotian inscription of the same period, there was a grain shortage throughout Boiotia (T33 ll. 4–5). Localized strains on production, such as drought and flooding, are expected and figure into Mediterranean extractive techniques and the social relations on which individuals rely for help when crops fail.[256] It is, however, generally believed that such shortages rarely affected an entire region unless ecological stress was compounded by the devastation of crops associated with war, or by loss of a harvest due to the absence of men fighting in a campaign. Associated with the latter problem is the social phenomenon of land abandonment, a result not only of the rise of mercenarism but also of changes in inheritance practices and declining birthrates, to name only a few causes. The grain shortage that existed throughout Boiotia in the early third century may thus have been one of the results of the bad state of Boiotian affairs described with something close to relish by Polybios in his narrative of the year 192/1 and was certainly in part a product of an extremely turbulent period in politics and military activity, with several major changes of alliance, a defeat on home territory at the hands of the Aitolians, and the annexation and subsequent loss of Megara.[257] The causes of this bad state of affairs have been discussed at length by Michel Feyel and others.[258] My interest is not so much in sorting out the hows and whys of the economic woes of Hellenistic Boiotia but in trying to make some sense of the responses we see to those troubles.

The document referred to above (T33), which mentions the grain shortage throughout Boiotia, is an honorary decree of Boiotian Chorsiai for one Kapon son of Brochas. He is clearly not a citizen of Chorsiai, since he is made proxenos of the city; his city ethnic is partly lost, and he may have been from another Boiotian city

253. *IG* XII.9.900A; Knoepfler 1990: 490–91.
254. *IThesp* 41 (*IG* VII.1719, 1744, plus three previously unedited fragments, all belonging to the same stele); cf. Roesch 1965b: 220–24; Migeotte 1985: 314–16 and 1990, 1991. M. Feyel 1942a: 45 placed the document in the period 191–172.
255. Athens: *IG* II² 903 with Gauthier 1982 (*SEG* 32.132). Thessaly: Helly 1973: II.41.
256. Gallant 1991; Halstead and O'Shea 1989.
257. Polyb. 20.6.1.
258. M. Feyel 1942b: 13–20. Walsh 2000 infers a drought or blight on crops in eastern central Greece and argues that this, and not the establishment of oligarchic regimes in the Greek cities after 197, is to blame for the economic hardship attested in the region in this period.

or perhaps from a nearby city of Phokis.[259] The nature of Kapon's good deed toward the city is explained in detail: in response to this panregional grain shortage, "all the poleis of Boiotia had voted to prohibit the export of grain," but Kapon advanced two hundred *kophinoi* of grain to Chorsiai, apparently free of interest. There has been debate about whether the embargo was voted by the poleis individually or by the koinon as a whole, but in my view it stretches the limits of plausibility to imagine that all the poleis in Boiotia would unanimously have decided to prohibit exports in the absence of some centralized decision-making body like the koinon, a forum in which regional interests could be balanced against local ones. There are, I believe, good reasons for thinking that the decree itself was passed shortly after the dissolution of the Boiotian koinon by the Romans in 171, but it reflects a considerable passage of time since Kapon's advance during the grain shortage, which must have occurred at the same time as the other shortages well attested in the region, the period between about 180 and 170: that is, precisely during the last years of the Boiotian koinon.[260] That the embargo reflects a decision of the koinon and not of a series of some fifteen poleis is further suggested by a similar measure taken by the Achaian koinon, which we learn about in a somewhat roundabout way from an honorific decree of Phokian Elateia for the city of Stymphalos.

Around the turn of the second century, the Elateians were driven out of their city, either by the occupying Roman army under Flamininus or by the Aitolians, who were given control of Phokis upon the departure of the Roman troops in 194 following Flamininus's declaration of the freedom of the Greeks.[261] In their distress they turned to the city of Stymphalos, which was at the time a member of the Achaian koinon and with which the Elateians claimed kinship. A somewhat later honorific decree of Elateia for Stymphalos (T43) records the details of the Elateians' peregrination. They were welcomed into Stymphalos, and although "there was a lengthy grain shortage everywhere," they were given "as much as was needed" by the Stymphalians and allowed to participate in cults and sacrifices, being treated as the Stymphalians' own fellow citizens, and were given besides plots of land on which they were allowed to live and work, free of taxes, for ten years (ll. 4–7). When, in 191, the Roman consul Manius Acilius Glabrio returned to Greece at the head of an army and took control of Elateia, the Achaian koinon, at the behest of Stymphalos, sent an embassy to Glabrio requesting permission for the Elateians to return (ll. 9–13). It was granted, but when they arrived home they were (or anticipated that they would be) without grain, since the fields of Elateia had lain fallow

259. For the restoration of the ethnic, see the commentary to T33.
260. For detailed argument about the date and the role of the koinon, as well as the nutritional impact of the advanced grain, see the commentary to T33.
261. For the disputed cause of expulsion see the commentary to T43. For the political context see above, pp. 125–26.

during their absence. There was at this time an embargo on the export of grain from Achaia because of a grain shortage (ll. 15–16), and it had clearly been imposed by the koinon: in order to help their friends out of their bind, the Stymphalians sent an embassy to the Achaians—that is, to the koinon—asking special permission for the Elateians who had lived in the city to export the grain that they had grown there (ll. 16–17). Permission was granted, and the Elateians were able to face their next set of challenges: rebuilding their walls and centralizing settlement, presumably with a view to safety in such turbulent times (ll. 18–22). There can be no doubt in this case that the Achaian koinon had prohibited the export of grain from the entire territory under its control, and that this prohibition arose in response to a grain shortage. The motive was clearly to prevent local supplies from being depleted; whether the koinon also undertook to assist in the fair redistribution of grain within the region is unknown. Probably like the Boiotian poleis in the 170s, each Achaian polis secured supplies to the best of its ability with the resources that it had.

The koinon's authority to impose embargoes that bound all member poleis can be viewed as the flip side of its authority to permit the export of surplus. Two documents of the Thessalian koinon in the second century highlight its control in this sphere. In the 190s, we learn from a recently published document, the Athenians sent officials, *sitōnai* in practice if not in name, to Thessaly (probably among other places) to see about purchasing grain for export to Athens. A decree of the city of Larisa agrees, in accordance with a prior resolution of the koinon, to export grain to Athens and to reduce the normal 5-percent export tax to a mere 1 percent.[262] A decree of the Thessalian koinon, issued in the third quarter of the second century, responds positively to a request from the Roman aedile Quintus Caecilius Metellus that "the koinon give as much grain as it has available to the senate and people."[263] This document is fascinating for the light it sheds on how such decisions were implemented: the koinon determines the total amount to be exported to the Romans, appoints its *stratēgos* and several lower magistrates to work out the apportionment of this burden to each city, and then places on its member poleis the burden and the cost of delivery to the Thessalian harbors. A heavy fine for noncompliance is established to enforce the decision, and the poleis are to be reimbursed from the sale of the grain at Rome. While we have no comparable evidence from other koina, the Thessalian koinon's exclusive authority to permit the export of grain from its entire territory is the logical corollary of the koinon's right in Boiotia and Achaia to prohibit such exports.

262. Helly 2008: Decree B ll. 39–42.

263. Garnsey, Gallant, and Rathbone 1984: 36 ll. 8–9. The date of this document has been debated: 151/0 (Garnsey, Gallant, and Rathbone 1984; Bresson 2007–8: II.192–95) or 129 (Garnsey and Rathbone 1985: 25). Helly 2008: 88 n. 134 is undecided.

The decrees of Chorsiai and Elateia, when read together, place the interventionist role of Hellenistic koina in regional crises beyond doubt. The clear record in the Elateia decree of the Achaian koinon's imposing an embargo on the export of grain from the entire region is so closely paralleled by the somewhat more elusive decree of Chorsiai that it encourages us to think that the koinon of the Boiotians did the exact same thing some twenty years later when their entire region was faced by a serious shortage of grain. In each case, the koinon's prohibition on grain exports was a measure designed to prevent anyone within the region who had a grain surplus from exporting it at a high price; it was, in other words, an antispeculation measure, which was probably made particularly necessary by the widespread nature of the grain shortage in this period, affecting not just Boiotia but also, as we have seen, Thessaly, Euboia, and Attica.[264] The decision to export the grain rather than simply to sell it to a neighboring community within the koinon would have been motivated by prices inflated in response to high demand and the existence of buyers with adequate funds to purchase a significant shipment. This is particularly important in light of the financial state in which we have already seen the poleis of central Boiotia laboring throughout this period. The embargoes imposed by the Achaian and Boiotian koina effectively forced any individual who did have a surplus to sell it within the region. The koinon, by sealing off its borders to prevent export, compelled its members to redistribute their grain within the region. There is no doubt whatsoever that in the impoverished conditions of third-century Boiotia regional sales (and advances) under such strictures would have been less lucrative than sales to a wealthier area. However advantageous these measures were to the citizens of a koinon, it is worth pointing out that the koinon could in principle have gone farther but to our knowledge never did. We have no evidence for actions taken by the koinon to secure an import of grain that might then have been distributed throughout the poleis on some proportional principle; such active measures were in Boiotia demonstrably left up to the poleis. The reason may have been that smaller purchases were easier to make and safer to convey.

The withdrawal of the Roman army from Greece in 194 had effects on the regional economies of central Greece beyond the expulsion of the Elateians already discussed, and it is from Livy's discussion of this impact that we learn of another way in which the Achaian koinon appears to have addressed an economic crisis that threatened all its member poleis. After announcing his intention to withdraw the Roman army from Greece within ten days, along with the Roman evacuation of the garrisons at Demetrias, Chalkis, and Akrocorinth, and after reaffirming the liberty

---

264. Regarding the Boiotian embargo Garnsey 1988: 75: "I believe that the law was an ad hoc measure issued in the context of a food crisis, and that the shortage had been aggravated by unscrupulous landowners who were sending their grain abroad in search of higher prices."

granted all the Greeks two years before at Isthmia, Flamininus asked in exchange that all Roman citizens who were held as slaves in the Greek states be released to him.[265] While the Greeks present at the council all readily agreed, this had serious financial implications, for Flamininus was not offering to buy them back; he was implicitly asking that they be returned gratis. Livy (34.50.5) claims that there was a large number of such slaves, who had been sold by Hannibal during the Second Punic War when they were not ransomed by their relatives. He goes on to cite Polybios, whose own account is lost, for the claim that this demand "cost the Achaians a hundred talents, since they had fixed the price per head to be paid to their owners as five hundred denarii."[266] The account implies that the Achaians—that is, the Achaian koinon—reimbursed those citizens who were owners of Roman slaves at a rate of five hundred denarii per slave surrendered. Plutarch confirms the account: "the Achaians ransomed them at five mnas [500 drachmas] per head, gathered them all together, and handed them over to Titus as he was about to sail" back to Italy.[267] That the measure was handled centrally is implied by the very fact that a net cost to the Achaians as a whole was known to Polybios and recorded by him; it is also implicit in Plutarch's account, which speaks of the Achaians doing the ransoming and then gathering all the freed slaves together to present them as a gift to Flamininus.

If this is correct, it shows us yet another way in which the Achaian koinon intervened to buffer economic hardships that might be experienced locally. In this case, the benefits accruing to the Achaians as a whole from the departure of the Roman army may have been a motive for the decision to reimburse individual citizens for losses sustained because of the Achaians' official assent to Flamininus's request. The koinon intervened again in the cost faced by citizens of liberating slaves in accordance with public mandate when Diaios, the same Achaian general who raised an atypical tax levy in 146, at the same moment ordered all member poleis to liberate in total twelve thousand home-born slaves who were to be armed and used to fight at Corinth against the Romans. Diaios, much scorned by Polybios, is reported to have "apportioned the number of slaves ordered to be sent by each city as he chose and unfairly, as he always did about other matters."[268] The implication is that under a better leader such a demand might still have been normal, but it would have been conducted on some fair and objective basis, probably relative to the size and resources of each city.

265. Livy 34.49.4–6, 50.3. Cf. Diod. Sic. 28.13.

266. Livy 34.50.6. Assuming the usual equivalence of denarius to drachma (F. W. Walbank 1957–79: I.176, III.63; Briscoe 1981: 126) the account implies that there were twelve hundred such slaves; this is the number given by Plut. *Flam.* 13.4. Cf. Val. Max. 5.2.6, who gives the suspiciously round total number of two thousand.

267. Plut. *Flam.* 13.5; cf. *Mor.* 197b.

268. Polyb. 38.15.3–5 with F. W. Walbank 1957–79: III.711.

Not only slaves but also money lay behind these episodes, but we are simply left to wonder how the payment of a hundred talents to Achaian citizens forced to surrender their Italian slaves affected the supply of coinage in the Peloponnese and how dire the cash shortage was that led to Diaios's collecting the women's jewelry as a tax in 146. Manipulation of the money supply to preserve vital state revenues during a period of crisis may have been another strategy of the Achaian koinon. A recent study of the bronze coinage issued by the Achaian poleis in the Hellenistic period has shown that these coins were all issued in a single (but not necessarily brief) episode around the time of the Third Macedonian War or shortly thereafter, circa 167–164. There are external reasons to think that silver supply in Greece was at a low after this war.[269] But it was urgently needed for paying the *eisphora* with which the Achaians' ongoing war efforts had to be funded. It has therefore been suggested that the Achaian bronze coinage was issued in accordance with a decree of the koinon that ordered the poleis to pay their *eisphora* in silver and to strike bronze coins for exchange purposes, at a volume correlated with their population size.[270] If this hypothesis is correct, it would suggest that the koinon was willing to manipulate the money supply, replacing precious-metal silver with fiduciary bronze, in order to preserve a limited supply of silver for high but necessary costs that would also frequently entail exchange with non-Achaians.

Interventionist actions of a rather different kind, still taken at the federal level, are attested in Aitolia as well as Achaia and point again to the management of economic crisis by the koinon. In a characteristically scornful tone, Polybios informs us that the Aitolians, in response to a mounting debt crisis in Aitolia at the end of the First Macedonian War, appointed two men, Dorimachos and Skopas, as lawgivers (*nomographoi*). One apparent aim of their appointment was that they would take measures—at the federal level—to alleviate the burden of debt under which many in the region were struggling.[271] Polybios's text is fragmentary here, and we know none of the details of the laws enacted by Dorimachos and Skopas; we know only that they incited stiff opposition and that Skopas failed to be elected *stratēgos* in the following year, a position for which, apparently, he had hoped the work as a lawgiver would have made him a shoo-in.[272] There is one piece of evidence suggesting that the federally sponsored program of debt cancellation did make some progress: at the end of the third century the polis of Pleuron dedicated a statue at Thermon of one Lykos son of Diokles, a Kalydonian, for having canceled its debt to him.[273] The

---

269. Much silver taken to Rome as booty: Larsen 1938. Macedonian silver mines closed 167–158: Livy 45.18.3–4, 29.11; Diod. Sic. 31.8.7.

270. Warren 2008.

271. Polyb. 13.1.1–3.

272. Polyb. 13.1a–2.1 with F. W. Walbank 1957–79: II.413–14.

273. *IG* IX.1² 70.

implication is that the indebtedness from which the Aitolians sought relief in this period was not only private, and in this respect the situation looks similar to the better-documented case of Boiotia. The fact that the Pleuronians made the dedication at Thermon rather than in their own city or perhaps at the sanctuary of Artemis in Kalydon is perhaps to be explained by the fact that the affair involved two cities within the koinon, and perhaps also that the measure was taken in accordance with the debt-relief laws enacted by Dorimachos and Skopas. Debt relief and the prohibition of imprisonment for debt were also undertaken by the Achaian koinon in 147, with the clear aim of bolstering support among the poor and indebted for the war against Rome and swelling the Achaian ranks at a moment of crisis.[274]

Arbitration among Friends

The picture I have presented so far of the regional economic systems of the koina of mainland Greece and the Peloponnese has been one characterized primarily by cooperation, regarded as a corollary of the interdependence that is a product of highly localized complementary resources. Yet this is only part of the story. Inscriptions recording the arbitration of disputes between poleis within a koinon frequently reveal conflicts over resources. These arbitrations, however, rarely mention foreign judges, third-party arbitrators in disputes who became a fixture in interpolis relations in the Hellenistic period.[275] In precisely the period when this remarkable experiment in interstate arbitration flourished, the koina of mainland Greece and the Peloponnese seem to have taken virtually no part.[276] That is, I shall

274. Polyb. 38.11.10 with Fuks 1970: 80–81.
275. See, e.g., Habicht 1987; Crowther 1995.
276. Cf. Habicht 1987; Cassayre 2010: 77–83. I know of two certain and two possible exceptions. The first certain exception is the new inscription recording arbitration of a series of disputes between Megalopolis and Messene when the latter was restored to the Achaian koinon in 182; the case went first to the Achaian koinon (thus confirming the general hypothesis), but when it went on and the Megalopolitans pressed their claims, it went to a tribunal of Milesians (Themelis 2008; Arnaoutoglou 2009–10; Luraghi, Magnetto, and Habicht 2012). The second certain exception is the late Hellenistic Thessalian koinon's use of arbitrators from Demetrias, not a member polis, to judge a dispute between two of its member poleis, Herakleia and Melitaia (Helly 2001; cf. Cassayre 2010: 78). The possible exceptions: the arbitration of a border dispute between Phanoteus and Steiris in Phokis was carried out by a board of *gaodikai* from Elis (Ager 1996: 74–75 no. 20) sometime in the third century, perhaps nearer the end than the beginning. Between 292 and 235, the communities of Phokis were gradually incorporated into the Aitolian koinon (and remained members until 191), and we might have expected the Aitolians to oversee the arbitration. But the Elians were close allies and kin of the Aitolians, and it seems likely that they were appointed by the Aitolians to conduct the arbitration as a neutral third party (compare T59, an Aitolian-sponsored arbitration by Thyrrheion of a dispute between Oiniadai and Matropolis, the only parallel for the *gaodikai* mentioned in Ager 1996: no. 20). The other possible exception is an arbitration involving Opous and the Epiknemidian Lokrians (Ager 1996: no. 23), but the arbitral body is not preserved, and the entire text is wholly obscure.

argue that koina rarely had recourse to true interstate arbitration because they created their own neutral authority with the goal of returning their members to full functionality. For this goal, as we saw with the case of western Achaia in 219, was in the best interest of the koinon itself. The role of the koinon as arbitrator is, however, fundamentally contingent upon the willing participation of its members. In Boiotia, it was a role into which the koinon had to grow: in the late sixth century, to the extent that regional integration of any kind existed, it was still too fraught with dispute for any centralized organization to achieve neutrality with respect to the conflicting interests of its members. Thus, when the Plataians opposed Thebes in 519 because they were not willing to contribute to the Boiotians, they sought the intervention first of the Spartans and then, following Spartan advice, of the Athenians. Eventually the Corinthians arbitrated.[277] So too the Akanthians and Apolloniates, wishing to avoid becoming part of the koinon of the Chalkideis, sought Spartan assistance and protection. Seeking external arbitration and protection was necessary when the dispute was over, precisely, the issue of whether or not to take part in a regional state. Yet there are signs that more ordinary disputes began to be adjudicated by koina in the fourth century.

Although the Arkadian koinon existed, in formal terms, for only eight years, during this period it undertook the arbitration of a dispute between Arkadian Orchomenos and one of its neighbors, either Torthyneion or Methydrion, which may have been prompted by the synoikism of Megalopolis and the consequent loss of some territory by Orchomenos.[278] A remarkable but difficult text found at the Laphrion in Kalydon shows that a dispute between two familial groups at Kalydon over seized goods was arbitrated by judges from the Elian city of Thraistos, chosen probably on the basis of the kinship between Elis and Aitolia.[279] The date of the document has not been determined with certainty, and both the early and the late fourth century have been proposed.[280] If it belongs to the end of the fourth century, we can be certain that the Aitolian koinon was in existence at the time of the arbitration, but that it was not involved would be an indication of the limited reach of that state in its early years.

Two brief texts document the role of the Boiotian koinon in the direct arbitration of border disputes between its neighbors. The first (T14), from the late fourth

277. See above, p. 27.

278. Schwyzer 1923: 664; C. D. Buck 1955: 18; Daverio Rocchi 1988: 96–99 no. 2; Thür and Taeuber 1994: 124–29 no. 14. Nielsen 2002: 352–53 suggests that the incorporation of Methydrion, apparently a dependent polis of Orchomenos, into Megalopolis (Paus. 8.27.4) may have sparked the dispute; cf. Nielsen in Hansen and Nielsen 2004: 522–23.

279. IG IX.1² 1.138 with addendum; Poulsen 1929: 84. Poulsen 1930 publishes a new edition, with text, translation, commentary, and a photograph of the inscribed bronze plaque. Cf. Daux 1932: 325–26; Bravo 1980: 726–27. Syngeneia between Elis and Aitolia: Ephoros FGrHist 70 F 122 ap. Str. 10.3.2.

280. Rhomaios 1926: 40 (early fourth century) with Klaffenbach, addendum to IG IX.1² 1.138; Poulsen 1930: 44 (late fourth century, based on letter forms).

or early third century, establishing a border between Lebadeia and Koroneia, seems not only to have recorded the decision made by the Boiotian koinon but to have demarcated the boundary as well. The text is inscribed on a round pillar that was found at Granitsa, about four kilometers southeast of Lebadeia in the direction of ancient Koroneia, and very likely functioned as a boundary marker. Behind a territorial dispute like this we must read a struggle for control of resources, but the specifics are obscure; one of the demarcation points is "the summit," certainly of Laphystion, so the dispute may have been over grazing rights on the mountain. Some of the disputed land was sacred to Trophonios and as such may have been a source of revenue for the city of Lebadeia. In the early third century the koinon also arbitrated in a territorial dispute between Kopai and Akraiphia, neighbors on the northeastern shore of Lake Kopaïs. Again the arbitration is recorded on what certainly functioned as a boundary stone, in this case an enormous and unmistakable one, four meters high and almost as wide (T31). The stone was found, apparently in situ, between Cape Phtelia and the outcropping of Gla, which in antiquity was an island in the lake. The position of the stone suggests something about the dispute: not only was the lake itself a valuable resource because of its *pescosità*, but pasturage was also highly valued here, where fluctuating water levels periodically revealed fertile grazing land. The capacity of the marginal landscape in the Kopaïc Basin was high enough that it may have become an object of dispute.[281] The same boundary was demarcated in the late sixth or early fifth century, and though we do not know the mechanisms behind that demarcation, it was probably motivated by a similar dispute over access to the resources of Kopaïs and its surrounding wetlands.[282] Resolving the conflict was both in the interest and in the power of the Boiotian koinon in the early Hellenistic period, although we do not know the precise institutional mechanisms by which the arbitrations were carried out.[283] Paul Roesch argued that in the Hellenistic period the Boiotian *tethmophylakes* mentioned in several documents constituted a federal appeals court for disputes between citizens of different member poleis and between member poleis themselves.[284] If this interpretation is correct, then the appearance of a college of

281. Roesch 1965b: 64. On the underestimated wetland see Horden and Purcell 2000: 186–90.

282. *Ed.pr.* Lauffer 1976: 40 (Lauffer 1980: 161–62 with photo, pl. 3.1; *SEG* 30.440); Roesch, *Teiresias Epigraphica* 1980: 2 no. 1; Knoepfler 1992: 499 no. 178 (best text). The stone was found at Palaiokastro, 0.5 km NW of Cape Phtelia.

283. The language of both inscriptions is similar: "the Boiotians demarcated the boundary" (T14. l. 3; T31 l. 3). But they do not provide us with adequate information to make inferences about the composition of the judicial board or the direct involvement of the Boiotian council (rightly Ager 1996: 71), *contra* Raeder 1912: 78–79; Dittenberger, comm. to *Syll.*² 454.

284. Roesch 1965b: 145–52. A *tethmophylax* appears in the Thespiai magistrate list (Roesch 1965b: 9 l. 66) between the *synedroi* for the federal council and the aphedriate (on whose role see above pp. 221–24). Plut. *Quaest. Graec.* 292d8 mentions a *tethmophyla‹k›ikos nomos*.

tethmophylakes in a long dossier of documents pertaining to a large loan made by one Nikareta of Thespiai to the city of Orchomenos and her struggle to be repaid would suggest that the Boiotian koinon had a board of magistrates that oversaw the arbitration of internal disputes.[285]

More detailed and plentiful evidence comes from the epigraphic records of both the Achaian and the Aitolian koinon. The Achaian documents, beginning in the mid-third century, are particularly interesting in their indications that when the Achaian koinon expanded to include new members, it took measures to see that any new member would resolve all outstanding disputes with other communities before its integration into the koinon.[286] This policy (if we can call it that) was astute: a new member with a simmering conflict with another community could open the Pandora's box of war for the koinon. In 243, when Epidauros joined the Achaians, the city's outstanding conflict with the Corinthians appears to have been countenanced (T37 ll. 17–18), and measures were probably taken immediately for its resolution, for another document (T38) records the arbitration of this boundary dispute by a board of Megarians "in accordance with the request of the Achaians" (ll. 4–5, 9–10). By the time of the arbitration, Megara, Corinth, and Epidauros were all members of the koinon, which requested that Megara appoint judges to hear the case. The land in dispute appears to have been entirely mountainous: the judges delineated a border that ran across ridges and peaks and down wagon tracks; there is perhaps no better indication that, while economic mobility within the region was promoted by the koinon, each polis retained its de iure autonomy over its territory and strenuously objected to violations of its boundaries.

When Arkadian Orchomenos became a member about a decade later, the koinon had a clear interest in seeing this new member's disputes resolved upon entrance, as is clear from the decree that establishes the terms of its membership (T39). Residual strife internal to Orchomenos over Nearchos, probably a deposed local tyrant, was quelled by an order putting a stop to litigations between him and his sons on the one hand and the citizens of Orchomenos on the other. A dispute over monies owed to Megalopolis, apparently by citizens of Methydrion, a subject polis of Orchomenos, was recognized, and terms for its resolution were

---

285. *IG* VII.3172 (dated to 225–223, on the basis of the federal archon Onasimos in l. 22: Étienne and Knoepfler 1976: 301–2, 349–50 with *IG* VII.209–18), with mention of "the secretary of the *tethmophy-lakes*" in l. 178, just before the stone breaks off. The mention in ll. 28–29 of repayment "according to the law" (*kata ton nomon*) seems to point to a federal law, perhaps regarding the repayment of debts, since the lender, Nikareta, is a citizen of Thespiai and the borrower is the city of Orchomenos. Only a federal law could in actuality span these two jurisdictions. Cf. Roesch 1982: 299–300, 388–91.

286. Tod 1913: 74–75 believed that the Achaian koinon required its member states to submit their differences to the koinon for arbitration, but there is no clear evidence for strict obligation, as Ager 1996: 116 rightly points out.

established. The Achaian koinon wanted the participation of the major cities of Arkadia, but certainly did not want their quarrels or their debts. The same concern over avoiding the introduction of economic disputes to the koinon when admitting new members is reflected in the koinon's arbitration of disputes in newly restored cities: the Achaians judged the internal economic disputes of the Megalopolitans when the city was restored to the koinon in 217, after being seized and depopulated by Kleomenes, as well as a territorial dispute between Megalopolis and Messene on the occasion of the latter's restoration to the koinon in 182.[287]

The extent and variety of the political constituents of the koinon made feasible the appointment of an internal board of arbitrators whose only bias, in theory, was to see that any disputes between member poleis were resolved. This was sometimes done, as in the case of the dispute between Epidauros and Arsinoe (previously Methana, not a member), by selecting representatives from several poleis (T40; cf. T36 l. 16), and in other cases, as in the dispute between Corinth and Epidauros (T38), by asking a single member polis to arrange for arbitrators. The dispute between Epidauros and Arsinoe was territorial (T40, ll. 5–6), and although the inscription certainly contained a detailed delineation of the boundary between the two poleis, virtually none of it survives. It is generally thought that the territory of Arsinoe was restricted to the small volcanic peninsula on which it was situated, but this arbitration raises the possibility that it had control over (or at least claimed rights to) pasture along the mountainous ridge that runs along the coast between the Methana Peninsula and Epidauros.[288] Although nothing survives in the text to this effect, comparison with the arbitration of a dispute between Arsinoe and Troizen suggests that access to fisheries and saltworks in the bay between Arsinoe and Epidauros may also have been at issue.[289] The agreement reached between Arsinoe and Troizen authorized that "the common proceeds from the tuna traps" should be used to compensate victims of seizures that had taken place in the course of the territorial dispute. Remains of these fisheries (or of their successors) are still visible in the bay to the west of the Methana Peninsula.[290] Whatever the details, the

287. Megalopolis in 217: Polyb. 5.93.9–10 seems to attribute the resolution to Aratos but also alludes to an inscribed agreement, and this may have recorded procedural details that were not of interest to Polybios. Messene and Megalopolis: Themelis 2008.

288. Gill, Foxhall, and Bowden in Mee and Forbes 1997: 75 remark that "possibly the inhabitants of Methana took advantage of their privileged position of royal favour to indulge in disputes with their larger and more powerful neighbours, against whom they would not be likely to win on their own." If this is correct, it would explain the spate of arbitration decrees involving Methana during its Ptolemaic period.

289. So Dixon 2000: 176–92.

290. IG IV² 1.76 + 77, joined by Peek 1969: no. 31 (complete composite text given by Ager 1996: no. 138); copy found at Troizen: IG IV.752. Hiller placed the document between 163 and 146, but Dixon 2003: 85 argues for the early second century. Remains of tuna trap: Mee and Forbes 1997: 272.

overall picture is clear: the Achaians, who had promoted economic mobility within the koinon by extending property rights to all member citizens throughout its territory, went to lengths to resolve territorial squabbles that could obstruct the access to economic resources that was afforded and protected by the koinon.

The same basic principle appears to have operated in the Aitolian koinon. When the Aitolians struck their ephemeral alliance with Akarnania, probably in the late 260s, the agreement included resolution of a series of simmering territorial disputes along the border of the two koina. The Achelöos River always functioned as the border between the two regions, but it never remained still for long. Strabo explains that the silt from the river was constantly obliterating the boundary markers between Aitolia and Akarnania; the two koina addressed their disputes in arms, because, he says, they had no arbitrators.[291] When they came to their agreement in the 260s, then, it is no surprise that the control of several communities was an object of difference. The alliance reinforced the old arrangement, that the land to the east of the river should be Aitolian, that to the west Akarnanian, with the exception of Pras and Demphis (T57 ll. 5–8).[292] Pras lay west of the river, between Stratos and Aitolian Agrai (map 5); its chief importance may have been that it provided the Aitolians with access to the Ambrakian Gulf, to the northwest.[293] Since at this stage Oiniadai, with its superlative harbor and harbor facilities (not to mention its good lands), remained in Akarnanian hands, the Akarnanians may have allowed the Aitolians to keep Pras and Demphis as a concession.[294]

We have already seen that a concerted and systematic push toward the coast was an important feature of the story of Aitolian territorial expansion in the third century and that it was probably motivated by a desire to access maritime resources. The terms of the Aitolian-Akarnanian alliance make it clear that Aitolian control of Pras and Demphis was nonnegotiable. However, room was made for fine-tuning, apparently on the specific boundaries of the territory of Pras. If the citizens of

---

291. Str. 10.2.19. See Fouache 1999, 2000 for recent archaeological and geological studies of the alluviation of the Achelöos. Compare *Syll.*³ 588.28–38 (Ager 1996: 292–96 no. 109), the arbitration of a dispute between Magnesia and Miletos over the territory of Myous in Ionia, which establishes the Hybandos River as the boundary between the territories of Magnesia and Miletos, with the specific order that boundary stones be erected and inscribed to delimit the boundary, which would be permanent, regardless of whether the course of the river changed in future.

292. Larsen 1968: 267, followed by Ager 1996: 106, assumes that Pras and Demphis were captured by the Aitolians when they seized Agrinion in 314 (Diod. Sic. 19.68.1), but Agrinion, east of the Achelöos, is far from the western Akarnanian site of Pras, and the two cannot be associated with any confidence.

293. Pras has been identified with the ruins at Kastrakion: Berktold, Schmidt, and Wacker 1996: 127–28; Schoch 1997: 77–78; cf. Antonetti 1987b: 99–100. Demphis remains unlocated.

294. Paus. 4.25.1 gives the good quality of the soil at Oiniadai as the motivation for the Messenian attack on the place, probably in the 450s. For the date see Hornblower 1991–2008: I.178 *ad* Th. 1.111.3.

Stratos (Akarnanian) and the Agraioi (Aitolian) agreed to boundaries that were apparently stipulated by the parties drawing up the alliance, they were to be ratified and considered official. If, however, there was a dispute, then a board of arbitrators was to be elected, comprised of ten men from each of the two communities (T57 ll. 8–11). Evidently, Pras was uncomfortably sandwiched between the two communities, one Aitolian and one Akarnanian, but the old pattern of resolving territorial disputes by force was, in theory, broken by the terms set up for arbitration in the event that it should prove necessary. For the Aitolians, apparently, what mattered was having control of Pras, regardless of the precise delineation of its territory, and avoiding armed conflict that might threaten that control. As we have already seen, the Akarnanians and Aitolians by this agreement had mutual rights of property ownership, intermarriage, and potential citizenship or *isopoliteia* (ll. 11–13).

But the alliance did not last long, and in the 240s the Aitolians joined Alexander II of Epeiros in seizing and partitioning among themselves the territory of their neighbors.[295] Even after this settlement, the Aitolians appear to have expended considerable effort to gain some access to the Ambrakian Gulf. A highly fragmentary inscription found at Pagai in the Megarid, which appears to belong precisely to the period between the partitioning and the Aitolians' outright seizure of southern Akarnania, seems to record the arbitration of a dispute between Thyrrheion and Kassope on the one hand, both cities in the Epeirote part of Akarnania, and the Aitolians on the other, over the harbor of Panormos.[296] Some years after the seizure of southern Akarnania by the Aitolians, a dispute arose between Oiniadai and Matropolis (T59, map 5), probably over the fertile alluvial territory between them, for the demarcation includes a straight line that runs "from the marsh to the sea." The Aitolians appear to have asked the city of Thyrrheion to arbitrate in the dispute, and the decision of its land judges became

---

295. See above, p. 105.

296. *IG* VII.188–89. This was the position of Dittenberger, and it was widely accepted: Bérard 1894: 29–30; Raeder 1912: 83–84; Tod 1913: 21–22. But it was for many years supplanted by the interpretation of Robert 1939, who saw that *IG* VII.188 and 189 were two fragments of the same stone and restored it as the arbitration of a dispute between Aigosthena, then a member of the Boiotian koinon, and Pagai, a member of the Achaian koinon, over a small harbor situated between them called Panormos. The arbitrators, on this restoration, came from the Akarnanian cities of Thyrrheion and Kassope; this situation fit only in the historical context of ca. 192, when Pagai had returned to the Achaian koinon. Wacker 1996 has argued that Dittenberger was correct and by the involvement of Boiotian and Achaian arbitrators dates it to the period 245–239, after the partitioning of Akarnania by the Aitolians and Epeirotes but before the Achaian-Aitolian alliance struck in 239 (Polyb. 2.44.1; Str. 8.7.3), while the Boiotian koinon was formally part of the Aitolian. He proposes that Panormos, otherwise unattested in Akarnania, be sought along the southeast coast of the Ambrakian Gulf. Harter-Uibopuu 1998: 110–11 is right to denote the interpretation uncertain; everything depends upon restorations. If Robert's interpretation is correct it becomes the only known instance of the interesting case in which a territorial dispute erupted between the members of two different koina.

a matter of permanent public record not only in the poleis of both parties to the dispute but also in Thermon.

There is one hint that when the Aitolian koinon admitted new members, it required them to submit any differences they had with other communities (whether members or not) to the koinon for arbitration, just as the Achaians did. Between 214 and 212 the Aitolians arbitrated in two disputes that the Thessalian polis Melitaia had with its neighbors, Xyniai and Pereia.[297] The resolution of the dispute with Pereia, which we have already seen revealing important facts about the taxation structure of the Aitolian koinon, mentions that the judges (three men from Kalydon) were selected "in accordance with the agreements" (T60 l. 3), possibly a reference to an agreement made when the cities joined the koinon, in an arrangement similar to that we have seen in Achaia.[298] In light of regional property rights and other measures that promoted economic mobility within the region, it may seem odd that these territorial disputes should have mattered so much, but it is perhaps worth stating explicitly that no matter how strongly economic interactions affected political relationships, the political integrity of every member community was an essential feature of the koinon system. The disintegration of member communities would have led to the highly centralized structure of a large polis with an extensive territory, a structure in which the ability to exploit and manage resources on a regional rather than a local scale would have become virtually impossible.

The Evanescent Polis: Regional Responses to Localized Stress

It should be clear by now that by the Hellenistic period the koina of mainland Greece took their role as managers of regional economies quite seriously. They took measures to gain and protect regional economic resources, including coinage, to address debt crises, and to end disputes between member poleis that frequently arose over access to a variety of resources, principally but not only land and harbors. In all these ways, the koinon can be seen as an institution that dramatically increased the capacity of its member states to cope with stress, whether induced by ecological or by social factors, and in so doing it decreased their vulnerability.[299] There is one additional strategy, stemming still from the basic principle of regional mobility, by which some koina mitigated the vulnerability of

---

297. Arbitration of dispute between Melitaia and Xyniai: *IG* IX.1² 1.177 (Ager 1996: no. 55); dispute between Melitaia and Pereia: T60.

298. So Raeder 1912: 222–23. This is indeed a conjecture (Ager 1996: 156), but it is difficult to see what other meaning the phrase could have. It should be noted that in the arbitration for Melitaia and Xyniai, the logical place for a similar phrase would be precisely in ll. 6–7, which are lacunose.

299. Cf. Watts and Bohle 1993: 45–46, who outline the three coordinates of vulnerability: exposure to stress, high potential risk, and limited coping capacity.

their small member states. Settlement mobility, perhaps best understood as the extreme form of economic mobility, became an option to communities under severe stress that could rely either on close social relations with other communities (above all, those that were expressed in the form of kinship, however fictive) or on formal, institutional ties such as those provided by membership in a koinon.[300] Ancient sources suggest that under strain, some poleis evanesced, being abandoned by their inhabitants for more salubrious places or for communities within the koinon in which survival, if not prosperity, would be easier.

When the Helikeans refused the requests of the Ionians' sacred ambassadors in 373 and subsequently disturbed their sacrifice at the altar of Poseidon Helikonios, they probably did not realize that they were perched on a spot of land that was highly vulnerable to catastrophe (map 3).[301] A coastal delta fed by the alluvial silting of three rivers, resting directly above the highly active Helike Fault, and shadowed by the Achaian mountains, which reach nearly 1,800 meters, Helike was vulnerable not only to earthquakes but also to two of their more insidious and deadly counterparts: soil liquefaction and tsunami.[302] Ancient literary sources report that an earthquake followed by a massive sea wave destroyed the city in a single night.[303] Strabo, citing the fourth-century philosopher Herakleides Pontikos, reports that "two thousand men were sent by the Achaians to collect the bodies of the dead, but they were unable to do so. They divided up the territory among the neighbors."[304] Ongoing archaeological investigations appear to confirm the claim that Helike was not inhabited during the early Hellenistic period, as does its complete absence from the literary and numismatic record after the 370s.[305] "The Achaians" in Herakleides' report can only be the Achaian koinon. That their rescue and retrieval effort was unsuccessful is less important than the fact that they made it in the first place. We must likewise see the koinon's hand in the distribution of that portion of Helike's territory that was still above water: a land grab by Aigion or Boura or Aigai would surely have been contested by the other Achaian poleis, and the koinon would likely have become involved in arbitration to resolve the issue. The sources are ambiguous on the question of survivors, but they are in a sense the most interesting factor in all this. If the territory was divided up among

300. I have studied this phenomenon in detail elsewhere (Mackil 2004) and focus my remarks here on settlement mobility within the koinon and the institutions that facilitated it.
301. See above, pp. 194–98, for the religious dispute.
302. Ambraseys and Jackson 1997; Soter 1998.
303. Herakleides Pontikos apud Str. 8.7.2 (Gottschalk 1980; Wehrli 1953); Diod. Sic. 15.48.1–49.4; Paus. 7.24.5–13; Ael. NA 11.9. Cf. Lafond 1998a for a detailed survey of the literary sources.
304. Str. 8.7.2.
305. Signs of settlement have been detected for the Bronze Age, and the archaic, classical, late Hellenistic, Roman, and Byzantine periods: Soter and Katsonopoulou 1998, 1999: 559–61.

neighbors, any surviving Helikeans would probably have become citizens of those poleis. This issue is clearer in other, rather less spectacular cases.

Pausanias's description of Achaia is littered with references to poleis that were abandoned "because of weakness," and he gives the same explanation for the abandonment of several poleis in Phokis.[306] Aigai, situated on the Achaian coast between Aigeira and Aigion (map 3), was abandoned sometime between the fifth century and the third; the only cause given is "weakness."[307] Strabo tells us that its territory belonged to Aigion.[308] The few archaeological indicators that we have confirm the impression that Aigai was abandoned in the late classical or the Hellenistic period; the end of the city's once plentiful coinage in the first half of the fourth century narrows down the date of abandonment further. That coinage was characterized by the appearance of a goat, a pun on the city's name and certainly an allusion to the importance of pastoralism in its economy. It may be that, with Aigai abandoned, Aigeira, another goatish city, felt free to pick up the punning type for its coins, but its sudden appearance there may also indicate that some of the inhabitants of Aigai went to Aigeira.[309] Far from any catastrophic incident, Aigai was abandoned sometime in the first half of the fourth century "because of weakness," perhaps through a lack of local resources, or a lack of effective fortification, or a lack of population, or some combination of the above. Its inhabitants were able, it appears, to join Aigion and perhaps Aigeira, fellow members of the Achaian koinon. It is possible that the synoikism of Aigai with Aigion (and Aigeira) was associated with the development of the formal institutions of the Achaian koinon, which we see emerging for the first time in these years. It is also possible that the inhabitants of Aigai took advantage of rights of property ownership throughout the koinon (if indeed these rights existed in fourth-century Achaia) to simply relocate. The polis itself was abandoned, but there was nothing catastrophic about it, a fact due almost certainly to the safety net created by the institutions of the koinon.

The poleis of Phokis, notoriously small, suffered severely in the course of Xerxes' invasion and again in the aftermath of the Third Sacred War. Among them, Pausanias mentions that, with the exception of about seventy souls, the inhabitants of Ledon had by his time abandoned their city "because of weakness."[310] The abandonment of Ledon was probably associated with the punishment that the city experienced at the hands of Greek allies in 346, for it was the home of Philomelos, chief

306. Compare Paus. 7.18.1 (Olenos), 10.33.1 (Phokian Ledon).

307. Paus. 7.25.12; cf. 8.15.9. Its presence in Herodotos's list of Achaian *merea* (1.145) and its absence from Polybios's list of Achaian poleis (2.41.8) provide chronological boundaries for the abandonment.

308. Str. 8.7.5.

309. Coinage of Aigai and Aigeira: Mackil 2004: 500–501 with nn. 42, 47.

310. Paus. 10.33.1.

sacrilegious villain of the Third Sacred War.[311] It had been a member of the Phokian koinon, and if events in Achaia are any guide, its surviving inhabitants probably went to neighboring poleis that had fared less badly. This is certainly what happened at Parapotamioi, which was among the Phokian poleis burned by Xerxes.[312] It was resettled then but dismantled in 346, and shortly thereafter its inhabitants, according to Pausanias, "being poverty stricken and few in number, were distributed among the other cities."[313] Here, as at Olenos and Helike, and probably Ledon, the koinon absorbed the shock of settlement failure. That the Elateians were forced to look to their non-Phokian kin in Stymphalos after 192 attests the extremely harsh treatment the entire region must have suffered. Across the Aegean, as a final example, it is instructive to note that when the inhabitants of Ionian Myous were driven out of their small polis by a malaria problem caused by the progressive silting of its harbor, its territory was divided between neighboring Magnesia and Miletos, which latter also received Myous's vote in the Ionian koinon.[314]

It was not at all unusual for the communities of the ancient Mediterranean to experience pressure on their economic resources. Yet it tends to be assumed that measures were taken to counteract or cope with such pressures only at the level of the individual or of the polis, which with the exception of a few very large poleis operated at scales small enough to make the beneficial impact of such remedial measures negligible. There is, however, plentiful evidence for measures being taken by a koinon to ensure the economic welfare of its inhabitants, which I have explored in this section: the Achaians and Boiotians used their regional state power to prohibit the export of grain during periods of severe regional shortage; the Boiotians undertook the large-scale infrastructural project of draining Lake Kopaïs, which bordered on several poleis in the region, in order to gain agricultural land; in virtually every region we can see the koinon arbitrating in disputes between member poleis over resources; and when the tide of threats could no longer be stemmed, the institutions of the koina made it easy for member poleis simply to open their doors to the inhabitants of other member poleis who could no longer remain in their homes.

This chapter has attempted to chart a path through terra incognita, the relationship between the political institutions of the koina and the economic behavior of

---

311. Paus. 10.3.2, 33.2.

312. Hdt. 8.33.

313. Paus. 10.33.8.

314. Paus. 7.2.11. Myous had become subordinate to Miletos by 234/3 (*Milet* I.3.33e), was given to Magnesia by Philip V in 201 (Polyb. 16.24.9), and was finally divided between the two (*Syll.*³ 588 with Rehm, *Milet* I.3.148; F. W. Walbank 1957–79: II.532; Ager 1996: 292–96 no. 109). Vitr. *De arch.* 4.1.4 for representation in the Ionian koinon going to Miletos.

their member communities and individual citizens. Like every early attempt to map a particular reality, it will inevitably contain distortions and miss important information. The exploration that I have undertaken through this unfamiliar land has, however, revealed a series of important facts and phenomena, which I hope will serve as a starting point, if not a foundation, for future work on the public economy of the koinon in particular and on public economy in the ancient Mediterranean in general.

The appearance of cooperative coinage among many groups of poleis prior to the emergence of state institutions at the regional level that bound them into a koinon suggests that there was intense economic interaction between them and a cooperative commitment to facilitating it. In light of this, and of the adoption of similar monetary systems in other regions more or less simultaneous with the adoption of regional state institutions, it is difficult to suppose that there was no economic incentive for the creation of a koinon. This impression is supported by the fact that most koina of mainland Greece and the Peloponnese established legal rights for their citizens that tended to promote economic mobility within the region, whether by formal rights of property ownership throughout the koinon (certainly the most common solution) or by bilateral agreements between member poleis that tended toward the same end (in places like Ozolian Lokris, where the koinon was a relatively loose structure with limited capacities). The economic mobility promoted by these measures is certainly a response to the general need for mobility in the ancient Mediterranean, where resources were highly localized and production capacities irregular. It has been possible to sketch some ways in which this Mediterranean fragmentation was configured in regions governed by koina and to suggest that the mobility promoted by state measures was advantageous because it gave individual inhabitants as well as member poleis access to a wide array of highly differentiated but complementary resources.

If one of the advantages of membership in a koinon lay precisely in legally ensured access to varied resources, then it is not surprising to find some evidence of economic motives for expansion beyond the original boundaries of a koinon. Beyond capturing a set of resources that would supply a population with most (if not all) of its needs and using the legal authority of the regional state to facilitate access to those resources, koina in several cases generated state revenues from goods being imported to and exported from their territory as a whole while extracting taxes directly from their member communities only to raise funds for war. A koinon thus created a highly advantageous economic system for its citizens and member communities, which it took pains to protect by managing regional economic crises like grain shortage and arbitrating those disputes between member poleis that threatened to undermine the system. We see, in short, the koinon emerging partly in response to economic needs and developing institutions over time that sought in increasingly sophisticated ways to capture the benefits of cooperation.

The economic picture is quite rosy. I began with the speech attributed by Xenophon to Kleigenes of Akanthos, who despite outlining all the economic benefits of a koinon had gone to Sparta seeking help for his city's desire to resist incorporation in the koinon of the Chalkideis. The Akanthians were accompanied in their mission by the Apolloniates. Many other poleis preferred to remain outside of a koinon: Plataia, Thespiai, and Orchomenos in Boiotia and Sparta and Messene in the Peloponnese, to name just a few. If the advantages were as great as I (drawing on Xenophon's hints) have suggested, then why did they resist? There may have been economic grounds for concern: that the koinon would exploit its authority to collect taxes or to pool resources in an inequitable way, taking away local resources from a community that had always enjoyed them and giving nothing (or less) in exchange. We have no evidence for either form of behavior. I have suggested that koina were concerned with private debt, but we have no evidence for their involvement with public debt, an arena in which the perils of fiscal federalism have become immediately apparent in the sovereign debt crisis that is currently plaguing Europe. Member poleis of a koinon that went into public debt handled the situation like any other polis, borrowing from private creditors and raising public subscriptions; they did not, to our knowledge, look to the koinon for bailouts, nor do we see that a koinon was ever successful in an attempt to leverage polis revenues for the aims and activities of the koinon, beyond the licit collection of taxes from member communities. This may be because doing so would have been politically explosive; the relatively good fiscal behavior of koina may be a function of their political fragility.

For Xenophon, the grounds of opposition were political, not economic: the Akanthians, he has Kleigenes say, wish to be *autopolitai*, to be fully independent politically and not to participate in a *sympoliteia*.[315] If Xenophon presents the issue as an ideological commitment to the polis, underlying the desire to be *autopolitai* there must have been fears that the central power of a koinon could and would easily abuse its authority and exploit its member states. We need to consider how, and how frequently, such abuses occurred. Despite the strong resistance of some poleis, the fact remains that almost half the poleis of mainland Greece and the Peloponnese had joined a koinon before the end of the classical period, and this suggests that for many the koinon was, if not highly attractive, then perhaps their least worst option. These are the questions to which I shall turn in the final chapter.

---

315. Xen. *Hell.* 5.2.12, 14. See Bearzot 1994: 174–79 and 2004: 47–52; Lehmann 2000: 22–23; Beck 2001: 360–62.

6

Political Communities

If the religious and economic origins of the koinon and the state's ongoing engagement with those spheres of social action highlight its complexity and suggest that it was more multifaceted than what we tend to think of as a federal state, its political structures are indubitably akin to those we recognize in modern federal states. We need now to turn to this arena, where the label "federal" is more immediately applicable than it has been until this point in the argument.

At the heart of the Greek koinon, as in all federal political structures, lies a pair of dilemmas. First, if the central government has enough power to rule over the member states, what prevents it from overawing them and subordinating them as mere parts of a unitary state? Second, if the member states have enough power to govern themselves, what prevents them from undermining the koinon by refusing to cooperate with one another and with the central government? If a federal state is to survive, it must solve both dilemmas.[1] And this is particularly difficult, for the resolution of one tends only to exacerbate the other. Rules and practices that restrict the power of the central government tend to do so by strengthening member states, with the result that federal structures are undermined by fragmentation and the failure of member states to cooperate. Restrictions on the power of member states, on the other hand, tend to yield an increase in the capacities of the central government, with the result that federal structures are undermined by the centralization of power. For this reason federal states tend to be highly unstable—unless their institutions are self-enforcing, configured in such a way that they

1. Riker 1964: 7–8; Weingast 2005: 149–50.

provide incentives for both member states and central government to remain within the circumscribed limits of their power.[2]

Federal institutions are by necessity the result of a compromise, for they provide the rules and structure according to which sovereignty is divided among member states and the central government, and represent attempts, whether conscious or not, to resolve the twin dilemmas of federalism.[3] In order to complete our analysis, we need to ask how these two dilemmas were resolved by the poleis and koina of Boiotia, Achaia, and Aitolia, which involves looking carefully at the terms of the federal compromise in each state, developing as full a picture as possible of the competencies and powers of each level of government. Yet a simple survey of the distribution of authority in these states would fail to capture the essence of the problem, for it would necessarily take the institutions of each koinon as static entities, as analytical givens. We need to understand how and why these institutions emerged in the first place, how they responded to changing pressures and opportunities presented over time by both exogenous and endogenous developments, and how they interacted with one another.

The previous two chapters gave partial answers to this question. Chapter 4 considered the religious and economic contexts in which communities interacted, giving them a sense of shared identity and material incentives for cooperation. We saw that as the koinon emerged as a state, religious and economic interactions among its member communities continued to be of tremendous importance, so much so that formal institutions were developed to protect and promote those interactions. The tension between integration and differentiation that characterized these institutions is a hallmark of Greek federalism. It played out in the sphere of religion in the form of festivals sponsored by the koinon and including all of its member states, which participated in the rituals not as individuals but as poleis; and in the appointment of individuals to represent their communities in religious acts undertaken by the koinon as a whole, such as sacrifice, dedication, and the enactment of sacred laws. We see the same basic tension in the koinon's economic institutions. The economic gains to be captured by the pooling of resources, the promotion of regional mobility, and the facilitation of regional trade by the production of a common coinage all certainly contributed to poleis' willingness to join a koinon. But a view of federalism seen through a purely fiscal lens is certainly too rosy to be entirely correct—"a Candidian view of institutions as 'the best of all possible worlds.'"[4] For the economic exploitation of member states was not, in

---

2. Instability of federalism: Riker 1964; Bednar, Eskridge, and Ferejohn 2001. Stability through the correct structuring of incentives: De Figueiredo and Weingast 2005.

3. Federal institutions as bargain: Riker 1964: 11–16. Cf. Levi 1990: 410: "Institutions represent a social bargain in which there are returns for compliance."

4. Levi 1990: 406.

theory, difficult for the koinon to accomplish. The emphasis in the preceding chapters has been on cooperation and on the peaceful maintenance of polis identity and local autonomy in the face of regional integration. Yet despite this optimistic view, there have been glimmers of serious tension: the Boiotian communities known as the Thebageneis probably did not incur their obligation to provide a tripod to Apollo Ismenios at Thebes voluntarily; the Theban drive to incorporate Plataia into the new Boiotian koinon may have been motivated at least in part by land hunger; and the western Achaian poleis were outraged that the koinon was taking their tax revenues but failing to provide defensive assistance in exchange. These are only a few examples, chosen for their clarity and variety. When brought together, however, they highlight the presence of asymmetrical power relations and the use of coercion alongside voluntary cooperation in the development of the koinon.

This darker side of federalism has not been neglected in scholarship on the koinon, which has sometimes been perceived as yet another mechanism for garnering power not entirely dissimilar from the imperial leagues set up by Athens and Sparta in the fifth and early fourth centuries, a deeply hierarchical structure marked by the centralization of both power and resources. This is certainly the implication of Adalberto Giovannini's argument that the Greek koinon was in reality a unitary, not a federal, state.[5] Athanasios Rizakis, while recognizing the federal nature of the koinon, takes Polybios literally when he claims (2.37.11) that the Achaian koinon had made of the entire Peloponnese virtually a single polis, suggesting that "l'évolution naturelle de tout État fédéral territorial était l'incorporation et la subordination de la polis."[6] Both arguments rest on the belief that member poleis were politically powerless, forced to endure the legislative whims of the central government and to follow wherever it led in interstate relations. Careful scrutiny of the terms of the federal compromise and the ways in which it was negotiated over time will, however, suggest that in most cases this belief is ill founded.

This does not mean that the koinon was the best of all political worlds. The pessimistic view is also suggested by the developmental trajectory of the political institutions themselves that lay at the heart of the koinon, a process that was marked in some regions by coercion and the use of force or nonviolent exercises of power. The emergence of formal institutions is an extremely difficult problem to tackle from a purely historical perspective when we lack clear accounts of the pressures, opportunities, discourses, and conflicts that contributed to the establishment of formal institutions by individual actors, as we do for the Greek koinon in

---

5. Giovannini 1971.
6. Rizakis 1990b: 109. This position has implicitly been revised: Rizakis 2008b.

every instance prior to the late Hellenistic period. Yet we can, and must, piece together the evidence that sheds light on the conditions and processes by which the formal political institutions of the koinon were developed. As soon as we do, the role of power and coercion becomes evident, but it also becomes apparent that cooperation played an equally significant role.[7] We need to encompass both modes of behavior in our analysis.

Purely theoretical approaches to this problem are equally difficult. Ever since Hobbes, political scientists have tended to rely on some variety of the social contract to understand the emergence of political institutions, but there are serious problems with this approach.[8] And most of the work in the new institutionalism takes the existence of particular institutions as a starting point and then deploys a rational-choice perspective, which assumes the voluntary participation of all agents (or players in the game, of which institutions are the rules) to analyze how institutions facilitate cooperation in order to achieve material gains.[9] While this approach is well suited to explaining how the formal structuring of a polity can lead to particular outcomes, it occludes entirely the complex process of how institutions are put in place, as well as the possibility that participation may not always be entirely voluntary. William Riker, devoting himself explicitly to the problem of the origins of federalism, assumed that all parties made the federal bargain on a strictly voluntary basis.[10] Nevertheless, it is clear that institutions determine the distribution of power in a society, and are thus both a product of the deployment of power in the past and a means of deploying it in the future. Political institutions are in fact the product of power asymmetries, structures that tend to protect and

7. The distinction between koina driven by cooperation and those driven by coercion is similar to Consolo Langher's (2004) distinction between the sympolitical koinon and the hegemonic koinon. She views the former as the norm for Greek federal states as Greek authors understood them, the latter being a deviation ("fenomeno degenerativo") from that norm. While this distinction captures a highly significant difference, the argument about deviation from a norm suffers from anachronism: the Boiotian koinon is presented as the primary exemplar of the hegemonic model already in the late sixth century, but there is no evidence for normative thinking about the koinon, let alone a view that the sympolitical model was the norm, before the fourth century with Xenophon and the Oxyrhynchos Historian.

8. Hardin 1990.

9. Shepsle 1986; Weingast 2002. The emphasis on cooperation is particularly striking in the literature on the relationship between institutions and economic growth: North 1981, 1990; Weingast 1993, 1995, 1997.

10. Riker 1964: 12: "As bargains, the acts of making federal constitutions should display the main feature of bargains generally, which is that all parties are willing to make them." Riker's argument, couched in universal terms, is clearly based on the U.S. experience. Stepan 1999: 20–23 calls this "coming-together federalism" and observes that it is historically quite rare; in most instances—for example, in India in 1948–49—federal states emerge rather from a process of holding together, in which a state with strong unitary features develops federal institutions to keep it from breaking apart.

promote those asymmetrical relationships.[11] And while they are uniquely effective at facilitating cooperation, they "are also weapons of coercion and redistribution. They are the structural means by which political winners pursue their own interests, often at the great expense of political losers."[12] Indeed what may look like voluntary participation is frequently participation driven by a response to institutional changes imposed unilaterally by the powerful on weaker states; seen in this light, participation takes on a radically different significance.[13] Thus it is undeniable that power plays a significant role in both the emergence and the maintenance of formal institutions. When read in conjunction with the voluntarist, choice-based literature on institutions as mechanisms for the facilitation of cooperation, such observations suggest a basic logic of institutional emergence and change that helps us to tease out of the ancient evidence the roles of both coercion and cooperation in the formation of koinon institutions.

The current chapter is an attempt to do just that, by considering the historical emergence of the political institutions themselves that lay at the heart of the koinon and by studying the terms of the federal compromise, the precise ways in which power was distributed among the koinon itself, its member poleis, and its districts. While the historical context of each piece of evidence for the terms of the federal compromise in each state will be taken into account, it is nevertheless possible to approach the issue as a single subject because federal institutions, like all formal institutions, tend to exhibit path dependence: tremendously difficult to set up, once the compromise has been accepted and the rules applied, they tend to persist until major changes in circumstance occur, whether endogenous or exogenous to the state itself.[14] Changes in circumstance did occur, and while these sometimes resulted in actual institutional change, they resulted just as frequently in bargaining between member states and the central government that had the effect of reinforcing existing institutional arrangements and thereby achieving resilience.

COERCION AND COOPERATION
IN THE FORMATION OF THE KOINON

While the development of formal political institutions—state formation in the strictest sense of the term—is always a difficult and frequently violent process, the development of federal institutions binding together a group of previously

---

11. Levi 1981, 1988, 1990. Related to this idea is Knight's argument (1992: 19) that institutions are "best explained . . . as a by-product of conflicts over distributional gains."

12. Moe 1990: 213; cf. 2005.

13. Gruber 2000.

14. On institutional stickiness and path dependence, see North 1990: 92–104; Levi 1997: 28; Pierson 2000: 251. See also Thelen 2003.

independent states, as was clearly the case in ancient Greece, poses a particular challenge.[15] For it presupposes the existence of multiple states and requires the coordination of their interests and actions. But until institutions are formed that provide them with rules about how they should relate to each other and, at least ostensibly, with information about what the other member states as well as the central government are doing now and will do in the future, these states will struggle to understand and to agree upon what it means to participate and what it means to transgress.[16] By what process do states overcome the confusion, distrust, and lack of information that hinder political coordination? There are in essence only two paths to the development of federal institutions: they can be built from the bottom up, with states voluntarily "designing rules to sustain cooperation" among themselves, or they can be built from the top down, with one state that wields inordinate power over others imposing such rules, using coercion if necessary.[17] The outcomes will inevitably be different, with the institutions in a top-down federal state favoring the interests of the power holder, while those formed from the bottom up are predicted to be more equitable.[18] The trajectory followed in any particular historical context depends almost entirely on the conditions that facilitated, or perhaps necessitated, the development of such institutions.

Five such conditions can be isolated. In an important theoretical study, Rui de Figueiredo and Barry Weingast have suggested that two conditions must be present for federal institutions to emerge: there must exist some gains from cooperation among what they call "subnational units," and these gains must not be available in other institutional forms.[19] Although the authors' focus is on bottom-up federalism, these conditions certainly also apply to top-down situations. No hegemonic state will create a federation if it can create an empire, for federal institutions, requiring a division of powers among multiple state actors, naturally dilute the power of even the strongest member state.[20] These conditions are certainly applicable to the contexts in which koina developed in mainland Greece and the

---

15. Historically, this situation is rare (Stepan 1999), but it does apply to ancient Greece.

16. For political institutions as coordinating devices that determine rules and provide definitions of loyalty, transgressions, and the like, see Hardin 1989; Weingast 1997. The political importance of the coordination of knowledge has recently been explored for the case of classical Athens by Ober 2008.

17. On bottom-up federalism see De Figueiredo and Weingast 2005: 114.

18. Cf. Riker 1964: 7–8, whose centralized and peripheralized federalisms are essentially the same as my top-down and bottom-up federalisms, with the same predicted outcomes.

19. De Figueiredo and Weingast 2005: 108.

20. Cf. Riker 1964: 12, who suggests that the federal bargain is offered by "politicians who . . . desire to expand their territorial control, usually either to meet an external military or diplomatic threat or to prepare for military or diplomatic aggression and aggrandizement. But, though they desire to expand, they are not able to do so by conquest, because of either military incapacity or ideological distaste."

332   INTERACTIONS AND INSTITUTIONS

Peloponnese. That there were material gains to be had from cooperation has already become apparent in our analysis of the economic interactions of communities prior to the development of federal institutions, and no other form of state feasible in the classical Greek world was capable of capturing them.[21] Cooperation was also advantageous for defensive purposes, as is particularly evident in the early histories of Phokis, Boiotia, and Aitolia. But we can observe three further conditions particular to the Greek case that were always present. First, in every instance, the communities that became members of a koinon shared a sense of group identity, which was forged and articulated especially if not exclusively through myths of common origin, frequently performed in rituals at shared sanctuaries.[22] This sense of group identity appears to have suggested the logical boundaries of the group of states that would (or should, or could be persuaded to) participate in the koinon. Second, within these groups state entities existed prior to the emergence of federal institutions, usually in the form of poleis, a condition that generated significant resistance to the possibility of surrendering power at the local level in order to capture the gains to be had from cooperation with neighboring poleis.[23] Third, and finally, in the ancient Greek world it appears to have been exceedingly difficult for a single state to exercise power over a very large territory unless it assumed the shape of an empire or a hegemonic league like the Peloponnesian, which required as a precondition the existence of a tremendous asymmetry of power.[24] That is certainly a function, at least in part, of what geographers call distance decay, the weakening of power relations over spatial extent.[25] The enervating effects of distance can be mitigated by the construction of lateral relationships between individuals and groups, which have the effect of imbricating power "in overlapping and coexisting spatial arrangements."[26] These relationships need not take the shape of formal institutions, although in many instances they do; nor must they be characterized by a symmetrical distribution of power. In this context it is striking that the territory of Attica was roughly the same size as the entire

21. Ténékidès 1954: 113: "On peut tenir pour acquis que l'organisation fédérative des États répond à un besoin majeur des groupements nationaux, pour cette raison bien simple qu'il existe des tâches essentielles qui dépassent les capacités de l'État isolé."

22. See pp. 157–206 and, for further discussion, Mackil forthcoming.

23. While poleis were certainly slower to form in Aitolia than in Boiotia or even Achaia, at least some of the Aitolian communities were poleis by the time the koinon becomes visible as a formal institution in 369. See Funke 1991, and above, pp. 55, 77–78.

24. It is only from a very particular perspective that the Athenian empire can be considered a unitary state: I. Morris 2008. On the asymmetry of the treaties between Sparta and most members of the Peloponnesian League, see Bolmarcich 2005. The value of federalism to ruling large territories is underscored by Riker 1964: 2–5 from a theoretical and modern historical perspective.

25. See Sheppard 1984.

26. Amin and Thrift 1995; quote from J. Allen 1997: 69.

region of Boiotia, although the former belonged to a single polis whereas the latter belonged to twenty-five poleis.[27] Attica is the largest territory ever governed by a single polis in the Greek world, a feat that was certainly facilitated, if not fundamentally made possible, by the creation of the Kleisthenic deme system, which exhibits striking structural similarities to the koinon. This restriction made it unlikely for a unitary state to succeed in capturing the material and strategic gains to be had from cooperation and in overcoming the resistance of entrenched state interests at the polis level.

Under these conditions the development of federal institutions became both feasible and, at least to some communities, extremely attractive. The coordination of the interests and actions of poleis within a particular group and its institutionalization in the form of a koinon were accomplished by two developmental trajectories characterized by coercion and cooperation, which despite being analytically distinct partly overlap in practice.

The disproportionate strength of both Thebes and Orchomenos relative to the other Boiotian poleis is evident as early as the sixth century, a period characterized by competition between these communities. Dedications at Olympia attest armed conflict within Boiotia, with victories won by Orchomenos (over Koroneia, or at a battle fought in Koroneia against an unknown enemy), by Thebes (over Hyettos), and by Tanagra (over an unknown enemy). Tanagra suffered defeat in its turn, at the hands of an unknown enemy.[28] The source of the conflicts remains unclear. While it may have been a simple matter of seeking a position of regional dominance, unpublished epigraphical evidence raises the possibility that territorial disputes fueled these conflicts.[29] It is possible that both issues were associated with an attempt to coordinate the actions and resources of the Boiotian poleis. This is the impression given by the early cooperative coinage issued first by Thebes, Tanagra, and Hyettos, to which Akraiphia, Koroneia, Mykalessos, and Pharai soon contributed.[30] Orchomenos did not, and the participation of its near neighbor Hyettos, combined with the epigraphic evidence for a Theban victory over Hyettos, suggests that the impetus for this coordination effort came from Thebes. Tanagra's

27. The territory of Attica was about 2,550 km² (excluding Oropos but including the small islands: Busolt and Swoboda 1920–26: II.758), while Boiotia was 2,580 km² (Bintliff and Snodgrass 1985: 142; cf. González 2006: 44, who calculates 2,554 km²).

28. See above, p. 25.

29. Four inscribed bronze plaques found at Pyri, in the outskirts of Thebes, and now in the Thebes Museum: Whitley 2004–5: 46; Aravantinos 2006: 371; Angelos Matthaiou *per epist.* and a paper presented in Berkeley in September 2011. Photographs of two of these plaques are published in Aravantinos 2010: 166–67. See above, p. 25 and n. 23.

30. Above, pp. 247–49; Mackil and van Alfen 2006.

role—ally or subordinate?—is unclear. The impression that Thebes was the driving force behind all this is further supported by the city's attempt in 519 to "press" (*piezeumenoi*) the Plataians. When that pressure was resisted by the Plataians, a Theban invasion was stayed only by an eleventh-hour Corinthian arbitration that required the Thebans to "leave alone those of the Boiotians who did not wish to contribute to the Boiotians." This pressing is to be distinguished from outright military force, for that was the next step taken by the Thebans as they invaded Plataian territory.[31]

Plataia was for a time left alone, but the work that the Thebans had already done was not wasted. When they decided to support Kleomenes' invasion of Attica in 506, the Thebans had the assistance of Tanagra, Koroneia, and Thespiai but clearly played a leadership role in the affair.[32] For in the disastrous aftermath of the campaign it was the Thebans who consulted the Delphic oracle for advice about revenge. They brought the oracle's response before a meeting of the assembly. The meeting place is not specified, but the reported deliberations suggest strongly that some other Boiotian cities were cooperating with the Thebans. The oracle had told the Thebans to "ask those who are nearest" for assistance, and in the assembly they deliberated the meaning of this utterance: "Are not those who live nearest to us the Tanagrans and Koroneians and Thespians? And these, already fighting eagerly, wage war with us."[33] Herodotos is not one to downplay the brutality of the Thebans, but this passage gives us no room to argue that Tanagra, Koroneia, and Thespiai were acting under coercion. It is possible that the coordination we see in 506 was accomplished by the violent conflicts reflected in the dedications at Olympia, but by the time the Thebans and other communities of the Boiotian *ethnos* (T1) decided to help Kleomenes, they were supporting the Thebans eagerly. If they were initially forced by the Thebans to coordinate their actions with them by joining them on military expeditions and perhaps by paying some kind of tax (for this is the implication of the Corinthians' arbitration in the dispute between Thebes and Plataia in 519), that compulsion will have changed the status quo for those communities subjected to it, making voluntary compliance in the new circumstances a more attractive option. The late sixth century, then, was marked by attempts, clearly spearheaded by Thebes, to coordinate the poleis of Boiotia. This does not necessarily imply an attempt to impose federal institutions; the boiotarchs mentioned by Herodotos in 479 may be anachronistic, and if they are not they may simply reflect the regional aspirations of the Thebans rather than the existence of an actual regional state.[34] But the

31. Hdt. 6.108.2–5.
32. Hdt. 5.79.2.
33. Hdt. 5.79.2.
34. Hdt. 9.15.1, and see above, p. 30 n. 39.

coordination attempt, which had limited success, clearly laid the groundwork for later developments in the region.

The Medism of most of Boiotia during the Persian Wars, and the sack of Thebes by allied Greek forces after the battle of Plataia in 479, may have weakened the position of Thebes within the region. This period is notoriously poorly attested, but one source imputes to the Thebans a rather dirty deal made with the Spartans in 457, that they would harry Attica on behalf of the Spartans if they, in exchange, would help the Thebans gain "the complete hegemony of Boiotia." They agreed, and proceeded to help the Thebans fortify their city, and "compelled the poleis in Boiotia to submit themselves to the Thebans."[35] An isolated report, the claim is perhaps just plausible but utterly unverifiable. The Athenian victory at Oinophyta in the same year put an abrupt end to whatever plans the Thebans may have had, the surviving traces of which suggest a strong move toward the centralization of power in Theban hands, perhaps by violent means.

Yet when the Athenians were expelled from the region in 446, the Boiotians created a rich set of formal institutions that provided rules for their cooperation and attempted to restrict the power of Thebes, if not to alter the structural tendency toward greater centralization of power in the hands of a single polis. How do we account for the change? Certainly, as Larsen pointed out, the record of Theban leadership was not stellar: the defeats suffered at the hands of the Athenians in 506 and 457, and at the hands of the allies after the Persian Wars in 479, did nothing to bolster Theban claims to a right to their leadership position.[36] But it also seems clear that the poleis of Boiotia had grasped the advantages of cooperation as well as the fact that these would be attained only with tremendous difficulty if one polis assumed significantly greater power than the others. If it were simply a matter of Orchomenos attempting to supplant Thebes as hegemon of Boiotia, as Larsen argued, the other poleis would not have been given significant powers in the new state. The Orchomenians could have used their leadership role in expelling the Athenians as justification for assuming the hegemonic position within Boiotia that the Thebans had been attempting to carve out for themselves. Yet this was evidently not the case. The institutions outlined by the Oxyrhynchos Historian in his narrative of the events of 395 probably stem ultimately from the aftermath of the battle of Koroneia, although they exhibit some features that were certainly not in place at that time.[37] (These will be discussed in the next section.) What is important to note here is that these institutions appear to have been created at a time when no single polis had the strength to coerce others into joining; it is therefore almost

35. Diod. Sic. 11.81.1, 3.
36. Larsen 1960b: 11.
37. *Hell.Oxy.* 16.2–4 (Bartoletti); Larsen 1960b: 11.

certain that they were created from the bottom up by those poleis that agreed to participate.

This impression is corroborated by clear signs of bargaining between the participating poleis. Although in 395 the Thebans controlled four of the eleven districts of Boiotia, the Oxyrhynchos Historian reports that two of those four had previously been under the control of Plataia, Skolos, Erythrai, Skaphai, "and the other places previously in *sympoliteia* with them."[38] He does not say when Thebes gained control of those additional two districts, but it can only have been with the Theban war on Plataia, 431–427. Prior to that, we have to infer, Plataia and the small communities of the Parasopia were members of the Boiotian koinon with representation in the federal council and courts, the power to appoint (together) two boiotarchs, and obligations to meet military levies and pay taxes.[39] This arrangement implicitly protected the territory of Plataia and upheld the Corinthian arbitration of 519. A formal institutional arrangement of this sort, which guaranteed the Plataians some power via representation and participation in the

38. *Hell.Oxy.* 16.3 (Bartoletti). On the grounds of T3 it appears that the Thespian *sympoliteia* predates the Persian Wars; cf. Siewert 1977.

39. Most scholars have accepted the inference from *Hell.Oxy.* 16.3 (Bartoletti) that Plataia and the communities in its *sympoliteia* belonged to the Boiotian koinon in this period: Kirsten 1950: 2302–3; Larsen 1960b: 12 and 1968: 34, 132–33; Roesch 1965b: 40; Amit 1971: 63 and 1973: 87; Hansen 2004: 450. This inference is further supported by Thucydides' report that the Thebans defended their attack on Plataia in 431 on the grounds that they had been invited by some Plataians "to restore [καταστῆσαι] [the city] to the ancestral traditions of all the Boiotians." It has been doubted by a few (Bruce 1968: 190; Sordi 1968: 70; Prandi 1988: 79–91) on the grounds of Plataia's continued alliance with Athens in these years (Th. 3.68.5), which is taken to be incompatible with being a member of the koinon, while the rest of the Boiotian cities were allies of the Spartan-led Peloponnesian League. However, in the very earliest years of the koinon's existence, as its formal institutions were still being developed, such rigid rules may not have been in place; it is even possible that the Plataians' alliance with Athens was allowed to continue after 446 as a concession to persuade the city to join. There is a further problem with the assumption that Plataia never joined the koinon in the fifth century: Why would Thebes have gained an additional two districts after destroying the city, expelling the inhabitants, and annexing its territory? Bruce 1968 argues that representation in the koinon was based entirely on a proportional basis to the population of full citizens who met property qualifications and that the leasing of Plataian land to Theban citizens after 427 (Th. 3.68.3; cf. 3.58.5, 5.17.2) newly enriched a sufficient number of Thebans to qualify them as citizens, thereby justifying the expansion of Theban representation in the federal government. But this is unnecessarily complex as well as being economically questionable. Those authors who reject the inference of Plataia's participation in the koinon do not countenance the very real possibility, accepted here (cf. Hansen 2004: 450), that its participation was relatively ephemeral. Once two districts were created for Plataia and the communities in its *sympoliteia*, they would more likely have been transferred to Thebes upon annexation of the territory rather than simply dissolved; 446 thus emerges as a critical juncture, after which the district system persisted despite endogenous changes as a function of path dependence. It is very difficult to accept the proposal (Sordi 1968: 71–72) that those two additional districts were simply created by the Thebans following the annexation of the territory of Plataia.

decision-making procedures, judicial system, and magistracies of the federal government, would have been a powerful incentive for bringing this hesitant border city within the koinon. We have no account of the process by which these institutions were formed and accepted, but the initial participation of Plataia points ineluctably toward voluntary participation in an active compromise.

The formal political institutions that emerged in the aftermath of the battle of Koroneia in 446 established the Boiotian koinon as a state characterized by the voluntary participation of member poleis and their equitable representation in the central government. Yet these very institutions quickly became the framework upon which the Thebans reestablished their regional hegemony. At some point between 446 and the spring of 431, the Plataians must have left the koinon, for at that time the Thebans led an attack on the city with the aim of restoring it as a member state (Th. 2.24). Yet despite this Boiotian aim, there is no evidence that any member poleis of the koinon joined the Thebans in the attack. If Thucydides' language does not reflect a misleading slippage between "Thebans" and "Boiotians," then it was the Thebans, not the Boiotians, who were the Plataians' enemies (Th. 3.58–59). It was the Thebans who razed the city to the ground, annexed the land, and leased it to Theban citizens. And it was the Thebans who assumed control of the two Plataian districts in order to double their representation in the organs of the federal government (*Hell.Oxy.* 16.3 [Bartoletti]). As a result, by 424 the Thebans controlled four of eleven districts; the Theban Kadmeia served as the meeting place of both the federal council (*synedrion*) and assembly, and the Thebans commanded a military contingent that outperformed those of the other member poleis.[40] The aggressive leadership position of Thebes within the koinon by 427 is indubitable. The Plataians were clearly not regarded as being free to leave the state, but it is difficult to say whether this was a function of the fact that Boiotia was dragged into the undertow of Athenian-Spartan hostilities, with security concerns leaving it little room for tolerance of fragmentation, or whether the Thebans had what would later become, as we shall see, a typical response to the secession of a member polis of a koinon. What is clear is that the Boiotian koinon formed in or shortly after 446 was founded by the voluntary participation of poleis that understood the value of cooperation and needed formal institutions to provide them with clear rules about how, in practical terms, that would occur. While these institutions did not prevent Thebes from regaining its customary position of leadership within the region, they did prevent the city from assuming complete hegemonic control—for a while.

The tumultuous history of Boiotia allows us two further glimpses into the formation of federal institutions. The combination of the King's Peace and the

---

40. Districts and meeting place: *Hell.Oxy.* 16.4 (Bartoletti). Theban military prowess: Th. 4.96.3–4 (Delion).

Spartan occupation, not only of the Theban Kadmeia but of many other Boiotian cities as well, temporarily crippled the koinon. It is clear that the impetus and the agency behind the establishment of new political institutions following the occupation lay with the Thebans rather than in a cooperative effort of multiple Boiotian cities. In the years leading up to the peace the Thebans had claimed a position of leadership over the entire region, and by taking the lead in expelling the Spartan occupying forces from Thebes and the other poleis, they could resume their former position with an added source of legitimacy.[41] Yet the reconstruction of the koinon in the years after 379 was nevertheless accomplished largely by coercion. Violence was of course used to dislodge Spartan forces from the Boiotian cities. In some cases, including Tanagra, Orchomenos, and Tegyra, the inhabitants then appear to have rejoined the Boiotian koinon on at least a quasi-voluntary basis; the sources obscure nuances of orientation and policy.[42] At Plataia and Thespiai, old animosities toward Thebes caused the citizens to cleave to their alliance with Sparta, and this resistance led to their destruction at the hands of the Thebans.[43] If this story of coercive origins were not enough on its own to allow us to conclude that the Boiotian koinon of the period from 378 to 335 was highly centralized, its institutions make it clear beyond any reasonable doubt. The highest magistrates of the state, the boiotarchs, were in this period exclusively Theban.[44] In place of the eleven there were only seven, and they no longer represented the member poleis in a formal manner.[45] The legislative body of the state was the *damos,* a primary

41. Xen. *Hell.* 5.1.32–33, 5.4.1–9.

42. Tanagra: Isocr. 14.9. Orchomenos: Diod. Sic. 15.37.1–2, Plut. *Pelop.* 16.2–3. Tegyra: Plut. *Pelop.* 16–17.10, *Ages.* 27.3; Diod. Sic. 15.81.2. Other Boiotian poleis: Xen. *Hell.* 5.4.63. The initial adherence of Orchomenos is to be distinguished from the city's destruction by Thebes in 364, an act of retaliation for the attempted oligarchic coup of the Orchomenian cavalry (Diod. Sic. 15.79.3–6; cf. Dem. 20.109; Paus. 9.15.3).

43. Xen. *Hell.* 5.4.42–45, 6.3.1, 5; Diod. Sic. 15.46.6, 51.3; Isocr. 6.27; Dem. 16.4, 25, 28 (Thespiai); Xen. *Hell.* 6.3.1, 5; Plut. *Pelop.* 25.7; Diod. Sic. 15.46.6; Paus. 9.1.8; Isocr. 14 passim (Plataia).

44. Sordi 1973: 79–82 emphasizes the Theban election of boiotarchs immediately after the murder of the Spartans' polemarchs as establishing a pattern that persisted well beyond the immediate military crisis.

45. Seven boiotarchs at Leuktra: Diod. Sic. 15.53.3, Paus. 9.13.7. The proxeny decrees issued by the koinon in the 360s include lists of seven boiotarchs, and they never include patronymic or ethnic: T7.12–15, T9.12–16, T11.12–15. See also Knoepfler 1978: 379 and 2000; Bakhuizen 1994: 326 and n. 71. Buckler 1979: 57 (followed by Beck 1997: 102–4) insists that there were non-Theban boiotarchs in the period 378–338 but relies for his argument on *SEG* 25.553 (T13) and *SEG* 27.60 (T12), which both belong after 338 (*contra* Gehrke 1985: 180 n. 97) and tell us nothing about the earlier period. Buckler 1980b: 28 is more cautious but concludes that "all citizens were probably eligible for the office." Larsen 1955: 72 implies that the boiotarchs in this period still represented the various Boiotian communities, but he is compelled to admit that by virtue of voting procedures and meeting place, the Thebans dominated political decision making in the koinon. Roesch 1965b: 46 (followed by Vottéro 1995) argues that the seven boiotarchs were four Thebans, one Tanagran, and one from each of the remaining two districts,

assembly that met in Thebes and clearly supplanted the old council, which had been attended only by representatives appointed or elected by member poleis via the districts.[46] The meeting place alone privileged Theban attendance and therefore Theban representation in the assembly; despite the appearance of a stronger democratic leaning in this new government, the Thebans clearly exercised greater political privileges than the citizens of other Boiotian poleis.[47]

These new political institutions clearly enshrined and protected the concentration of power in Theban hands, a fact that raises three important questions. First, did the other Boiotian cities possess any rights at all? In other words, was this new state in any meaningful sense federal?[48] It was, in the sense that each Boiotian polis retained its own local government; but the role of each polis in the conduct of the central government appears to have been restricted to the right to attend assemblies in Thebes, having beyond this no formal representation. The obligations of the Boiotian poleis, furthermore, appear to have far outweighed their rights: they were expected to contribute manpower to the Boiotian army, to pay taxes, and to adhere to the foreign-policy decisions made by the central government in the hands of the boiotarchs and the assembly. Dio Chrysostom's comparison of Thebes under Epameinondas to Athens synoikized under Theseus may be hyperbolic, but it captures well the significance of the concentration of power in Theban hands.[49] This point raises the second question: If the Thebans had such inordinate power relative to the other Boiotian cities, why did they bother with the trappings of federal government at all? Answers to this question are necessarily hypothetical, but path dependence must be part of the explanation: federal institutions had worked before to promote and facilitate the coordination and cooperation of the Boiotian cities, so they would be easier to impose and more acceptable than a radical centralization of power akin to what happened in Kleisthenic Athens. Third, if some, like Tanagra, Orchomenos, and Tegyra, initially adhered in a quasi-voluntary way, why did they do so? Again

---

Haliartos-Lebadeia-Koroneia and Akraiphia-Kopai-Chaironeia; cf. Ducrey and Calame 2006: 73. P. Salmon 1995: 369 hints in the same direction. The reduction from eleven to seven occurred, according to Roesch, when Thebes annexed Thespiai and Orchomenos, each of which had previously sent two boiotarchs. However, the annexation of Orchomenos did not occur until after the battle of Leuktra, at which already there were only seven boiotarchs. It is most likely that Thebes had exclusive control over the college of boiotarchs in this period. There has been much speculation about why there were seven boiotarchs in place of the old eleven: Sordi 1973; Knoepfler 2000; Rzepka 2010.

46. The sovereignty of the *damos* is reflected in decrees of the period: T6.2, T7.2, T9.1, T11.3; Vlachogianni 2004-9.

47. Sordi 1973: 82-85, who also emphasizes the military character of this assembly.

48. Jehne 1999 views the Boiotian koinon in this period as effectively an extension of the Theban state; for the most part I would agree, but the persistence within this state of poleis with local autonomy is significant.

49. Dio Chrys. *Or.* 45.13.

an answer to this question must be hypothetical, but it becomes more comprehensible if we recognize that their options were limited; the status quo ante had been removed by the violent Spartan occupation of the region, which had been facilitated by internal discord—a function, it may have been argued by the Thebans, of the significant power that lay in the hands of the other Boiotian cities in that period. The Spartan occupation exposed the principal danger of distributed authority, and the Thebans were unwilling to run that risk a second time. So a return to prior arrangements became impossible, and membership on the new terms was clearly preferable to the complete destruction that the Thebans could wreak on them, as evidenced by the razing of Plataia in 427.

The situation was radically changed in 335, when Thebes in turn was razed to the ground by Alexander, with assistance from the exiled Plataians, Orchomenians, and Thespians. The Boiotian koinon was established once again, but for the first time without the participation of Thebes, let alone its leadership or control. Although the city was rebuilt by Cassander in 316/5, it became essentially a Macedonian garrison; but when the Thebans attempted to revolt from Demetrios Poliorketes in 293, they appear to have had the support of the entire koinon.[50] And when Demetrios liberated Thebes in 287, "return[ing] to the Thebans their *politeia*," we know that the Boiotian cavalry was engaged in protecting its territory, along with that of Oropos, which was returned to Boiotia in the same year, signifying voluntary Boiotian support for Thebes and a probable reintegration into the koinon in this year.[51] We have virtually no information about the process by which Thebes was restored, but the institutions that were implemented reflect a strikingly equitable distribution of authority, which points to cooperation rather than coercion as the driving force behind it. The boiotarchs were again representatives of all the poleis in the region.[52] The districts attested by the Oxyrhynchos Historian were effectively reinstated, though they were now seven in number rather than eleven, serving as a mechanism for political representation, taxation, and military levies across Boiotia. They may in fact have been created in tandem with the readmission of Thebes in the koinon, perhaps as a structural mechanism for preventing the repetition of the Thebans' political abuses of the period 379–335. The principal deliberative body in this period, the *koinon synedrion*, comprised representatives of all the poleis and met at Onchestos.[53] A Boiotian assembly also gathered there, and

50. Plut. *Demetr.* 39.2, 5; Polyaenus, *Strat.* 4.7.1; Roesch 1982: 432–33.

51. Plut. *Demetr.* 46.1. The phrase appears to signal the Thebans' autonomous return to the koinon: see above, pp. 97–98; Roesch 1982: 435–39; Knoepfler 2001c. Cavalry protection: T15.

52. This was true from 335, not just 287: T13.13–15.

53. Roesch 1965b: 126–33; cf. 1982: 266–82, 369–70. Cf. Livy 33.2.6. These representatives may have been sent according to the same principle of proportionality by which the districts were determined (Knoepfler 1999b). The meeting place appears to have returned to Thebes by 197 (C. Müller 2011: 275–80).

although it appears to have been open to all citizens, we do not know how votes were taken or counted.[54] It is, however, clear that Theban claims to leadership were no longer rooted in an inequitable hold on the political structures of the koinon.

In Achaia and in Aitolia the dynamics of regional state formation are much more difficult to discern. We lack any evidence for a single polis with hegemonic aspirations attempting to impose federal institutions on its neighbors in either region. The silence of our sources does not necessarily imply the absence of a dynamic like that we see in Boiotia in the classical period, but it is quite likely that in both regions cooperation rather than coercion lay behind the formation of federal institutions. This is suggested by sources that shed light on interpolis relations shortly before and shortly after we receive our first notice about the formal existence of a koinon in both regions. Xenophon's report that in 389 the Achaians were in possession of Kalydon, formerly an Aitolian city, and had made its inhabitants Achaian citizens indirectly informs us of the existence of an Achaian state bestowing double citizenship, at the level of the polis and of the koinon.[55] While the existence of Achaian citizenship on its own points to the existence of a regional state incorporating multiple Achaian poleis, literary sources for this period refer rather loosely to "the Achaians," and it is only with a late fourth-century inscription (T34) that we discover the existence of a council of the Achaians with *damiorgoi* (referred to as *damiourgoi* in literary sources) as regional magistrates. Although there was serious political tension in Achaia in 367, we have seen that it pertained not to the question of whether (or how) the poleis should participate in a koinon but rather to the question of whether Achaia should be ruled by oligarchs or democrats.[56] We have only one hint that an Achaian polis was forced to participate in the koinon, and that is a reference to the purported liberation of Dyme by the Thebans under Epameinondas in 367, along with the expulsion of Achaian garrisons from Naupaktos and Kalydon, in Aitolia.[57] If Dyme was indeed compelled to participate, the agents of that compulsion are invisible to us. We find resistance by a polis to a decree of the koinon in Helike's refusal, in 373, to allow the Ionians to take some sacred object from the sanctuary of Poseidon Helikonios, which they wished to use in refounding the Panionion on Mount Mykale, but the episode reveals more about what happens when a koinon tries to intervene in the affairs of a polis cult than it does about tension over regional integration per se or the process by which that integration occurs.[58] When Helike was destroyed later in the same year by

54. Roesch 1965b: 125–26; C. Müller 2011: 276.

55. Xen. *Hell.* 4.6.14. The significance of the double citizenship is discussed by Larsen 1953: 809–10; Beck 1997: 55–66; Freitag 2009: 17–18.

56. See above, p. 75.

57. Diod. Sic. 15.75.2.

58. See above, pp. 195–98.

earthquake and tsunami, the Achaian koinon divided up its territory "among the neighbors," probably meaning Aigion and Aigeira.[59] The absorption by neighboring communities of the population and territory of failing cities in the Achaian koinon is attested for Rhypes, Aigai, and Olenos. At what date these absorptions occurred is not clear, but in the case of Rhypes and Aigai, Aigion was the major beneficiary.[60] There is no evidence that this was the result of predation or hostility; it is probably better seen as a synoikism, and no political struggle like that we see playing out in classical Boiotia between Thebes and the other Boiotian poleis can be detected in fourth-century Achaia.

The Achaian koinon was effectively dismantled by the imposition of a series of tyrants by the early Macedonian rulers, but when the opportunity arose to rebuild the regional political institutions founded in the fourth century, the Achaian poleis seized it, although doing so gradually and cooperatively.[61] According to Polybios, in the period 284–280 "the Patraians and the Dymaians began to agree," and then the Tritaians and Pharaians "stood together with them."[62] By the narrative that interrupts these two statements, which recounts in rapid succession the early (mythic to classical) history of Achaian cooperation, Polybios makes it clear that he means nothing less than a gradual rebuilding of the koinon. It appears to have assumed something like its former shape by about 275, including as members all the poleis along the north shore of the Peloponnese as far east as Pellene.[63] There is no doubt that the voluntary participation of the Achaian poleis in the new koinon is partly to be explained by their shared desire to gain complete independence from Macedonia after a period in which most of them had directly experienced the rule of tyrants installed by Alexander and his successors. They clearly realized that this would be possible only by cooperation; their previous experience of a koinon certainly suggested its reconstruction as an immediate solution rather than a looser, purely military alliance. The institutions of the Hellenistic Achaian koinon bear the distinctive stamp of a federation created from the bottom up. A popular assembly open to all citizen males of military age met four times a year at the sanctuary of Zeus Homarios at Aigion from 275, along with a smaller council.[64] The highest magistrates of the koinon were a secretary and two generals, stratēgoi, elected by the poleis on a rotating basis, probably designed to ensure that these high officials came from different poleis each year. In 255/4, the two generals were

---

59. Str. 8.7.2; cf. Mackil 2004: 511.
60. Rhypes: Str. 8.7.5. Aigai: Str. 8.7.5; Paus. 7.25.12, 8.15.9. Olenos: Polyb. 2.41.7 (which allows us to give only a terminus ante quem of the early second century for the absorption of Olenos); Str. 8.7.4; Paus. 7.18.1.
61. Cf. Larsen 1968: 216.
62. Polyb. 2.41.1, 11–12; cf. 4.60.10. Str. 8.7.1, while less detailed, implies the same process.
63. Polyb. 2.41.13–15; see above, pp. 99–101.
64. Polyb. 2.43.1–2. Cf. Larsen 1968: 217.

POLITICAL COMMUNITIES   343

replaced with one.[65] This single general was then supported by a college of Achaian magistrates together known as the *synarchiai*, which probably included the *damiourgoi*, the secretary, and other high military officials.[66] These magistracies were never the exclusive domain of a single polis, as was the college of boiotarchs in Boiotia during the period 379–335. There is some evidence to suggest, however, that the political leaders of the Achaian koinon came from a few major cities, notably Sikyon, Megalopolis, and the four western Achaian cities with whom the refoundation in 280 originated.[67] While the mechanics of the elections of such magistrates are obscure to us, it is clear that in practice the offices rotated among member communities. Nevertheless, voting in these assemblies was done by city rather than individually, which meant that although an assembly held in Corinth, for example, would likely have a greater proportion of Corinthians in attendance than one held at Megalopolis, the Corinthians would have no greater influence on the vote itself.[68] These institutions all bear the marks of having been designed by a group of poleis cooperating on a voluntary basis to produce rules and practices that would tend to sustain their cooperation in the future.

In Aitolia federal institutions seem to be a product of cooperation among communities in the region, although the process by which this occurred is again obscure. While the fifth-century alliance and treaty between the Aitolians and Lakedaimonians (T48) shows that the Aitolians were recognized as a single entity by outsiders in diplomatic contexts, it does not tell us anything about the internal organization of the Aitolians. It is only in 367 that we discover a koinon in Aitolia (T52), but we have no information about how it was formed. Insofar as we can discern it, however, the prior history of internal Aitolian affairs is marked by cooperation; that implicit in the treaty with the Lakedaimonians was probably motivated by a desire to prevent the Athenians, Messenians, and Naupaktians from making any further seizures of their territories.[69] Thucydides' detailed narrative of Demosthenes' invasion of Aitolia in 426 exposes the cooperative response of the Aitolian communities to his attack: they "all assisted with great strength," even those Ophiones who lived near the Malian Gulf, far from the hills immediately north of the Corinthian Gulf.[70] The Aitolians then joined to defend Aigition, which was targeted by Demosthenes, and

65. Polyb. 2.43.1 with Aymard 1933. On the sanctuary of Zeus Homarios as meeting place see Str. 8.7.3 with Aymard 1935, 1936, 1938.

66. *Synarchiai*: Polyb. 4.4.2; 27.2.11; 38.13.4. The *stratēgos* and ten *damiourgoi* certainly formed a board: Polyb. 23.5.16; T34.35; Livy 32.22.2. The other magistrates who probably composed the board referred to as the *synarchiai* by Polybios are the hipparch (Polyb. 5.95.7), *hypostratēgos* (4.59.2, 5.94.1), and admiral (5.94.7, 95.11).

67. O'Neil 1984–86.

68. Livy 32.22.8–9, 32.23.1 with O'Neil 1980: 46–47; Lehmann 1983a: 257–58 n. 51.

69. See above, pp. 54–57.

70. Th. 3.96.3.

here were successful in expelling the invading force.[71] In the aftermath of the attack, they chose one representative from each of the three major population groups (*merē*) to go as ambassadors to Corinth and Sparta in search of aid, which they then used to regain Makyneia, just west of Naupaktos.[72] This response points to cooperation in the service of defending the region as a whole and of attempting to regain parts of it that had previously been lost. The institutional mechanisms behind all this are wholly obscure, but there is no evidence whatsoever for any asymmetry of power among the communities of Aitolia in this period. The existence of federal institutions here is attested only by an Athenian decree of 367 (T52) that dispatched a herald to complain to the koinon of the Aitolians about the seizure of sacred ambassadors by citizens of Aitolian Trichoneion. It was certainly this same koinon that granted citizenship to an Athenian sometime in the fourth century (T49). Elections were held at Thermon, and the sanctuary was also apparently used as an archive for public documents; the complete absence of any indication that a single Aitolian community controlled Thermon or drove any of this cooperation points us ineluctably toward the conclusion that the federal institutions of the Aitolian koinon in the classical period, despite being known only in their barest outlines, were the product of bottom-up federalism.[73] There is no need to see in this process the influence of Epameinondas; the history of Aitolian cooperation predates the Boiotian statesman by several generations, and the politics of ethnicity had, as has recently been argued, a life of its own in this period.[74] The institutions of the Aitolian koinon as they can be discerned for the Hellenistic period reveal no shift toward a concentration of power in the hands of a single member community. Indeed, the full and speedy political integration of new members alone precludes this possibility. It is further attested by the fact that extraordinary meetings of the Aitolian assembly were held quite frequently and were not tied to a particular location; one regular meeting was always held in connection with the Thermika festival at Thermon, a perfect federal capital by virtue of the fact that it was a sanctuary unconnected to any single polis or other Aitolian community. The other regular meeting, dubbed the Panaitolika, appears to have been held in different locations from year to year; additional, extraordinary assemblies were likewise held wherever the right combination of need and opportunity arose.[75] The practice of voting individually rather

71. Th. 3.97.3–98.5.

72. Th. 3.100.1.

73. Elections in the classical period: Ephoros, *FGrHist* 70 F 122; cf. Soph. *Inachos, TrGF* IV F 288 (Radt), *Meleager* 404 (Radt) with Hsch. κ4343. The practice is better attested for the Hellenistic period: Polyb. 4.37.2, 5.8.5.

74. Epameinondas was given a founding role by Schweigert 1939. On the politics of ethnicity see Funke and Luraghi 2009.

75. Here I follow the view of Larsen 1952 and 1968: 198–99, *contra* Mitsos 1947. See also Scholten 2000: 26–27 and 2003: 71.

than by community in the assemblies further attests a cooperative federalism in which local interests were intentionally subordinated to regional ones.[76] Representation of local communities was not, however, left to the chance of assembly attendance, which would vary depending upon the location. The council (*boulē, synedrion*) of the Aitolians was composed of representatives of member communities, appointed according to some principle of proportional representation.[77]

The emergence of federal institutions in Aitolia can be seen only as a response to the region's experience of significant territorial losses and invasions by predatory neighbors. The communities of Aitolia, probably a mixture of poleis and villages organized in large population groups that had clearly demarcated territories, needed to defend themselves and could do so only by cooperation. Behind their willingness to cooperate in order to achieve an effective defense of their territory, and to do so by creating federal institutions rather than a much simpler multilateral military alliance, lay a long history of ritual interactions at shared sanctuaries, above all Thermon, and a highly interconnected regional economy. But the rules that the Aitolians designed to promote and sustain their cooperative efforts—the political institutions they created—were also directly influenced by the settlement history of Aitolia, which yielded distinct and apparently relatively equitable communities, and by the ethnic unity of the Aitolians, which generated a sense of belonging that traversed the boundaries of individual settlements, however politicized they may have been.

This systematic assessment of the conditions in which federal institutions emerged in Boiotia, Achaia, and Aitolia has suggested that the voluntary cooperation of political communities, rather than coercion exercised by one asymmetrically strong polis over others, was the main path leading to their development. The history of the Boiotian koinon in the period from 379 to 335 appears in this light to be far from typical, yet it dominates perceptions of Greek federalism because it is so extraordinarily well documented. Although in Aitolia and Achaia the processes that led to the emergence of federal institutions are quite poorly documented by comparison, yet the nature of the institutions themselves—achieving and protecting an equitable distribution of power among the constituent members by representation and by rotation of magistracies and of meeting places—confirms the impression that they were created from the bottom up by means of cooperation. And the contrast between these institutions and those that governed the Boiotian koinon in the period known as the Theban hegemony could not be stronger. The Theban seizure of the college of boiotarchs during this period is but the clearest example of their use of a central political institution as a weapon

76. Funke 1985: 86–88; Scholten 2003: 71.
77. T60.32–37.

of coercion, a way of pursuing purely Theban interests at the expense of the other Boiotian poleis. This result is particularly striking because cooperation is so difficult to achieve. The background conditions of group identity, shared religious practices, and interdependent economies go a long way toward explaining how it was possible in every instance, while in the cases of mid-fifth-century Boiotia and Aitolia, the exogenous shock of foreign invasion was clearly the immediate catalyst for the creation of institutions that would promote and sustain cooperation.

THE TERMS OF THE FEDERAL COMPROMISE

Once the cooperation of multiple states had been achieved by the creation of a single federal state, its preservation and stability were largely determined by its institutions, for these provided the rules and structures according to which authority was distributed among the poleis and the koinon. The vital importance of institutions to the success of a state was not lost on those who were most closely involved in them. So Lykortas, the father of Polybios, reminded the Achaians in 181/0 that it was the oaths, laws, and inscribed agreements that bound together their state (*koinē sympoliteia*).[78] The power of institutions to promote cooperation on an ongoing basis rather than simply in moments of exceptional danger or risk is likewise alluded to by Polybios when he claims that by sharing "the same laws, weights, measures, and coins, magistrates, councillors, and judges, the whole Peloponnese differs from being a single city only by virtue of the fact that its inhabitants are not enclosed by a single defensive circuit."[79] Several centuries earlier, Xenophon had Kleigenes of Akanthos warn the Spartans that the member poleis of the koinon of the Chalkideis would become strongly united by common laws.[80] This ideology of common laws was clearly central to the experience of the koinon, but the precise nature of those laws was tremendously important. In order to understand how the koinon functioned, we need to determine as fully as possible the range of powers held by the regional government. We also need, however, to understand what political role the member poleis played, for laws common to the entire region—that is, federal institutions—were only part of the story. This means understanding in detail the terms of the federal compromise, the institutions that were put in place as a result of the negotiations by which cooperation was originally achieved. Our focus will be on the powers of the koinon and its poleis, with

78. Polyb. 24.8.3. Cf. Livy 38.34.3: in 188 the Achaians, in the process of integrating Sparta into the koinon, required that they surrender their Lykourgan laws and accept the Achaian ones, "for thus they would become one body and would more easily agree about all things."
79. Polyb. 2.37.10–11. Cf. F. W. Walbank 1957–79: I.218–21 and Lehmann 2000: 97–100.
80. Xen. *Hell.* 5.2.19.

attention also drawn to the district, a median level of political organization that served as an instrument for the coordination of member poleis to act in the interests of the koinon.

The Powers of the Koinon

In the most general terms, the koinon itself was responsible for the provision of public goods that could not be delivered by member poleis. These were public goods that were accomplished by scale effects, most significantly defense and diplomacy, goods that relied upon the cooperation of member poleis. But they were also goods that actually facilitated cooperation by establishing the common laws, binding on all member poleis, that were so central to the ideology of the koinon. Koinon legislation coexisted with polis legislation, and although there are only hints about the respective spheres of each, they point toward a careful delineation in which the koinon could only impose laws pertaining to defense, interstate relations, the regional economy, and religious practices of interest to the entire koinon. The koinon was also responsible for handling the inclusion of new members and the separation or secession of existing member states, processes that demanded a tremendous amount of energy and attention during periods of growth and conflict, and that provide us with a window onto the priorities of the koinon as a political entity.

Public Goods.   That federal states were responsible for waging war on behalf of their member poleis is so obvious as not to require comment. What is both more important and less well known is how the work of getting an army into the field or of protecting any part of a koinon's territory from attack was done off the battlefield. Insofar as we have repeatedly seen defense serving as a motive for the cooperation of individual poleis as well as being a catalyst for the formalization of koinon institutions, it is not surprising that the koinon should have undertaken legislation aimed at organizing and training its armed forces and protecting its member poleis. In the early fourth century the Boiotian koinon had a law that established the obligations of each community to send troops to the Boiotian army at a level proportional to its population.[81] In the third century, at least, the responsibility for training these troops was also placed in the hands of the cities that provided them, but this responsibility was imposed from above. A decree of Thespiai bestowing proxeny on an Athenian in the mid-third century preserves the reason for the honor, unusually for this class of documents: "There is a law of the koinon of the Boiotians that the poleis must provide trainers who will teach the boys and the youths to shoot bows, to hurl javelins, and to draw up ranks in battle array for wartime situations," and the honoree took charge of training the youths

---

81. *Hell.Oxy.* 16.4 (Bartoletti). See Bruce 1967: 161–63 for some speculations about how this worked in practice, with references to earlier scholarship.

of Thespiai for war.[82] In Achaia in the later third century, a law of the koinon made provision for reimbursement from the federal treasury of any expenses met by member poleis in defending their own territories against enemy attack.[83] Polybios reports that interesting detail in the course of his narrative of the costly Social War: it was certainly in response to their experience of manpower shortage and defensive failures in that war that the koinon undertook a major reform of its military, implementing now for the first time a standing army of Achaian citizens, with some specification about how many men would be contributed by each polis as well as a commitment to funding a mercenary army of a fixed size.[84] A few years later, it is clear that the *stratēgos* himself became occupied with training the Achaian troops, and this seems to represent a shift from the earlier arrangement, which would have been more like the Boiotian.[85]

Logically if not temporally prior to military training was the process of making decisions about going to war and concluding peace, and these decisions were always and exclusively in the hands of the koinon. Typically such decisions were made in assemblies, the composition of which is crucially important, for it demonstrates the extent to which member poleis played an active part in decision making at the federal level. Thanks to Polybios there is a good deal of detailed evidence about this point for the Hellenistic Achaian koinon. From the beginning it is clear that matters of war and peace were decided by the Achaian assembly, but further restrictions were put in place when a law was passed, probably at the end of the third century, that required a special meeting of the Achaian assembly to discuss matters of war and peace. This means that an irregular meeting would be called to discuss only the specific issue, but the body that met was nevertheless a general assembly open to all Achaian citizens of military age; the only factor limiting attendance was probably the geographical location of the meeting in question.[86]

82. T27.10–16.

83. Polyb. 4.60.10.

84. Polyb. 5.91.4–8. Argos and Megalopolis are the two cities singled out for specific levels of troop contribution: each is to provide five hundred infantry and fifty cavalry to the combined Achaian standing army of three thousand infantry and three hundred cavalry. This means that one-third of the total military burden was to be shouldered by these two member poleis.

85. Polyb. 11.10.9; Plut. *Philop.* 9.13–14; Paus. 8.50.1 (Philopoimen, in 207). See Anderson 1967 and Errington 1969: 64–66 for Philopoimen's military reforms.

86. E.g., Polyb. 4.22.2, 25.1 for the earlier situation. Polyb. 22.12.6 with Livy 39.33.7; Polyb. 23.5.16, 29.23.8–9, 29.45.5 for circumstances under the new law requiring a special meeting. Polybios's terminological variations led to a heated debate over the nature and composition of the Achaian assemblies and its change over time: Aymard 1938; Larsen 1955: 165–88 and 1972; Giovannini 1969; F. W. Walbank 1970b; O'Neil 1980; Lehmann 1983a: 251–61 and 2000: 70–81. The debate to 1979 is well analyzed by F. W. Walbank 1957–79: III.406–14, whose conclusions seem to me most satisfactory. Cf. Rizakis 2003: 97–98; Roy 2003: 84–85. There is no longer any real debate that throughout most of the third century the assembly met regularly and was (potentially) attended by all citizens of military age.

For Boiotia the evidence is much less detailed; we simply find the Boiotians accepting or refusing peace.[87] But the famous negotiations held at Sparta to renew the common peace in 371 are illustrative of the broader principle: although the Boiotians wished to renew their oath, the other Greeks were unwilling to recognize the validity of a koinon signing on behalf of all its member poleis. They were shut out, and the battle of Leuktra ensued. The episode is typically taken as emblematic of Theban stubbornness and aggressiveness, but it is certain that the Thebans were effectively faced with a legal challenge. Under Boiotian law, only the koinon had the authority to agree to matters of war and peace, and for this reason they insisted on signing the treaty as the Boiotians or not signing it at all.[88] According to Diodoros, the Theban ambassador (who happened to be Epameinondas himself) did not sign the treaty, "for [the Thebans] alone, leading Boiotia under a single *synteleia,* were not accepted by the Greeks, out of a general desire that the oaths and treaties be made city by city."[89] The only thing that makes this episode atypical is that the Boiotian koinon was in this period tightly controlled by Thebes, with little evidence for significant representation of the member cities in leadership positions or decision-making processes. Yet the legal position was clear: only the koinon (however it was internally constituted) could draw up a peace agreement or declare war.

Cooperation in matters of war and peace appears in Aitolia to have preceded the emergence of federal institutions by at least a few decades; if indeed the peace treaty drawn up between the Spartans and Aitolians belongs to the fifth century, there is no evidence for the existence of any formal federal institutions at that time, but the treaty was made with "the Aitolians" (T48.1–3). The peace treaty concluded between the Aitolians and Demetrios Poliorketes circa 289 was clearly made with the Aitolians as a koinon, although the details are lost in the many lacunae on the stone.[90]

The authority of the koinon to conduct war as well as to decide upon when (and when not) to do so leads to the broader issue of diplomacy, of the way in which Greek federal states interacted with other states. Here too power lay in the hands of the koinon; poleis were free to conduct relations with other states only of a nonpolitical and nonmilitary kind. The Argive attempt to drum up allies to combat Sparta in 421 reveals the machinations of this process in Boiotia: Argive ambassadors made a formal proposal of alliance to the boiotarchs, who were in favor. They

87. E.g., Th. 5.17.2, 26.2, 32.5.
88. Xen. *Hell.* 6.3.18–4.3; cf. Plut. *Ages.* 28.2–3.
89. Diod. Sic. 15.50.4. Compared to Xenophon's own account of this episode, the language of Diodoros is strikingly technical, which may suggest that he was drawing on the fourth-century historian Ephoros here.
90. Lefèvre 1998.

then "communicated these proposals to the four councils of the Boiotians, which had complete authority [over the decision], and advised them to exchange oaths with whatever cities were willing to lend them aid. But the members of the Boiotian councils did not accept this proposal."[91] Thucydides here seems to refer to the existence of four federal councils, which met in rotation, a replication at the regional scale of the system of local government that was in place in all the Boiotian poleis in this period, as described by the Oxyrhynchos Historian.[92] With final authority for making decisions about the conduct of relations with other states, the Boiotian councils, at this point probably composed of representatives of each of the member poleis of the koinon, rejected the Argive proposal. In fourth-century Aitolia it appears likewise to have been the koinon alone that had the right to conduct diplomatic relations with other states. It was the koinon that initially accepted the Eleusinian truce declared by the Athenians' sacred heralds (T52.8), and it was to the koinon of the Aitolians that the Athenians sent their ambassadors to demand the return of the heralds who had been seized by some Trichonian citizens (T52.16–17). When Polyperchon sought Aitolian support in 310 for the restoration of Alexander's son Herakles to the Macedonian throne, he "wrote to the koinon of the Aitolians."[93]

It is clear that the Achaian koinon likewise had the exclusive authority to conduct diplomatic relations with other states. In the first half of the fourth century we find the Achaians engaging in cooperative diplomacy by using the koinon itself (or, in practice, its representatives) to send and receive embassies.[94] When it joined an alliance of Athens, Arkadia, Elis, and Phleious in 362, it was "the Achaians" who were signatories to the alliance. According to a plausible restoration of the text, amendments of the agreement were possible but required resolution by "all the cities," and as an extra precautionary step, it appears that the oath of adherence to the treaty had to be sworn by each member polis individually.[95] For the Hellenistic period a tremendous amount of detail is preserved about negotiations in the Achaian assembly about diplomatic issues, from all of which it is clear that this body, composed theoretically of all Achaian citizens along with the high magistrates of the koinon, had full authority to make decisions about how the koinon would relate to other states. One particularly detailed account will serve as an example. In 198 the Achaians faced the choice of accepting a proposed alliance with Rome or

---

91. Th. 5.38.2–3.

92. *Hell.Oxy.* 16.2 (Bartoletti) with Andrewes in Gomme, Andrewes, and Dover 1945–81: IV.42–43 and Hornblower 1991–2008: III.89–90 for a proposed textual emendation of the papyrus that would make the implicit analogy between local and regional institutions explicit.

93. Diod. Sic. 20.20.3.

94. Xen. *Hell.* 4.6.1 for an Achaian embassy sent to Sparta in 389. Diod. Sic. 15.49.2 for the koinon of the Achaians receiving Ionian ambassadors in or shortly before 371.

95. RO 41.35–38.

of retaining their existing alliance with the Romans' enemy Philip V. Livy describes an assembly deeply divided on the question of whether to join Rome and abandon their now-traditional alliance with Macedon, or to remain loyal to an old benefactor: "Soon not only individuals but whole communities were at odds with one another," and the college of ten *damiourgoi* was itself divided on the question.⁹⁶ But Achaian law required that a vote be held by the end of the third day of debate on a specific issue, and the outcome of that vote reveals a great deal about the continuing challenge of concerted action and interests in a regional state as large as the Achaian: realizing that a continued alliance with Philip would represent a very serious threat to the Achaians' collective safety, but not being willing to abandon an ally who had been responsible for restoring their cities, the citizens of Dyme, Megalopolis, and Argos in attendance walked out of the assembly, abstaining from the vote. An overwhelming majority then voted in the council to conclude an alliance with the Romans, Attalos, and the Rhodians.⁹⁷ This episode is striking: because the stakes of the decision were so high, and because so many communities, as well as individuals, felt an allegiance to the Macedonian king despite realizing that he was now on the losing side, it was extraordinarily difficult to achieve consensus on the issue. Yet after three days of active debate, a coordinated response was achieved, and this was precisely what was required of the koinon and what its institutions were designed to produce. There is perhaps no other report of a debate held in a Greek federal assembly that is reported in such detail, but Livy's account of the Achaian debate in 198 exposes not only the authority of the koinon over issues of diplomacy but also the difficulties that perhaps not infrequently accompanied the process of reaching a single decision that would affect so many communities at once.

The koinon also had legislative and judicial powers. That the koinon should undertake legislation that would be binding on every member polis and its citizens was vitally important, for it was only by this means that the coordination and cooperation of member poleis could be regularized, protected, and mandated. When the Boiotian koinon withdrew its long-standing support for the Spartans in 404 and sought to help the embattled Athenian democrats regain control of their city from the Thirty Tyrants, a decree was issued that every household and polis in Boiotia should be open to Athenians in exile; that failure to help an Athenian fugitive would incur a one-talent fine; and that all actions hostile to the tyrants in

96. Livy 32.19.1–22.2.

97. Livy 32.22.4–23.3. Champion 2004: 127 sees this episode as evidence that contradicts Polybios's own claim (2.37.9–11) that the Achaian koinon united the Peloponnese. While Polybios's claim is certainly exaggerated, it is important to note that the outcome was a single decision; the representatives of these cities voluntarily left the assembly. Dissent is no enemy to political process (Ober 1998); the Achaian koinon appears to have been quite effective in handling it.

Athens would go unpunished.[98] Federal legislation was sometimes used to support diplomacy in more positive ways, particularly by the conclusion of *symbola,* conventions establishing the legal procedures to be followed in disputes arising between citizens of different states. Concluded by the koinon and an independent state, these agreements were binding on all member poleis and their citizens.[99] Federal legislation was thus used not only to promote uniform behavior among the poleis internally but also in their interactions with other states, and in this respect it can be seen as an important instrument for the promotion of federal political aims. None of this could be done by polis legislation, but the political character of such legislation was profoundly affected by the composition of boards of legislators and judges at the federal level.

We have seen that Polybios's summary description of the Achaian koinon mentions common laws and courts as one of the state's distinctive and highly advantageous features. These certainly included the laws that have already been mentioned, limiting special meetings of the assembly and requiring that decisions be made about such matters after three days of deliberation.[100] We also know that in all three regions, the koinon occasionally passed laws intended to protect the regional economy during periods of crisis and shortage, a response to crisis that was only effective because of the scale effect of the koinon.[101] Two inscriptions provide us with an indication of how such laws were made, for they attest the existence of a college of lawgivers, *nomographoi,* apparently composed of representatives sent by groups of poleis, perhaps as members of a district.[102] The first (T41) records a law establishing as a regular part of the festival of Asklepios a sacrifice to Hygieia; the legislative outcome that must have been recorded on the second (T44) is lost. But it was certainly the *nomographoi,* representing all the member poleis of the koinon, who enacted the Achaian laws of which Polybios wrote so

98. Plut. *Lys.* 27.6; cf. *Pelop.* 6.5; Diod. Sic. 14.6.3.

99. Several Athenian decrees attest a *symbolon* between the Boiotian koinon and Athens in the mid-third century (*IG* II² 778, 779, 861). The Aitolian koinon concluded a *symbolon* with Delphi sometime before the end of the third century (*FDelph* III.1.451); it must have been nullified by the crippling of the Aitolian koinon in 189, for after this we find several former member poleis concluding *symbola* with Delphi: Daux 1936: 275–79; Gauthier 1972: 96–100. Cf. Cassayre 2010: 72–73, taking the view that the poleis had these agreements imposed upon them by the koinon, representation in federal councils being largely insignificant. The true political importance of representation is difficult to measure, but *symbola* are hardly instruments for oppression, rather promoting extraregional economic interactions and profit for individual citizens.

100. Cf. Polyb. 24.8.4–5.

101. Achaia: T43.15–16. Boiotia: T33.4–7 (a *psēphisma*). In Aitolia this took a different form, viz. the appointment of lawgivers to oversee financial reforms that may have included some measure for the cancellation of debts (Polyb. 13.1.1). See above, pp. 305–313.

102. The testimony of these inscriptions bearing on the question of districts in Achaia will be discussed below.

enthusiastically, which, as we have seen, regulated deliberative processes, military activity, and diplomacy, among other things. They appear also to have performed the vital function of recording legal decisions of the koinon, an act distinct from that of inscribing or commissioning the inscription of a decision on a stone.[103]

Judicial proceedings at the federal level are somewhat more obscure. It is clear that in early fourth-century Boiotia federal judges were chosen by districts and served on the juries as representatives of the poleis comprised within the district that appointed them.[104] Although the method of appointing judges to the federal courts may have changed by the 360s, with Theban control in the judicial sphere matching its stranglehold on the college of boiotarchs after circa 379, it is virtually axiomatic that the federal courts heard trials of federal magistrates charged with misconduct.[105] We can say a bit more about the system in Hellenistic Boiotia thanks to Polybios's description of its almost complete breakdown in the late third and early second century. "For the administration of justice had been dragging on slowly for nearly twenty-five years, and now there was talk among the poleis to the effect that it was necessary to put an end to the disputes between them."[106] While this may point to a widespread problem affecting all the courts in Boiotia, it is much more likely to apply to the federal judicial system in particular, for the outstanding cases, as Polybios notes, were those between poleis and probably, by extension, between individuals of different poleis.[107] He goes on to explain that large numbers of legal cases between individual Boiotians and Achaians were also outstanding and that the Achaian koinon sent ambassadors exhorting the Boiotians to resolve these cases. When they failed to do so, the Achaians granted to all citizens the right to seize

103. *I.Magn.* 39 (Rizakis 1995: no. 690A; Rigsby 1996: no. 89). It is worth noting that the Achaian koinon received the *theōroi* from Magnesia, as we might expect given the Achaian koinon's exclusive authority to deal with interstate relations, while the Aitolians received them polis by polis: *I.Magn.* 28. I shall return to this issue below.

104. *Hell.Oxy.* 16.4 (Bartoletti).

105. The trials of Epameinondas and Pelopidas for refusing to relinquish control at the end of their terms as boiotarchs are the best attested, but there were others: Plut. *Pelop.* 25.2; Nep. *Epam.* 7.3–8.5. That the trials were conducted by a federal court was recognized by Cary 1924; cf. Bonner and Smith 1945: 18–19.

106. Polyb. 22.4.2. Compare Her. Krit. *BNJ* 369A F 1.15–16 for withering remarks about the Boiotian justice system in the early third century. Bonner and Smith 1945 have virtually nothing to say about the Hellenistic period.

107. The role of the federal court as a court of appeal in disputes between individuals of different cities, and between individuals and cities themselves, is shown by the famous case of Nikareta of Thespiai, who struggled to get the polis of Orchomenos to repay its debt to her and was successful only when a federal ruling found in her favor: *IG* VII.3172 (Migeotte 1984: 53–69). For recent discussion see Cassayre 2010: 74–77, whose interpretation of the judicial system in Boiotia as corrupted by an inappropriate intervention by the koinon in affairs of the city and by the personal interests of federal magistrates is not supported by the evidence.

Boiotian property as redress for the wrongs they claimed to have suffered at the hands of individual Boiotians.[108] In addition, then, to cases between member poleis of the Boiotian koinon, cases between Boiotians and Achaians were outstanding, and this points once again to the federal courts in Boiotia and indirectly to another facet of their jurisdiction, namely cases between citizens and foreigners. But Polybios's own narrative, along with epigraphic evidence, allows us to say more. It was certainly a Boiotian federal court that tried the pro-Roman Zeuxippos in 188 in a criminal and political trial for the murder of the boiotarch Brachylles in 192.[109] That the federal courts did crucial work, despite the problems that may have plagued them, is suggested by a decree of Akraiphia improvising an arbitration for the settlement of disputes with its neighbors in the years immediately after the dissolution of the koinon.[110] Alongside the federal courts attested by Polybios was a federal board of *tethmophylakes*, guardians of the law, who were appointed by poleis (perhaps via the districts), and whose jurisdiction included the enforcement of laws and agreements affecting the relations between individual citizens of different Boiotian poleis.[111] Their exact relationship to the courts is unclear, but it is likely that the details of their jurisdiction were established by a federal law attested by Plutarch.[112]

The establishment and enforcement of laws as well as the conduct of trials were public goods provided by both the Achaian and the Boiotian koina, and they differed in both form and content from the legal systems of member poleis with which they coexisted. The manner in which the legal system was conducted at the federal level was carefully constrained to ensure the participation and representation of member poleis. And the issues over which federal legislators and judiciaries had authority were carefully restricted to matters affecting the entire koinon, disputes between member poleis and individual citizens of different member poleis, and disputes between individual citizens and citizens of foreign states.[113]

In its limited but strong jurisdiction the federal legal system was closely analogous to the koinon's political and diplomatic powers, focusing on relations with foreign states, relations between member states, and the provision of public goods

---

108. Polyb. 22.4.10–13.

109. Murder: Polyb. 18.43.3. Trial: Polyb. 22.4.6–8 with Roesch 1982: 404–5; Roesch 1985: 127–28; Cassayre 2010: 77.

110. *IG* VII.4130 (Gauthier 1972: 343–44).

111. *Tethmophylakes* appointed by the polis: Roesch 1965b: ll. 66–67 (*SEG* 23.271; *IThesp* 84). Jurisdiction involving disputes between citizens of different poleis: *IG* VII.3172.77. For discussion see Roesch 1965b: 145–52.

112. Plut. *Quaest. Graec.* 292d: θεσμοφυλακι‹κ›οῦ νόμου (emendation by Roesch 1965b: 149 n. 4).

113. The explicit distinction between judiciaries of the koinon and of the polis is made in inscriptions from other regions: *IG* IX.2.8 with Robert 1925: 221–28 (Ainianes); *Syll.*³ 647 (Phokis, *sympoliteia* of Steiris and Medeon). See Cassayre 2010: 79.

that could not be delivered, or delivered with equal efficacy, by individual poleis alone. In the historical record it becomes evident that the other major power of the koinon, and one that at times occupied tremendous resources, was regulation of the koinon's membership, the loyalty of member poleis, and their disputes with one another—in short, protection of the very fabric of the koinon.

Expansion and Integration. The very nature and existence of the koinon was predicated on the idea that cooperation promoted material, military, and political welfare. Cooperation among communities that already have a sense of belonging together, of sharing an identity expressed through claims about a common past or through the performance of shared rituals, is easier to accomplish than cooperation among communities with little sense of connectedness, and it was perhaps for this reason that ethnic belonging was so often advanced as an argument for participation in a koinon.[114] But in the Hellenistic period in particular these ethnic boundaries were broken, and koina grew to incorporate as member states communities with fewer ties to the original group. This process of expansion was overseen by the koinon itself—its high magistrates and assemblies—and the several modalities by which it was accomplished reveal a great deal about the priorities, concerns, and powers of the koinon.

While the infamous episode of Plataia at the outbreak of the Peloponnesian War could on its own be taken to suggest otherwise, the integration of new members into a koinon rarely occurred by coercion. In fact, the vast majority of cases about which we are meaningfully informed pertain to circumstances in which a new polis voluntarily joined a koinon. Again the most detailed information comes from Hellenistic Achaia. Here expansion occurred in tandem with the expulsion, and then the voluntary resignation, of pro-Macedonian tyrants in the small poleis of the Peloponnese, followed by the choice of their citizen populations to join Achaia: first Sikyon in 251, followed in 243 by Corinth, Megara, Troizen, and Epidauros, then Megalopolis in 235, and Argos, Hermione, and Phleious in 229.[115] A fragmentary inscription found at the Asklepieion in Epidauros (T37) preserves some of the terms upon which that city was introduced into the koinon: it appears to have been decided by a vote (l. 2), probably of the Achaians, for this is elsewhere attested as part of the process by which Argos was integrated, and it was probably regular.[116] From the inscription we also find that Epidauros is to be ungarrisoned and, according to a probable restoration, autonomous (ll. 3–4); the legal system of the polis is to remain in place (ll. 7–9); and an existing territorial dispute with

---

114. Mackil forthcoming.

115. Sikyon: Polyb. 2.43.3. Corinth, Megara, Troizen, and Epidauros: Polyb. 2.43.4–5, Plut. *Arat.* 24.3 with T37–45. Megalopolis: Polyb. 2.44.5. Argos, Hermione, Phleious: Polyb. 2.44.6.

116. Argos: Plut. *Arat.* 35.1–5.

Corinth is to be resolved by Achaian arbitration (ll. 17–19), a decision that is also preserved epigraphically (T38).[117] The Achaians experienced a period of remarkable growth over a little more than two decades, during which time the addition of eight new poleis doubled the number of members of the koinon and probably more than doubled its territorial extent. The expansion was, so far as we can tell, entirely fueled by the voluntary participation of communities as a palatable alternative to tyranny. But history does not always yield such an optimistic narrative.

Political divisions within cities led to resistance by one group when another sought membership in the koinon. In such cases, the Achaians tended either to impose garrisons, sometimes at the request of their supporters, or to exile their opponents at the moment when the city became a member.[118] Mantineia joined the koinon around 233 but shortly afterward was taken by the Aitolians.[119] When the Achaians managed to regain control of Mantineia in 227, it received a garrison of Achaian mercenaries, according to Polybios at the request of the Mantineians themselves, who "foresaw conflicts among themselves and plots by the Aitolians and Lakedaimonians."[120] Aratos awarded citizenship to the metics in the city, a power normally reserved for the polis, in an attempt to reward pro-Achaian groups within Mantineia.[121] The Achaians likewise furnished a garrison and an Achaian general to hold Kynaitha when the pro-Achaian party gained the upper hand after a period of violent stasis in or before 219.[122] These security measures were almost certainly provided at the request of the Kynaithans, just as they were at Mantineia, for shortly thereafter, wishing to end the stasis and restore exiled Kynaithans, "those in control of the city sent an embassy to the Achaian *ethnos*, wishing to effect the reconciliation with their consent."[123] The Achaians readily agreed, and the garrison and commander were withdrawn; the entire

117. See pp. 313–20 for discussion of the koinon's role in the resolution of internal interpolis disputes.

118. Rizakis 2008b: 280 suggests, following Aymard 1938: 172 n. 5, that garrisons were imposed by the Achaians on "cités stratégiques, intégrées récemment à l'union mais dont la fidélité n'était pas encore totalement acquise." This does not, however, take account of the evidence for garrisons being sent at the request of the citizens of these new member poleis, an important distinction; the evidence is presented below. Rizakis further suggests that the garrisoning of Kalydon in the early fourth century is the earliest example of this dynamic, but Xenophon (*Hell.* 4.6.1) makes it clear that the Achaians "were forced to garrison Kalydon, for the Akarnanians had marched against it, and some Athenians and Boiotians were present with them as allies." The problem here is evidently not suspicion of loyalty (though that may have been an added factor, particularly in the presence of those who had the strength to liberate the city from the Achaians) but of providing assistance to a member polis under attack.

119. Polyb. 2.46.2, 2.57.1 with Scholten 2000: 159–61 for the likely context of the transfer.

120. Polyb. 2.57–58, with quote at 2.58.1; Plut. *Arat.* 36.2–3, *Cleom.* 5.1. Cf. Rizakis 2008b: 280. See further the commentary to T39.

121. Plut. *Arat.* 36.3.

122. Polyb. 4.17.4–5.

123. Polyb. 4.17.9.

arrangement appears to have been voluntary, intended to support but not to force the adherence of the polis to the koinon.[124]

Sparta represents the most complex case in which we can see the Achaians struggling to integrate a polis whose citizens were in fact divided on the question of membership. With a history of Spartan opposition to the Achaian koinon going back at least as far as Kleomenes, a considerable portion of the population remained hostile to the Achaians despite their apparently fair handling of the Lakonian coastal poleis that were handed to them by Flamininus in 195 following the Roman war against Nabis.[125] But when Nabis was assassinated three years later and Sparta was left in total disarray, Philopoimen seized the opportunity to make Sparta a member of the Achaian koinon. It is clear that despite the long history of hostility to Achaia, there was some support within Sparta for becoming a member: Philopoimen "fell upon the city with his army, and while some were unwilling, he brought over those who were sympathetic and attached the polis to the Achaians."[126] Those who were unwilling were exiled, and this group became a constant problem for the Achaians.[127]

Divided sympathies in the context of civil strife also lay behind the quasi-compulsory integration of Oropos into the Boiotian koinon at the end of the fifth century. The polis of Oropos with its important healing sanctuary of Amphiaraos, which sat on the regional border between Attica and Boiotia, was a locus of contention between the two states for years. Subordinated to Athens, it became independent in 412, during which time stasis erupted and some citizens were exiled.[128] Unable to effect their own restoration, the exiles appealed to the Thebans for military assistance. The Thebans gained control of the city and after moving the city inland allowed it to be autonomous, but sometime later "they gave them citizenship and made the territory Boiotian."[129] Force was indeed applied, but it was at the request of exiled citizens; unfortunately we know neither how large that group was nor any details of the manner in which Oropos participated in the koinon in these years.[130] In any case, the King's Peace appears to have signaled renewed

124. Withdrawal: Polyb. 4.17.8–9.
125. Livy 34.35.5; 35.12.7, 13.2, 35.2; and see above, p. 128.
126. Plut. *Philop.* 15.4. Further details about pro-Achaians in Sparta: Plut. *Philop.* 15.5. Livy 35.37.1–3 and Paus. 8.51.1 are less detailed. Cf. Errington 1969: 109–12; Cartledge and Spawforth 2002: 77.
127. Plut. *Philop.* 16.1–3, 17.4; Livy 36.35.7; Paus. 8.51.1, 4.
128. See Petrakos 1997: 489–93 for the evidence; Hansen and Nielsen 2004: 449 for an overview.
129. Diod. Sic. 14.17.1–3. Cf. Theopomp. *FGrHist* 115 F 12.
130. González 2006: 31–32 infers from the absence of Oropos from the Oxyrhynchos Historian's description of the Boiotian districts that the city was not part of the koinon until 395 or shortly after, when Orchomenos revolted from the Boiotian koinon. His hypothesis (p. 32) that "Oropos was ... included in the Boiotian Confederation as compensation in place of Orchomenos" obscures, however, the crucial question of agency.

independence for the Oropians, and they joined Athens again. For the next century they suffered being taken by one ruler after another and handed over to either
Athens or Boiotia. We know virtually nothing about the Oropians' attitude toward
all this. But when Oropos again became a full member of the Boiotian koinon, in
287, it appears to have done so voluntarily, for Demetrios Poliorketes, who had last
rendered the city to Athens in 304, had now lost power, so there was no one to
force the Oropians to become members of the Boiotian koinon, yet they remained
such until the koinon was dismantled by the Romans in 171.[131] Whether it was
because the loyalty of the Oropians was not regarded as a sure thing or because the
Boiotians felt that the territory of its new member was particularly vulnerable to
attacks, the koinon deployed cavalry forces in the area in the years immediately
after 287.[132]

Cases in which a koinon attempted to integrate a new member polis by pure
coercion were exceptionally rare and almost never successful, a fact that attests the
centrality of consent and cooperation to the functioning of the koinon. The most
famous example is the Boiotian attempt to compel the Plataians to join: in some
sense the effort stems back to the late sixth century; but at that time, as we have
seen, the Boiotians were a rather loose group bound together by military and some
economic cooperation, though without any formal institutions or rules governing
their interactions.[133] When the Boiotians renewed their attempt in the spring of
431, the institutional framework was entirely different: a koinon with elaborate and
detailed rules guiding the cooperation and coordination of member poleis, characterized by a relatively equitable principle of proportional representation. The
Thebans' attempt to force Plataia to join the koinon was an utter failure, leading
after a three-year siege to the complete destruction of the city rather than its
integration in the larger Boiotian state.[134] In Achaia our only clear instance of
a city's being integrated into the koinon by pure coercion is that of Messene.[135]
After Sparta became a member in 192, the only Peloponnesian states outside the
koinon were Messene and Elis, and the Achaians were eager to bring them in.
Embassies were sent to both poleis, and while the Elians accepted the overtures,

131. Evidence for the integration of Oropos: T15.34–37; T18.5, T23.12. See Roesch 1982: 439.
132. T15.34–37.
133. Hdt. 6.108.2–4; see above, p. 27.
134. For the narrative see above, pp. 38–39.
135. In light of the extreme rarity and limited success of compulsory integration of a polis into a
koinon, I find it difficult to accept the argument (Rizakis 2008b: 280 with n. 56) that Orchomenos must
have been compelled to join the Achaian koinon between 235 and 229 only on the grounds of the mention of plots of land in the city being offered to Achaians on the condition that they not be sold for
twenty years (T39.11–13; see the commentary in the epigraphic dossier). The underlying concerns here
appear to be the same as those behind the Aitolian settlement at Same on Kephallenia ca. 223 (*IG* IX.1²
1.2 and above, pp. 114–15).

the Messenians resisted, and the Achaians began to attack their territory. Without so much as a battle, the Messenians applied to Flamininus, who ordered them to join the Achaians.[136] It is remarkable that it took eight years for Messene, effectively forced into the koinon, to attempt to rebel.[137] It is the first clear case of an even partly successful coercive integration in the history of the koinon, with no internal support in evidence. The success of this integration is perhaps a function of the fact that with Messene and Elis, the Achaian koinon now included the entire Peloponnese, creating little opportunity for restiveness. It is not surprising that coercion was so unsuccessful as a strategy for the expansion of a koinon, given the fragility of the federal structure in general and the degree of direct or indirect participation required by member states. Federalism was not, and could not be, a form of imperialism. Federal states expanded by voluntary cooperation and participation, not by coercion—with a few exceptions that prove the rule.

The Aitolian koinon expanded rapidly in the Hellenistic period, as is well known, but has thus far remained outside this analysis. This is because the growth of the Aitolian koinon is for the most part charted by the growth of the Aitolian delegation to the council of the Delphic Amphiktyony and the disappearance of delegates from old members; we can, in other words, detect the outcome but not the process by which the Aitolians expanded their state. In a few cases we know a bit more, but not enough to analyze the integration of new members in terms of voluntary adherence and coercion. The Aitolian-Boiotian alliance of the early third century makes mention of "the Phokians with the Aitolians" (T53.A10), but we know nothing about what this meant in practice, what the actual political status of individual Phokians or of whole Phokian communities was in the Aitolian koinon in the early third century.[138] In the treaty between the Aitolian koinon and Demetrios Poliorketes, concluded probably in late 289, we find a distinction between Aitolians and those in *sympoliteia* with them, but the document is highly fragmentary, and it is difficult to tell whether individuals or whole communities are meant, much less what the status of being in *sympoliteia* with the Aitolians entailed.[139] It is possible that the treaty refers to the Phokians, who were simply with the Aitolians in the alliance concluded with Boiotia a decade before; there may have been other communities in a similar position.[140]

<hr/>

136. Livy 36.31.1–9. See now Luraghi 2008: 262.

137. The revolt of Messene in 183 will be discussed in detail below. There were signs of discontent at Messene by 185 (Polyb. 22.10.6), but it would be surprising if it had not been there earlier.

138. See McInerney 1999: 242–43.

139. Lefèvre 1998 l. 23: μήτ᾽ Αἰτωλοῖς μήτε τοῖς σ]υμπολιτευομένοις μετ᾽ αὐτῶν. Buraselis 2003: 44 translates the phrase as "the Aetolians and those politically belonging to the Aetolians." Scholten 2003: 72–73.

140. Lefèvre 1998: 124; Buraselis 2003: 44.

But these are frustratingly elliptical hints; what we want to know is how communities came to be in that position and, furthermore, what it meant to be with the
Aitolians or in *sympoliteia* with the Aitolians, in practical political terms. Were they
forced to join, or did they do so voluntarily? What were the local, legal implications
of participation? Did all citizens of such new member communities automatically
become full Aitolian citizens with rights to participate in the workings of the Aitolian federal state? We can piece together a slightly more satisfying answer for the
case of Herakleia Trachinia, the old Spartan colony in Doris that was "compelled to
contribute (*syntelein*) to the Aitolian koinon" in 280.[141] By 272, a citizen of Herakleia
had become *grammateus* of the Aitolian koinon; it is possible that a decade later,
another citizen had become *stratēgos*.[142] It is, however, unclear whether this was
possible because the entire citizen body of Herakleia received full political rights in
the Aitolian koinon or because these individuals were enfranchised as a privilege.[143]
The Aitolians' integration of Herakleia gave them a seat on the Amphiktyonic
council, which they had taken by 278, along with the seat that formerly belonged to
Ozolian Lokris, signaling the integration of that region into the koinon as well.[144] In
272, when Polycharmos of Herakleia was *grammateus* of the Aitolian koinon, several citizens of Amphissa in Ozolian Lokris received a grant of *isopoliteia* from it.[145]
This apparently minor detail is of tremendous importance, for it implies that when
Amphissa and the other Ozolian Lokrian communities were integrated into the
Aitolian koinon, their citizens did not receive a universal grant of Aitolian citizenship.[146] This has been seen as a sign of autonomy granted to the Ozolian Lokrian
communities, which is contrasted with the apparently full integration of Herakleia.[147] But it does seem possible that the individual Herakleians who achieved high
offices in the koinon did so by virtue of having exercised a grant of *isopoliteia* made
to them as individuals, just as we see it being made to Amphissan citizens.[148] Our
first clear evidence for something close to the full political integration of an entire

141. Paus. 10.20.9.

142. Herakleian *grammateus:* IG IX.1² 1.10a, b; 11a–e, 12a. Herakleian *stratēgos:* Klaffenbach, *IG* IX.1²
1, p. xlix. Cf. Scholten 2000: 52.

143. Scholten 2000: 52 sees the election of a Herakleian as *grammateus* as confirmation "that, at
some time before their passage, the members of the Aitolian League had voted to give full citizenship
rights to the Oitaian population of Trachinian Herakleia and subsequently had seen fit to elect one of
these nonethnic Aitolians to what was then the League's second most prestigious office."

144. *CID* IV.12 = *FDelph* III.2.68.

145. *IG* IX.1² 1.12.A1. Another inscription of the same period, *IG* IX.1² 1.5.3 records a grant of proxeny to a Chaleian.

146. Scholten 2000: 55 and 2003: 73.

147. Scholten 2000: 29, 45, 55.

148. I am thus sympathetic to the skepticism of Lerat 1952: II.65, who doubts whether these inscriptions can tell us anything about the status of these communities.

community by the Aitolians is the grant of *isopoliteia* to all Akarnanians in the alliance reached in the late 260s or early 250s (T57.11–13). If such documents point to a lingering resistance to the complete integration of non-Aitolian communities into the koinon on an equal footing with the original members, that resistance eventually faded. Phthiotic Achaia probably became part of the koinon in the 230s, and in the following decade citizens of the Phthiotic polis Melitaia appear as high-ranking Aitolian magistrates.[149] In 213/2, we find that Melitaia and its neighbor Pereia were sending councillors to the Aitolian *boulē* according to some principle of representation proportional to the population of each polis (T60.16–21).[150] Here at last we have clear evidence that the familiar but only superficially understood phenomenon of Aitolian expansion in the third century entailed the extension of full political participation to entire communities rather than only to individuals. It may very well have happened before 213/2, but how much earlier we simply cannot tell given the state of the evidence.

Whether on a purely voluntary basis, by the voluntary participation of one faction within a polis, or by total coercion, the integration of a new polis into a koinon inevitably demanded the resolution of a whole host of issues. Rarely does our evidence afford us any insight into this process, but there are some hints from the relatively rich documentation of Hellenistic Achaia. Two general principles appear to be at work: if a new member polis had any outstanding disputes with another polis, those disputes were to be resolved as part of the process of integration; and if a new member polis had any dependent poleis of its own, they were to be separated from it and become members in their own right.

First, dispute resolution.[151] When Epidauros joined the koinon in 243, it had an outstanding territorial dispute with Corinth, another new member, and the Achaians passed a decree calling for its resolution; this was accomplished by a board of arbitrators from Megara.[152] Arkadian Orchomenos joined a few years later, circa

149. *IG* IX.1² 1.31.28–43 (f), 99–104 (m).

150. Integration of Phthiotic Achaia: Scholten 2000: 155. See also Scholten 2003: 71–72.

151. Tod 1913: 74–75 argued that the Achaian koinon at all times required that disputes between its members be referred to the koinon for arbitration, but Moretti 1967–76: I.131 and Harter-Uibopuu 1998: 119–29 have shown that the procedure was voluntary, for it is also clear that it was not always the koinon or its delegate carrying out the arbitration. Cf. Ager 1996: 116. The moment of integration is, however, a different and altogether more fragile context, and it is striking that the only two decrees recording the integration of new members preserve measures taken by the koinon toward the resolution of disputes between member poleis. It is quite possible that the koinon allowed nonmembers to act as arbitrators; the overriding principle was that disputes be resolved before integration, to prevent the koinon from assuming a conflict that could escalate to war or otherwise lead to trouble and expense.

152. T38 ll. 4–5. The dispute between Epidauros and Corinth was recognized at the time when Epidauros joined the koinon, for it is mentioned in the fragmentary decree recording Epidauros's entrance (T37.10–12, 17–19), and although lacunae make it uncertain, it is likely that this decree provided for an arbitration to be carried out (Mitsos 1937).

235–229, and the Achaians took measures to end ongoing disputes between the citizens of Orchomenos and Methydrion, a dependent polis of Megalopolis, as well as between the Orchomenians and an individual named Nearchos, plausibly identified as a former tyrant of the city.[153]

Second, the disintegration of structures of dependency at the level of the polis. Although this sounds highly intrusive, it appears not to have been employed as a mechanism for punishing communities that resisted joining the koinon. Indeed Messene, the only successful case of integration by coercion, was required to dissolve its own koinon in 191, but when the Elians joined voluntarily in the same year, they were also required to abandon their dependent poleis, which themselves became members of the Achaian koinon.[154] This condition appears not to have been applied in a complete or rigorous fashion, for we know of several exceptions.[155] Messene revolted from the Achaians in 182 (an event to which I shall return shortly), and when it was reintegrated, several cities that had remained dependencies of Messene, including Abai, Thouria, and Pharai, were now made independent members of the koinon with "the erection of a stele for each city participating in the koinē sympoliteia."[156] The clear implication is that although the Messenian koinon was dissolved in 191, some dependent poleis were left in place; it is logical to suppose that this position was the outcome of negotiations between the prospective member polis and the koinon.[157] Overwhelming force had after all not been applied, and it was due primarily to the diplomatic orders from Flamininus that Messene became a member, creating a situation in which there would have been room for negotiation. When Megalopolis joined in 235, it appears that the status of its dependent polis Methydrion was not to change, but the Methydrians viewed

153. T39 ll. 17–21 (Methydrion), ll. 13–17 (Nearchos).

154. The Messenian koinon is attested for 207/6: *I.Magn.* 43. Whether this reflects a federal arrangement or a polis and its dependents remains a matter of debate. See Lazenby 1972: 90; E. Meyer 1978: 283; McDonald and Hope Simpson 1972: 145; Luraghi 2008: 267. The integration of Messene in 191 may also have prompted Achaian arbitration of its old territorial dispute with its neighbor Phigaleia: *IG* V.1.1430 records an arbitration between these partners, but it is fragmentary and has been dated as early as ca. 240, contemporary with the *isopoliteia* treaty concluded between Messene and Phigaleia (*IG* V.2.419), and as late as ca. 191. See Ager 1996: 123–24, who is agnostic about the date, and Harter-Uibopuu 1998: 46–52, who places it after 191. Elis: Livy 36.35.7 with 36.31.3. See Rizakis 2008b: 277 with n. 26.

155. Niccolini 1914: 245–46.

156. Polyb. 23.17.1–2. These communities were probably attached to Messene at the time of its foundation: Luraghi 2008: 229. The separation of Abai, Thouria, and Pharai from Messene triggered a series of boundary disputes that were arbitrated by the Achaian koinon: Ager 1996: nos. 116 (*IVO* 46), 145 (Moretti, *ISE* 51; Rizakis 1995: no. 699). A new inscription from Messene records three stages in an arbitration of a boundary dispute between Messene and Megalopolis, which involves the Achaian koinon and is to be dated to 182: Themelis 2008; Arnaoutoglou 2009-10; Luraghi, Magnetlo, and Habicht 2012.

157. Roebuck 1941: 93 attributed the exception in this case to Flamininus's personal intervention, but there is no evidence in support of the hypothesis. See Luraghi 2008: 262.

things differently and tried to break away.[158] Plutarch suggests that Philopoimen allowed Megalopolis to retain some of its dependent poleis for purely personal reasons, but the parallel with Messene suggests that something else may have been going on here. One wonders whether the koinon deliberately left in their existing relationships some communities that were regarded as being too small to pose a threat to the strength of the koinon by coordinating opposition to it.

It is likely that additional issues were addressed in the process of integrating a new polis into the Achaian koinon. The establishment of local and federal jurisdictions appears to have been a significant concern in the integration of Epidauros in 243, but the inscription recording the process is so fragmentary that the contexts in which the laws of the polis are repeatedly mentioned (T37.7–8, 34; cf. ll. 5–6) are entirely obscure. With Orchomenos the primary concern appears to have been about dispute resolution, as we have just seen, but that inscription makes it clear that all the terms were inscribed on a stele (T39.8–10); it would then have been set up, most likely, in the polis as well as in Aigion, probably at the sanctuary of Zeus Homarios. The integration of formerly dependent poleis of Messene as full members of the Achaian koinon in 182 likewise involved the erection of stelai recording the specifics of each case. And when Sparta was reintegrated in the same year, "a stele was inscribed for public notice, and Sparta became a member of the Achaian koinon."[159] The process of recording and disseminating the terms of membership for each city was vital, for it ensured clarity about the rights and obligations of both polis and koinon. It may well have been these inscriptions to which Lykortas referred when he reminded the Achaian assembly that the koinon was held together by oaths, laws, and stelai.[160]

Although details are scarce, it is clear that the integration of new members into a koinon entailed numerous challenges and the need to resolve disputes between new members and other communities as well as between new members and the koinon itself. Such disputes were difficult to resolve completely, particularly when a city was brought into the koinon without the consent of its entire citizen body.

Responses to Separation.   Failure to resolve existing disputes contributed to subsequent attempts by such cities to break away. The koinon's responsibility for dealing with these secession attempts is part of its broader engagement in self-regulation. The dynamics of fission in this context are as interesting and revealing as those of fusion. Separations occasionally took place with the consent of both koinon and

---

158. T39 for Methydrion. Plut. *Philop.* 13.4–5 with Errington 1969: 90–91; Moggi 1974: 82–84; Rizakis 2008b: 277. There are numismatic reflections of this situation: Warren 2007.

159. Polyb. 23.18.1.

160. Polyb. 24.8.4.

member polis, but it is much more typical to see a koinon fighting to retain its member poleis. The case of Megara provides an illuminating example. From a position of independence it became a member of the Achaian koinon in 243, following the integration of Corinth, but in 224 it was cut off from the rest of Achaia by Kleomenes' control of the isthmos of Corinth, and as a result they joined the Boiotian koinon instead, "with the consent of the Achaians."[161] The only other possible case of separation accepted by the koinon without any resistance is the temporary separation of Orchomenos, Mantineia, and Tegea from Achaia in the period 234–229.[162] When Kleomenes attacked these places in 229, they "were not only allies of the Aitolians but were also members of their koinon at the time."[163] We know that they had briefly been members of the Achaian koinon before going over to Aitolia, but the conditions under which they shifted their participation are unclear.[164] It has, however, been suggested that the Achaians voluntarily ceded these poleis to the Aitolians after the attack of Demetrios II on Arkadian Phylake around 233; the shift would have been made in a momentary panic about the Achaians' ability to defend eastern Arkadia after this attack and in the broader context of the alliance forged between the Achaians and Aitolians in 239.[165] But details are lost, and the bizarre temporary shift from one koinon to the other may not have been made with the consent of the Achaians at all; the evidence is too thin for certainty.

The voluntary concession of a member polis to another koinon was, however, quite rare. Once a community was integrated, the koinon became vitally interested in maintaining its participation, for secession tended to produce military vulnerability as well as a diminution of resources flowing to the koinon in the form of both tax revenues and fighting men. As a result, secession threats, whether evident

---

161. Joining in 243: Polyb. 2.43.5; Plut. *Arat.* 24.3; cf. above n. 114. Separating in 223 to join the Boiotian koinon: Polyb. 20.6.8. M. Feyel 1942b: 127 supposed that the transfer of Megara from Achaia to Boiotia contributed significantly to the Achaian hostility toward Boiotia reflected in Polybios's rather scathing description of the collapse of morals and the failure of the legal system in Boiotia in the late third century (Polyb. 20.6.1–6), but it very likely has more to do with Boiotia's longtime alliance with Aitolia. Megara was, after all, separated from the Achaian koinon with the consent of the Achaians at a time when Kleomenes' overwhelming strength at the isthmos put Megara in real danger.

162. Pausanias's report (7.11.3) that Aitolian Pleuron, which had been given to the Achaians as a reward for their loyalty to Rome at Pydna, separated from Achaia with the support of Sulpicius Gallus in 164 and after a consultation with the Achaian *synedrion,* cannot be verified, although it is not intrinsically implausible. See Gruen 1976: 50–51 for strong hesitation; caution is also heeded by Nottmeyer 1995b: 201 with n. 20. Rizakis 2008b: 280 accepts Pausanias's report at face value and suggests that the separation of Pleuron is another example of peaceful separation from the Achaian koinon.

163. Polyb. 2.46.2.

164. Mantineia as Achaian before it became Aitolian: Polyb. 2.57.1. Orchomenos: Polyb. 4.6.5; Livy 32.5.4.

165. Alliance: Polyb. 2.44.1; Plut. *Arat.* 33.1. Cf. Scholten 2000: 134–36. Demetrios's attack on Phylake: Plut. *Arat.* 34.2–3.

or only suspected, usually prompted the koinon to find some means of diminishing the suspect city's local military strength, either by destroying its walls or by imposing a garrison. The first strategy is exemplified by the Theban response to the democratizing movement in Boiotia in 424 led by Orchomenos and Thespiai but involving other cities as well. Democratizing Boiotia of course meant seeking Athenian support, and insofar as this was done by the poleis rather than the koinon, it was a clear breach of the terms of the federal compromise. The pro-Athenians' plan was botched, but the invasion of Athenian troops led to the battle of Delion. From their position as victors in that battle, the Thebans destroyed the city walls of Thespiai, a measure clearly designed to ensure that it would not in future be able to harbor traitors to the Boiotian cause.[166]

The imposition of garrisons appears to have been a favored strategy of the Achaian koinon when there were suspicions that a member polis might attempt to break away. The garrisons imposed at Mantineia and Kynaitha after these cities were brought back into the koinon are certainly to be understood in this context.[167] The most revealing case, however, is that of Argos in 198. Shortly after the Argives joined the Megalopolitans and Dymaians in walking out of the assembly meeting at which the Achaians decided to repudiate their alliance with Philip V in favor of one with Rome, we find that an Achaian garrison "recently imposed, comprising five hundred young men chosen from all the cities," had been installed at Argos with, significantly, a Dymaian in command.[168] The Dymaians had, of course, joined the Argives in their opposition to the Roman alliance; the Dymaian garrison commander at Argos was probably a dissenting pro-Roman within his own polis. The garrison was clearly put in place to prevent the city from going over to Philip and thereby breaking from the koinon; Achaian suspicion was in fact well grounded, for the Argives soon after opened their gates to an agent of Philip. Most of the garrison departed under a truce when it became evident that they did not have enough force to hold the city in the face of united opposition, but the Dymaian garrison commander, one of a minority of pro-Romans at Dyme, preferred to die in defense of his post.[169] Argive dissent was obvious to everyone, and the stakes were high. But when allegiances were murkier, the Achaians did have recourse to more subtle methods of surveillance and protection. During the Kleomenean War,

166. Th. 4.133.1. Larsen 1960b: 16 assumes that behind the charge of Atticism "there must have been some action on the part of the federal government, some sort of trial and condemnation of the Thespians." I agree with R. J. Buck 1994: 18 that the aim in destroying the walls was "League security rather than Theban imperialism," but his own argument, citing events of 413–401, is hardly relevant or persuasive. It is quite clear that destroying the walls of a city that had harbored traitors was a wise move for a state that cherished its own independence.

167. See above, p. 356.

168. Livy 32.22.8–12, 25.6.

169. Livy 32.25.1–12.

not itself a low-stakes conflict, allegations of disaffection in Sikyon and Corinth began to circulate. In the dire circumstances of the war, Aratos was given absolute power, received a bodyguard of Sikyonians, and was invested with special judicial authority to investigate the rumors of disaffection in his home city as well as in Corinth. In Sikyon those found guilty were executed, but in Corinth Aratos, "trying to seek out and punish the disaffected, only enraged the populace, already suffering and weighed down by the Achaian *politeia.*"[170] Aratos and the Achaian forces were shut out of Corinth, a loss severe enough to prompt the Achaians to make concessions to Antigonos and formally seek his assistance.[171]

Full-fledged secession from a koinon, achieved by violence, elicited a coercive response. The intention was always to return the polis to membership if at all possible. The Theban response to disaffection among Boiotian poleis in the 370s, after the expulsion of the Spartans from the Kadmeia and other Boiotian strongholds, provides an illustrative set of examples. Comparison with Achaian responses to violent secession in the Hellenistic period will suggest that although the Boiotian koinon in the period 386–334 was exceptionally centralized, its responses to this problem were not atypical and should not be taken as a product of the extreme concentration of political power in the hands of Thebes at the expense of its member poleis.

The process of rebuilding Boiotian institutions after 379 was gradual, performed in tandem with the expulsion of lingering Spartan garrisons from Boiotian poleis. Orchomenos, Thespiai, Tanagra, and Plataia were the four that continued to support a Spartan presence. In 375 the garrison at Orchomenos was defeated by Theban forces, and the city appears to have again become a member of the koinon.[172] Sometime in the next two years, Thespiai and Tanagra were also reintegrated, but by 373 Thespiai and Plataia were attacked by Thebes and their cities completely destroyed.[173] We can only infer that Thespiai had effectively seceded, while Plataia

170. Plut. *Arat.* 40.1–2.
171. See above, p. 111 for the broader context.
172. Diod. Sic. 15.37.1–2 (who places the event, probably wrongly, in 376/5; cf. Beloch 1912–27: III.1.155); Plut. *Pelop.* 16.2–3. Tegyra: Plut. *Pelop.* 16–17.10, *Ages.* 27.3; Diod. Sic. 15.81.2.
173. Reintegration is hinted at by Isocr. 14.9: συντελεῖν μόνον εἰς τὰς Θήβας, which should mean that they became members of the koinon who would contribute taxes and soldiers according to agreed-upon principles. Hansen (in Hansen and Nielsen 2004: 457) argues that from 375 to 373 Thespiai was indeed a member of the Boiotian koinon, but this relies on acceptance of the mid-fourth-century date for T13 (*SEG* 25.553), which is virtually impossible; see the commentary in the epigraphic dossier. Isokrates is thus the only source pointing in this direction, and his claim may have been made only to portray the Theban attack of 373 in a more villainous light. Destruction of Thespiai: Xen. *Hell.* 6.3.1, 5; Diod. Sic. 15.46.6, 51.3; Isocr. 6.27; Dem. 16.4, 25, 28. Destruction of Plataia: Xen. *Hell.* 6.3.1, 5; Plut. *Pelop.* 25.7; Diod. Sic. 15.46.6; Paus. 9.1.8; Isocr. 14 passim. For discussion of the fate of Plataia see Amit 1973: 114–18; Tuplin 1986.

had, until 373, resisted any attempts at integration. During this same period the Thebans appear to have been struggling to bring Orchomenos back into the koinon, but it was only after Leuktra, in 370, that they "reckoned the Orchomenians among the territory of their allies."[174] The exact meaning of this phrase is elusive, but it seems to allude to membership in the koinon.[175] In 364, however, some Orchomenians became involved in a plot with Theban exiles to overthrow the Theban democracy and install an aristocracy, an act tantamount to secession. The plot was exposed before it came to fruition, but the Thebans punished the betrayal of Orchomenos by executing the conspirators, destroying the city, and enslaving its remaining inhabitants.[176] More than a matter of revenge, the destruction of Orchomenos sent a signal to other members of the koinon that attacks on the Theban state, which in this period was in one sense coterminous with the Boiotian state, would not be tolerated.[177] If we accept the Theban perspective that "the Thebans" were unproblematically identical to "the Boiotians," these three attacks on member poleis of the koinon appear as federal responses to secession by a member polis atypical only in their severity. And that severity may in fact be explained not as an example of Theban aggression and bloody-mindedness but rather as a product of the radical concentration of political power in the hands of the Thebans. In a less centralized koinon, an attack by one city on another can be met with less extreme forms of violence, and the city preserved for the koinon, precisely because a state in which power is more widely distributed is far less vulnerable. This is best exemplified by the responses of the Hellenistic Achaian koinon to secession by several of its member poleis.

The most radical Achaian response to the secession of a member city was the enslavement of the population of Mantineia in the spring or summer of 223. Having temporarily been ceded to the Aitolian koinon, as we saw, it was brought back into the Achaian in 227 and held with a garrison but revolted again in the next year, this time to Kleomenes. Both Polybios and Plutarch make it clear that the city was not forcibly taken by Kleomenes but handed over to him by its inhabitants. The Achaian garrison was massacred, and on the same day Kleomenes "restored to them their own laws and constitution [politeia]."[178] The political separation from the Achaian koinon was absolutely clear, and the Achaians responded with overwhelming force, taking the city by siege, pillaging the Mantineians'

---

174. Xen. Hell. 4.6.10 for war. Diod. Sic. 15.57.1 for status of Orchomenos in 370. Bakhuizen 1994: 316 takes this passage as stating that the communities of the chōra of Orchomenos were "now to contribute military contingents to the Thebans."

175. So Hansen 2004: 447.

176. Diod. Sic. 15.79.3–6; cf. Dem. 20.109; Paus. 9.15.3.

177. The episode is reduced to an act of vengeance by Buckler 1980b: 184.

178. Polyb. 2.57.1 (voluntary secession), 58.4–8 (massacre of the Achaian garrison); Plut. Cleom. 14.1 (for quote). Cf. Plut. Arat. 39.1, 45.6 (critical of the Achaians).

property, and enslaving the population.[179] Polybios strenuously defends the Achaians' treatment of the Mantineians on the grounds that they betrayed the Achaians and massacred the very garrison that they had requested in the previous year; they suffered only the typical punishment meted out to those who are defeated in war—whereas, he maintains, they deserved something worse. This argument is part of a Polybian diatribe against Phylarchos that is not relevant to our concerns, but that it was exceptionally severe in comparison with the Achaians' other responses to complete secession is clear. Without diminishing the severity of the Achaians' treatment of Mantineia, it is apparently to be explained by the Achaians' sense of outrage at having previous merciful acts rewarded with betrayal.[180]

For when Messene separated itself from the koinon in 183, in circumstances that are lost to us, the Achaians responded with a full-scale military attack.[181] Polybios claims that the Messenian revolt had been led by the city's political leaders, while the populace dared only to voice its support for Achaia and its wish that Messene again become a member of the koinon, as the Achaian military presence lent them a sense of security. The conflict, he implies, was resolved when pro-Achaian Messenians made diplomatic overtures. The terms of the initial settlement were simple: the Messenians were to surrender those responsible for the defection and for the death of the Achaian general Philopoimen (who died in captivity in Messene and was believed to have been poisoned), to accept a garrison on the akropolis, and to refer all other matters to the koinon.[182] The Messenians agreed and "returned to their original position in the state."[183] The final settlement was worked out by the koinon in 181. This involved the separation of several dependent communities of Messene and their integration as independent members of the koinon.[184] If the Messenians had been allowed to retain these dependent communities in 191 in recognition of the fact that the Messenians had not joined the koinon on an entirely voluntary basis, they were now stripped away, probably to weaken the manpower base of a city that now had a history of rebellion. Yet a board of Achaian arbitrators at the same time upheld Messene's claim to the "cities

179. Polyb. 2.58.12, 62.12; Plut. *Arat.* 45.6.

180. Champion 2004: 125 argues that Polybios's account of the punishment of Mantineia "compromises the [Polybian] image of the Achaean *koinon* as a smoothly functioning, disinterested polity based on law and order" when it is compared with the apparently lighter punishment suffered by the Tegeans (2.58.14–15). While the Mantineia episode certainly does not portray the Achaians in a flattering light, Polybios's refusal to occlude it entirely is surely also to be credited.

181. Polyb. 23.12.3, 16.1. Cf. Livy 39.49.1–50.9; Plut. *Philop.* 20; Paus. 8.51.7, mostly focusing on the death of Philopoimen at Messene.

182. Polyb. 23.16.6–7.

183. Polyb. 23.17.1.

184. Polyb. 23.17.2.

POLITICAL COMMUNITIES 369

and territory around Andania and Pylana" against Megalopolis, so this argument cannot be taken too far.[185]

The Achaian response to two secessions by the Spartans, one in 189/8 and the other in 181, expose as the Achaians' primary motive the restoration of the polis to the koinon, which was accomplished both by reducing the Spartans' ability to rebel in future and also by replacing Spartan with Achaian institutions. As in Mantineia, so at Sparta the populace itself was divided, and pro-Achaians were exiled from Sparta in 189 only to join the ranks of the Achaian army.[186] The Spartans then "decreed that the koinon of the Achaians should be renounced" and sought to hand over their city instead to the Romans, attacking those coastal cities of Lakonia that had been separated from Sparta in 191, when it first joined the koinon.[187] When the rebels were defeated, those responsible for the revolt were executed, following a nearly universal practice, the city wall was destroyed, and Sparta was stripped of its control of the Belbinatis, which was ceded to Megalopolis.[188] The second step was to ensure that Sparta became more closely connected with Achaia, and this was attempted by replacing the so-called Lykourgan constitution established by Agis and Kleomenes with Achaian institutions, "for thus they would become of a single body and would more easily reach consensus on all things."[189] This measure was probably not exceptional, if when Kleomenes took over Mantineia in 226 he "restored to them their own laws and constitution." We shall see below that the poleis within koina typically preserved at least some of their local laws, while nevertheless also accepting all the laws of their koinon; it is likely that where local laws did not conflict or interfere with federal laws, they were left in place. So the laws and constitution of Mantineia that were restored by Kleomenes were probably those that pertained to interstate relations, warfare, and the like, which had been suspended in favor of Achaian laws as a necessary step in the process of becoming a member polis. The Spartan constitution, on the other hand, would have been an obvious target for the Achaians, primarily because ever since the reforms of Agis and Kleomenes it had become so strongly associated with the cause of Spartan independence and a return to the city's past glories.[190] This

185. Themelis 2008: col. I.1–24. The Megalopolitans also claimed that the Messenians had given them the right to control two other territories in exchange for payment of half the harvest collected from this land and that this claim was rejected by a tribunal of Milesians.

186. Livy 38.33.6

187. Livy 38.31.5: *decreverunt renuntiandam societatem Achaeis*. With *societatem* here Livy means not "alliance" but "membership in the Achaian koinon," as Briscoe 2008: 113 realizes. Cf. Livy 35.37.2 for a similar usage; Livy 39.36.9–12.

188. Livy 38.33.10–34.9; 39.36.13–37.1.

189. Livy 38.34.4.

190. Cartledge and Spawforth 2002: 45–47, 51–53 on the legal reforms at Sparta under Agis and Kleomenes. Livy 39.37.7–8 for the Achaians' association of these laws with the tyrants.

settlement was more effective, although the Spartans were never unanimous in their support for Achaia and quarrels frequently arose over the fate of pro-Achaians who had been exiled by the Spartans in 189/8, as well as over the disposition of the Belbinatis. It is remarkable and significant that the Achaians responded to such irredentism with equanimity, supporting resolution of the conflicts by arbitration rather than by force.[191] For this reason the Spartans remained members of the koinon until 146, when their quarrel effectively brought about the Roman war that put an end to its history.[192]

The broad powers of the koinon to conduct relations with other states on behalf of its members are widely recognized, and it is the surrender of authority over interstate relations by member poleis that is usually taken as the basic outcome of what I have called the federal compromise. But to suggest that the powers of the koinon stop here would be an unrealistically minimalist analysis of its powers. For the presentation of a united exterior front entails a tremendous amount of internal work. The provision of defense and the conduct of a kind of cooperative diplomacy were only the beginning; the creation of common and binding laws and institutions, which governed everything from participation in religious rituals to the protection of the regional economy to the arbitration of disputes between member poleis, the integration of new members, and the management of attempted and actual secession by member poleis, were the major tasks belonging to the koinon. If the majority of our detailed evidence for the internal workings of a koinon comes from Hellenistic Achaia, there are nevertheless enough parallels from classical and Hellenistic Boiotia to suggest that the situation there was closely parallel. So little is known about the internal organization of the Aitolian koinon as to make comparison there virtually impossible. What is striking, however, is that in Boiotia and Achaia, and probably in Aitolia as well, the koinon relied heavily on the poleis to coordinate their own actions on behalf of the koinon and seems to have facilitated this process by the creation of what modern scholars call districts.

The Powers of the District

Clusters of poleis with distinct sets of responsibilities, districts are best understood as mechanisms of coordination for the member poleis of the koinon, facilitating their participation in the regional state on an equitable and regular basis. The phenomenon of median-scale political organization has recently received welcome attention after several decades of neglect, but it has not been fully considered in relation to the polis and the koinon as part of a complex, multiscalar political

191. See T45 for Spartan resistance even to the process of arbitration, apparently ordered (or facilitated) by the koinon.

192. On the Spartan exiles see Cartledge and Spawforth 2002: 82–84.

system.[193] The work that has been done on the phenomenon of districts proceeds from an implicit assumption that the district is only another artifice of politicians and countenances neither the nonpolitical aspects of subregional interpolis interaction nor the possibility that the districts may represent the formal institutionalization of a whole complex of processes.[194] What is needed is an analysis of the functions of the district in each region as well as a consideration of how districts participate in the regional political system as a whole.

The most explicit ancient description that we have of the extent and functions of districts within a koinon comes from the Oxyrhynchos Historian, who tells us that in Boiotia circa 395 there were eleven *merē*—literally "parts," but we can simply call them districts—each comprised of one large or several smaller poleis.[195] Thebes itself, and together with it the small communities of the Parasopia that were by now integrated into Thebes, made up four districts (map 8, Districts I–IV). Orchomenos and Hyettos formed two (V, VI); Thespiai, Eutresis, and Thisbe combined to make up two (VII, VIII); Tanagra alone was a single district (IX); Haliartos, Lebadeia, and Koroneia made up another one (X), and Akraiphia, Kopai, and Chaironeia combined to form a single district (XI). How precisely the composition of the districts was determined is unclear, but it appears likely that it was based on some principle of proportion in relation to total population; thus the sheer size of Thebes and its integration of several formerly independent poleis would explain why it had four districts.[196]

The fundamental purpose of the districts in Boiotia circa 395 was to coordinate the participation of poleis in the koinon and to ensure that the opportunities and burdens of participation were equitably distributed across the entire state. The opportunity was political; the burdens were economic and military. Political functions first. Each district appointed one boiotarch and sixty councillors, with the result that the highest college of magistrates in the Boiotian koinon as well as its council was always composed of individuals from all parts of the region in proportion to the population size of member poleis.[197] They also sent judges to serve in the federal courts, but the size of these judicial delegations is unknown.[198] The appointment process will have been relatively straightforward for those districts controlled by a single city, like Thebes, Tanagra, and probably Orchomenos and

193. Corsten 1999 has studied the phenomenon in detail, but he does not consider the functions of the districts in relation to those of the koinon and the polis or the ways in which these functions fit together to form a complex but complete polity.

194. E.g., Corsten 1999: 161; Gschnitzer 1954: 452–56.

195. For detailed arguments attempting to establish the precise dates when particular communities entered the various districts, see P. Salmon 1956; Roesch 1965b: 36–43; Dull 1985; Corsten 1999: 27–33.

196. On the Hyettos (or Hysiai) and Orchomenos districts see González 2006: 39–43.

197. *Hell.Oxy.* 16.3–4 (Bartoletti).

198. *Hell.Oxy.* 16.4 (Bartoletti).

Hysiai. But in multicity districts that sent only one boiotarch and sixty councillors, such an arrangement entailed an extraordinary degree of cooperation among poleis for identifying eligible candidates and electing or appointing them.[199] With this privilege of political participation went fiscal and manpower burdens. The districts were required to provide for their councillors' daily expenses during periods of active service, and it was they, rather than the poleis, that paid *eisphora* to the koinon.[200] Finally, each district had to meet a federal military levy of a thousand hoplites and one hundred cavalry.[201]

The districts, then, served as a vital mechanism for the equitable participation of poleis in the koinon, ensuring that the scale of their obligations was correlated to the scale of their privileges, both being placed in some relationship to population size. One implication of this system is that it placed on small poleis the burden of coordinating with their fellow district members in order to meet their obligations. We shall see some details of this process at work in the Hellenistic period. But there is one hint that the Boiotian districts may also have served as instruments for the coordination of rebellion from the koinon. We know that in 395 Chaironeia formed a district with Kopai and Akraiphia (map 8, District XI), which is odd, because unlike all the other districts, this one does not form a territorial unity; it is broken in two by Orchomenos and Hyettos, which make up districts V and VI. In 424, however, Chaironeia was in *synteleia* to Orchomenos.[202] In that year, of course, Orchomenos along with Thespiai led the movement to betray Boiotia to the Athenians. After the Athenians were defeated at Delion, the Boiotians destroyed the walls of Thespiai. But what happened to Orchomenos? It would be surprising indeed if the Boiotians left them unpunished. One way to prevent secession was to break up clusters of allegiance that existed between the polis and the koinon, and the districts may have been a context in which such allegiances could have formed. Might the Boiotians have reorganized the districts to separate Orchomenos from Chaironeia? This is the best explanation I can find for the bizarre District XI attested by the Oxyrhynchos Historian, and it would suggest that although the districts were implemented to facilitate the constructive coordination of poleis on behalf of the koinon, they could also be deployed for subversive ends.

As the Oxyrhynchos Historian introduced his account of the internal organization of Boiotia circa 395, he implied that it had already changed by the time he was writing.[203] When the Boiotian koinon was rebuilt under Theban leadership

199. The precise selection process is unknown, but we can safely assume it to have been undertaken in an oligarchic framework in which eligibility was determined by wealth, probably landed.

200. *Hell.Oxy.* 16.4 (Bartoletti). On the *eisphora* see above, pp. 295–98.

201. *Hell.Oxy.* 16.4 (Bartoletti).

202. Th. 4.76.3.

203. *Hell.Oxy.* 16.2 (Bartoletti).

after 379, the college of boiotarchs was composed entirely of Thebans, and in place of the eleven attested by the Oxyrhynchos Historian, we now find only seven. There is no evidence that the districts were retained; contributions to the Boiotian military and its treasury appear to have been made by individual poleis.[204] The absence of districts in the period 379–335 is a symptom of the complete centralization of power in Theban hands. In the Hellenistic period the districts were restored, probably at the same time that Thebes again became a member of the koinon, in 287. Given that the broad function of the districts was to facilitate an equitable distribution of rights and obligations across the member poleis, it is likely that their recreation was a condition for the renewed membership of Thebes, designed to prevent a repetition of the Thebans' fourth-century abuses.[205] But the Hellenistic districts were only seven, and briefly eight to recognize the integration of new members of the koinon, and this number was certainly suggested by the size of the Theban college of boiotarchs in the fourth century, itself perhaps a function of Theban ideology.[206] Our picture of the districts in Hellenistic Boiotia is drawn entirely from the epigraphic record, but for this period we have so many inscriptions that the conclusions we can draw from them are quite sound.[207]

In chapter 4 we considered ten dedications made by the aphedriates in the name of the Boiotoi (T16–25) as evidence for the existence and functioning

204. C. Müller 2011: 263–66. To the extent that relationships between poleis within the koinon took an institutional form in this period, they were relationships between individual member poleis and Thebes. So Orchomenos is "placed in the category of territory of the allies" (Diod. Sic. 15.57.1) by the Thebans in 370; Chorsiai, for many years a dependent polis of Thespiai, appears to have become an independent member of the koinon (Theopomp. FGrHist 115 F 167; cf. Diod. Sic. 16.58.1; Hansen 2004: 440); Thespiai is described as being in a relationship of *synteleia* to Thebes (Isocr. 14.9). The dismantling of the districts, or at least the decoupling of Chorsiai from Thespiai, may be indicated by two inventories of *hestiatorion* equipment from Hera shrines in each polis (Chorsiai: SEG 24.361, 30.441; Thespiai: Michaud 1974a: 645). Vottéro 1996: 166–70, however, argues that the text long attributed to Chorsiai actually came from Thespiai and proposes that the fragment published by Michaud belongs to the same stone. Vottéro also brings down the traditional date of the texts by a decade. The date has less effect on the evidence of these two stones for the dismantling of sub-Boiotian structures of interpolis cooperation than does the suggestion that they in fact come from the same stone. If they are indeed distinct the inscriptions may have been motivated by the forcible disintegration of the district that had bound them together.
205. Knoepfler 2001c: 19; C. Müller 2011: 266–74.
206. Seven gates of Thebes, etc.: Knoepfler 2000: 358–59.
207. Until quite recently, *communis opinio* held that there were no districts in Hellenistic Boiotia: e.g., Roesch 1982: 501; Gullath 1982: 48–60 (cf. 1989). Fraser 1954, drawing comparisons between Aitolian (T59, T61) and Boiotian documents and literary evidence from Achaia (Polyb. 5.94.1), raised the possibility that both had districts (*telē*). But the case in favor has been presented again, several times, by Knoepfler (1999b: 37–42; 2000; 2001b: 352–62), whose careful arguments have in my judgment established the existence of the districts as a fact.

of districts in the Boiotian koinon after 338. Another series of texts shows cities coordinating their participation in pan-Boiotian festivals, where ephebes displayed their readiness for war, ultimately a federal concern. This coordination, we saw, maps directly onto the hints of district organization implied by the aphedriate dedications.[208] Each group of cities is now called a *telos* rather than a *meros*, as the Oxyrhynchos Historian called them in the fourth century. The evidence of three additional inscriptions, considered together with these, shows clearly and incontrovertibly that the districts played significant political and military roles in addition to the cultic one already discussed.

The only inscription that preserves a complete list of boiotarchs from the Hellenistic period is a proxeny decree of the koinon for one Ophelas of Amphipolis, found at the Amphiareion and dated, very roughly, to the period between 287 and about 225 (T26). The boiotarchs are a Theban (line 1), a Thespian (l. 3), and a Tanagran (l. 3), each of which poleis is always represented in the aphedriate texts, and which accordingly seem each to have commanded a district of its own; an Oropian (l. 2) but not a Plataian; a citizen of Thisbe (l. 4) but no representatives of Lebadeia or Koroneia; an Akraiphian (l. 2) but no representatives of Anthedon, Haliartos, Hyettos, or Kopai; an Opountian (l. 2), and an Orchomenian (l. 3). A Chaironeian serves as secretary of the college (l. 4). The Chaironeian secretary might be taken, with the Orchomenian boiotarch, to over-represent District IV, but with this possible exception this pattern fits precisely into the map of the districts suggested by the aphedriate texts (table 2 and map 9). In the aphedriate texts, we never find representatives of both Orchomenos and Chaironeia in the same year, suggesting that they together made up a single district and that one of their obligations as a district was to send a single aphedriate to the koinon every year. Without additional full boiotarch lists it is impossible to know whether there was some temporary shift in district boundaries or the creation of an additional district that put Chaironeia with Lebadeia, perhaps, or whether the secretary of the college is not included in the district's representation.

If it is correct that the district system was formed in or shortly after 287, then we can be certain that Orchomenos and Chaironeia were originally members of the same district (District IV). A remarkable document from that period, dated by the eponymous archon Philokomos, records an agreement between the two poleis on supplying cavalry to the Boiotian military (T15).[209] It records a distinction between prior and future campaigns (ll. 9–12); the terms of the agreement are to apply to all future campaigns. This distinction may suggest that the agreement stems from the reestablishment, during the archonship of Philokomos, of the

---

208. See above, pp. 221–24.

209. Note that the provision of troops was to be accomplished by districts, but by federal law training was the responsibility of individual poleis: T27.10–16.

TABLE 2 The districts of Hellenistic Boiotia as inferred from epigraphic evidence for patterns of representation by aphedriates in appendix texts 16–25, boiotarchs in appendix text 26, and hostages sent to guarantee a treaty in appendix text 42

Polis	T16	T17	T18	T19	T20	T21	T22	T23	T24	T25	T26	T42	District[a]
Thebes	•	•	•	•	•	•	•	•	•	•	•	•	I
Thespiai	•	•	•	•	•		•	•	•	•	•		II
Tanagra	•	•	•	•	•	•	•	•		•	•		III
Orchomenos	•	•		•		•	•	•		•	•		IV
Chaironeia					•								
Plataia	•	•	•	•	•		•		•		•		V
Oropos								•		•	•		
Lebadeia	•												VI
Koroneia	•	•		•	•	•					•		
Thisbe				•	•						•		
Anthedon	•							•	•				VII
Haliartos	•	•			•						•		
Akraiphia	•	•							•				
Hyettos										•			
Kopai				•									
Opous										•			VIII
Chalkis			•										

[a] The districts as defined by these data are represented in map 9.

district system.[210] From this agreement we learn that Orchomenos appointed three commanders and Chaironeia supplied one; attached to each commander was apparently a contingent of cavalry of the same size. An order for service among the four squadrons is established for duty inside and outside Boiotia. They are to keep track for themselves of the time they serve, because they are evidently to be paid for it, by the district itself, and presumably at different rates depending on whether they served inside Boiotia or outside the region (ll. 26–29). We know from the Oxyrhynchos Historian that in the early fourth century groups of cities cooperated to provide a single contingent for the Boiotian military, but we have for that period no evidence of the mechanisms by which that joint provision was made. From the agreement between Orchomenos and Chaironeia we have just that, though we lack the explicit statement that the districts were used in the Hellenistic period as a means of pooling resources to meet military contributions. Coordination for the provision of troops to the federal military is probably also reflected in a dedication made by a *telos* composed of citizens from Koroneia, Lebadeia, and Thisbe (District VI), another made, simply, by "the *telos* of Koroneia" (District VI again),

210. C. Müller 2011: 269–70.

and a third made by the various teams from Thespiai, which made up its own district (II).[211]

The list of boiotarchs on the proxeny decree for Ophelas of Amphipolis and the agreement between Orchomenos and Chaironeia on the provision of cavalry to the koinon, when understood against the framework supplied by the more plentiful aphedriate dedications, suggest that the districts served again in the Hellenistic period as mechanisms that required smaller poleis to coordinate with one another and participate in the political, military, and religious life of the koinon as a unit. Again this system of coordination promoted an equitable distribution of power that encompassed the radically different sizes of member poleis. Small communities were able to pool their resources to provide cavalry and infantry contingents of a regular size to the federal army, which would certainly have facilitated its administration.[212] If it is correct that the districts were created in 287, when Thebes was reintegrated into the Boiotian koinon, we would be justified in concluding that the Boiotian poleis themselves saw them as a mechanism for the protection of that equitable distribution of power against Theban encroachments.

Our final piece of epigraphic evidence for the existence and functioning of districts in Hellenistic Boiotia is an inscription recording the bestowal of proxeny by the Achaian koinon upon hostages taken from the Boiotian and Phokian koina sometime in the 220s (T42). Eight Boiotian hostages are listed, with patronymic. With only one exception (Plataia and Oropos, District V), no two poleis from the same district are represented (table 2).[213] Existing social structures may regularly have influenced the process by which hostages were taken when a state sought to bind a regional polity to it by this means. So when the Athenians took hostages from Opountian Lokris in 457 after the battle of Oinophyta, they demanded one

---

211. Dedication by *peltophoroi* from Koroneia, Lebadeia, and Thisbe competing in the Pamboiotia: *SEG* 26.551–52 with Knoepfler 1992: 484 no. 145. Dedication by the *telos* of Koroneia after participation in the Pamboiotia: *SEG* 3.354. Dedication commemorating Thespian victory in the Pamboiotia: *IThesp* 201.

212. It is highly unlikely that many of these small communities could have met substantial troop levies on their own. Individual muster lists for Lebadeia and Thisbe, and recently published ephebic lists from Chaironeia, record remarkably small numbers: *SEG* 3.351–53; *IG* VII.3065–68, 3070. Chaironeia: Kalliontzis 2007. Roesch 1979: 247–48 saw these numbers as a product of population decline and assumed that the cooperative military contingents reflected in T15 and *SEG* 26.551–52 were ad hoc measures adopted in the particular context of population shortage, but he had not countenanced the possibility that the pattern of representation seen in the aphedriate texts could bear on the functioning of districts. Rather, these communities were always small (though population decline from the early second century has been suggested by Bintliff 1999, so they may even have been waning) and the functioning of a political scale between the individual polis and the regional koinon provided them with the ability to maintain their small towns—probably the most economically advantageous form of settlement—while still securing a tolerable measure of physical safety.

213. Knoepfler 2000: 362.

hundred of the richest men of the region, probably responding to their knowledge of the existence of the aristocratic Lokrian institution of the Hundred Houses.[214] Similarly the Achaian demand for hostages may have been suggested by the existence of the districts; knowing they were there, and not feeling a need for a hostage from every small polis in Boiotia but still wishing to bind the entire region to its obligation, the Achaians could have demanded a single hostage from every district.

The districts in Boiotia were endowed with political power: they elected, by some unknown mechanism, the highest political and military magistrates of the koinon as their representatives rather than as representatives of individual poleis. The importance of creating political power at this median scale is, however, perhaps best understood when we consider the nonrepresentative aspects of the districts' participation in the koinon. They provided men, arms, and horses for the region's army, and they met the expenses of feeding and provisioning them. No single polis of Boiotia had the human and financial resources to defend itself independently, but the conditions of landscape fragmentation and localized resource specialization made agglomeration impossible, the synoikism of all Boiotia into a single polis. It is in these twin parameters, of interdependence and the need for dispersed settlement, that one of the principal reasons for the creation of a koinon with its distinctive multiscalar political landscape can be found. The deployment of this strategy of representation in the sphere of religion as a means of ensuring the participation of all communities in collective dedications to the gods is not paralleled in any source for the functioning of the districts in the early fourth century. Nor do we have any evidence that the districts had religious lives of their own with, for example, clusters of cults that do not appear elsewhere in the region. For this reason it is more plausible to suggest that the districts were ritualized as an additional means of protecting the institution from change and as a strategy for ensuring the participation of the entire region in the religious activities of the koinon, rather than to suppose that they were initially created in response to existing religious patterns and then took on other kinds of functions. The districts were, in other words, political institutions from the beginning and were at some point—probably in the early Hellenistic period—appropriated to facilitate koinonwide participation in religious activities.

In Achaia and in Aitolia the evidence for political organization at the median scale of the district is rather poorer than it is for Boiotia, and the picture that does emerge from the few indications we possess suggests that the districts here may have played a slightly different role in the larger regional political structures of which they were a part. Despite the difference in details, however, the overarching

214. Th. 1.108.3; Polyb. 12.5.6–8. See Oldfather, *RE* XIII.1 s.v. "Lokris," col. 1244; F. W. Walbank 1957–79: II.334; Hornblower 1991–2008: I.173.

function appears to be the same: facilitating the coordination of poleis in their contributions to the koinon.

In Hellenistic Achaia we find hints of a district comprising a number of poleis. In the previous chapter, we saw that three cities in western Achaia—Dyme, Pharai, and Tritaia—refused to pay their taxes when the koinon failed to meet their request for defensive forces during the Social War.[215] There are good reasons to believe that these three communities formed a district through which they coordinated to meet their military and fiscal obligations to the koinon, just as was clearly the case in Boiotia in the early fourth century and the Hellenistic period. For before they made their appeal to the koinon, full levies were gathered from each of these three cities by the *hypostratēgos* of the koinon, one Mikkos of Dyme.[216] Mikkos clearly had a special interest in protecting the territory of his own city, but he would have been able to levy from all three if they belonged to a single district that typically cooperated to meet a single federal levy. This hunch seems to be confirmed by the fact that two years later one Lykos of Pharai is attested as the *hypostratēgos* "of the *synteleia Patrikē*"—a phrase that is plausibly translated as "the Patraian district."[217] Pharai is of course one of the poleis that withdrew its contributions to the koinon just two years earlier, under the leadership of a *hypostratēgos* from Dyme. Patrai did not emerge as part of the episode in 219, but it would not be at all surprising if it belonged with the smaller cities of western Achaia in a single district, perhaps named after the largest polis included in it. Much later, in 146, an Achaian force was fighting in Phokis against the Romans. The contingent is described as "the Patraians and the force that contributed [*syntelikon*] with them," perhaps an allusion to forces from Pharai, Tritaia, and Dyme that were mustered with the Patraians.[218] Polybios occasionally refers to certain magistrates called *apoteleioi* who are clearly subordinate to the *hypostratēgos* and who seem to be military magistrates within the district system.[219] All this makes it clear that the *synteleia* had a role very similar to what we have seen for the districts in early fourth-century Boiotia: it facilitated the coordination of poleis to meet military levies and taxes imposed by the koinon. But the coordinated refusal of Pharai, Tritaia, and Dyme to pay their taxes when the koinon failed to send troops to defend their territory points to the fact that an institution designed to facilitate the equitable participation of poleis in the koinon could also become a mechanism for the coordination of revolt, echoing

215. Polyb. 4.60.4–5; and see above, pp. 299–300.

216. Polyb. 4.59.2.

217. Polyb. 5.94.1 with F. W. Walbank 1957–79: I.624–25 for a crucial textual emendation.

218. Polyb. 38.16.4.

219. Polyb. 10.23.9 (with F. W. Walbank 1957–79: II.228), 16.36.3. Cf. Aymard 1938: 90 n. 1; Larsen 1968: 221; Corsten 1999: 166–69.

the hint, explored above, of coordinated revolt on the part of Orchomenos and Chaironeia in Boiotia in 424.

Are there good reasons for thinking that the Patraian *synteleia* was one of several, and that these districts could have had some political function as they did in Boiotia? It has been argued that it was the only one in existence, but this is not especially compelling, for there is nothing so unique about western Achaia that would demand it, nor does it seem consistent with any other evidence to suppose that the koinon would tolerate formal interpolis organization so strong that it could foster secession in just one part of its territory.[220] We do have one inscription that has been cited as evidence for district organization in Achaia: the late third-century law of the *nomographoi* on procedures for sacrifices to Hygieia at Epidauros (T41). Thomas Corsten has argued that this list is a product of representation on the college of *nomographoi* by district and not by polis.[221] Twenty-four lawgivers from a total of seventeen communities are listed; some of those communities (e.g., Argos, Megalopolis, Sikyon, Aigion, and Dyme) have more than one representative on the college. The four cities that we already know to have made up a *synteleia* in western Achaia, namely Patrai, Dyme, Pharai, and Tritaia, are listed together (lines 18–23), and they together contribute five *nomographoi*. The list is composed in roughly geographical order, from the east (Epidauros) to the west (Dyme) and then south (Ascheion). On the basis of the pattern of representation for the sole attested district in Achaia, Corsten divides the list into units so that each has five representatives, explaining the odd one with only four by hypothesizing that the fifth was the secretary whose name is lost in lines 29–30. Corsten's divisions are arbitrary, however, and it is difficult see how some of the larger poleis like Corinth would go entirely unrepresented.[222] It is impossible to suppose that within the districts the number of representatives sent by each polis was determined by the luck of the draw, for we find the largest cities sending three representatives (Megalopolis and Argos), the medium-sized ones sending two (Sikyon, Aigion, Dyme), and the small ones sending one.[223]

220. Larsen 1968: 220–21 and 497 with n. 3. Larsen 1971: 85 argues that the *synteleia* of Patrai was the only one in existence; he explains this oddity as a result of the fact that the four poleis that it comprised were the four founding members of the revivified koinon in 280, as well as a product of the vulnerability of western Achaia with respect to Elis. I agree with Corsten 1999: 169–70 that although the *synteleia* of Patrai is the only one of which we are informed, there were probably others.

221. Corsten 1999: 170–72.

222. E.g., Corsten 1999: 171 assumes that Pheneos, Pellene, Boura, and Aigion constituted a district with five *nomographoi* to represent it (ll. 13–17), and that Kleonai, Sikyon, and Phleious, which have together only four, would have made up a district along with the fifth *nomographos*, who was also secretary. It is, however, equally possible to divide these names so that Kleonai, Sikyon, Phleious, and Pheneos together made up a district represented by five lawgivers, while Pellene, Boura, and Aigion had only four (plus the secretary).

223. Lehmann 1983a: 246–47.

One wishes in a case like this for another, similar inscription that might clarify matters. After all, the district system in Hellenistic Boiotia can be discerned only by compiling data from a dozen different texts. Our wish has been granted, but our hopes dashed, by the recent publication of a new list of names believed to belong to the Achaian *nomographoi* (T44). Unfortunately, it does not allow us either to refute or to confirm Corsten's hypothesis: the stone is broken at the top, and thus the list of names is incomplete. It lists twenty-one representatives from seventeen cities in Arkadia, Messenia, Triphylia, and Lakonia; clearly the cities of old Achaia are missing, as are the cities of Elis, the Argolid, and the Corinthia. For this reason, a total of some forty to forty-four members have been postulated for the college of *nomographoi* in this period.[224] The growth of the college is clearly a result of the growth of the koinon itself; both Lakedaimon and Messene are represented on the college, which places the stone certainly after 191. But the only cities that appear on both lists are Lousoi and Ascheion (which on both occasions send one representative) and Megalopolis (which first has three and later only two representatives). The only clear consistency between the lists is the principle of granting three representatives to the largest, two to the medium-sized, and one to the smaller cities. There remain, then, good reasons for being cautious about the existence of districts in Achaia directly analogous to those in Boiotia, despite the fact that the case of western Achaia appears so strikingly comparable.[225]

Epigraphic evidence from third-century Aitolia points to the existence of districts within the koinon that had their own council, led by a boularch. These documents show that the Aitolian districts had a considerable degree of independence within the larger regional system in which they participated, and though the evidence for their role in the mustering of troops and administration of the region's military is less clear than in Boiotia and even Achaia, there are compelling hints that the situation was similar. They may thus have shared with the districts of these other states the fundamental role of serving as a mechanism for the coordination of member communities in their participation in the koinon.

Aitolian documents attest two *telē*—the same term as is used in Hellenistic Boiotia, and clearly akin to the third-century Achaian *synteleia*. The two *telē* attested for Aitolia are centered on Ozolian Lokris and Akarnanian Stratos. The *Lokrikon telos* is known from a series of second-century manumission decrees. The first, found at Delphi (T61), records a boularch of the *Lokrikon telos* from the Lokrian polis Physkeis; the individual who freed his slave was a citizen of Amphissa, and the manumission took place at Delphi. We can thus presume that each of these three poleis was part of the Lokrian district. Two additional decrees found at Naupaktos make it clear that this important coastal city was likewise

---

224. Rizakis 2008a: 169.
225. Cf. Rizakis 2003: 104 and 2008a: 169.

part of the Lokrian district.[226] In these texts, the boularch is a citizen of Agrinion, which allows us to add that important city to the district.[227] The title of the eponymous magistrate itself implies that the district had a council in which to deliberate matters pertaining to its own political authority and administrative responsibilities. Regrettably we are ill informed as to just what those responsibilities were.

The other epigraphically attested Aitolian district was centered on the old Akarnanian city of Stratos, situated on the western bank of the Achelöos River, which marked the division between Akarnania and Aitolia until the partitioning of Akarnania in the 240s, after which Stratos and the southwestern part of the region, as far as Oiniadai, became part of Aitolia.[228] A document recorded at Thermon preserves the outcome of an arbitration in a territorial dispute between Oiniadai and Matropolis (T59) that was carried out by the *Stratikon telos* in the 230s. The provenance of the stele suggests that this Stratian district was authorized by the Aitolian koinon to undertake the arbitration. Oiniadai and Matropolis, like Stratos, are both west of the Achelöos and prior to the partitioning were firmly Akarnanian cities.[229] It is unclear whether the Aitolian koinon ordered the arbitration process and delegated the task of judgment to the Stratian district or whether the decision was inscribed at Thermon simply to publish an act that was by definition under the authority of the district. But for all its autonomy in strictly local matters, the district is inextricably bound up with the Aitolian koinon: the two parties to the dispute are obliged to pay for the inscription of the decision, to be set up in the sanctuary of Apollo at Thermon, along with all the decrees of the koinon itself.[230]

It is striking that both of the clearly attested districts within the Aitolian koinon seem to be comprised of groups that were not originally Aitolian, and it has been suggested that the creation of *telē* along those old group lines was effectively a "concession" made by the Aitolians to "preexisting regional structures," perhaps to respect feelings of ethnic unity.[231] This is certainly correct but probably an oversimplification. First, Aitolia itself comprised subregional groups in the fifth and fourth centuries, at least some of them incorporating multiple communities (map 5), and insofar as the koinon emerged out of a process of cooperation it is likely that these groups pressed to retain a distinct existence as they transformed themselves into

---

226. *IG* IX.1² 3.618 and 625.

227. Membership of Agrinion in the Lokrian district is problematic: see Corsten 1999: 149–50.

228. For the Achelöos River as boundary T57.5–7. For the partitioning of Akarnania see above, p. 105, and Scholten 2000: 88–92.

229. The judges in the case (*gaodikai*) came from Thyrrheion; it is unclear whether this was part of the Aitolian koinon or not. See Scholten 2000: 91 n. 110 with references.

230. Corsten 1999: 155–56.

231. Quote from Scholten 2000: 64; Funke 1985: 26–27 (*non vidi*).

members of a larger state.[232] Second, feelings of ethnic unity were certainly not all that bound these groups together. The Ophiones, comprising the Kallieis—the people living around Kallion—and the Bomieis, are one of the parts of the Aitolian *ethnos* attested by Thucydides in 426.[233] And we have seen that the region around Kallion or Kallipolis, known today as the Strouza region, was bound together by resource specialization and economic interdependence (map 6).[234]

Another illuminating example of the economic integration of these subregional groups in Aitolia comes from the area around Agrinion, the territory of the Agraioi. This group lived to the northwest of Aitolia on the east bank of the Acheloös River and were ruled by a king in the fifth century.[235] They were still independent in 338, but by 314 they seem to have become part of the Aitolian koinon.[236] Their membership did not, however, erase their identity as a group, for in the 260s the Agraioi, clearly as Aitolian representatives, along with the Stratioi as Akarnanian representatives, were asked to arbitrate in any dispute that might arise over the boundaries of Pras after the alliance between Aitolia and Akarnania (T57.8, 10). In the early second century they retained a distinct group identity, which suggests that when the Agraioi became members of the koinon, they were treated for administrative purposes as a unit, perhaps as a district like the Stratian and Lokrian *telē*.[237] We have no narrative in the ancient sources of the process whereby the Agraioi became part of the Aitolian koinon in the late fourth century,

232. Th. 3.94.3 for the Eurytanes, Ophiones, and Apodotoi as *merē* of the Aitolian *ethnos*. T48 for the Erxadieis, who appear to act with complete political autonomy. Their territory is unknown; see the commentary in the epigraphic dossier. T50, T51 for four additional population groups with distinct and demarcated territories in the fourth century, documents that make unlikely the theory that these three groups alone comprised all Aitolia in the classical period: Gschnitzer 1978: 22–23; Hansen 1997a: 175. Bommeljé, Doorn, Deylius, et al. 1987: 15 are more cautious: "The written sources indicate that the Aetolian *ethnos* comprised in late Classical times *at least three* major territorial groups ... : the Ophioneis, the Apodotoi, and the Eurytanes" (my emphasis). Cf. Larsen 1968: 79. See Antonetti 1990: 28 and Antonetti's map 1 for this disposition of population groups. The exact location of the Apodotoi and Ophiones is debated; cf. Antonetti 1988; Klaffenbach 1939a.

233. Th. 3.96.3.

234. See above, pp. 278–81. It is possible that these communities were further united by a common sanctuary at Kallion. A fifth-century *lex sacra* found built into the wall of a house in modern Kallion provides our most explicit evidence for organized cult activity here (Sokolowski 1969: 214 n. 128). Beneath the fourth-century temple excavators found a geometric-period structure of some kind and figurines, including a bronze horse very similar to that found at nearby Halikyrna: Themelis 1983; cf. *AD* 27 (1972) *Chron.* 439. But the catchment area of the cult cannot be determined with any certainty.

235. Th. 3.106.2; cf. 4.77.2, 101.3. The general location of the Agraioi can be deduced from Th. 2.102.2.

236. In 338 they are listed apart from the Aitolians as members of the League of Corinth: *Staatsverträge* III.403b. Their incorporation in the Aitolian koinon by 314 is suggested by Diod. Sic. 19.67.3–68.1, provided that Agrinion really was part of the territory of the Agraioi.

237. Polyb. 18.5.7–8.

but economic and strategic considerations may have played a significant role. The territory of the Agraioi comprised the northeastern portion of the central Aitolo-Akarnanian plain, carved out and well watered by the Achelöos. The plain itself is valuable, but its relationship to the coast and to the mountains that rise into the Pindos make it of crucial importance. In chapter 5 we saw in detail how much more effectively the resources of the mountains could be harnessed when brought into conjunction with the sea. It was only through the Agraid that passage could be made between Aitolia and Akarnania on the one hand, and Amphilochia and Ambrakia on the other. To the east of the Agraid were the Eurytanian communities that controlled access to the Spercheios Valley.[238] It was, then, a crossroads for transportation, certainly as important for traders and pastoralists as for generals and their armies.

Two coin hoards found at Agrinion provide an index of the economic importance of the region. A hoard buried in the fifth century contained a total of thirty-two didrachmas of Tanagra, Aigina, and Elis, suggesting that at least some of the people who lived in the area were far more connected to the economic system of the wider Corinthian Gulf than has been realized.[239] The enormous Hellenistic Agrinion hoard shows that the area became even more heavily integrated economically.[240] It is highly unlikely that when the Aitolians brought the Agraioi within their koinon they were ignorant of the economic importance of the territory or unmotivated by it. When the Agraioi became a part of the Aitolian koinon in the late fourth century, it appears that they retained a certain degree of coherence as a territorial entity, acting in concert in a judicial capacity in the context of the territorial dispute over Pras in the 260s. Their territory was strategically and economically valuable, and it had functioned as a unit for several centuries before incorporation; that it was allowed to continue functioning in that way suggests that the Aitolians were keenly interested in harnessing its resources without disrupting the regional structure. This may have been the purpose of the creation of districts, attested clearly only for Lokris and the area around Stratos. If this is correct, the Aitolians' motivation may have been as much the economic one of facilitating the incorporation of flourishing subregional economies into their koinon as it was a concession to feelings of ethnic unity. We do not know whether the telē of the Aitolian koinon served as a mechanism for the coordination of multiple member communities in their fiscal contributions to the koinon, as was certainly the case in Boiotia in the early fourth century and in western Achaian in the late third, but if the treasurers (tamiai) of the Aitolian koinon are in fact representatives of

---

238. See Lévêque 1957: I.362 n. and Hammond 1976: 31–32 for discussion of the communication routes in this area.

239. Agrinion 1931? (*IGCH* 37).

240. For the Hellenistic Agrinion hoard see Thompson 1968.

districts, as has been suggested, it would appear highly likely.[241] And in this respect the institutionalization of old ethnic groups as districts of the koinon would have served precisely to make the economic resources of these groups more available to the koinon as a whole.

In Achaia and Boiotia the functions of the districts seem to have been very much alike: mustering troops and leaders for those military contingents, all to be sent to the army of the koinon; paying contributions in wartime (and perhaps in peace as well, though we have no record for it); and electing magistrates for the various colleges and boards of the koinon itself, ranging from lawgivers to dedicators to arbitrators. The only evidence we have for deliberative competence at the scale of the district in any region is the mention of a boularch of the Lokrian *telos* in early second-century Aitolia. In general, then, the districts seem to have been formalizations of long-standing intercommunal relationships driven by economic need and in many cases articulated and reinforced by common cults. The role of the districts in each case was primarily to muster financial and human resources for the koinon, bridging the gap between poleis and other small member communities and the larger regional state.

The Powers of the Polis

Although it is widely accepted that poleis within a koinon had authority over local affairs but none over relations with other states, control of which belonged exclusively to the koinon, attempts to test or to nuance this claim are rare.[242] It was once argued that the Achaian poleis had wide latitude in making agreements and conducting relations with other, nonmember states, but the evidence cited in support of this position has since been dramatically redated and shown to be irrelevant to the question.[243] Others take the view that it was the fate of the member polis to gradually lose its rights until it became completely subordinated to the koinon, a blow that was softened only by the concession of privileges like landownership (*enktēsis*) and intermarriage (*epigamia*) that could be exercised throughout the territory of the koinon.[244] The right of cities to be represented in the magistracies and deliberative bodies of the koinon has also been cited as a vital component of

241. Corsten 1999: 144–48. See the commentary to T57 for discussion of the problems associated with this interpretation.

242. Clearest is *Hell.Oxy.* 16.2 (Bartoletti).

243. Larsen 1971, based heavily on *Staatsverträge* III.567, then thought to be a *symbolon* between Stymphalos and Aigeira and dated to 219, when both poleis were part of the Achaian koinon. But a new reading of the stone shows it to be a *symbolon* between Stymphalos and Demetrias, the name given to Sikyon in the brief period ca. 303–300 (Taeuber 1981; Thür and Taeuber 1994: 158–251 no. 17; Thür 1995) when neither was a member of the Achaian koinon. No wonder the cities were so remarkably free to make agreements with each other.

244. Rizakis 1990b: 109.

their autonomy.[245] In principle, of course, polis autonomy of some kind is vital to the very existence of the federal compromise; without it, the federal state would become a unitary state or an empire.[246] But the nature and shape of this autonomy, the actual powers of the member poleis of a koinon, and the ways in which these intersected with the powers of the koinon, remain badly known.[247] There is, however, enough evidence at least to begin to answer the question, by outlining the nature of the autonomy of poleis within a koinon. This appears to have had five facets: control of the polis over its own sanctuaries; control of the polis over its own finances; the preservation of local magistracies, laws, and courts, insofar as these did not conflict with federal laws; control of the polis over its own citizenship rolls; and interaction by the polis with other states in ways that had neither military nor political implications. I shall treat these five facets of polis autonomy within the koinon in turn.

The right of poleis to control their own sanctuaries is in effect a subset of the general right to control their own resources.[248] But the sanctuary is the local resource about which we are best informed, and because it was so efficacious, in ways that we have already seen, it occasionally became a point of contention between polis and koinon as they negotiated the terms of the federal compromise. One example should suffice for illustration of such a basic point: in the 220s the Boiotian polis Akraiphia reorganized its festival for Apollo Ptoios and sent ambassadors to all the other poleis in Boiotia, inviting them to participate in the expanded celebration, which now included rites for Athena Itonia and Zeus Karaios as well.[249] There is no sign of the koinon in this gesture of inclusion, and the polis of Akraiphia is in full control of its festival and sanctuary. This was certainly the normal state of affairs.

Member poleis of a koinon were also in full control of their public finances. Once they had met their fiscal obligations to the koinon, they were completely free to conduct a fiscal policy of their choice. This means that they were free to tax or not to tax, to spend, and to borrow in whatever way they wished. But one result of this freedom was that they would receive no help from the koinon if they became indebted; this, at least, is the implication of several documents from Hellenistic Boiotia that record the public indebtedness of member poleis of a koinon.

245. P. Salmon 1985.

246. Thus Ténékidès 1954: 45–46 cites polis autonomy as the second law of federalism, along with the law requiring the participation of poleis in the deliberative organs of the federal government and the law that all member states must have an equal interest in the federal government.

247. Roesch 1973: 259.

248. Cf. R. Parker 1998: 184: "Membership of a federation or an alliance . . . normally had no impact on the cults of a city even when such membership severely restricted its freedom of action in other areas."

249. SEG 3.354; IThesp 201.

Orchomenos, Akraiphia (T29, T30), and Chorsiai (T32) all had to borrow money—in the first two cases from individuals and in the third from another polis (Thisbe).[250] It is remarkable that nowhere do we have evidence of member poleis borrowing from the koinon—receiving what we might call a federal bailout. On the contrary, the koinon could, in extreme circumstances, be brought in to enforce the terms of the loan made by the lender to the polis.[251] Autonomy had its price.

Several literary sources lend the impression that poleis had very little room to craft and retain their own laws and magistrates. The Oxyrhynchos Historian reports that circa 395 each polis in Boiotia had four councils (boulai, membership in which was determined by wealth), that these four councils sat in rotation, and that decisions were made only in consultation with the other three councils. The anonymous historian admits no local differences in bouleutic structure, and the implied uniformity has about it a strong whiff of centralized decision making.[252] In a similar vein, Polybios remarks that the Achaian poleis of the Hellenistic period all used the same laws, councillors, magistrates, and judges, but to interpret that as an indication of complete uniformity of political organization at the local level would be a mistake.[253] Polybios is referring here to the legal and political institutions of the koinon, in which each of the cities participates. Although abundant evidence is lacking, there are enough indications of legal autonomy and local variation in polis magistracies and organization to justify real suspicion of this generalized impression of regional uniformity.

The legal autonomy of member poleis is evident in each of the three regions that form the focus of this study. When Epidauros became part of the Achaian koinon in 243, it appears that its laws and judicial system were maintained (T37.7–9). Megalopolis, as we have seen, became a member of the Achaian koinon in 235, but its population was expelled by Kleomenes in 223 and then brought back by the Achaians in 217. In the process of refoundation the Megalopolitans fell into dispute with one another over various matters, including "the laws written by Prytanis, an illustrious member of the Peripatetic School, whom Antigonos [Doson] had sent to them as a lawgiver."[254] The koinon had clearly stayed out of the process, allowing the Megalopolitans to make their own arrangements, seeking the help of the Achaians' Macedonian ally. It was only in arbitration of the dispute that the Achaians became involved.[255] We have only one record of a specific law of an individual

---

250. Orchomenos borrowed from Eubolos, a Phokian: Migeotte 1984: no. 12 (Chandezon 2003: no. 7).

251. *IG* VII.3172 with Roesch 1965b: 146–52 and 1973: 262–63.

252. *Hell.Oxy.* 16.2 (Bartoletti).

253. Polyb. 2.37.10–11.

254. Polyb. 5.93.8. Prytanis of Karystos, the Peripatetic, is honored by the Athenians in 226: *IG* II² 838 l. 32.

255. Cf. Roy 2003: 83.

member polis of the Achaian koinon, and it reveals that the polis's jurisdiction was not restricted to, for example, crimes of a noncapital nature. An inscription records the execution by the polis of Dyme of six individuals who were convicted of producing counterfeit coins; there is no sign that the koinon was in any way involved.[256] In Aitolia too member poleis retained their local laws: when the koinon appointed judges to arbitrate a territorial dispute between the member cities Melitaia and Pereia in the late third century, the result was something like a political synoikism for the two communities, with the provision that they would use the same laws (T60.28–29). For Boiotia the principle can be easily illustrated by the remarkable magistrate list from late third-century Thespiai, which includes offices otherwise unknown in Boiotia, including overseers of children (*paidonomoi*) and of women (*gynaikonomoi*), a *hendekarchos*, an official in charge of roads (*hodagos*), and one in charge of the harbor at Kreusis (*limenarchos*).[257] Likewise at Orchomenos a *nomōnas*, a magistrate apparently in charge of regulating use of the city's pasturable land, is unattested elsewhere.[258] So although it is possible that in early fourth-century Boiotia the local governments were all organized at the highest level in the same way, we should remain aware of the possibility that then, as was demonstrably the case in the Hellenistic period, there was a great deal of local variation in administrative structures and, by extension, local laws.

Control by member poleis over their own citizenship rolls—determining who could and who could not become a citizen—is clearly attested by three documents from Hellenistic Achaia. At some point in the third century Dyme engaged in the sale of citizenship to foreign residents (T35), certainly as a means of boosting both population and public revenues. The process was clearly sanctioned by the koinon, for the new Dymaian citizens became eligible, it is explicitly stated, to hold the magistracies of both polis and koinon (ll. 32–34). A text from Achaian Tritaia likewise records the sale of citizenship to foreigners in the third century, and despite its fragmentary state it is clear that the polis was in complete control of the process from deliberation to execution.[259] Another text from Dyme records the bestowal of citizenship on "those who fought the war with us and together saved the city."[260] It is likely that the recipients of this award were the mercenaries hired by the Dymaians in 219/8 to defend their territory against Aitolian attacks during the Social War, when the Achaian koinon failed to send the forces to which Dyme was entitled.[261]

256. *Syll.*³ 530 with Thür and Stumpf 1989.

257. Roesch 1965b: 231–45.

258. Migeotte 1984: no. 12 (Chandezon 2003: no. 7), ll. 43–44.

259. Rizakis 1990b: 129–34 no. 3 (*SEG* 40.400); Rizakis 2008a: 134–37 no. 94.

260. *SEG* 40.393; Rizakis 2008a: no. 4 ll. 6–10.

261. Polyb. 4.60.4–5; see above, pp. 119 and 299–300. The document provides no internal clues about its date, which is based entirely on context: Hiller von Gaertringen, *Syll.*³ 529 n. 8; M. Feyel 1942b: 295; Launey 1949–50: II.657; F. W. Walbank 1957–79: I.536; Gauthier 1985: 200; Rizakis 1990b: 127 and 2008a: 53.

It is in a certain way surprising that member poleis of a koinon had the right to grant citizenship to foreigners. For, as the record of the sale of citizenship to foreigners at Dyme makes clear (T35), citizens of poleis that were members of a koinon automatically became citizens of the koinon too, eligible for all its privileges but also subject to all its demands. The poleis' right to bestow citizenship on foreigners thus affected the shape of the koinon's own citizenship, showing that at least in one small way the exercise of power was multidirectional in the koinon, more a lateral than a hierarchical politics, and in this way the frequent descriptions of the koinon as a system ring especially true.[262]

If member poleis could bestow citizenship on individual foreigners, in what ways could they interact with foreign states and their representatives? The evidence suggests that they were free to do so in matters that had no military or overtly political implications. First, they were free to bestow proxeny on foreigners, and did so regularly. These honored individuals usually received the right to purchase land and real estate, tax freedom, and security in war and peace (which amounted to immunity from seizure), but they received no political privileges.[263] Member poleis were also generally free to receive *theōroi*, sacred ambassadors, representing foreign states. So when ambassadors from Magnesia on the Maeander went to Aitolia in the late third century seeking recognition of the inviolability and elevated status of the local festival in honor of Artemis Leukophryene, they were received by individual poleis.[264] Whether this was a gray area in polis authority or whether the Achaians simply took a different view than the Aitolians is unclear, but when the same *theōroi* went to Achaia, they were received by the koinon and made no visits to the several Achaian poleis.[265] We have one case in which a member polis of a koinon itself sent ambassadors to foreign states, but again the business they had to conduct was neither military nor political. When Dorian Kytenion sought

262. The koinon had a limited reciprocal impact on the fabric of the poleis, for its grants of proxeny to foreigners usually included the included the right for the proxenos to acquire land and real estate, a right that could be exercised anywhere in the koinon (e.g., T6, T7, T9, T11–T12 for fourth-century Boiotia; T13, T26 for Hellenistic Boiotia; T42 for Hellenistic Achaia; T49 for fourth-century Aitolia; T54 for Hellenistic Aitolia; see Marek 1984: 23, 26, 46–48 for lists, complete as of 1984, of proxeny decrees issued by each of our koina). It is quite rare (e.g., T49.3) that the honors bestowed on a proxenos by a koinon include citizenship (shown by Marek 1984: 152–55 to be potential citizenship). The koinon might indirectly have power over the citizenship rolls of a polis if it could be proved that a citizen of one member polis had the right to relocate to another member polis and become a full citizen there, but this cannot be proved. Ehrenberg 1960: 127–28 is too confident.

263. Examples are abundant: T27 for a Thespian proxeny decree for an Athenian; Kalliontzis 2007 for proxeny decrees of Chaironeia for Aitolians. Rousset 2006 publishes a dossier of eighteen proxeny decrees issued by Kallion (Kallipolis) in Aitolia, probably in the early second century; these are the first known proxeny decrees issued by an Aitolian polis.

264. *I.Magn.* 28.

265. *I.Magn.* 39; Rigsby 1996: no. 89.

contributions for the rebuilding of its city walls in the 220s, the city planned a tour to multiple states to make its appeal; but before it did so, it sought and received the approval of the Aitolian koinon, of which it was then a member.[266] It is unclear whether Kytenion sought approval from the Aitolian koinon because the right of the polis to send ambassadors on the mission was in doubt or whether it was looking for an endorsement that would carry some weight with intended audiences. But one final episode suggests that in gray areas poleis did indeed seek the permission of the koinon and enlisted its help before engaging directly with foreign states. When the Elateians, who had been harbored at Stymphalos for several years in the early second century, sought permission from the Roman consul Manius Acilius Glabrio to go home again, the Stymphalians assisted them not by sending an embassy directly to Glabrio but by enlisting the Achaian koinon to do so (T43.10–13). For although they apparently had the right to welcome foreigners into their city on a quasi-temporary basis (just as they had the right to grant citizenship to foreigners), embassies to foreign states or their representatives on nonreligious matters was clearly within the purview of the koinon alone. The episode over the return of the Elateians to their city reveals the limits of a member polis's ability to interact with a foreign state or its representatives.

If the evidence is fragmentary, scattered, and nowhere as full as we would want, it is nevertheless adequate to provide a clear sketch of the terms of the federal compromise, of how political power was distributed across the koinon, the district, and the polis. From it we see that although the koinon had exclusive control over deliberation and decision making in matters of war, peace, alliance, and interactions with foreign powers that might lead in one of those crucial directions, the poleis were by no means excluded from interacting with foreign states; and the koinon, as we have seen, extended its purview also to domestic matters such as legislation, management of the region's economy, its cultic activities, and the resolution of disputes between member poleis and between poleis and the koinon itself. The koinon as a political entity was emphatically not, in other words, functional only in its relations with foreign states, nor were its member poleis politically irrelevant.[267] Rather, the political power of the koinon was intricately interwoven with the power of the poleis and districts that, together with the koinon, created a complex and multifaceted political system for the governance and protection of an entire region. Yet we have already seen that the koinon exerted considerable effort in responding to attempts at secession and rebellion by member poleis. That is not surprising, given that the poleis were not entirely stripped of power but were instead given vital functions within the koinon. The powers they

266. Bousquet 1988b: ll. 73–110; cf. Scholten 2003: 77.
267. *Contra* Giovannini 1971. Cf. F. W. Walbank 1976–77: 25–37.

held gave them some willingness and ability to seek complete autonomy, to refuse to recognize the koinon's right to exercise any power at all over them. The koinon's response to those secession attempts was occasionally overwhelming: member poleis were entirely obliterated. These instabilities on their own may suggest that the terms of the federal compromise were in the Greek case inadequate to prevent the entire fragile structure from being undermined. Yet the koinon was, broadly speaking, a remarkably long-lasting political structure in the Greek world, under-mined not from within but from without, by the Roman conquest of Greece. Given the signs of instability we have detected in our study of the terms of the federal compromise, how can we explain the koinon's longevity?

ENFORCEMENT, NEGOTIATION, AND INSTITUTIONAL STABILITY

The twin dilemmas that lie at the heart of every federal state make political stability remarkably tricky. In observing this fact, Riker argued that it could be achieved only when a state's institutions granted the federal government enough power to provide those public goods that could not be delivered by lower levels of political organization, and to keep the member states in line with their obligations, but not so much power that it became capable of usurping the authority vested in the member states.[268] But the allocation of powers is not, on its own, enough: a federal government and member states need to have incentives to adhere to the terms of the federal compromise, and both parties need to have ways to check the abuses of the other, to enforce those terms.[269] These conditions, yielding what has been called "self-enforcing federalism," are central to the stability of federal institutions.[270] Yet political stability does not mean the rigid persistence of a fixed set of institutions, the complete absence of institutional change. Indeed the ability of a state to respond to both endogenous and exogenous change over time is crucial to its overall stabil-ity; constant, gradual, and incremental institutional change is well known to mod-ern historians and political scientists.[271] For the koinon our evidence is not usually fine-grained enough to detect such frequent adjustments, but significant changes are occasionally attested, and analysis of them should contribute to an explanation of how the terms of the federal compromise were negotiated over time and how the koinon, despite its intrinsic fragility, survived for such an implausibly long time.

268. Riker 1964.

269. Incentives: Bednar, Eskridge, and Ferejohn 2001: 226 for the federal case; cf. Greif, Milgrom, and Weingast 1994; Greif 1998 for the importance of incentives for maintaining institutional equilib-rium in other contexts. Checks as well as incentives: De Figueiredo and Weingast 2005.

270. De Figueiredo and Weingast 2005.

271. Levi 1990; North 1995; Ferejohn and Weingast 1997; Greif 2006; Shepsle 2006.

We have seen that responding to suspected and actual secession by member poleis was a major facet of the koinon's political power and occupied a good deal of its time in periods of tension. This is a form of policing, one of the ways in which the koinon was authorized to keep the poleis within the terms of the federal compromise to which they had agreed by becoming members. When the koinon responded to suspicions of disloyalty, it not only checked the temptation of an individual polis to renege on its commitments, but it did so as well for other poleis that were looking on. That it had this ripple effect is perhaps suggested by the presence of a Dymaian garrison commander at Argos in 198, put in place shortly after Argos, along with Dyme and Mantineia, refused to go along with the Achaian vote to repudiate the Macedonian alliance in favor of a new one with Rome: the Dymaians may have recognized the value of sticking to their federal obligations when they saw that fighting the koinon to remain independent would be worse than having to surrender the Macedonian alliance in order to remain loyal to Achaia.[272] The Thebans' attack on Plataia in 431 and their destruction of the walls of Thespiai in 423 after the city was found to have been colluding with Athenian democrats, and the Achaian attack on Messene in 182 following its revolt, are all clear examples of the koinon's ability to penalize member states for noncompliance. Although we have no evidence for the way a koinon responded to a member polis that refused to meet its fiscal or military obligations, for example, or that failed to send a magistrate but still expected to be a part of the koinon, it is almost certain that such attempts at free riding happened and that the koinon found ways to keep the polis in line with the terms of the agreement.

Polybios suggests that there was a legal basis for this kind of policing in Achaia: member poleis were obligated to obey the common decisions of the Achaians.[273] So when the Spartans refused to accept the findings of a board of arbitrators in its boundary dispute with Megalopolis in 163, the Achaians imposed a fine on them for noncompliance.[274] In this way what began as a conflict between two member states over territory was transformed into a conflict between a member state and the koinon over noncompliance with an arbitration process that had apparently been endorsed by all parties. The conflict was resolved by legal rather than military means. Foreign states also knew that poleis were obligated to abide by the laws and decisions of the koinon, as is implied by the Athenian embassy sent to the Aitolian koinon in 367, complaining of the failure of several Trichonians to adhere to the koinon's official recognition of the sacred truce for the Eleusinian Mysteries (T52).

272. See above, p. 365.
273. Polyb. 22.12.3, reported by the disgruntled Spartans to the Roman Senate in 185/4.
274. Referred first to Roman legates (Polyb. 31.1.6–7; T45.41–46) and then perhaps to the Achaian koinon (Paus. 7.11.1–2); cf. Ager 1996: 374–80, esp. 379–80.

The legal structures were in place to create and communicate a standard of behavior, and coercive measures existed to enforce those laws. In Boiotia, at least, the koinon had recourse to other, equally powerful but far more subtle means of enforcing the terms of the federal compromise. The board of aphedriates allowed the koinon to ensure that every polis within the koinon, through the presence of its representative, participated in collective dedications made by the koinon.[275] By facilitating their participation the koinon elicited from all its member poleis an expression of contingent consent to the terms of the federal compromise every time a sacrifice was made by the koinon. The fact that the Achaian *nomographoi* were involved in religious legislation suggests that the Achaians may have had similar strategies; although the law regarding sacrifices to Hygieia at Epidauros is fragmentary (T41), and we do not know whether it regulated Achaian participation in particular or sacrifices by the general public, the apparently representative nature of the board of *nomographoi* suggests that in Achaia too the koinon ritualized its institutions in order to elicit expressions of contingent consent to the terms of the federal compromise by its member poleis.

Despite the fact that member poleis and districts held significant forms of power, the koinon by virtue of their cooperation held a preponderance of the military and fiscal power of the state, so the instances in which it elicited expressions of contingent consent or undertook to police its member states for failure to uphold their obligations are not especially surprising. The koinon was in a much more favorable position for policing and enforcing the terms of the federal compromise.

What is more interesting but has gone largely unnoticed is the way in which member poleis could check abuses of the federal arrangement by the koinon. Our only clear evidence for this comes from Achaia, and that may turn out to be significant. One last time, that illuminating episode of 219 when Dyme, Tritaia, and Pharai requested a defensive force from the Achaian koinon to counter Aitolian depredations in their territory: the request was refused, and the cities decided to join together in refusing to pay their taxes to the Achaians, using the money thus saved to hire a mercenary force of their own.[276] Insofar as the successful implementation of extraction policies by a state are actually a means of creating the compliance of subjects and political subunits, refusal to pay is a powerful means of removing the contingent consent granted by acquiescence to a state's demands.[277] This was not an act of secession; it was a means of checking the koinon's failure to deliver defensive support to its member poleis, one of its central functions and the

275. See above, pp. 221–24.
276. Polyb. 4.60.4–5. See above, pp. 299–300.
277. On revenue-extraction policies as a means of creating compliance, see Levi 1988: 48–70. On the concept of contingent consent see Levi 1990.

justification for its ability to collect taxes and levy troops from those poleis. Here the koinon failed to meet one of its most fundamental obligations, reneging on the federal bargain that had been struck. The move was clearly successful, for within two years a citizen of Pharai held the position of *hypostratēgos* of the koinon, effectively the second in command; Pharai and certainly along with it Dyme and Tritaia were active members of the koinon, and we have to assume that in the interim the dispute had been resolved, the koinon called to account for its failure. If the cities once again agreed to contribute their soldiers (and probably also their taxes), they were complying with the koinon's demands and must have received satisfaction that the koinon would again meet its obligations to its member cities. One reason why the dispute appears to have been resolved so easily may be that these cities, on the western edge of Achaian territory, had a credible exit threat. Sharing a border with Elis, a longtime ally of the Aitolians, who had in the recent past made several Peloponnesian cities members of their koinon, the cities of western Achaia could quite plausibly have gone over to them, and the Achaians were certainly aware of that fact, making them perhaps more willing to make amends, or to provide incentives not to decamp, than they might have been with a polis entirely surrounded by other members.[278]

A second example comes from fourth-century Achaia. We have already seen that poleis were normally left in control of their local sanctuaries as part of the federal bargain. Thus when the Ionians were hoping for sacred relics of the cult of Poseidon Helikonios with which they could effect a transfer of the cult to Ionia, they approached the polis of Helike. When their request was refused, the Ionians took it to the Achaian koinon, which voted in favor of granting it—but the Helikeans again refused.[279] Another version suggests a different process with the same implication: the Ionians went directly to the Achaian koinon, which granted their request, but the Helikeans refused to comply on the grounds that "the sanctuary was not common [*koinon*] to the Achaians but was their own. The inhabitants of Boura also joined with them in this."[280] The Ionians attempted their sacrifice, supposing the Achaian consent to be sufficient, but the Helikeans interrupted the sacrifice and seized the sacred ambassadors. Their objection appears to have been twofold: a religious scruple stemming from an oracle warning against Ionians sacrificing at the altar of Poseidon and a political scruple stemming from the sense that by granting the Ionians' request the Achaians had violated the terms of the

---

278. Compare Treisman 1999 for an explanation, along similar lines but from a theoretical perspective, of the willingness of central governments in modern states to provide better economic incentives to states on the margins to combat the political fragmentation associated with economic decentralization.

279. Herakleides Pontikos fr. 46a (Wehrli 1953); see above, pp. 195–99.

280. Diod. Sic. 15.49.1.

federal compromise, assuming control over a polis sanctuary. The Achaians prob-ably had several motivations. The first was certainly the religious motive of want-ing to associate with the ancient cult of Poseidon Helikonios, which was remem-bered as having regional significance before the Achaians inhabited the territory; claiming Achaian control over the sanctuary was a means of aligning the new political order with the conquerors who took the territory in the past and thus laid the foundations for the regional state.[281] But there was certainly also a political motive: it was the koinon that had authority over interstate relations, and insofar as representatives of a foreign state were involved in this episode, it seems likely that they deemed it appropriate to usurp the polis's authority over its local sanctu-ary in order to maintain its own exclusive control over interstate relations. We have seen that poleis were free to interact with foreign states and their representa-tives in matters that had no obvious political significance or implications. Had the Ionians come on a more routine religious errand, the koinon would likely have been uninterested in their presence (although Diodorus hints that the Helikeans would not have allowed the Ionians even to make a normal sacrifice to Poseidon). But the request for relics with which to transfer the cult to Ionia seems to have transformed the embassy, at least in the eyes of the koinon, into a matter of inter-state relations. There was probably the additional concern to present Achaia to the outside world as a unified entity, to assume a posture of integration in its dealings with foreign states. Similar interventions by a koinon in the cults of one of its member poleis are attested for Boiotia, but we have no evidence of the polis's response in these cases.[282] Helike's staunch resistance to Achaian intervention in its local sanctuary can be understood as an attempt to check the koinon's abuse of its power and its failure to uphold the federal bargain.

If our only clear evidence for this dynamic comes from Achaia, it is perhaps not surprising that it is also here that we find the koinon itself resisting temptations to abuse its power, enforcing its own adherence to the terms of the federal compro-mise when it could quite easily have broken that agreement. When Messene was brought back into the koinon in 181 by a combination of force and diplomacy, the city was required to surrender those responsible for the revolt and to accept an Achaian garrison, and it lost several subordinate communities over which it had retained control when it first joined the koinon in 193.[283] But what is striking and

281. Morgan and Hall 1996: 196 suggest that the koinon may have claimed the right to determine the Ionians' access to the sanctuary on the grounds that it had always been a sanctuary in which Acha-ians from other communities participated. Indeed, but we have no evidence whatsoever for the catch-ment area or use patterns of the sanctuary prior to 373.

282. E.g., the Boiotian response to Agesilaos's attempted sacrifice to Artemis at Aulis in 395 (Xen. *Hell.* 3.4.3–4) and the Theban effort to restore the gilded statue of Apollo that had been pilfered by Mardonios's troops from Tanagra in 479 (Hdt. 6.118.2–3).

283. See above, p. 368.

unusual, and for our purposes tremendously important, is that the Achaians granted them a special exemption from paying taxes to the koinon for three years, "so that the destruction of their territory would harm the Achaians no less than the Messenians."[284] Collecting taxes from Messene would not actually have been an abuse of federal power; it was a central power of the koinon, enabling it to provide for the defense of its entire territory. In the normal course of affairs, however, it was not within the koinon's prerogative to cut down the crops and ravage the territory of a member polis, and yet this was part of its strategy in forcing Messene to return.[285] The economic damage was long-lasting, and it is safe to assume that the Messenians' ability to pay their taxes stemmed ultimately from their agricultural activities, which would be severely curtailed for several years as a result of war damage. The koinon itself evidently realized that not granting the special exemption could have seemed like an abuse of federal power, and it chose to avoid giving that impression. The exemption also functioned as a kind of incentive for the Messenians to remain; having already lost almost everything in the war, there would have been very little cost for them to revolt again, and in order to counterbalance this the Achaians sought to make it a little more attractive for them to stay. In this way the koinon worked to gain (or perhaps regain) the Messenians' trust. Without strategies of this kind, the contingent consent central to the maintenance of political institutions crumbles, and significant change becomes more likely.[286]

We can also detect a kind of self-regulating response by the Achaian koinon to its own remarkable growth in the Hellenistic period. Rather than preserving unchanged the institutions and practices that had served the koinon in its first few decades, when it comprised only ethnically Achaian cities, we find significant adjustments that enabled new members to acquire power and influence equal to that held by the original members. One result of the massive expansion that occurred in the late third and early second centuries was that Aigion, for nearly a century the exclusive meeting place of the Achaian assemblies, was no longer geographically central. Apparently at the impetus of Philopoimen, and despite resistance from Aigion, which fought to preserve its special status, after 188 the

284. Polyb. 24.2.3. See above, p. 301.
285. Plut. *Philop.* 21.1; Polyb. 24.9.13. Cf. Polyb. 23.15.1–3, a fragment in which the historian condemns the practice of destroying crops and agricultural systems in warfare—despite the fact that it was his father, Lykortas, who did so at Messene. The fragment probably comes from Polybios's lost account of the Achaians' war against Messene. His reason for condemning the practice is that it does long-lasting damage disproportionate to the commitment of a single offense, and such behavior leads to hatred. Within a federal state, opposition to the federal government by a member state is particularly dangerous; this may have been what Polybios was seeing in the case of Messene. It is tempting to suppose that he was responsible (or other, like-minded individuals were) for the special exemption granted in the final negotiation of terms in 181.
286. Levi 1990.

assemblies were held in various cities on a rotating if not regular or completely inclusive basis.[287] The change was not radical: the assemblies continued to meet on their regular schedule, and the same men were eligible to participate; but now they were held in various cities throughout the koinon, and the preponderant political influence of old Achaia, and of Aigion in particular, was broken. Under the leadership of the koinon's highest-ranking and most respected magistrate, the Achaians sought to ensure that their new members would receive political privileges equal to those held by their original member communities. This concern is also reflected in the considerable expansion of the size of the college of *nomographoi* between the late third (T41) and the early second (T44) century; on the latter occasion the college included representatives of Sparta, Messene, and a number of other Messenian cities, all new members of the koinon. In the Hellenistic period we see the Boiotian koinon taking similar steps, creating a new, eighth district in which to enroll non-Boiotian members like Euboian Chalkis and Lokrian Opous.[288] Insofar as the districts were mechanisms for participation in koinon-wide activities like sacrifice as well as for the provision of obligatory military levies and taxes to the koinon, the extension of this system to incorporate new members was a means of extending power to new members equal to that held by the original member communities. We can detect the same basic process at work in Aitolia, even if it was realized only gradually, for here new, non-Aitolian members were given more and more political rights over time, until at last they appear to have had all the same privileges as the original Aitolian citizens.[289]

The full enfranchisement of new member communities and individual citizens provides us with clear evidence that the koinon did not resist extending the original terms of the federal compromise as it expanded. This is evident in Aitolia as in Achaia, the two koina that grew farthest beyond their original ethnic boundaries, but it also appears to be true in Hellenistic Boiotia, where the koinon grew to encompass only a few additional neighboring communities in Lokris, Euboia, and Megara. Nowhere, however, is there such detailed evidence for the subtle self-restraint of the koinon, its commitment to enforcing its own adherence to the federal compromise even beyond the letter of the law, as there is in Achaia. And this very fact may help to explain its remarkable ability to attract new members, its longevity, and its resilience. Highly adaptable to exogenous pressures and changes, and keenly aware of the need to uphold its end of the federal bargain, the Achaian koinon preserved the contingent consent of its member poleis and achieved a remarkable stability throughout the notoriously tumultuous Hellenistic period.

287. Livy 38.30.3.
288. T19.6, T26.1–2 with map 9.
289. Scholten 2000: 44–45, 63–66, 90–91.

The importance of this kind of institutional self-enforcement in creating overall political stability is also illustrated by considering the implications of its absence. If after 446 the Boiotian poleis cooperated with one another to create a koinon governed by fair and equitable institutions, subsequent history reveals a marked failure to enforce those terms as the Thebans used the koinon as an instrument for polis-based hegemony over the region. After their destruction of Plataia, which can be seen as the result of a battle by a koinon to regain a secessionist member polis or as an unjustified attack by one overwhelmingly strong polis on a smaller neighbor, the Theban assumption of control over the two formerly Plataian districts shows the city attempting to use the institutions of the koinon while at the same time riding roughshod over the compromise that had been struck by all the cities when they first formed the koinon after expelling the Athenians. The federal institution of the boiotarchs was even more badly abused by the Thebans after 379, when they assumed complete control of that college of magistrates, purporting to lead in the name of all Boiotia despite having effectively undermined any meaningful form of political representation. Our evidence does not allow us to determine whether non-Thebans were allowed to or actually did attend meetings of the Boiotian assembly in this period, but it was always held in Thebes, and it is almost certain that no citizen of a polis other than Thebes had a leadership position in the wider Boiotian state, a koinon in name only. Signs of internal resistance to this usurpation of power, this breach of the federal bargain, were crushed. The evident stability in Boiotian politics after 379 was a product of overweening force, not institutional self-enforcement. Change was brought about only when Alexander destroyed Thebes in 335. The fact that the Boiotian koinon was held together essentially by force for nearly half a century explains why several other Boiotian poleis cheerfully assisted him.[290] The reestablishment of the old federal compromise, with appropriate checks imposed on Thebes, ushered in the longest and most stable period of the Boiotian koinon's existence, from the destruction of Thebes until the dismantling of the koinon by the Romans after Pydna.

A careful and realistic analysis of what it takes for several communities to cooperate with one another in the absence of any coercive strategies and to forge institutions of a federal kind to guide them in their interactions with one another has suggested that it is a remarkably difficult process, the outcome of which is highly susceptible to failure. The terms of the federal compromise are as easily undermined by a central government that has the ability to control its member states as they are by a member state that has the ability to govern itself. The stability and success of a federal political arrangement are predicated, then, on the voluntary adherence of each party to the obligations and privileges defined for it.

290. See above, pp. 87–88.

The voluntary participation of communities in the initial forging of federal institutions thus appears to be crucial to the success of the enterprise; true federalism is a poor vehicle for hegemony and imperialism. And indeed our evidence suggests that it was present in virtually every such compromise in Achaia, Aitolia, and Boiotia, with the striking exception of the period from 379 until 335, when the Thebans used the shell of the old Boiotian koinon to impose a strong polis-based hegemony over the entire region that gave other poleis little or no political power. Yet in fifth- and early fourth-century Boiotia, the institutions themselves bespeak the voluntary participation and significant political power of member poleis; this picture is even clearer for Hellenistic Achaia. For Aitolia, we have only hints.

Surveying the terms of the federal compromise—the powers allocated to the koinon, its districts, and its member poleis—has revealed, in as much detail as is possible, the character of the koinon as a state in which power is carefully and fully distributed and the koinon and its poleis are profoundly interdependent. The poleis' surrender of local autonomy over interstate relations of a political and military kind was compensated by a mixture of their representation (via magistrates, military leaders, and the council) and direct participation (in assemblies) in the koinon's governing bodies. The political power of member poleis in a koinon was not, however, restricted to representation and participation in deliberative assemblies. In addition to controlling local affairs and being free to interact with foreign states and their representatives in matters that had no evident military or political ramifications, the poleis had considerable latitude in determining precisely how they would meet their fiscal and military obligations to the koinon, particularly when they did so by coordination with other poleis in a district. It is only when coercion was deployed to impose federal institutions from the top down, as in Boiotia after 379, that those institutions strongly favored the interests of the power holder (Thebes) and severely restricted the political power of member poleis while nevertheless placing heavy demands on them to man the armies that fought to make the fatherland prevail by the might of a spear over the rest of Hellas (T5).

However, not even voluntary participation ab origine ensures on its own the stability of whatever compromise was reached. Its terms can be easily undermined and are preserved, even with modulations, when all parties not only remain bound by their own obligations but also work actively to check abuses of power by the other. This condition of institutional self-enforcement is difficult to detect in the ancient evidence; minor checks, and successful attempts to prevent one community or power from violating its obligations to another, tend not to be reported by literary sources preoccupied with grand narratives of war and conquest. But although Polybios is no less interested in those themes than the other major Greek historians, his vital secondary interest in the Achaian koinon encouraged him to preserve details of this kind of internal policing that simply do not survive from other periods. So it is difficult to tell whether this is a function of the evidence or whether the Achaian koinon was in fact more self-enforcing than others. Here, however, we find three western Achaian communities policing the koinon when it attempted to renege on its obligations to its member communities during the Social War; Helike's resistance to the Achaians' attempt to usurp their authority over the local sanctuary of Poseidon in 373 suggests that the poleis had a good record of keeping the central government in its place in the region. The political culture of restraint and adherence to the terms of the federal compromise became so entrenched that even when Messene (led by part of its citizen population) seceded from the koinon and was forced back in, the koinon avoided even the appearance of abuse of power, granting tax exemptions in recognition of hardship imposed by hostilities waged by the koinon itself. The longevity, stability, and extraordinary growth of the Achaian koinon during a period of tremendous political upheaval together suggest, however, that the nature of the state's political institutions had something to do with it.

With the exception of fourth-century Boiotia, the koinon as it developed in central Greece and the Peloponnese appears, then, to be a state in which power was equitably distributed, in which the regional government and its member poleis were fully interdependent. The true significance of the political power of member poleis was never more evident than when it was used to check abuses of federal power. The Greek koinon was not, then, a unitary state, nor was it an instrument for the subordination of member poleis.[291] The careful, equitable distribution of power, and the efforts made internally to enforce the terms on which a group of communities agreed to cooperate with one another, examined in detail for the Boiotian, Achaian, and Aitolian koina, may not be atypical for Greek federal states. And if that is correct, we may have an explanation for the remarkable spread and longevity of federal institutions in the Greek world. But in order to address that question fully we need to draw together all the threads, weaving the political considerations of this chapter with the religious and economic conditions that contributed to a willingness to strike the compromise in the first place, and to a final assessment of the nature of the koinon as something much more complex and multifaceted than a narrowly political experiment.

291. *Contra* Giovannini 1971 (unitary state); Rizakis 1990b (instrument for subordination).

Conclusion

The origins of this book lie in two simple observations. The first is the fact that nearly half the poleis of the classical Greek world for some time participated in koina, a number that certainly increased in the Hellenistic period. The second is that we have had no compelling understanding of why they did so. For membership in a koinon entailed the surrender of partial autonomy by the polis, which can be construed either as a dilution or as a loss of significant state power. Yet refusal to surrender autonomy, a state's power of self-determination, lies at the heart of the major political battles of the classical and indeed of the Hellenistic period. Major and minor examples abound: the Greeks' collective refusal to allow their states to be subordinated to the Persian empire; the refusal of the Kerkyraians to allow their metropolis, Corinth, to continue to determine their political affairs; the struggle of the Argives to avoid having to follow wherever the Spartans might lead; the desire of the citizens of the tiny volcanic island of Melos to remain neutral in the totalizing conflict between Athens and Sparta known as the Peloponnesian War. These were all struggles against different kinds of encroachment on polis autonomy, yet the threatened result was strikingly similar in each case: the way each state would interact with the wider Greek world would be determined by another. The violent struggles that ensued against these end results have given us the impression that total autonomy was prized above all else by the Greek poleis. One could add to this list the struggle of Plataia to avoid becoming part of the Boiotian koinon, or later the struggle of Sparta to avoid becoming part of the Achaian koinon, and conclude that the koinon was not at all unlike these other imperial and quasi-imperial powers that wished to break polis autonomy by force. Yet the focus of our sources on the stubborn resistance of places like Plataia and Sparta conceals a fact that is perhaps more interesting, and more difficult to explain: hundreds of poleis joined koina, most of them willingly. Why did they do so? Answering that question has been the central project of this book, and it has entailed thinking about both the developmental trajectory of the koinon and the way this innovative new state actually functioned, in as much detail and with as much clarity as possible.

I have attempted both to expose the process by which poleis within a region joined a koinon and to reveal the koinon as a far more complex entity than was ever realized when koina were taken simply as examples of federal states like those of the modern era. But doing so has required the isolation and analysis of different factors in turn—the religious, the economic, and the political backgrounds, motives for participation, and practices as the koinon developed over time. It may be helpful now to draw these threads together, to express, in a succinct narrative, the interaction of particular pressures, opportunities, and bargains that seems to have created the Greek koinon.

Given that every koinon with its origins in the classical period originally comprised poleis belonging to a single ethnic group, it is reasonable to suppose that the existence of a shared ethnic identity tended to make poleis more willing to cooperate with one another by giving them a sense that they had more in common with one another than they did with outsiders to the group. This sense of belonging was promulgated above all by shared rituals articulating myths of migration and descent from a common ancestor. Our earliest evidence for this phenomenon comes from late sixth-century Boiotia, where the cult of Athena Itonia at Koroneia received a temple and worshippers drawn from an area well beyond the boundaries of the polis of Koroneia. By the fifth century (if not earlier) the Boiotians claimed that they had taken this cult with them when they migrated from Thessaly in the upheavals that followed the capture of Troy. The Itonion was, however, by the early fifth century linked to a series of other Boiotian cults, including those of Poseidon at Onchestos and Apollo Ismenios at Thebes, by the overlap of worshipping groups and the interactions of individuals at their sanctuaries. These overlapping cultic networks tended to create distinct but tightly imbricated tiers of identity at the level of the polis and at the level of the region. While these mythic articulations of a Boiotian identity gave the inhabitants of distinct Boiotian poleis a sense of belonging together, economic interactions between these communities and the production of a cooperative coinage to facilitate those interactions as early as the late sixth century bound them more closely together and created a material incentive for continued if not further cooperation. Yet in this period there was as much conflict as there was cooperation: a series of inscribed dedications at Olympia reveals armed conflict between Boiotian poleis, but at least some of these poleis were also able to make joint diplomatic and military responses to specific events. These responses, like that of Thebes, Tanagra, Koroneia, and Thespiai against the Athenians in 506, were certainly ad hoc; there is no evidence for formal institutions that obligated each polis to participate or determined how it would do so. A sense of belonging and a common material interest, as well certainly as shared risk when the enemy was at the border, as the Athenians were in 506, were the background conditions that facilitated this ad hoc political and military cooperation.

Although there is much less evidence, we can see the outlines of a strikingly similar process at work in Achaia and in Aitolia. The early fifth-century Achaian dedication at Olympia of the statue group depicting Nestor and the Achaian warriors drawing lots for the duel with Hektor suggests that an Achaian ethnic identity, articulated around descent from the Homeric Achaians, was bound up with joint religious actions. But it is not until the first half of the fourth century that we can see the interaction of different Achaian communities at shared Achaian sanctuaries. The cult of Poseidon Helikonios, associated by the Achaians with their victorious seizure of the northern Peloponnese from the Ionians, was a common Achaian shrine at least by the early fourth century, as was the cult of Zeus Homarios, a god of assemblies associated with the Homeric Achaians. The crystallization of Achaia as a region in the fifth century may have been articulated around these cults, but our evidence for regional participation in them is contemporaneous with our earliest evidence for economic cooperation in the form, again, of a cooperative coinage and with the bestowal of Achaian citizenship on the Aitolian communities of Kalydon and Naupaktos, our earliest evidence for the existence of formal koinon institutions in Achaia. The process by which all this came about is extremely obscure, but it is important to recognize that religious and economic ties are central to the Achaians' experience at the first moment when we see that they have formed a common polity in 389. That they provided background conditions that made the Achaian poleis willing to strike the federal bargain is necessarily a hypothesis, but one that is supported by comparanda from Boiotia as well as from Aitolia.

In mountainous western Greece the Aitolians cooperated militarily on what appears to be an ad hoc basis in the fifth century, much as the Boiotians did in the late sixth. The sanctuary at Thermon, despite never belonging to a single community, was so richly elaborated in the archaic period that we must conclude that its cult drew worshippers from much of Aitolia, and close readings of the myths associated with it suggest this; by the second half of the fifth century it was the site of elections, but for what kind of officials is entirely unknown. Although the Aitolians did not mint their own coins until the late fourth or early third century, the economic practices they seem to have pursued—a combination of pastoralism and grain and olive production—required significant levels of mobility and exchange within their region, and this situation must go back at least to the fifth century. Again, it appears that religious and economic interactions provided background conditions that facilitated the cooperation of politically independent communities on an ad hoc basis to respond to exogenous threats.

Such situations might have gone on indefinitely had these regions not faced new pressures, both external and internal, that could be alleviated by the creation of a common polity that would incorporate all the communities of the ethnic group that had for so long interacted with one another without actually obliterating their political and social identities. The Athenian occupation and control of Boiotia from 457 to 446 clarified the costs of ongoing political fragmentation and motivated the Boiotian poleis to formalize and regularize, with a strong set of institutions, the irregular ad hoc cooperative arrangements that had prevailed among them for several generations. The fact that the western Boiotian poleis rather than the Thebans instigated the revolt that led to the expulsion of the Athenians meant that the creation of the koinon was the result of cooperation rather than coercion, with Thebes initially receiving representation not at all disproportionate to its size and the size of the other member poleis. The political cost of striking the federal bargain at this point, the surrender by poleis of their absolute autonomy, was alleviated by the creation of a central political system in which each member polis was represented in deliberative, judicial, legislative, military, and fiscal contexts. Ritual played a vital role in justifying the creation of this new regional state while at the same time protecting the integrity and identity of its member poleis. It is highly probable that a material incentive to participation was now offered in the form of the extension to all poleis of rights of property ownership and intermarriage throughout the koinon, a means of protecting and promoting old patterns of economic mobility within the region. Clear evidence for such rights in Boiotia dates only to the third quarter of the fourth century but is well attested for the koinon of the Chalkideis in 382, and while it is possible that this was a Chalkidian innovation that was later borrowed by the Boiotians, this seems unlikely.

The formation of koinon institutions in Aitolia was probably also catalyzed by the need to regain access to the coast, lost before 426 and regained only in 367, precisely the year in which we first have explicit evidence for the existence of an Aitolian koinon. For Achaia catalyzing pressures are deeply uncertain: hostility toward Aitolia may have been a factor (the first act of the Achaian koinon about which we are informed is its seizure of Kalydon and Naupaktos), but more immediately the experience of living on the border of the central zone of conflict in the potentially totalizing Corinthian War may have created a sense of urgency about regularizing cooperation among the Achaian poleis. As in Boiotia, so too in Aitolia and Achaia the earliest clear evidence for the koinon's extension of regional property rights to all citizens belongs about a century after the emergence of the koinon itself, but it would not be surprising if new evidence were to show that such rights were a feature of the early years as well, for they would have provided a significant incentive to participation that could have alleviated somewhat the cost of the political bargain struck.

Once established, the institutions of the koinon were remarkably stable in each of the three cases at the heart of this book. Religion, part of the process of integration from the start, played a major role in achieving this stability. A venue for the legitimation of the koinon in periods of strain and for the celebration of its successes, it was perhaps most crucially a means of securing regular commitments from the member poleis to participation in the regional polity. This was accomplished by deploying the pervasive political strategy of representation in the ritual sphere, designating official representatives of poleis and districts to participate in dedications made to gods throughout the region by the entire koinon. If participants realized that the economic gains stemming from the breakdown of political barriers between poleis were considerable in the early years of the koinon, it is clear that they sought to extend those advantages over time. In the Hellenistic period we can see the Boiotian, Aitolian, and Achaian koina intervening to arbitrate in economic disputes between members and to minimize economic crises, for example by prohibiting the export of grain from the entire territory of the koinon during periods of shortage and by undertaking legislation on debt. If the logic of resource complementarity was intrinsic to the koinon from its origin, it is not surprising to see it applied to the process of expanding the koinon's territory. While economic motives were certainly not the only ones driving expansion, they were nevertheless highly significant. Yet evidence for predatory fiscal regimes among the koina is nonexistent. Taxes were collected regularly from member poleis, but when in Achaia the koinon failed to provide defense to a vulnerable border area under attack by the Aitolians, one of the public goods it promised to fund from these tax revenues, the cities affected simply refused to pay. And the Achaian koinon itself exercised remarkable restraint: for example, in granting Messene tax immunity for three years after having waged a destructive war to bring the rebel city back into the koinon in 182/1.

These two instances of bargaining over taxes within the context of a fully developed koinon point to a larger phenomenon that contributed significantly to the stability of the koinon and its institutions, namely a kind of reciprocal policing by member poleis and the koinon of the terms of the federal bargain struck by both parties. It was this that prevented the koinon from becoming, with one important exception, an instrument of empire and subordination. That one exception, of course, is the position of Thebes within the Boiotian koinon in the late fifth and the fourth century. Although the institutional arrangements made after 446 sought initially to keep Theban power within bounds and all members participating in the koinon on an equitable basis, the emergency of the Peloponnesian War gave the Thebans the opportunity to acquire additional representation by the synoikism of the cities of the Parasopia into Thebes, certainly on the grounds of their vulnerability. The Theban attack on Plataia in 431, which ultimately yielded even greater representation for Thebes in the koinon, should be seen as part of this anxiety about the Attic-Boiotian frontier on the eve of the Peloponnesian War. After the war the Thebans sought to extend the formal advantages they had thus gained by directing Boiotian policy in the Corinthian War. When the Thebans successfully expelled the Spartans from their akropolis in 379 and worked to eradicate pro-Spartan sentiments and regimes from all Boiotia, they appear to have seized control of the college of boiotarchs, the highest magistrates in the koinon, formerly composed of representatives of the member communities. As a result, the Boiotian koinon in the period from 379 until the destruction of Thebes in 335 was a koinon in name only. Although the city was rebuilt by Cassander in 316, it appears that the other Boiotian poleis did not allow it to become a member of the koinon again until 287, and vigilance against a repetition of this scenario together with robust representative institutions held Thebes in check, making the Hellenistic koinon a truly federal state. Although the disparity in size and power between Thebes and most other Boiotian poleis was rare and the problem therefore less likely to be replicated elsewhere, it is also likely that the koina that developed later, including the Achaian and Aitolian, were on the lookout to prevent similar abuses.

I have, in short, argued that the koinon developed in the Greek world against a background of intensive religious and economic interactions between communities within a region, which contributed to a sense of ethnic identity and regional cohesiveness and made the prospect of surrendering partial autonomy to a newly created regional state more palatable to the poleis that participated. Religion became central to the structure and stability of the koinon, because it provided a means of legitimating the existence of this new power and of articulating and reinforcing the integration of the entire region while at the same time protecting the distinct identities of its constituent poleis. The protection and promotion of old patterns of regional exchange and economic mobility by the koinon may have offered a material incentive for poleis to join, as was certainly the case in the Chalkidike around 382. One of the aims here was to capture a broad array of complementary resources within the territory of the koinon, vital in the highly fragmented Mediterranean, and this motive can be seen in the history of the expansion of koina beyond their original ethnic boundaries.

The result of this inquiry is a picture of the koinon as a state so deeply imbricated from its origins in the religious and economic interactions of its individual citizens and member communities as to be inseparable from them. The koinon, as it first developed in mainland Greece and the Peloponnese, emerges as the product of countless interactions at sanctuaries, mountaintops, markets, and harbors. The formal institutions that emerged from this process bear the stamp of their origins: they served to promote and protect old patterns of economic interaction and the coherence of the region as an economic entity; they promoted the participation of the entire koinon in rituals both for gods who were associated with the unity and integrity of the entire ethnic group and its control over the koinon's territory as well as in rituals for the gods of individual member poleis. In the process of trying to understand the emergence and nature of a particular kind of state in ancient Greece, I have developed a new way of thinking about state formation that may be more widely applicable in the ancient world. This view of states as the products of social interactions shares some observations made recently by the sociologist John Levi Martin, although Martin's conclusion—that the modern nation-state is built on social structures marked by inequality—is strikingly different from my own and exposes one of the most distinctive and fascinating things about the emergence of the koinon, namely its role in limiting political hierarchy and subordination while facilitating cooperation.[1] Two recent publications in ancient history suggest that the idea of states as the products of social interaction may gain some traction. Athens has been dubbed "la cité des réseaux" by Paulin Ismard, advancing the view that Athenian civic society was a complex network of distinct but interrelated entities that were themselves highly complex—not only the demes, trittyes, and phylai from which the democracy was constructed but also cultic associations (the genē and orgeōnes), legal and financial associations, and even philosophical associations.[2] Connectivity has been stressed as a distinctive feature of the Mediterranean from antiquity to modernity, and this fact has served as one of the foundations of my inquiry.[3] If connectivity has been a powerful tool for describing the Mediterranean world, its potential as an analytical tool has recently been explored by applying network theory to the ancient Mediterranean.[4] Still in its infancy, this set of ideas has not yet been applied to the problem of the emergence of particular political institutions; it is hoped that this book may contribute to this nascent dialogue.

The results of this book also have significant implications for the narrower field of Greek political history. Careful examination of the political structures of the koinon has revealed a highly distinctive kind of state, a political innovation deeply situated in a world of small city-states and other independent communities, relatively highly urbanized and intensely interconnected with one another, unable or unwilling to sacrifice their integrity yet unable to impose their political will on

1. J. L. Martin 2009.
2. Ismard 2010.
3. Braudel 1973; Horden and Purcell 2000. I. Morris 2003: 51 calls (inter alia) for the need, in pursuing an approach that emphasizes connectedness over the "static, cellular theories" that characterized earlier work in ancient history, to think about processes, to take institutions seriously, not to forget about power ("Mediterraneanization created winners and losers"), and to be precise about definitions. Although I did not happen to read this article until this book had been completely written, and although I do not agree with everything Morris says in it, I do agree with these points and think that my book has at least attempted to do all these things.
4. Malkin, Constantakopoulou, and Panagopoulou 2009.

others, surviving in a competitive military and political environment only by cooperation with neighbors with whom they felt closer ties as a result of both religious and economic interactions than they did with other Greeks. From these conditions emerged a state in which political organization takes on a fractal quality, with small-scale institutions replicated at the larger scales of both district and region, facilitating a careful distribution of powers that simultaneously protects the integrity of the member poleis and unifies them into a single state. I have argued that the koinon was a poor instrument for empire and that it was more complex and more robust than a system of alliances. It is, it seems to me, time to lose the "league" in ancient Greek history, to confront directly the distinctions between "the Boiotian League," "the Peloponnesian League," "the Delian League," and "the Second Athenian League," to cite only a few of the most commonly used examples. This means, in a sense, returning to the study of institutions, avoiding the descriptive trap of the old institutionalism and thinking hard about the evolution, development, and impact of the formal institutional arrangements in which the Greeks were so remarkably innovative. The koinon, like the systems of bilateral alliances undertaken by the Spartans and Athenians during their periods of military hegemony, was an attempt to overcome the limitations imposed by the political fragmentation of the Greek world as it emerged out of the archaic period. But unlike the Spartan and Athenian systems of alliance, the koinon was a response not only to the political and military limitations of that fragmentation but also to the restrictions it imposed on religious and economic life. It was, in its original form in mainland Greece and the Peloponnese, created from the bottom up by poleis that responded to their very real fear that participation would effectively yield annihilation of their local state and local culture by creating institutions that would protect their ability to participate directly in the political process and thereby to protect their very existence as social and political entities. This, it seems to me, is why politics beyond the polis really mattered to the Greeks, and why it should really matter to us.

Epigraphic Dossier

CONTENTS

INTRODUCTION

This dossier is divided geographically. Part I comprises texts (T1–T33) from or pertaining to Boiotia; part II (T34–T46), Achaian texts; part III (T47–T61), Aitolian texts. Within each part, the texts are presented in chronological order. For most texts a complete genetic lemma is provided, from which the textual history of each document can be reconstructed. For texts that are included in relatively recent editions of the major corpora, especially *Inscriptiones Graecae*, where consultation of those editions will provide the reader with the same information, a simple reference to that edition suffices. An asterisk indicates the edition on which the text printed is based. I have attempted, however, to impose a uniform set of sigla (below) on all the Greek texts, despite differing systems adopted by different editors. Where relevant, an apparatus criticus is included, and every text is accompanied by an original translation and commentary, with bibliographic references, on the issues raised by each text that pertain to the historical issues explored in this book. As a result, problems of language, dialect, meter, and poetic style, and issues stemming from a text that are of particular relevance to other problems, receive little attention here. Discussion of these issues can easily be tracked in the *Supplementum Epigraphicum Graecum* and *Bulletin épigraphique*.

SIGLA

[ ]	enclose letters that are not now preserved but that are believed to have been inscribed
‹ ›	enclose letters supplied by the editor either because the stonecutter omitted them or because the stonecutter mistakenly inscribed other letters
{ }	enclose letters inscribed by the stonecutter in error and deleted by the editor
[[ ]]	enclose an erasure or letters inscribed by the stonecutter over an erasure
[. . . .]	lost letters, equal in number to the number of dots
[– – –]	lost letters that cannot be restored, of an uncertain number; more than three dashes are sometimes used to give a visual representation of the length of the lacuna
[–ca. 6–]	lost letters that cannot be restored, of the estimated number indicated
αβγ	letters (dotted) that survive in part; readings given are likely, but alternatives are possible
h	aspirate, if the original text contained an inscribed aspirate character
ᵛ	a single letter space left vacant by the stonecutter
vacat	line, or remainder of line, uninscribed

I. BOIOTIA

1. Athenian Monument Commemorating Victory over Boiotians and Chalkidians

a. Found on the Athenian akropolis. Now in the Epigraphical Museum (inv. 6286). Original monument ca. 506.

IG I² 394; Raubitschek 1949: 191–94 no. 168 with photos and drawing; ML 15A. *IG* I³ 2.501A.

[δεσμ̑οι ἐν ἀχνύεντι(?) σιδερέοι ἔσβεσαν *hύβ*]ριν ⋮
παῖδε[ς Ἀθεναίον ἔργμασιν ἐμ πολέμο]
[ἔθνεα Βοιοτ̑ον καὶ Χαλκιδέον δαμάσαντες] ⋮
4   τὸν *híππος* δ̣[εκάτεν Παλλάδι τάσδ᾽ ἔθεσαν].

b. Found on the Athenian akropolis. Now in the Epigraphical Museum (inv. 6287, 6287a, 12410). Replacement monument, ca. 457. *IG* I² 394; Raubitschek 1949: 201–5 no. 173 with photo and drawing; ML 15B. *IG I³ 2.501B.

[ἔθνεα Βοιοτῶν καὶ Χαλκιδέον δαμά]σαν[τες]
[παῖδ]ες Ἀθεναίον ἔργμα[σιν ἐμ πολέμο]
[δεσμῶι ἐν ἀχνύεντι(?) σιδερέοι ἔσβε]σαν[ḥύβριν·]
4   [τ]ὸν ḥίππος δεκάτ[εν Παλλάδι τάσδ᾿ ἔθεσαν]·

Taming the *ethnea* of the Boiotians and Chalkidians,
the sons of the Athenians in works of war
with grief-laden iron bonds quenched their arrogance,
and dedicated these horses as a tithe for Pallas.

The replacement monument was seen and copied by Herodotos (5.77.4), on the basis of whose text the restorations are made. The *quadriga* itself may have been seen by Pausanias, who also quotes the inscription (1.28.2); see Modenesi 2001: 27–30; S. West 1985: 283–85 (but see Pritchett 1993: 150–59); Dinsmoor 1980: 43 n. 25, 61. The epigram is sometimes ascribed to Simonides; for discussion see Molyneux 1992: 84–87.

Most scholars believe that the original monument was erected shortly after the defeat of the Boiotians and Chalkidians in 506, with the replacement set up after Oinophyta (Hauvette-Besnault 1894: 51–52; Raubitschek 1949: 203; ML p. 29). Mattingly 1982: 383–84 argues that there were two changes: the original statue group, destroyed by the Persians, was replaced by a new one, on the old base, in the 470s. In the summer of 431, after the Theban attempt to seize Plataia, the Athenians moved the group outside the akropolis to the Propylaia (where Herodotos saw it) and gave it a new base. The shackles, however, were left inside, near the Promachos statue, prompting the need to change the emphatic word order of the old inscription. See also Keesling 2003: 50–55.

2. Theban Dedication after Battle with Athens

Found in a cist to the northwest of ancient Thebes, perhaps just within the enceinte, in the area of modern Pyri. Now in the Thebes Museum, inv. 35900. Ca. 506 BCE.

Fluted kioniskos of whitish poros. The cist in which the kioniskos was found contained objects dating from the second half of the sixth century to the end of the fifth. The column is inscribed with a text of four lines in epichoric alphabet, in as many flutings of the column, which is broken at the top. The column is reportedly 57.02 cm high, 19.3 cm in diameter at the top and 19.8 cm in diameter at the bottom. Aravantinos reports that the letters are 0.33 to 0.21 cm high, but this is

impossible if the reported height of the column is correct, and 0.33 to 0.21 m (3.3–2.1 cm) must be meant. Color photograph in Aravantinos 2010: 148.
Preliminary reports by Aravantinos, *AD* 52 (1998 [2004]): 355–56; *AR* 2005–6: 46 (with provisional text). Knoepfler, *BE* 2006.203 presents a preliminary text based on a provisional transcription by Aravantinos in the Thebes Museum (*SEG* 54.518). *Ed.pr.* Aravantinos 2006. The text below is based on my reading of the photograph and facsimile in Aravantinos 2006; both published texts seem to contain errors.

> [- - - - - - - -]ος Φοινόας καὶ Φυλᾶς
> [- - - - - - - - -] ℎελόντες κ᾿ Ἐλευσῖνα
> [- - -]αι Χαλκίδα λυσαμενοι
> 4   [- - -]μοι ἀνέθειαν

1 ος Οἰνόας καὶ Φυλᾶς Knoepfler ος Φοινόας αἱ Φυλᾶς Aravantinos   2 ℎελόντες καὶ Ἐλευσῖνα Knoepfler ℎελόντες κ̇έλευσῖνα Aravantinos   4 μōι ἀνέθειαν Knoepfler μοι ἀνέθειαν Aravantinos

... Oinoe and Phyle ... taking Eleusis also ... liberating Chalkis [*or* Chalkis, fulfilling] ... dedicated it.

The column served as the base for some object, probably a tripod (Aravantinos 2006: 375 also suggests a statue; Knoepfler *BE* 2006.203, 2008.236). The monument and the letter forms are comparable to an inscribed and fluted kioniskos from the Ptoion, ca. 550: Ducat 1971: 391 no. 241, with fig. 40 and pl. CXXXII (though this earlier document is in false boustrophedon). The particular combination of place names and the general date of the monument (based on letter forms and comparable material from the Ptoion) points ineluctably to the Boiotians' involvement in Kleomenes' abortive invasion of Attica in 506, as reported by Herodotos (5.72–77). Knoepfler (*BE* 2006), taking λυσάμενοι as a nominative plural participle, suggests that with the dedication of this monument the Thebans would have felt themselves acquitted of their vow to a deity whose name has been lost. This is one way to explain the otherwise strange fact that, if Herodotos's account is correct, the Boiotians would here be making a dedication to commemorate a signal defeat. The other possibility—not incompatible with Knoepfler's suggestion—is that the Boiotians enjoyed significant success at Oinoe and Phyle (Herodotos has Oinoe and Hysiai) and dedicated this monument to commemorate it. It is worth noting that according to Herodotos some (indeterminate) period of time passed between the Boiotians' seizure of Oinoe and Hysiai (Hdt. 5.74.2) and the Athenians' defeat of their forces (5.77.1–2). In the interim the Boiotians would likely have wished to celebrate their seizure of the Attic frontier and to secure their control by symbolically transferring it to a god. However, although it is less likely, it is possible that λυσαμενοι is the dative singular and should be accented λυσαμενōι (Knoepfler *BE*

2008.236 p. 627). Aravantinos 2006 suggests several possible restorations of line 4 construing -]μοι as either a nominative plural (so, e.g., δᾶ]μοι) or a dative singular (in which case it would need to be the name of the recipient of the dedication) but notes (p. 376) that "none . . . can be taken as more than speculative." In *AR* 2005-6 Aravantinos proposed [Κάδ]μωι, and in *BE* 2006.203 Knoepfler suggested [Διονύσωι Κάδ]μωι, citing Paus. 9.12.4. I prefer to restore nothing; the votive character of the monument seems to me beyond doubt.

3. Elian Arbitration(?) Regarding the Boiotians,
Athenians, Thespians, and Thessalians

Found at Olympia. Now in the Olympia Museum, B6362. Ca. 476–472(?).
Inscribed on a bronze tablet.

Ed.pr. Siewert 1977: 463 n. 4 (*SEG* 26.475); reprinted by Roesch, *Teiresias AE* (1978): 14 no. E78.20, with textual changes suggested by Siewert; then appearing in *Siewert 1981 with photo, plate 24 (*SEG* 31.358; Siewert 2006: 46 no. 2).

> Ἄγαλμα Διός· Πύρρο‹γ› γρ[α]φέας *vacat*
> καὶ Χαρίξενος καὶ τοὶ μαστροὶ *vacat*
> [τ]αὶρ δίκαις, ταὶρ κὰ‹τ› τὸν Βοιοτὸν Μένανδρος
> 4 [κ]᾿ Ἀριστόλοχος τοῖρ Ἀθαναίος ἐδικαξάταν, *vacat*
> [ἀ]πέγνον καὶ τοῖ‹ρ› Θεσπιέσσιν καὶ τοῖρ σὺν αὐτὸς
> [μ]ὲ δικαίος δικαστᾶμεν, κἀπὸ τὸν Θεσαλὸν *vacat*
> [ἀ]πεδίκαξαν. *vacat*

5 [ἐ]πέγγον Siewert 1977   6 [σφ]ὲ Siewert 1977   7 [ἐ]πεδίκαξαν Siewert 1977

Delight of Zeus. Pyrrho(n) was the secretary. Charixenos and the *mastroi* rejected the judgments that Menandros and Aristolochos brought against the Boiotians in favor of the Athenians, and also in favor of the Thespians and those with them, on the grounds that the charge against them was not rightly judged, and they revoked the decision against the Thessalians.

Line 2: μαστροὶ are also attested in Olympia (*IVO* 2.6.7) and as political officials elsewhere in the Peloponnese as well as at Delphi: Pellene (Arist. *Pell.Pol. ap.* Harpokration s.v. μαστῆρες); Stymphalos (*IG* V.2.357 lines 37–38); Andania (*IG* V.1.1390); Delphi (Haussoulier 1917: 132–33). They are compared by F. W. Walbank 1957–79: III.260 to the δοκιμαστῆρες τῶν κοινῶν at Sparta.

Line 3: [τ]αὶρ δίκαις is accusative plural, -αις being a common Elian variant (cf. *IvO* 2.4, 3.4), until the fourth century, of the ending -ας (cf. *IvO* 4.3, 5.4). It is taken as the object of [ἀ]πέγνον in line 5. The rhotacism evident in the article's ending appears inconsistently in the earliest Elian documents: *IVO* 1, 9, 10, 11.

Line 5: Θεσπιέσσιν καὶ τοῖρ σὺν αὐτὸς. The phrase is similar to that in *Hell. Oxy.* 16.3 (Bartoletti), where δύο δὲ [βοιωτάρχους παρείχοντο] Θεσπιεῖς σὺν Εὐτρήσει καὶ Θίσβαις, and δύο δὲ ὑπὲρ Πλαταιέων καὶ Σκώλου καὶ Ἐρ[υ]θρῶ[ν] καὶ Σκαφῶν καὶ τῶν ἄλλων χωρίων τῶν πρότερον μὲν ἐκείνοις συμπολιτευομένων. It is similar to phrases in which a state name is followed not by σύν and another name in the dative but by μετά and the place name in the genitive. Precisely this locution is used by Thucydides in the Thebans' speech to the Spartans in defense of their attack on Plataia in 427: ἡμῶν κτισάντων Πλάταιαν ὕστερον τῆς ἄλλης Βοιωτίας καὶ ἄλλα χωρία μετ᾽ αὐτῆς (Th. 3.61.2). Both locutions are typical in formulas associated with *sympoliteia*: A.T. Edwards 2004; cf. Siewert 1981: 239 and 2006: 47. See also Schmitt 1994; Dreher 2003; Rzepka 2002 on *sympoliteia* generally. The resonance with the *Hellenica Oxyrhynchia* makes it tempting to suggest that the Boiotian districts may have been formed at least in part by the incorporation of existing clusters of communities, like "the Thespians and those with them."

Siewert 1981 (cf. Siewert 2006: 46–47) suggests that the text constitutes the outcome of an appellate deliberation on a decision made earlier by Menandros and Aristolochos, who he suggests may have been *hellanodikai;* the earlier decision apparently found against Boiotia and Thessaly, and in favor of Athens and Thespiai. The only practical change brought about by this reconsideration seems to have been that the decision against the Thessalians was revoked, which probably implies that they were freed of an obligation to pay damages (Siewert 1981: 237 interprets δίκαις in line 3 to mean *Strafgeld*) to Athens and Thespiai.

The date of the document is indicated by letter forms (which point to a date ca. 475) and the historical background, which is probably as follows: shortly after 479 the Elians punished the Boiotians and Thessalians for breaking the Olympic truce of 480 when they participated in the sacking of Athens and Thespiai. Siewert accordingly dates the document to the following Olympiad, 476–472.

The document is discussed by Thür 1987: 469 (no. 1) in his study of the pronouncement of verdicts in legal proceedings, where it is cited as evidence that the final votes of judges were all that was required for the pronouncement of a verdict in Greek law.

4. Grave Stele with Epigram
for the Boiotian Generals at Leuktra

Found at Pyri, near Thebes. Now in Thebes Museum, inv. 88. 371/0 BCE.

Limestone stele, 0.86 m (h), 0.48 m (w), 0.36 m (d).

IG VII.2462 (Larfeld 1883: no. 308); Tod 130; *RO 30. For photo, Demakopoulou and Konsola 1981: 31 fig. 1; Aravantinos 2010: 230.

    Ξενοκράτης,
    Θεόπομπος,
    Μνασίλαος.
4   ἀνίκα τὸ Σπάρτας ἐκράτει δόρυ, τηνάκις εἷλεν
     Ξεινοκράτης κλάρωι Ζηνὶ τρόπαια φέρειν,

οὐ τὸν ἀπ᾽ Εὐρώτα δείσας στόλον οὐδὲ Λάκαιναν
ἀσπίδα· Θηβαῖοι κρείσσονες ἐν πολέμωι,
8   καρύσσει Λεύκτροις νικαφόρα δουρὶ τρόπαια,
οὐδ᾽ Ἐπαμεινώνδα δεύτεροι ἐδράμομεν.

Xenokrates, Theopompos, Mnasilaos. When the Spartan spear was dominant, at that
time Xeinokrates took by lot the task of presenting a trophy to Zeus, not fearing the
army from the Eurotas, nor the Lakonian shield. "The Thebans are superior in war,"
proclaims the victory-bearing trophy won by the spear at Leuktra, nor did we run
second to Epameinondas.

Pausanias (9.13.6) mentions Xenokrates as one of the boiotarchs in office at
the time of Leuktra. Beister 1973 argues that the story reported in Pausanias
(4.32.5–6) of the Boiotians' demoralizing the Spartans before Leuktra by setting
up a trophy of the Messenian hero Aristomenes is an elaborated (distorted) version of the story recorded in these verses. But the story is late, and certainly
postdates the Boiotian-led liberation of Messenia (Diod. Sic. 15.62.1–66.1).
Tuplin 1987: 94–107 argues that these lines should refer only to the usual erection of a trophy after battle, despite the fact that φέρειν is an unusual verb for
that action.

For the ideology here expressed, Θηβαῖοι κρείσσονες ἐν πολέμωι, compare the
first line of T5.

5. Inscribed Base of a Statue by Lysippos Honoring
a Theban Military Commander

Reportedly found in Thebes. Now in the Archaeological Museum of Thebes, inv.
21393. 371–360 BCE.

Statue base in gray limestone, broken at the right and bottom. 32.5 cm (h), 51 cm
(w), 43.5 cm (d).

Preliminary publication (without Greek text) by Ducrey 1999. *Ed. pr.* *Ducrey
and Calame 2006 (with comments and some textual emendation by Knoepfler in
BE 2009: 259, in places following suggestions made by Chamoux).

[Π]ατρὶς ἀριστεύουσ᾽ ἀλκῆι δορὸς Ἑλλά[δος ἄλλης]
[ε]ἵλετο τόνδ᾽ αὐτῆς ἡγεμόν᾽ ἐμ πολέ[μωι]
[ὅ]ς ποτε κινδύνοις πλείστοις Ἄρεως ἐ[ν ἀγῶσιν]
4   [τ]ὰς ἀφόβους Θήβας μείσζονας ηὔκλε[ισεν]
vacat
Ἱππίας Ἐροτιώγιος Διὶ Σαώτη ἀνέθη[κε]
Λύσιππος Σικυώνιος ἐπόησε

3 ἐ[ν ἀγῶσιν] Calame ἐ[πάγοντος] Chamoux, Knoepfler

The fatherland, prevailing by the might of a spear over the rest of Hellas
has chosen this man as its leader in war,

who, when there were many dangers in the contests of Ares,
brought greater honor to fearless Thebes.
Hippias son of Erotion dedicated it to Zeus Saotas.
Lysippos of Sikyon made it.

The provenance of the stone is uncertain; reports that it was found at Akraiphia may be misleading, and it is more likely to have been found in Thebes itself, honored by the victories of "this man" who was chosen "as its leader in war" by "the fatherland," which we should understand as Thebes. The language of the epigram seems to make a dedication in another city unlikely (Ducrey in Ducrey and Calame 2006: 72; Knoepfler, *BE*). Ducrey, however, raises the possibility that it was dedicated in Thespiai, where we know there was a cult of Zeus Saotas (Paus. 9.26.7), and where Lysippos was commissioned to produce a statue of Eros (Paus. 9.27.3). Yet this is highly unlikely, for Thespiai was hostile to Thebes from 386 to 373, when it was finally destroyed for its intransigence. What is more, Zeus Saotas is simply the Boiotian form of Zeus Soter, a god worshipped widely and in no way particularly local (Knoepfler).

Hippias the son of Erotion was not previously known. But he may be the same Hippias who appears in two boiotarch lists of the same period: T9, T11. If this is correct, then he was certainly a Theban, and the Theban provenance becomes even more likely (Knoepfler, *contra* Ducrey in Ducrey and Calame 2006: 73).

Cuttings in the preserved part of the upper surface of the base reveal that Hippias dedicated a statue of an armed man holding a lance (Ducrey in Ducrey and Calame 2006: 74–78, with figs. 2–6). But who was he? Certainly not Hippias himself. The text is situated at the left edge of the stone, rather than having been centered, which strongly suggests that it was one of a series of connected bases and its statue part of a group. Knoepfler suggests that the statue depicted Pelopidas (depicted in another statue by Lysippos, commissioned by the Thessalians: T10) and was adjoined by the statue of Epameinondas, which Pausanias saw (9.15.6). That statue, too, was accompanied by an epigram emphasizing the military might of Thebes. Yet where the new epigram boasts the predominance of the Theban spear "over the rest of Hellas," the epigram for Epameinondas, highlighting the defeat of Sparta and the foundation of Messene, boasts that "all Hellas became autonomous in freedom." It is an interesting hypothesis; the epigram for Epameinondas is known only from Pausanias.

The monument certainly belongs after 371, when for the first time the Thebans could speak without any hesitation of military predominance "over the rest of Hellas." Prior to Leuktra, "the Spartan spear was dominant" (T4.4). If Hippias the son of Erotion is the same Hippias who appears in the boiotarch lists of T9 and T11, the stone must belong in the 360s. Historical context does not tolerate its being placed much later. Ducrey (Ducrey and Calame 2006: 79–81) places it in the period 372–364.

6. Proxeny Decree of the Boiotian Koinon
for Timeas Son of Cheirikrates of Lakonia

Reportedly found in Thebes. Now in the Museum of Fine Arts, Boston, inv. 1987.297. Ca. 369–363 BCE.

Stele of white marble, 65 cm (h), 32.5 cm (w), 20 cm (d).

Preliminary publication of the stele, with no Greek text, by Vermeule and Comstock 1988: 27–28 no. 16 (photo). *Ed.pr.* *Mackil 2008 (*SEG* 55.564; Knoepfler *BE* 2009.260, with some textual emendations).

```
     Πολυδεύκες· Κάστορ· Ἀθάνα{ς} Ἀλέα·
     Θεός· ἔδοξε τôι δάμοι. Ἐργοτέλεος
     ἄρχοντος, Ἰσμεινίας ἔλεξε· Τιμέα[ν]
4    Χειρικράτεος Λάκωνα πρό[ξε]-
     νον εἶμεν κὴ εὐεργέτα[ν Βοιω]-
     τῶν κὴ αὐτὸγ κὴ ἐκγό[νους]
     κὴ εἶμέν [ϝοι] γᾶς κ[ὴ ϝοικίας]
8    ΕΠΩΝ[- - - - - - - - - - - - -]
```

1 Ἀθάνα{ς} Ἀλέα Mackil Ἀθανᾶς Ἀλέα[ς] Knoepfler   3 Ἰσμεινίας Mackil Ἰσμεινίας Knoepfler

Polydeukes, Kastor, Athana Alea. God. Resolved by the people. Ergoteles was archon; Ismeinias proposed. Let Timea[s] son of Cheirikrates the Lakonian be pro[xenos] and benefacto[r of the Boio]tians, both him and his descen[dants], and let him have the right to (purchase) land a[nd a house] . . .

The relief depicts the infant Herakles strangling snakes, an image that appears on Theban coins in the fifth and fourth centuries (*BMC Central Greece* 72 with pl. XII.7–8, 79 with pl. XIV.7–8; Kraay 1976: 111–13 with pll. 19.354, 20.361.) and conveys a civic message of aggression against attackers that well represents the Thebans' stance after 379. The image is discussed from an art-historical perspective by Vermeule 1998. The Dioskouroi are depicted as "riders of white horses" (Pind. *Pyth.* 1.66–67; Eur. *Hel.* 638) and as Lakonian deities (Alcman fr. 19 Calame; Pind. *Nem.* 10.55–57, *Isthm.* 1.30–31, *Pyth.* 11.61–64; *Hymn.Hom.* 17, 33) are probably representative of the honorand, Timeas. Athena Alea, normally associated with the shrine at Tegea, also had a home near Therapne in Lakonia (Xen. *Hell.* 6.5.27; Paus. 3.19.7), which was probably not a minor affair, to judge from a recently published throne of the first quarter of the fourth century, inscribed with a dedication to Halea by one Hippansidas as a memorial of his service in the *gerousia* (Kourinou 1992–98 [*SEG* 46.400]; Kourinou 2000: 153–67). Knoepfler's alternative restoration of the goddess's name in line 1 would render it a genitive, which he believes to be an indication that the Dioskouroi, with a sanctuary near that of Athena Alea in Therapne, were "in service" to her (*BE* 2009.465; Chapouthier 1935). To judge from the three-pronged ram, the vessel is a warship, but it is

depicted with neither sails nor oars, and the class of the vessel cannot be determined with certainty.

Nothing certain is known about the archon, Ergoteles. Ismeinias (Hismeinias),
a common enough name in Boiotia with a variant spelling (*LGPN* IIIB.212), may
be the Ismenias who accompanied Pelopidas on his expedition to Thessaly in 367
and was "admired for his virtue" (Diod. Sic. 15.71.2). Timeas himself is not otherwise known, but the only Spartan known to have the name Cheirikrates was a
Spartan nauarch in 395 (*Hell.Oxy.* 19.1, 22.4 [Bartoletti]), and it is very likely that
the Timeas honored here was this man's son.

Knoepfler 2005: 77–79, without producing a text of the inscription, discusses
the stele as a whole. He argues that the ethnic Λάκωνα signifies Timeas's perioikic
status and suggests that the decree was promulgated by the Boiotians to honor him
for his assistance in the Boiotian-Arkadian invasion of Lakonia in winter 370/69.
He connects Athena Alea on the stele with the Lakonian shrine to the goddess
mentioned by Xenophon in connection with the invasion, and the ship with the
attack on Gytheion (Xen. *Hell.* 6.5.32). Knoepfler infers from Polyainos (*Strat.* 2.9)
that there was a Boiotian garrison at Gytheion for many years and speculates that
the Boiotians tried to turn it into a settlement for the perioikoi just as they created
Messene for the helots during the same year. There are several problems with this
argument. First, the ethnic Λάκωνα does not necessarily denote a perioikos;
although Λακεδαιμόνιος is certainly more common, the two are interchangeable
(Shipley in Hansen and Nielsen 2004: 588–89), and when perioikoi are listed on
inscriptions, they tend to be named along with the city ethnic of their perioikic
polis (*SEG* 13.239, with Androtion, *FGrHist* 324 F49; *IG* XII.5.542.20–23). Second,
although the new throne suggests that the shrine of Athena Alea in Lakonia was a
larger affair than we had realized, Athena Alea at Tegea cannot be ruled out, particularly in light of the Tegeans' close involvement with the invasion (note the
Arkadian, and perhaps specifically Tegean, dedication at Delphi in commemoration of the event: *FDelph* III.1.3 with Paus. 10.9.5) and the goddess's record of providing asylum to Spartans, among others (Hdt. 6.72 with Paus. 3.7.10; Paus. 3.5.6
with Xen. *Hell.* 3.5.18–19; Diod. 14.81.1–3, 14.89; Plut. *Lys.* 28.1–30.1). Third, it is
certainly pressing Polyainos too hard to conclude that there was a Boiotian garrison at Gytheion for many years, and the idea that the Boiotians attempted to transform the Spartan port into a polis for the perioikoi who had revolted in the course
of the invasion is unsupported by any evidence. Despite these specific problems
with the interpretation, the invasion of 370/69 remains a plausible historical context for the decree.

However, Knoepfler further asserts that the name of the archon in this decree,
Ergoteles, allows us to restore the fragmentary archon's name in T11.1–2, the
proxeny decree for Nobas of Carthage, not as [. .]οτέ[λι]|ος but as [Εργ]
οτέ[λε]|ος. The stele for Nobas is lost, so there is no way of measuring the lacuna;

the text is based on Pococke's transcription, which was indeed problematic, but the first lacuna has always been restored as being two letters in length. If that restoration of the archon's name in T11 is accepted, it has significant implications for the date of our decree, for the boiotarch list of T11.12–15 would have to be restored on the stele for Timeas as well. The question hinges on whether Epameinondas was a boiotarch in 369 or not, for he is absent from the boiotarch list in T11. My reading of the sources suggests that he was (Mackil 2008: 178–80), but others have concluded that he was not (Wiseman 1969, followed by Knoepfler, BE 2009.260 p. 465). If we were to associate the bestowal of proxeny on Timeas with the invasion of 370/69, we would then have to assume a significant lapse of time before the decree was passed, which seems rather unlikely. If we relax the assumption that the stele for Timeas provides the restoration of the archon's name in the stele for Nobas of Carthage, this problem disappears. But we cannot have it both ways.

In light of the chronological uncertainties surrounding all the Boiotian proxeny decrees of this period, it remains worth considering the possibility that the decree for Timeas belongs to the Boiotian naval building program of 365–363, which would make excellent sense of the ship on the stele. If Timeas's father was in fact the Spartan nauarch of 395, it would suggest that the Boiotians sought to establish relations with a maritime family, a practice that is also followed in the decree for Athaneos of Macedon (T7), whose son, Demonikos son of Athenaios, was an admiral in Alexander's fleet (Arr. Ind. 18.3; cf. Roesch 1984: 58–59). For detailed discussion of this possibility see Mackil 2008: 181–85.

7. Proxeny Decree of the Boiotian Koinon
for Athaneos of Macedon

Beige limestone block built into the wall above the southern entrance of the Chapel of St. Peter and St. Paul at Leuktra (near Parapoungia). 365 or 364 BCE.

The stele was recut at the top, with the result that the first three lines are lost. The surviving part of the stele has a maximum height of 57 cm; width, 39 cm; its depth cannot be measured. The letters have an average height of 1.5 cm; round letters and omega are 0.8 cm high; the interlinear space is 1 cm.

Ed.pr. *Roesch 1984 (*SEG* 34.355).

> [Θεός· Τύχα· – – – ἄρ]-
> [χοντος, ἔδοξε τοῖ δάμοι]
> [πρόξενον εἶμεν Βοιω]-
> 4   [τῶν κὴ εὐεργέταν] Ἀθ[αν]-
> [ῆο]ν Δαμονί[κο]υ Μακεδ-
> όνα καὶ εἶμεν αὐτοῖ γᾶς
> καὶ ϝοικίας ἔππασιν κὴ
> 8   ἐνώναν κὴ ἀσυλίαν κ-

ἢ πολέμω κὴ ἰράνας ἰώ-
σας κὴ κατὰ γᾶν κὴ κὰτ θ-
άλαττ[α]ν κὴ αὐτοῖ κ[ὴ] γέ-
12 νι, βο[ιωταρ]χιόντων [Πελο]-
πίδα[ο, Τι]μολάω, Δαμ[οφίλ]ω,
[Π]άτρων[ος], Ἀσωποτέλ[εο]ς,
Ἡσχύλω, Παντακλεῖος.
vacat

[God. Good fortune. When – – – was archon, it was resolved by the people that]
Ath[aneo]s son of Damoni[ko]s the Macedonian shall be [proxenos of the Boiotians
and benefactor], and he shall have the right to own land and houses and the right to
purchase, and he shall have *asylia* both in war and in peace going by land and by sea.
These rights shall belong both to him and to his descendants. The boiotarchs were
Pelopida[s, Ti]molaos, Dam[ophil]os, [P]atron, Asopotel[e]s, Eschylos, Pantakles.

Roesch 1984 compares the text with the two federal proxeny decrees, *IG*
VII.2407 (T11) and 2408 (T9), voted at approximately the same time, honoring a
Carthaginian and a citizen of Byzantium, respectively, and after revision of the
stone gives (p. 48) a new text of 2408.

Damophilos was also a boiotarch in 371 (Paus. 9.13.6). The inclusion of Pelopidas
in the boiotarch list, without Epameinondas, allows us to date the decree to 365 or
364 (Rhodes and Osborne 2003: 218). We know Patron served again as boiotarch in
361 (*IG* VII.2407.15). Roesch associates this decree, along with those for the Carthaginian and Byzantian, with the experimental naval program of 365 led by Epameinondas. One Demonikos son of Athenaios, probably the son of our honorand, was
appointed trierarch by Alexander in 326 (Arr. *Ind.* 18.3; cf. Hornblower 2000: 140;
Tataki 1998: 148 no. 6). This supports the idea that the family was involved in ships,
and Roesch proposes that Athaneos son of Demonikos was honored for providing
Macedonian timber for some of the one hundred Boiotian triremes.

8. Proxeny Decree of Knidos for Epameinondas the Theban
Found in Burgaz in 1991. 363 BCE.
Ed.pr. *W. Blümel 1994 with photo and German translation (*SEG* 44.901).
Buckler 1998.

['Έδο]ξε [Κνιδί]οις·Ἐ-
[πα]μειν[ών]δαν Πο-
[λύ]μμη Θηβαῖον κ-
4 [αὶ ἐ]κγόνος προξ-
[ένο]ς ἦμεν τᾶς πό-
[λιος] καὶ ὑπάρχεν α-
[ὐτοῖ]ς ἔσπ[λο]υν ἐ-
8 [ς Κνίδον καὶ ἔκπλουν]

Resolved by the Knidians, that Epameinondas son of Polymmis the Theban and his descendants shall be proxenoi of the city, and that they shall have the right to sail in and out of Knidos.

This inscription provides the first evidence that Epameinondas had any dealings with Knidos during his Aegean naval campaign of 364. Diodoros 15.79.1 alludes vaguely to successful Boiotian overtures toward Byzantion, Rhodes, and Chios (the problem lies in the interpretation of the phrase ἰδίας τὰς πόλεις τοῖς Θηβαίοις ἐποίησεν), but Justin (16.3.1–4.5) indicates that he met with no concrete success. This decree reveals the (unsurprising) limits of our literary sources (all late and derivative) for this important episode of Boiotian history. Knidos, situated just north of Rhodes, would have been of real importance to the Boiotians if they were attempting to create a bloc of allies in the region. Buckler 1998: 204–5 underscores the alignment of Knidos's grant of proxeny to Epameinondas with the stance of Mausollos, who as satrap had recognized the status of Knidos as a polis and had recently realigned himself with Artaxerxes (cf. Hornblower 1982: 116–19). So it cost the Knidians nothing to make Epameinondas their proxenos, and the detail in the last two lines (admittedly heavily restored, but plausible) suggests that they took his naval presence in the region seriously. Knoepfler 2007b (*BE* 2008.237) challenges the restoration of Epameinondas's patronymic in line 3, proposing Πο|[λέ]μμη instead of Πο|[λύ]μμη.

9. Proxeny Decree of the Boiotian
Koinon for a Byzantian

Found at Thebes, now in the Thebes Museum. 364/3 BCE.
IG VII.2408, revised by *Roesch 1984 (*SEG* 34.355).

[- - -]
[ἔδοξε] τοῖ δ[άμοι, - - -]
[- - -]λωνος Βυζ[άντιον]
[Βοι]ωτῶν πρόξενον εἶ[μεν]
4   [κ]αὶ εὐεργέταν, καὶ ε[ἶμ]-
[εν] αὐτοῖ ἀτέλε[ιαν] κα[ὶ ἀσ]-
[φά]λιαν καὶ ἀσ[υλίαν]
[καὶ π]ολέμ[ω καὶ ἰράνας]
8   [ἰώ]σας καὶ κατ[ὰ γᾶν καὶ]
[κατ]ὰ θάλασσαν κα[ὶ]
[γ]ᾶς καὶ οἰκίας ἔγκτησι-
[ν] καὶ αὐτῶι καὶ ἐγγόνο-
12   [ι]ς ‡ βοιωταρχιόντων
Ἀσωποδώρω, Μαληκί-
δαο, Διογίτ[ο]νος, Μιξί-
[λ]αο, Ἀμινά[δ]αο, Ἱππίαο,
16   Δαιτώνδαο.

Resolved by the people, . . . [. .]lon the Byzantian shall be proxenos and benefactor of the Boiotians, and he shall have freedom from taxation, security and freedom from seizure both in war and in peace, by land and by sea, and he shall have the right to own land and house. These privileges shall belong both to him and to his descendants. The boiotarchs were Asopodoros, Malekidas, Diogiton, Mixilas, Aminadas, Hippias, Daitondas.

Roesch 1965b: 75–77 and 1966: 65 n. 4 places the document in 364/3 on the following grounds. Two of the men who are boiotarchs here, Hippias and Daitondas, also appear in the boiotarch list of T11 (ll. 12–13). T11 in turn has several points of overlap with that in T7. Neither of these lists includes Epameinondas or Pelopidas, who both held the office of boiotarch for most of the 360s. Pelopidas died in 364 (Plut. *Pelop.* 34; Diod. Sic. 15.81). The only years in which he was not boiotarch were 371 (Paus. 9.13.6–7), and possibly 369 and 368, when both he and Epameinondas were tried for illegal extension of their office during the invasion of Lakonia in the winter of 370/69. (But for caution on this assumption see Mackil 2008: 179–80.) But a proxeny decree for a Byzantian fits logically with those for the Macedonian (T7) and the Carthaginian (T11) in a context of intense maritime activity on the part of the Boiotians (Mackil 2008: 182–83). These considerations together place our document most likely in 364, after the death of Pelopidas, or in 363. Cf. Fossey 1994: 35.

See the commentary to T11 for the issue of the identification of Daitondas.

10. The Thessalians Dedicate a Statue
of Pelopidas at Delphi

Delphi inv. 6758 + 7710. 369–364 BCE.

Irregular stoichedon 13+. Full line length not known, though from the preserved left side of the stone it is clear that lines corresponded with word breaks, making an irregular line length inevitable..

Ed.pr. Bousquet 1939; Wilhelm 1941 proposes alternative restorations; *Bousquet 1963: 206–8 (ph.) incorporates a new fragment, and produces a new text (*SEG* 22.460). Gallavotti 1985: 55–57 proposes an alternative restoration (*SEG* 35.480).

> Σπάρτημ μὲγ χήρ[ωσας – – –]
> εὐλογίαι πιστ[– – – – – – – –]
> [πλε]ιστάκι ΔΗ[– – – – – – –]
> 4 [στῆ]σαι Βοιω[τ– – – – – – –]
> Πελοπίδαν Ἱπ[πόκλου Θηβαῖον]
> Θεσσαλοὶ ἀνέ[θηκαν Ἀπόλλωνι Πυθίωι]·
> Λύσιππος Λυσ[– – Σικυώνιος ἐποίησε].

1 χήρ[ωσας – – – Bousquet χήρ[ωσε σὺν] Gallavotti   2 πίστ[ει τε] Gallavotti   3 ΔΗ Bousquet δ᾽ ἡ[λθε πόλεις] Gallavotti   4 [στῆ]σαι Βοιω[τ– – –] Bousquet [σῶι]σαι Βοιώ[τιος ἀρχός]· Gallavotti   5 Πελοπίδαν Ἱπ[πόκλου

Θηβαῖον] Bousquet Πελοπίδαν ἱπ[πηλάταν] Gallavotti   6 Θεσσαλοὶ ἀνέ[θηκαν
Ἀπόλλωνι Πυθίωι] Bousquet Θεσσαλοὶ ἀνέ[θηκαν] Gallavotti   7 Λύσιππος
Λυσ[- - Σικυώνιος ἐποίησε] Bousquet Λύσιππος λύσ[ατο τόνδε] Gallavotti

You depr[ived] Sparta . . . eulogy trust[y? . . .] very often . . . to erect (a statue of) the
Boio[tian? -tarch? . . .] Pelopidas son of Hip[poklos the Theban]. The Thessalians
dedi[cated it to Apollo Pythios]. Lysippos son of Lys[- - - of Sikyon made it].

Line 4 could be restored in several ways: στῆσαι Βοιω[τῶν ἄρχοντα], στῆσαι
Βοιω[τάρχοντα], στῆσαι Βοιω[τῶν στρατηγόν]. Line 3 should include some clause
about the resolution to erect the statue, and somewhere we need mention of an *agalma*.

The statue must have been dedicated between 369, Pelopidas's first mission to
Thessaly, and ca. 364, when he died trying to help them at Kynoskephalai. It may
or may not have been posthumous.

The base is included in Jacquemin's study of the monumental offerings at
Delphi (Jacquemin 1999: 355 no. 465).

11. Proxeny Decree of the Boiotian Koinon for Nobas of Carthage

Stele found at Thebes, now lost. 360s or 350s BCE.

Larfeld 1883: no. 316; *IG* VII.2407 (*Syll*[3] 179); *Roesch 1984; RO 43. Knoepfler,
BE 2009.261 proposes several restorations.

[θ]εός· τύχα. [- - -]οτέ[λι]-
ος ἄρχοντος. ἔδοξε
τοῖ δάμοι. πρόξενον
4   εἶμεν Βοιωτῶν καὶ εὐεργέταν Νώβαν Ἀξι-
ούβω Καρχαδόνιον, καὶ
εἶμεν ϝοι γᾶς καὶ ϝοικία-
8   ς ἔπ‹π›ασιν καὶ ἀτέλιαν
καὶ ἀσουλίαν καὶ κατὰ γᾶν
καὶ κατ θάλατταν καὶ πο-
λέμω καὶ ἰράνας ἰώσας.
12   [Β]οιωταρχιόντων Τίμων[ος],
[Δ]αιτώνδαο, Θίωνος, Μέ[λ]-
ωνος, Ἱππίαο, Εὐμαρί[δ]αο,
Πάτρωνος.

1 [Θι]οτέ[λι]|ος Dittenberger, *IG* [Δι]οτέ[λι]|ος Larfeld, Dittenberger *Syll.*[3] [Εργ]-
οτέλεος Knoepfler   6 Καρχαδόνιον Dittenberger Καραχαδόνιον Rhodes, Osborne
12 Τίμ‹ων›[ος] Dittenberger Τιμων[ος] Rhodes, Osborne Τιμολά[ω] Knoepfler
13 Αἰτώνδαο Dittenberger Δαιτώνδαο Wilhelm

God. Good fortune. [- - -]oteles was archon. Resolved by the people. Nobas son of
Axioubas of Carthage shall be proxenos and benefactor of the Boiotians, and he
shall have the right to acquire land and house, freedom from taxation and freedom

from seizure both by land and by sea, during both war and peace. The boiotarchs were Timon, Daitondas, Thion, Melon, Hippias, Eumaridas, and Patron.

Wilhelm 1974: II.293–99. Glotz 1933 suggested that the Boiotians granted proxeny to Nobas in their search for naval expertise in the wake of their decision, made in 365/4, to build a fleet of one hundred ships. Roesch built on this suggestion and connected the decree for Atheneos of Macedon (T7) and the citizen of Byzantium (T9) to the same program; Macedon would have been valuable as a source for timber, and it is known from Diodoros (15.79.1) that Epameinondas secured the allegiance of Byzantium in the 360s. Many have dismissed this association, primarily on the grounds that the Boiotian shipbuilding project never got very far, and that Carthaginians were neither unusual in the fourth-century Mediterranean nor possessors of special knowledge as shipwrights (Cawkwell 1972: 272 n. 1; cf. Buckler 1980b: 308 n. 27; Chandezon and Krings 2001: 38–40; Rhodes and Osborne 2003: 219). The regular presence of Carthaginians has recently been reconfirmed (Chandezon and Krings 2001), and they performed many other economic functions. Thus Manganaro 2000: 258 suggests that Nobas may have been a grain merchant. But the Boiotian shipbuilding program appears to have been more successful than Cawkwell and others were prepared to admit (Mackil 2008: 182), and whether Nobas was a shipwright or not, many of the Boiotian proxeny decrees of the 360s seem to be associated with maritime activity (Fossey 1994).

None of the other individuals can be identified with certainty. Knoepfler 1989: 47–48 (cf. Knoepfler 2000) suggests that Daitondas, who appears as one of the boiotarchs here and in T9, is the author of a law forbidding nocturnal religious rites, known to Cicero (*De leg.* 2.37) as Diagondas. Vottéro 1995: 130–31 thinks this legislator belonged rather to the Solonian period. We know that Melon, one of the other boiotarchs, was one of the seven men who launched the attack on the Spartan garrison in the Kadmeia in 379 (Xen. *Hell.* 5.4.2–3; Plut. *Pel.* 8). The boiotarch Hippias in line 14 is probably the same Hippias who appears as boiotarch in *IG* VII.2408 (T9) and may be the same Hippias son of Erotion who dedicated to Zeus Saotas a large statue by Lysippos: T5. Knoepfler has proposed alternative restorations of two names in this list, which he argues date this document, as well as T6, to the year 369. Knoepfler 2005: 81–83 suggests that the name of the archon in lines 1–2 should be restored [Εργ]οτέ[λε]|ος after the archon in T6, but this is quite uncertain, and impossible if Knoepfler's date of 369 is accepted for T6 (Mackil 2008). The name of the first boiotarch in the list was long restored as Τίμ‹ων›[ος], but Knoepfler (*BE* 2009.261) proposes instead Τιμολά[ω] and identification with the [Τι]μολάω who appears in T7.13. This could have the effect of raising the date of this text, as Knoepfler would have it, to 369, on the assumption of identity between the eponymous archons of this text and T6: "C'est donc une nouvelle preuve que tous ces décrets fédéraux de la Ligue thébaine sont à placer dans une fourchette réduite, guère plus d'une dizaine d'années" (Knoepfler, *BE* 2009.261 p. 466).

12. *Proxeny Decree of the Boiotian Koinon for Kallippidas of Athens*

Onchestos. 335–ca. 300 BCE.

Ed.pr. Spyropoulos 1973: 381, majuscule only (Ioannidou 1973: 270). Michaud 1974a: 644 no. 3; *BE* 73.212; Roesch, *Teiresias, Epigraphica* (1976) 10 no. 24 and (1978) 25 no. 39 (*SEG* 27.60).

   Θιός· Ὀλυμπίχω ἄρχοντος,
   ἔδοξε τῶι κοινῶι Βοιωτῶν
   Καλλιππίδαν Θεόκλειον
4 Ἀθανῆον πρόξενον εἶμεν
   κὴ εὐεργέταν τῶ κοινῶ
   Βοιωτῶν κὴ αὐτὸν κὴ ἐκγόνως κὴ εἶμεν αὐτ[ὶ γᾶς κῆ]
8 [ϝοικίας ἔππασιν – – –]

7 αὐτ[ὶ Spyropoulos, Michaud αὐ[τὸν Ioannidou αὐτ[οῖ γᾶς κῆ] Roesch
8 [ϝοικίας ἔππασιν – – –] Roesch

God. When Olympichos was archon, resolved by the koinon of the Boiotians. Kallippidas son of Theokles of Athens shall be proxenos and benefactor of the koinon of the Boiotians, both himself and his descendants, and he shall have the right [to own land and a house . . .]

Spyropoulos does not venture to date the text, but Roesch (1976) places it shortly after 338, on the grounds of the provenance of the stone; it is only after the destruction of Thebes that the sanctuary seems to have become a political meeting place and repository of decrees. For this role we can compare *IG* XII.9.912, a late fourth- or early third-century decree from Chalkis, of which only the preamble and a partial list of names is preserved; the preamble includes (ll. 5–6) the eponymous archon, ἄρχοντος ἐν Ὀν[χηστῶι]‖ Νείανδρος Νειάνδρ[ου]. At the time of the decree, Chalkis must have been a member of the Boiotian koinon. However, Onchestos can have become the political meeting place only after the destruction of Thebes in 335, giving a terminus post quem. Letter forms suggest a date before the end of the fourth century (C. Müller 2011: 268).

13. *Proxeny Decree of the Boiotian Koinon*
for Oïkles Son of Antiphatas of Pellene

Found at Onchestos. 335–ca. 300 BCE.

Marble stele, 0.60 m (h), 0.34 m (w), 0.08 m (d).

Ed.pr. *Touloupa 1964: 200–201 with photo, pl. 237B (*SEG* 25.553; Roesch 1982: 271–72 with photo pl. XVI.1). Vottéro 1995: 122–28 proposes a textual emendation.

Θεοί.
ἔδοξε τôι κοινôι Βοιω-
τῶν, [[Πιστολάω]] ἄρχοντος
4   Ὀϊκλῆν Ἀντιφάταο Πελ-
λανῆα πρόξενον κὴ εὐ-
εργέταν ἦμεν Βοιωτῶν,
αὐτὸν καὶ ἐσγόνους, καὶ
8   ἦμεν ⟨ϝ⟩οι ἀτέλειαν καὶ ἀ-
συλίαν καὶ ἐν ἱράναι καὶ
ἐν πολέμωι καὶ γᾶς καὶ οἰκίας ἔνπασιν καὶ τὰ ἄλλα
12   καθάπερ τοῖς ἄλλοις προξένοις ἄπαντα. Βοιωταρχε-
όντων [[Κλέωνος]] Θεσπιῆος, [– – –]
ρίδα Ταναγραίῳ, [– – –]

7 ἐκγόνους Touloupa ἐσγόνους Roesch   8 ἦμεν{ν} οἰ Touloupa ἦμεν ⟨ϝ⟩οἰ Vottéro

Gods. Resolved by the koinon of the Boiotians, when [[Pistolaos]] was archon, Oïkles son of Antiphatas of Pellene shall be proxenos and benefactor of the Boiotians, himself and his descendants, and they shall have freedom from taxes and asylia, in peace and in war, the right to acquire land and property, and all the other privileges belonging to the other proxenoi. The boiotarchs were [[Kleon]] of Thespiai, [. . .]ris of Tanagra, [. . .]

The monogram ΠΕ is inscribed in the pediment above the stele.

Date. The letter forms seem to be no earlier than the mid-fourth century (Roesch 1982: 271–72; cf. Vottéro 2001: 71), but the formula of lines 2–3, ἔδοξε τôι κοινôι Βοιω|τῶν, is unparalleled before 338; decrees of the earlier fourth century (e.g., SEG 28.466) use ἔδοξε τôι δάμοι Βοιωτῶν (Knoepfler 2000: 354; cf. Knoepfler 1978: 393). The presence of a Thespian boiotarch also mandates against a date before 335: Thespiai was destroyed in 373, and we have no evidence for its restoration before the destruction of Thebes (Tuplin 1986). Touloupa's suggested mid-fourth-century date for this inscription (accepted without argument by Buckler 1979: 57; Gehrke 1985: 179 n. 97; R. J. Buck 1994: 107; Beck 1997: 101–3 passim and 2000: 334–35; Hansen 2004: 457) is thus impossible. Furthermore, we have no evidence for non-Theban boiotarchs in the period between 378 and 335, and the conclusion has been drawn that in this period Thebes had exclusive control of the college of boiotarchs (Knoepfler 1978: 379; Bakhuizen 1994: 326 and n. 71; Knoepfler 2000: 351 and n. 22 with new [unpublished] evidence in support of the argument). It also appears that the Thebans exclusively occupied the two Boiotian seats on the council of the Delphic Amphiktyony in the same period (Knoepfler 2000: 354 with n. 34). The presence of a Thespian boiotarch thus requires a date shortly after 335 (Roesch 1965b: 45, 87, 93 and 1982: 271–72; Knoepfler 1978: 379; Gullath

1982: 16 n. 1; Fossey 1994: 37). Vottéro 1995: 121–22 n. 2 rejects the relevance of the historical argument. The mounting evidence that Thebes had exclusive control of the college of boiotarchs in this period, and the thorough and compelling case for the complete physical and political dismemberment of the Thespian polis in this period are strong arguments against Vottéro's position. Guarducci 1969: 602–3 (with photo but no text) proposes a date in the third century, without further comment. The provenance of the stone is a final piece of evidence in support of the post-338 date; there is no evidence to suggest that the sanctuary at Onchestos had any political significance before then.

Knoepfler 1988: 234 suggests that the honorand, Oïkles son of Antiphatas, was a seer, perhaps of the family of Melampous. Oïkles is mentioned by Homer (*Od.* 15.243) as the son of Antiphatas; the brother of the heroic Antiphatas was Mantios, and their father was Melampous (Aesch. *Sept.* 611). Pellenean seers seem to have enjoyed some repute: one is found in the court of the Lykian dynast Arbinas in the early fourth century (Bousquet 1975: lines 18–19; Robert 1978b [*SEG* 28.1245]; Herrenschmidt 1985; Rizakis 1995: 386 no. 727).

14. The Boiotian Koinon Arbitrates in a Boundary Dispute
between Koroneia and Lebadeia

Found at Granitsa, 4 kilometers southeast of Lebadeia and a thirty-minute walk from the Trophonion, toward Koroneia; late fourth or early third century.

Ed.pr. Vollgraff 1902 (majuscule); Wilhelm 1911: 13–19, no. 3 with different readings; Pappadakis 1916: 259 with new restorations; *Roesch 1965b: 62 with new restorations (*SEG* 23.297; Ager 1996: no. 16). Alternative restorations of lines 6–7 proposed by Schachter 1981–94: III.108 n. 3 (*SEG* 44.412).

> [Ὅρια τᾶς Τροφ]ωνιάδος γᾶς
> [ἱαρᾶς κὴ Λεβα]δειήωμ ποτὶ
> [Κορωνείας ὡς] Βοιωτοὶ ὥριτταγ
> 4   [κὰτ τὰν ὁδὸν τὰ]ν ἐς τὰμ παγάων
> [ἄγωσαν ἔττε] ὡς τὰ ἄκρα ὡς ὕ-
> [δωρ ῥέει(?) ἐπὶ τ]ὸμ βωμὸν τῶ Δι-
> [ὸς τῶ Λαφουστί]ω.

1 [Ὅρια Ἑλικ]ωνιάδος Wilhelm, Pappadakis [Ὅρια τᾶς Τροφ]ωνιάδος Roesch 2 [πόλι Λεβα]δειήων Wilhelm, Pappadakis [ἱαρᾶς κὴ Λεβα]δειήωμ Roesch 3 [Κορωνῆας Wilhelm, Pappadakis, Roesch 4 [καὶ ἐτερμάξα]ν Pappadakis [κὰτ τὰν ὁδὸν τὰ]ν Roesch 5 [τῶν θερμάων …] Pappadakis [ἄγωσαν ἔττε] Roesch 6 ὕ|[δωρ ῥέει(?) ἐπὶ τ]ὸμ Wilhelm, Pappadakis, Roesch πὰρ τ]ὸμ βωμὸν Schachter 7 Δι|[ὸς τῶ Ἑλικωνί]ω *or* Δι|[ὸς τῶ Λαφουστί]ω Wilhelm, Pappadakis Δι|[ὸς τῶ Λαφουστί]ω Roesch Δι|[ὸς τῶ Ἀκρή]ω Schachter

[Boundaries of the] land sacred to [Troph]onios and belonging to [Leba]deia in the direction of [Koroneia, as] the Boiotians delimited it. [Along the road] to the [rising?] of the springs, to the summit where the wa[ter flows to t]he altar of Ze[us Laphysti]os.

The altar of Zeus Laphystios is described by Pausanias (9.34.5) as being below the altar of Herakles Charops on the summit of Mount Laphystion, which lies between Koroneia and Lebadeia (cf. Schachter 1981–94: III.107–8); he also mentions that the river Phalaros flows down the mountain toward the sanctuary of Athena Itonia. These two topographic descriptions make the restoration Δι|[ὸς τῶ Λαφουστί]ω more likely than Δι[ὸς τῶ Ἑλικωνί]ω, the two alternatives proposed by Wilhelm and followed by Pappadakis. The latter option makes little topographic sense: Zeus Helikonios had an altar on Helikon (Σ Hes. *Theog.* 1), probably below the sanctuary of the Muses, which is at a considerable distance from Lebadeia. Schachter 1981–94: III.108 n. 3 proposes a restoration of line 7 that would make the altar belong to Zeus Akraios, at the top of Mount Laphystios. The restoration of line 3 is mandated by geography, assuming that the stone was found in situ. The restoration of ὅρια in line 1 is required by the nature of the document.

15. Agreement Between Orchomenos and Chaironeia
on Supplying Cavalry to the Boiotian Army

Found at Orchomenos, now in the collection near the tholos tomb in Orchomenos, inv. no. 64 (Lauffer 1980: 179–80). 287 BCE or shortly after.

Ed.pr. Spyropoulos 1971: 222–23 (majuscule). Michaud 1974a: 641 revises the text without commentary (Roesch, *Teiresias Epigraphica* 1976: 11–12, no. 27). *Étienne and Roesch 1978 (*SEG* 28.461) reproduce the revised text of Michaud with slight variations, translation, commentary, and photo of the stone.

    [Θιός. Τούχα]ν ἀγαθάν.
    [Φιλοκώμω] ἄρχοντος Βοιωτοῖς, Ἐρχομενί-
    [οις δὲ Θιογ]νειτίδαο, ἱππαρχίοντος Τιμα-
4   [σιθίω Ἀρι]στομαχίω, ἀγιομένων Σαυκλέ-
    [αο – – – – – –]ω, Ἀριστίωνος Ἑρμαίω, Πουθο-
    [δώρω – – –]ικλέαο· Χηρωνείων Εὐμείλω
    Εὐνομίω· ὁμόλογα τοῖς ἱππότης τοῖς Ἐρ-
8   χομενίων κὴ Χηρωνείων ὑπὲρ τᾶν
    στροτειάων. τὰς μὲν προτεινὶ στρο-
    τείας Θιογνειτίδαο ἄρχοντος Ἐρχο-
    μενίοις, Βοιωτοῖς δὲ Φιλοκώμω, ἀφι-
12 [εμ]ένας εἶμεν, ἀρχέμεν δὲ τὰς στρο-
    [τε]ιίας τὰς ἐπὶ Θιογνειτίδαο ἄρχον-
    [τος] Ἐρχομενίοις, Βοιωτοῖς δὲ Φιλο-
    [κώ]μω· στροτευθεῖμεν δὲ ἐχθόν-
16 [δ]ε τᾶς Βοιωτίας πράταν τὰν Σαυκλ-
    [έα]ο, δευτέραν τὰν Πουθοδώρω, τ-

[ρ]ίταν τὰν Χηρωνείων Εὐμειλίαν,
[π]ετράταν Ἀριστίωνος, ἐν δὲ τῆ
20 [Βο]ιωτίη πράταν τὰν Ἀριστίωνος,
[δ]ευτέραν Πουθοδώρω, τρίταν
[Χ]ηρωνείων Εὐμείλω, πετράταν
[Σ]αυκλίαο· ἡ δὲ κά τινες Ϝίλη Ϝίσα
24 [στρ]οτευθείωνθι, κλαροέτω ὁ ἵπ-
[πα]ρχος τὰς Ϝίσα ἐσστροτευμέ-
νας Ϝίλας· τιθέσθη δὲ τὰς στροτει-
ίας τάς τε ἐν τῆ Βοιωτίη κὴ τὰς ἐ-
28 χθόνδε τὰς Βοιωτίας χωρὶς ἑκατέ-
[ρ]ας ἃς κα τὰ ἐφόδια λάβωνθι. ⌐
[Θ]ι[ο]γνειτ[ί]δαο ἄρχοντος, Τιμασιθίω ἱππαρ-
[χίον]τος, ἐσστρότευθεν τοὶ ἱππότη ἐν τῆ
32 Βοιωτίη Σαυκλέαο Ϝίλα ἐν Θειβὰς ἁμέρας ἕξ,
Ἀριστίωνος ἐν Θειβὰς ἁμέρας ἕνδεκα, Ε[ὐ]-
μείλω ἐ[ν Θ]ειβὰς ἁμέρας ἕξ, Πουθοδώρω
[ἐν Θειβ]ὰς ἁμέρας ὀκτό, ἐν Ὡρωπὸν Σαυ-
36 [κλ]έαο ἁμέρας δέκα, Εὐμείλω ἐν Ὡρωπ[ὸν]
ἁμέρας δέκα, Πουθοδώρω ἐν Ὡρ[ωπὸν]
ἁμέρας ὀκτό. ⌐ ἐχθόνδε τ[ᾶς Βοιωτίας]
[- - - - - - - Σα]υκλέαο Ε[- - -]
[- - -]

1 τύχα]ν ἀγαθάν Spyropoulos [Θιὸς τούχα]ν Michaud [Θιός. Τούχα]ν Étienne, Roesch
2]ἄρχοντος Spyropoulos Φιλοκώμω] ἄρχοντος Michaud, Étienne, Roesch 3 [οις
δε Θιογ]νειτίδαο Spyropoulos, Michaud, Étienne, Roesch 4 [σιθίω....]τομαχίω
Spyropoulos [σιθίω Ἀρι]στομαχίω Michaud [σιθίω Ἀρι]στομαχίω Étienne, Roesch
5 τ]ῳ Spyropoulos [αο - - -]ω Michaud [αο .....]ω Étienne, Roesch 6 [δώρω
Σαυκ]λεαο Spyropoulos [δώρω - - -]ικλέαο Michaud [δώρω...]ικλέαο Étienne, Roesch 7 Εἰν...ὁμόλογα Spyropoulos Εὐνωμί[ω] Michaud Εὐνομίω Étienne, Roesch 12 [.]ενιας Spyropoulos [εμ]ένας Michaud, Étienne, Roesch 16 ... τᾶς
Spyropoulos [δὲ] τᾶς Michaud [δ]ε τᾶς Étienne, Roesch 16–17 Σαυκλ̣|[α]ο Spyro-
poulos Σαυκλί|[α]ο Michaud Σαυκλ|[έα]ο Étienne, Roesch 18 [πρά]ταν ταν Spy-
ropoulos [τρί]ταν ταν Michaud τ|[ρ]ίταν τὰν Étienne, Roesch 19 [τε]τράταν Spy-
ropoulos [π]ετράταν Michaud, Étienne, Roesch 20 [Β]ιωτίη Spyropoulos
[Βο]ιωτίη Michaud [Βο]ιωτίη Étienne, Roesch 22 τετράταν Spyropoulos πετράταν
Michaud, Étienne, Roesch 23 [Σαυ]κλιαον δέκα τινες ϝιληείσα Spyropoulos [Σ]αυ-
κλίαο· ἡ δὲ κά τινες ϝίλη ϝίσα Michaud, Étienne, Roesch 24 [στρ]οτευθείων οἱ
κλαροετωο ἵπ- Spyropoulos [στρ]οτευθείωνθι, κλαροέτω ὁ ἵπ- Michaud, Étienne, Roesch 26 [τ]ας ϝίλας Spyropoulos [ν]ας ϝίλας Michaud, Étienne, Roesch 27 ιας
τάς ἐν Spyropoulos ιας τάς τε ἐν Michaud, Étienne, Roesch 28 -[χ]θόνδε Spyropoulos -χθόνδε Michaud, Étienne Roesch 29 λάβωνοι Spyropoulos λάβωνθι Michaud,
Étienne, Roesch 30 [Θ]ιογνειτίδαο Spyropoulos [Θ]ι[ο]γνειτ[ί]δαο Michaud,
Étienne, Roesch 32 Βιωτίη Spyropoulos Βοιωτίη Michaud, Étienne, Roesch ἕξ

Spyropoulos, Étienne, Roesch ἔ[ξ] Michaud   34 ἐν Θειβᾶς Spyropoulos ἐ[ν Θ]ειβᾶς
Michaud, Étienne, Roesch   Θουθοδώρω Spyropoulos Πουθοδώρω Michaud, Étienne,
Roesch   35 ἐν Ὠρωπὸ Σαυ[κ]- Spyropoulos ἐν Ὠρωπὸν Σαυ- Michaud ἐν Ὠρωπὸν
Étienne, Roesch   36 [λε]αο Spyropoulos [κλ]έαο Michaud, Étienne, Roesch
Ὠρωπ[ω] Spyropoulos Ὠρωπὸν Michaud Ὠρωπ[ὸν] Étienne, Roesch   37 Ὠ[ρωπω]
Spyropoulos Ὠ[ρωπὸν] Michaud Ὠρ[ωπὸν] Étienne, Roesch   39 ΚΛΕΑΩΝ Spyro-
poulos [Σα]υκλέαο [ἀμέρας] Michaud [Σα]υκλέαο E- - - - - Étienne, Roesch

[God.] Good [fortun]e. When [Philokomos] was archon of the Boiotians, and
[Thiog]neitidas was archon of the Orchomenians, and the hipparch was
Tima[sithios son of Ari]stomachos, the squadron commanders were Saukle[as son
of . . .], Aristion son of Hermaios, Poutho[doros son of . . .]ikleas, and at Chaironeia Eumeilos son of Eunomios. Agreement between the cavalry forces of
Orchomenos and of Chaironeia, regarding military service. Because the preceding
campaigns during the archonship of Thiogneitidas at Orchomenos and of Philokomos in Boiotia have been concluded, let the campaigns begin during the archonship of Thiogneitidas at Orchomenos, and of Philokomos in Boiotia. Let the
following take part in the campaign: outsi[d]e Boiotia, first the squadron of Sau-
kl[ea]s, second the squadron of Pouthodoros, t[h]ird the Chaironeian squadron of
Eumeilos, [f]ourth the squadron of Aristion; within Boiotia, first the squadron of
Aristion, [s]econd the squadron of Pouthodoros, third the Chaironeian squadron
of Eumeilos, fourth the squadron of Sauklias. If some squadrons have served equal
time on campaign, let the hip[par]ch draw lots among the squadrons who have
served equal time. Let them keep track of the time they serve inside Boiotia and
outside it separately, for which they have accepted traveling expenses. When
[Th]i[o]gneit[i]das was archon, and Timasithios was hippar[ch], the following cavalry squadrons served in Boiotia: the squadron of Saukleas in Thebes, six days; the
squadron of Aristion in Thebes, nine days; the squadron of E[u]meilos i[n Th]ebes,
six days; the squadron of Pouthodoros [in Theb]es, eight days; in Oropos the
squadron of Sau[kl]eas, ten days; the squadron of Eumeilos in Or[opos], eight
days. Outside [Boiotia] [. . . of Sa]ukleas . . .

Lines 1–29 and 30–38 are inscribed by two different hands, though clearly in the
same year.

Date. The Boiotian archonship of Philokomos is dated to the period 285–280
by M. Feyel 1942b: 28 (cf. Roesch 1965b: 87 and 1982: 439; Knoepfler 2001b: 15–16)
primarily on the basis of linguistic and prosopographic considerations. This
coheres with the hints of historical context given by the document itself, which
indicates that at the time of the agreement Oropos was part of the Boiotian
koinon. We know it was from 313 to 304 (Diod. Sic. 19.78.3, 20.100; Plut. Demetr.
23), and again from 287 to 172 (Robert 1940–65: XI–XII.201; Petrakos 1968:
29–33). Although Thebes was rebuilt after 316, it received its full political autonomy from Demetrios Poliorketes only in 287 (Plut. Demetr. 46.1; cf. Roesch 1979:
246 and 1982: 436–38), when it was reintegrated into the koinon (Knoepfler

2001b). In this text it appears as part of Boiotia, and the Boiotians' concern to keep it a part of the koinon is implicit in the expectation of deployment in the territory of the city (ll. 35–36); around the same time the city of Oropos borrowed money for the construction of a wall (*IG* VII.4263; Migeotte 1984: 38 no. 9; Petrakos 1997: no. 303), implying significant defense needs (Knoepfler 2002: 131–43). Philokomos appears as archon of the Boiotians likewise in T16 and in a military catalogue from Orchomenos (*IG* VII.3175). Hennig 1977: 147–48 raises the possibility that the document should be associated with the second revolt of Boiotia against Demetrios in 292/1 or with the defeat of Antigonos Doson in the naval battle against Ptolemy Keraunos in 281 (Memnon 13.3; Just. 24.1.1–8). But the fact that Thebes and Oropos are the focus of the Boiotians' defensive concerns suggests a date closer to 287, when both had been recently reintegrated into the koinon and whose security may therefore have been seen to be especially vulnerable. Roesch 1982: 439 places the document in the period 287–285. C. Müller 2011: 270–71 suggests 287, on the grounds that it seems to represent two communities adjusting their practices to a new regulation, namely the reestablishment of the district system that governed military contributions inter alia, which was probably a response to, if not a condition of, the reintegration of Thebes into the koinon. This date has the effect of placing T16, also passed in the archonship of Philokomos, at the beginning of the series of aphedriate dedications, which are also products of the district system.

The agreement. Roesch 1979: 247 supposes that Chaironeia was grouped with Orchomenos in this year only because low population rendered it unable to contribute a full contingent on its own. But as Knoepfler 2000: 362–63 shows, there is nothing exceptional about the arrangement: Orchomenos and Chaironeia formed a district for the purposes of participation in regional sacrifices (through the agency of the aphedriates), and this document is best understood if we assume the same districts to have formed the basis for military levies, as they did in the fourth century (*Hell.Oxy.* 16.4 [Bartoletti]). The document allows us to see the mechanism by which the member poleis of a district fulfilled their military obligations to the koinon, and we should not be surprised, with Hennig 1977: 146–47, to see two poleis making an arrangement for their joint deployment of troops.

16. *Dedication of a Tripod by the Boiotoi to Apollo Ptoios*

Tripod base found at the Ptoion (Guillon 1943: I.13 Base III). 287 BCE or shortly after.

IG VII.2723.

Βοιωτοὶ Ἀπόλλωνι Πτωΐοι ἀνέθιαν, ἄρχοντος Βοιωτοῖς Φιλοκώμω [Ἀντ]ιγ[ενει]–
ίω Θε[ι]σπιε[ῖος],
ἀφεδριατευόντων Ἐμπεδο[κ]λεῖος Ἀθανοκριτίω Ταναγρήω, Πούθωνος Α[ὐ]–
τομει[δ]ε[ιι]ω Ἐρχομενίω,

Ἱπποτίωνος Ϝαστυμειδοντίω Κορωνεῖος,Ἐπιϝά[λτ]ιος Μαχωνίω Θειβήω,
Νικίωνος Γ[ρ]υλ[ί]ωνος Πλαταεῖος,
4   Ἀριστοκλεῖος Ἀγασιήω Ἀνθαδονίω, Σάωνος [Θ]ιο[τ]ιμίω Θεισπιεῖος,
μαντευομένω [Ὀ]νυμάστω Νικολαῖω Θεισπιεῖος.

The Boiotoi dedicated (this tripod) to Apollo Ptoios when Philokomos son of
[Ant]ig[ene]s of Thespia[i] was archon. The aphedriates were Empedo[k]les son of
Athanokritos of Tanagra, Pouthon son of A[u]tomei[d]es of Orchomenos,
Hippotion son of Wastumeidon of Koroneia, Epiwa[lt]es son of Machon of Thebes,
Nikion son of G[r]yl[i]on of Plataia, Aristokles son of Agasies of Anthedon, Saon
son of [Th]io[t]imos of Thespiai. [O]nymastos son of Nikolaos of Thespiai was the
mantis.

Roesch 1965b: 137 (cf. Roesch 1982: 424–25) placed this text slightly later than
T17–T19 on grounds of letter forms and his incorrect belief that it "n'a aucun lien
prosopographique avec les troies autres dédicaces": Onymastos son of Nikolaos is
also the *mantis* in the next three documents. Dated by the eponymous Boiotian
archon Philokomos, this text must belong to the same year as T15, probably 287.
Despite the identity of the *mantis*, each of the following dedications was made in a
different archon year.

This text, along with T17–T25, is our primary evidence for the magistrate college of aphedriates (see also *IG* VII.2724e with Guillon 1962), long known but the
subject of a significantly revised interpretation: see above, pp. 221–24, for full
discussion. Representatives of districts, the aphedriates can have been created
only when the district system was revived for the Boiotian koinon, probably in or
shortly after 287, when Thebes was restored to the koinon (C. Müller 2011: 270–
71). The *mantis* in these texts has been seen as the regular prophet who was
charged by the koinon to consult the oracle, as he was by other comers (Holleaux
1889b: 22, Busolt and Swoboda 1920–26: II.1437, and Roesch 1965b: 141), but he is
more likely to be "a delegate of the koinon, who consulted the oracle ... on its
behalf" (Schachter 1981–94: I.67 n. 3), and is thus to be distinguished from the
prophet himself.

17. Dedication of a Tripod by the Boiotoi to Apollo Ptoios
Tripod base found at the Ptoion (Guillon 1943: I.15 Base IV). After 287 BCE.
IG VII.2724.

Εὐμείλω ἄρχοντος Ἐπικουδείω Κορωνεῖ[ο]ς,
τοῖ Ἀπόλλωνι τὸν τρίποδα ἀνέθειαν Βοιωτοί, μαντευσ-
αμένω τῶ θεῶ καὶ ἀποδόντος τὰν ἀγαθὰν μαντείαν
4   Βοιωτοῖς, ἀφεδριατευόντων Εὐωνυμοδώρω Πυθορμίω Ἁλι-
αρτίω, Φιλίππω Ἀριστοκρατείω Θεισπιεῖος, Μοιρίχω Εὐκώμω Πλατ-
αιεῖος, Τρίακος Ἀντιδωρίω Θειβ[ε]ίω, Τερψίαο Φορυσκίω Ἐρχομενίω,
Μοσχίνω Θεδωρίδαο Λεπαδείηω, Ἀμεινοκλεῖος Ἀμεινίαο Ταν-

8   αγρήω, Ὀνουμάστω Νικολαῖω Θεισπιεῖος μάντιος.

5 Εὐβω‹λί›ω Dittenberger Εὐκώμω Knoepfler 1981: 317 n. 116

When Eumeilos son of Epikoudeos of Koroneia was archon, the Boiotoi dedicated this tripod to Apollo, for the god prophesied and gave a prophesy that was favorable to the Boiotoi. The aphedriates were Euonymodoros son of Pythormos of Haliartos, Philip son of Aristokrates of Thespiai, Moirichos son of Eukomos of Plataia, Triax son of Antidoros of Thebes, Terpsias son of Phoryskos of Orchomenos, Moschinos son of Thedoridas of Lebadeia, Ameinokles son of Ameinias of Tanagra. Onymastos son of Nikolaos of Thespiai was the *mantis*.

Date. This dedication and the following three, connected by the *mantis* Onymastos, were dated by Holleaux 1889b to the period 312–304, because the third in the group (T19) includes an aphedriate from Chalkis. Holleaux argued that Chalkis could have become a member of the Boiotian koinon only in 312, when it was liberated from Cassander's garrison (Diod. Sic. 19.77.4–6), and that it would have been lost in 304 when the Boiotians were driven from the city by Demetrios Poliorketes (Diod. Sic. 20.100.5–6). Holleaux's date was accepted by Roesch 1965b: 135–41 and Gullath 1982: 50–54, inter alios. Guillon 1943: 75 argued that this group belonged to the period ca. 280–240. But the mantic link between the documents, with Philokomos at the start of the series, puts this as well as T18 and T19 after 287.

·   *18. Dedication of a Tripod by the Boiotoi to Apollo Ptoios*

Tripod base found at the Ptoion (Guillon 1943: I.16–17 Base VI). After 287 BCE. *IG* VII.2724a.

[Βοιω]τοὶ Ἀπόλλωνι Πτ[ωῖο]ι ἄρχοντος Τρίακος Ἀντ[ι]δωρ[ίω Θειβήω],
ἀφεδριατευόντων Ὀλυνπίχω Ἀθαναγιτ[ο]νίω [Ἀ]κρηφ[ιεῖος],
Εὐμείλω Ἐπικουδείω Κορωνεῖος, Εὐπόρω Πολυκλείω [Θεισπιεῖος],
4   [.]ωρίμαο Πολυκλείω Ταναγρήω, Ἠσχριώνδαο Θιομναστ[ίω Θειβή]ω,
[Κ]ρατύλλω Ἀμφιδαμίω Ὠρωπίω, μαντευομένω Ὀνυμάστω Νικο[λαῖω]
Θεισπιεῖος,
Πάτρωνος Μιττίω Ἐρχομενίω.

The [Boio]toi (dedicated it) to Apollo Pt[oio]s when Triax son of Ant[i]dor[os of Thebes] was archon. The aphedriates were Olynpichos son of Athanagit[o]nos of [A]kraiph[ia], Eumeilos son of Epikoudeos of Koroneia, Euporos son of Polykles of [Thespiai], [.]orimas son of Polykles of Tanagra, Eschriondas son of Thiomnast[os of Theb]es, [K]ratyllos son of Amphidamos of Oropos. Onymastos son of Niko[laos] of Thespiai and Patron son of Mittos of Orchomenos were the *manteis*.

19. Dedication of a Tripod by the Boiotoi to Apollo Ptoios

Tripod base found at the Ptoion (Guillon 1943: I.16 Base V). After 287 BCE, perhaps 280–270.

IG VII.2724b.

Βοιωτοὶ Ἀπόλλωνι Πτωΐ[οι], ἄρχοντος Ἠσχρώνδαο Θιομνάστ[ω]
Θειβῆω, ἀφεδριατευόντων Κρισάδαο Ἀγχιαρίω Ἀριαρτίω,
Θηράρχω Στρωσιήω Θεισπιεῖος, Ἡροδώρω Εὐκώμω Πλαταεῖος,
4   Ἀπολλοδώρω Βροχχίω Θειβῆω, Νίωνος Ἀριστωνυμίω
Ταναγρήω, Θοίνωνος Τιμογιτονίω Ἐρχομενίω, Περιπόλ[ω]
Μικουλίω Χαλκιδεῖος, Πύρρακος Ἰθουδαμίω Θισβεῖος,
μαντευ[ο]μένω Ὀνυμάστω Νικολαΐω Θεισπιεῖος.

3 Εὐ‹β›ω‹λί›ω Dittenberger Εὐκώμω Knoepfler

The Boiotoi (dedicated it) to Apollo Ptoi[os] when Eschrondas son of Thiomnast[os] of Thebes was archon. The aphedriates were Krisadas son of Anchiaros of Haliartos, Therarchos son of Stroses of Thespiai, Herodoros son of Eukomos of Plataia, Apollodoros son of Bronchos of Thebes, Nion son of Aristonymos of Tanagra, Thoinon son of Timogiton of Orchomenos, Peripol[os] son of Mikoulos of Chalkis, Pyrrhax son of Ithoudamos of Thisbe. Onymastos son of Nikolaos of Thespiai was the *mantis*.

Knoepfler 1981: 317 n. 116 reports that Anne Jacquemin, after studying a squeeze of the stone made by Holleaux, confirms the reading Περιπόλ[ω]| Μικουλίω Χαλκιδεῖος in lines 5–6. Knoepfler gives his new reading of line 3 on the basis of a study of the squeeze.

Knoepfler 1991b: 210 places the archonship of Eschrondas (Aischrondas) in the period ca. 280–270; we would then associate Chalkis's participation with its liberation from Macedonia ca. 284–281. Cf. Knoepfler 1992: 450–51, 1995: 147, and 1998: 202–3, 207.

20. Dedication of a Tripod by the Boiotoi to Apollo Ptoios

Tripod base found at the Ptoion (Guillon 1943: I.20 Base XV). Mid-third century BCE (ca. 240–235).

IG VII.2724c.

Ἀχέλωνος ἄρχοντος Θειβῆω Βοιωτὺ
Ἀπόλ‹λ›ωνι Πτωΐυ κατ τὰν μαντείαν Ἀπόλ‹λ›ωνος τῶ Πτωΐω,
ἀφεδριατευόντων Πτωϊοκλεῖος Δεξιλάω Ἀκρηφειῖος,
4   Ἀριστοδίκω Ἀντικράτιος Θειβῆω, Τριακαδ‹ί›ωνος Ἀριστοκρίτω Ταναγρήω,
Δολίχω Σμίκρωνος Πλαταεῖος, Λανόμω Γλαυκίαο Θεισπιεῖος,
Θοινάρχω Καλλισθένιος Θισβεῖος, Βωτύλω Ἰσμεινοδώρω Χηρωνεῖος,
γραμ‹μ›ατίδ‹δ›οντος Θ‹ι›ογίτονος Ὀνασίμω Ὀρχομενίω.

When Achelon the Theban was archon, the Boiotians (dedicated it) to Apollo Ptoios in accordance with an oracle of Apollo Ptoios. The aphedriates were Ptoiokles son of Dexilaos of Akraiphia, Aristodikos son of Antikrates of Thebes, Triakadion son of Aristokritos of Tanagra, Dolichos son of Smikron of Plataia, Lanomos son of Glaukias of Thespiai, Thoinarchos son of Kallisthenes of Thisbe, Botylos son of Hismeino-doros of Chaironeia. The secretary was Thiogiton son of Onasimos of Orchomenos.

This text and T22, T23, and T25 all mention a secretary to the aphedriates, which office is taken to mark an evolution of the college, placing these texts later than the previous four. It is assumed that in the lacuna of T24 a secretary would have been mentioned, and it is possible that such a reference is also missing from T21. See Knoepfler 2000: 360 with n. 61.

21. Dedication of a Tripod by the Boiotoi to Apollo Ptoios

Tripod base found at the Ptoion (Guillon 1943: I.22 Base XIX). Mid-third century BCE. *IG* VII.2724d.

> Μνάσωνος [ἄρχοντος] Βοιωτὺ Ἀπόλλωνι Πτωῖυ
> κατ τὰν μαντεί[αν, ἀφε]δριατευόντων
> Εὐφαμίδαο Θιογέν[ιος Κο]ρωνεῖος,
> 4   [Σω]σστρότω Νίκων[ος] Ἐρχομενίω,
> Ἀρισστοκράτιος [Εμ]πέδωνος Κωπήω,
> [F]ίλλωνος Τειλε[φ]άνιος Θειβήω,
> Δαμηνέτω Ἰσσχί[ν]αο Ταναγρήω.

3 Θιογέ[νιος . . .]ρωνεῖος Dittenberger

When Mnason was [archon], the Boiotians (dedicated it) to Apollo Ptoios in accordance with an oracl[e. The aphe]driates were Euphamidas son of Thiogen[es of Ko]roneia, [So]sstrotos son of Nikon of Orchomenos, Arisstokrates son of [Em]pedon of Kop[a]i, [W]illon son of Teile[ph]aneis of Thebes, and Damenetos son of Isschi[n]as of Tanagra.

The ethnic of Thiogen[es] in line 3 could be either Chai]roneia (cf. T20 line 6) or Ko]roneia (cf. T16 line 3). Since, however, Orchomenos (which appears in line 4) and Chaironeia functioned as a district and are never otherwise represented by an aphedriate in the same year, it is much more likely to be Koroneia, and I have restored it accordingly. That there are a total of five spaces (not six, as Chai]roneia would require) in the lacuna is supported by Dittenberger's majuscule copy (*IG* VII.2724d): ΘΙΟΓΕΙ. . . . . ΡΩΝΕΙΟΣ. Holleaux 1889a (*ed.pr.*) reports that the stone is intact to the right. Neither *mantis* nor secretary is mentioned on this stone; this omission, along with the reduced number of aphedriates (five rather than the usual seven), may be grounds for placing it later in the series than the others; indeed M. Feyel 1942b: 50 n. 1 and Guillon 1943: II.73 (cf. Holleaux 1889a: 227) place the archonship of Mnason ca. 230.

22. Dedication of a Tripod by the Boiotoi to the Muses

Tripod base found in the church of Agia Triada on Mount Helikon, now in the Thebes Museum (inv. 2014). Mid-third century BCE. *IG* VII.1795. *Roesch *IThesp* 287 (based on squeeze).

[Βοιωτοὶ τὸν] τρίποδ[α ἀνέθεικαν] τῆς
[Μώσης τῆς Ἑ]λικ[ωνιά]δεσσι κὰτ τ[ὰν μαντείαν τῶ] Ἀπόλλω-
[νος τῶ Πτοίω, ἄρχοντος] Ξένωνος Διοδ[ω]ρίω Θειβήω, ἀφεδρια-
4   [τευόντων – – – name – – – – –] Φίλ[ω]νος Θεισπιεῖος, Ἑρμαίω Ἀμεινίαο
     Ὀρχ[ο]–
     [μενίω, – – – – – name – – – – –]νος Πλαταιέος, Ἀντιγενίδαο Εὐμόλπω
     Ἀριαρτ[ίω],
     [– – – – name – – –patronymic– Θει]βήω, Στρότωνος Τιμοξενίω Ταναγρήω, ᵛ
     Θεοζότω
     [– – – – patronymic – – – – –]κλε[ῖο]ς Κορωνεῖος, γραμματίδδοντος
     Φερεν[ίκω]
8   [– patronymic, ethnic – – –, μαντευο]μένω [Ἀ]γωνος Ἀριστονοίω Θεισπιεῖος.

[The Boiotoi dedicated the trip]od [to the Muses of He]lik[on] in accordance with
a[n oracle of] Apollo [Ptoios] when Xenon son of Diod[o]ros of Thebes was [archon].
The aphedria[tes were . . .] son of Philon of Thespiai, Hermaios son of Ameinias of
Orch[omenos, [. . .] son of [. . .]n of Plataia, Antigenidas son of Eumolpos of
Haliart[os], [. . . son of . . .] of Thebes, Stroton son of Timoxenos of Tanagra, Theozo-
tos [son of . . .]kles of Koroneia. The secretary was Pheren[ikos son of . . . of . . .]; the
[*mantis*] was [A]gon son of Ariston of Thespiai.

Knoepfler 2000: 361 n. 67, relying on Dittenberger's text, restores the ethnic of
Θεοζότω (l. 6), which is lost in the end of the lacuna in line 7, as Ὠ[ρω]πί[ω], on
the basis of the appearance of a Θεοζότος at Oropos (Petrakos 1997: 69, 135, 151–52,
174). But Roesch's study of the stone and squeeze, on which the text in *IThesp* is
based, seems to rule out that reading.

23. Dedication of a Tripod by the Boiotoi to the Graces

Semicircular tripod base found in the church at Orchomenos. Mid-third century
BCE.

IG VII.3207.

     Βοιωτοὶ τὸν τρίποδα ἀνέθεικαν
     τῆς Χαρίτεσσι κατ τὰν μαντεῖαν
     τῶ Ἀπόλλωνος, ἄρχοντος
4   Σαμίαο Ἰσμεινικέταο Θειβήω,
      ἀφεδριατευόντων
     Μελάννιος Νικοκλεῖος Ἐρχομενίω
     Ἡσχρίωνος Θερσανδρίχω Κορωνεῖος
8   Ἀρνοκλεῖος Ἀνιοχίδαο Ἀνθαδονίω
     Ἀρίστωνος Μεννίδαο Θεισπιεῖος
     Πραξιτέλιος Ἀριστοκλίδαο Θειβήω
     Θιομνάστω Ἑρμαΐχω Ταναγρήω
12   Πούθωνος Καλλιγίτονος Ὠρωπίω
      γραμματεύοντος

Διοκλεῖος Διοφάντω Πλαταεῖος
μαντευομένω
16   Δινίαο Ἐροτίωνος Θεισπιεῖος
θι[ο]προπίοντος
Οἰνοχίδαο Εὐμενίδαο Ἐρχομενίω
[ἰαρ]ατεύοντος
20   Λαμπρίαο Θιοδότω Ἐρχομενίω.

The Boiotoi dedicated the tripod to the Graces in accordance with an oracle of Apollo, when the archon was Samias son of Hismeiniketas of Thebes. The aphedriates were Melannios son of Nikokles of Orchomenos, Eschrion son of Thersandrichos of Koroneia, Arnokles son of Haniochidas of Anthedon, Ariston son of Mennidas of Thespiai, Praxiteles son of Aristoklidas of Thebes, Thiomnastos son of Hermaichos of Tanagra, Pouthon son of Kalligiton of Oropos. The secretary was Diokles son of Diophantos of Plataia. The *mantis* was Dinias son of Erotion of Thespiai. The one sent to consult the oracle was Oinochidas son of Eumenidas of Orchomenos. The priest was Lamprias son of Thiodotos of Orchomenos.

24. Dedication of a Tripod by the Boiotoi to Zeus Eleutherios

Semicircular tripod base of white marble, found in the Byzantine church near Plataia. Mid-third century BCE.
IG VII.1672.

Βοιωτοὶ Διὶ Ἐλευθερίοι τὸν [τρίποδα ἀνέθεικαν]
κατὰ τὰν μαντείαν τῶ Ἀπόλλω[νος – – –]
ἄρχοντος Βοιωτοῖς Λουσιμνάστ[ω, – – –]
4   ἀφεδριατευόντων·
Δωρόθεος Ἀριστέαο Πλατηεύς, Ε[–ca. 8 –]
Ἰσμηνίχω Θειβῆος, Εὐρούμει Διοσκο[ρί]-
[δα]ο Θεισπιεύς, Καφισόδωρος Ἐρμα[ῖω –ca. 6 –]
8   Μαντίας Νικοκλείδαο Ἀνθ[αδόνιος].
μαντευομένω Ὁμολωΐχω.

1 τὸν[τρίποδα ἀνέθεικαν – – –]Girard τὸν[τρίποδα]|Dittenberger   2 Ἀπόλ[λωνος Girard Ἀπόλλω[νος] Dittenberger   6 Εὐρουμείδιος Κο... Girard Εὐρούμει Διοσκο[ρί] Dittenberger   7 ..ο Θεισπιεύς, Καφισόδωρος Ἐρμα[ῖχω... Girard [δα]ο Θεισπιεύς, Καφισόδωρος Ἐρμα[ῖω ....] Dittenberger   8 [Ἀ]νθ[αδόνιος Girard Ἀνθ[αδόνιος] Dittenberger

The Boiotoi (dedicated) the [tripod] to Zeus Eleutherios in accordance with an oracle of Apollo when the archon of the Boiotians was Lousimnast[os]. The aphedriates were Dorotheos son of Aristeas of Plataia, E[...] son of Hismenichos of Thebes, Euroumes son of Diosko[rida]s of Thespiai, Kaphisodoros son of Herma[ios ...], Mantias son of Nikokleidas of Anth[edon]. The *mantis* was Homoloichos.

The stone must be broken at the right, and the facsimile made by Girard 1887: 208 no. 1 shows that a considerable amount of text is lost. This is not reflected in Dittenberger's *IG* text. The lost ethnic in line 7 is likely to be Θισβεῖος (T19 l. 6, T20 l. 6) or Θισβέως (T26 l. 4), the shortest of the five ethnics that could be restored given that we have no representative from either District IV (Orchomenos, Chaironeia) or District VI (Lebdaeia, Koroneia, Thisbe).

25. Dedication of a Tripod by the Boiotoi to Zeus Eleutherios

Semicircular tripod base of white marble found in the Byzantine church near Plataia. Mid-third century BCE.

IG VII.1673.

[– ᶜᵃ· ³ –]δότω Πυρράλω Θεισπιεῖο[ς, – ᶜᵃ· ³ –]
[– ᶜᵃ· ⁴ –νί]κω Ἰσμεινικέταο Θειβή[ω, – ᶜᵃ· ³ –]
[–ᶜᵃ· ⁴ –] Ἀριστίωνος Ἐρχομεν[ίω – ᶜᵃ· ³ –]
4   [– ᶜᵃ· ⁴ –] Ἀριστομάχω Ὑειττίω, [– ᶜᵃ· ³ –]
[Θιοπρ]οπίοντος Δινίαο Ἐροτ[ίωνος]
[Θεισπιεῖος, Ἀ]ντιγενείδαο γραμματίδδον[τος].

[. . .]dotos son of Pyrrhalos of Thespiai, [. . .ni]kos son of Hismeniketas of Thebes, [. . .] son of Aristion of Orchomen[os, . . .] son of Aristomachos of Hyettos, [. . .]; [the one who consulted] the prophet was Dinias son of Erot[ion of Thespiai. A]ntigeneidas was secretar[y].

At least two lines are entirely missing from the top of the stone; Dittenberger restored them following *IG* VII.1672 (T24), but given the variety of formulations found in the tripod dedications at the Ptoion, it is more prudent simply to signal their necessary presence. The stone is likewise broken at the left and the right. The ethnic of Dinias son of Erotion in line 6 is restored by Dittenberger on the basis of *IG* VII.3207 (T23), where the same individual appears.

26. Proxeny Decree of the Boiotian Koinon for Ophelas of Amphipolis

Found at the Amphiareion. 287–ca. 225 BCE.

Ed.pr. Mitsos 1952: 181 no. 14 with photo of a squeeze, fig. 8 (*SEG* 15.282; Moretti 1967–76: I.63). Petrakos 1967: 8–9 no. 3 prints a new text on the basis of a squeeze made by Leonardos (*SEG* 24.347). *Petrakos 1997: no. 21 based on a new study of the stone, with photo, plate 45.

[Α]ἰσχρίωνος ἄρχοντος Βοιωτοῖς, βοιωταρχούντων Καφισοδώρου Χάρητος
    Θηβαίου, Μηλίου
[Ἀ]ριστοδήμου Ὀπουντίου, Εὐαρχίδου Πτωϊοτίμου Ἀκραιφιέως, Λυσάνδρου
    Φανοστράτου Ὠρωπίου,
[Θηβ]αγγέλου Ἰσμηνίου Θεσπιέως, Διογένου Οἰνίωνος Ταναγραίου, Θύρρωνος
    Λυσίνου Ὀρχομενίου,

4   [Τι]μοκρίτου Θεο[πόμ]που Θισβέως, γραμματεύοντος Εὐρυφάοντος Καλλι[έ]-
     ρωνος Χαιρωνέως,
     [μην]ὸς Πανάμου, ἐπεψήφι[ζ]ε Κηφισόδωρος Χάρητος, Λύσανδρος
     Φανοστράτου ἔλεξεν· δεδό-
     [χθαι] τῶι δήμωι· Ὀφέλ[α]ν Φιλή[μ]ονος Ἀμφιπολίτην πρόξενον εἶναι καὶ
     εὐεργέτην τοῦ κοινοῦ Βοιωτῶ[ν]
     [κα]ὶ αὐτὸν καὶ ἐκγόνους καὶ εἶναι αὐτοῖς γῆς καὶ οἰκίας ἔγκτησιν καὶ
     ἰσοτέλειαν καὶ ἀσφάλειαν
8   καὶ ἀσυλία[γ?] καὶ πολέμου καὶ εἰρήνης καὶ τὰ ἄλλα πάντα καθάπερ καὶ τοῖς
     ἄλλοις προξένοις καὶ
     εὐεργέταις τοῦ κοινοῦ Βοιωτῶν.

1 Κηφισοδώρου Mitsos Καφισοδώρου Petrakos   3 [Θη]βαγγέλου Mitsos [Θηβ]-
ανγέλου Petrakos   4 . .μοκρίτου E.... . .ου Mitsos [Τι]μοκρίτου Θεο[πόμ]που
Petrakos   Καλλίφρονος Mitsos Καλλι[έ]ρωνος Petrakos   5 ἐπε[ψ]ήφιζε Mitsos ἐπεψήφι[ζ]ε Petrakos   6 Ὀφέλα Ὠφελίωνος Mitsos Ὀφέλ[α]ν Φιλή[μ]ονος
Petrakos   Βοιωτῶν Mitsos   Βοιωτῶ[ν] Petrakos   7 Mitsos leaves out initial [κα]ὶ
read by Petrakos   8 τἆλλα Mitsos τὰ ἄλλα Petrakos   9 τῶν Βοιωτῶν Mitsos τοῦ κοινοῦ Βοιωτῶν Petrakos

When [A]ischrion was archon of the Boiotians, the boiotarchs were Kaphisodoros
son of Chares of Thebes, Melios son of Aristodemos of Opous, Euarchidos son of
Ptoiotimos of Akraiphia, Lysandros son of Phanostratos of Oropos, Thebangelos son
of Ismenios of Thespiai, Diogenes son of Oinion of Tanagra, Thyrrhon son of Lysinos
of Orchomenos, [Ti]mokritos son of Theo[pom]pos of Thisbe, and the secretary was
Euryphaon son of Kallieron of Chaironeia; in the month of Panamos, Kephisodoros
son of Chares voted, and Lysandros son of Phanostratos spoke. Reso[lved] by the
dēmos: Ophel[a]s son of Phile[m]on of Amphipolis shall be proxenos and benefactor
of the koinon of the Boiotians, himself and his descendants, and they shall have the
right to own land and houses, *isoteleia, asphaleia,* and *asylia,* in war and in peace, and
all the other rights and privileges that belong to other proxenoi and benefactors of
the koinon of the Boiotians.

Date. Roesch 1965b: 83 and 88 places the archonship of Aischrion ca. 280–245, and
more particularly 263–257, because following Mitsos's reading of line 6 he assumed it
had to be contemporary with a decree of Rhamnous (*SEG* 3.122) that names the individual Ophelas son of Ophelion. Petrakos's new reading of the stone, however, dis-
sociates the text from that individual, and he argues that it should be placed simply
in the period between 287, when Oropos joined the Boiotian koinon, and 245, when
Opous went over to the Aitolian koinon (an opinion offered by Beloch 1912–27:
IV.2.429–32, which was long accepted uniformly). However, Scholten 2000: 259–60
has shown that Beloch's assumption is not supported by subsequent epigraphic discoveries and suggests that Opous remained part of the Boiotian koinon until it was
seized by Antigonos Doson in the early 220s; Knoepfler 1995: 148 n. 62 suggests that
he is in agreement. I accordingly date the text to the period 287–ca. 225.

Roesch 1965b: 83 (*SEG* 23.269 and *BE* 68.281) notes that the reading Θύρρωνος in line 3 allows us to restore this name at the head of the Boiotian decree recognizing the *asylia* of the festival of Artemis Leukophryene at Magnesia (*IMagn.* 25B line 1).

27. *Thespian Proxeny Decree and Law of the Boiotian Koinon on Military Training*

Found in a field on the site of ancient Thespiai, spring 1967. Ca. 250–240 BCE.
Ed.pr. *Roesch 1971 (Roesch 1982: 307–54; *SEG* 32.496; *IThesp* 29).

Φαείνω ἄρχοντος, ἔδοξε τοῖ δάμοι
πρόξενον εἶμεν τᾶς πόλιος Θεισ-
πιείων Σώστρατον Βατράχω Ἀθανῆ-
4   ον κὴ αὐτὸν κὴ ἐκγόνως κὴ εἶμεν αὐ-
[τ]οῖς γᾶς κὴ ϝοικίας ἔππασιν κὴ ϝι-
[σο]τέλειαν κὴ ἀσφάλιαν κὴ ἀσουλί-
[αν] κὴ πολέμω κὴ ἰράνας ἰώσας κὴ κα-
8   τὰ γᾶν κὴ κατὰ θάλατταν κὴ τἆλλα
πάντα καθάπερ κὴ τοῖς ἄλλοις προ-
ξένοις· Ἐπειδεὶ νόμος ἐστὶ ἐν τοῖ κοι-
νοῖ Βοιωτῶν τὰς πόλις παρεχέμεν
12   διδασκάλως οἵτινες διδάξονθι
τώς τε παῖδας κὴ τὼς νιανίσκως
τοξευέμεν κὴ ἀκοντιδδέμεν
κὴ τάδδεσθη συντάξις τὰς περὶ
16   τὸν πόλεμον, κὴ Σώστροτος φιλο-
τίμως ἐπιμεμέλειτη τῶν τε παίδων
κὴ τῶν νεανίσκων, ὑπαρχέμεν Σωσ-
στράτοι τὸ ϝέργον πὰρ τᾶς πόλιος ἄως
20   κα βείλειτη, ἐπιμελομένοι τῶν τε παίδων κὴ τῶν νεανίσκων κὴ διδάσκον-
τι καθὰ ὁ νόμος κέλετη· μισθὸν δ᾽ εἶμεν αὐτοῖ τῶ ἐνιαυτῶ πέτταρας
24   μνᾶς.

When Phaeinos was archon, resolved by the people that Sostratos son of Batrachos the Athenian should be proxenos of the polis of Thespiai, he and his descendants, and they should have the right to acquire land and houses, along with *i[so]teleia*, *asphaleia*, and *asylia* in war and peace, by land and by sea, and all the other rights and privileges belonging to the other proxenoi. Because there is a law of the koinon of the Boiotians that the poleis must provide trainers who will teach the boys and the youths to shoot bows, to hurl javelins and to draw up ranks in battle array for wartime situations, and because Sostratos zealously took charge of the boys and youths, it was resolved by the polis for Sostratos to undertake the task, having charge of the boys and youths and teaching them as the law requires. Let him be paid annually four mnas.

This inscription is our only evidence that there was a federal law on military preparation (Roesch). Cassayre 2010: 70–71 takes the federal law as a marker of the relative weakness of member poleis. What is equally interesting is that the decree was issued by the polis of Thespiai and shows it to be exercising a considerable degree of freedom in the way it meets the requirement imposed by the "law of the koinon of the Boiotians." Sostratos the Athenian seems to have been resident at Thespiai, fully enough integrated into the community to be entrusted with training the boys who would become the city's future infantry contingent.

28. Treaty between Boiotia and Phokis

Elateia. 228–224 BCE.

Ed.pr. Lolling 1878. *IG* IX.1.98 (*Moretti 1967–76: II.83).

 [ἐὰν δέ τι ὑπεκ]τίθεσθαι βο[ύλω]ν[τ]α[ι Βοιωτοὶ εἰς τὴν Φωκίδα ἢ]
 [Φωκεῖς εἰς Βοι]ω[τ]ίαν, ἀτέλειαν εἶναι αὐτοῖς εἰ[σάγουσί τε καὶ]
 [ἐὰν πάλιν ἐ]ξάγωνται· ἐν δὲ τῆι χώραι διδόναι τ[ὰ τέλη - - -]
4 [- - -]ναιτο δίκαιον διδόναι αὐτοὺς καὶ λ[αμβάνειν - - -]
 [ἐὰν δέ τις] γίνηται ἀπὸ τῶν ὑπεκτιθεμένων κα[ρπός, ἀτελῆ εἶναι]
 [παντὸς τέλους π]αρ' ἑκατέροις· ὑπὲρ δὲ τῶν ἄλλων ἁπάντ[ων τὰ νόμι]-
 [μα τέλη λ]αμβάνειν Βοιωτοὺς καὶ Φωκεῖς παρ' ἀλλή[λων - - -]
8 [- - - ἐξ]εῖναι δὲ Βοιωτοῖς καὶ Φωκεῦσι διορθώσασ[θαι ἐν ταῖς συν]-
 [θήκαις] ὃ ἂν δόξηι κοινῆι ἀμφοτέροις. ὀμνύειν δὲ τὰ [ἀμφοτέρων ἀρ]-
 [χεῖα τά τε κοι]νὰ καὶ τὰ κατὰ πόλεις καθ' ἕκαστον ἐνιαυτὸν ἐφ[- - -]
 [- - -]λην ἐπειδὰν αἱρεθῆι, τὰ μὲν Βοιωτῶν ἐν Ὀγχηστ[ῶι, τὰ δὲ Φω]-
12 [κέων ἐν Ἐ]λατείαι· ἐξορκιζέτωσαν δὲ τοὺς μὲν βοιωτάρχ[ας οἱ τῶν]
 [Φωκέων κο]ινοὶ στρατηγοί, τοὺς δὲ στρατηγοὺς καὶ τὰ κατὰ π[όλεις]
 [ἀρχεῖα οἱ] βοιωτάρχαι· τὸ δὲ ὅρκιον ἑκάτεροι παρεχόντων. ὅρκος·
 [ὀμνύω τ]ὸν Δία τὸμ Βασιλέα καὶ τὴν Ἥραν τὴμ Βασίλειαν καὶ τὸμ Ποσει-
16 [δῶνα καὶ τὴ]ν Ἀθηνᾶν καὶ τοὺς ἄλλους θεοὺς πάντας καὶ πάσας ἐμ[μενεῖν τῆι]
 [συμμαχίαι Βο]ιωτοῖς καὶ Φωκεῦσι κατὰ τὰς ὁμολογίας ἀδόλως εἰς τὸν
 [πάντα χρ]όνον· εὐορκοῦντι μέμ μοι εἴη πολλὰ κἀγαθά, εἰ δ' ἐφιορκοίην, τἀ-
 [ναντία. το]ὺς δὲ βοιωτάρχας καὶ τοὺς στρατηγοὺς ἀνα-
20 [γράψαι τὴ]ν συμμαχίαν εἰς στήλην καὶ ἀναθεῖναι ἑκατέρους
 [παρ' ἑαυτο]ῖς ἐν ἱερῶι, οὗ ἂν δοκῆι ἐγ καλλίστωι εἶναι.

8–9 διορθώσασ[θαι - - -|- - -] ὃ Dittenberger   διορθώσασ[θαι ἐν ταῖς συν|θήκαις]
ὃ Moretti 14 βοιωτάρχαι Dittenberger   βοιώταρχαι Moretti

If the Boiotians wish to bring anything into Phokis for safety, or the Phokians into Boiotia, they shall be allowed to import it, and to export it again if they wish, free of taxes. . . . to pay taxes in the territory . . . they shall give what is due and t[ake. . . . If some fr]uit is borne from goods deposited for safety, [it shall be free of all tax] imposed by either (the Boiotians or the Phokians). The Boiotians and Phokians may exact the usual taxes on all other goods from each other. . . . Both the Boiotians and the Phokians may revise . . . whatever is resolved by both in common. Let them both swear the official joint oaths in each polis individually . . . whenever one is elected, the (oaths?) of the Boiotians in Onchest[os, those of the Phokians in E]lateia. Let the common generals [of the Phokians] administer the oaths to the boiotarchs, and let the boiotarchs administer the oaths to the (Phokian) generals and the (Boiotian) cities. Each shall provide the following oath. Oath: [I swear b]y Zeus Basileus and Hera Basileia and Posei[don and] Athena and all the other gods and goddesses to re[main loyal to the alliance] between the Boiotians and the Phokians, according to the agreements, without guile and for [all t]ime. If I remain true to the oath, may all good things come to me, but if I violate the oath, the [opposite. Th]e boiotarchs and the generals shall in[scribe th]e alliance on a stele, and each shall set up a copy in their own shrine, in whatever place seems best.

This treaty has been gradually downdated since it was first published by Lolling, who placed it in the mid-third century on paleographical grounds. It has been placed a little before the battle of Chaironeia in 245 (Schober, *RE* s.v. Phokis col. 493), in the year 228 (M. Feyel 1942b: 124–25), in 221 or 206 (Flacelière 1937: 289 n. 2), after 196, again on paleographical grounds (Dittenberger, *IG* IX.1.98, followed by McInerney 1999: 252), and after 189 (Moretti 1967–76: II.83). In my view, it is more likely to belong to the period 228–224: Roesch 1982: 359–64 (228 or 227); Nafissi 1995 (perhaps more likely 224). For the complete reciprocity of the terms of the alliance point not to subordination but to equality between the two koina, which can have occurred only after Phokis was liberated from Aitolia between 228 and 224 by Antigonos Doson. Doson's raid on central Greece, now attested by the Xanthian inscription recording an embassy from Dorian Kytenion (Bousquet 1988b; F. W. Walbank 1989), appears to have separated eastern Phokis, including Elateia, from the Aitolian koinon (M. Feyel 1942b: 114–16). By 224 both Phokis and Boiotia had joined Antigonos's Hellenic Alliance: Polyb. 4.9.4, 15.1; 11.5.4, with Hammond, Griffith, and Walbank 1972–88: III.341; Scholten 2000: 175. That the alliance was not concluded much after that is necessitated by the reconquest of Phokis by Philip V in 218, from whom Flamininus liberated it in 198; he then handed it over to the Aitolians again in 196. And after 196, Boiotia remained loyal to Macedonia and hostile to Rome, making an alliance after 196 unlikely. Cf. Roesch 1982: 359–60. The document seems to best fit the historical context of Doson's liberation of central Greece in the period 228–224; we have no other grounds on which to date it.

29. Public Debt at Akraiphia

Akraiphia. Third century BCE.

The text is inscribed on the left side of a quadrangular block of white marble, below two military catalogues, and opposite the text below (T30).

Ed.pr. Pappadakis 1923: 190 with photograph, fig. 2 (*SEG* 3.356; Schwahn 1931a: 342–46; Pleket 1964: no. 30; *NCIG* 24A, with translation and commentary;

*Migeotte 1984: no. 16A, with translation and commentary; Chandezon 2003: no. 8).

[Κ]άλλων Σωσιφάνιος ἀφεῖκε τὰν
[π]όλιν ἀφ᾽ ὡῶφειλε αὐτῦ, ἀπὸ δρ[α]-
[χ]μάων χειλιάων ἑξακατιάων
4   ἑβδομείκοντα διοὺ πέντ᾽ ὀβολ[ῶ]ν
[ἑ]μνιωβελίω, ἀφ᾽ οὕτω ἀφεῖκε δρα-
[χ]μὰς ἑξακατίας ἑβδομείκοντα
διοὺ πέντ᾽ ὀβολὼς ἑμνιωβέλιον
8   [κ]ὴ τόκον παντὸς τῶ ἀργουρίω ‹ὣ›
[ἀν]εγέγραπτο ἁ πόλις ϝετίων
[πέ]ντε, δραχμὰς ὀκτακατίας
[τρι]άκοντα πέντε.
12   [ἁ π]όλις Ἀκρηφιείων ἔδωκε Κάλ-
[λ]ωνι Σωσιφάνιος αὐτῦ κὴ ἐγγό-
[ν]υς ἐπινομίαν βοτῦ ϛ ϝιδίυς
πεντείκοντα.

[K]allon son of Sosiphanos released the [p]olis from its debt to him, namely 1,672 dra[ch]mas, 5 ob[o]ls and a [h]alf; from this total he released them (from the obligation of paying) six hundred seventy-two dra[ch]mas, five obols and a half, as well as the interest on the total amount [that] the polis had [re]corded for five years, 835 drachmas. The polis of the Akraiphians gave to Kal[l]on son of Sosiphanos and to his descen[da]nts the right to pasture fifty of their own animals (on public land).

Bogaert 1979: 126–28 points out that the debt owed by Akraiphia to Kallon may have been the result not of a loan but of a purchase made by them on credit. However, the number of texts indicating a rather severe financial crisis in Boiotia in the third century puts this decree in a clear context: the cities were in dire financial straits, compelled to take out loans that many were unable to repay. For the general picture see Schwahn 1931a and M. Feyel 1942a: 148–55. On *epinomia*, the right of pasturage, in Boiotia see M. Feyel 1942a: 151–52; Roesch 1965b: 212–13. It is a privilege extended to proxenoi in Thessaly in the early third century: *SEG* 36.549 (Pharsalos); *SEG* 48.660 (Mopseion). Gabrielsen 2005 draws attention to the increasing importance of private, nonprofessional lenders in providing credit to cities in the Hellenistic period, a dossier into which both this and the next document fit very well.

30. Akraiphia Borrows from a Theban

Akraiphia. Third century BCE.

Inscribed on the right side of a quadrangular block of white marble, opposite the text above (T29).

Ed.pr. Pappadakis 1923: 192–94 (Schwahn 1931a: 343–46 [*SEG* 3.359]); Pleket 1964: no. 31 (*NCIG* 24B); *Migeotte 1984: no. 16B, with translation and commentary.

[Φ]ρουνίχ[ω] ἄρχοντος, Ε[ὐκ]-
[λ]ίδας Θεοπόμπω Θειβ[ῆος]
ἀφεῖκε τὰν πόλιν ἀπὸ [τῶ]
4   δανεί[ω], τῶ ὤφειλε αὐτ[ῦ ἁ]
πόλις ἐπὶ τῇ ἱαρῇ γῇ τ[ῶ]
Ἀπόλλωνος κὰτ τὸ ψάφισ-
μα τῶ δάμω, ἀπὸ δραχμά-
8   ων πεντάκις χειλιάων
διακατιάων ἑξείκοντα
ἱᾶς δύ᾽ ὀβολῶν ἐμνιωβελί[ω],
ἀφ᾽ οὕτω ἀφεῖκε ἀργουρίω δρα-
12 χμὰς τρισ[χ]ειλίας ἑ-
κατὸν ἑξ[είκον]τα τρῖς
ὀβολόν.

5 [τῇ] Pappadakis, Pleket   13 ἑξ[ήκον]τα Pappadakis ἑξ[είκον]τα Pleket, Migeotte

When [Ph]rounik[os] was archon, E[ukl]idas son of Theopompos the Theb[an] released the city from [the] loan that [the] polis owed to him on security of the sacred land [of] Apollo according to the vote of the people of 5,261 drachmas, 2 obols and a half. He has reduced this loan by 3,163 drachmas, 1 obol.

Migeotte 1984: 76 notes that letter forms suggest this document to be slightly later than T29, but with so few chronologically fixed local documents in this period the argument is necessarily impressionistic. The document has attracted the interest of Migeotte 1980 and Dignas 2002: 27–28 for its evidence of a city mortgaging sacred land for a loan made by a private individual. Knoepfler 1992: 478–79 points out that the name of the lender, which has been reprinted as Ε[ὐκλ]ίδας since it was thus restored in the *editio princeps,* could be any number of other names.

31. Boiotian Arbitration of a Boundary Dispute between Akraiphia and Kopai

Found in the Kopaic Plain, 500 meters northwest of Cape Phtelia, 500 meters southwest of Gla. Third century BCE.

Inscribed on a large cubic stone (4.0 m high, 3.90 m wide). Photo Lauffer 1985: 106 no. 19.

*Ed.pr. *IG* VII.2792 (*Syll.*³ 933; Daverio Rocchi 1988: 120–22 no. 9; Ager 1996: no. 17; Magnetto 1997: no. 63).

Ὅρια Κ[ω]πήων
πὸτ᾽ Ἀκρηφιεῖα[ς]
ὀριττ[ά]ντων Βοιω[τῶν].

Borders of Kopai toward Akraiphia. The Boiotians arbitrated.

The text is mentioned by Roesch 1965b: 64 in a discussion of the representational district of Kopai and Akraiphia. Roesch 1982: 397 notes the complete absence of foreign judges in the Boiotian epigraphic record, as here, suggesting that the Boiotians used the koinon where completely autonomous and independent poleis would have had recourse to foreign arbitrators. Daverio Rocchi 1988: 120–22 discusses the nature of this border, following Roesch (1965b: 64) in suggesting that the dispute was primarily economic: the sale of fish from Lake Kopaïs, including eel and a variety of freshwater fish (see Lytle 2010), was a mainstay of the local economy, and the position of the inscribed stone suggests that the dispute may have arisen over fishing rights and the extent of each community's territory in the lake.

32. Agreement between Chorsiai and Thisbe Regarding Public Debt

Found at Thisbe, now in the Thebes Museum. 200–190 BCE.

Ed.pr. Pappadakis 1923: no. 1 with photograph p. 183 (*SEG* 3.342, with restorations suggested by Crönert and Haussoullier *per epist.*). *Roesch 1965a: 252–56 (*SEG* 22.407; *Staatsverträge* III.565, 25.513; Moretti 1967–76: I.65; Migeotte 1984: no. 11).

[Θεο]ῖς.
ὁμόλο[γον τῆ πό]λι Θισβείων πὸτ τὰν πόλιν
Χορσιείω[ν ο]ὑπὲρ ὧν ἀξίωσε ἁ πόλις Χορσιε[ίων]
4   τὰμ πόλιν Θισβείων περὶ τῶν χρειμάτ[ων, τὰ]
ὦφλε ἁ πόλις Χορσιείων τῆ πόλι Θισβε[ίων, δρα]-
χμάων μουριάων χειλιάων πεντακατ[ιάων]
τριάκοντα ὀκτὸ πέντε ὀβολῶν, κὴ ὁ ἐπίθωσ[ε ποτ]-
8   θέσθη τῶν χρόνων, τρισχειλιάων ἐξακα[τιάων]
πεντείκοντα δύ' ὀβολῶν, ὥστε ὁμολόγοι π[ιθο]-
μέναν ἀποδιδόμεν οὗτα τὰ χρείματα [τὰμ πό]-
λιν Χορσιείων τῆ πόλι Θισβείων διὰ ἔνδεκα ἐ[τέ]-
12   ων, τὸ ἐπιβάλλον τῶ ἐνιαυτῶ ἑκάστω δραχμ[ὰς]
χειλίας τριακατίας ὀγδοείκοντα πέντ' ὀβ[ολῶς· κὴ]
τὰμ μὲν πόλιν Χορσιείων καταβαλλέμεν [τῆ πό]-
λι Θισβείων τὰν ἐπαβολὰν κατ' ἐνιαυτὸν ἔκ[αστον],
16   καθ' ἃ αὐτὰ ἀξίωσε, ἐπ' χ' ὁ ταμίας τὰς ἀπ[ολογί]-
ας ἄγει ὁ ἐν Θίσβης, τῶ Δαματρίω μεινός, πα[ρεόν]-
των τῶν πολεμάρχων κὴ τῶν κατοπτάων πε[δὰ τᾶς]
[π]λείθας· ἀρχέμεν δὲ τῶ χρόνω τᾶς καταβολ[ᾶς]
20   [τ]ὸν ἐνιαυτὸν τὸν ἐπὶ Ἐμπεδιώνδαο ἄρ[χον]-
τος Βοιωτοῖς. ἁ δὲ πόλις Θισβείων ἰαέτω τὰν [πό]-
λιν Χορσιείων καρπίδδεσθη τὰν χώραν εἴ κ[α κατα]-
βάλλει τὰς καταβολὰς τὰς ἐν τοῖ ὁμολ[όγοι γεγραμ]-
24   μένας ἐν τοῖς χρόνοις τοῖς γεγραμμ[ένοις, κὴ μεὶ]
ἐπικωλυέτω κὰτ τὰν οὑπεραμερίαν. ἐπ[ὶ δέ κα οἱ]-
κονομείσει ἁ πόλις Χορσιείων τῆ πόλι Θι[σβείων]
τὰ χρείματα οὗτα τὰ ἐν τοῖ ὁμολόγοι γ[εγραμμένα],

28 ἐσλιανάτω ἁ πόλις Θισβείων τὰν οὐπ[ε]ρ[αμε]-
    ρίαν τὰν κὰτ τᾶς πόλιος Χορσιείων· [εἰ δέ κα]
    μεὶ ἐσλιήνει τὰν οὐπεραμερίαν κα[ταβε]-
    βλειώσας τ[ᾶ]ς πόλιος Χορσιείων τὰ [χρείμα]-
32 τα κὰτ τὰ γεγραμμένα, ἅ τε οὐπεραμ[ερία]
    ἄκουρος ἔστω κὴ ἀποπισάτω ἁ πόλις [Θισβείων]
    τῆ πόλι Χορσιείων διπλάσια τὰ χρεί[ματα].

1 [Χορσιεί]οις Pappadakis, Schwahn [Θεο]ῖς Roesch   2 ὁμολ[ογὰ Pappadakis
ὁμόλο[γον Roesch   7–8 [ποτ]‖θέσθη Pappadakis, Roesch [συν]‖θέσθη Haussoulier   8 ἐξακ[ατιάων] Pappadakis ἐξακα[τιάων] Roesch ("la moitié gauche de l'alpha
pointé est visible")   9–10 [ὥ]στε ὁμ[ολ]όγο[ι λελαμ]‖μέναν or σουνθε]‖μέναν Pappadakis πιθο]‖μέναν Haussoulier ὥστε ὁμόλογοι π[ιθο]‖μέναν Roesch   18 καὶ
Pappadakis κὴ Roesch   18–19 π[ὸτ ἐπι‖με]λει(τ)άς Pappadakis, Schwahn π[ὸτ τὼς‖
πο]λεί(τ)ας Haussoulier πε[δὰ τᾶς‖ π]λείθας Crönert, Roesch π[ρὸ‖ π]λείθας Feyel
22–23 [ἄς κα κατα]‖βάλλει Pappadakis εἴκ[α κατα]‖βάλλει Roesch   27 ἐ[γραμμένα]
Pappadakis, Schwahn ἐ[κκίμενα] Crönert, Roesch   28–29 οὐπ[εραμε]‖ρίαν Pappadakis οὐπ[ε]ρ[αμε]‖ρίαν Roesch   29 [ἢ δέ κα] Pappadakis [εἰ δέ κα] Roesch
30–31 κ[αταβε]‖βλειώσας Pappadakis κα[ταβε]‖βλειώσας Roesch   34 χρε[ίματα]
Pappadakis χρεί[ματα] Roesch

To the gods. Agreement between the polis of Thisbe and the polis of Chorsiai
regarding the request made by the polis of Chorsiai to the polis of Thisbe, regarding
the money that the polis of Chorsiai owes to the polis of Thisbe, 11,538 drachmas,
5 obols, and the supplementary amount that was added for the time, 3,650 drachmas, 2 obols. Conforming ourselves to the agreement, the polis of Chorsiai shall pay
back this money to the polis of Thisbe in eleven years, the annual payment being
1,380 drachmas, 5 obols. And the polis of Chorsiai shall return this payment to the
polis of Thisbe every year, as it has requested, when the treasurer does the accounts
in Thisbe in the month of Damatrios, in the presence of the polemarchs and the
controllers of finances before a full assembly. The period of reimbursement shall
begin in the year when Empediondas is archon of the Boiotians. The city of Thisbe
shall allow the polis of Chorsiai to cultivate its territory if it makes the payments
specified in the agreement within the specified time, and it shall not prohibit it
because of the default caused by nonobservance of the latest term for payment.
When the polis of Chorsiai has repaid to the polis of Thisbe the sums recorded in
the agreement, the polis of Thisbe shall cease pursuing the funds that had been
defaulted on by the city of Chorsiai. And if it does not cease the pursuit when the
polis of Chorsiai has repaid the recorded sums, then the agreement arising out of
the original default shall be null and void, and the polis of Thisbe shall owe the polis
of Chorsiai double the sum.

The federal archonship of Empediondas (l. 20) is placed ca. 200–190 by Étienne
and Knoepfler 1976: 350. See the commentary to T33 for the relationship of this
text to the decree of Chorsiai for Kapon son of Brochas.

The document informs us that Chorsiai had borrowed money from its neighbor and fellow member of the Boiotian koinon, Thisbe, and struggled to repay its debt. This agreement appears to revise terms for repayment that were previously reached. The amount originally borrowed is not known; the debt of 11,538 drachmas, 5 obols, owed by Chorsiai to Thisbe represents principal and accumulated unpaid interest. Attempts have been made to calculate the original amount of the loan (e.g., Schwahn 1931a, followed by Moretti and Schmitt), but they are highly problematic (Migeotte 1984: 47).

33. Honorific Decree of Chorsiai for Kapon Son of Brochas

Discovered in the 1850s encased in a wall of the monastery of Taxiarchis near Chostia. Now in the Epigraphical Museum (EM 11538). Ca. 171–160 BCE. *IG* VII.2383. Gaheis 1902 offers several new readings based on autopsy of the stone. Roesch 1965a: 256–61 provides a number of new readings based on inspection of the stone and a squeeze (*SEG* 22.410; Moretti 1967–76: I.66 with translation and commentary); *Migeotte 1984: no. 10 (with translation and commentary) bases his text on Roesch's but proposes several alternative restorations.

```
        [Καλ]λιξένω ἄρχοντος,
     [- - - - - - - - - - - - -]κ[λ]εῖος ἔλεξε· ἐπιδεὶ Κάπων Βρόχαο
     [- - - - - εὔν]οος ἐὼν [διατ]ελῆ τῆ πόλι Χορσιείων,
 4    [ἐν παντὶ κ]ηρῦ, κὴ [σ]πανοσιτίας γενομένας περὶ
      [τὰν Βοιωτ]ίαν κὴ τὰν πολίων πασ[ά]ων ἀπεψαφισμέ-
      [νων τ]ὰν τῶ [σ]ίτω [ἀπο]στ[ο]λάν, προέχρεισε τῆ πό-
      [λι πο]υρῶν κοφίνως διακατίω[ς κ]ὴ κατέστασε
 8    [τὸν] σῖτον τῆ πόλι· [κὴ] οὔ[σ]τερ[ον] δίκας ἐώσας τῆ πό-
      [λι] ἁμέων [κ]ὰτ τὸ σού[μ]βο[λ]ον τὸ πὸτ α[ὐτ]ώς, βειλόμε-
      [ν]ος ἐκ παντὸς τρό[πω] ἀποδί[κ]νουσθη τὰν εὔνυ-
      αν κὴ ἥρεσιν ἂν ἔχ[ι π]οτὶ Χορσιείας, οὐκ ἐόντων
12    χρειμάτων ἐν τ[ῦ] κ[υ]ν[ῦ], προέ[χρ]εισε [τ]ῆ πόλι χρεί-
      ματα οὐκ ὀλίγα, κὴ δανίω μεγάλω γενομένω,
      κὴ τῶν πολιτά[ω]ν πιθόντων αὐτόν, ἀφεῖκε τὰν
      πόλιν δραχμὰς πεντακατίας· ἔτι δὲ κὴ τῶν ἰ[δ]ι-
16    ωτάων τὺς κ[α] χρείαν ἐχόντυς εὐχ[ρ]ειστέων
      διατελῆ ἐν παντὶ κηρῦ· ὅπως ὦν κὴ ἁ πόλις φή-
      νειτη εὐ[χ]άριστος ἐῶσα κὴ τιμεῶσα καθόλου
      [κ]ὰτ ἀξίαν [τ]ὼς ἀγαθόν τι ποιέ[ο]ντας αὐτάν· δ[ε]-
20    [δό]χθη τῦ δάμυ· πρόξενόν τε εἶμεν κὴ εὐεργέ-
      [τ]α τᾶς πόλιος Χο[ρσιεί]ω[ν αὐτὸν κὴ] ἐκγ[όν]ως
     [- - - - - - - - - - - - - - - - - - - - - - - - - - -]
```

3 [Θισβεὺς Gaheis [Θειβῆος? Migeotte   5 [τὰν πόλιν Dittenberger [τὰν χώρ]-
αν Gaheis, Roesch [τὰν Βοιωτ]ίαν Migeotte   16 κ[α] Roesch

In the archonship of [Kal]lixenos, [. . . son of . . .]k[l]eis proposed: since Kapon son of Brochas of [. . .] has [con]stantly been [well dis]posed toward the polis of Chorsiai [for all t]ime, and there being a [g]rain shortage throughout [Boiot]ia, and all the poleis having vot[ed] against the [ex]port of [g]rain, he made an advance to the po[lis] of two hundre[d] *kophinoi*, and he brought [the] grain to the polis. Since our po[lis] was engaged in a suit according to an agr[e]em[e]nt with them, wish[i]ng to pro[v]e in every w[ay] his goodwill and the favor he has [fo]r the people of Chorsiai, there being no money in t[he] tr[ea]s[u]ry, he made an advance to [t]he polis of a not inconsiderable sum of money, and the loan being great, some citi[ze]ns acting as guarantors, he remitted to the polis five hundred drachmas of that loan. And he continued to be useful with regard to the needs of pr[i]vate individuals all the time. So that the polis may appear gr[a]teful and honor fully [acc]ording to worth those who do any good deed, it was r[eso]lved by the *damos* that he should be proxenos and benefact[or] of the polis of Cho[rsia]i, both he and his desc[en]dants [. . .]

The date of this document will perhaps not be established with certainty on present evidence, but the issues at stake and the arguments marshaled need to be laid out clearly. The absence of any mention of the koinon and the bestowal of proxeny by one Boiotian polis on a citizen of another have led several scholars to place it in the decade after the dissolution of the koinon in 171. When Roesch reedited the text in 1965, this was his interpretation, and he was followed by Étienne and Knoepfler 1976: 209 n. 705, 244 n. 908. Later, however, he reversed his opinion, thinking it unlikely that all the Boiotian cities would unanimously have decided, independently and without the central decision-making apparatus of the koinon, to prohibit the export of grain, and instead saw in it a decision of the koinon (Roesch 1973: 260–61). This view was widely rejected (F. Gschnitzer and H. Müller, in a note appended to Roesch's 1973 paper; Jean and Louis Robert, *BE* 74.266; Étienne and Knoepfler 1976: 209 n. 705, 244 n. 908; Migeotte 1984: 43), but no reasons were given. The document's relation to the activities of the koinon depends upon its date, arguments for which have been made on three interrelated grounds: first, the civic identity of Kapon; second, the practice of one Boiotian polis bestowing proxeny on a citizen of another and the question of whether this was done at all when the koinon was in existence, before 171; and third, the relationship of this document to T32, the convention between Chorsiai and Thisbe. There are two additional considerations, which have barely been mentioned: the relationship of this document to others attesting a severe grain shortage in central Greece; and parallel actions taken by other koina. To the extent that they can be separated out, each of these points needs to be addressed in turn.

First, Kapon's civic identity. Gaheis's restoration of line 3 is based on the presence of one Brochas son of Kapon attested at Thisbe ca. 120 (*IG* VII.4139 l. 132), who may be the son of the Kapon attested in our text. However, the lacuna at the beginning of the line has space for 9 or 10 letters (C. Müller 2005: 101–2 n. 33, based on recent autopsy of the stone; Migeotte 1984: 43 estimated 6 or 7, following the implications of Gaheis's restoration). Knoepfler 1992: 473 no. 110 remarks that "cette . . . inscription, qui mentionne un embargo sur le blé décrété par toutes les cités béotiennes, s'explique beaucoup mieux si le personnage honoré n'est pas de Thisbè, comme on l'admis jusqu'ici, mais d'une ville phocidienne toute proche de la Béotie." Kapon did provide both grain and a loan to the city, but Knoepfler seems to imply that the embargo on export would have prohibited him, as a citizen of another Boiotian city, from doing that legally. (Cf. C. Müller 2005: 100–104.) C. Müller 2007: 37–38 avoids the problem of import by assuming that Kapon had stockpiled grain, which in this moment of shortage he now advanced to the city. The embargo may have prevented the export from each city, or from the territory of the koinon as a whole; unfortunately the text is simply not clear on this point, and we have no other evidence of interpolis grain sales within Boiotia in this period. But the embargo certainly did not prevent the import of grain and its distribution within the koinon. Kapon may well have been a merchant who acquired the grain outside the area of central Greece, which was demonstrably so hard hit by a shortage in this period (see above, pp. 306–307, and Walsh 2000), and sold or advanced it to several communities in Boiotia or elsewhere. We need not assume, as Knoepfler seems to, that he himself produced, within the territory of his own city, the grain he advanced to Chorsiai. The embargo would not have stood in the way of a mercantile transaction of this sort.

There is a better reason, perhaps, for supposing that he was a citizen of a non-Boiotian polis, and that is that we have no clear evidence for one Boiotian city bestowing proxeny on a citizen of another Boiotian city in the period before 171, when the koinon was dismantled by the Romans, which brings us to the second set of arguments. Roesch 1973 believed that Boiotian cities did bestow proxeny upon one another's citizens while the koinon was intact; the significance, for him, was that such decrees seemed not to grant the new proxenoi the right of property ownership (eppasis/enktēsis) that was typical in grants to foreigners. He inferred that the documents were silent on this point because the Boiotian recipients of proxeny from other Boiotian cities already had the right of property ownership by virtue of their membership in the koinon. The corpus of decrees in which one Boiotian polis bestows proxeny on a citizen of another is small: (i) Perdrizet 1899: 93 (ll. 17–21), a decree of Akraiphia for a Theban; (ii) Perdrizet 1899: 95 (ll. 1–2), a decree of Akraiphia for a Haliartian; (iii) IG VII.3059, a decree of Lebadeia for a citizen of Chaironeia; (iv) IG VII.2708, a decree of Akraiphia for a citizen of Kopai; and (v) perhaps the present decree of Chorsiai for Kapon, depending upon the restoration of his ethnic. For Roesch, (ii) was the smoking gun: Haliartos was destroyed by the Romans in 171 (Livy 42.63), so the decree must have preceded that date, and therefore seemed to provide firm evidence for the practice of proxeny bestowal by one Boiotian polis on citizens of another while the koinon was in existence. Decrees (i) and (ii) were inscribed on the same stele, by the same mason, along with four other proxeny decrees and an ephebic list, a collocation meaning that they all belong to the same period. However, Habicht 1993 has shown that the entire dossier must belong to the period ca. 140–120: there are compelling prosopographical links between one of the other proxeny decrees on the stele (Perdrizet 1899: 93 no. 2) for three individuals whose ethnics are lost but who appear in no fewer than twenty-two Delphic inscriptions from ca. 152 through ca. 120, with most belonging to the 130s. The proxeny decree for a Haliartian so many years after the destruction of Haliartos is not, Habicht suggests, as bizarre as it may seem. He cites the appearance of Ὀλύνθιοι long after the destruction of Olynthos by Philip in 342 (Habicht 1993: 41), and one can also compare the appearance of an Orchomenian *thearodokos* who hosted a sacred ambassador from Epidauros in 359 (*IG* IV² 1.94a.8), five years after Orchomenos was destroyed by the Thebans. In other words, documents (i) and (ii) must belong to the period 140–120; there are no clear criteria by which to date (iii) or (iv), though Dittenberger placed them after 171 (*IG* VII.3059, commentary), on the assumption that such bestowals would not have been made when the koinon was in existence. It appears, then, that Roesch was probably wrong: we have no firm evidence for a bestowal of proxeny by one Boiotian polis on a citizen of another before 171. (Cf. C. Müller 2005 and 2007.)

If, therefore, Gaheis was correct and Kapon was indeed a citizen of Thisbe, it would follow that the document should be placed after 171. Prosopography provides reasons for thinking that he was a Boiotian, but the evidence is, frustratingly, still not decisive. A highly fragmentary decree of the Boiotian koinon found near the sanctuary of Athena Itonia at Koroneia honors one –]αλμον [Βρ]οχαο Φω[κεα? (Pritchett 1969: 85–95; cf. Robert, *BE* 69.299; Knoepfler, *BE* 2006.194), suggesting that a son of Brochas may have been from Phokis. However, Brochas and Kapon are resolutely Boiotian names. Βροχᾶς is attested once at Thisbe (*IG* VII.4139) in addition to its appearance in this text, once in Thessaly (*SEG* 35.664), and not at all in Phokis, unless the present individual is assigned to Phokis. (So Knoepfler, *BE* 2006.194.) Furthermore, the name Κάπων is attested twenty-three times in Boiotia and nowhere else.

It is tempting to associate this decree with T32, the agreement (*homologon*) between Thisbe and Chorsiai that establishes the terms according to which Chorsiai will repay its debt to Thisbe, but the nature of the relationship between the two documents is elusive. Although he ultimately concludes that the two documents refer to distinct affairs, Migeotte 1984: 46 suggests that the agreement (T32) may have been drawn up as a result of Chorsiai's failure to repay Kapon; the Chorsiaians' struggle to do so would thus be implicit in this decree (T33). C. Müller 2005: 103–4 envisions the opposite: if Chorsiai was already indebted to Thisbe, "on n'est guère étonné de voir un Thisbéen se porter au secours des Chorsiéens." In lines 8–9 there seems to be reference to a preexisting agreement, a *symbolon*, between the two cities: [κὴ] οὔ[σ]τερ[ον] δίκας ἑώσας τῆ πό||[λι] ἀμέων [κ]ὰτ τὸ σού[μ]βο[λ]ον τὸ πὸτ α[ὐτ]ώς. (I interpret πὸτ α[ὐτ]ώς to mean "with them," namely the Thisbeans, and not "regarding the two hundred *kophinoi* of grain," κοφίνως διακατίω[ς], as Moretti 1967–76: I.170 n. 5, followed by Gauthier 1972: 382–83 thought; so too Roesch 1965a: 260; C, Müller 2005: 103–4 n. 42.) The surviving agreement is called a *homologon*, but "malgré la différence de vocabulaire, ne faut-il pas voir dans le *symbolon* du décret une allusion à la convention liant les deux cités à propos des dettes de Chorsiai?" (C. Müller 2005: 103–4). The lawsuit alluded to in this line must be to a suit existing between the two poleis in accordance with the terms of an agreement, and the one recorded in T32 seems to fit the bill. It is likely (though not certain) that the decree for Kapon postdates the agreement between Chorsiai and Thisbe, which is dated by the federal archon Empediondas to the period 200–190, and refers to that agreement.

The result of these three arguments is somewhat inconclusive: it probably belongs after 200–190; if Kapon is a Thisbean, it probably has to be placed after 171, namely after the dissolution of the koinon; but he may after all be a Phokian, in which case there would be no reason to push it beyond 171 except for the absence of an explicit reference to the koinon in lines 5 and 6; and that, after all, is a weak argument from silence. I see two further historical reasons for thinking that Kapon's initial advance of grain to the city, during the shortage and the period of embargo, occurred before 171. The first is that a massive grain shortage in central Greece is abundantly attested for the period ca. 180–175: Petrakos 1997: 210; *IG* XII.9.900A; *IThesp* 41; Walsh 2000. The second is the clear and uncomplicated fact that the Achaian koinon in the 190s took precisely the same measure, namely a prohibition on the export of grain from the entire region (T43), suggesting that this was the sort of thing a koinon was likely to do, indeed better able to do than a string of individual poleis. Finally, there are several indications in the decree that some significant amount of time has passed between Kapon's advance of grain to the polis during the period of shortage and embargo and the bestowal of honors by the city recorded in this decree: after the record of this advance, [κὴ] οὔ[σ]τερ[ον], "and later," indicates that the loan he made to the city "when there was no money in the treasury" occurred well after the advance of grain. He made the loan (ll. 12–13), but then canceled a portion of it (ll. 14–15), which can have happened only after the passage of enough time for the polis to feel the pinch of its debt. Record of Kapon's cancellation of part of the debt is followed by the phrase διατελῆ ἐν παντὶ κηρῦ, "he continued all the time" being helpful to private citizens. There is no explicit record of how much time has passed, but it seems that Kapon is being honored for services rendered over a period of many years. If the "grain shortage throughout Boiotia" (ll. 4–5) is in fact part of the severe and widespread grain shortage attested in central Greece between 180 and 175, which I think is an inescapable conclusion, then it is likely that the honorific decree itself was passed after 171, although some of the facts recorded in it pertain to the previous decade. This would explain why one Boiotian polis is bestowing proxeny on a citizen of another (for the onomastic and prosopographic evidence makes it overwhelmingly likely that Kapon is indeed a Boiotian, not a Phokian) but would also explain how "all the poleis" of Boiotia could unanimously have decided to prohibit the export of grain from the region, a measure that, if taken by each individual polis with no central decision-making body or capacity for enforcement, stretches the bounds of plausibility.

Economic implications. The Boiotian *kophinos* was equivalent to 3/16 of an Attic *medimnos* (M. Feyel 1942a: 84–85)—that is, 9.85 liters. The Athenian estimate of a *choinix* (1.09 liters) as a daily ration would suggest that Kapon's advance yielded around 1,870 daily rations. The population of Chorsiai has been estimated (on admittedly meager evidence) to have been around 250 in this period (Roesch 1965a: 259–60). If this is correct, then two hundred *kophinoi* of grain would have provided adequate grain for the city for just 7.5 days. The advance was not a long-term solution, but it was also a not-inconsiderable stopgap measure. For individual grain consumption rates see Reger 1994: 85–95, with references.

II. ACHAIA

34. *Treaty(?) between the Achaian Koinon and Koroneia*

Found at Aigion in 1933. Late fourth century BCE. Now in the Aigion Museum, inv. no. 1.

White marble stele, of which only the left side is preserved. Rough stoichedon. Letter forms are highly angular.

Ed.pr. Bingen 1954: 402–7 with photograph (*BE* 55.221 no. 117; *SEG* 14.375). Åström 1955. Stavropoulos 1954: 192. *Rizakis 2008a: 176–78 no. 120, with photo, pl. XXVII.

```
      [- - - - - - - εὐορκέοντι μέν μοι εἴη τἀγαθά, ἐ]-
      φιορκέον[τι δὲ τἀναντία - - - - - - - - - - - - -]-
      ε δὲ ἅ τε βου[λὰ] τῶν Ἀχα[ιῶν καὶ - - - δα]-
4     μιοργοὶ καὶ Κορωνεῖς [- - - - - - - - - - - - - κα]-
      τ᾽ ταὐτὰ ἐπὶ δαμιοργῶ[ν? - - - - - - - - - - - -]
      Εὐφάτας, Κλ[ε]ώνυμος [- - - - - - - - - - - - -]-
      ίοχος, Κλεόμβροτο[ς - - - - - - - - - - - - - - - -]-
8     ίας, Ἀριστοκράτ[ης - - - - - - - - - - - - - - - -]-
      [-]ης, Σιμίας· ῾Ρύπ[ες· - - - - - - - - - - - - -]-
      [-]ος· Πατρεῖς· Λ[- - - - - - - - - - - - - - -]-
      [- -]ς· Ὠλένιοι ·[- - - - - - - - - - - - - - - - -]-
12    [- - -]ος· Δυμα[ῖοι- - - - - - - - - - - - - - -]
```

1 [- - - - - - - - εὐορκέοντι μέν μοι εἴη τἀγαθά, ἐ] Åström, Rizakis   2 φιορκέον[τι δὲ τἀναντία Åström φιορκέον[τι δὲ τἀναντία Rizakis   4 ΚΟΡΩΝΕΙΣ Stavropoulos Κορωνεί[ων Bingen Κορωνεῖς Rizakis   5 ΔΑΜΙΟΡΓΟΥ Stavropoulos δαμιοργῶ[ν or δαμιοργο[ῦ Bingen δαμιοργ[ῶν] Åström δαμιοργῶ[ν? Rizakis   10 Πατρεῖς· Μ[Åström Πατρεῖς Λ[Bingen, Rizakis   11 [- -]ς Ὠλένιοι· Åström, Rizakis οος· Ὠλένιοι Bingen   12 [- - -]ος. Δυμ[αῖοι· Åström [- - -]ος· Δυμα[ῖοι Bingen, Rizakis

. . . those swearing the oath[s . . .] the council of the Achaians and [. . . the *da*]*miorgoi* and [. . .] of the Koronei[ans . . . accord]ing to these (regulations?) to those of the *damiorg*[*oi* . . .] Euphatas, Kl[e]onymos [. . .]iochos, Kleombroto[s . . .]ias, Aristokrat[es . . .]es Simias: the people of Rhyp[es. . . .]os: the people of Patrai. L[. . .] [. .]s: the people of Olenos. [. . .]os: the people of Dym[e. . .]

The chief importance of this text lies in the fact that it is the earliest surviving document of the Achaian koinon; it is also the first epigraphic reference to an Achaian *boula* and to the *damiorgoi*. Larsen 1968: 221 n. 3 argues that the preserved names, all in the nominative, must belong to a list of officials other than the *damiorgoi*, who, if listed, would have appeared in the genitive. I do not find this argument compelling. The names, listed in the nominative, follow nominative plural ethnics and certainly give the *damiorgoi* from each of the member cities; we can infer that there was more than one per city in this period. On the federal *damiorgoi* see Aymard 1938: 173–76, 370 n. 1. The inclusion of *damiorgoi* from Rhypes and Olenos secures a date for the document before 280, for neither of these cities appears in the list of members of the koinon newly reconstituted in that year (Polyb. 2.41.7–8, 12–15). Despite Polybios's claim (2.41.7) that Olenos was destroyed at the same time as Helike (373), Strabo (8.7.1) implies that it still existed ca. 280 but actively refused to join the koinon. Giangiulio 1989: 172 suggests that the *damiorgoi* of Kroton may have been influenced by the magistrates of the Achaian metropolis attested here.

It is generally believed, following a suggestion of Bingen 1954: 402, that the stone derived from the Homarion; cf. Robert and Robert (*BE* 55.221); R. Parker 1998: 31 n. 76; F. W. Walbank 2000: 26; Rizakis 2008a: 177.

The Koroneians of line 4 are something of a puzzle. Bingen 1954: 407 (followed by Larsen 1968: 86 n. 2; Wiseman 1978: 108; Rizakis 2008a: 177 with 326–27 n. 123) raises the possibility that they are not Koroneians of Boiotia but citizens of a Peloponnesian Koroneia situated between Sikyon and Corinth (Steph. Byz. s.v. Κορωνεία). Boiotian Koroneia is an unlikely candidate, for it would not have been free, as a member polis of the Boiotian koinon, to conclude an agreement (whether a treaty or some other arrangement—the exact nature of the text is not clear) with a foreign state. Another possible candidate for the Koroneia of this text is Messenian Korone or Koroneia (Hansen and Nielsen 2004: no. 316). Literary and numismatic evidence for the existence of this polis begins only in the second century BCE, but if Korone is to be identified with the modern site of Petalidhi, the substantial fourth-century walls would suggest that the polis was flourishing much earlier. Indeed, according to Pausanias (4.34.5), the polis was founded (or refounded) by an oikist from Thebes named Epimelides after the liberation of Messene in the 360s. This would fit very well with the archaeological remains at Petalidhi.

The oath clause partly preserved in line 4 is perhaps loosely paralleled by the late third-century decree of the Achaian koinon by which Arkadian Orchomenos became a member (T39).

35. Dyme Enrolls New Citizens

Found built into the staircase of a private house in Kato Achaïa (ancient Dyme). Third century BCE.

Ed.pr. Martha 1878: 94–96 no. 2 from a copy of the stone and a squeeze. Various corrections were suggested by Fick 1880: 321–23 no. 2 (*GDI* 1614; *Syll.*³ 531). Bingen rediscovered the stone but found its surface much effaced; he republished the first six lines (Bingen 1954: 86–87 no. 4) on the basis of the stone itself, earlier editions, and a copy made by a local scholar, Zikidis (Νέα Ἐφημερίς, Athens, 19 August 1892 [*SEG* 13.273]), who gave readings for the first four lines, which were hidden by a ramp in the staircase at the time when the copy and squeeze from which Martha worked were made. Rizakis 1990b: 110–23 publishes a complete new edition, based on Martha's majuscule copy, with translation and ample commentary (*BE* 91.303; *SEG* 40.394, q.v. for apparatus criticus). *Rizakis 2008a: 44–49 no. 3 gives a slightly revised edition.

[Θεοί. ἐπὶ τ]οῖσδε εἶμεν τὰν πολιτ[είαν] τοῖς ἐποί-
[κοις - - - ἐν τᾶι π]όλι· τὸν θέλοντα κοινωνεῖν τᾶς πολι-
[τείας - - - - - -]α ἐλεύθερον καὶ ἐξ ἐλευθέρων δόντα
4   [- - - - - - ἐπὶ γρα]μματέος τοῖς Ἀχαιοῖς Μενανδρίδα

[– – – – – – – ἐν] τᾶι πρώται ἑξαμήνωι, τὸ δὲ λοιπὸν
[ἐν τῶι – – – – – – μ]ηνί, ὡς οἱ Ἀχαιοὶ ἄγοντι, εἰ δὲ μὴ δοίη
[τὸ ὅλον ἐν τῶι ἐνι]αυτῶι τῶι ἐπὶ Μενανδρίδα, ἀλλὰ
8 [καθυστερίζοι], μὴ ἔστω αὐτῶι ἀ πολιτεία. εἰ δέ τις
[ἔχοι ὑὸν νεώτερον] ἑπτακαίδεκα ἐ{ε}τέων ἢ θυγατέρα
[ἀνέκδοτον, ὀμοσ]άσθω ἐμ βουλᾷ ὁ πατὴρ τὸν νόμιμον ὅρκ-
[ον· ἦ μὰν εἶμεν α]ὐτοῦ γενεὰν καὶ [νεώ]τερον ἑπτα-
12 [καίδεκα ἐτέων] τὸν ὑὸν παῖδ[α γνήσιον]. ἐξομοσα-
[μένου δὲ τὰν τοῦ ὑο]ῦ ἁ[λ]ικίαν [– – – – – – – – – – –]Η ὀρθῶς
[καὶ δικαίως ὀμοσ]άσθω ΚΑΙ [– – – – – – – – –]ΟΒΟΥΛΑΙ
[– – – τὸν νόμιμον ὅρ]κον ἄνπα[λιν – – – – – – – –] ΔΟΞΑΙ
16 [– – – – – – – – – – – – – – –]ΑΙΕΣΤ[– – – – – – – – – – – – – –]ς αὐ-
[τῶι καὶ γενεᾶι. εἰ δὲ] χήρα ἐλευ[θέρα καὶ ἐξ] ἐλευθέ-
[ρων θελήσει κοι]νωνεῖ[ν τᾶς πολιτείας – – – – – ἔ]στω
[– – – – – – – – – – – – – – –] τᾶι γυν[αικὶ – – – – – – – – – πο]λι-
20 [τείαν αὐτᾶι καὶ] γενεᾶι. ε[ἰ δὲ ἔχοι ὑὸν νεώτερον] ἑπτα-
[καίδεκα ἐτέων] ἢ θυγατέρ[α ἀνέκδοτον, ὀμο]σαμ-
[έναν τὸν νόμιμον ὅ]ρκον ἐμ [βο]υλ[ᾶι· ἦ μὰν α]ὐτᾶ[ς] εἶμε-
[ν γενεὰν καὶ νεώτ]ε[ρον] τ[ὸ]ν [ὑὸν ἑπτακαίδεκα] ἐτέ-
24 [ων καὶ παῖδα γνήσιον? ἐπομνυ]όμενος [– – – – – –] ἀνάπ[α]-
[λιν – – – – – – – – – – – – – –]ον καὶ γυναῖκα κα[ὶ γεν]εάν. ἀ-
[πογραφέντω δὲ] ποτὶ τὸμ βούλαρχον καὶ [προσ]τάταν δα-
[μοσιοφυλάκω]ν καὶ γραμματιστάν. τοὺς δὲ ἀπογ-
28 [ραφέντες καὶ ὑῶ]ν ὀμοσαμένους τὰν ἡλικίαν καὶ δόν-
[τες τὸ ἀργύριον] καθὼς γέγραπται, διακλαρωσάν-
[τω αἱ συναρ]χίαι ὡς ἰσότατα ἐπὶ τὰς φυλάς, καὶ λα-
[χόντω ἐπὶ τὰν] Στρατίδα, ἐπὶ τὰν Δυμαίαν, ἐπὶ τὰν Θεσμι-
32 [αίαν· καὶ κοινω]νεόντω θεοκολιᾶν, ἂν ἀ πόλις καθιστᾶι ἐν
[τᾶι φυλᾶι τᾶι] ἑαυτῶν, καὶ ἀρχείων τῶν τε εἰς τὸ κοινὸν
[καὶ τὰν πόλιν – – – – – – –]ας τάς τε εἰς τὸ κοινὸν ΚΑΙΓ[–]

[Gods. It was resolved?] to give citizenship to those liv[ing in the c]ity. Let the free
man who is a son of free parents and who wishes to have citi[zenship] pay [(sum) to
the sec]retary of the Achaians, Menandris, [. . . in] the first six months, the remainder
[in the (lacuna) m]onth on the Achaian calendar. If anyone fails to pay [the entire
amount in the] year to Menandris, but [is late], let him not be granted citizenship. If a
father [has a son who is younger] than seventeen years or a daughter [who is unmarried, let him sw]ear in the council the legal oa[th to the effect that they are h]is offspring and that the boy is [you]nger than seven[teen years] and a [legitimate] son.
After having sworn [the oath regarding the] age [of his son] [lacuna] let him swear
correctly [and justly] and [lacuna] [the legal oa]th over aga[in (lacuna)] [lacuna]|
[lacuna] to hi[m and his offspring. If a] freeborn widow born of free [parents wishes
to re]ceive [citizenship, (lacuna)] let [lacuna] to the wom[an (lacuna) ci]-
ti[zenship to her and to her] offspring. I[f she has a son who is younger] than
seven[teen years] or a daughter [who is unmarried, let her] swear [the legal o]ath in

the counc[il to the effect that they are her children and that the boy is younger than seventeen y]ears and is a legitimate son [*lacuna*] agai[n (*lacuna*)] both the woman and her offspring (shall have citizenship?). [Let them register] with the boularch and the [pre]sident of the *da[mosiophylake]s* and the secretary. Let [the *synar*]*chiai* distribute equally among the *phylai* those who have regi[stered], taken an oath regarding the age [of their sons], and paid [the money] in accordance with what has been recorded, pla[cing them in] Stratis, Dymaia, and Thesmi[aia. Let them also take] part in the priesthoods that the polis established in [their own *phyla*] and the magistracies belonging to the koinon [and to the polis (*lacuna*)] in the koinon . . .

Fick proposed the restoration ἐξ ἐλευθέρων τά[λαντον in lines 3 and 4; this has been widely accepted (e.g., *Syll.*³ 531; Robert 1940: 40; Ogden 1996: 296–97), but the figure is simply not preserved on the stone (Bingen 1954: 86; Rizakis 1990b: 112). Fick restored the beginning of line 5 as [τὸ μὲν ἥμισυ ἐν] τᾶι; this cannot be supported by any direct formulaic parallel, but the sense it conveys is probably correct, for a text from Achaian Tritaia concerned with enrolling new citizens likewise demands payment in multiple installments (Rizakis 1990b: 130, lines 8–11). This implies that the sum was relatively high in both cases. Rizakis 1990b: 115–16 discusses parallel evidence for the payment of sums of money as part of the registration process in other cities. Sales of citizenship to foreigners in the Hellenistic period were in some cases clearly motivated by the city's need to raise revenues (Gauthier 1985: 199–201 following Robert 1940: 37–41), but in other cases the city's need was to raise manpower (Ogden 1996: 296–99). Oliver 2011: 359–60 observes that the practice is also a strategy for persuading the resident noncitizen population to remain in the city.

Dittenberger proposed to restore the beginning of line 34 [φόρων καὶ τᾶς εἰσφορ]ᾶς τᾶς. However, without any other epigraphic—and indeed nonmilitary—evidence for *eisphora* in the Achaian koinon, the restoration remains hypothetical. The *phylai* of Dyme attested in lines 31 and 32 have drawn some attention. N. F. Jones 1987: 130–32 wrongly claims that Demeter, whom Szántó saw behind the *phylē* Thesmiaia, had no presence in Dyme: Sokolowski 1969: suppl. no. 33, a third-century sacred law of Demeter found at Alissos, near ancient Dyme; Lakakis 1991 and Rizakis et al. 1992: site 67, a sanctuary in the village of Petrochori in the territory of Dyme, which surveyors believe belonged to Demeter. (Cf. Rizakis 1990b: 122 n. 62.) Jones also suggests that, since three *phylai* are listed, while the citizens of Dyme certainly knew the names of their *phylai*, it is likely that these were not the only *phylai* of the city but the only ones into which new citizens were integrated on this occasion. The enrollment of new citizens in *phylai* is well attested at Athens in the closing years of the fifth century (*IG* I³ 127 ll. 33–34; *IG* II² 10 l. 6). Rizakis 1990b: 120–21, citing other instances of the distribution of new citizens into existing *phylai*, suggests that "ces précautions . . . étaient probablement destinées à maintenir l'équilibre entre vieux et nouveaux citoyens dans les cadres civiques et à prévenir l'isolement des citoyens de fraîche date."

The text is dated by the Achaian *grammateus* Menandris, but he is otherwise unknown. On paleographical grounds it has been placed in the third century, but no more precise date can be given (Rizakis 2008a: 49).

36. Arbitration of a Frontier by the Achaian Koinon

Found near modern Aigion, on the bank of the river Meganeitas, just before World War II. Aigion Museum, inv. 66. Ca. 250–200 BCE.

Limestone stele, broken on top, left, and bottom. 36.6 cm (h), 26 cm (w), 10.2 cm (d).

Ed.pr. Bingen 1953: no. 1 with photo and full commentary (*SEG* 13.278; Ager 1996: 110–11 no. 36 (ll. 1–7 only); Magnetto 1997: no. 33; Harter-Uibopuu 1998: 11–14 no. 1 (ll. 1–7 only); *Rizakis 2008a: 178–81 no. 121 with photo, pl. XXIX.

```
    [- - - - - - - - - τὸ ἱερ]ὸν τᾶς Νικε[ίας - - -]
    [- - - - - - - - - - - - - - - - - - - - - ἐπὶ τὰν σ]υμβολὰν τοῦ ' Ριγο-
    [στασίου - - - - καὶ τοῦ - - - - - - - - ποτ]αμοῦ καὶ ἀπὸ τᾶς σ-
4   [υμβολᾶς - - - - - ἐπὶ - - - - - - - - - - - -] τὸν ' Ριγοστάσιον κ-
    [αὶ ἀπὸ - - - - - - - - - - - - - - - - -] ἐπὶ τὸ ἱερὸν τᾶς Νικείας τᾶ-
    [ς - - καὶ ἀπὸ τοῦ ἱεροῦ τᾶς Νικείας ἐπὶ τὰ]ν δέραν τοῦ ΙΠΕΙΟΥ : δικασταὶ
    [τοὶ κρίναντες τοίδε·- - -]ης Σίλωνος, Εὐχέας Εὐφράντω,
8   [- - - - - - - - - - - - - - - - - -]νιας Λαχάριος, Ἀθάναιος Δαμα-
    [- - - - - - - - - - - - - - - -] Ἀλεξίδαμος Αἰγίνα, Ἄνδριος Βρευ-
    [- - - - - - - - - - - - -]στωνος, Φίλυς Μεθίκωνος, Λίχας Εὐαγόρα,
    [- - - - - - - - - - - -]ω, Φαῖδρος Τίμωνος, Ἀλεξ[ίω]ν Ἀριστέα, Κριτ-
12  [- - - - - - - - - - - -]ς Γοργάσω, Δαμάρετος Α[λκ]ιμάχω, Μετω-
    [- - - - - - - - - - - -] Κλειονοξένω, Εὐχύλος Εὐβιότω, Δᾶμυς Θα-
    [- - - - - - - - - - - -]ς, Ἀρίστων Δαμάρχω, Ἀγέμαχος Σάωνος,
    [- - - - - - - - - - - - -]ς Σθένωνος, Ξενοκλῆς Τιμοθέω, Αἰσχ-
16  [- - - - - - - - - - - - -]ς Ἀνδραγάθω : Δυμαῖοι Καλλίας Πε-
    [- - - - - - - - - - - -] Ἀγήσανδρος Ἀριστοδάμω, Τιμόμα-
    [χος - - - - - - - - - - - -]χμω, Αἰσχρίων Ἀνδρίω, Στρατόλαος
    [- - - - - - - - - - - -]κλεος, Ἀθανάδας Μεθίκοντος, Εὐφρι-
20  [- - - - - - - - - - - -]νος, Ἀρχῖνος Σατυρίωνος, Ἄλκιμος Σω-
    [- - - - - - - - - - - - - - -] Φιλοκλείδα, Αἰσχρίων Φίλωνος, Σω-
    [- - - - - - - - - - - - - -] Σώσιμος Πετάλω, Νεόπατρος Σω-
    [- - - - - - - - - - - Σ]ατυρίων Φυλλάρω, Λεοντομένης Αἰ-
24  [- - - - - - - - - - - -]ιεὺς Θρασυξένω, Ταυρίας Φίλωνος,
    [- - - - - - - - - - - -] Ἀριστέας Τιμαίω, Ὀμφαλίων ᵛᵛ
    [- - - - - - - - - - - Ἀν]τιγένης Ξενοτίμω, Τεισαμεν-
    [ὸς - - - - - - - - - - - - - -]ένης Χαρόπω, Θράσων Θρασίω,
28  [- - - - - - - - - - - - - - - -]μοφίλω, Γόργις Δρακοντίω,
    [- - - - - - - - - - - - - - - -]ος, Ξένων Νικάνδρω,
    [- - - - - - - - - - - - - - - -]ος Ἀντάνδρω, Ἀντι-
    [- - - - - - - - - - - - - - - - - - - - - - - - - - -]ος
```

... the sanctuary of Nikeia ... to the confluence of the Rigo[stasios ... and of... ri]ver and from the confluence ... to ... the Rigostasios and from ... to the sanctuary of Nikeia [and from the sanctuary of Nikeia to th]e dale of *ipeios*. The judges who arbitrated in this case were [. . .]es son of Silon, Eucheas son of Euphrantos, [. . .]nias son of Lacharis, Athanaios son of Dama[. . .], Alexidamos son of Aiginos, Andrios son of Bre|[. . .]stonos, Philys son of Methikon, Lichas son of Evagoras, [. . .]os, Phaidros son of Timon, Alex[io]n son of Aristeas, Krit[. . .]s son of Gorgasos, Damaretos son of A[. . .]imachos, Meto[. . .] son of Kleinoxenos, Euchylos son of Eubiotos, Damus son of Tha[. . .]s, Ariston son of Damarchos, Agemachos son of Saon, [. . .]s son of Sthenon, Xenokles son of Timotheos, Aisch[. . .]s son of Andragathos. Dymaians: Kallias son of Pe[. . .], Hagesandros son of Aristodamos, Timoma[chos . . .]chmos, Aischrion son of Andrios, Stratolaos [. . .]kleos, Athanadas son of Methikon, Euphri[. . .]nos, Archinos son of Satyrion, Alkimos son of So[. . .] son of Philokleidas, Aischrion son of Philon, So[. . .] Sosimos son of Petalos, Neopatros son of So[. . . S]atyrion son of Phyllaros, Leontomenes son of Ai[. . .]ieus son of Thrasyxenos, Taurias son of Philon, [. . .] Aristeas son of Timaios, Omphalion [. . . An]tigenes son of Xenotimos, Teisamen[os . . .] enes son of Charops, Thrason son of Thrasion, [. . .]mophilos, Gorgis son of Drakontis, [. . .]os, Xenon son of Nikandros, [. . .]os son of Antandros, Anti[. . .]os

The text consists of two parts: lines 1–6 record the delimitation of the disputed boundary; lines 6–31 are a list of judges. Δυμαῖοι in line 16 indicates that the judges were listed according to their poleis; if the left side of the stone were preserved we would probably find judicial delegations from several other poleis of the Achaian koinon, an interpretation strengthened considerably by the provenance of the fragment. It is of course possible that it is a *pierre errante*, but the appearance of a delegation of Dymaians in a much longer list of judges speaks strongly for the idea that the stone represents a boundary delimitation arbitrated by the Achaian koinon. Bingen indeed believes that the stone was originally set up in the Homarion; Rizakis 2008a: 180 remarks with confidence that "ce texte faisait partie de la documentation fédérale d'Hamarion." The organization of the text is similar to *IG* IV² 1.72, an arbitration in a dispute between Epidauros and Methana (Arsinoe) from shortly after 228. The decision is dated by the Achaian *stratagos*, and delegations from Pellene, Aigion, and Telphousa are listed. The parallel is so close between these two roughly contemporaneous texts as to reinforce Bingen's suggestion. Harter-Uibopuu 1998: 119–29 discusses the role of the Achaian koinon in arbitration, noting that there is no indication that arbitration by the koinon was obligatory in the event of disputes between members; most of the cases she discusses (with the exception of the present one) belong to the second century.

37. Epidauros Joins the Achaian Koinon

Found at the Asklepieion, Epidauros. 243 BCE.

Upper part of an ornate stele, broken at the right. Stoichedon.

IG IV² 1.70 (Hiller von Gaertringen); Mitsos 1937 (*SEG* 11.401; *Staatsverträge* III.489). New fragment (ll. 27–41) added by *Peek 1969: 23–25 no. 25, with photo, pl. IV fig. 7 (Ager 1996: 113–14 no. 38.I, following Mitsos's restorations for ll. 1–24 but including Peek's new fragment for ll. 27–40; Magnetto 1997: no. 36.I, ll. 1–24 only).

Ἀγαθᾶι τύχαι. [ἐ]πὶ [– – – – – – – – – – – – τοῖς Ἐπιδαυ]-
ρίοις καὶ τοῖς Ἀ[χ]αιοῖς [ἐ]ψαφίσ[θ]α[ι – – – – – – – – – – – – κα]-
θὰ ποτῆλθον ποτὶ τὰν τῶν Ἀχαιῶν σ[ύνοδον – – – – αὐτόνομοι ὄν]-
4   τες καὶ ἀφρούρατοι καὶ πολιτείαι [χ]ρώμ[ενοι τᾶι πατρίωι – – – ἄνευ ὅ]-
πλων παραπορευομένους εἰς τὰν πόλιν ἐλ[θ– – – – – – – – – – – κατὰ νό]-
μους διακωλύοντας π[ο]ρείας [– – – – – – – – – – – – – τῶν ἀρ]-
χείων τῶν ἐπὶ πόλιος [– – – – – – – – – – – – – – – – – – – πόλι]-
8   ος νόμοις καὶ ταῖς δίκαις καὶ ταῖς [– – – – – – – – – – – – – – – δι]-
καστηρίοις περί τε [τ]ῶν ἱαρῶ[ν κ]αὶ [– – – – – – – – – – – – –]
καὶ περὶ γένεος κρίσιος καὶ περὶ τᾶν [– – – – – – – τῶν ἐγ]-
κλημάτων τῶν ποτ᾽ ἀλλάλους κατὰ τοὺς [– – – – καὶ τὰς]
12   στάλας τὰς ἐν τοῖς ἱεροῖς τοῖς ἀνα[τεθεῖσι – – – – – – – ἁ τῶν Ἐπι]-
δαυρίων βουλά. ἵνα [δὲ] γί[νηται π]ᾶσι κα[– – – – – – – – – – – – – – –]
τῶν Ἐπιδαυρίων, δι[ότι] ἔσται ἁ φιλία [– – – – – – – – – – – – – – – δύ]-
ναται καὶ τὰν χώραν, ἂν τοὶ Ἀργεῖοι τ[– – – – – – – – – – – – – – – –]
16   μεν τοὺς Ἀχαιοὺς ΙΙ[– – – –]ΙΣΟΝ [– – – – – – – – – – – – – – – – – – τοὶ]
Κορίνθιοι ἔχοντι [χ]ώρας τοὺς π[– – – – – – – – – – – – – – – – εἰ]
μὴ ἀντιλέγοντι τοὶ Ἐπιδ[α]ύρι[οι – – – – – – – – – – – – –]
[– –]τοὶ Ἀχαιοὶ ἢ ἀ[ν]ακριθ[– – – – – – – – – – – – – – – – – – –]
20   [– – – – –]αι τοὺς ἐπὶ τας [– – – – – – – – – – – – – – – – – – –]
[ἀποστελ]λομένους μὴ [– – – – – – – – – – – – – – – – – – –]
[– – – – – – – – ἀ]ποστελλ[– – – – – – – – – – – – – – – – – –]
[– – – – – – – – – – – –]λει κ[– – – – – – – – – – – – – – – – –]
24   [– –]
[– –]
[– –]
[– – – – – – – – –]δε[– – – – – – – – – – – – – – – – – – – –]
28   [– – – – – – –]αν ἐν Ἐπιδαύρωι [– – – – – – – – – –]
[– – –]ει καὶ ὑπέχετ[αι – – – – – – – – – – – – – – – – – – –]
[– – –]α καὶ ἁ γενεὰ αὐ[τ– – – – – – – – – – – – – – – – – –]
κὰτ᾽ ταὐτὰ ποιείτω[– – – – – – – – – – – – – εἰ δέ κα – – – εἰς]
32   Ἐπίδαυρον γαμῆται, δ[– – – – – – – – – – – – – – – – – –]
τῶν ἐν Ἀχαίαι συναλ[λαγμάτων – – – – – – – – – – – – κὰτ]
τοὺς τᾶς πόλιος νόμους [– – – – – – – – – – – – – – – – τῶν]
συναλλαγμάτων ἁ κὰτ τ[– – – – – – – – – – – – – – – – ὧι]-
36   κησε ἐν Ἐπιδαύρωι, ὕστε[ρον δὲ – – – – – – – – – – – – –]
ἐν τᾶι βουλᾶι τῶν Ἐπιδα[υρίων – – – – – – – – – – – – τὰν]
μὲν συμπολίτευσιν μὴ σ[υγχωρῆσαι – – – – – – – εἴ κα ἐμ]-
πολιτεύσηται κατὰ χρέος [– – – – – – – – – – – – – – – – –]

40   [- -]ει ἔστε κα παύσητ[α]ι [- - - - - - - - - - - - - - - - - - -]
      [- -]

1 [ἐ]πὶ τοῖσδε [ἐπόησ]αν [ὁμολογίαν τοὶ Ἀχαιοὶ καὶ τοὶ Ἐπιδαύριοι· συμπολιτείαν εἶμεν τοῖς Ἐπιδαυ]|ρίοις Peek   [ἐ]πὶ [στραταγοῦ τῶν Ἀχαιῶν Ἀράτου, ἐν δ ᾿Ἐπιδαύρωι ἐπ᾿ ἱαρεῦς τοῦ Ἀσκλαπιοῦ - - - - ὁμολογία? τοῖς Ἐπιδαυ]|ρίοις Mitsos

Too much of the stone is missing to justify attempts at continuous translation. Hiller thought that this document recorded the initial arbitration between Corinth and Epidauros mentioned in T38, which the Corinthians disputed (ll. 3–8). But Mitsos showed that the document established the terms according to which Epidauros would join the koinon in 243, which involved taking cognizance of the outstanding dispute between Epidauros and Corinth, and probably (though this is lost in the lacunae of ll. 15–20) setting out a procedure for its resolution, which we see realized in T38.

38. Megarian Arbitration of a Dispute
between Corinth and Epidauros

Found at the Asklepieion in Epidauros. 242/1–238/7 BCE.

IG IV² 1.71 (*Syll.*³ 471; C. D. Buck 1955: no. 99 [ll. 1–32 only]; Daverio Rocchi 1988: 156–61 no. 15.1 [ll. 2–15 only]; *Ager 1996: 113–17 no. 38.II [ll. 1–32 only]; Magnetto 1997: no. 36.II [ll. 1–32, 49, 67, 85 only]; Harter-Uibopuu 1998: no. 3).

[ἐ]πὶ στραταγ[οῦ τῶν] Ἀχαιῶν Αἰγιαλεύς, ἐν δ ᾿Ἐπιδαύρωι ἐπ᾿ ἱαρεῦς
[το]ῦ Ἀσκλαπι[οῦ Δι]ονυσίου· κατὰ τάδε ἔκριναν τοὶ Μεγαρεῖς τοῖς
[Ἐπ]ιδαυρίοις καὶ Κορινθίοις περὶ τᾶς χώρας ἇς ἀμφέλλεγον, καὶ
4   [περ]ὶ τοῦ Σελλᾶντος καὶ τοῦ Σπιραίου, κατὰ τὸν αἶνον τὸν τῶν Ἀ-
      [χαι]ῶν δικαστήριον ἀποστείλαντες ἄνδρας ἑκατὸν πεντήκοντα
      [ἕν]α καὶ ἐπελθόντων ἐπ᾿ αὐτὰν τὰν χώραν τῶν δικαστᾶν καὶ κρινάν-
      [τω]ν Ἐπιδαυρίων εἶμεν τὰν χώραν, ἀντιλεγόντων δὲ τῶν Κορινθί-
8   [ων τ]ῶι τερμονισμῶι, πάλιν ἀπέστειλαν τοὶ Μεγαρεῖς τοὺς τερμο-
      ν[ιξ]οῦντας ἐκ τῶν αὐτῶν δικαστᾶν ἄνδρας τριάκοντα καὶ ἕνα κα-
      [τὰ] τὸν αἶνον τὸν τῶν Ἀχαιῶν. οὗτοι δὲ ἐπελθόντες ἐπὶ τὰν χώραν
      ἐτερμόνιξαν κατὰ τάδε· ᵛ ἀπὸ τᾶς κορυφᾶς τοῦ Κορδυλείου ἐπὶ
12   [τ]ὰν κορυφὰν τοῦ Ἁλιείου. ᵛ ἀπὸ τοῦ Ἁλιείου ἐπὶ τὰν κορυφὰν τοῦ
      [Κ]εραυνίου. ᵛ ἀπὸ τοῦ Κεραυνίου ἐπὶ τὰν κορυφὰν τοῦ Κορνιάτα.
      ἀπὸ τᾶς κορυφᾶς τοῦ Κορνιάτα ἐπὶ τὰν ὁδὸν ἐπὶ τὸν ῥάχιν τὸν τοῦ
      Κορνιάτα. ἀπὸ τοῦ ῥάχιος τοῦ Κορνιάτα ἐπὶ τὸν ῥάχιν τὸν ἐπὶ ταῖ-
16   ς Ἀνείαις ὑπὲρ τὰν Σκολλειάν. ᵛ ἀπὸ τοῦ ῥάχιος τοῦ ὑπὲρ τὰν Σκολ-
      λειὰν [ὑ]πὸ τὰς Ἀνείας ἐπὶ τὸν κορυφὸν τὸν ὑπὲρ τᾶς ὁδοῦ τᾶς ἁμα-
      ξιτο[ῦ τᾶ]ς καταγούσας ἐπὶ τὸ Σπιραῖον. ᵛ ἀπὸ τοῦ κορυφοῦ τοῦ ὑπὲ-
      ρ τᾶς [ὁ]δοῦ τᾶς ἁμαξιτοῦ ἐπὶ τὸν κορυφὸν τὸν ἐπὶ τοῦ Φάγας. ᵛ ἀπὸ
20   τοῦ κορυφοῦ τοῦ ἐπὶ τοῦ Φάγας ἐπὶ τὸν κορυφὸν τὸν ἐπὶ τοῦ Αἰγι-
      πύρας. ᵛ ἀπὸ τοῦ κορυφοῦ τοῦ ἐπὶ τᾶς Αἰγιπύρας ἐπὶ τὸν κορυφὸν
      τὸν τ[οῦ] Ἀραίας. ᵛ ἀπὸ τοῦ Ἀραίας ἐπὶ τὸν κορυφὸν τὸν ὑπὸ ταῖ Πέτρ-

αι. ^ν ἀπὸ τοῦ ὑπὸ τᾶι Πέτραι ἐπὶ τὸν κορυφὸν τὸν ἐπὶ τοῦ Σχοινοῦν-
24   τος. ἀπὸ τοῦ κορυφοῦ τοῦ ὑπὲρ τοῦ Σχοινοῦντος ἐπὶ τὸν κορυφὸ[ν]
τὸν κατὰ τὰν Εὐόργαν. ^ν ἀπὸ τοῦ κορυφοῦ τοῦ ὑπὲρ τᾶς Εὐόργας ἐ[πὶ]
τὸν ῥάχ[ιν] τὸν ὑπὲρ τᾶς Συκουσίας. ^ν ἀπὸ τοῦ ῥάχιος τοῦ ὑπὲρ τᾶς
Συκουσίας ἐπὶ τὸν κορυφὸν τὸν ὑπὲρ τᾶς Πελλερίτιος. ^ν ἀπὸ τοῦ
28   [κ]ορυφοῦ τοῦ ὑπὲρ τᾶς Πελλερίτιος ἐπὶ τὸν κορυφὸν τὸν τοῦ Παν-
[ίο]υ. ἀπὸ τοῦ Πανίου ἐπὶ τὸν ῥάχιν τὸν ὑπὲρ τοῦ Ὄλκοῦ. ^ν ἀπὸ τοῦ ῥά-
[χιο]ς τοῦ ὑπὲρ τοῦ Ὄλκοῦ ἐπὶ τὸν ῥάχιν τὸν ‹ὑπὲρ› τοῦ Ἀπολλωνίου. ἀπὸ
[τοῦ] ῥάχιος τοῦ ὑπὲρ τοῦ Ἀπολλωνίου ἐπὶ τὸ Ἀπολλώνιον. ^ν δικασ-
32   [ταὶ τ]οὶ κρίναντες τοίδε·
*The names of the 151 Megarian citizens who comprised the board of arbitrators
follow in an additional 64 lines.*

When Aigialeos was *stratagos* of the Achaians and Dionysios was priest of Asklapios in
Epidauros, the Megarians arbitrated the dispute between the Epidaurians and Corinthians over territory, and around Sellas and Spiraion, in accordance with the resolution of
the Achaians. They sent as a court 151 men, who arrived at the territory and judged it to
belong to the Epidaurians. The Corinthians, however, disputed the boundary delimitation, and again the Megarians sent boundary delimiters from their own citizens, this
time 31 men, in accordance with the resolution of the Achaians. These went to the territory and drew the following boundaries. From the peak of Kordyleion to the peak of
Halieios. From the peak of Halieios to the peak of Keraunios. From the peak of
Keraunios to the peak of Kornias. From the peak of Kornias to the road, to the ridge of
Kornias. From the ridge of Kornias to the ridge on Aneia above Skolleia. From the ridge
above Skolleia under Aneia to the peak above the wagon road leading to Spiraion. From
the peak above the wagon road to the peak on Phaga. From the peak on Phaga to the
peak on Aigipyra. From the peak on Aigipyra to the peak of Araia. From the peak of
Araia to the peak below Petra. From the peak below Petra to the peak on Schoinous.
From the peak above Schoinous to the peak at Euorga. From the peak above Euorga to
the ridge above Sykousia. From the ridge above Sykousia to the peak above Pelleritis.
From the peak above Pelleritis to the peak of Panion. From the peak of Panion to the
ridge above Holkos. From the ridge above Holkos to the ridge above Apollonios. From
the ridge above Apollonios to the Apollonion. The following were the judges . . .

The topographical details of this inscription are discussed by Bölte, *RE* s.v.
Speiraion, and by Wiseman 1978: 136–42. Dixon 2005 associates this arbitration
with the settlement whose remains are located at Agia Paraskevi, 2 kilometers
northeast of the modern village of Sophiko in the southeastern Corinthia, and suggests (p. 141) that the Panion mentioned in lines 28 and 29 may be associated with
niches carved in the rock face on either side of a modern quarry southeast of Agia
Paraskevi.

39. Arkadian Orchomenos Joins the Achaian Koinon

Found built into the wall of a house in Kalpaki, near ancient Orchomenos.
235–229 BCE.

Ed.pr. Foucart 1876 (Foucart in LeBas 1847–88: II.353; Hicks 1882: 187). Dittenberger *Syll.*² 229. Hoffmann *GDI* 1634 (Michel 1900: 199). Hiller von Gaertringen *IG* V.2.344 (*Syll.*³ 490; Schwyzer 1923: 428; Schmitt *Staatsverträge* 499; Rizakis 1995: 340–41 no. 599 reproduces lines 1–11; Ager 1996: 129–31 no. 43). *Thür and Taeuber 1994: no. 16.

[– – – – – – –] παραβαίνηι [– – –]
μον πέμπηι εἴτε ἄρχω[ν – – – εἴ]-
πέοι εἴτε ἰδιώτας ψαφοφορέοι [– – – ὀφλέτω]
4   τριάκοντα τάλαντα ἱερὰ τοῦ Διὸ[ς τοῦ Ἀμαρίου, καὶ ἐξέστω τῶι στραταγῶι
       δίκαν]
     [θ]ανάτου εἰσάγειν εἰς τὸ κοινὸν τ[ῶν Ἀχαιῶν. ᵛ κατὰ τάδε ὀμνυόντων τὸν
       ὅρκον τὸν]
     αὐτὸν οἱ Ὀρχομένιοι καὶ οἱ Ἀχαιοί, ἐμ μὲ[ν Αἰγίωι οἱ δαμιοργοὶ τῶν Ἀχαιῶν καὶ
       ὁ στρα]-
     [τ]αγὸς καὶ ἵππαρχος καὶ ναύαρχος, ἐν δὲ [Ὀρχομενῶι οἱ ἄρχοντες τῶν
       Ὀρχομενί]-
8   [ων]· ὀ[μ]νύω Δία Ἀμάριον, Ἀθάναν Ἀμαρίαν, Ἀφρ[οδ]ίτα[ν καὶ τοὺ]ς θ[εοὺς
       πάντας, ἦ μὴν ἐν]
     πᾶσιν ἐμμε[ν]εῖν ἐν τᾶι στάλαι καὶ τᾶι ὁμολογίαι καὶ τῶι ψαφίσματι [τῶι
       γεγονότι τῶι]
     [κοι]ν[ῶι] τῶι τ[ῶ]ν Ἀχαιῶν, καὶ εἴ τίς κα μὴ ἐμμένηι, οὐκ ἐπιτρέψω εἰς δύναμ[ιν,
       καὶ εὐορ]-
     [κέ]οντι μέν μοι εἴη τἀγαθά, ἐπιορκέοντι δὲ τἀναντία. ᵛ τῶν δὲ λαβόντων ἐν
       Ὀρ[χο]-
12 [μενῶι] κλᾶρον ἢ οἰκίαν, ἀφ’ οὗ Ἀχαιοὶ ἐγένοντο, μὴ ἐξέστω μηθενὶ
       ἀπαλλοτριῶ-
     [σα]ι ἐτέων εἴκοσι. ᵛ εἰ δέ τι ἐκ τῶν ἔμπροσθε χρόνων ἢ οἱ Ὀρχομένιοι Ἀχαιοὶ
       ἐγέ-
     [νον]το Νεάρχ[ω]ι ἔγκλημα γέγονεν ἢ τοῖς υἱοῖς, ὑπότομα εἶμεν πάντα,
       καὶ μ[ὴ]
     [δικαζέ]σθω μήτε Νεάρχωι μηθεὶς μήτε τοῖς υἱοῖς αὐτοῦ μηδὲ Νέαρχος μηδὲ
       [τῶν]
16 [υἱ]ῶν αὐτοῦ μηθεὶς περὶ τῶμ πρότερον ἐγκλημάτων ἢ οἱ Ὀρχομένιοι Ἀχαιοὶ
       ἐγ[έ]-
     [νο]ν[τ]ο· [ὃς δ]ὲ δικάζοιτο, ὀφλέτω χιλίας δραχμάς, καὶ ἁ δίκα ἀτελὴς ἔστω. ᵛ
       περ[ὶ]
     [δὲ τᾶς Νί]κας τᾶς χρυσέ[α]ς τοῦ Διὸς τοῦ Ὁπλοσμίου, ἃγ καταθέντες ἐνέχυρα
       οἱ Μεθυ[δρι]-
     [εῖς οἱ μετοική]σαντες ε[ἰ]ς Ὀρχομενὸν διείλοντο τὸ ἀργύριον καί τινες αὐτῶν
       ἀπήν[εγ]-
20 [καν εἰς Μεθύδρ]ι[ο]ν, ἐὰμ μὴ ἀποδιδῶντι τὸ ἀργύριον τοῖς Μεγαλοπολίταις,
       καθὼς ἐξ[ε]-
     [χώρησεν ἁ πό]λις τῶν Ὀρχομενίων, ὑποδίκους εἶμεν τοὺς μὴ ποιοῦντας τὰ
       δίκαια. ᵛ

4–5 τῶι βουλομένωι αὐ|τῶι δίκαν θ]ανάτου Foucart τῶι στραταγῶι δίκαν] Thür
6 μὲ[ν Αἰγίωι οἱ σύνεδροι Foucart (*regarded as impossible by Larsen 1968: 220 n. 5, who
prefers* οἱ δαμίοργοι)   9 ψαφίσματ[ι τῶι γενομένωι τῶι] Foucart ψαφίσματ[ι τῶι
γεγονότι τῶι] Dittenberger(?)   11–12 Ὀρ[χο|μένωι γᾶν ἐπί]κλαρ[ο]ν Foucart
Ὀρ[χο|μενῶι γᾶς] κλᾶρ[ο]ν Dittenberger Ὀρ[χο|μενίοις ἢ] κλᾶρ[ο]ν Hoffmann
Ὀρ[χο|μενῶι] Hiller   12–13 ἀπαλλοτριῶ|[σαι πλέον χρυσέ]ων Foucart ἀπ-
αλλοτριῶ|[σαι ἐντὸς ἐτ]έων Dittenberger ἀπαλλοτριῶ|[σα]ι ἐτέων Hiller
13–14 ἐγ|[γένοντο, ἤ τοι] Νεάρχ[ω]ι Dittenberger ἐγ[έ|νον]τοHiller   14–15 μ[η|θὲν
ἐγκαλεί]σθω Foucart μ[ὴ| δικαζέ]σθω Hiller   15–16 μήτε τοῖς ... αὐτοῦ μηθεὶς
omitted by Hoffmann   17 [ἐνοντο καὶ] ὅ[στι]ς δικάζοιτο Foucart [νο]γ[τ]ο· [ὃς δ]ὲ
δικάζοιτο Hiller   18 [ἱ δὲ τὰς τραπέζα]ς τὰς Foucart [ἱ δὲ τὰς Νί]κας τὰς
Hiller Μεθυ| Foucart Μεθυ[δρι] Hiller   19 [δριεῖς οἱ μεταστή]σαντες Foucart [εἶς
οἱ μετοική]σαντες Hiller ἀπέ- Foucart ἀπήν[εγ]- Hiller   20 [φυγον, παρέχειν
αὐτοὺς ἐ]ὰμ Foucart [καν εἰς Μεθύδρ]ι[ο]ν, ἐὰμ Hiller   20–21 καθὼς ἐ|ψήφισται,
τὰμ πό]λιν Foucart ἐ|[παγγείλαντο ποτὶ τὰμ πό]λιν Dittenberger ε|[ἱκός, ποτὶ τὰμ πό]
λιν Hoffman ἐξ[ε|χώρησεν ἁ πό]λις Hiller

... if anyone shall violate ... or if an archon should send ... or a private individual
should vote [. . . let him owe] thirty talents as sacred funds of Zeu[s Hamarios, and let
the *stratagos* bring a capital charge before the koinon of the Achaians. In accordance
with these regulations the Orchomenians and the Achaians [shall swear] the same
[oath], in [Aigion the *damiorgoi* of the Achaians and the *strat]agos,* hipparch, and
nauarch, while in [Orchomenos the archons of the Orchomenians (shall swear it):] "I
s[w]ear by Zeus Hamarios, Athana Hamaria, Aphr[od]ita, and [all the other] g[ods
that I shall] rem[a]in within all the terms stipulated on the stele and the agreement
and the vote [that was passed by the [koi]n[on] of t[h]e Achaians. And if anyone does
not obey these stipulations, I shall not entrust him with political authority. May all
good things come if I obey the oath I have sworn, but if I violate the oath, the opposite." Any of the Achaians who take up a parcel of land or a house in Or[chomenos]
may not sell it for twenty years. If there are any Orchomenians who became Achaians
before the accusation was brought against Nearchos or his sons, all charges (against
them) shall be rescinded, and they shall no[t have actions] brought against them by
Nearchos or by his sons, nor shall Nearchos or any [of] his [so]ns have actions brought
against them by any Orchomenians who be[ca]me Achaians. If anyone should con-
demn them, he shall owe one thousand drachmas, and the penalty shall not be subject
to reduction. Regarding the golden Nike of Zeus Hoplosmios, which the Methydrians
[who mo]ved to Orchomenos put down as a pledge in exchange for which they
received money, and some of them who have now retu[rned to Methydr]i[o]n: if they
do not return the money to the Megalopolitans just as the po[lis] of the Orchomenians conc[ceded], they shall be liable for not doing what is just.

Restoration of line 6. Larsen 1968: 220 n. 3 suggests that Foucart's unanimously
accepted restoration of line 6, ἐμ μὲ[ν Αἰγίωι οἱ σύνεδροι τῶν Ἀχαιῶν, ought rather
to read ἐμ μὲ[ν Αἰγίωι οἱ δαμιοργοὶ τῶν Ἀχαιῶν. The only direct association
between *damiorgoi* and oath taking appears in the fourth-century decree of the

koinon (T34). Other evidence pertaining to these officials is less conclusive. When Aratos allied the Achaians with Antigonos Doson in 224 he was accompanied by the *damiourgoi* (Plut. *Arat.* 43.1); while a formal alliance was made, there is mention neither of an oath nor of the other officials (*stratagos*, hipparch, nauarch) who participate in swearing the oath that binds Orchomenos to the koinon. In 184/3, Flamininus wrote to the *stratagos* and the *damiourgoi* asking them to summon the Achaian *ekklēsia*, to which they replied that they needed first to know on what subject he wished to address the assembly, since, Polybios says, the laws bound the magistrates to do that (Polyb. 23.5.16–17, showing that the *damiourgoi* had a probouleutic function). The fourth-century decree strongly indicates that, if the responsibilities of the highest magistrates were roughly the same after the resuscitation of the koinon in 280, we ought to read δαμίοργοι rather than σύνεδροι. For further discussion of the text as evidence for the formalities of the Achaian assemblies see Aymard 1938: 284–314.

The date. The text must belong in or after 235, when Megalopolis, which is so favorably treated (lines 20 and 21), joined the Achaian koinon (Polyb. 2.44.5; Plut. *Arat.* 30.4), and before 229, when Orchomenos, along with Mantineia and Tegea, went over to the Aitolian koinon (Polyb. 2.46.2 with F. W. Walbank 1957–79: I.242). Cf. Errington 1969: 10 n. 1 (ca. 234/3); Urban 1979: 84–85.

Administration in the Achaian koinon. Giovannini 1971: 33 n. 2 suggested that the text records mere ad hoc regulations between the two communities. Lehmann 1983a: 238 n. 2 rejects this interpretation, arguing that the basic constitutional regulations would have been contained in the lines that are now lost. The agreement (*homologia*) clearly spelled out the details according to which Orchomenos would be integrated into the koinon; this process was probably typical whenever a new member was added (Rizakis 2008b: 276–77 and above, pp. 361–62). The sense of δύναμ[ιν is somewhat unclear: "power" as military forces (LSJ s.v. I.3) is unlikely, for violation of the oaths would surely entail political punishment, not just exclusion from military service; "power" as political authority (LSJ s.v. I.2) is more likely and suggests disenfranchisement or at least ineligibility for public office. Lines 11–13 suggest that the koinon sent Achaian citizens as settlers to Orchomenos, receiving a plot of land or a house, which were inalienable for twenty years. This is clearly a measure designed to ensure the loyalty of the polis to the koinon, to make it more thoroughly Achaian. Rizakis 2008b: 280 n. 56 distinguishes the Achaian settlers at Orchomenos from those sent to repopulate a city after a disaster (e.g., Megalopolis after the expulsion of the inhabitants by Kleomenes: Plut. *Cleom.* 23; Polyb. 5.93.6–7), seeing them as rather more similar to the "colons Achéens installés à Mantinée par Aratos en 227" (Polyb. 2.58.1–2). This is indeed the more apt comparison, but it speaks against Rizakis's further conclusion, namely that the colonists at Orchomenos were installed arbitrarily and are a sign that Orchomenos was brought into the koinon by coercion. For Polybios tells us that at Mantineia it was the citizens themselves who requested an Achaian garrison; the Achaian response was not simply to send soldiers to man fortifications, but rather they "chose by lot [ἀπεκλήρωσαν] three hundred citizens who, leaving behind their own hometowns and their ways of life, settled in Mantineia, standing guard over the freedom and safety of its citizens" (2.58.2). While in Polybios's hands the Achaian garrison troops are made to look like selfless devotees of the cause of Achaian justice and protection of the oppressed, and while it is certain that their presence significantly advanced Achaian interests, there is no reason to doubt that the Mantineians requested the garrison. Why should we jump to the conclusion that the situation was significantly different in Orchomenos, where we know only that the settlers were sent and prevented from leaving by the prohibition on the sale of real estate for two decades? Population shortage may have exacerbated the security problem (Roy 2000: 341–42), but it was not the principal motive behind these settlements.

Methydrion. Methydrion was an Arkadian polis whose territory abutted those of Orchomenos and Torthyneion (Thür and Taeuber 1994: no. 14); in 371 it was dependent on Orchomenos (Paus. 8.27.4: ἐκ δὲ τῶν συντελούντων ἐς Ὀρχομενὸν Θισόα, Μεθύδριον, Τεῦθις; cf. Nielsen 1996a: 84–86), but it may have been politically integrated into Megalopolis when that city was founded by synoikism (Paus. 8.27.4; Moggi 1974: 93–94). It can be inferred from the present document that Methydrion was by the third century a dependent polis of Megalopolis but tried to break away, perhaps when Megalopolis became a member of the Achaian koinon in 235, with the hope of remaining independent. The Methydrians apparently put down a golden statue of Nike as security on a loan from their own citizens, probably motivated by the need for cash to fund their secession effort. At the moment when Orchomenos became a member of the Achaian koinon, some of the lenders, perhaps the leaders of the secession effort, fled to Orchomenos, apparently taking the Nike with them. Whether Methydrion was brought back under the control of Megalopolis is unclear, but Megalopolis certainly demanded the return of the money or of the golden Nike from Orchomenos. So when Orchomenos joined the Achaian koinon, it had an outstanding dispute with Megalopolis, which had become a member of the koinon in 235, and the issue had to be resolved as part of the process of the integration of Orchomenos into the koinon. The money for which the Nike was pledged was deemed by the Achaians to belong to Megalopolis, and they required its return. This decision implies an arbitration process: Ager 1996: 131; Harter-Uibopuu 1998: 30, 125 n. 41.

Nearchos was probably a deposed local tyrant (Larsen 1968: 310 n. 2).

*40. The Achaian Koinon Oversees Arbitration of a Dispute
between Arsinoe and Epidauros*

Found in the Asklepieion at Epidauros. 236–225 BCE.

Ed.pr. Kavvadias 1918 (*IG IV² 1.72; SEG 13.251; Rizakis 1995: 376 no. 695 [ll. 1–18 only]; Ager 1996: 135–36 no. 46; Foxhall, Gill, and Forbes in Mee and Forbes 1997:

272–73 no. 11; Harter-Uibopuu 1998: no. 5). Knoepfler 1983: 54 n. 27 suggests some revised restorations.

Side A
θεός.

[ἐπὶ στρ]αταγοῦ τοῖς Ἀχαιοῖ[ς ----------]
[------]ος, ἐν δὲ Ἐπιδαύρωι ἐ[π᾽ ἱαρεὺς ----]
4   [Ἐπιδαυ]ρίοις καὶ Ἀρσινοε[ύσιν ----------]
[------]εν περὶ τᾶς χώρα[ς, ἃς ἀμφέλλεγον --]
[κρίσις] ἔστω ἐπὶ τᾶς χώ[ρας -----------]
[πόλεις] ἔνδεκα προβληθ[εῖσαι ----------]
8   [------] ᵛ Πελλάνα ᵛ Αἴγ[ιον --------------]
[Θελποῦ]σσα ᵛ οἱ δὲ λαχό[ντες ----------]
[------]ς ἄχρι κα τρεῖς [----------------]
[------] ποιήσονται γ[----------------]
12   [ἐν δὲ τῶ]ι Τρίτωι μην[ὶ -------------]
[----πα]ραγενέσθωσα[ν -------------]
[τῶν ἡρώ]ων ἢ θεῶν τι[μ------------]
[-------] εἰς τὰς πό[λεις -----------]
16   [--------κ]αιρ[-------------------]
[-------]ταε[-------------------]

Side B
[δικασταὶ ἔκρι]ναν τοίδε
[Θελπ]ούσσ[ιοι]·
20   Ὀξυτίων ᵛ Διύλλ[ου]
Παυσανίας ᵛ Τρο[---]
Θεοίτας ᵛ Κλεισ[--]
Φιλόξενος ᵛ Δαϊ[--]
24   Στράτιππος ᵛ Ἀν[---]
Μελανκόμας ᵛ Φι[---]
Πολύστρατος ᵛ [---]
Σώστρατος ᵛ Ἀν[---]
28   Ἐμαυτίων ᵛ Σταδ[---]
Ἀριστόδαμος ᵛ Δ[---]
Εὐθυμένης ᵛ Λάκ[ωνος]
[-]έρις ᵛ Κρίθωνο[ς]
32   [Λε?]ωνίδας ᵛ Πειθ[---]
[----]ίων ᵛ Κλε[---]

8 Αἴγ[ιον] Kavvadias Αἴ[γιον] or Αἴ[γειρα] Rizakis   9 [Θελποῦ]σσα Kavvadias [Θελφοῦ]σσα Knoepfler   19 [Θελπ]ούσσ[ιοι] Kavvadias [Θελφ]ούσσ[ιοι] Knoepfler

God. When [---] was general of the Achaians ... and in Epidauros the [priest was ...]. [The Epidau]rians and Arsinoe[ans ...] regarding the territory [that was being

disputed . . .]. Let this be the [judgment] about the terri[tory . . .] eleven [poleis] were
propos[ed . . .] . . . Pellana, Aig[- - -] [Telphou]sa. Those who were selec[ted . . .] . . .
and until three . . . let them be made . . . [in the] month of Triton . . . were present . . .
of the heroes or the gods . . . to the po[leis . . .]. . . . The following [judges de]cided.
[Telph]ousi[ans]: Oxytion son of Diyll[os], Pausanias son of Tro[. . .], Theoitas son of
Kleis[. . .], Philoxenos son of Daï[. . .], Stratippos son of An[. . .], Melankomas son of
Phi[. . .], Polystratos [son of . . .], Sostratos son of An[. . .], Emaution son of Stad[. . .],
Aristodamos son of D[. . .], Euthymenes son of Lak[on], [. . .]eris son of Krithon,
[Le?]onidas son of Peith[. . .], [. . .]ion son of Kle[. . .]

Kavvadias's restoration of line 7 is usually taken to mean that the Achaians had
asked eleven poleis to put forward representatives who would form the arbitral
board (Ager 1996: 136). In lines 8 and 9 it is clear that Pellana, Aig[ion] or Aig[eira],
and Telphousa (or Thelpoussa) were involved, but there is hardly room in the
remaining lacunae of lines 7–9 for the mention of another eight poleis (rightly
Robertson 1976: 266 n. 29). The number of cities that sent representatives cannot
be ascertained with confidence. Perhaps line 7 provided the time frame within
which the arbitration had to be completed (e.g., [ἡμέρας] ἕνδεκα προβληθ[εῖσαι)?
Or perhaps, as Ager 1996: 136 n. 3 suggests, "the names of eleven cities were put
forward [by the disputing states], and a selection (of three?) was made among
them."

The inscription was dated to the second half of the third century by Kavvadias
1918, on the basis of the stoichedon style of the inscription and its letter forms.
Hiller von Gaertringen 1925–26: 71 simply placed it in the third century, but in *IG*
IV.1² 72 he put it after 228 without further comment, and this has been generally
accepted (most recently by Ager 1996: 135–36). However, Dixon 2003: 82–83
shows that a date after 228, the beginning of the Kleomenean War, is unlikely, and
one after 225 is impossible, for in this year Kleomenes seized both Pellene and
Epidauros (Polyb. 2.52.2; Plut. *Cleom.* 19.3). The logical terminus post quem is
236–234, when Telphousa (or Thelpoussa) probably joined the Achaian koinon
along with its neighbor Heraia (Polyaenus, *Strat.* 2.36; see above, p. 107). Arsinoe
was never a member of the Achaian koinon but was rather a Ptolemaic possession, and an Achaian arbitration of the dispute between Arsinoe and its member
Epidauros makes sense, as Dixon shows, only in the period before the Kleomenean War when the Achaians had an alliance with Ptolemy (Plut. *Arat.* 24.4;
Polyb. 2.47.2–3).

41. Law of the Achaian Nomographoi Regarding Sacrifices to Hygieia
Found at the Asklepieion, Epidauros. After 229/8 BCE.
    White marble stele, in two fragments. Stoichedon 22 lines 1–11, 23 lines 12–36.
    Hiller von Gaertringen, *IG* IV.1² 73 (*SEG* 1.74; Moretti 1967–76: vol. I no. 48;
Rizakis 1995: 340–41 no. 597 reprints fragment A with some commentary).

Fragment A
Θεός. τύχα ἀγαθά.
νομογράφοι Ἀχαιῶν οἱ τὸν ν-
όμον τᾶι Ὑγιείαι θέντες. ᵛᵛ
4   Ἐπιδαύριος· Ἀρχέλοχος ᵛ Τι-
μαΐδα. ᵛἙρμιονεύς· ᵛ Ἀμφαίν-
ετος ᵛ Μνάμονος. ᵛ Ἀργεῖοι· ᵛ
Λύσιππος ᵛ Δαμοκρίτου, ᵛ Τι-
8   μοκράτης ᵛ Τίμωνος, ᵛ Φιλό- ᵛ
δαμος ᵛ Φιλάρχου. ᵛ Κλεωναῖ-
ος· Νικίας Ξενοκλέος. ᵛ Σικυ-
ώνιοι· Δεξίας Δέξιος, Πυθο- ᵛ
12   κλῆς Πυθοδώρου. ᵛ Φλειάσιος·
Ἀρχέας Εὐτελείδα. ᵛ Φενεά- ᵛᵛ
τας· Πανταίνετος Διοφάνεος.
Πελλανεύς· Αἰσχύλος Ἀρχιμή-
16   δεος. ᵛ Βούριος· Δίφιλος Δαμο-
κράτεος. ᵛ Αἰγιεῖς· Τεισίας ᵛ
Ἐχεκράτεος, Νεολαΐδας. ᵛ Πα- ᵛ
τρεύς· Ἀγανορίδας Τιμανορί-
20   δα. ᵛ Δυμαῖοι· Θυῖων Λύκωνος, ᵛ
Σαμοφάνης Θευξένου. ᵛ Φαραι-
εύς· Ξένων Σατύρου. ᵛ Τριται-
εύς· Ἀριστέας Ἀριστέος. ᵛ Λου-
24   σιάτας· Ἀκράγας Κλέϊος. ᵛ Με- ᵛ
γαλοπολῖται· Πύρρανθος Ἱε- ᵛ
ρωνύμου, Λυσίμαχος Λυσίπ[ου],
Καλλίδαμος Καλλιμά[χου. ᵛᵛᵛ],
28   Ἀσχεύς· Ἀριστόβου[λος Λεον]- ᵛ
[τ]ίχου. ᵛ γραμματε[ύς.– ᶜᵃ· ⁷ –]
[–]λευσ[ι– ᶜᵃ· ⁴ –]ρ[– – –]

Fragment B
τᾶι Ὑγιεί[αι τοὺς ἱερέας τοῦ]
32   Ἀσκλαπιοῦ [τᾶι παναγύρι θύ]-
ειν βοῦν.ᵛ μγ[– ᶜᵃ· ¹⁰ –]τὰν
βύρσαν κατα[ναλίσκειν.ᵛ προ]-
στατεύειν [τᾶς θυσίας πάσας]
36   τοὺς τοῦ Ἀσ[κλαπιοῦ ἱερέας.ᵛ]

26 Λυσίπ[ου] Hiller   27 Καλλιμά[χου Hiller   28 Ἀριστόβου[λος Λεον]-
Hiller   29 [τ]ίχου. γραμματε[ύς Hiller   30 [Κ]λευσ[θ]έ[νης] Ῥυπ[αῖος
Hiller (*vestigia dubia; fortasse*)   31–36 *All printed restorations are Hiller's*

God. Good fortune. The Achaian lawgivers establish this law regarding Hygieia. The
representative of Epidauros was Archelochos son of Timais; of Hermione, Amphainetos

son of Mnamon; of Argos, Lysippos son of Damokritos, Timokrates son of Timon, and Philodamos son of Philarchos; of Kleonai, Nikias son of Xenokles; of Sikyon, Dexias son of Dexis and Pythokles son of Pythodoros; of Phleious, Archeas son of Euteleidas; of Pheneos, Pantainetos son of Diophanes; of Pellene, Aischylos son of Archimedes; of Boura, Diphilos son of Damokrates; of Aigion, Teisias son of Echekrates and Neolaidas; of Patrai, Aganoridas son of Timanoridas; of Dyme, Thyion son of Lykon and Samophanes son of Theuxenos; of Pharai, Xenon son of Satyros; of Tritaia, Aristeas son of Aristes; of Lousoi, Akragas son of Kleïs; of Megalopolis, Pyrranthos son of Hieronymos, Lysimachos son of Lysip[os], and Kallidamos son of Kallima[chos]; of Ascheion, Aristobou[los son of Leont]ichos. The secretar[y . . .]leus[i]. . . . Let [the priests of] Asklepios [sa]crifice to Hygiei[a] at the festival a cow . . . and bu[rn] the skin. Let [the priests] of As[klepios] [pre]side [over all the] sacrifices.

This text provides important evidence for the manner in which member cities of the Achaian koinon were represented on the board of lawgivers. Swoboda 1922: 521–22 suggested that the cities sent representatives in proportion to their population. Aymard 1938: 383–84 observes, however, that the pattern of representation shown by the text does not seem to map onto what we know about the relative populations of the cities involved at this time, proposing instead that individuals were elected to the college from the entire citizen population of the koinon, regardless of their city of origin. This was accepted by both Larsen 1955: 217 n. 22 (cf. Larsen 1968: 231) and Moretti 1967–76: vol. I no. 48 but has since been challenged. Lehmann 1983a: 245–46 (cf. Lehmann 2000: 82–89) observed that the college as here composed preserves perfect parity between the large and medium cities on the one hand, which sent three and two representatives, respectively (12 representatives total), and the small cities on the other, which sent only one (12 representatives total). Like Lehmann, Gschnitzer 1985 returns to Swoboda's argument, taking the list as indicative of patterns of representation based on polis size. Corsten 1999: 170–72 suggests that because some communities known to have been members of the koinon are not listed, they probably took turns with those communities represented in this list by a single representative, in the same way that the aphedriates and boiotarchs (and on one occasion hostages) were sent in the Hellenistic Boiotian koinon. While noting that Corsten's hypothesis is not supported by any conclusive evidence, Rizakis 2003: 106 confesses sympathy with his solution. See above, p. 379, for further discussion.

The text must postdate the entry of Epidauros to the koinon in 243 and of Argos, Hermione, and Phleious to the koinon in 229/8. Gschnitzer 1985: 112–16 argues, from the pattern of representatives indicated by the text and what we know from external sources about the membership of different cities in the koinon, that the law must have been passed between 210, when the Achaians lost Aigina to the Aitolians (Polyb. 9.42.5–8), and 207, when Tegea rejoined the koinon (Polyb. 11.18.8); for both these poleis were large enough that we would have expected them to be represented if they were then members of the koinon. The lower date is accepted by Corsten 1999: 171. A fragmentary inscription recently found at Aigion (T44) is probably another law of the Achaian *nomographoi*.

42. The Achaian Koinon Grants Proxeny to Hostages from Boiotia and Phokis

Copied at Aigion (then Vostizza) by Cyriac of Ancona. Now lost. Ca. 228–224 BCE. Dittenberger *Syll.*³ 519, based on Cyriac; some new readings proposed by Knoepfler 2004.

    ἔδοξε τῶι κοινῶι Ἀχαιῶν· τοῖς ὁμήροις τῶν
    Βοιωτῶν καὶ Φωκέων προξενίαν δόμεν αὐτοῖς
    καὶ ἐκγόνοις, Εὐδάμωι Βρύχωνος Πλαταιεῖ, Ἀρχέαι
4 Ὀλυμπίωνος Ταναγραίωι, Ἀριστομένει Μειλίχου
    Ὠρωπίωι, Ἀπολλοδώρωι Ἀσκληπιοδώρου Κορωνεῖ,
    Ἀκροτάτωι Ἰσμηνοδώρου Θηβαίωι, Ῥόδωνι Τιμο-
    κράτους Ἁλιαρτίωι, Ἀριστίωνι Καλλιππίδος Ὀρχο-
8 μενίωι, Νικέαι Κορρινάδου Θεσπιεῖ, Κλεαρέτωι
    Ἀντιλέοντος Φανοτεῖ, Λεοντιάδηι Νικοβούλου Ἐ-
    λατεῖ, καὶ εἶμεν αὐτοῖς ἀτέλειαν καὶ ἀσυλίαν καὶ πολέ-
    μου καὶ εἰρήνης καὶ κατὰ γῆν καὶ κατὰ θάλατταν
12 καὶ τἄλλα πάντα, ὅσα καὶ τοῖς ἄλλοις προξένοις
    ‹κ›αὶ εὐεργέταις δίδοται. ἐπὶ δαμιορ[γῶν – – –]ῆγα Βου-
    ρίου, Νικανδρίδα [– – –]

3 Ἀρχέαι Dittenberger Ἀρχε[λαΐδαι?] Knoepfler

Resolved by the koinon of the Achaians to grant to the hostages of the Boiotians and Phokians proxeny, to them and their descendants, Eudamos son of Brychon of Plataia, Archeas son of Olympion of Tanagra, Aristomenes son of Meilichos of Oropos, Apollodoros son of Asklepiodoros of Koroneia, Akrotatos son of Hismenodoros of Thebes, Rhodon son of Timokrates of Haliartos, Aristion son of Kallippidos of Orchomenos, Nikeas son of Korrinados of Thespiai, Klearetos son of Antileon of Phanoteus, Leontiades son of Nikoboulos of Elateia. Let them have *ateleia* and *asylia*, in war and peace, by land and by sea, and all the other things that are given to other proxenoi and benefactors. The *damior[goi* were . . .]egas of Boura, Nikandris [. . .]

Hostages. The practice of taking hostages to secure the clauses of a treaty between Athens and Chalkis (*IG* I³ 40) is discussed by Garlan 1965: 332–38, though no reference is made to the Achaian koinon decree, apparently the only other epigraphic attestation of the practice. Hostage-taking practices in Greece are discussed by Aymard 1967: 418–35, focusing in particular on Philip II's stay at Thebes. Amit 1970 studies the phenomenon in the classical period. Roesch (1965b: 104, 139) notes the connection between the cities represented by these hostages and the representation of boiotarchs and aphedriates in the same period and takes this text as support for his argument that there were two ranks of cities in Hellenistic Boiotia. Knoepfler 2000: 362 compares the pattern of representation to that attested by the aphedriate inscriptions (T16–T25) and the one complete list of boiotarchs of the third century that identifies the individuals also by their city ethnic (T26), drawing the conclusion that they are district, not polis, representatives. Knoepfler 2004 resumes the same argument and through prosopographic links demonstrates that the men who served as hostages in this decree were all elites in their own communities, themselves involved in politics, high-profile lending, civic benefaction, and service in priesthoods, or coming from families in which such activities are attested.

Date. Holleaux 1938–68: I.94–95 places the document in the late third or early second century on grounds of prosopography. Hiller von Gaertringen in the note to *Syll.*[3] 519 first suggested that the decree should be associated with the rapprochement between Achaia and Boiotia (inter alia) in 224 in an attempt to combat the threat of Kleomenes; cf. Treves 1934: 407. M. Feyel 1942b: 124–25 suggested that it should be associated with the Phokian-Boiotian alliance (T28) and early resistance to Kleomenes, between summer 228 and winter 227/6, and interpreted Phokian participation as a sign that they feared being attacked by the Aitolians after having been detached from their league by Antigonos. In 228/7 Kleomenes first began attacking Peloponnesian towns that were part of the Achaian koinon (Polyb. 2.46.2; see above, p. 110), and it would make sense to place the alliance implied by this document in that year, because the Phokian-Boiotian alliance of 228 would explain why both koina participated in the alliance with Achaia.

43. Honorary Decree of Elateia for the City of Stymphalos

Found at Kionia, northwest of Lake Stymphalos, in 1947. Now in the Epigraphical Museum, Athens, inv. 13053. Ca. 189–186 BCE.

Ed.pr. Mitsos 1946–47 (*SEG* 11.1107). Accame 1949 publishes a new text based on squeezes and photographs, with translation and commentary. Maier 1959–61: I.132–36 no. 30 produces a new edition incorporating a number of new readings, with commentary; Moretti 1967–76: vol. I no. 55, with translation, bases his text on Maier but includes several different restorations (*SEG* 25.445, with several improved readings from Klaffenbach 1968; Garlan 1969: 159–60; Michaud 1974b: 275–76; Lehmann 1999: 79–81; *AEph* 1999.1470). *Thür and Taeuber 1994: 252–60 no. 18.

> [- - -]HK[- - -]IP[- - -]
> [- - - - - -]νοι καὶ ἐκτενεί[αν φιλα]νθρωπίας τᾶι σ̣[υγγενείαι καθ]ακοῦσαν καὶ κατα
> [- - - - - -]αις ὑπεδέξαντο ἕ[κ]αστος ἐπὶ τὰν ἰδί[αν] ἑστίαν μετὰ πάσας φι-
> 4   [λανθρωπίας(?), ἀπό τε τ]οῦ δαμοσίου ἐσειτομέτρησαν πᾶσιν ἐν πλείονα χρόνον καὶ ὅσων
> [χρεία ἦν μετέδωκα(?)]ν πάντων· καὶ ἱερῶν καὶ θυσιᾶν ἐκοινώνησαν, νομί-
> [ξ]αντες ἰδίους

[πολίτας εἶναι· καὶ τ]ᾶς αὐτῶν χώρας ἀπεμέριξαν καὶ {καὶ} διέδωκαν Ἐλατέοις καὶ ἀτέ-

[λειαν πάντων ἐτέω]ν δέκα· καὶ περὶ τούτων πάντων γράψαντες εἰστάλαν χαλκέαν

8   [ἀνέθεσαν ἐν τῶι ἱερῶι] τᾶς Ἀρτέμιτος τᾶς [Βραυρ]ωνίας, οὐθὲν ἐνλείποντες πάσας εὐερ-

[γεσίας ποτ' αὐτούς· ὕστερον δ]ὲ πάλιν μετὰ ἔτη τινὰ παραγενομένων Ῥωμαίων ἐν τὰν Ἑλλάδα

[μετὰ στρατοῦ(?) καὶ κυριε]ύσαντος Μανίου τῶν κατ' [Ἐ]λάτεαν τόπων, ἐπρόσβευσαν Στυμφάλιοι πο-

[τὶ τοὺς Ἀχαιούς, ὅπω]ς ἐκπεμφθῇ προσβεία ποτὶ Μάνιον περὶ τᾶς Ἐλατέων καθόδου ἐν τὰν [ἰδί]-

12   [αν, τῶν δ' Ἀχαιῶν ἀπο]στειλάντω‹ν› προσβευτὰς Διοφάνη κάθ[αν]οκλῆ καὶ Μανίου ἐπιχωρ[ή]-

[σαντος ἀποδοθήμεν] Ἐλατέοις τάν τε π[ό]λιν καὶ τ[ὰν] χ[ώ]ραν καὶ τοὺς νόμους, Ἐλατέων δὲ ἐ-

[πιμεινάντων ἐν Στυ]μφάλωι πλείονα χρόνον [ἀνε]γκλήτως [κ]αὶ καταξίως τῶν προγό[νων]

[πρὶν ἀπελθεῖν ἐν] τὰν ἰδίαν, οὐκ οὔσας σίτου ἐξαγωγᾶς τοῖς Ἀχαιοῖς διὰ τὸν περιεσ[τῶτα]

16   [καιρὸν(?) καὶ τὰν σι]τοδείαν, Στυμφάλιοι διεπρεσβεύσαντο ποτὶ τοὺς Ἀχαιούς, ὅπως ἀπέλθων-

[τι Ἐλατεῖς τὸ]ν ἴδιον σῖτον ἐνείκαντες καὶ ἐκ τᾶς Στυμφαλίων χώρας εὐχάριστοι ΟΠ[– – –]

[– – – – – –]μένοι τοῦ συνστᾶμεν καὶ οἰκισθῆμεν τὰν [– – –]Ι[–]ΩΙ· καὶ μετὰ τ[ὰν]

[κάθοδον ἐν τὰ]ν ἰδίαν διαπορειομένων Ἐλατέων [κα]θ' αὐτο[ὺς] περὶ τοῦ συνοικισμοῦ καὶ

20   [πεμψάντων περὶ τού]του ποτὶ Στυμφαλίους, ἐ[ξ]απέστειλαν Στυμφ[άλιοι] ἄνδρας καλοὺς καὶ ἀγα-

[θοὺς – – –]ου, Εὐρήμονα, Θεαρίδαν Ἰ[σ]αγόρα, οἵτινες πα[ρ]αγεν[ό]μενοι [εἰς Ἐλ]άτειαν τὰν

[κρίσιν περὶ τοῦ τοῦ(?)] διατειχίσματος τόπου [ἐποι]ήσαντο ὀρθῶ[ς] καὶ δικαίω[ς]· ὅπως οὖν φαίνηται

[καὶ ἁ πόλις ἡμῶν μνημ]ονεύουσα τῶν παρὰ Στυμφαλίων φιλανθρώπων καὶ ἀντ[απο]διδοῦσα χ[ά]-

24   [ριτας τοῖς εὐεργέται]ς, δεδόχθαι τ[οῖ]ς Ἐλατέοις τοὺς ἐσταμένους ἄνδ[ρας] Δαφναῖον

[Ἀριστωνύμου, – –]κράτεος, Θεώνδαν Πύθωνος, Ἄγωνα Θεοκλέ[ο]ς, Αἰτωλὸν Ἀριστολάου, Κρίτω-

[να Ἀριστωνύμου, ἐπιμέλειαν ποι]ήσασθαι ὅπως ἀν[α]γ[ρ]αφῇ τὰ φιλάνθ[ρωπα Ἐλ]ατέοις καὶ Στυμφαλίοι[ς]

[εἰς στάλαν λιθίναν καὶ ἀν]ατεθῇ ἐν Ἐλατείαι ἐν τᾶι ἀγορᾶι παρὰ τὸν βωμὸν τοῦ Διὸς τοῦ Σωτῆρος,

28   [ἐν δὲ Στυμφάλωι ἐν τῶι ἱ]ερῶι τᾶς Ἀρτέμιτος τᾶς Βραυρωνίας· ὑπάρχειν δὲ
Στυμφαλίοις ἐν Ἐ-
[λατείαι ἀσφάλειαν καὶ ἀσυλ]ίαν καὶ πόθοδον ποτὶ βουλὰν καὶ ἐκκλησίαν
πρώτοις μετὰ τὰ προϊερά, καὶ
[μετέχειν αὐτοὺς ἐν Ἐλατ]είαι τᾶν κοινᾶν θυσιᾶν καὶ τῶν ἄλλων τιμίων καὶ
φιλανθρώπων πάν-
[των· στεφανῶσαι δὲ τὸν δᾶμον τ]ὸν Στυμφαλίων στεφάνωι χρυσέωι καὶ
ἀνακαρύσσειν κατ᾽ ἐνι-
32   [αυτὸν τοὺς ἱεροκήρυκας ἐν τῷ]ι ἄγωνι τῶι γυμ[νικῶι] τῶν Βοαδρομίων,
διασ[α]φέοντας ὅτι [ἁ]
[πόλις τῶν Ἐλατέων στεφανοῖ τὰν πόλιν τὰν Στυμφαλίων στεφάνωι χρυσ]έωι,
ἀριστείωι, ἀρε[τᾶς]
[ἕνεκεν καὶ φιλανθρωπίας τᾶς ποθ᾽ αὑτάν - - -]ΝΟΝΕΣ[- - -]
[- - -]

2 ἐκτένει[αν   φιλανθρ(?)]ωπίας Mitsos ἐκτενεί[ας   καὶ   φιλανθρ]ωπίας Moretti
σ[υγγενείαι καθ]ακούσαν Accame   σ[υγγενείαι καθ]ακοῦσαν Thür   12 κ᾽ Ἀθα[νο]-
κλῆ Accame, Moretti κἀθ[αν]οκλῆ Thür   13 τοὺς δούλους Mitsos τοὺς νόμους
Klaffenbach   15 ἀ[ν]αγωγᾶς Mitsos ἐξαγωγᾶς Garlan   16–17 ἀπελθών|[τες
Mitsos ἀπέλθων|[τι Klaffenbach   17 ΕΙΚΑΡΥΞΑ . . . [ἀπ]ὸ Mitsos ἐνείκαντες
καὶ ἐκ Garlan   χώρα[ς] εὐχαριστε ΥΟΠΩ. Mitsos χώρας εὐχάριστοι οπ . .
Garlan   18 καριμισθῆμεν Mitsos καὶ οἰκισθῆμεν Klaffenbach   25 [Ἀριστωνύμου
Michaud Πυθ[ω]νος Mitsos Πύθονος Maier Πυθωνος Garlan Ἀγ[έ]αν Mit-
sos Ἀγ[ων]α Klaffenbach Ἄγωνα Garlan   26 Ἀριστωνύμου Michaud   πρόνοιαν
Mitsos ἐπιμέλειαν Moretti   29 ἀτέλειαν(?), ἀσυλ]ίαν Mitsos, Thür ἀσφάλειαν καὶ
ἀσυλ]ίαν Follett (AEph 1999: 1470)   29–30 καὶ [μ|ετέχειν Mitsos καὶ| [μετέχειν
Taeuber   32 τὸν ἱεροκήρυκα Mitsos τοὺς ἱεροκήρυκας Accame

. . . and because of the extension of kindness, befitting our kinship, and in accordance with . . . each one of them displayed . . . at his own hearth with complete
ki[ndness(?), at the] public expense, when there was a lengthy shortage of grain
everywhere, and [they gave as much] as was needed. They allowed us to participate
in their cults and sacrifices, treating us as their own [citizens. And] they divided up
their own territory and distributed it among the Elateians, exempt from taxation for
ten years. They wrote about all these things on a bronze stele [and placed it in the
temple] of Artemis [Braur]onia, omitting no part of their bene[faction toward them
(the Elateians). Later], after several years, when the Romans came to Greece [with
an army?] and Manios was in control of the territory of the Elateians, the Stymphalians sent an embassy to the Achaians so that] an embassy would be sent to Manios
regarding the restoration of the Elateians to their own land. The Achaians sent as
ambassadors Diophanes and Atha[no]kles; Manios consented to the return of the
Elateians to their city, their territory, and their laws, the Elateians having re[mained
in Sty]mphalos for a long time, giving no grounds for reproach and quite worthily
of their ancest[ors, before going back to] their own (territory). There being a prohibition on the export of grain among the Achaians as a result of the critical [state of

things and the gr]ain shortage, the Stymphalians sent an embassy to the Achaians
so that the [Elateians] who had left could take their own grain from the territory of
the Stymphalians as a favor . . . we gathered together and settled ourselves. . . . After
t[he return to our] own territory, the Elateians were at a loss regarding the synoikism and [sent] to the Stymphalians [about it]. The Stymphalians dispatched good
and honest men . . . Euremon, Thearidas, and Isagoras, who came [to El]ateia and
made a correct and just judgment about the fortification of the place. In order,
therefore, that [our polis] may seem mindful of the kindnesses of the Stymphalians
and inclined to repay with g[ratitude their benefaction]s, it was resolved by the
Elateians (to thank) the men who stood by us(?), Daphnaios [son of Aristonymos
. . . , . . . son of . . .]krates, Theondas son of Python, Agon son of Theokles, Aitolos
son of Aristolaos, Krito[n son of Aristonymos, who took so much thought for us],
to record the kindnesses between the Elateians and the Stymphalians [on a stone
stele and set] it up in Elateia in the marketplace by the altar of Zeus Soter, and in
Stymphalos in the s]anctuary of Artemis Brauronia. It was also resolved to provide
the Stymphalians in E[lateia with security and *asyl*]*ia*, and the right of first approach
to the council and assembly after the initial sacrifices, and to [take part in Elat]eia
in the common sacrifice, and all the other honors belonging to benefact[ors. It was
also resolved to crown the *dēmos*] of the Stymphalians with a gold crown and to
have a sacred herald announce it every year at the athletic contest of the Boadromia,
making it clear that [the polis of the Elateians would crown the polis of the Stymphalians with a gold cr]own, the best, because [of their virtue and their kindness
toward it . . .]

The references to "Manios," Manius Acilius Glabrio, date the text after 191, the
year of Glabrio's consulship. There has been much debate about whether the cruel
treatment of Elateia implicit in this decree was the work of Flamininus in 198,
when the Romans took the city of Elateia (Livy 32.24.1–2; Paus. 10.34.4), or of the
Aitolians, who were given control of Phokis in the settlement of 196 (Livy 33.34.8).
Most favor the latter position: Passerini 1948 (cf. *BE* 49.72, 51.108; and Accame
1949); Lehmann 1967: 120–25 and 1999; Larsen 1968: 405–6 (*BE* 68.267) and 1971:
82 with n. 5. Accame 1949, Maier 1959–61: I.132–36, Klaffenbach 1968, and McInerney 1999: 251 support the former view.

Kinship between Elateia and Stymphalos was articulated in myth (Paus.
8.4.2–6, 10.34.2); the claim can be traced back to the first half of the fourth century
(Paus. 10.9.6 with *FDelph* III.1.3–11 with Habicht 1998: 68).

44. Law(?) of the Achaian Nomographoi

Found in Aigion in 1999; now in the Aigion Museum, inv. ΑΛ 540. Early second
century BCE.

Limestone stele, broken at the top.

Discovery reported in *AD* 52 (1997) *Chron*. B1: 297 (*SEG* 50.470). *Ed.pr.* *Rizakis
2008a: 168–70 no. 116 with photo, pl. XXVI.

[- - -]
Ἡραιεύς· Λυ[- - - - - - -]
[Φι]αλεύς· Κλεόξενος
[Ὑπ]ανεύς· Θεαρίδας
4 [Κυ]παρισσεύς·
[Ἀρ]ιστομένης
Μεσσάνιοι· Ἄριστις,
Κλεῖππος
8 Ἀσιναῖος· Ἀριστόμαχ[ος]
Κορωναεύς· Καλλιάδ[ας]
Μεγαλοπολῖται· Ἄψιπ[πος],
Πολυήρατος
12 Παλλαντεύς· Τιμοτέλ[ης]
[Λ]ακεδαιμόνιοι· Εὐκλείδα[ς],
[Τ]ιμοτέλης, Πολύλαος
Τεγεάτας· Σῖμος
16 Ἀντιγονεύς· Νίκις
[Ὀρ]χομένιος· Ἐχέτιμος
[Κ]αφυεύς· Σῖμος
Κλειτόριος· Κελευθίω[ν]
20 Λουσιάτας· Σακράτης
Ἀσχεύς· Ἀρχῖνος
γραμματεύς
Ἀλιφειρεύς· Νίκανδρο[ς]

Heraia: Ly[- - -]. Phigaleia: Kleoxenos. Hypanai: Thearidas. Kyparissia: Aris-
tomenes. Messene: Aristis, Kleippos. Asine: Aristomachos. Korone: Kalliadas.
Megalopolis: Hapsippos, Polyeratos. Pallantion: Timoteles. Lakedaimon: Eukleidas,
Timoteles, Polylaos. Tegea: Simos. Antigoneia: Nikis. Orchomenos: Echetimos.
Kaphyaia: Simos. Kleitor: Keleuthion. Lousoi: Sakrates. Ascheion: Archinos, the sec-
retary. Alipheira: Nikandros.

Rizakis (2008a: 168–70; cf. 2003: 104–7) has shown that this text likely preserves
the end of a law of the Achaian *nomographoi;* the only previously known example
is T41. Only part of the list of the *nomographoi* is preserved; we have lost the law
that was in fact passed and have only the section listing representatives from northwestern Arkadia, Messenia, and southern Arkadia. Like the Epidauros list (T41),
this one follows a geographical order in listing the members of the college of
nomographoi. The other important similarity between the two lists is that the largest cities are represented by three individuals (here only Sparta; in T41 Megalopolis,
l. 24, and Argos, l. 6), medium-sized cities by two (here Messene and Megalopolis,
in T41 Sikyon, ll. 10–12; Aigion, ll. 17–18; Dyme, ll. 20–21), and small cities by one.
The list of cities represented reflects the Achaian koinon at its maximum extent,
in the early second century. The cities of Orchomenos and Heraia were restored to

the Achaians by Philip V in 199 (Livy 32.5.4–5). Antigoneia (l. 16) is the name given to Mantineia after the battle of Sellasia in 222; it was retained until the second century CE (Polyb. 2.56.6–7, 58.12; Plut. *Arat.* 45; Paus. 8.8.12 with Pretzler 2005). [Φι]αλεύς (l. 2) is the ethnic of Φιάλεια (*IG* V.2.419 l. 6, ca. 240; Diod. Sic. 15.40.2), more commonly known as Φιγάλεια (e.g., Polyb. 4.3.8).

45. Arbitration between the Achaian Koinon and Sparta

Fragmentary inscription found at Olympia. After 163 BCE.

Dittenberger and Purgold *IVO* 47; *Dittenberger *Syll.*³ 665 (Ager 1996: no. 137; Harter-Uibopuu 1998: 80–97 no. 11; Camia 2009: 22–31, no. 2, with Italian translation).

      ἀπόφασις δικαστᾶν π[ερὶ χώρας ἀμφιλλεγομένας, τῶν αἱρεθέντων]
      δικάσαι τοῖς Ἀχαιοῖς κ[αὶ τοῖς Λακεδαιμονίοις,– ^{ca. 13} –]
      τοῦ Ἐπιγόνου, Ἀριστάρχου [τοῦ – – –, – – – τοῦ – – – ἀν]-
4   δρου, Πολυκράτευς τοῦ Πολυ[– – –, – – – τοῦ – – –, καὶ]
      περὶ τὰς ζαμίας ἃς ἐζαμίωσα[ν – ^{ca. 15} – τὸν δᾶμον τὸν Λα]-
      κεδαιμονίων, ὅτι ἀντιποεῖτ[αι – ^{ca. 16} – τῶι δάμωι τῶι]
      Μεγαλοπολιτᾶν ταύτας τὰς [χώρας– ^{ca. 17} – λόγων δὲ]
8   πλειόνων ῥηθέντων, ἐπεὶ πολ[– ^{ca. 29} –]
      τας διὰ τῶν συνδίκων, καὶ τὰμ [μὲν ὑπάρχουσαν ἐκ πολλοῦ χρόνου]
      διαφορὰν ταῖς πόλεσι δι' [ὅλ]ο[υ – ^{ca. 7} – διαλῦσαι ἐπειρασάμεθα],
      προθυμίας καὶ σπουδᾶς οὐθὲν [ἐλλείποντες·– ^{ca. 14} – οὐκ ἀ]-
12   πηνέγκαμεν ἐπιγραφὰν διὰ πο[λλ]οῦ, ἕνεκεν τοῦ χρόνον ἱκα[νὸν]
      δοθῆμεν εἰς σύλλυσιν τοῖς δια[φερ]ομέ[ν]οις· ἐπε[ὶ] δὲ ἀναγκαῖόν [τε]
      καὶ ἀκόλουθ[ον τῶι ὅρ]κωι ὃν ὠμ[όσα]μεν καὶ τοῖς νόμοις τοῖς τῶν Ἀ-
      χαιῶν σ[υ]ντε[λ]εσθεῖσαν τὰν κρίσιν [εἰς] τὰ γράμματα τὰ δαμόσια
      ἀπενεγχθῆ-
16   μεν, ἕνεκεν τοῦ μήτε τὰ ποτιδε[ό]μενα κρίσιος ἄκ[ρ]ιτα γίνεσθαι μή-
      τε τὰ κεκριμένα ἄκυρα, ὅπως δα[μ]οκρατούμενοι καὶ τὰ ποθ' αὑτοὺς
      ὁμονοοῦντες οἱ Ἀχαιοὶ διατε[λ]ῶντι εἰς τὸν ἀεὶ χρόνον ὄντες ἐν εἰ-
      ράναι καὶ εὐνομίαι, αἵ τ' ἐν τοῖ[ς] Ἕλλασιν καὶ συμμάχοις γεγενημέ-
20   ναι πρότερον [κ]ρ[ί]σεις βέβαια[ι] καὶ ἀκήρατοι δ[ι]αμένωντι εἰς τὸ[ν]
      ἀεὶ χρόνον κα[ὶ] αἱ στάλαι καὶ τ[ὰ ὅρι]α τὰ τεθέ[ντα] ὑπὲρ τᾶν κρισ[ί]-
      ωμ μένη κύρια δι' ὅλου καὶ μηδὲ[ν αὐτῶν ἦι] ἰσχυ[ρότ]ερον, γεγεν[ημέ]-
      νας καὶ πρότε[ρ]ον κρίσιος Μεγ[αλοπολίταις καὶ Λακεδ]αιμο[νίοις]
24   [ὑπὲ]ρ ταύ[τας τᾶ]ς χώρας, ὑπὲρ ἃς [νῦν διαφέρονται, – ^{ca. 14} –]
      [– – –]ων τῶι προδίκωι [– – –]
      [– – –]στα κατακολουθ[– – –]
      [– – – ἐν] Μεγάλαι πόλει ἐ[ν τῶι ἀρχείωι – – –]
28   [– – – ἐ]ν τῶι ἀσύλ[ω]ι κ[αὶ – ––]
      [– – –μ]έναις εὖ ὑ[πὸ] Με[γαλοπολιτᾶν – – –]
      [– – – οἱ ὑπὸ τῶ]ν συμμάχων αἱρε[θέντες – ^{ca. 9} – κρ]ιτα[ὶ – ^{ca. 6} –]
      [– – – ἀμφοτ]έ[ρ]ων ἐπιτρε[ψάντων, εἰ δοκεῖ τὰ]ν Σκιρί[τιν κατέ]-

32   [χεσθαι ὑπὸ Μεγαλοπο]λιτᾶν, ἐν αἷ κ[αὶ ἁ Αἰγῦτι]ς χώρα, ἢ ὑ[πὸ Λακεδαι]-
      [μονίων, καὶ ὁρισ]μὸς τᾶς χώρας ἀπ[ογεγραμμένο]ς, καὶ ὅτι ὤμοσ[αν αἱρῆσε]-
      [σθαι ἐκ πά]ντων ἀριστίνδαν, κ[αὶ ὅτι ἔκριν]αν οἱ δικασταὶ [γενέσθαι]
      [τὰν Σκιρ]ῖτιν καὶ τὰν Αἰγῦτιν Ἀρ[κάδων ἀπὸ] τοῦ τοὺς Ἡρακλείδας εἰς
36   [Π]ελοπόννασον κατελθεῖν, καὶ [ὁ ὅρκο]ς τὸν [ὁ]μόσαντες οἱ δικασταὶ ἐ-
      [δ]ίκασαν, καὶ τῶν δικασάντων τὰ [ὀνό]ματα, οἳ ἦσαν τῶι πλήθει ἑκατὸν
      [κα]ὶ εἷς, καὶ οἱ παρόντες Λακεδα[ιμ]ονίων ἐπὶ τοῦ ὅρκου. κρίνοντες
      [οὖν ο]ὔ[τ]ω κα μάλιστα μένειν [τὰ ποθ'] αὐτοὺς τοὺς Ἀχαιοὺς ὁμονοοῦν-
40   [τας, εἰ] τὰ κριθέντα παρ' αὐτοῖς μηκέτι γίνοιτο ἄκυρα δι' ἑτέρων ἐγ-
      [κλημά]των, ἀλλ' ὅρον ἔχοι τᾶς ποθ' αὐτοὺς διαφορᾶς κρίσιν δικ[αστ]η-
      [ρίου, ἐ]γνωκότες δὲ ἐκ τ[ῶ]ν παρατεθέντων ἁμῖν παρ' ἀμφοτέρ[ων γραμ]-
      [μάτων] καὶ Ῥωμαίους τοὺς προεστακότας τᾶς τῶν Ἑλλάν[ων εὐνομί]-
44   [ας καὶ ὁμο]νοίας, ὅκ[α π]αρεγενήθησαν ποθ' αὐτοὺς Μεγ[αλοπολῖται]
      [καὶ Λακεδαιμόνιοι ὑπ]ὲρ ταύτας τᾶς χώρας διαφε[ρόμενοι, ταύταν]
      [ἀποφάνασθαι τὰν γνώμα]ν, διότι δεῖ τὰ [κεκριμένα εἶμεν κύρια – – –]
      [– – –]αι[– – –]
48   [– – – κρ]ί[σ]ιν κα[ὶ – – –]
      [– – –μ]ένας πόλιο[ς – – –]
      [– – – κ]ρίσεις πα[– – –]
      [– – – τὰν ζα]μίαν ἂν ἐζ[αμίωσαν – – –]
52   [– – – ὑπό]δικον εἶμε[ν – – –]
      [τᾶι πόλει τ]ᾶι Λακεδαιμ[ονίων].

Decision of the judges re[garding the disputed land. The following were chosen] to
adjudicate between the Achaians a[nd the Lakedaimonians . . .] son of Epigonos,
Aristarchos [son of . . . , . . . son of . . . an]dros, Polykrates son of Poly[. . . , . . . son
of . . . , and] regarding the penalty that they impose[d . . . the people of the La]-
kedaimonians, because they contend[ed with . . . the people of] Megalopolis for
these [lands . . . more speeches] having been given, since . . . by the *syndikoi,* and
the dispute [that has existed for a long time] between the poleis g[enerally . . . we
tried to resolve], [lacking] nothing in eagerness and zeal. We did [not] deliver the
inscription for a long time, in order to allow sufficient time for reconciliation of
the disputants. Since it is necessary both in accordance with the oath that we swore
and with the laws of the Achaians, we delivered the final decision to the public
records, because neither were the cases that needed judgment left undecided, nor
were the judgments invalid. So that the Achaians, governing themselves demo-
cratically and being in agreement among themselves, may continue for all time to
live in peace and good order, the judgments that were previously rendered among
the Greeks and allies shall remain firm and undamaged for all time, and the stelai
and boundary markers that were erected by the judges shall remain entirely valid
and nothing shall su[per]sede [them], and the judgment that was previously rendered between the Megalopolitans and Lakedaimonians about these lands over
which they [are now in dispute . . . (*five lines are too fragmentary to render any
continuous sense*) . . .] cho[sen by th]e allies . . . judg[es. . . bot]h sides having
entr[usted . . . if] the Skiri[tis seems to be occupied by the Megalopo]litans, in

which [the Aigyti]s is also situated . . . or b[y the Lakedaimonians, and the delim-
ita]tion of the land [having been written] down, and that those [who were selected
from the who]le populace on the basis of their merit swore an oath, a[nd that] the
judges [have decid]ed that [the Skir]itis and the Aigytis have belonged to the
Ar[kadians since] the time when the Herakleidai returned to the Peloponnese; and
[the oat]h that the judges in the case swore, and the [na]mes of the judges, who
were one hundred and one in number, and those Lakedaimonians who were
present at the oath. Judgments were made so that above all else the Achaians could
remain in agreement among themselves. If their decisions should become no
longer valid as a result of other [accu]sations, but the boundary of the land disputed by them should receive the judgment of a co[urt, r]ecognizing from what
was previously [written] down by us for both sides, and what the Romans put
forward about the [lawfulness and har]mony of the Greeks, when the
Meg[alopolitans and Lakedaimonians] went to them about the land over which
they were in dis[pute, this resolution shall be publicized], because it is necessary
that [judgments be valid . . .] (*seven lines are too fragmentary to render any continuous sense*).

The appeal made by Megalopolis and Sparta to the Romans in their land
dispute (ll. 44–45) is mentioned by Polybios (31.1.6–7) in the year 163, and by
Pausanias (7.11.1–3) in more detail, some of it questionable (see Bowman 1992;
Höghammar 2000–2001; Camia 2009: 28–29). Whether all three incidents are
identical is not certain (Pausanias actually mentions a dispute between Sparta and
Argos, not Sparta and Megalopolis), but the Polybian reference seems to fit quite
well with the Olympia text. See above, pp. 139–40.

The land under dispute, including the Skiritis and Aigytis, was situated in the
upper Eurotas Valley (*Barr.* map 58 C3) and had long been a bone of contention
between Arkadians and Spartans (Gruen 1976: 50 n. 35; Shipley 2000: 374; Camia
2009: 25–26). The arbitration by the Romans in 163 clearly awarded the disputed
land to the Megalopolitans. The Spartans failed to comply with the conclusion of
that judgment and as a result were fined (l. 5), probably by the Achaian koinon.
Their apparent refusal to pay that fine is what gave rise to the arbitration between
the Achaian koinon itself and its member polis Sparta that is recorded in this
text. The arbitrators evidently affirmed the previous judgment that the land
belonged to Megalopolis and probably also the validity of the Achaian fine (l. 53).
The central concern is to restore and protect the internal peace of the Achaian
koinon (ll. 18–19, 39–40). It is not clear how the board of arbitrators in this dispute between the koinon and Sparta was composed (Ager 1996: 380; Camia
2009: 27).

The extent of Roman involvement in this dispute appears to have been minimal: if Pausanias (7.11.2) is correct, the Roman legate Gaius Sulpicius Gallus
handed the matter over to the Achaian leader Kallikrates, which was probably

tantamount to the Romans telling the Achaians that they would not intervene in
internal Achaian disputes (Gruen 1976: 50–51; Harter-Uibopuu 1998: 192; Camia
2009: 30).

46. Oropos Honors Hieron of Aigeira

Found at the Amphiareion. Ca. 154–149 BCE.
IG VII.411 (*Syll.*[3] 675; Petrakos 1968: 187–88 no. 44, with pl. 62a, and *1997: no.
307 with photo, pl. 29; Rizakis 1995: 347–48 no. 619).

Ὀλύμπιχος Ἑρμοδώρου εἶπεν· ἐπειδὴ Ἱέρων
Τηλεκλέους Αἰγειράτης εὔνους ὢν διατελε[ῖ]
τῶι δήμωι τῶι Ὠρωπίων ἐμ παντὶ καιρῶι καὶ λέγων
4 καὶ πράττων τὰ συμφέροντα, γενομένων τε συμ-
πτωμάτων καὶ παρασπονδημάτων τῶμ μεγίστων
περὶ Ὠρωπίους καὶ τῶν ἀρχόντων καὶ ἡμῶν παραγενομένων εἰς τὴν ἐν Κορίνθωι σύνοδον ἠρά-
8 νισέν τε ἡμῖν καὶ συμβουλεύσας παρεστήσατο
τοὺς Ἀχαιοὺς τὴν πᾶσαν πρόνοιαν ποιήσασθαι ὑ-
πέρ τε τῆς πόλεως ἡμῶν καὶ τοῦ ἱεροῦ τοῦ Ἀμφιαράου, ἐπεὶ καὶ ἐν τεῖ Ῥωμαίων φιλίαι καὶ πίστει διατε-
12 λοῦμεν ὑπάρχοντες· δόξαντος δὲ τοῖς Ἀχαιοῖς
συναγαγεῖν σύγκλητον ἐν Ἄργει περὶ τούτων,
Ἱέρων ἐμ παντὶ καιρῶι βουλόμενος ἐκφανῆ π[οι]-
εῖν τὴν αὑτοῦ εὔνοιαν καὶ καλοκἀγαθίαν ὑπ[ε]-
16 δέξατο πάντας τοὺς παραγενομένους Ὠρωπίων ἐπὶ τὴν ἰδίαν ἑστίαν, ἔθυσέν τε τῶι Δ[ιὶ]
τῶι Σωτῆρι ὑπὲρ ἡμῶν, πρός τε Ἀθηναίους κα[ὶ]
τοὺς ἄλλους τοὺς ἀντιπρεσβεύοντας ὑπέ[σ]-
20 τη καὶ παρεστήσατο τοὺς Ἀχαιοὺς μὴ περιιδε[ῖν]
πόλιν Ἑλληνίδα ἐξανδραποδισθεῖσαν, οὐσάν
γε ἐν τεῖ Ῥωμαίων φιλίαι καὶ πίστει, καὶ διὰ τὴν
τούτου πρόνοιαν καὶ καλοκἀγαθίαν συμβέβηκε
24 κεκομίσθαι ἡμᾶς τὴν πατρίδα καὶ κατεληλ[υ]-
θέναι μετὰ τέκνων καὶ γυναικῶν· ὅπως οὖν κ[αὶ]
Ὠρώπιοι φαίνωνται μνημονεύοντες ὧν ἂν εὐε[ρ]-
γετηθῶσιν ὑπό τινος, γίνωνται δὲ καὶ ἄλλοι ζ[η]-
28 [λ]ωταὶ τῆς αὐτῆς αἱρέσεως εἰδότες ὅτι τιμηθ[ή]-
σονται ἀξίως ὧν ἂν εὐεργετήσωσιν, ἀγαθε[ῖ]
τύχει, δεδόχθαι τῶι δήμωι Ὠρωπίων· στεφαν[ῶ]-
σαι Ἱέρω[ν]α Τηλεκλέους Αἰγειράτην εἰκόν[ι]
32 χαλκεῖ ἀρετῆς ἕνεκεν καὶ καλοκἀγαθίας ἣν
ἔχων διατελεῖ εἰς τὸν δῆμον τὸν Ὠρωπίων, ἀν[α]-
γορεῦσαι δὲ τὴν τῆς εἰκ[ό]νος στάσιν Ἀμφιαρά[ων]
τῶμ μεγάλων τῶι γυμνικῶι ἀγῶνι.

Olympichos son of Hermodoros spoke: since Hieron son of Telekles of Aigeira has always been well disposed toward the people of Oropos on every occasion, saying and doing what is advantageous, the greatest mischances and breaches of faith befalling the Oropians, and with our archons having attended the meeting in Corinth, he made collections for our benefit, and giving advice he showed the Achaians that complete foresight ought to be given on behalf of our city and of the sanctuary of Amphiaraos, especially since we remain in the friendship and loyalty of the Romans. When the Achaians resolved to gather an assembly in Argos to discuss the matter, Hieron wishing always to make apparent his goodwill and grace, entertained all the Oropians who were present at his own hearth, and sacrificed to Zeus Soter on our behalf. Speaking to the Athenians and the other ambassadors who were hostile toward us, he showed the Achaians that they must not stand by and watch a Greek polis be reduced to utter slavery, which is in the friendship and loyalty of the Romans. Through his foresight and grace he ensured that our fatherland was provided for and liberated, along with our children and women. Therefore so that the Oropians may also be seen commemorating the good deeds done by someone, so that others may become eager for the same course of action, knowing that they will be honored properly for their good deeds, therefore, good fortune, it is resolved by the *dēmos* of the Oropians to honor Hieron son of Telekles of Aigeira with a bronze statue for the sake of the virtue and grace that he always exhibits toward the *dēmos* of the Oropians. (It was also resolved) to proclaim publicly the erection of the statue at the athletic contest of the Greater Amphiaraia.

It is usually thought that this inscription records the same Athenian attack on Oropos described by Pausanias (7.11.4–8), but there are so many discrepancies between them that it is necessary either to accuse Pausanias of bias and error (Gruen 1976: 51–53) or to suppose that he was describing an altogether different event (Bastini 1987: 195, 269 n. 1). Knoepfler 1991a: 274–78 discusses the attitudes of the eastern Boiotians and Euboians toward Rome in this period and the pressure they suffered from both sides; cf. Lafond 1991: 33 n. 15.

Telekles of Aigeira, the father of Hieron, is probably identical with the man sent to Rome to appeal for the return of exiles in 160/59 (Polyb. 32.3.14) and again in 155 (Polyb. 33.1.3); cf. Gruen 1976: 53 with n. 61. These efforts imply hostility to the policy of Kallikrates, who according to Polybios was chiefly responsible for encouraging the dispatch of the detainees to Rome (Polyb. 30.7.5–7, 13.8–10), and who according to Pausanias (7.11.7–8) was a primary agent in the failed Achaian attempt to help Oropos. Telekles' active resistance suggests that "Callicrates did not run a monolithic regime in Achaea" (Gruen 1976: 53).

Lines 13–17 imply that Hieron, a citizen of Aigeira, owned a house at Argos, one of several pieces of evidence for the right of citizens of the Achaian koinon to own property in other member cities (Larsen 1968: 239 and 1971). Aymard 1938: 26–35 discusses the evidence of the inscription for the Achaian assembly.

III. AITOLIA

47. Dedication of Messenians and Naupaktians
after Victory over Kalydon

Found at Delphi. Mid-fifth century BCE.

Delphi inv. 295, 455, 2195.

Two discontinuous fragments were long known: *Syll.*³ 81a; *FDelph* III.4 no. 1; *FDelph* II.2: 297–302; *RE* Suppl. IV 1308–10; Pomtow *JDAI* 37 (1922 [1924]): 55–112; Tod 65; Lerat 1952: II.34–36. Bousquet 1961: 69–71 (*SEG* 19.392) published a new fragment of the dedication and provided two possible restorations, which he regarded as equally likely. *Jacquemin and Laroche 1982 (*SEG* 32.550) found an additional fragment (uninscribed) that secures the relative placement of the three inscribed pieces, and they find other evidence to support the following textual restoration, initially (but tentatively) proposed by Bousquet.

[Μ]εσσάνιο[ι καὶ Ναυπάκτιοι] ἀνέθ[εσαν]
[ἀ]πὸ Καλ[υδωνίων δεκάταν τ]ῶι Ἀπ[όλωνι]

The [M]essanian[s and Naupaktians] dedi[cated] it to Ap[ollo as a tithe] (of spoils taken) [f]rom the Kal[ydonians].

The fragmentary inscription is part of a large pillar monument erected just to the south of the temple of Apollo at Delphi: Jacquemin 1999: no. 362. For a reconstruction see Jacquemin and Laroche 1982 (followed by Luraghi 2008: 192 fig. 4). It appears to be the result of an important act of Messenian self-promotion in a pan-Hellenic context immediately after their settlement at Naupaktos (Figueira 1999: 215 and Luraghi 2008: 191).

The date of the dedication has been debated. Dittenberger (*Syll.*[3] 81a) associated it rather with Demosthenes' campaign against the Aitolians in 426/5. Thucydides' narrative of Demosthenes' campaign against Aitolia in 426, and of the retaliatory invasion of Naupaktos by the Aitolians and their Spartan allies, makes it clear that Kalydon was at the very least sympathetic to the Aitolian-Spartan side, for the army retreated there after the attack on Naupaktos (Thuc. 3.102.5). But the monument as a whole looks to be somewhat earlier than the rather similar pillar monument dedicated by the Messenians and Naupaktians at Olympia, crowned with the stunning Nike of Paionios (*IVO* 259 = *IG* IX.1² 3.656 for the dedicatory inscription; Herrmann 1972 for reconstruction of the pillar; Hölscher 1974 for the statue), which belongs to the period of the Peloponnesian War (Jacquemin and Laroche 1982: 204 for the relative dating of the two monuments). It is more likely to belong to the period 456–446 (Jacquemin and Laroche 1982: 199, 204), when the Athenians, with assistance from the Messenians at Naupaktos and the Naupaktians themselves, pushed to gain control of the central northern coast of the Corinthian Gulf. The seizure of Chalkis in 456/5 (Thuc. 1.108.5), after the Athenians had gained sufficient control of Naupaktos to settle the Messenians there, may have entailed the capture of Molykreion and Makyneia, small communities between them that were later regained by the Aitolians (maps 4, 5). Kalydon, just west of Chalkis, would have been a likely target as well.

48. Treaty between Sparta and the Aitolians

Found on the Spartan akropolis. Now in the Sparta Museum (inv. 6265). Mid-fifth century or ca. 426/5 BCE.

Ed.pr. Peek 1974 with a sketch of the stone (Cartledge 1976 with Peek's sketch, English translation, and commentary; SEG 26.461; Cozzoli 1985). Gschnitzer 1978: 41 prints a new text, after detailed discussion of Peek's edition, with full commentary (*SEG* 28.408; *BE* 1982.179; van Effenterre and Ruzé 1994: I no. 55; Panessa 1999: no. 30). Luppe 1982 offers a new reading of lines 12 and 13 based on examination of Peek's squeeze (*SEG* 32.398, where the heading erroneously reads "Alliance with the Arkadians"; *BE* 1984.205). Meiggs and Lewis 1988: 312 (addenda, 67 *bis*) "print a composite text, without textual commentary and with much hesitation" (Bolmarcich 2005: 22). *Pikoulas 2000–2003 presents a new text based on autopsy of the stone (*SEG* 51.449).

[Συνθêκ]αι Αἰτολοîς. κ[αττάδε]
[φιλία]ν καì *h*ιράναν Ἰ[- - ποτ']
[Αἰτολ]òς καì συνμαχ[ίαν ἀίδιο]-
4   [ν πλ(?)]ὰν μόνος Μαν[- - - - -, (?)*h*επο]-
[μ]ένος *h*όπυι κα Λα[κεδαιμόνι]-

[ο]ι ḥαγίονται καὶ κα̣[τὰ γᾶν]
καὶ καθάλαθαν, τὸ[ν αὐτὸν]
8 φίλον καὶ τὸνν αὐτ[ὸν ἐχθρὸν]
ἔχοντες ḥόγ̣ περ [καὶ Λακε]-
δαιμόνιοι. μ[ε]δὲ [κατάλυḥιν]
ποιἐθαι ἄνευ Λα[κεδαιμονίον]
12 μεδενί, ἀνḥιέν[τας τὸν πόλεμον?]
ἐπὶ ταὐτὸν π̣οθ᾽ ὅν̣ [περ Λακεδαι]-
μονίος. φεύγον[τας δὲ μὲ δεκέθο]-
ḥαν κεκοινανεκ[ότας ἀδικε(?)]-
16 μάτον. αἐ δέ τίς κα̣ [ἐπὶ τὰν τὸν]
[.]ρ̣ξαδιέον χόραγ̣ [στρατεύει]
ἐπὶ πολέμοι, ἐπικ[ορὲν Λακεδαιμο]-
ν̣ίος παντὶ σθένε[ι - - - - - - - -]
20 α̣ἰ δέ τίς κα ἐπὶ τὰ[ν τὸν Λακεδαιμο]-
νίον χόραν στρα̣[τεύει ἐπὶ πολέ]-
μοι, ἐπικορὲν Ἐ[- - - - - - - - - -]
[- - - - - - - - - - - - - - - - - - - -]

1 κ[αττάδε] Peek, Meiggs and Lewis, Pikoulas Ἐ[ρξαδιεῦḥι·] Gschnitzer   2 [φιλία]ν
Peek, Cartledge, Meiggs and Lewis [φιλία]γ Pikoulas [σπονδὰ]ς Griffith *apud*
Kelly εἶ [μεν ποτ] Peek, Meiggs and Lewis ἔ[χεν αἰὲς] Gschnitzer Ι[- - ποτ᾽] Pikoulas   3 [Αἰτο]λὸς Peek, Meiggs and Lewis [Αἰτολ]ὸς Pikoulas [ἀδό]λος Gschnitzer
συνμα[χίαν . ³⁻⁴ .] Peek συνμα[χίαν ἐπ᾽ ἄ(λ)λος] Gschnitzer συνμαχ[ίαν αἴδιο]- Pikoulas   4 [. ³⁻⁴ .]νμονος μαν[τι . ¹⁻² . ḥεπο]- - Peek, Meiggs and Lewis [πλ]ὰ̣ν μόνος
Μαν[τινες, ḥεπο]- Gschnitzer [ν πλ(?)]ὰν μόνος Μαν[- - - - -, (?)ḥεπο]- Pikoulas   5 ḥόποι Peek ḥόπυι Gschnitzer, Pikoulas   7 καθάλαθαν Peek, Pikoulas κὰ(θ)
θάλα(θ)θαν Gschnitzer   9 ḥόν περ Gschnitzer, Meiggs and Lewis ḥόγ̣ περ Pikoulas   10 μεδὲ κ[ατάλυḥιν Gschnitzer μ[ε]δὲ [κατάλυḥιν] Pikoulas   11 ποιἐθαι
Peek, Pikoulas ποιἐ(θ)θαι Gschnitzer   12 μεδενίαν ḥιέντ[ας πρέσβες] Peek μεδενί,
ἀνḥιέντ[ας πολεμεν] Gschnitzer ἀνḥιέμε[ν δὲ μαχομένος Luppe   13 ποθόν [περ
Λακεδαι]- Peek ποθ᾽ ὅν[περ Λακεδαι]- Gschnitzer πόθ᾽ ὅ Λ[ακεδαι]- Luppe, Meiggs
and Lewis   14 φεύγον[τας μὲ] Peek [δεκέθο]- Peek [δεκέ(θ)θο]- Gschnitzer
15 κεκοινανεκ[ότ . ⁷⁻⁸ .] Peek κεκοινανεκ[ότας ἀδικε]- Peek   17 Ἐρξαδιέον
Peek [Ἐ . .]ερξαδιέον Jeffery   19 σθένε[ι καττὸ δυνατόν] Peek σθένε[ι κὰ(τ) τὸ
δυνατόν] Gschnitzer   20–21 τὰ[ν τὸν Λακεδαιμο]|νίον Matthaiou and Pikoulas τὰ[ν
Λακεδαιμο]|νίον Peek   22 Ἐ[ρξαδιες παντὶ] Peek   23 [σθένει καττὸ δυνατόν - -
-] Peek [σθένει κὰ(τ) τὸ δυνατόν - - -] Gschnitzer [σθένει κὰ τὸ δύνατον - - -] Lewis

[Trea]ty with the Aitolians. Let there b[e] [friendshi]p and peace [with the Aitolia]ns,
and allia[nce for all time with one another] [ex]cept for the Man[- - -(?), follo]wing
wherever the La[kedaimonian]s should lead, by [land] and by sea, having th[e
same] friends and [enemies] as the [Lake]daimonians. Let no one make a s[eparate
peace] without the La[kedaimonians], but they may leave off [fighting] when the
L[akedai]monians (do so). They shall not [recei]ve fugit[ives] who have commit[ted

any wrong]doing. If someone [marches against] the territory of the [-]rxadieis
in war, the [Lakedaimo]nians shall hel[p] with all their streng[th . . .]. But if someone
ma[rches] against the territory of th[e Lakedaimo]nians [in wa]r, the E[- - -] shall
help. . . .

Kelly 1978 rejects Peek's restoration [φιλία]ν in line 2 because of lack of contemporary comparanda, suggesting instead (with Griffith) [σπονδὰ]ς, for which compare Th. 5.29.1, the treaty between Sparta and Argos of 418. Peek's reading is supported by Cartledge 1979: 189, citing Th. 4.19.1. Jeffery 1988: 181 argues that the stele
was probably wider (to the left) than Peek believed, but reexamination of the stone
has ruled out the possibility that anything is lost on the left side except the upper
left corner (Pikoulas 2000–2003: 455 with the drawing on p. 461).

Cartledge 1976: 91 highlights the subject condition of the Aitolians with respect
to the Spartans, noting in particular the lack of reciprocal clauses in lines 5–16. On
this point see too Graeber 1992: 141–43 (who consistently and erroneously refers to
the Aitolian partners to the alliance as Erxardieis); van Wees 2004: 14; Pikoulas
2000–2003: 465; Bolmarcich 2005: 24 (who takes the asymmetry as evidence that
the Aitolians became what she calls "subject-allies" of the Peloponnesian League).
Kelly 1978 regards the specific mention of the [-]rxadieis as an indication that the
Spartans were attempting to dismantle the Aitolian koinon by making separate
alliances with its members, as they did in Arkadia (Xen. Hell. 5.2.7, 16, 34). That
observation, however, proceeds on the assumption that there was a formally institutionalized Aitolian koinon in the latter part of the fifth century (or the early
fourth, to which Kelly dates the document), for which we have no evidence.

The identity of the [-]rxadieis (l. 17) has been a subject of debate, but the issue
defies secure conclusions. Gschnitzer's reading of the end of line 1 made the problem particularly important for him, for he took the entire treaty to be with the
"Aitoloi Erxadieis." He took them to be "der Teil, oder der Splitter, des wohlbekann-
ten mittelgriechischen Stammes der Aitoler" (Gschnitzer 1978: 23), drawing a comparison with the Ἀχαιοὶ Φθιῶται, Λοκροὶ Ὑποκναμίδιοι, Λυγκησταὶ Μακεδόνες
(Thuc. 4.83.1), and the Ἰμφέες Περραιβοί (Hekataios, FGrHist 1 F 137). He raises the
possibility (p. 23) that they could be a separate Peloponnesian group, supporting
that suggestion with his belief that Thucydides' reference (3.100.1) to three Aitolian
territorial groups is comprehensive—that, in effect, "hier ist für einen weiteren
Teilstamm kein Platz." From that conclusion he argues for a conjectural "Splitter"
of the Aitolians living in the Peloponnese. However, a more attentive reading of
Thucydides, along with recent epigraphic evidence, suggests that there were more
territorial groups in Aitolia than Thucydides himself tells us about. Gschnitzer is
correct that Thucydides mentions only the Ophiones, Apodotoi, and Eurytanes in
3.100.1; they are also the only three groups he mentions in 3.94.5. In the latter
passage, Thucydides is reporting the suggestions made by the Messenians of

Naupaktos to Demosthenes regarding how he should go about attacking the Aitolians. The Messenians are concerned only with eastern Aitolia, north of Naupaktos, and it is therefore to be expected that they should mention only the groups that would logically be involved in an attack on that area. In Thuc. 3.100.1, ambassadors of the same three groups go to Corinth and Sparta seeking aid against Demosthenes and the Messenians at Naupaktos; again the list should be regarded as not exhaustive but merely a reflection of the parties involved in this localized territorial conflict. Further, the epigraphic evidence: two boundary markers of the fourth century prove the existence of four territorial groups in Aitolia that are otherwise entirely unattested: Vokotopoulos 1967: 322 for the Arysaes and Nomenaies (T50), and *IG* IX.1² 1.116, for the Eiteaies and Eoitanes (T51). These texts are a salutary reminder of how much we do not know about the various territorial groups of Aitolia. They may be subgroups of the Agraioi or Aperantoi, or they may be independent. Gschnitzer's assumption that Thucydides tells us all there is to know about Aitolia is thus not sound; cf. Pikoulas 2000–2003: 466. For different reasons Siewert 1994b (cf. Siewert 1994a) thinks these may be Aitolians living in the Peloponnese, perhaps to be identified with τοὶ Ϝαλεῖοι καὶ ἁ συμαχία, the formal name for the Elian perioikoi. Pikoulas 2000–2003: 466–67 conjectures that the [-]rxadieis are either a part of the Aitolian *ethnos* or a distinct group inhabiting the coastal region in the direction of Naupaktos whose territory bordered the Aitolians'.

Peek 1974 dated the inscription ca. 500–470 on the basis of letter forms. (Cf. Graeber 1992: 141; Tausend 1992: 174–80; Panessa 1999: 111.) Van Effenterre and Ruzé 1994: 234–36 no. 55 place it even earlier, at the end of the sixth century, likewise on the basis of letter forms, though they concede that the formulas contained in the treaty appear to fit better in a fifth-century context. Overall, however, the tendency has been to downdate the text from Peek's initial suggestion. So Cozzoli 1985 places it in the period 455–446 on the supposition that the letter forms require a date before the mid-fifth century. Jeffery 1988: 181, after a detailed comparison of letter forms from fifth- and early fourth-century Sparta, concluded that he saw "no epigraphic reason why Peek's stele should go above 426." Meiggs and Lewis 1988: 312 are of the same opinion, though for unspecified reasons. Matthaiou and Pikoulas 1989: 120 (cf. Pikoulas 2000–2003: 464–66), after studying the stone for the first time since Peek's edition, compare the letter forms to those of the Spartan war fund, which they date to the period 427/4–414, and argue that on paleographic grounds the current treaty is earlier, belonging to the period before the Peloponnesian War, and in particular to the decade 456/5–446, following the settlement of the Messenians at Naupaktos, to whom they see reference in the φεύγον[τας of line 14 (on this point following Peek and most other scholars).

Cartledge 1976: 90 notes the perils of attempting to date Lakonian inscriptions by letter forms and regards the retention of archaic forms in the fifth century in other attested documents of Lakonia (cf. Jeffery 1990: 187) as grounds for countenancing the possibility that the text may belong much later in the fifth century than Peek believed. He proposes that the treaty should be associated with the Athenian attempt in 426 to gain a foothold in northwestern Greece and the consequent Aitolian need for allies (Thuc. 3.100.1; cf. Cartledge 1979: 189–90; Beck 1997: 46–47 n. 17), proposing that the reference to exiles in line 14 may be to Messenian helots settled at Naupaktos by the Athenians (ML 74). As an alternative to summer 426, Cartledge raises the possibility of a context immediately after Pylos in 425/4, "when Sparta was thrashing around for allies in all sensitive quarters." There may be another reason to place the treaty ca. 426. By that time the Spartans had made an alliance with the Agraioi, who lived in the territory to the northwest of Aitolia, on the east bank of the Acheloos (Thuc. 3.106.2); it is generally believed (though not firmly demonstrated) that Agrinion was a polis in their territory. By 424 the Agraioi had been won over by Demosthenes and were pressed into service for the Athenian attack on Sikyon in that year, which led to heavy losses for the invaders (Thuc. 4.77.2, 101.3). While the Agraioi and their king, Salynthios, were clearly independent of the Aitolians in the 420s (and continued to be until sometime between 338 and 314: Staatsverträge III.403b; Diod. Sic. 19.67.3–68.1; cf. Antonetti 1987a: 201 with n. 18), their territory bordered Aitolia, and it would be only logical for the Spartans to collect as many allies in the region as they could.

   There have been a few proponents of a date after the Peloponnesian War. Mosley 1979: 228 places the document in the late fifth century on the grounds of the subordinate role of the Aitolians and the appearance of diplomatic terminology common in this period (though he provides no specifics). The subordinate position of the Aitolians likewise suggests a late date to Sordi (1991), who argues in particular that the treaty was made under Spartan compulsion and reflects the defeat of the Aitolians allied with Elis in the latter's struggle against Sparta in 402 (Diod. Sic. 14.17.9–10). The exiles of line 16 are in her analysis the Messenians driven from Naupaktos by the Spartans in 401 after the conclusion of the war with Elis (Diod. Sic. 14.34.1–3). She suggests that this treaty explains why the Aitolians granted Agesilaos permission to traverse their territory in 389/8, as reported by Xen. Hell. 4.6.14. (The same argument is presented by Bolmarcich 2005: 27, who seems unaware of Sordi's article.) Indeed the permission granted by the Aitolians is taken by Kelly 1978 to provide the context for the conclusion of the treaty; cf. Yates 2005: 66 n. 4. However, Xenophon's text implies that there was considerable uncertainty as to whether permission would be granted (ἂν ἀκόντων Αἰτωλῶν πορεύεσθαι· ἐκεῖνον μέντοι εἴασαν διελθεῖν), and he explains that it was only because the Aitolians were hoping for restoration of Naupaktos (ἤλπιζον γὰρ Ναύπακτον αὐτοῖς συμπράξειν ὥστ' ἀπολαβεῖν) that they might permit the Spartans to cross their territory. That is a far cry from the position envisioned by Sordi of complete subordination resulting from a peace treaty imposed on a defeated party by victorious Spartans. Baltrusch 1994: 22–24 argues that "vom

Vertragsformular her kann der Vertrag nicht anders als in das beginnende 4. Jh. datiert werden" (p. 22). But of the four purportedly indicative formulas, three are used from the mid-fifth century; only the fourth, the mention of εἰρήνη (hιράναν, l. 2), is not attested epigraphically before 387/6. But the state of those few fifth-century treaties that do survive epigraphically is so lacunose (e.g., ML 47, 56, 87) that this does not seem a particularly compelling argument.

49. Proxeny Decree of the Aitolian Koinon for an Athenian

Found at Thermon. Fourth century BCE.

Three fragments of a bronze tablet, in the form of a stele with a narrow pediment at the top. The pediment carries an image of an owl. A single fragment was published by Klaffenbach as IG IX.1² 1.91.3, and two additional joining fragments were discovered among the debris from the early excavations of Sotiriades. The new fragments were associated with IG IX.1² 1.91.3, and a combined text was published by Mastrokostas 1965: 152, with photo, fig. 60. Klaffenbach suggested alternative restorations to those given by Mastrokostas in his text, and these were printed as *SEG 25.615.

> [Θεοί. Α]ἰτωλοὶ ἔδωκαν Σω[– – – – – – – – – – –]
> [– – – – Ἀ]θηναίωι αὐ[τῶ]ι καὶ ἐγ[γόνοις πρό]-
> [ξενί]α‹ν›, πολιτ[είαν, ἀ]τέλε[ιαν, – – – – – – – –]
> 4 [– – – –]νας, ἀσφ[άλεια]ν, ἀσ[υλίαν, – – – – – – –]
> [– –]

1 [Ἀγαθᾶι τύχαι. Α]ἰτωλοὶ ἔδωκαν Σω[– – – Mastrokostas   2 ἐγ[γόνοις προξενίαν] Mastrokostas   3 [εἰς ἄματα πάντ]α πολιτ[είαν, ἀ]τέλε[ιαν καὶ πολέμου] Mastrokostas   4 [καὶ εἰρά]νας, ἀσφ[άλεια]ν, ἀσ[υλίαν – –] Mastrokostas

[Gods. The A]itolians gave to So[– – – the A]thenian, to him[se]lf and his de[scendants, proxen]ly, citiz[enship,] immunity from tax[ation, – – –], secu[rity], immunity from sei[zure, – – –]

The text is discussed by Petsas 1991: 129–30; Antonetti 1999: 302, 304.

50. Boundary Stone Demarcating the Territory of the Arysaes and Nomenaeis

Found just off the road between Agrinion and Agios Vlasios. Fourth century BCE. Ed.pr. *Vokotopoulos 1967: 322 (SEG 37.435 n. A).

> Τέρμων [– – –]
> Ἀρυσάων
> Νωμεναίων

Boundaries [– – –] of the Arysaes (and) Nomenaies.

Comparison with T51 would suggest that the space at the end of line 1, marked by Vokotopoulos as lacunose, may well have been left blank. I have not been able to see a photo of the stone or the stone itself. Νουμεναιεϣύς is attested as an ethnic on a third-century-BCE grave marker found at Palairos in Akarnania (Antonetti 1987b: 97; SEG 37.435).

51. Boundary Stone Demarcating the Territory of the Eiteaies and Eoitanes

Found on the left bank of the Ermitsas River, one hour east of Neo Chorio (Rhomaios). (See map 4, Eiteia[?], for estimated findspot.) Fourth century BCE.
Large bronze stele, 1.90 m (h), 1.40 m (w). The letters in lines 1–3 are larger than the rest.
Ed.pr. Rhomaios 1924–25: 8–9 with drawing (*IG IX 1² 1.116).

Τέρμων
Εἰτεαίων
Ἐοιτάνω[ν].
4   Δασστῆρε[ς - - -]
Εὔαρχος [- - -]
Ο[- - -]
[- - -]

Boundaries of the Eiteaies (and the) Eoitanes. The judges in the land dispute (were) Euarchos . . .

Rhomaios 1924–25: 8 compares the δασστῆρες (from δάσσω = δατέομαι) of line 4 to the γαοδίκαι of IG IX 1² 1.3B (T59) and to the τερμαστῆρας of IG IV² 1.71 (T38) line 85. Their function is beyond doubt. Rousset 1994: 104–5 suggests that the δασστῆρες are, like the γαοδίκαι in T59, unusual among individuals performing arbitrations of territorial disputes in being professionals rather than simply eminent citizens, but while the judges have clearly been given a collective title that reflects their activity in this case, they need not have been professionals in land division.

52. Athens Sends a Herald to the Aitolian Koinon

Found in the Athenian agora near the Eleusinion. 367/6 BCE.
Three contiguous fragments of a stele found in the vicinity of the Eleusinion in the Athenian agora; now in the Agora Museum (inv. I 4384a-b, I 7259). Stoichedon 32.
Ed.pr. Schweigert 1939: no. 3 with photo, p. 6 (frr. a and b only); Tod 137. Woodhead 1997: 75–78 no. 48 with photo, pl. 4, publishes a composite text of all three fragments; *RO 35.

Θ[ε]οί.
Δημόφιλος Θεώρο Κεφαλῆ-
θεν ἐγραμμάτ[ε]υε. vacat
4   ἔδοξεν τῆι βουλῆι καὶ τῶ[ι] δήμωι. Οἰνηὶς
ἐπρυτάνε[υ]ε· Δημόφιλος Θεώρο Κεφαλῆθε-

ν ἐγραμμάτευεν· Φί[λι]ππος Σημαχίδης ἐπ-
εστάτει· [Π]ολύζηλος [ἦρχ]ε. Κηφισόδοτος ε-
8   [ἶ]πεν· ἐπε[ι]δὴ Αἰτωλῶν [τ]οῦ κ[ο]ινοῦ δεξαμέ-
[ν]ων τὰς μ[υ]στηριώτιδ[α]ς [σ]π[ο]νδὰς τῆς Δήμ-
[η]τρος τῆς [Ἐ]λευσινίας καὶ τῆς Κόρης τοὺ-
[ς] ἐπαγγείλαντας τὰς σπονδὰς Εὐμολπιδ-
12   ῶν καὶ Κηρύκων δεδέκασι Τ[ρ]ιχονειῆς Πρ-
[ό]μαχον καὶ Ἐπιγένην παρὰ τοὺς νόμους τ-
[ο]ὺς κοι[ν]οὺς τῶν Ἑλλήνων· ἐλέσθαι τὴμ βο-
[υ]λὴν αὐ[τ]ίκα μάλα κήρυκα ἐξ Ἀθηναίων ἀπ-
16   άντων ὅσ[τ]ις ἀφικόμενος πρὸς τὸ κοινὸν
[τὸ Αἰ]τω[λῶν] ἀ[παιτήσει τοὺς] ἄνδρας ἀφεῖ-
[ναι] καὶ [.................. δικ]άζειν
[ὅ]πως ἄν μ[.....................]ς κα-
20   ὶ Αἰτωλο[.....................]ρ-
οι εἰς το[........................]
αν οἵ ἂν τ[.................... Εὐμολ]-
πίδας κ[αὶ Κήρυκας.................]
24   ας βουλ[.......................]
ἤσοντ[αι........................]
ους δώσ[ουσι(?).....................]
ἐς ἐφόδ[ια τὸν ταμίαν τοῦ δήμου ΔΔΔ δραχ]-
28   μὰς ἐκ τ[ῶν κατὰ ψηφίσματα ἀναλισκομέν]-
ων τῶι [δήμωι. vacat?]
vacat?

[Go]ds. [Demo]philos son of Theoros of Kephale was secretary. [Resolved by th]e council and the *dēmos;* Oineis [held the prytan]y; Demophilos son of Theoros of Kephale [was secre]tary. Phi[li]p of Semachidai pre[sided; P]olyzelos was [arch]on; Kephisodotos s[poke: Where]as the Aitolian k[o]inon accep[ted the s]acred [t]r[u]-ce of Dem[eter E]leusinia and Kore, and whereas the T[r]ichonians [sei]zed those of the Eumolpid[ae and Ke]rykes who announced the truce, Pr[o]machos and Epigenes, contrary to t[h]e co[m]mon laws of the Greeks, let the coun[cil imm]ediately elect from a[ll] the Athenians a herald [who] is to go to the koinon [of the Aito]l[ians to demand the] release of the men ...

The document is our earliest evidence for a formal Aitolian koinon, to which the Eumolpidae and Kerykes went for official acceptance of the truce (ll. 8–10). That probably means that they approached the council or general assembly of the koinon, but because we do not know in what month the embassy was sent, and we do know that the assembly met only twice a year, it is impossible to determine which body received them. Their initial approach to the koinon itself suggests that it was known to be responsible for determining the behavior of its member communities in their relations with other states. The Athenians clearly expected the koinon to be likewise responsible for enforcing adherence to its decisions by member communities and for punishing disobedience, but we cannot be sure this was the case when it came to seizure in Aitolia. Schweigert proposed that a koinon appearing for the first time in 367 could have been created only by Epameinondas, but there are serious problems with this view, and archaeological evidence points to ongoing endogenous changes in Aitolia throughout the first half of the fourth century to which the development of the koinon must be connected; see above, pp. 77–78.

53. Alliance of the Boiotians and Aitolians

Found at Delphi. Ca. 301–298 or after 278 BCE.

Delphi inv. 1846 (fr. A), 5769 (fr. B), 4220 (fr. C).

Fragment A: edd.pr. Walek 1913 and Pomtow Syll.³ 366 (Pomtow 1918: 51 no. 34; Klaffenbach, IG IX.1² 1.170), published independently and apparently without knowledge of each other's editions; republication of lines 16–18 by Roesch 1965b: 80–82 (photo pl. XI.1). Fragments B and C: ed. pr. Flacelière 1930. Emendations to fragment B in Roesch 1965b: 80–82. A composite text is provided by *Staatsverträge III.463.

Fragment B

[– – –]ε[– – –]

[– – –]ας ὄτα[ν – – –]

[– – –]ων ἐφόδια [– – –]

4   [– – – παρ'(?) Αἰτω]λῶν Βοιωτοὺς [– – –]

[– – – ὅσον δ' ἂν χρόν]ον δέωνται, χρῆσ[θαι τᾶι συμμαχίαι(?) – – –]

[– – – Αἰτωλοὶ παρὰ Βοιωτ]ῶν ἢ Βοιωτοὶ παρ' Αἰτω[λῶν – – –]

[– – –]τι ἀφῶσιν Αἰτωλοὶ Βοιω[τοὺς – – –]

8   [– – – ἤ(?) Βοιωτοὶ] Αἰτωλούς· διδόναι δὲ ὅτι [– – –]

[– – – ἐπ]ειδὰν προαν[α]λώσωσιν Βοι[ωτοὶ – – –]

[– – – ἀποδ]οῦναι τοὺς βουλάρχους ἐντ[– – –]

[– – –]ειν καὶ ἐν τῶι ἐπιστήσοντι συ[νεδρίωι(?) – – –]

12   [– – – ο]υ. κατὰ ταὐτὰ δὲ καὶ ὅτι ἂν Αἰτ[ωλοὶ – – –]

[– – – προαναλώσω]σιν, [ἀ]ποδ[ο]ῦναι τὰ[ς ἀρχὰς τῶν Βοιωτῶν – – –]

[– – – – – – – – – – –]

Fragment A

[– –]

[– ᶜᵃ· ²⁰ –]ν τῶι κοινῶ[ι – – – – – – – –]αι τοὺς ὁπλ[ί]-

[τας –ᶜᵃ· ¹²–]ς· στήλας δὲ στῆσαι ἀναγράψαντας·

[τήν τε συμμαχ]ίαν καὶ τὸν ὅρκον ἐμ μὲν Αἰτωλίαι ἐν Θέρμωι

4   [– – – – – – – – – Α]ἰτωλίαι καὶ ἐλ Λοφρίωι, ἐν δὲ Βοιωτοῖς ἐν τῶι ἱερῶι

[τοῦ Ποσει]δ[ῶ]νος ἐν Ὀγχηστῶι καὶ ἐν Ἀλαλκομενείωι καὶ ἐγ Κο-

[ρωνείαι] ἐν τῶι ἱερῶι τῆς Ἀθηνᾶς, καὶ κοινὴν ἐν Δελφοῖς. ὀμό-

[σαι δὲ] τὸν ὅρκον ἑκατέρους τόνδε· ὀμνύω Δία, Γῆν, Ἥλιον, Πο-

8   [σειδ]ῶ, Ἄρη, Ἀθηνᾶν Ἀρείαν, θ[εο]ὺς πάντας καὶ πάσας· συμμα-

[χῆσ]ω κατὰ τοὺς ὅρκους καὶ τὰς συνθήκας τὰς γεγενημένας
[Βοιωτ]οῖς καὶ Αἰτωλοῖς καὶ Φωκεῦσιν τοῖς μετ᾽ Αἰτωλῶν ἀδόλως
[καὶ οὐκ] ἐνκαταλείψω οὔτε πολέμου ὄντος οὔτε εἰρήνης,ᵛ

12   [ἀλλὰ βο]ηθήσω παντὶ σθένει καθότι ἂν παρακαλῶσι· εἰ μὲν εὐ-
[ορκέω] πολλά μοι κἀγαθὰ εἴησαν, εἰ δ᾽ ἐφιορκοίην, ἐξώλης εἴην
[αὐτὸς καὶ] γένος. εἰ δέ τις ὅπλα ἐπιφέροι ἐπὶ Βοιωτοὺς ἐπὶ πο-
[λέμωι ἢ ἐπ᾽ Αἰ]τωλούς, βοηθεῖν ἀλλήλοις παντὶ σθένει. vacat.

16   [– ᶜᵃ· ⁶⁻⁷ – ἄρχον]τος Βοιωτοῖς, ἢ συμμαχί[α ἐκυρώθη] βοιω[ταρχόν]-
[των – – – – – – –ο]υ Θεσπιέος [– –]
[– – – – – – – – – – – –]α Τανα[γραίου – – –]

Fragment C
[– – – – – –]
[– – –]του κ[– – –]
[– – – ἐ]ν Αἰτ[ω]λίαι του [– – –]
[– – –]ίας καὶ τἀπί[λοιπα(?) – – –]

4   [– – – τὰ]ς ἀρχὰς [– – –]
[– – – – – –]

4 [– – – – – – – – – A]ἰτωλίαι Pomtow [παρὰ τῆι Α]ἰτωλίαι Knoepfler   16 – – –]
Βοιωτοῖς ἢ συμμάχ[Klaffenbach ἄρχον]τος Βοιωτοῖς ἢ συμμαχί[α ἐκυρώθη]
βοιω[ταρχόν]- Roesch   17 [– – –ο]υ Θεσπιέος [– Klaffenbach, Flacelière
1937 [των – – – – – – –ο]υ Θεσπιέος [– Roesch   18 –]ατανα[– Klaffenbach,
Flacèliere 1937 –]α Τανα[γραίου – Roesch

Fragment A: ... the koinon ... the hopli[tes ...]. (Resolved) to erect stelai
on which are to be recorded [the alli]ance and the oath, in Aitolia in Thermon
[... A]itolia and in the Laphrion; in Boiotia in the sanctuary [of Posei]don in
Onchestos, in the Alalkomenion and in Ko[roneia] in the sanctuary of Athena; and
in common at Delphi. Let them swear the following oath to one another: I swear by
Zeus, Earth, Sun, Po[seid]on, Ares, Athena Areia, and all the gods and goddesses.
I shall make an alliance according to the oaths and treaties made [between the
Boiot]ians and the Aitolians and the Phokians with the Aitolians without deceit,
[and I shall not] abandon it either in war or in peace, [but I will he]lp them with all
my strength whenever they should request it. If I swear the oath properly, may
many good things come to me, but if I swear deceitfully, let me and my kin be
utterly destroyed. If someone should bear arms against the Boiotians in wa[r, or
against the Ai]tolians, let them help each other with all their strength. [...
was arch]on of the Boiotians; the allianc[e was ratified] by the boio[tarchs ...] of
Thespiai, ... of Tanagra ...

Flacelière 1937: 57–68 discusses the date of the alliance in detail, with a review
of earlier opinions, and argues on the basis of B.14–16 that it represents a defensive alliance made during a period of peace (cf. the commentary of Schmitt in
Staatsverträge ad loc.; Gullath 1982: 195); this suggests a date between 301 and

298, immediately after the Aitolian occupation of Phokis. Knoepfler 2007a: 1250 proposes a date after 278 on the grounds that his proposed restoration of A.4, [παρα τῆι Α]ἰτωλίαι, would require that a statue of Aitolia already existed in Thermon to serve as a geographical reference point for the erection of a copy of the treaty. The fragments of a statue base taking the form of a pile of Gallic shields discovered between the east and west stoas at Thermon (Rhomaios 1916: 188–89 with figs. 10 and 11; Béquignon 1931: 485; Rhomaios 1931: 66; BCH 108 (1984) 781 with photo, p. 783 fig. 83) have long been associated with a statue of Aitolia like the one dedicated at Delphi after 279, and the shields require that the Thermon statue must also postdate 279/8. Knoepfler suggests, more specifically, the period 274–272, when the Aitolians were caught up in the conflict between Pyrrhos and Antigonos Gonatas. The suggestion is attractive from an epigraphic perspective, but it raises more historical questions than it answers: if the Aitolians did not have an alliance with the Boiotians until the later 270s, we need another explanation of their coordination with the Boiotians in the war against Demetrios in 293 and their support for the Boiotians in the matter of the Athenian inscription accompanying the rededication of Persian shields at Delphi, which recalled Boiotian Medism during the Persian Wars. (See above, pp. 96–97.)

That the alliance was made on Aitolian initiative is suggested by A.10: the alliance is made according to the oaths and treaties made "between the Boiotians and the Aitolians and the Phokians with the Aitolians."

54. Proxeny Decree of the Aitolian Koinon

Found at Thermon. 273/2 BCE.

*IG IX 1² 1.10b. Inscribed on the same stone as IG IX 1² 1.10a.

```
        καὶ γᾶς καὶ οἰ[κίας] ἔγ[κτησιν καὶ ἀσυ]-
        λίαν καὶ πολέμο[υ καὶ εἰράνας καὶ]
        τἆλλα ὅσα καὶ τοῖς [ἄλλοις προξέ]-
4       νοις. στραταγοῦντος Δορκ[ί]να Ναυπ-
        ακτίου, γραμματεύον[τος Πολυχάρ]-
        μου Ἡρακλειώτα. ἔγγυ[οι - - - - - - -]
        Εὐπαλιεύς [- - - - - - - - - - - - - -]
```

... and the ri[ght to own] land and hou[ses], [and asy]lia in war [and in peace, and] all the other rights and privileges belonging to the [other proxe]noi. Dorkinas of Naupaktos was general; the secreta[ry was Polychar]mos of Herakleia. The guar[antors . . .] Eupalieus [. . .]

This text is highly lacunose, and the portions that survive are not easily legible. However, line 1 can be restored with relative confidence by comparison with the similar formula in T58, lines 7–8. The attribution to the koinon rather than to any single polis is based entirely (and securely) on the provenance of the stone.

*55. The Delphic Amphiktyony Honors Sokrates of Knidos
and Alexeinides of Elis*

Found at Delphi. 272/1 BCE.

Ed.pr. Foucart 1883: 409 I, 415 (Michel 1900: 247; *GDI* 2516, 2564–65). **Syll.*³ 418A.

ἐπὶ Εὐδόκου ἄρχοντος, πυλαίας ὀπωρινῆς, ἱερομ[νημο]νούντων· Αἰτωλῶν
Γαύ[σου],
Τριχᾶ, Πολύφρονος, Πολυχάρμου, Τεισάρχου· Δελφ[ῶν] Κρίτωνος,Ἡρακλε[ί-
δο]υ· Φωκέων
Δωροθέου, Πεισίωνος· Βοιωτῶν Θηβαγγέλου, Μοιρίχου, Φαντία· Ε[ὐβο]ιέων
Ἐπηράστ[ου]·
4   Ἀθηναίων Ἀσωποδώρου· Σικυωνίων Εὐθυδάμου· ἐπειδὴ Σωκράτης Τελεσία
Κνίδιος καὶ Ἀλεξεινίδης Φιλωνίδου Ἡλεῖος ἐν Αἰτωλίαι οἰκῶν ἐμήνυσαν
ἱερὰ χρήματα τῶι θεῶι καὶ κρίναντες ἐπὶ τῶν ἱερομνημόνων φανερὰ ἐποίησαν
τὰ χρήματα καὶ ἐνέβαλον εἰς τὸ κιβώτιον κατάδικον μυρίων στατήρων Ζήνωνα
8   Σολέα, δεδόχθαι τοῖς ἱερομνήμοσιν, δοῦναι Σωκράτει καὶ Ἀλεξεινίδηι προ[δι]κίαν
καὶ ἀσφάλειαν καὶ ἐπιτιμὰν καὶ αὐτοῖς καὶ ἐκγόνοις καθὰ καὶ τοῖς ἄλλοις
δίδονται [αἱ]
προδικίαι, ἐπειδὴ φαίνονται εὐεργετηκότες τὸν θεὸν ἄξια αὐτοῦ.

In the archonship of Eudokos, at the autumn Pylaia, the sacred representatives were:
of the Aitolians, Gau[son], Trichas, Polyphron, Polycharmos, and Teisarchos; of the
Delph[ians], Kriton and Herakle[ide]s; of the Phokians, Dorotheos and Peision; of the
Boiotians, Thebangelos, Moirichos, and Phantias; of the E[ubo]ians, Eperast[os]; of
the Athenians, Asopodoros; of the Sikyonians, Euthydamos. Because Sokrates son of
Telesias of Knidos and Alexeinides son of Philonidos, the Elian living in Aitolia, presented sacred monies to the god, and dividing it in the presence of the sacred representatives made the money visible and deposited in the chest the ten thousand staters
in fines (owed by) Zenon of Soli, it was resolved by the sacred representatives to give
to Sokrates and Alexeinides the right to priority of trial, security and honor, to them
and their descendants, just as the right to priority of trial is given to others, since they,
having done a good deed to the god, show themselves worthy of the privilege.

Scholten 2000: 45 n. 52 sees Alexeinides the Elian ἐν Αἰτωλίαι οἰκῶν (l. 5) as
evidence for a "variety of categories of privilege and responsibility" within the
expanding koinon, which variety attests a process of negotiation whereby the role
of these newly incorporated populations in the political life of Aitolia was gradually worked out. For the date see Klaffenbach *IG* IX.1² 1 p. liii and Flacelière 1937:
389 app. I.8.

*56. Proxeny Decree of the Aitolian Koinon
for Four Citizens of Phthiotic Achaia*

Found at Thermon. 269/8–265/4 or 251/0–249/8 BCE.

Ed.pr. Sotiriadis 1905: 99 no. 17 (**IG* IX 1² 1.6).

ἀγαθῆι τύχηι. τὸ κοινὸν τῶν Αἰτωλῶν ἔδ[ωκεν]
Ἀφθονή^γ τωι Χαρ⟨ι⟩δήμου καὶ τοῖς υἱοῖς [αὐτοῦ]
[Π]ολυστράτωι, Ἀναξάνδρωι, Χαριδήμ[ωι]
4   [π]ροξενίαν, ἰσοπολιτείαν, ἀσφάλεια[ν, ἀσυ]-
λίαν καὶ πολέμου καὶ εἰρήνης αὐτῶι [καὶ ἐγγό]-
νοις καὶ κατὰ γῆν καὶ κατὰ θάλασσα[ν καὶ]
ἔκκτησιν καὶ γῆς καὶ οἰκίας καὶ τἆλ[λα, ὅσ]-
8   α καὶ τοῖς ἄλλοις προξένοις καὶ εὐε[ργέ]-
ταις δίδοται, Ἀχαιοῖς ἀπὸ Φθίας ἐξ Αἰ[- - -]-
ρων. βουλαρχούντων Φύσκου Ναυπακτίο[υ, - - -]-
μαδέα Φαξ⟨ί⟩ου, στρατάγου Φυταιέως Καλλ[ία‛Ηρα]-
12   κλειώτα, γραμματεύοντος Μνασιμά[χου]
Ο̣[ἰ]να⟨ί⟩ου. ἔγγυος τῆς προξενίας Πολέ[μαρ]-
χος ἐξ‛Υποσιρίας.

Good fortune. The koinon of the Aitolians ga[ve] to Aphthones son of Charidemos and to [his] sons, [P]olystratos, Anaxandros and Charidemos, [p]roxeny, *isopoliteia*, *asphaleia*, [*asy*]*lia* in war and in peace, for him [and for his descen]dants, by land and by se[a, and] the right to own land and houses and the oth[er privileges] given to other proxenoi and bene[fa]ctors of the Phthiotic Achaians from Ai[. . .]ron. The boularchs were Physkos of Naupaktos and [. . .]mades of Axos; the general was Phytaieus son of Kall[ias of Hera]kleia; the secretary was Mnasima[chos] son of O[i]-naios. The guarantor of the grant of proxeny was Pole[mar]chos from Hyposiria.

Klaffenbach places the generalship of Physkos of Naupaktos in the early third century, but we can perhaps be more precise. Herakleia Trachinia (ll. 11–12) was annexed by the Aitolian koinon only in 280 (Paus. 10.20.9; Scholten 2000: 120 n. 108), which date provides us with a terminus post quem. The only blanks in the Aitolian *stratagia* list for this period are 278/7–274/3, 269/8–265/4 and 251/0–249/8. Physkos of Naupaktos, one of the boularchs in our text, was general in 257/6 and was honored with a statue at Olympia (*IVO* 295) that may have been associated with his assistance to the Elians during the Social War (Scholten 2000: 120 n. 108). Although a twenty-year career in high offices is not unthinkable, it seems more likely that Physkos was boularch and Phytaieus archon in one of the later gaps. It is difficult to imagine a native son of Herakleia achieving the highest office in the koinon within just two to six years of the annexation of the city. I therefore suggest that the *stratēgia* of Phytaieus should be placed in the period 269/8–265/4 or 251/0–249/8, the latter being more likely.

57. Alliance between Aitolia and Akarnania

Found at Thermon. Late 260s or early 250s BCE.

Inscribed on both sides of a hollow bronze stele.

Ed.pr. Sotiriadis 1905 with photo, plate 2 (*IG* IX 1² 1.3A; *Syll.*³ 421; C. D. Buck 1955: 67; *Staatsverträge* III.480; Hainsworth 1972: II.10; Ager 1996: no. 33 (ll. 1–11 only); Daverio Rocchi 1988: 115–17 no. 7 (ll. 1–16 only).

συνθήκα καὶ συμμαχία
Αἰτωλοῖς καὶ Ἀκαρνάνοις.

ἀγαθᾶι τύχαι. συνθήκα Αἰτωλοῖς καὶ Ἀκαρνάνοις ὁμόλογος· εἰρήναν

4   εἶμεν καὶ φιλίαν ποτ' ἀλλάλους, φίλους ἐόντας καὶ συμμάχους ἅματα τὸμ πάντα χρόνον, ὅρια ἔχοντας τᾶς χώρας τὸν Ἀχελῶιον ποταμ-
ὸν ἄχρι εἰς θάλασσαν. τὰ μὲν ποτ' ἀῶ τοῦ Ἀχελώιου ποταμοῦ Αἰτωλῶν εἶμεν, τὰ δὲ
ποθ' ἑσπέραν Ἀκαρνάνων πλὰν τοῦ Πραντὸς καὶ τᾶς Δεμφίδος. ταύτας δὲ
Ἀκαρνᾶν-

8   ες οὐκ ἀντιποιοῦνται. ὑπὲρ δὲ τῶν τερμόνων τοῦ Πραντός, εἰ μέγ κα Στράτιοι
καὶ Ἀγραῖ-
οι συγχωρέωντι αὐτοὶ ποτ' αὐτούς, τοῦτο κύριον ἔστω· εἰ δὲ μή, Ἀκαρνᾶνες καὶ
Αἰτωλοὶ
τερμαξάντω τὰμ Πραντίδα χώραν, αἱρεθέντας ἑκατέρων δέκα πλὰν Στρατίων
καὶ Ἀγρα⟨ί⟩-
ων· καθὼς δέ κα τερμάξωντι, τέλειον ἔστω. εἶμεν δὲ καὶ ἐπιγαμίαν ποτ'
ἀλλάλους καὶ γ-

12   ᾶς ἔγκτησιν τῶι τε Αἰτωλῶι ἐν Ἀκαρνανίαι καὶ τῶι Ἀκαρνᾶνι ἐν Αἰτωλίαι καὶ
πολίταν εἶμε-
ν τὸν Αἰτωλὸν ἐν Ἀκαρνανίαι καὶ τὸν Ἀκαρνᾶνα ἐν ⟨Α⟩ἰτωλίαι ἴσον καὶ ὅμοιον.
ἀναγραψάν-
τω δὲ ταῦτα ἐν στάλαις χαλκέαις ἐπ' Ἀκτίωι μὲν οἱ ἄρχοντες τῶν Ἀκαρνάνων,
ἐν δὲ Θέρμ-
ωι τοὶ ἄρχοντες τῶν Αἰτωλῶν, ἐν Ὀλυμπίαι δὲ καὶ ἐν Δελφοῖς καὶ ἐν Δω[δ]ώναι
κοινᾶι ἑκάτ-

16   εροι. ἐπὶ ἀρχόντων ἐμ μὲν Αἰτωλίαι στραταγέοντος Πολυκρίτου Καλλιέος τὸ
δεύτε-
ρον, ἱππαρχέοντος Φίλωνος Πλευρωνίου, γραμματεύοντος Νεοπτολέμου
Ναυπακτίου,
ἐπιλεκταρχεόντων Λαμέδωνος Καλυδωνίου, Ἀριστάρχου Ἐρταίου, Λέωνος Κα-
φρέος, Καλλία Καλλιέος, Τιμολόχου Ποτειδανιέος, Παμφαΐδα Φυσκέος, Σίμου

20   Φυταιέος, ταμιευόντων Κυδρίωνος Λυσιμαχέος, Δωριμάχου Τριχονίου, Ἀρίστ-
ωνος Δαιάνος, Ἀριστέα Ἱστωρίου, Ἀγήσωνος Δεξιέος, Τιμάνδρου Ἐριναῖος,
Ἀγρίου Σωσθενέος, ἐν δὲ Ἀκαρνανίαι στραταγῶν Βυνθάρου Οἰνιάδα, Ἐπιλ-
άου Δηριέος, Ἀγήσωνος Στρατίου, Ἀλκέτα Φοιτιᾶνος, Ἀλκίνου Θυρρείου, Θέων-

24   ος Ἀνακτοριέος, Πολυκλέος Λευκαδίου, ἱππαρχέοντος Ἱππολάου Οἰνιάδα,
γραμματεύοντος Περικλέος Οἰνιάδα, ταμία Ἀγε⟨λ⟩άου Στρατικοῦ.
συμμαχία Αἰτωλοῖς καὶ Ἀκαρνάνοις ἅματα τὸμ πάντα χρόνον.
εἴ τίς κα ἐμβάλλῃ εἰς τὰν Αἰτωλίαν ἐπὶ πολέμωι, βοαθεῖν τοὺς

28   Ἀκαρνᾶνας πεζοῖς μὲν χιλίοις, ἱππεῦσι δὲ ἑκατόν, οὕς κα τοὶ ἄρχοντε-
ς πέμπωντι, ἐν ἁμέραις ἕξ. καὶ εἴ τις ἐν Ἀκαρνανίαν ἐμβάλλοι ἐπὶ πολέμωι,
βοαθεῖν Αἰτωλοὺς πεζοῖς μὲν χιλίοις, ἱππέοις δὲ ἑκατὸν ἐν ἁμέραις ἕξ, οὕς
κα τοὶ ἄρχοντες πέμπωντι. εἰ δὲ πλειόνων χρείαν ἔχοιεν ἄτεροι πότεροι,

32   βοαθοούντω τρισχιλίοις ἑκάτεροι ἑκατέροις ἐν ἁμέραις δέκα. τᾶς δὲ βοαθοίας τ-
ᾶς ἀποστελλομένας ἔστω τὸ τρίτομ μέρος ὁπλῖται. πεμπόντω δὲ τὰμ βοάθοιαν

ἐγ μὲν Ἀκαρνανίας οἱ στραταγοὶ τῶν Ἀκαρνάνων καὶ οἱ σύνεδροι, ἐγ δὲ
Αἰτωλίας
οἱ ἄρχοντες τῶν Αἰτωλῶν. σιταρχούντω δὲ τοὺς [ἀπ]οστελλομένους στρατιώτ-
36 ας ἑκάτεροι τοὺς αὐτῶν ἁμερᾶν τριάκοντ[α. εἰ δὲ πλεί]ονα χρόνον ἔχοιεν τᾶς
βοα-
θοίας χρείαν οἱ μεταπεμψάμενοι τ[ὰμ βοάθοια]ν, διδόντω τὰς σιταρχίας, ἔστε κα
ἐν οἶκον ἀποστείλωντι τοὺς [στρατιώ]τας. σιταρχία δ' ἔστω τοῦ πλείονος χρόν-
ου τῶ[ι ἱππεῖ στα]τὴρ Κορίν[θιος τᾶς] ἁμέρας ἑκάστας, τῶι δὲ τὰμ πανοπλίαν
ἔχο-
40 [ντι δύο δραχμαί], τῶι δὲ τὸ [ἡμιθωρ]άκιον ἐννέ' ὀβολοί, ψιλῶι ἕπτ' ὀβολοί.
ἀγείσθων
[δὲ ἐμ μὲν Αἰτω]λί«α»ι οἱ Αἰ[τωλο]ί, ἐν δὲ Ἀκαρνανίαι οἱ Ἀκαρνᾶνε[ς – – – – –]οι
δὲ μ-
The last four lines are highly fragmentary.

Agreement and alliance between the Aitolians and Akarnanians. Good fortune.
Agreement reached between the Aitolians and Akarnanians. Let there be peace and
friendship between them, being friends and allies without deception for all time,
having the boundaries of their territory defined by the Achelöos River and the sea.
Let that land to the east of the Achelöos River belong to the Aitolians, while that to
the west shall belong to the Akarnanians, except for Pras and Demphis. These shall
not be made Akarnanian again. Regarding the boundaries of Pras, if the Stratioi and
Agraioi agree to these boundaries, let them be official. If not, the Akarnanians and
Aitolians shall delimit the territory of Pras, selecting ten men each from the Stratioi
and the Agraioi. And as they delimit it, let it be final. Let there be the right of intermarriage between them, and the right to acquire land for an Aitolian in Akarnania,
and for an Akarnanian in Aitolia, and let every Aitolian have equal and identical
citizenship in Akarnania, and every Akarnanian in Aitolia. Let these things be written in a bronze stele at Aktion by the archons of the Akarnanians, and in Thermon
by the archons of the Aitolians, in Olympia and in Delphi and in Dodona in common
by both. Of the archons in Aitolia, Polykritos of Kallion was *stratēgos* for a second
time, Philon of Pleuron was hipparch, Neoptolemos of Naupaktos was secretary; the
epilektarchai were Lamedon of Kalydon, Aristarchos of Ertaia, Leon of Kaphrai,
Kallias of Kallion, Timolochos of Poteidania, Pamphaïs of Physkeis, Simos of Phytai;
the treasurers were Kydrion of Lysimacheia, Dorimachos of Trichoneion, Ariston of
Daias, Aristeas of Istorion, Hageson of Dexiai, Timandros of Erineos, Agrios of
Sosthenis. In Akarnania the generals were Byntharos of Oiniadai, Epilaos of Deriai,
Hageson of Stratos, Alketas of Phoitianai, Alkinos of Thyrrheion, Theon of Anakto-
rion, Polykles of Leukas; the hipparch was Hippolaos of Oiniadai; the secretary was
Perikles of Oiniadai; the treasurer was Hagelaos of Stratos. Alliance between the
Aitolians and Akarnanians, without deceit, for all time; if anyone should attack Aitolia with hostile intent, the Akarnanians shall come to their aid with a thousand infantry and a hundred cavalry, which the archons will send, within six days. And if someone attacks Akarnania with hostile intent, the Aitolians shall come to their aid with
a thousand infantry and a hundred cavalry in six days, which the archons will send.

If any others have need for more, let them each send three thousand additional troops, in ten days. Let the assistance that has been sent consist of one-third hoplites. Let the generals and councillors of the Akarnanians send the reinforcements from Akarnania, and let the archons of the Aitolians send them from Aitolia. Let each pay their own soldiers that have been sent out for thirty days. If those who have sent for reinforcements need assistance for longer than thirty days, let them provide pay to the houses of the soldiers who have been sent out. Let the pay for any additional time be one Corinthian stater per cavalryman per day, and twelve obols to a fully armed foot soldier, nine obols to a hemithorax, and seven obols to a light-armed man. Let the Aitolians be mustered in Aitolia, the Akarnanians in Akarnania, but the others . . .

Klaffenbach 1931 and *IG* IX.1^2 p. xlix placed the document in the year 263/2 in the belief that, by studying the other *stratagia* lists, he could pin Polykritos of Kallion's second term of office to that year, but Scholten 2000: 253–56 has stressed how uncertain the reconstruction of that list is for the third century, based often upon circular arguments. Klaffenbach 1955 revisited the question, concluding that the treaty is best understood in the context of the end of the Chremonidean War, when Alexander of Epeiros, seeking revenge on Antigonos for the death of his father, Pyrrhos, in Argos in 272, invaded Macedonia while the king was in southern Greece. But Alexander was quickly driven out and stripped of his own kingdom, at which time he took refuge in Akarnania (Justin 26.2.9–3.1). Klaffenbach now proposed that the agreement between two old enemies could be seen only as the product of arbitration by Alexander, who could play on widespread fears of Macedonia and needed local support to regain his kingdom. This would place the treaty around 261. Furthermore, a small fragment of a copy of the alliance was found at Olympia (*IVO* 40). The Olympia copy and the instructions in this text (line 15) to set it up may imply Elian involvement in the agreement. Deeply hostile to Antigonos during the Chremonidean War, the Elians may have been particularly keen to advertise and support such an alliance in its aftermath, at a time when Antigonos remained a threat to northwestern Greece. (Cf. the remarks of Scholten 2000: 255–56.) Scholten 2000: 263–66 argues persuasively against the attempt by Grainger 1995: 327–330 to place this document ca. 270 (for which see now Dany 1999: 69–86) or in the early 260s; cf. Corsten 1999: 145.

The Stratioi and Agraioi appear (ll. 8–9) as quasi-autonomous groups whose approval of the proposed delimitation of the boundary between Pras and Demphis is required. The Agraioi created their own koinon probably shortly after the death of Alexander but were by this period part of the Aitolian koinon (Antonetti 1987a: 216 n. 18). The integrity of their group within the Aitolian koinon is to be explained only partly as a function of the strategic importance of their territory (Antonetti 1987a: 201); it was simply the normal procedure adopted by the Aitolians as they expanded their koinon.

Several of the communities represented by an *epilektarchēs* or a treasurer are otherwise unknown or have not been located. In line 18 Ertaia is nowhere else attested. In line 21 Daias, Istorion, and Dexiai are similarly unknown. Sosthenis (l. 22) was situated in southern Thessaly at the western end of the Malian Gulf: Ptol. *Geogr.* 3.12.42; Plassart 1921: 20 III ll. 128, 137; cf. Béquignon 1937: 306–7 and Kontogiannis 1994. There is a Kaphrai in Aitolia and another in Ozolian Lokris: Lerat 1952: I.66. It is not certain which of these two is represented in the document (ll. 18–19), but it is not safe to assume (as Corsten 1999: 147 does) that it must be the Aitolian Kaphrai simply because one Lokrian community (Physkeis, l. 19) is already represented. Poteidania (l. 19), east of Naupaktos, is certainly Lokrian, so we have at least two Lokrian communities represented (though precisely what such labels mean in this period is difficult to pin down), and there is nothing to mandate against a third.

Our inability to locate these communities is a hindrance to Corsten's (1999: 140–48) attempt to deduce the existence of districts and their precise configuration in third-century Aitolia from this document. It is not impossible (*pace* Scholten 2003: 75) to detect geographic patterns from the demotics of the colleges of *epilektarchai* and *tamiai*, but only five districts can be hypothetically outlined thus, and our ignorance of the location of the other four communities represented by these magistrates makes even these five deeply uncertain. And if these two colleges did in fact imply the existence of districts in Aitolia, there would be a conflict between the single *Lokrikon telos* attested in T61, which comprises both Naupaktos and Amphissa, and the districts in this region implied by the magistrate lists, for here Physkeis and Poteidania, which lie between Naupaktos and Amphissa (Map 5), both send an *epilektarchēs* (l. 19). Corsten's assumption that each district sent only one *epilektarchēs* would thus require the division of Lokris into at least two districts. It is possible, of course, that there was a change in the organization of the districts between the 240s and the early third century, but there are enough difficulties with the implementation of the theory to leave it aside as an interesting hypothesis. It is hoped that the discovery of additional documents may shed some light here.

The *epilektarchēs* is a military magistrate, literally a commander of picked troops. Whether the *epilektoi* are picked because of their excellence and superior training, making them elite troops (cf. Xen. *Hell.* 5.3.23, *Anab.* 3.4.43), or whether they are picked by the districts to fulfill their troop levies for the army of the Aitolian koinon, is not known. Corsten 1999 assumes that the office is directly comparable to the *hypostratēgos* of the Achaian koinon, explicitly associated with the Patraian *synteleia* or district (Polyb. 5.94.1).

58. Proxeny Decree of the Aitolian Koinon for Kallippos and Kephallas of Pronnon
Found at Thermon. Mid-third century BCE.
*IG IX 1² 1.8.

[ἀγαθῆι τύ]χηι. τὸ κοινὸν τῶν
[Αἰτωλῶν ἔ]δωκε Καλλίππωι
[- - - - - - - - -] Κεφαλλᾶνι ἐκ Πρ-
4   [ώννων πρ]οξενίαν, ἰσοπολιτ-
[είαν, ἀσφά]λειαν αὐτῶι καὶ ἐγ-
[γόνοις κ]αὶ πολέμου καὶ εἰρή-
[νης] καὶ γῆς ἔγκτησιν καὶ οἰ-
8   [κία]ς καὶ εἰσάγουσι καὶ ἐξάγο-
[υσι] καὶ τἆλλα, ὅσα καὶ τοῖς
[λοιπ]οῖς δίδοται προξένο-
[ι]ς. βουλαρχοῦντος Λυκέα
12   Δυμαίου, ἱππαρχοῦντος
Δράκοντος Πολιέος, γρα-
[μ]ματεύοντος Ἀγέα Καλ-
[λι]έος. ἔγγυος τᾶς προξενί-
16   [α]ς Σφοδρίας [[- - -]]
[[- - -]] Ναυπάκτιος.

[Good for]tune. The koinon of the [Aitolians g]ave to Kallippos [. . .] and Kephallas from Pr[onnon pr]oxeny, *isopolit*[*eia*, and *aspha*]*leia*, to them and their de[scendants, i]n war and in pea[ce], and the right to own land and hou[ses], to import and expo[rt] (goods) and all the other rights and privileges given to the [oth]er proxenoi. The boularch was Lykeas son of Dymaios; the hipparch was Drakon son of Polias; the sec[r]etary was Ageas of Kal[li]on. The guarantor of the bestowal of proxeny was Sphodrias [[*rasura*]] of Naupaktos.

59. Arbitration of the Aitolian Koinon in a Boundary Dispute between Oiniadai and Matropolis

Found at Thermon. Ca. 239–231 BCE.
Inscribed on a hollow bronze stele, on the other side of which is T57.
IG IX 1² 1.3B (Daverio Rocchi 1988: 118–19 no. 8; Ager 1996: 124–26 no. 41; Corsten 1999: 155).

στραταγέοντος Χαριξένου τὸ τέταρτον.
κρῖμα γαϊκὸν Στρατικοῦ τέλεος. τάδε
ἔκριναν Θυρρείων οἱ γαοδίκαι· ὅρια τᾶς χώ-
4   ρας Οἰνιά‹δα›ις ποτὶ Ματροπολίταις τὸ δια-
τ‹ε›ίχισμα καὶ ἀπὸ τοῦ διατειχίσματος
εὐθυωρίαι διὰ τοῦ ἔλεος εἰς θάλασ‹σ›αν.
ἀναγραψάτω δὲ τὸ κρῖμα ἁ πόλις τῶν Ο[ἰ]-
8   νιαδᾶν, πόλις τῶν Ματροπολιτᾶν ἐν
Θέρμωι ἐν τῶι ἱερῶι τοῦ Ἀπόλ‹λ›ωνος.

When Charixenos was *stratēgos* for the fourth time. Territorial judgment of the district of Stratos [*Stratikon telos*]. These things the *gaodikai* of the Thyrrheians judged:

the boundaries of the territory of Oiniadai facing Matropolis are the fortification and from the fortification in a straight line from the marsh to the sea. Let the polis of O[i]-niadai inscribe this judgment, and the polis of Matropolis, in Thermon in the sanctuary of Apollo.

Date. Reinach 1911: 236, followed by Dittenberger *Syll.*[3] 659 and Préaux 1962: 260, placed this document within a few years of the conclusion of the alliance between Akarnania and Aitolia (T57), which he dated to 268. However, the precise date of that document is itself uncertain (see above, favoring a date at the end of the Chremonidean War), and the letter forms seem to require a gap of some decades between the two. Beyond this, we seek some historical context into which the arbitration would seem to fit. Klaffenbach 1931: 233-34 originally placed it in the period 235-230 (followed by Wacker 1996: 212) but later revised his view (Klaffenbach 1954: 23-24 n. 2), suggesting rather the period 239-231, shortly after the Aitolian invasion of Epeirote Akarnania in 239/8 (Justin 28.1.1) but before 231, when the Aitolians lost Thyrrheion again (cf. Klaffenbach *IG* IX.1[2] 1 p. xxi); he is followed by Ager 1996: 125-26. Daverio Rocchi dates the text to 258; Scholten 2000: 64 n. 20 places it after the partitioning of Akarnania by Epeiros and Aitolia, which he dates, following scholarly consensus, to the late 240s. The arbitration clearly reflects Aitolian control of Akarnania west of the Achelöos River, the boundary recognized by the treaty T57; as a result it only makes sense to read it as a product of the agreement with Alexander of Epeiros to partition Akarnania, which effectively discarded the older treaty.

Arbitration. Préaux 1962, Rousset and Katzouros 1992, and Rousset 1994 all discuss the γαοδίκαι. Whether or not they were specialists in territorial disputes (see commentary to T51), that was their competency in this particular arbitration. It is doubtful that these judges were actually foreign. Klaffenbach (*IG* IX.1[2] 1.3A) and Larsen 1968: 267 n. 3 believe that Thyrrheion must have been part of the Aitolian koinon in order for its γαοδίκαι to have arbitrated in the dispute, since we have no other evidence for Aitolians appealing to foreign judges to settle internal disputes. Habicht 1987 echoes the sentiment in his assertion that the Aitolians did not use foreign judges. However, Thyrrheion was not Aitolian in 220 (Polyb. 4.6.2-3) but rather was part of Epeirote Akarnania: Wacker 1996: 212; Scholten 2000: 91 n. 110. What is perhaps most compelling is the weight of epigraphic evidence tilting toward the Aitolian tendency to arbitrate disputes within the koinon's boundaries by appointing representatives or communities within the regional system.

Topography and political landscape. Pritchett 1965-92: VII.14-15 discusses topographical problems relating to the text, suggesting that ἕλος in line 6 refers to what was then Lake Melite (cf. Strabo 10.2.21), in the territory of Oiniadai at the mouth of the Achelöos, and that the word διατείχισμα "may have been used metaphorically" for a dike extending from some point on the Achelöos between the modern village of Pentalopho and Mount Panagia; he identifies the village of Palaiomanina as ancient Matropolis. Funke 1991 places the document in the context of the development of nucleated settlements in Aitolia with extensive territories, a change that he argues occurred throughout the fourth century, representing a shift away from the dominant pattern of scattered settlement in this area in the archaic period and the fifth century.

60. The Aitolian Koinon Arbitrates in a Dispute between Melitaia and Pereia

Marble stele found at Avaritsa, the site of ancient Melitaia. 213/2 BCE.

*IG IX 1² 1.188 (Syll.³ 546b; Migeotte 1984: 111–13 no. 31 [ll. 16–23 only]; Ager 1996: no. 56; Magnetto 1997: 339–48 no. 55).

Μελιταιέοις καὶ Πηρέοις ἔκριναν οἱ ὑπὸ τῶν Αἰτωλῶν αἱρεθέν-
τες δικασταὶ Δωρίμαχος, Πολεμαῖος, Ἀργεῖος Καλυδώνιοι αὐτῶν
ἐπιχωρησάντων ἐξ ὁμολόγων· ὅρια μὲν εἶμεν τᾶς χώρας Μελιταιέ-
4   οις καὶ Πηρέοις, ὡς ὁ Ἀκμεὺς ἐμβάλλει ἐν τὸν Εὐρωπόν, καὶ ἀπὸ τοῦ
Ἀκμέος ἐν τὰν παγὰν τοῦ Γαλαίου, καὶ ἀπὸ τοῦ Γαλαίου ἐν τὰν Κολώ-
ναν, καὶ ἀπὸ τᾶς Κολώνας ἐπὶ τὸ Ἑρμαῖον ἐπὶ τὰ Εὐρύνια, καὶ ἀπὸ τῶν Ε[ὐ]-
ρυνίων κατὰ τῶν ἄκρων, ὡς ὕδωρ ῥεῖ ἐν τὸν Εὐρωπόν, ἐκ τοῦ Εὐρω-
8   ποῦ ἐν τὸν Ἐλιπῆ, ἐκ τοῦ Ἐλιπέος ἐν τὸ νέμος τὸ ἄγον ἐν τὰν Ἄ[μπε]-
λον, ἀπὸ τᾶς Ἀμπέλου κατὰ τῶν ἄκρων ἐπὶ τὸ Ὕπατον, ἀπὸ
ᵛ τοῦ Ὑπάτου ἐν τὸν Κερκινῆ, ἀπὸ τοῦ Κερκινέος ἐν
ᵛ τὰν Μύνιν, ἀπὸ τᾶς Μύνιος ἐν τὸν Εὐρωπόν, τοῦ Σκαπεταίου
12   καὶ τοῦ Εὐρωποῦ ἐν τὰν συμβολάν. τὰν δὲ δαμοσίαν χώραν, τούς τε Καράνδας καὶ τὰν Φυλιαδόνα, μὴ ἀποδόσθων Μελιταεῖς ὥστε πατρῴαν ἔχειν τὸν πριάμενον πολιτευόντω[ν]
Πηρέων μετὰ Μελιταιέων, ἀλλὰ κατ’ ἄνπαλον μισθούντω κα-
16   θὼς καὶ τὸ πρότερον. εἰ δέ κα ἀποπολιτεύωντι Πηρεῖς ἀπὸ Μελ[ι]-
ταέων, περὶ μὲν τᾶς χώρας ὅροις χρήσθων τοῖς γεγραμμένοις καὶ ἔ-
χοντες ἀποπορευέσθων βουλευτὰν ἕνα καὶ τὰ δάνεια συναπο-
τινόντω, ὅσα κα ἁ πόλις ὀφείλῃ, κατὰ τὸ ἐπιβάλλον μέρος
20   τοῦ βουλευτᾶ καὶ ἐμφερόντω τὰ ἐ[ν] τοὺς Αἰτωλοὺς γινόμε-
να κατὰ τὸν βουλευτάν. ἀποδόντων δὲ οἱ Πηρεῖς τὰς δεκάτας
τὰς γινομένας τοῖς δανεισταῖς, ἃς ὀφείλοντι ἐτέων τριῶν, ἀ-
ναβολὰν λαβόντες ἔτη τρία. ὅσα δὲ καὶ πρότερον ἐλάμβανον ο[ἱ]
24   Πηρεῖς πὰρ τᾶς πόλιος κατ’ ἐνιαυτόν, τοῖς τε ἀρχόντοις ἀργυρίου
μνᾶς τρεῖς καὶ κάρυκι στατῆρας δέκα καὶ εἰς τὸ ἔλαιον τοῖς νεανί-
οις στατῆρας δέκα καὶ εἰς τὰν θυσίαν τῶν Σωτηρίων στατῆρας πέντε,
καὶ νῦν λανβανόντω, καὶ τὰ λοιπὰ ἐπιμελέσθω ἁ πόλις τῶν Μελιτα-
28   έων τῶν κοινῶν ἐμ Πηρέοις καθὼς καὶ τὸ πρότερον. νόμοις δὲ χρήσθων Πηρεῖς τοῖς αὐτοῖς καὶ Μελιταεῖς. τὰς δὲ ἐν ἀγορανόμοις δίκας γινομένας Πηρέοις ποτὶ Πηρεῖς κατὰ τετράμηνον δικαζόντω ἐμ Πηρέοις οἱ ἐγ Με-
λιτείας ἀγορανόμοι. ἀναγραφήτω δὲ ταῦτα ἐν στάλας ἔν τε Μελιτείαι

32   καὶ ἐν Δελφοῖς καὶ ἐν Καλυδῶνι καὶ ἐν Θέρμωι. μάρτυρες· τὸ συνέδριον ἅ-
παν τὸ ἐπὶ γραμματέος Λύκου καὶ οἱ προστάται τοῦ συνεδρίου [Πει]-
θόλαος Σπάττιος, Δύσωπος Ἀπολλωνιεὺς καὶ ὁ γραμματεὺς [Λύ]-
κος Ἐρυθραῖος καὶ ὁ ἱππάρχας Ἀλέξων Ἑρμάττιος, Πανταλέω[ν Πε]-
36   τάλου Πλευρώνιος, Νικόστρατος Νικοστράτου Ναυπάκτιος,
Δαμόξενος Θεοδώρου Ἡρακλεώτας.

The judges selected by the Aitolians, who arbitrated in the dispute between the Melitaians and Pereians, were the Kalydonians Dorimachos, Polemaios, and Argeios, in
accordance with the agreements. The boundaries of the territory of the Melitaians
and Pereians shall be as follows: as the Akmeus empties into the Europos, and from
the Akmeus to the spring of Galaios, and from Galaios to Kolona, and from Kolona
to Hermaion and Eurynia, and from Eurynia down from the peaks, as the water
flows into the Europos, from the Europos to Elipe, from Elipe to the sacred grove in
Ampelos, from Ampelos down from the peaks to Hypaton, from Hypaton to Kerkines, from Kerkines to Mynis, from Mynis to Europos, in the confluence of the Ska-
petaios and Europos rivers. The Melitaians shall not sell the public land, Karandai
and Phyliadon, for they hold it as ancestral land, the Pereians having bought it when
they were governed in common with Melitaia. However, they may lease it by repeated
auction, just as before. If the Pereians should separate themselves from the Melitaians, they shall use as the boundaries of their territory those that have been recorded
(here). Having departed, they shall have one councillor and shall join in paying
whatever expenses the polis may owe, according to the proportion of their representation on the council, and they shall pay these expenses to the Aitolians in proportion to their representation on the council. The Pereians shall pay to their creditors
the 10-percent interest that they have been owed for three years, for they took a
three-year payment deferral. Whatever the Pereians previously took from the polis
each year, three mnas of silver for the archons, ten staters for the herald, ten staters
for the olive oil for the youths, and five staters for the sacrifice on behalf of the Sav-
iors, let them take it now too, and let the polis of the Melitaians sharing with the
Pereians look after the remaining expenses just as before. The Pereians shall use the
same laws as the Melitaians. The *agoranomoi* from Melitaia shall judge trials having
arisen among the Pereian *agoranomoi* against Pereians every four months among the
Pereians. These terms shall be recorded on stelai in Melitaia, Delphi, Kalydon, and
Thermon. Witnesses: the entire synedrion, when Lykos was secretary, and the presi-
dents of the *synedrion* [Pei]tholaos of Spattioi, Dusopos of Apollonia, and the secretary Lykos of Erythrai, and the hipparchs Alexon of Hermattioi, Pantaleon son of
Petalos of Pleuron, Nikostratos son of Nikostratos of Naupaktos, Damoxenos son of
Theodoros of Herakleia.

61. Manumission Decree of the Lokrian Telos

GDI 2070. Found at Delphi. Early second century BCE.

βουλαρχέοντος τοῦ Λοκρικοῦ τέλεος Δαμοτέλεος Φυσκέος μηνὸς Ἀγυείου, ἐν Δελφοῖς δὲ ἄρχοντος Ξένωνος

τοῦ Ἀτεισίδα μηνὸς Ἡρακλείου, ἐπὶ τοῖσδε ἀπέδοτο Ἀγή-
4   σανδρος Πύθωνος Ἀμφισσεὺς τῶι Ἀπόλλωνι τῶι Πυθίωι
σῶμα ἀνδρεῖον ὧι ὄνομα Νίκων τὸ γένος Μεγαρέα, τιμᾶς
ἀργυρίου μνᾶν τεσσάρων, καθὼς ἐπίστευσε Νίκων τῶι
θεῶι τὰν ὠνάν, ἐφ᾽ ὧιτε αὐτὸν ἐλεύθερον εἶμεν καὶ ἀνέ-
8   φαπτον, ποέοντα ὅ κα θέληι. βεβαιωτὴρ κατὰ τὸν νόμον·
Σωκράτης Εὐάρχου Ἀμφισσεύς. μάρτυρες· ὁ ἱερεὺς Ξένων, τῶν δὲ ἀρχόντων Ξένων, ἰδιῶται Δαμοχάρης,
Πραξίας, Ἀρχέλας Δελφοί, Ξένων, Θεύτιμος Ἀμφισσεῖς.

When Damoteles of Physkeis was boularch of the Lokrian *telos*| in the month of Agyeios, and in Delphi the archon was Xenon| son of Ateisidas in the month of Herakleios, at that time Hage||sandros son of Python of Amphissa gave to Apollo Pythios| the male slave whose name is Nikon of Megara, worth| four mnas of silver, because Nikon entrusted| his purchase money to the god. For which reason let him be free and not|| be claimed as a slave, doing whatever he wishes. The guarantor was, according to law:| Sokrates son of Euarchos of Amphissa. Witnesses: the priest Xen|on, of the archons Xenon, and the private citizens Domachares,| Praxias, and Archelas, all Delphians, and Xenon and Theutimos of Amphissa.

The document is dated by the Delphic archon listed in line 10 (Daux 1936: 189). It is a key piece of evidence for the territorial organization of the Aitolian koinon. (See Scholten 2000: 64 n. 19; Corsten 1999: 149–52.) Cf. *IG* IX.1² 3.618, 625, for other manumission decrees sponsored by the boularch of the *Lokrikon telos* in the first two decades of the second century; both were found in the vicinity of Naupaktos. Only slightly earlier than these texts are several manumissions "to Asklepios in Naupaktos" dated by the *stratagos* of the Aitolian koinon and not mentioning the *Lokrikon telos* (*IG* IX.1² 3.612–17; 613–17 range in date from 205/4 to 193/2, while 612 is lacunose in the dating prescript and cannot be placed more precisely than the second half of the third century). The same officials mentioned in lines 1–3 appear in *GDI* 2139, though in that text there is no mention of the *Lokrikon telos*.

BIBLIOGRAPHY

Accame, S. 1949. "Elatea e la nuova epigrafe di Stinfalo." *Riv. Fil.* 27: 217–48.

———. 1972 [1946]. *Il dominio romano in Grecia dalla guerra acaica ad Augusto*. Rome.

Adger, W. N. 2000. "Social and Ecological Resilience: Are They Related?" *Progress in Human Geography* 24: 347–64.

Ager, S. 1994. "Hellenistic Crete and the *Koinodikion*." *JHS* 114: 1–18.

———. 1996. *Interstate Arbitrations in the Greek World, 337–90 B.C.* Berkeley and Los Angeles.

Aigner Foresti, L., A. Barzanò, C. Bearzot, L. Prandi, and G. Zecchini, eds. 1994. *Federazioni e federalismo nell'Europa antica: Alle radici della casa comune europea*. Milan.

Alcock, S. E. 1992. *Graecia Capta: The Landscapes of Roman Greece*. Cambridge.

———. 1995. "Pausanias and the *Polis*: Use and Abuse." In M. H. Hansen, ed., *Sources for the Ancient Greek City-State*, 326–44. Copenhagen.

Alcock, S. E., J. F. Cherry, and J. Elsner, eds. 2001. *Pausanias: Travel and Memory in Roman Greece*. Oxford.

Allen, J. 1997. "Economies of Power and Space." In R. Lee and J. Wills, eds., *Geographies of Economies*, 59–70. London.

Allen, N. J. 1998. "Effervescence and the Origins of Human Society." In N. J. Allen, W. S. F. Pickering, and W. Watts Miller, eds., *On Durkheim's Elementary Forms of Religious Life*, 149–61. London.

Allen, R. E. 1971. "Attalos I and Aigina." *ABSA* 66: 1–12.

Amandry, P. 1978a. "Bases de trépied à Coronée." *BCH* 102: 565–69.

———. 1978b. "Consécration d'armes galates à Delphes." *BCH* 102: 571–86.

———. 1981. "Chronique delphique (1970–1981)." *BCH* 105: 673–769.

Ambraseys, N. N., and J. A. Jackson. 1997. "Seismicity and Strain in the Gulf of Corinth (Greece) since 1694." *Journal of Earthquake Engineering* 1: 433–74.

Amin, A., and N.J. Thrift. 1995. "Institutional Issues for the European Regions: From Markets and Plans to Socioeconomics and Powers of Association." *Economy and Society* 24: 41–66.

Amit, M. 1970. "Hostages in Ancient Greece." *Riv. Fil.* 98: 129–47.

———. 1971. "The Boeotian Confederation during the Pentekontaetia." *RSA* 1: 49–64.

———. 1973. *Great and Small Poleis: A Study in the Relations between the Great Powers and the Small Cities in Ancient Greece.* Brussels.

Anderson, J.K. 1954. "A Topographical and Historical Study of Achaea." *ABSA* 49: 72–92.

———. 1967. "Philopoemen's Reform of the Achaean Army." *CP* 62: 104–6.

Andreau, J. 2002. "Markets, Fairs and Monetary Loans: Cultural History and Economic History in Roman Italy and Hellenistic Greece." In P. Cartledge, E.E. Cohen, and L. Foxhall, eds., *Money, Labour and Land: Approaches to the Economies of Ancient Greece,* 113–29. London.

Andreau, J., P. Briant, and R. Descat, eds. 1994. In *Les échanges dans l'antiquité: Le rôle de l'état.* Saint-Bertrand-des-Comminges.

Andrewes, A.A. 1978. "Spartan Imperialism?" In P. Garnsey and C.R. Whittaker, eds., *Imperialism in the Ancient World,* 91–102. Cambridge.

Anguissola, A. 2006a. "Note on *Aphidruma,* 1: Statues and Their Function." *CQ* 56: 641–43.

———. 2006b. "Note on *Aphidruma,* 2: Strabo on the Transfer of Cults." *CQ* 56: 643–46.

Antonetti, C. 1987a. "*AGRAIOI* et *AGRIOI*: Montagnards et bergers: Un prototype diachronique de sauvagerie." *DHA* 13: 199–236.

———. 1987b. "Le popolazioni settentrionali dell'Etolia: Difficoltà di localizzazione e problema dei limiti terrioriali, alla luce della documentazione epigrafica." In P. Cabanes, ed., *L'Illyrie méridionale et l'Épire dans l'antiquité I: Actes du colloque international de Clermont-Ferrand, 22–25 octobre 1994,* 95–115. Clermont-Ferrand.

———. 1988. "Problemi di geografia storica del territorio etolo-acarnano: Appunti sulla base di nuove testimonianze epigrafiche." In *Geographia: Atti del II convegno maceratese su geografia e cartografia antica,* 11–38. Rome.

———. 1990. *Les Étoliens: Image et religion.* Paris.

———. 1994. "Un decreto etolico inedito del 165/4 per un Acheo di Dime." *ZPE* 101: 127–35.

———. 1999. "Termo (Etolia): Scoperte epigrafiche degli anni 1969–1972." In *XI congresso internazionale di epigrafia greca e latina, Roma, 18–24 settembre 1997,* 301–10. Rome.

Antonetti, C., and E. Cavalli. 2004. "La composita facies culturale dell'Etolia méridionale in epoca arcaica." In P. Cabanes and J.-L. Lamboley, eds., *L'Illyrie méridionale et l'Épire dans l'antiquité, IV: Actes du IVᵉ colloque international de Grenoble, 10–12 octobre 2002,* 92–113. Paris.

Aravantinos, V.L. 2006. "A New Inscribed *Kioniskos* from Thebes." *ABSA* 101: 369–77.

———. 2010. *The Archaeological Museum of Thebes.* Athens.

Aravantinos, V., and N. Papazarkadas. 2012. "Ηαγεμονία: A New Treaty from Classical Thebes." *Chiron* 42: 239–54.

Archibald, Z.H. 2000. "Space, Hierarchy, and Community in Archaic and Classical Macedonia, Thessaly, and Thrace." In R. Brock and S. Hodkinson, eds., *Alternatives to Athens: Varieties of Political Organization and Community in Ancient Greece,* 212–33. Oxford.

———. 2011. "Mobility and Innovation in Hellenistic Economies: The Causes and Consequences of Human Traffic." In Z.H. Archibald, J.K. Davies, and V. Gabrielsen, eds., *The Economies of Hellenistic Societies, Third to First Centuries BC,* 42–65. Oxford.

Arenz, A. 2006. *Herakleides Kritikos «Über die Städte in Hellas»: Eine Periegese Griechen-lands am Vorabend des chremonideischen Krieges.* Munich.

Argoud, G. 1987. "Eau et agriculture en Grèce." In P. Louis, F. Métral, and J. Métral, eds., *L'homme et l'eau en Méditerranée et au Proche-Orient,* vol. IV, *L'eau dans l'agriculture,* 25–43. Lyon.

Arnaoutoglou, I. 2009–10. "Dispute Settlement between *Poleis*-Members of the Achaean League: A New Source." *Dike* 12–13: 181–201.

Arnush, M. 1995. "The Archonship of Sarpadon at Delphi." *ZPE* 105: 95–104.

———. 2000. "Argead and Aetolian Relations with the Delphic Polis in the Late Fourth Century BC." In R. Brock and S. Hodkinson, eds., *Alternatives to Athens: Varieties of Political Organization and Community in Ancient Greece,* 293–307. Oxford.

Arthur, W. B. 1994. *Increasing Returns and Path Dependence in the Economy.* Ann Arbor.

Åström, P. 1955. "Une inscription d'Aigion." *OAth* 2: 4–9.

Auffarth, C. 2006. "Das Heraion von Argos oder das Heraion der Argolis? Religion im Prozeß der Polisbildung." In K. Freitag, P. Funke, and M. Haake, eds., *Kult—Politik—Ethnos: Überregionale Heiligtümer im Spannungsfeld von Kult und Politik,* 73–87. Stuttgart.

Austin, R. P. 1926–27. "Excavations at Haliartos, 1926." *ABSA* 28: 128–41.

Aymard, A. 1933. "Recherches sur les secrétaires des confédérations aitolienne et achaïenne." In *Mélanges offerts à M. Nicolas Iorga,* 71–108. Paris.

———. 1935. "Le Zeus fédéral achaïen Hamarios-Homarios." In *Mélanges offerts à M. Octave Navarre par ses élèves et ses amis,* 453–70. Toulouse.

———. 1936. "Le rôle politique du sanctuaire fédéral achaïen." In *Mélanges offerts à Franz Cumont, Annuaire de l'Institut de Philologie et d'Histoire Orientales et Slaves,* 1–26. Brussels.

———. 1938. *Les assemblées de la confédération achaïenne.* Bordeaux.

———. 1967. *Études d'histoire ancienne.* Paris.

Babelon, E. 1907. *Traité des monnaies grecques et romaines.* Paris.

———. 1925. *Catalogue de la Collection de Luynes: Monnaies grecques.* Vol. II, *Grèce conti-nentale et îles.* Paris.

Badian, E. 1958. *Foreign Clientelae (264–70 BC).* Oxford.

———. 1989. "Plataea between Athens and Sparta." In H. Beister and J. Buckler, eds., *Boiotika: Vorträge vom 5. internationalen Böotien-Kolloquium zu Ehren von Professor Dr. Siegfried Lauffer,* 95–111. Munich.

———. 1990. "Athens, the Locrians and Naupactus." *CQ* 40: 364–69.

———. 1991. "The King's Peace." In M. Flower and M. Toher, eds., *Georgica: Studies in Honour of George Cawkwell,* 25–48. London.

———. 1993. *From Plataea to Potidaea: Studies in the History and Historiography of the Pentekontaetia.* Baltimore.

———. 1995. "The Ghost of Empire." In W. Eder, ed., *Die athenische Demokratie im 4. Jahrhundert v. Chr.: Vollendung oder Verfall einer Verfassungsform?* 75–106. Stuttgart.

Bakhuizen, S. C. 1982. "De Vikingen van Hellas; Strooptochten van de Aetoliërs, een Grieks bergvolk." *Utrechtse Historische Cahiers* 3: 21–39.

———. 1988. "A Note on Syntely: The Case of Boeotia." *Επετηρίς της Εταιρείας Βοιωτικών Μελετών* vol. IA, 279–89.

————. 1992. "The Town Wall of Aitolian Kallipolis." In S. van de Maele and J. M. Fossey, eds., *Fortificationes Antiquae: Including the Papers of a Conference Held at Ottawa University, October 1988*, 171–83. Amsterdam.

————. 1994. "Thebes and Boeotia in the Fourth Century BC." *Phoenix* 48: 307–30.

Baltrusch, E. 1994. *Symmachie und Spondai: Untersuchungen zum griechischen Völkerrecht der archaischen und klassischen Zeit (8.–5. Jahrhundert v. Chr.)*. Berlin.

Bammer, A. 1996. "Aigeira." *JÖAI* 65: 33–39.

————. 2002. "Aigeira e Hyperesia." In E. Greco, ed., *Gli Achei e l'identità etnica degli Achei d'occidente*, 235–56. Paestum and Athens.

Barber, G. L. 1935. *The Historian Ephorus*. Cambridge.

Barratt, C. 1932. "The Chronology of the Eponymous Archons of Boiotia." *JHS* 52: 72–115.

Bastini, A. 1987. *Der achäische Bund als hellenistische Mittelmacht: Geschichte des achäischen Koinon in der Symmachie mit Rom*. Frankfurt.

Bearzot, C. 1994. "Un'ideologia del federalismo nel pensiero politico greco?" In L. Aigner Foresti, A. Barzanò, C. Bearzot, L. Prandi, and G. Zecchini, eds., *Federazioni e federalismo nell'Europa antica: Alle radici della casa comune europea*, 161–80. Milan.

————. 1997. "Cassandro e la ricostruzione di Tebe: Propaganda filellenica e interessi peloponnesiaci." In J. Bintliff, ed., *Recent Developments in the History and Archaeology of Central Greece: Proceedings of the 6th International Boeotian Conference*, 265–76. Oxford.

————. 2001. "La nozione di *koinon* in Pausania." In D. Knoepfler and M. Piérart, eds., *Éditer, traduire, commenter: Pausanias en l'an 2000*, 93–108. Geneva.

————. 2004. *Federalismo e autonomia nelle Elleniche di Senofonte*. Milan.

Beck, H. 1997. *Polis und Koinon: Untersuchungen zur Geschichte und Struktur der griechischen Budesstaaten im 4. Jahrhundert v. Chr.* Stuttgart.

————. 2000. "Thebes, the Boeotian League and the 'Rise of Federalism' in Fourth Century Greece." In P. A. Bernardini, ed., *Presenza e funzione della città di Tebe nella cultura greca: Atti del convegno internazionale, Urbino, 7–9 iuglio 1997*, 331–44. Pisa and Rome.

————. 2001. "'The Laws of the Fathers' versus 'The Laws of the League': Xenophon on Federalism." *CP* 96: 355–75.

————. 2003. "New Approaches to Federalism in Ancient Greece: Perceptions and Perspectives." In K. Buraselis and K. Zoumboulakis, eds., *The Idea of European Community in History: Conference Proceedings*, vol. II, *Aspects of Connecting Poleis and Ethnē in Ancient Greece*, 177–90. Athens.

Beck, H., and P. Funke, eds. Forthcoming. *Greek Federal States*. Cambridge.

Bednar, J. L., W. Eskridge, and J. A. Ferejohn. 2001. "A Political Theory of Federalism." In J. A. Ferejohn, J. Rakove, and J. Riley, eds., *Constitutional Culture and Democratic Rule*, 223–67. New York.

Behrwald, R. 2000. *Der lykische Bund: Untersuchungen zur Geschichte und Verfassung*. Bonn.

Beister, H. 1973. "Ein thebanisches Tropaion bereits vor Beginn der Schlacht bei Leuktra: Zu Interpretation von IG VII.2463 und Paus. 4.32.5f." *Chiron* 3: 65–84.

————. 1989. "Hegemoniales Denken in Theben." In H. Beister and J. Buckler, eds., *Boiotika: Vorträge vom 5. internationalen Böotien-Kolloquium zu Ehren von Professor Dr. Siegfried Lauffer*, 131–53. Munich.

Bell, C. 1992. *Ritual Theory, Ritual Practice*. Oxford.

————. 1997. *Ritual: Perspectives and Dimensions.* Oxford.

Beloch, K. J. 1906. "Griechische Aufgebote, II." *Klio* 6: 34–78.

————. 1912–27. *Griechische Geschichte.* 4 vols. Berlin.

Béquignon, Y. 1931. "Chronique des fouilles et découvertes archéologiques dans l'Orient hellénique (1931)." *BCH* 55: 450–522.

————. 1937. *La vallée du Spercheios des origines au IVᵉ siècle: Études d'archéologie et de topographie.* Paris.

Bérard, V. 1894. *De arbitrio inter liberas Graecorum civitates.* Paris.

Berktold, P., J. Schmidt, and C. Wacker, eds. 1996. *Akarnanien: Eine Landschaft im antiken Griechenland.* Würzburg.

Bernardini, P. A. 1989. "Il proemio della *Pitica* XI di Pindaro e culti tebani." In H. Beister and J. Buckler, eds., *Boiotika: Vorträge vom 5. internationalen Böotien-Kolloquium zu Ehren von Professor Dr. Siegfried Lauffer,* 39–47. Munich.

Bickerman, E. J. 1958. "*Autonomia:* Sur un passage de Thucydide (1.144.2)." *RIDA* 5: 313–44.

Billows, R. 1990. *Antigonos the One-Eyed and the Creation of the Hellenistic State.* Berkeley and Los Angeles.

Bingen, J. 1953. "Inscriptions du Péloponnèse." *BCH* 77: 616–46.

————. 1954. "Inscriptions d'Achaïe." *BCH* 78: 74–88, 395–409.

Bintliff, J. L. 1977. *Natural Environment and Human Settlement in Prehistoric Greece.* Oxford.

————. 1994. "Territorial Behaviour and the Natural History of the Greek Polis." In E. Olshausen and H. Sonnabend, eds., *Stuttgarter Kolloquium zur historischen Geographie des Altertums,* vol. IV, *Grenze und Grenzland,* 207–49. Amsterdam.

————. 1996. "The Archaeological Survey of the Valley of the Muses and Its Significance for Boeotian History." In A. Hurst and A. Schachter, eds., *La montagne des Muses,* 193–210. Geneva.

————. 1997. "Further Considerations on the Population of Ancient Boeotia." In J. Bintliff, ed., *Recent Developments in the History and Archaeology of Central Greece: Proceedings of the 6th International Boeotian Conference,* 231–52. Oxford.

————. 1999. "Pattern and Process in the City Landscape of Boeotia from Geometric to Late Roman Times." In M. Brunet, ed., *Territoires des cités grecques,* 15–33. Paris.

————. 2002. "Going to Market in Antiquity." In E. Olshausen and H. Sonnabend, eds., *Stuttgarter Kolloquium zur historischen Geographie des Altertums,* vol. VII, *Zu Wasser und zu Land: Verkehrswege in der antiken Welt,* 209–50. Stuttgart.

————. 2005. "Explorations in Boeotian Population History." *Ancient World* 36: 5–15.

Bintliff, J., P. Howard, and A. M. Snodgrass. 2007. *Testing the Hinterland: The Work of the Boeotia Survey (1989–1991) in the Southern Approaches to the City of Thespiai.* Cambridge.

Bintliff, J. L., and A. M. Snodgrass. 1985. "The Cambridge/Bradford Boeotia Expedition: The First Four Years." *JFA* 12: 123–61.

Bissa, E. M. A. 2009. *Governmental Intervention in Foreign Trade in Archaic and Classical Greece.* Leiden.

Bizard, L. 1920. "Fouilles du Ptoïon (1903), II: Inscriptions." *BCH* 44: 227–62.

Bloch, M. 1974. "Symbols, Song, Dance and Features of Articulation: Is Religion an Extreme Form of Traditional Authority?" *Archives européennes de sociologie* 15: 55–81.

———. 1977. "The Disconnection between Power and Rank as a Process: An Outline of the Development of Kingdoms in Central Madagascar." *Archives européennes de sociologie* 18: 107–48.

Block, F., and P. Evans. 2005. "The State and the Economy." In N. J. Smelser and R. Swedberg, eds., *The Handbook of Economic Sociology*, 505–26. Princeton and New York.

Bloesch, H. 1987. *Griechische Münzen in Winterthur.* Winterthur.

Blum, G. 1914. "Nouvelles inscriptions de Delphes." *BCH* 38: 21–37.

Blum, G., and A. Plassart. 1914. "Orchomène d'Arcadie: Fouilles de 1913; Inscriptions." *BCH* 38: 447–78.

Blümel, C. 1940. *Katalog der Sammlungen antiker Skulpturen, Berlin,* vol. II.1, *Griechische Skulpturen: Des sechsten und fünften Jahrhunderts v. Chr.* Berlin.

Blümel, W. 1994. "Two New Inscriptions from the Cnidian Peninsula: Proxeny Decree for Epaminondas and a Funeral Epigram." *EA* 23: 157–59.

Boedeker, D. 1993. "Hero Cult and Politics in Herodotus: The Bones of Orestes." In C. Dougherty and L. Kurke, eds., *Cultural Poetics in Archaic Greece,* 164–77. Cambridge.

Bogaert, R. 1979. "Remarques sur deux inscriptions grecques concernant le crédit public." *ZPE* 33: 126–30.

Bolmarcich, S. 2005. "Thucydides I.19.1 and the Peloponnesian League." *GRBS* 45: 5–34.

Bolton, P., and G. Roland. 1997. "The Breakup of Nations: A Political Economy Analysis." *Quarterly Journal of Economics* 112: 1057–90.

Bommelaer, B., and J.-F. Bommelaer. 1983. "Eschine et le temple d'Apollon à Delphes." In *Mélanges E. Delebecque,* 19–31. Aix-en-Provence.

Bommeljé, S. 1981–82. "Strouza (Aigition): An Historical-Topographical Fieldwork." *AD* 36: 236–48.

———. 1988. "Aeolis in Aetolia: Thuk. III.102.5 and the Origins of the Aetolian Ethnos." *Historia* 37: 297–316.

Bommeljé, S., and P. K. Doorn, eds. 1984. *Stroúza Region Project (1981–1983): An Historical-Topographical Fieldwork; Second Interim Report.* Utrecht.

———. 1985. *Stroúza Region Project (1981–1984): An Historical-Topographical Fieldwork; Third Interim Report.* Utrecht.

Bommeljé, S., P. K. Doorn, M. Deylius, et al., eds. 1987. *Aetolia and the Aetolians: Towards the Interdisciplinary Study of a Greek Region.* Utrecht.

Bommeljé, S., P. K. Doorn, R. P. Fagel, K G. A. M. van Gulik, and H. van Wijngaarden. 1981. *Stroúza Region Project (1981): An Historical-Topographical Fieldwork; First Interim Report.* Utrecht.

Bonnechere, P. 2003. *Trophonios de Lébadée: Cultes et mythes d'une cité béotienne au miroir de la mentalité antique.* Leiden.

Bonner, J. R., and G. Smith. 1945. "The Administration of Justice in Boeotia." *CP* 40: 11–23.

Bookidis, N. 1976. "Thermos." In R. Stillwell, ed., *The Princeton Encyclopedia of Classical Sites,* 910–11. Princeton.

Bosworth, A. B. 1976. "Early Relations between Aetolia and Macedon." *AJAH* 1: 164–81.

Bourdieu, P. 1977. *Outline of a Theory of Practice.* Cambridge.

Bourguet, É. 1899. "Inscriptions de Delphes, I: Sur trois archontes du IVe siècle." *BCH* 23: 353–69.

———. 1929. *Fouilles de Delphes*. Vol. III.1, *Inscriptions de l'entrée du sanctuaire au trésor des Athéniens*. Paris.

Bousquet, J. 1939. "Une statue de Pélopidas à Delphes signée de Lysippe." *RA* 14: 125–32.

———. 1958. "Inscriptions de Delphes." *BCH* 82: 61–91.

———. 1961. "Inscriptions de Delphes." *BCH* 85: 69–97.

———. 1963. "Inscriptions de Delphes." *BCH* 87: 188–208.

———. 1975. "Arbinas, fils de Gergis, dynaste de Xanthos." *CRAI*: 138–48.

———. 1977. "Inscriptions de Delphes: Notes sur les comptes des naopes." In *Études delphiques*, 91–101. Paris.

———. 1985. "L'hoplothèque de Delphes." *BCH* 109: 717–27.

———. 1988a. *Études sur les comptes de Delphes*. Paris.

———. 1988b. "La stèle des Kyténiens au Létôon de Xanthos." *REG* 101: 12–53.

———. 1991. "Inscriptions de Delphes." *BCH* 115: 167–81.

Boutin, S. 1979. *Catalogue des monnaies grecques antiques de l'ancienne collection Pozzi: Monnaies frappées en Europe*. Maastricht.

Bowman, D. A. 1992. "Pausanias 7.11.1–2 and the Identity of *ho Gallos*." *AHB* 6: 95–102.

Bowra, C. M. 1938. "The Epigram on the Fallen of Coronea." *CQ* 32: 80–88.

Bradeen, D. W. 1964. "Athenian Casualty Lists." *Hesperia* 33: 19–62.

———. 1969. "Athenian Casualty Lists." *CQ* 19: 145–59.

Braudel, F. 1973. *The Mediterranean and the Mediterranean World in the Age of Philip II*. Berkeley and Los Angeles.

Bravo, B. 1980. "Sulan: Représailles et justice privée contre des étrangers dans les cités grecques." *ASNP* 10: 675–988.

Breccia, E. 1911. *Iscrizioni greche e latine: Service des antiquités de l'Égypte; Catalogue géneral des antiquités égyptiennes du Musée d'Alexandrie*. Cairo.

Breglia Pulci Doria, L. 1984. "Demetra tra Eubea e Beozia e i suoi rapporti con Artemis." In *Recherches sur les cultes grecs et l'occident*, 69–88. Naples.

Brélaz, C., A. K. Andreiomenou, and P. Ducrey. 2007. "Les premiers comptes du sanctuaire d'Apollo à Delion et le concours pan-béotien des Delia." *BCH* 131: 235–308.

Brennan, G., and J. M. Buchanan. 1980. *The Power to Tax: Analytical Foundations of a Fiscal Constitution*. Cambridge.

Bresson, A. 1987. "Aristote et la commerce extérieur." *REA* 89: 217–38.

———. 2000. *La cité marchande*. Bordeaux.

———. 2005. "Coinage and Money Supply in the Hellenistic Age." In Z. H. Archibald, J. K. Davies, and V. Gabrielsen, eds., *Making, Moving and Managing: The New World of Ancient Ecoomies, 323–31 BC*, 44–72. Oxford.

———. 2007. "L' entrée dans les ports en Grèce ancienne: Le cadre juridique." In C. Moatti and W. Kaiser, eds., *Gens de passage en Méditerranée de l'antiquité à l'époque modern: Procedures de contrôle et d'identification*, 37–78. Paris.

———. 2007–8. *L' économies de la Grèce des cités*. Paris.

———. 2011. "Grain from Cyrene." In Z. H. Archibald, J. K. Davies, and V. Gabrielsen, eds., *The Economies of Hellenistic Societies, Third to First Centuries BC*, 66–95. Oxford.

Brett, A. B. 1955. *Catalogue of Greek Coins, Museum of Fine Arts, Boston*. Boston.

Bringmann, K. 2001. "Grain, Timber and Money: Hellenistic Kings, Finance, Buildings, and Foundations in Greek Cities." In Z. H. Archibald, J. K. Davies, V. Gabrielsen, and G. J. Oliver, eds., *Hellenistic Economies*, 205–14. London.

Briscoe, J. 1981. *A Commentary on Livy, Books 34–37*. Oxford.

———. 2008. *A Commentary on Livy, Books 38–40*. Oxford.

Bruce, I. A. F. 1967. *An Historical Commentary on the Hellenica Oxyrhynchia*. Cambridge.

———. 1968. "Plataea and the Fifth-Century Boeotian Confederacy." *Phoenix* 22: 190–99.

Brun, P. 1983. *Eisphora–syntaxis stratiotika: Recherches sur les finances militaires d'Athènes au IVᵉ siècle*. Paris.

———. 1989. "L'île de Kéos et ses cités au IVᵉ siècle av. J.-C." *ZPE* 76: 121–38.

Brunel, J. 1953. "À propos des transferts de cultes: Un sens méconnu du mot ἀφίδρυμα." *RPh* 27: 21–33.

Brunt, P. A. 1967. "Athenian Settlements Abroad in the Fifth Century B.C." In E. Badian, ed., *Ancient Society and Institutions: Studies Presented to Victor Ehrenberg on His 75th Birthday*, 71–92. New York.

Buck, C. D. 1955. *Introduction to the Study of the Greek Dialects: Grammar, Selected Inscriptions, Glossary*. Chicago.

Buck, R. J. 1970. "The Athenian Domination of Boeotia." *CP* 65: 217–27.

———. 1979. *A History of Boeotia*. Edmonton.

———. 1994. *Boeotia and the Boeotian League, 432–371*. Edmonton.

———. 2008. "Boeotian Federalism." In V. Aravantinos, ed., *Ἐπετηρίς τῆς Ἑταιρείας Βοιωτικῶν Μελετῶν*, vol. IV A, 25–39. Athens.

Buckler, J. 1978. "The Alleged Achaian Arbitration after Leuktra." *SO* 53: 85–96.

———. 1979. "The Re-establishment of the Boiotarchia (378 B.C.)." *AJAH* 4: 50–64.

———. 1980a. "The Alleged Theban-Spartan Alliance of 386 B.C." *Eranos* 78: 179–85.

———. 1980b. *The Theban Hegemony, 371–362 B.C.* Cambridge, Mass.

———. 1985. "Thebes, Delphoi, and the Outbreak of the Third Sacred War." In P. Roesch and G. Argoud, eds., *La Béotie antique, Lyon–Saint-Étienne, 16–20 mai 1983*, 237–46. Paris.

———. 1989. *Philip II and the Sacred War*. Leiden.

———. 1998. "Epameinondas and the New Inscription from Knidos." *Mnemosyne* 51: 192–205.

———. 2000a. "A Survey of Theban and Athenian Relations between 403 and 371 B.C." In P. A. Bernardini, ed., *Presenza e funzione della città di Tebe nella cultura greca: Atti del convegno internazionale, Urbino, 7–9 iuglio 1997*, 319–29. Pisa and Rome.

———. 2000b. "The Phantom *Synedrion* of the Boiotian Confederacy, 378–335 B.C." In P. Flensted-Jensen, T. H. Nielsen, and L. Rubinstein, eds., *Polis and Politics: Studies in Greek History Presented to Mogens Herman Hansen on His Sixtieth Birthday, August 20, 2000*, 431–46. Copenhagen.

———. 2004. "The Incident at Mt. Parnassus, 395 BC." In C. Tuplin, ed., *Xenophon and His World: Papers from a Conference Held in Liverpool in July 1999*, 397–412. Stuttgart.

Buckler, J., and H. Beck. 2008. *Central Greece and the Politics of Power in the Fourth Century BC*. Cambridge.

Bundgaard, J. A. 1946. "À propos de la date de la péristasis du Mégaron B à Thermos." *BCH* 70: 51–57.

Buraselis, K. 1982. *Das hellenistische Makedonien und die Ägäis: Forschungen zur Politik des Kassandros und der drei ersten Antigoniden im ägäischen Meer und in Westkleinasien*. Munich.

————, ed. 1994. *Unity and Units of Antiquity: Papers from a Colloquium at Delphi, 5–8.4.1992.* Athens.

————. 2003. "Considerations on Symmachia and Sympoliteia in the Hellenistic Period." In K. Buraselis and K. Zoumboulakis, eds., *The Idea of European Community in History: Conference Proceedings*, vol. II, *Aspects of Connecting Poleis and Ethnē in Ancient Greece*, 39–50. Athens.

Buraselis, K., and K. Zoumboulakis, eds. 2003. *The Idea of European Community in History: Conference Proceedings*. Vol. II, *Aspects of Connecting Poleis and Ethnē in Ancient Greece*. Athens.

Burkert, W. 1985. *Greek Religion*. Cambridge, Mass.

Burr Carter, J. 1987. "The Masks of Orthia." *AJA* 91: 355–83.

Busolt, G. 1897. *Griechische Geschichte bis zur Schlacht bei Chaironeia*. Vol. III.1, *Die Pentekontaëtie*. Gotha.

————. 1908. "Der neue Historiker und Xenophon." *Hermes* 43: 276–77.

Busolt, G., and H. Swoboda. 1920–26. *Griechische Staatskunde*. Munich.

Buxton, R. G. A. 1992. "Imaginary Greek Mountains." *JHS* 112: 1–15.

————. 1994. *Imaginary Greece: The Contexts of Mythology*. Cambridge.

Cabanes, P. 1976. *L'Épire de la mort de Pyrrhos à la conquête romaine, 272–167 av. J.-C.* Paris.

————. 2004. "L'Épire et le royaume des Molosses à l'époque d'Alexandre le Molosse." In *Alessandro il Molosso e i "Condottieri" in Magna Grecia: Atti del quarantatressimo convegno di studi sulla Magna Grecia, Taranto-Cosenza, 26–30 settembre 2003*, 11–52. Taranto.

Cahill, N. 2002. *Household and City Organization at Olynthus*. New Haven.

Calame, C. 1997. *Choruses of Young Women in Ancient Greece: Their Morphology, Religious Role, and Social Function*. Lanham, Md.

Cameron, A. 1995. *Callimachus and His Critics*. Princeton.

Camia, F. 2009. *Roma e le poleis: L'intervento di Roma nelle controversie territoriali tra le comunità greche di Grecia e d'Asia Minore nel secondo secolo a.C.; Le testimonianze epigrafiche*. Athens.

Camp, J. M. 1974. "Greek Inscriptions." *Hesperia* 43: 314–24.

Campbell, D. A. 1982. *Greek Lyric Poetry: A Selection of Early Greek Lyric, Elegiac and Iambic Poetry*. Bristol.

Cannadine, D. 1987. "Introduction: Divine Rites of Kings." In D. Cannadine and S. Price, eds., *Rituals of Royalty: Power and Ceremonial in Traditional Societies*, 1–19. Cambridge.

Cargill, J. 1981. *The Second Athenian League*. Berkeley and Los Angeles.

Cartledge, P. 1976. "A New 5th-Century Spartan Treaty." *LCM* 1: 87–92.

————. 1979. "The New 5th-Century Spartan Treaty Again." *LCM* 3: 189–90.

Cartledge, P., and A. Spawforth. 2002 [1989]. *Hellenistic and Roman Sparta: A Tale of Two Cities*, 2nd ed. London.

Cary, M. 1924. "The Trial of Epaminondas." *CQ* 18: 182–84.

————. 1925. "The Alleged Achaean Arbitration after Leuctra." *CQ* 19: 165–66.

Cassayre, A. 2010. *La justice dans les cités grecques: De la formation des royaumes hellénistiques au legs d'Attale*. Rennes.

Catling, R. W. V. 2004–9. "Attalid Troops at Thermon: A Reappraisal of *IG* IX 1(2).1.60." *Horos* 17–21: 397–439.

Cawkwell, G. 1961. "The Common Peace of 366/5 B.C." *CQ* 11: 80–86.

———. 1962. "Notes on the Social War." *C&M* 23: 34–49.

———. 1972. "Epaminondas and Thebes." *CQ* 22: 254–78.

———. 1973. "The Foundation of the Second Athenian Confederacy." *CQ* 23: 47–60.

———. 1976. "The Imperialism of Thrasybulus." *CQ* 26: 270–77.

———. 1981. "The King's Peace." *CQ* 31: 69–83.

———. 2005. *The Greek Wars: The Failure of Persia.* Oxford.

Champion, C. 1995. "The Soteria at Delphi: Aetolian Propaganda in the Epigraphical Record." *AJP* 116: 213–20.

———. 1996. "Polybius, Aetolia, and the Gallic Attack on Delphi (279 B.C.)." *Historia* 45: 315–28.

———. 2004. *Cultural Politics in Polybius's Histories.* Berkeley and Los Angeles.

———. 2007. "Polybius and Aetolia: A Historiographical Approach." In J. Marincola, ed., *A Companion to Greek and Roman Historiography*, 356–62. Oxford.

Chandezon, C. 2003. *L' élevage en Grèce (fin V^e-fin Ier s. a.C.): L'apport des sources épigraphiques.* Bordeaux.

Chandezon, C., and V. Krings. 2001. "À propos des Carthaginois en Égée (IVe–IIe siècle av. J.-C.)." In C. Hamdoune, ed., *«Ubique amici»: Mélanges offerts à Jean-Marie Lassère*, 35–53. Montpellier.

Chaniotis, A. 1995. "Problems of 'Pastoralism' and 'Transhumance' in Classical and Hellenistic Crete." *Orbis Terrarum* 1: 39–89.

———. 1996a. "Die kretischen Berge als Wirtschaftsraum." In E. Olshausen and H. Sonnabend, eds., *Stuttgarter Kolloquium zur historischen Geographie des Altertums*, vol. V, *Gebirgsland als Lebensraum*, 255–66. Amsterdam.

———. 1996b. "Von Hirten, Kräutersammlern, Epheben und Pilgern: Leben auf den Bergen im antiken Kreta." In G. Siebert, ed., *Nature et paysage dans la pensée et l'environnement des civilisations antiques: Actes du colloque de Strasbourg, 11–12 juin 1992*, 91–108. Paris.

———. 1999. "Milking the Mountains: Economic Activities on the Cretan Uplands in the Classical and Hellenistic Period." In A. Chaniotis, ed., *From Minoan Farmers to Roman Traders: Sidelights on the Economy of Ancient Crete*, 181–220. Stuttgart.

———. 2002. "Ritual Dynamics: The Boiotian Festival of the Daidala." In H.F.J. Horstmannshoff, H.W. Singor, F.T. van Straten, and J.H.M. Strubbe, eds., *Kykeon: Studies in Honor of H.S. Versnel*, 23–48. Leiden.

———. 2004. "Justifying Territorial Claims in Classical and Hellenistic Greece: The Beginnings of International Law." In E. M. Harris and L. Rubinstein, eds., *The Law and the Courts in Ancient Greece*, 185–228. London.

———. 2005. "Ritual Dynamics in the Eastern Mediterranean: Case Studies in Ancient Greece and Asia Minor." In W.V. Harris, ed., *Rethinking the Mediterranean*, 141–66. Oxford.

Chantraine, H. 1972. "Der Beginn der jüngeren achäischen Bundesprägung." *Chiron* 2: 175–90.

Chapouthier, F. 1935. *Les Dioscures au service d'une déesse: Étude d'iconographie religieuse.* Paris.

Clairmont, C. 1983. *Patrios Nomos: Public Burial in Athens during the Fifth and Fourth Centuries BC; The Archaeological, Epigraphic-Literary and Historical Evidence.* Oxford.

Clark, I. 1998. "The Gamos of Hera: Myth and Ritual." In S. Blundell and M. Williamson, eds., *The Sacred and the Feminine in Ancient Greece,* 13–26. London.

Cloché, P. 1918. "La politique thébaine de 404 à 396 av. J.-C." *REG* 31: 315–43.

———. 1952. *Thèbes de Béotie des origines à la conquête romaine.* Namur.

Cohen, E. E. 1973. *Ancient Athenian Maritime Courts.* Princeton.

———. 1992. *Athenian Economy and Society: A Banking Perspective.* Princeton.

———. 2005. "Commercial Law." In M. Gagarin and D. Cohen, eds., *The Cambridge Companion to Ancient Greek Law,* 290–302. Cambridge.

Consolo Langher, S. N. 2004. "Natura giuridica e valori del federalismo greco: Il conflitto fra autonomia ed egemonia." In S. Cataldi, ed., *Poleis e politeiai: Esperienze politiche, tradizioni letterarie, progetti costituzionali; Atti del convegno internazionale di storia greca, Torino, 29–31 maggio 2002,* 315–33. Alexandria.

Cook, R. M. 1970. "The Archetypal Doric Temple." *ABSA* 65: 17–19.

Cooper, F. A. 2000. "The Fortifications of Epaminondas and the Rise of the Monumental Greek City." In J. D. Tracy, ed., *City Walls: The Urban Enceinte in Global Perspective,* 155–91. Cambridge.

Corsten, T. 1999. *Von Stamm zum Bund: Gründung und territoriale Organisation griechischer Bundesstaaten.* Munich.

———. 2000. "Stammeskult und Bundeskult: Die einigende Rolle der Religion am Beispiel Akarnaniens." *Achelöos* 2: 17–32.

———. 2006. "Stammes- und Bundeskulte in Akarnanien." In K. Freitag, P. Funke, and M. Haake, eds., *Kult—Politik—Ethnos: Überregionale Heiligtümer im Spannungsfeld von Kult und Politik,* 157–68. Stuttgart.

Corvisier, J.-N., and W. Suder. 2000. *La population de l'antiquité classique.* Paris.

Costabile, F. 1992. *Polis ed Olympieion a Locri Epizefiri: Costituzione, economia e finanze di una città della Magna Graecia; Editio altera e traduzione delle tabelle locresi.* Catanzaro.

Cottier, M., M. H. Crawford, C. V. Crowther, et al., eds. 2008. *The Customs Law of Asia.* Oxford.

Cozzoli, U. 1985. "Sul nuovo documento di alleanza tra Sparta e gli Etoli." In F. Broilo, ed., *Xenia: Scritti in onore di Piero Treves,* 67–76. Rome.

Crawford, M. 1970. "Money and Exchange in the Roman World." *JRS* 60: 40–48.

Crowther, C. 1995. "Iasos in the Second Century BC, III: Foreign Judges from Priene." *BICS* 91–136.

Crugnola, A. 1971. *Scholia in Nicandri Theriaka.* Milan.

D'Alessio, G. B. 1997. "Pindar's *Prosodia* and the Classification of Pindaric Papyrus Fragments." *ZPE* 118: 23–60.

———. 2005. "Il primo *Inno* di Pindaro." In S. Grandolini, ed., *Lirica e teatro in Grecia: Il testo e la sua ricezione; Atti del II incontro di studi, Perugia, 23–24 gennaio 2003,* 113–49. Naples.

———. 2009a. "Defining Local Identities in Greek Lyric Poetry." In R. L. Hunter and I. Rutherford, eds., *Wandering Poets in Ancient Greek Culture: Travel, Locality and Pan-Hellenism,* 137–67. Cambridge.

———. 2009b. "Reconstructing Pindar's *First Hymn:* The Theban "Theogony" and the Birth of Apollo." In L. Athanassaki, R. P. Martin, and J. F. Miller, eds., *Apolline Poetics and Politics: Proceedings of a Conference Held at Delphi, 4–11 July 2003,* 129–47. Athens.

Dany, O. 1999. *Akarnanien im Hellenismus: Geschichte und Völkerrecht in Nordwestgriechen-land*. Munich.

Daux, G. 1932. "Notes étoliennes." *BCH* 56: 313–30.

———. 1936. *Delphes au IIe et au Ier siècle*. Paris.

Daverio Rocchi, G. 1988. *Frontiera e confini nella Grecia antica*. Rome.

———. 1993. *Città-stato e stati federali della Grecia classica: Lineamenti di storia delle istituz-ioni politiche*. Milan.

Davidson, J. 1997. *Courtesans and Fishcakes: The Consuming Passions of Classical Athens*. London.

Davies, J. K. 1994. "The Tradition about the First Sacred War." In S. Hornblower, ed., *Greek Historiography*, 193–212. Oxford.

———. 1998. "Ancient Economies: Models and Muddles." In H. Parkins and C. Smith, eds., *Trade, Traders, and the Ancient City*, 225–56. London.

———. 2000. "A Wholly Non-Aristotelian Universe: The Molossians as Ethnos, State and Monarchy." In R. Brock and S. Hodkinson, eds., *Alternatives to Athens: Varieties of Polit-ical Organization and Community in Ancient Greece*, 234–58. Oxford.

Dawkins, R. M., ed. 1929. *The Sanctuary of Artemis Orthia*. London.

De Figueiredo, R. J. P., and B. Weingast. 2005. "Self-Enforcing Federalism." *Journal of Law, Economics, and Organization* 21: 103–35.

de Franciscis, A. 1972. *Stato e società in Locri Epizefiri: L'archivio dell'Olympieion locrese*. Naples.

de Laix, R. A. 1973. "The Silver Coinage of the Aetolian League." *CSCA* 6: 47–75.

de Ligt, L. 1993. *Fairs and Markets in the Roman Empire*. Amsterdam.

de Sanctis, G. 1930. "I molpi di Mileto." In *Studi in onore di P. Bonfante*, 671–79. Pavia.

de Schutter, H. 2011. "Federalism as Fairness." *Journal of Political Philosophy* 19: 167–89.

de Souza, P. 1999. *Piracy in the Graeco-Roman World*. Cambridge.

Debord, P. 2003. "Cité grecque—village carien: Des usages du mot *koinon*." In B. Virgilio, ed., *Studi ellenistici* 15: 115–80. Pisa.

Deininger, J. 1971. *Der politische Widerstand gegen Rom in Griechenland, 217–86 v. Chr*. Berlin.

Demakopoulou, K., and D. Konsola. 1981. *Archaeological Museum of Thebes: Guide*. Athens.

Demand, N. H. 1982. *Thebes in the Fifth Century: Heracles Resurgent*. London.

———. 1990. *Urban Relocation in Archaic and Classical Greece*. Norman and London.

Demandt, A. 1995. *Antike Staatsformen: Eine vergleichende Verfassungsgeschichte der Alten Welt*. Berlin.

Derks, T., and N. Roymans, eds. 2009. *Ethnic Constructs in Antiquity: The Role of Power and Tradition*. Amsterdam.

Diehl, E. 1949–52. *Anthologia Lyrica Graeca*. 3 vols. Leipzig.

Dietz, S., L. Kolonas, S. Houby-Nielsen, and I. Moschos. 2000. "Greek-Danish Excavations in Aetolian Chalkis, 1997–1998: Second Preliminary Report." *Proceedings of the Danish Institute at Athens* 3: 219–307.

Dietz, S., L. Kolonas, I. Moschos, and S. Houby-Nielsen. 1998. "Surveys and Excavations in Chalkis, Aetolia, 1995–1996: First Preliminary Report." *Proceedings of the Danish Institute at Athens* 2: 233–317.

Dietz, S., L. Kolonas, I. Moschos, and M. Stavropoulou-Gatsi. 2007. "Archaeological Fieldwork in Ancient Kalydon, 2001–2004: First Preliminary Report." *Proceedings of the Danish Institute at Athens* 5: 35–60.

Dietz, S., and M. Stavropoulou-Gatsi. 2009. "Archaeological Fieldwork in Ancient Kalydon 2005: Second Preliminary Report." *Proceedings of the Danish Institute at Athens* 6: 161–66.

Dignas, B. 2002. *The Economy of the Sacred in Hellenistic and Roman Asia Minor.* Oxford.

Dillery, J. 1995. *Xenophon and the History of His Times.* London.

Dillon, M. P. J. 1994. "The Didactic Nature of the Epidaurian Iamata." *ZPE* 101: 239–60.

DiMaggio, P. J., and W. W. Powell. 1991. *The New Institutionalism in Organization Analysis.* Chicago.

Dinsmoor, W. B. 1980. *The Propylaia to the Athenian Akropolis.* Vol. I: *The Predecessors.* Princeton.

Dixon, M. D. 2000. "Disputed Territories: Interstate Arbitrations in the Northeast Peloponnese, ca. 250–150 B.C." Ph.D. dissertation, History, The Ohio State University, Columbus.

———. 2003. "Hellenistic Arbitration: The Achaian League and Ptolemaic Arsinoë." In E. Konsolaki, ed., *ΑΡΓΟΣΑΡΩΝΙΚΟΣ· Πρακτικά του διεθνούς συνεδρίου ιστορίας και αρχαιολογίας του Αργοσαρονικού, Πόρος, 26–29 ιουνίου 1998*, 81–87. Athens.

———. 2005. "Epigraphy and Topographical Survey: The Case of the Corinthian-Epidaurian Border in the Hellenistic Period." In N. M. Kennell and J. Tomlinson, eds., *Ancient Greece at the Turn of the Millennium: Recent Work and Future Perspectives; Proceedings of the Athens Symposium*, 137–45. Athens.

Domingo Gygax, M. 2001. *Untersuchungen zu den lykischen Gemeinwesen in klassischer und hellenistischer Zeit.* Bonn.

Doorn, P. K., and S. Bommeljé. 1990. "Transhumance in Aetolia, Central Greece: A Mountain Economy Caught between Storage and Mobility." *Rivista di studi liguri* 56: 81–97.

Dörig, J. 1962. "Lysippe und Iphianassa." *MDAI(A)* 71: 72–92.

———. 1977. *Onatas of Aegina.* Leiden.

Dreher, M. 2003. "*Symmachia* und *sympoliteia* in der griechischen Welt bis 323 v. Chr." In K. Buraselis and K. Zoumboulakis, eds., *The Idea of European Community in History: Conference Proceedings*, vol. II, *Aspects of Connecting Poleis and Ethnē in Ancient Greece*, 27–38. Athens.

Drerup, H. 1969. *Griechische Baukunst in geometrischer Zeit.* Göttingen.

Ducat, J. 1964. "Le Ptoion et l'histoire de la Béotie a l'époque archaïque: À propos d'un livre récent." *REG* 77: 283–90.

———. 1971. *Les kouroi du Ptoion.* Paris.

———. 1973. "La confédération béotienne et l'expansion thébaine à l'époque archaïque." *BCH* 97: 59–73.

Ducrey, P. 1999. "Une base de statue portant la signature de Lysippe de Sicyone à Thèbes." *CRAI*: 7–20.

Ducrey, P., and C. Calame. 2006. "Notes de sculpture et d'épigraphie en Béotie, II: Une base de statue portant la signature de Lysippe de Sicyone à Thèbes." *BCH* 130: 63–81.

Dull, C. J. 1977. "Thucydides I.113 and the Leadership of Orchomenos." *CP* 72: 305–14.

———. 1985. "A Reassessment of the Boiotian Districts." In J.M. Fossey and H. Giroux, eds., *Proceedings of the Third International Conference on Boiotian Antiquities*, 33–40. Amsterdam.

Dumke, R. 1984. "Der deutsche Zollverein als Modell ökonomischer Integration." In H. Berding, ed., *Wirtschaftliche und politische Integration in Europa im 19. und 20. Jahrhundert*, 71–101. Göttingen.

Durkheim, E. 1915 [1947]. *The Elementary Forms of Religious Life: A Study in Religious Sociology*. Glencoe.

Dyggve, E., and F. Poulsen. 1948. *Das Laphrion, der Tempelbezirk von Kalydon*. Copenhagen.

Ebert, J. 1972. *Griechische Epigramme auf Sieger an gymnischen und hippischen Agonen*. Berlin.

Ebert, J., and P. Siewert. 1997. "Eine archaische Bronzeurkunde aus Olympia mit Vorschriften für Ringkämpfer und Kampfrichter." In J. Ebert, ed., *Agonismata: Kleine philologische Schriften zur Literatur, Geschichte und Kultur der Antike*, 200–236. Stuttgart.

———. 1999. "Eine archaische Bronzeurkunde aus Olympia mit Vorschriften für Ringkämpfer und Kampfrichter." In A. Mallwitz and K. Herrmann, eds., *Bericht über die Ausgrabungen in Olympia*, vol. XI, 391–412. Berlin.

Eckstein, A.M. 2006. *Mediterranean Anarchy, Interstate War, and the Rise of Rome*. Berkeley and Los Angeles.

Eckstein, F. 1969. *ΑΝΑΘΗΜΑΤΑ· Studien zu den Weihgeschenken strengen Stils im Heiligtum von Olympia*. Berlin.

Edwards, A. T. 2004. *Hesiod's Ascra*. Berkeley and Los Angeles.

Edwards, G. P. 1971. *The Language of Hesiod in Its Traditional Context*. Oxford.

Ehrenberg, V. 1960. *The Greek State*. Oxford.

Eich, A. 2006. *Die politische Ökonomie des antiken Griechenland (6.–3. Jahrhundert v. Chr.)*. Cologne.

Einhorn, R. L. 2006a. *American Taxation, American Slavery*. Chicago.

———. 2006b. "Institutional Reality in the Age of Slavery: Taxation and Democracy in the States." *Journal of Policy History* 18: 21–43.

Ellinger, P. 1987. "Hyampolis et la sanctuaire d'Artémis Elaphébolos dans l'histoire, la légende et l'espace de la Phocide." *AA*: 88–99.

Elwyn, S. 1990. "The Recognition Decrees for the Delphian Soteria and the Date of Smyrna's Inviolability." *JHS* 110: 177–80.

Errington, R. M. 1969. *Philopoemen*. Oxford.

Erxleben, E. 1975. "Die Kleruchien auf Euböa und Lesbos und die Methoden der attischen Herrschaft im 5. Jh." *Klio* 57: 83–100.

Étienne, R., and D. Knoepfler. 1976. *Hyettos de Béotie et la chronologie des archontes fédéraux entre 250 et 171 avant J.-C.* Paris.

Étienne, R., and P. Roesch. 1978. "Convention militaire entre les cavaliers d'Orchomène et ceux de Chéronée." *BCH* 102: 359–74.

Faraguna, M. 1995. "Note di storia milesia arcaica: I Γέργιθες e la στάσις di VI secolo." *SMEA* 36: 37–89.

———. 2005. "La figura dell'aisymnetes tra realtà storica e teoria politica." In R. W. Wallace and M. Gagarin, eds., *Symposion 2001: Vorträge zur griechischen und hellenistischen Rechtsgeschichte*, 321–38. Vienna.

Farinetti, E. 2008. "Orchomenos in the Archaic Period: A Pathway Towards a *Polis* Model." In V. Aravantinos, ed., *Επετηρίς της Εταιρείας Βοιωτικών Μελετών*, vol. IVA, 279–91. Athens.

Ferejohn, J., and B. R. Weingast, eds. 1997. *The New Federalism: Can the States Be Trusted?* Stanford.

Ferrary, J.-L. 1988. *Philhellénisme et impérialisme: Aspects idéologiques de la conquête romaine du monde hellénistique, de la seconde guerre de Macédoine à la guerre contre Mithridate.* Rome.

Feyel, C. 2006. *Les artisans dans les sanctuaires grecs aux époques classique et hellénistique à travers la documentation financière en Grèce.* Paris.

———. 2007. "Le monde du travail à travers les comptes de construction des grands sanctuaires grecs." *Pallas* 74: 77–92.

Feyel, M. 1936a. "Études d'épigraphie béotienne." *BCH* 60: 175–83, 389–415.

———. 1936b. "Nouvelles inscriptions d'Akraiphia." *BCH* 60: 11–36.

———. 1937. "Études d'épigraphie béotienne." *BCH* 61: 217–35.

———. 1942a. *Contribution à l'épigraphie béotienne.* Le Puy.

———. 1942b. *Polybe et l'histoire de Béotie au IIIe siècle avant notre ère.* Paris.

Fick, A. 1880. "Die neu aufgefundenen Inschriften von Dyme (Achaja)." *Beiträge zur Kunde der indogermanischen Sprachen* 5: 320–25.

Figueira, T. J. 1999. "The Evolution of the Messenian Identity." In S. Hodkinson and A. Powell, eds., *Sparta: New Perspectives*, 211–44. London.

Fine, J. V. A. 1932. "The Problem of Macedonian Holdings in Epirus and Thessaly in 221 B.C." *TAPA* 63: 126–55.

———. 1940. "The Background of the Social War of 220–217 B.C." *AJP* 61: 129–65.

Finley, M. I. 1985. *The Ancient Economy.* London.

Fischer, W. 1960. "The German *Zollverein*: A Case Study in Customs Union." *Kyklos* 13: 65–89.

Flacelière, R. 1930. "Les rapports de l'Aitolie et de la Béotie de 301 à 278 av. J.-C." *BCH* 54: 75–94.

———. 1937. *Les Aitoliens à Delphes.* Paris.

Flensted-Jensen, P., and M. H. Hansen. 1996. "Pseudo-Skylax' Use of the Term *Polis*." In M. H. Hansen and K. Raaflaub, eds., *More Studies in the Ancient Greek Polis*, 137–67. Stuttgart.

Forbes, H. A. 1994. "Pastoralism and Settlement Structures in Ancient Greece." In P. N. Doukellis and L G. Mendoni, eds., *Structures rurales et sociétés antiques: Actes du colloque de Corfou, 14–16 mai 1992*, 187–96. Paris.

Forrest, W. G. 1956. "The First Sacred War." *BCH* 80: 33–52.

Fossey, J. M. 1971. "Early Boiotian Temples." *AJA* 75: 201.

———. 1981–82. "The City Archive at Koroneia, Boiotia." *Euphrosyne* 11: 44–59.

———. 1988. *Topography and Population of Ancient Boiotia.* Chicago.

———. 1990. *The Ancient Topography of Opountian Lokris.* Amsterdam.

———. 1994. "Boiotian Decrees of Proxenia." In J. M. Fossey, ed., *Boeotia Antiqua*, 35–59. Amsterdam.

Fossey, J. M., and G. Gauvin. 1985. "Les fortifications de l'acropole de Chéronée." In J. M. Fossey and H. Giroux, eds., *Proceedings of the Third International Conference on Boiotian Antiquities*, 41–75. Amsterdam.

Fouache, E. 1999. *L'alluvionnement historique en Grèce occidentale et au Péloponnèse: Géo-morphologie, archéologie, histoire.* Athens.

———. 2000. "Les preuves géomorphologiques de la mobilité historique du delta de l'Achéloos." In A. D. Rizakis, ed., *Paysages d'Achaïe, II, Dymé et son territoire: Actes du colloque international; Dymaia et Bouprasia, Katô Achaïa, 6–8 octobre 1995,* 21–30. Athens and Paris.

Foucart, P. 1876. "Fragment inédit d'un décret de la Ligue achéenne." *RA* 32: 96–103.

———. 1883. "Décrets des amphictionies de Delphes." *BCH* 7: 409–39.

Fowler, B. 1957. "Thucydides I.107–8 and the Tanagran Federal Issues." *Phoenix* 11: 164–70.

Foxhall, L. 1992. "The Control of the Attic Landscape." In B. Wells, ed., *Agriculture in Ancient Greece: Proceedings of the Seventh International Symposium at the Swedish Institute at Athens, 16–17 May 1990,* 155–59. Stockholm.

———. 2002. "Access to Resources in Classical Greece: The Egalitarianism of the Polis in Practice." In P. Cartledge, E. E. Cohen, and L. Foxhall, eds., *Money, Labour and Land: Approaches to the Economies of Ancient Greece,* 209–20. London.

Fraser, P. M. 1954. "Review of Lerat, *Les Locriens de l'Ouest.*" *Gnomon* 26: 246–56.

Frazer, J. G. 1921. *Apollodorus: The Library.* London.

Freeman, E. A. 1893. *History of Federal Government in Greece and Italy.* London.

Freitag, K. 1996. "Eine vergessene Notiz zur Geschichte Achaias im 5. Jahrhundert v. Chr. bei Herodot (8,36,2)." *Historia* 45: 124–26.

———. 2000. *Der Golf von Korinth: Historisch-topographische Untersuchungen von der Archaik bis in das 1. Jh. v. Chr.* Munich.

———. 2006. "Ein Schiedsvertrag zwischen Halos und Thebai aus Delphi." In K. Freitag, P. Funke, and M. Haake, eds., *Kult—Politik—Ethnos: Überregionale Heiligtümer im Spannungsfeld von Kult und Politik,* 211–38. Stuttgart.

———. 2009. "Achaea and the Peloponnese in the Late Fifth–Early Fourth Centuries." In P. Funke and N. Luraghi, eds., *The Politics of Ethnicity and the Crisis of the Peloponnesian League,* 15–29. Cambridge, Mass.

Freitag, K., P. Funke, and M. Haake, eds. 2006. *Kult—Politik—Ethnos: Überregionale Heiligtümer im Spannungsfeld von Kult und Politik.* Stuttgart.

Freitag, K., P. Funke, and N. Moustakis. 2004. "Aitolia." In M. H. Hansen and T. H. Nielsen, eds., *An Inventory of Archaic and Classical Poleis,* 379–90. Oxford.

Fried, M. H. 1968. "On the Concepts of 'Tribe' and 'Tribal Society.'" In J. Helm, ed., *Essays on the Problem of Tribe: Proceedings of the 1967 Annual Spring Meeting of the American Ethnological Society,* 3–20. Seattle and London.

———. 1975. *The Notion of Tribe.* Menlo Park.

Friedlaender, J. 1861a. "A Coin of Helike." *NC,* n.s., 1: 216–17.

———. 1861b. "Eine Münze von Helice." *Archäologische Zeitung* 18: 163–66.

Frier, B., and D. P. Kehoe. 2007. "Law and Economic Institutions." In W. Scheidel, I. Morris, and R. P. Saller, eds., *The Cambridge Economic History of the Greco-Roman World,* 113–43. Cambridge.

Frontisi-Ducroux, F. 1975. *Dédale: Mythologie de l'artisan en grèce ancienne.* Paris.

Fuks, A. 1970. "The Bellum Achaicum and Its Social Aspect." *JHS* 90: 78–89.

Funke, P. 1980. *Homónoia und Arché: Athen und die griechische Staatenwelt vom Ende des peloponnesischen Krieges bis zum Königsfrieden (404/3–387/6 v. Chr.).* Wiesbaden.

———. 1985. *Untersuchungen zur Geschichte und Struktur des aitolischen Bundes.* Habilitationsschrift, Cologne.

———. 1987. "Zur Datierungen befestigter Stadtanlagen in Aitolien." *Boreas* 10: 87–96.

———. 1991. "Zur Ausbildung städtischer Siedlungszentren in Aitolien." In E. Olshausen and H. Sonnabend, eds., *Raum und Bevölkerung in der antiken Stadtkultur,* 313–32. Bonn.

———. 1993. "Stamm und Polis." In J. Bleicken, ed., *Colloquium aus Anlaß des 80. Geburtstages von Alfred Heuß,* 29–48. Kallmünz.

———. 1997. "Polisgenese und Urbanisierung in Aitolien im 5. und 4. Jh. v. Chr." In M. H. Hansen, ed., *The Polis as an Urban Centre and as a Political Community: Symposium, August 29–31, 1996,* 145–88. Copenhagen.

———. 1998. "Die Bedeutung der griechischen Bundesstaaten in der politischen Theorie und Praxis des 5. und 4. Jh. v. Chr.: Auch eine Anmerkung zu Aristot. *Pol.* 1261a22–29." In W. Schuller, ed., *Politische Theorie und Praxis im Altertum,* 59–71. Darmstadt.

———. 2008. "Die Aitoler in der Ägais: Untersuchungen zur sogenannten Seepolitik der Aitoler im 3. Jh. v. Chr." In E. Winter, ed., *Vom Euphrat bis zum Bosporus: Kleinasien in der Antike; Festschrift für Elmar Schwertheim zum 65. Geburtstag,* vol. I, 253–67. Bonn.

Funke, P., and N. Luraghi, eds. 2009. *The Politics of Ethnicity and the Crisis of the Peloponnesian League.* Washington, D.C.

Fustel de Coulanges, N. D. 1980 [1864]. *The Ancient City: A Study on the Religion, Laws, and Institutions of Greece and Rome.* Baltimore.

Gabrielsen, V. 2005. "Banking and Credit Operations in Hellenistic Times." In Z. H. Archibald, J. K. Davies, and V. Gabrielsen, eds., *Making, Moving, and Managing: The New World of Ancient Economies, 323–31 BC,* 136–64. Oxford.

Gadolou, A. 1996–97. "Χάλκινα και σιδερένια όπλα από το ιερό Άνω Μαζαράκι (Ρακίτα) Αχαΐας." In *Πρακτικά του Ε΄ διεθνούς συνεδρίου πελοποννησιακών σπουδών,* vol. II, 51–72.

———. 2000. "Η Αχαΐα στους πρώιμους ιστορικούς χρόνους· Κεραμεική παραγωγή και έθιμα ταφής." Doctoral dissertation, University of Athens.

———. 2002. "The Pottery Fabrics and Workshops from Ano Mazaraki: The 1979 Excavation Season." In E. Greco, ed., *Gli Achei e l'identità degli Achei d'occidente,* 165–204. Paestum and Athens.

———. 2003. "Achaean Pottery of the Late Geometric Period: The Impressed Ware Workshop." *ABSA* 98: 307–29.

Gagarin, M. 1974. "Hesiod's Dispute with Perses." *TAPA* 104: 103–11.

Gaheis, A. 1902. "Das Proxeniedekret des Kapon." *Wiener Studien* 24: 279–82.

Gallant, T. 1985. *A Fisherman's Tale.* Ghent.

———. 1991. *Risk and Survival in Ancient Greece: Reconstructing the Rural Domestic Economy.* Stanford.

Gallavotti, C. 1985. "Revisione di testi epigrafici." *BollClass* 6: 28–57.

Game, J. 2008. *Actes de vente dans le monde grec: Témoignages épigraphiques des ventes immobilières.* Lyon.

Garlan, Y. 1965. "Études d'histoire militaire et diplomatique, I–IV." *BCH* 89: 332–48.

———. 1969. "Études d'histoire militaire et diplomatique, V: À propos des «Griechische Mauerbauinschriften» de F. G. Maier." *BCH* 93: 152–61.

Garnsey, P. 1985. "Grain for Athens." In P. Cartledge and F. D. Harvey, eds., *Crux: Essays Presented to G. E. M. de Ste Croix on His 75th Birthday*, 62–75. Exeter.

———. 1988. *Famine and Food Supply in the Graeco-Roman World: Responses to Risk and Crisis.* Cambridge.

Garnsey, P., T. Gallant, and D. Rathbone. 1984. "Thessaly and the Grain Supply of Rome during the Second Century BC." *JRS* 74: 30–44.

Garnsey, P., and D. Rathbone. 1985. "The Background to the Grain Law of Gaius Gracchus." *JRS* 75: 20–25.

Gauthier, P. 1972. *Symbola: Les étrangers et la justice des cités grecques.* Nancy.

———. 1982. "Les villes athéniennes et un décret pour un commerçant (*IG* II² 903)." *REG* 95: 275–90.

———. 1985. *Les cités grecques et leurs bienfaiteurs.* Paris.

Geertz, C. 1980. *Negara: The Theatre State in Nineteenth-Century Bali.* Princeton.

Gehrke, H.-J. 1980. "Zur Geschichte Milets in der Mitte des 5. Jahrhunderts v. Chr." *Historia* 29: 20–24.

———. 1985. *Stasis: Untersuchungen zu den inneren Kriegen in den griechischen Staaten des 5. und 4. Jahrhunderts v. Chr.* Munich.

Gercke, P. 1975. "Die Weihgeschenke aus dem Bothros." In U. Jantzen, ed., *Führer durch Tiryns*, 159–61. Athens.

Giangiulio, M. 1989. *Ricerche su Crotone arcaica.* Pisa.

Giddens, A. 1984. *The Constitution of Society.* Cambridge.

Giovannini, A. 1969. "Polybe et les assemblées achéennes." *MH* 26: 7–15.

———. 1971. *Untersuchungen über die Natur und die Anfänge der bundesstaatlichen Sympolitie in Griechenland.* Göttingen.

Girard, P. 1887. "Inscriptions de Béotie." *BCH* 1: 208–11.

Gitti, A. 1939. "I perieci di Sparta e le origini del Κοινὸν τῶν Λακεδαιμονίων." *RAL* 15: 189–203.

Glotz, G. 1908. "Le conseil fédéral des Béotiens." *BCH* 32: 271–78.

———. 1925–41. *Histoire grecque.* 4 vols. Paris.

———. 1933. "Un Carthaginois à Thebes en 365 av. J.-C." In *Mélanges offerts à M. Nicolas Iorga par ses amis de France et des pays de langue française*, 331–39. Paris.

Gómez Espelosín, F.-J. 1989. "Estrategía política y supervivencia: Consideraciones sobre una valoración histórica del fenómeno etolio en el siglo III a. de C." *Polis* 1: 63–80.

Gomme, A. W., A. Andrewes, and K. J. Dover. 1945–81. *A Historical Commentary on Thucydides.* 5 vols. Oxford.

González, J. P. 2006. "Poleis and Confederacy in Boiotia in the Early Fourth Century B.C." *Ancient World* 37: 22–45.

Gottschalk, H. B. 1980. *Heraclides of Pontus.* Oxford.

Gould, S. J. 1985. *The Flamingo's Smile: Reflections in Natural History.* New York.

Graeber, A. 1992. "Friedensvorstellung und Friedensbegriff bei den Griechen bis zum peloponnesischen Krieg." *ZRG* 19: 116–62.

Graham, A. J. 1983. *Colony and Mother City in Ancient Greece.* Chicago.

Grainger, J. D. 1995. "The Expansion of the Aetolian League, 280–260 B.C." *Mnemosyne* 48: 313–43.

———. 1999. *The League of the Aitolians*. Leiden.

Grandjean, C. 2000. "Guerre et monnaie en Grèce ancienne: Le cas du *koinon* achaïen." In J. Andreau, P. Briant, and R. Descat, eds., *Économie antique: La guerre dans les economies antiques*, 315–36. Saint-Bertrand-de-Comminges.

Graninger, C D. 2011. *Cult and Koinon in Hellenistic Thessaly*. Leiden.

Granovetter, M. 1985. "Economic Action and Social Structure: The Problem of Embeddedness." *American Journal of Sociology* 91: 481–510.

Green, P. 2006. *Diodorus Siculus, Books 11–12.37.1: Greek History, 480–431 B.C.; The Alternative Version*. Austin.

Greif, A. 1989. "Reputation and Coalitions in Medieval Trade: Evidence on the Maghribi Traders." *Journal of Economic History* 49: 857–882.

———. 1993. "Contract Enforceability and Economic Institutions in Early Trade: The Maghribi Traders' Coalition." *American Economic Review* 83: 525–48.

———. 1998. "Self-Enforcing Political Systems and Economic Growth: Late Medieval Genoa." In R. H. Bates, A. Greif, M. Levi, J.-L. Rosenthal, and B. Weingast, eds., *Analytic Narratives*, 23–63. Princeton.

———. 2006. *Institutions and the Path to the Modern Economy: Lessons from Medieval Trade*. Cambridge.

Greif, A., P. Milgrom, and B. R. Weingast. 1994. "Coordination, Commitment, and Enforcement: The Case of the Merchant Guild." *Journal of Political Economy* 102: 745–76.

Grenfell, B. P., and A. S. Hunt, eds. 1904. *The Oxyrhynchus Papyri*. Part IV. London.

———. 1908. *The Oxyrhynchus Papyri*. Part V. London.

Grose, S. W. 1926. *Fitzwilliam Museum: Catalogue of the McClean Collection of Greek Coins; Vol. 2, The Greek Mainland, the Aegean Islands, Crete*. Cambridge.

Grote, G. 1906. *A History of Greece*. London.

Gruber, L. 2000. *Ruling the World: Power Politics and the Rise of Supranational Institutions*. Princeton.

Gruen, E. S. 1972. "Aratus and the Achaean Alliance with Macedon." *Historia* 21: 609–25.

———. 1976. "The Origins of the Achaean War." *JHS* 96: 46–69.

———. 1984. *The Hellenistic World and the Coming of Rome*. Berkeley and Los Angeles.

Gschnitzer, F. 1954. "Namen und Wesen der thessalischen Tetraden." *Hermes* 82: 451–64.

———. 1955. "Stammes- und Ortsgemeinden im alten Griechenland." *Wiener Studien* 68: 120–44.

———. 1978. *Ein neuer spartanischer Staatsvertrag und die Verfassung des peloponnesischen Bundes*. Meisenheim am Glan.

———. 1985. "Die Nomographen Liste von Epidauros (*IG* IV.12, 73) und der achäische Bund im späten 3. Jh. v. Chr." *ZPE* 58: 103–16.

Guarducci, M. 1929. "Poeti vaganti e conferenzieri dell'età ellenistica: Ricerche di epigrafia greca nel campo della letterature e del costume." *MAL* 6: 627–65.

———. 1969. *Epigrafia greca*. Vol. II, *Epigrafi di carattere pubblico*. Rome.

Guillon, P. 1943. *Les trépieds du Ptoion*. Paris.

———. 1962. "Offrandes et dédicaces du Ptoion." *BCH* 86: 569–77.

———. 1963. *Le Bouclier d'Héraclès et l'histoire de la Grèce centrale dans la période de la première guerre sacrée*. Aix and Marseille.

Guizzi, F. 1999. "Private Economic Activities in Hellenistic Crete: The Evidence of the *Isopoliteia* Treaties." In A. Chaniotis, ed., *From Minoan Farmers to Roman Traders: Sidelights on the Economy of Ancient Crete*, 235–45. Stuttgart.

Gullath, B. 1982. *Untersuchungen zur Geschichte Boiotiens in der Zeit Alexanders und der Diadochen.* Frankfurt.

———. 1989. "Veränderungen der Territorien boiotischer Städte zu Beginn der hellenistischen Zeit am Beispeil Thebens." In H. Beister and J. Buckler, eds., *Boiotika: Vorträge vom 5. internationalen Böotien-Kolloquium zu Ehren von Professor Dr. Siegfried Lauffer*, 163–68. Munich.

Habicht, C. 1957. "Eine Urkunde des akarnanischen Bundes." *Hermes* 85: 86–122.

———. 1970. *Gottmenschentum und die griechische Städte.* Munich.

———. 1979. *Untersuchungen zur politischen Geschichte Athens im 3. Jahrhundert v. Chr.* Munich.

———. 1987. "Fremde Richter im ätolischen Delphi?" *Chiron* 17: 87–95.

———. 1993. "Proxeniedekrete von Akraiphia." *Grazer Beiträge* 19: 39–43.

———. 1997. *Athens from Alexander to Antony.* Trans. Deborah Lucas Schneider. Cambridge, Mass.

———. 1998. *Pausanias' Guide to Ancient Greece.* Berkeley and Los Angeles.

Hackens, T. 1969. "La circulation monétaire dans la Béotie hellénistique: Trésors de Thèbes 1935 et 1965." *BCH* 93: 701–29.

Hainsworth, J. B. 1972. *Tituli ad Dialectos Graecas Illustrandas Selecti.* Leiden.

Hall, J. M. 1995. "How Argive Was the 'Argive' Heraion? The Political and Cultic Geography of the Argive Plain, 900–400 B.C." *AJA* 99: 577–613.

———. 1997. *Ethnic Identity in Ancient Greece.* Cambridge.

———. 2002. *Hellenicity: Between Ethnicity and Culture.* Chicago.

Hall, P. A., and R. C. R. Taylor. 1996. "Political Science and the Three New Institutionalisms." *Political Studies* 44: 936–57.

Halstead, P., and J. O'Shea, eds. 1989. *Bad Year Economics: Cultural Responses to Risk and Uncertainty.* Cambridge.

Hamilton, A., J. Jay, and J. Madison. 1937 [1788]. *The Federalist: A Commentary on the Constitution of the United States.* New York.

Hammond, N. G. L. 1967. *A History of Greece to 322 BC.* Oxford.

———. 1976. *Migrations and Invasions in Greece and Adjacent Areas.* Park Ridge, N.J.

———. 1986. *A History of Greece.* Oxford.

Hammond, N. G. L., G. T. Griffith, and F. W. Walbank. 1972–88. A *History of Macedonia.* 3 vols. Oxford.

Hampl, F. 1935. "Olynth und der chalkidische Staat." *Hermes* 70: 177–96.

Hansen, M. H. 1995a. "Boiotian *Poleis*: A Test Case." In M. H. Hansen, ed., *Sources for the Ancient Greek City-State*, 13–63. Copenhagen.

———. 1995b. "The 'Autonomous City-State': Ancient Fact or Modern Fiction?" In M. H. Hansen and K. Raaflaub, eds., *Studies in the Ancient Greek Polis*, 21–43. Stuttgart.

———. 1996. "Were the Boiotian *Poleis* Deprived of Their *Autonomia* during the First and Second Boiotian Federations? A Reply." In M. H. Hansen and K. Raaflaub, eds., *More Studies in the Ancient Greek Polis*, 127–36. Stuttgart.

———. 1997a. "A Note on the Classification of Aigition as a *Polis*." In M. H. Hansen, ed., *The Polis as an Urban Centre and as a Political Community: Symposium, August 29–31 1996*, 173–75. Copenhagen.

————. 1997b. "A Typology of Dependent *Poleis*." In T. H. Nielsen, ed., *Yet More Studies in the Ancient Greek Polis*, 29–37. Stuttgart.

————. 2000a. "A Survey of the Use of *Polis* in Archaic and Classical Sources." In P. Flensted-Jensen, ed., *Further Studies in the Ancient Greek Polis*, 173–215. Stuttgart.

————. 2000b. "Aristotle's Reference to the Arkadian Federation at *Pol.* 1261a29." In T. H. Nielsen and J. Roy, eds., *Defining Ancient Arkadia*, 80–88. Copenhagen.

————. 2004. "Boiotia." In M. H. Hansen and T. H. Nielsen, eds., *An Inventory of Archaic and Classical Poleis*, 431–61. Oxford.

Hansen, M. H., and T. H. Nielsen, eds. 2004. *An Inventory of Archaic and Classical Poleis:. An Investigation Conducted by the Copenhagen Polis Centre for the Danish National Research Foundation.* Oxford.

Hanson, V. D. 1995. *The Other Greeks: The Family Farm and the Agrarian Roots of Western Civilization.* New York.

Hardin, R. 1989. "Why a Constitution?" In B. Grofman and D. Wittman, eds., *The Federalist Papers and the New Institutionalism*, 100–120. New York.

————. 1990. "Contractarianism: Wistful Thinking." *Constitutional Political Economy* 1: 35–52.

Harris, E. M. 1995. *Aeschines and Athenian Politics.* New York.

————. 2006. *Democracy and the Rule of Law in Classical Athens.* Cambridge.

Harrison, E. B. 1986. "Charis, Charites." In *Lexicon Iconographicum Mythologiae Classicae*, vol. III, 191–203. Zurich and Munich.

Harter-Uibopuu, K. 1998. *Das zwischenstaatliche Schiedsverfahren im achäischen Koinon.* Cologne.

Hatzopoulos, M. B. 1988. *Actes de vente de la Chalcidique centrale.* Paris.

————. 1996. *Macedonian Institutions under the Kings: A Historical and Epigraphic Study.* Athens and Paris.

Haussoulier, B. 1917. *Traité entre Delphes et Pellana: Étude de droit grec.* Paris.

Hauvette, A. 1894. *Hérodote, historien des guerres médiques.* Paris.

Hayek, F. 1948. "The Economic Conditions of Interstate Federalism." In F. Hayek, ed., *Individualism and the Economic Order*, 255–72. Chicago.

Head, B. V. 1881. *On the Chronological Sequence of the Coins of Boeotia.* London.

————. 1911. *Historia Numorum.* Oxford.

Heinen, H. 1972. *Untersuchungen zur hellenistischen Geschichte des 3. Jh. v. Chr.: Zur Geschichte der Zeit des Ptolemaios Keraunos und zum chremonideischen Krieg.* Wiesbaden.

Helly, B. 1973. *Gonnoi.* Amsterdam.

————. 1979. "Une liste des cités de Perrhébie dans la premiere moitié du IVe siècle avant J.-C." In B. Helly, ed., *La Thessalie: Actes de la table-ronde, 21–24 juillet 1975*, 165–200. Lyon.

————. 1995. *L' État thessalien: Aleuas le Roux, les tetrades et les tagoi.* Lyon.

————. 2001. "Un décret fédéral des Thessaliens méconnu dans une cité d'Achaïe phthiotide (*IG* IX, 2, 103)." *BCH* 125: 239–87.

————. 2008. "Encore le blé thessalien: Trois décrets de Larisa (*IG* IX 2, 506) accordant aux Athéniens licence d'exportation et réduction des droits de douane sur leurs achats de blé." *Studi ellenistici* 20: 25–108.

Hennig, D. 1977. "Der Bericht des Polybios über Boiotien und die Lage von Orchomenos in der 2. Hälfte des 3. Jahrhunderts v. Chr." *Chiron* 7: 119–48.

———. 1994. "Immobilienerwerb durch Nichtbürger in der klassischen und hellenistischen Polis." *Chiron* 24: 305–44.

———. 1995. "Staatliche Ansprüche an privaten Immobilienbesitz in der klassischen und hellenistischen Polis." *Chiron* 25: 235–82.

Hepworth, R. G. 1989. "Epaminondas' Coinage." In I. Carradice and P. Attwood, eds., *Proceedings of the 10th International Congress of Numismatics*, 35–40. London.

———. 1998. "The 4th-Century-BC Magistrate Coinage of the Boiotian Confederacy." Νομισμάτικα χρόνικα 17: 61–90.

Herman, G. 1987. *Ritualised Friendship and the Greek City*. Cambridge.

Herrenschmidt, C. 1985. "Une lecture iranisante du poème de Symmachos dédié à Arbinas dynaste de Xanthos." *REA* 87: 125–35.

Herrmann, K. 1972. "Der Pfeiler der Paionios-Nike in Olympia." *JDAI* 87: 232–57.

Hicks, E. L. 1882. *Manual of Greek Historical Inscriptions*. Oxford.

Higgins, R. A. 1954. *Catalogue of the Terracottas in the Department of Greek and Roman Antiquities, British Museum*. London.

Hiller von Gaertringen, F. 1925–26. "Ἐπιγραφαὶ ἐκ τοῦ ἱεροῦ τῆς Ἐπιδαύρου." *AEph*, ser. 3, 43–44: 67–86.

Hodkinson, S. 2007. "The Episode of Sphodrias as a Source for Spartan Social History." In N. Sekunda, ed., *Corolla Cosmo Rodewald*, 43–65. Gdansk.

Hofstetter, J. 1978. *Die Griechen in Persien*. Berlin.

Höghammar, K. 2000–2001. "A Note on the Border Conflict between Argos and Sparta in the Second Century BC." *OAth* 25–26: 67–70.

Hölkeskamp, K.-J. 1999. *Schiedsrichter, Gesetzgeber und Gesetzgebung im archaischen Griechenland*. Stuttgart.

Holleaux, M. 1885. "Fouilles au temple d'Apollon Ptoos." *BCH* 9: 520–24.

———. 1889a. "Dedicace nouvelle de la confédération béotienne." *BCH* 13: 225–29.

———. 1889b. "Dédicaces nouvelles de la confédération béotienne." *BCH* 13: 1–23.

———. 1921. *Rome, la Grèce et les monarchies hellénistiques au IIIe siècle avant J.-C. (273–205)*. Paris.

———. 1938–68. *Études d'épigraphie et d'histoire grecques*. 6 vols. Paris.

Hollis, A. S. 1990. *Callimachus: Hecale*. Oxford.

Hölscher, T. 1974. "Die Nike der Messenier und Naupaktier in Olympia." *JDAI* 89: 70–111.

Horden, P., and N. Purcell. 2000. *The Corrupting Sea: A Study of Mediterranean History*. Oxford.

Hornblower, S. 1982. *Mausolus*. Oxford.

———. 1990. "When Was Megalopolis Founded?" *ABSA* 85: 71–77.

———. 1991–2008. *A Commentary on Thucydides*. 3 vols. Oxford.

———. 2000. "Personal Names and the Study of the Ancient Greek Historians." In S. Hornblower and E. Matthews, eds., *Greek Personal Names: Their Value as Evidence*, 129–43. Oxford.

———. 2002. *The Greek World, 479–323 BC*. London.

———. 2004. *Thucydides and Pindar: Historical Narrative and the World of Epinician Poetry*. Oxford.

———. 2007. "Did the Delphic Amphiktyony Play a Political Role in the Classical Period?" *MHR* 22: 39–56.

How, W. W., and J. Wells. 1912. *A Commentary on Herodotus.* 2 vols. Oxford.

Howgego, C. 1990. "Why Did Ancient States Strike Coins?" *NC* 150: 1–26.

Humphreys, S. 1983. "Fustel de Coulanges and the Greek Genos." *Sociologica del diritto* 8: 35–44.

Hurst, A. 1989. "La prise de Thèbes par Alexandre selon Arrien." In H. Beister and J. Buckler, eds., *Boiotika: Vorträge vom 5. internationalen Böotien-Kolloquium zu Ehren von Professor Dr. Siegfried Lauffer,* 183–92. Munich.

———. 1996. "La stèle de l'Helicon." In A. Hurst and A. Schachter, eds., *La montagne des Muses,* 57–71. Geneva.

Imhoof-Blumer, F. 1883. *Monnaies grecques.* Amsterdam.

Imhoof-Blumer, F., and P. Gardner. 1886. "Numismatic Commentary on Pausanias, Part 2." *JHS* 7: 57–113.

Inman, R. P., and D. L. Rubinfeld. 1998. "Subsidiarity and the European Union." In P. Newman, ed., *The New Palgrave Dictionary of Economics and the Law,* 545–51. London.

Ioannidou, A. 1973. "Ἀρχαιότητες καὶ μνημεῖα Βοιωτίας-Φθιώτιδος." *AD* 28: 247–83.

Ismard, P. 2010. *La cité des réseaux: Athènes et ses associations VIᵉ-Iᵉʳ siècle av. J.-C.* Paris.

Iversen, P. A. 2007. "The Small and Great Daidala in Boiotian History." *Historia* 56: 381–418.

Jacquemin, A. 1985. "Aitolia et Aristaineta: Offrandes monumentales étoliennes à Delphes au IIIᵉ s. av. J.-C." *Ktema* 10: 27–35.

———. 1999. *Offrandes monumentales à Delphes.* Paris.

———. 2000. *Guerre et religion dans le monde grec (490–322 av. J.-C.).* Paris.

Jacquemin, A., and D. Laroche. 1982. "Notes sur trois piliers delphiques." *BCH* 106: 191–218.

Jameson, M. H., C. N. Runnels, and T. H. van Andel. 1994. *A Greek Countryside: The Southern Argolid from Prehistory to the Present Day.* Stanford.

Janko, R. 1982. *Homer, Hesiod, and the Hymns: Diachronic Development in Epic Diction.* Cambridge.

———. 1986. "The *Shield of Heracles* and the Legend of Cycnus." *CQ* 36: 38–59.

Jannoray, J. 1937. "Krisa, Kirrha, et la première guerre sacrée." *BCH* 61: 33–43.

Jeffery, L. H. 1976. *Archaic Greece: The City-States c. 700–500 BC.* London.

———. 1988. "The Development of Lakonian Lettering: A Reconsideration." *ABSA* 83: 179–81.

———. 1990. *The Local Scripts of Archaic Greece.* Oxford.

Jehne, M. 1994. *Koine Eirene: Untersuchungen zu den Befriedungs- und Stabilisierungsbemühungen in der griechischen Poliswelt des 4. Jahrhunderts v. Chr.* Suttgart.

———. 1999. "Formen der thebanischen Hegemonialpolitik zwischen Leuktra und Chaironeia." *Klio* 81: 317–58.

Jones, C. P. 1996. ""Εθνος and γένος in Herodotus." *CQ* 46: 315–20.

Jones, N. F. 1987. *Public Organization in Ancient Greece: A Documentary Study.* Philadelphia.

Jost, M. 1985. *Sanctuaries et cultes d'Arcadie.* Paris.

———. 1997. "Le thème des disputes entre Héra et Zeus en Arcadie et en Béotie." *Héra: Images, espaces, cultes; Actes du colloque international de Lille,* 87–92. Naples.

Jucker, H. 1967. "Helike." *GNS* 17: 63–65.

Kagan, D. 1961. "The Economic Origins of the Corinthian War." *PP* 16: 321–41.

Kallet, L. 2004. "Epigraphic Geography: The Tribute Quota Fragments Assigned to 421/0–415/4 B.C." *Hesperia* 73: 465–96.

Kallet-Marx, R.M. 1985. "Athens, Thebes, and the Foundation of the Second Athenian League." *ClAnt* 4: 127–51.

———. 1989. "The Evangelistria Watchtower and the Defense of the Zagara Pass." In H. Beister and J. Buckler, eds., *Boiotika: Vorträge vom 5. internationalen Böotien-Kolloquium zu Ehren von Professor Dr. Siegfried Lauffer*, 301–11. Munich.

Kalliontzis, Y. 2007. "Décrets de proxénie et catalogues militaires de Chéronée trouvés lors des fouilles de la basilique paléochrétienne d'Haghia Paraskévi." *BCH* 131: 475–514.

Kase, E. W., and G. J. Szemler. 1984. "The Amphiktyonic League and the First Sacred War: A New Perspective." In J. Harmatta, ed., *Actes du VIIᵉ congrès de la fédération internationale des associations d'études classiques*, 107–16. Budapest.

Kasperson, R. E., J. X. Kasperson, B. L. Turner, K. Dow, and W. B. Meyer. 1995. "Critical Environmental Regions: Concepts, Distinctions and Issues." In J. X. Kasperson, R. E. Kasperson, and B. L. Turner, eds., *Regions at Risk: Comparisons of Threatened Environments*, 1–41. Tokyo.

Katsonopoulou, D. 1998. "Η λατρεία του Ελικωνίου Ποσειδῶνος· Μια νέα θεώρηση." In D. Katsonopoulou, S. Soter, and D. Schilardi, eds., *Helike*, vol. II: *Ancient Helike and Aigialeia: Proceedings of the Second International Conference, Aigion, 1–3 December 1995*, 251–65. Athens.

———. 2002. "Helike and Her Territory in the Light of New Discoveries." In E. Greco, ed., *Gli Achei e l'identità etnica degli Achei d'occidente*, 205–16. Paestum and Athens.

Kavvadias, P. 1918. "Ἡ ἀχαϊκὴ συμπολιτεία κατ᾽ ἐπιγραφὰς ἐξ᾽Ἐπιδαύρου." *AEph*, ser. 3, 36: 115–54.

Kearns, E. 1992. "Between God and Man: Status and Functions of Heroes and Their Sanctuaries." In A. Schachter and J. Bingen, eds., *Le sanctuaire grec*, 65–99. Geneva.

Keen, A. G. 1996. "Were the Boiotian *Poleis Autonomoi*?" In M. H. Hansen and K. Raaflaub, eds., *More Studies in the Ancient Greek Polis*, 113–25. Stuttgart.

Keesling, C. M. 2003. *The Votive Statues of the Athenian Acropolis*. Cambridge.

Kelly, D. H. 1978. "The New Spartan Treaty." *LCM* 3: 133–41.

Kennell, N. M. 1999. "From Perioikoi to Poleis: The Laconian Cities in the Late Hellenistic Period." In S. Hodkinson and A. Powell, eds., *Sparta: New Perspectives*, 189–210. London.

Keramopoullos, A. D. 1917. "Ὁ ναός τοῦ Ἰσμηνίου Ἀπόλλωνος." *AD* 3: 33–79.

———. 1920. "Εἰκόνες πολεμιστῶν τῆς ἐν Δηλίῳ μάχης (424 π.Χ.)." *AEph*, ser. 3, 38: 1–36.

———. 1930–31. "Ἀνάθημα [Κορω]νέων ἐν Θήβαις." *AD* 13: 105–18.

———. 1931–32. "Ἐπιγραφαὶ Θεσπιῶν." *AD* 14: 12–40.

Kertzer, D. 1988. *Ritual, Politics, and Power*. New Haven.

Kim, H. 2001. "Archaic Coinage as Evidence for the Use of Money." In A. Meadows and K. Shipton, eds., *Money and Its Uses in the Ancient Greek World*, 7–22. Oxford.

———. 2002. "Small Change and the Moneyed Economy." In P. Cartledge, E. E. Cohen, and L. Foxhall, eds., *Money, Labour and Land: Approaches to the Economies of Ancient Greece*, 44–51. London.

Kim, H., and J. H. Kroll. 2008. "A Hoard of Archaic Coins of Colophon and Unminted Silver (*CH* I.3)." *AJN* 20: 53–104.

Kindt, J. 2009. "Polis Religion: A Critical Appreciation." *Kernos* 22: 1–21.

Kirsten, E. 1950. "Plataiai." *RE* 20: 2255–2331. Stuttgart.

Klaffenbach, G. 1931. "Die Zeit des ätolisch-akarnanischen Bündnisvertrages." *Klio* 24: 223–34.

———. 1939a. "Ophieis." *RE* 18: 640–43. Stuttgart.

———. 1939b. "Zur Geschichte Ätoliens und Delphis im 3. Jahrhundert v. Chr." *Klio* 32: 189–209.

———. 1954. "Der römisch-ätolische Bündnisvertrag vom Jahre 212 v. Chr." *SAWDDR*, 1–26.

———. 1955. "Die Zeit des ätolisch-akarnanischen Bündnisvertrages: Δεύτεραι φροντίδες." *Historia* 4: 46–51.

———. 1968. "Die Sklaven von Elateia." *BCH* 92: 257–59.

Kleiner, G., P. Hommel, and W. Müller-Wiener. 1967. *Panionion und Melie.* Berlin.

Knauss, J. 1990. *Wasserbau und Geschichte: Minische Epoche–bayerische Zeit.* Munich.

Knight, J. 1992. *Institutions and Social Conflict.* Cambridge.

Knoepfler, D. 1978. "Proxénies béotiennes du IVᵉ siècle." *BCH* 102: 375–93.

———. 1981. "Argoura: Un toponyme eubéen dans la Midienne de Démosthène." *BCH* 105: 289–329.

———. 1983. "Un témoignage épigraphique méconnu sur Argous(s)a, ville de Thessalie." *RPh* 57: 47–57.

———. 1988. "Review of H. W. Pleket and R. S. Stroud, *Supplementum Epigraphicum Graecum*, 31–33." *Gnomon* 60: 222–35.

———. 1989. "Un législateur thébain chez Cicéron (De legibus II, XV, 37)." In M. Piérart and O. Curty, eds., *Historia Testis: Mélanges d'épigraphie, d'histoire ancienne et de philologie offerts à Tadeusz Zawadzki*, 37–60. Fribourg.

———. 1990. "Contributions à l'épigraphie de Chalcis." *BCH* 114: 473–98.

———. 1991a. "L. Mummius Achaicus et les cités du golfe euboïque: À propos d'une nouvelle inscription d'Erétrie." *MH* 48: 252–80.

———. 1991b. *La vie de Ménédème d'Erétrie de Diogène Laërce: Contribution à l'histoire et à la critique du texte des Vies des philosophes.* Basel.

———. 1992. "Sept années de recherches sur l'épigraphie de la Béotie (1985–1991)." *Chiron* 22: 411–503.

———. 1993a. "Adolf Wilhelm et la *pentétèris* des Amphiaraia d'Oropos." In M. Piérart, ed., *Aristote et Athènes,* 279–302. Paris.

———. 1993b. "Les kryptoi du stratège Épicharès à Rhamnonte et le début de la guerre de Chrémonides." *BCH* 117: 327–41.

———. 1995. "Les relations des cités eubéennes avec Antigone Gonatas et la chronologie delphique au début de l'époque étolienne." *BCH* 119: 137–59.

———. 1998. "Chronologie delphique et histoire eubéenne." *Topoi: Orient–Occident* 8: 197–214.

———. 1999a. "L'épigraphie de la Grèce centro-méridionale (Eubée, Béotie, Phocide et pays voisins, Delphes): Publications récentes, documents inédits, travaux en cours." In *XI congresso internazionale di epigrafia greca e latina, Roma, 18–24 settembre 1997,* 229–55. Rome.

———. 1999b. "La confédération béotienne au IIIᵉ s. avant J.-C.: Un modèle pour la Suisse du 3ᵉ millénaire?" In P. Henry and M. Tribolet, eds., *In Dubiis Libertas: Mélanges d'histoire offerts au professeur Rémy Scheurer,* 27–45. Hauterive.

———. 2000. "La loi de Daitôndas, les femmes de Thèbes et le collège des béotarques au IVᵉ et au IIIᵉ siècle avant J.-C." In P. A. Bernardini, ed., *Presenza e funzione della città di Tebe nella cultura greca: Atti del convegno internazionale, Urbino 7–9 iuglio 1997*, 345–66. Pisa and Rome.

———. 2001a. *Décrets érétriens de proxénie et de citoyenneté.* Lausanne.

———. 2001b. "La fête des Daidala de Platées chez Pausanias: Une clef pour l'histoire de la Béotie hellénistique." In D. Knoepfler and M. Piérart, eds., *Éditer, traduire, commenter: Pausanias en l'an 2000*, 343–74. Geneva.

———. 2001c. "La réintégration de Thèbes dans le *koinon* béotien apres son relèvement par Cassandre; ou, Les surprises de la chronologie épigraphique." In R. Frei-Stolba and K. Gex, eds., *Recherches recentes sur le monde hellenistique: Actes en l'honneur de Pierre Ducrey*, 11–26. Bern.

———. 2002. "Oropos et la confédération béotienne à la lumière de quelques inscriptions «revisitées»." *Chiron* 32: 119–56.

———. 2004. "Huit otages béotiens proxènes de l'Achaïe: Une image de l'élite sociale et des institutions du KOINON BOIOTON hellénistique (*Syll.*[³], 519)." In M. Cébeillac-Gervasoni, L. Lamoine, and F. Trément, eds., *Autocélébration des élites locales dans le monde romain: Contextes, images, textes, IIᵉ s. av. J.-C.–IIIᵉ ap. J.-C.; Actes du colloque qui s'est tenu à Clermont-Ferrand du 21 au 23 novembre 2003*, 85–106. Clermont-Ferrand.

———. 2005. *Apports récents des inscriptions grecques à l'histoire de l'antiquité.* Paris.

———. 2007a. "De Delphes à Thermos: Un témoignage épigraphique méconnu sur le trophée galate des Étoliens dans leur capitale (le traité étolo-béotien)." *CRAI*, fasc. 3: 1215–53.

———. 2007b. "ΠΟΛΥΜΝΙΣ est-il l'authentique patronyme d'Épaminondas? Réexamen critique de la tradition à la lumière d'un décret de Cnide récemment publié." In M. B. Hatzopoulos, ed., *Φωνής χαρακτήρ εθνικός· Actes du Vᵉ congrès international de dialectologie grecque, Athènes, 28–30 septembre 2006*, 117–35. Athens.

Koerner, R. 1974. "Die staatliche Entwicklung in alt-Achaia." *Klio* 56: 457–95.

Kolbe, W. 1929. "Das griechische Bundesbürgerrecht der hellenistischen Zeit." *Zeitschrift der Savigny-Stiftung für Rechtsgeschichte* 49: 129–54.

Kolia, E. 2011. "A Temple of the Geometric Period in Ancient Helike–Nikoleïka: The Excavation Seasons 2004–2009." *ABSA* 106: 201–46.

Konecny, A., M. J. Boyd, R. T. Marchese, and V. L. Aravantinos. 2008. "Plataiai in Boiotia: A Preliminary Report on Geophysical and Field Surveys Conducted in 2002–2005." *Hesperia* 77: 43–71.

Kontogiannis, A. 1994. "Σωσθενίς." In *Θεσσαλία· Δεκαπέντε χρόνια αρχαιολογικής έρευνας, 1975–1990—Αποτελέσματα και προοπτικές· Πρακτικά διεθνούς συνεδρίου, Λύων, 17–22 απριλίου 1990*, vol. II: 239–44. Athens.

Kossatz-Deismann, A. 1988. "Hera." In *Lexicon Iconographicum Mythologiae Classicae*, vol. IV, 659–719. Zurich and Munich.

Koumanoudes, S. N. 1964. "Τὸ μνημεῖον τῶν ἐν Σικελίᾳ θανόντων Ἀθηναίων." *AEph*, ser. 3, 103: 83–86.

Kourinou, E. 1992–98. "Μνᾶμα γεροντείας." *Horos* 10–12: 259–76.

———. 2000. *Σπάρτη· Συμβολή στη μνημειακή τοπογραφία της.* Athens.

Kowalzig, B. 2007. *Singing for the Gods: Performances of Myth and Ritual in Archaic and Classical Greece.* Oxford.

Kraay, C.M. 1976. *Archaic and Classical Greek Coins.* Berkeley and Los Angeles.

Kramolisch, H. 1978. *Die Strategen des thessalischen Bundes vom Jahr 196 v. Chr. bis zum Ausgang der römischen Republik.* Bonn.

Krasner, S. 1988. "Sovereignty: An Institutional Perspective." *Comparative Political Studies* 21: 66–94.

Krentz, P. 1989. "Athena Itonia and the Battle of Koroneia." In H. Beister and J. Buckler, eds., *Boiotika: Vorträge vom 5. internationalen Böotien-Kolloquium zu Ehren von Professor Dr. Siegfried Lauffer,* 314–17. Munich.

Kritzas, C. 2006. "Nouvelles inscriptions d'Argos: Les archives des comptes du trésor sacré (IVᵉ av. J.-C.)." *CRAI:* 397–434.

Kroll, J.H. 1971. "Three Inscribed Greek Bronze Weights." In D.G. Mitten, J.G. Pedley, and J.A. Scott, eds., *Studies Presented to George M.A. Hanfmann,* 87–93. Cambridge, Mass.

———. 1996. "Hemiobols to Assaria: The Bronze Coinage of Roman Aigion." *NC* 156: 49–78.

———. 1998. "Silver in Solon's Laws." In R. Ashton and S. Hurter, eds., *Studies in Greek Numismatics in Memory of Martin Jessop Price,* 225–32. London.

———. 2008. "The Monetary Use of Weighed Bullion in Archaic Greece." In W.V. Harris, ed., *The Monetary Systems of the Greeks and Romans,* 12–37. Oxford.

Kuhn, A.B. 2006. "Ritual Change during the Reign of Demetrius Poliorcetes." In E. Stavrianopoulou, ed., *Ritual and Communication in the Graeco-Roman World,* 265–81. Liège.

Kühr, A. 2006a. *Als Kadmos nach Boiotien kam: Polis und Ethnos im Spiegel thebanischer Gründungsmythen.* Stuttgart.

———. 2006b. "Invading Boeotia: *Polis* and *Ethnos* in the Mirror of Theban Foundation Myths." *Hermes* 134: 367–72.

Kunze, E. 1967. *Olympische Forschungen.* Vol. VIII, *Bericht über die Ausgrabungen in Olympia.* Berlin.

———. 1991. *Olympische Forschungen.* Vol. XXI, *Beinschienen.* Berlin.

Kurke, L. 1988. "The Poet's Pentathlon: Genre in Pindar's First *Isthmian.*" *GRBS* 29: 97–113.

———. 1992. "The Politics of *habrosunē* in Archaic Greece." *ClAnt* 11: 91–120.

———. 2007. "Visualizing the Choral: Epichoric Poetry, Ritual, and Elite Negotiation in Fifth-Century Thebes." In C. Kraus, S. Goldhill, H.P. Foley, and J. Elsner, eds., *Visualizing the Tragic: Drama, Myth, and Ritual in Greek Art and Literature; Essays in Honour of Froma Zeitlin,* 63–101. Oxford.

Kymlicka, W. 2007. "Multi-National Federalism." In B. He, B. Galligan, and T. Inogushi, eds., *Federalism in Asia,* 33–56. Cheltenham.

La Coste-Messelière, P. 1949. "Listes amphictioniques du IVᵉ siècle." *BCH* 73: 201–47.

Laani, A. 2006. *Law and Justice in the Courts of Classical Athens.* Cambridge.

Lafond, Y. 1991. "Pausanias historien dans le livre VII de la Périégèse." *JSav,* 27–45.

———. 1998a. "Die Katastrophe von 373 v. Chr. und das Verschwinden der Stadt Helike in Achaia." In E. Olshausen and H. Sonnabend, eds., *Naturkatastrophen in der antiken Welt,* 118–23. Stuttgart.

———. 1998b. "Review of Massimo Osanna, *Santuari e culti dell'Acaica antica* (1996)." *Kernos* 11: 396–99.

Lagos, C. 2001. "Athena Itonia at Koroneia (Boiotia) and in Cilicia." *NC* 161: 1–10.

Lakakis, M. 1991. "Αγροτικοί οικισμοί στη Δυμαία χώρα· Η περίπτωση του Πετροχωρίου."
In A. D. Rizakis, ed., *Αρχαία Αχαΐα και Ηλεία*, 241–46. Athens and Paris.

Lakakis, M., and A. D. Rizakis. 1990. "Polis et chora: L'organisation de l'espace urbain et
rural en Achaïe occidentale." *Akten des XIII. internationalen Kongresses für klassiche
Archäologie, Berlin, 1988*, 551–52. Mainz.

———. 1992a. "Dyme, cité achéenne: Son histoire à la lumière des fouilles récentes." In A. D.
Rizakis, ed., *Paysages d'Achaïe, I: Le bassin du Peiros et la plaine occidentale*, 77–100.
Athens and Paris.

———. 1992b. "Les grandes étapes de l'occupation du sol de l'âge de pierre à l'époque con-
temporaine." In A. D. Rizakis, ed., *Paysages d'Achaïe I : Le bassin du Peiros et la plaine
occidentale*, 59–76. Athens and Paris.

Lambros, P. 1891. *Ἀναγραφὴ τῶν νομισμάτων τῆς κυρίως Ἑλλάδος*. Athens.

Landucci Gattinoni, F. 2000. "Ismenia di Tebe tra opposizione e governo nella Beozia della
prima metà del IV secolo." In M. Sordi, ed., *L'opposizione nel mondo antico*, 135–54.
Milan.

Langdon, M. 1987. "An Attic Decree Concerning Oropos." *Hesperia* 56: 47–58.

Lapatin, K. D. S. 2001. *Chryselephantine Statuary in the Ancient Mediterranean World*.
Oxford.

Laqueur, R. 1931. "Mnaseas (6)." *RE* 15: 2250–52. Stuttgart.

Larfeld, W. 1883. *Sylloge Inscriptionum Boeoticarum Dialectum Popularem Exhibentium*.
Berlin.

Larsen, J. A. O. 1938. "Roman Greece." In T. Frank, ed., *An Economic Survey of Ancient
Rome*, vol. IV: 259–498. Baltimore.

———. 1952. "The Assembly of the Aetolian League." *TAPA* 83: 1–33.

———. 1953. "The Early Achaean League." In G. E. Mylonas and D. Raymond, eds., *Studies
Presented to David Moore Robinson, 797–815*. St. Louis.

———. 1955. *Representative Government in Greek and Roman History*. Berkeley and Los
Angeles.

———. 1957. "Lycia and Greek Federal Citizenship." *SO* 33: 5–26.

———. 1960a. "A New Interpretation of the Thessalian Confederacy." *CP* 55: 229–48.

———. 1960b. "Orchomenus and the Formation of the Boeotian Confederacy in 447 B.C."
CP 50: 9–18.

———. 1968. *Greek Federal States: Their Institutions and History*. Oxford.

———. 1971. "The Rights of Cities within the Achaean Confederacy." *CP* 66: 81–86.

———. 1972. "A Recent Interpretation of the Achaean Assemblies." *CP* 67: 178–85.

———. 1975. "The Aetolian-Achaean Alliance of ca. 238–220 B.C." *CP* 70: 159–79.

Larson, S. L. 2007. *Tales of Epic Ancestry: Boiotian Collective Identity in the Late Archaic and
Early Classical Periods*. Stuttgart.

Lauffer, S. 1976. "Inschriften aus Boeotien." *Chiron* 6: 11–51.

———. 1980. "Inschriften aus Boiotien (II)." *Chiron* 10: 161–82.

———. 1985. "Problèmes de Copaïs: Solutions et énigmes." In G. Argoud and P. Roesch, eds.,
La Béotie antique, Lyon–Saint-Étienne, 16–20 mai 1983, 101–8. Paris.

———. 1986. *Kopais: Untersuchungen zur historischen Landeskunde Mittelgriechenlands*.
Frankfurt.

Launey, M. 1949–50. *Recherches sur les armées hellénistiques*. 2 vols. Paris.

Lazenby, J. F. 1972. "The Literary Tradition." In W. A. McDonald and G. R. Rapp, eds., *The Minnesota Messenia Expedition: Reconstructing a Bronze Age Regional Environment,* 81–93. Minneapolis.

Lazzarini, M. L. 1976. *Le formule delle dediche votive nella Grecia arcaica.* Rome.

Le Bohec, S. 1993. *Antigone Doson, roi de Macédoine.* Nancy.

Leahy, D. M. 1955. "The Bones of Tisamenus." *Historia* 5: 26–38.

Leake, W. M. 1835. *Travels in Northern Greece.* London.

LeBas, P. 1847–88. *Voyage archéologique en Grèce et Asie Mineure.* With contributions by P. Foucart, W. H. Waddington, and S. Reinach. 3 vols. Paris.

Lefèvre, F. 1994. "Un document amphictyonique inédit du IVᵉ siécle." *BCH* 118: 99–112.

———. 1995. "La chronologie du IIIᵉ siècle à Delphes, d'après les actes amphictioniques (280–200)." *BCH* 119: 161–206.

———. 1998. "Traité de paix entre Démétrios Poliorcète et la confédération étolienne (fin 289?)." *BCH* 122: 109–41.

———. 2002. *Corpus des Inscriptions de Delphes.* Vol. IV, *Documents amphictioniques.* Paris.

Lehmann, G. A. 1967. *Untersuchungen zur historischen Glaubwürdigkeit des Polybios.* Münster.

———. 1983a. "Erwägungen zur Struktur des achaiischen Bundesstaates." *ZPE* 51: 237–61.

———. 1983b. "Thessaliens Hegemonie über Mittelgriechenland im 6. Jhdt. v. Chr." *Boreas* 6: 35–43.

———. 1999. "Elateia, Aitolien und Rom nach der Entscheidung des 2. makedonischen Krieges." *ZPE* 127: 69–83.

———. 2000. *Ansätze zu einer Theorie des griechischen Bundesstaates bei Aristoteles und Polybios.* Göttingen.

Lehnus, L. 1984. "Pindaro: Il *Dafneforico per Agasicle* (Fr. 94b Sn.–M.)." *BICS* 31: 61–92.

Lejeune, M. 1945. "En marge d'inscriptions grecques dialectales, II–IV." *REA* 47: 97–115.

Lendon, J. C. 1989. "The Oxyrhynchus Historian and the Outbreak of the Corinthian War." *Historia* 38: 300–313.

Lerat, L. 1952. *Les Locriens de l'ouest.* Paris.

Lévêque, P. 1957. *Pyrrhos.* Paris.

Levi, M. 1981. "The Predatory Theory of Rule." *Politics and Society* 10: 431–65.

———. 1988. *Of Rule and Revenue.* Berkeley and Los Angeles.

———. 1990. "A Logic of Institutional Change." In K. S. Cook and M. Levi, eds., *The Limits of Rationality,* 402–18. Chicago.

———. 1997. "A Model, a Method, and a Map: Rational Choice in Comparative and Historical Analysis." In M. I. Lichbach and A. S. Zuckerman, eds., *Comparative Politics: Rationality, Culture, and Structure,* 19–41. Cambridge.

Lévy, E. 1994. "Le discours d'Agélaos de Naupacte." In L. Aigner Foresti, A. Barzanò, C. Bearzot, L. Prandi, and G. Zecchini, eds., *Federazioni e federalismo nell'Europa antica: Alle radici della casa comune europea,* 33–50. Milan.

Lewis, D. M. 1981. "The Origins of the First Peloponnesian War." In G. S. Shrimpton and D. J. McCargar, eds., *Classical Contributions: Studies in Honour of Malcolm Francis McGregor,* 71–78. Locust Valley, N.Y.

———. 1990a. "Public Property in the City." In O. Murray and S. Price, eds., *The Greek City from Homer to Alexander,* 245–64. Oxford.

————. 1990b. "The *Synedrion* of the Boeotian Alliance." In A. Schachter, ed., *Essays in the Topography, History and Culture of Boiotia*, 71–73. Montreal.

Liampi, K. 1994. "Ein Beitrag zur Münzprägung der Ainianen." In Θεσσαλία· Δεκαπέντε χρόνια αρχαιολογικής έρευνας, 1975–1990—Αποτελέσματα και προοπτικές· Πρακτικά διεθνούς συνεδρίου, Λύων, 17–22 απριλίου 1990, vol. II: 327–334. Athens.

————. 1995–96 [1998]. "On the Chronology of the Bronze Coinages of the Aetolian League and Its Members (Spearhead and Jawbone types)." *Archaiognosia* 9: 83–109.

————. 1996. "Η νομισματική παραγωγή της Ποτιδανίας, πόλεως των Αποδότων." In Χαρακτήρ· Αφιέρωμα στη Μάντω Οικονομίδου, 157–64. Athens.

Lobel, E., and D. Page. 1955. *Poetarum Lesbiorum Fragmenta.* Oxford.

Lolling, H. G. 1878. "Symmachievertrag der Phoker und Böoter." *MDAI(A)* 3: 19–27.

Loomis, W. T. 1992. *The Spartan War Fund: IG V.1.1 and a New Fragment.* Stuttgart.

Low, P. 2003. "Remembering War in Fifth-Century Greece: Ideologies, Societies, and Commemoration beyond Democratic Athens." *World Archaeology* 35: 98–111.

Lucas, G. 1997. *Les cités antiques de la haute vallée du Titarèse: Étude de topographie et de géographie historique.* Lyon.

Lukes, S. 1975. "Political Ritual and Social Integration." *Sociology: Journal of the British Sociological Association* 9: 289–308.

Luppe, W. 1982. "Zum spartanischen Staatsvertrag mit den ΑΙΤΩΛΟΙ ΕΡΞΑΔΙΕΙΣ." *ZPE* 49: 23–24.

Lupu, E. 2005. *Greek Sacred Law: A Collection of New Documents (NGSL).* Leiden.

Luraghi, N. 2008. *The Ancient Messenians: Constructions of Ethnicity and Memory.* Cambridge.

————. 2009. "Messenian Ethnicity and the Free Messenians." In P. Funke and N. Luraghi, eds., *The Politics of Ethnicity and the Crisis of the Peloponnesian League*, 110–34. Washington, D.C.

Luraghi, N., A. Magnetto, and C. Habicht. 2012. "The Controversy between Megalopolis and Messene in a New Inscription from Messene." *Chiron* 42: 509–50.

Lytle, E. 2010. "Fish Lists in the Wilderness: The Social and Economic History of a Boiotian Price Decree." *Hesperia* 79: 253–303.

Ma, J. 2008. "Chaironeia 338: Topographies of Commemoration." *JHS* 128: 72–91.

MacDonald, D. 1987–88. "The Significance of the 'Boiotian League/Chalkis' Silver Issue." *JNG* 37–38: 23–29.

Mackil, E. 2004. "Wandering Cities: Alternatives to Catastrophe in the Greek Polis." *AJA* 108: 493–516.

————. 2008. "A Boiotian Proxeny Decree and Relief of the Fourth Century in the Museum of Fine Arts, Boston, and Boiotian-Lakonian Relations in the 360s." *Chiron* 38: 157–94.

————. 2012. "The Greek *Koinon.*" In P. Bang and W. Scheidel, eds., *The Oxford Handbook of the State in the Ancient Near East and Mediterranean*, 304–23. Oxford.

————. Forthcoming. "Ethnos and Koinon." In J. McInerney, ed., *A Companion to Ethnicity in the Ancient Mediterranean.* Oxford.

Mackil, E., and P. van Alfen. 2006. "Cooperative Coinage." In P. van Alfen, ed., *Agoranomia: Studies in Money and Exchange Presented to John H. Kroll*, 201–46. New York.

Mafodda, G. 2000. *Il koinon beotico in età arcaica e classica: Storia ed istituzioni.* Rome.

Magnetto, A. 1997. *Gli arbitrati interstatali greci.* Vol. II, *Dal 337 al 196 a.C.* Pisa.

Maier, F. G. 1959–61. *Griechische Mauerbauinschriften*. 2 vols. Heidelberg.

Malkin, I. 1987. *Religion and Colonization in Ancient Greece*. Leiden.

———. 1991. "What is an *Aphidruma?*" *ClAnt* 10: 77–96.

———. 1994. *Myth and Territory in the Spartan Mediterranean*. Cambridge.

———. 1996. "Territorial Domination and the Greek Sanctuary." In P. Hellström and B. Alroth, eds., *Religion and Power in the Ancient Greek World: Proceedings of the Uppsala Symposium, 1993*, 75–81. Uppsala.

———. 1998. *The Returns of Odysseus: Colonization and Ethnicity*. Berkeley and Los Angeles.

———, ed. 2001. *Ancient Perceptions of Greek Ethnicity*. Cambridge, Mass.

Malkin, I., C. Constantakopoulou, and K. Panagopoulou, eds. 2009. *Greek and Roman Networks in the Mediterranean*. London.

Manganaro, G. 2000. "Fenici, Cartaginesi, Numidi tra i Greci (IV–I sec. a.C.)." *NAC* 29: 255–68.

Marcellesi, M.-C. 2000. "Commerce, monnaies locales et monnaies communes dans les états hellénistiques." *REG* 113: 326–57.

Marek, C. 1984. *Die Proxenie*. Frankfurt.

Markle, M. M. 1994. "Diodorus' Sources for the Sacred War." In I. Worthington, ed., *Ventures into Greek History*, 43–69. Oxford.

Martha, J. 1878. "Inscriptions d'Achaïe." *BCH* 2: 40–44, 94–101.

Martin, J. L. 2009. *Social Structures*. Princeton.

Martin, R. P. 2005. "Pulp Epic: The *Catalogue* and the *Shield*." In R. L. Hunter, ed., *The Hesiodic Catalogue of Women: Constructions and Reconstructions*, 153–75. Cambridge.

Martin, T. R. 1985. *Sovereignty and Coinage in Classical Greece*. Princeton.

———. 1995. "Coins, Mints, and the *Polis*." In M. H. Hansen, ed., *Sources for the Ancient Greek City-State: Symposium, August 24–27, 1994*, vol. II, 257–91. Copenhagen.

Martin, V. 1944. "Le traitement de l'histoire diplomatique dans la tradition littéraire du IVe siècle avant J.-C." *MH* 1: 13–30.

Masaracchia, A. 1978. *Erodoto: La sconfitta dei Persiani; Libro IX delle Storie*. Milan.

Massenzio, M. 1968. "La festa di Artemis Triclaria e Dionysos Aisymnetes a Patrai." *Studi e materiali di storia delle religioni* 39: 101–32.

Mastrokostas, E. 1955a. "Ἡ στήλη τῶν ἐν Σικελίᾳ πεσόντων." *AEph*, ser. 3, 94: , 180–202.

———. 1955b [1961]. "Ἐπιγραφαὶ Ἑσπερίας Λοκρίδος, Αἰτωλίας, Φωκίδος, Δωρίδος καὶ Μαλίδος." *AEph*, ser. 3, 94:, 51–89.

———. 1965. "Inschriften aus Ätolien, Akarnanien und Westlokris." *MDAI(A)* 80: 152–59.

Matthaiou, A. P., and E. Mastrokostas. 2000–2003. "Συνθήκη Μεσσηνίων και Ναυπακτίων." *Horos* 14–16: 433–54.

Matthaiou, A. P., and G. A. Pikoulas. 1989. "Ἔδον τοῖς Λακεδαιμονίοις ποττὸν πόλεμον." *Horos* 7: 77–124.

Mattingly, H. B. 1963. "The Growth of Athenian Imperialism." *Historia* 12: 257–73.

———. 1966a. "Athenian Imperialism and the Foundation of Brea." *CQ* 16: 172–92.

———. 1966b. "Periclean Imperialism." In *Ancient Society and Institutions: Studies Presented to Victor Ehrenberg on His 75th Birthday*, 193–224. Oxford.

———. 1982. "The Athena Nike Temple Reconsidered." *AJA* 86: 381–85.

Mazarakis Ainian, A. 1997a. *From Rulers' Dwellings to Temples: Architecture, Religion, and Society in Early Iron Age Greece*. Jonsered.

————. 1997b [1998]. "Σκάλα Ωρωπού." Το έργον της αρχαιολογικής εταιρείας 44: 24–34.
Mazarakis Ainian, A., and A. P. Matthaiou. 1999. "Ενεπίγραφο αλιευτικό βάρος των γεωμετρικών χρόνων." AEph ser. 3 vol. 138: 143–53.
McDonald, W. A., and R. Hope Simpson. 1972. "Archaeological Exploration." In W. A. McDonald and G. R. Rapp, eds., The Minnesota Messenia Expedition: Reconstructing a Bronze Age Regional Environment, 117–47. Minneapolis.
McGregor, M. F. 1976. "The Attic Quota-List of 453/2 B.C." Hesperia 45: 280–82.
McInerney, J. 1997. "The Phokikon and the Hero Archegetes." Hesperia 66: 193–207.
————. 1999. The Folds of Parnassos: Land and Ethnicity in Ancient Phokis. Austin.
McKechnie, P. R., and S. J. Kern. 1988. Hellenica Oxyrynchia, Edited with Translation and Commentary. Warminster.
McKinnon, R., and T. Nechyba. 1997. "Competition in Federal Systems: The Role of Political and Financial Constraints." In J. Ferejohn and B. R. Weingast, eds., The New Federalism: Can the States Be Trusted?, 3–61. Stanford.
Mee, C., and H. Forbes, eds. 1997. A Rough and Rocky Place: The Landscape and Settlement History of the Methana Peninsula. Liverpool.
Meiggs, R. 1966. "The Dating of Fifth-Century Attic Inscriptions." JHS 86: 86–98.
————. 1972. The Athenian Empire. Oxford.
————. 1982. Trees and Timber in the Ancient Mediterranean World. Oxford.
Meiggs, R., and D. M. Lewis. 1988. A Selection of Greek Historical Inscriptions to the End of the Fifth Century BC. Oxford.
Mele, A. 1983. "Crotone e la sua storia." Crotone: Atti del XXIII convegno di studi sulla Magna Grecia, Taranto, 7–10 ottobre 1983: 33–80. Taranto.
Meloni, P. 1953. Perseo e la fine della monarchia macedone. Rome.
Mendels, D. 1984. "Aetolia 331–301: Frustration, Political Power, and Survival." Historia 33: 129–80.
Merker, I. L. 1989. "The Achaians in Naupaktos and Kalydon in the Fourth Century." Hesperia 58: 303–11.
Mertens Horn, M. 1978. "Beobachtungen an dädalischen Tondächern." JDAI 93: 30–65.
Meyer, E. 1978. Messenien und die Stadt Messene. Munich.
Meyer, E., and H. E. Stier. 1958. Geschichte des Altertums. Vol. 5, Das Perserreich und die Griechen: Der Ausgang der griechischen Geschichte 404–350 v. Chr. Basel.
Meyer, J. W., and B. Rowan. 1977. "Institutionalized Organizations: Formal Structure as Myth and Ceremony." American Journal of Sociology 83: 340–63.
Meyer, J. W., and W. R. Scott. 1983. Organizational Environments: Ritual and Rationality. Beverly Hills.
Michaud, J.-P. 1974a. "Chronique des fouilles et découvertes archéologiques en Grèce en 1973." BCH 98: 579–722.
————. 1974b. "Deux notes d'épigraphie phocidienne." In Mélanges helléniques offerts à Georges Daux, 269–78. Paris.
Michaud, J.-P., and J. Blecon. 1973. Fouilles de Delphes. Vol. II.15, Topographie et architecture: Le trésor de Thèbes. Paris.
Michel, C. 1900. Recueil d'inscriptions grecques. Brussels.
Migdal, J. 2001. State in Society: Studying How States and Societies Transform and Constitute One Another. Cambridge.

Migeotte, L. 1980. "Engagement et saisie de biens publics dans les cités grecques." In *Mélanges d'études anciennes offerts à M. Lebel*, 161–71. Quebec.

———. 1984. *L'emprunt public dans les cités grecques: Recueil des documents et analyse critique.* Quebec.

———. 1985. "Souscriptions publiques en Béotie." In P. Roesch and G. Argoud, eds., *La Béotie antique, Lyon–Saint-Étienne, 16–20 mai 1983*, 311–16. Paris.

———. 1990. "Le pain quotidien dans les cités hellénistiques: Une 'affaire d'État'?" *CEA* 24: 291–300.

———. 1991. "Le pain quotidien dans les cités hellénistiques: À propos des fonds permanents pour l'approvisionnement en grain." *CCG* 2: 19–41.

———. 1994. "Ressources financières des cités béotiennes." In J. M. Fossey, ed., *Boeotia Antiqua IV: Proceedings of the 7th International Congress on Boiotian Antiquities*, 3–15. Amsterdam.

———. 1995. "Les finances publiques des cités grecques: Bilan et perspectives de recherche." *Topoi: Orient–Occident* 5: 7–32.

———. 1997. "Le contrôle des prix dans les cités grecques." In J. Andreau, P. Briant, and R. Descat, eds., *Prix et formation des prix dans les économies antiques*, 33–52. Saint-Bertrand-de-Comminges.

———. 2002. "La cité grecque, les citoyens et les finances publiques." *Les études classiques* 70: 13–26.

———. 2003. "Taxation directe en Grèce ancienne." In G. Thür and F. J. F. Nieto, eds., *Symposion 1999: Vorträge zur griechischen und hellenistischen Rechtsgeschichte*, 297–313. Cologne.

———. 2004. "La mobilité des étrangers en temps de paix en Grèce ancienne." In C. Moatti, ed., *La mobilité des personnes en Méditerranée de l'antiquité à l'époque moderne: Procédures de contrôle et documents d'identification*, 615–48. Rome.

———. 2005. "Les pouvoirs des agoranomes dans les cités grecques." In R. W. Wallace and M. Gagarin, eds., *Symposion 2001: Vorträge zur griechischen und hellenistischen Rechtsgeschichte*, 287–301. Vienna.

Milne, J. G. 1953. "Unpublished Greek Coins in the Oxford Collection." *NC*, ser. 6, 13: 21–26.

Mitsos, M. 1937. "Εἰς *IG* IV.2 1, 170." *AEph*, ser. 3, 76: 708–14.

———. 1946–47. "Inscription de Stymphale." *REG* 59–60: 150–74.

———. 1947. "Thermika and Panaetolika." *Hesperia* 16: 256–61.

———. 1952. "Ἐπιγραφαὶ ἐξ Ἀμφιαρείου." *AEph*, ser. 3, 91:, 167–204.

———. 1979. "Εἰς *IG* IV.2 1, 75." *AEph*, ser. 3, 118: 214–17.

Modenesi, N. 2001. "Pausania «epigrafista» nell'itinerario della «Periegesis.»" *Acme* 54: 3–37.

Moe, T. 1990. "Political Institutions: The Neglected Side of the Story." *Journal of Law, Economics and Organization* 6: 213–53.

———. 2005. "Power and Political Institutions." *Perspectives on Politics* 3: 215–33.

Moggi, M. 1974. "Il sinecismo di Megalopoli (Diod. XV,72,4 ; Paus. VIII,27,1–8)." *ASNP* 4: 71–107.

———. 1976. *I sinecismi interstatali greci: Introduzione, edizione critica, traduzione, commento e indici.* Pisa.

———. 2002. "Sulle origine della lega achea." In E. Greco, ed., *Gli Achei e l'identità etnica degli Achei d'occidente*, 117–32. Paestum and Athens.

Mollard-Besques, S. 1954. *Musée National du Louvre: Catalogue raisonné des figurines et reliefs en terre-cuite grecs, étrusques, et romains.* Paris.

Möller, A. 2007. "Classical Greece: Distribution." In W. Scheidel, I. Morris, and R. P. Saller, eds., *The Cambridge Economic History of the Greco-Roman World,* 362–84. Cambridge.

Molyneux, J. H. 1992. *Simonides: A Historical Study.* Wauconda, Ill.

Momigliano, A. 1935. "L'egemonia tebana in Senofonte e in Eforo." *A&R,* 101–17.

Moreau, A. 1990. "Le retour des cendres: Oreste et Thésée, deux cadavres (ou deux mythes) au service de la propagande politique." In F. Jouan and A. Motte, eds., *Mythe et politique: Actes du colloque de Liège, 14–16 septembre 1989,* 209–18. Paris.

Moreno, A. 2007. *Feeding the Democracy: The Athenian Grain Supply in the Fifth and Fourth Centuries BC.* Oxford.

Moretti, L. 1953. *Iscrizioni agonistiche greche.* Rome.

———. 1957. *Olympionikai: I vincitori negli antichi agoni olimpici.* Rome.

———. 1962. *Ricerche sulle leghe greche (Peloponnesiaca, Beotica, Licia).* Rome.

———. 1967–76. *Iscrizioni storiche ellenistiche.* 3 vols. Florence.

Morgan, C. 1991. "Ethnicity and the Early Greek States: Historical and Material Perspectives." *PCPS* 37: 131–159.

———. 1997. "The Archaeology of Sanctuaries in Early Iron Age and Archaic *Ethnē*: A Preliminary View." In L. G. Mitchell and P. J. Rhodes, eds., *The Development of the Polis in Archaic Greece,* 168–98. London and New York.

———. 2000a. "Cultural Subzones in Early Iron Age and Archaic Arkadia?" In T. H. Nielsen and J. Roy, eds., *Defining Ancient Arkadia,* 382–456. Copenhagen.

———. 2000b. "Politics without the Polis: Cities and the Achaean Ethnos, *c.* 800–500 BC." In R. Brock and S. Hodkinson, eds., *Alternatives to Athens: Varieties of Political Organization and Community in Ancient Greece,* 189–211. Oxford.

———. 2002. "Ethnicity: The Example of Achaia." In E. Greco, ed., *Gli Achei e l'identità degli Achei d'occidente,* 95–116. Paestum and Athens.

———. 2003. *Early Greek States beyond the Polis.* London and New York.

Morgan, C., and J. Hall. 1996. "Achaian Poleis and Achaian Colonisation." In M. H. Hansen, ed., *Introduction to an Inventory of Poleis: Symposium, August 23–26, 1995,* 164–231. Copenhagen.

———. 2000. "Αχαϊκές πόλεις και αχαϊκός αποικισμός." *Paysages d'Achaïe, II: Dymé et son territoire,* 105–12. Athens and Paris.

———. 2004. "Achaia." In M. H. Hansen and T. H. Nielsen, eds., *An Inventory of Archaic and Classical Poleis,* 472–88. Oxford.

Mørkholm, O. 1991. *Early Hellenistic Coinage.* Cambridge.

Morris, I. 1994. "The Athenian Economy Twenty Years after *The Ancient Economy.*" *CP* 89: 351–66.

———. 1996. "The Strong Principle of Equality and the Archaic Origins of Greek Democracy." In J. Ober and C. W. Hedrick, eds., *Demokratia: A Conversation on Democracies, Ancient and Modern,* 19–48. Princeton.

———. 2003. "Mediterraneanization." *MHR* 18: 30–55.

———. 2008. "The Greater Athenian State." In I. Morris and W. Scheidel, eds., *The Dynamics of Ancient Empires: State Power from Assyria to Byzantium.* Oxford, 99–177.

Morris, I., R. P. Saller, and W. Scheidel. 2007. "Introduction." In W. Scheidel, I. Morris, and R. P. Saller, eds., *The Cambridge Economic History of the Greco-Roman World*, 1–12. Cambridge.

Morris, S. 1992. *Daidalos and the Origins of Greek Art*. Princeton.

Morrison, J. S. 1942. "Meno of Pharsalus, Polycrates, and Ismenias." *CQ* 36: 57–78.

Mosley, D. J. 1979. "Bericht über die Forschung zur Diplomatie im klassischen Griechenland." In E. Olshausen and H. Biller, eds., *Antike Diplomatie*, 204–35. Darmstadt.

Müller, C. 2005. "La procédure d'adoption des décrets en Béotie de la fin du IIIe s. av. J.-C. au Ier s. apr. J.-C." In P. Fröhlich and C. Müller, eds., *Citoyenneté et participation à la basse epoque hellénistique*, 95–119. Paris.

———. 2007. "La dissolution du koinon béotien en 171 av. J.-C. et ses conséquences territoriales." In P. Rodriguez, ed., *Pouvoir et territoire*, vol. I, *Antiquité et Moyen-Âge*, 31–46. Saint-Étienne.

———. 2011. "ΠΕΡΙ ΤΕΛΩΝ: Quelques réflexions autour des districts de la confédération béotienne à l'époque hellénistique." In N. Badoud, ed., *Philologos Dionysios: Mélanges offerts au Professeur Denis Knoepfler*, 261–82. Geneva.

Müller, D. 1987. *Topographischer Bildkommentar zu den Historien Herodots*. Tübingen.

Munn, M. 1998. "The First Excavations at Panakton on the Attic-Boiotian Frontier." In *Boeotia Antiqua VI: Proceedings of the 8th International Conference on Boiotian Antiquities, Loyola University of Chicago, 24–26 May 1995*, 47–58. Amsterdam.

Murray, O. 1990. "Cities of Reason." In O. Murray and S. R. F. Price, eds., *The Greek City from Homer to Alexander*, 1–25. Oxford.

Musgrave, R. 1959. *Public Finance*. New York.

Mylonopoulos, I. 2003. *Πελοπόννησος οἰκητήριον Ποσειδῶνος· Heiligtumer und Kulte des Poseidon auf der Peloponnes*. Liège.

———. 2006. "Von Helike nach Tainaron und von Kalaureia nach Samikon: Amphiktyonische Heiligtümer des Poseidon auf der Peloponnes." In K. Freitag, P. Funke, and M. Haake, eds., *Kult—Politik—Ethnos: Überregionale Heiligtümer im Spannungsfeld von Kult und Politik*, 121–56. Stuttgart.

Nachtergael, G. 1977. *Les Galates en Grèce et les Sôtèria de Delphes: Recherches d'histoire et d'epigraphie hellénistiques*. Brussels.

Nafissi, M. 1991–93. "Un decreto da Haliartos ed il culto di Athena Itonia (a proposito di *SEG* XXXVII.380)." *AFLPer (Class)*, n.s., 15–16: 109–20.

———. 1995. "Zeus Basileus di Lebadea: La politica religiosa del *koinon* beotico durante la guerra cleomenica." *Klio* 77: 149–69.

Neer, R. 2001. "Framing the Gift: The Politics of the Siphnian Treasury at Delphi." *ClAnt* 20: 273–336.

Nerantzis, Y. Y. 1991. "Οψείς της φυλετικής κοινωνίας στην προϊστορική Αιτωλία και Ακαρνανία." In *Α΄ αρχαιολογικό και ιστορικό συνέδριο Αιτωλοακαρνανίας· Μνημειακή κληρονομία και ιστορία της Αιτωλοακαρνανίας*, 27–34. Agrinion.

Niccolini, G. 1914. *La confederazione achea*. Pavia.

Nielsen, T. H. 1996a. "A Survey of Dependent Poleis in Classical Arkadia." In M. H. Hansen and K. Raaflaub, eds., *More Studies in the Ancient Greek Polis*, 63–106. Stuttgart.

———. 1996b. "Arkadia: City-Ethnics and Tribalism." In M. H. Hansen, ed., *Introduction to an Inventory of Poleis: Symposium, August 23–26, 1995*, 117–63. Copenhagen.

———. 1996c. "Was There an Arkadian Confederacy in the Fifth Century B.C.?" In M. H. Hansen and K. Raaflaub, eds., *More Studies in the Ancient Greek Polis*, 39–61. Stuttgart.

———. 1997. *"Triphylia*: An Experiment in Ethnic Construction and Political Organisation." In T. H. Nielsen, ed., *Yet More Studies in the Ancient Greek Polis*, 129–62. Stuttgart.

———. 2000. "Epiknemidian, Hypoknemidian, and Opountian Lokrians: Reflections on the Political Organisation of East Lokris in the Classical Period." In P. Flensted-Jensen, ed., *Further Studies in the Ancient Greek Polis*, 91–120. Stuttgart.

———. 2002. *Arkadia and Its Poleis in the Archaic and Classical Periods*. Göttingen.

Nielsen, T. H., and J. Roy. 1998. "The Azanians of Northern Arkadia." *C&M* 49: 5–44.

Niese, B. 1893–1903. *Geschichte der griechischen und makedonischen Staaten seit der Schlacht bei Chaeronea*. 3 vols. Gotha.

Nilsson, M. P. 1906. *Griechische Feste von religiöser Bedeutung*. Leipzig.

———. 1951. *Cults, Myths, Oracles, and Politics in Ancient Greece*. Lund.

———. 1967. *Geschichte der griechischen Religion*. Munich.

North, D. C. 1981. *Structure and Change in Economic History*. New York.

———. 1990. *Institutions, Institutional Change, and Economic Performance*. Cambridge.

———. 1995. "Five Propositions about Institutional Change." In J. Knight and I. Sened, eds., *Explaining Social Institutions*, 15–26. Ann Arbor.

Nottmeyer, H. 1995a. *Polybios und das Ende des Achaierbundes: Untersuchungen zu den römische-achaiischen Beziehungen, ausgehend von der Mission des Kallikrates bis zur Zerstörung Korinths*. Munich.

———. 1995b. "Römische Gebietspolitik im 2. Jhd. v. Chr. am Beispiel des achaiischen Koinons." In C. Schubert and K. Brodersen, eds., *Rom und der griechische Osten: Festschrift für Hatto H. Schmitt zum 65. Geburtstag*, 199–208. Stuttgart.

O'Neil, J. L. 1980. "Who Attended Achaean Assemblies?" *MH* 37: 41–49.

———. 1984–86. "The Political Elites of the Achaian and Aitolian Leagues." *AncSoc* 15–17: 33–61.

Oates, W. 1972. *Fiscal Federalism*. New York.

———, ed. 1991. *Studies in Fiscal Federalism*. Worcester.

———. 1999. "An Essay on Fiscal Federalism." *Journal of Economic Literature* 37: 1120–49.

Ober, J. 1989. *Mass and Elite in Democratic Athens: Rhetoric, Ideology, and the Power of the People*. Princeton.

———. 1992. "Towards a Typology of Greek Artillery Towers: The First and Second Generations (c. 375–275 B.C.)." In S. van de Maele and J. M. Fossey, eds., *Fortificationes Antiquae: Including the Papers of a Conference Held at Ottawa University, October 1988*, 147–69. Amsterdam.

———. 1998. *Political Dissent in Democratic Athens: Intellectual Critics of Popular Rule*. Princeton.

———. 2008. *Democracy and Knowledge: Innovation and Learning in Classical Athens*. Princeton.

Ogden, D. 1996. *Greek Bastardy in the Classical and Hellenistic Periods*. Oxford.

———. 2004. *Aristomenes of Messene: Legends of Sparta's Nemesis*. Swansea.

Oliver, G. J. 2007. *War, Food, and Politics in Early Hellenistic Athens*. Oxford.

———. 2011. "Mobility, Society, and Economy in the Hellenistic Period." In Z. H. Archibald, J. K. Davies, and V. Gabrielsen, eds., *The Economies of Hellenistic Societies: Third to First Centuries BC*, 345–67. Oxford.

Osanna, M. 1996. *Santuari e culti dell'Acaia antica*. Naples.

Osborne, R. 1985. "The Land-Leases from Hellenistic Thespiai: A Re-examination." In G. Argoud and P. Roesch, eds., *La Béotie antique, Lyon–Saint-Étienne, 16–20 mai 1983*, 317–23. Paris.

———. 1992. "Is It a Farm? A Definition of the Agricultural Sites and Settlements in Ancient Greece." In B. Wells, ed., *Agriculture in Ancient Greece: Proceedings of the Seventh International Symposium at the Swedish Institute at Athens*, 21–28. Stockholm.

Ostwald, M. 1982. *Autonomia: Its Genesis and Early History*. Chico, Calif.

Palaiopanou, B. 1991. "Οι μετοπές του αρχαϊκού ναού του Θερμίου Απόλλωνος." In *Α΄ αρχαιολογικό και ιστορικό συνεδρίο Αιτωλοακαρνανίας· Μνημειακή κληρονομία και ιστορία της Αιτωλοακαρνανίας*, 144–48. Agrinion.

Panessa, G. 1999. *Philiai: L'amicizia nelle relazioni interstatali dei Greci*. Vol. I, *Dalle origini alla fine della guerra del Peloponneso*. Pisa.

Papagiannopoulos-Palaios, A. 1965–66. "Ἐπίγραμμα τοῦ Εὐριπίδου τοῖς ἐν Σικελίᾳ ἀποθανοῦσιν Ἀθηναίοις ἐκ τοῦ δημοσίου σήματος." *Polemon* 8: 5–26.

Papahatzis, N. 1981. "Προθεσσαλικὲς λατρείες στὴ Θεσσαλία τῶν ἱστορικῶν χρονῶν." *Ἀνθρωπολόγικα* 2: 33–37.

———. 1992. "Η φύση και η καταγωγή της Θεσσαλικής Ιτωνίας και της Πανελλήνιας Αθήνας." In Ε. Kypraiou, ed., *Πρακτικά του διεθνού συνεδρίου για την αρχαία Θεσσαλία· Στη μνημή του Δημήτρη Ρ. Θεοχάρη*, 321–25. Athens.

Papakosta, L. 1991. "Παρατηρήσεις σχετικά με την τοπογραφία του αρχαίου Αιγίου." In A. D. Rizakis, ed., *Αρχαία Αχαΐα και Ηλεία*, 235–40. Athens and Paris.

Papalexandrou, N. 2005. *The Visual Poetics of Power: Warriors, Youths, and Tripods in Early Greece*. Lanham, Md.

———. 2008. "Boiotian Tripods: The Tenacity of a Panhellenic Symbol in a Regional Context." *Hesperia* 77: 251–82.

Papapostolou, I. A. 1982. "Ἀνασκαφὴ ὑστερογεωμετρικοῦ ἀποθέτη στὴ Ρακίτα Παναχαϊκοῦ." *PAAH* 138: 187–88.

———. 2004. "Η ανασκαφή υπό τον ναό του Απόλλωνος στον Θέρμο." *Β΄ διεθνές ιστορικό και αρχαιολογικό συνεδρίο Αιτωλοακαρνανίας, Αγρίνιο, 29–31 μαρτιού, 2002*, 193–97. Agrinion.

Papazarkadas, N. 2009a. "Epigraphy and the Athenian Empire: Re-shuffling the Chronological Cards." In J. Ma, N. Papazarkadas, and R. Parker, eds., *Interpreting the Athenian Empire*, 67–88. London.

———. 2009b. "The Decree of Aigeis and Aiantis (*Agora* I 6793) Revisited." In N. Papazarkadas and A. A. Themos, eds., *Αττικά επιγραφικά· Μελέτες προς τιμήν του Christian Habicht*, 165–81. Athens.

Papazarkadas, N., and D. Sourlas. 2012. "The Funerary Monument for the Argives Who Fell at Tanagra (*IG* I³ 1149): A New Fragment." *Hesperia* 81: 585–616.

Pappadakis, N. G. 1916. "Περὶ τὸ Χαροπείον τῆς Κορωνείας." *AD* 2: 217–72.

———. 1923. "Ἐκ Βοιωτίας." *AD* 8: 182–256.

Parker, R. 1996. *Athenian Religion: A History*. Oxford.

———. 1998. *Cleomenes on the Acropolis: An Inaugural Lecture Delivered before the University of Oxford on 12 May 1997*. Oxford.

———. 2005. *Polytheism and Society at Athens*. Oxford.

———. 2009. "Subjection, Synoecism and Religious Life." In P. Funke and N. Luraghi, eds., *The Politics of Ethnicity and the Crisis of the Peloponnesian League*, 183–214. Washington, D.C.

Parker, R., and D. Obbink. 2001. "Aus der Arbeit der «Inscriptiones Graecae» VIII: Three Further Inscriptions Concerning Coan Cults." *Chiron* 31: 253–75.

Parker, V. 2003. "Sparta, Amyntas, and the Olynthians in 383 B.C.: A Comparison of Xenophon and Diodorus." *RhM* 146: 113–37.

———. 2007. "Sphodrias' Raid and the Liberation of Thebes: A Study of Ephorus and Xenophon." *Hermes* 135: 13–33.

Parsons, T. 1990. "Prolegomena to a Theory of Institutions." *American Sociological Review* 55: 319–33.

Partida, E. C. 2000. *The Treasuries at Delphi: An Architectural Study*. Jonsered.

Pasquali, G. 1913. "I due Nicandri." *SIFC* 20: 55–111.

Passerini, A. 1948. "La condizione della città di Elatea dopo la seconda guerra macedonica in una nuova iscrizione." *Athenaeum* 26: 83–95.

Peek, W. 1933. "Das Epigramm auf die Gefallenen von Koroneia." *Hermes* 68: 353–56.

———. 1955. *Griechische Versinschriften*. Vol. I, *Grab-Epigramme*. Berlin.

———. 1969. *Inschriften aus dem Asklepieion von Epidauros*. Berlin.

———. 1974. "Ein neuer spartanischer Staatsvertrag." *Abhandlungen der Sächsischen Akademie der Wissenschaften zu Leipzig, Phil.-Hist. Klasse* 65: 3–15.

———. 1977. "Hesiod und der Helikon." *Philologus* 121: 173–75.

Pelekides, S. 1924–25. "Περὶ τῆς ἀνασκαφῆς τῶν Βραστινῶν Καλυβιῶν." *AD* 9: 36–40.

Perdrizet, P. 1898. "Inscriptions d'Acraephiae." *BCH* 22: 241–60.

———. 1899. "Inscriptions d'Acraephiae." *BCH* 23: 90–96.

———. 1921. "Miscellenea XIII: La ligue achéenne et les Lagides." *REA* 23: 281–83.

Perlman, S. 1964. "The Causes and Outbreak of the Corinthian War." *CQ* 58: 64–81.

Pernice, E. 1894. *Griechische Gewichte*. Berlin.

Pernin, I. 2004. "Les baux de Thespies (Béotie): Essai d'analyse économique." In C. Chandezon, ed., *Les hommes et la terre dans la Méditerranée gréco-romaine*, 221–32. Toulouse.

Petrakos, V. H. 1967. "Τὸ Ἀμφιάρειον τοῦ Ὠρωποῦ." *AEph*, ser. 3, 106: 1–13.

———. 1968. *Ὁ Ὠρωπὸς καὶ τὸ ἱερὸν τοῦ Ἀμφιαράου*. Athens.

———. 1997. *Οι επιγραφές του Ὠρωπού*. Athens.

Petropoulos, M. 1987–88. "Τρίτη ανασκαφική περίοδος στο Άνω Μαζαράκι (Ρακίτα) Αχαΐας." In *Πρακτικά του Γ' διεθνούς συνεδρίου Πελοποννησιακών σπουδών, Καλαμάτα, 8–15 σεπτεμβρίου 1985*, vol. II, 81–96. Athens.

———. 1991. "Τοπογραφικά της χώρας των Πατρέων." In A. D. Rizakis, ed., *Αρχαία Αχαΐα και Ηλεία*, 249–58. Athens and Paris.

———. 1992–93. "Περίπτερος αψιδωτός γεωμετρικός ναός στο Άνω Μαζαράκι (Ρακίτα) Πατρών." In *Πρακτικά του Δ' διεθνούς συνεδρίου Πελοποννησιακών σπουδών, Κόρινθος, 9–16 σεπτεμβρίου 1990*, vol. II, 141–58. Athens.

———. 2001. "Γεωμετρικός ναός Ρακίτας· Λατρευομένη θεότητα." In V. Mitsopoulos-Leon, ed., *Forschungen in der Peloponnes: Akten des Symposions anläßlich der Feier «100 Jahre Österreichisches Archäologisches Institut Athen», Athen 5.3–7.3.1998*, 39–45. Athens.

———. 2001–2. "Η αρχαία Μεσάτις της Πάτρας." In *Πρακτικά του ς' διεθνούς συνεδρίου Πελοποννησιακών σπουδών, Τρίπολις, 24–29 σεπτεμβρίου 2000*, vol. II, 399–422. Athens.

———. 2002. "The Geometric Temple at Ano Mazaraki (Rakita) in Achaia during the Period of Colonisation." In E. Greco, ed., *Gli Achei e l'identità etnica degli Achei d'occidente*, 143–64. Paestum and Athens.

Petropoulos, M., and A. D. Rizakis. 1994. "Settlement Patterns and Landscape in the Coastal Area of Patras: Preliminary Report." *JRA* 7: 183–207.

Petsas, P. 1991. "Αμνημόνευτα από την Αιτωλοακαρνανία." In *Πρακτικά του Α´ αρχαιολογικού και ιστορικού συνεδρίου Αιτωλοακαρνανίας, Αγρίνιο, 21–22–23 οκτωβρίου 1988*, 129–30. Agrinion.

Pfeiffer, R. 1949. *Callimachus*. Vol. I, *Fragmenta*. Oxford.

Pfister, F. 1951. *Die Reisebilder des Herakleides: Einleitung, Text, Übersetzung und Kommentar, mit einer Übersicht über die Geschichte der griechischen Volkskunde*. Vienna.

Picard, O. 1979. *Chalcis et la confédération eubéenne*. Paris.

———. 1984. "Monnaies." In *L'antre corycien*, vol. II, 281–306. Paris.

———. 1989. "Innovations monétaires dans la Grèce du IV e siècle." *CRAI*: 673–87.

Pierson, P. 2000. "Increasing Returns, Path Dependence, and the Study of Politics." *American Political Science Review* 94: 251–67.

Pierson, P., and T. Skocpol. 2002. "Historical Institutionalism in Political Science." In I. Katznelson and H. Milner, eds., *Political Science: The State of the Discipline*, 693–721. New York.

Pikoulas, G. A. 2000–2003. "Λακεδαιμονίων συνθεκαι Αιτολοῖς." *Horos* 14–16: 455–67.

Pirenne-Delforge, V. 1994. *L'Aphrodite grecque: Contribution à l'étude de ses cultes et de sa personnalité dans le panthéon archaïque et classique*. Athens and Liège.

Plassart, A. 1921. "Inscriptions de Delphes: La liste des théorodoques." *BCH* 45: 1–85.

———. 1926. "Fouilles de Thespies et de l'hiéron des Muses de l'Hélicon: Inscriptions." *BCH* 50: 383–462.

Platon, N., and M. Feyel. 1938. "Inventaire sacré de Thespies trouvé a Chostia (Béotie)." *BCH* 62: 149–66.

Pleket, H. W. 1964. *Epigraphica*. Vol. I, *Texts on the Economic History of the Greek World*. Leiden.

Polignac, F. 1994. "Mediation, Competition, and Sovereignty: The Evolution of Rural Sanctuaries in Geometric Greece." In S. E. Alcock and R. Osborne, eds., *Placing the Gods: Sanctuaries and Sacred Space in Ancient Greece*, 3–18. Oxford.

———. 1995 [1984]. *Cults, Territory, and the Origins of the Greek City-State*. Chicago.

Pollhammer, E. 2002. "Das Kap Kolonna: Eine Festung der Attaliden auf Aigina." In B. Asamer, ed., *Temenos: Festgabe für Florens Felten und Stefan Hiller*, 99–108. Vienna.

Pomtow, H. 1918. "Delphische Neufunde, II: Neue delphische Inschriften." *Klio* 15: 1–77.

Poulsen, F. 1929. "La deuxième campagne de fouilles gréco-danoise à Calydon." *CRAI*: 76–87.

———. 1930. "Inscription de Kalydon relative à une affaire de succession." *BCH* 54: 42–50.

Powell, J. U. 1925. *Collectanea Alexandrina*. Oxford.

Prandi, L. 1982. "Platea e la Parasopiade in età arcaica." *Giornale filologico ferrarese* 5: 3–16, 49–52.

———. 1983. "L'Heraion di Platea e la festa dei Daidala." In M. Sordi, ed., *Santuari e politica nel mondo antico*, 82–94. Milan.

———. 1988. *Platea: Momenti e problemi della storia di una polis*. Padua.

———. 1989. "La rifondazione de 'Panionion' e la catastrofe di Elice (373 a.C.)." *Contributi dell'istituto di storia antica dell' Università di Milano* 15: 43–59.

Préaux, C. 1962. "La paix à l'époque hellénistique." In *La paix: Recueils de la Societé J. Bodin*, 227–301. Brussels.

Pretzler, M. 2005. "Pausanias at Mantinea: Invention and Manipulation of Local History." *PCPS* 51: 21–34.

Price, M. J., and N. M. Waggoner. 1975. *Archaic Greek Coinage: The Asyut Hoard*. London.

Pritchett, W. K. 1965–92. *Studies in Ancient Greek Topography* 8 vols. Berkeley and Los Angeles.

———. 1974–91. *The Greek State at War*. 5 vols. Berkeley and Los Angeles.

———. 1993. *The Liar School of Herodotus*. Amsterdam.

Prott, I., and L. Ziehen. 1896–1906. *Leges Graecorum Sacrae e Titulis Collectae*. Leipzig.

Psoma, S. 1999. "Ἀρκαδικόν." *Horos* 13: 81–96.

———. 2001. *Olynthe et les Chalcidiens de Thrace: Études de numismatique et d'histoire*. Stuttgart.

Psoma, S., and D. Tsangari. 2003. "Monnaie commune et états fédéraux: La circulation des monnayages frappés par les états fédéraux du monde grec." In K. Buraselis and K. Zoumboulakis, eds., *The Idea of European Community in History: Conference Proceedings*, vol. II, *Aspects of Connecting Poleis and Ethnē in Ancient Greece*, 111–42. Athens.

Purcell, N. 1995a. "Eating Fish: The Paradoxes of Seafood." In J. Wilkins, D. Harvey, and M. Dobson, eds., *Food in Antiquity*, 132–49. Exeter.

———. 1995b. "On the Sacking of Carthage and Corinth." In D. Innis, H. Hine, and C. Pelling, eds., *Ethics and Rhetoric: Classical Essays for Donald Russell on His Seventy-Fifth Birthday*, 133–48. Oxford.

———. 2005. "The Ancient Mediterranean: The View from the Customs House." In W. V. Harris, ed., *Rethinking the Mediterranean*, 200–234. Oxford.

Raaflaub, K. 2004. *The Discovery of Freedom in Ancient Greece*. Chicago.

Rackham, O. 1983. "Observations on the Historical Ecology of Boeotia." *ABSA* 78: 291–351.

Raeder, A. 1912. *L'arbitrage international chez les Hellènes*. New York.

Ramp, W. 1998. "Effervescence, Differentiation, and Representation in *The Elementary Forms*." In N. J. Allen, W. S. F. Pickering, and W. Watts Miller, eds., *On Durkheim's Elementary Forms of Religious Life*, 136–48. London.

Rappaport, R. A. 1999. *Ritual and Religion in the Making of Humanity*. Cambridge.

Raubitschek, A. E. 1949. *Dedications from the Athenian Akropolis*. Cambridge, Mass.

Redfield, J. 1990. "From Sex to Politics: The Rites of Artemis Triklaria and Dionysos Aisymnetes at Patras." In D. M. Halperin, J. J. Winkler, and F. Zeitlin, eds., *Before Sexuality: The Construction of Erotic Experience in the Ancient Greek World*, 115–34. Princeton.

Reger, G. 1994. *Regionalism and Change in the Economy of Independent Delos, 314–167 B.C.* Berkeley and Los Angeles.

———. 2003. "The Economy." In A. Erskine, ed., *A Companion to the Hellenistic World*, 331–53. Oxford.

———. 2004. "Sympoliteia in Hellenistic Asia Minor." In S. Colvin, ed., *The Greco-Roman East: Politics, Culture, Society*, 145–180. Cambridge.

———. 2007. "Hellenistic Greece and Western Asia Minor." In W. Scheidel, I. Morris, and R. P. Saller, eds., *The Cambridge Economic History of the Greco-Roman World*, 460–83. Cambridge.

Reger, G., and M. Risser. 1991. "Coinage and Federation in Hellenistic Keos." In J. F. Cherry, J. L. Davis, and E. Mantzourani, eds., *Landscape Archaeology as Long-Term History: Northern Keos in the Cycladic Islands from Earliest Settlement until Modern Times*, 305–17. Los Angeles.

Reinach, A.-J. 1911. "Un monument delphien: L'Étolie sur les trophées gaulois de Kallion." *Journal international d'archéologie numismatique* 13: 177–240.

Rhodes, P. J. 1981. *A Commentary on the Aristotelian Athenaiōn Politeia*. Oxford.

———. 1999. "Sparta, Thebes and *Autonomia*." *Eirene* 35: 33–40.

Rhodes, P. J., and R. Osborne. 2003. *Greek Historical Inscriptions, 404–323 BC*. Oxford.

Rhomaios, K. A. 1915. "Περὶ τῶν ἐν τοῖς μουσείοις τῆς 8ης ἀρχαιολογικῆς περιφερείας." *AD* 1 Παράρτημα: 45–49.

———. 1916. " Ἔρευναι ἐν Θέρμῳ." *AD* 2: 179–89.

———. 1924–25. "Εἰδήσεις ἐκ τῆς 8ης ἀρχαιολογικῆς περιφερείας κατὰ τὰ ἔτη 1922–25." *AD* 9 Παράρτημα: 1–12.

———. 1926 [1929]. "Ἁι Ἑλληνοδανικαὶ ἀνασκαφαὶ τῆς Καλυδῶνος." *AD* 10 Παράρτημα: 24–40.

———. 1931. "Ἀνασκαφή ἐν Θέρμῳ." *PAAH* 61–70.

Rice, D. G. 1975. "Xenophon, Diodorus and the Year 379–378 B.C.: Reconstruction and Reappraisal." *YCS* 24: 95–130.

Richter, G. M. A. 1960. *Kouroi: Archaic Greek Youths; A Study of the Development of the Kouros Type in Greek Sculpture*. London.

Riele, G.-J., and M.-J. Riele. 1966. "Une terre-cuite de Platées et son parentage." *Mnemosyne* 19: 261–68.

Rigsby, K. 1987. "A Decree of Haliartos on Cult." *AJP* 108: 729–40.

———. 1996. *Asylia: Territorial Inviolability in the Hellenistic World*. Berkeley and Los Angeles.

Riker, W. H. 1964. *Federalism: Origin, Operation, Significance*. Boston and Toronto.

———. 1987. *The Development of American Federalism*. Boston.

Rizakis, A. D. 1990a. "Cadastres et espace rural dans le nord-ouest du Péloponnèse." *DHA* 16: 259–80.

———. 1990b. "La *politeia* dans les cités de la confédération achéenne." *Tyche* 5: 109–34.

———. 1995. *Achaïe. Vol. I, Sources textuelles et histoire régionale*. Athens and Paris.

———. 2003. "Le collège des nomographes et le système de représentation dans le koinon Achéen." In K. Buraselis and K. Zoumboulakis, eds., *The Idea of European Community in History: Conference Proceedings*, vol. II, *Aspects of Connecting Poleis and Ethnē in Ancient Greece*, 97–109. Athens.

———. 2008a. *Achaïe. Vol. III, Les cités achéennes: Épigraphie et histoire*. Athens and Paris.

———. 2008b. "L'expérience de l'organisation intercivique et supracivique dans la confédération achéenne." In M. Lombardo and F. Frisone, eds., *Forme sovrapoleiche e interpoleiche di organizzazione nel mondo greco antico: Atti del convegno internazionale, Lecce, 17–20 settembre 2008*, 274–85. Lecce.

———. Forthcoming. "États fédéraux et sanctuaires: Le cas du *koinon* achéen." In P. Funke and M. Haake, eds., *Greek Federal States and Their Sanctuaries: Identity and Integration*. Stuttgart.

Rizakis, A. D., R. Dalongeville, M. Lakakis, L. Kallivretakis, A. Moutzali, and V. Panayo-topoulos. 1992. *Paysages d'Achaïe.* Vol. I, *Le bassin du Peiros et la plaine occidentale.* Athens and Paris.

Robert, L. 1925. "Notes d'épigraphie hellénistique." *BCH* 49: 219–38.

———. 1933. "Sur les inscriptions de Chios." *BCH* 57: 505–43.

———. 1935a. *Collection Froehner.* Vol. I, *Inscriptions grecques.* Paris.

———. 1935b. "Études sur les inscriptions et la topographie de la Grèce centrale." *BCH* 59: 193–209.

———. 1939. "Hellenica, I: Inscriptions de Pagai en Mégaride relatives à un arbitrage." *RPh* 65: 97–122.

———. 1940–65. *Hellenica: Recueil d'épigraphie, de numismatique et d'antiquités grecques.* 13 vols. Limoges and Paris.

———. 1978a. "Documents d'Asie Mineure." *BCH* 102: 395–543.

———. 1978b. "Les conquêtes du dynaste lycien Arbinas." *JSav* 3–48.

Robertson, N. 1976. "A Corinthian Inscription Recording Honors at Elis for Corinthian Judges." *Hesperia* 45: 253–66.

———. 1978. "The Myth of the First Sacred War." *CQ* 28: 38–73.

———. 1986. "A Point of Precedence at Plataia: The Dispute between Athens and Sparta over Leading the Procession." *Hesperia* 55: 88–102.

———. 1987. "Government and Society at Miletus, 525–442 B.C." *Phoenix* 41: 356–98.

Robinson, D. M. 1931. "New Inscriptions from Olynthus and Environs." *TAPA* 62: 40–56.

———. 1934. "Inscriptions from Olynthus, 1934." *TAPA* 65: 103–37.

Robinson, D. M., and P. A. Clement. 1938. *Excavations at Olynthus.* Vol. IX, *The Chalcidic Mint and the Excavation Coins Found in 1928–1934.* Baltimore.

Rodden, J. 2007. *Hamilton's Paradox: The Promise and Peril of Fiscal Federalism.* Cambridge.

Roebuck, C. 1941. *A History of Messenia from 369 to 146 B.C.* Chicago.

Roesch, P. 1965a. "Notes d'épigraphie béotienne." *RPh* 39: 252–63.

———. 1965b. *Thespies et la confédération béotienne.* Paris.

———. 1966. "Inscriptions du Musée de Thèbes." *REA* 68: 61–85.

———. 1971. "Une loi fédérale béotienne sur la préparation militaire." In *Acta of the Fifth Congress of Greek and Latin Epigraphy, Cambridge, 1967,* 81–88. Oxford.

———. 1973. "Pouvoir fédéral et vie économique des cités dans la Béotie hellénistique." In *Akten des VI. internationalen Kongresses für griechische und lateinische Epigraphik, München, 1972,* 259–70. Munich.

———. 1979. "La cavalerie béotienne à l'époque hellénistique (338–172)." In D. M. Pippidi, ed., *Actes du VIIᵉ congrès international d'épigraphie grecque et latine, Constanza, 9–15 septembre 1977,* 243–54. Bucharest and Paris.

———. 1982. *Études béotiennes.* Paris.

———. 1984. "Un décret inédit de la ligue thébaine et la flotte d'Épaminondas." *REG* 97: 45–60.

———. 1985. "La justice en Béotie à l'époque hellénistique." In J. M. Fossey and H. Giroux, eds., *Proceedings of the Third International Conference on Boiotian Antiquities,* 127–34. Amsterdam.

Rougement, G. 1991. "Complémentarité entre les différentes parties du territoire dans les cités grecques de l'antiquité classique." In M.-C. Cauvin, ed., *Rites et rythmes agraires,* 127–33. Lyon.

Roussel, D. 1976. *Tribu et cité: Études sur les groupes sociaux dans les cités grecques aux époques archaïque et classique.* Paris.

Rousset, D. 1994. "Les frontières des cités grecques: Premières réflexions à partir du recueil des documents épigraphiques." *CCG* 5: 97–126.

———. 2002. *Le territoire de Delphes et la terre d'Apollon.* Paris.

———. 2004. "West Lokris." In M. H. Hansen and T. H. Nielsen, eds., *An Inventory of Archaic and Classical Poleis,* 391–98. Oxford.

———. 2006. "Les inscriptions de Kallipolis d'Étolie." *BCH* 130: 381–434.

Rousset, D., and P. Katzouros. 1992. "Une délimitation de frontière en Phocide." *BCH* 116: 197–215.

Roux, G. 1989. "Problèmes delphiques d'architecture et d'épigraphie." *RA,* 29–56.

Roy, J. 1971. "Arcadia and Boiotia in Peloponnesian Affairs, 370–362 B.C." *Historia* 20: 569–99.

———. 2000. "The Economies of Arkadia." In T. H. Nielsen and J. Roy, eds., *Defining Ancient Arkadia,* 320–81. Copenhagen.

———. 2003. "The Achaian League." In K. Buraselis and K. Zoumboulakis, eds., *The Idea of European Community in History: Conference Proceedings,* vol. II, *Aspects of Connecting Poleis and Ethnē in Ancient Greece,* 81–95. Athens.

Rubel, A. 2000. *Stadt in Angst: Religion und Politik in Athen während des peloponnesischen Krieges.* Darmstadt.

Rung, E. 2004. "Xenophon, the Oxyrhynchus Historian and the Mission of Timocrates to Greece." In C. Tuplin, ed., *Xenophon and His World: Papers from a Conference Held in Liverpool in July 1999,* 413–25. Stuttgart.

Russo, C. F., ed. 1965. *Hesiodi Scutum: Introduzione, testo critico e commento con traduzione e indici.* Florence.

Rutherford, I. 2001. *Pindar's Paeans: A Reading of the Fragments, with a Survey of the Genre.* Oxford.

———. 2009. "Aristodama and the Aetolians: An Itinerant Poetess and Her Agenda." In R. L. Hunter and I. Rutherford, eds., *Wandering Poets in Ancient Greek Culture: Travel, Locality and Pan-Hellenism,* 237–48. Cambridge.

Ryder, T. T. B. 1965. *Koinē Eirēnē: General Peace and Local Independence in Ancient Greece.* Oxford.

Rzepka, J. 2002. "Ethnos, Koinon, Sympoliteia, and Greek Federal States." In T. Derda, J. Urbanik, and M. Weçowski, eds., *Εὐεργεσίας Χάριν· Studies Presented to Benedetto Bravo and Ewa Wipszycka by Their Disciples,* 225–47. Warsaw.

———. 2010. "Plutarch on the Theban Uprising of 379 B.C. and the *Boiotarchoi* of the Boeotian Confederacy under the Principate." *Historia* 59: 115–18.

Sahlins, M. 1976. *Culture and Practical Reason.* Chicago.

Sakellariou, M. 1991. "Le peuplement de l'Achaïe à la fin de l'âge du bronze et le début de l'âge de fer." In A. D. Rizakis, ed., *Αρχαία Αχαΐα και Ηλεία,* 13–18. Athens and Paris.

Salmon, J. 1984. *Wealthy Corinth: A History of the City to 338 BC.* Oxford.

Salmon, P. 1956. "Les districts béotiens." *REA* 58: 51–70.

———. 1978. *Étude sur la confédération béotienne (447/6–386).* Brussels.

———. 1985. "Droits et devoirs des cités dans la confédération béotienne (447/6–386)." In G. Argoud and P. Roesch, eds., *La Béotie antique, Lyon–Saint-Étienne, 16–20 mai 1983,* 301–6. Paris.

———. 1995. "Le rôle des béotarques dans la confédération béotienne." In E. Frézouls and A. Jacquemin, eds., *Les relations internationales: Actes du colloque de Strasbourg, 15–17 juin 1993*, 365–83. Strasbourg.

Salviat, F., and C. Vatin, eds. 1971. *Inscriptions de Grèce centrale*. Paris.

Sánchez, P. 2001. *L'amphictionie des Pyles et de Delphes: Recherches sur son rôle historique, des origines au IIe siècle de notre ère*. Stuttgart.

Sandbach, F. H., ed. 1967. *Plutarchi Moralia*. Vol. VII, *Fragmenta*. Leipzig.

Sargent, T., and F. Velde. 2002. *The Big Problem of Small Change*. Princeton.

Savalli, I. 1985. "I neocittadini nella città ellenistiche: Note sulla concessione e l'acquisizione della 'politeia.'" *Historia* 34: 387–431.

Schachter, A. 1967. "A Boeotian Cult-Type." *BICS* 14: 1–16.

———. 1976. "*Homeric Hymn to Apollo*, lines 213–8 (The Onchestos Episode): Another Interpretation." *BICS* 23: 102–14.

———. 1978. "La fête des *Pamboiotia*: Le dossier épigraphique." *CEA* 8: 81–107.

———. 1981–94. *Cults of Boiotia*. 4 vols. London.

———. 1989. "Boeotia in the Sixth Century." In H. Beister and J. Buckler, eds., *Boiotika: Vorträge vom 5. internationalen Böotien-Kolloquium zu Ehren von Professor Dr. Siegfried Lauffer*, 73–86. Munich.

———. 1994. "Gods in the Service of the State: The Boiotian Experience." In L. Aigner Foresti, A. Barzanò, C. Bearzot, L. Prandi, and G. Zecchini, eds., *Federazioni e federalismo nell'Europa antica: Alle radici della casa comune europea*, 67–86. Milan.

———. 1997. "The Daphnephoria of Thebes." In P. A. Bernardini, ed., *Presenza e funzione della città di Tebe nella cultura greca: Atti del convegno internazionale, Urbino, 7–9 iuglio 1997*, 99–123. Pisa and Rome.

Schaps, D. M. 1987. "Small Change in Boeotia." *ZPE* 69: 293–96.

———. 2004. *The Invention of Coinage and the Monetization of Ancient Greece*. Ann Arbor.

Scheffer, C. 1992. "Boeotian Festival Scenes: Competition, Consumption, and Cult in Archaic Black Figure." In R. Hägg, ed., *The Iconography of Greek Cult in the Archaic and Classical Periods*, 117–41. Athens and Liège.

Scheidel, W. 2003. "The Greek Demographic Expansion: Models and Comparisons." *JHS* 103: 120–40.

Scherberich, K. 2009. *Koinè symmachía: Untersuchungen zum Hellenenbund Antigonos' III. Doson und Philipps V. (224–197 v. Chr.)*. Stuttgart.

Scheu, F. 1960. "Coinage Systems of Aetolia." *NC*, ser. 6, 20: 38–52.

Schilardi, D. 1977. "The Thespian Polyandrion (424 B.C.): The Excavations and Finds from a Thespian State Burial." Ph.D. dissertation, Princeton University.

Schmitt, H. H. 1994. "Überlegungen zur Sympolitie." In G. Thür, ed., *Symposion 1993: Vorträge zur griechischen und hellenistischen Rechtsgeschichte, Graz-Andritz, 12.–16. September 1993*, 35–44. Cologne.

Schoch, M. 1996. "Die Einrichtung des zweiten akarnanischen Bundes." In P. Berktold, J. Schmid, and C. Wacker, eds., *Akarnanien: Eine Landschaft im antiken Griechenland*, 129–31. Würzburg.

———. 1997. *Beiträge zur Topographie Akarnaniens in klassischer und hellenistischer Zeit*. Munich.

Schoch, M., and C. Wacker. 1996. "Die Teilung Akarnaniens." In P. Berktold, J. Schmid, and C. Wacker, eds., *Akarnanien: Eine Landschaft im antiken Griechenland*, 125–28. Würzburg.

Scholten, J. B. 2000. *The Politics of Plunder: The Aitolians and Their Koinon in the Early Hellenistic Era, 279–217 B.C.* Berkeley and Los Angeles.

———. 2003. "The Internal Structure of the Aitolian Union: A Case Study in Ancient Greek Sympoliteia." In K. Buraselis and K. Zoumboulakis, eds., *The Idea of European Community in History: Conference Proceedings*, vol. II, *Aspects of Connecting Poleis and Ethnē in Ancient Greece*, 66–80. Athens.

Schwahn, W. 1931a. "Boiotische Stadtanleihen aus dem dritten Jahrhundert v. Chr." *Hermes* 66: 337–46.

———. 1931b. "Das Bürgerrecht der sympolitischen Bundesstaaten bei den Griechen." *Hermes* 66: 97–118.

Schweigert, E. 1939. "The American Excavations in the Athenian Agora, Fifteenth Report: Greek Inscriptions (1–13)." *Hesperia* 8: 1–47.

Schweighäuser, J. 1792. *Polybii Megalopolitani Historiarum Quidquid Superest*, vol. V. Leipzig.

Schwertfeger, T. 1974. *Der achäische Bund von 146 bis 27 v. Chr.* Munich.

Schwyzer, E. 1923. *Dialectorum Graecarum Exempla Epigraphica Potiora*. Leipzig.

Scott, L. 2005. *Historical Commentary on Herodotus Book 6*. Leiden.

Seibert, J. 1979. *Die politischen Flüchtlinge und Verbannten in der griechischen Geschichte*. Darmstadt.

Severyns, A. 1938. *Recherches sur la Chrestomathie de Proclos, première partie: Le Codex 239 de Photius*. Paris.

Shapiro, H. A. 1984a. "Herakles and Kyknos." *AJA* 88: 523–29.

———. 1984b. "Herakles, Kyknos, and Delphi." In H. A. G. Brijder, ed., *Ancient Greek and Related Pottery: Proceedings of the International Vase Symposium, Amsterdam, 12–15 April 1984*, 271–74. Amsterdam.

Sheets, G. A. 1994. "Conceptualizing International Law in Thucydides." *AJP* 115: 51–76.

Sheppard, E. S. 1984. "The Distance Decay Gravity Model Debate." In G. L. Gaile and C. J. Willmott, eds., *Spatial Statistics and Models*, 367–88. Dordrecht.

Shepsle, K. A. 1986. "Institutional Equilibrium and Equilibrium Institutions." In H. F. Weisberg, ed., *Political Science: The Science of Politics*, 51–81. New York.

———. 2006. "Old Questions and New Answers about Institutions: The Riker Objection Revisited." In B. R. Weingast and D. A. Wittman, eds., *The Oxford Handbook of Political Economy*, 1031–49. Oxford.

Sherwin-White, S. 1978. *Ancient Cos: An Historical Study from the Dorian Settlement to the Imperial Period*. Göttingen.

Shipley, G. 2000. "The Extent of Spartan Territory in the Late Classical and Hellenistic Periods." *ABSA* 95: 367–90.

Siewert, P. 1977. "L'autonomie de Hyettos et la sympolitie thespienne dans les Helléniques d'Oxyrhynchos." *REG* 90: 462–64.

———. 1981. "Eine Bronze-Urkunde mit elischen Urteilen über Böoter, Thessaler, Athen und Thespiai." In A. Mallwitz, ed., *Bericht über die Ausgrabungen in Olympia*, vol. X, 228–48. Berlin.

———. 1994a. "Eine archaische Rechtsaufzeichnung aus der antiken Stadt Elis." In G. Thür, ed., *Symposion 1993: Vorträge zur griechischen und hellenistischen Rechtsgeschichte, Graz-Andritz, 12.–16. September 1993*, 17–32. Cologne.

———. 1994b. "Symmachien in den neuen Inschriften von Olympia: Zu den sogennanten Periöken der Eleer." In L. Aigner Foresti, A. Barzanò, C. Bearzot, L. Prandi, and G. Zecchini, eds., *Federazioni e federalismo nell'Europa antica: Alle radici della casa comune europea*, 257–64. Milan.

———. 2006. "Kultische und politische Organisationsformen im frühen Olympia und in seiner Umgebung." In K. Freitag, P. Funke, and M. Haake, eds., *Kult—Politik—Ethnos: Überregionale Heiligtümer in Spannungsfeld von Kult und Politik*, 43–54. Stuttgart.

Simon, E. 1997. "Héra en Béotie et en Thessalie." In J. de la Genière, ed., *Héra: Images, espaces, cults; Actes du colloque international du centre de recherches archéologiques de l'Université de Lille III et de l'Association P.R.A.C., Lille, 29–30 novembre 1993*, 83–86. Naples.

Simpson, R. H. 1958. "Aetolian Policy in the Late Fourth Century B.C." *AC* 27: 357–62.

Sinn, U. 1992. "The 'Sacred Herd' of Artemis at Lusoi." In R. Hägg, ed., *The Iconography of Greek Cult in the Archaic and Classical Periods*, 177–88. Athens and Liège.

Skias, A. N. 1917. "Ἐπιγραφαὶ ἐκ Πλαταιῶν." *AEph*, ser. 3, 35: 157–67.

Smarczyk, B. 1990. *Untersuchungen zur Religionspolitik und politischen Propaganda Athens im delisch-attischen Seebund*. Munich.

Smart, J. D. 1986. "Thucydides and Hellanicus." In I. S. Moxon, J. D. Smart, and A. J. Woodman, eds., *Past Perspectives: Studies in Greek and Roman Historical Writing; Papers Presented at a Conference in Leeds, 6–8 April 1983*, 19–35. Cambridge.

Smith, A. D. 1986. *The Ethnic Origins of Nations*. Oxford.

Smith, G., ed. 1995. *Federalism: The Multiethnic Challenge*. London and New York.

Snell, B. 1946. "Pindars Hymnus auf Zeus." *Antike und Abendland* 2: 180–92.

Sokolowski, F. 1969. *Lois sacrées des cités grecques*. Paris.

———. 1970. "Règlement relatif à la célébration des Panionia." *BCH* 94: 109–12.

Sordi, M. 1953a. "La prima guerra sacra." *Riv. Fil.* 81: 320–46.

———. 1953b. "Le origini del koinon etolico." *Acme* 6: 419–45.

———. 1957. "La fondation du collège des naopes et le renouveau politique de l'amphictionie au IV e siècle." *BCH* 81: 38–75.

———. 1958. *La lega tessala fino ad Alessandro Magno*. Rome.

———. 1968. "Aspetti del federalismo greco arcaico: Autonomia ed egemonia nel koinón beotico." *A&R* 13: 66–75.

———. 1969. "Die Anfänge des aitolischen Koinon." In F. Gschnitzer, ed., *Zur griechischen Staatskunde*, 343–74. Darmstadt.

———. 1973. "La restaurazione della lega beotica nel 379–8 a.C." *Athenaeum* 51: 79–91.

———. 1991. "Il trattato fra Sparta e gli Etoli e la guerra d'Elide." *Aevum* 64: 35–38.

———. 1994. "Il federalismo greco nell'età classica." In L. Aigner Foresti, A. Barzanò, C. Bearzot, L. Prandi, and G. Zecchini, eds., *Federazioni e federalismo nell'Europa antica: Alle radici della casa comune europea*, 3–22. Milan.

———. 2005. "L'egemonia beotica in Diodoro, libro XV." In C. Bearzot and F. Landucci, eds., *Diodoro e l'altra Grecia: Macedonia, occidente, ellenismo nella Biblioteca storica; Atti del convegno, Milano, 15–16 gennaio 2004*, 3–15. Milan.

Sosin, J. 2004. "Acraephia Counts." *ZPE* 148: 193–95.

Soter, S. 1998. "Holocene Uplift and Subsidence of the Helike Delta, Gulf of Corinth, Greece." In I. Stewart and C. Vita-Finzi, eds., *Coastal Tectonics*, 41–56. London.

Soter, S. and D. Katsonopoulou. 1998. "The Search for Ancient Helike, 1988–1995: Geological, Sonar, and Bore Hole Studies." In D. Katsonopoulou, S. Soter, and D. Schilardi, eds., *Helike*, vol. II: *Ancient Helike and Aigialeia: Proceedings of the Second International Conference, Aigion, 1–3 December 1995*, 67–124. Athens.

————. 1999. "Occupation Horizons Found in the Search for the Ancient Greek City of Helike." *Geoarchaeology* 14: 531–63.

Sotiriadis, G. 1905. "Ἀνασκαφαὶ ἐν Θερμῷ." *AEph*, ser. 3, 23: 57–100.

Sourvinou-Inwood, C. 1988. "Further Aspects of Polis Religion." *Annali dell'istituto orientale di Napoli* 10: 259–74.

————. 1990. "What Is *Polis* Religion?" In O. Murray and S. Price, eds., *The Greek City from Homer to Alexander*, 295–322. Oxford.

Southall, A. W. 1969. "The Illusion of Tribe." *Journal of Asian and African Studies* 5: 28–50.

————. 1996. "Tribes." In D. Levinson and M. Ember, eds., *Encyclopedia of Cultural Anthropology*, 1329–36. New York.

Spyropoulos, T. 1971. "Ἀρχαιότητες καὶ μνημεία Βοιωτίας-Φθιωτίδος." *AD* 26: 195–238.

————. 1973. "Εἰδήσεις ἐκ Βοιωτίας." *AAA* 6: 375–99.

————. 1975 [1977]. "Ἀνασκαφὴ παρὰ τὴν Κορωνείαν Βοιωτίας." *PAAH*, 392–414.

Stavropoulos, A. 1954. *Αἴγιον· Ἱστορία τῆς πόλεως Αἰγίου ἀπὸ ἀρχαιοτάτων χρόνων μέχρι τῶν ἡμερῶν μας*. Patras.

Stepan, A. 1999. "Federalism and Democracy: Beyond the U.S. Model." *Journal of Democracy* 10: 19–34.

Stephanis, I. E. 1982–83. "Ἡ Συμμετοχὴ τῶν Ἁλιαρτίων στὰ Πτώια." *Ἑλληνικά* 34: 220–22.

Stewart, A. F. 1990. *Greek Sculpture*. New Haven.

Stylianou, P. J. 1998. *A Historical Commentary on Diodorus Siculus, Book 15*. Oxford.

Svoronos, J.-N. 1911. "Νομισματικὴ Συλλογὴ Ἑλένης Ν. Μαυροκορδάτου ἀνήκουσα νῦν τῷ Γ. Ν. Μπαλατζῇ." *Journal international d'archéologie numismatique* 13: 241–300.

————. 1916. "Θησαυρὸς νομισματῶν ἐκ τοῦ χωρίου Μυροῦ Καρδίτσης τῆς Θεσσαλίας." *AD* 2: 273–335.

Swoboda, H. 1913. *Lehrbuch der griechischen Staatsaltertümer*. Freiburg.

————. 1922. "Die neuen Urkunden von Epidauros." *Hermes* 57: 518–34.

————. 1924. *Zwei Kapitel aus dem griechischen Bundesrecht*. Vienna.

Symeonoglou, S. 1985. *The Topography of Thebes from the Bronze Age to Modern Times*. Princeton.

Szántó, E. 1892. *Das griechische Bürgerrecht*. Freiburg.

Taeuber, H. 1981. "Sikyon statt Aigeira: Neue Beobachtungen zur Stele von Stymphalos (*IG* V/2, 351–7)." *ZPE* 42: 179–92.

Taillardat, J., and P. Roesch. 1966. "L'inventaire sacré de Thespies: L'alphabet attique en Béotie." *RPh* 40: 70–87.

Taita, J. 2000. "Gli Αἰτωλοί di Olimpia: L'identità etnica delle communità di vicinato del santuario olimpico." *Tyche* 15: 147–88.

Tandy, D. W. 1997. *Warriors into Traders: The Power of the Market in Early Greece*. Berkeley and Los Angeles.

Tataki, A. B. 1998. *Macedonians Abroad: A Contribution to the Prosopography of Ancient Macedonia.* Athens.

Tausend, K. 1992. *Amphiktyonie und Symmachie: Formen zwischenstaatlicher Beziehungen im archaischen Griechenland.* Stuttgart.

Teffeteller, A. 2001. "The Chariot Rite at Onchestos: Homeric Hymn to Apollo 229–38." *JHS* 121: 159–66.

Ténékidès, G. 1954. *La notion juridique d'indépendance et la tradition hellénique: Autonomie et fédéralisme aux Ve et IVe siècles av. J.-C.* Athens.

Thelen, K. 2003. "How Institutions Evolve: Insights from Comparative Historical Analysis." In J. Mahoney and D. Reuschmeyer, eds., *Comparative Historical Analysis in the Social Sciences,* 208–40. Cambridge.

Themelis, P. 1979. "Ausgrabungen in Kallipolis (ost-Aetolien) 1977–1978." *AAA* 12: 245–79.

———. 1983. "Δελφοί και περιοχή των 8° και 7° π.Χ. αιώνα (Φωκίδα–Δυτική Λοκρίδα)." *ASAA* 61: 213–56.

———. 1996. "Damophon." In O. Palagia and J. J. Pollitt, eds., *Personal Styles in Greek Sculpture,* 154–85. Cambridge.

———. 1999. "Ausgrabungen in Kallipolis (ost-Aetolien)." In W. Hoepfner, ed., *Geschichte des Wohnens,* vol. I, 427–40. Stuttgart.

———. 2004 [2007]. "Ανασκαφή Μεσσήνης." *PAAH* 159: 27–53.

———. 2008. "Κρίμα περὶ χώρας Μεσσηνίων καὶ Μεγαλοπολιτῶν." In I. A. Pikoulas, ed., *Ιστορίες για την αρχαία Αρκαδία· Proceedings of the International Symposium in Honour of James Roy, 50 χρόνια Ἀρκάς (1958–2008),* 211–22. Stemnitsa.

Thompson, M. 1939. "A Hoard of Greek Federal Silver." *Hesperia* 8: 116–54.

———. 1968. *The Agrinion Hoard.* New York.

Thür, G. 1987. "Neuere Untersuchungen zum Prozeßrecht der griechischen Poleis: Formen des Urteils." In D. Simon, ed., *Akten des 26. deutschen Rechtshistorikertages,* 467–84. Frankfurt.

———. 1995. "Zu den Hintergründen des 'Rechtswährungsvertrags zwischen Stymphalos und Demetrias' (IPArk 17)." In C. Schubert, K. Brodersen, and U. Huttner, eds., *Rom und der griechische Osten: Festschrift für Hatto H. Schmitt zum 65. Geburtstag, dargebracht von Schulern, Freunden und münchner Kollegen,* 267–72. Stuttgart.

Thür, G., and G. Stumpf. 1989. "Sechs Todesurteile und zwei plattierte Hemidrachmen aus Dyme: Zu *Syll.*³ 530, Munzkabinette Athen Nr. 4046 und München, Dyme 12." *Tyche* 4: 171–83.

Thür, G., and H. Taeuber. 1994. *Prozeßrechtliche Inschriften der griechischen Poleis: Arkadien (IPArk).* Vienna.

Tod, M. N. 1913. *International Arbitration amongst the Greeks.* Oxford.

———. 1946–48. *Greek Historical Inscriptions.* Oxford.

Todd, S. C. 1993. *The Shape of Athenian Law.* Oxford.

Touloumakos, J. 1971. *Zum Geschichtsbewußtsein der Griechen in der Zeit der römischen Herrschaft.* Bonn.

Touloupa, E. 1964. "Ἀρχαιότητες καὶ Μνημεία Βοιωτίας." *AD* 19: 191–203.

Tréheux, J. 1987. "Koinon." *REA* 89: 39–46.

Treisman, D. 1999. "Political Decentralization and Economic Reform: A Game-Theoretic Analysis." *American Journal of Political Science* 43: 488–517.

Treves, P. 1934. "Studi su Antiogono Dosone." *Athenaeum*, n.s., 12: 381–411.

Tsangari, D. I. 2007. *Corpus des monnaies d'or, d'argent et de bronze de la confédération étolienne*. Athens.

Tsirigoti-Drakotou, I. 2000. "Νέα στήλη πεσόντων από το δημόσιον σήμα· Μια πρώτη παρουσίαση." *AD* 55: 87–112.

Tsouvara-Souli, C. 1991. "Κορινθιακές λατρείες στην Ήπειρο και την Αιτωλοακαρνανία." In *Α΄ αρχαιολογικό και ιστορικό συνεδρίο Αιτωλοακαρνανίας· Μνημειακή κληρονομία και ιστορία της Αιτωλοακαρνανίας*, 149–61. Agrinion.

Tuplin, C. J. 1986. "The Fate of Thespiai during the Theban Hegemony." *Athenaeum* 64: 321–41.

———. 1987. "The Leuctra Campaign: Some Outstanding Problems." *Klio* 69: 72–107.

Turner, L. A. 1996. "The Basileia at Lebadeia." *Boeotia Antiqua VI: Proceedings of the 8th International Conference on Boiotian Antiquities, Loyola University of Chicago, 24–26 May 1995*, 105–26. Amsterdam.

Turner, V. 1967. *The Forest of Symbols: Aspects of Ndembu Ritual*. Ithaca.

Typaldou-Fakiris, C. 2004. *Villes fortifiées de Phocide et la IIIᵉ guerre sacrée, 356–346 av. J.-C.* Aix-en-Provence.

Ulrichs, H. N. 1840–63. *Reisen und Forschungen in Griechenland*. 2 vols. Bremen.

Urban, R. 1979. *Wachstum und Krise des achäischen Bundes: Quellenstudien zur Entwicklung des Bundes von 280 bis 222 v. Chr.* Wiesbaden.

———. 1991. *Der Königsfrieden von 387/6 v. Chr: Vorgeschichte, Zustandekommen, Ergebnis und politische Umsetzung*. Stuttgart.

Ure, A. D. 1929. "Boeotian Geometricising Vases." *JHS* 49: 160–71.

van Alfen, P. 2011. "Social Controls, Institutions, and the Regulation of Commodities in Classical Aegean Markets." *Marburger Beiträge zur antiken Handels-, Wirtschafts- und Sozialgeschichte* 28: 197–229.

van Effenterre, H., and F. Ruzé. 1994. *Nomima: Recueil d'inscriptions politiques et juridiques de l'archaïsme grec*. Rome.

van Groningen, B. A. 1933. *Aristote: Le second livre de l'Économique*. Leiden.

van Wees, H. 2004. *Greek Warfare: Myths and Realities*. London.

Vatin, C. 1966. "Un tarif des poissons à Delphes." *BCH* 80: 274–80.

———. 1968. "La convention Chaleion-Tritea." *BCH* 92: 29–36.

Velissaropoulos-Karakostas, J. 2002. "Merchants, Prostitutes and the 'New Poor': Forms of Contract and Social Status." In P. Cartledge, E. E. Cohen, and L. Foxhall, eds., *Money, Labour, and Land: Approaches to the Economies of Ancient Greece*, 130–39. London.

Vélissaropoulos, J. 1980. *Les nauclères grecs*. Paris.

Veneri, A. 1990. "Poseidone e l'Elicona: Alcuni osservazioni sull'antichità e la continuità di una tradizione mitica beotica." In A. Schachter, ed., *Essays in the Topography, History, and Culture of Boiotia*, 129–34. Montreal.

———. 1996. "L'Elicona nella cultura tespiese intorno al III sec. a.C.: La stele di Euthy[kl]es." In A. Hurst and A. Schachter, eds., *La montagne des Muses*, 73–86. Geneva.

Vermeule, C. C. 1998. "Baby Herakles and the Snakes: Three Phases of His Development." In G. Capecchi, O. Paoletti, C. Cianferoni, A. M. Esposito, and A. Romualdi, eds., *In Memoria di Enrico Paribeni*, 505–13. Rome.

Vermeule, C. C., and M. B. Comstock. 1988. *Sculpture in Stone and Bronze in the Museum of Fine Arts, Boston: Additions to the Collections of Greek, Etruscan, and Roman Art, 1971–1988*. Boston.

Vidal-Naquet, P. 1986. *The Black Hunter: Forms of Thought and Forms of Society in the Greek World*. Baltimore.

Vika, E., V. L. Aravantinos, and M. P. Richards. 2009. "Aristophanes and Stable Isotopes: A Taste for Freshwater Fish in Classical Thebes (Greece)?" *Antiquity* 83: 1076–83.

Vimercati, E. 2003. "Il concetto di 'ethnos' nella terminologia politica ellenistica." In C. Bearzot, F. Landucci, and G. Zecchini, eds., *Gli stati territoriali nel mondo antico*, 111–26. Milan.

Vlachogianni, E. 2004–9. "Προξενικό ψήφισμα του κοινού των Βοιωτών." *Horos* 17–21: 361–72.

Vokotopoulos, P. A. 1967. "Ἀρχαιότητες καὶ μνημεία Αἰτωλοακαρνανίας." *AD* 22 B2: 318–36.

Vollgraff, W. 1902. "Inscription de Béotie." *BCH* 26: 570.

von Stern, E. 1884. *Geschichte der spartanischen und thebanischen Hegemonie vom Königsfrieden zur Schlacht bei Mantinea*. Dorpat.

Vordos, A. G. 2001. "Τραπεζά Αιγίου· Επιφανειακή έρευνα του αρχαιολογικού χώρου—Τα πρώτα συμπεράσματα." In V. Mitsopoulos-Leon, ed., *Forschungen in der Peloponnes: Akten des Symposions anläßlich der Feier «100 Jahre Österreichisches Archäologisches Institut Athen», Athen, 5.3.–7.3.1998*, 47–54. Athens.

———. 2002. "Rhypes: À la recherche de la métropole achéenne." In E. Greco, ed., *Gli Achei e l'identità etnica degli Achei d'occidente*, 217–34. Paestum and Athens.

Vottéro, G. 1995. "Boeotica varia." In C. Brixhe, ed., *Héllenika symmikta: Histoire, linguistique, épigraphie*, 121–32. Nancy.

———. 1996. "L'alphabet ionien-attique en Béotie." In P. Carlier, ed., *Le IV* siècle av. J.-C.: Approches historiographiques*, 157–81. Nancy and Paris.

———. 1998. *Le dialecte béotien (7* s.-2* s. av. J.-C.)*. Vol. I, *L'écologie du dialecte*. Nancy and Paris.

———. 2001. *Le dialecte béotien (7* s.-2* s. av. J.-C.)*. Vol. II, *Répertoire raisonné des inscriptions dialectales*. Nancy and Paris.

Vroom, J. 1993. "The Kastro of Veloukovo (Kallion): A Note on the Surface Finds." *Pharos* 1: 113–38.

Waanders, F. M. J. 1983. *The History of τέλος and τελέω in Ancient Greek*. Amsterdam.

Wacker, C. 1996. "Der akarnanische Hafenplatz Panormos." In P. Berktold, J. Schmid, and C. Wacker, eds., *Akarnanien: Eine Landschaft im antiken Griechenland*, 209–13. Würzburg.

Walbank, F. W. 1933. *Aratos of Sicyon*. Cambridge.

———. 1936. "Aratos' Attack on Cynaetha." *JHS* 56: 64–71.

———. 1940. *Philip V of Macedon*. Cambridge.

———. 1957–79. *A Historical Commentary on Polybius*. 3 vols. Oxford.

———. 1970a. "An Experiment in Greek Union." *PCA* 67: 13–27.

———. 1970b. "The Achaean Assemblies Again." *MH* 27: 129–43.

———. 1976–77. "Were There Greek Federal States?" *SCI* 3: 27–51.

———. 1984a. "Macedonia and Greece." In F. W. Walbank, A. E. Astin, M. W. Frederiksen, and R. M. Ogilvie, eds., *The Cambridge Ancient History*, vol. VII.1, *The Hellenistic World*, 221–56. Cambridge.

———. 1984b. "Macedonia and the Greek Leagues." In F. W. Walbank, A. E. Astin, M. W. Frederiksen, and R. M. Ogilvie, eds., *The Cambridge Ancient History,* vol. VII.1, *The Hellenistic World,* 446–81. Cambridge.

———. 1989. "Antigonus Doson's Attack on Cytinium (*REG* 101 [1988], 12–53)." *ZPE* 76: 184–92.

———. 2000. "Hellenes and Achaians: 'Greek Nationality' Revisited." In P. Flensted-Jensen, ed., *Further Studies in the Ancient Greek Polis,* 19–34. Stuttgart.

Walbank, M. B. 1978. *Athenian Proxenies of the Fifth Century B.C.* Toronto and Sarasota.

Walek, T. 1913. "Inscription inédite de Delphes: Traité d'alliance entre les Étoliens et les Béotiens." *RPh* 37: 262–70.

Walker, A. 2006. *Coins of Peloponnesos: The BCD Collection. LHS Numismatics: Auction 96, 8–9 May 2006.* Zurich.

Walker, E. M. 1913. *The Hellenica Oxyrynchia.* Oxford.

Wallace, P. W. 1979. *Strabo's Description of Boiotia.* Heidelberg.

Wallace, W. P. 1962. "The Early Coinages of Athens and Euboia." *NC,* ser. 7, 2: 23–42.

Walsh, J. J. 2000. "The Disorders of the 170s B.C. and Roman Intervention in the Class Struggle in Greece." *CQ* 50: 300–303.

Walter-Karydi, E. 1987. *Die äginetische Bildhauerschule: Werke und schriftliche Quellen.* Mainz.

Warren, J. A. W. 1991. "The Bronze Coinage of the Achaian League: The Mints of Achaia and Elis." In A. D. Rizakis, ed., *Αρχαία Αχαΐα και Ηλεία,* 151–54. Athens and Paris.

———. 1993. "Towards a Resolution of the Achaian League Silver Coinage Controversy: Some Observations on Methodology." In M. Price, A. Burnett, and R. Bland, eds., *Essays in Honour of Robert Carson and Kenneth Jenkins,* 87–99. London.

———. 1999. "The Achaian League Silver Coinage Controversy Resolved: A Summary." *NC* 159: 99–109.

———. 2007. *The Bronze Coinage of the Achaian Koinon: The Currency of a Federal Ideal.* London.

———. 2008. "The Framework of the Achaian Koinon." In C. Grandjean, ed., *La Péloponnèse d'Épaminondas à Hadrien,* 91–100. Bordeaux.

Washington, H. S. 1891. "Excavations by the American School at Plataia in 1891: Discovery of a Temple of Archaic Plan." *AJA* 7: 390–405.

Waterfield, R. 1998. *Herodotus: The Histories.* Oxford.

Watts, M. J., and H. G. Bohle. 1993. "The Space of Vulnerability: The Causal Structure of Hunger and Famine." *Progress in Human Geography* 17: 43–67.

Wehrli, F., ed. 1953. *Die Schule des Aristoteles: Herakleides Pontikos.* Basel.

Weiler, A. J. M. 1987. "Herders en kudden in griekse inscripties." *Lampas* 20: 16–22.

Weingast, B. R. 1993. "Constitutions as Governance Structures: The Political Foundations of Secure Markets." *Journal of Institutional and Theoretical Economics* 149: 286–311.

———. 1995. "The Economic Role of Political Institutions: Market-Preserving Federalism and Economic Development." *Journal of Law, Economics, and Organization* 11: 1–31.

———. 1997. "The Political Foundations of Democracy and the Rule of Law." *American Political Science Review* 91: 245–63.

———. 2002. "Rational-Choice Institutionalism." In I. Katznelson and H. Milner, eds., *Political Science: The State of the Discipline,* 660–92. New York.

———. 2005. "The Performance and Stability of Federalism: An Institutional Perspective." In C. Ménard and M. Shirley, eds., *Handbook of New Institutional Economics*, 149–72. Dordrecht.

Welcker, F O. 1865. *Der epische Cyclus*. Bonn.

Wells, J. "Some Points as to the Chronology of the Reign of Cleomenes I." *JHS* 25: 193–203.

Wesenberg, B. 1982. "Thermos B1." *AA*, 149–57.

West, M. L. 1972. *Iambi et elegi Graeci ante Alexandrum cantati*. Vol. 2, *Callinus, Mimnermus, Semonides, Solon, Tyrtaeus, Minora adespota*. Oxford.

———. 1978. *Hesiod: Works and Days, Edited with Prolegomena and Commentary*. Oxford.

———. 1985. *The Hesiodic Catalogue of Women: Its Nature, Structure, and Origins*. Oxford.

West, S. 1985. "Herodotus' Epigraphical Interests." *CQ* 35: 278–305.

Westlake, H. D. 1985. "The Sources for the Spartan Debacle at Haliartos." *Phoenix* 39: 119–33.

Whitby, M. 1998. "The Grain Trade of Athens in the Fourth Century BC." In H. Parkins and C. Smith, eds., *Trade, Traders, and the Ancient City*, 102–28. London.

Whitley, J. 20045. "Archaeology in Greece, 2004–2005." *AR* 51: 1–118.

Wickersham, J. M. 2007. "Spartan Garrisons in Boeotia in 382–379/8 B.C." *Historia* 56: 243–46.

Wilamowitz-Moellendorff, U. von. 1874. "Abrechnung eines boiotischen Hipparchen." *Hermes* 8: 431–41.

———. 1921. "Ein vergessenes Homerscholien." *SPAW* 729–35.

———. 1922. *Pindaros*. Berlin.

Wilhelm, A. 1911. *Neue Beiträge zur griechischen Inschriftenkunde*. Vienna.

———. 1940. "Rudolf Heberdeys neue Lesung des Rechtshilfevertrages der Städte Stymphalos und Aigeira, *IG* V 2, 357." *JÖAI* 32: 68–78.

———. 1941. "Zu Ehren des Pelopidas." *JÖAI* 33: 35–45.

———. 1974. *Akademieschriften zur griechischen Inschriftenkunde (1895–1951)*. Leipzig.

Will, E. 1955. *Korinthiaka: Recherches sur l'histoire et la civilisation de Corinthe des origines aux guerres médiques*. Paris.

———. 1977. "Bulletin historique." *Revue historique* 257: 190–91.

———. 1979–82. *Histoire politique du monde hellénistique*. 2 vols. Nancy.

Williams, H. 1996. "Excavations at Stymphalos." *EMC* 40: 75–98.

Williams, R. T. 1965. *The Confederate Coinage of the Arcadians in the Fifth Century B.C.* New York.

———. 1972. *Silver Coinage of the Phokians*. London.

Williamson, O. 1975. *Markets and Hierarchies: Analysis and Antitrust Implications; A Study in the Economics of Internal Organization*. New York.

Winter, N. A. 1990. "Defining Regional Styles in Archaic Greek Architectural Terracottas." *Hesperia* 59: 13–32.

———. 1993. *Greek Architectural Terracottas from the Prehistoric to the End of the Archaic Period*. Oxford.

Wiseman, J. 1969. "Epaminondas and the Theban Invasions." *Klio* 51: 186–99.

———. 1978. *The Land of the Ancient Corinthians*. Göteborg.

Woodhead, A. G. 1997. *The Athenian Agora*. Vol. XVI, *Inscriptions: The Decrees*. Princeton.

Woodhouse, W. J. 1897. *Aetolia: Its Geography, Topography and Antiquities*. Oxford.

Wroth, W. 1902. "Greek Coins Acquired by the British Museum in 1901." *NC*, ser. 4, 2: 313–44.

Yates, D.C. 2005. "The Archaic Treaties between the Spartans and Their Allies." *CQ* 55: 65–76.

Yoffee, N. 2005. *Myths of the Archaic State: Evolution of the Earliest Cities, States, and Civilizations*. Cambridge.

Zahrnt, M. 1971. *Olynth und die Chalkidier: Untersuchungen zur Staatenbildung auf der chalkidischen Halbinsel im 5. und 4. Jahrhundert v. Chr.* Munich.

Zunino, M.L. 1994. "Del buon uso del sacrificio." *QS* 40: 33–57.

INDEX OF SUBJECTS

Page references in italics refer to illustrations.

Hiller von Gaertringen, F., 261n87, 317n290, 468;
on Epidauros, 461
Hippias (boiotarch), 423, 425
Hippias (son of Erotion), 417
Hobbes, Thomas, 153, 329
Holleaux, M., 95n23, 434, 435, 436, 472
Homeric Hymn to Apollo, 190; Onchestos in,
164–65
Horden, Peregrine, 150n15, 257; *The Corrupting
Sea,* 244; on regional economies, 244
Hornblower, Simon, 40n86, 296n218
hostages: to Achaian koinon, 376, 471–72; from
Opountian Lokris, 376–77; to Rome, 138,
139, 481
Hyettos, representational district of, 372
Hygieia: cult at Epidauros, 232, 233, 469–71;
sacrifices to, 233, 352, 468–71
Hymettos: coinage of, 26, 248; Theban victory
over, 333
Hyperbatos (Achaian), 134
Hysiai, Boiotian seizure of, 188

Illyrian War, 110; Aitolian-Achaian involvement
in, 109
infrastructure, development of, 240
institutionalism, new, 4, 11, 329
institutions: cooperative, 330; cultural norms of,
11; dynamics of, 12; informal elements of, 12;
path-dependent, 13; power distribution in, 11,
156; as rules, 12; self-enforcing, 326–27; stickiness of, 330n14; structure of, 11, 12n41; as
systems, 12
institutions, Aitolian, 77, 341, 343, 349;
Hellenistic, 344; political, 58
institutions, Boiotian: Hellenistic, 89; koinon,
10–11, 14, 22–46, 185, 335, 337; of poleis,
22–46; political, 338–39; rituals, 223–24, 231
institutions, Greek: coinage predating, 247;
control over natural resources, 239;
development of, 22–46, 243–44, 284;
economic, 4, 15–16, 239–40; effect on
economic behavior, 240; emergence of,
10–13, 328–29; of poleis, 10n31, 22–46, 244;
religious, 15–16, 147–48; ritualization of, 215,
216–17, 233–36; role of ecology in, 281;
self-enforcing, 301; stability through, 346. *See
also* political institutions, Greek
institutions, koinon, 10, 12, 15; Achaian, 22, 76,
233, 341, 342, 346, 369, 392; cellular theories
of, 406n3; cooperative, 100; emergence of,
328–29, 405; entities preceding, 332; religious,
15–16, 147–48, 401; ritualization of, 215,

216–17, 233–36; socio-political entities of, 336,
407; stability of, 390–99, 404; voluntary
participation in, 397–98
intermarriage rights: in Boiotian koinon, 273,
403; Chalkidic, 266; integrative effect of, 264;
within koina, 102, 238, 246, 255–57; in poleis,
384
Ionians: expulsion from Achaia, 194, 195, 202; at
Helike, 194, 195, 197, 198, 321; sacrifice to
Poseidon Helikonios, 197, 206, 321, 393,
394n281; sanctuary of Artemis Triklaria, 218
Ismard, Paulin, 406
Ismenias (pro-Athenian), 60; control of Thebes,
45; execution of, 67
Ismenias (pro-Macedonian), 135
Ismenion: poetry of, 160–61; shared cult at, 170,
186–87; tripod dedication at, 168, 186–88. *See
also* Apollo Ismenios; Daphnephoria
Isocrates, *Plataikos,* 67n48
isopoliteia rights, 102; Aitolian, 360–61; for
individuals, 360
Isthmian Games, 165; proxeny at, 166
Iton (son of Amphiktyon), 158
Itonion: *asylia* decree for, 224n286; black-figure
vase depicting, 160n51; Delphic decree on,
224; group identity at, 163, 401; multi-com-
munity celebrations at, 166; pan-Boiotian
celebration of, 224, 225; participations in,
160; procession of, 160; ritual games at, 161,
162; rituals of, 159–60; social environment of,
163. *See also* Athena Itonia

Jacquemin, Anne, 435
Jason of Pherai, 211
Jeffery, L. H., 485
Jehne, M., 339n48
Jones, F. N., 457

Kadmeia, Theban: Boiotian treasury at, 296;
federal meetings at, 337; Spartan occupation
of, 67, 68, 69n61, 83, 209, 210, 305, 338, 425
Kalapodi, sanctuary at, 151n17Kallieis (Aitolians),
54, 56; territory of, 280
Kallikrates (Achaian *stratēgos*), 134, 138, 141, 479,
481; bribing of, 140n297; vilification of,
139n290
Kallimachos, Hera statue of, 226, 227
Kallipolis (Kallion): cult activity at, 279, 382n234;
economic resources of, 287; excavation of,
278, 279–80; proxeny decree of, 263n93; sack
of, 211, 214
Kallippidas of Athens, proxeny decree for, 426

INDEX LOCORUM

www.ingramcontent.com/pod-product-compliance
Lightning Source LLC
Chambersburg PA
CBHW020329270326
41926CB00007B/97